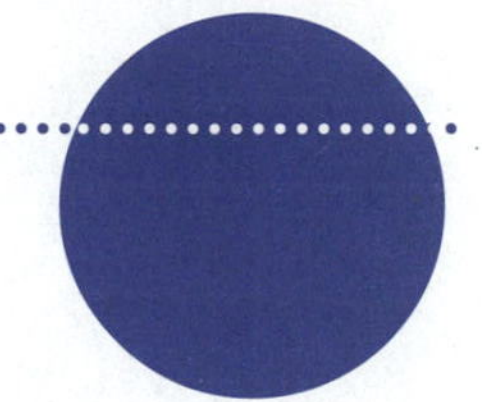

Price Theory and Applications

FOURTH EDITION

Price Theory and Applications

FOURTH EDITION

STEVEN E. LANDSBURG

University of Rochester

SOUTH-WESTERN College Publishing

An International Thomson Publishing Company

Team Director/Publisher: Jack W. Calhoun
Acquisitions Editor: Keri Witman
Developmental Editor: Susanna Smart
Production Editor: Peggy K. Buskey
Marketing Manager: Lisa L. Lysne
Production House: Maryland Composition Company, Inc.
Internal Design: Meighan Depke, Depke Design
Cover: Tin Box Studio

0-538-88206-9

Landsburg, Steven E., 1954-
Price theory and applications / Steven E. Landsburg.—4th ed.
p. cm.
Includes bibliographical references and index.
ISBN 0-538-88206-9
1. Prices. 2. Microeconomics. I. Title.
HB172.L34 1998
338.5—dc21
98-4436
CIP

4 5 6 7 8 C5 5 4 3 2 1 0
Printed in the United States of America

I(T)P®
International Thomson Publishing
South-Western College Publishing is an ITP Company.
The ITP trademark is used under license.

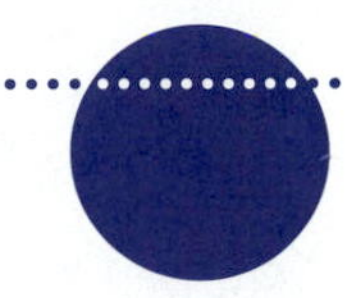

About the Author

Steven E. Landsburg teaches economics at the University of Rochester. His articles have appeared in the *Journal of Political Economy,* the *Journal of Economic Theory,* and many other journals of economics, mathematics, and philosophy. He is the author of *The Armchair Economist* (Free Press/Macmillan, 1993), *Fair Play* (Free Press, 1997), and co-author of the textbook *Macroeconomics* (McGraw-Hill, 1997). He writes a monthly column in *Slate Magazine* and serves on the board of directors of Hutchinson Technology.

To Lauren and Cayley

Preface

TO THE STUDENT

Price theory is a challenging and rewarding subject. The student who masters price theory acquires a powerful tool for understanding a remarkable range of social phenomena. How does a sales tax affect the price of coffee? Why do people trade? What happens to ticket prices when a baseball player gets a raise? How does free agency affect the allocation of baseball players to teams? Why might the revenue of orange growers increase when there is an unexpected frost—and what may we infer about the existence of monopoly power if it does?

Price theory teaches you how to solve similar puzzles. Better yet, it poses new ones. You will learn to be intrigued by phenomena you might previously have considered unremarkable. When rock concerts predictably sell out in advance, why don't the promoters raise prices? Why are bank buildings fancier than supermarkets? Why do ski resorts sell lift tickets on a per-day basis rather than a per-ride basis?

Throughout this book, such questions are used to motivate a careful and rigorous development of microeconomic theory. New concepts are immediately illustrated with entertaining and informative examples, both verbal and numerical. Ideas and techniques are allowed to arise naturally in the discussion, and they are given names (like "marginal rate of substitution") only after you have discovered their usefulness. You are encouraged to develop a strong economic intuition and then to test your intuition by submitting it to rigorous graphical and verbal analysis.

I think that you will find this book inviting. There are no mathematical demands nor prerequisites and no lists of axioms to memorize. At the same time, the level of economic rigor and sophistication is quite high. In many cases, I have carried analysis beyond what is found in most other books at this level. There are digressions, examples, and especially problems that will challenge even the most ambitious and talented students.

Using this Book

Many books begin by telling you, at some length, what price theory is. This book begins by showing you. When you finish the first chapter, you will know how to analyze the effects of sales and excise taxes, and you will have discovered the surprising result that a tax on buyers and a tax on sellers have exactly the same effects. When you finish the second chapter, you will understand why oranges, on average, taste better in New York than in Florida. In each succeeding chapter, you will be exposed to new ideas in economics and to their surprising consequences for the world around you.

To learn what price theory is, dig in and begin reading. The next few paragraphs give you a hint of what it's all about.

Price theory, or *microeconomics,* is the study of the ways in which individuals and firms make choices, and the ways in which these choices interact with each other. We assume that individuals have certain well-defined preferences and limits to their behavior. For example, you might enjoy eating both cake and ice cream, but the size of your stomach limits your ability to pursue these pleasures; moreover, the amount of cake that you eat affects the amount of ice cream you can eat and vice versa.

In predicting behavior, we assume that individuals behave *rationally,* which is to say that they make themselves as well-off as possible, as measured by their own preferences, and within the limitations imposed on them. While this assumption (like any assumption in any science) is only an approximation to reality, it is an extraordinarily powerful one, and it leads to many profound and surprising conclusions.

Price theory is made richer by the fact that each individual's choices can affect the opportunities available to others. If you decide to eat all of the cake, your roommate cannot decide to eat some too. An *equilibrium* is an outcome in which each person's behavior is compatible with the restrictions imposed by everybody else's behavior. In many situations, it is possible to say both that there is only one possible equilibrium and that there are good reasons to expect that equilibrium to actually come about. This enables the economist to make predictions about the world.

Thus, price theory is most often concerned with two sorts of questions: those that are **positive** and those that are **normative.** A positive question is a question about what *is* or *will be,* whereas a normative question is a question about what *ought*-to be. Positive questions have definite, correct answers (which may or may not be known), whereas the answers to normative questions depend on values. For example, suppose that a law is proposed that would prohibit any bank from foreclosing on any farmer's mortgage. Some positive questions are: How will this law affect the incomes of bankers? How will it affect the incomes of farmers? What effect will it have on the number of people who decide to become farmers and on the number of people who decide to start banks? Will it indirectly affect the average size of farms or of banks? Will it indirectly affect the price of land? How will it affect the price of food and the well-being of people who are neither farmers nor bankers? And so forth. A normative question is: Is this law, on balance, a good thing?

Economics can, at least in principle, provide answers to the positive questions. Economics by itself can never answer a normative question; in this case your answer to the normative question must depend on how you feel about the relative merits of helping farmers and helping bankers.

Therefore, we will be concerned in this book primarily with positive questions. However, price theory is relevant in the consideration of normative questions as well. This is so in two ways. First, even if you are quite sure of your own values, it is often impossible to decide whether you consider some course of action desirable unless you know its consequences. Your decision about whether to support the antiforeclosure law will depend not only on your feelings about farmers and bankers, but also on what effects you believe the law will have. Thus, it can be important to study positive questions even when the questions of ultimate interest are normative ones.

For another example, suppose that you have decided to start recycling newspapers to help preserve large forests. One of your friends tells you that in fact recycling leads to *smaller* forests because it lowers the demand for trees and induces paper companies to do less planting. Whether or not your friend is correct is a positive question. You might want the answer to that positive question before returning to the normative question: Should I continue to recycle?

The second way in which price theory can assist us in thinking about normative questions is by showing us the consequences of consistently applying a given normative criterion. For example, if your criterion is "I am always for anything that will benefit farmers, provided that it does not drive any bankers out of business," the price theorist might be able to respond, "In that case, you must support such-and-such a law, because I can use economic reasoning to show that such-and-such a law will indeed benefit farmers without driving any bankers out of business." If such-and-such a law does not sound like a good idea to you, you might want to rethink your normative criterion.

In the first seven chapters of this book, you will receive a thorough grounding in the positive aspects of price theory. You will learn how consumers make decisions, how firms make decisions, and how these decisions interact in the competitive marketplace. In Chapter 8, you will examine the desirability of these outcomes from the viewpoints of various normative criteria. Chapter 9 rounds out the discussion of the competitive price system by examining the role of prices as conveyors of information.

In Chapters 10 through 14, you will learn about various situations in which the competitive model does not fully apply. These include conditions of monopoly and oligopoly, and circumstances in which the activities of one person or firm affect others involuntarily (for example, factories create pollution that their neighbors must breathe).

The first 14 chapters complete the discussion of the market for goods, which are supplied by firms and purchased by individuals. In Chapters 15 through 17 you will learn about the other side of the economy: The market for inputs to the production process (such as labor) that are supplied by individuals and purchased by firms. In Chapter 17, you will study the market for the productive input called *capital* and examine the way that individuals allocate goods across time, consuming less on one day so that they can consume more on another.

Chapter 18 concerns a special topic: the role of risk.

Chapter 19 provides an overview of what economics in general, and price theory in particular, is all about. Most of the discussion in that final chapter could have been included here. However, we believe that the discussion will be more meaningful *after* you have seen some examples of price theory in action, rather than before. Therefore, we make the following suggestion: Dip into Chapter 19. Not all of it will make sense at this point, but much of it will. After you have been through a few chapters of the book, dip into Chapter 19 again. Even the parts you understood the first time will be more meaningful now. Later on—say, after you have finished Chapter 7—try it yet again. You will get the most from the final chapter if you read it one last time, thoroughly, at the end of the course.

Features

This book provides many tools to help you learn. Here are a few hints on how to use them.

Exhibits

Most of the exhibits have extensive explanatory captions that summarize key points from the discussion in the text.

Exercises

Exercises are sprinkled throughout the text and, with a few exceptions (marked with two square bullets), they are routine. They are intended to slow you down and make sure that you understand one paragraph before going on to the next. If you cannot do an exercise quickly and accurately, you have probably missed an important point. In that case, it is wise to pause and reread the preceding few paragraphs. Answers to all of the exercises are provided in Appendix B at the back of the book.

Dangerous Curves

The dangerous curve symbol appears periodically to warn you against the most common misunderstandings. Passages marked with this symbol describe mistakes that students and theorists often make and explain how to avoid them.

Margin Glossary

Each new term is defined both in the text (in bold) and in the margin, where you can easily find it. All of the definitions in the margin glossary are gathered in alphabetical order in the Glossary at the back of the book.

Internet Margin Notes

Throughout each chapter, internet margin notes point to web sites where you can find more information relevant to the examples in the text.

Chapter Summaries

The summaries at the end of each chapter provide concise descriptions of the main ideas. You will find them useful in organizing your studying.

Review Questions

The Review Questions at the end of each chapter test to see whether you have learned and can repeat the main ideas of the chapter.

Numerical Exercises

About half of the chapters have Numerical Exercises at the end. By working these, you apply economic theory to data to make precise predictions. For example, at the end of Chapter 7, you are given some information about the costs of producing kites and the demand for kites. Using this and the theory that you have learned, you will be able to deduce the price of kites, the number of kites sold by each firm, and the number of firms in the industry.

Problem Sets

The extensive Problem Sets at the end of each chapter occupy a wide range of difficulty. Some are quite straightforward. Others are challenging and open-ended and give you the opportunity to think deeply and creatively. A few of the most difficult are labeled "hard problems."

Often, problems require additional assumptions that are not explicitly stated. Learning to make additional assumptions is a large part of learning to do economics. In some cases there will be more than one correct answer, depending on what assumptions you made. Thus, in answering problems you should always spell out your reasoning very carefully. This is particularly so of "true or false" problems, where the quality of your explanations will usually matter far more than your conclusion.

About one third of the problems are discussed in Appendix C at the end of the book; answers are provided for the Problem Set questions indicated by the QA icon. The discussions in Appendix C range from hints to complete answers. In many cases, the answer section lists only conclusions without the reasoning necessary to support them; your instructor will probably require you to provide that reasoning.

If your instructor allows it, you will learn a lot by working on problems together with your classmates. You may find that you and they have different answers to the same problem, and that both you and they are equally sure of your answers. In attempting to convince each other, and in trying to pinpoint the spot at which your thinking diverged, you will be forced to clarify your ideas and you will discover which concepts you need to study further.

Internet Activities

Projects designed by Steven C. Hackett of Humboldt State University encourage you to analyze information from the internet in light of the theory you've been learning from the text.

Now you are ready to begin.

TO THE INSTRUCTOR

One advantage of teaching the same course every semester is that you constantly discover new ways to help students understand and enjoy the subject. I've taught price theory 40 times now, and am eager to share the best of my recent discoveries.

The first three editions of this textbook have gathered an extremely positive response from both students and professors. In light of that, I've been careful to retain the book's basic structure and the many features that have been recognized as highlights—the clarity of the writing, the careful pedagogy (including "dangerous curve" signals to warn students against the most common misunderstandings), the lively examples, and the wide range of exercises and problems. But at the same time, I've rewritten parts of several chapters to incorporate new explanations that have proved exceptionally successful in the classroom.

Thus, long-term users will find substantial improvements in the presentation of basic consumer theory (in Chapter 3), income and substitution effects (Chapter 4), the theory of the firm (in Chapter 6), the theory of the competitive industry (Chapter 7), welfare economics (Chapter 8), Pareto optimality (Chapter 12) and labor economics (Chapter 16). In Chapter 4 I've highlighted the contrast between inferior goods and Giffen goods; in Chapter 7 I've streamlined and simplified the discussion of profits, and used numerical examples to clarify the zero-profit condition; in Chapter 8 I've been more explicit about the hidden assumptions underlying various forms of welfare analysis; and in Chapter 16 I have drastically streamlined the analysis of labor supply—without, I think, sacrificing anything of real importance.

There are also many new examples, including Microsoft versus Netscape (to illustrate the advantages and disadvantages of vertical integration), Amazon versus Barnes & Noble (to illustrate the issues involved with retail price maintenance) and mob control of New York concrete pouring (to illustrate the enforcement of cartels). There is new material on multiple equilibria (in contexts ranging from role of social status of imperfections in the auto insurance market), the regulation of airplanes, pesticides and prescription drugs, the origin of pantomime and the supply of jokes.

But while I am very pleased with these improvements and innovations, I have not tampered with the fundamental structure and content of the book, which I expect will be as satisfactory to the next generation of students as it was to the last. The standard topics of intermediate price theory are covered in this edition, and in the previous versions. I have retained all of the book's unique features, of which the following are the most important:

The Use of Social Welfare (via Triangles of Consumers' and Producers' Surplus) as a Unifying Concept

Consumers' and producers' surplus are introduced in Chapter 8, immediately following the theory of the competitive industry. There, they are used to analyze the effects of various forms of market interference. Thereafter, most new concepts are related to social welfare and analyzed in this light.

The Economics of Information

Chapter 9 (Knowledge and Information) surveys the key role of prices in disseminating information and relates this to their key role in equilibrating markets. Section 9.1 emphasizes the price system's remarkable success in this regard while Section 9.3 surveys some of its equally remarkable failures. Section 9.2 studies information in financial markets.

Treatment of the Theory of the Firm

It is often difficult for students to understand the importance of production functions, average cost curves, and the like until after they have been asked to study them for several weeks. To remedy this, Chapter 5 (The Behavior of Firms) provides an overview of how firms make decisions, introducing the general principle of equating marginal costs with marginal benefits and relating this principle back to the consumer theory that the student has just learned. Having seen the importance of cost curves, students may be more motivated to study their derivation in Chapter 6 (Production and Costs).

The material on firms is presented in a manner that gives a lot of flexibility to the instructor. Those who prefer the more traditional approach of starting immediately with production can easily skip Chapter 5 or postpone it until after Chapter 6. Chapter 6 itself has been extensively reorganized for this edition, to rigorously separate the short-run theory (in Section 6.1) from the long-run theory (in Section 6.2). Relations between the short and the long run are thoroughly explored in Section 6.3. Instructors who want to defer the more difficult topic of long-run production will find it easy to simply cover Section 6.1 and then move directly on to Chapter 7.

An Extended Analysis of Market Failures, Property Rights, and Rules of Law

This is the material of Chapter 13, which I have found to be very popular with students. The theory of externalities is developed in great detail, using a series of extended examples and illustrated with actual court cases. Section 13.4 (The Law and Economics) analyzes various legal theories from the point of view of economic efficiency.

Relationships to Macroeconomics

The topic coverage provides a solid preparation for a rigorous course in macroeconomics. In addition, several purely "micro" topics are illustrated with "macro" applications. (None of these applications is central to the book, and all can be easily skipped by instructors who wish to do so.) There are sections on information, intertemporal decision making, labor markets in general equilibrium, and rational expectations. In the chapter on interest rates, there is a purely microeconomic analysis of the effects of federal deficits, including Ricardian Equivalence, the hypotheses necessary for it to hold, and the consequences of relaxing these hypotheses. (This material has been extensively rewritten and simplified for this edition.) The section on rational expectations, in Chapter 18, is presented in the context of a purely micro problem, involving agricultural prices, but it includes a discussion of "why economists make wrong predictions" with a moral that applies to macroeconomics.

Other Nontraditional Topics

There are extensive sections devoted to topics excluded from many standard intermediate textbooks. Among these are alternative normative criteria, efficient asset markets, contestable markets, antitrust law, mechanisms for eliciting private information about the demand for public goods, human capital (including the external effects of human capital accumulation), the role of increasing returns in economic growth, the Capital Asset Pricing Model, and the pricing of stock options. The book concludes with a chapter on the methods and scope of economic analysis (titled What Is Economics?), with examples drawn from biology, sociology, and history.

Supplements

The *Instructor's Manual* contains the following features in each chapter: general discussion, teaching suggestions, suggested additional problems, and solutions to all of the end-of-chapter problems in the textbook.

The *Test bank,* prepared by William V. Weber, Eastern Illinois University, offers True/False questions, multiple-choice questions, and essay questions for each chapter. This is an entirely new testbank prepared for this edition.

The *Study Guide,* prepared by William V. Weber, Eastern Illinois University, has chapters that correspond to the textbook. Each chapter contains key terms, key ideas, completion exercises, graphical analyses, multiple-choice questions, questions for review, and problems for analysis. Artwork from the text is reprinted in the *Study Guide,* with ample space to take notes during classroom discussion.

Acknowledgments

I first learned economics at the University of Chicago in the 1970s, which means that I learned most of it, directly or indirectly, from Dee McCloskey. Generations of Chicago graduate students were infected by Dee's enthusiasm for economics as a tool for understanding the world, and the members of one generation communicated their exuberance to me. They, and consequently I, learned from Dee that the world is full of puzzles—not the abstract or technical puzzles of formal economic theory, but puzzles like: Could the advent of free public education cause less education to be consumed? We learned to see puzzles everywhere and to delight in their solutions. Later, I had the privilege to know Dee as a friend, a colleague, and the greatest of my teachers. Without Dee, this book would not exist.

The exuberance that Dee personifies is endemic at Chicago, and I had the great good fortune to encounter it every day. I absorbed ideas and garnered examples in cafeterias, the library's coffee lounge, and especially in all-night seminars at Jimmy's Woodlawn Tap. Many of those ideas and examples appear in this book, their exact sources long forgotten. To all who contributed, thank you.

Among the many Chicago students who deserve explicit mention are Craig Hakkio, Eric Hirschhorn, and Maury Wolff, who were there from the beginning. John Martin and Russell Roberts taught me much and contributed many valuable suggestions specifically for this book. Ken Judd gave me a theory of executive compensation. Dan Gressell taught me the two ways to get a chicken to lay more eggs.

I received further education, and much encouragement, from the Chicago faculty. I thank Gary Becker, who enticed me to think more seriously about economics; Sherwin Rosen, who had planted the seeds of all this years before; and José Scheinkman, who listened to my ideas even when they were foolish. Above all, Bob Lucas can have no idea of how grateful I have been for his many gracious kindnesses. I remember them all, and value his generosity as I value the inspiration of his intellectual depth, honesty, and rigor.

Since leaving Chicago, my good fortune in colleagues followed me to Iowa and Cornell, and especially to Rochester, where this book was written. There is no faculty member in economics at Rochester who did not contribute to this book in one way or another. Some suggested examples and problems; others helped me learn material that I had thought I understood until I tried to write about it; and many did both. I should name them all, but have space for only a few. William Thomson taught me about mechanisms for revealing the demand for public goods and suggested that they belonged in a book at this level. Walter Oi contributed more entertaining ideas and illustrations than I can remember and told me how Chinese bargemen were paid. Alan Stockman and Ken McLaughlin come in for special mention. Alan has been teaching me both economics and the joys of economics for almost fifteen years; when I first met Ken he crammed fifteen years of teaching into two.

I must also mention the contributions of the daily lunch group at the Hillside Restaurant, where no subject is off limits and no opinion too outrageous for consideration. The daily discussions about how society is or should be structured were punctuated by numerous tangential discussions of how various ideas could best be presented in an intermediate textbook. I thank especially Stockman, McLaughlin, Mark Bils, John Boyd, Jim Kahn, Marvin Goodfriend (the first inductee into the Hillside Hall of Fame), and various parttime members.

Lauren Feinstone should have been mentioned in nearly all of the above categories, as a Chicago student, a Rochester faculty member, and a sometime Hillsider. She taught me how to think about Ricardian Equivalence and told me the best way to present it to students. For that, I thank her here. For so much more, no words can be enough.

Harold Winter's extensive written criticism of Chapter 11 led to substantial improvements. Wendy Betts gave me the epigram for Section 9.3.

We gratefully acknowledge the contributions of the following reviewers whose comments and suggestions have improved this project:

Ted Amato
University of North Carolina—Charlotte

John Antel
University of Houston

Charles A. Berry
University of Cincinnati

Jay Bloom
SUNY—New Paltz

Victor Brajer
California State University—Fullerton

Satyajit Chatterjee
University of Iowa

John Conant
Indiana State University

John P. Conley
University of Illinois

John Devereux
University of Miami

Arthur M. Diamond
University of Nebraska—Omaha

John Dodge
Calvin College

Richard Eastin
University of Southern California

Carl E. Enomoto
New Mexico State University

Claire Holton Hammond
Wake Forest University

Dean Hiebert
Illinois State University

John B. Horowitz
Ball State University

Roberto Ifill
Williams College

Paul Jonas
University of New Mexico

Kenneth Judd
University of Chicago

Elizabeth Sawyer Kelly
University of Wisconsin—Madison

Edward R. Kittrell
Northern Illinois University

Daniel Y. Lee
Shippensburg University

Chris Brown Mahoney
University of Minnesota

Devinder Malhotra
University of Akron

Joseph A. Martellaro
Northern Illinois University

John Martin
Baruch College

Scott Masten
University of Michigan

J. Peter Mattila
Iowa State University

Sharon Megdal
Northern Arizona University

Jack Meyer
Michigan State University

John Miller
Clarkson University

David Mills
University of Virginia

H. Brian Moehring
Ball State University

Robert Molina
Colorado State University

John Mullen
Clarkson University

Kathryn A. Nantz
Fairfield University

Jon P. Nelson
Penn State University

Craig M. Newmark
North Carolina State University

Margaret Oppenheimer
De Paul University

Lydia Ortega
San Jose State University

Michael Peddle
Holy Cross College

James Pinto
Northern Arizona University

Anil Puri
California State University—Fullerton

Libby Rittenberg
Colorado College

Russell Roberts
Washington University—Los Angeles

Peter Rupert
SUNY—Buffalo

David Sisk
San Francisco State University

Hubert Spraberry
Howard Payne University

Annette Steinacker
University of Rochester

Douglas O. Stewart
Cleveland State University

Vasant Sukhatme
Macalester College

Paul Thistle
University of Alabama

Mark Walbert
Illinois State University

Paula Worthington
Northwestern University

Gregory D. Wozniak
University of Tulsa

David Zervos
University of Rochester

Finally, I am grateful to the people at ITP/South-Western College Publishing: to Susan Smart, for seeing this project through from beginning to end with great wisdom and a great deal of patience, and to Peggy Buskey, for her attention to the many details involved in producing this final textbook.

Steven E. Landsburg

Brief Contents

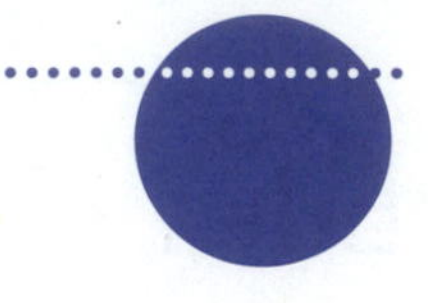

Contents

chapter I

Supply, Demand, and Equilibrium

Visit the slide show on supply, demand and market equilibrium at: http://price.bus.okstate.edu/archive/Econ3113_963/Shows/Chapter2/chap_02.htm

You have undoubtedly heard at some time in your life that economics is all about "supply" and "demand," and that statement is true. So our first task is to understand these two crucial concepts. In this chapter we will discuss the meanings and the applications of supply and demand. Using these tools, we will see how prices and quantities are determined in the marketplace. We will then be able to see how these prices and quantities change in response to changes in other economic variables. As an example, we will be able to analyze the effects of various kinds of taxes, and will discover that these effects can be very different from what you might at first expect.

1.1 Demand

Law of demand The observation that when the price of a good goes up, people will buy less of that good.

When the price of a good goes up, people generally choose to purchase less (or at least not more) of it. This statement is known as the **law of demand** and can be summarized as: "When the price goes up, the quantity demanded goes down." Economists believe that the law of demand is always (or very nearly always) true, and believe so primarily on the basis of observation. In Chapter 3, we will see that this law is also a logical consequence of certain fundamental assumptions about human behavior. Here we shall examine some of its consequences.

Demand versus Quantity Demanded

As an example, suppose that the good in question is coffee. The number of cups of coffee that you choose to purchase on a typical day might be given by a table like this:

Price	Quantity
20¢/cup	5 cups/day
30¢	4
40¢	2
50¢	1

Quantity demanded The amount of a good that a given individual or group of individuals will choose to consume at a given price.

We say that when the price is 20¢ per cup, your **quantity demanded** is 5 cups per day. When the price is 30¢ per cup, your quantity demanded is 4 cups per day, and so on. Notice that the price is measured **per cup** and the quantity is measured in **cups per day.** If we had selected different units of measurement, we would have had different entries in the table. For example, if we measured quantity in cups per week, the numbers in the right-hand column would be 35, 28, 14, and 7. In order to speak meaningfully about demand, we must specify our units and we must use them consistently.

Demand A family of numbers that lists the quantity demanded corresponding to each possible price.

The information in the table is collectively referred to as your **demand** for coffee. Notice the difference between *demand* and *quantity demanded.* Quantity demanded is a number, and it changes when the price does. Demand is a whole family of numbers, listing the quantities you would demand in a variety of hypothetical situations. The demand table asserts that if the price of coffee were 50¢ per cup, then you would buy 1 cup per day. It does not assert that the price of coffee actually is, or ever has been, or will be, 50¢ per cup.

If the price of coffee rises from 30¢ to 40¢ per cup, then your quantity demanded falls from 4 cups to 2 cups. However, your demand for coffee is unchanged, because the same table is still in effect. It remains true that if the price of coffee were 20¢ per cup, you would be demanding 5 cups per day, if the price of coffee were 30¢ per cup, you would be demanding 4 cups per day, and so on. The sequence of "if statements" is what describes your demand for coffee.

A change in price leads to a change in quantity demanded. A change in price does *not* lead to a change in demand.

Demand Curves

Unfortunately, when we represent demand by a table, we do not provide a complete picture. Our table does not tell us, for example, how much coffee you will purchase when the price is 22¢ per cup, or 33½¢. Therefore, we usually represent demand by a graph. We plot price on the vertical axis and quantity on the horizontal, always specifying our units.

Demand curve A graph illustrating demand, with prices on the vertical axis and quantities demanded on the horizontal axis.

Exhibit 1–1 provides an example. There, the information in your demand table for coffee has been translated into the black points in the graph. The curve through the points is called your **demand curve** for coffee. It fills in the additional information corresponding to prices that do not appear in the table. If we were to fill in enough rows of the table (and only space prevents us from

Exhibit 1-1 The Demand Curve

Price	Quantity
20¢/cup	5 cups/day
30¢	4
40¢	2
50¢	1

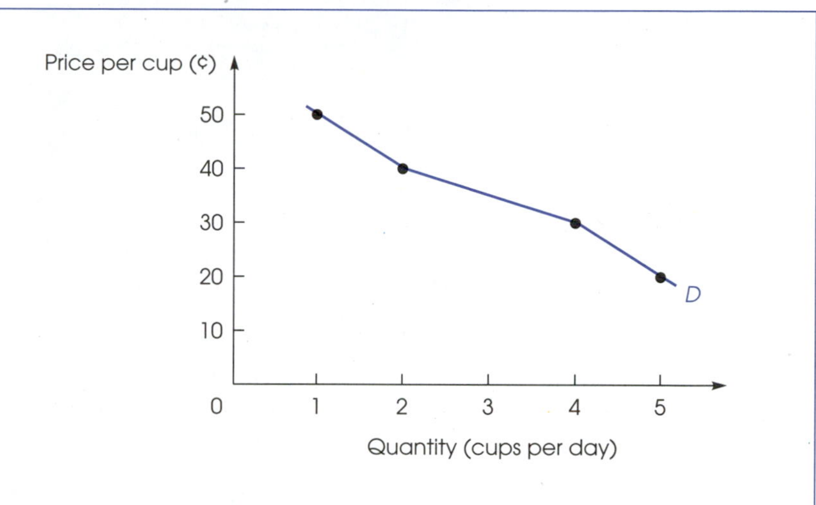

The demand table shows how many cups of coffee you would buy per day at each of several prices. The black points in the graph correspond precisely to the information in the table. The curve connecting the points is your demand curve for coffee. It conveys more information than the table because it shows how many cups of coffee you would buy at intermediate prices like 22¢ or 33½¢ per cup. If the table were enlarged to include enough intermediate prices, then the table and the graph would convey exactly the same information.

doing so), then the demand table and the demand curve in Exhibit 1–1 would convey exactly the same information. The demand curve is a picture of your demand for coffee.

Because the demand curve is a picture of demand, every statement that we can make about demand can be "seen" in the curve. For example, consider the law of demand: "When the price goes up, the quantity demanded goes down." This fact is reflected in the downward slope of the demand curve. It is important to remember both of these statements:

When the price goes up, the quantity demanded goes down.

and

Demand curves slope downward.

But it is even more important to recognize that these two statements are just two different ways of saying the same thing, and to understand *why* they are just two different ways of saying the same thing.

Changes in Demand

If a change in price does not lead to a change in demand, does this mean that demand can never change? Absolutely not. Suppose, for example, that your doctor has advised you to cut back on coffee for medical reasons. You might then choose to buy coffee according to a different table such as this:

Price	Quantity
20¢/cup	3 cups/day
30¢	2
40¢	1
50¢	0

Now your rule for deciding how many cups of coffee to purchase at different prices has changed—and this rule is just what we have called *demand*.

We can also use demand curves to illustrate the difference between a change in quantity demanded and a change in demand. A change in quantity demanded is represented by a movement along the demand curve from one point to another. A change in demand is represented by a shift of the curve itself to a new position.

The curve labeled D in Exhibit 1–2 is the same as the demand curve in Exhibit 1–1. The curve labeled D' illustrates your demand after medical advice to reduce your caffeine intake. Because you now want fewer cups of coffee at any given price, the new demand curve lies to the left of (and consequently below) the old demand curve. We describe this situation as a **fall in demand.**

Fall in demand A decision by demanders to buy a smaller quantity at each given price.

Rise in demand A decision by demanders to buy a larger quantity at each given price.

The opposite situation, a **rise in demand,** results in a rightward shift of the demand curve. If you enrolled in a class that required a lot of late-night studying, you might experience a rise in your demand for coffee.

There are many other possible reasons for a shift in demand. If the price of tea were to fall, you might decide to drink more tea and less coffee. The amount of coffee you would choose to buy at any given price would go down. This is an example of a fall in demand. On the other hand, if your aunt gives you a snazzy new coffeemaker for your birthday, your demand for coffee might rise.

A change in anything *other* than price can lead to a change in demand.

Visit the Federation of Tax Administrators at: http://www.taxadmin.org/fta/rate/sales.html

EXERCISE 1.1 If the price of donuts were to fall, what do you think would happen to your demand for coffee? Does a fall in the price of a related good always affect your demand in the same way, or does it depend on what related good we are talking about?

EXERCISE 1.2 How might a rise in your income affect your demand for coffee?

example

A Sales Tax

Sales tax In this book, a tax that is paid directly by consumers to the government. Other texts use this phrase in different ways.

One thing that could change your demand for coffee is the imposition of a **sales tax.**[1] Suppose that a new law requires you to pay a tax of 10¢ per cup of coffee that you buy. What happens to your demand curve?

---

[1] In this book we will use the phrase *sales tax* to refer to a tax that is paid to the government by consumers. Some other texts use this phrase in a different way.

Exhibit 1-2 Shifting The Demand Curve

Table A. Your Original Demand for Coffee

Price	Quantity
20¢/cup	5 cups/day
30¢	4
40¢	2
50¢	1

Table B. Your New Demand for Coffee after Medical Advice to Cut Back

Price	Quantity
20¢/cup	3 cups/day
30¢	2
40¢	1
50¢	0

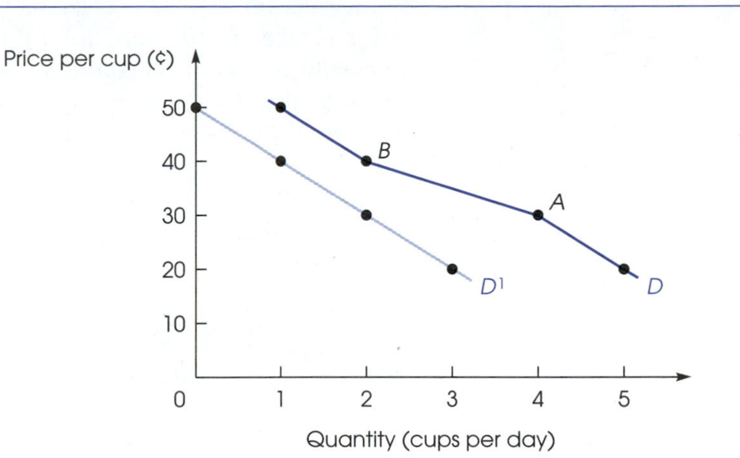

Your original demand curve for coffee is the curve labeled *D*. A change in price, say from 30¢ per cup to 40¢ per cup, would cause a movement along the curve from point *A* to point *B*. A change in something other than price, such as a doctor's suggestion that caffeine is bad for your health, can lead to a change in demand, represented by a shift to an entirely new demand curve. In this case the doctor's advice leads to a fall in demand, which is represented by a leftward shift of the curve.

Before we can begin to think about how a sales tax affects your demand curve, we have to decide what the word *price* means in a world with sales taxes. If a cup of coffee carries a price tag of "50 cents plus tax" and the tax is a nickel, should we say that the price is 50 cents or should we say that the price is 55 cents? It doesn't matter which choice we make, but it *does* matter that we make a choice and stick with it. In this book, we will consistently use the word *price* to mean the pretax price, so that the price of that cup of coffee is 50 cents. We think of the sales tax as something that you pay *in addition to* the market price. Therefore a new sales tax is a change in something *other* than the price, and therefore a new sales tax can affect the location of the demand curve.

A sales tax makes buying coffee less desirable; at any given (pretax) price, you now want to buy less coffee than before. Your demand curve shifts to the left and downward. In fact, we can even figure out how far it shifts.

Let us suppose that your demand for coffee in a world without taxes is given by the table in Exhibit 1–1. Let us figure out your demand in a world where coffee is taxed at 10¢ per cup. If the (pretax) price of coffee is 10¢, what will it actually cost you to acquire a cup of coffee? It will cost you 10¢ plus 10¢ tax—a total of 20¢. How many cups of coffee do you choose to buy when they cost you 20¢ apiece? According to the table in Exhibit 1–1, you will buy 5.

Using this information, we can begin to tabulate your demand for coffee in a world with taxes. We know that, with taxes, if the price of coffee is 10¢ per cup, you will choose to buy 5 cups per day. This is the first row of your new demand table:

Price	Quantity
10¢/cup	5 cups/day

We can continue in this way. When the price of coffee is 20¢, the actual cost to you will be 30¢. We know from Exhibit 1–1 that you will then choose to buy 4 cups. Thus, we can fill in another row of our table:

Price	Quantity
10¢/cup	5 cups/day
20¢	4

If we complete the argument at other prices, we finally arrive at your new demand for coffee, which is shown in Exhibit 1–3. Compare the entries in the two demand tables of that exhibit. Notice that the same quantities appear in each but the corresponding prices are all 10¢ lower in the new demand schedule (Table B). What can we conclude about the demand curves that illustrate these tables? For every point on the original demand curve *(D),* a corresponding point on the new demand curve *(D′)* represents the same quantity but a price that is lower by 10¢. This corresponding point lies a vertical distance exactly 10¢ below the original point.

We can summarize by saying that the sales tax causes each point of the demand curve to shift downward by the vertical distance 10¢. Because each point shifts downward the same distance, we can say that the demand curve shifts downward parallel to itself by the vertical distance 10¢. This gives us a precise prediction of how a sales tax affects demand.

A sales tax causes the demand curve to shift downward parallel to itself by the amount of the tax.

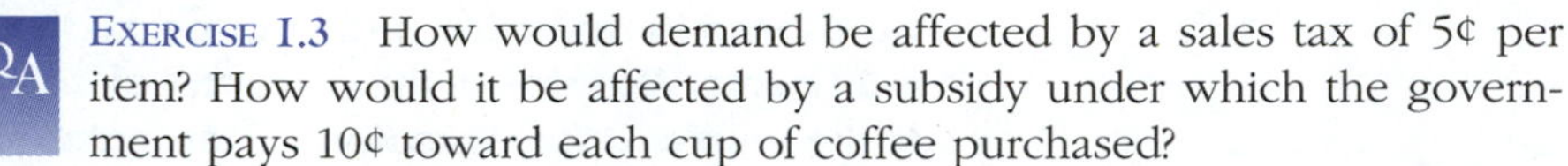

QA EXERCISE I.3 How would demand be affected by a sales tax of 5¢ per item? How would it be affected by a subsidy under which the government pays 10¢ toward each cup of coffee purchased?

QA EXERCISE I.4 How would demand be affected by a percentage sales tax—say, a tax equal to 10% of the price paid?

Exhibit 1-3 **The Effect of a Sales Tax on Demand**

Table A. Demand for Coffee without Tax

Price	Quantity
20¢/cup	5 cups/day
30¢	4
40¢	2
50¢	1

Table B. Demand for Coffee with Sales Tax of 10¢ per Cup

Price	Quantity
10¢/cup	5 cups/day
20¢	4
30¢	2
40¢	1

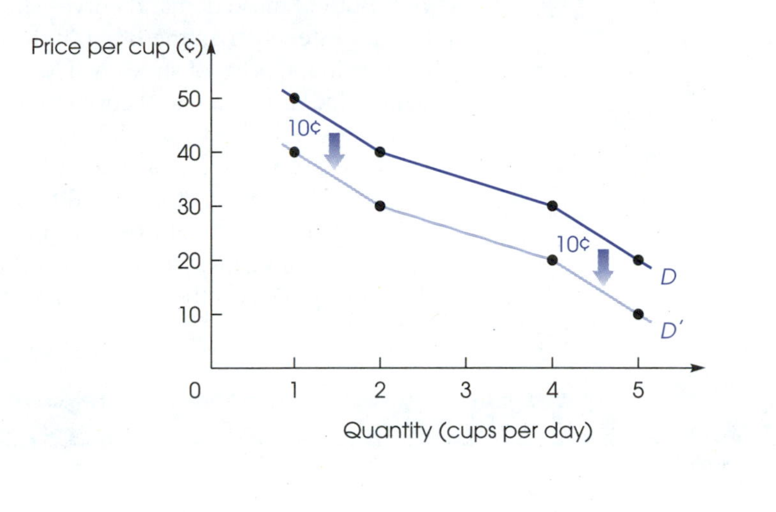

If the price of coffee is 10¢ per cup and there is a sales tax of 10¢, then it will actually cost you 20¢ to acquire a cup of coffee. Table A shows that under these circumstances you would purchase 5 cups per day. This is recorded in the first row of Table B. The other rows in that table are generated in a similar manner.

The rows of Table B contain the same quantities as the rows of Table A, but the corresponding prices are all 10¢ lower. Another way to say this is that each point on the new demand curve lies exactly 10¢ below a corresponding point on the original demand curve. Therefore, the new demand curve lies exactly 10¢ below the original demand curve in vertical distance. The sales tax causes the demand curve to shift downward parallel to itself by the amount of the tax.

Market Demand

Until now we have been discussing your demand for coffee or the demand by some individual. We can just as well discuss the demand for coffee by some *group* of individuals. We can speak of the demand by your family, your city, your country, or the entire world. The quantity associated with a given price is the total number of cups per day that the group members would demand.

Of course, since we can speak of a group's demand for coffee, we can speak of that group's demand curve as well. And, of course, this demand curve slopes downward.

The Shape of the Demand Curve

We have discussed the meaning of the demand curve's downward slope, but have not yet discussed how steeply the demand curve slopes downward. Your community's demand curve for shoes might look like either panel of Exhibit 1–4. Both of these demand curves slope downward, but one slopes downward far more steeply than the other. If the demand curve looks like panel A, a small change in the price of shoes will lead to a small change in the quantity of shoes demanded. If the demand curve looks like panel B, a small change in the price of shoes will lead to a much larger change in the quantity of shoes demanded.

There are many circumstances in which it is desirable to have information about the steepness of a particular demand curve. For example, if you owned a shoe store, you would be very interested in knowing whether a small price rise would drive away only a few customers or a great many. This is the same thing as asking whether the demand curve for your shoes is very steep or very flat.[2]

Exhibit 1-4 The Shape of the Demand Curve

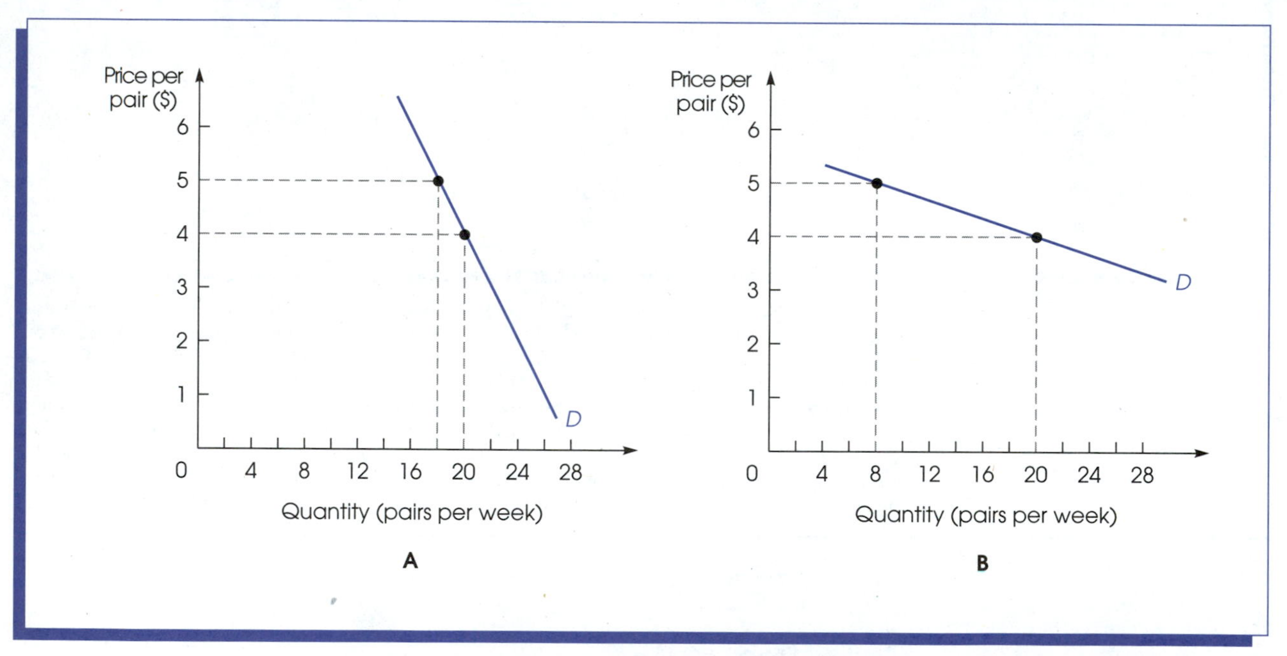

The two panels depict two possible demand curves for shoes. In panel A a given change in price (say from $4 per pair to $5 per pair) leads to a small change in quantity demanded (from 20 pairs of shoes per week to 18 pairs per week). In panel B the same change in price leads to a large change in quantity demanded (from 20 pairs per week to 8 pairs per week).

---

[2] The simplest measure of a demand curve's steepness is its slope. An alternative measure, more widely used in economics, is its *elasticity*. The elasticity is the ratio (percentage change in quantity)/(percentage change in price) between any two points. In panel A of Exhibit 1–4, where the price rises from $4 to $5 (a 25% increase), the quantity falls from 20 to 18 (a 10% decrease). Thus, the elasticity is $-10\%/25\%$, or $-.4$. We will have more to say about elasticity in Chapter 4.

Econometrics A family of statistical techniques used by economists.

To help resolve such questions, economists have developed a variety of statistical techniques known collectively as **econometrics.** These techniques allow us (among other things) to estimate the slopes of various demand curves on the basis of direct observations in the marketplace. In this book we will not study any econometrics, but it is important for you to know that the techniques exist and work tolerably well. In many circumstances economists can estimate the slopes of demand curves with considerable accuracy.

example

The Demand for Murder

Many economists have applied the successful techniques of econometrics to the study of demand curves for a variety of interesting "goods" that were previously viewed as outside the realm of economic analysis. Consider, for example, the demand curve for murder.

Visit FindLaw at: http://www.findlaw.com/lawecon/

Murder is an activity that some people choose to engage in for a variety of reasons. We can view murder as a "good" for these people, and the commission of murder as the act of consuming that good. The price of consuming the good is paid in many forms. One of these forms is the risk of capital punishment.

This means that we can draw a demand curve for murder, plotting the probability of capital punishment on the vertical axis and the quantity of murders committed on the horizontal axis. We can ask how steep this demand curve is, which is the same thing as asking whether a small increase in the probability of capital punishment will lead to a small or a large decrease in the number of murders committed. In other words, measuring the slope of this demand curve is the same thing as measuring the deterrent effect of capital punishment.

Now, on the one hand, the deterrent effect of capital punishment is something about which there is much discussion and much interest. On the other hand, the slope of a demand curve is something that economists know how to measure. In the early 1970s Isaac Ehrlich set out to measure the slope of the demand curve for murder, using the same sort of techniques that economists had used for many years to measure things like the slope of the demand curve for shoes.

His results were striking.[3] He found that the demand curve for murder was remarkably flat. A small increase in the price of murder could be expected to lead to a large decrease in the quantity of murders committed. In fact, he estimated that over the period 1935–1969, one additional execution per year in the United States would have prevented, on average, about eight murders per year.[4]

[3] I. Ehrlich, "The Deterrent Effect of Capital Punishment: A Question of Life and Death," *American Economic Review* 65 (1975): 397–417.

[4] Other researchers have questioned this result. See B. Forst, "The Deterrent Effect of Capital Punishment: A Cross State Analysis of the 1960s," *Minnesota Law Review* 61 (1977): 743–767; A. Blumstein, J. Cohen, and D. Nagin, *Deterrence and Incapacitation: Estimating the Effects of Criminal Sanctions on Crime Rates* (National Academy of Sciences, 1968); and P. Passell, "The Deterrent Effect of the Death Penalty: A Statistical Test," *Stanford Law Review* 28 (1975): 61–80.

The disagreements expressed in these articles do not involve attitudes toward capital punishment or attitudes toward econometrics; they are primarily concerned with highly technical matters of statistical theory and implementation. In principle, such issues can be settled on strictly technical grounds.

However, for a warning about how a researcher's prior expectations can affect his results, see E. Leamer, "Let's Take the `Con' Out of Econometrics," *American Economic Review* 73 (1983): 31–43.

This is a remarkable example of an application of economics to a positive question: "What is the deterrent effect of capital punishment?" It is emphatically *not* an answer to the related normative question: "Is capital punishment a good thing?" It is entirely possible to believe Ehrlich's results and still oppose capital punishment on a variety of ethical grounds. However, knowing the answer to the positive question is undoubtedly helpful in thinking about the normative one. The size of the deterrent effect of the death penalty will certainly affect our assessment of its desirability, even though our assessment depends on many other things as well.

example

The Demand for Reckless Driving

Visit the National Center for Statistics and Analysis at: http://www.nhtsa.dot.gov/people/ncsa/

Reckless driving is another good that people choose to "consume." For this consumption they pay a price, partly by risking death in an accident. When that price is reduced—say, by the installation of safety equipment in cars—we should expect the quantity of reckless driving to increase.

This implies that safety equipment (such as seat belts, energy-absorbing steering columns, penetration-resistant windshields, dual braking systems, and padded instrument panels) could lead to either an increase or a decrease in the number of driver deaths. Each individual accident would have a lower probability of being fatal. But the reduction in price (that is, the risk of death per accident) would lead to more reckless driving and therefore to more accidents. Whether the number of driver deaths decreased, increased, or stayed the same as a result of the safety equipment would depend on whether the rise in the quantity of reckless driving was small or large compared to the reduction in the probability of fatality. It would depend on whether the demand curve for reckless driving was steep or flat.

When Sam Peltzman investigated this question, he found that the advent of automobile safety regulation in the 1960s (mandating the installation of safety equipment in all new cars) led to no change in the quantity of driver deaths.[5] Unless the demand curve for reckless driving was moving for some reason, we may conclude that it was remarkably flat. People chose to engage in enough additional reckless driving as to completely offset the advantages of the new safety equipment. On this interpretation, one would expect to see increases in the number of pedestrian deaths and the amount of property damage. Peltzman found evidence of these results as well.

The Expanding Realm of Economics

Measurements of the demand curves for murder and for reckless driving are examples of the application of economic reasoning to social phenomena once considered to be outside the realm of economics. One of the pioneers in this activity was Gary Becker. In his book, *The Economics of Discrimination* (University of Chicago Press, 1957), Becker investigated the effects of racial discrimination on things like wage rates and employment. By applying fundamental economic reasoning, he was able to reach many surprising conclusions

[5] S. Peltzman, "The Effects of Automobile Safety Regulation," *Journal of Political Economy* 83 (1975): 677–725.

about who gained and who lost from the effects of discrimination. Many of the tools that he used will be developed in this book. Since that time, Becker has developed economic theories of love, marriage, and fertility, and his students have written about topics ranging from the economics of religious belief to the economics of cannibalism. Others have used economic theory to achieve startling new insights in the areas of political science, sociology, philosophy, and law. The broad applicability of economic reasoning will be a recurrent theme in this book.

1.2 Supply

Law of supply The observation that when the price of a good goes up, the quantity supplied goes up.

Quantity supplied The amount of a good that suppliers will provide at a given price.

The law of demand states that "when the price goes up, the quantity demanded goes down." The **law of supply** states that "when the price goes up, the quantity supplied goes up." By **quantity supplied** we mean the quantity of some good that a specified individual or group of individuals wants to supply to others per specified unit of time.

The law of supply is not as ironclad as the law of demand. Imagine a manufacturer of bicycles who works 12 hours a day to produce one bicycle that he can sell for $40. If the price of bicycles were to go up to $500, he might choose to work harder and produce more bicycles—but he might choose instead to cut back on production, make one bicycle per week, and spend more time at the beach.[6]

Nevertheless, economists have found that in most circumstances an increase in price leads to an increase in quantity supplied. Throughout this chapter, therefore, we shall assume the validity of the law of supply.

Supply versus Quantity Supplied

Supply A family of numbers giving the quantities supplied at each possible price.

Consider the supply of coffee in your city. It might be given by Table A of Exhibit 1–5. According to the table, if the price is 20¢ per cup, then the individuals who supply coffee to your city will wish to supply a total of 100 cups per day. If the price is 30¢ per cup, then they will wish to supply a total of 300 cups, and so forth. All of these hypothetical statements taken together constitute the **supply** of coffee to your city.

As with demand, a change in price leads to a change in the quantity supplied (which is a single number). Such changes are represented by movements along the supply curve. A change in anything other than price can lead to a change in supply—that is, to a change in the entries in the supply schedule. Such changes are represented by shifts in the supply curve itself.

For example, imagine an innovation in agricultural techniques that allows growers to produce coffee less expensively. This innovation might take the form of a new hybrid coffee plant that produces more beans, or a new idea for organizing harvesting chores so that more beans can be picked in a given amount of time. Such an innovation would make supplying coffee more desirable, and suppliers would supply more at each price than they did before.

[6] However, we will see in Chapter 6 that when the supplier is a profit-maximizing firm, the law of supply must hold.

Table B of Exhibit 1–5 shows what the new supply schedule might look like. The new supply curve is the curve labeled S' in Exhibit 1–5.

Rise in supply An increase in the quantities that suppliers will provide at each given price.

Fall in supply A decrease in the quantities that suppliers will provide at each given price.

The shift in supply due to improved agricultural techniques is an example of a **rise in supply.** It is represented by a rightward shift of the supply curve. The opposite situation is a **fall in supply.** If the wages of coffee bean pickers went up, growers would want to provide less coffee at any given price, which is another way of saying that supply would fall. A fall in supply is represented by a leftward shift of the supply curve.

In Exhibit 1-5 the new supply curve *S′*, with its higher quantities, lies to the right of the old supply curve *S*. This is because quantity is measured in the horizontal direction, so *higher* translates geometrically into *rightward*. In the vertical direction, *S′* lies below *S*, even though it represents a rise in supply. This is the opposite of what you might at first expect, and you should be on your guard against possible confusion.

EXERCISE 1.5 How would the supply of shoes be affected by an increase in the price of leather? How would it be affected by an increase in the price of leather belts?

example

The Supply of Check Cashing

The July 1990 issue of *Spy* magazine reported the results of a remarkable experiment. Writer Julius Lowenthal sent checks for \$1.11 to 58 of the wealthiest Americans, including entertainers such as Woody Allen, Cher, Michael Douglas, and Billy Joel; successful entrepreneurs such as the late Harry Helmsley and Bob Guccione; sports figures such as John McEnroe; and a variety of others, including politicians, writers, and fashion designers. Of the 58, there were 26 who took the trouble to cash the check. These 26 were then sent checks for \$0.64. Now only 13 of the recipients cashed their checks. Each of these 13 was sent a final check for \$0.13. Only 2 of the 13 were cashed.[7]

These results are consistent with an upward-sloping supply curve for check cashing. When the reward for cashing a check is small, relatively few celebrities supply the effort necessary to obtain that reward. When the reward is relatively greater—even though it might still be as small as \$1.11—a substantially larger number of checks get cashed.[8]

---

[7] The two recipients who cashed checks for 13¢ were Donald Trump and Adnan Kashoggi. Interestingly, these two experienced major financial difficulties in 1990.

[8] Presumably, those celebrities who did not cash the checks for \$1.11 would also not have cashed the checks for \$0.64. It is unfortunate that *Spy* didn't send \$0.64 checks to everyone on its original list of 58, which would have provided an interesting test of this proposition.

Exhibit 1-5 The Supply of Coffee

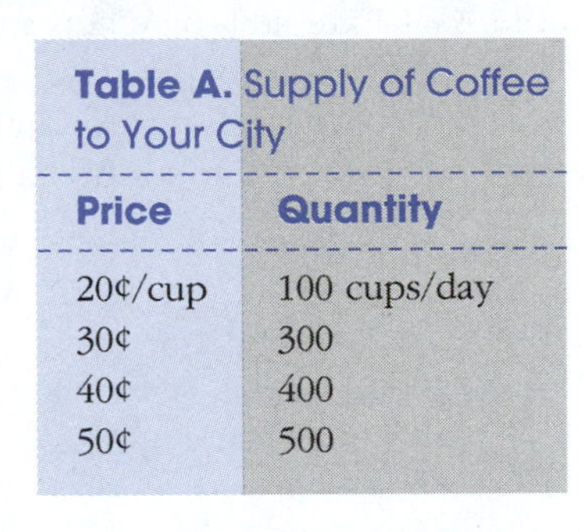

Table A. Supply of Coffee to Your City

Price	Quantity
20¢/cup	100 cups/day
30¢	300
40¢	400
50¢	500

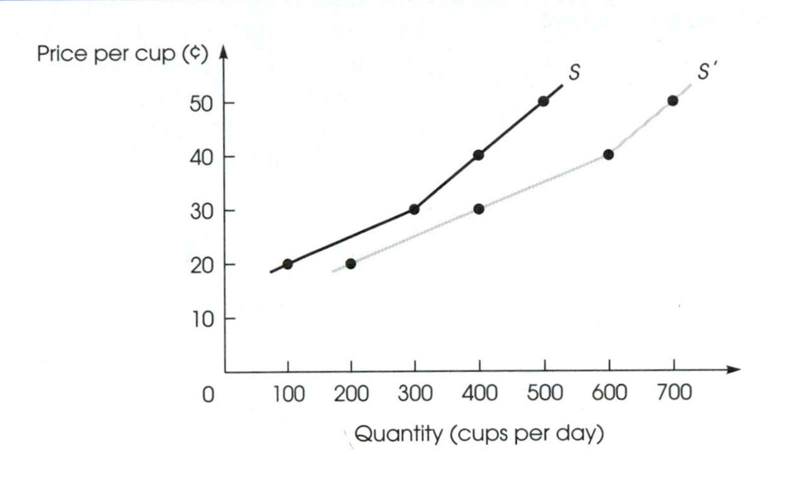

Table B. Supply of Coffee to Your City Following the Development of Better Farming Methods

Price	Quantity
20¢/cup	200 cups/day
30¢	400
40¢	600
50¢	700

Table A shows, for each price, how much coffee would be supplied to your city. The same information is illustrated by the points in the graph. The curve labeled *S* is the corresponding supply curve. It conveys more information than the table by displaying the quantities supplied at intermediate prices. The law of supply is illustrated by the upward slope of the supply curve.

The invention of a cheaper way to produce coffee increases the willingness of suppliers to provide coffee at any given price. The new supply is shown in Table B and is illustrated by the curve *S′*. Although a change in price leads to a movement along the supply curve, a change in something other than price causes the entire curve to shift.

The curve *S′* lies to the right of *S*, indicating that the supply has increased.

example

An Excise Tax

Excise tax In this book, a tax that is paid directly by suppliers to the government.

One thing that could lead to a change in supply is the imposition of an **excise tax**—that is, a tax on suppliers of goods.[9] Suppose that a new tax is instituted requiring suppliers to pay 10¢ per cup of coffee sold. Suppose also that in the absence of this tax the supply of coffee in your city is given by Table A of Ex-

[9] We shall use the phrase *excise tax* to refer to a tax that is paid to the government by suppliers. As with the phrase *sales tax*, this phrase is not used the same way in all textbooks.

hibit 1–6 (which is identical to Table A of Exhibit 1–5). Let us compute the supply of coffee in your city after the tax takes effect.

Visit the Federation of Tax Administrators at: http://www.taxadmin.org/fta/rate/tax_stru.html

Suppose first that the price of a cup of coffee is 30¢. Then a supplier gets to keep 20¢ for every cup of coffee sold (the supplier collects 30¢ and gives a dime to the tax collector). We want to know what quantity will be supplied under these circumstances. The answer is in Table A of Exhibit 1–6: When suppliers receive 20¢ per cup of coffee sold, they provide 100 cups per day.

Therefore, in a world with an excise tax, a price of 30¢ leads to a quantity supplied of 100 cups per day. This gives us the first row of our supply table for a world with an excise tax:

Price	Quantity
30¢/cup	100 cups/day

The entire new supply schedule is displayed in Table B of Exhibit 1–6.

EXERCISE 1.6 Explain how we got the entries in the last three rows of Table B in Exhibit 1–6.

Notice that both of the tables in Exhibit 1–6 list the same quantities, but that the associated prices are 10¢ higher in Table B. This means that the supply curve associated with Table B will lie a vertical distance 10¢ above the supply curve associated with Table A. The graph in Exhibit 1–6 illustrates this relationship.

Notice that the supply curve with the tax (curve S' in the exhibit) is geometrically above and to the left of the old supply curve S. This is what we have called a lower supply curve (it is lower because, for example, a price of 30¢ calls forth a quantity supplied of only 100, instead of 300).

We can summarize as follows:

An excise tax causes the supply curve to shift upward parallel to itself (to a new, *lower* supply curve) by the amount of the tax.

1.3 Equilibrium

Visit David Friedman's Internet textbook at: http://www.best.com/~ddfr/Academic/Price_Theory/PThy_Chapter_7/PThy_Chapter_7.html

The language of demand and supply curves enables us to express how buyers and sellers would like to behave in response to various hypothetical prices. We have said nothing about what prices these buyers and sellers will actually face, or whether they will be able to trade their desired quantities at those prices. Demanders cannot purchase more coffee than suppliers are willing to sell them, and suppliers cannot sell more coffee than demanders are willing to buy. In this section we will examine the interaction between suppliers and demanders and the way in which this interaction determines both the prices and the quantities of goods traded in the marketplace.

Exhibit 1-6 Effect of an Excise Tax

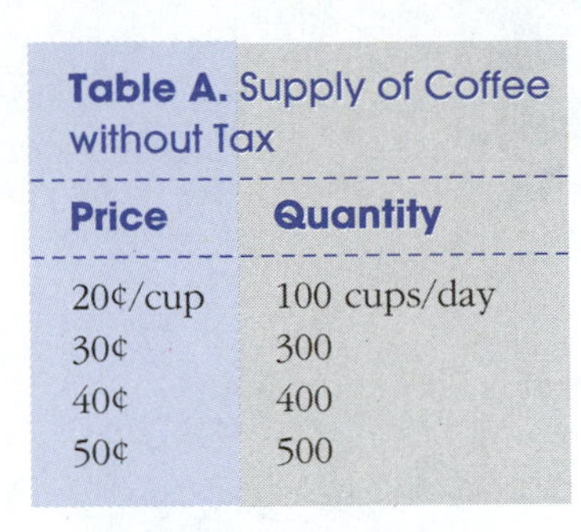

Table A. Supply of Coffee without Tax

Price	Quantity
20¢/cup	100 cups/day
30¢	300
40¢	400
50¢	500

Table B. Supply of Coffee with Excise Tax of 10¢ per Cup

Price	Quantity
30¢/cup	100 cups/day
40¢	300
50¢	400
60¢	500

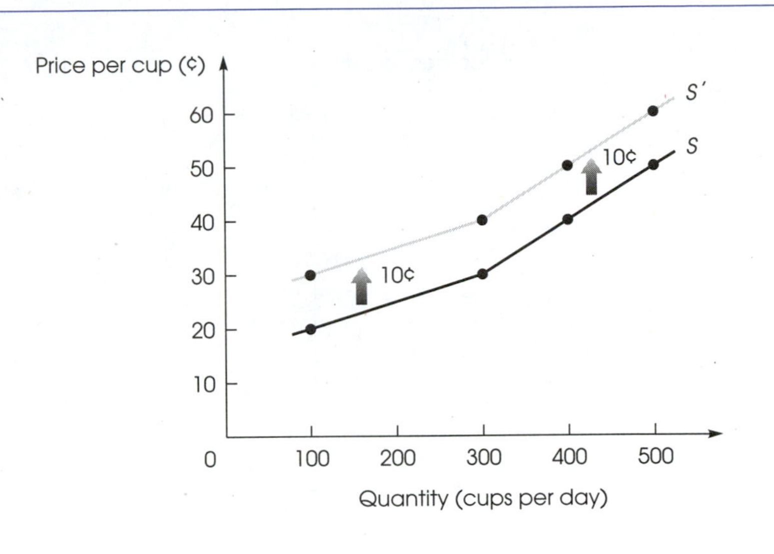

If the price of coffee is 30¢ per cup and there is an excise tax of 10¢, then a seller of coffee will actually get to keep 20¢ per cup sold. The original supply schedule (Table A) shows that under these circumstances suppliers would provide 100 cups per day. This is recorded in the first row of Table B. The other rows in that table are generated in a similar manner.

The rows of Table B contain the same quantities as the rows of Table A, but the corresponding prices are all 10¢ higher. Thus, each point on the new supply curve S' lies exactly 10¢ above a corresponding point on the old supply curve S. Therefore, S' lies exactly 10¢ above S in vertical distance. The excise tax causes the supply curve to shift upward parallel to itself a distance of 10¢.

The Point of Equilibrium

Exhibit 1–7 shows the demand and supply curves for cement in your city. We want to find the point on the graph that describes the price of cement and the quantity of cement that is sold at that price.

The first thing to notice is that there is only one price at which the quantity supplied and the quantity demanded are equal. That price is $4.50 per bag, where the quantities supplied and demanded are each equal to 300 bags per week. The corresponding point on the graph is called the **equilibrium point.** The equilibrium point is the point at which the supply and demand curves cross.

Equilibrium point The point where the supply and demand curves intersect.

Exhibit 1-7 Equilibrium in the Market for Cement

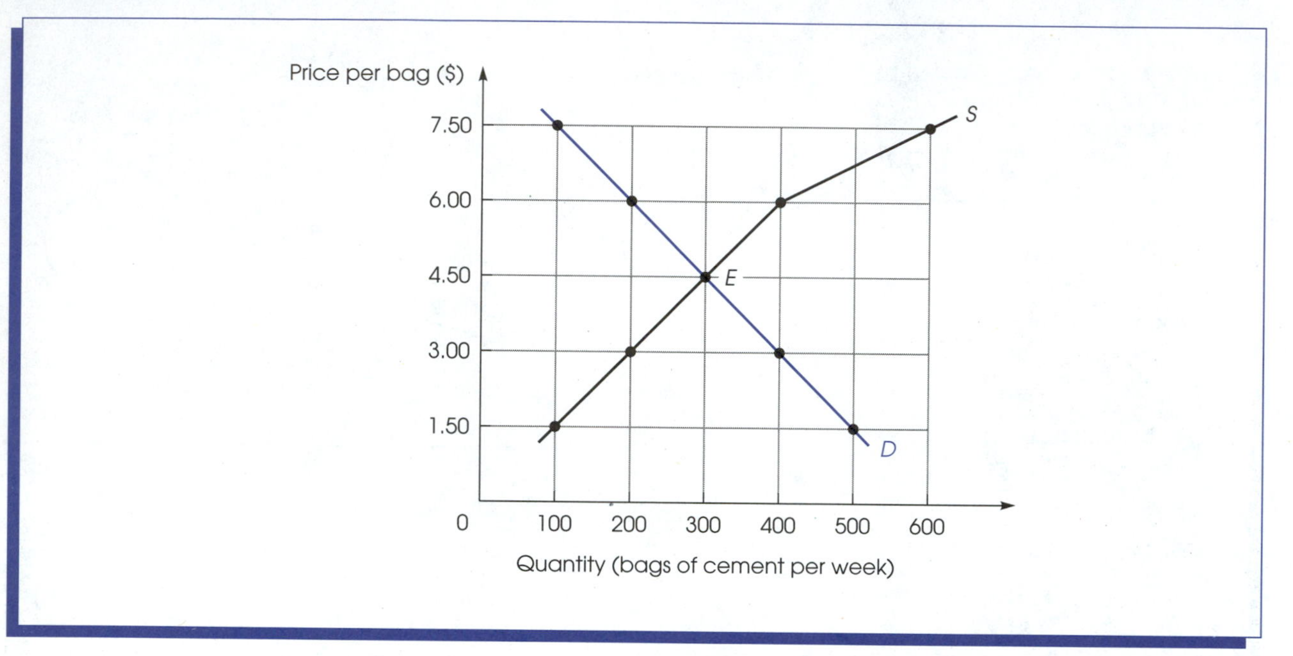

The graph shows the supply and demand curves for cement. The equilibrium point, *E,* is located at the intersection of the two curves. The equilibrium price, $4.50 per bag, is the only price at which quantity supplied and quantity demanded are equal.

To understand the significance of the equilibrium point, we will first imagine what would happen if the market were not at the equilibrium—that is, if the price were something other than $4.50.

Suppose, for example, that the price is $7.50. We see from the demand curve that all demanders taken together want a total of 100 bags of cement each week, while suppliers want to provide 600 bags of cement. The demanders purchase the 100 bags that they want and refuse to buy any more. At least some of the suppliers are not able to sell all of the cement that they want to. Those suppliers are unhappy.

Of course, some demanders may be unhappy too. They may be unhappy because the price of cement is so high. They would prefer a price of $4.50 per bag, and they would prefer even more a price of $0 per bag. But the demanders are perfectly happy in one limited sense: Given the current price of cement, they are buying precisely the quantity that they want to buy. We choose to describe this situation by saying that the demanders are **satisfied.**

Satisfied Able to behave as one wants to, taking market prices as given.

In general, a satisfied individual is one who is able to behave as he wants, taking the prices he faces as given. This is so regardless of how he feels about the prices themselves. We take this as a definition. It is the only definition that really makes sense in this context. Nobody is ever completely happy about the prices themselves: Buyers always wish they were lower and sellers always wish they were higher.

So, when the price is $7.50 per bag, the demanders buy 100 bags per week and are satisfied. The suppliers, who want to sell 600 bags per week, sell only 100 bags per week and are unsatisfied. When some suppliers discover that they cannot sell as much cement as they would like at the going price, they lower their prices to attract more demanders.

Suppose that they lower their prices to $6 per bag. Referring again to Exhibit 1–7, we see that demanders want to buy 200 bags of cement per week and suppliers want to sell 400 bags. After 200 bags are sold, the demanders go home satisfied, and some suppliers are still left unsatisfied. They lower their prices further.

We may expect this process to continue as long as the quantity supplied exceeds the quantity demanded. That is, we expect it to continue until the market reaches the equilibrium price of $4.50 per bag.

If the price of cement starts out below $4.50, we can expect the same process to work in reverse. For example, when the price is $1.50, demanders want to buy 500 bags of cement per week, but suppliers want to provide only 100 bags. The suppliers, having provided 100 bags, will go home, leaving some demanders unsatisfied. In order to lure the suppliers back to the marketplace, demanders will offer a higher price for cement. This process will continue until the quantity demanded no longer exceeds the quantity supplied. It will continue until the market reaches the equilibrium price of $4.50 per bag.

The story we have just told gives a reason to expect the market to be in equilibrium. The reason is that if the market were not in equilibrium, buyers and sellers would change their behavior in ways that would cause the market to move toward equilibrium. We still have to ask how realistic our story is. Later in this book we will see that there are some markets for which it is substantially accurate, and other markets for which it may not be accurate at all. For the time being, we will focus on the first type of market. That is, for the remainder of this chapter we will assume that the markets we are studying are always in equilibrium. For a wide range of economic problems, this is a safe and useful assumption to make.

Changes in the Equilibrium Point

Suppose there is an increase in the cost of feed corn for pigs. What happens to the price and quantity of pork chops?

Here is a *wrong* way to approach this question. First, farmers respond to the cost increase by raising fewer pigs. This means that there are fewer pork chops in the supermarkets, so demanders bid their price up. Next the rise in price induces farmers to raise *more* pigs. This in turn causes the price to be bid back down, whereupon farmers cut back their production again, whereupon....

The problem with this kind of approach is that it never reaches a conclusion. Each step in the analysis is correct, but there are infinitely many steps, and it takes forever to consider them one at a time. Therefore we need a device that accounts for all of the steps in the argument simultaneously.

Consequently, and perhaps paradoxically, when you want to figure out how a change in circumstances affects price and quantity, you should never begin by thinking about price and quantity. Instead, think about how the change in circumstances affects the demand curve and how it affects the supply curve (these are two separate questions). Imbedded in the supply and demand shifts are all of the infinitely many responses and counter-responses that we failed to completely list above. Once you have shifted the curves, you can see what happens to the equilibrium point.

So let's try the same problem again. First, when there is an increase in the cost of feed corn, what happens to the *demand* for pork chops? The answer is nothing; changes in the cost of feed corn have no effect at all on the number of pork chops that a demander wants to buy at a given price. To convince yourself of this, imagine entering a supermarket where pork chops are on sale for $8 a pound and trying to decide how many pounds you want to buy. In that situation, it is unlikely that you feel compelled to inquire how much it cost to feed the pigs before you can make your decision. That cost is quite irrelevant to you as a demander.

On the other hand, the *supply* of pork chops shifts to the left. Suppliers do care about the cost of feed corn, and are willing to produce fewer pork chops at a given price when that cost goes up.

If we plot the demand and supply for pork chops on the same graph, then demand stays fixed while supply shifts to the left, as illustrated in the last panel of Exhibit 1–8. The new equilibrium point lies above and to the left of the old one. Thus the price of pork chops is up, and the quantity is down.

Because the equilibrium price and quantity are determined by the supply and demand curves, anything that affects the curves will affect the equilibrium price and quantity. The panels of Exhibit 1–8 show a variety of ways in which changes in demand or supply can affect the point of equilibrium.

EXERCISE I.7 Taking the panels of Exhibit 1–8 to represent the market for pork chops, which panel shows the effect of a rise in the price of beef? How does a rise in the price of beef affect the equilibrium price and quantity of pork chops?

Keep in mind that *the only way that anything can affect the equilibrium price and quantity is by causing a shift in either the supply curve or the demand curve (or both)*. That is why any analysis of a change in equilibrium must begin with the question of how the curves have shifted.

It is important to distinguish causes from effects. For an individual demander or supplier, the price is taken as given and determines the quantity demanded or supplied. For the market as a whole, the demand and supply curves determine both price and quantity simultaneously.

The Nature of Equilibrium: Some Common Mistakes

A standard reference work on the taming and training of parrots reports that "when popular demand for a species exceeds the available supply, prices remain high."[10] A barrage of news reports warns that a frost in Florida could lead

[10] E. J. Maluka, *Taming and Training Parrots* (T. F. H. Publications Inc., 1981).

Exhibit 1-8 The Effects of Supply and Demand Shifts

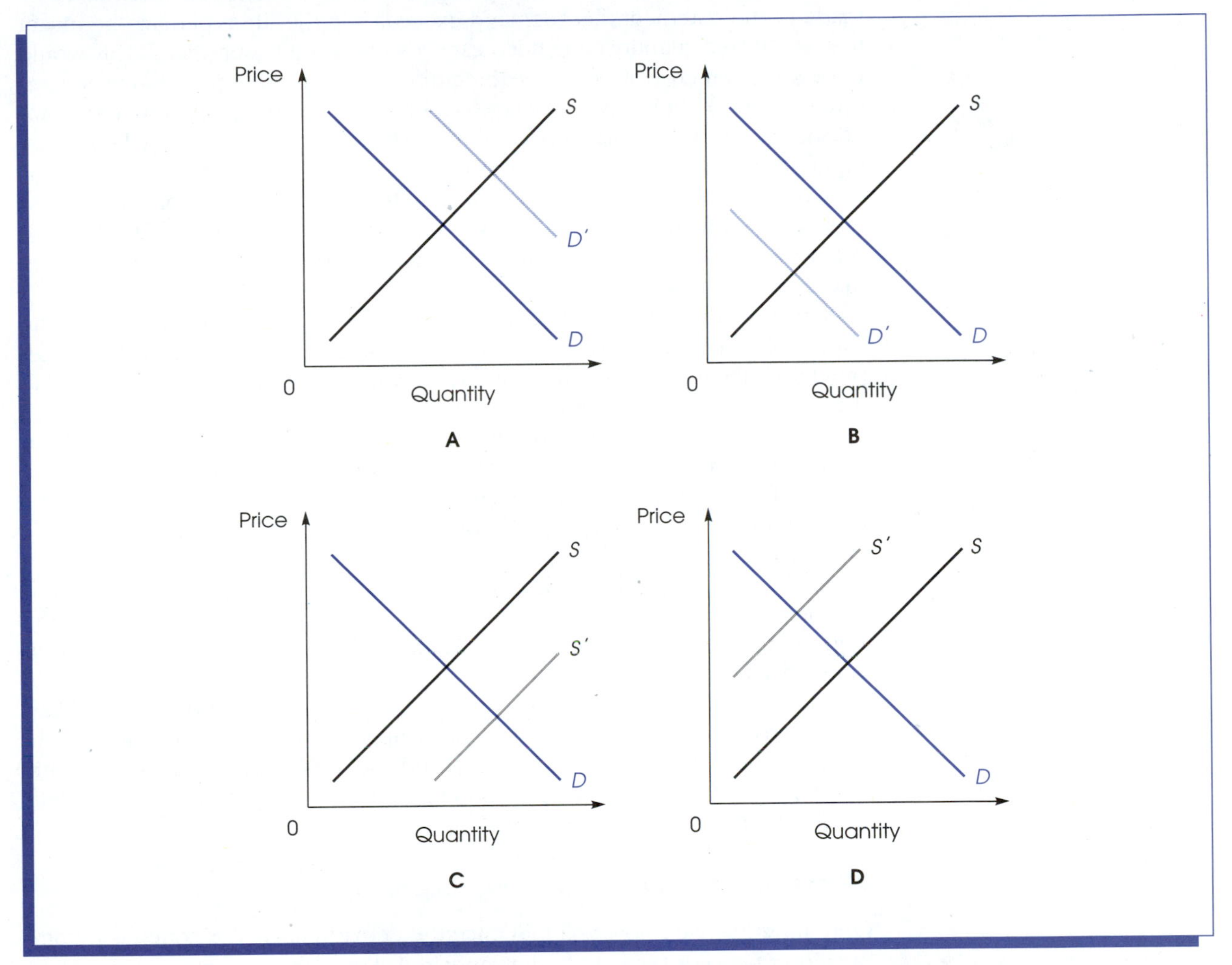

The graphs show the effects of various shifts in demand and supply. For example, in panel A we see that a rise in demand leads to a rise in price and a rise in quantity.

to a "shortage" of oranges, with people unable to buy as many as they want. The well-known columnist Michael Kinsley, explaining the market for art, reports in the *New Republic* that "when the price of something goes up, the supply of it increases." Columnist Jack Mabley of the *Chicago Tribune* reports that "General Motors just increased prices another 2.5%" even after a "bad year," and concludes that "if the law of supply and demand were working, GM would reduce prices, not raise them."

Like most people, these writers might benefit from a course in economics. Statements like "demand exceeds supply" make no sense, because demand and supply are not numbers but curves. A glance back at Exhibit 1–7 will remind you that there are always some prices (such as $1.50 in the exhibit) at which the quantity demanded exceeds the quantity supplied, and others (such as $7.50) at which the quantity supplied exceeds the quantity demanded.

What, then, does the parrot expert mean to say? If there is no sense to be made of the statement that "demand exceeds supply," then perhaps he meant to say that "the quantity demanded exceeds the quantity supplied." This would have the advantage of being meaningful (a number *can,* after all, exceed another number) but the disadvantage of being wrong. In equilibrium, the quantities supplied and demanded are equal. This is so regardless of whether the equilibrium price is high, low, or in between.

When the demand curve for parrots shifts rightward (as in panel A of Exhibit 1–8), or when the supply curve shifts leftward (as in panel D), then the price rises to a new equilibrium at which the quantities supplied and demanded again coincide.

Similarly, a frost in the Florida orange groves causes a leftward shift in the supply of oranges and a new, higher equilibrium price at which demanders can purchase all the oranges they want. (They will want fewer than they wanted at the old price.) No shortage need occur.

Michael Kinsley's analysis of the art market is wrong because a change in price causes a change in the quantity supplied, not in the supply. But we can go further and ask what causes the change in price. The answer: The price change itself must be caused by either a change in supply or a change in demand.

Finally, let us examine Jack Mabley's analysis of the rising price of cars. If we interpret Mabley's report of a "bad year" to mean that fewer cars are being sold, then by examining the possibilities in Exhibit 1–8 we can see that either demand has fallen (as in panel B of the exhibit) or supply has fallen (as in panel D). In the first case, the price falls, while in the second it rises. Since Mabley reports that the price has risen, the supply curve must have shifted as in panel D. A simultaneous fall in quantity and rise in price is nothing so dramatic as a failure of the "law of supply and demand"; it is simply evidence of a leftward shift in supply.

Effect of a Sales Tax

One thing that we know will influence the demand curve for coffee is the imposition of a sales tax paid by demanders. Let's see how such a tax would affect the equilibrium.

Exhibit 1–9 shows the market for lettuce before and after the imposition of a sales tax of 5¢ per head. The curve labeled D is the original demand curve, and the one labeled D' is the demand curve after the tax is imposed. Recall from our discussion of sales taxes in Section 1.1 that D' lies a vertical distance 5¢ below D.

Prior to the imposition of the tax, the market is in equilibrium at point E. When the sales tax is imposed, the downward shift in demand moves the equilibrium to point F. How does point F compare with point E? The first thing to notice is that it is to the left of point E. It corresponds to a smaller quantity than point E does. This gives our first conclusion:

Imposing a sales tax reduces the equilibrium quantity.

Exhibit 1-9 The Effect of a Sales Tax in the Lettuce Market

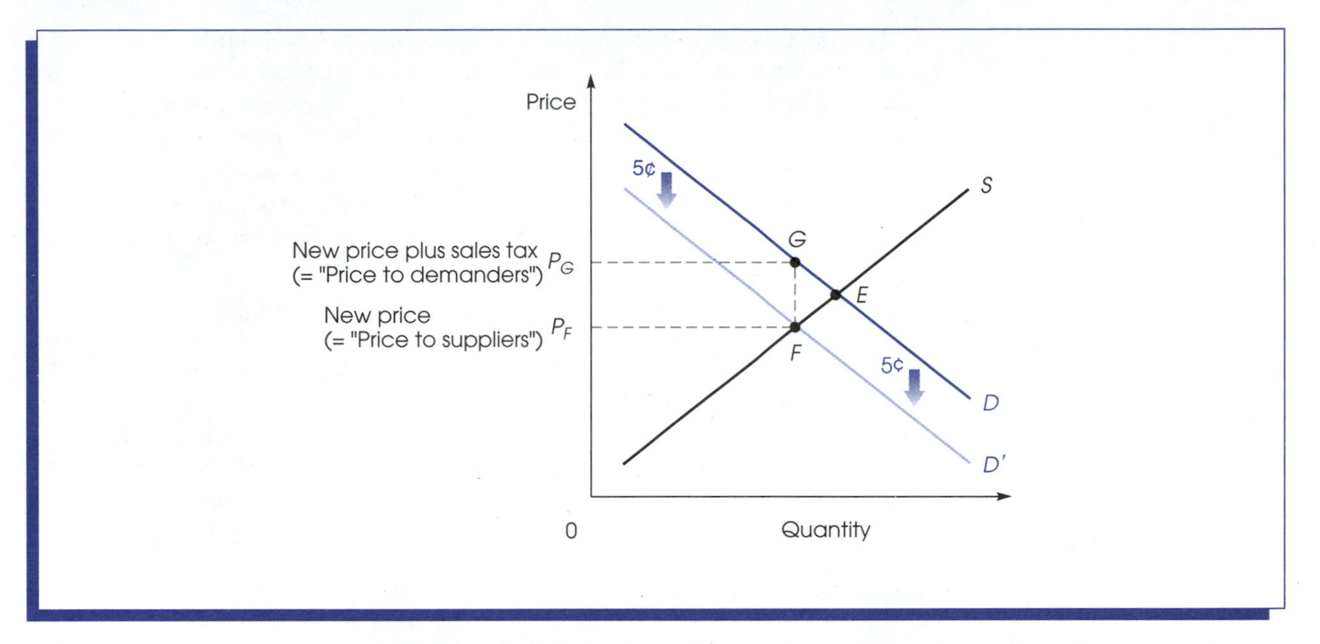

The graph shows the market for lettuce before and after the imposition of a sales tax of 5¢ per head. The original demand curve *(D)* intersects the supply curve at *E*, which is the point of equilibrium before the tax. When the tax is instituted, the demand curve moves down vertically a distance 5¢, to *D′*. The new equilibrium point is *F*, and the new equilibrium price for lettuce is P_F. However, demanders must pay more than P_F for a head of lettuce—they must pay P_F plus 5¢ tax. Thus, to buy a head of lettuce consumers must pay P_F *plus* the 5¢ sales tax. To find this amount, begin at *F* and move up a distance 5¢ to *G*. Since *F* is on the curve *D′*, *G* must be on the curve *D*. The price to demanders is—that is, the price plus the sales tax—is P_G.

What about the equilibrium price? We can see immediately from the diagram that point *F* is lower than point *E*. In other words, imposing a sales tax causes the equilibrium price to fall. We can even say something about how far the equilibrium price will fall. You should be able to see from the graph in Exhibit 1–9 that the vertical drop from point *E* to point *F* is smaller than the vertical distance between the old and the new demand curves. In other words, it is a drop of less than 5¢. (The vertical distance from point *G* to point *F* is 5¢, and the vertical distance from point *E* to point *F* is clearly less than this.) In other words:

A sales tax of 5¢ per item causes the equilibrium price to fall by some amount less than 5¢ per item.

The exact amount of the fall in price depends on the exact shapes of the supply and demand curves, but it is always somewhere between 0¢ and 5¢.

EXERCISE 1.8 Draw some diagrams in which either the demand or the supply curve is either unusually steep or unusually flat. In which cases will a 5¢ sales tax cause the price to drop very little? In which cases will the tax cause the price to drop by nearly 5¢?

The price P_F shown in Exhibit 1–9 is the new price of lettuce. However, a consumer wishing to acquire a head of lettuce must pay more than P_F. He must pay P_F plus 5¢ tax. To find this amount, we must look for a point 5¢ higher than point *F*. Because point *F* is on the new demand curve *D′*, a point 5¢ higher than *F* will be on the old demand curve *D*. (This is because the vertical distance between the demand curves is exactly 5¢.) That point has been labeled *G* in the exhibit. The full amount that the consumer must pay to get a head of lettuce is the corresponding price P_G.

Let us summarize: By shifting the equilibrium from point *E* to point *F*, a sales tax of 5¢ per head lowers the quantity sold. It lowers the price that sellers collect from the original equilibrium price P_E to P_F. It raises the amount that demanders pay from P_E to P_G.

In the exhibit, we have called the new price P_F the *price to suppliers*, because P_F is the only "price" that suppliers care about. We have called the amount P_G—the new price plus sales tax—the *price to demanders*, because this is the amount that demanders must pay to get a head of lettuce.

Effect of an Excise Tax

Now that we have analyzed the effect of a sales tax, let us turn to a different problem: the effect of a 5¢ excise tax. This effect is illustrated in panel B of Exhibit 1–10. The sales tax has disappeared now, so the demand curve has returned to its original position. However, as we discovered in Section 1.2, the 5¢ excise tax will shift the supply curve by a vertical distance 5¢. The new supply curve is labeled *S′* in panel B. With the excise tax, the new market equilibrium is at point *H*. The quantity traded has fallen, and the price has risen by an amount less than 5¢.

EXERCISE 1.9 How do we know that the price rise is less than 5¢?

In everyday language, this situation is described by saying that the suppliers have "passed on" part of the excise tax to consumers through the rise in the market price of lettuce. This is analogous to the situation brought on by the sales tax: In that case, demanders "passed on" a portion of the tax to producers through the fall in the market price of coffee.

Referring again to panel B of Exhibit 1–10, the market price has risen to P_H, and that is the price that demanders pay for a head of lettuce. But a supplier who sells a head of lettuce does not get to keep P_H—he can keep only P_H minus the 5¢ that goes to the tax collector. In order to find the amount that the supplier gets to keep, we must drop a vertical distance 5¢ below point *H*. Because point *H* is on the curve *S′*, this vertical drop will land us on the curve *S* at the point marked *J*. This gives a *price to suppliers* of P_J, below the original equilibrium price that was given by point *E*.

Exhibit 1-10 A Sales Tax versus an Excise Tax

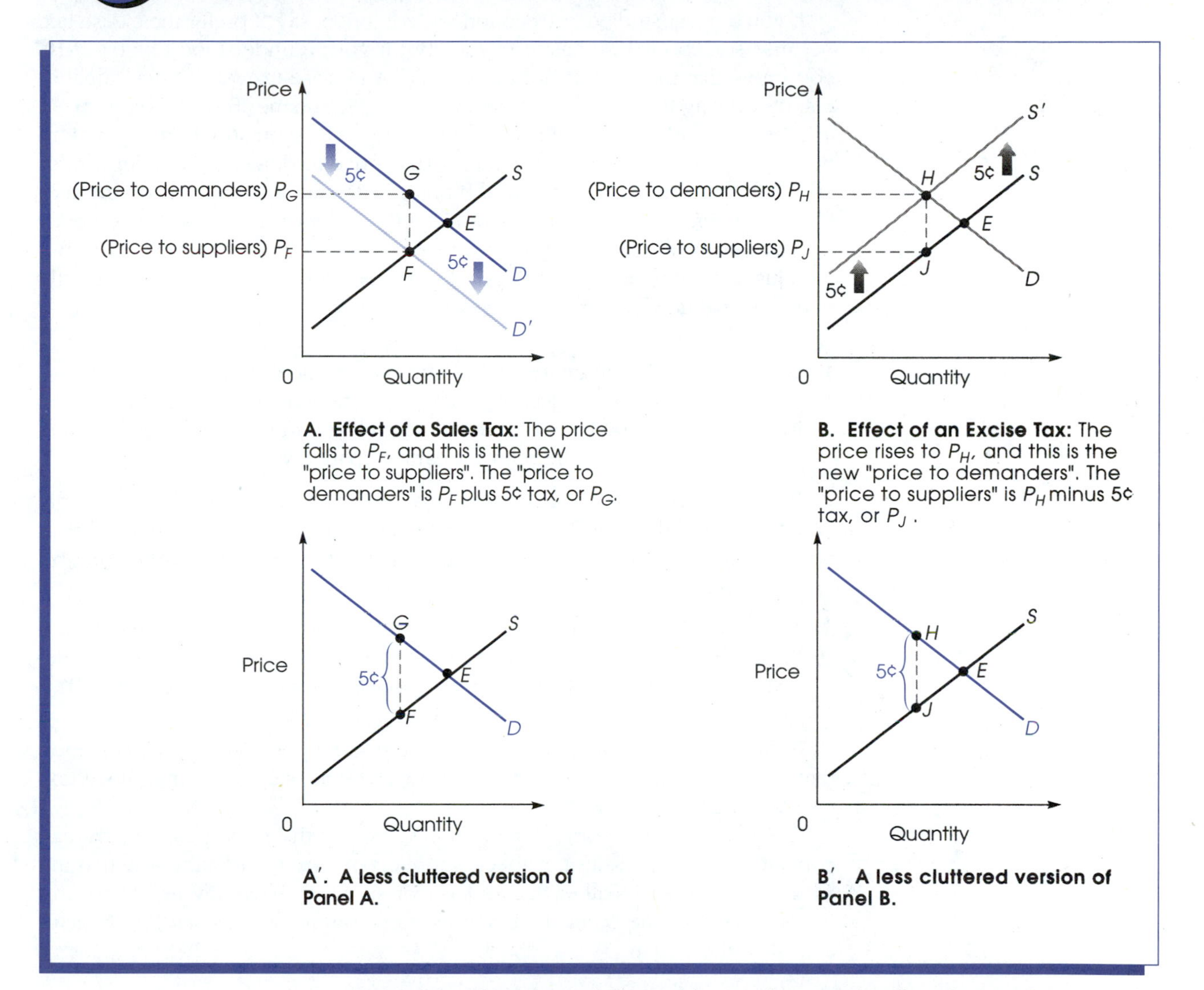

Panel A reproduces the graph from Exhibit 1–9, illustrating the effect of a 5¢ excise tax. Panel B illustrates the effect of a 5¢ excise tax: The supply curve shifts upward a vertical distance 5¢, leading to a new market equilibrium at point *H*. The corresponding price, P_H, is what demanders have to pay; the amount that suppliers get to keep is P_H *minus* 5¢, which is P_J. (Because *H* is on the curve *S′*, *J* must be on the curve *S*.)

Panels A′ and B′ are less cluttered versions of panels A and B. In each of these panels, we see two darkened points, one on the original demand curve *D* and one on the original supply curve *S*, separated by a vertical distance 5¢. There is only one possible location for such a pair of points.

It follows that points *G* and *F* in panel A′ (or panel A) are identical with points *H* and *J* in panel B′ (or panel B). In other words, the effects of the excise tax are identical with the effects of the sales tax, from the viewpoint of either demanders or suppliers.

Comparing Two Taxes

Suppose you're a demander of lettuce. Would you rather live in a world with a 5¢ sales tax or a world with a 5¢ excise tax?

If you'd never studied any economics, you might say "I prefer the excise tax, because somebody else has to pay it." But if you've understood Exhibit 1–10, you know that the issue is not that simple. An excise tax *does* affect demanders, by causing the price of lettuce to rise (to P_H in panel B of the exhibit).

So when you're asked which tax you prefer, what you should really seek to do is compare the price P_G in panel A (the price to demanders under a sales tax) with the price P_H in panel B (the price to demanders under an excise tax). If P_G is higher, the sales tax is worse and if P_H is higher, the excise tax is worse.

Based on what we've said so far, there's no way to decide this question. But with just a bit more analysis, we can discover that in fact P_G and P_H are exactly equal! All we need is three observations:

1. Point *G* is on the original demand curve *D*, point *F* is on the original supply curve *S*, and the vertical distance between them is 5¢. (You can see this in panel A, and you can see it even more clearly in the less cluttered panel A′, which reproduces the relevant parts of panel A.)
2. Point *H* is on the original demand curve *D*, point *J* is on the original supply curve *S*, and the vertical distance between them is 5¢. (You can see this in panel B, and you can see it even more clearly in the less cluttered panel B′, which reproduces the relevant parts of panel B.)
3. There is only one place to the left of *E* where the vertical distance between the curves *D* and *S* is exactly 5¢. This means that points *G* and *F* in panel A′ must occupy exactly the same positions as points *H* and *J* in panel B′.

Because points *G* and *H* are in exactly the same position, we can conclude that the 5¢ sales tax affects demanders in exactly the same way that the 5¢ excise tax does.

Likewise, because points *F* and *J* are in exactly the same position, we can conclude that the 5¢ sales tax affects suppliers in exactly the same way that the 5¢ excise tax does. Neither demanders nor suppliers have any reason to prefer one tax over the other. Economists often summarize this startling conclusion with the slogan:

The economic incidence of a tax is independent of its legal incidence.

Economic incidence The division of a tax burden according to who actually pays the tax.

Legal incidence The division of a tax burden according to who is required under the law to pay the tax.

In this statement, the **economic incidence** of a tax refers to the distribution of the actual tax burden. The **legal incidence** of the tax is the distribution of the tax burden in legal theory. The sales tax places the legal incidence entirely on demanders, because it is they who are required by law to pay the tax. The excise tax places the legal incidence entirely on suppliers. However, the economic incidence of the sales tax and the economic incidence of the excise tax are the same, because the actual prices paid by suppliers and demanders are the same in both cases.

Students sometimes misunderstand the conclusion we have drawn by thinking that the sales tax (or the excise tax) imposes equal burdens on demanders and suppliers. This is not correct. The division of the tax burden depends on the shapes of the supply and demand curves. In Exhibit 1-10, point *F* might be 4¢ below the original equilibrium *(E)* and point *G* 1¢ above the original equilibrium; in this case, 4/5 of the tax is being passed on to suppliers and 1/5 is being paid by demanders. With differently shaped curves, the suppliers might be paying 1/5 and the demanders 4/5. What we have argued is that the division of the tax burden will be the same under an excise tax as it is under a sales tax. If suppliers pay 4/5 of the sales tax, they will also pay 4/5 of the excise tax; if they pay 1/5 of the sales tax, they will also pay 1/5 of the excise tax.

EXERCISE 1.10 Suppose that an excise tax of 2¢ per head of lettuce and a sales tax of 3¢ per head of lettuce were simultaneously imposed. Show that the combined economic incidence of these taxes will be the same as the economic incidence of either the pure 5¢ sales tax or the pure 5¢ excise tax.

An interesting application involves Social Security taxes. We can view Social Security as a tax on hours worked. "Hours worked" are demanded by firms and supplied by their employees. A Social Security tax that is paid directly by the employees is an excise tax. One that is paid by firms is a sales tax. Whenever Social Security taxes are raised, there is a furor in the legislature about how to divide the legal incidence of the two taxes: Should they be paid entirely by employees, entirely by firms, divided equally, or divided in some other way? The analysis of this section shows that the resolution of this conflict ultimately makes not one bit of difference to anybody.

summary

The law of demand says that when the price of a good goes up, the quantity demanded goes down. For any individual or any group of individuals, and for any particular good, such as coffee, we can draw a demand curve. The demand curve shows, for each possible price, how much of the good those individuals or groups will purchase in a specified period of time. Another way to state the law of demand is: Demand curves slope downward.

A change in price leads to a change in quantity demanded, which is the same as a movement along the demand curve. A change in something other than price can lead to a change in demand, which is a shift of the demand curve itself.

One example of a change in something other than price is the imposition of a sales tax, paid directly by consumers to the government. (For purposes of drawing the demand curve, we do *not* view the tax as a form of price increase. When coffee sells for 50¢ plus 10¢ tax per cup, we say that the price is 50¢, not 60¢.) Consider the effect of a sales tax on coffee. The sales tax makes coffee less desirable at any given (pretax) price and so causes the demand curve to shift downward. In fact, we can calculate that the demand curve will shift downward by a vertical distance equal to the amount of the tax.

The law of supply says that when the price of a good goes up, the quantity supplied goes up. For any individual or any group of individuals, and for any particular good, we can draw a supply curve. The supply curve shows, for each possible price, how much of the good those individuals will provide in a specified period of time. Another way to state the law of supply is: Supply curves slope upward.

A change in price leads to a change in quantity supplied, which is the same as a movement along the supply curve. A change in something other than price can lead to a change in supply, which is a shift of the supply curve itself.

One example of a change in something other than price is the imposition of an excise tax, paid directly by suppliers to the government. Consider the effect of an excise tax on coffee. The excise tax makes providing coffee less desirable at any given price and so causes the supply curve to shift leftward. (The resulting curve is called a lower supply curve, because it has shifted leftward. Geometrically, it lies above and to the left of the original supply curve.) In fact, we can calculate that the supply curve will shift upward by a vertical distance equal to the amount of the tax.

The equilibrium point is the point at which the supply and demand curves intersect. The corresponding equilibrium price is the only price at which the quantity supplied is equal to the quantity demanded. Therefore, it is reasonable to expect that this will be the price prevailing in the market. We make the assumption that this is indeed the case. Later in the book, we will discover that there are many circumstances in which this assumption is well warranted.

Because the point of equilibrium is determined by the supply and demand curves, it can change only if either the supply or the demand curve changes. To see how a change in circumstances affects market prices and quantities, we first decide how it affects the supply and demand curves and then see where the equilibrium point has moved.

As an example, we can examine the effects of a sales tax on coffee. The sales tax causes the demand curve to shift down by the amount of the tax. This leads to a reduction in quantity and a reduction in the market price. The market price is reduced by less than the amount of the tax. To acquire a cup of coffee, a demander must now pay the new market price plus tax; this adds up to a new posttax *price to demanders* that is higher than the old equilibrium price.

Another example is the effect of an excise tax on coffee. This shifts the supply curve to the left (vertically, it shifts it up by the amount of the tax), leading to a smaller quantity and an increase in the market price. The market price goes up by less than the amount of the tax. When a supplier sells a cup of coffee, he earns the market price minus the amount of the tax; this leaves him with a new posttax *price to suppliers* that is less than the old equilibrium price.

The sales and excise taxes both reduce quantity, reduce the posttax price to suppliers, and raise the posttax price to demanders. A simple geometric argument shows that the magnitudes of these effects are all the same regardless of whether the tax is legally imposed on demanders or on suppliers. We summarize this by saying that the economic incidence of a tax is independent of its legal incidence. For example, an increase in the Social Security tax will affect both employers and employees in exactly the same way regardless of whether the employers or the employees are required to pay the tax.

Review Questions

R1. What can cause a movement along the demand curve? What can cause the demand curve itself to shift? Which of these is a change in demand and which is a change in quantity demanded?

R2. Explain why a sales tax of $100 per automobile would cause the demand curve for automobiles to shift down a vertical distance $100. Explain why an excise tax of $100 per automobile would cause the supply curve to shift up a vertical distance $100.

R3. How are the equilibrium price and quantity of compact discs affected by a rise in demand? A fall in demand? A rise in supply? A fall in supply? Give examples of possible causes for rises and falls in the supply and demand for compact discs.

R4. Explain what is meant by the statement "The economic incidence of a tax is independent of its legal incidence." Explain the geometric argument that leads to this conclusion.

Numerical Exercises

N1. Suppose that the demand curve for oranges is given by the equation

$$Q = -200 \cdot P + 1{,}000$$

with quantity *(Q)* measured in oranges per day and price *(P)* measured in dollars per orange. The supply curve is given by

$$Q = 800 \cdot P$$

Compute the equilibrium price and quantity of oranges.

N2. Suppose that an excise tax of 50¢ apiece is imposed on oranges. If the original supply and demand curves are as in Exercise N1, what are the equations for the new supply and demand curves? What is the new equilibrium price and quantity of oranges? What is the new posttax price from the supplier's point of view? Illustrate your answer by drawing supply and demand curves.

N3. Repeat Exercise N2 for a 50¢ sales tax instead of a 50¢ excise tax.

N4. Suppose that an excise tax of 20¢ apiece and a sales tax of 30¢ apiece are imposed simultaneously. Answer again all of the questions in Exercise N2.

Problem Set

1. **True or False** If a law were passed requiring all cars sold in the United States to get at least 40 miles per gallon of gasoline, then Americans would surely use less gasoline.
2. **True or False** The discovery of a new method of birth control that is safer, cheaper, more effective, and easier to use than any other method would reduce the number of unwanted pregnancies.

3. Can you think of some other "goods," such as murder and reckless driving, that are not traded in the traditional economic marketplace but for which people nevertheless have demand curves? For each of these goods, what would it mean for the demand curve to be unusually steep? Unusually flat?

4. True or False A sharp rise in the price of oranges would be unlikely to last very long; after all, the rise in price would lead to a fall in demand, and this fall in demand would then cause the price to fall.

5. Suppose that the enrollment at your university unexpectedly declines. True or False: Apartment owners in the area will face higher vacancy rates and might raise their rents to compensate.

6. A socially conscious student has decided to reduce his meat consumption by one pound per week. True or False: That way, there will be one more pound of meat each week for somebody else to eat.

7. Nosmo King is an anti-smoking crusader who finds that people who don't recognize him sometimes offer him a cigarette. He always takes the cigarette and throws it away. This happens ten times a year, and Nosmo figures that this way there are ten fewer cigarettes for other people to smoke.

   a. How does Nosmo's policy affect the demand and supply curves for cigarettes?

   b. How does Nosmo's policy affect the equilibrium quantity of cigarettes?

   c. Is Nosmo correct in believing that he reduces the number of cigarettes that other people smoke? Is he correct in believing that he reduces it by ten per year? How do you know?

8. The following item appeared in a major daily newspaper:

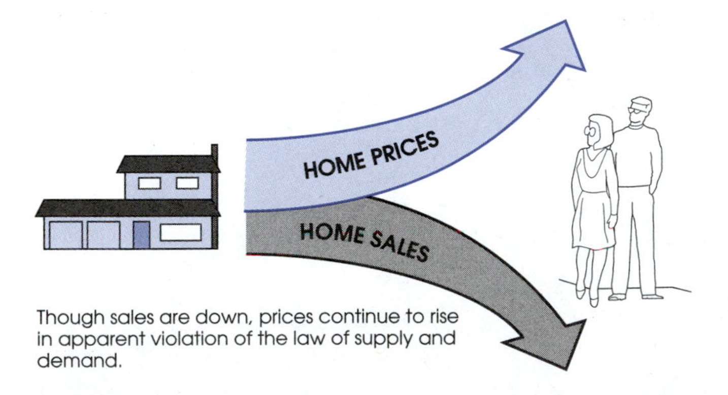

Does this observation in fact violate the laws of supply and demand?

9. True or False If we observe more ice cream being purchased this year than last year, then we may conclude that the demand has risen and the price must rise.

10. The demand and supply for catnip are given by the following tables:

Demand	
Price	**Quantity**
$.50/lb.	10 lb.
1.00	9
1.50	8
2.00	7
2.50	6
3.00	5

Supply	
Price	**Quantity**
$.50/lb.	3 lb.
1.00	4
1.50	5
2.00	7
2.50	9
3.00	10

What quantity is sold in equilibrium, and at what price?

11. **a.** Suppose in problem 10 that a sales tax of $1.50 per pound is imposed on catnip. What is the new market price of catnip? What price do demanders actually pay? What is the new equilibrium quantity?

b. Suppose instead that an excise tax of $1.50 per pound is imposed on catnip. What is the new market price of catnip? What price do suppliers actually collect? What is the new equilibrium quantity?

c. As a consumer of catnip, would you prefer to live in a world with a sales tax or with an excise tax? How about if you were a supplier of catnip?

12. In each of the following circumstances, what would happen to the price and the quantity consumed of corn?

a. The price of wheat goes up.

b. The price of fertilizer goes up.

c. An epidemic wipes out half the population.

d. The wages of industrial workers go up.

13. How would each of the following circumstances affect the price and quantity of beef sold?

a. The price of chicken falls.

b. The price of grazing land falls.

c. There is a report that beef consumption increases longevity.

d. Average incomes rise.

e. The price of leather, which is produced from the hides of beef cattle after they are slaughtered, rises.

14. True or False: Suppliers' ability to pass on an excise tax to demanders depends on the strength of demand. If the demand curve is very high, a large percentage of the excise tax will be passed on; whereas if demand is very low, suppliers will have to pay most of the tax themselves.

15. True or False: If the demand curve for avocados is perfectly vertical, then an excise tax on avocados would be entirely passed on to consumers.

16. Suppose that the supply curve for wheat is perfectly horizontal. How will a sales tax on wheat affect the market price? What about an excise tax?

17. At a price of $10,000 apiece, Japanese producers are willing to sell any quantity of compact cars that Americans want to buy. True or False: An excise tax on Toyotas sold in the United States would be paid entirely by Americans.

18. Upper Slobbovians smoke 10 million cigarettes per year; so do Lower Slobbovians. To discourage smoking, each country imposes an excise tax of 50 cents per pack. As a result, the price of cigarettes rises by 35 cents per pack in Upper Slobbovia, but by only 15 cents per pack in Lower Slobbovia. True or False: The Upper Slobbovian excise tax discourages smoking more effectively (that is, it leads to a bigger decrease in smoking) than the Lower Slobbovian excise tax. *Answer on the assumption that the supply curves for cigarettes are identical in both countries.* Justify your answer.

19. Suppose that donuts sell for 50 cents apiece. Now a sales tax of 20 cents per donut is imposed, and the market price of donuts falls to 35 cents apiece. Now the sales tax is eliminated, and in its place an excise tax of 20 cents per donut is imposed. What can you say about the new price of donuts?

20. Suppose that the government wants to increase Social Security taxes by $1 per hour of work, and is undecided between increasing the tax on workers and increasing the tax on employers. According to the last sentence of this chapter, "the resolution of this conflict ultimately makes not one bit of difference to anybody."

- **a.** Explain the *meaning* of the quoted sentence, in terms that could be understood by a person who had never taken an economics course.
- **b.** Use graphs to explain why the quoted sentence must be true, in terms that could be understood by your fellow students.

21. The federal government wants to improve the fortunes of domestic car manufacturers and is considering two plans to accomplish this. Under Plan A, every purchaser of a domestic car would receive a $100 rebate from the government. Under Plan B, the car manufacturers would receive a $100 rebate from the government for every car they sell.

- **a.** How does Plan A affect the demand for cars?
- **b.** How does Plan B affect the supply of cars?
- **c.** Compare and contrast the effects of the two plans.

22. A new law is passed requiring every landlord to give each of his tenants

$10 per month. Illustrate the effects on the supply and demand curves for rental apartments.

a. What happens to the supply curve for apartments?

b. What happens to the demand curve for apartments? (*Hint:* It does *not* stay fixed.)

c. What happens to the price at which apartments are rented?

d. What happens to the quantity of apartments that are rented?

e. Who gains and who loses as a result of this law?

23. Apples currently sell for 50 cents apiece. The government is experimenting with three different plans. Plan A is to subsidize apple purchases: every time you buy an apple, you get a dime back from the government. Plan B is to subsidize apple sales: every time you *sell* an apple, you get a dime from the government. Plan C is to tax apple sales: every time you sell an apple you pay a dime to the government. When Plan A is instituted, the price of apples rises to 57 cents.

a. What would have happened to the price of apples if the government had instituted Plan B instead of Plan A? Justify your answer.

b. What would have happened to the price of apples if the government had instituted Plans A and C simultaneously instead of Plan A alone? Justify your answer.

24. Suppose that a law requires every college professor in your city to wear a special uniform while teaching. These uniforms must be rented from the mayor's brother at a cost of $1 per hour. With the law in effect, universities pay professors $5.40 an hour.

a. If the law were repealed, how much would professors get paid?

b. If the law were replaced by a new law requiring the *universities* to pay for the uniforms (at the same $1 per hour), how much would professors get paid?

For each part, your answer should be an exact number if possible, or a range of numbers otherwise. (*Hint:* Remember that professors are the *suppliers* of teaching services and universities are the *demanders*.)

25. Suppose that a new law requires every firm to provide its workers with free parking spaces. These spaces are worth $200 a year to the workers and cost the firms $500 a year to provide.

a. Show how this law affects the workers' labor supply curve, the firms' labor demand curve, and the equilibrium wage rate.

b. When the law is enacted, does the equilibrium wage rate go up or down? Does it go up or down by more or by less than $200? Does it go up or down by more or by less than $500?

c. Is this law good for firms? Is it good for workers? Explain your reasons carefully.

Note: Colored numbers indicate that the discussion of the problem appears in Appendix C.

Internet Exercise

Colorado and New Mexico charge both excise and sales taxes on distilled spirits. Using the information on the Federation of Tax Administrators' Website (http://www.taxadmin.org/fta/rate/tax_stru.html), and assuming that other demand and supply characteristics are the same, predict which side of the Colorado–New Mexico border will tend to have the higher proportion of out-of-state liquor sales.

chapter 2

Prices, Costs, and the Gains from Trade

The supply and demand curves of Chapter 1 arose from the desires of individuals to trade with one another. Suppliers offered goods to demanders in exchange for money, which they themselves presumably exchanged for other goods. We studied various aspects of those exchanges: the quantities that were traded, the prices at which those trades took place, and the ways in which these exchanges were affected by external influences such as various forms of taxation.

Our main goal in this chapter is to understand some of the reasons why people want to trade with each other in the first place. We will begin in Section 2.1 with a more precise discussion of what is meant by the term *price*. Then in Section 2.2 we will relate prices to the more general notion of costs. We will see how differences in costs create opportunities for people to gain from trade. Another source of such opportunities—differences in tastes—will be discussed in Chapter 3.

2.1 Prices

In Chapter 1 we had much to say about prices, on the assumption that everybody knows what prices are. Now it is time for a more precise discussion. In this section we will study alternative interpretations of the word *price*, and will specify exactly what is meant by the concept of price in microeconomics.

Absolute versus Relative Prices

Imagine a world without money. In such a world, people would still trade, and it would make perfectly good sense to talk about prices. For example, if you gave your neighbor 2 loaves of bread in exchange for 1 bottle of wine, we would say that the price you paid for the wine was 2 loaves of bread per bottle. At the same time, we would say that your neighbor had purchased 2 loaves of bread at the price of ½ bottle of wine per loaf.

In the real world we use money to make purchases. Consequently, we usually measure the price of wine in terms of dollars rather than in terms of loaves of bread. However, it is still possible to measure the price of wine in terms of bread. If bread sells for $1 per loaf and wine sells for $2 per bottle, it follows that you can exchange 2 loaves of bread for 1 bottle of wine.[1] We can still say that the price of wine is 2 loaves of bread per bottle or that the price of bread is ½ bottle of wine per loaf.

We now have two different meanings for the word *price*, and we must distinguish between them. The number of dollars necessary to purchase a bottle of wine is called the **absolute price** of the bottle, whereas the number of loaves of bread necessary to purchase a bottle of wine is called the **relative price** of wine in terms of bread. In general, the absolute price of a good is measured in dollars and the relative price of a good is measured in units of some other good.

Absolute price The number of dollars that can be exchanged for a specified quantity of a given good.

Relative price The quantity of some other good that can be exchanged for a specified quantity of a given good.

Of course, there are many different relative prices of wine. We could measure the relative price of wine in terms of chickens, the relative price of wine in terms of steel, or the relative price of wine in terms of hours of labor.

To illustrate the difference between relative and absolute prices, suppose that the absolute prices of bread and wine in two different years are given by the following table:

	1995	2000
Bread	$ 1/loaf	$ 3/loaf
Wine	$ 2/bottle	$ 6/bottle

In this example, the absolute price of wine has tripled over a five-year period. However, the relative price of wine in terms of bread has remained fixed at ½ bottle of wine per loaf. This illustrates the important point that changes in absolute prices are not the same thing as changes in relative prices.

In microeconomics, the prices that we study are relative prices. This means that the price of wine should always be measured in terms of other goods, such as bread. However, we can still use dollars to measure the relative price of wine—provided we assume that the dollar price of bread does not change. We simply must remember that the dollars in which we express the price of wine are really just stand-ins for loaves of bread.

[1] In order to do this, you might first have to sell the bread for $2 cash and then use the cash to buy the wine. But the end result is the same as if you had exchanged the bread for the wine directly.

In microeconomics the single word *price* always refers to a relative price.

Relative Prices When There Are More than Two Goods

If we imagine a world with only two goods, such as bread and wine, the *price of wine* refers to something unambiguous: namely, a certain number of loaves of bread. In the real world there are many different relative prices for wine: one in terms of bread, one in terms of chickens, and so on. We can also consider the price of wine relative to a basket containing representative quantities of all goods in the economy. Sometimes we will speak of *the* price of wine, in which case we will be referring to the price relative to that representative basket. Often we will measure this relative price in dollars, keeping in mind that the word *dollar* is being used to refer not to a piece of green paper but to a basket of goods.

Changing Prices

Suppose that in 1998 the absolute price of bread is $1 per loaf, the absolute price of wine is $2 per bottle, and that these are the only two items you consume. Now suppose that because bad weather has damaged the vineyards, you are led to expect that the price of wine will double in 1999. Because we are studying relative prices, this means that in 1999, 1 bottle of wine will trade for 4 loaves of bread rather than for the 1998 price of 2 loaves. The table in Exhibit 2–1 shows only a few of the many different absolute prices at which this could happen.

If in 1999 any of the last four columns of the table describes the prices correctly, then we will be able to say that the price of wine has doubled, just as we predicted it would. All four of these columns fit our prediction equally well. Because microeconomics is concerned only with relative prices, from our point of view there is no real difference between those columns. If you woke up tomorrow morning to discover that all absolute prices (including wages) had

Exhibit 2-1 **Absolute and Relative Price Changes in a World with Two Goods**

	1998	1999(a)	1999(b)	1999(c)	1999(d)
Bread	$1/loaf	$1/loaf	50¢/loaf	$5/loaf	25¢/loaf
Wine	$2/bottle	$4/bottle	$2/bottle	$20/bottle	$1/bottle

The table shows the absolute prices of bread and wine in 1998 and four possibilities for the absolute prices in 1999. In each of the four cases the relative price of a bottle of wine has risen from 2 loaves of bread to 4 loaves of bread. In each case we can correctly assert that "the price of wine has doubled," because in microeconomics the *price* always means *the relative price*.

doubled (or halved), the world would not really be different in any significant way.

Relative Price Changes and Inflation

Because relative prices and absolute prices are determined independently of each other, it is always misleading to attribute an absolute price change to a relative price change. It is quite common to hear that there has been inflation (a rise in the level of absolute prices) because of a rise in the price of a particular commodity such as oil, housing, or wine. But we can see from Exhibit 2–1 that a rise in the relative price of wine is equally consistent with either a rise or a fall in the absolute price level.

In fact, when the relative price of wine increases to 4 loaves of bread per bottle, what happens to the relative price of bread? It decreases, from ½ to ¼ bottle of wine per loaf. Any increase in the relative price of wine must be accompanied by a decrease in the relative price of bread.

EXERCISE 2.1 Explain why the preceding statement is true.

Inflation An ongoing rise in the average level of absolute prices.

Price indices from which inflation can be calculated are at the Economic Statistics Briefing Room Site at: http://www.whitehouse.gov/fsbr/prices.html

Inflation is an ongoing rise in the average level of absolute prices. When you hear the commentator on the nightly news program attribute the latest burst of inflation to a rise in the price of gasoline, reflect on what he means. He means that gasoline is now more expensive relative to, say, shoes than it was before. Another way to say the same thing is to state that shoes are now cheaper, relative to gasoline, than they were before. If the rise in the relative price of gasoline causes inflation, why doesn't the fall in the relative price of shoes cause deflation? In fact, relative price changes do not cause absolute price changes—and you now know more than the commentator on the nightly news.

Some Applications

The Quality of Oranges

Oranges are grown in Florida and shipped to places like New York. In which state do you suppose that people, on average, eat better oranges?[2]

Most noneconomists guess Florida. But a little understanding of relative prices leads to the surprising conclusion that the answer is New York.

To see why, suppose for simplicity that there are only two kinds of oranges: "good" oranges, which cost $1 in Florida, and "bad" oranges, which cost 50¢ there. When we speak of "bad" oranges, we don't mean to imply that these oranges are entirely undesirable, only that they are not quite so desirable—not so sweet or so juicy—as the "good" ones are.

What, then, is the relative price of a good orange in Florida? The answer is: two bad oranges. The Floridian who chooses to eat a good orange passes up the opportunity to eat two bad ones.

[2] The example in this section is adapted from A. Alchian and W. Allen, *Exchange and Production: Theory in Use* (Belmont, CA: Wadsworth, 1969).

Now let us calculate the relative price of a good orange in New York. The key observation is that it is impossible for a New Yorker to buy just an orange. What he buys, implicitly, is a combination package consisting of an orange and a train ticket to transport that orange to New York. Suppose for illustration that it costs 50¢ to transport an orange to New York. The New Yorker must pay $1.50 for a good orange ($1 for the orange and 50¢ for the transportation) and $1 for a bad orange. The relative price of a good orange in New York is only 1.5 bad oranges. A New Yorker who chooses to eat a good orange passes up the opportunity to eat just 1.5 bad ones.

Who, then, is more likely to select a good orange: the New Yorker facing a relative price of 1.5 bad oranges, or the Floridian facing a relative price of 2 bad oranges? Clearly the New Yorker, since he faces the lower relative price.

Of course the relative price of *oranges* (in terms of, say, apples) is higher in New York than in Florida, and New Yorkers will therefore buy fewer oranges than they would at Florida prices. But once the New Yorker has made the decision to consume an orange, he faces a lower relative price than the Floridian does for choosing a good orange rather than a bad one.

Because orange-eating New Yorkers are more likely to choose good oranges than their compatriots in Florida, the average quality of oranges bought in New York is higher than in Florida. Because every orange bought is an orange sold, we can express the same thing by saying that the average quality of oranges sold is higher in New York than in Florida: New York supermarkets carry better oranges, on average, than Florida supermarkets do.

2.2 Costs, Efficiency, and the Gains from Trade

In the preceding section we discussed the concept of *price*. In this section we will discuss the related concept of *cost*. Once we understand what costs are, we will be able to see how everyone can benefit when activities are carried out at the lowest possible cost. This will provide us with a powerful example of the gains from trade.

Costs and Efficiency

When you decide to spend an evening at the opera, you must forgo a number of other things. First, you pay a price, say $50, for the ticket. Of course, the money itself is valuable only insofar as you could have used it to buy something else. That "something else"—perhaps 10 movie tickets or 5 pizzas—represents some of the cost of going to the opera.

The ticket price is only part of the cost, because your evening at the opera entails many other sacrifices as well. There is the gasoline that you use to drive to the opera. There is also the time spent actually attending the performance.

That time could have been spent doing something else, and the value of that something else is also part of the cost of going to the opera.

Cost A forgone opportunity.

In summary, a **cost** is a forgone opportunity. The cost of engaging in an activity is the totality of all the opportunities that the activity requires you to forgo.

You may have heard the term *opportunity cost* used to describe such costs as the time sacrificed in attending the opera. This term is quite misleading because it implies that an "opportunity cost" is one of several types of cost. In reality, *every cost is an opportunity cost*. The dollars that you pay for the opera ticket are valuable only insofar as they represent forgone opportunities to purchase other goods. They are of exactly the same nature as the costs represented by your time and your gasoline—forgone opportunities all.

In calculating costs, it is important not to double-count. The time spent at the opera could have been used to go to the movies or to study for exams, but not both. Therefore, it would not be correct to count both the forgone movie and the forgone studying as costs. The only activities that should be counted as costs are those you would have actually engaged in if you had not gone to the opera.

How much does it cost your college to maintain a football team? The most obvious costs are those such as coaches' salaries and transportation to games. But other, less obvious costs can be equally important. What, for example, is the cost of using the football stadium? You might think it is zero if the college owns the football stadium, but this overlooks the forgone opportunity to put that land to other uses. If a developer who wants to build a shopping center would be willing to pay $500,000 for the land, then that $500,000 is part of the cost of having a team.

It is sometimes argued that we should pay higher salaries to our elected officials in order to ensure that the most talented and creative individuals run for office. This argument also overlooks an opportunity cost: If a brilliant corporate executive becomes a brilliant U.S. senator, then the nation must make do with one less brilliant corporate executive. It is not obvious that a genius can do more good as 1 of 100 U.S. senators than as the chairman of the board of General Motors. Perhaps we should *lower* Senate salaries precisely in order to avoid the cost of attracting talented people into politics!

example

The Electrician and the Carpenter

Imagine an electrician and a carpenter, each of whom wants his house rewired and his den paneled. As shown in Table A of Exhibit 2–2, the electrician requires 10 hours to rewire his house and 15 hours to panel his den. The carpenter knows how to do his own rewiring, but because he is less skilled at it than the electrician, it takes him 20 hours instead of 10. And what about paneling? The electrician can panel his den in 15 hours, so you might expect a professional carpenter to be able to do it in a shorter time. But we forgot to tell

Exhibit 2–2 The Electrician and the Carpenter

Table A			Table B		
	Electrician	*Carpenter*		*Electrician*	*Carpenter*
Rewiring	10 hours	20 hours	*Rewiring*	2/3 paneling	10/9 panelings
Paneling	15 hours	18 hours	*Paneling*	3/2 rewirings	9/10 rewiring

Table A shows the amount of time needed for the electrician and the carpenter to rewire and to panel. Notice that the electrician can complete either job in less time than the carpenter can. We express this by saying that the electrician has an absolute advantage at each task.

Table B shows the costs of rewiring and paneling jobs performed by each individual. The costs are measured in terms of forgone opportunities; thus the cost of a rewiring job must be measured in terms of paneling jobs and vice versa. All of the information in Table B can be derived from the information in Table A.

Notice that the electrician can rewire at a lower cost than the carpenter, but that the carpenter can panel at a lower cost than the electrician. We express this by saying that the electrician has a comparative advantage at rewiring, whereas the carpenter has a comparative advantage at paneling.

Suppose that each individual wants his house rewired and his den paneled. Table C below shows the total amount of time that each will have to work in order to accomplish both jobs. In the first column we assume that each does all of the work on his own house. For example, the electrician spends 10 hours rewiring and 15 hours paneling, for a total of 25 hours. In the second column, we assume that each specializes in the area of his comparative advantage: The electrician rewires both houses and the carpenter panels both dens.

It is apparent from Table C that trade makes both parties better off. In particular, the electrician can gain from trade with the carpenter, despite his absolute advantages in both areas. This illustrates the general fact that everyone can be made better off whenever each concentrates in his area of comparative advantage and then trades for the goods he wants to have.

Table C		
	Without Trade	*With Trade*
Electrician	25 hours	20 hours
Carpenter	38 hours	36 hours

you that this particular carpenter is a tad on the doltish side, and has some paralysis in his left arm to boot. As a result, paneling his den takes him 18 hours to complete. All of these numbers are summarized in Table A of Exhibit 2–2.

Because the electrician can both rewire and panel faster than the carpenter can, you might think that it is correct to say that he can perform both tasks at a lower cost than the carpenter can. But this is definitely not true. To see why not, we have to remember that costs are defined in terms of forgone opportunities. The electrician needs 10 hours to rewire his house. Alternatively, he could use that same 10 hours to complete $\frac{2}{3}$ of a 15-hour paneling job. That $\frac{2}{3}$ of a paneling job is the *cost* of his rewiring. Similarly, a paneling job costs him $\frac{3}{2}$ rewirings.

We can do the same kind of calculations for the carpenter. The results are displayed in Table B of Exhibit 2–2.

QA EXERCISE 2.2 Explain how we got the entries in the second column of Table B.

The electrician can produce a rewiring job more cheaply than the carpenter can because he rewires a house at a cost of $\frac{2}{3}$ of a paneling job, whereas the carpenter rewires at a cost of $\frac{10}{9}$ paneling jobs. We express this by saying that the electrician has a **comparative advantage** at rewiring. This simply means that he can do the job at a lower cost than the carpenter can. Another way to say the same thing is that the electrician is **more efficient** at rewiring than the carpenter is.

Comparative advantage The ability to perform a given task at a lower cost.

More efficient Able to perform a given task at lower cost; having a comparative advantage.

It is a bit more surprising, but equally true, that the carpenter is more efficient than the electrician at paneling. This statement may surprise you, since the carpenter takes 18 hours to do a paneling job that the electrician can do in 15 hours. Nevertheless, it is true. The cost to the carpenter of performing a paneling job is only $\frac{9}{10}$ of a rewiring job, whereas the cost to the electrician of performing a paneling job is $\frac{3}{2}$ rewiring jobs. This follows from our definition of cost as a forgone opportunity. The cost of paneling is not the number of hours devoted to the job, but the use to which those hours could have been put. The carpenter is therefore a more efficient paneler than the electrician. He has a comparative advantage at paneling.

Students often make statements like, "The electrician is more efficient at rewiring than he is at paneling," or "The electrician has a comparative advantage at rewiring over paneling." Such statements are not only wrong; they are without meaning. The correct statements are, "The electrician is more efficient at rewiring than the carpenter is, and less efficient at paneling than the carpenter is," and "The electrician has a comparative advantage over the carpenter at rewiring, whereas the carpenter has a comparative advantage over the electrician at paneling." The *comparative* in *comparative advantage* refers to a comparison of two individuals performing the same task, and never to a comparison of different tasks performed by the same individual.

Specialization and the Gains from Trade

Visit David Friedman's Internet textbook at: http://www.best.com/~ddfr/Academic/Price_Theory/Pthy_Chapter_6/Pthy_Chapter_6.html

We have chosen to define *efficiency* in such a way that the most efficient producer of a good is the one who produces it at the lowest cost, where costs are defined in terms of forgone opportunities. According to this definition, the carpenter is more efficient at paneling than the electrician is. Perhaps this definition strikes you as strange. Why have we chosen it? The answer is that it is the only definition of efficiency that makes the following statement true:

Everyone in society can be made better off if each specializes in the area where he is most efficient, and then trades for the goods he wants to have.

We can illustrate this with the example of the electrician and the carpenter. Suppose that each of these individuals elects to make his own home improvements. Then the electrician spends 10 hours rewiring and 15 hours paneling, for a total of 25 hours. At the same time, the carpenter spends 20 hours and 18 hours for a total of 38 hours.

Suppose, on the other hand, that each specializes in his area of comparative advantage, and that they trade services. The electrician specializes in rewiring, and does both his own house and the carpenter's. These two 10-hour jobs take him 20 hours. In exchange for this, the carpenter panels both dens. These two 18-hour jobs take him 36 hours. All of this is summarized in Table C of Exhibit 2–2.

As you can see, everybody in this society is better off when each exploits his comparative advantage by specializing in the area in which he is the more efficient producer.

When you first looked at Table A in Exhibit 2–2, you might have thought that the electrician could not possibly have anything to gain by trading with the carpenter. You might have thought that this was so because the electrician appeared to be better than the carpenter at everything. Now you know that the carpenter is actually "better" than the electrician at paneling, in the sense that he panels at a lower cost than the electrician does, giving him a comparative advantage. This is the reason that trade can be a profitable activity for both.

An individual's preferences are not sufficient (or even necessarily relevant) for determining what he should produce. The electrician wants both rewiring and paneling, but he is better off when he produces two rewirings than when he produces exactly what he wants. The same is true of groups of individuals. The people of Finland might collectively love grapefruit, but it would not be intelligent for Finland to specialize in domestic grapefruit production. The Finns can have more grapefruit by specializing in the areas of their comparative advantage (in this case, timber and timber products) and then trading for grapefruit and the other commodities they wish to consume.

The benefits of specialization and trade account for most of the material wealth that you see in the world. Wherever you go in the United States, you will find small towns of 500 or 2,000 or 3,000 people. The residents of these towns consume fresh fruit and power tools and air-conditioning and comic books and Hollywood movies and catcher's mitts and artwork. None of the towns produces such a wide variety of goods on its own. Typically, the residents of the town specialize in a few areas of comparative advantage and acquire the goods they want to have by trading with people in other towns who have specialized in other areas. If a town of 2,000 people attempted to produce its own fresh fruit and power tools and Hollywood movies, very little of anything would be accomplished. The difference between the standard of living in that imaginary isolated town and the standards of living actually observed in the United States is due entirely to the principle of comparative advantage. The enormous magnitude of that difference is almost impossible to contemplate.

example

The Middleman

One important task in society is the transfer of goods from producers to consumers. The complexity of this task is often overlooked or underestimated: Somebody has to figure out who wants which products, where these products are to be found, which producers can be relied upon to provide a certain level of quality, what is the most efficient means of transporting those goods, and the solutions to many other problems of this sort. According to the principles we have just established, everybody can benefit when this task is accomplished by specialists with an appropriate comparative advantage. Those specialists are often called *middlemen*.

The middleman is much maligned in popular mythology for his alleged tendency to increase the costs of the products in which he deals. In fact, he does the opposite. Suppose that a bicycle manufacturer is able to make three bicycles per day, from which he earns a net income of $30. One day a week, he delivers the bicycles, using $10 worth of gasoline. The total cost to him of making deliveries is $40: $10 in gasoline plus $30 worth of forgone opportunities to earn income. If he can hire a middleman to make deliveries for him, and if that middleman can produce that service at a cost of less than $40, then the cost of a delivered bicycle will go down, not up.

The middleman might be an employee, or he might be an independent contractor who buys the bicycles and then resells them. The analysis is the same in either case.

Notice that even if the middleman has a poor sense of direction and requires $15 worth of gasoline instead of $10 to make the deliveries, he can still be more efficient at delivering bicycles than the manufacturer is. He is more efficient, and is reducing costs, as long as he has a comparative advantage at bicycle delivery.

The fact that the manufacturer chooses to use the middleman's services is already good evidence that those services reduce costs. If this weren't the case, the middleman would soon be eliminated.

We have said that the middleman performs many tasks that would otherwise be performed by the producer. It is also true that he performs many tasks that would otherwise be performed (more expensively) by the consumer. When you go to the sporting-goods store to buy a canoe, the store is acting as a middleman between you and the canoe maker. The three or four brands that are available at the store have been chosen from among the dozens that are manufactured. The store owner has performed an extensive search to find the brands with characteristics that are most likely to appeal to his customers. For this service you pay a premium when you buy the canoe. The alternative would be to conduct the search yourself, a process almost surely more expensive than paying the premium. Indeed, it would be fair for an observer to conclude that this is the case, since he sees you choosing to shop at the store. By exercising his comparative advantage as a middleman, the store owner is able to make everybody—the producer, the consumer, and himself—a beneficiary.

Why People Trade

People trade for two reasons, either one of which would be sufficient for trade to take place. They trade because they have different tastes and because they have different abilities.

Imagine a world with only two goods: apples and gasoline. Suppose that the only way in which these goods are produced is that once a week each individual receives 5 apples and 5 gallons of gasoline as a gift from heaven. In that world everyone has equal abilities in production—we each "produce" 5 apples and 5 gallons of gasoline per week and can do nothing to increase or decrease that production—but we might still trade with one another because of differences in tastes. If you preferred to stay home every night eating apples while your friend preferred to spend his evenings driving through the countryside, you would have an excellent opportunity for a mutually beneficial exchange.

At the other extreme, imagine a world in which everyone has the same preferences regarding apples and gasoline, but some people only know how to grow apples while others only know how to manufacture gasoline. The apple growers will grow apples, the gasoline manufacturers will make gasoline, and then they will trade so that each has a mix of apples and gasoline that is preferable to what the individual could produce for himself.

In each of these imaginary worlds, trade takes place for a different reason. People with identical abilities might trade because of differing tastes, and people with identical tastes might trade because of differing abilities. In a world in which both tastes and abilities differ, people will trade for both reasons.

It Pays To Be Different

One moral to be drawn from this discussion is that to benefit from trade, *it pays to be different* from everyone else. If you and your neighbor have identical collections of baseball cards, and if you both have all the same favorite players, then you might as well not have a neighbor, at least for the purpose of improving your baseball card collection. But if either your collection (that is, your *ability* to provide certain baseball cards) or your *taste* is unusual in any way, you and your neighbor should probably talk.

The more different you are, the more you have to gain. If you are the only person in your neighborhood who likes liver, you'll be able to buy it at a very low price and be happy. If you are the only one who hates liver, your neighbors' preferences will leave more prime rib for you. If you are the only person in your neighborhood who hates gardening, you'll be able to hire gardeners at a very low price; if you are the only one who loves it, you can be very happy in the gardening business. These benefits result from differences in tastes; the carpenter and the electrician benefited from differences in abilities. In trading, any difference is an opportunity for mutual gain.

This observation has an important consequence for international trade. All countries benefit from trade, but which countries benefit the most? The answer is: those countries whose citizens are most different from the rest of the world. By and large, these are the small countries. For purely numerical reasons, the average citizen of the United States is not too different from the average North American (counting U.S. and Canadian citizens as North Americans). There are just so many more people south of the U.S.-Canadian border that they dominate the continent-wide average. But the average Canadian may differ substantially, in both tastes and abilities, from the average North American. Because it pays to be different, the Canadians gain more from trade between the two countries.

Trade Without Differences

The great nineteenth century economist David Ricardo was the first to recognize the importance of comparative advantage and to analyze its consequences for mutually beneficial trade. Earlier, the great eighteenth century economist Adam Smith had described another, completely different, way in which trade can benefit all parties.

Sometimes goods can be produced more effectively when they are produced in large quantities. You might be able to bake 2 dozen cupcakes in less than twice the time that it takes you to produce just 1 dozen. If you bake alone, you spend an hour producing a dozen cupcakes and another hour making frosting. If you trade with your neighbor, you can spend 1½ hours making two dozen cupcakes while your neighbor spends 1½ hours making a double recipe of frosting. After the appropriate trade, you each have a dozen frosted cupcakes and you have each worked only 1½ hours instead of 2 hours.

This gain from trade is quite different from the others we have discussed in this chapter, since it does not arise from any differences in tastes or abilities. Instead, it is a consequence of the increased productivity that can result when goods are produced in greater quantities. Trade enables each partner to expand the scale of his activities and take advantage of this phenomenon.

What's Next

Despite the example of the cupcakes, you should not lose sight of our main theme: Trading is beneficial whenever people differ in their abilities or in their tastes. In this chapter we have explored the meaning of *differing abilities* and have made the term more precise through the concept of comparative advantage. We have seen quite explicitly how individuals with different comparative advantages can gain from trade. Our next task is to make a thorough study of tastes and to incorporate them into our study of market behavior. That will be the subject of Chapter 3.

summary

In microeconomics, the word *price* is always used to refer to the *relative price* of a good. Thus, the price of a potato is the quantity of some other good or collection of goods that can be exchanged for a potato. The relative price must be distinguished from the *absolute price*, which measures the number of dollars that can be exchanged for a potato. Nevertheless, we often measure relative prices in "dollars." In doing so, we must remember that these dollars are not pieces of green paper but simply a convenient shorthand for referring to collections of other goods in the economy.

The price of a good or of an activity is typically only one component of the cost of acquiring that good or participating in that activity. The full cost of participation is the totality of all alternative opportunities that must be forgone. In calculating this cost, we must be careful to count only those alternatives that we would have actually pursued.

An individual is said to perform a task more efficiently than another if he performs it at a lower cost. An individual is said to have a comparative advantage at a task if he performs it more efficiently than anyone else. In determining who is the most efficient producer of a good, we must keep in mind that all costs are forgone opportunities. Thus we do not count, for example, time and raw materials, but instead the alternative uses of that time and those raw materials.

Everyone benefits when each person specializes in his area of comparative advantage and then engages in trade. Therefore, an individual's preferences need not enter into his decisions about what to produce.

Differences in ability (in other words, differences in comparative advantage) are one reason for trade. Another reason is differences in taste, which will be examined in Chapter 3.

Review Questions

R1. Explain the difference between absolute and relative prices. Which one are we referring to when we use the single word *price?*

R2. Suppose that the absolute prices of bread and wine are $2 per loaf and $6 per bottle in 1997, and that they change to $4 per loaf and $8 per bottle in 1999. Assuming that bread and wine are the only two goods in the world, would you say that the price of wine has gone up or down? Why?

R3. List some of the costs of going to college.

R4. How is efficiency defined in economics? Why do economists choose this definition?

R5. Why might a person who loves potatoes and hates squash nevertheless choose to grow squash in his garden?

R6. What are the reasons that people trade?

Numerical Exercise

N1. Suppose that the amount of time required for the electrician or the carpenter to complete a job of rewiring or paneling is given by the following table:

	Rewiring	Paneling
Electrician	5 hours	10 hours
Carpenter	10 hours	15 hours

a. Compute the costs of performing each of these tasks for each individual.

b. Who has the comparative advantage at rewiring? At paneling?

c. Suppose that the more efficient rewirer does all of the rewiring and the more efficient paneler does all of the paneling. Does this trade benefit the electrician? Does it benefit the carpenter?

d. Suppose that a different trade is worked out whereby the electrician rewires the carpenter's entire house in exchange for the carpenter's doing ⅗ of the electrician's paneling job. Now how much time does each spend working? Do they each benefit?

Note: This problem illustrates the fact that when different parties have different comparative advantages, there is always some trade that will benefit both. However, not *any* trade will benefit both; the trade must take place at an appropriate relative price.

Problem Set

1. In 1993, the absolute price of tea was $12 a pound and the absolute price of a Honda Civic was $8,000. In 1994, the absolute price of tea rose to $15 per pound and the absolute price of a Honda Civic rose to $12,000. Did the relative price of tea in terms of Civics increase or decrease? What about the relative price of Civics in terms of tea?

2. If somebody tells you that all of the relative prices in the economy have increased over the past year, what can you conclude?

3. The price of personal computers has fallen dramatically in recent years. True or False: If it were not for this fact, inflation in the United States would have been higher than it has been.

4. Suppose that there is a fall in the cost of shipping goods by railroad. What will happen to the difference between the average quality of oranges sold in Florida and the average quality of oranges sold in New York?

5. At a football stadium where some fans live nearby and others travel great distances to attend, where would you expect to find a higher percentage of long-distance travelers: in the cheap seats or in the expensive seats? Why?

6. Suppose that an acre of land in Iowa can yield either 50 bushels of wheat or 100 bushels of corn, while an acre of land in Oklahoma can yield either 20 bushels of wheat or 30 bushels of corn.

   a. What is the cost of growing 200 bushels of wheat in Iowa? What is the cost of growing 200 bushels of wheat in Oklahoma? Which state has a comparative advantage in growing wheat?

   b. Which state has a comparative advantage in growing corn?

   c. Suppose that the residents of Iowa eat 200 bushels of wheat and 360 bushels of corn, and that the residents of Oklahoma also eat 200 bushels of wheat and 360 bushels of corn. If there is no trade between the states, how many acres must each state devote to agriculture?

   d. In part c, suppose that the states begin to trade, with each specializing in its area of comparative advantage. How many acres of Iowa farmland are freed up for other uses? How many acres of Oklahoma farmland?

7. True or False: A farmer with a lot of children will find it less costly to harvest his crops than a farmer with no children, since he can put his children to work without pay.

8. True or False: If George types 50 words per minute and Mary types 120, then it certainly makes more sense for Mary to be employed as a secretary than for George to be.

9. True or False: It would be a good thing if only those students with the most talent for medicine were allowed to become doctors. (Assume that there

are enough such students so that we could still have the same number of doctors that we have today.)

10. True or False: A small country with widespread starvation would be well advised to concentrate its resources in the production of food rather than in the production of decorative jewelry.

11. True or False: A country that is poor in natural resources and has an unskilled population may be unable to trade profitably because it has no comparative advantage at anything.

12. Suppose that the Winkies and the Munchkins are initially identical in terms of their abilities to produce a wide variety of goods, including food and automobiles. One day the Munchkins discover a new, cheaper way to make automobiles. True or False: This puts the Winkies at a comparative disadvantage, and therefore makes them worse off.

13. Sears typewriters are made by Smith-Corona. True or False: If Sears made its own typewriters, they would be cheaper for consumers to buy.

14. Explain exactly where the following argument goes wrong: The Anderson Little clothing store buys clothes directly from the manufacturers, whereas Brand X clothing stores buy from middlemen. In each case there are the same costs of producing, shipping, and marketing the clothes, but with Brand X's system there is also the additional cost of supporting the middlemen. Therefore, clothes will be cheaper at Anderson-Little.

15. True or False: If everyone had the same income, substandard housing would disappear.

Internet Exercise

It has been argued by some that by allowing direct purchases and sales, information technologies such as the Internet will substantially reduce or eliminate the role of the middleman, a process referred to as disintermediation (see, for example, Nicholas Imparato, *Jumping the Curve: Innovation and Strategic Choice in an Age of Transition* (Jossey-Bass Inc. Publishers, 1994), and Duke University Professor John McCann's Web site: (http://www.duke.edu/~mccann/q-mkting.htm)).

Use the Internet to visit some of the following Internet middlemen sites: Amazon.com, Virtual Vineyards, BargainFinder, Filmfinder, Auto-By-Tel, StoneAge, Onsale, InsWeb, TPN Register, Unibex, FastParts, TechnologyNet, and pcOrder. Use Yahoo! or some other search engine to find the Internet addresses. How has information technology and the Internet changed the role of the middleman? Describe the economies of middleman-intermediated exchange relative to direct exchange for those products and services offered on the Internet middleman sites that you visited.

chapter 3

The Behavior of Consumers

Access a slide show on consumer behavior at: http://price.bus.okstate.edu/archive/Econ3113_963/Shows/Chapter3/chap_03.htm

A consumer's demand curve for a product displays the quantities he will choose to purchase at various possible prices. Our next goal is to dig a little deeper and ask where the demand curve comes from. How, for example, does a consumer decide to buy 5 cups of coffee per day when the price is 50¢ per cup but only 3 cups per day when the price is 60 cents?

The answer to this question lies in the interplay between *tastes* and *opportunities*. Consumers' choices are limited by factors that are largely beyond their control, such as their income and the market prices of goods. From the available choices (their opportunities), consumers make selections on the basis of their tastes.

In Section 3.1 we will discuss the tastes (or preferences) of the consumer. In Section 3.2 we will examine the opportunities available to the consumer, and how the interaction between tastes and opportunities leads to the consumer's choice. In Section 3.3 we will practice applying these tools. Then in Chapter 4 we will be in a position to use what we have learned to analyze consumer behavior in the marketplace.

3.1 Tastes

The Latin proverb "*De gustibus non est disputandum*" can be translated as "There's no accounting for tastes." Some people like antique wooden furniture, whereas others prefer brass. You are likely to get a variety of answers if you ask different friends whether they would prefer to live in a world without Bach or in a world without clean sheets.

Economists accept the wisdom of the proverb and make no attempt to account for tastes. Why people prefer the things that they do is an interesting topic, but it is not one that we will explore. We take people's tastes as given and see what can be said about them.

Indifference Curves

Imagine a consumer named Beth who lives in a world with only two goods: eggs and root beer. You might imagine asking Beth which of these two goods she likes better. But although this question sounds sensible at first, it really isn't. There are many reasons why not. First, the answer is likely to depend on what quantities of eggs and root beer are being compared. Second, the answer is likely to depend on how much of each Beth happens to own already. The question is open to several interpretations: Are we asking which good Beth would least like to do without altogether, or are we asking which she would rather receive for her birthday?

See David Friedman's Web site at: http://www.best.com/~ddfr/Academic/Price_Theory/PThy_Chapter_3/PThy_Chapter_3.html

Here is a better question: We can ask Beth whether she'd rather own a basket of 3 eggs and 5 root beers or a basket with 4 eggs and 2 root beers. In principle, we could discover the answer by taking away all of Beth's possessions and then offering her a choice between the two baskets. A question makes sense when some (possibly imaginary) experiment is capable of revealing the answer.

Of course, there are many possible baskets besides the ones we've described. We can display all of them simultaneously on a graph, as in Exhibit 3–1. Each point on that graph represents a basket containing a certain number of eggs and a certain number of root beers. For example, point A represents a basket with 3 eggs and 5 root beers—the first of the 2 baskets we offered to Beth.

QA EXERCISE 3.1 Describe the baskets represented by points *B, C*, and *D*. Which represents the second basket of our imaginary experiment?

What can we say about Beth's preferences among these baskets? Compare basket *A* to basket *B*, for example. Which would she prefer to own? Basket *B* contains more eggs than basket *A* (4 units instead of 3) and also more root beers (7 instead of 5). *If we assume that food and clothing are both* **goods**—items that Beth would prefer to have more of whenever she can—then the choice is unambiguous. Basket *B* is better than basket *A*.

Goods Items of which the consumer would prefer to have more rather than less.

EXERCISE 3.2 Which is preferable, basket *A* or basket *C*? How do you know?

When it comes to comparing basket *A* with basket *D*, the choice is less clear. Basket *D* has more eggs (4 units versus 3) but less root beer (2 versus 5). Which will Beth prefer? At this point we cannot possibly say. She might like *A* better than *D*, or *D* better than *A*. It is also possible (though not necessary or even likely) that she would happen to like them both equally.

Now consider this question: Where should we look to find the baskets that Beth likes exactly as much as *A*? They can't be to the "northeast" of *A* (like *B*) because the baskets there are all preferred to *A*. They can't be to the "southwest" of *A* (like *C*) because *A* is preferred to all of those baskets. They must

Exhibit 3-1 Baskets of Goods

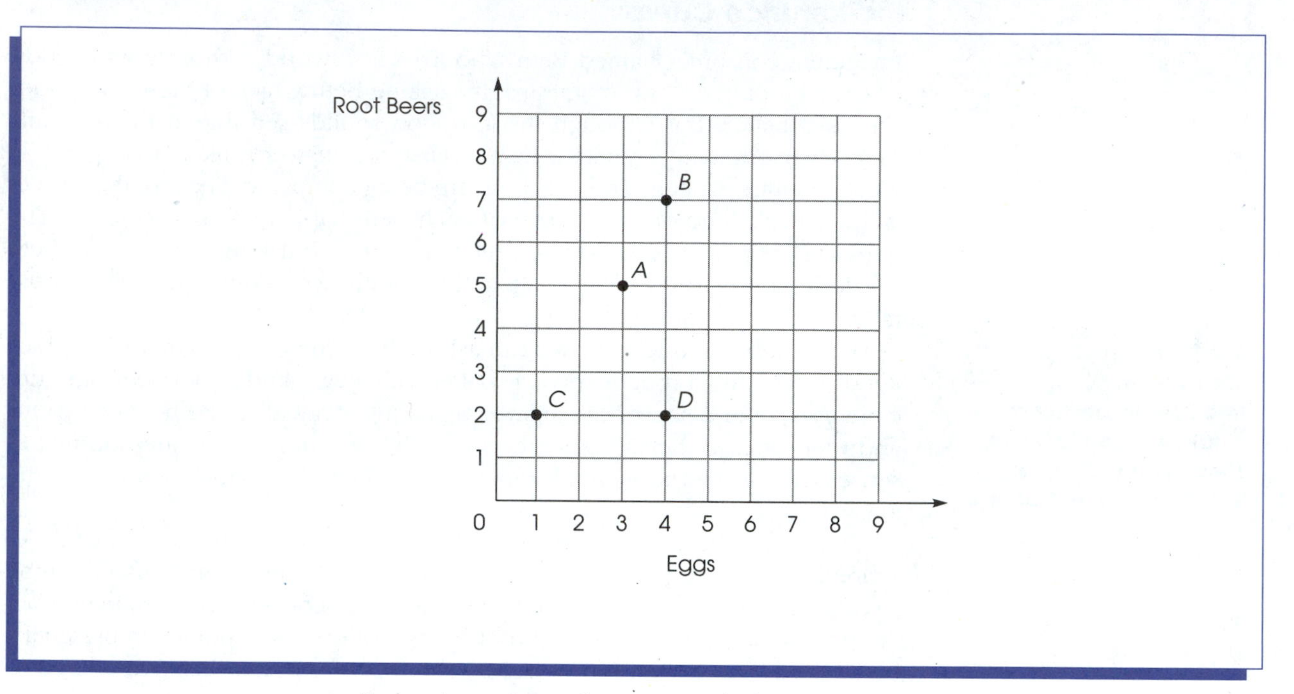

Each point on the graph represents a basket containing a certain number of eggs and a certain number of root beers. For example, point *A* corresponds to 3 eggs and 5 root beers.

all be to either the "northwest" or the "southeast" of *A* (like *D*). This doesn't mean that *D* is necessarily one of them, just that they lie in the same general direction from *A* that *D* does.

If we draw in a few of the baskets that Beth likes just as well as she likes *A*, they might look like the points shown in panel A of Exhibit 3–2. Because each of these baskets is *exactly as good* as *A*, they must all be *exactly as good* as each other. This means that each one must lie either to the northwest or to the southeast of each other one, which accounts for the downward slope that is apparent in the picture.

The baskets shown in panel A of Exhibit 3–2 are only a few of those that Beth likes just as well as *A*. There are many other such baskets as well. The collection of all such baskets forms a curve, shown in black in panel B of the exhibit. From our discussion in the preceding paragraph, we know that the curve will be downward sloping. Because Beth is indifferent between any two points on this curve, it is called an **indifference curve**.

Indifference curve A collection of baskets, all of which the consumer considers equally desirable.

There is nothing special about basket *A*. We could as easily have begun with a different basket, such as *A′* in panel B of Exhibit 3–2. That panel depicts both the indifference curve through *A* (in black) and the indifference curve through *A′* (in color).

Exhibit 3-2 Comparing Baskets

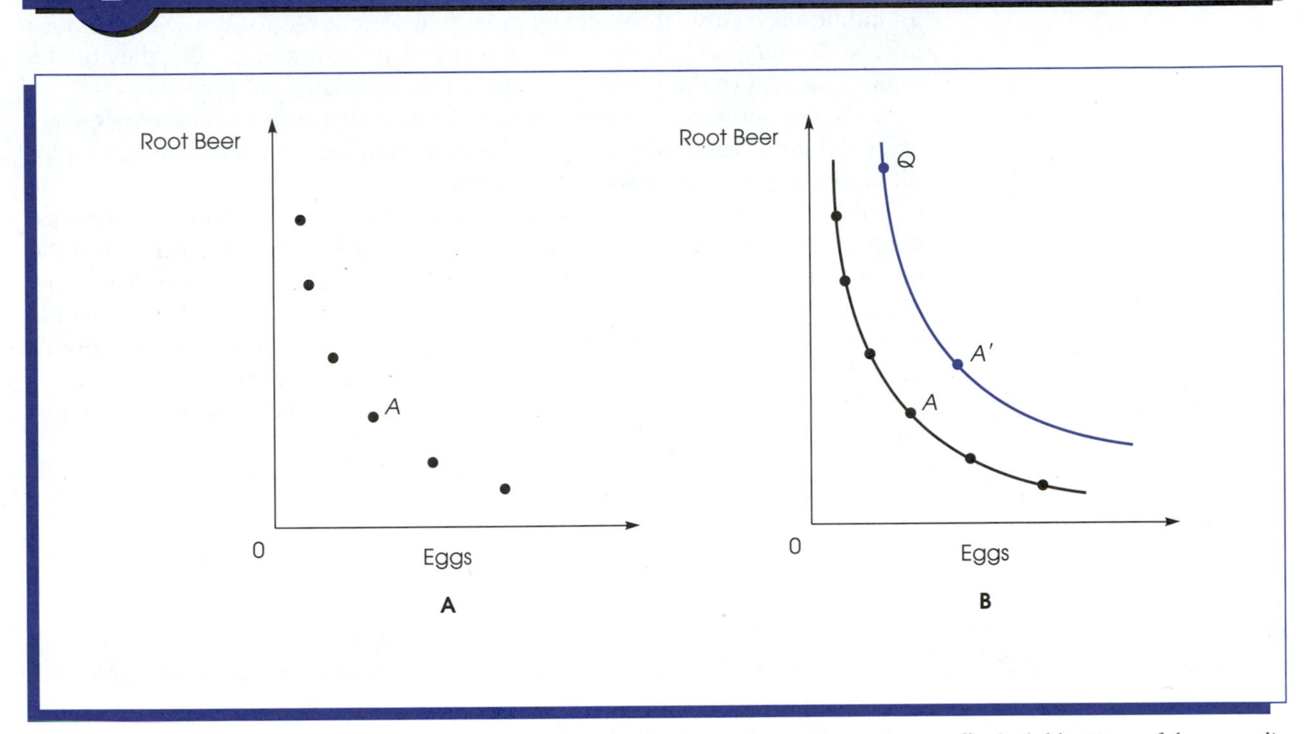

Panel A shows several baskets that Beth considers to be equally desirable. None of these can lie to the northeast or southwest of any other one, because if it did, one would be clearly preferable to the other. As a result, they all lie to the northwest and southeast of each other, accounting for the downward slope.

The black indifference curve in panel B includes the points from panel A, as well as all of the other baskets that Beth considers equally as desirable as these. The colored indifference curve shows a different set of baskets, all of which are equally as desirable as each other. Knowledge of Beth's indifference curves allows us to make inferences about her preferences that would otherwise be impossible. For example, we know that Beth likes *Q* and *A′* equally because they are on the same indifference curve, and that *A′* is preferable to *A* because it contains more of everything. We may infer that Beth prefers *Q* to *A*.

The indifference curves do not have to have the same shape, but they do both have to slope downward.

If we know a consumer's indifference curves, we can make inferences that would not be possible otherwise. Try comparing basket *A* to basket *Q* in panel B of Exhibit 3–2. Basket *A* has more eggs than basket *Q*, but basket *Q* has more root beer than basket *A*. Without more information, we cannot say which one Beth will prefer. But the indifference curves provide that additional information. We know that Beth likes *Q* and *A′* equally, because they are on the same indifference curve. We know that she likes *A′* better than she likes *A*, because it is to the northeast of *A* and therefore contains more of everything than *A* does. We may infer that she likes *Q* better than she likes *A*.

In general, a basket is preferable to another precisely when it is on a higher indifference curve, where *higher* means "above and to the right."

Relationships among Indifference Curves

Of course, Beth has more than two indifference curves. Indeed, we can draw an indifference curve through any point that we choose to start with. Because of this, *the indifference curves fill the entire plane.* (More precisely, they fill the entire quadrant of the plane in which both coordinates are positive.)

An important feature of indifference curves is that *indifference curves never cross.* To understand why this must be true, imagine a consumer with two indifference curves that cross, as in Exhibit 3–3.

From the fact that baskets *P* and *Q* are on the same (black) indifference curve, we know that the consumer likes these baskets equally well. From the fact that baskets *R* and *Q* are on the same (blue) indifference curve, we know that he also likes these equally well. Putting these facts together, we conclude that he likes *P* and *R* equally well. But this is impossible, since *R* is to the northeast of *P* and therefore contains more of both goods. In other words, if indifference curves cross, impossible things will happen. We conclude that indifference curves don't cross.

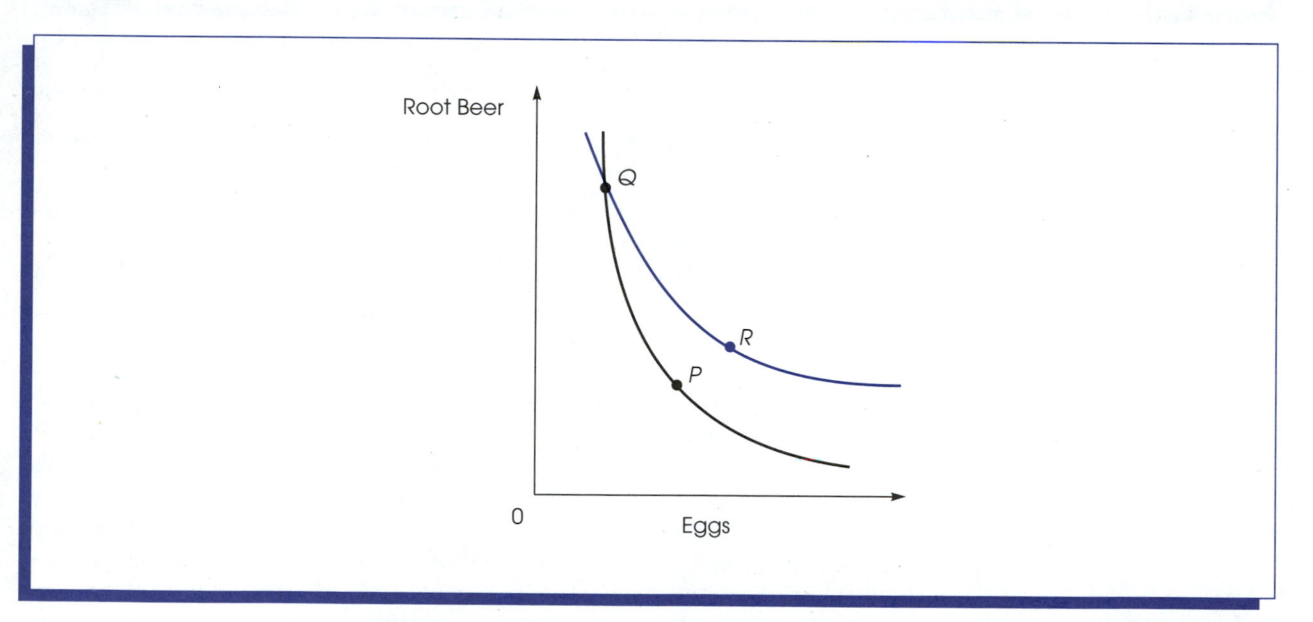

Crossing indifference curves, such as those shown in the graph, cannot occur. The consumer likes *P* and *Q* equally well because they are both on the same (black) indifference curve. He also likes *R* and *Q* equally well because they are both on the same (colored) indifference curve. We may infer that he likes *P* and *R* equally well, which we know to be false (in fact, *R* is preferred to *P*). Thus, the graph cannot be correct.

Marginal Values

We have said that indifference curves slope downward, but we haven't yet said anything about how steep the slope is. In this section we will interpret the slope of the indifference curve. The first step is to understand how indifference curves can tell us whether certain trades are desirable.

Desirable and Undesirable Trades

Suppose you have 7 eggs and 2 root beers; this basket is represented by point *C* in Exhibit 3–4. Your friend Jeremy offers to trade you 2 root beers for an egg. If you accept his offer, you'll end up at point *P*. (That is, you'll give Jeremy an egg, leaving you with 6 eggs, and he'll give you 2 root beers, leaving you with 4 root beers. Point *P* illustrates your new basket.)

Will you accept Jeremy's offer? It depends on your preferences. Suppose, for example, that you have the indifference curve shown in Exhibit 3–4. Then you will *not* accept Jeremy's offer, because—according to your preferences—point *P* is inferior to point *C*.

Marginal Value

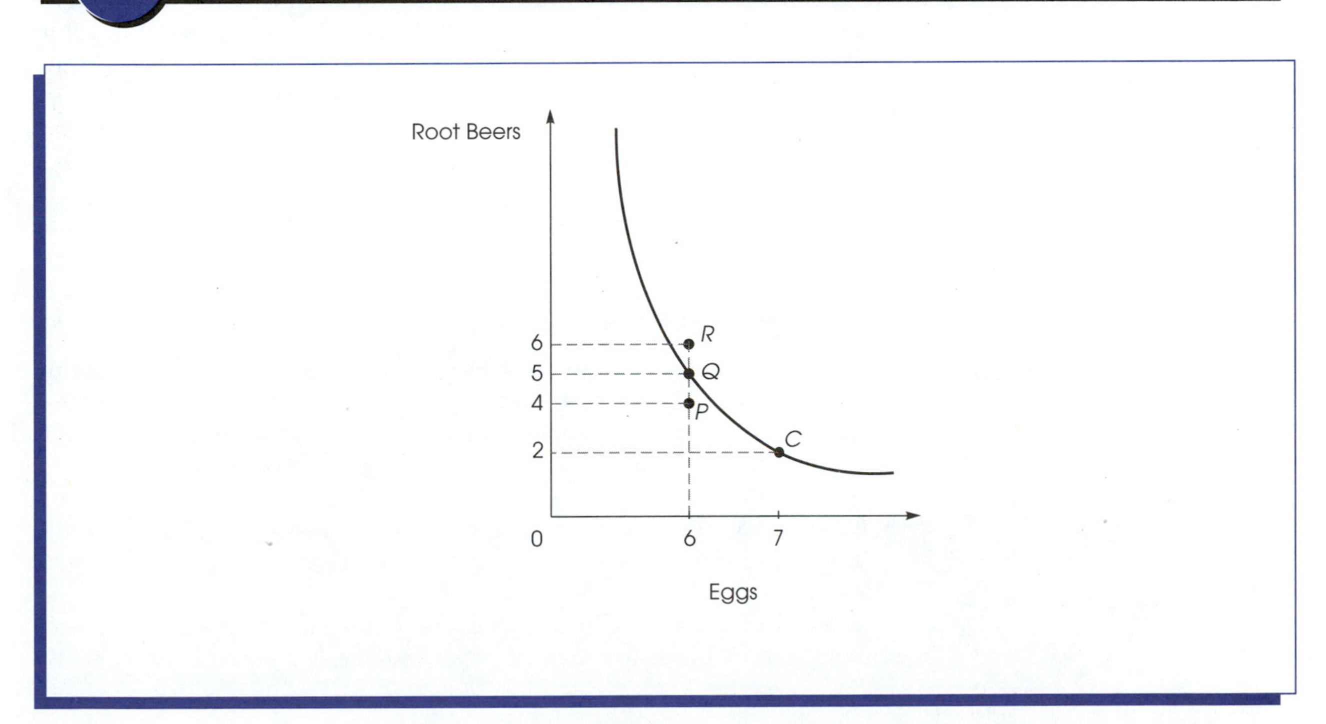

Suppose you start with basket *C*. If someone offers to trade you 2 root beers for an egg, you can move to basket *P*, which is worse; so you'll reject this trade. The minimum price you'd accept for an egg is 3 root beers, moving you to basket *Q*. Thus (to you), the marginal value of an egg is 3 root beers.

In other words, when Jeremy says, "I'll give you 2 root beers for an egg," you'll say, "No thanks; I'd rather keep the egg." In ordinary language, we'd say that your seventh egg is worth more to you than 2 root beers.

Suppose Jeremy tries again, by offering you 4 root beers for an egg instead of 2 root beers. Now do you accept the trade? If you do, you'll end up at point *R*, above your original indifference curve. This trade is desirable; it makes you happier; you got more for your egg than you thought it was worth.

QA EXERCISE 3.3 Explain why Jeremy's new offer brings you to point *R*.

Finally, what if Jeremy had offered you exactly 3 root beers for your seventh egg? This brings you to point *Q*, which is exactly as desirable as your original point *C*. That is, trading an egg for 3 root beers makes you neither better nor worse off than you were to begin with. This makes it reasonable to say that your seventh egg is *worth* exactly 3 root beers (to you). We say that (to you) the **marginal value** of an egg is 3 root beers.

Marginal value of *X* in terms of *Y* The number of *Y*s for which the consumer would be just willing to trade one *X*.

In general, the marginal value that you place on good *X* (in terms of good *Y*) is defined to be the number of *Y*s for which you'd be just willing to trade one *X*.[1] (The adjective *marginal* refers to the fact that this you are trading just *one X*.)

Given a consumer's initial basket and the indifference curve through that basket, you can always compute the marginal value of the horizontal good by traveling leftward 1 unit and then seeing how far upward you must travel to reach the indifference curve. In Exhibit 3–4, this means starting at point *C*, traveling leftward 1 egg (from 7 to 6) and then observing that you must travel upward 3 root beers (from 2 to 5); thus—as we have already said—the marginal value of an egg is 3 root beers.

EXERCISE 3.4 How can you use the indifference curve of Exhibit 3–4 to illustrate the marginal value of *root beers* in terms of *eggs*?

Marginal Value as a Slope

Exhibit 3–5 illustrates the indifference curves of two consumers, each starting with basket *C*. We can use these indifference curves to compute the marginal value of an apple to each consumer. For Jack, the marginal value of an egg is 6 root beers, for Jill, the marginal value of an egg is 1 root beer.

QA EXERCISE 3.5 Explain how to compute these marginal values from the graphs in Exhibit 3–5.

Now let's forget about marginal values for a moment and ask a purely geometric question: What is the *slope* of Jack's indifference curve at point *C*? By

[1] In many textbooks, the marginal value is called the *marginal rate of substitution* or *MRS*. Unfortunately, there is quite a bit of confusion associated with this term. The quantity that we've called the marginal value of *X* in terms of *Y* is sometimes called the marginal rate of substitution between *X* and *Y*, and sometimes called the marginal rate of substitution between *Y* and *X*. To avoid this confusion, we will stick with the term *marginal value*.

Exhibit 3-5 Marginal Value as a Slope

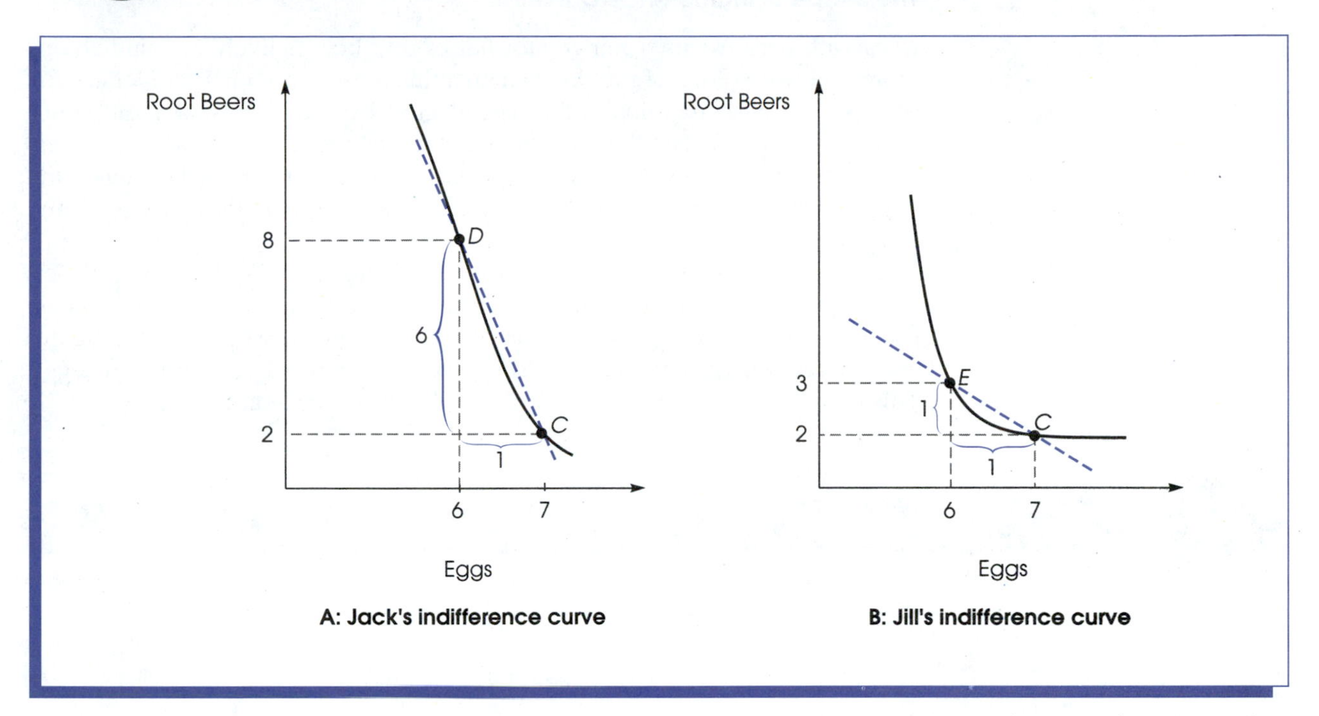

Jack and Jill each start with basket C. To Jack, the marginal value of an egg is 6 root beers. Thus, trading 1 egg for 6 root beers leaves him on the same indifference curve; in other words, his indifference curve goes through point D and so has slope -6. To Jill, the marginal value of an egg is 1 root beer, so her indifference curve goes through point E and has slope -1. In general, the marginal value of an egg is equal to the absolute value of the slope of the indifference curve.

the slope of a curve we mean the slope of a line tangent to that curve. The tangent line at C is well approximated by the illustrated line through C and D. So we want to compute the slope of that line.

Recalling that the slope of a line is given by the *rise over the run*, we see that in this case the slope is $-6/1 = -6$. The numerator 6 is the vertical distance between points C and D, the denominator 1 is the horizontal distance, and there is a minus sign because the curve is downward sloping. The absolute value of this slope is 6 (or, more precisely, 6 root beers per egg). Recall that according to Jack, this is exactly the marginal value of an egg.

Likewise, in panel B the line through C and E has a slope with absolute value 1, which according to Jill is the marginal value of an egg.

It is no coincidence that these slopes are equal to the corresponding marginal values. In panel A, for example, we compute the marginal value of an egg as the vertical distance from D to C (that is, 6), while we compute the absolute value of the slope as that same vertical distance divided by the horizontal distance, which is 1. But dividing by 1 leaves the number 6 unchanged.

In general, then, **for a consumer with basket *C*, the marginal value of an egg is equal to the slope of the indifference curve at point C.** Consequently, **the steeper the indifference curve, the greater the marginal value of an egg**.

The Shape of Indifference Curves

A starving person with a refrigerator full of root beer is likely to value an egg more highly (in terms of root beer) than a thirsty person with a refrigerator full of eggs. Because marginal value is reflected by the slopes of indifference curves, we can translate this statement into geometry: As a general rule, we expect indifference curves to be steep near baskets containing few eggs and many root beers, and to be shallow near baskets containing many eggs and few root beers.

Consider the two sets of indifference curves shown in Exhibit 3–6. Both sets slope downward. The first set slopes steeply in the area where baskets contain few eggs and many root beers (that is, in the "northwest" part of the figure) and shallowly in the area where baskets contain few root beers and many eggs. This consumer conforms to the general rule of the preceding paragraph.

Exhibit 3-6 The Curvature of Indifference Curves

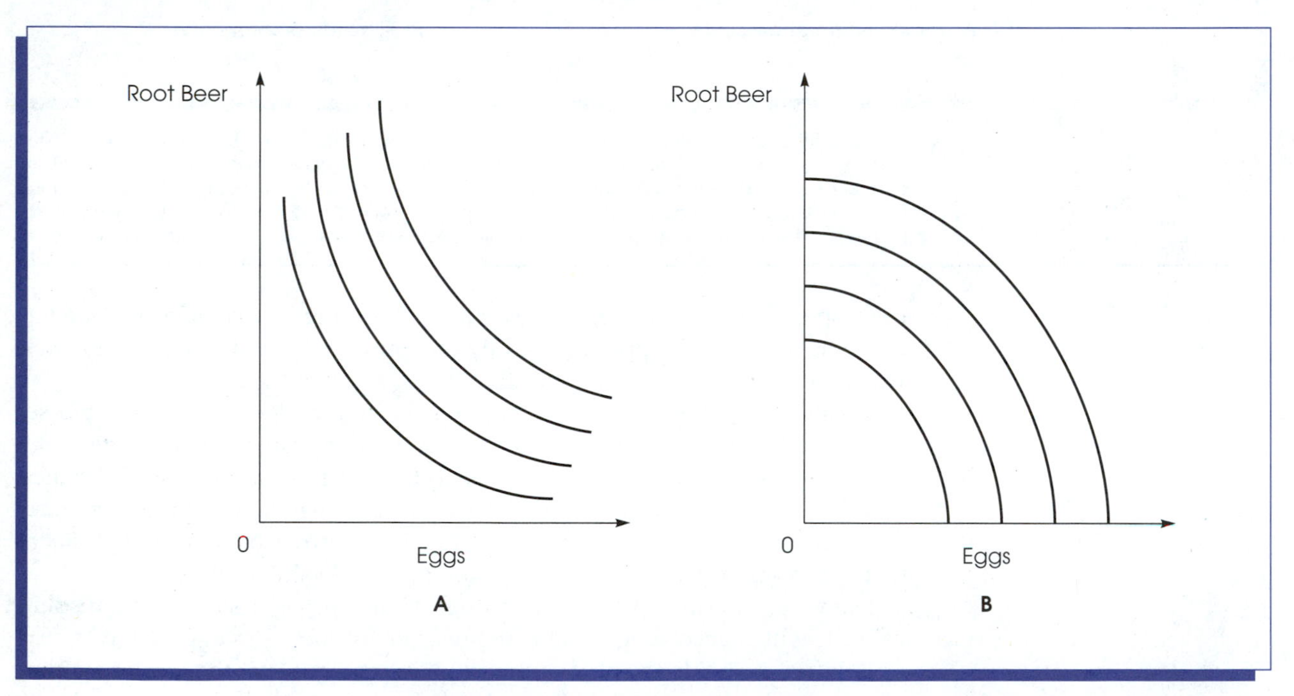

The indifference curves in panel A are convex (bowed in toward the origin), indicating that when the consumer has few eggs and many root beers (in the "northwest" part of the diagram), she places a high marginal value on eggs—that is, you'd have to offer her a lot of root beer to get her to part with an egg. We assume that indifference curves have this shape, rather than the alternative shape illustrated in panel B.

Another consumer might have the indifference curves shown in panel B of Exhibit 3–6. This consumer values eggs highly when she has many eggs and few root beers, but values eggs much less when she has few eggs and many root beers. Such tastes are possible, but they seem unlikely.

For this reason we will always assume that indifference curves are shaped like those in panel A rather than like those in panel B. That is, we assume that indifference curves bow inward toward the origin. This property is expressed by saying that indifference curves are **convex**. At the end of Section 3.2 we will give another, independent justification for assuming convexity.

Convex Bowed in toward the origin, like the curves in panel A of Exhibit 3–6.

EXERCISE 3.6 Under what circumstances do you expect the consumer to value additional root beers highly relative to additional eggs? Combine this answer with your answer to Exercise 3.4 to draw a conclusion about where the indifference curves should be steep and where they should be shallow. Does your conclusion give further support to our assumption that indifference curves are convex, or does it suggest a reason to doubt that assumption?

More on Indifference Curves

Properties of Indifference Curves: A Summary

Here are the fundamental facts about a given consumer's indifference curves:

Indifference curves slope downward, they fill the plane, they never cross, and they are convex.

A consumer's indifference curves between two goods encode everything that there is to say about the consumer's tastes regarding those goods. A different consumer is likely to have a different family of indifference curves (also satisfying the fundamental facts). This is just another way of saying that tastes may differ across individuals.

We have assumed that eggs and root beer are both *goods*—items you'd always prefer to have more of—and we've concluded that indifference curves are downward sloping and convex. A different assumption would lead to different conclusions. End-of-chapter problems 3 and 4 will lead you through the analysis when one or both of the goods is replaced by a *bad*—something you'd prefer to have less of. (In problems 6 and 7, you'll encounter other special circumstances in which the shapes of indifference curves can differ from what is pictured in Exhibit 3-6a).

The Composite-Good Convention

In order to draw indifference curve diagrams, we must assume that there are only two goods in the world. This might appear to be a severe limitation, yet in fact it is not. In many applications we will want to concentrate our attention on a single good—say, eggs. In that case we divide the world into two classes of goods, namely, "eggs" and "things that are not eggs," otherwise known as "all other goods." This allows us to draw indifference curves between eggs (on the horizontal axis) and all other goods (on the vertical).

There remains the problem of units. What is a single unit of *all other goods*? The simplest solution to this problem is to measure all other goods in terms of their dollar value.

Composite-good convention The lumping together of all goods but one into a single portmanteau good.

When we lump together all things that are not eggs and measure it in a single unit like dollars, we say that we are using the **composite-good convention.**

In the presence of the composite-good convention, the slope of an indifference curve is the marginal value of an egg in terms of other goods, with the other goods measured in dollars. Thus, it is the minimum number of dollars for which the consumer would be willing to trade an egg.

3.2 The Budget Line and the Consumer's Choice

In order to predict a consumer's behavior, we need to know two things. First, we need to know the consumer's tastes, which is the same thing as saying that we need to know his indifference curves. Second, we need to know the options available to the consumer. In other words, we need to know his budget.

The Budget Line

Continue to assume a world with two goods. Instead of calling them eggs and root beers, we're going to start calling them X and Y. You may continue to think of them as eggs and root beers if you wish. In order to determine which baskets our consumer can afford, we need to know three things: the price of X, the price of Y, and the consumer's income.

Rather than make up specific numbers, let's make up names for the three things we need to know:

$$P_X = \text{the price of } X \text{ in dollars}$$
$$P_Y = \text{the price of } Y \text{ in dollars}$$
$$I = \text{the consumer's income in dollars}$$

Now let's suppose that the consumer is considering the purchase of a particular basket. Suppose that the basket contains x units of X and y units of Y. (Keep in mind that the capital letters X and Y are the *names* of the goods and the small letters x and y are the *quantities*.) How much will it cost the consumer to acquire this basket? The x units of X at a price of P_X dollars apiece will cost $P_X \cdot x$ dollars. The y units of Y at a price of P_Y dollars apiece will cost $P_Y \cdot y$ dollars. The total price of the basket is:

$$P_X \cdot x + P_Y \cdot y \text{ dollars}$$

Under what circumstances can the consumer afford to acquire this particular basket? Clearly he can acquire it only if the price of the basket does not exceed his income. In other words, he can afford the basket precisely if:

$$P_X \cdot x + P_Y \cdot y < I$$

In fact, we can say a little more. Let's take seriously our assumption that X and Y are the only goods in the world. (In view of the composite-good convention, this assumption is not as outrageous as it seems.) Then the consumer will have to spend his entire income on X and Y,[2] and must choose a basket that costs exactly I dollars. The consumer can have the basket in question precisely if:

$$P_X \cdot x + P_Y \cdot y = I$$

It is important to distinguish the meanings of the various symbols in this equation. P_X, P_Y, and I are particular, fixed numbers that the consumer faces. The letters x and y are variables that can represent the contents of any basket. As the consumer considers purchasing various baskets, the values of x and y change. For each basket he plugs the relevant values of x and y into the equation, and he asks if the equation is true. Asking "Does this basket make the equation true?" is exactly the same as asking "Can I afford to purchase this basket?"

Budget line The set of all baskets that the consumer can afford, given prices and his or her income.

The line described by the equation $P_X \cdot x + P_Y \cdot y = I$ is a picture of all the baskets that the consumer can afford. It is called the consumer's **budget line.**

Another way to write the equation of the budget line (using some simple algebraic manipulations) is:

$$y = -\frac{P_X}{P_Y} \cdot x + \frac{I}{P_Y}$$

If you remember that P_X, P_Y, and I are constants and that x and y are variables, you may recognize this as the equation of a line with slope $-P_X/P_Y$ and y-intercept I/P_Y. The points on that line are those that satisfy the equation, and are therefore those that represent baskets that the consumer can buy. Exhibit 3–7 shows the budget line.

Here is an easy way to remember how to draw the budget line. If you were the consumer and you bought no Xs at all, how many Ys could you afford? Since your income is I and Ys sell at a price of P_Y apiece, the answer is I/P_Y. This means that the point $(0, I/P_Y)$ must be on the budget line. If you bought no Ys at all, how many Xs could you afford? The answer is I/P_X. This means that the point $(I/P_X,0)$ must be on the budget line. The budget line must be the line connecting the points $(0,I/P_Y)$ and $(I/P_X,0)$.

[2] It is possible that the consumer would want to save some income, but in that case we would want to consider savings as another good. If we are using the composite-good convention, we can include savings along with "all other goods."

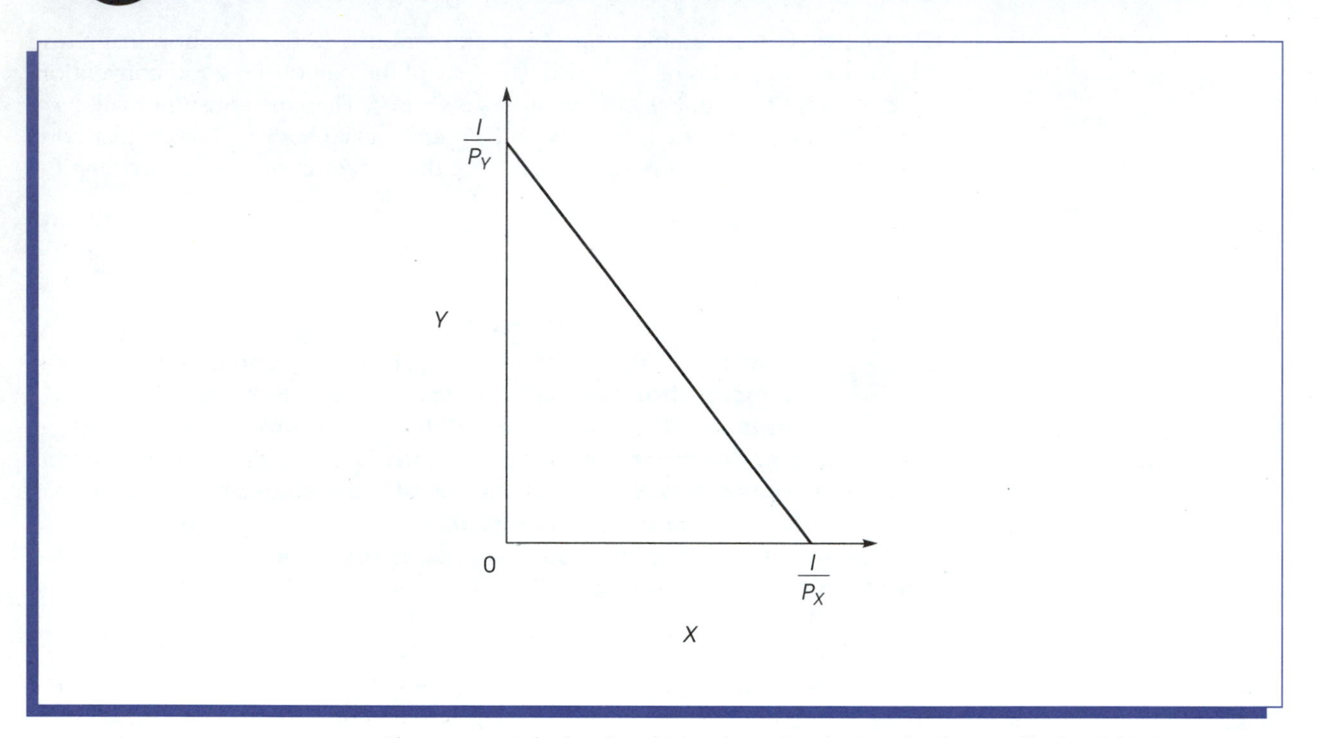

The consumer's budget line depicts the various baskets that he can afford with his income.

What if P_X, P_Y, and I were all to double simultaneously? This would have no effect on the ratios I/P_Y and I/P_X. It follows that a simultaneous doubling of all prices and income would have no effect on the budget line. This accords with our expectation that only relative prices matter.

The geometry of the budget line reflects everything there is to know about the opportunities facing the consumer. For example, the slope of the budget line is $-P_X/P_Y$, and the ratio P_X/P_Y is the relative price of X in terms of Y. Therefore, the budget line will be steep when X is expensive relative to Y, and it will be shallow when X is inexpensive relative to Y.

The Consumer's Choice

The Geometry of the Consumer's Choice

The budget line conveys an entirely different kind of information than the indifference curves do. The indifference curves reflect the consumer's preferences without regard to what he can actually afford to buy. The budget line shows which baskets he can afford to buy (that is, it shows his opportunities) without regard to his preferences. To determine how the consumer will actually behave, we must combine these two kinds of information. To this end, we have drawn the indifference curves and the budget line on the same graph, as in Exhibit 3–8.

We now have enough information to determine which basket this consumer will choose. Look at the baskets pictured. Of these, *F* is on the highest indifference curve and the one that the consumer would most like to own. (There are also many baskets not pictured that the consumer would like even more than *F*.) Unfortunately, he can't afford basket *F*—it's outside the budget line. By contrast, point *E* is inside the budget line and would fail to exhaust his income; therefore, *E* is ruled out as well. The baskets that the consumer can acquire are the ones on his budget line. In Exhibit 3–8 these include *A, B, O, C,* and *D*.

Of these, he will choose the one on the highest possible indifference curve. It is clear from the picture that this choice is *O*. In fact, *O* is not just the best

Exhibit 3-8 The Consumer's Optimum

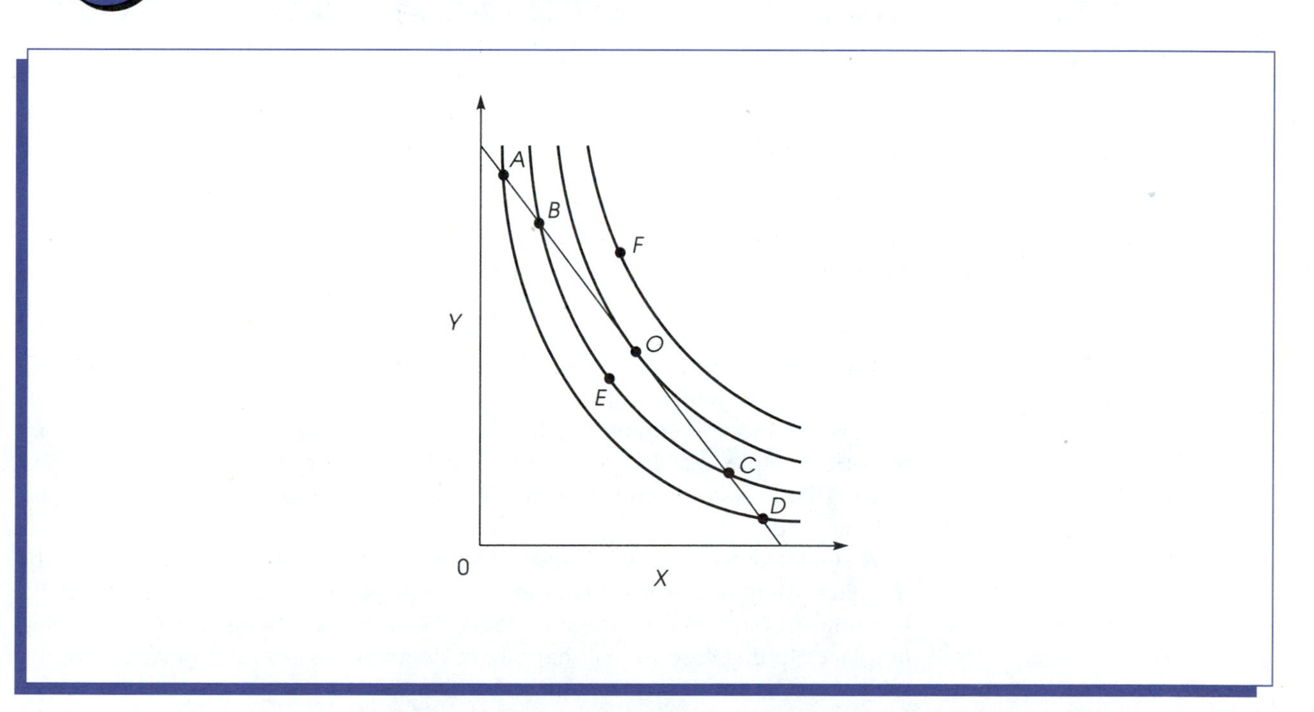

The consumer must choose one of the baskets that is on his budget line, such as *A, B, O, C,* or *D*. Of these, he will choose the one that is on the highest indifference curve, namely, *O*. Thus, the consumer is led to choose the basket at the point where his budget line is tangent to an indifference curve. This point is called the consumer's optimum.

At the consumer's optimum, the relative price of *X* in terms of *Y* (given by the slope of the budget line) and the marginal value of *X* in terms of *Y* (given by the slope of the tangent line to the indifference curve) are equal. The geometric reason for this is that the budget line is the tangent line to the indifference curve. The economic reason for it is that whenever the relative price is different from the marginal value, the consumer will continue to make exchanges until the two become equal.

choice among the five baskets we have considered, but the best choice of any basket on the budget line. From the picture, the following is clear:

The basket the consumer chooses will always be located where his budget line is tangent to one of his indifference curves.

Optimum (plural: optima) The most preferred of the baskets on the budget line.

This basket is called the consumer's **optimum**. Because there is only one such point, the budget line and the indifference curves give sufficient information for us to predict which basket the consumer will choose.

The Economics of the Consumer's Choice

We can analyze the consumer's problem from a different perspective and still reach the same conclusion about the location of his optimum.

Referring to Exhibit 3–8, suppose that the consumer owns basket *A*. How much *Y* would this consumer be willing to trade for an additional unit of *X*? The answer is given by the marginal value of a unit of *X* (in terms of *Y*), which is measured by the absolute value of the slope of his or her indifference curve at *A*.

How much *Y* would this consumer actually have to sacrifice in order to acquire an additional unit of *X*? The answer is given by the relative price of *X* in terms of *Y*, which is the ratio P_X/P_Y, the absolute value of the slope of his budget line.

Of these two, which is greater, the marginal value or the relative price? At point *A* the indifference curve is steeper than the budget line. Consequently, the amount of *Y* that the consumer is *willing* to pay for a unit of *X* exceeds the amount of *Y* that he actually *has to* pay for a unit of *X*. In such a situation, buying a unit of *X* is an attractive proposition. The consumer will exchange *Y*s for *X*s at the going relative price, ending up with more *X* and less *Y* than he started with. This will bring him to a point like *B*.

Now the same reasoning applies again. At *B* it is still the case that the marginal value exceeds the relative price. The consumer will want to buy another unit of X, which will move him further down the budget line.

This process will continue until the consumer reaches point *O*. At that point the price that he is willing to pay for *X* and the price at which he is able to purchase *X* have become equal. There is no longer anything to be gained from additional trades.

A similar process occurs if the consumer starts out with basket *D*. Here the marginal value of *X* is less than the relative price of *X*; the consumer values his last unit of *X* at less than the number of *Y*s he can exchange it for in the marketplace. In this case he will happily trade away his last unit of *X*, ending up with more *Y*s and fewer *X*s, at a point like *C*.

As long as the marginal value of *X* is less than the relative price of *X*, the consumer will trade *X*s for *Y*s. This process stops when the marginal value and the relative price become equal, at point *O*.

Whenever the marginal value of *X* exceeds the relative price of *X*, the consumer will want to buy *X*s, moving down the budget line. Whenever the marginal value is less than the relative price, the consumer will want to sell *X*s, moving up the budget line. The only point at which he can settle is *O*, where the marginal value and the relative price are exactly equal. Thus, the economic reasoning leads to the same conclusion as the geometric reasoning: Of the points available to the consumer, the optimum occurs where his budget line is tangent to one of his indifference curves.

Corner Solutions

There is an exception to the rule that the consumer's optimum always occurs at a tangency. This exception is illustrated in Exhibit 3–9. In this case there is no tangency for the consumer to choose.

To predict the consumer's choice in this situation, we can use simple geometry. We know that the consumer must choose a basket on his budget line. Of all of these baskets, we can see from the picture that the one lying on the highest indifference curve is *P*. Therefore, this is the basket that the consumer will choose.

Here is an alternative path to the same conclusion: Suppose that the consumer begins with basket *S*. At this point his indifference curve is less steep than his budget line. To this consumer the marginal value of *X* in terms of *Y* is less than the relative price of *X* in terms of *Y*. The last unit of *X* is worth less

Exhibit 3-9 A Corner Solution

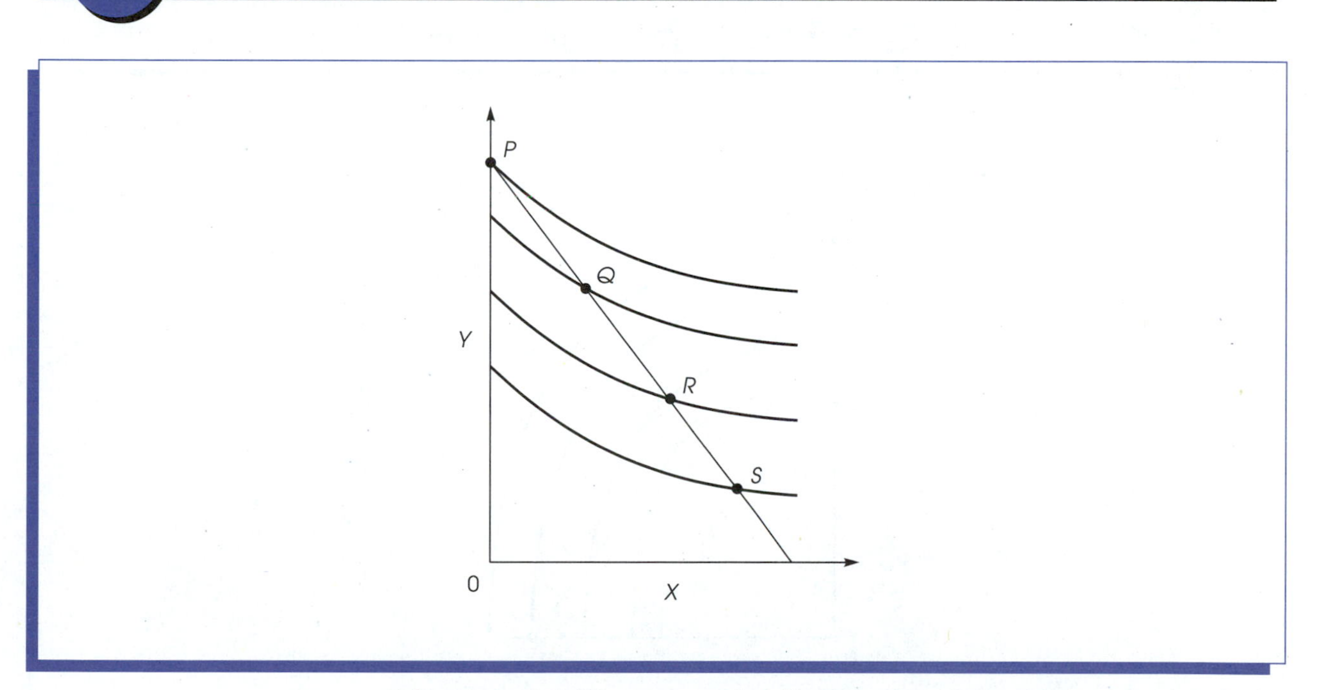

If the consumer's indifference curves look like those pictured, there is no tangency between his budget line and any of his indifference curves. Of all the points on the budget line, the consumer will choose the most desirable, namely, *P*. At any other point on the budget line the marginal value of *X* in terms of *Y* is less than the relative price, so the consumer can sell *X*s for more than they are worth to him, and will continue to do so until he has sold all of his *X*s, ending up in the corner at *P*.

to him than it will bring in the marketplace. Therefore, he trades X for Y, moving to a point like R. Now the same reasoning applies again, leading the consumer to move first to Q and then to P. The same reasoning would apply no matter what the original basket was.

Corner solution An optimum occurring on one of the axes when there is no tangency between the budget line and an indifference curve.

The situation depicted in Exhibit 3–9 is called a **corner solution** because the consumer's optimum occurs in a corner of the diagram. As you can see from the picture, he consumes no X whatsoever; and spends all of his income on Y.

More on the Shape of Indifference Curves

In Section 3.1 we justified the assumption that indifference curves are convex with an appeal to the idea of marginal value. Now we can give an additional reason for making this assumption.

Suppose that a consumer has the indifference curves illustrated in Exhibit 3–10. Will this consumer choose to purchase the basket at point O? No! He can do better. Points C and D are both available to him (they are on his budget line) and they are on a higher indifference curve than O. And can he do better than C and D? Yes. Every movement "outward" along the budget line, away from O and toward one of the axes, improves the consumer's welfare. For this

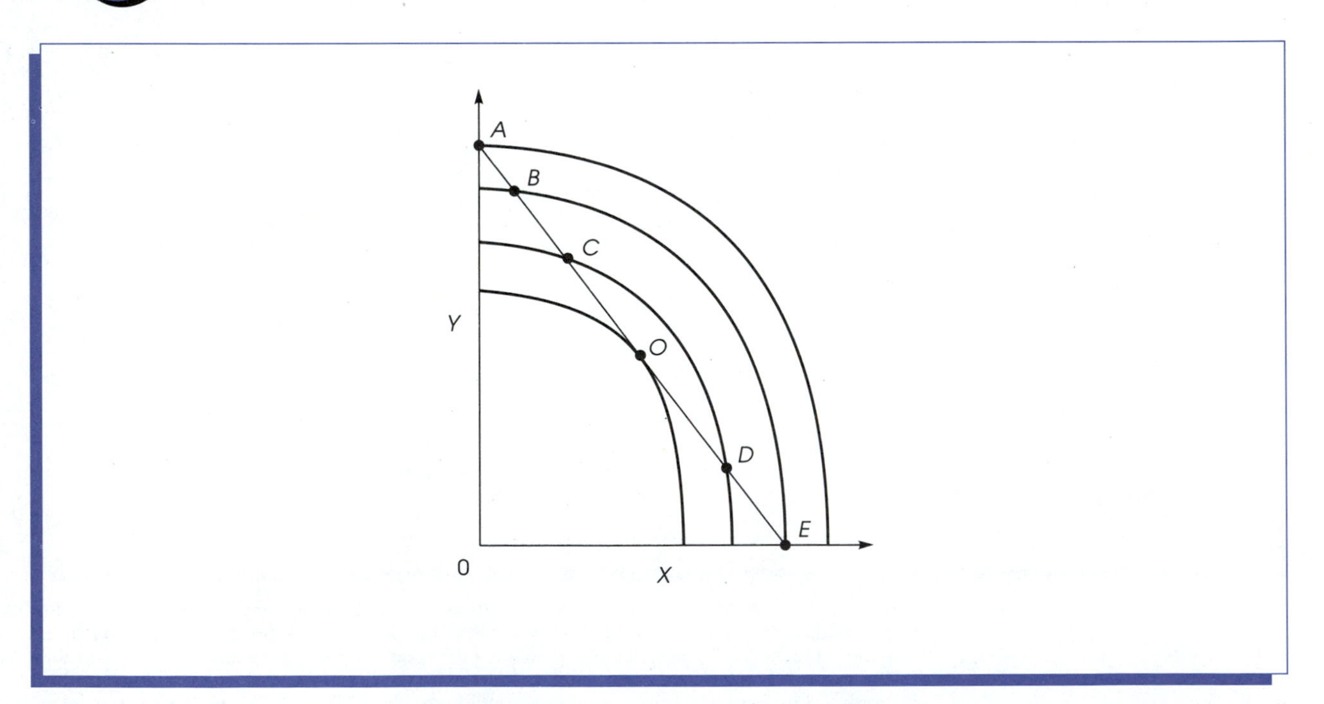

Nonconvex indifference curves always lead to a corner solution. The consumer pictured here will choose point A, which is on the highest possible indifference curve.

reason he will always want to choose a basket on one of the axes—a corner solution. In this case he will choose basket *A*.

EXERCISE 3.7 Why does the consumer choose basket *A* rather than basket *E*? How would the budget line have to look for him to choose a point on the *X* axis rather than the *Y* axis?

Because this consumer always selects a corner solution, he consumes either zero units of *X* or zero units of *Y*. But goods that consumers choose to purchase none of are not very interesting from the viewpoint of economics. So now we have our additional reason for assuming that indifference curves are convex. They might not be—but in this case one of the goods in question would not be consumed at all, and we would prefer to turn our attention to goods that *are* consumed. Therefore, we usually confine our attention to convex indifference curves.

3.3 Applications of Indifference Curves

Indifference curve analysis is a powerful tool for understanding consumer behavior. The two ways to become proficient with a tool are to observe it in use and to use it. In this section we present three solved problems that illustrate some of the applications of indifference curves. You might want to attempt the problems yourself before reading the solutions. By working through them, you can acquire the ability to work similar problems quickly and accurately. After you have practiced on these, you can test your new skills on the problems at the end of the chapter.

Price Indices

A Problem

Suppose that the only goods you consume are *X* and *Y*. Suppose further that the price of *X* is $3 (per unit), the price of *Y* is $4, and at these prices you choose to purchase 4 units of *X* and 2 units of *Y*, exhausting your total income of $20. One day the price of *X* goes up to $4, the price of *Y* falls to $2, and your income stays fixed at $20. Are you better off or worse off than before?

The Solution

We begin by graphing your original budget line. We are told that (originally) your income is $20, the price of *X* is $3, and the price of *Y* is $4. This means that if you buy no *X*s at all, you can afford exactly 5 *Y*s, and if you buy no *Y*s at all, you can afford exactly 6⅔ *X*s. Your original budget line is the one labeled *original* in Exhibit 3–11. The basket (4,2) is on this line. Because this is the basket you choose with the *original* budget line, it must be where the *original* line is tangent to an indifference curve (that is, it must be your original optimum). The basket (4,2) is labeled *O* in the exhibit. The graph shows the indifference curve that is tangent there.

Now let's figure out your *new* budget line. The price of *X* is now $4, the

Exhibit 3-11 Your Original and New Budget Lines

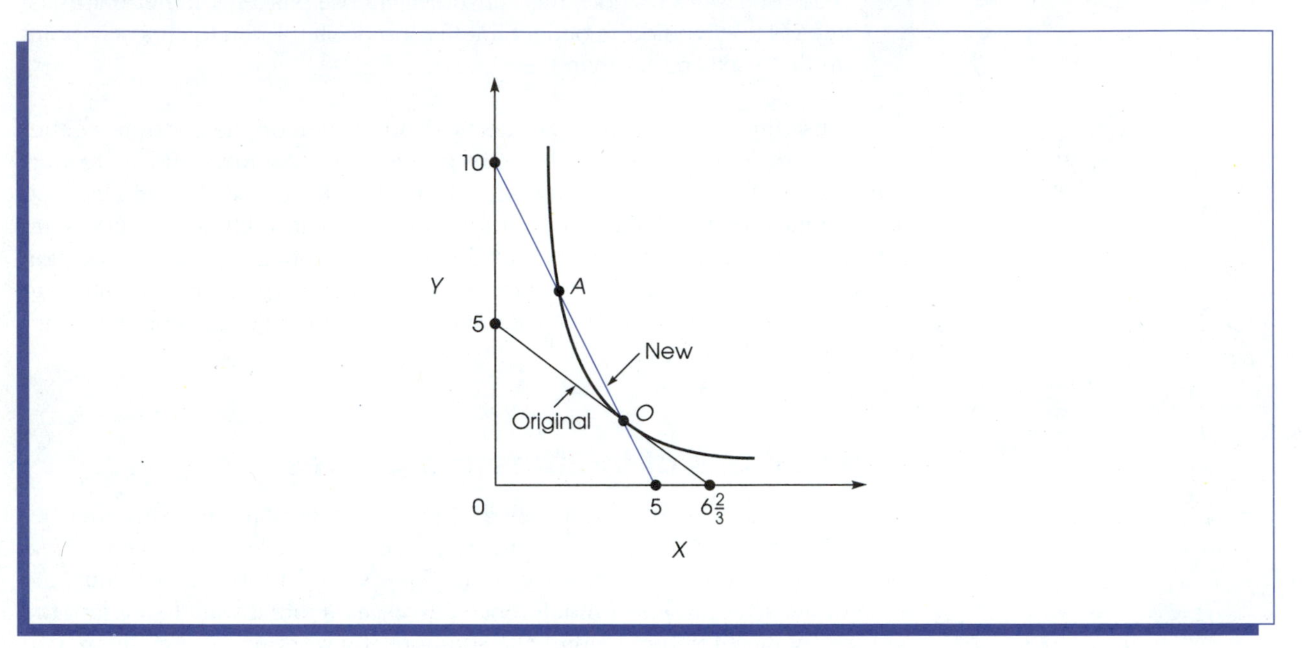

The graph shows the original and new budget lines that are specified in the problem. We know that an indifference curve is tangent to the original line at the point *O*. We can calculate that the new budget line passes through the point *O*.

price of *Y* is \$2, and your income is still \$20. If you buy no *Y*s you get 5 *X*s, and if you buy no *X*s you get 10 *Y*s. The *new* budget line goes through (5,0) and (0,10).

If we are drawing the *new* budget line freehand and want to draw it accurately, we have to figure out whether point *O* is above, below, or on the *new* budget line. That is, we must determine whether basket *O* would cost more than your income, less than your income, or exactly the same as your income at the new prices. At the new prices of \$4 for *X* and \$2 for *Y*, basket *O* will cost (\$4 × 4) + (\$2 × 2) = \$20, so that you can exactly afford it. This means that the *new* budget line goes right through *O*, and it is drawn that way in Exhibit 3–11.

Now let's figure out where your *new* budget line is tangent to an indifference curve, that is, the location of your new optimum. First, we can rule out point *O*. The indifference curve through *O* is already tangent to the *original* line, so it can't be tangent to the *new* line. (This is because *a smooth curve cannot be tangent to two different lines at the same point*—an important fact about geometry that will be useful to keep in mind.)

Where, then, is your new optimum? It cannot be anywhere between point *A* and the *Y* axis. If it were tangent in that region, it would be forced by geometry to cross the indifference curve that passes through *O*—and this is not allowed. For the same reason there cannot be a tangency anywhere between point O and the X axis. In panel A of Exhibit 3–12 we reproduce the graph from Exhibit 3–11 with two dashed indifference curves in the forbidden regions. The pictures are dashed precisely because there cannot really be any indifference curves tangent there. They are illustrated only to show you what they would look like if they were there—and to show you that they would be forced to cross the curve passing through O.

The only possible locations for the new optimum are the points between A and O, such as at P in panel B of Exhibit 3–12. If you look at that panel, you will see that P must be on a higher indifference curve than O is. In other words, your new basket is preferable to your old basket.

This solves the problem that began this section. The price change unquestionably makes you better off. It allows you to move to a higher indifference curve. Your old basket O is still as expensive as it ever was, but you can now afford better baskets (like P) that were previously outside your budget constraint.

Consumer Price Index Internet site: http://stats.bls.gov/cpihome.htm

Measuring the Cost of Living

Now let's ask another interesting question. What has happened to the *cost of living* (or the *price level*) in this problem? When the price of X goes from $3 to

Exhibit 3-12 Finding the New Optimum

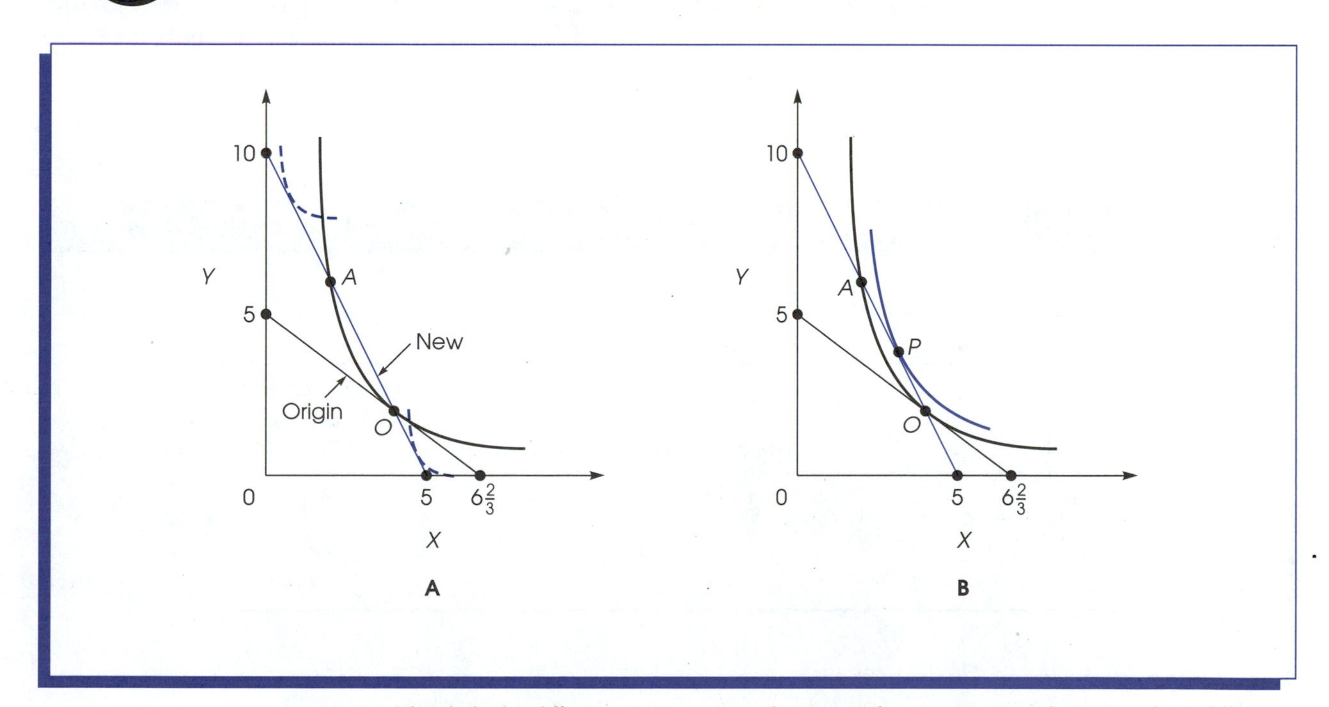

The dashed indifference curves in panel A cannot be correct, since they cross the indifference curve through O. The only correct way to draw an indifference curve tangent to the *new* budget line is with the tangency between A and O, at a point like P as in panel B. The new indifference curve is then necessarily higher than the old one, so you are better off at the new optimum.

$4 and the price of *Y* goes from $4 to $2, will the newspapers report *inflation* or *deflation*?

The answer is not obvious. The prices of different baskets have changed in different ways. A basket consisting entirely of *X* will have risen in price and a basket consisting entirely of *Y* will have fallen in price. In order to report the change in the *cost of living*, we must choose a basket and report the change in the cost of that basket. The answer that we get will depend on what basket we choose. This choice is known as selecting a **price index.**

Price index A measure of the cost of living, based on changes in the cost of some basket of goods.

Consumer price index (CPI) The price index officially reported by the U.S. Department of Labor.

In practice the most commonly quoted price index is the **consumer price index (CPI)** compiled by the Bureau of Labor Statistics of the U.S. Department of Labor. Roughly, the CPI chooses the basket consumed by a typical consumer in the earlier period and reports changes in the price of that basket.

In the situation of Exhibit 3–12, the CPI would report the change in the price of basket *O*, because that is the basket consumed in the *original* period. Recall that $O = (4,2)$ costs exactly $20 at both the *original* and the *new* prices. Therefore, the CPI will report no change in the price level. This is so despite the fact that an income of $20 will now buy you more "happiness" than it did before.

Here is another example. Suppose that the only two items you consume are steak and potatoes. You consider buying 4 possible baskets, which we call *A*, *B*, *C*, and *D*. These baskets are described in Exhibit 3–13. For example, *A* contains 2 steaks and 2 potatoes. Suppose, also, that the baskets are listed in your order of preference (*A* being the best and *D* the worst). Finally, suppose that in 1994 steaks cost $2 apiece and potatoes cost $1 apiece, whereas in 1998 these prices are reversed. The last two columns in Exhibit 3–13 show the prices of the baskets in each of the two years.

Exhibit 3-13 Changing Prices and the Consumer Price Index

Basket	No. of Steaks	No. of Potatoes	1994 Basket Price (Steak = $2, Potato = $1)	1998 Basket Price (Steak = $1, Potato = $2)
A	2	2	$6	$6
B	2	1	5	4
C	1	2	4	5
D	1	1	3	3

We assume that the 4 baskets in the exhibit are listed in the order of your preference. With a $4 income, you will choose basket *C* in 1994 and basket *B* in 1998, making you better off in 1994. However, a Laspeyres price index such as the CPI will report a 25% rise in the cost of living from 1994 to 1998, because basket *C* costs 25% more in the later year.

QA EXERCISE 3.8 Verify the last two columns of Exhibit 3–13.

For more about Laspeyres price indices visit: http://stats.bls.gov/blshome.html

Now assume that your income is $4 per year and that in each year you buy the most desirable basket you can afford. In 1994 you will buy basket *C* and in 1998 you will buy basket *B*. In which year are you happier? Clearly 1998.

What has happened to the officially reported cost of living in the four-year period from 1994 to 1998? The consumer price index focuses on the basket purchased in the earlier year—in this case basket *C*. The price of *C* has gone up, from $4 to $5. The CPI will report that the price level has risen 25%, implying that you are worse off than before. Indeed, a naïve observer might think that you are worse off, because you can no longer afford basket *C* in 1998. In fact, you are better off, because you can now afford basket *B*, which you like better.

Laspeyres price index A price index based on the basket consumed in the earlier period.

Paasche price index A price index based on the basket consumed in the later period.

A price index that focuses on the basket purchased in the earlier year is called a **Laspeyres[3] price index**. Whenever there is a change in relative prices, a Laspeyres index makes the price changes seem worse for consumers than they really are. Does this mean that the Bureau of Labor Statistics is foolish for choosing such an index? No, it only reflects the fact that there is no such thing as a perfect measure of the cost of living. For example, a **Paasche[4] price index** is one that focuses on the basket purchased in the later period. In Exhibit 3–13 a Paasche price index will focus on basket *B* and report a 20% drop in the cost of living. A Paasche price index always makes price changes seem better for consumers than they really are. Every price index contains some information, but it must be interpreted with care.

QA EXERCISE 3.9 The examples of Exhibits 3–12 and 3–13 are not perfectly analogous. In Exhibit 3–12 there is no change in the Laspeyres price index, whereas in Exhibit 3–13 the Laspeyres price index rises by 25%. The goal of this exercise is to construct a graphical representation of the tabular example in 3–13 and a tabular representation of the graphical example in 3–13.

Draw a figure like the ones in Exhibit 3–12 that reflects the situation described in Exhibit 3–13. Be sure to draw indifference curves that reflect the order of presence given in Exhibit 3–13. Show the *original* and *new* budget lines, and the points where they are tangent to indifference curves.

Nobody blames the Bureau of Labor Statistics for the fact that there is no such thing as a perfect price index. However, the CPI has been criticized for a number of reasons unrelated to its being a Laspeyres index. An entertaining catalog of reasons for being skeptical of the CPI can be found in an article by William Kruskal and Lester Telser.[5] A number of these problems have been corrected since the article appeared.

---

[3] Pronounced "La-spears."

[4] Pronounced "Posh."

[5] W. Kruskal and L. Telser, "Food Prices and the Bureau of Labor Statistics," *Journal of Business* 33 (1960):258–279.

Differences in Tastes

A Problem

Albert lives in New York City, where almonds sell for $2 a pound and cashews sell for $1 a pound. He earns $10 a day, with which he buys 4 pounds of almonds and 2 pounds of cashews.

Betty lives in Los Angeles, where almonds sell for $3 a pound and cashews sell for $6 a pound. She earns $45 a day, with which she buys 1 pound of almonds and 7 pounds of cashews.

Is it possible to tell from this information whether Albert and Betty have the same tastes?

The Solution

If two people—like Albert and Betty—choose different consumption baskets, it must be either because they have different tastes (represented by different families of indifference curves), or because they face different budget lines, or both. It is certainly true that Albert and Betty face different budget lines, as you can see in Exhibit 3–14. So the question is whether they must *also* have different tastes.

Exhibit 3-14 Comparing Preferences

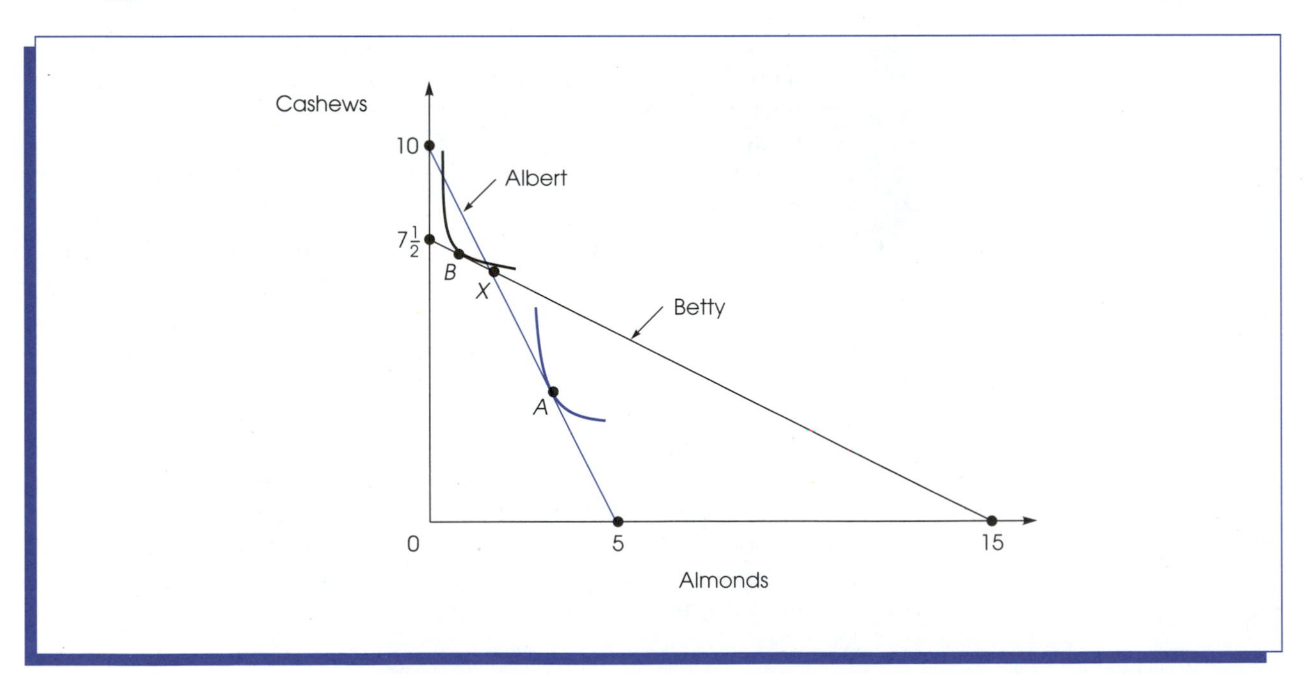

Albert's indifference curve (tangent at *A*) must eventually cross Betty's indifference curve (tangent at *B*). Therefore, Albert and Betty cannot possibly have the same tastes.

QA EXERCISE 3.10 Make sure the budget lines in Exhibit 3–14 are drawn correctly.

The next step is to illustrate both consumers' optimum points. Albert's optimum is shown at the point $A = (4,2)$ on his (blue) budget line. To make sure the picture is accurate, we must pause to consider whether (4,2) is located outside Betty's budget line (above and to the left of the cross-point X) or inside Betty's budget line (below and to the right of the cross-point X). This is the same as asking whether Betty could afford to purchase basket A. The answer is yes: At the prices she pays, basket A would cost $(4 \times \$3) + (2 \times \$6) = \$24$, which is less than her \$45 income. Therefore, point A is inside Betty's budget line, below and to the right of X, which is how it's drawn in Exhibit 3–14.

Betty's optimum is shown at the point $B = (1,7)$ on her black budget line. Albert could afford this basket: At the prices he pays, it would cost $(1 \times \$2) + (7 \times \$1) = \$9$. Thus, the basket is inside Albert's budget line, above and to the left of X.

Next, we draw in some indifference curves. Because Albert chooses point A, he must have an indifference curve tangent to his (blue) budget line at A; that indifference curve is shown in color. Because Betty chooses point B, we must have an indifference curve tangent to her (black) budget line at B; that indifference curve is shown in black.

Now: Could Albert and Betty have the same tastes? That is the same as asking; Could Albert's (blue) indifference curve and Betty's (black) indifference curve both be from the same *family* of indifference curves. The answer is no, because it is clear from the picture that the two illustrated indifference curves must eventually cross. There is no possibility that Albert and Betty have the same tastes.

Students sometimes misunderstand this analysis and think that the crucial point is that the two indifference curves in Exhibit 3–14 are not identical. Those students have missed an important point. The key fact is not that the curves are different; it is that they are incapable of belonging to the same *family* of indifference curves. The observation leading to this key fact is that the two curves must cross.

Do Tastes Change over Time?

The method that we have used to discover taste differences across individuals can also be used to discover changes in taste over time. In Exhibit 3–14 replace Albert and Betty with "Mr. Jones in 1997" and "Mr. Jones in 1998." Suppose that Mr. Jones in 1997 had the black budget line and chose point A, and Mr. Jones in 1998 had the colored budget line and chose point B. We would then be entitled to conclude that Mr. Jones in 1998 had different tastes from Mr. Jones in 1997. In other words, we could conclude that Mr. Jones's tastes changed.

Whenever possible, economists prefer to assume that people's tastes are rel-

Exhibit 3-15 An Income Tax versus a Head Tax

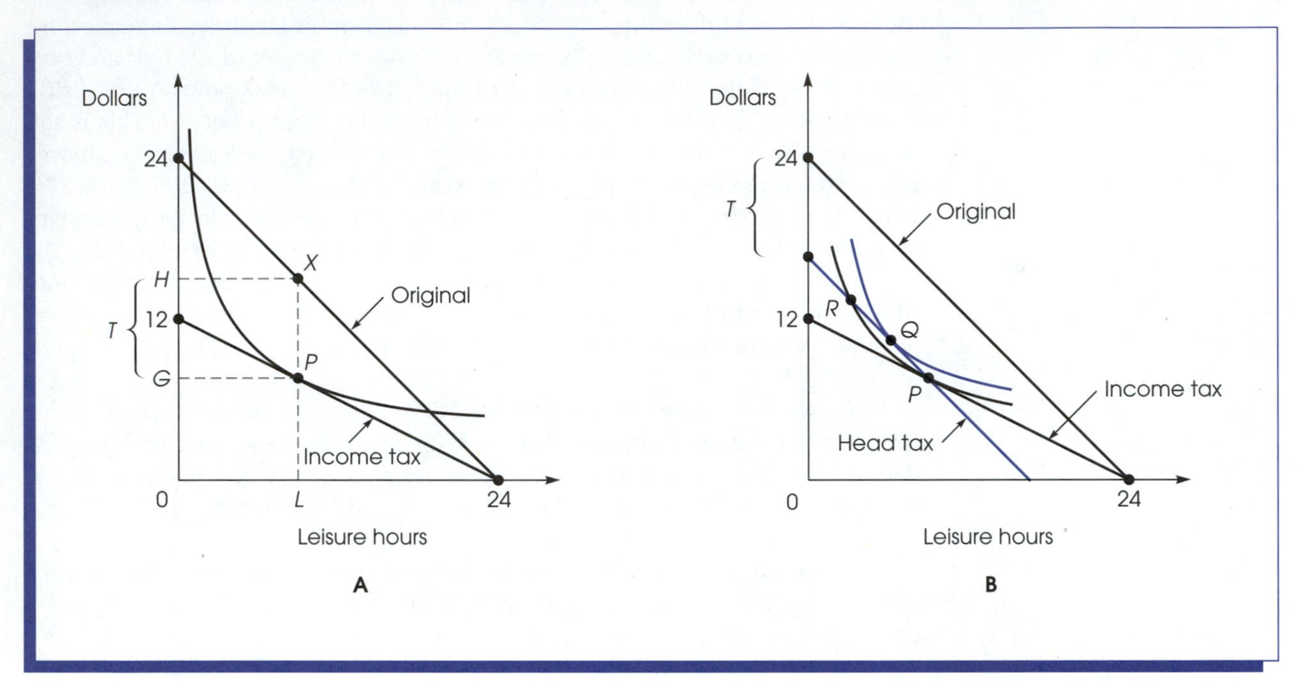

Panel A shows your *original* (untaxed) budget line and your *income tax* budget line. The optimum on the *income tax* line is at *P*. Your after-tax income is *$G*. Your before-tax income is equal to what you would earn if you were on your *original* budget line and working *L* hours, that is, *$H*. Your tax bill is the difference, or *$T*.

Panel B shows the *head tax* budget line, which lies a vertical distance *$T* below the *original* budget line and consequently passes through point *P*. The optimum on the *head tax* line must be at a point like *Q* between *P* and *R*, and it is consequently on a higher indifference curve. The head tax is thus preferable to the income tax.

atively constant over time, and that changes in their behavior are due primarily to changes in prices and changes in income (that is, changes in the budget constraint). The reason for this is that tastes are unobservable, and theories that allow for significant changes in unobservable variables are very hard to test. In fact, the economists Gary Becker and George Stigler have gone so far as to argue for the assumption that all individuals have the same tastes in all things at all times and they never change![6] It is important to know whether such assumptions are consistent with the observable facts about the world. One way to find out is to plot a single consumer's budget lines in different years, draw the consumer's optimal points, and see if the picture ever looks like panel B of Exhibit 3–14. If it does, the assumption of constant tastes is in trouble.

[6] G. Becker and G. Stigler, "De Gustibus Non Est Disputandum," *American Economic Review* 67 (1977): 76–90.

This test has been performed via an examination of the behavior of the "typical" British consumer in the years 1900–1955.[7] Using 127 goods in every possible pairing, and plotting budget lines for each pair of successive years, there were hundreds of cases in which the budget lines crossed. Each of these was potentially a source of evidence for taste change. If in any of these cases, the optima had been located like those in Exhibit 3–15, a taste change would have been revealed. In fact, there were no such cases.

Looking for a taste change and not finding it does not prove that no taste changes exist. But looking very extensively for a thing and not finding it entitles one to doubt its existence. The tests described here are only a fraction of those that were performed and reported in the paper. Many of these tests had the potential to reveal a taste change, but none of them did so.

Head Taxes versus Income Taxes

Which would you rather pay: a percentage income tax (under which the government takes a certain percentage of your earnings) or a head tax (under which the government takes a certain number of dollars per day, regardless of your earnings)? Obviously, the answer depends at least partly on the size of the taxes. A 1% income tax is probably better than $10,000 daily head tax, whereas a 2¢ daily head tax is probably better than a 90% income tax.

So let's make the comparison fair by assuming that the taxes are set at such levels that your tax bill will be the same under either tax. Now which would you rather pay? The following problem is designed to lead you through an analysis of this question.

A Problem

a. Suppose that you can work up to 24 hours per day at a wage of $1 per hour, with the remainder of your time available for leisure. Draw your budget constraint between "dollars" and "leisure hours."

b. Now suppose that the government institutes a 50% income tax. Draw your new budget constraint. Depict your new optimum. Call it *P*.

c. Show the number of dollars that you get to keep. Show the number of dollars that you earn before you pay your taxes. Show the size of your tax bill. Call it *$T*.

d. Now suppose that the income tax is abolished and replaced by a head tax of *$T* per day. Draw your new budget line. Does it pass over, under, or through point *P*? How do you know?

e. Which would you rather pay: the income tax or the head tax? Why?

---

[7] S. Landsburg, "Taste Change in the United Kingdom," *Journal of Political Economy* 89 (1981): 92–104.

The Solution

a. If you consume no leisure, you will be able to earn \$24 per day, whereas if you earn no income, you will be able to consume 24 hours of leisure per day. Therefore, your budget line is the line labeled *original* in each of the two panels of Exhibit 3–15.

b. Now if you consume no leisure, you will be able to earn only \$12 per day. Therefore, your new budget line is the one labeled *income tax* in each of the two panels of Exhibit 3–15. Your new optimum occurs where this line is tangent to an indifference curve. Such a tangency is depicted in the exhibit and labeled *P*.

c. The number of dollars you get to keep is the number of dollars in basket *P*. That number of dollars is labeled *G* in panel A of Exhibit 3–15. With basket *P* you consume *L* leisure hours and receive *\$G* in after-tax income.

To compute your before-tax income, you must ask yourself this question: If the income tax were abolished, and if I kept working the same number of hours I am working now, how many dollars would I get to keep? (Notice that this question is entirely hypothetical. If the income tax were abolished, you would probably choose to work some different number of hours.)

If the income tax were abolished, you would be back on the *original* budget line. If you continued to work the same number of hours, you would continue to have the same number of leisure hours, namely, *L*. Putting these two facts together, you would be consuming basket *X* in panel A of Exhibit 3–16, and you would earn *\$H*. *\$H* is your before-tax income.

Since you earn *\$H* before taxes and keep *\$G* after taxes, the difference must be the size of your tax bill. This difference is represented by the vertical distance from *G* to *H*, labeled *T* in the exhibit.

Sometimes students think that *X* must be the optimum on the *original* budget line. There is no reason to believe that is true. As we have pointed out, you would quite likely work some different number of hours if the income tax were abolished, which is the same as saying that the optimum is elsewhere than at *X*.

d. First the abolition of the income tax returns you to your *original* budget line. Then the institution of the head tax reduces your income by *\$T* regardless of how many hours you work. Therefore, we can get your *head tax* budget line by removing *\$T* from each basket on the *original* budget line; this causes a parallel downward shift by the amount *\$T*. The *head tax* budget line is shown in panel B of Exhibit 3–15.

Since point *P* lies a distance *\$T* below the *original* budget line, and since the *head tax* budget line lies a distance *\$T* below the *original* budget line, the *head tax* line must pass through the point *P*.

e. The optimum along the *head tax* line must be between *P* and *R* (at a point like *Q*). If this were not true, the indifference curves would cross. It is clear from the exhibit that Q must be on a higher indifference curve than P. The best basket that you can acquire under a head tax *(Q)* is superior to the best basket that you can acquire under an income tax *(P)*. The head tax is preferable to the income tax.

Discussion

Since your head tax bill is the same size as your income tax bill, you might be tempted to think that either tax is equally unpleasant. To see why this is false, consider your position at point P under the income tax. Here your marginal rate of substitution is such that your last hour of leisure is worth 50¢. If you forgo that last hour of leisure by working another hour, you will take home 50¢ in wages, gaining nothing. However, when the income tax is abolished and replaced by the head tax, you have the opportunity to forgo an hour of leisure in exchange for an additional $1 in wages. This new opportunity is an attractive one. By accepting it, you move up and to the left along the *head tax* budget line, improving your situation. You continue to move in that direction until you reach point Q, where your marginal rate of substitution between leisure and income is exactly $1 per hour.

summary

A consumer's behavior depends on his tastes and his opportunities. His tastes are encoded in his indifference curves and his opportunities are encoded in his budget line. By combining this information in a single graph, we can predict the consumer's behavior.

Each consumer has a family of indifference curves. Each curve in the family consists of baskets between which he is indifferent. His indifference curves slope downward, fill the plane, never cross, and are convex. A different consumer will have a different family of indifference curves, also satisfying these properties.

The slope of an indifference curve is equal (in absolute value) to the marginal value of X in terms of Y. That is, it is the number of units of Y for which the consumer is just willing to trade one unit of X.

As the consumer moves along an indifference curve in the direction of more X and less Y, we expect that the marginal value of X will decrease. This accounts for the convexity of indifference curves.

The consumer's budget line depends on his income and the prices of the goods that he buys. Its equation is:

$$P_X \cdot x + P_Y \cdot y = I$$

where P_X and P_Y are the prices of X and Y and I is the consumer's income. The slope of the budget line is equal (in absolute value) to the relative price of X in terms of Y.

The consumer's optimum occurs where his budget line is tangent to one of his indifference curves. This is the point at which he attains the highest indifference curve that is available to him. At this point the marginal value of X in terms of Y is equal to the relative price of X in terms of Y. At any other point either the marginal value would exceed the relative price, in which case the consumer would trade Y for X, or the relative price would exceed the marginal value, in which case the consumer would trade X for Y. Only at his optimum point is he satisfied not to trade any further.

Review Questions

R1. Explain why indifference curves slope downward.

R2. Explain why two of a consumer's indifference curves can never cross. Can two indifference curves belonging to different consumers ever cross?

R3. What is the meaning of the marginal value of X in terms of Y? How is it reflected geometrically?

R4. What is the equation for the consumer's budget line? What is the economic interpretation of the slope of the budget line?

R5. Where does the consumer's optimum occur? What two important quantities are equal at the optimum point?

R6. Suppose that the marginal value of X in terms of Y is greater than the relative price of X in terms of Y. Is the consumer's basket to the left or to the right of his optimum point? Will the consumer want to buy or sell X? Explain how you know. In which direction will this cause the consumer to move along the budget line?

Numerical Exercise

N1. Every day Fred buys wax lips and candy cigarettes. After deciding how many of each to buy, he multiplies the number of sets of wax lips times the number of packs of candy cigarettes. The higher this number comes out to be, the happier he is. For example, 3 sets of wax lips and 5 packs of candy cigarettes will make him happier than 2 sets of wax lips and 7 packs of candy cigarettes, because 3×5 is greater than 2×7. Wax lips sell for $2 a pair and candy cigarettes for $1 a pack. Fred has $20 to spend each day.

a. Make a table that looks like this:

Pairs of Wax Lips	Packs of Candy Cigarettes
0	
1	
2	
.	
.	
.	
10	

where each row of the chart corresponds to a basket on Fred's budget line. Fill in the second column.

b. Draw a graph showing Fred's budget line and marking the baskets described by your table. Draw Fred's indifference curves through these baskets. If he must select among these baskets, which one will Fred choose?

c. Add to your table a third column labeled *MV* for the marginal value of wax lips in terms of candy cigarettes. Fill in the *MV* for each basket. (*Hint:* For each basket construct another basket that has one less pair of wax lips but enough more packs of candy cigarettes to be equally desirable. How many packs of candy cigarettes have been added to the basket?) For which basket is the marginal value closest to the relative price of wax lips? Is this consistent with your answer to part (b)?

Problem Set

1. Herman buys 10 turnips each year. True or False: If the price of turnips goes up by 10¢ apiece, and if Herman's tastes and income remain unchanged, then he will have $1 a year less to spend on other things.

2. True or False: If crime prevention is a costly activity, then it is possible for New York City to have too *little* crime.

3. Suppose that you hate typing and hate filing.

   a. Draw a graph with "hours of typing" on the horizontal axis and "hours of filing" on the vertical. Do your indifference curves slope upward or downward? Why?

   b. Suppose you currently type for 3 hours a day and file for 5, but you'd be just as happy typing for 2 hours a day and filing for 7. What is the slope of your indifference curve at the point (3,5)? If you hated typing even more than you do, would you expect the indifference curve to be steeper or shallower?

   c. Would you expect the indifference curve to be steeper or shallower at points that represent a lot of typing and very little filing? What does this say about the shape of the indifference curves?

   d. Suppose your boss tells you that henceforth, you may divide your 8-hour day any way you wish between these two activities, but the number of hours you spend typing and the number of hours you spend filing must add up to 8. Draw the relevant budget constraint.

   e. Given the information in part b, will you now choose to type more or less than 3 hours a day? Illustrate your new optimum and explain why it is your optimum.

4. Suppose you like driving fast but you hate getting injured.

   a. Draw a graph with "speed" on the horizontal axis and "probability of injury" on the vertical. Do your indifference curves slope upward or downward? Why?

   b. Suppose you drive to work every day at 40 miles per hour (m.p.h.) and have a 5% annual chance of being injured. You are aware that in general, your annual chance of being injured (measured in percent) is always equal to ⅛ of your driving speed (measured in m.p.h.). Draw the relevant budget constraint, and draw a set of indifference curves that could have led to your decision to drive at 40 m.p.h.

   c. In order for your chosen speed to be an optimum, what must be true about the shape of the indifference curves?

   d. Suppose that because of a new kind of safety device, the probability of injury falls to ⅒ of your driving speed. Draw the new budget constraint and the new optimum. Can you determine whether the device causes a fall in your probability of being injured? Can you determine whether the device causes an increase in your happiness?

5. Suppose your indifference curves between food and clothing were nonconvex as in Exhibit 3-10. True or False: In this case a very small change in price could lead to either no change at all in your consumption of X or to a very large change in your consumption of X.

6. Suppose that you like to own both left and right shoes, but that a right shoe is of no use to you unless you own a matching left one, and vice versa. Draw your indifference curves between left and right shoes.

7. Draw your indifference curves between nickels and dimes, assuming that you are always willing to trade 2 nickels for 1 dime, or vice versa. What is the marginal value of nickels in terms of dimes?

8. Amanda consumes only two goods, X and Y. Her indifference curves have the usual shape. Consider the baskets (1,3), (2,2), and (3,1) (notice that these all lie along a straight line). Amanda is exactly indifferent between (1,3) and (3,1). Which does she prefer between (2,2) and (3,1)? Carefully justify your answer.

9. Suppose that you consume nothing but beer and pizza. In 1995, your income is $10 per week, beer costs $1 per bottle, pizza costs $1 per slice, and you buy 6 bottles of beer and 4 slices of pizza per week. In 1996, your income rises to $20 per week, the price of beer rises to $2.50 per bottle, and the price of pizza rises to $1.25 per slice.

   a. In which year are you happier?

   b. In which year do you eat more pizza? Justify and illustrate your answer with indifference curves.

10. Suppose that the only two goods you consume are bread and circus tickets. When bread sells for $1 a loaf and circus tickets sell for $1 apiece, you buy 7 loaves of bread and 3 circus tickets to exhaust your income of $10. One day the price of bread falls to 50¢ a loaf while the price of circus tickets rises to $2 apiece and your income remains unchanged. You now buy 12 loaves of bread and 2 circus tickets. Is it possible to say with certainty whether you are better off? Why or why not?

11. Recently the price of cheese has risen from $4 per pound to $6 per pound, the price of meat has fallen from $5 per pound to $2 per pound, and Susan's income has stayed fixed at $22 per week. Since the price changes, Susan has been buying 3 pounds of cheese and 2 pounds of meat every week. Is Susan happier now than she was before?

12. Suppose that you live in a world with two goods, X and Y. There is no money in this world, but Xs and Ys can be exchanged directly at a relative price of 1 X per Y. You currently choose to own 3 Xs and 2 Ys.

   a. Draw your budget constraint.

   b. Suppose that the relative price of X goes up to 2 Ys per X. Use a graph to show how this would make you better off.

   c. True or False: Since a rise in the relative price of X would make you better off, a fall in the relative price of X would make you worse off.

d. Suppose that the relative price of X goes up to 2 Ys per X, stays there for a while, and then returns to 1 Y per X. True or False: At the end of this process, you are neither better nor worse off than you were at the beginning.

13. In 1998, you buy shoes for $2 a pair and socks for $1 a pair, and your income is $30, with which you buy 12 pairs of shoes and 6 pairs of socks. In 1999, you buy shoes for $1 a pair and socks for $2 a pair, and your income is still $30.

a. Draw both years' budget lines. Notice that they cross at the point (10, 10).

b. True or False: In 1999, you will surely buy more than 10 pairs of shoes.

c. True or False: In 1999, you will surely buy more than 12 pairs of shoes.

14. In 1998, you buy shoes for $2 a pair and socks for $1 a pair, and your income is $30, with which you buy 6 pairs of shoes and 18 pairs of socks. In 1999, you buy shoes for $1 a pair and socks for $2 a pair, and your income is still $30.

a. True or False: In 1999, you can still afford your 1998 basket.

b. True or False: In 1999, you might or might not be happier than in 1998.

c. True or False: In 1999, you certainly buy more than 6 pairs of shoes.

d. True or False: *If* in 1999 you are happier than in 1998, *then* in 1999 you buy more than 6 pairs of shoes.

15. Amelia buys coffee for $1 per cup and tea for 50¢ per cup; every day she drinks 1 cup of coffee and 2 cups of tea. Bernard buys coffee for 50¢ per cup and tea for $1 per cup; every day he drinks 2 cups of coffee and 1 cup of tea. Can you determine whether Amelia and Bernard have identical tastes?

16. Chris buys coffee for $1 per cup and tea for 50¢ per cup; every day she drinks 2 cups of coffee and 1 cup of tea. David buys coffee for 50¢ per cup and tea for $1 per cup; every day he drinks 1 cup of coffee and 2 cups of tea. Can you determine whether Chris and David have identical tastes?

17. Evelyn buys coffee for $1 per cup and tea for 50¢ per cup; every day she drinks 1 cup of coffee and 2 cups of tea. Frederick buys coffee for 50¢ per cup and tea for $1 per cup; every day he drinks 1 cup of coffee and 1 cup of tea. Can you determine whether Evelyn and Frederick have identical tastes?

18. Amanda is indifferent between baskets (4,1) and (2,3). Bernard is indifferent between baskets (3,2) and (1,4). Notice that all four baskets lie along a straight line.

a. Can you determine whether Amanda and Bernard have identical tastes?

b. Suppose that Amanda chooses basket (4,1) and Bernard chooses basket (1,4). Can you determine whether Amanda and Bernard pay the same prices for the goods they buy?

19. Herman has an income of $10, which he spends on fish heads and all other goods. Fishheads cost $1 apiece.

a. Suppose that the government agrees to pay half of Herman's fishhead bill, so that fishheads now cost him only 50¢ apiece. He now chooses to buy 8 fishheads. Show how the government program affects Herman's budget line, and show his new optimum point. Call it *P*. What are the coordinates of the point *P*?

b. Now suppose the government ends the program in part a and replaces it with a new and simpler program: Herman just gets a cash gift of $4. Show his new budget line. Does it go above, below, or through point *P*? How do you know?

c. Of the two programs in parts a and b, which is more expensive for the government? Which does Herman prefer? Justify your answer.

20. Mr. Smith has a very low income and Mr. Jones has a very high income. They both purchase education from the same private school.

a. In a single diagram, draw budget lines between "education" and "all other goods" for both Mr. Smith and Mr. Jones.

b. Now suppose that the government offers a certain quantity of free education with the proviso that if you accept the offer, you must consume exactly the quantity that the government offers, no more and no less. Draw Mr. Smith's new budget constraint and Mr. Jones's new budget constraint. (*Hint:* Mr. Smith's new budget constraint is no longer a line, but a line plus a point; the same is true for Mr. Jones.)

c. Suppose that Mr. Smith accepts the government's offer and Mr. Jones rejects it. Is it possible that Mr. Smith and Mr. Jones have the same tastes?

21. Suppose that you are a government policymaker and your goal is to make poor people happier. You can do so by subsidizing their food, education, and medical care; or you can do so by giving them cash.

a. On the basis of your answer to problem 19, make an argument in favor of giving cash.

b. Now suppose that although you want to help only the poor, it is difficult for you to tell who is poor and who is rich, and you are worried that some rich people will claim a share of the cash giveaways. On the basis of your answer to problem 20, make an argument for subsidizing education instead of giving away cash.

c. Can you think of a reason why governments would want to deliberately limit the amount of education available at public schools?

22. Mr. Jones can purchase varying quantities of education from private schools at a going price. One day there opens in Mr. Jones's neighborhood a public school that he may attend for free if he wants to. However, if he attends the public school, he must accept the amount of education that it offers. He can no longer take any private school classes because the public and private schools are in session at the same time of day.

a. Draw Mr. Jones's old and new budget constraints.

b. Draw a set of indifference curves that implies that Mr. Jones will increase his consumption of education as a result of the opening of the public school. Draw a set that implies that Mr. Jones will not change his level of education. Draw a set that implies that Mr. Jones will now buy less education than before. Call these the indifference curves of Mr. A. Jones, Mr. B. Jones, and Mr. C. Jones, respectively. Can you rank Mr. A., Mr. B., and Mr. C. in terms of how much they seem to like education?

c. True or False: If most people are reasonably fond of education but not fanatically so, then an offer of free public education could reduce the quantity of education consumed.

23. Suppose that you can work anywhere from 0 to 24 hours per day at a wage of $1 per hour. You are subject to a tax of 50% on all income over $5 per day (the first $5 per day is untaxed). You elect to work 10 hours per day.

a. Show your budget constraint and your optimum point.

b. Suppose that the tax law is changed, so that *all* income is subject to a 25% tax. Do you now work more or less than 10 hours? Does the government collect more or less tax revenue than before?

c. Which do you prefer: the old tax law or the new one?

24. Suppose that you have 24 hours per day to allocate between leisure and working at a wage of $1 per hour. Draw your budget line between leisure and dollars. One day the government simultaneously institutes two new programs: a 50% income tax and a plan whereby everybody in the country receives a gift from the government of $6 each year.

a. Draw your new budget line.

b. Suppose that the government chose the level of $6 for the gift because it precisely exhausts the income from the tax. Explain why this means that the average taxpayer must be paying exactly $6 in tax.

c. Assume that you are the average taxpayer and draw your new optimum. Is it on, above, or below your original budget line?

d. As the average taxpayer, are you working harder or less hard than before the programs went into effect? Are you happier or less happy? How do you know?

25. You have an income of $120 per week and own a car that costs $2 per mile to drive. You choose to drive 50 miles per week.

a. Draw your budget constraint between "miles driven" and "all other goods," with "all other goods" measured in dollars. Show your optimum point.

b. Suppose that you are offered the opportunity to purchase for $60 a car that costs 50¢ a mile to drive. Draw that budget constraint that would result if you bought the new car. Note that the two budget constraints cross at (40,40).

c. Would you buy the new car? Defend your answer using indifference curves.

26. Suppose that you get rid of your old gas-guzzler and buy a new, fuel-efficient car. Driving is now cheaper, but on the other hand you have to make monthly car payments. You find that, on balance, you are exactly as happy as you were before. Illustrate this situation using indifference curves between "Car Rides" and "All Other Goods." Are you driving more or less than you were before?

27. Dizzyland Amusement Park has begun selling a "VIP pass" that costs $20 and entitles the bearer to a discount price on rides. Mickey Duck, a Dizzyland patron, has decided he is definitely happier with a VIP pass than without one.

a. In a diagram with "rides" on the horizontal axis and "all other goods" on the vertical axis, illustrate the shift in Mickey's budget line when he buys his pass.

b. True or False: Mickey will certainly go on more rides now that he has a VIP pass.

28. Kramden's Grocery advertises, "We randomly chose 10 of our customers and calculated the costs of their market baskets at Norton's Supermarket. At Norton's, they were an average of 6% higher." Does this convince you that wise shoppers will shop at Kramden's? Why or why not?

Internet Exercise

Recently the method of calculating Consumer Price Index (CPI) has been criticized for leading to overstated consumer price inflation. There are several sources of information on this bias on the Internet. One of these is the testimony of Federal Reserve Bank Chairman Alan Greenspan before the Committee on the Budget, U.S. House of Representatives March 4, 1997 (http://www.bog.frb.fed.us/BOARDDOCS/TESTIMONY/19970304.htm).

Another is the final report of the Advisory Committee to Study the Consumer Price Index (also known as the Boskin Commission) (http://www.stat-usa.gov/BEN/boskin.pdf). After accessing these Internet sites, summarize the key sources of bias in the CPI, and the effects of a downward revision in the CPI on inflation-indexed programs such as Social Security.

Appendix to Chapter 3

Cardinal Utility

The theory of cardinal utility is an alternative approach to consumer behavior. It has the advantage of sometimes being easier to work with and the disadvantage that it introduces a new quantity—called *utility*—that can never actually be measured. However, it turns out to be the case that *the cardinal utility approach has exactly the same implications as the indifference curve approach.* Thus, the choice between the two is largely a matter of convenience and of taste.

The Utility Function

Utility A measure of pleasure or satisfaction.

In the cardinal utility approach, we assume that the consumer can associate to each basket a number, called the **utility** derived from that basket, that measures how much pleasure or satisfaction he would get from owning that basket. For the basket containing x units of X and y units of Y, the utility is often denoted $U(x,y)$. Thus, for example, if we write

$$U(5,7) = 6$$

what we mean is that a basket containing 5 *X*s and 7 *Y*s gives the consumer 6 units of utility. The rule for going from baskets to utilities is called the consumer's *utility function.* An example of a utility function is

$$U(x,y) = \sqrt{xy + 1},$$

which would yield the value $U(5,7) = 6$, as above.

We assume that, given a choice between two baskets, the consumer always chooses the one that yields higher utility. Thus, if the consumer with the above utility function were given a choice between basket *A*, with 5 units of *X* and 7 units of *Y*, and basket *B*, with 6 units of *X* and 4 units of *Y*, then he would choose basket *A*, since $U(5,7) = 6$ but $U(6,4) = 5$.

The assumption that consumers seek to maximize utility enables us to pass from utility functions to indifference curves. The consumer with this utility function is indifferent between the baskets (6,4), (8,3), (12,2), and (4,6), since they all yield utilities of 5. Thus, all of these baskets must lie on the same indifference curve. More generally, all of the baskets (x,y) that satisfy.

$$U(x,y) = 5$$

lie on a single indifference curve, so that the equation of that indifference curve is given by $U(x,y) = 5$. Similarly, there is another indifference curve whose equation is given by $U(x,y) = 6$.

If a consumer has the utility function $U(x,y)$, then his indifference curves are the curves with equations $U(x,y) = c$, where c is any constant.

Marginal Utility

Marginal utility of X (MU_X) The amount of additional utility derived from an additional unit of *X*, when the quantity of *Y* is held constant.

The consumer's **marginal utility of X (MU_X)** is defined to be the amount of additional utility he acquires when the amount of *X* is increased by one unit and the amount of *Y* is held constant. For example, consider a consumer whose utility function is as above and who consumes 5 units of *X* and 7 units of *Y*. His utility is $U(5,7) = 6$. If we increase his consumption of *X* by one unit, his utility will be $U(6,7) \approx 6.557$. Thus, the marginal utility of *X* for this consumer is about .557.

We define the marginal utility of *Y* (MU_Y) in a similar way. For this consumer, increasing *Y* by one unit would yield utility $U(5,8) \approx 6.403$. The marginal utility of *Y* for this consumer is about .403.

We assume that the marginal utility of *X* is always positive (more is preferred to less) but that each additional unit of *X* yields less marginal utility than the previous unit (always holding fixed the consumption of *Y*). This is known as the principle of *diminishing marginal utility*. For example, we have seen that a consumer who starts with basket (5,7) has $MU_X \approx .557$. After acquiring a unit of *X* and moving to basket (6,7), his marginal utility of *X* is reduced to $MU_X \approx .514$, as you can verify with your calculator.

Marginal Utility versus Marginal Value

We can relate the concept of marginal utility to the concept of marginal value. Suppose that we reduce your consumption of *X* by one unit. This reduces your utility by the amount MU_X. Now suppose that we increase your consumption of *Y* by ΔY units. This increases your utility by $MU_Y \cdot \Delta Y$. Finally, suppose that ΔY is chosen to leave you just as happy as you were before the changes in your consumption. Then ΔY is the marginal value (to you) of *X* in terms of *Y*. Since you are equally happy before and after the changes, the loss of utility from consuming less *X* must equal the gain in utility from consuming more *Y*;

in other words,

$$MU_X = MU_Y \cdot \Delta Y$$

Rearranging terms, we get

$$\frac{MU_X}{MU_Y} = \Delta Y = MV_{XY}$$

where MV_X denotes the marginal value of X in terms of Y.

The Marginal Utility of Income

Suppose that a consumer facing prices P_X and P_Y finds that his income goes up by a dollar. How much additional utility can he achieve?

First, suppose that he spends the additional dollar entirely on X. Then he can purchase $1/P_X$ units of X, each of which yields an additional MU_X units of utility. By spending an additional dollar on X, the consumer increases his utility by the amount $MU_X \cdot (1/P_X) = MU_X/P_X$. Similarly, by spending an additional dollar on Y, the consumer increases his utility by the amount MU_Y/P_Y. We can think of MU_X/P_X and MU_Y/P_Y as the marginal utility of a dollar spent on X and of a dollar spent on Y.

The Consumer's Optimum

The consumer allocates his income across X and Y so as to achieve the highest possible level of utility. We will determine the conditions that describe this optimum.

Consider the marginal utility of a dollar spent on X, MU_X/P_X, and the marginal utility of a dollar spent on Y, MU_Y/P_Y. We will argue that at the consumer's optimum these two quantities must be equal.

To see why, suppose first that MU_X/P_X, is greater than MU_Y/P_Y. Then there is a way for the consumer to increase his utility. He can spend one dollar less on Y and use that dollar to buy more of X. In doing so, he will sacrifice MU_Y/P_Y units of utility and gain the greater quantity MU_X/P_X, thus, he becomes better off. Having increased his consumption of X, the consumer finds, due to decreasing marginal utility, that MU_X is reduced; and having decreased his consumption of Y, he finds that MU_Y is increased. This brings the quantities MU_X/P_X and MU_Y/P_Y closer together. If MU_X/P_X still exceeds MU_Y/P_Y, the consumer will again cut his expenditures on Y and use the freed-up income to buy more of X. This continues until MU_X/P_X and MU_Y/P_Y become equal.

The same sort of thing happens if MU_Y/P_Y starts out greater than MU_X/P_X. In this case the consumer can increase his utility by spending less on X and more on Y, which brings MU_X/P_X and MU_Y/P_Y closer together. Again, the process continues until the two are equal.

Thus, at the consumer's optimum we must have

$$MU_X/P_X = MU_Y/P_Y$$

Rearranging terms, we get

$$MU_X/MU_Y = P_X/P_Y$$

We have encountered the term on the left before in this appendix; we determined that it is equal to the marginal value of X in terms of Y. The term on the right is the relative price of X in terms of Y. So our cardinal utility analysis leads us to conclude that the consumer's optimum occurs at that point on his budget line where the marginal value of X in terms of Y is equated to the relative price of X in terms of Y—exactly the same conclusion that we reached from the indifference curve analysis in Chapter 3!

c h a p t e r 4

Consumers in the Marketplace

Visit Beverage Digest Online at: http://www.beverage-digest.com/

The average American drinks about 50 gallons of soft drinks a year. Why 50, and not 40 or 60? And why does this number change from year to year? In just two years, from 1992 to 1994, per-capita soft-drink consumption rose by more than 7.5% (from 48.5 gallons to 52.2). The explanation isn't that Americans were getting thirstier; over the same two years, coffee consumption fell by 18%.

We know from Chapter 3 that consumption choices depend on the budget line, and the budget line depends on income and prices. A change in income or a change in price causes the budget line to shift; this, in turn, causes the consumer's optimum to change. In Section 3.3 we saw some isolated examples of such changes; in this chapter we shall investigate them more systematically.

In order to focus on a single good—call it *X*, which might stand for soft drinks or coffee or eggs—we will use the composite-good convention, lumping together everything except *X* into a single category called *all other goods*. This allows us to maintain the useful fiction that there are only two goods in the economy: There is *X*, and there is "all other goods," which we label *Y*.

4.1 Changes in Income

In this section we consider the effects of a change in income.

Changes in Income and Changes in the Budget Line

Let's think about how your budget line moves when your income rises.

Suppose you start with the *original* budget line in Exhibit 4–1. You can afford any basket on this budget line, including, for example, the illustrated basket G.

If your income rises by $5, you can now afford to buy basket *G plus* $5 worth of good *Y*. That is, you can afford point *H*. So point *H* is on your new budget line.

(If the price of *Y* is $1 per unit, then the vertical arrow in Exhibit 4–1 has length 5; if the price of *Y* is $2 per unit, then the vertical arrow has length 2½; if the price of *Y* is 1¢ per unit, then the vertical arrow has length 500.)

More generally, given *any* point on your old budget line, you can add $5 worth of *Y* and get a point on your new budget line. So the vertical distance between the two budget lines is always the same "$5 worth". Because this distance is always the same, it follows that the new budget line is parallel to the original.

A change in income causes a parallel shift of the budget line.

QA EXERCISE 4.1 Draw the new budget line that would result from a $5 *fall* in income.

There is another way to see that a change in income causes a parallel shift of the budget line. Recall from Section 3.2 that the equation of the budget line can be written

$$y = -\frac{P_X}{P_Y} \cdot x + \frac{I}{P_Y}$$

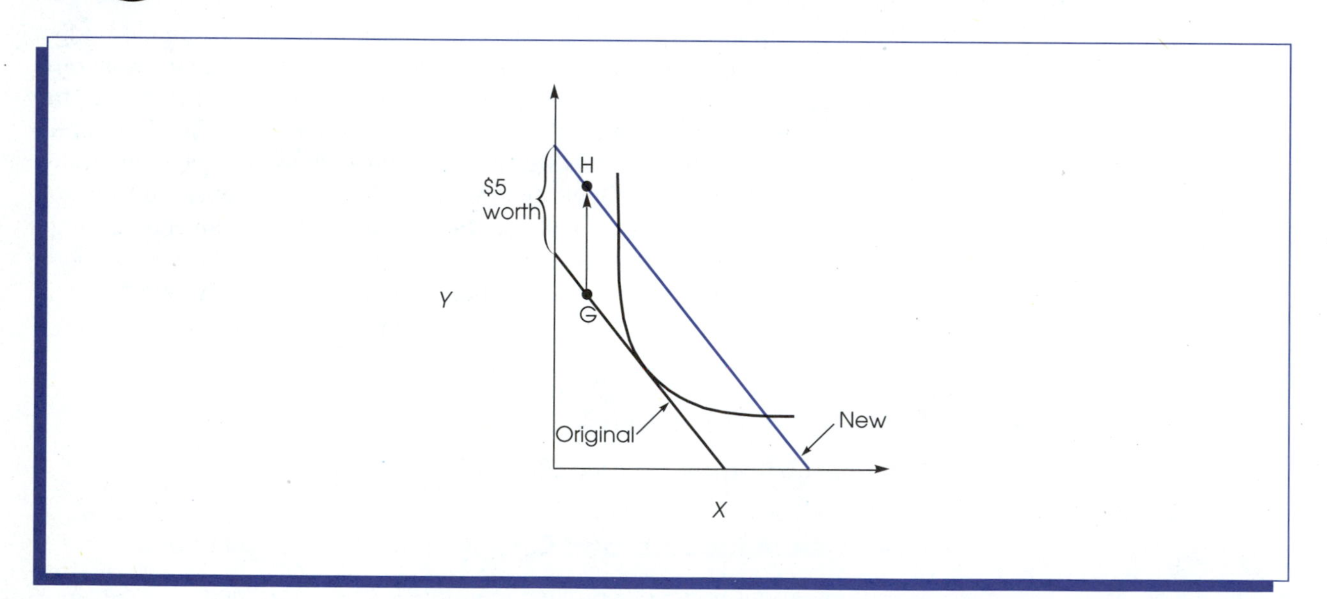

When your income increases by $5, the budget line shifts out parallel to itself. For each point on the original budget line (like *G*), there is a point on the new budget line (like *H*) which consists of basket *G* plus an additional $5 worth of *Y*.

Exhibit 4-2 A Rise In Income

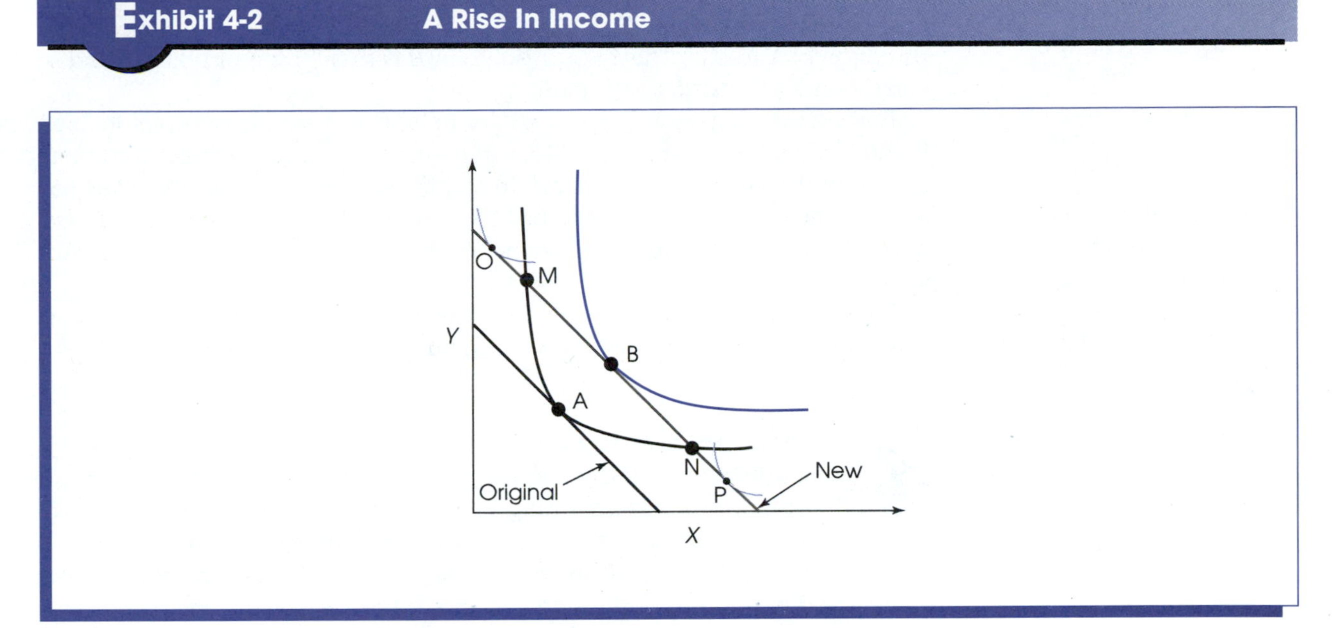

An increase in income causes the budget line to shift outward. If the original tangency is at *A*, then the new tangency cannot be at *O* or *P*, as either possibility would require two indifference curves to cross. (The curves that are shown tangent at these points cannot be indifference curves because they must cross the original black indifference curve.) Instead, the new tangency is at a point like *B*.

so that a change in income (I) does not affect the slope ($-P_X/P_Y$). A change in income affects only the *Y*-intercept of the budget line, which is another way of saying that a change in income causes a parallel shift.

Changes in Income and Changes in the Optimum Point

When your income rises by $5, your budget line shifts out as in Exhibit 4–1. What happens to your optimum point?

In Exhibit 4–2, we suppose that your original optimum point is *A*, where the original budget line (in black) is tangent to the black indifference curve. Now your income rises $5, causing your budget line to shift out; the new budget line is shown in blue. Where can the new tangency be?

The tangency *cannot* be at point *O*. Here's why: If an indifference curve were tangent at *O*, it would be forced to cross the black indifference curve, which cannot happen. (The lightly colored curve shown tangent at *O* can *not* be an indifference curve, because it crosses the black indifference curve that is tangent at *A*.) Likewise, the tangency cannot be at point *P*. Instead, the tangency must occur somewhere between points *M* and *N* on the new budget line, at a point like *B*.

Normal good A good that you consume more of when your income rises.

Inferior good A good that you consume less of when your income rises.

Normal and Inferior Goods

If point *B* is located as in Exhibit 4–2, then a rise in income causes your consumption of *X* to rise. This is because point *B* is to the right of point *A*, and so corresponds to a basket with more *X*.

But alternative pictures are possible. Exhibit 4–3 shows two possibilities. Point *B* could be to the right of *A*, as in the first panel, or point *B* could be to the left of *A*, as in the second panel. In the first case, a rise in income leads you to consume more *X*, and we say that *X* is a **normal good**. In the second case, a rise in income leads you to consume *less X*, and we say that *X* is an **inferior good**.

For example, it is entirely likely that if your income rises, you will consume less Hamburger Helper. That makes Hamburger Helper an inferior good.

The word *inferior* is used differently here than in ordinary English. In ordinary English, *inferior* is a term of comparison; you can't call something inferior without saying what it is inferior *to*; as a student, you can be inferior to some of your classmates and superior to others. But in economics, a good either is or is not inferior, and inferiority does not have the negative connotations that it has in everyday speech.

Exhibit 4-3 Normal and Inferior Goods

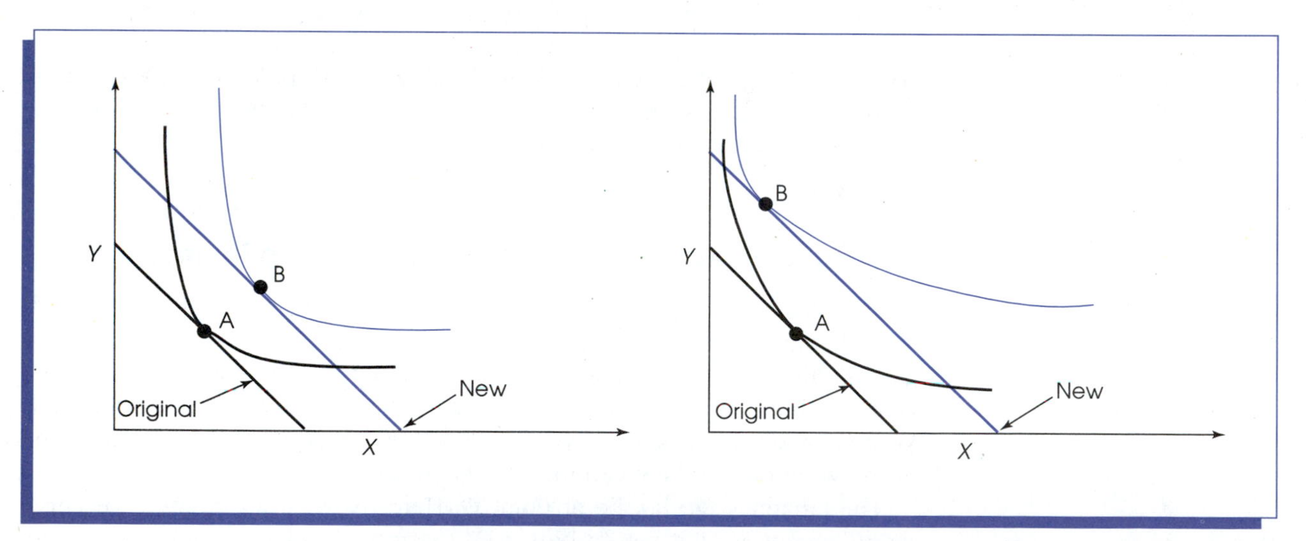

Suppose your original tangency is at *A* and your income increases. Then your new tangency *B* could be either to the right of *A* (as in the first panel) or to the left of *A* (as in the second panel). In the first case, a rise in income leads you to consume more *X* and we call *X* a normal good. In the second case, a rise in income leads you to consume less *X* and we call *X* an inferior good.

EXERCISE 4.2 In the first panel of Exhibit 4–3, is Y an inferior good? What about in the second panel? Where must the tangency B be located if Y is an inferior good?

The Engel Curve

Engel curve A curve showing, for fixed prices, the relationship between income and the quantity of a good consumed.

Beth is a consumer who buys eggs and root beer. Her **Engel curve** for eggs is a graph that shows how many eggs she'll consume at each level of income. You can see her Engel curve in the second panel of Exhibit 4–4. When her income is $4, she consumes 3 eggs; when her income is $8, she consumes 6 eggs, and so on.

It turns out that if we know the prices of eggs and root beer, and if we know Beth's indifference curves, then we can *figure out* the coordinates of the points on her Engel curve. For example, suppose we know that the price of an egg is 50¢, the price of a root beer is $1, and Beth's indifference curves are the curves shown in Exhibit 4-4A.

Exhibit 4-4 Constructing the Engel Curve

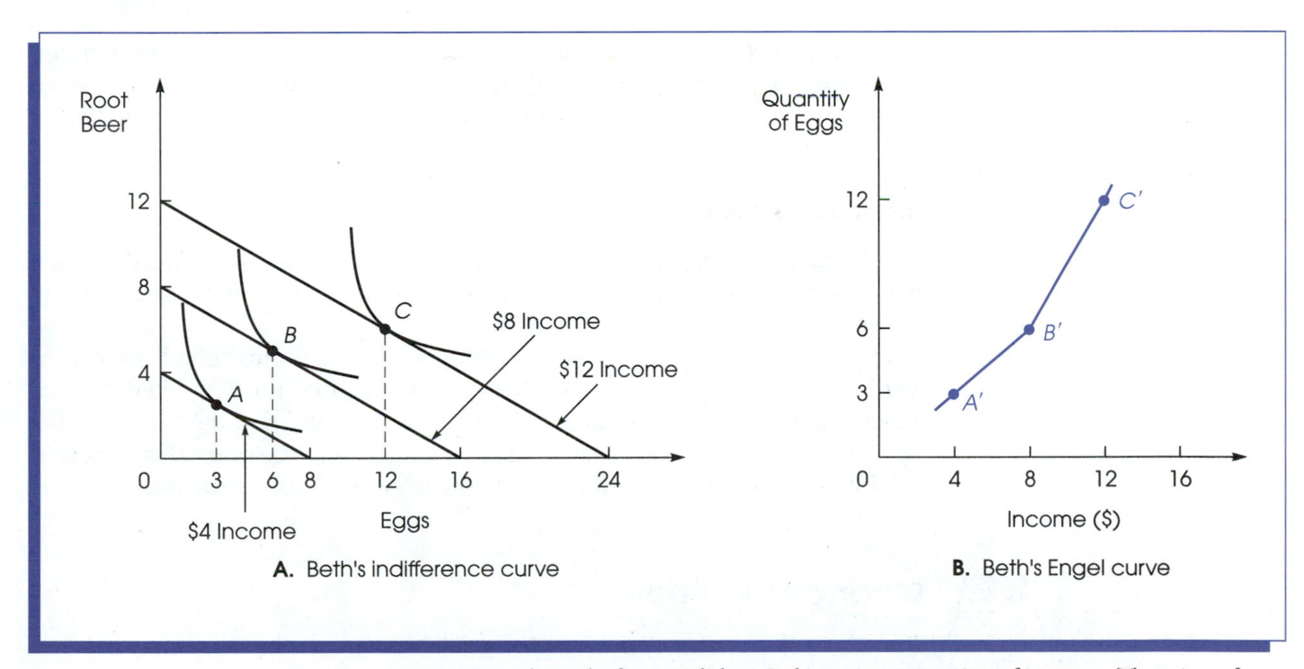

Points A, B, and C in the first panel show Beth's optima at a variety of incomes. (The prices of eggs and root beer are held fixed at 50¢ and $1 respectively). Points A', B', and C' in the second panel record the quantity of eggs that Beth consumes for each of three incomes; these quantities are the horizontal coordinates of points A, B and C. The curve through A', B' and C' is Beth's Engel curve for eggs.

To construct a point on Beth's Engel curve, we follow a five-step process:

1. Imagine an income for Beth—say, \$4.
2. Draw the corresponding budget line. In this case, given our assumptions about the prices of eggs and root beer, Beth can afford up to 8 eggs (with no root beer) or 4 root beers (with no eggs). Therefore her budget line is the one labeled "\$4 income" in Exhibit 4-4A.
3. Find the tangency between this budget line and an indifference curve. (We can do this because we've assumed that we *know* Beth's indifference curves.) In this case, the tangency occurs at point A.
4. Read off the corresponding quantity of eggs—in this case, 3.
5. Plot the point on the Engel curve, relating the income in Step 1 to the quantity in Step 4. In this case we get the point $A' = (\$4,3)$, illustrated in Exhibit 4-4B.

To get *another* point on Beth's Engel curve, repeat the entire five-step process, beginning with a different income. If you imagine the income \$8 in step one, you'll be led to the quantity 6 in step 4, and you'll plot the point B' in step 5.

EXERCISE 4.3 Explain how to derive the coordinates of point C' in Exhibit 4-4B.

The moral of this story is that *the Engel curve contains no information that is not already encoded in the indifference curve diagram.* Once we know the indifference curves, we can generate the Engel curve by a purely mechanical process.

The Shape of the Engel Curve

The Engel curve in Exhibit 4-4B is upward sloping. In other words, when Beth's income rises, she consumes more eggs. Thus, eggs are a normal good for Beth.

In general, the Engel curve will slope upward for a normal good and downward for an inferior good. If eggs were an inferior good for Beth, then the tangency B in Exhibit 4-4A would occur somewhere to the *left* of the tangency A—say, with a horizontal coordinate of 2. This would yield the point $B' = (\$8,2)$ in Exhibit 4-4B, and the curve through A' and B' would slope downward.

4.2 Changes in Price

We now shift our attention from changes in income to changes in the price of X.

Changes in Price and Changes in the Budget Line

To focus attention on changes in the price of X, we assume that your income and the price of Y remain fixed. For example, suppose the price of Y remains

Exhibit 4-5 Changes in the Price of *X*

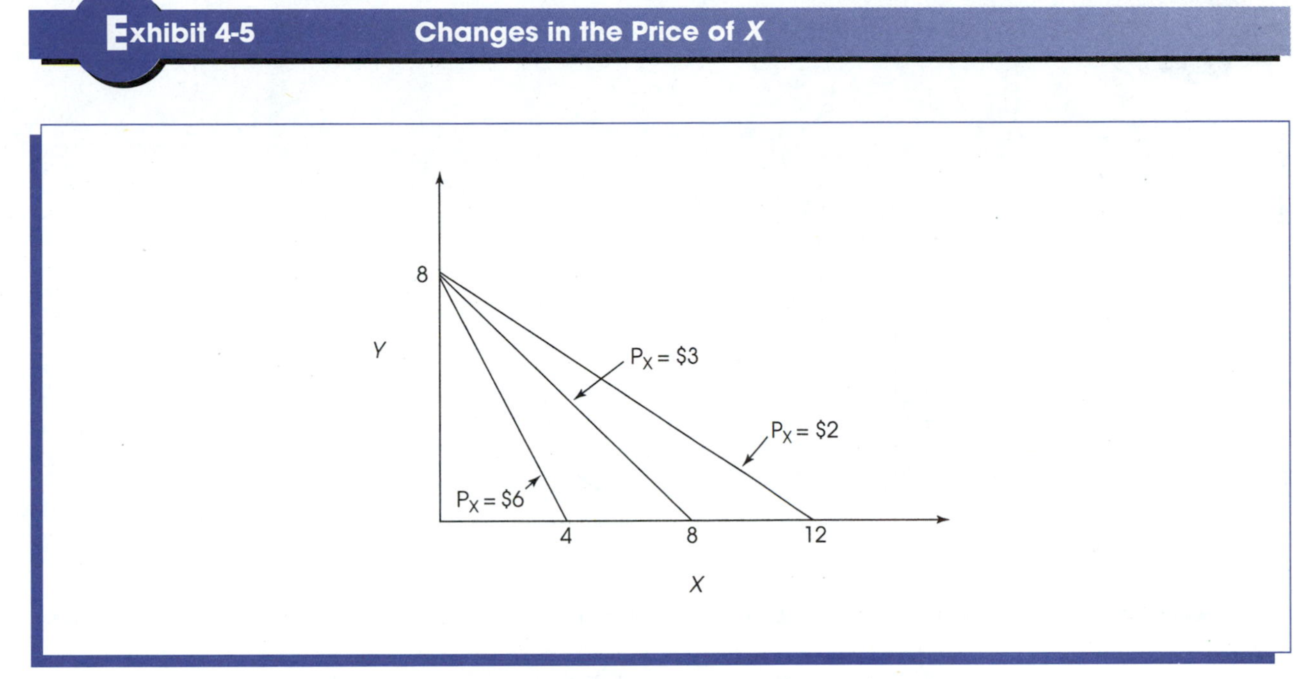

The price of *Y* is fixed at $3 and income is fixed at $24. A rise in the price of *X* causes the budget line to pivot inward around its *Y*-intercept, and a fall in price causes the budget line to pivot outward around its *Y*-intercept.

fixed at $3 per unit and your income remains fixed at $24. Exhibit 4–5 shows the budget lines that result when the price of *X* is $2, $3, and $6.

 EXERCISE 4.4 Verify that the budget lines have been drawn correctly.

There are two important things to notice in Exhibit 4–5. First, a change in the price of *X* has no effect on the *Y*-intercept of the budget line. When you buy zero *X*s, you can always afford exactly 8 *Y*s, regardless of what happens to the price of *X*. Thus:

A change in the price of *X* causes the budget line to pivot around its *Y*-intercept.

The second important thing to notice is the direction in which the budget line pivots. When the price of *X* is low (like $2), the budget line extends out to a high quantity of *X* (in this case, 12); when the price of *X* is high (like $6), the budget line extends out only to a low quantity of *X* (in this case, 4). Thus:

A rise in the price of *X* causes the budget line to pivot inward. A fall in the price of *X* causes the budget line to pivot outward.

Changes in Price and Changes in the Optimum Point

When the price of *X* rises, your budget line pivots inward as shown in Exhibit 4–6.

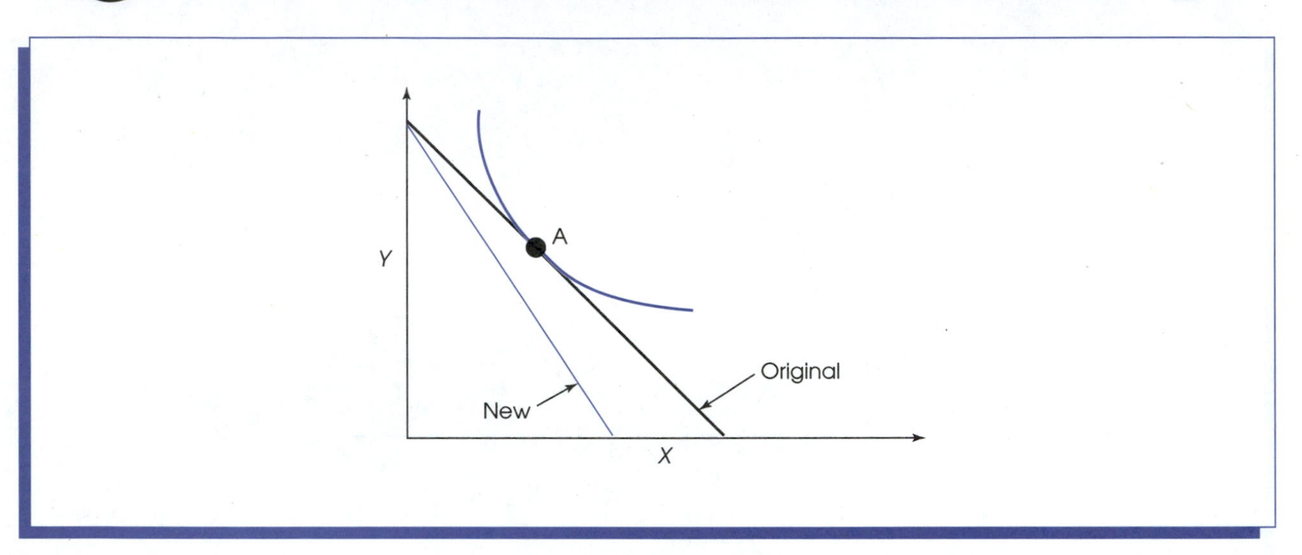

A rise in price causes the budget line to pivot inward. The original optimum is at A, and the new optimum could be anywhere at all on the new (blue) budget line.

The geometry of Exhibit 4–6 places no restrictions on the location of the new optimum point; it could be anywhere at all on the new budget line. Now we're going to think a little more deeply about the location of that new optimum.

Giffen and Non-Giffen Goods

Exhibit 4–7 illustrates two possibilities. In both cases, a rise in the price of X causes the optimum point to shift from A to B. In the first panel, B lies to the left of A; in the second panel, B lies to the right of A.

In the first panel, you can see that when the price of X goes up, the quantity demanded goes down (from Q_A to Q_B). That statement should sound familiar; it is the same law of demand that we met in Chapter 1.

In the second panel, you can see that when the price of X goes up, the quantity demanded goes *up*! In this case, X violates the law of demand.

Goods that violate the law of demand (like good X in the second panel of Exhibit 4-7) are called **Giffen goods**. Goods that obey the law of demand (like good X in the first panel of Exhibit 4-7) are called **non-Giffen goods**.

Giffen Good A good that violates the law of demand, so that when the price goes up, the quantity demanded goes up.

Non-Giffen good A good that obeys the law of demand: When the price goes up, the quantity demanded goes down.

Do not confuse the question "Is *X* Giffen?" with the question "Is *X* inferior?" To determine whether *X* is inferior, you must ask what happens when *income* changes, so that the budget line undergoes a parallel shift (as in the two panels of Exhibit 4-3). To determine whether *X* is Giffen, you must ask what happens when the *price of X* changes, so that the budget line pivots around its *Y*-intercept, as in the two panels of Exhibit 4-7.

Exhibit 4-7 Non-Giffen Goods and Giffen Goods

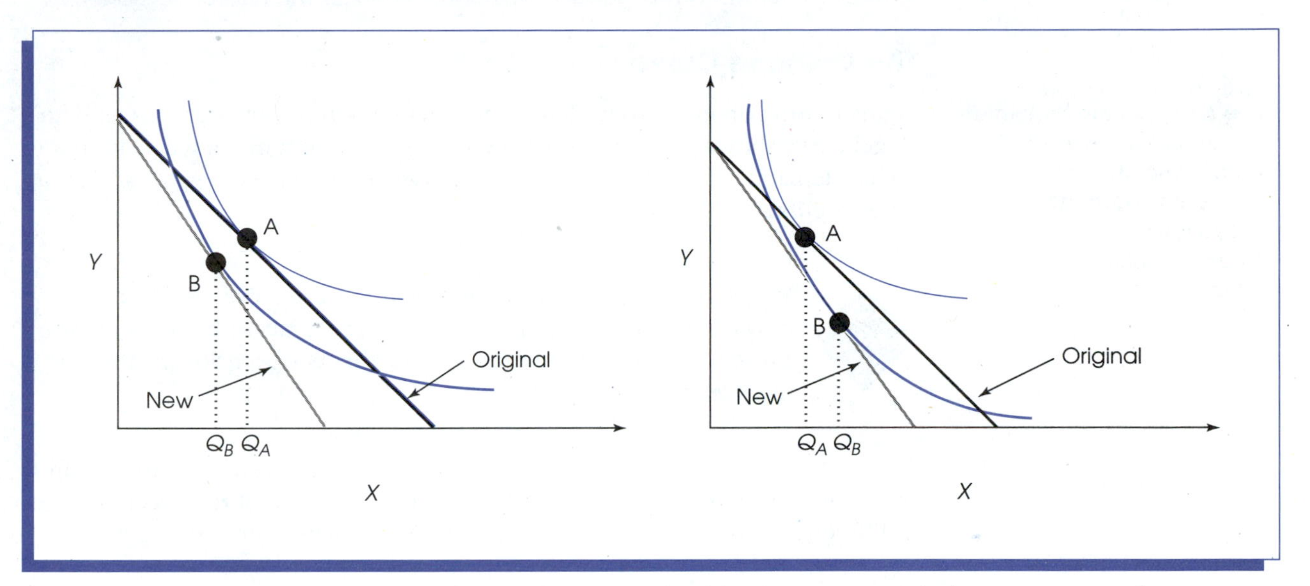

When the price of X goes up, the budget line pivots inward. The optimum moves from point A to point B and the quantity of X that you demand changes from Q_A to Q_B. In the first panel, Q_B is less than Q_A; in other words "when the price goes up the quantity demanded goes down", as required by the law of demand. In the second panel, Q_B is greater than Q_A, so that "when the price goes up the quantity demanded goes *up*," in violation of the law of demand. When the law of demand is violated, X is called a Giffen good.

In the panels of Exhibit 4-7, it is not possible to tell by inspection whether *Y* is a Giffen good. To determine whether *Y* is Giffen, we have to ask what happens to the consumption of *Y* when there is a change in the price of *Y*. But the graphs in Exhibit 4-7 illustrate a change in the price of *X*, not a change in the price of *Y*.

EXERCISE 4.5 Draw a graph illustrating how the budget line shifts when the price of Y rises. Draw the original optimum. Where is the new optimum located if Y is not a Giffen good? Where is the new optimum located if Y is a Giffen good?

A Puzzle: Why Are Giffen Goods So Rare?

Giffen goods are extremely uncommon; in fact, they are so uncommon that the author of your textbook does not know of a single actual instance. That's why the law of demand is called a *law*—it is virtually always obeyed.

The theory of indifference curves tells us that there *can* be exceptions to the law of demand—in other words, it is possible to draw a picture like the second panel of Exhibit 4-7. But experience tells us that although such exceptions are possible, they are either extremely rare or completely nonexistent. And therein lies a puzzle. If the theory allows Giffen goods to exist, why don't they?

We will return to this puzzle—and solve it—near the end of Section 4.3.

The Demand Curve

See slides on the derivation of consumer demand at: http://price.bus.okstate.edu/archive/Econ3113_963/Shows/Chapter4/chap_04.htm

Let us return our attention to Beth, who buys eggs and root beer. Just as Beth's Engel curve shows the relation between her income and her egg consumption, so her demand curve shows the relation between the price of eggs and her egg consumption.

The Engel curve plots income on the horizontal axis versus egg consumption on the vertical; the demand curve plots the price of eggs on the vertical axis versus egg consumption on the horizontal.

Like the Engel curve, the demand curve can be derived from the indifference curve diagram. If we know Beth's income, the price of root beer, and her indifference curves, then we can construct her demand curve for eggs.

Exhibit 4-8 Constructing the Demand Curve

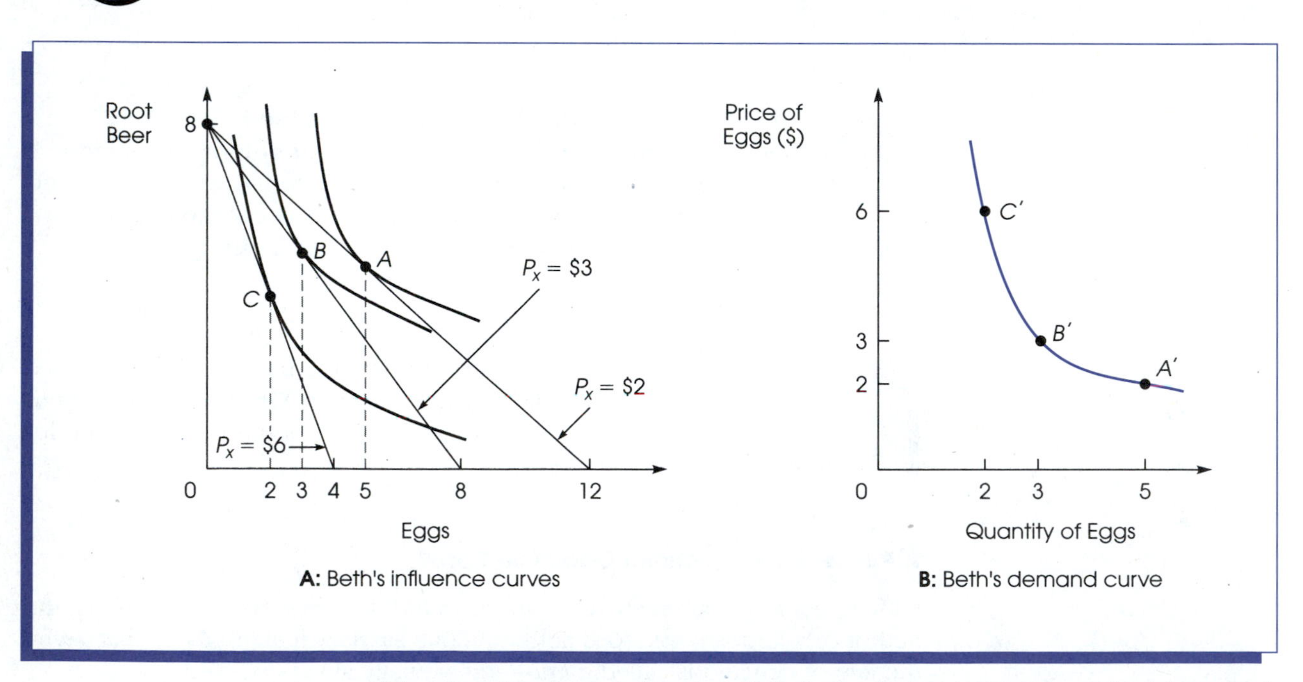

When the price of eggs is \$2 apiece, Beth chooses basket A, with 5 eggs. This information is recorded by point A' in the second panel. Points B' and C' are derived similarly. The curve through A', B' and C' is Beth's demand curve for eggs.

The process is illustrated in Exhibit 4-8, where we assume that the price of root beer is $3 and Beth's income is $24; thus, the vertical intercept of her budget line is at 8 root beers.

To construct a point on Beth's demand curve, we follow a five-step process:

1. Imagine a price for eggs—say, $2.
2. Draw the corresponding budget line. Given our assumption that Beth's income is $24, she can afford up to 12 eggs (with no root beer). Thus, her budget line has horizontal intercept 12, as illustrated in Exhibit 4-8A.
3. Find the tangency between this budget line and an indifference curve. In this case, the tangency occurs at point *A*.
4. Read off the corresponding quantity of eggs—in this case, 5.
5. Plot a point on the demand curve, relating the price in Step 1 to the quantity in Step 4. In this case we get the point *A′* in Exhibit 4-8B.

To get *another* point on Beth's demand curve, repeat the entire five-step process, beginning with a different price for eggs. If you imagine the price $3 in step 1, you'll be led to the quantity 3 in step 4, and you'll plot the point *B′* in step 5.

EXERCISE 4.6 Explain how to derive the coordinates of point *C′* in Exhibit 4–8B.

As with the Engel curve, we now know that *the demand curve contains no information that is not already encoded in the indifference curve diagram.* Once we know the indifference curves, we can generate the demand curve by a purely mechanical process.

The Shape of the Demand Curve

In Exhibit 4–8, eggs obey the law of demand; therefore, the demand curve for eggs slopes down. If eggs were a Giffen good, then the tangency *B* would be to the *right* of *A*, say, at a quantity of 7. Then the point *B′* on the demand curve would have horizontal coordinate 7 and the demand curve would slope upward.

Students sometimes attempt to draw the demand curve and the indifference curves on the same graph. This cannot be done correctly, because the two diagrams require different axes (quantities of goods *X* and *Y* for the indifference curves; quantity and price of good *X* for the demand curve).

Other students sometimes think that the labeled points in Exhibit 4–8A illustrate the shape of the demand curve. This is also incorrect. It *is* true that each point on the demand curve arises from a point in the indifference curve diagram, but translating from one diagram to the other is not simply a matter of copying points. The only way to go from one diagram to the other is via the five-step process just described.

4.3 Income and Substitution Effects

See David Friedman's Web site at: http://www.best.com/~ddfr/Academic/Price_Theory/PThy_Chapter_3/PThy_Chapter_3.html

We have a puzzle to solve: Why, in the real world, do there seem to be essentially no Giffen goods? It would be very satisfying to answer this question by saying that the geometry of indifference curves makes Giffen goods impossible. Unfortunately, that's not the case. Exhibit 4–7 showed that there is no geometric obstruction to the existence of a Giffen good.

So the solution to our puzzle will require an argument that goes beyond geometry. We will start with a purely verbal discussion of two distinct reasons why the law of demand "ought" to hold. After we've understood these effects in words, we will translate our words into geometry, and then tie the two approaches together.

Two Effects of a Price Increase

When the price of a good goes up, we typically expect the quantity demanded to fall. There are two separate good reasons for this expectation, called the *substitution effect* and the *income effect.*

The Substitution Effect

We will begin by describing the substitution effect of a price increase.

Suppose hamburgers sell for $2 each, and you are in the habit of buying 5 hamburgers per day. We know that each of those hamburgers has a marginal value (to you) of at least $2 or you wouldn't buy them. But their marginal values are probably not all identical; the second hamburger is worth less than the first, and the fifth is worth the least of all.

Now let's suppose that the price of hamburgers rises from $2 to $3. Then you'll decide to forego any hamburger with a marginal value of less than $3. For example, you might decide that your fourth and fifth daily hamburgers are each worth less than $3 to you, so you'll now buy only 3 hamburgers per day.

Substitution effect of a price increase A change in consumption due to the fact that you won't buy goods whose marginal value is below the new price.

That's the **substitution effect** of the price increase: When the price of a good rises, you adjust the quantity downward so that you're not buying goods whose marginal values are below their prices.

When the price of a good goes up, the substitution effect leads you to consume less of it.

The Income Effect

Now we will describe the income effect of a price increase.

Suppose the price of hamburgers rises. Then, because you can't spend more than your entire income, you'll have to consume less of *something.* (Another way to say this is that your old basket is outside your new budget line, so you'll have to choose a new basket.) It's then quite likely—though not certain—that hamburgers themselves will be among the goods you cut back on.

We can be more precise about this: The fact that you can no longer afford your original basket is tantamount to a change in *income;* in a very real sense, a price increase makes you *poorer.* When you become poorer, you reduce your consumption of all normal goods, though you increase your consumption of inferior goods.

Income effect of a price increase A change in consumption due to the fact that you can no longer afford your original basket, and are therefore effectively poorer.

That's the **income effect** of a price increase: When the price of hamburgers rises, you are effectively poorer, and therefore consume either fewer hamburgers (if hamburgers are a normal good) or more hamburgers (if hamburgers are an inferior good).

When the price of a good goes up, the income effect leads you to consume either less of it (this happens if the good is normal), or more of it (this happens if the good is inferior).

Exhibit 4-9 Income and Substitution Effects

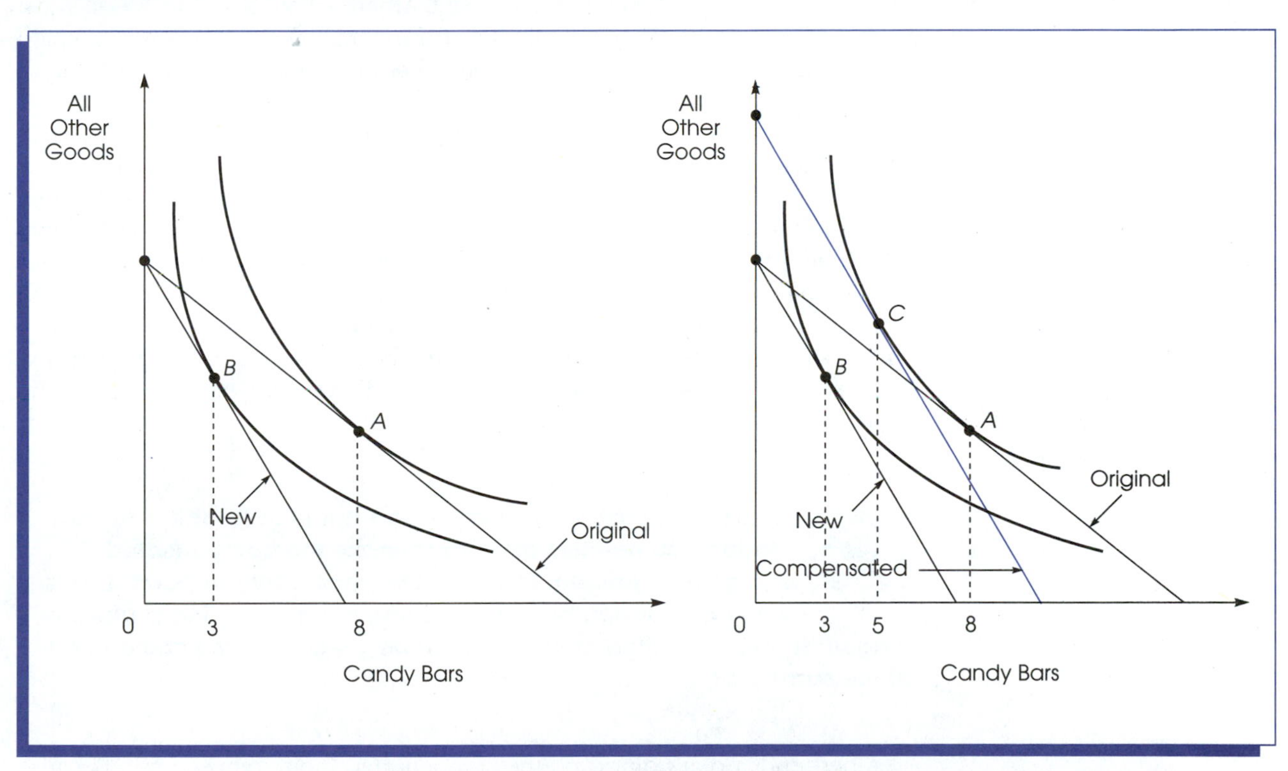

When the price of candy bars rises, Albert moves from point *A* on his *original* budget line to point *B* on his new budget line. His consumption falls from 8 candy bars to 3. Part of this fall is due to the substitution effect and part is due to the income effect.

In the second panel, we imagine that the price increase is accompanied by an increase in Albert's income, just large enough to make him exactly as happy as he was originally. This gives Albert the *compensated* budget line, which is parallel to the *new* line (to reflect the new prices) and tangent to the original indifference curve (to reflect Albert's level of happiness). In this case, the income effect is eliminated and Albert moves to point *C*, where he consumes 5 candy bars. Therefore, when the price goes up and Albert moves from *A* to *B*, we can imagine the move taking place in two steps: A pure substitution effect (from *A* to *C*) followed by a pure income effect (from *C* to *B*).

Isolating the Substitution Effect: A Hypothetical Scenario

The first panel of Exhibit 4–9 illustrates a rise in the price of candy bars. When the price goes up, Albert's budget line pivots inward (from the *original* line to the *new* line) and his consumption falls from 8 candy bars a day to 3 candy bars a day—the quantity demanded falls by 5. Our immediate goal is to determine how much of that change is due to the substitution effect and how much is due to the income effect.

To accomplish that goal, let's imagine a hypothetical scenario. Suppose Albert walks down to the vending machine and discovers that the price of candy bars has risen. This makes him less happy than he was a moment ago. But now suppose Albert discovers a $5 bill lying on the ground. This makes him *more* happy. And suppose that—just by coincidence—the combination of these two surprises leaves Albert exactly as happy as he was when he woke up this morning.

In that hypothetical scenario, Albert feels no income effect. The income effect is the result of "feeling poorer," but Albert—thanks to the $5 he's just found—does not feel poorer at all. Thus the income effect has been eliminated so we can now observe the substitution effect in isolation. Now we will incorporate this idea into our graph.

The second panel of Exhibit 4–9 illustrates the hypothetical scenario. First, Albert discovers that the price of candy bars has risen; this causes his budget line to pivot inward (from the *original* to the *new*) just as in the first panel. Then, he discovers the $5 bill on the floor. This is a pure increase in income, so it causes his *new* budget line to shift out parallel to itself.

The final position of the budget line is labeled *compensated* in Exhibit 4–9. Notice that the compensated line is tangent to the original (black) indifference curve. That's because we assumed that the combined changes leave Albert exactly as happy as he was at the beginning, which means he ends up on the same indifference curve he started out on.

In drawing graphs like the second panel of Exhibit 4-9, students sometimes attempt to make the compensated budget line tangent to the indifference curve at point *A*. This can't be correct, because the original budget line is already tangent there. Two different lines cannot be tangent to the same curve at the same point.

Albert ends up at point *C* on the compensated indifference curve. Because we have eliminated the income effect, the move from *A* to *C* is a pure substitution effect. Thus, we can see from the graph that the substitution effect causes Albert to reduce his consumption of candy bars from 8 to 5.

Combining the Effects

Now let's reconsider what happens when the price of candy bars goes up. We know that Albert moves from point *A* to point *B* in either panel of Exhibit 4–9. (We have now discarded the hypothetical scenario and are no longer supposing that Albert gets lucky and finds money on the floor.) The move from *A* to *B* is due partly to the substitution effect and partly to the income effect.

We have already figured out (by imagining the hypothetical scenario) that the substitution effect moves Albert from *A* to *C*. Thus, the remainder of the move—from *C* to *B*—must be due to the income effect. So in this case, our experiment has revealed that when the price of candy bars rises as in the first panel of Exhibit 4–9, Albert cuts out 3 candy bars because of the substitution effect (moving from 8 to 5) and 2 candy bars because of the income effect (moving from 5 to 3), for a total cutback of 5 candy bars.

An Imaginary Experiment

In real life, we rarely get to observe income and substitution effects separately. A rise in price causes both effects to happen simultaneously, and it's generally impossible for an observer to disentangle them. Thus, when Albert discovers the price increase and cuts back from 8 candy bars to 3, it's not at all obvious how much of that cutback we should attribute to each of the effects.

However, in principle, an experimenter can always disentangle the effects by first giving Albert extra income and then taking it away. If you wanted to observe a pure substitution effect, you could leave a $5 bill under the machine for Albert to find, and then watch to see how many candy bars he wants to buy. According to Exhibit 4–9, you'll see him choose 5 (at point *C*). Then, just as he's about to make his selections, you can whisk by him and grab the $5 out of his hand. Now he's returned to his *new* budget line, and he chooses 3 candy bars (at point *B*).

To do this experiment properly, you can't just give Albert a random amount of additional income; you have to give him just enough to compensate him for the price change—that is, just enough to allow him to achieve his original indifference curve.

Notice that the income effect is well named; it occurs because you take away some of Albert's income.

In real life, Albert never gets the extra income. But whenever the price of candy bars goes up, you can *imagine* that Albert first finds, and then loses, some extra income. This lets you imagine that the move from *A* to *B* takes place in two steps, with a stop at *C* along the way. In that way, you can separate the substitution effect from the income effect.

EXERCISE 4.7 Suppose the price of candy bars were to fall. Draw a diagram analogous to Exhibit 4–9 showing how Albert's consumption changes and separating the change into a substitution effect and an income effect. (*Hint:* When the price of candy bars falls, Albert feels happier than before. To eliminate the income effect, you have to "compensate" him negatively, by taking income away until he is no happier than before.

Why Demand Curves Slope Downward

The first panel of Exhibit 4–10 illustrates the income and substitution effects of a rise in the price of *X*. The substitution effect is the move from *A* to *C* and the income effect is the move from *C* to *B*.

Some Geometric Observations

Here are three key observations about the points in Exhibit 4–10:

1. *C* is always to the left of *A*. Here's why: *C* and *A* are on the same indifference curve, but *C* is the tangency with a steeper line, so *C* must be on a steeper part of the curve. Steeper parts of the curve are always to the left.

Exhibit 4-10 Income and Substitution Effects

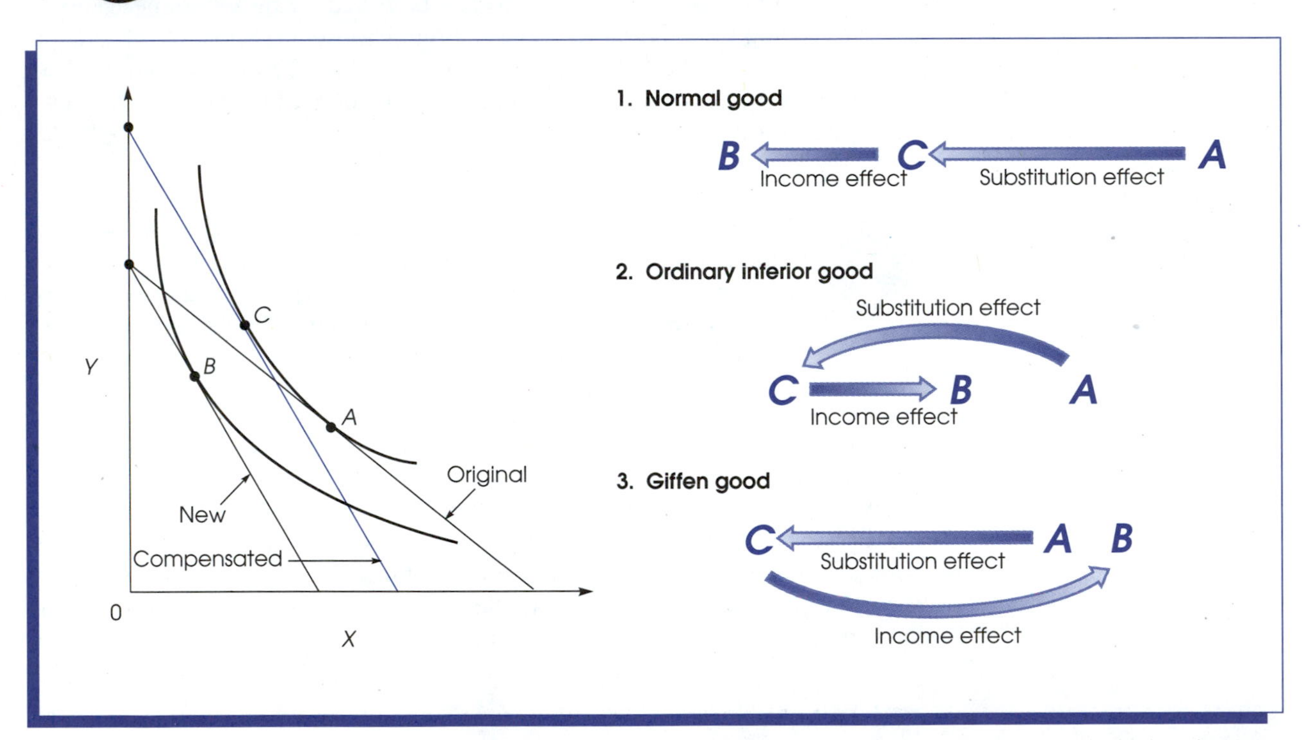

When the price of *X* rises, the consumer moves from *A* to *B*. This move can be broken down into a substitution effect (from *A* to *C*) followed by an income effect (from *C* to *B*). The move from *A* to *C* is always leftward. If *X* is normal, the move from *C* to *B* is also leftward, so the move from *A* to *B* is leftward; therefore, *X* is not Giffen. If *X* is inferior, the move from *C* to *B* is rightward. This allows two possibilities: Either *B* is to the left of *A* (this happens when the income effect is small), so that *X* is not Giffen, or *B* is to the right of *A* (this happens when the income effect is large), so that *X* is Giffen.

(Notice that this purely geometric observation is equivalent to something we observed earlier: When the price of a good goes up, the substitution effect always leads you to consume less of it.)

2. If X is a normal good, then B is to the left of C. Here's why: The move from C to B represents a pure change in income (C and B are tangencies with parallel budget lines). When you move from the *compensated* line to the *new* line, income falls, so you consume less X; that is, you move to the left.

3. If X is an inferior good, then B is to the right of C. In other words, when income falls, you consume *more* of the inferior good X.

(In Exhibit 4–10, B is drawn to the left of C, so in this case X is a normal good.)

The Demand Curve for a Normal Good

Suppose that X is a normal good. When the price of X goes up, the consumer in Exhibit 4–10 moves from A to B. What is the direction of that move?

We know from the first of our geometric observations that C is to the left of A. Because we've assumed that X is normal, we know from the second observation that B is to the left of C. Using your best IQ-test skills, what can you conclude about the relative positions of A and B?

The answer is revealed in the top row of the right-hand panel in Exhibit 4–10, where you can see that B must be to the left of A. In other words, when the price of X goes up, the quantity demanded goes down. In still other words, X is not a Giffen good. Because this argument applies whenever X is normal, we can summarize our conclusion as follows:

A normal good cannot be Giffen.

We've just discovered something truly remarkable. To say that a good is normal is to say something about the response to an *income* change. To say that a good is Giffen is to say something about the response to a *price* change. There is no obvious reason why these conditions should have anything to do with one another. But our analysis reveals that they are closely related nevertheless: No normal good can ever be Giffen. The demand curve for a normal good is sure to slope downward.

Although we've phrased the argument in terms of geometry, we can translate it into economics. When the price of X goes up, the substitution effect (from A to C) must cause the quantity demanded to fall. At the same time, the income effect (from C to B) *also* causes the quantity demanded to fall. These effects reinforce each other, and the quantity demanded certainly falls.

The Demand Curve for an Inferior Good

Now suppose that X is an inferior good. When the price of X goes up, the consumer in Exhibit 4–10 moves from A to B. What is the direction of that move?

We know from the first geometric observation that C is to the left of A. Because we've assumed that X is inferior, we know from the second observation that B is to the right of C.

Bringing your IQ-test skills to bear on this problem, you'll quickly discover that you can draw no certain conclusion about the relative locations of points *A* and *B*. There are two possibilities, illustrated in the second and third rows of the right-hand panel in Exhibit 4–10. When the substitution effect is larger than the income effect, *B* is to the left of *A* (so that *X* is not Giffen) but when the income effect is larger than the substitution effect, *B* is to the right of *A* (so that *X* is Giffen).

The two panels of Exhibit 4–11 show that each of these possibilities can occur. Therefore:

An inferior good is non-Giffen if the substitution effect exceeds the income effect, but Giffen if the income effect exceeds the substitution effect.

The economic interpretation is straightforward: When the price of *X* goes up, the substitution effect (from *A* to *C*) causes the quantity demanded to fall. At the same time, the income effect (from *C* to *B*) causes the quantity demanded to *rise* (because *X* is an inferior good). These effects work in opposite directions, so the quantity demanded of *X* can fall or rise, depending on which effect is bigger.

Exhibit 4-11 Income and Substitution Effects for an Inferior Good

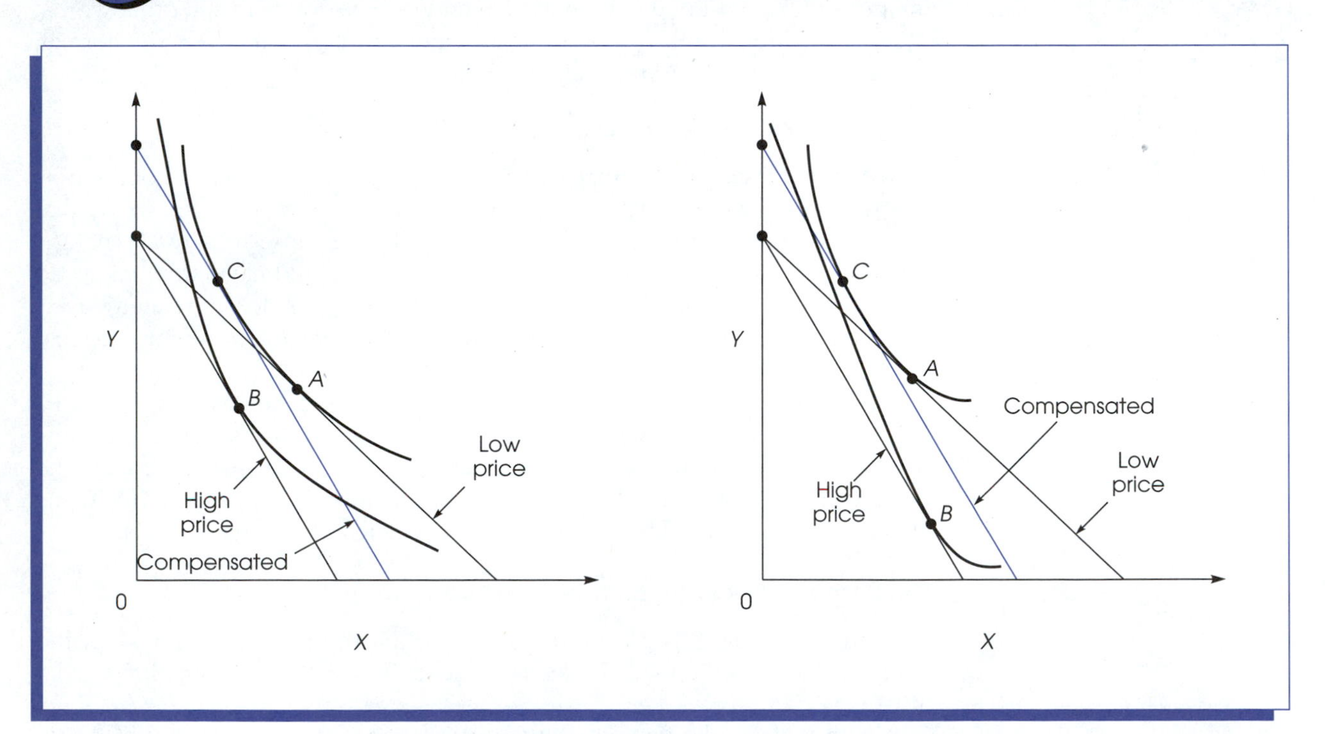

In both panels, *X* is an inferior good; that is, *B* is to the right of *C*. In the first panel, *X* is not Giffen; that is, *B* is to the left of *A*. In the second panel, *X* is Giffen; that is, *B* is to the right of *A*.

The Size of the Income Effect

Suppose the price of bubble gum rises. Will you feel slightly poorer or a lot poorer? Unless you are a very unusual person—that is, unless you spend a very substantial portion of your income on bubble gum—you will feel only slightly poorer. Therefore, the income effect, which is caused by that sense of being poorer, is likely to be small.

On the other hand, suppose the price of college tuition rises. Depending on who's paying for your education, there's a good chance you'll now feel quite substantially poorer. If tuition expenses account for a substantial fraction of your income, the income effect might be considerable.

In general, the income effect of a price change is large only for goods that account for a large fraction of your expenditure. The laws of arithmetic dictate that there can't be very many such goods (for example, there can be no more than 3 goods that account for at least ⅓ of your expenditure). So large income effects are relatively rare.

Giffen Goods Revisited

A Giffen good must satisfy two conditions. First, it must be inferior (because a normal good cannot be Giffen). Second, it must account for a substantial fraction of your expenditure (because an inferior good is Giffen only when the income effect exceeds the substitution effect).

Each of these conditions is unusual. Many goods are inferior, but most are not. And only very few goods can account for substantial fractions of your expenditure. Thus, in order to be Giffen, a good must satisfy *two* unusual conditions at once. This explains why Giffen goods are rare.

In fact, one can make an even stronger argument. We've said that a randomly chosen good is likely to be normal. But we can also say that if the randomly chosen good accounts for a large fraction of your expenditure, then it's *particularly* likely to be normal. Here's why: When your income increases, you have to spend the excess on *something*, and the goods on which you spend relatively little are unlikely to soak up much of that excess. For example, if your income rises by $100 per week, it is unlikely that you'll devote the entire $100 to bubble gum—to do so would require an implausibly large percentage increase in your bubble gum expenditures. Instead, some of the $100 will probably go toward the goods that account for the bulk of your expenditure—which means that those goods are probably normal. So not only do Giffen goods have to satisfy two improbable conditions, but one of those improbable conditions causes the other to become even *more* improbable.

Here's a hypothetical example. Suppose you eat hamburger 6 days a week and steak on Sunday; suppose also that hamburger is an inferior good. One day the price of hamburger rises. Because you eat so much hamburger, this makes you feel a lot poorer. Because you are now so much poorer, you decide to cut out steak entirely and eat hamburgers 7 days a week. When the price of hamburgers goes up, the quantity demanded goes *up*. In this case, hamburgers are a Giffen good.

For this story to work, hamburgers must be inferior *and* you must spend so much on hamburger that the price increase has a major impact on your lifestyle. The moral of Exhibit 4–10 is that this story about hamburgers is essentially the *only* story that could ever produce a Giffen good.

The Compensated Demand Curve

For more on regular and compensated demand curves, go to: http://www.best.com/~ddfr/Academic/Price_Theory/PThy_Chapter_3/PThy_Chapter_3.html

When the price of lettuce rises from $1 to $3, Bugs reduces his consumption from 7 heads of lettuce per day to 1 head of lettuce per day. You can see in the first panel of Exhibit 4–12 that his consumption is reduced from 7 to 3 by the substitution effect and from 3 to 1 by the income effect. Bugs's demand curve, shown in the third panel, records the combined effect by showing that his consumption falls from 7 to 1.

But for some applications, it is useful to keep track of the substitution effect independent of the income effect. (We will meet some of these applications in

Exhibit 4-12 Compensated and Uncompensated Demand Curve

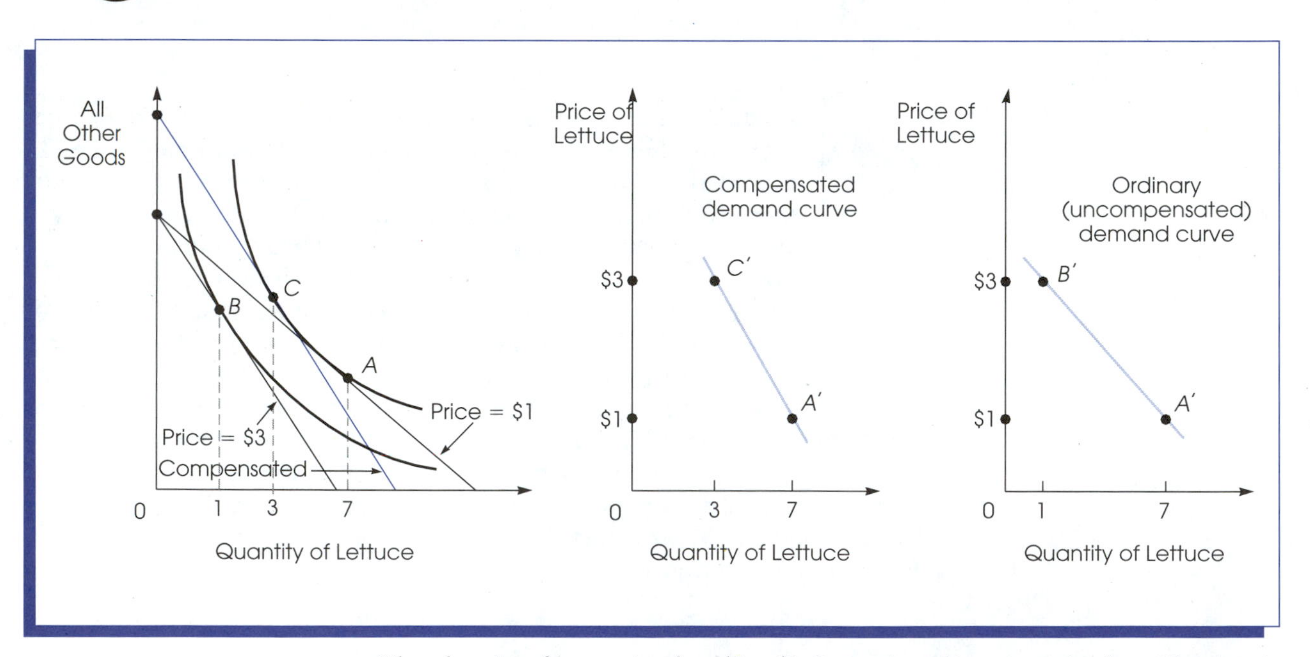

When the price of lettuce rises from $1 to $3, Bugs reduces his consumption from 7 heads to 1; this is recorded by the ordinary demand curve in the rightmost panel. If he were income-compensated for the price change, he would reduce his consumption from 7 heads to 3; this is recorded by the compensated demand curve in the center panel.

Compensated demand curve
A curve showing, for each price, what the quantity demanded would be if the consumer were income-compensated for all price changes.

Chapter 8.) In order to do that, we can draw Bugs **compensated demand curve**, which shows that at a price of \$3, he would consume 3 heads of lettuce—in the hypothetical circumstance where he feels no income effect.

You can imagine Bugs as the subject of an imaginary experiment, where every time the price of lettuce changes, experimenters adjust his income to keep him on his original indifference curve; we summarize this condition by saying that Bugs is income-compensated for all price changes. The compensated demand curve shows how much lettuce Bugs would consume if he were the subject of that experiment.

Because the substitution effect of a price change always reduces the quantity demanded, it follows that the compensated demand curve must slope down. In terms of Exhibit 4–11, point C in the first panel is always to the left of point A; therefore, point C' in the second panel is always to the left of point A'. Again, the conclusion is that the compensated demand curve slopes downward. This is in contrast to the ordinary (uncompensated) demand curve, which slopes upward in the case of a Giffen good.

The ordinary (uncompensated) demand curve describes the behavior of actual consumers in actual markets. *Whenever we use the unqualified phrase "demand curve," we always mean the ordinary (uncompensated) demand curve.*

4.4 Elasticities

For more on price elasticities, visit Rothstein-Tauber, Inc., at: http://www.rtimarketresearch.com/rt03008.htm

If you owned a clothing store, you'd want to be able to anticipate changes in your customers' buying habits. From the material we have developed so far, you'd be able to draw two general conclusions. First, if their income increases, your customers will probably spend more on clothes. Second, if the price of clothing falls, your customers will almost certainly buy more of it.

As the owner of a business who is trying to foresee market conditions, you might find these revelations unsatisfying. Although they predict the *directions* of change, they say nothing about the *magnitude* of change. What you really want to know is: If my customers' incomes increase by a certain amount, by *how much* will they increase their expenditures on clothing? If the price falls by a certain amount, by *how much* will the quantity demanded increase?

Elasticities are numbers that answer these questions. In this section we will learn what elasticities are and see some sample estimates.

Income Elasticity of Demand

First we will consider the response to a change in income. This response is depicted by the Engel curve, and one way to measure it is by the *slope* of that curve. We ask: If your income increased by \$1, by how many units would you increase your consumption of X? That number is the slope of your Engel curve.

Unfortunately, this slope is arbitrary. For one thing, it depends on the units in which X is measured. When your income goes up by \$1, your yearly coffee consumption might go up by 6 cups, which is the same as 1 pot. If coffee is measured in cups, your Engel curve has slope 6; if coffee is measured in pots, it has slope 1.

For another thing, the slope depends on the units in which your income is measured. Your coffee consumption will respond differently if your income increases by one Italian lire instead of one U.S. dollar.

Therefore, we adopt a different measure, one that does not depend on the choice of units. Instead of asking, "If your income increased by *one dollar* by how many *units* would you increase your consumption of X?" we ask, "If your income increased by *one percent,* by what *percentage* would you increase your consumption of X?" The answer to this question is a number that does not depend on the choice of units. That number is called the elasticity of your Engel curve, or your **income elasticity of demand.**

Income elasticity of demand The percentage change in consumption that results from a 1% increase in income.

If your income I changes by an amount ΔI, then the percentage change in your income is given by $100 \times \Delta I/I$. If the quantity of X that you consume, Q, changes by an amount ΔQ, then the percentage change in consumption is $100 \times \Delta Q/Q$. The formula for income elasticity is

$$\text{Income elasticy} = \frac{\text{Percentage change in quantity}}{\text{Percentage change in income}}$$

$$= \frac{100 \cdot \Delta Q/Q}{100 \cdot \Delta I/I}$$

$$= \frac{I \cdot \Delta Q}{Q \cdot \Delta I}$$

Suppose, for example, that your Engel curve for X is the one depicted in panel B of Exhibit 4–4. When your income increases from \$8 to \$12 (a 50% increase), your consumption of X increases from 6 to 12 (a 100% increase). In this region, your income elasticity of demand is 100%/50% = 2.

On the other hand, when your income increases from \$4 to \$8, your consumption of X increases from 3 to 6; a 100% increase in income yields a 100% increase in quantity, so your income elasticity of demand in this region is 1.

QA EXERCISE 4.8 What would it mean for your income elasticity of demand for X to be negative?

examples

Let us suppose again that you own a clothing store, you foresee an increase in your customers' incomes, and you want to anticipate the change in their clothing expenditures. The critical bit of information is the income elasticity of demand for clothing. In fact, that elasticity has been estimated at about .95.[1] If your customers' incomes increase by 10%, you may expect them to increase their expenditures on clothing by about 9.5%.

[1] H. Houthakker and L. Taylor, *Consumer Demand in the United States,* Cambridge: Harvard University Press, 1970. All further elasticity estimates in this chapter are taken from this source.

Following an increase in income, it usually takes time for people to fully adjust their spending patterns. Thus, we can estimate both a short-run and a long-run income elasticity, reflecting an initial partial response to an income increase and the ultimate full response. We expect the long-run elasticity to exceed the short-run elasticity, and for clothing this is indeed the case. Although the short-run elasticity is .95, the long-run elasticity is 1.17. Following a 10% increase in income, people initially increase expenditures on clothing by 9.5%, but ultimately increase expenditures by 11.7%.

Income elasticities take a wide range of values. The income elasticity of demand for an inferior good is negative. The income elasticity of demand for alcoholic beverages is only about .29. (A 10% increase in income leads to a 2.9% increase in expenditure on alcohol.) The income elasticity of demand for jewelry is about 1, so that expenditure on jewelry increases roughly in proportion with income. The income elasticity of demand for household appliances is 2.72. When income increases 10%, expenditure on appliances increases 27.2%. (The estimates in this paragraph are all short-run elasticities.)

Price Elasticity of Demand

Price elasticity of demand The percentage change in consumption that results from a 1% increase in price.

Your **price elasticity of demand** for X (also called the elasticity of your demand curve) measures how sensitively your consumption of X responds to a change in the price.

As with income elasticity, it is convenient to measure everything in percentage terms so the outcomes do not depend on the choice of units.

Therefore, the price elasticity is defined as the answer to the question: If the price of X goes up by 1%, by what percentage will you change your consumption of X? It can be computed from the formula:

$$\text{Price elasticity} = \frac{\text{Percentage change in quantity}}{\text{Percentage change in price}}$$

$$= \frac{100 \cdot \Delta Q/Q}{100 \cdot \Delta P/P}$$

$$= \frac{P \cdot \Delta Q}{Q \cdot \Delta P}$$

The elasticity of a downward-sloping demand curve is negative, because an increase in price (that is, a positive percentage change in price) yields a decrease (a negative percentage change) in quantity. For example, suppose that a price of 20¢ corresponds to a quantity of 3 and a price of 30¢ corresponds to a quantity of 2. In this case, a 50% change in price yields a 33% fall in Q, so the price elasticity is $(-33\%)/50\% = -.67$.

There is a price elasticity associated with any demand curve. Therefore, we should distinguish in principle between the compensated and uncompensated price elasticities for any particular good. In each case we can use the formula $(P \cdot \Delta Q)/(Q \cdot \Delta P)$, but in one case the quantities are read off the compensated demand curve, while in the other they are read off the uncompensated demand curve. When income effects are small, there is very little difference between the two demand curves and the two price elasticities are close to equal.

Market Elasticities

Just as we can talk about your personal price elasticity of demand for X, we can talk about the market's price elasticity of demand. Again, we divide the percentage change in quantity by the percentage change in price, only this time we take quantities from the market demand curve.

We say that the demand for a good is highly elastic if the price elasticity of demand for that good has a large absolute value. When the demand for a good is highly elastic, people are willing to reduce their consumption significantly in response to a given price rise. This is most likely to be the case when the good has a large number of close substitutes.

It is reasonable to expect that the demand for Hostess Twinkies is more elastic than the demand for packaged cakes; the demand for packaged cakes is more elastic than the demand for snack foods; and the demand for snack foods is more elastic than the demand for food generally.

For a given income and quantity of *X*, high income elasticity is reflected in a relatively steep Engel curve. For a given price and quantity of *X*, high price elasticity is reflected in a relatively flat demand curve. The apparent paradox occurs because the quantity of *X* is plotted on the vertical axis for an Engel curve and on the horizontal axis for a demand curve.

The price elasticity of demand for electricity is −.13, for water −.20, for jewelry −.41, for shoes −.73, and for tobacco −1.4. If the price of electricity rises by 10%, the quantity demanded falls by 1.3%. If the price of water rises by 10%, the quantity demanded falls by 2%.

EXERCISE 4.9 If the price of jewelry rises by 10%, by how much does the quantity demanded fall? How about for shoes? For tobacco?

Cross Elasticities

Cross elasticity of demand The percentage change in consumption that results from a 1% increase in the price of a related good.

One other circumstance that can affect your demand for X is a change in the price of some other good Y. The **cross elasticity of demand** for X with respect to Y is a measure of the size of this effect; it is the percentage change in consumption of X divided by the percentage change in the price of Y.

A change in the price of Y could cause your consumption of X to either rise or fall. In the first case, your cross elasticity of demand is positive and in the second it is negative. If X is coffee and Y is tea, the cross elasticity is likely to be positive: When the price of tea increases by 1%, your coffee consumption is likely to increase. The percentage by which it increases (a positive number) is the cross elasticity of demand. But if X is coffee and Y is cream, a 1% increase in the price of cream is likely to lead to a *decrease* (that is, a *negative* percentage change) in the demand for coffee, and so in this case the cross elasticity of demand is negative.

Substitutes Goods for which the cross elasticity of demand is positive.

Complements Goods for which the cross elasticity of demand is negative.

When the cross elasticity of demand for X with respect to Y is positive, we say that X and Y are **substitutes.** When it is negative, we say that they are **complements.** Substitutes, as the name indicates, tend to be goods that can be substituted for each other, as in our example of tea and coffee. Other examples might be Coke and Pepsi, or train tickets and airline tickets. Complements tend to be goods that are used together—each complements the other. We have seen the example of coffee and cream. Other pairs of complements might be computers and floppy disks, or textbooks and college courses.

Elasticities and Monopoly Power

Does the McDonald's hamburger chain have a monopoly on the products it sells? If consumers think that there is no close substitute for a McDonald's hamburger, then the answer is yes. On the other hand, if consumers think that a Burger King hamburger and a McDonald's hamburger are indistinguishable, then McDonald's faces heavy competition.

When courts are called upon to decide whether a firm has monopoly power, they must ask whether competing firms offer products that are close substitutes in the minds of consumers. But how is the court to tell whether an alternative product is viewed as a close substitute? A solution is to examine the cross elasticity of demand.

Suppose that the cross elasticity of demand between McDonald's and Burger King hamburgers is positive and large. Then the goods are close substitutes and Burger King competes in essentially the same market as McDonald's. The large cross elasticity means that if McDonald's tries to raise its prices, a lot of customers will switch to Burger King, so that McDonald's monopoly power is severely limited. On the other hand, if the cross elasticity is small, McDonald's needs to worry much less about this kind of competition. Large cross elasticities are evidence of competition and small cross elasticities are evidence of monopoly. Cross elasticities routinely play major roles in antitrust cases.

summary

Changes in the consumer's opportunities lead to changes in the optimal consumption basket. Changes in opportunities arise from changes in income and changes in prices.

A change in income causes a parallel shift in the budget line. When income rises, consumption of the good X can either rise (in which case X is called a normal good) or fall (in which case X is called an inferior good).

If we fix the prices of goods X and Y, we can draw budget lines corresponding to various levels of income. If we also know the consumer's indifference curves, we can find the optimal basket corresponding to each level of income and read off the quantity of X associated with each level of income. We can plot this information on a graph, with income on the horizontal axis and quantity of X on the vertical. The resulting curve is called an Engel curve. The Engel curve slopes upward for a normal good and downward for an inferior good.

A change in the price of X causes the budget line to pivot around its Y-intercept, outward for a fall in price and inward for a rise in price. A rise in price can cause the quantity of X demanded to fall (in which case X is called a non-Giffen good) or rise (in which case X is called a Giffen good).

If we fix the price of Y and the consumer's income, we can draw budget lines corresponding to various prices of X. If we also know the consumer's indifference curves, we can find the optimal basket associated with each price of X and read off the quantity of X associated with each price. We can plot this information on a graph, with price on the vertical axis and quantity on the horizontal. The resulting curve is the demand curve for X. The demand curve slopes downward if X is not Giffen and upward if X is Giffen.

When the price of X goes up, the consumer changes his consumption of X for two reasons. First, there is the substitution effect: Consumers will not purchase goods whose marginal value is below the price. Second, there is the income effect: Consumers are made effectively poorer when a price goes up. The substitution effect always reduces consumption of X. The income effect reduce consumption of X if X is a normal good, but increases consumption of X if X is an inferior good.

For a normal good, the substitution and income effects work in the same direction, ensuring that when the price goes up the quantity demanded goes down. Thus, a normal good cannot be Giffen. For an inferior good, the substitution and income effects work in opposite directions: If the substitution effect is greater, the good is not Giffen, but if the income effect is greater, the good is Giffen.

The compensated demand curve shows, for each price, the quantity of X the consumer would demand if he were income-compensated for every price change. Thus, the compensated demand curve shows only the substitution effect and so must slope downward.

Review Questions

R1. How does a change in income affect the budget line?

R2. What is the definition of an inferior good? What is the definition of a normal good?

R3. Explain how to use the indifference curve diagram to construct a point on the Engel curve.

R4. How does a change in price affect the budget line?

R5. What is the definition of a Giffen good?

R6. Explain how to use the indifference curve diagram to construct a point on the demand curve.

R7. Describe the income and substitution effects of a price increase. Illustrate these effects in an indifference curve diagram.

R8. When the price of a good increases, what is the direction of the substitution effect? Use the geometry of indifference curves to explain your answer.

R9. When the price of a normal good increases, what is the direction of the income effect? When the price of an inferior good increases, what is the direction of the income effect?

R10. Are all Giffen goods inferior? Are all inferior goods Giffen? Justify your answers in terms of the substitution and income effects.

R11. What is the compensated demand curve? Does it always slope downward? Why or why not?

R12. Give the formulas for income elasticity of demand and price elasticity of demand.

Numerical Exercises

N1. Suppose your indifference curves are all described by equations of the form $x \cdot y =$ constant, with a different constant for each indifference curve.

a. Show that for any point $P = (x,y)$, the indifference curve through P has slope $-y/x$ at P. (This requires calculus. If you don't know enough calculus, you can just pretend you've solved this part and go on to part b.)

b. Suppose that your income is \$40, the price of X is \$1, and the price of Y is \$1. How much X do you buy? *Hint:* The problem is to find your optimal basket (x,y). First write down an equation that says (x,y) is on the budget line. Next write down an equation that says the slope of the indifference curve at (x,y) is equal to the slope of the budget line at (x,y). (Remember that you have a formula for the slope of the budget line from part a, and that you can compute the slope of the budget line from the prices of X and Y.) Then solve these two equations simultaneously.

c. Suppose your income and the price of Y remain as above, but the price of X rises to \$4. Now how much X do you consume? (Use the same hint as in part b.)

d. Based on your answers to parts b and c, draw two points on your demand curve for X.

e. After the price of X rises from \$1 to \$4, suppose that your income rises by just enough to bring you back to your original indifference curve. Now how much X do you buy? *Hint:* The problem is to find the basket (x,y) where the compensated budget line is tangent to the original indifference curve. First write down the equation of the original indifference curve (remember that it is of the form $xy =$ constant, and you can figure out the constant because you already know the coordinates of one point on that curve). Next write down an equation that expresses the condition that the slope of the indifference curve must equal the slope of the compensated budget line. Then solve these two equations simultaneously.

f. When the price of X rises from \$1 to \$4, how much of the change in your consumption is due to the substitution effect? How much is due to the income effect?

N2. Suppose that your Engel curve for X is given by the equation

$$X = a + bI$$

where I is income and a and b are constants.

a. If your income increases from I to $I + \Delta I$, by how much does X increase?

b. Write down a formula, in terms of X and I, for your income elasticity of demand for X.

c. Use the equation $X = a + bI$ to eliminate I from your formula, and write a formula for income elasticity in terms of X alone.

d. As your consumption of X increases, what happens to your income elasticity of demand for X?

e. If your Engel curve is a line through the origin, what is your income elasticity of demand for X?

N3. Suppose that your demand curve for X is given by the equation

$$X = c - dP$$

where P is price and c and d are positive constants.

a. Derive a formula for your price elasticity of demand for X, and write your formula in terms of X alone.

b. When you consume zero units of X, what is your price elasticity of demand? When the price of X is zero, what is your price elasticity of demand?

N4. Suppose that your demand curve for X is given by the equation

$$X = \frac{e}{P}$$

where P is price and e is a positive constant. Derive a formula for your price elasticity of demand for X.

Problem Set

1. **True or False:** It is unlikely that a consumer would view all goods as inferior goods.

2. The only good that Herman consumes is Munster cheese. What is the shape of his Engel curve for Munster cheese? What is the shape of his demand curve for Munster cheese?

3. Suppose your indifference curves between X and Y are shaped, somewhat unusually, as in Exhibit 3–10. What is the shape of your Engel curve for X? What is the shape of your demand curve for X?

4. Suppose the only goods you consume are cakes and ale. You have chosen an optimal basket containing 5 cakes and 7 ales. Now suppose that someone starts giving you additional cakes, but you are unable to adjust your consumption of ales. In this circumstances, you find that each additional cake has a lower marginal value to you than the previous one. **True or False:** Ale cannot possibly be an inferior good.

5. Suppose the only two goods you buy are food and clothing. One day the price of clothing and your income both increase by 10%, while the price of food remains fixed. How does your budget line move?

6. Suppose that the only goods you consume are wine and roses. On Tuesday the price of wine goes up, and at the same time your income increases by just enough so that you are equally as happy as you were on Monday.

   a. What happens to the quantity of wine that you consume? Illustrate your answer with indifference curves.

   b. On Tuesday would you still be able to afford the same basket that you were buying on Monday? How do you know?

   On Wednesday there are no new price changes (so the Tuesday prices are still in effect), but your income changes to the point where you can just exactly afford Monday's basket.

   c. Are you happier on Wednesday or on Monday?

d. Is it possible to say with certainty whether you buy more wine on Wednesday than on Monday? If not, on what would your answer depend?

e. Is it possible to say with certainty whether you buy more wine on Wednesday than Tuesday? If not, on what would your answer depend?

7. When the price of shoes goes up, Tara goes right on buying as many shoes as she did before. **True or False:** Shoes could not possibly be an inferior good for Tara.

8. Suppose that the only two goods you purchase are X and Y. One day the price of X goes down.

a. Illustrate your old and new budget lines.

b. Illustrate the substitution and income effects on your consumption of X.

c. What is the direction of the substitution effect? Why?

d. If X is a normal good, what is the direction of the income effect? Why?

e. If X is an inferior good, what is the direction of the income effect? Why?

f. True or False: If X is an inferior good, then a fall in price must lead to a rise in consumption, but if X is a normal good, then a fall in price might lead to a fall in consumption. Justify your answer carefully in terms of income and substitution effects.

9. Suppose the only goods you buy are wine and roses.

a. Between Monday and Tuesday, the price of wine goes up (while your income remains fixed). Draw a diagram, with wine on the horizontal axis and roses on the vertical, to illustrate how your budget line moves. Illustrate your optimum points on the two budget lines, labeling Monday's optimum M and Tuesday's optimum T.

b. On Wednesday, the price of wine returns to its Monday level, but at the same moment your income falls by just enough so that you are just as happy on Wednesday as on Tuesday. Illustrate your new budget line and your new optimum point. Label the optimum point W.

In each of parts c, d, and e, determine whether the statement is (1) true always, (2) false always, (3) true if wine is an inferior good, but otherwise false, (4) false if wine is an inferior good but otherwise true, (5) true if wine is a Giffen good, but otherwise false, or (6) false if wine is a Giffen good but otherwise true.

c. M is to the left of T.

d. T is to the left of W.

e. M is to the left of W.

f. True or False: Every Giffen good is an inferior good. Justify your answers by **using the earlier parts of this problem**, *not* by using the argument given in the text.

10. Suppose the only two goods you consume are *X* and *Y*. On Tuesday, the price of *Y* (*not X!*) goes up. On Wednesday, there are no new price changes, but your income rises by just enough so that you can exactly afford Monday's basket.

a. Use a diagram, with *X* on the horizontal axis and *Y* on the vertical, to illustrate your budget lines and optimum points on Monday, Tuesday, and Wednesday. Label the optimum points *M, T,* and *W*.

b. In terms of the locations of points *M, T,* and *W*, what would it mean for *X* to be an inferior good?

c. Is it true that *W* is always to the right of *M*? If so, how do you know? If not, what would your answer depend on?

d. *X* is called a *gross complement* for *Y* if it is true that "when the price of *Y* goes up, the quantity demanded of *X* goes up." In terms of points *M, T,* and *W*, what would it mean for *X* to be a gross complement for *Y*?

e. True or False: If *X* is an inferior good, then it must be a gross complement for *Y*. Fully justify your answer.

f. True or False: If *X* is a Giffen good, then it must be a gross complement for *Y*. Fully justify your answer.

11. Sam consumes only green eggs and ham. Ham is an inferior good for Sam. One day the price of green eggs goes up.

a. Illustrate Sam's old and new optimum points, and show both the substitution and the income effects. How does this graph reflect the fact that ham is an inferior good?

b. True or False: When the price of green eggs goes up, Sam certainly buys more ham than before. Justify your answer carefully, by considering the directions of both the substitution and income effects.

12. Bugs consumes only carrots and lettuce, both of which are normal goods for Bugs. One day the price of carrots goes up.

a. Illustrate Bugs's old and new optimum points, and show both the substitution and income effects. How does your graph reflect the fact that carrots are a normal good? How does it reflect the fact that lettuce is a normal good?

b. Can you say for certain whether the substitution effect causes Bugs to buy more or less lettuce than before? If you can, use your graph to explain why. If you cannot, explain on what the answer would depend. (*Warning:* Notice that although the price of carrots has fallen, you are being asked about the effect on consumption of lettuce, not of carrots.)

c. Can you say for certain whether the income effect causes Bugs to buy more or less lettuce than before? If you can, use your graph to explain why; if you cannot, explain on what the answer would depend.

d. When the price of carrots goes up, can you say for certain whether Bugs would buy more or less lettuce than before? If you can, carefully justify your answer; if you cannot, explain on what the answer would depend.

e. Suppose that almost all of Bugs's income is spent on lettuce. Now when the price of carrots goes up, do you expect him to buy more or less lettuce than before? Carefully justify your answer in terms of the income and substitution effects.

13. Leopold consumes only kidneys and liver. When the price of kidneys rises, Leopold reduces his consumption of liver.

a. Illustrate the substitution and income effects from a rise in the price of kidneys. Be sure that your diagram shows that Leopold now consumes less liver than before.

b. Can you determine whether liver is an inferior good for Leopold?

c. Can you determine whether liver is a Giffen good for Leopold?

14. Suppose that without a seat belt, drivers who travel at 0 m.p.h. have a 100% chance of staying alive, while drivers who travel at 100 m.p.h. have 0% chance of staying alive. Suppose that with a seat belt, drivers who travel at 0 m.p.h. have a 100% chance of staying alive, drivers who travel at 100 m.p.h. have a 50% chance of staying alive, and drivers who travel at 200 m.p.h. have a 0% chance of staying alive.

a. Draw an indifference curve diagram relating safety (measured by chance of staying alive) on the horizontal axis and speed (measured in m.p.h.) on the vertical. Draw the budget constraints of a driver with a seat belt and a driver without a seat belt. (You may assume these constraints are straight lines.)

b. True or False: If speed and safety are both normal goods, then the invention of seat belts will certainly make people drive faster, but might or might not save lives. Explain your answer in terms of substitution and income effects.

15. Suppose you have 24 hours per day that you can allocate between leisure and working at a wage of $2 per hour.

a. Draw your budget constraint between "leisure hours" on the horizontal axis and "income" on the vertical.

b. Draw in your optimum point. Keeping in mind that the number of hours you spend working is equal to 24 minus the number of hours that you spend at leisure, plot a corresponding point on your labor supply curve.

c. Now suppose that the wage rate rises to $3 per hour. Draw your new budget constraint, your new optimum, and a new point on your labor supply curve.

d. On your indifference curve diagram, decompose the effect of the wage increase into a substitution effect and an income effect. What is the direction of the substitution effect? What is the direction of the income effect if leisure is a normal good? What is the direction of the income effect if leisure is an inferior good?

e. True or False: If leisure is an inferior good, the labor supply curve must slope upward, but if leisure is a normal good, the labor supply curve could slope either direction.

f. Whose labor supply curve is likely to slope upward more steeply: Somebody whose income is derived entirely from wages, or somebody who has a large nonwage income? Why?

16. You start with $500,000 to spend on housing and other goods. Housing costs $100 a square foot. You choose to purchase a 3,000-square-foot house. Assume that it costs nothing (in terms of attorney's fees, advertising, and so on) to buy and sell houses.

a. Draw an indifference curve diagram between "size of house" and "all other goods." Draw your budget line and indicate your optimum point.

b. Suppose that after you have bought your 3,000-square-foot house, the price of housing drops to $50 per square foot. Show your new budget line. (*Hint:* You can keep your existing house if you want to.)

c. Having recently bought a house, are you made better or worse off by a fall in the price of housing?

d. Suppose that after the price of housing falls, you move from your 3,000-square-foot house to house *A*. If the price of housing had fallen before you bought your 3,000-square-foot house, you would have chosen house *B*. Can you say for certain which house is bigger, *A* or *B*? If you can, why? If you cannot, on what would the answer depend?

17. Suppose you have $1,000 today and expect to receive another $1,000 one year from today. Your savings account pays an annual interest rate of 25%, and your bank is willing to lend you money at that same interest rate.

a. Suppose that you save all of your money to spend next year. How much will you be able to spend next year? How much will you be able to spend today?

b. Suppose you borrow $800 and spend $1,800 today. How much will you be able to spend next year?

c. Draw your budget constraint between "spending today" and "spending next year." What is its slope? How does the slope reflect the relative price of spending today in terms of spending next year?

d. How would your budget line shift in each of the following circumstances?

You find $400 that you'd forgotten was in your desk drawer.
Your boss informs you that you will receive a $500 bonus next year.
The interest rate rises to 50%.

e. Under which circumstance would you spend more today: finding a forgotten $400 in a desk drawer or being told that you will receive a $500 bonus next year? Under which circumstance would you spend more tomorrow?

f. Returning to the assumption that you have $1,000 today and expect to receive $1,000 next year, suppose that you choose neither to borrow nor to lend. Illustrate the tangency of your budget line with an indifference curve.

g. In part f, suppose that the interest rate rises to 50%. Show how your budget line shifts. Do you increase or decrease your current spending? Do you increase or decrease your future spending? Are you better off or worse off than before?

h. In part g, decompose the change in your consumption into a substitution effect followed by an income effect. Can you determine the direction of the substitution effect? Can you determine the direction of the income effect?

18. If you consume only one good, what is the shape of your compensated demand curve for that good?

19. If your indifference curves between X and Y are shaped as in Exhibit 3–10, what is the shape of your compensated demand curve for X?

20. True or False: For a normal good, the compensated demand curve is steeper than the uncompensated demand curve, but for an inferior good the reverse is true.

21. True or False: Your compensated and uncompensated demand curves for bubble gum are likely to be very similar to each other, but your compensated and uncompensated demand curves for college tuition might be very different.

22. Suppose the only good you ever consume is Nestle's Crunch bars. What is your income elasticity of demand for Nestle's Crunch bars? What is your price elasticity of demand for Nestle's Crunch bars?

23. A *luxury* is defined to be a good with income elasticity greater than 1. Explain what this means without the technical jargon. Is it possible for all the goods you consume to be luxuries? Why or why not?

Internet Exercise

The Federal Trade Commission and the Department of Justice evaluate the potential anticompetitive effects from mergers of rival firms using the 1992 Horizontal Merger Guidelines. You can access the Horizontal Merger Guidelines on the Internet (http://www.ftc.gov/bc/docs/horizmer.htm). Once you have done so, review the material in Section 1.1 pertaining to the way that antitrust authorities are to define the relevant product market. Use what you have learned about elasticity of demand to describe how antitrust authorities might use estimates of price and cross elasticity of demand to determine the relevant product market in an antitrust case.

chapter 5

The Behavior of Firms

More on firm behavior can be found at:
http://www.best.com/~ddfr/Academic/Price_Theory/PThy_Chapter_9/PThy_Chapter_9.html

In this chapter we will turn our attention from the behavior of individuals to the behavior of firms. Firms are the institutions that produce and supply the goods that individuals demand. Just as our study of individual consumers' behavior led us to a deeper understanding of demand, our study of firms' behavior will lead us to a deeper understanding of supply.

All firms are created and owned by individuals. Some, like many corner grocery stores, have one owner; whereas others, like the General Motors Corporation, have many thousands of owners (in this case the General Motors stockholders). In some firms the owner or owners exert considerable day-to-day control over operations, whereas in others salaried managers serve these functions. With such diversity in the size, nature, and organization of firms, you might wonder how it could be possible to make any statements at all about the behavior of firms in general.

There is, however, one grand generalization about firms that economists have found to be extraordinarily powerful: We assume that firms act to maximize profits. There are reasons to question this assumption. Why should individuals, who are interested in many things other than profits, choose to organize firms that pursue profits single-mindedly? Even if the owners view profit maximization as desirable, does it follow that the managers will behave accordingly? Economists have given much thought to these and related questions.[1] However, most economists also believe that the assumption of profit maximization, while only an approximation to the truth, leads to deep insights into the ways in which goods are supplied.

Firm An entity that produces and sells goods, with the goal of maximizing its profits.

Therefore, we will use the word **firm** to refer to an entity that produces and

[1] One of the earliest and most enlightening contributions to this literature is R. H. Coase, "On the Nature of the Firm," *Economica* 4 (1937):386–405.

supplies goods and that seeks to do so in such a way as to maximize the profits that it earns in any given time period. The goal of profit maximization will enter into every decision that the firm makes. In Section 5.1 we will study a simple problem in which a firm must weigh costs against benefits. This will lead us to the equimarginal principle, which is one of the most fundamental concepts in economics and the key to profit maximization. In Section 5.2 we will see how firms use this principle in deciding how much to produce.

5.1 Weighing Costs and Benefits

In this section we will examine how firms make decisions by imagining a simple problem that a farmer might face: How many acres of her land should she spray with insecticide? The solution to this problem will reveal one of the key concepts in economics, known as the equimarginal principle. Once this principle has been made explicit, we will see that it applies both to the behavior of firms and to the behavior of individuals.

A Farmer's Problem

To begin to understand how firms make decisions, let us imagine a problem Farmer Adams faces in operating her farm as a firm (that is, as a profit-maximizing enterprise). Farmer Adams owns 6 acres of land planted with wheat. Her problem is to decide how many acres to spray with insecticide.

Suppose that spraying 1 acre saves $7 worth of crops. What then will be the value of the crops saved when 2 acres are sprayed? Your first guess might be $14, but a more reasonable guess would be something less. Why? Because the 6 acres of land on the farm are not identical. Some acres are more fertile than others, and some acres are more susceptible to insect damage than others. When Farmer Adams sprays only 1 acre, she chooses that acre where spraying yields the greatest benefit. When she sprays 2 acres, she chooses the one where spraying yields the greatest benefit and the one where spraying yields the second greatest benefit. We can expect this to generate less than twice the gain from spraying the first acre.

So a reasonable assumption would be that if spraying 1 acre saves $7 worth of crops, then spraying 2 acres saves $13 worth of crops. We record these numbers in the second column of the following table, along with the total benefit when 3, 4, 5, or 6 acres are sprayed.

No. of Acres Sprayed	Total Benefit	Marginal Benefit
0	$ 0	
1	7	$7/acre
2	13	6
3	18	5
4	22	4
5	25	3
6	27	2

Marginal benefit The additional benefit gained from the last unit of an activity.

The third column of the table, labeled **marginal benefit**, refers to the value of crops saved on the last acre sprayed. For example, since spraying 2 acres saves $13 worth of crops, of which $7 worth are saved on the first acre, it follows that $6 worth are saved on the second acre. So when 2 acres are sprayed, we say that the marginal benefit from spraying the second acre is $6 worth of crops saved per acre. If Farmer Adams sprays 3 acres, she will save $18 worth of crops. Because we know that spraying has saved $13 on the first two acres, we can calculate a marginal benefit of $5 per acre for the third acre sprayed.

EXERCISE 5.1 Verify the other numbers in the third column of the table. Explain why it is reasonable for these numbers to be decreasing. Explain why the sum of the first 3 (or 4 or 5) entries in the "marginal" column is equal to the third (or fourth or fifth) entry in the "total" column.

In order to decide how many acres Farmer Adams should spray, we also need to know something about the costs of spraying. Let us suppose that the farmer can hire a crop duster for a fee of $5 per acre. The second column of the following table shows the total cost of spraying various numbers of acres.

No. of Acres Sprayed	Total Cost	Marginal Cost
0	$ 0	
1	5	$5/acre
2	10	5
3	15	5
4	20	5
5	25	5
6	30	5

Marginal cost The additional cost associated with the last unit of an activity.

The third column of the table shows the **marginal cost** associated with each acre sprayed; that is, it shows the additional cost incurred as a result of spraying each acre. If Farmer Adams sprays 4 acres, the spraying bill is $20, of which $15 pays for the first 3 acres sprayed. Therefore, the marginal cost of spraying the fourth acre is $5 per acre.

EXERCISE 5.2 Explain why the marginal cost of spraying is $5 per acre regardless of how many acres are sprayed.

In Exhibit 5–1 all of our information is gathered together and displayed on graphs. The only new column in the table, labeled "Net Gain," is the total value of crops saved through spraying minus the total cost of spraying.

The graphs in the exhibit display the information from the table. The values in the "Net Gain" column are illustrated by the lengths of the vertical lines in the first graph, indicating the distance between total cost and total benefit.

The net gain from spraying adds to the farmer's profits, so she wants this net gain to be as large as possible. Looking at the last column of the table, we see that this occurs when the number of acres sprayed is either 2 or 3. To remove the ambiguity, let us arbitrarily suppose that whenever the farmer is indifferent between two options, she chooses the larger one. In that case the number of acres sprayed will be 3.[2]

Farmer Adams has an easy way of deciding how many acres to spray: Scan the "Net Gain" column, find the largest possible net gain, and spray the corresponding number of acres. We will call this process *Method 1*. There is an alternative, equally valid process available to Farmer Adams, which we will call *Method 2*.

To use Method 2, focus on the row of the table corresponding to 1 acre sprayed and look only at the "Marginal" columns. Now ask yourself which is greater—the marginal benefit of spraying the first acre or the marginal cost? Since $7 is greater than $5, the marginal benefit is greater, and so spraying that first acre is a good deal. On this basis we decide to spray the first acre.

Next, inspect the row of the table corresponding to 2 acres sprayed, again looking at only the "Marginal" columns. Does the marginal gain from spraying a second acre exceed the marginal cost of doing so? Since $6 is greater than $5, the answer is yes, and so it is a good idea to spray the second acre as well.

When we get to the next row of the table, we find that the marginal gain from spraying a third acre is equal to the marginal cost of spraying that acre. Having already decided to spray the first 2 acres, the farmer is indifferent about spraying the third. As before, we arbitrarily eliminate the ambiguity by assuming the farmer always moves forward when she is indifferent, and so she sprays a third acre as well.

When we consider spraying a fourth acre, we find that the marginal value of the crops saved is only $4. This is less than the marginal cost of saving them. Farmer Adams would be $1-poorer after spraying this fourth acre. Spraying the fourth acre is *not* a good idea, and so Farmer Adams stops after spraying 3 acres.

Method 2 can be summarized as follows: Continue spraying as long as the marginal benefit from spraying is greater than or equal to the marginal cost; stop spraying when the marginal value and the marginal cost become equal. Here is an even briefer summary of Method 2: Scan the "Marginal" columns until you find the row in which the marginal benefit is equal to the marginal cost; then spray the corresponding number of acres. In terms of the graph, Method 2 says to choose the quantity at which the marginal benefit curve and the marginal cost curve cross.

Notice that Method 1 and Method 2 both yield the same answer: Spray 3 acres. They *must* yield the same answer, since each is a perfectly valid way of determining the optimal behavior. In view of this, you may wonder why we

---

[2] In real life the farmer would have many more than six choices. In addition to the possibilities displayed in Exhibit 5–1, she could choose to spray exactly 3½ acres, or 1.7894 acres, or any other number of acres between 0 and 6. If we had been able to display all of these possibilities, we would have found that the net gain was maximized by only one of them, rather than two. The optimal number of acres to spray might have been somewhere between 2 and 3. You might have been disturbed by our arbitrary rule that the farmer always chooses the larger of the two options that maximize net gain. If so, you should be relieved by the observation that this was necessitated only by the simplicity of our example, and that if we displayed more options, no such arbitrary choice would be required.

Exhibit 5-1 Maximizing Net Gain

No. of Acres Sprayed	Total Benefit	Marginal Benefit	Total Cost	Marginal Cost	Net Gain
0	$ 0		$0		$0
1	7	$7/acre	5	$5/acre	2
2	13	6	10	5	3
3	18	5	15	5	3
4	22	4	20	5	2
5	25	3	25	5	0
6	27	2	30	5	−3

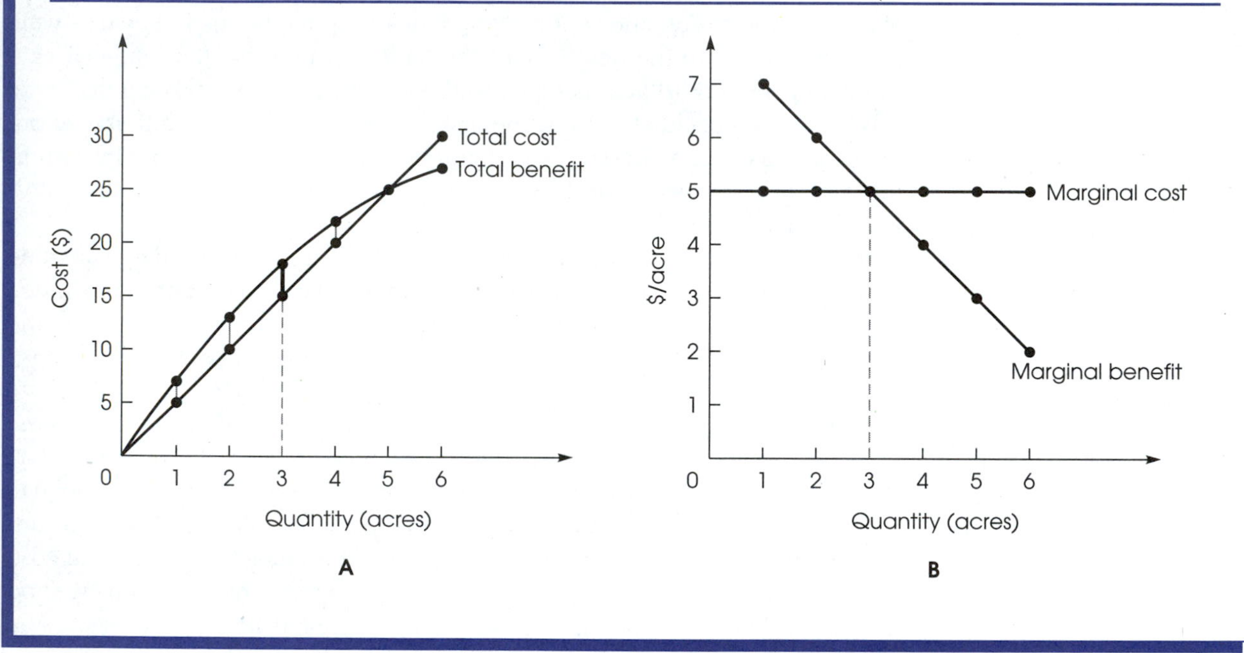

The graphs display the information in the table. Because Net gain = Total benefit − Total cost, the net gain is equal to the distance between the total cost and total benefit curves in panel A. For example, the heavy vertical line has length $3, representing the net gain of $3 when 3 acres are sprayed. Because the heavy line is the longest of the vertical lines, the farmer will maximize her net gain by spraying 3 acres. An alternative way to reach the same conclusion is to continue spraying as long as marginal benefit exceeds marginal cost and to stop when they become equal, at 3 acres.

went to the trouble of developing Method 2 when Method 1 works perfectly well. The reason for studying Method 2 is that it demonstrates the importance of the "Marginal" columns. It shows that the "Marginal" information alone is enough to determine the optimal decision. We can say the same thing in a slightly different way: A change in circumstances will not affect Farmer Adams's behavior unless it causes a change in a "Marginal" column.

Exhibit 5-2 Maximizing Net Gain

No. of Acres Sprayed	Total Benefit	Marginal Benefit	Total Cost	Marginal Cost	Net Gain
1	$ 7	$7/acre	6	$5/acre	$ 1
2	13	6	11	5	2
3	18	5	16	5	2
4	22	4	21	5	1
5	25	3	26	5	−1
6	27	2	31	5	−4

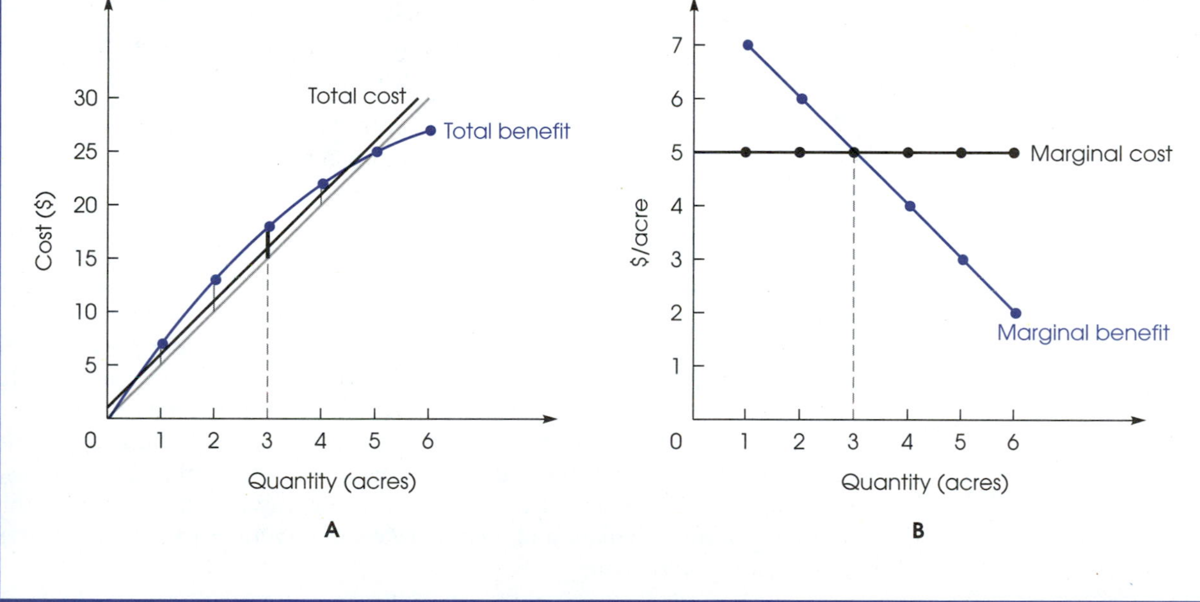

The table describes the situation after the crop duster institutes a $1 flat fee for coming out to the farm. The data from the table are displayed in the graphs. The light-colored curve in panel A is the old Total Cost curve from Exhibit 5-1 and is reproduced here for comparison. The marginal curves are the same as those in Exhibit 5-1. Therefore, the optimal number of acres to spray, which is determined by the intersection of the marginal cost and the marginal benefit curves, is unchanged.

An example will illustrate this last point. Suppose that the crop duster changes his pricing policy. He now charges a $1 flat fee for coming out to the farm, plus $5 for each acre sprayed. (One dollar is the fee for spraying *zero* acres!) Exhibit 5–2 illustrates the new situation.

The marginal costs and marginal benefits in Exhibit 5–2 are the same as those in Exhibit 5–1. Therefore, Method 2 still gives the same result as before: Marginal cost equals marginal benefit when 3 acres are sprayed, and so 3 acres is the optimal number to spray. We can confirm this using Method 1. Net gain is still maximized when 3 acres are sprayed. Graphically, the total cost curve has shifted up parallel to itself a distance $1, so that the maximal distance between it and the total benefit curve still occurs at a quantity of 3 acres.

Now here is the key observation: We really could have predicted this result without ever building the table in Exhibit 5–2. All we had to observe was that the change in the crop duster's pricing policy does not change either of the "Marginal" columns in the table, and that only these columns are necessary for predicting the farmer's behavior. Therefore, the farmer's behavior will not change under the new pricing policy.

It is true that the crop duster's new pricing policy makes the farmer worse off than before: She used to realize a net gain of $3 when she sprayed 3 acres, and now she realizes a net gain of only $2. What remains unchanged is the number of acres that the farmer chooses to spray: 3 in either case.

EXERCISE 5.3 Suppose that the crop duster changes his policy again, so that he now charges $2 to come out to the farm, plus $5 per acre sprayed. How many acres will the farmer spray now? Figure out the answer without building a table, and explain how you know that your answer is correct. Now build a table and check that your answer really is correct.

EXERCISE 5.4 Suppose now that the crop duster lowers his price to $4 per acre sprayed. Does this affect anything marginal? Does it change the farmer's decision about how many acres to spray?

There is one exception to the rule we have just learned. The rule is: If nothing marginal changes, then Farmer Adams's behavior won't change. The exception is: If the only possible net gains from spraying become negative, Farmer Adams will quit spraying altogether. For example, suppose that the crop duster changes his pricing scheme to: $100 to come out to the farm plus $5 per acre sprayed. If you construct a table like those in Exhibits 5–1 and 5–2, you will see that the "marginal" columns remain unchanged but that the farmer loses money by spraying no matter how many acres she sprays. In this case, she will spray not 3 acres but 0 acres. So a better way to state the rule is this: If nothing marginal changes and if Farmer Adams continues to spray at all, then her behavior won't change.

The Equimarginal Principle

Equimarginal principle
The principle that an activity should be pursued to the point where marginal cost equals marginal benefit.

Farmer Adams has discovered the **equimarginal principle,** which is the essence of Method 2 for deciding how many acres to spray:

If an activity is worth pursuing at all, then it should be pursued up to the point where marginal cost equals marginal benefit.

She has also discovered an important consequence of the principle:

If circumstances change in a way that does not affect anything marginal and if an activity remains worth pursuing at all, then the optimal amount of that activity is unchanged.

The equimarginal principle has broad applicability. It applies not only to firms but also to individuals. Indeed, we have already met the equimarginal principle in Chapter 3, where we studied the consumer's optimum. The consumer moves along his budget line, trading Y for X until the relative price of a unit of X (which is the marginal cost of that unit measured in terms of Y) is equal to the marginal rate of substitution between X and Y (which is the marginal value of that unit measured in terms of Y). Since the benefit to a consumer from owning a unit of X is the same thing as the value to him of that unit, equating marginal cost to marginal value is the same as equating marginal cost to marginal benefit.

Applying the Principle

Occasionally you will read a newspaper editorial that makes an argument along the following lines: "Our town spends only $100,000 per year to run its police department, and the benefits we get from the police are worth far more than that. Police services are a good deal in our town. We should be expanding the police department, not cutting back on it as Mayor McDonald has proposed." This argument is wrong. The editorial writer has observed (we assume correctly) that the total benefit derived from the police department exceeds the total cost of acquiring those benefits. But this is not relevant to the decision between expanding the department or contracting it. For this decision, only marginal quantities matter.

Reconsider Exhibit 5-1. When Farmer Adams sprays 3 acres, she is getting a good deal: Her gains from spraying exceed her costs by $3. Does it follow that she should expand her spraying program and spray a fourth acre? No, because the *marginal* cost of spraying that fourth acre exceeds the *marginal* gain from doing so. It is true that Farmer Adam's gains exceeded her costs on each of the first 3 acres she decided to spray. However, if she sprayed a fourth acre, the marginal cost of doing so would exceed the marginal gain by $1, reducing her total net gain from $3 to $2. Spraying the fourth acre is a bad idea.

Imagine Farmer Jefferson, faced with the same opportunities as Farmer Adams, who has foolishly decided to spray 4 acres. He is considering cutting back his spraying program. The logic of the editorial would have us say: "Your spraying program is costing you only $20 and the value of the crops it saves is far more than that [$2 more, to be exact]. Your spraying program is a good deal. If anything, you should be expanding it, not cutting back." It is true that Farmer Jefferson's spraying program is a good deal overall, but it is also true that spraying the fourth acre is a bad deal (a $5 marginal cost exceeds a $4 marginal benefit). His spraying program will be an even better deal if that fourth acre is eliminated. Although his total gains exceed his total costs, this is beside the point, because for a decision like this only marginal quantities matter.

5.2 Firms in the Marketplace

We are now prepared to study the market behavior of firms, armed with our key observation that "only marginal quantities matter." The Tailor Dress Company produces dresses and sells them in the marketplace. This firm (like all firms in this book) is interested only in maximizing its profits. The firm's profit for any given period is equal to its revenues in that period minus its costs of production in that period. So to understand profits, we first have to understand revenues and costs. We begin with costs.

Costs

The production of dresses requires many inputs: fabric, thread, labor, the use of various types of machinery, and so on. The cost of producing a dress is the sum total of the costs of all these inputs.

Suppose that Tailor Dress Company can produce 1 dress for a cost of $4. How much will it cost to produce 2 dresses? Your first guess might be $8, but this need not actually be the case. When the firm produces its first dress, it does so at the lowest possible cost. This means that of all the resources available to it, it uses precisely those that can produce a dress most efficiently. It will choose the fabric that is most appropriate for the pattern, hire the best possible dressmakers, and put them to work on the firm's most efficient sewing machines.

When Tailor decides to produce a second dress, the most efficient inputs will have been used up and the firm will have to resort to its second most efficient production process. Perhaps all of the large pieces of fabric have been used up and it will now be necessary to work with odd-shaped pieces. Perhaps it will be necessary to hire additional, less skillful dressmakers. Perhaps the firm will find that its best sewing machines cannot be run all day without damage, and so will make the dress on its second most efficient machines. Alternatively, the firm might go ahead and use the first machines again, but it would incur more repair bills in the process, adding to costs.

The same sort of phenomenon might occur in any industry. The farmer producing 1 acre of wheat plants his most fertile acre of land, resorting to his second most fertile acre when he decides to increase his production to 2 acres. A writer producing one short story will work at the time of day when she is most productive and will use her best ideas. When she produces her second story, she will have to work harder.

For such reasons it is plausible to conclude that the cost of producing 2 dresses could well be *more* than $8. Suppose that the cost is $9. Then the marginal cost of producing the second dress is $5, because this is how much it costs to produce the second dress given that the first one has already been produced.

If 3 dresses can be produced for a total cost of $15, then the marginal cost of producing the third is $6. This is the additional cost incurred when the third dress is produced, given that the first 2 dresses have already been produced at a total cost of $9. We have assumed that the marginal cost of the third dress is higher than that of the second, just as the marginal cost of the second is higher than that of the first.

Increasing marginal cost The condition where each additional unit of an activity is more expensive than the last.

We say that the Tailor Dress Company faces the condition of **increasing marginal cost.** In the preceding few paragraphs we have argued for the plausibility of this assumption. There are also arguments to be made against it; perhaps you can construct some. In Chapter 6 we will make a careful study of how marginal costs arise from the production processes available to the firm. There we will have much to say about the circumstances in which marginal costs can be expected to increase. Here we will simply make the assumption of increasing marginal cost so that we can study the behavior of firms in the context of a simple example.

Exhibit 5–3 illustrates Tailor's total cost and marginal cost curves. Notice the units used; when total cost is measured in dollars, marginal cost is measured in dollars *per item produced*. There must also be a unit of time agreed on in advance. The table shows the company's costs per week, for each possible quantity of output per week.

Exhibit 5-3 Total and Marginal Costs at the Tailor Dress Company

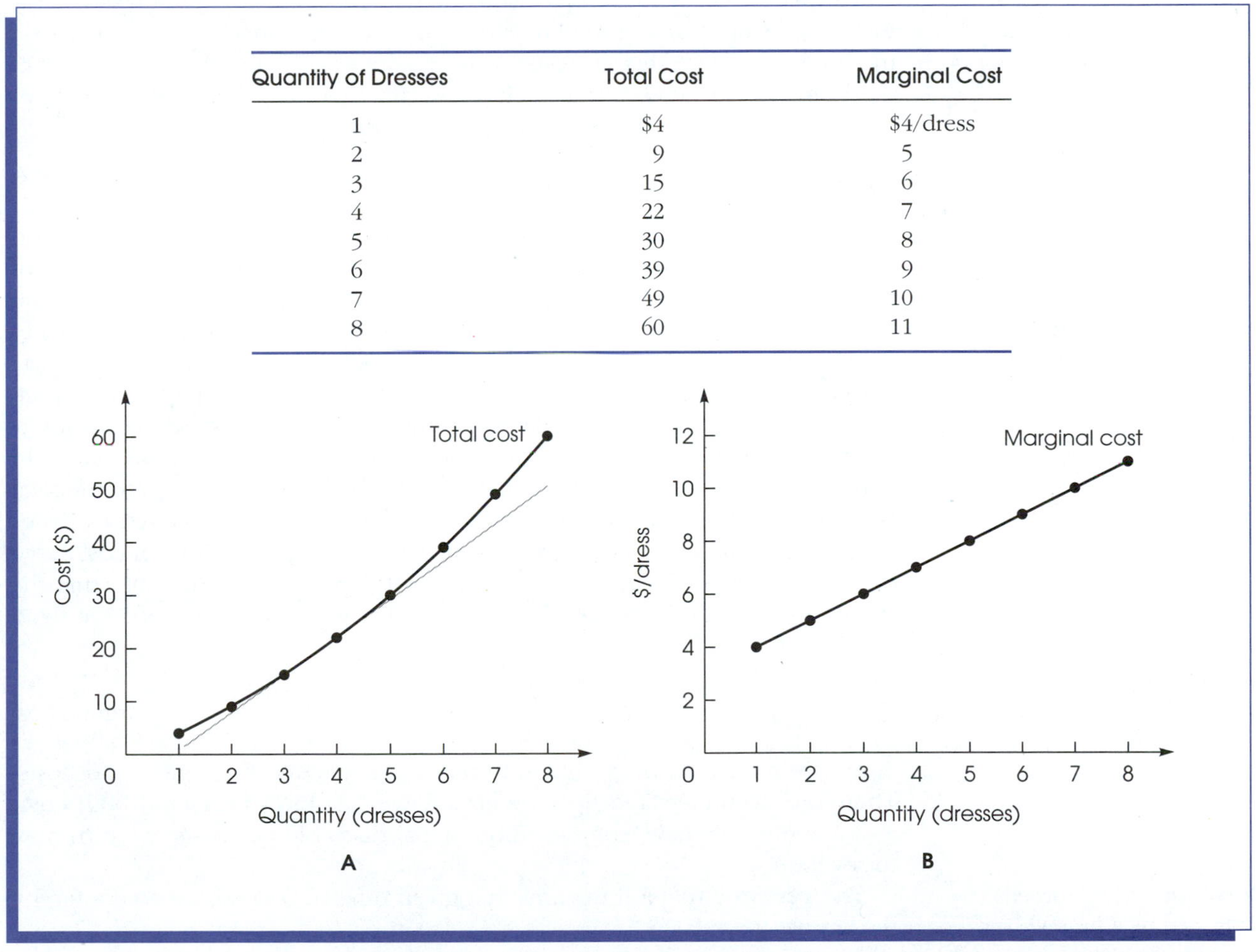

Quantity of Dresses	Total Cost	Marginal Cost
1	$4	$4/dress
2	9	5
3	15	6
4	22	7
5	30	8
6	39	9
7	49	10
8	60	11

When 4 dresses are produced, the marginal cost is $7 per dress, which is the total cost of producing 4 dresses minus the total cost of producing 3 dresses. That difference is also the slope of the line that connects the 2 points on the total cost curve at quantities of 3 and 4. When the unit of quantity is small, such a line is nearly tangent to the total cost curve. Thus, we say that marginal cost is the slope of total cost.

EXERCISE 5.5 In Exhibit 5–3 explain how you could derive the numbers in the marginal cost column from those in the total cost column. Explain how you could derive the numbers in the total cost column from those in the marginal cost column.

In Exhibit 5-3 we plotted total cost on one graph and marginal cost on another. It is necessary to do so because they require different vertical axes: dollars for total cost and dollars per dress for marginal cost. For this reason it is never correct to plot total cost and marginal cost on the same graph.

As the exhibit demonstrates, marginal cost is the slope of total cost. For example, when 4 dresses are produced, the marginal cost is $7 per dress. That is the same as the slope of the line shown in panel A, connecting the points on the total cost curve that correspond to quantities of 3 and 4. When the standard unit of quantity is small, such points are close together, and the line approximates the tangent line to the total cost curve.

Fixed Costs

Fixed cost A cost that does not vary with the level of output.

Some of the costs of operating a firm may not appear in the marginal cost column at all. These are the costs that are necessary to maintain the existence of the firm; they are costs that have to be met even if the firm produces nothing. These costs are called the **fixed costs** of the firm. They are called *fixed* because they do not depend on the quantity produced. For example, the Tailor Dress Company may find itself in a position where it has to pay $2 per week rent for the factory that it uses. Alternatively, if the firm owns the factory, it forgoes the opportunity to rent that factory to someone else for $2 per week. In either case it has $2 per week of fixed costs, which must be added to the total costs of the firm even though they are not part of the marginal cost of producing any item. Exhibit 5–4 displays such a situation. The marginal cost curve of Exhibit 5–4 is identical to that of Exhibit 5–3, but the total cost curve is shifted upward a distance of $2 because of the new assumption of $2 in fixed costs.

Revenue

Firms are motivated by profit, and profit is the excess of revenue over costs. Therefore, to understand firms' behavior, we need to understand both costs and revenue. We have completed our initial discussion of costs; we turn now to revenue.

Revenue The proceeds collected by a firm when it sells its products.

The **revenue** that a firm earns in a given time period can be computed by the simple formula:

$$\text{Revenue} = \text{Price} \times \text{Quantity}$$

In this formula *price* refers to the price per unit at which the firm sells its product. *Quantity* refers to the number of units that the firm sells in the time pe-

Exhibit 5-4 Total and Marginal Costs at the Tailor Dress Company

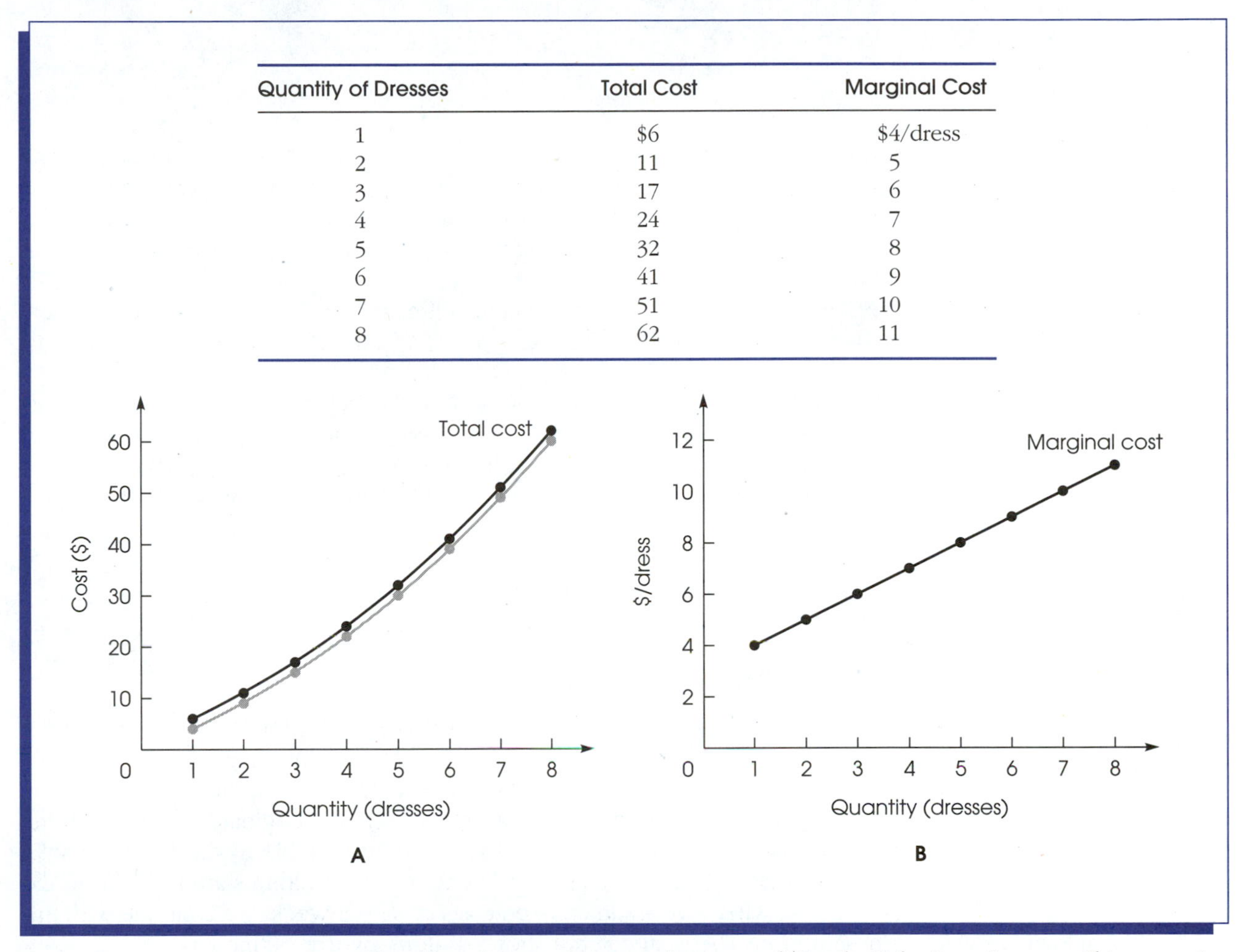

Quantity of Dresses	Total Cost	Marginal Cost
1	$6	$4/dress
2	11	5
3	17	6
4	24	7
5	32	8
6	41	9
7	51	10
8	62	11

The table and the graphs assume fixed costs of $2 at the Tailor Dress Company. This assumption has no effect on marginal costs, so the marginal cost curve is identical to that of Exhibit 5–3. The new $2 fixed cost does cause the total cost curve to shift upward a distance $2. Since the vertical shift is the same everywhere, the shape of the total cost curve remains unchanged. Another way to see that the slope remains unchanged is to recall that marginal cost is the slope of total cost, and this slope has not changed.

riod under consideration. The firm can choose either the price it wants to charge or the quantity it wants to sell, but it cannot choose both independently. The Tailor Dress Company can decide to sell exactly 9 dresses this week, or it can decide to sell dresses at a price of $100 apiece. But it can't decide to sell 9 dresses at $100 apiece, because it may not find demanders willing to purchase 9 dresses at that price. Tailor's options are limited by the quantity of Tailor dresses that demanders are willing to purchase at any given price. That is, its options are limited by the demand curve for Tailor dresses.

Suppose that the demand curve is given by the following table:

Price	Quantity	Price	Quantity
$1	10	$5	6
2	9	6	5
3	8	7	4
4	7	8	3

(Remember that this table is not the demand curve for dresses. It is the demand curve for *Tailor* dresses.) If Tailor wants to sell 9 dresses, it cannot charge a price of more than $2. In fact, if it wants to sell 9 dresses, it should charge a price of *exactly* $2. This is the highest price it can charge and still sell 9 dresses.

EXERCISE 5.6 If Tailor wants to sell exactly 5 dresses, what price should it charge? Why?

For any given quantity of dresses, Tailor selects the highest price at which it can sell them by reading the demand curve backward. That is, Tailor finds the point on the demand curve with the desired quantity and reads off the corresponding price. Its total revenue from the sales of these dresses is then given by this formula:

$$\text{Revenue} = \text{Price} \times \text{Quantity}$$

Maximizing Profits

Exhibit 5–5 displays the options available to the Tailor Dress Company. For each quantity the "Price" column shows the maximum price at which that quantity can be sold. The "Total Revenue" column shows how much revenue the company will earn if it sells that quantity. The "Marginal Revenue" column indicates the amount of additional revenue attributable to the last item sold. (Notice that this can be negative!) The two "Cost" columns are taken from Exhibit 5–4, where we assumed fixed costs of $2 per week; we continue with this assumption. The final column shows Tailor's **profit,** defined as:

Profit The amount by which revenue exceeds costs.

$$\text{Profit} = \text{Revenue} - \text{Cost}$$

EXERCISE 5.7 Verify all of the entries in Exhibit 5–5.

To choose the quantity that will maximize profits, Tailor can use either Method 1 or Method 2. Method 1 is the direct method: Scan the profit column and choose the maximum possible profit. Graphically, this is equivalent to finding the point where the distance between total cost and total revenue is greatest. This occurs at a quantity of either 2 or 3, where the profit is $7. As in Section 5.1, we assume that when firms are indifferent between two choices they take the larger of the two. Therefore, Tailor produces 3 dresses and sells them at $8 apiece, the highest price at which demanders are willing to buy 3 dresses.

Exhibit 5-5 Maximizing Profits at the Tailor Dress Company

Quantity of Dresses	Price	Total Revenue	Marginal Revenue	Total Cost	Marginal Cost	Profit
1	$10/dress	$10	$10/dress	$6	$4/dress	$4
2	9	18	8	11	5	7
3	8	24	6	17	6	7
4	7	28	4	24	7	4
5	6	30	2	32	8	−2
6	5	30	0	41	9	−11
7	4	28	−2	51	10	−23
8	3	24	−4	62	11	−38

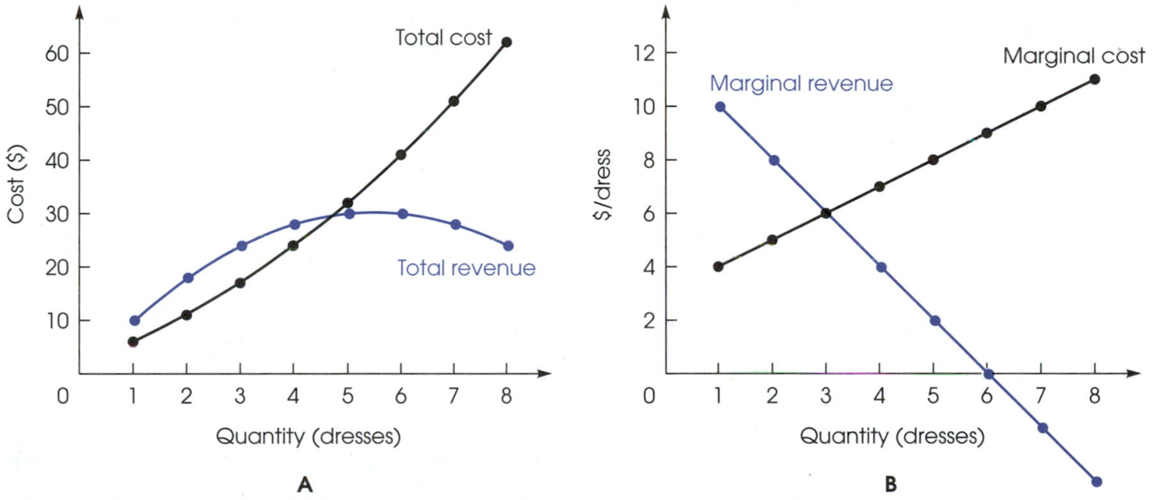

There are two ways for the Tailor Dress Company to choose a profit-maximizing quantity, each of which leads to the same outcome. Using Method 1, Tailor scans the profit column looking for the largest entry. This is the same as looking for the point of maximum distance between the total cost and total revenue curves. Using Method 2, Tailor scans the marginal columns and chooses the quantity at which marginal cost and marginal revenue are equal. This is the same as looking for the point where the marginal cost and marginal revenue curves cross. Using either method, Tailor will be led to produce 3 dresses and will earn a profit of $7.

Method 2 is the method of scanning only the marginal columns. Taking them row by row, the Tailor Dress Company first asks: Is the first dress worth making? The answer is yes, because the marginal revenue earned from selling that dress exceeds the marginal cost of producing it ($10 is greater than $4). Next the company asks if the second dress is worth making. Here again, comparing a marginal revenue of $8 with a marginal cost of $5, we find that the answer is yes. What about a third dress? Now the marginal revenue is equal to the marginal cost, so it is a matter of indifference whether to provide the third dress. In accordance with our conventions, we assume that Tailor goes ahead and produces the third dress. Now when we come to the fourth row in the column, Tailor finds that marginal cost exceeds marginal revenue. Making the fourth dress is a bad idea, so Tailor stops after three.

Graphically, Method 2 consists of looking for the point where the marginal cost and marginal revenue curves cross.

The validity of Method 2 is an application of the equimarginal principle. It reveals that:

Any firm produces that quantity at which marginal cost equals marginal revenue.

In Exhibit 5-2, the farmer chooses the point where marginal cost equals marginal *benefit*. In Exhibit 5-5, the firm chooses the point where marginal cost equals marginal *revenue*. The firm is doing the same thing the farmer is doing, because to a profit-maximizing firm, revenue *is* the benefit that is derived from supplying goods.

Changes in Cost Schedules

From the validity of Method 2, it follows that:

Any change in circumstances that does not affect anything marginal will not affect the behavior of the firm.

(There is one exception: A change in circumstances that causes the firm to go out of business will certainly affect its behavior, in that it will produce a quantity of zero. The firm will want to go out of business if it can earn only negative profits.)

To illustrate this point, suppose that the owner of the building where the Tailor Dress Company is located announces a rent increase from $2 to $5 per week. How does this affect the firm's costs? It raises the total cost by $3 per week regardless of how many dresses the firm manufactures and sells. However, marginal costs are unaffected because the additional rent is paid even before the first dress is sewn. The cost of producing each additional dress is the same as it was before this rent increase. Exhibit 5–6 illustrates the new situation.

EXERCISE 5.8 Verify the entries in the table in Exhibit 5–6.

Using Method 2 to maximize profits, the Tailor Dress Company chooses the quantity where marginal cost equals marginal revenue. That quantity is 3, just as it was before the rent increase. The price it charges is $8, the highest price at which demanders will buy 3 dresses, just as it was before the rent increase.

We can verify this result by using Method 1: Scan the profit column and look for the largest possible profit. We find that this occurs at a quantity of 3, with a profit of $4 (per week).

Exhibit 5–6 The Effect of a Rent Increase

Quantity of Dresses	Price	Total Revenue	Marginal Revenue	Total Cost	Marginal Cost	Profit
1	$10/dress	$10	$10/dress	$ 9	$ 4/dress	$ 1
2	9	18	8	14	5	4
3	8	24	6	20	6	4
4	7	28	4	27	7	1
5	6	30	2	35	8	−5
6	5	30	0	44	9	−14
7	4	28	−2	54	10	−26
8	3	24	−4	65	11	−41

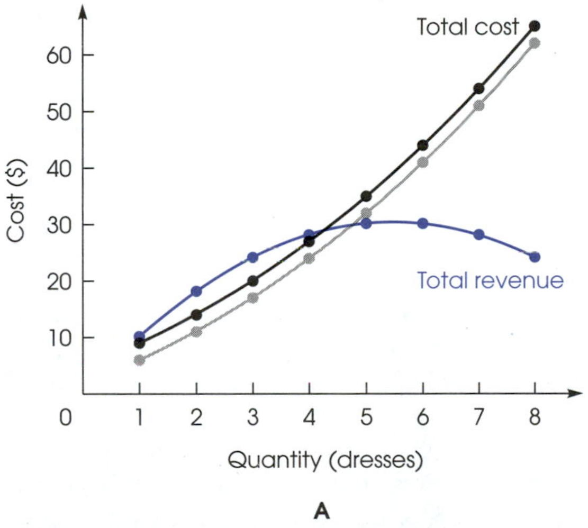

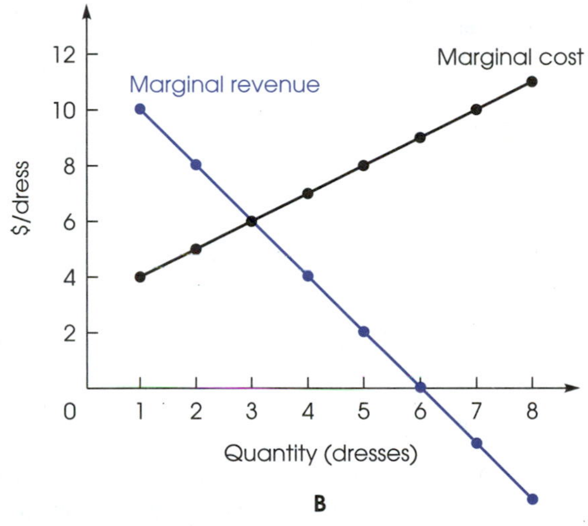

The table is derived from the table in Exhibit 5–5 by incorporating a $3 increase in rent. This increases total cost by $3 everywhere, but does not affect marginal cost. Therefore, the point of maximum profit is unaffected. The light-colored curve in panel A is the old total cost curve, from Exhibit 5–5. Although the distance between total cost and total revenue has decreased, the point of maximum distance is still at a quantity of 3.

The most important point of this example is that we could have predicted in advance that the rent increase would not affect price or quantity, simply on the basis of the observation that the rent increase did not affect anything marginal and the fact that only marginal quantities matter. Therefore, we know that the same result will hold for any change in costs that does not affect marginal costs.

QA EXERCISE 5.9 Predict what will happen if the rent increases by $4 per week rather than by $3 per week. Make a table to verify your prediction.

Sunk Costs Are Sunk

Prior to the rent increase, Tailor earned a profit of $7. The rent increase leaves Mr. Tailor, the owner, poorer by the amount of $3 per week. You might wonder why Tailor does not attempt to compensate for this loss by changing his price. The answer to this question can be found in Exhibit 5–6: There *is* no price that brings Tailor a profit of more than $4 per week. No change in pricing policy can benefit Mr. Tailor; he can only make himself worse off if he tries.

If this seems counterintuitive, ask yourself the following question: If Tailor could make greater profits by producing some quantity other than 3, or by charging some price other than $8, then why wasn't he already doing so before the rent was increased? If he has been profit-maximizing all along, why would a rent increase cause him to alter his strategy?

If you still aren't convinced, ask yourself these questions: If Tailor had accidentally lost a dollar bill down a sewer, would he change his business practices as a result? If he *did* change his business practices because of this bad luck, wouldn't you wonder whether those practices had been especially well thought out in the first place? Now, is the rent increase any different from losing a dollar bill in a sewer?[3]

Economists sum up the moral of this fable in this slogan:

Sunk costs are sunk.

Sunk cost A cost that can no longer be avoided.

The dollar rent increase is a **sunk cost** from the moment that the Tailor Dress Company decides to continue producing dresses at all; from that moment it is irretrievable. Once a cost has been sunk, it becomes irrelevant to any future decision making.

However, before you learn too well the lesson that a rent increase does not affect a company's behavior, note one exception: A sufficiently large rent increase might simply drive the firm out of business altogether. Only after the firm is committed to staying in business does the rent become a sunk cost.

Here is another example of the principle that sunk costs are sunk: Suppose the video you've spent $5 to rent turns out to be lousy; you're thinking about turning it off in the middle and watching a TV show instead. How should you decide what to do? Would your decision be any different if you'd gotten the video for free? Would it be any different if the video had cost you $10 instead of $5?

The answer is that the cost of the video is sunk and should therefore be irrelevant to your decision. If you expect the second half of the video to be better than the TV show, you should stick with the video. If you expect the TV show to be better, you should switch to the TV show.

[3] There is one way in which the lost dollar is different from the rent increase. Mr. Tailor might be able to avoid the rent increase by going out of business entirely, but there is no way for him to recover his dollar. However, once Tailor decides to remain in business, either dollar is lost irretrievably.

It's true that if you switch to the TV show, you'll lose $5. But it's equally true that if you stick with the video, you'll lose $5. The $5 (or $10, or whatever you paid for the video) is lost no matter what you do; that's exactly what it means to say that this cost is sunk. Once a cost is sunk, it can be a cause for regret, but it should not affect your future behavior.

Changes in Marginal Cost

Of course, marginal costs can also change. Suppose, for example, that the price of fabric goes up. In this case the cost of making a dress will certainly rise. The Tailor Dress Company's *total* costs will go up, and its *marginal* costs will go up as well. This example is very different from the example of the rent increase, where only fixed costs changed. Returning to Exhibit 5–5 (where the rent is still $2 per week), assume that the price of fabric goes up by $3 per square yard, and each dress requires exactly 1 square yard of cloth. Now the total cost of making 1 dress will be $3 higher than before, the total cost of making 2 dresses will be $6 higher, and so on. The marginal cost of making any given dress will be $3 higher than before. The new situation is illustrated in Exhibit 5–7.

In this circumstance the marginal cost curve shifts from its original position in Exhibit 5–5, so that it now crosses the marginal revenue curve at a quantity of 2. This is the new point of maximum profit. Since marginal cost is the slope of total cost, the change in marginal cost is equivalent to a nonparallel shift in total cost. This nonparallel shift allows a change in the point of maximum distance between total cost and total revenue. The new maximum is now at 2, where marginal cost crosses marginal revenue.

Tailor will now sell 2 dresses at a price of $9 apiece. The change in marginal costs will affect the firm's behavior, even though the earlier change in fixed costs could not.

Changes in the Revenue Schedule

We now understand a great deal about how and when changes in a firm's schedule of costs will affect its economic behavior. However, it is important to realize that this is not the whole story: Changes in the firm's marginal revenue schedule can affect its behavior as well. This is because both marginal revenue and marginal cost are used in the Method 2 calculations for maximizing profits. Therefore, it is important to understand the circumstances under which a firm's marginal revenue schedule might change.

Referring to Exhibit 5–5, you will see that when we computed marginal revenue, it was determined completely by the demand curve for Tailor dresses. We used the demand curve to determine the right price to charge for any given quantity, then calculated total revenue by multiplying price times quantity, then calculated marginal value revenue from that. What can affect marginal revenue? The answer is: anything that affects the demand curve.

Our question then becomes: What can affect the demand curve for the Tailor Dress Company? First, anything that affects the demand curve for dresses in general—changes in income, changes in the prices of related goods, and so on. But there are other factors as well. Suppose the Seamstress Dress Company down the street closes up shop for good and its customers have to look else-

Exhibit 5-7 An Increase in the Price of Fabric

Quantity of Dresses	Price	Total Revenue	Marginal Revenue	Total Cost	Marginal Cost	Profit
1	$10/dress	$10	$10/dress	$ 9	$7/dress	$ 1
2	9	18	8	17	8	1
3	8	24	6	26	9	−2
4	7	28	4	36	10	−8
5	6	30	2	47	11	−17
6	5	30	0	59	12	−29
7	4	28	−2	72	13	−44
8	3	24	−4	86	14	−62

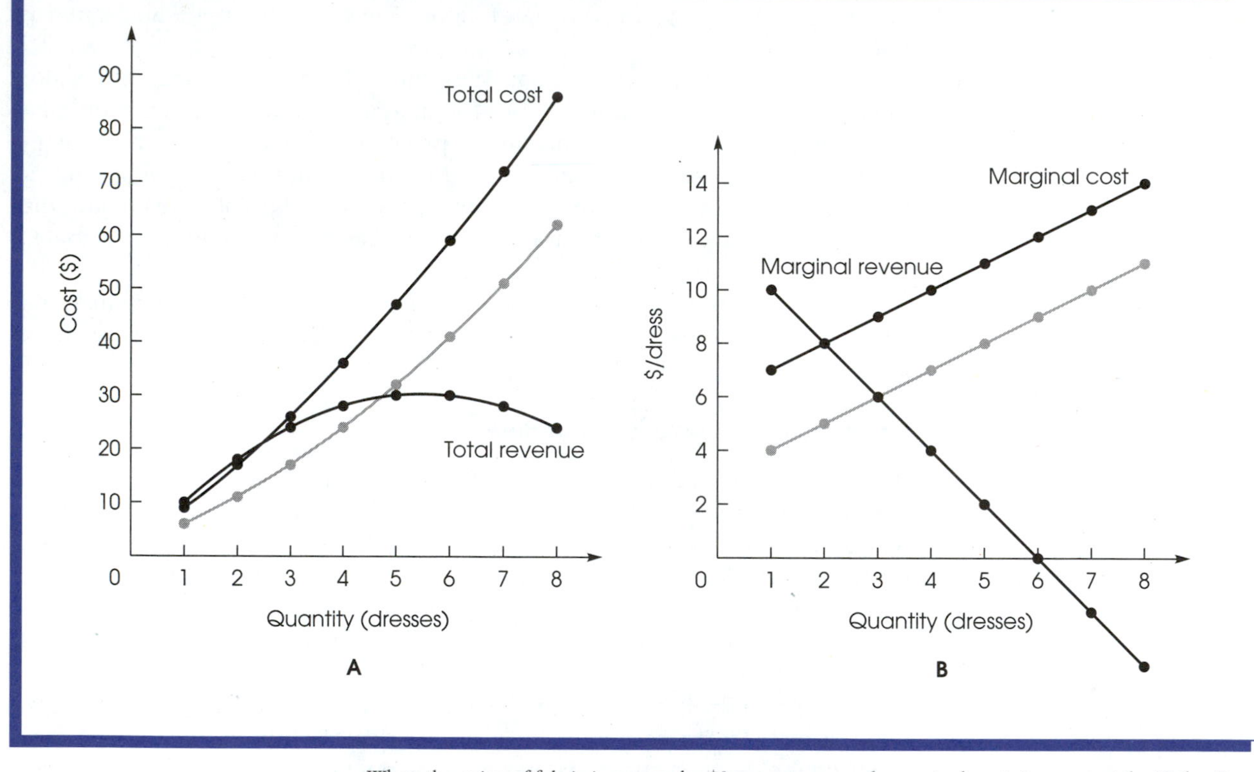

When the price of fabric increases by $3 per square yard, marginal costs increase at the Tailor Dress Company. The new cost curves can be compared with the original (light-colored) curves reproduced from Exhibit 5–6. The shift in total cost is no longer parallel, so the point of maximum distance between it and total revenue is able to shift. The new point of maximum profit occurs at a quantity of 2 and a price of $9.

where for dresses. In that case, the demand for Tailor's product will probably rise, and so will its marginal revenue curve. It is likely to produce a different number of dresses at a different price.

We can continue this line of inquiry one step further back and ask what might have driven the Seamstress Dress Company out of business. One possibility is a very large increase in rent at the Seamstress building. So we have the remarkable conclusion that although a rise in the Tailor Dress Company's rent will not lead to a change in Tailor's prices, a rise in someone *else's* rent very well *could* have that effect—provided that the "someone else" is a competitor who is driven out of business by the rent increase.

summary

We assume that firms act to maximize profits. This implies that they will act in accordance with the equimarginal principle; that is, they will engage in any activity up to the point where marginal cost equals marginal benefit.

When the firm sells goods in the marketplace, it chooses the profit-maximizing quantity. In accordance with the equimarginal principle, this is the quantity at which marginal cost equals marginal revenue. The firm sells this quantity at a price determined by the demand curve for its product.

The total revenue derived from selling a given quantity is given by the formula Revenue = Price × Quantity, where the price is read off the demand curve. Thus, the total revenue curve, and consequently the marginal revenue curve, are determined by the demand curve for the firm's product.

A change in the firm's fixed costs, because it affects nothing marginal, will not affect the quantity or price of the firm's output. There is one exception: A sufficiently large increase in fixed costs will cause the firm to shut down or leave the industry entirely.

A change in marginal costs can lead to a change in the firm's behavior. So can a change in marginal revenue. Any change in the demand curve facing the firm can lead to a change in marginal revenue. For example, a change in the availability of competing products can affect demand and, consequently, marginal revenue and, consequently, the behavior of the firm.

Review Questions

R1. State and explain the equimarginal principle.

R2. What formula defines a firm's profits? What formula defines its revenue?

R3. How might each of the following affect the behavior of a firm? (a) a change in marginal costs, (b) a change in fixed costs, (c) a change in the demand for the firm's product, (d) a competitor leaving the industry.

Numerical Exercises

In the following exercises suppose that x liters of orange juice can be produced for a total cost of $\$x^2$.

N1. Write down a formula for the marginal cost of production when x liters of orange juice are produced. Simplify your formula algebraically.

N2. Suppose now that orange juice is measured in centiliters (there are 100 centiliters in a liter). Write a formula for the total cost of producing y centiliters of orange juice. (*Hint:* When you produce y centiliters, how many liters are you producing? What is the associated cost?)

N3. Write a formula for the marginal cost of production when y centiliters are produced. Your formula gives the marginal cost in dollars per centiliter. Express the same formula in terms of dollars per liter.

N4. On the basis of your answer to Exercise N3, would you be willing to say that the marginal cost when x liters are produced is about $\$2x$ per liter? Why or why not?

N5. Now measure orange juice in milliliters (there are 1,000 milliliters in a liter). Write formulas for total cost and marginal cost when orange juice is measured in milliliters. Convert your marginal cost formula from dollars per milliliter to dollars per liter. Are you now more confident of your answer to Exercise N4? What do you think will happen if you measure orange juice in even smaller units?

Problem Set

1. The government has undertaken a highway project that was originally projected to cost $1 billion and provide benefits of $1.5 billion. Unfortunately, the costs have been much higher than anticipated. The government has spent $1.2 billion so far and now expects that it will cost an additional $1.2 billion to finish the project. Should the project be abandoned or completed?

2. The ABC company has a problem with vandals, who throw bricks through its windows at random times. The XYZ company has a problem with pilferage: Of everything it produces, about 10% is stolen. **True or False:** Although the vandalism problem will not affect prices at ABC, the pilferage problem might cause XYZ's prices to rise.

3. Bobo runs a one-man taxi service in a tiny town where there will never be room for more than one taxicab. He rents a cab, pays for gas, and charges passengers for rides. To express its appreciation for Bobo, the town council is thinking of paying either half his cab rental expenses or half his gasoline expenses. Which choice would have a bigger effect on the price of cab rides, and why?

4. In the town of Smallville, there are many dentists but just one eye doctor. Suppose the town institutes a new rule requiring every doctor and every dentist to take an expensive retraining course once a year. Which is more likely to increase: the price of a dental exam or the price of an eye exam?

5. Suppose that a new law requires every department store in Springfield to carry $10 million worth of fire insurance. **True or False:** If there is only one department store in Springfield, then none of the insurance costs will be passed on to consumers, but if there are many stores, then some of the costs might be passed on.

6. Suppose that Pat and Sandy's restaurant has just installed fancy new decor costing $10,000. Suppose also that in a distant solar system, there is a planet identical to earth in every way except that at this planet's Pat and Sandy's, the same redecoration cost $20,000. True or False: Pat and Sandy's hamburgers will be more expensive in the distant solar system than on earth.

7. Which of the following might affect the price of a hamburger at Waldo's Lunch Counter and why?

a. The price of meat goes up.

b. A new restaurant tax of 50¢ per hamburger is imposed.

c. Waldo's is discovered to be in violation of a safety code, and the violation is one that would be prohibitively expensive to correct. As a result, Waldo is certain to incur a fine of $500 per year from now on.

d. A new restaurant tax of $500 per year is imposed.

e. Waldo recalculates and realizes that the redecoration he did last month cost him 15% more than he thought it had.

f. Word gets around that a lot of Waldo's customers have been having stomach problems lately.

8. a. Suppose that a famous Chicago Cubs baseball player threatens to quit unless his salary is doubled, and the management accedes to his demand. True or False: The fans will have to pay for this through higher ticket prices.

b. Now suppose that the Cubs hire a famous and popular player away from the Philadelphia Phillies. Explain what will happen to ticket prices now.

9. A firm faces the following demand and total cost schedules.

Demand		Total Cost	
P	*Q*	*Q*	*TC*
$20	1	1	$ 2
18	2	2	6
16	3	3	11
14	4	4	18
12	5	5	26

Suppose that the firm is required to produce a whole number of items each month. How much does it produce and at what price? How do you know?

10. A firm faces the following demand and total cost schedules, with all quantities listed on a per-month basis. Suppose that it is required to produce a whole number of items each month.

Demand		Total Cost	
P	*Q*	*Q*	*TC*
$20	1	1	$ 5
18	2	2	15
15	3	3	30
12	4	4	50
8	5	5	75

a. How much does the firm produce, and at what price? How do you know?

b. Suppose that the firm is subject to an excise tax of $5 per item sold. How much does it produce, and at what price? How do you know?

c. Suppose, instead, that the firm is subject to a tax of $20 per month, regardless of how much it produces. How much does it produce, and at what price? How do you know?

d. Suppose, instead, that the firm is subject to a tax of $25 per month, regardless of how much it produces. How much does it produce, and at what price? How do you know?

11. Fred and Wilma have noticed that prices tend to be higher in stores that are located in high-rent districts. Fred thinks that the high rents cause the high prices, whereas Wilma thinks that the high prices cause the high rents. Under what circumstances is Fred correct? Under what circumstances is Wilma correct?

Internet Exercise

Oak Ridge National Labs performed a study in which researchers estimated the marginal cost of delivered wood chips as an input for biomass energy generating facilities in Tennessee. Access their Internet site (http://www.esd.ornl.gov/bfdp/papers/bioam95/graham2.html). Figure 2 shows estimated marginal cost of wood chips delivered from each of three regions in Tennessee. Figures 7 and 8 show how these marginal cost estimates vary based on farmer participation rates. Which region of Tennessee offers the best location for a small-scale biomass energy generating facility (of capacity less than 3 million tons/year), from the perspective of the delivered marginal cost of woodchip feedstocks? Why do higher farmer participation rates lower the marginal cost of delivered wood chips?

chapter 6

Production and Costs

How much does it cost to watch a movie? It depends on how you watch. You can adopt a "high-tech" strategy, investing several hundred dollars in a VCR and renting movies for $2 apiece, or a "low-tech" strategy, paying $6 each time you go to the theater. (The low-tech strategy might cost you more in time and transportation costs as well.)

Which strategy is less expensive? A lot depends on how many movies you plan to watch. If you spend almost all of your evenings in the gym or the library and treat yourself to a movie just once a semester, you'll save money by going to theaters. If you are a film buff who is determined to see every movie ever made before you turn 30, a VCR might be a good investment.

There is, however, more to consider. Suppose that you have been in the habit of seeing two movies per year at the theaters and have just decided for some reason to change your lifestyle and see two movies per night instead. This makes it optimal to get a VCR. Unfortunately, you've made this momentous decision at 7:00 P.M. on a Friday evening and the appliance stores are not open on weekends. In that case, you will continue to visit the high-priced theaters, at least until Monday morning.

There is another reason why you might not buy a VCR right away, even though you have planned a massive increase in your movie consumption. The reason is that you might not expect your change in habits to be permanent. It is a good idea for a heavy movie watcher to own a VCR and for a light movie watcher not to. But if you plan to be a heavy movie watcher for just one month and then return to a schedule of two movies per year, it might not be worth the trouble to buy a VCR today and sell it a month from now.

Business executives and managers face this sort of problem all the time. Imagine that you run a word-processing service, hiring typists who use computers to produce manuscripts for clients. There is more than one way to produce a given number of manuscripts: You can hire a lot of typists to work on slow, inexpensive computers, or you can hire fewer typists to work on the fastest machines available.

What is the least expensive way to produce manuscripts? It depends on how many manuscripts you produce each week. If business is slow and there is a lot of idle time around the office, it might not pay to invest too much in fancy machinery. If you are turning customers away because you can't handle any more business, your best option might be to upgrade your technology.

However, if the high demand for your services is a recent phenomenon, or if you are uncertain of its permanence, it might be unwise or impossible to upgrade your technology immediately. Therefore, the question "How can we best produce 100 manuscripts per week?" might have two very different answers. There is a *short-run* solution, applicable over periods in which changing the number of computers is not an option, and a *long-run* solution, applicable in situations where it is feasible to adjust every aspect of your operation.

In this chapter, we will study the firm's approach to such problems in both the short run and the long run. We will begin in Section 6.1 by studying production and costs in the short run, when some factors cannot be varied. In later sections, we will consider the same issues in the long run, when everything is variable.

In Chapter 5 we began to see the importance of understanding costs if we are to understand the behavior of firms. The purpose of this chapter is to advance that understanding. We will see exactly how the firm's cost curves arise from the technology it has available. In Chapter 7 we will be able to apply this knowledge to the foundations of supply behavior in a large class of firms and industries.

6.1 Production and Costs in the Short Run

Visit http://price.bus.okstate.edu/archive/Econ3113_963/Shows/Chapter6/index.htm for a slide show on production and costs

In the short run a firm has limited options. The Chrysler Corporation cannot instantly change the number of assembly lines that it operates; it takes time to build a new one and it takes time to sell one off. Union contracts might prevent immediate adjustments in the amount of labor employed. The short-run analysis of production and costs is designed to take account of this phenomenon.

Factors of Production

Consumption goods (or **outputs**) Goods that individuals want to consume.

Factors of production (or **inputs**) Goods that are used to produce outputs.

Capital Physical assets used as factors of production.

The goods in an economy can be roughly classified into two sorts: **consumption goods** (or **outputs**), which contribute directly to individuals' utility, and **factors of production** (or **inputs**), which are combined to create consumption goods. The firm's task is to convert factors of production into consumption goods.

Factors of production are typically classified into the three broad categories of land, labor, and capital. Of these, land and labor need no further explanation, but capital does. To a first approximation, **capital** in economics refers to physical assets, such as machinery and factories, that enter directly into the production process.[1]

Students are often confused by the way the word *capital* is used in their economics courses, because the same word is used quite differently in everyday speech, where it refers to financial assets such as stocks and bonds. In economics, stocks and bonds are not considered capital. Examples of capital include a handyman's van, a secretary's word processor, a professor's library, and a cowboy's lariat.

For concreteness, we will consider a good that is produced with exactly two inputs, *labor* and *capital*. The analysis we give would apply equally well to any other two inputs. We could also study goods produced with three or more inputs. When one of these inputs (say labor) is the immediate focus of attention, it is often productive to treat labor as one input and "all other inputs" as another.

Fixed and Variable Factors

Fixed factor of production One that the firm must employ in a given quantity.

Variable factor of production One that the firm can employ in varying quantities.

We say that a factor of production is **fixed** if the firm cannot change the quantity of that factor it employs. A factor is **variable** when the firm can make such changes. A power plant cannot easily change the number of dams that it operates, but it might be able to adjust the size of its work force at a moment's notice. In this case dams are a fixed factor and labor is a variable factor. To a farmer, land might be a fixed factor.

The distinction between fixed and variable factors is a vague one, and a given factor can be either fixed or variable, depending on the time period in which changes must be made. A new dam cannot be constructed in five minutes, but it can be in five years. Over five minutes, dams are a fixed factor, but over five years they are a variable factor.

It is a standard assumption in economic theory that given a sufficiently long time period, every factor is variable. For the most part we shall adopt this assumption. There are, however, circumstances in which an alternative assumption might be called for. Alcatraz Island is itself an input into the production of Alcatraz Island tours. Try as he might, and no matter how long he works at it, no entrepreneur can increase the number of Alcatraz islands.

Short run A period of time over which some factors are fixed.

Long run A period of time over which all factors are variable.

In many circumstances, one factor is more easily variable than another over some important period of time, and much insight can be gained from a simplified model that treats one factor as completely variable and the others as completely fixed. Any time period over which such a model applies is referred to by economists as the **short run**. The short run is to be distinguished from the **long run**, which is a period of time sufficient for all factors to be considered variable.

[1] Later in this book we will adopt a more general definition.

The Total, Marginal, and Average Products of Labor

For purposes of illustration, we will adopt a vision of the short run in which labor is variable and all other factors of production are fixed. Thus, the firm's output depends only on the quantity of labor that it hires.

Total product (*TP*) The quantity of output produced by the firm in a given amount of time. Total product depends on the quantity of labor the firm hires.

Short-run production function The function that associates to each quantity of labor its total product.

The firm's **total product** (abbreviated *TP*) is the quantity of output it produces in a given amount of time (say an hour). Total product depends on how much labor the firm hires. For example, in Exhibit 6–1, we assume that in a given hour, 1 worker can produce 5 units of output, 2 workers can produce 12 units, 3 workers can produce 21 units, and so on. In Exhibit 6–1, this information is recorded both in the "Total Product" column of the chart and in the graph below it. The total product curve is also called the firm's **short-run production function**.

Marginal product of labor (*MPL*) The increase in total product due to hiring one additional worker (assuming that capital is held fixed).

When a firm hires an additional worker, it can produce more output—that is, its total product increases. (That's why the total product curve slopes upward.) The amount of the increase is called the **marginal product of labor** (*MPL*). For example, when the firm in Exhibit 6–1 hires its sixth worker, the total product increases by 3 units (from 33 to 36), so the marginal product of the sixth worker is 3 units of output. Each worker's marginal product is recorded in the "Marginal Product" column of the chart and graphed in the right-hand panel.

EXERCISE 6.1 Check that all the marginal products have been computed correctly in Exhibit 6–1.

In order to talk about the marginal product of labor, we must hold the quantity of capital fixed. Imagine a firm where five tailors work with five sewing machines to produce 125 dresses per year. Suppose the firm hires a sixth tailor and buys a sixth sewing machine for that tailor to work on, thereby increasing its output to 150 dresses per year. Then the marginal product of the sixth tailor is *not* 25 dresses! To compute the sixth tailor's marginal product correctly, you must ask how many additional dresses the firm can produce by hiring a sixth tailor *while keeping the number of machines fixed at five.* If, for example, that number is 130, then the sixth tailor's marginal product is 130 − 125 = 5 dresses.

Average product of labor (*APL*) Total product divided by the number of workers.

The **average product of labor**, *APL*, is the firm's total product divided by the number of workers; in other words, it is given by the formula

$$APL = TP/L$$

where *L* (which stands for labor) is the number of workers employed. Thus, for example, when 4 workers produce 28 units of output, the average product of labor is 7 units of output per worker. In Exhibit 6–1, the average product of labor is computed in the "Average Product" column of the chart and graphed in panel B.

Exhibit 6-1 Total, Marginal and Average Products

Quantity of Labor	Total Product (*TP*)	Marginal Product of Labor (*MPL*)	Average Product of Labor (*APL*)
1 worker	5 units	5 units per worker	5 units per worker
2	12	7	6
3	21	9	7
4	28	7	7
5	33	5	6.6
6	36	3	6
7	37	1	5.3

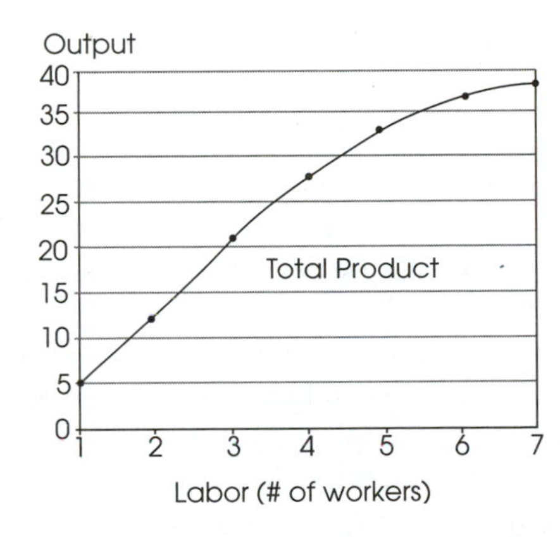

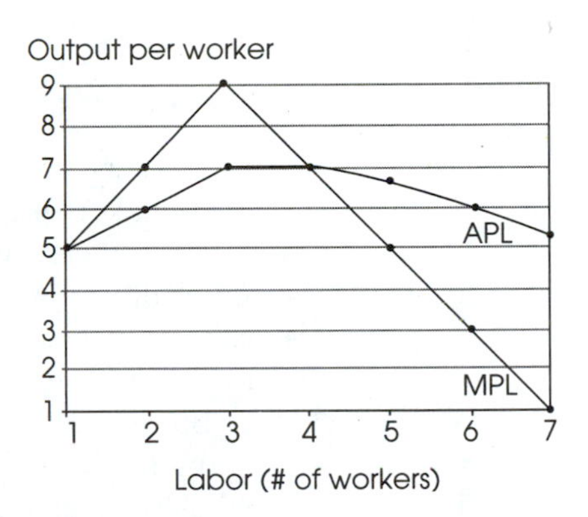

Total product (*TP*) is the quantity of output that a given number of workers can produce (in a prespecified amount of time). The marginal product of labor (*MPL*) is the additional output due to one additional worker, and the average product of labor is the total product divided by the number of workers. In this example, when there are fewer than 4 workers, the marginal product exceeds the average product, so the average product is rising (the first stage of production). When there are more than 4 workers, marginal product is less than average product, so average product is falling (the second stage of production).

EXERCISE 6.2 Check that all of the average products have been computed correctly in Exhibit 6–1.

Marginal product and average product can both be plotted on the same graph—as in panel B of Exhibit 6-1. But total product must be plotted separately, because it requires a different kind of unit on the vertical axis. Total product is measured in units of output, whereas the marginal and average products of labor are measured in units of output *per worker*.

The shapes of the total product and marginal product curves are related: Marginal product gives the *slope* of total product. For example, when the number of workers increases from 5 to 6 (an increase of 1), output increases from 33 to 36 (an increase of 3). The ratio 3/1 is the slope of the total product curve near the point (6, 36), and 3 is also the height of the marginal product curve at 6.

The Stages of Production

If 5 bakers can produce 500 cupcakes per day, how many cupcakes per day can 6 bakers produce?

If this were a word problem in elementary school, the answer would be 600. After all, the average product of labor—that is, the average number of cupcakes per baker—is 100. That answer implicitly assumes that all bakers are identical, so that all bakers are average. Thus 6 bakers produce 600 cupcakes.

But in real life, there is an additional complication: The sixth baker is likely to interact with the first 5 bakers, making them either more or less productive. So as soon as the sixth baker joins the crew, the average product of labor is likely to change to something other than 100.

The interaction can take many forms. One possibility is that additional bakers create more opportunities for *specialization*: One baker can grease the pans while another mixes the batter, another prepares the frosting, another explores new recipes, and so forth. In this case, 6 bakers can probably produce *more* than 600 cupcakes—say, 630. We can describe this outcome in either of two ways:

1. When the sixth baker arrives, the average product of labor increases (from 100 to 105).
2. The marginal product of the sixth baker (130) is greater than the average product of labor.

EXERCISE 6.3 Explain where we got the numbers 105 and 130 for the marginal and average products when there are 6 bakers.

In general, an additional baker raises the average product if (and only if) his marginal product exceeds the average product—just as an additional baseball player raises the team's average performance if and only if his personal contribution exceeds the team's average.

It's easy to see how specialization can be advantageous in other industries besides baking. A few auto workers located at strategic points along an assembly line, or a few farmhands with specific duties, can each be far more productive than a single worker trying to accomplish too many tasks at once.

Even beyond specialization, there are a variety of ways in which workers can assist each other and thereby increase each others' productivity. Two lumberjacks working together with a two-handled whipsaw will cut down a lot more than twice as many trees as either one of them could harvest individually.

In any of these cases, average product is increasing (as a function of the number of workers) and marginal product exceeds average product.

But workers don't *always* make each other more productive; in fact, sometimes the reverse is true. The sixth baker might compete for counter space with the first five and thereby slow them down; it might be that where 5 bakers can produce 500 cupcakes, 6 can produce not 600 but only 540. We can describe this in two equivalent ways:

1. The sixth baker lowers the average product (from 100 to 90).
2. The marginal product of the sixth baker (40) is below the average product.

QA EXERCISE 6.4 Explain where we got the numbers 90 and 40 for the average and marginal products.

QA EXERCISE 6.5 Explain why a worker will lower the average product of labor if and only if the marginal product is below the average product.

There are many other examples of the same phenomenon. The Roman poet Virgil tells us that his army was so crowded that many soldiers had no room to use their weapons. The 11th secretary added to an office with only 10 computer terminals will not be as productive as the 10th (though the 11th is still of *some* value, being available to run errands or to fill in while someone else is on break).

First stage of production
Production with relatively few workers, so that each additional worker increases the productivity of his colleages. Therefore, the average product of labor is increasing and the marginal product exceeds the average product.

Second stage of production
Production with enough workers so that each additional worker decreases the productivity of his colleagues. Therefore, the average product of labor is decreasing and the marginal product is below the average product.

What, then, is the general rule? Do additional workers usually help or hinder the productivity of the others?

Typically, the answer is this: When there are relatively few workers, the advantages of additional specialization are so great that each worker makes the others more productive. When there are more workers, the disadvantages of additional crowding are so great that each worker makes the others *less* productive.

Economists call these stages the **first stage of production** and the **second stage of production**. In the first stage of production, there are relatively few workers and their average product increases as additional workers are added; equivalently, each worker's marginal product exceeds the average product. In the second stage of production, there are many workers and their average product falls as additional workers are added; equivalently, each worker's marginal product is below the average product.

You can see both the first and second stages of production if you turn back to Exhibit 6–1. When the firm has between 1 and 4 workers, it is in the first stage of production: The average product curve is increasing (meaning that each additional worker raises the average product of all workers) and the marginal product of labor is above the average product. When the firm has more than 4 workers it is in the second stage of production: The average product curve is decreasing, and the marginal product of labor is below the average product.

Keep in mind that, like all the analysis in this section, "stages of production" are a *short-run* concept. A sixth baker will not crowd out the first five if the bakery itself is expanded. It is only in the short run that we assume such expansions (and other additions to capital) are impossible.

For diagrams of various product curves, see: http://www.bus.okstate.edu/oamos/course/2023graphs.html

The Shapes of the Product Curves

The shapes of the product curves are largely determined by the stages of production.

Average product must rise throughout the first stage of production and then fall throughout the second stage; therefore it has roughly the shape of an inverted U. You can see this in Exhibit 6–1 or in the second panel of Exhibit 6–2, where the curves are smoother and perhaps easier to look at than the choppy curves in Exhibit 6–1.

Marginal product must lie above average product through the first stage of production and below average product thereafter. Therefore, marginal product must cut through average product just at the point when average product starts to turn downward—that is, at the top of the inverted U.

Diminishing marginal returns The condition in which the *MPL* curve slopes downward.

Point of diminishing marginal returns That quantity of labor beyond which the firm experiences diminishing marginal returns.

Typically, marginal product, like average product, has an inverted U shape. At the point where the marginal product of labor begins to fall, we say that the firm has begun to experience **diminishing marginal returns to labor** or that it has passed the **point of diminishing returns**. In Exhibit 6–2, the point of diminishing marginal returns occurs at L_0 units of output.

Finally, consider the total product curve. Recall that the slope of the total product curve is given by the value of the marginal product curve. Thus, in the range where marginal product is increasing (from 0 to L_0 in Exhibit 6–2), total product is becoming steeper, in the range where marginal product is decreasing, total product is becoming flatter.

Costs in the Short Run

Rental rate The price of renting capital.

Wage rate The price of hiring labor.

Firms care about the costs of the inputs they use. We will assume that firms can rent capital at a going market price P_K (called the **rental rate** of capital) and hire labor at a going market P_L (called the **wage rate** of labor).

For example, suppose that it costs $10 per hour to rent a machine and $15 per hour to hire a worker; then we write $P_K = 10$ and $P_L = 15$.

Exhibit 6-2 The Stages of Production

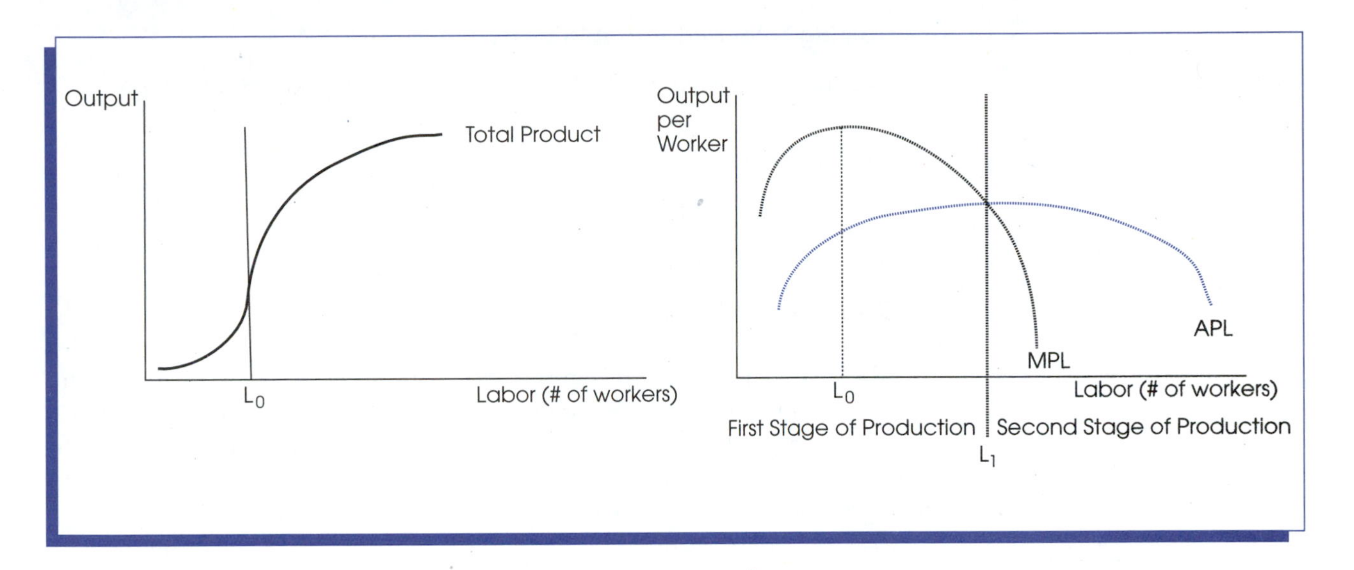

In the first stage of production (up to L_1 workers), marginal product (*MPL*) exceeds average product (*APL*) and average product is rising. In the second stage of production (beyond L_1 workers), marginal product is less than average product and average product is falling. Therefore, average product has the shape of an inverted U and marginal product cuts through average product at the top of the U. The marginal product curve also has an inverted U shape, rising until the point of diminishing marginal returns (at L_0 workers), and then falling. The total product curve becomes successively steeper up to the point of diminishing marginal returns and then begins to flatten out.

When you calculate costs, remember to include opportunity costs. For example, suppose the rental rate for printing presses is $10 per hour. Then the Smith Publishing Company, which rents time on other people's presses, incurs a cost of $10 per hour to use a printing press. But the Jones Publishing Company, which owns its own presses, *also* incurs a cost of $10 per hour per press, because Jones forgoes the opportunity to rent its presses to Smith.

Fixed cost The cost of renting a fixed factor.

Variable cost The cost of hiring a variable factor.

In the short run, the firm uses a fixed quantity of capital. In other words, there are a fixed number of machines on the premises, and that number can neither be increased nor decreased. The cost of renting those machines is therefore a **fixed cost** (abbreviated *FC*); it remains unchanged no matter how much or how little the firm produces.

By contrast, the firm can adjust the size of its labor force, and therefore its expenditures on labor can change when the quantity of output changes. Those expenditures are thus **variable costs** (abbreviated *VC*).

Total cost The sum of fixed costs and variable costs.

Total cost (*TC*) is the sum of fixed costs and variable costs. That is,

$$TC = FC + VC$$

Computing Total and Variable Costs

To compute the cost of producing output, we need to know four things:

1. The rental rate on capital (P_K)
2. The wage rate of labor (P_L)
3. The (fixed) quantity of capital that the firm employs
4. The firm's total product curve

Exhibit 6–3 shows how this information can be combined to compute variable costs and total costs. We assume: (1) P_K = \$10 per machine per hour; (2) P_L = \$15 per worker per hour; (3) the firm employs 5 machines; and (4) the total product curve is the same as in Exhibit 6–1. That total product curve is reproduced in the left half of Exhibit 6–3, both as a chart and as a graph.

Now we want to construct the firm's variable cost curve, showing the variable cost of producing each quantity of output. (Because we have assumed that labor is the only variable factor, variable costs will be the same thing as labor costs.) We construct the curve one point at a time, as follows:

Begin with a quantity of output that the firm might want to produce—say 5 units. (Remember that there is always a unit of time lurking in the background; when we say that output equals 5 units, we mean that the firm produces 5 units *per hour*.) Use the total product curve to determine how many workers (per hour) are necessary to produce that output; in this case the answer is 1 worker. Multiply 1 worker times the \$15 per hour wage rate to get a variable cost of \$15. Record this calculation by plotting the point (5, \$15) on the variable cost curve in the right half of Exhibit 6–3.

To get another point, repeat the procedure: To produce 12 units of output requires 2 workers at \$15 an hour, so the variable cost of 12 units of output is \$30. Thus the point (12, \$30) appears on the variable cost curve.

EXERCISE 6.6 In Exhibit 6–3, verify that all of the points on the variable cost curve have been computed correctly. (The exact coordinates of these points are listed in the chart above the graph.)

Next, we turn our attention to the total cost curve. Remember that $TC = FC + VC$. In this case, we have assumed that the firm employs 5 machines at \$10 apiece, so the fixed cost comes to 5 × \$10 = \$50. Thus, in Exhibit 6–3, the listed total costs are all \$50 higher than the corresponding variable costs. For example, for 5 units of output the variable cost is \$15, so the total cost is \$65.

These points are plotted on the total cost curve, which is parallel to the vari-

Exhibit 6-3 Variable Cost Curve

Quantity of Labor	Total Product (TP)
1 worker	5 units
2	12
3	21
4	28
5	33
6	36
7	37

Quantity of Output	Variable Cost (VC)	Total Cost (TC)
5	15	65
12	30	80
21	45	95
28	60	110
33	75	125
36	90	140
37	105	155

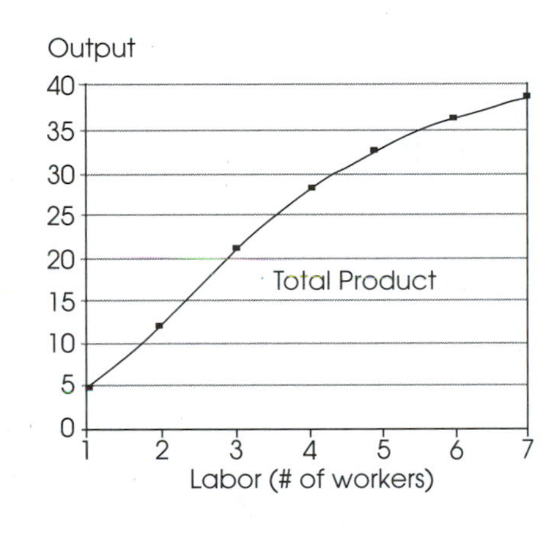

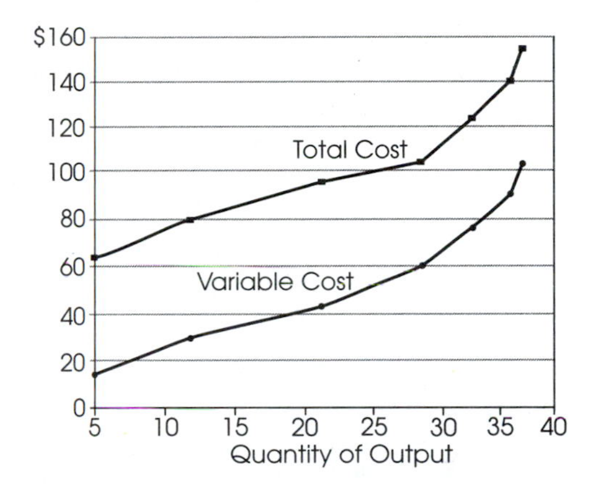

We take as given: the price of capital ($10 per machine), the price of labor ($15 per worker), the quantity of capital (5 machines) and the total product curve (shown on the left half of the exhibit). From this information, we compute points on the variable cost (*VC*) and total cost (*TC*) curves as follows: Given a quantity of output, use the total product curve to find the corresponding number of workers. Multiply by the wage rate ($15 per worker) to get variable cost. Take variable cost and add fixed costs (in this case, 5 machines times $10 per machine, or $50) to get total cost.

able cost curve. The vertical distance between the two curves is equal to the fixed cost, which in this case is $50.

Computing Average Costs

Average variable cost
Variable cost divided by the quantity of output.

The firm's **average variable cost** (*AVC*) is defined by the formula

$$AVC = VC/TP$$

Average cost, or **average total cost** Total cost divided by the quantity of output.

where VC is variable cost and TP is the quantity of output (the firm's total product). The firm's **average cost** (AC) is defined by the formula

$$AC = TC/TP$$

where TC is total cost. Average cost is sometimes called **average total cost.**

In Exhibit 6–4, we compute AVC and AC for the same firm we studied in Exhibits 6–1 and 6–3. The left half of Exhibit 6–4 reproduces information on total, average and marginal products from Exhibit 6–1. On the right side, the chart reproduces the variable cost and total cost columns from Exhibit 6–3. Average variable cost and average cost are computed directly from those columns. For example, at 5 units of output we have

$$AVC = VC/Q = \$15/5 = \$3 \text{ per unit of output}$$

and

$$AC = TC/TP = \$65/5 = \$13 \text{ per unit of output.}$$

All of the AVC and AC numbers are recorded on the curves below the chart.

QA EXERCISE 6.7 In Exhibit 6–4, verify that all the numbers in the AVC and AC columns have been computed correctly.

When labor is the only variable factor (as we have been assuming), there is another formula for average variable cost. Notice first that if the firm hires L units of labor, then its variable costs come to $P_L \cdot L$, where P_L is the wage rate of labor. Therefore,

$$AVC = \frac{VC}{TP} = \frac{(P_L \cdot L)}{TP} = \frac{P_L}{(TP/L)} = \frac{P_L}{APL},$$

or, more briefly,

$$AVC = P_L/APL$$

where $APL = TP/L$ is the average product of labor.

QA EXERCISE 6.8 Verify that $AVC = P_L/APL$ in every row of the charts in Exhibit 6–4. (Keep in mind that in this example, $P_L = \$15$.)

The Marginal Cost Curve

Now we want to construct the firm's marginal cost curve. Recall from Chapter 5 that marginal cost is the additional cost attributable to the last unit of output produced.

Thus, for example, we see in Exhibit 6–4 that the total cost of producing 36 units of output is \$140 and the total cost of producing 37 units of output is \$155. The difference, \$15 per unit, is the marginal cost when 37 units are pro-

Exhibit 6-4 Deriving the Average and Marginal Cost Curves

Quantity of Labor	Total Product	Marginal Product of Labor (MPL)	Average Product of Labor (APL)
1 worker	5 units	5 units per worker	5 units per worker
2	12	7	6
3	21	9	7
4	28	7	7
5	33	5	6.6
6	36	3	6
7	37	1	5.3

Quantity (TP)	Variable Cost (VC)	Total Cost (TC)	Average Variable Cost (AVC)	Average Cost (AC)	Marginal Cost (MC)
5	$15	$65	$3 per unit	$13 per unit	$3 per unit
12	30	80	2.50	6.67	2.14
21	45	95	2.14	4.52	1.67
28	60	110	2.14	3.93	2.14
33	75	125	2.27	3.79	3.00
36	90	140	2.50	3.89	5.00
37	105	155	2.84	4.19	15.00

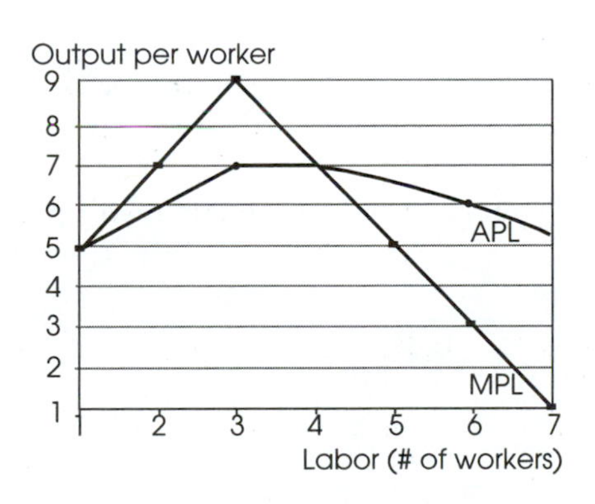

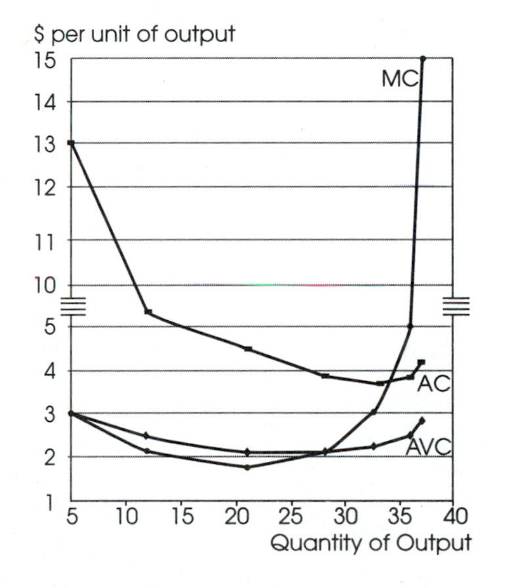

The product curves on the left are taken from Exhibit 6-1. On the right, the variable cost and total cost data are taken from Exhibit 6-3. We compute *AVC, AC,* and *MC* from their definitions; namely, $AVC = VC/TP$ and $AC = TC/TP$. It turns out that we can also write $AVC = P_l/APL$. To compute *MC*, we use the formula $MC = P_L/MPL$.

duced. We have recorded the result of that calculation in the marginal cost column across from the quantity 37.

But how can we get the other numbers in the marginal cost column? For example, how we can we compute marginal cost when the firm produces 33 units of output? In principle, we need to take the total cost of producing 33 units—which, according to the chart, is $125—and subtract the cost of producing 32 units. Unfortunately, that information is missing from our incomplete chart, which lists only the quantities 5, 12, 21, 28, 33, 36, and 37.

But fortunately, there is another way to compute marginal cost. Here's the trick: First, use the total and marginal product curves to determine that when the total product is 33 units of output, the marginal product is 5 additional units of output per additional worker. Second, notice that "5 additional units of output per additional worker" is the same thing as "⅕ additional workers per additional unit of output." So the marginal cost of producing an additional unit of output is equal to the cost of hiring ⅕ of a worker. At the assumed going wage rate of $15 per worker, that comes to $3. So we record $3 as the marginal cost of producing 33 units of output.

You might object that there is no such thing as ⅕ of a worker. But don't forget that everything in our charts is implicitly measured "per hour." That makes it easy to hire ⅕ of a worker—you hire someone to work 12 minutes out of every hour, or one day out of every five.

Similarly, we compute the marginal cost at a quantity of, say, 12: The marginal product of labor is now 7 units of output per worker, so it takes ⅐ of a worker to produce an additional unit of output. Therefore, the marginal cost is $15 × ⅐, or about $2.14.

This method of calculating marginal costs can be summed up in a simple formula:

$$MC = P_L \times \frac{1}{MPL}$$

or

$$MC = \frac{P_L}{MPL}$$

QA **EXERCISE 6.9** Check that all of the marginal cost numbers in Exhibit 6–4 have been derived correctly.

The Shapes of the Cost Curves

The right half of Exhibit 6–5 shows the shapes of the cost curves at a typical firm. The left half of the exhibit reproduces the product curves from Exhibit 6–2 for comparison. Here are the key facts about the geometry of the cost curves:

Exhibit 6-5 The Geometry of Product Curves and Cost Curves

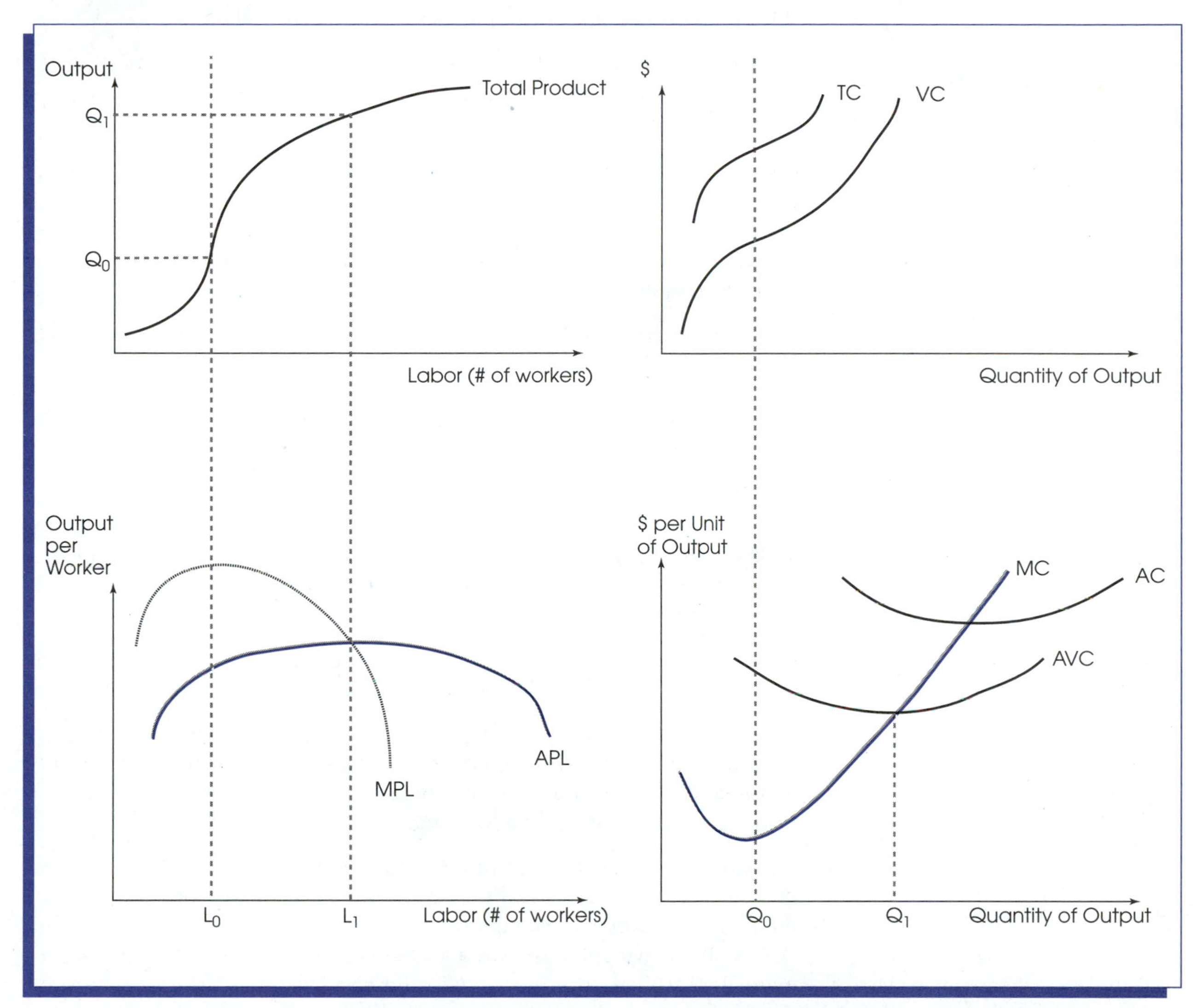

The product curves on the left are reproduced from Exhibit 6–2. Diminishing marginal returns set in when there are L_0 workers and Q_0 units of output. Up to this point, the total product curve becomes steeper, the variable and total cost curves become flatter, the marginal product curve rises, and the marginal cost curve falls; thereafter, the total product curve becomes flatter, the variable and total cost curves become steeper, and the marginal cost curve rises. The first stage of production continues until there are L_1 workers and Q_1 units of output. Up to this point, marginal product exceeds average product, average product rises, marginal cost is below average variable cost, and average variable cost falls. Thereafter, marginal product is below average product, average product falls, marginal cost is above average variable cost, and average variable cost rises. Marginal cost cuts through both average variable cost and average cost at the bottom of the respective U's.

1. The variable cost (VC) curve is always increasing, because more output requires more labor and hence higher costs. As output increases from 0 to Q_0, the variable cost curve flattens out, reflecting gains from specialization as more labor is added. At Q_0, diminishing marginal returns set in and additional units of output require successively greater increments of labor, so the VC curve becomes progressively steeper.
2. The total cost (TC) curve is determined by the formula $TC = FC + VC$ where FC (fixed cost) is constant. Therefore, it has exactly the same shape as the VC curve.
3. The marginal cost (MC) curve is U-shaped. Remember that marginal cost is the slope of total cost, so the U shape of the MC curve reflects the changing slope of the TC curve. Marginal cost falls in the region where total cost is becoming flatter (up to Q_0) and rises in the region where total cost is becoming steeper (beyond Q_0).
4. The average cost (AC) and average variable cost (AVC) curves are also U-shaped.
5. When marginal cost is below average variable cost, average variable cost is falling. In Exhibit 6–5, this refers to the region to the left of Q_1. (This region represents the first stage of production, where the firm hires fewer than L_1 workers.) To see why, consider a situation where you've already produced, say, 10 items at an average variable cost of $12 apiece. If the 11th item has a marginal cost below $12 (that is, if MC is below AVC), then it will lower the average variable cost below $12 (that is, average cost falls as the quantity increases from 10 to 11).
6. When marginal cost is above average variable cost, average variable cost is rising. In Exhibit 6–5, this occurs in the region to the right of Q_1.
7. Marginal cost crosses average variable cost at the bottom of the average variable cost "U". This is a geometric consequence of points 5 and 6. When marginal cost is just equal to average variable cost, average variable cost is just changing from falling to rising.
8. The analogs of points 5, 6, and 7 hold when average variable cost is replaced by average cost, and they hold for the same reasons. Thus, when marginal cost is below average cost, average cost is falling; when marginal cost is above average cost, average cost is rising; marginal cost crosses average cost at the bottom of the average cost U.
9. The shapes of the cost curves are related to the shapes of the product curves. For example, we have $AVC = P_L/APL$ and $MC = P_L/MPL$ where P_L (the wage rate of labor) is a constant. These formulas convert the inverted "U" shapes of APL and MPL to the U shapes of AVC and MC.

In drawing the cost curves, remember that *TC* and *VC* belong on a graph whose vertical axis shows "dollars," while *AVC*, *AC*, and *MC* belong on a graph whose vertical axis shows "dollars per unit of output." Remember, also, that *all* of these

curves have an implicit unit of time built into them; thus, when we say that it takes 2 workers to produce 6 units of output, we really mean that it takes 2 workers to produce 6 units of output *in a given, prespecified period of time.*

6.2 Production and Costs in the Long Run

Typically, there are many ways to produce a unit of output. What can be done by 3 workers with 5 machines can perhaps also be done by 6 workers with only 1 machine. In the long run, the firm can adjust its employment of both labor and capital so as to achieve the least expensive method of producing a given quantity of output. Our first task will be to develop some geometry to help clarify the firm's considerations.

Isoquants

Exhibit 6–6 shows the set of all combinations that suffice to produce one unit of a certain good, which we will call X, in a given period of time. The vertical axis, labeled K, represents capital, and the horizontal axis, labeled L, represents

Exhibit 6-6 The Unit Isoquant

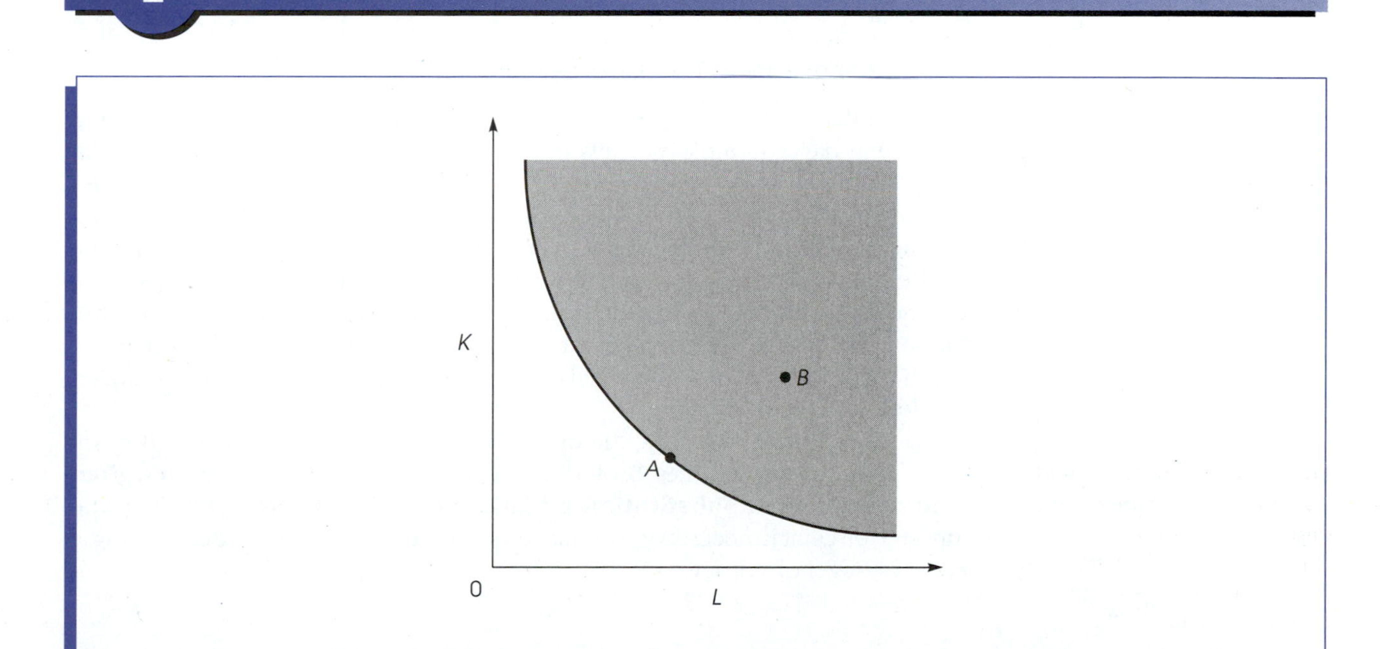

The shaded region represents all of the different baskets of capital and labor that can be used to produce one unit of X. Baskets that are off the boundary, like B, are technologically inefficient, in that a unit of X can be produced by a different basket (like A) containing smaller quantities of both inputs. The technologically efficient baskets for producing a unit of X are those on the unit isoquant, which is the heavy curve that bounds the shaded region.

labor. (K is traditionally used instead of C for *capital* in order to avoid any possible confusion with *consumption*.) The period of time is implicitly fixed; for example, we might be speaking of producing one unit of X per day. Appropriate units for labor and capital are, for example, "man-hours per day" and "machine-hours per day."

In Exhibit 6–6 every basket of inputs in the shaded part of the graph suffices to produce a unit of X. However, points that are off the boundary (like B) are **technologically inefficient**, in that there are other baskets of inputs, containing both less capital and less labor, that will also suffice to produce a unit of X. (For example, basket A contains smaller quantities of both inputs than basket B does.) No firm would want to produce a unit of X using a technologically inefficient basket of inputs. Thus, we will ignore these baskets and concentrate on the technologically efficient ones. In Exhibit 6–6 the technologically efficient baskets for producing a unit of X are represented by the heavy curve that bounds the shaded region. That curve is called the **unit isoquant.**

Technologically inefficient A production process that uses more inputs than necessary to produce a given output.

Unit isoquant The set of all technically efficient ways to produce one unit of output.

Why is the unit isoquant shaped as it is? Note first that no point to the northeast of A can be on the unit isoquant, because any such point (like B) is technologically inefficient. For the same reason, no point to the northeast of *any* point on the unit isoquant can also lie on the unit isoquant. It follows that the points on the isoquant must all be to either the northwest or the southeast of each other. Another way to say this is:

The unit isoquant is downward sloping.

The Marginal Rate of Technical Substitution

Suppose that each day a firm uses the basket of inputs A to produce one unit of X. One day an employee calls in sick, making it necessary to get by with one less unit of labor. How much additional capital will the firm need in order to maintain the daily output level? The answer is shown in Exhibit 6–7. Reducing labor input by one unit corresponds geometrically to moving one unit to the left; maintaining the output level corresponds geometrically to staying on the isoquant. Taken together, these requirements mandate that the firm move to point A'. The vertical distance between A and A' is the additional capital that must be added to the usual daily ration. That vertical distance has been labeled ΔK in Exhibit 6–7.

For all practical purposes, the distance ΔK is equal to the slope of the isoquant at the point A.[2] The absolute value of this slope is called the **marginal rate of technical substitution of labor for capital ($MRTS_{LK}$)**; it is the amount of capital necessary to replace one unit of labor while maintaining a constant level of output.[3]

Marginal rate of technical substitution of labor for capital The amount of capital that can be substituted for one unit of labor, holding output constant.

---

[2] The line through A and A' is nearly tangent to the isoquant, and can be made more nearly tangent by measuring labor in smaller units when it is desirable to do so. Its slope is equal to the rise over the run, which is $-\Delta K/1$, or $-\Delta K$.

[3] Some books call this the marginal rate of technical substitution of capital for labor; unfortunately, there is no standard accepted terminology.

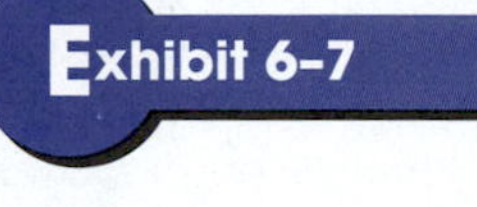

Exhibit 6-7 The Marginal Rate of Technical Substitution

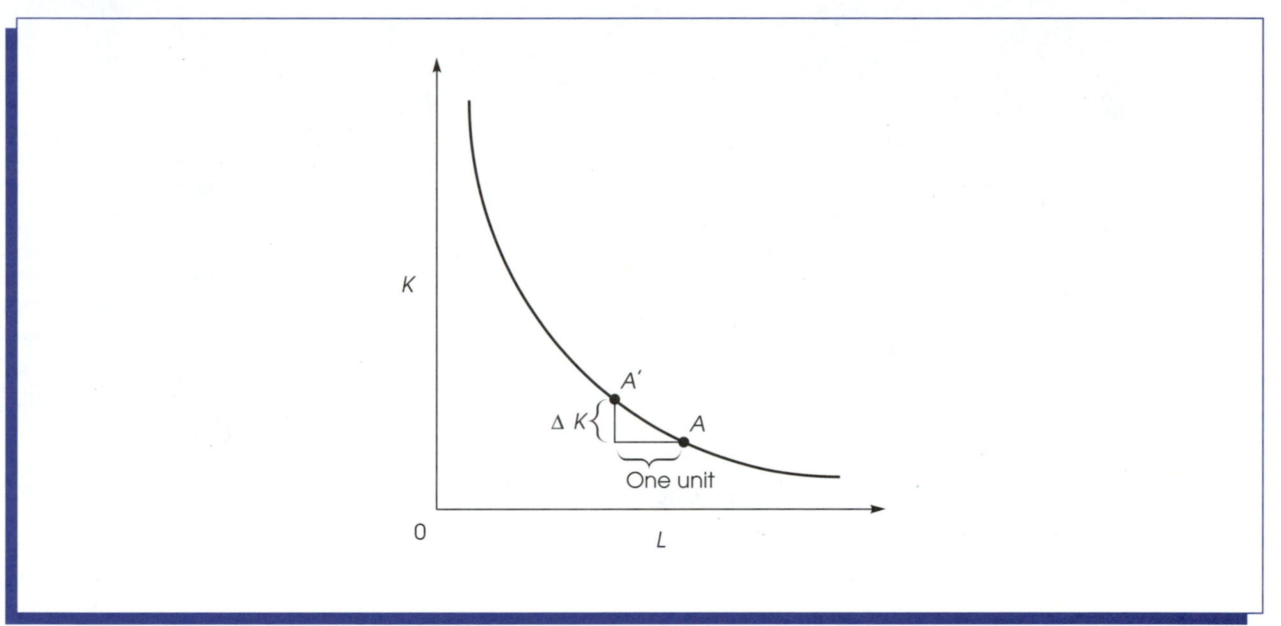

The firm produces one unit of X per day using basket A of inputs. When labor input is reduced by one unit, capital input must be increased by ΔK units in order for the firm to remain on the isoquant and maintain its level of output. The number ΔK is the marginal rate of technical substitution of labor for capital.

Suppose that a construction firm produces 1 house per day by employing 100 carpenters and 10 power tools. Then it is reasonable to think that when a carpenter calls in sick, the firm can maintain its level of production through a small increase in power tool usage. On the other hand, if the same firm produces the same 1 house per day by employing 10 carpenters and 100 power tools, we expect it to need a much larger increase in tool usage to compensate for the same absent carpenter. In other words, when much labor and little capital are employed to produce a unit of output, $MRTS_{LK}$ is small, but when little labor and much capital are employed to produce the same unit of output, $MRTS_{LK}$ is large. Geometrically, this means that at points far to the southeast, the isoquant is shallow, while at points far to the northwest it is steep. That is, the isoquant is convex.

Marginal Products and the MRTS

The marginal products of labor and capital are related to the marginal rate of technical substitution. Suppose labor input is reduced by one unit and capital input is increased by ΔK units, where ΔK is just enough to maintain the existing level of output. Then $\Delta K = MRTS_{LK}$.

Consider the two steps in this experiment separately. When one unit of labor is sacrificed, output goes down by the marginal product of labor *MPL*. When ΔK units of capital are hired, output goes up by $\Delta K \cdot MPK$ where *MPK* is the marginal product of capital. Since the existing level of output does not change, we must have

$$MPL = \Delta K \cdot MPK = MRTS_{LK} \cdot MPK$$

or

$$MRTS_{LK} = MPL/MPK$$

Thus, the marginal rate of technical substitution is closely related to the marginal products of labor and capital. Keep in mind the conceptual distinction, though: To measure $MRTS_{LK}$, we hold *output* fixed, vary *L* by one unit, and ask how much *K* must vary. To measure *MPL* we hold *capital* (*K*) fixed, vary *L* by one unit, and ask how much output varies. To measure *MPK* we hold *labor* (*L*) fixed, vary *K* by one unit, and ask how much output varies.[4]

The Production Function

Suppose that the firm wants to produce 2 units of *X* instead of 1. We can draw an isoquant representing all of the technologically efficient input combinations that the firm can use. This "2-unit" isoquant lies above and to the right of the original "1-unit" isoquant. We can go on to draw isoquants for any given level of output, generating a family of isoquants such as the one shown in Exhibit 6–8.

The important facts about isoquants are these:

Isoquants slope downward, they fill the plane, they never cross, and they are convex.

You should recognize this list of properties; it characterizes families of indifference curves as well.

EXERCISE 6.10 Explain why isoquants never cross. Explain why they fill the plane.

Suppose that we want to know how much output the firm can produce with a given basket of inputs. We can use the family of isoquants to answer this question. For example, suppose that we want to know how much the firm can

[4] The discussion in this section assumed a one-unit change in labor. More generally, if labor had changed by some amount ΔL, the equation would have been

$$\Delta L \cdot MPL = \Delta K \cdot MPK$$

and we would still have reached the conclusion

$$MRTS_{LK} = \frac{\Delta K}{\Delta L} = \frac{MPL}{MPK}$$

Exhibit 6-8 The Production Function

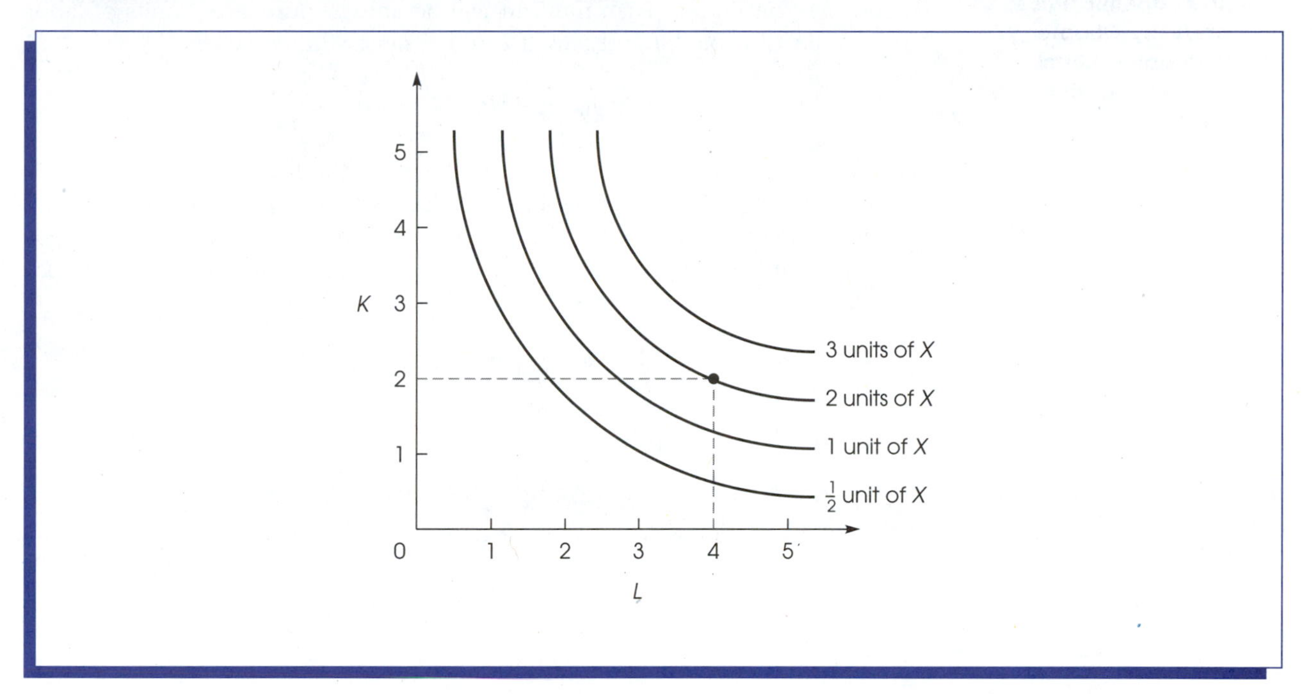

The family of isoquants can be used to determine the maximum level of production that can be attained with any given level of inputs. For example, if the firm uses 4 units of labor and 2 of capital, then it can produce 2 units of output and no more. This rule for calculating the output that can be produced from a given basket of inputs is the firm's production function.

produce using 4 units of labor and 2 units of capital. From Exhibit 6–8 we see that this basket lies on the 2-unit isoquant; thus, the firm can use this basket to produce 2 units of *X*.

Production function The rule for determining how much output can be produced with a given basket of inputs.

The rule for determining how much output can be produced with a given basket of inputs is called the firm's **production function.** If we know the family of isoquants, then we know the production function, and vice versa. Therefore, we can think of the graph in Exhibit 6–8 as providing a picture of the firm's production function.

Choosing a Production Process

In the long run no factor of production is fixed, and the firm is free to use any production process. Given a level of output, the corresponding isoquant presents the firm with a menu of ways to produce that output, from which it chooses the option with the lowest cost. We will now develop a geometric device for keeping track of those costs.

For more on isoquants, isocosts, and production visit: http://www.best.com/~ddfr/Academic/Price_Theory/PThy_Chapter_9/PThy_Chapter_9.html Figure 9.3a is particularly relevant.

Isocost The set of all baskets of inputs that can be employed at a given cost.

Isocosts and Cost Minimization

Suppose that the firm can hire labor at a going wage rate of P_L and can hire capital at a going rental rate of P_K. Suppose also, for the moment, that the firm spends $10 on inputs. Then the firm will be able to purchase L units of labor and K units of capital if and only if L and K satisfy the equation

$$P_L \cdot L + P_K \cdot K = \$10$$

The collection of pairs (L,K) that satisfy this equation form a straight line with slope $-(P_L/P_K)$. That line, called the $10 **isocost**, is shown in Exhibit 6–9. Of the lines shown in the exhibit, the $10 isocost is the one closest to the origin.

If the firm is willing to spend $11 on inputs, then it can hire any combination of labor and capital that satisfies

$$P_L \cdot L + P_K \cdot K = \$11$$

Exhibit 6-9 Cost Minimization

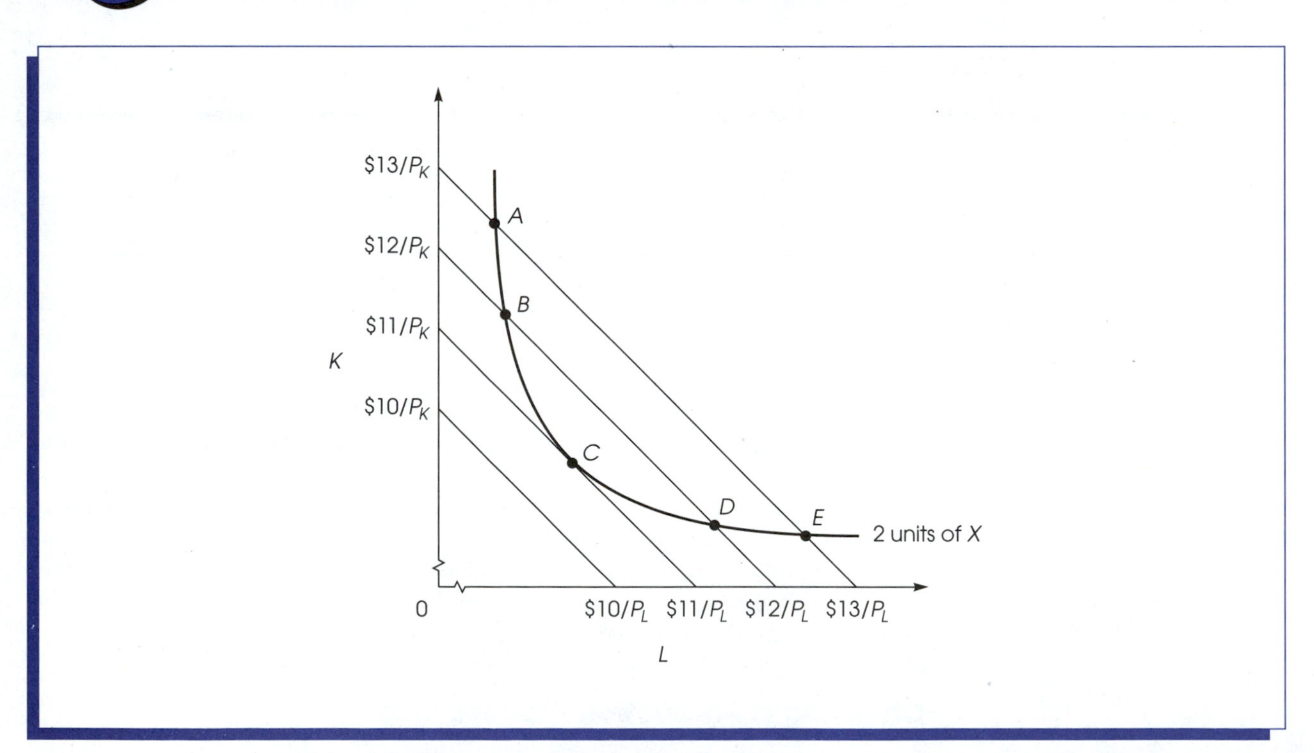

The isocost lines display all of the production processes that can be achieved for a given expenditure on inputs. Moving outward from the origin, the straight lines are the $10, $11, $12, and $13 isocosts. In order to produce 2 units of X, the firm must select a production process on the 2-unit isoquant. Of these processes, it will choose the one that is least costly, which is to say the one on the lowest isocost, namely, *C*.

The set of available points form another straight line, the \$11 isocost, which is also shown in Exhibit 6–9. The exhibit shows the \$12 and \$13 isocosts as well.

Now suppose that the firm wants to produce 2 units of output. Then it must select a production process that uses a basket of inputs on the 2-unit isoquant, shown in the exhibit. If it selects point A, on the \$13 isocost, then the cost of production is \$13. If it selects point B, the cost of production is \$12. If it selects point C, the cost of production is \$11. Of course, the firm wants to minimize its costs, and so it selects the production process corresponding to point C. The cost of producing 2 units of output is \$11.

Of course, the firm would prefer to spend only \$10 to produce its 2 units of output, but this is impossible: No point on the \$10 isocost is also on the 2-unit isoquant. The best it can do is to choose point C.

In order to minimize the cost of producing a given level of output, the firm always chooses a point of tangency between an isocost and the appropriate isoquant.

Cost Minimization and the Equimarginal Principle

There is another way to reach the same conclusion. Suppose that the firm considers hiring 1 less unit of labor and replacing it with sufficient capital so that it can continue producing 2 units of output. How much additional capital must it hire? The answer to this question is precisely the number that we have already called the marginal rate of technical substitution, or $MRTS_{LK}$. Recall that $MRTS_{LK}$ is also equal to the absolute value of the slope of the isoquant.

What are the marginal costs and benefits of such a decision? The marginal benefit is a saving of P_L when the firm hires 1 less unit of labor. The marginal cost arises from hiring $MRTS_{LK}$ additional units of capital at P_K each; the bill comes to $MRTS_{LK} \cdot P_K$.

The equimarginal principle tells us that the firm should seek to equate marginal cost with marginal benefit. That is, it should seek to set

$$MRTS_{LK} \cdot P_K = P_L$$

or

$$MRTS_{LK} = \frac{P_L}{P_K}$$

The left side of this equation is the absolute value of the slope of the isoquant and the right side is the absolute value of the slope of the isocost. So the equation tells us that the firm should seek a point where the slopes of the isoquant and the isocost are equal; that is, a point of tangency.

To understand this better, let us think about what the firm can do if it is *not* at a point of tangency. What if the firm makes the mistake of operating at point A in Exhibit 6–9? Here the isoquant is steeper than the isocost; that is,

$$MRTS_{LK} > \frac{P_L}{P_K}$$

If the firm hires 1 more unit of labor and $MRTS_{LK}$ fewer units of capital, it can stay on the isoquant, decrease its capital costs by $MRTS_{LK} \cdot P_K$, and increase its labor costs by P_L. Since the last displayed inequality can be rewritten $MRTS_{LK} \cdot P_K > P_L$, this is a wise move for the firm to make. It shifts to the right and down along the isoquant to a point like B. Here $MRTS_{LK}$ still exceeds P_L/P_K and the process is repeated; the firm keeps moving southeast along the isoquant until it reaches point C, where $MRTS_{LK}$ and P_L/P_K are equal.

EXERCISE 6.11 Explain the adjustment process if the firm starts at a point like E.

Output Maximization

We will describe one more way to see that the firm always chooses to operate at a tangency. Exhibit 6–9 illustrates the problem of a firm that has chosen its level of output (in this case 2 units) and seeks the least expensive way to produce it. Exhibit 6–10 illustrates the problem of a firm that has instead chosen its expenditure on inputs and is now deciding how much to produce.

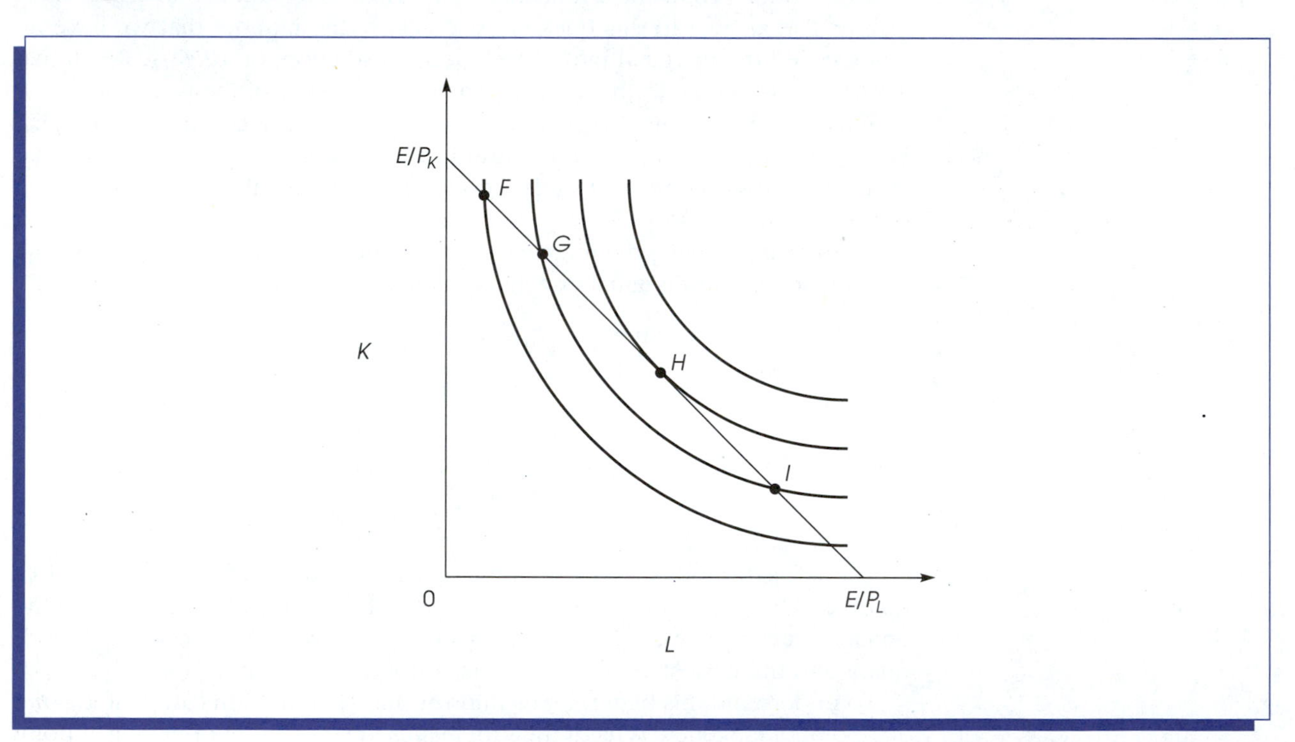

If the firm spends the amount E to hire inputs, it can choose any production process along the isocost line, such as F, G, H, or I. Of these it will choose the one that yields the greatest output, which is the point of tangency H.

If the chosen expenditure is E, then the firm must choose a production process on the E isocost, shown in Exhibit 6–10. How much does the firm want to produce? Surely the most that it possibly can, which is to say that it wants to be on the highest available isoquant. In the figure, it is clear that this occurs at point H, the point of tangency.

In summary, there are two ways of looking at the firm's problem, but both lead to the same conclusion. Whether the firm wants to minimize the cost of producing a given output (as in Exhibit 6–9), or to maximize its output for a given expenditure (as in Exhibit 6–10), it is led to the same conclusion: Produce at a point where an isocost is tangent to an isoquant.

The Expansion Path

All this should have a familiar ring to it; it is reminiscent of the way consumers choose bundles of output goods to purchase. However, the analogy is less close than it first appears. There is one critical difference between the consumer (who seeks a tangency between his budget line and an indifference curve) and the firm (which seeks a tangency between an isocost and an isoquant).

The difference is this: A consumer has a *given* income to divide among consumption goods, whereas a firm can *choose* its level of expenditure on inputs. Put another way, a consumer is constrained to only one budget line, whereas a firm has a whole *family* of isocosts (one for each level of expenditure) from which it can choose.

Unlike an individual, a firm has no budget constraint. The reason is that individuals pursue consumption, whereas firms pursue profits. As a result, the firm can "afford" to spend any amount on inputs that is appropriate to its goal. Even when there is a limited amount of cash on hand, a profit-maximizing firm can borrow against its future profits to achieve whatever is the optimal level of expenditure and output.[5] The same borrowing opportunities are not available to an individual who decides he wants to visit Hawaii.

In terms of our graphs, the consequence of all this is that we must consider the entire family of isocost lines available to the firm. They are parallel, since they all have the same slope $-(P_L/P_K)$, but those reflecting higher levels of expenditure are farther out than others.[6] This is shown in Exhibit 6–11.

Expansion path The set of tangencies between isoquants and isocosts.

The tangencies between isocosts and isoquants lie along a curve called the firm's **expansion path.** We know that the firm chooses one of these tangencies. However, we have not yet said anything that allows us to determine

[5] In practice, there might actually be limitations on the firm's ability to borrow that are not accounted for by our simple model. However, the standard assumption in elementary treatments of the theory of the firm is that all of the firm's profits from production are available for the purchase of inputs, even before production takes place. Economists are aware that firms can face borrowing constraints and have intensely studied the consequences of those constraints, but this is a more advanced topic.

[6] We are assuming that P_L and P_K are not affected by the actions of the firm. This assumption would fall only if the firm in question hired a significant proportion of either all the labor or all the capital in the economy.

Exhibit 6-11 Deriving Long-Run Total Cost

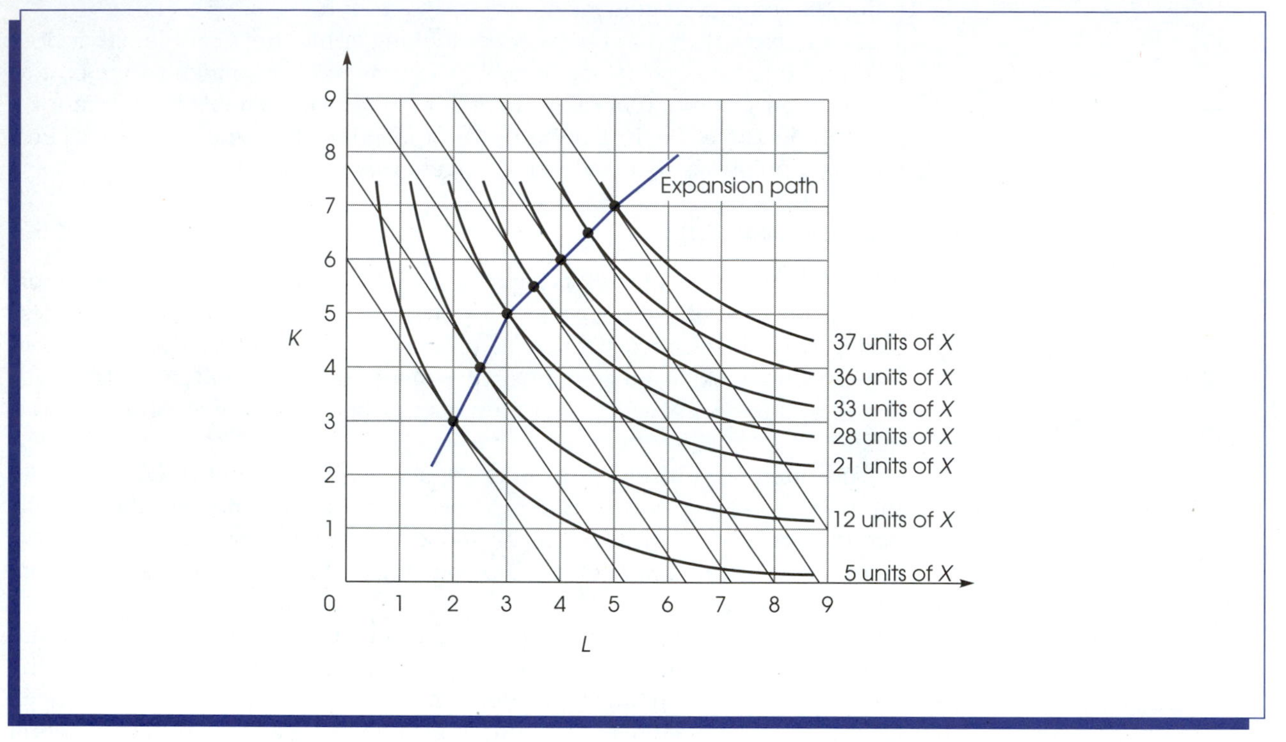

To produce 33 units of output, the firm selects the tangency, where $K = 6$ and $L = 4$. Because $P_K = \$10$ and $P_L = \$15$, the associated total cost is $(6 \times \$10) + (4 \times \$15) = \$120$.

which tangency the firm selects. In order to fully predict the firm's behavior, we know from Chapter 5 that we need to take account of the marginal revenue curve, which is derived from the demand for the firm's output. Since this information does not appear in the expansion path diagram, it is not surprising that we cannot use the diagram to predict the firm's behavior, at least with respect to its output decision. We will not return to this question until Chapter 7.

The Long-Run Cost Curves

To derive a firm's long-run cost curves, we need to know its production function (that is, the isoquants) and the input prices P_L and P_K (which determine the isocosts). By way of example, we will assume that the isoquants are as shown in Exhibit 6–11 and that the input prices are $P_K = \$10$, $P_L = \$15$. Given this information, we can plot the isocosts as in Exhibit 6–11 and draw in the expansion path by connecting the tangencies. All of this has been done in the exhibit.

Suppose the firm plans to produce 33 units of output per day. It selects a tangency on the 33 unit isoquant, which you can see from the exhibit occurs at the point where $K = 6$ and $L = 4$. Therefore, the firm hires 6 units of capital and 4 of labor for a total cost of $(6 \times \$10) + (4 \times \$15) = \$120$. This is the firm's **long-run total cost** of producing 33 units.

Long-run total cost The cost of producing a given amount of output when the firm is able to operate on its expansion path.

Similarly, if the firm wants to produce 21 units of output, then it uses 5 units of capital and 3 of labor for a total cost of $(5 \times \$10) + (3 \times \$15) = \$95$.

These points can be plotted on a long-run total cost curve with output on the horizontal axis and total cost on the vertical. There is a point at (33,$120) and another at (21,$95).

EXERCISE 6.12 What is the total cost of producing 37 units of output? 5 units of output? 12 units of output?

A study of returns to scale in agriculture is at: http://agecon.lib.umn.edu/mn/p97-02.html

Long-Run Average and Marginal Costs

In Exhibit 6–4 we constructed the (short-run) average and marginal cost curves from our knowledge of the (short-run) total cost curve. We can follow exactly the same procedure with long-run costs. The long-run total cost curve of Exhibit 6–12, panel A, gives rise to the long-run average and marginal cost curves shown in panel B. **Long-run average cost** is given by the equation and **long-run marginal cost** is the increment to long-run total cost attributable to the last unit of output produced. At a quantity of 33 units, we have $LRAC = TC/Q = \$120/(33 \text{ units}) = \$3.63$ per unit. At a quantity of 37 units, we have $LRMC = \$145 - \$132.50$ per unit $= \$12.50$ per unit. (All of the numbers here are taken from the table in Exhibit 6–12.)

Long-run average cost Long-run total cost divided by quantity.

Long-run marginal cost That part of long-run total cost attributable to the last unit produced.

If we want to compute the long-run marginal cost at a quantity of 28 units, we must subtract from $107.50 the long-run total cost of producing 27 units, a number that is not shown in the table. However, you could in principle determine this number from Exhibit 6–11, if the 27-unit isoquant were drawn in.

Comparing the long-run Exhibit 6–11 with the short-run Exhibit 6–4, you will find that there is one fewer curve in Exhibit 6–11: In the long run, the average variable cost curve has disappeared. This is because all costs are variable in the long run; therefore, in the long run there is no distinction between average cost and average variable cost.

Returns to Scale and the Shape of the Long-Run Cost Curves

Our goal is to determine the shape of the firm's long-run marginal and average cost curves. Since these curves are derived from the long-run total cost curve, which is in turn derived from the production function, it behooves us to start by thinking a little harder about the production function itself.

Here is an important question about the production function: When all input quantities are increased by 1%, does output go up by (1) more than 1%, (2) exactly 1%, or (3) less than 1%? Depending on the answer to this question, we say that the production function exhibits (1) **increasing returns to scale,** (2) **constant returns to scale,** or (3) **decreasing returns to scale**.

Increasing returns to scale A condition where increasing all input levels by the same proportion leads to a more than proportionate increase in output.

Constant returns to scale A condition where increasing all input levels by the same proportion leads to a proportionate increase in output.

Decreasing returns to scale A condition where increasing all input levels by the same proportion lead to a less than proportionate increase in output.

Exhibit 6–12 Long-Run Total, Marginal, and Average Costs

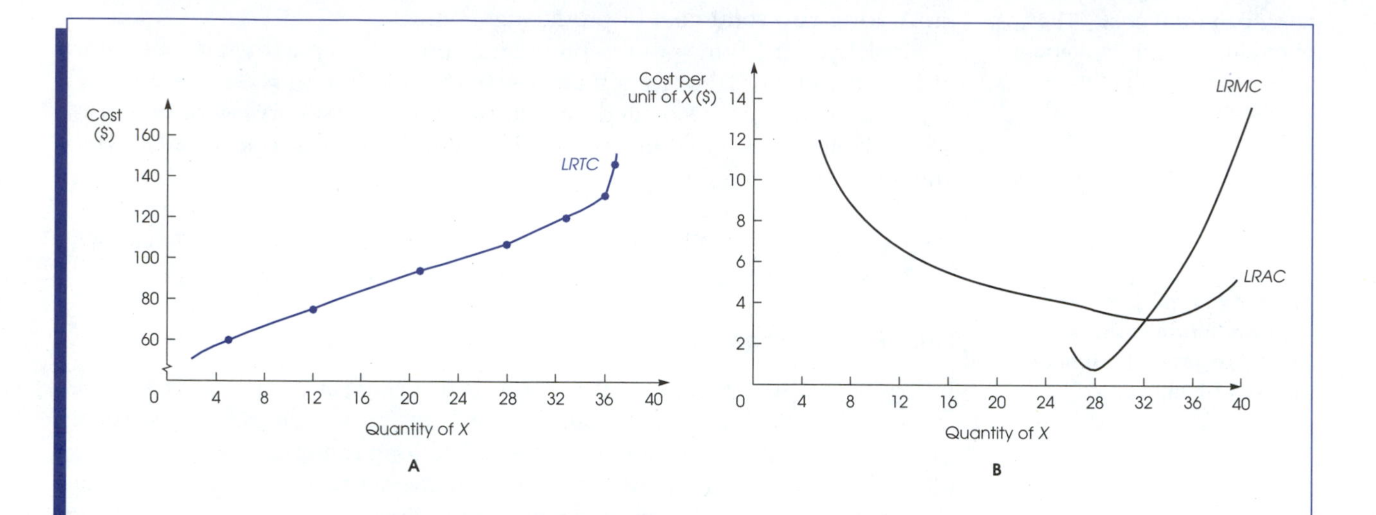

Quantity of Output	Factors Employed K	Factors Employed L	Cost of Factors K	Cost of Factors L	Total Cost
5	3	2	$30	$30	$60
12	4	2.5	40	37.50	77.50
21	5	3	50	45	95
28	5.5	3.5	55	52.50	107.50
33	6	4	60	60	120
36	6.5	4.5	65	67.50	132.50
37	7	5	70	75	145

These cost curves are all derived from the graph in Exhibit 6–11. The table illustrates computations like the one in the caption to Exhibit 6–11. These computations yield points on the total cost curve. Points on the average cost curve are computed by dividing total cost by quantity: When 33 units are produced, the average cost is $120/33 = $3.63. Points on the marginal cost curve are computed by taking differences in total cost: When 37 items are produced, the marginal cost is $145 − $132.50 = $12.50. To compute the marginal cost when 28 items are produced, we must start with $107.50 and subtract the total cost of producing 27 items. The latter number does not appear in the table but could be computed from the graph in Exhibit 6–11.

Students often confuse the concepts of diminishing marginal returns, on the one hand and decreasing returns to scale on the other. The two concepts are entirely different, and they are entirely different in each of two ways. The most important difference is that diminishing marginal returns is a short-run concept that describes the effect on output of increasing *one* input while holding other inputs fixed. Decreasing returns to scale is a long-run concept that describes the effect on output of increasing *all* inputs in the same proportion. The other difference is that the concept of diminishing marginal returns deals with marginal quantities, whereas the concept of decreasing returns to scale deals with total and average quantities. When we ask about diminishing marginal returns, we ask: "Will the next unit of this input yield more or less output *at the margin* than the last unit did?" When we ask about decreasing returns to scale, we ask: "Will a 1% increase in all inputs yield more or less than a 1% increase in *total* output?"

For given input prices, diminishing marginal returns are reflected by an increasing short-run marginal cost curve. Decreasing returns to scale, as we shall soon see, are reflected by an increasing long-run average cost curve.

Increasing Returns to Scale

Increasing returns to scale are likely to result when there are gains from specialization or when there are organizational advantages to size. Two men with two machines might be able to produce more than twice as much as one man with one machine, if each can occasionally use a helping hand from the other. At low levels of output, firms often experience increasing returns to scale.

Constant and Decreasing Returns to Scale

At higher levels of output, the gains from specialization and organization having been exhausted, firms tend to produce under conditions of constant or even decreasing returns to scale. Which of the two, constant or decreasing returns, is more likely? A good case can be made for constant returns. When a firm doubles all of its inputs, it can, if it chooses, simply set up a second plant, identical to the original one, and have each plant produce at the original level, yielding twice the original output. This strategy generates constant returns to scale and suggests that the firm should never have to settle for decreasing returns. This argument is often summed up in the slogan "What a firm can do once, it can do twice."

Students sometimes object to this argument for constant returns. They argue that doubling the number of workers and the number of machines can lead to congestion in the factory and consequently to less than a doubling of output. This objection overlooks the fact that factory space is itself a productive input. When we measure returns to scale, we assume that *all* inputs are increased in the same proportion. In particular, we must double the space in the factory as well as the numbers of workers and machines.

A related objection is that when the scale of an operation is doubled, the owners can no longer keep as watchful an eye on the entire enterprise as they could previously. But if we view the owners' supervisory talents as a productive input, this objection breaks down as well. Any measurement of returns to scale must involve the imaginary experiment of increasing these talents in the same proportion as all other productive inputs.

As long as *all* productive inputs are truly variable, the argument for constant returns is a convincing one. However, if there are some inputs (such as managerial skills or the owner's cleverness as an entrepreneur) that are truly *fixed even in the long run*, then there may be decreasing returns to scale with respect to changes in all of the variable inputs. As a result, most economists are comfortable with the assumption that firms experience decreasing returns to scale at sufficiently high levels of output.

We assumed at the outset that in the long run every input is variable. When we now admit the possibility that some inputs may not be variable in the long run, we are admitting that our original model might not be a fully adequate description of reality.

Returns to Scale and the Average Cost Curve

Under conditions of increasing returns to scale, the firm's long-run average cost curve is decreasing. This is because a 1% increase in output can be accomplished with less than a 1% increase in all inputs. It follows that an increase in output leads to a fall in the average cost of production.[7]

Under conditions of decreasing returns to scale, the firm's long-run average cost curve is increasing.

EXERCISE 6.13 Justify the assertion of the preceding paragraph.

Under conditions of constant returns to scale, the firm's long-run average cost curve is flat. This is the situation where "what a firm can do once it can do twice." If the firm wants to double its output, it does so by doubling all of its inputs. The average cost per unit of output never changes.

If we assume that firms experience increasing returns to scale at low levels of output and decreasing returns thereafter, the firm's long-run average cost curve is U shaped, as in panel B of Exhibit 6–12. Only at one level of output (the quantity at which long-run total cost is minimized) does the firm face constant returns to scale.

When long-run marginal cost is below long-run average cost, long-run average cost is decreasing, and when long-run marginal cost is above long-run average cost, long-run average cost is increasing. Consequently, when long-run

---

[7] This argument assumes that the firm can hire all of the inputs that it wants to at a going market price. Without this assumption, the long-run average cost curve could be increasing even in the presence of increasing returns to scale. The same caveat applies to all of our arguments in this subsection.

average cost is U shaped, it is cut by long-run marginal cost at the bottom of the U. This is true in the long run for the same reason that it is true in the short run.

In general, the upward-sloping part of the firm's long-run marginal cost curve will be much more elastic than the upward-sloping part of its short-run marginal cost curve. Marginal cost rises much more quickly when the firm is constrained not to vary certain inputs (in the short run) than when it can vary all inputs to minimize costs for each level of output (in the long run).

6.3 Relations Between the Short Run and the Long Run

In Section 6.1, we studied the firm's short-run production function and cost curves; in Section 6.2, we studied the firm's long-run production function and cost curves. Our remaining task is to relate the two points of view.

From Isoquants to Short-Run Total Cost

Consider a firm that rents capital at a rate of $P_K = \$10$ and hires labor at a rate of $P_L = \$15$. The firm's production function is illustrated in Exhibit 6–13. Its capital is fixed in the short run at 5 units (thus, if a "unit" is a machine, the firm has the use of 5 machines; if a "unit" is 100 square feet of office space, the firm has the use of 500 square feet).

In the short run, the firm can only choose input baskets that contain exactly 5 units of capital, which is to say that it can only choose baskets that are located on the blackened horizontal line. To produce 5 units of output, it must select a basket that is both on this line and on the 5-unit isoquant; that is, it must select the point with 5 units of capital and 1 unit of labor. The firm's total cost is then $5 \times \$10 = \$50$ for capital plus $1 \times \$15 = \$15$ for labor, or \$65. (Of this \$65, the \$50 spent on capital is a fixed cost and the \$15 spent on labor is a variable cost.) This calculation is recorded in the first row of the table, under the columns headed "Short Run."

Similarly, if the firm wants to produce 12 units of output it must select a point on both the blackened horizontal line and the 12-unit isoquant; that is, it must use 5 units of capital and 2 units of labor. Its total cost is \$80, as recorded in the second row of the table.

From the numbers in the "Short Run" half of the table, we can discover the firm's total product and total cost curves. The first column shows quantities of output and the third shows the quantity of labor needed to produce that output. The information here is identical to the information in the first two columns of the table in Exhibit 6–1. The moral is this: If you know the isoquants and the fixed quantity of capital, you can derive the (short-run) total product curve.

If, in addition, you know the factor prices, then you can also derive the short-run variable cost and total cost curves, as we showed in Exhibit 6–2 and Exhibit 6–3. The same computations are shown again in Exhibit 6–13, under the "Short Run" columns showing the cost of labor and total cost. The result-

Exhibit 6-13 Short-Run and Long-Run Total Cost Curves

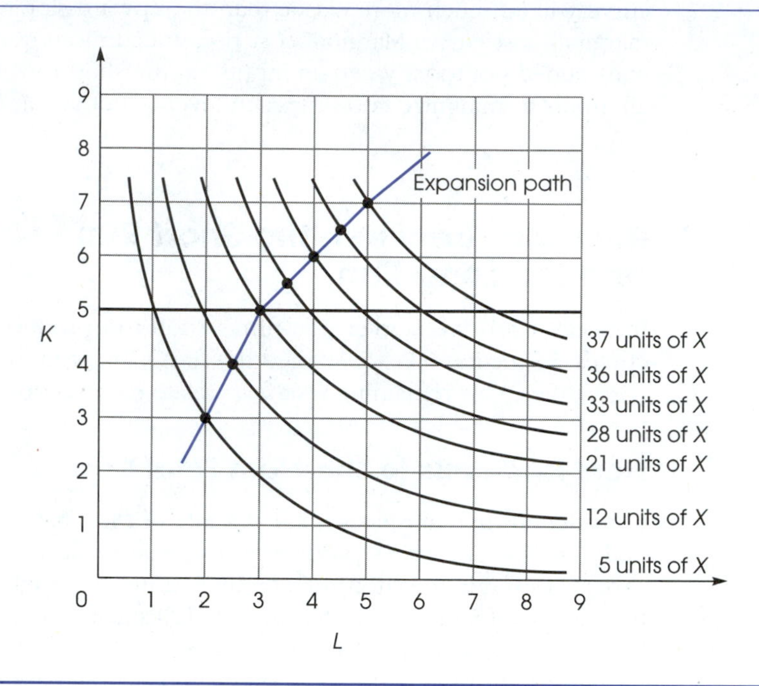

	Short Run					Long Run				
	Factors Employed		*Cost of Factors*			*Factors Employed*		*Cost of Factors*		
Quantity of Output	*K*	*L*	*K*	*L*	Total Cost	*K*	*L*	*K*	*L*	Total Cost
5	5	1	$50	$15	$65	3	2	$30	$30	$60
12	5	2	50	30	80	4	2.5	400	37.50	77.50
21	5	3	50	45	95	5	3	50	45	95
28	5	4	50	60	110	5.5	3.5	55	52.50	107.50
33	5	5	50	75	125	6	4	60	60	120
36	5	6	50	90	140	6.5	4.5	65	67.50	132.50
37	5	7	50	105	155	7	5	70	75	145

(Continues)

Exhibit 6-13 continued

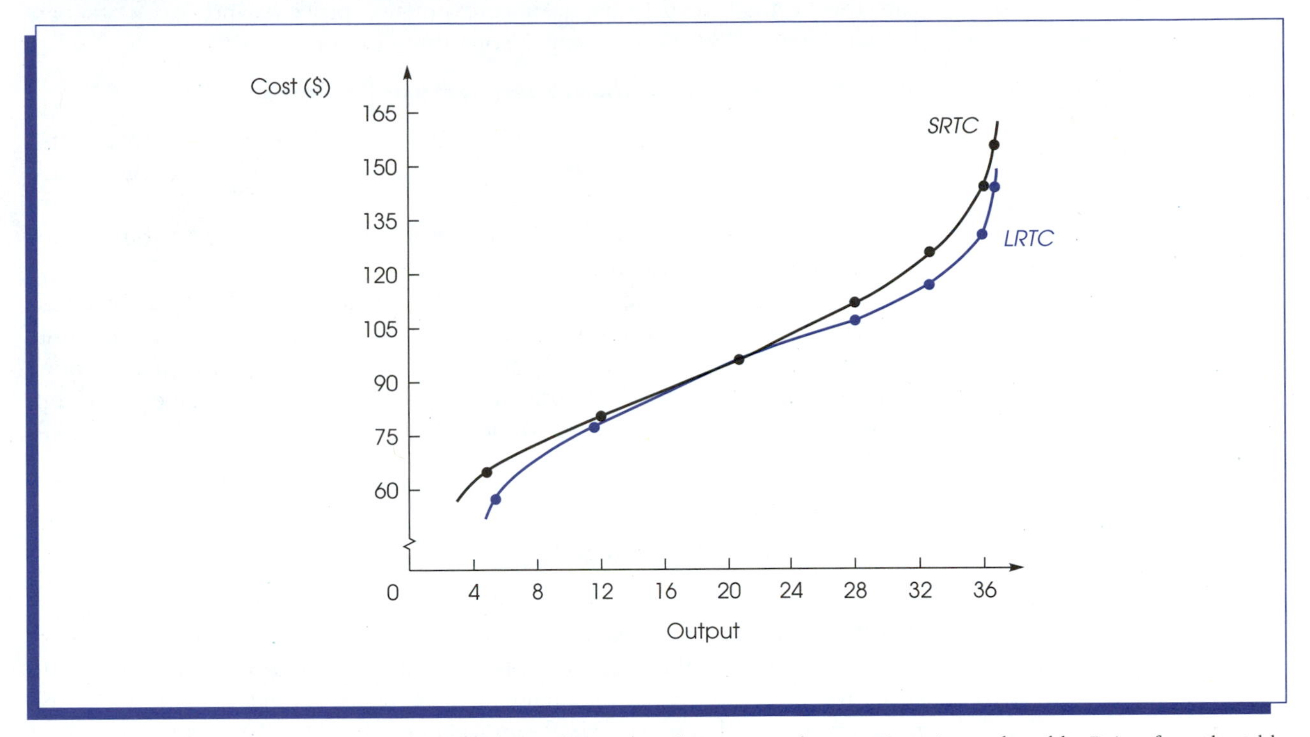

With P_K = \$10 and P_L = \$15, the isoquant diagram gives rise to the table. Points from the table are plotted on the graph. The short-run total cost (*SRTC*) curve is drawn on the assumption that capital employment is fixed at 5 units. It is the same curve that was constructed in Exhibit 6–3. Because the firm always chooses the least expensive production process in the long run, long-run total cost is never greater than short-run total cost. If the firm happens to want to produce exactly 21 units of output, then its desired long-run capital employment is equal to its existing capital employment of 5 units. In this fortunate circumstance, the firm can produce at the lowest possible cost even in the short run. For any other level of output, short-run total cost exceeds long-run total cost.

ing short-run total cost curve, labeled *SRTC* in the second panel of Exhibit 6–13, is identical to the one shown in Exhibit 6–3.[8]

From Isoquants to Long-Run Total Cost

Exhibits 6–11 and 6–12 already illustrated the derivation of long-run total cost from isoquants and factor prices. These computations are repeated in the "Long Run" columns of the table in Exhibit 6–13, and the resulting long-run total cost (*LRTC*) curve is redrawn in the second panel of that exhibit.

---

[8] In Section 6.1 we wrote *TC* for short-run total cost. We are now writing *SRTC* to distinguish the short-run total cost curve from the long-run total cost curve.

Short-Run Total Cost versus Long-Run Total Cost

To produce 12 units of output, the firm in Exhibit 6–13 selects the least expensive production process in the long run. Its costs total \$77.50. In the short run, the firm is forced to use a more expensive process, and so its costs are higher, totaling \$80. This illustrates something important:

Short-run total cost is always at least as great as long-run total cost.

The reason is simple. In the long run, the firm produces at the lowest possible cost. The short-run cost has no chance of being less than the lowest possible!

Geometrically, this means that *SRTC* never dips below *LRTC*. You can see that this is true in Exhibit 6–13.

We can say even more. There is exactly one quantity of output for which the short-run and long-run total costs are equal. In Exhibit 6–13, that quantity is 21. This is the quantity at which the firm's long-run desired capital employment (in this case 5 units) happens to precisely equal the fixed amount of capital it has available. You can see in the exhibit that the *SRTC* and *LRTC* curves touch at a quantity of 21.

A Multitude of Short Runs

All of the *short-run* numbers in Exhibit 6–13 are derived on the assumption that the firm's capital is fixed at 5 units. What if capital is fixed at 4 units instead? Now what is the short-run total cost of producing 5 units of output? In order to achieve the 5-unit isoquant with 4 units of capital, the firm must employ 1.5 units of labor. The short-run total cost is $(4 \times \$10) + (1.5 \times \$15) =$ \$62.50. To produce 12 units of output, the firm must employ 2.5 units of labor and the short-run total cost is \$77.50.

EXERCISE **6.14** With 4 units of capital, what is the *SRTC* when quantity is 28? When it is 33? When it is 36?

Plotting these points, we can construct a new short-run total cost curve, different from the one we constructed before. The new *SRTC* curve again touches the *LRTC* curve at exactly one point, this time at a quantity of 12.

For every quantity of capital, there is a corresponding *SRTC* curve, touching the *LRTC* curve at exactly one point. The geometry is illustrated in Exhibit 6–14.

Short-Run Average Cost versus Long-Run Average Cost

Instead of plotting total cost curves, we can plot average cost curves. There is a different short-run average cost curve for each quantity of capital. You can think of capital as a measure of "plant size," so that the short-run average cost curves in Exhibit 6–15 describe the situation for a small, a medium-size, and a large plant.

If the firm wants to produce quantity Q_1, average cost is minimized by the small plant represented by the curve $SRAC_1$. If the firm is required to operate with the medium-size plant represented by curve $SRAC_2$, its average cost is higher; if it operates with the large plant represented by $SRAC_3$, its average cost is even higher yet. In the long run, if Q_1 is the desired output, the firm chooses the small plant to minimize its average cost. Consequently, at Q_1 units, the long-run average cost is the same as the small plant's short-run average cost. That is why the $SRAC_1$ and $LRAC$ curves touch at Q_1.

If the firm wants to produce Q_3 units, it achieves the lowest average cost with the large plant, a somewhat higher average cost with the medium-size plant, and an even higher average cost with the small plant. In the long run, it chooses the large plant, so $LRAC$ is the same as $SRAC_3$ for Q_3 units of output.

EXERCISE 6.15 Suppose that the firm wants to produce Q_2 units of output. Which plant size is best? Which is second best? Which plant size will it choose in the long run? How is this fact reflected in the graph?

If the firm has only three possible plant sizes, then its long-run average cost curve consists of the black parts of the three short-run average cost curves. (For any quantity, the firm selects the optimal plant size and so achieves a point on

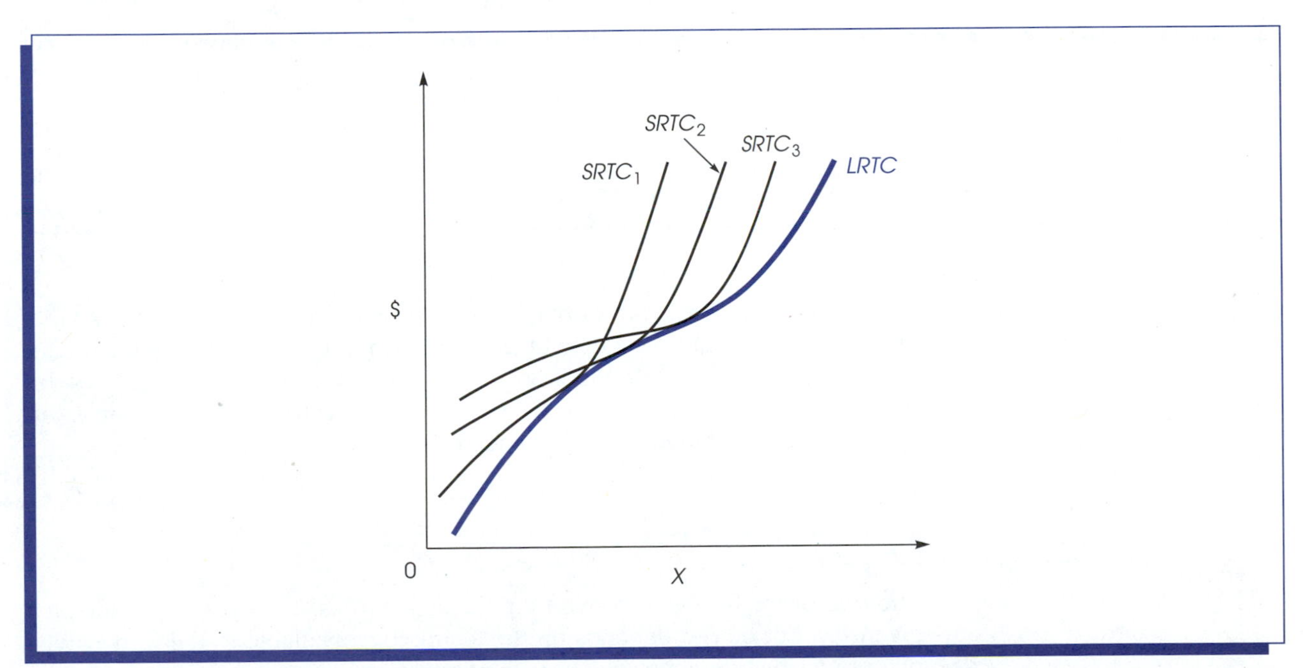

When we draw a short-run total cost curve, we assume a fixed level of capital employment. If we assume a different fixed level of capital employment, we get a different short-run total cost curve. The graph shows the short-run total cost curves that result from various assumptions.

Each total cost curve touches the long-run total cost curve in one place, at that level of output for which the fixed capital stock happens to be optimal. In that case the firm's long-run and short-run choices of production process coincide. The long-run total cost curve is the lower boundary of the region in which the various short-run total cost curves lie.

Exhibit 6–15 Many Short-Run Average Cost Curves

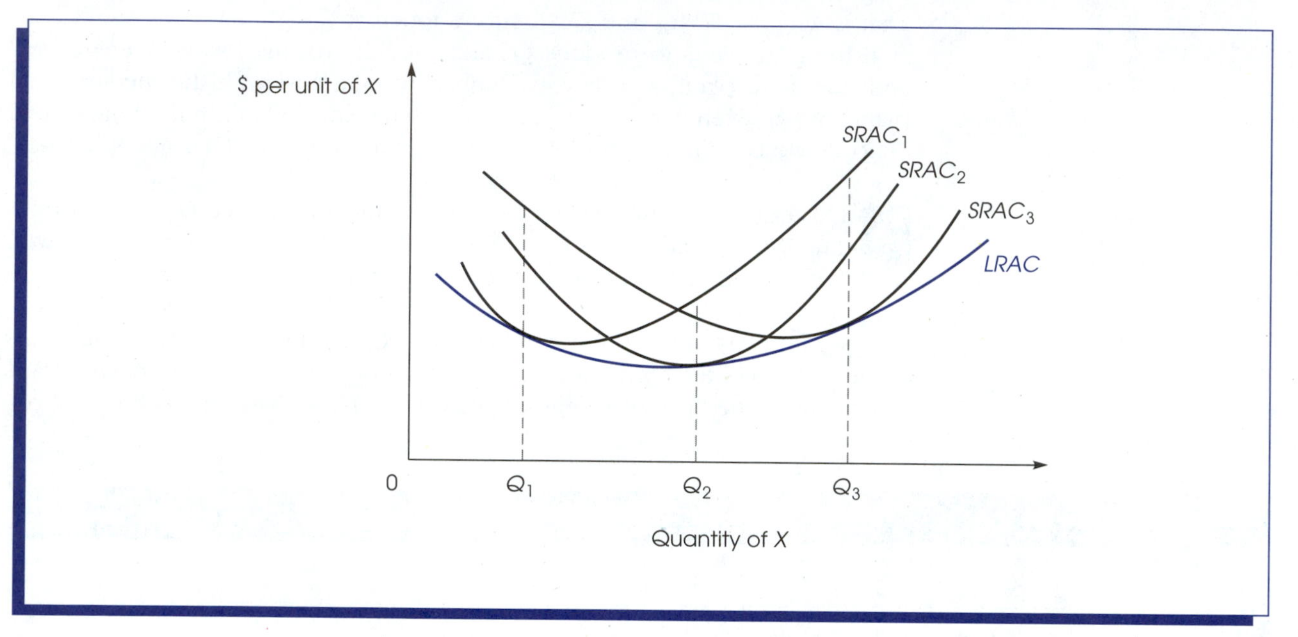

The curves $SRAC_1$, $SRAC_2$, and $SRAC_3$ show short-run average cost for a small, a medium-size, and a large plant. To produce Q_1 units, the firm finds that the small plant minimizes average cost, and so chooses that size plant in the long run. Thus, $LRAC = SRAC_1$ when quantity is Q_1. If only three plant sizes are available, the *LRAC* curve consists of the black portions of the *SRAC* curves shown. If a continuous range of plant sizes is available, there are many other *SRAC* curves, and the *LRAC* curve is the color curve shown.

one of the three *SRAC*s.) In most of this chapter, we have assumed instead that the firm has a continuous range of plant sizes (that is, it can choose any quantity of capital it desires). In this case, there are many other *SRAC* curves besides those pictured, and *LRAC* is the color curve in the graph. Each point on *LRAC* is then a point of tangency with some *SRAC* curve.

summary

The role of the firm is to convert inputs into outputs. The cost of producing a given level of output depends on the technology available to the firm (which determines the quantities of inputs the firm will need) and the prices of the inputs.

In the short run the firm is committed to employing some inputs in fixed amounts. In the long run it is free to vary its employment of every input, always producing at the lowest possible cost.

For illustrative purposes, we consider a firm that employs labor and capital, with capital fixed in the short run. The options available to the firm are then illustrated by its total product (*TP*) curve, also called its short-run production function. From the *TP* curve, we can derive the marginal product of labor (*MPL*) curve by computing the additional output derived from each additional unit of labor: The value of *MPL* is the slope of *TP*.

The average product of labor (*APL*) is defined to be TP/L where L is the amount of labor employed. At low levels of output (the first stage of production), each additional worker increases the productivity of his colleagues. Therefore, marginal product exceeds average product and average product is rising. At higher levels of output (the second stage of production), each additional worker reduces the productivity of his colleagues. Therefore, marginal product is below average product and average product is falling. The average product curve has the shape of an inverted U, with the marginal product curve cutting through it at the highest point.

For a given level of output, the firm faces a fixed cost (*FC*), which is the cost of renting capital, and a variable cost (*VC*), which is the cost of hiring labor. *FC* can be computed as $P_K \cdot K$ where P_K is the price of capital and K is the firm's (fixed) capital usage. *VC* can be computed as $P_L \cdot L$ where P_L is the wage rate of labor and L is the quantity of labor needed to produce the desired output; the value of L that corresponds to a given quantity of output can be found by examining the *TP* curve.

The firm's total cost (*TC*) is the sum of *FC* and *VC*. Its average cost (*AC*) is TC/Q, where Q is the quantity of its output. Its average variable cost (*AVC*) is VC/Q. Its marginal cost is the increment to total cost attributable to the last unit of output.

Typically, the average, average variable, and marginal cost curves are U-shaped. *MC* cuts through both *AC* and *AVC* at their minimum points.

In the long run the firm's technology is embodied in its production function, which is illustrated by the isoquant diagram. The slope of an isoquant is equal to the marginal rate of technical substitution between labor and capital. We expect $MRTS_{LK}$ to decrease as we move down and to the right along the isoquant, with the result that isoquants are convex.

In the long run the firm minimizes costs for a given level of output, which leads it to choose a point of tangency between an isocost and an isoquant. Alternatively, we can think of the firm as maximizing output for a given expenditure on inputs; this reasoning also leads to the conclusion that the firm operates at a tangency. The set of all such tangencies forms the firm's expansion path.

To compute the long-run total cost for Q units of output, find the tangency of the Q-unit isoquant with an isocost, and compute the price of the corresponding input basket.

Long-run average and marginal costs can be computed from long-run total cost.

The long-run average cost curve is downward sloping, flat, or upward sloping, depending on whether the firm experiences increasing, constant, or decreasing returns to scale. We expect increasing returns (decreasing average cost) at low levels of output because of the advantages of specialization. At higher levels of output there will be constant returns to scale unless some factor is fixed even in the long run; however, this case is very common because of limits on things like the skills and supervisory ability of the entrepreneur.

Therefore, we often draw the long-run average cost curve increasing at high levels of output, making the entire curve U-shaped. (That is, we assume decreasing returns to scale at high levels of output.) Long-run marginal cost cuts through long-run average cost at the bottom of the U.

The same isoquant diagram that is used to derive long-run total cost can be used to derive short-run total product and total cost curves as well. Each possible plant size for the firm results in a different short-run total cost curve, and consequently a different short-run average cost curve. The short-run cost curves never dip below the long-run cost curves. The short-run total cost curve associated with a given plant size touches the long-run total cost curve only at that quantity for which the plant size is optimal; the same is true for average cost curves.

Review Questions

R1. What are the first and second stages of production?

R2. What is the shape of the *APL* curve? Why?

R3. Where does the *MPL* curve cross the *APL* curve? Why?

R4. What is the relationship between the *MPL* curve and the total product curve?

R5. Explain how to derive the firm's *VC* and *TC* curves from its *TP* curve.

R6. Explain how to derive the firm's *AC*, *AVC*, and *MC* curves.

R7. What geometric relationships hold among *AC*, *AVC*, and *MC*? Why?

R8. Define the marginal rate of technical substitution.

R9. What is the relationship between the marginal products of the factors of production and the marginal rate of technical substitution?

R10. What are the geometric properties of isoquants? Why do we expect these properties to hold?

R11. Explain why firms want to operate at a tangency between an isoquant and an isocost.

R12. Explain how to derive a firm's long-run total cost curve from its isoquant diagram and knowledge of the factor prices.

R13. What are increasing, constant, and decreasing returns to scale? How are they related to the shape of the long-run average cost curve?

R14. Explain how to derive the firm's (short-run) total product and total cost curves from the isoquant diagram. How would these curves be affected by a change in the rental rate on capital? How would they be affected by a change in the wage rate of labor?

R15. What is the relationship between the firm's long-run and short-run total cost curves?

Numerical Exercise

N1. A firm discovers that when it uses K units of capital and L units of labor, it is able to produce $\sqrt{KL}$ units of output.

a. Draw the isoquants corresponding to 1, 2, 3, and 4 units of output.

b. Suppose that the firm produces 10 units of output using 20 units of capital and 5 units of labor. Compute the $MRTS_{LK}$. Compute the *MPL*. Compute the *MPK*.

c. On the basis of your answers to part (b), is the equation $MRTS_{LK} = MPL/MPK$ approximately true? (It would become closer to being true if we measured inputs in smaller units.)

d. Suppose that capital and labor can each be hired at $1 per unit and that the firm uses 20 units of capital in the short run. What is the short-run total cost to produce 10 units of output?

e. Continue to assume that capital and labor can each be hired at $1 per unit. Show that in the long run, if the firm produces 10 units of output, it will employ 10 units of capital and 10 units of labor. (*Hint:* Remember that in the long run the firm chooses to set $MPK/P_K = MPL/P_L$.) What is the long-run total cost to produce 10 units of output?

f. Does this production function exhibit constant, increasing, or decreasing returns to scale?

Problem Set

1. True or False: You should quit studying when you reach the point of diminishing marginal returns.
2. Suppose that you hire workers to address and stamp envelopes. Each worker earns $5 per hour and produces 50 addressed, stamped envelopes per hour. You have unlimited free office space and can therefore add as many workers as you want to with no fall-off in productivity. You have no expenses other than paying workers. Draw the total product, marginal product, average product, total cost, average cost, average variable cost, and marginal cost curves.
3. Suppose in the preceding problem that you rent a stamping machine with unlimited capacity, for $10 per hour. This makes it possible for workers to increase their output to 100 addressed, stamped envelopes per hour. Draw the new total product, marginal product, average product, total cost, average cost, average variable cost, and marginal cost curves.
4. In the situation of problems 2 and 3, suppose that you have a choice between renting the machine or not renting it. For what levels of output will you choose to rent the machine? For what levels of output will you choose not to? Suppose that in the long run you can decide whether or not to rent the machine. Draw your long-run total and average cost curves.

5. Suppose that your factory faces a total product curve that contains the following points:

Quantity of Labor	Total Product
6	1
10	2
13	3
15	4
18	5
23	6
30	7
40	8

a. If labor costs $2 per unit, and you have fixed costs of $30, construct tables showing your variable cost, total cost, average cost, and average variable cost curves.

b. At approximately what point does the second stage of production begin?

c. At approximately what point do diminishing marginal returns to labor set in?

6. Suppose that in the short run, capital is fixed and labor is variable. True or False: If the price of capital goes up, the firm's (short-run) average cost, average variable cost, and marginal cost curves will remain unaffected.

7. Suppose that in the short run, capital is fixed and labor is variable. True or False: If the price of labor goes up, the firm's (short-run) average cost, average variable cost, and marginal cost curves will all shift upward.

8. True or False: A wise entrepreneur will minimize costs for a given output rather than maximize output for a given cost.

9. Suppose that a firm is operating at a point off its expansion path, where

$$MRTS_{LK} > \frac{P_L}{P_K}$$

Explain how this firm could increase its output without changing its expenditure on inputs. Use this to give an additional argument for why a firm operating off its expansion path would want to move toward its expansion path.

10. Widgets are produced using thingamabobs and doohickeys. For some reason, a certain firm always produces exactly three widgets per day. True or False: If the price of thingamabobs increases, then in the long run the firm is certain to switch to a production process that uses fewer thingamabobs and more doohickeys.

11. A firm faces the following total product curves depending on how much capital it employs:

$K = 1$ Unit		$K = 2$ Units		$K = 3$ Units	
Quantity of Labor	Total Product	Quantity of Labor	Total Product	Quantity of Labor	Total Product
1	100	1	123	1	139
2	152	2	187	2	193
3	193	3	237	3	263
4	215	4	263	4	319
5	233	5	286	5	366
6	249	6	306	6	407
7	263	7	323	7	410

a. Suppose that the firm currently employs 1 unit of capital and 3 of labor. Compute $MRTS_{LK}$. Compute MPL. Compute MPK.

b. Suppose that the firm currently employs 2 units of capital. The price of capital is \$4 per unit and the price of labor is \$10 per unit. What is the short-run total cost of producing 263 units of output? What is the long-run total cost of producing 263 units of output?

c. Suppose that the price of capital increases to \$20 per unit and the price of labor falls to \$5 per unit. Now what is the long-run total cost of producing 263 units of output?

d. Beginning with 1 unit of capital and 2 units of labor, does this production function exhibit increasing, constant, or decreasing returns to scale? Which way does the long-run average cost curve slope?

12. Terry's Typing Service produces manuscripts. The only way to produce a manuscript is for 1 secretary to use 1 typewriter for 1 day. Two secretaries with 1 typewriter or 1 secretary with 2 typewriters can still produce only 1 manuscript per day.

a. Draw Terry's 1-unit isoquant.

b. Assuming that Terry's technology exhibits constant returns to scale, draw several more isoquants.

c. Assuming that Terry rents typewriters for \$4 apiece per day and pays secretaries \$6 apiece per day, draw some of Terry's isocosts. Draw the expansion path.

d. Terry has signed a contract to rent exactly 5 typewriters. Illustrate the following, using tables, graphs, or both: the total product and marginal product of labor; the short-run total cost, variable cost, average cost, average variable cost, and marginal cost; the long-run total cost, long-run average cost, and long-run marginal cost.

13. The desert town of Dry Gulch buys its water from LowTech Inc. LowTech hires residents to walk to the nearest oasis and carry back buckets of water. Thus, the inputs to the production of water are workers and buckets. The walk to the oasis and back takes one full day. Each worker can carry either 1 or 2 buckets of water but no more.

a. Draw some of LowTech's isoquants. With buckets renting for $1 a day and workers earning $2 per day, draw some of LowTech's isocosts. Draw the expansion path.

b. LowTech owns 5 buckets. It could rent these out to another firm at $1 per day, or it could rent additional buckets for $1 per day, but neither transaction could be arranged without some delay. Illustrate the following, using tables, graphs, or both: the total product and marginal product of labor; the short-run total cost, variable cost, average cost, average variable cost, and marginal cost; the long-run total cost, long-run average cost, and long-run marginal cost.

14. True or False: Diminishing marginal returns to labor need not imply decreasing returns to scale. However, increasing marginal returns to labor *would* imply increasing returns to scale.

15. True or False: If in agriculture there were increasing marginal returns to labor and constant returns to scale, then it would be possible for one farmer to feed the world from a flowerpot. (*Hint:* The inputs are labor and land. Start with one farmer and one full-size farm. Imagine the experiment of first doubling the number of workers, then halving both the number of workers and the amount of land.)

Internet Exercise

Access the Federal Reserve Bank of Minneapolis' Economics Challenge Playoff at the following site: (http://woodrow.mpls.frb.fed.us/econed/programs/chalque2.html). Work out answers to questions 5 and 6.

chapter 7

Competition

In the first chapter of this book we saw some of the power of supply and demand analysis. That analysis can be greatly strengthened and refined when we understand the sources of supply and demand. From that knowledge we can draw inferences about when supply and demand curves are likely to be more or less elastic, what will or will not cause them to shift, and when those shifts are likely to be relatively large or small.

Demand, as we saw in Chapter 4, arises from tastes. Supply, as we began to see in Chapter 5, arises from costs. In this chapter we will see exactly how information about costs can be used to derive the supply curves of a competitive firm and a competitive industry. We will study how prices and quantities are determined in such an industry and the circumstances under which those prices and quantities might change.

7.1 The Competitive Firm in the Short Run

Perfectly competitive firm One that can sell any quantity it wants to at some going market price.

A firm is said to be **perfectly competitive** if there is a market price at which consumers will buy whatever quantity the firm offers for sale. (Sometimes we abbreviate the phrase *perfectly competitive* to simply *competitive*.) The Tailor Dress Company, which we studied in Chapter 5, is not perfectly competitive because it faces a downward-sloping demand curve for its product. To increase sales, it must lower its price. A perfectly competitive firm, by contrast, faces a *horizontal* (infinitely elastic) demand curve, reflecting the fact that at the market price demanders will buy any quantity that the firm wants to sell.

This situation is most likely to occur when the firm is very small relative to its industry. No matter how much the firm produces, its productivity does not significantly affect the industry's total output. Therefore, there is no significant effect on the price at which that output can be sold.

To visit various U.S. wheat exchanges and markets visit the United States Department of Agriculture at: http://www.ams.usda.gov/lsg/mncs/ls_grain.htm

The best example to keep in mind is that of a wheat farmer, who provides a minuscule percentage of the wheat grown in the world. Regardless of whether he produces 10 bushels or 1,000, he remains too small to have any impact on the going market price. The demand curve for his wheat is horizontal, because the market will absorb whatever quantity he provides at the going price. If he tries to charge even a fraction of a penny more, he will sell no wheat, because buyers can just as easily buy from someone else. If he charges even a fraction of a penny less the public will demand more wheat than he can possibly produce—effectively, an infinite quantity.

Of course, the demand curve for *wheat* is still downward sloping; it is just the demand for *Farmer Adams's* wheat that is horizontal. To see how this can be, look at the two demand curves depicted in Exhibit 7–1. Notice in particular the units on the quantity axis. When Farmer Adams increases output from 1 bushel to 10 bushels, he is moving a long distance to the right on his quantity axis. At the same time he has moved the wheat industry a practically infinitesimal distance to the right, say from 10,000,000 bushels to 10,000,009 bushels. This tiny change in the industry's output requires essentially no change in price.

Farmer Adams's horizontal demand curve results from his being a very small part of a very large industry, in which all of the products produced are interchangeable and buyers can quite easily buy from another producer if Farmer

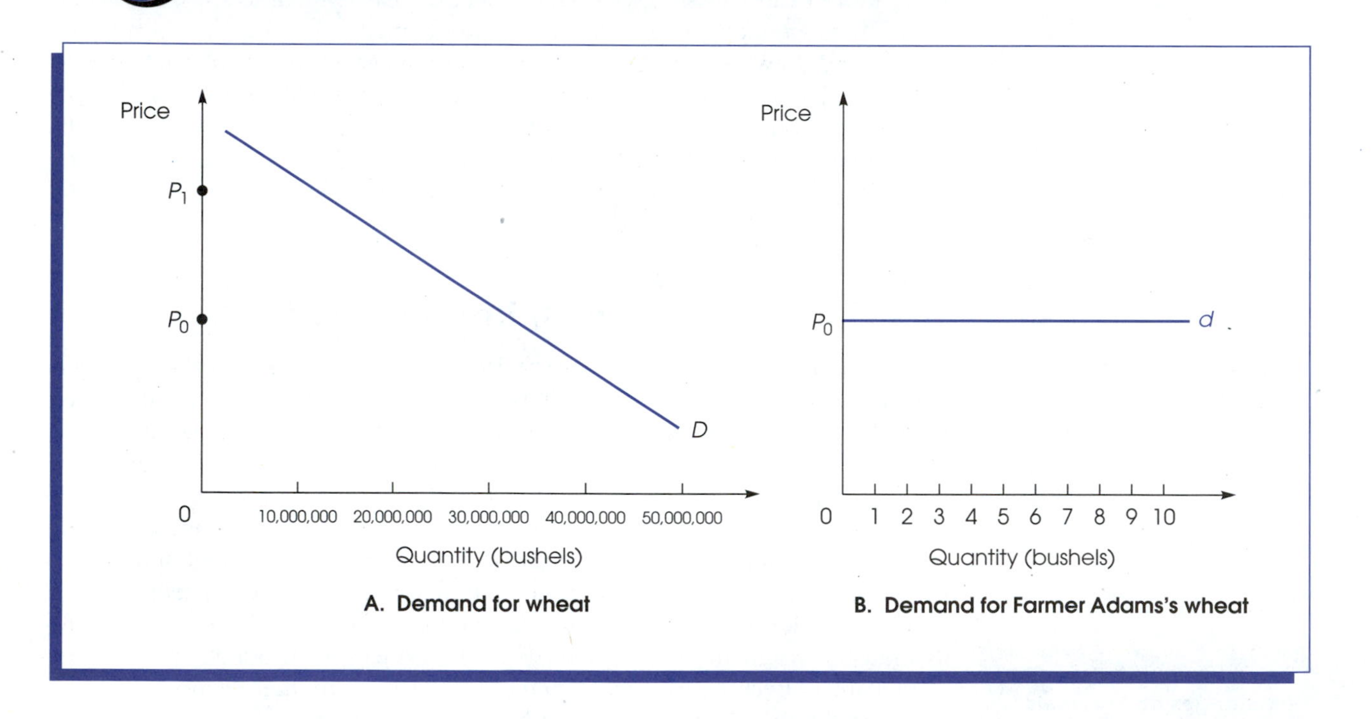

Panel A shows the downward-sloping demand curve for wheat. Panel B shows the horizontal demand curve for Farmer Adams's wheat. If the price of all wheat goes up from P_0 to P_1, consumers will buy less wheat. If the price of just Farmer Adams's wheat goes up from the market price of P_0 to P_1, consumers will buy none of it at all; they will shop elsewhere.

Adams tries to raise his price. All of these conditions tend to lead to perfect competition, but perfect competition can happen even without them. The only requirement for a firm to be called perfectly competitive is that the demand curve for its product be horizontal (for whatever reason).

Revenue

A perfectly competitive firm faces particularly simple total revenue and marginal revenue curves. If the going price for wheat is $5 per bushel, Farmer Adams's total revenue and marginal revenue are as shown in Exhibit 7–2.

Exhibit 7-2 **Total and Marginal Revenue at the Competitive Firm**

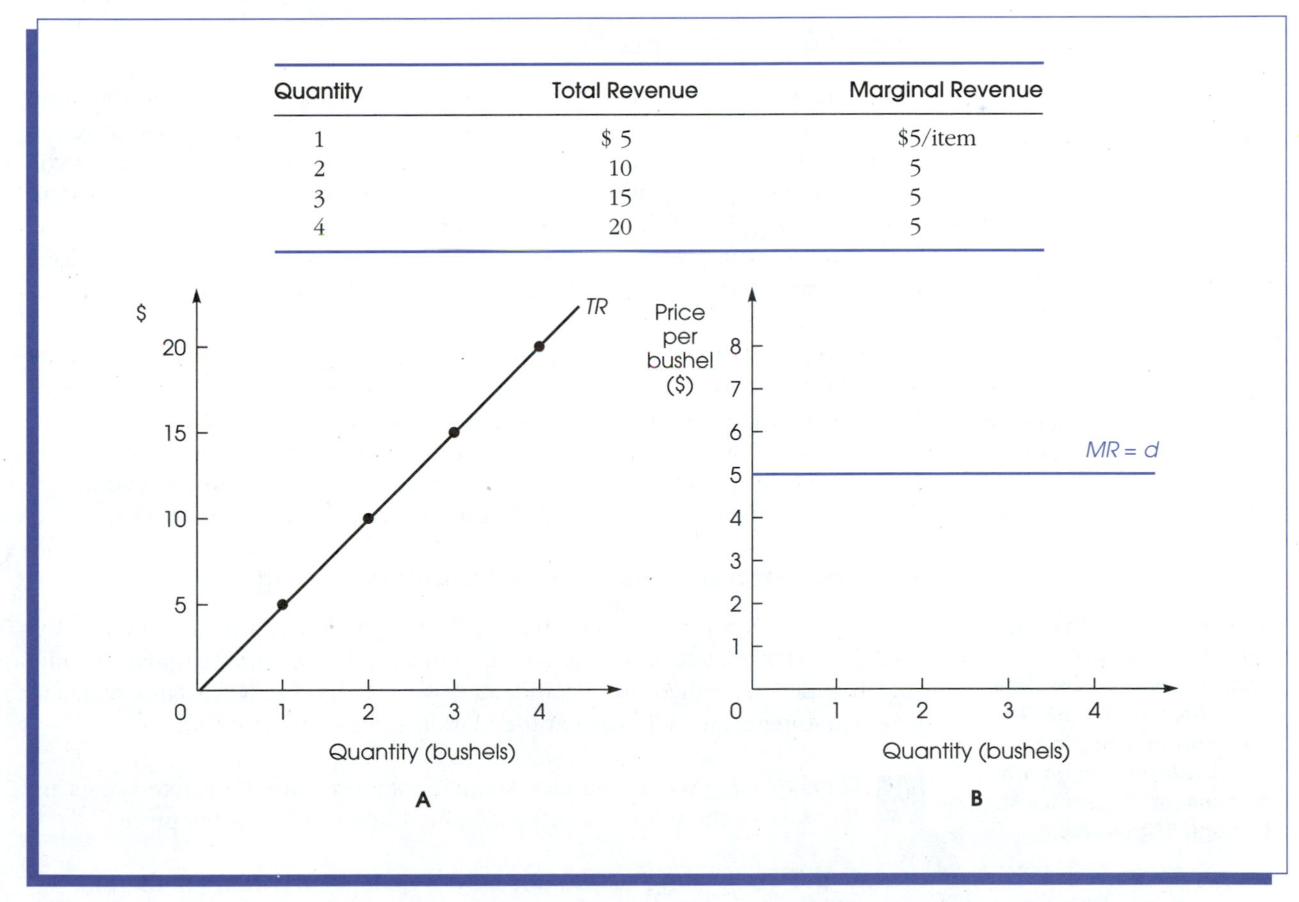

Quantity	Total Revenue	Marginal Revenue
1	$ 5	$5/item
2	10	5
3	15	5
4	20	5

If the going price of wheat is $5 per bushel, then Farmer Adams's total revenue is given by the equation $TR = \$5 \times Q$. The graph of this equation is a straight line through the origin. No matter what quantity he sells, his marginal revenue is $5 per bushel. The graph of marginal revenue is a horizontal line at $5, identical to the graph of the demand curve for Farmer Adams's wheat.

When Farmer Adams sells Q bushels of wheat, his total revenue is $\$5 \times Q$. The graph of this total revenue function is a straight line through the origin, shown in panel A of Exhibit 7–2.

Farmer Adams's marginal revenue is the same at every quantity; it is always equal to the going market price of $5 per bushel. Whenever he sells an additional bushel, he collects an additional $5. In general, for any competitive firm, we have the equation:

$$\text{Marginal revenue} = \text{Price}$$

Farmer Adams's marginal revenue curve is a horizontal line at the level of $5 per bushel. In other words, it looks exactly like the demand curve for Farmer Adams's wheat, which is also flat at the market price. The (identical) demand and marginal revenue curves are both shown in panel B of Exhibit 7–2.

The marginal revenue curve of a competitive firm is a horizontal line at the market price.

Short-Run Costs and Supply

We have seen in Chapter 6 that a firm's cost curves are different in the short run (when some factors of production are fixed) than they are in the long run (when all factors are variable). Consequently, the firm's supply responses will differ in the short run and the long run. Suppose that you run a pizza restaurant, employing both labor and pizza ovens. If the price of pizza goes up, you can increase your output in the short run by hiring more workers. In the long run you can build additional pizza ovens as well. In the long run you will produce more pizzas.

Short-run supply curve A curve that shows what quantity the firm will supply in the short run in response to any given price.

Long-run supply curve A curve that shows what quantity the firm will supply in the long run in response to any given price.

Therefore, we must distinguish two supply curves. For any given price, the **short-run supply curve** shows how the firm would respond to that price in the short run, and the **long-run supply curve** shows how the firm would respond to that price in the long run. In this section, we will concentrate on the firm's short-run behavior, returning to long-run considerations in Section 7.3. For this we must begin by considering the firm's short-run cost curves.

The Supply Decision when Marginal Cost Is Increasing

Access a slide show on quantity-setting at: (http://price.bus.okstate.edu/archive/Econ3113_963/Shows/Chapter8/index.htm). Click on the buttons for "Figure 8.4" through "Figure 8.6."

Suppose that Farmer Adams's (short-run) marginal costs are as shown in Exhibit 7–3. Maximizing profits by equating marginal cost with marginal revenue (in Chapter 5 we called this "Method 2"), we see that Farmer Adams wants to produce 4 items and sell them at the market price of $5 per item.

QA EXERCISE 7.1 What is Farmer Adams's total revenue? If his fixed costs are $2, what is the total cost of producing 4 items? What is his profit?

Any firm, competitive or not, chooses its quantity according to the rule:

$$\text{Marginal cost} = \text{Marginal revenue}$$

For a competitive firm the marginal revenue is equal to the market price. Thus,

Exhibit 7-3 The Optimum of the Competitive Firm

Quantity	Marginal Cost	Marginal Revenue
1	$2/item	$5/item
2	3	5
3	4	5
4	5	5
5	6	5
6	7	5

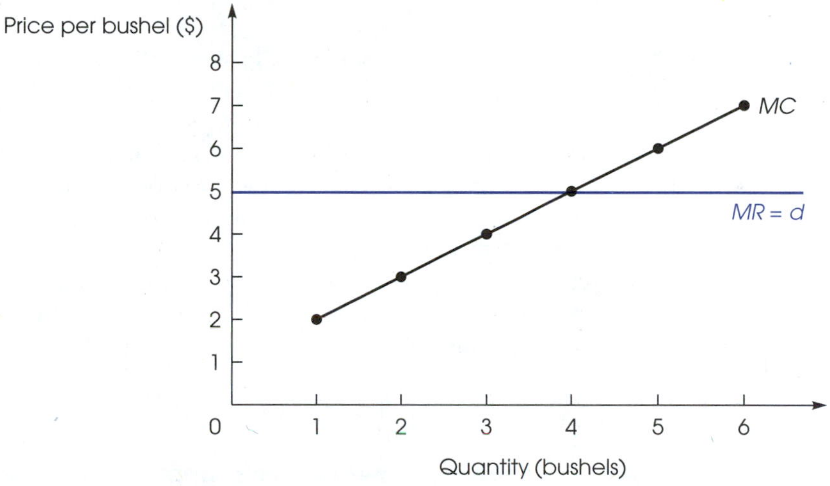

Farmer Adams, like any profit-maximizing producer (competitive or not), produces at the point where marginal cost equals marginal revenue. Because he is a competitive producer, Farmer Adams's marginal revenue curve is a horizontal line at the going market price. Thus, it is equally correct to say that he operates where marginal cost equals price. In this case he produces 4 bushels of wheat at the market price of $5 per bushel.

for a competitive firm (and only for a competitive firm) it is equally correct to say:

The competitive firm chooses its quantity according to the rule:

Marginal cost = Price

This rule for choosing quantities should make good intuitive sense. The firm faces a market price at which it can sell its goods. It produces goods as long as it can do so at a marginal cost that is lower than the market price. When marginal cost exceeds the market price, any additional items produced would subtract from the firm's profits. The time to stop producing is just before that happens, when the marginal cost of producing an item is exactly equal to the price at which that item can be sold.

Suppose that the market price of wheat were to rise to $6 a bushel. From the marginal cost curve in Exhibit 7–3, we see that Farmer Adams would now provide 5 bushels of wheat, the quantity at which marginal cost equals $6 per bushel. If the market price were to rise to $7, Farmer Adams would provide 6 bushels.

These facts are illustrated in Exhibit 7–4. Table A is Farmer Adams's marginal cost curve, reproduced from Exhibit 7–3. Table B shows the quantities Farmer Adams would produce at each price. We have already observed, and the graph illustrates, that at a price of $5 he would supply 4 bushels, at a price of $6 he would supply 5 bushels, and at a price of $7 he would supply 6 bushels. These observations are recorded in the last three rows of Table B. The other rows are deduced similarly.

QA EXERCISE 7.2 At a price of $4, how much wheat will Farmer Adams supply? Explain why.

At each given price, Table B tells us what quantity Farmer Adams will supply. We have a name for such a table. It is none other than Farmer Adams's supply schedule, and if we plot the same information on a graph we will get a picture of his supply curve!

In fact, we already have a picture of his supply curve. It is identical in appearance to his marginal cost curve, illustrated in Exhibit 7–4. The curves must be identical, because all of the numbers in Table B are the same as those in Table A.

Although Farmer Adams's supply and marginal cost curves appear identical, there is still an important conceptual difference between them. To use the marginal cost curve, you "input" a quantity (on the horizontal axis) and read off the corresponding marginal cost in dollars per item (on the vertical axis). To use the supply curve, you "input" a price (on the vertical axis) and read off the corresponding quantity (on the horizontal axis). The way to make this distinction mathematically precise is to say that marginal cost (*MC*) and supply (*S*) are *inverse functions*. In Exhibit 7-4, we have

$$MC\text{ (5 bushels)} = \$6\text{ per bushel}$$

and

$$S\text{ (\$6 per bushel)} = 5\text{ bushels.}$$

Notice that the marginal cost function *MC* is plotted just as it would be in a math class—with the input variable on the horizontal axis and the output variable on the vertical. By contrast, the supply function is plotted with the input on the vertical and the output on the horizontal—a reversal of the usual "math class" rules.

Exhibit 7-4 Marginal Cost and Supply

Table A		Table B	
Quantity	Marginal Cost	Price	Quantity
1	$2/item	$2/item	1
2	3	3	2
3	4	4	3
4	5	5	4
5	6	6	5
6	7	7	6

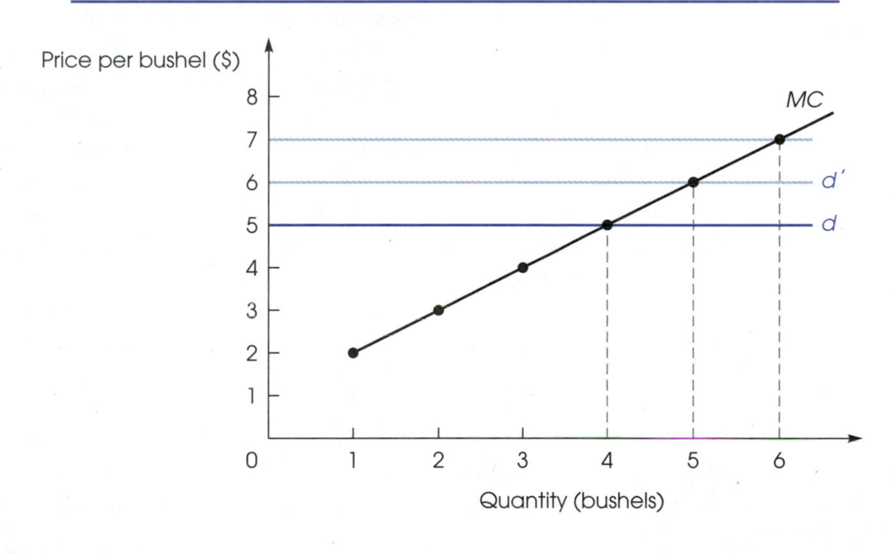

Table A is Farmer Adams's marginal cost schedule; the graph shows his marginal cost curve.

Table B shows the quantity Farmer Adams would supply at each price. Each entry is obtained by reading the marginal cost curve backward—we imagine a price, look for that price in the right-hand column of Table A (or on the vertical axis of the graph), and observe that the corresponding quantity is what Farmer Adams would produce at that price.

The horizontal lines in the graph represent hypothetical market prices of $5, $6, and $7. At these prices the quantities supplied, read off the marginal cost curve, are 4, 5, and 6. These are entered as the last three rows of Table B.

If we plot a graph of Farmer Adams's supply curve using the data points from Table B, it will look exactly like his marginal cost curve, because all of the numbers in Table B are the same as those in Table A.

Another thing you might recall from math class is that the graph of an inverse function is the *mirror image* (through a 45-degree line) of the graph of the original function. But the graph of the supply curve is mirror imaged a *second* time because of the reversal of the axes. Thus, the

supply curve is a *double* mirror image of the marginal cost curve (once because it is an inverse function and twice because it has the input on the vertical axis)—and a double mirror image looks exactly like the original. That's why the supply curve coincides with the marginal cost curve.

The Irrelevance of Fixed Costs

In the short run, fixed costs are unavoidable. As a result, they have no bearing on any economic decision.

Exhibit 7–5 shows the conditions on Farmer Adams's farm under two different assumptions about fixed costs. In the first example we assume fixed costs of \$2, and in the second example we assume fixed costs of \$20. In either case, he will produce at the point where marginal cost is equal to the market price of \$5; that is, he will produce 4 bushels of wheat.

In Example 1 Farmer Adams maximizes his profit at \$4; in Example 2, he maximizes it at −\$14. Even though −14 is a negative number (so that the farmer is suffering losses), Farmer Adams is still maximizing profits in the sense that any other level of output would lead to an even larger negative number.

A natural question now is this: In the second example wouldn't Farmer Adams quit farming altogether rather than continue to take losses? If we were examining his long-run behavior, the answer would be yes, but in the short run the answer is no. In the short run Farmer Adams is saddled with \$20 in fixed costs, which he cannot avoid even if he stops farming altogether. For example, the fixed factor of production might be the farm itself, leased on a yearly basis. Until the lease is up, there is nothing he can do about his fixed costs. If Farmer Adams decides not to plant crops at all, profits will be −\$20 instead of −\$14.

Because sunk costs are sunk, and because the firm's fixed costs are sunk in the short run, it follows that fixed costs are irrelevant to the firm's short-run supply decisions, including the decision about whether to shut down.

EXERCISE 7.3 Suppose that the price of wheat goes up to \$6 per bushel. Construct new tables to replace those in Exhibit 7–5. How much wheat will Farmer Adams produce, and what will his profit be, with fixed costs of \$2? With fixed costs of \$20?

The Supply Decision with a U-shaped Marginal Cost Curve

Farmer Adams has a marginal cost curve that is everywhere upward sloping. We saw in Chapter 6, however, that the firm's short-run marginal cost curve is typically U-shaped. We will now examine the supply decision for such a firm.

Exhibit 7–6 shows the U-shaped marginal cost curve of a competitive firm facing a market price of \$5. We know that such a firm, if it produces at all, will produce a quantity at which marginal cost and the market price are equal. We can see from the graph that there are two quantities at which this occurs: Q_1 and Q_2. Which will the firm choose?

Exhibit 7-5 The Irrelevance of Fixed Costs

Quantity	Total Revenue	Marginal Revenue	Total Cost	Marginal Cost	Profit
1 bushel	$ 5	$5/bu	$ 4	$2/bu	$1
2	10	5	7	3	3
3	15	5	11	4	4
4	20	5	16	5	4
5	25	5	22	6	3
6	30	5	29	7	1

Example 1: Fixed cost = $2

Quantity	Total Revenue	Marginal Revenue	Total Cost	Marginal Cost	Profit
1 bushel	$ 5	$5/bu	$22	$2/bu	−$17
2	10	5	25	3	−15
3	15	5	29	4	−14
4	20	5	34	5	−14
5	25	5	40	6	−15
6	30	5	47	7	−17

Example 2: Fixed cost = $20

In the first example we assume fixed costs of $2, and in the second example we assume fixed costs of $20. Marginal costs and marginal revenues are the same in each case. Consequently, optimal output is the same in each case: the quantity at which marginal cost equals marginal revenue, which is 4. In the first example the maximum attainable profit is $4, and in the second it is −$14, which is better than any of the alternatives.

Suppose that it produces Q_1 items. In that case it is possible to produce an additional item at a marginal cost that is less than the market price. This is because the marginal cost curve is downward sloping in the vicinity of Q_1. It follows that the firm can do better by producing another item. It continues producing as long as price exceeds marginal cost, and then stops; that is, it produces Q_2 items.

A competitive firm, if it produces at all, will always choose a quantity where price equals marginal cost *and* the marginal cost curve is upward sloping. Only the upward-sloping part of the marginal cost curve is relevant to the firm's supply decisions.

Exhibit 7-6 The Supply Decision with a U-Shaped Marginal Cost Curve

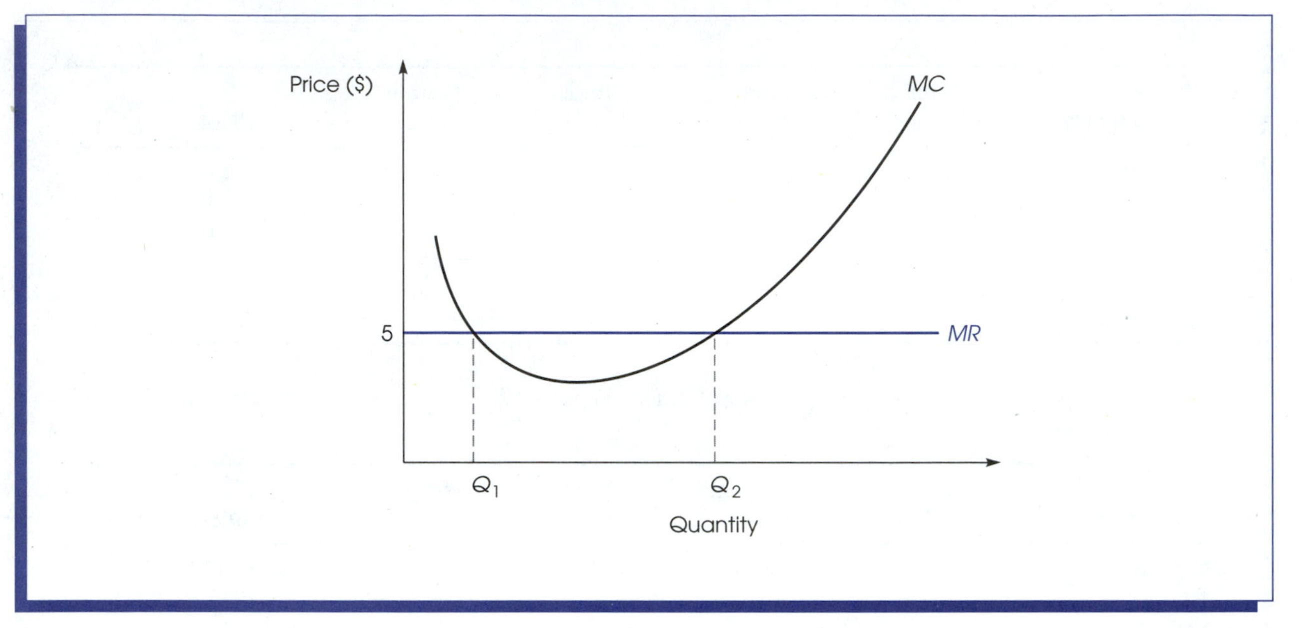

At a market price of $5 the firm produces Q_2 items (assuming it produces at all). It takes losses on the first Q_1 of these, all of which are produced at a marginal cost of more than $5, and it earns positive profits on the others. If those positive profits fail to outweigh the losses on the first Q_1 items, the firm will shut down.

The Shutdown Decision

We now know how much the firm will produce if it produces at all. We still must ask how the firm decides between remaining in operation and shutting down.[1]

In order to make this decision, the firm's owner must compare the profit to be earned from operating with the profit to be earned from shutting down. If the firm shuts down, it must still meet its fixed costs, while earning no revenue. Therefore, its profit is the negative number $-FC$, where FC stands for fixed costs. If the firm stays in business, producing a quantity Q, its profit is $TR - TC$, where TR is total revenue and TC is total cost. If $TR - TC$ is positive, it is certainly best to keep the business operating. Even if $TR - TC$ is negative, it might be better to operate than to shut down. The firm will want to operate if and only if

$$TR - TC > -FC$$

[1] We consider only temporary shutdowns, because we are considering only the short-run behavior of the firm. Permanent shutdowns (that is, exits from the industry) are usually treated as a long-run phenomenon.

Substituting the identity $TC = FC + VC$, this condition becomes

$$TR - FC - VC > -FC$$

or

$$TR > VC$$

The latter inequality should make good intuitive sense. Because the fixed costs of the firm are unavoidable in the short run, they are irrelevant to the decision of whether to shut down. The variable costs are the additional costs that the firm will incur if it continues to operate; they are avoidable and so are relevant to the shutdown decision. Staying in operation is a good idea precisely if the total revenue that the firm can earn outweighs these additional costs.

Remembering that $TR = P \cdot Q$ (P is price and Q is quantity), we can rewrite our inequality as

$$P \cdot Q > VC$$

Then if we divide each side by Q, the inequality becomes

$$P > AVC$$

In other words, the firm stays in operation if, after choosing the optimal quantity to produce, it finds that the price of output exceeds the average variable cost of production. We reiterate that only variable costs are relevant to the decision.

The Short-Run Supply Curve

A slide show on the short-run supply curve for a competitive firm is at: (http://price.bus.okstate.edu/archive/Econ3113_963/Shows/Chapter8/index.htm). Click on the buttons for "Figure 8.7" through "Short Run Supply."

In Exhibit 7–7 we see three possible market prices that a competitive firm might face. At a price of P_1, the firm produces a quantity of Q_1. At this quantity P_1 is greater than both average cost and average variable cost. The firm will stay in operation, producing Q_1 items and earning positive profits.

At a price of P_3, the firm's optimal output is Q_3. However, here the average variable cost of production exceeds P_3. Remaining in business would lead to a net reduction in profits, so the firm shuts down.

At a price of P_2, the firm's optimal output is Q_2. Here the average variable cost is less than P_2, so the firm stays in business. However, the average cost of production (including fixed costs) is *greater* than P_2, so the firm's profits are negative. Nevertheless, the firm loses less by continuing to produce than it would by shutting down.

Shutdown price The output price below which the firm could no longer cover its average variable costs and would therefore shut down.

The price P at which the marginal cost curve crosses the average variable cost curve is called the **shutdown price** of the firm. It is shown in Exhibit 7–8. When price is above the shutdown price, the firm produces a quantity read off the marginal cost curve. At prices lower than the shutdown price, the firm shuts down and produces nothing.

We conclude that:

The competitive firm's short-run supply curve is identical to that part of its marginal cost curve that lies above its average variable cost curve.

Exhibit 7-7 The Competitive Firm's Supply Responses

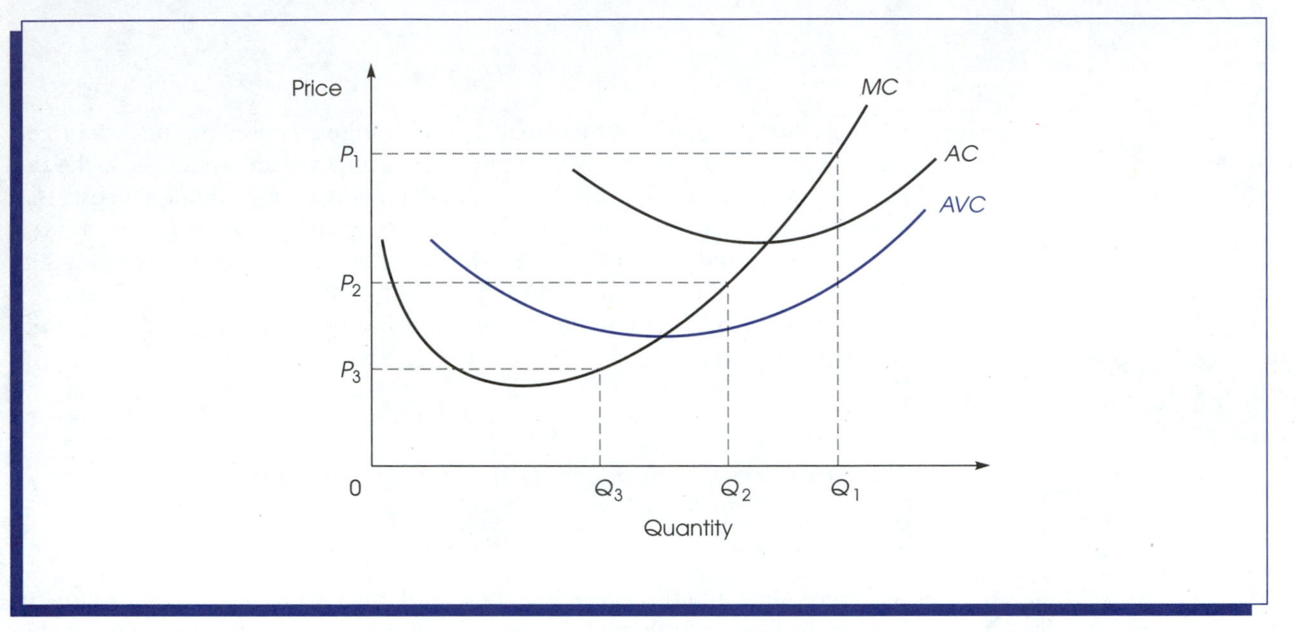

At price P_1, optimal output is Q_1. At Q_1, the average cost of production is less than P_1, so the firm earns positive profits.

At price P_3, the quantity Q_3 equates price with marginal cost. However, at this quantity the average variable cost is greater than the price P_3. Therefore, it is best for the firm to shut down.

At price P_2, optimal output is Q_2. Here the price exceeds average variable cost, so the firm earns more by producing than it does by shutting down. However, the price is less than average cost, so the firm is earning negative profits.

In Exhibit 7–8 this is the heavy portion of the marginal cost curve. A more complete description of the short-run supply curve is that it consists of two disconnected pieces, namely the two heavy segments in Exhibit 7–8.

Why Supply Curves Slope Up

When the competitive firm's marginal cost curve is U-shaped, its supply curve consists of that part of the marginal cost curve that lies above average variable cost. Since the marginal cost curve cuts the average variable cost curve from below, the entire supply curve is upward sloping.

To the question "Why do supply curves slope up?" we can answer "Because average and marginal cost curves are U-shaped." This is correct, but it raises another question: Why are the cost curves U-shaped? The answer, as we saw in Chapter 6, is that this is a consequence of diminishing marginal returns to the variable factors of production.

The technological fact of diminishing marginal returns suffices to account for the upward-sloping supply curves of competitive firms.

Exhibit 7-8 The Competitive Firm's Short-Run Supply Curve

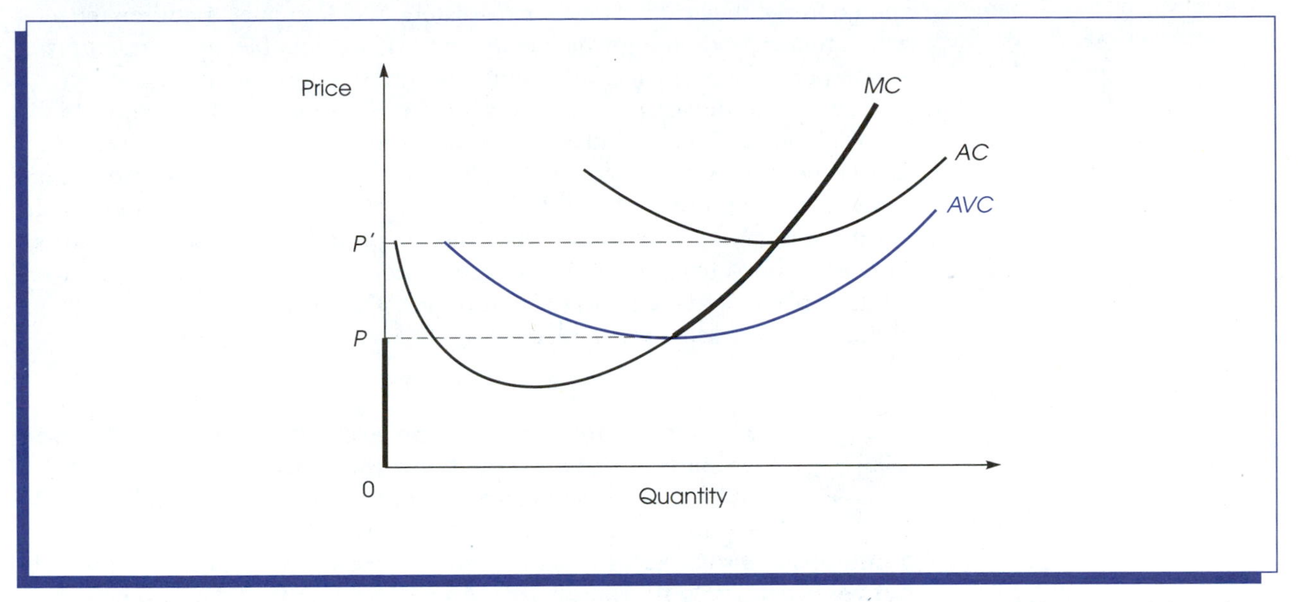

At prices below the shutdown price P, the firm cannot cover its variable costs and shuts down, producing zero output. At prices above P, it produces the quantity that equates price with marginal cost; this quantity can be read off the marginal cost curve. Thus, the two heavy segments constitute the firm's short-run supply curve. At prices above P', the price of an item exceeds the average cost of production, so the firm earns positive profits. At prices below P', profits are negative.

The Elasticity of Supply

Elasticity of supply The percentage change in quantity supplied resulting from a 1% increase in price.

We can compute the **elasticity of supply** at a firm using the same formula that we use to compute the elasticity of demand:

$$\text{Elasticity} = \frac{\text{Percentage change in quantity}}{\text{Percentage change in price}}$$

$$= \frac{100 \cdot \Delta Q/Q}{100 \cdot \Delta P/P}$$

$$= \frac{P \cdot \Delta Q}{Q \cdot \Delta P}$$

The elasticity of supply is positive because an increase in price brings forth an increase in the quantity supplied. Given two supply curves through the same point, the flatter one has the higher elasticity.

7.2 The Competitive Industry in the Short Run

Competitive industry An industry in which all firms are competitive and any firm can freely enter or exit.

A **competitive industry** is one in which all firms are competitive and in which firms can freely enter or exit from the industry. But although firms can come and go freely, they cannot do so immediately. We distinguish between the *long run*, a time period during which entry and exit are possible, and the *short run*, a time period during which the number of firms cannot change.

How long is the long run and how short is the short run? It depends. In the sidewalk flower vending industry, the short run is very short indeed (at least if there is no waiting time for a vendor's license). The time that it takes to acquire some flowers and walk down to the corner, or for an existing vendor to sell out his stock and go home, is already the long run. By contrast, when Eastern Airlines stopped flying in 1991, it began the lengthy process of finding buyers for its airplanes and the rights to fly its routes. The long run does not arrive until this exiting process is complete.

It is important not to confuse an *exit* with a *shutdown*. As soon as Eastern stopped flying, it had shut down, but as long as it remained in possession of valuable capital it had still not left the industry. When a firm shuts down, it stops producing but continues to incur fixed costs (in Eastern's case, the opportunity cost of not yet having sold its equipment). An exit implies that the firm has divested itself of all its fixed costs and thereby severed all of its ties with the industry. Shutdowns are a short-run phenomenon; exits are long-run.

In Section 7.1 we studied the firm's short-run supply curve. In this section we will study the industry's short-run supply curve. We will examine short-run competitive equilibrium and the interplay between the supply and demand curves for the industry and the supply and demand curves for the firm. This will enable us to understand how firms in a competitive industry react to changes in things like taxes, demand, costs, and the like.

The Short-Run Supply Curve of the Competitive Industry

For more on "Industry Supply Curve" visit David Friedman's Internet textbook at: http://www.best.com/~ddfr/Academic/Price_Theory/PThy_Chapter_9/PThy_Chapter_9.html

In the short run, entry and exit are not possible, so the number of firms in the industry is fixed. Given the short-run supply curves of the individual firms, we add them to construct the short-run supply curve for the entire industry. At a given price, we ask what quantities each of the firms will provide; then we add these numbers to get the quantity supplied by the industry.

Because different firms have different cost curves, different firms have different shut-down prices. Therefore, the number of firms in operation tends to be small at low prices and large at high prices. As a result, the industry supply curve tends to be more elastic than the supply curves of the individual firms. This can be seen in Exhibit 7–9. Here firms A, B, and C have the individual supply curves shown. At price P_1, only firm A produces, so the quantity supplied by the industry is the same as the quantity supplied by firm A. At the higher price P_2, firm B produces as well, and the industry supplies the sum of firm A's output and firm B's output. (In fact, firm A produces 2½ units and firm B produces 4½, for an industry total of 7.) At prices high enough for firm C to produce, industry output is correspondingly greater.

EXERCISE 7.4 At price P_3, how much does each firm produce? How much does the industry produce?

The industry supply curve in Exhibit 7–9 jumps rightward each time it passes a firm's shutdown price. In an industry with many firms, the effect of this is to greatly flatten the industry supply curve relative to those of the individual firms.

The Factor-Price Effect

Factor-price effect The effect that an expansion of industry output has on the price of a factor of production, thereby raising marginal costs in the industry.

We have said that the supply curve of a competitive industry is obtained by adding the supply curves of the individual firms. It is sometimes necessary to modify this statement to take account of the **factor-price effect.** This occurs when the industry in question represents a substantial fraction of the demand for the variable factor of production. For example, the steel industry represents a substantial fraction of the demand for iron. In this case, a rise in the price of output causes an increase in production, which raises the industry's demand

Exhibit 7–9 The Industry Supply Curve

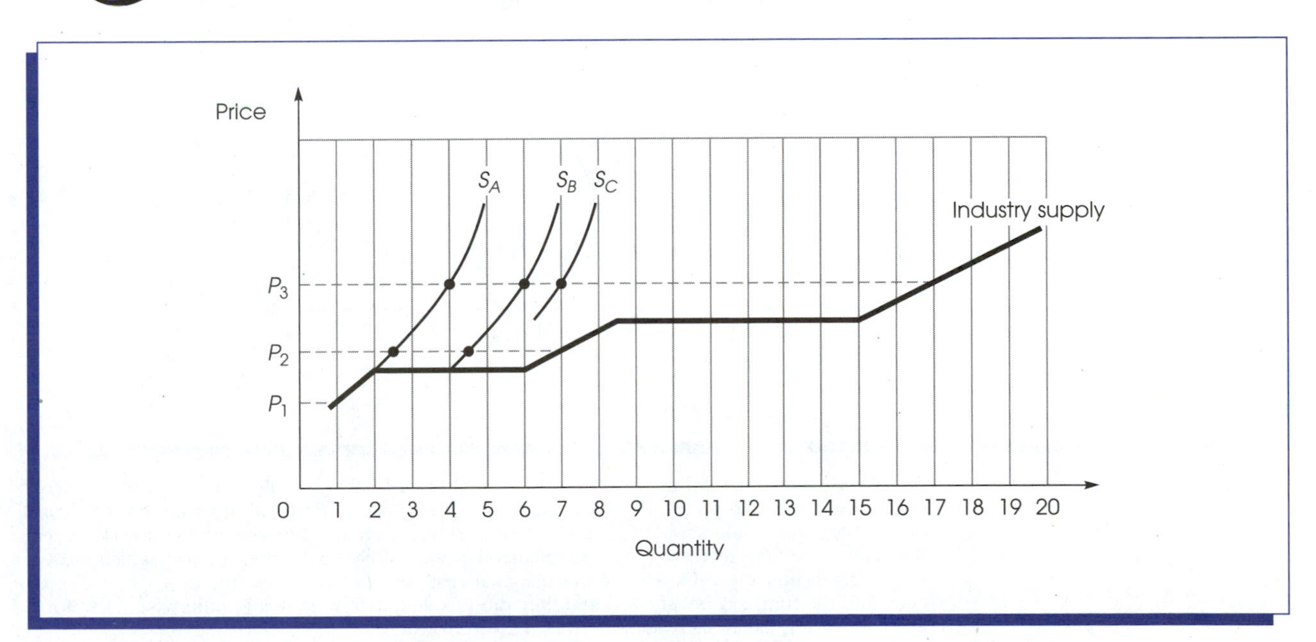

As the price goes up, two things happen. First, each firm that is producing increases its output. Second, firms that were not previously producing start up their operations. As a result, industry output increases more rapidly than that of any given firm, so the industry supply curve is more elastic than that of any given firm.

for the variable factor. Because this is a significant fraction of overall demand for the variable factor, that factor's price goes up. This factor-price increase raises the marginal cost curve of every firm in the industry, causing them to produce less than they otherwise would have.

In the presence of a factor-price effect, a rise in price will increase industry output, but by less than you might think if you naively added the individual firms' supply curves. Similarly, a fall in price will decrease industry output, but by less than might naively be expected.

EXERCISE 7.5 Explain carefully what happens to industry output when there is a factor-price effect and the output price falls.

Exhibit 7–10 contrasts the sum of the individual firms' supply curves with the industry supply curve in the presence of a factor-price effect. The factor-price effect tends to make the industry supply curve steeper (less elastic) than it would otherwise be.

Exhibit 7-10 The Factor-Price Effect

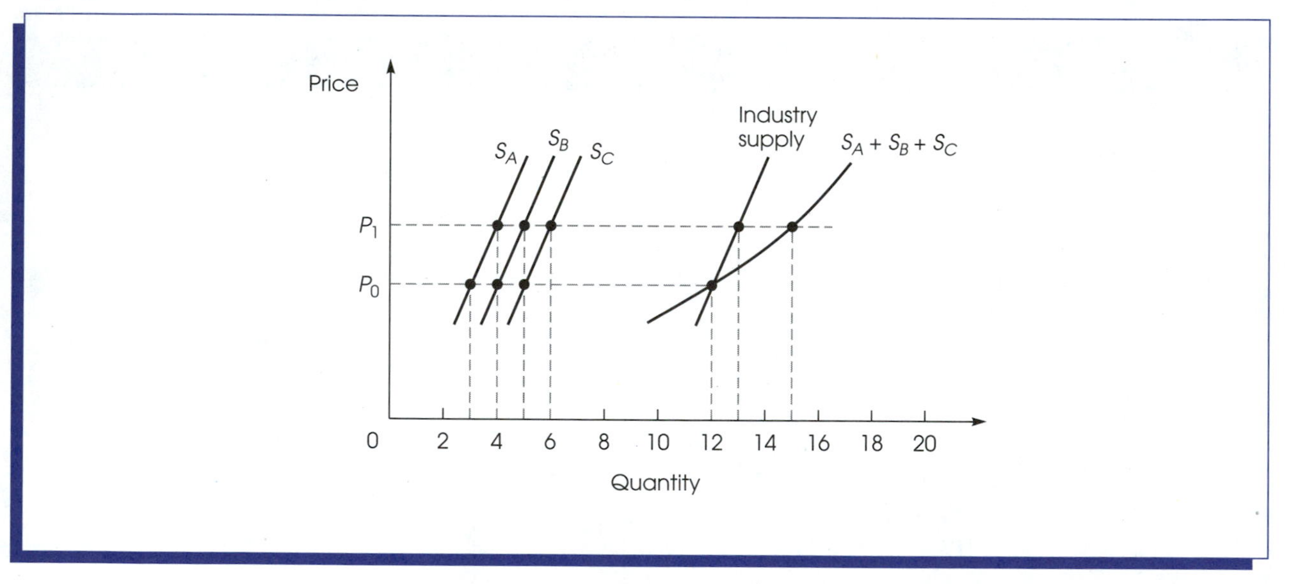

Firms A, B, and C are steel producers. At the current price P_0, they supply 3, 4, and 5 tons of steel, so that the industry supplies 12 tons. If the price were to rise to P_1, then under current cost conditions the firms would supply 4, 5, and 6 tons of steel for an industry total of 15 tons. However, when all of the firms increase output simultaneously, they drive up the price of iron, which is used in making steel. As a result, each firm's marginal cost curve moves back (the new marginal cost curves of the firms are not shown) and they produce less than they would otherwise. Therefore, at a price of P_1, the industry supplies only 13 tons instead of 15.

There is a factor-price effect when the industry in question represents a substantial fraction of the demand for one of its inputs. It causes the industry supply curve to be less elastic than the sum of the individual firm's supply curves.

Supply, Demand, and Equilibrium

In Chapter 5 we learned that any supplier, if he produces at all, chooses to operate where marginal cost is equal to marginal revenue. In Section 7.1 we learned that for a competitive producer the marginal revenue curve is the same as the demand curve, and, in the region where he produces at all, the marginal cost curve is the same as the supply curve. Therefore, we can just as well say that a competitive supplier chooses to operate at the point where supply is equal to demand.

In an industry in which all of the firms are competitive, each firm operates where supply equals demand, and so the industry-wide supply (which is the sum of the individual firms' supplies) must equal the industry-wide demand (which is the sum of the demands from the individual firms). In other words, such an industry will be at equilibrium, simply as a consequence of optimizing behavior on the part of individuals and firms.

In Chapter 1 we gave some "plausibility arguments" for the notion that in many industries prices and quantities would be determined by the intersection of supply and demand. Now we have a much stronger reason to believe the

Exhibit 7-11 The Competitive Industry and the Competitive Firm

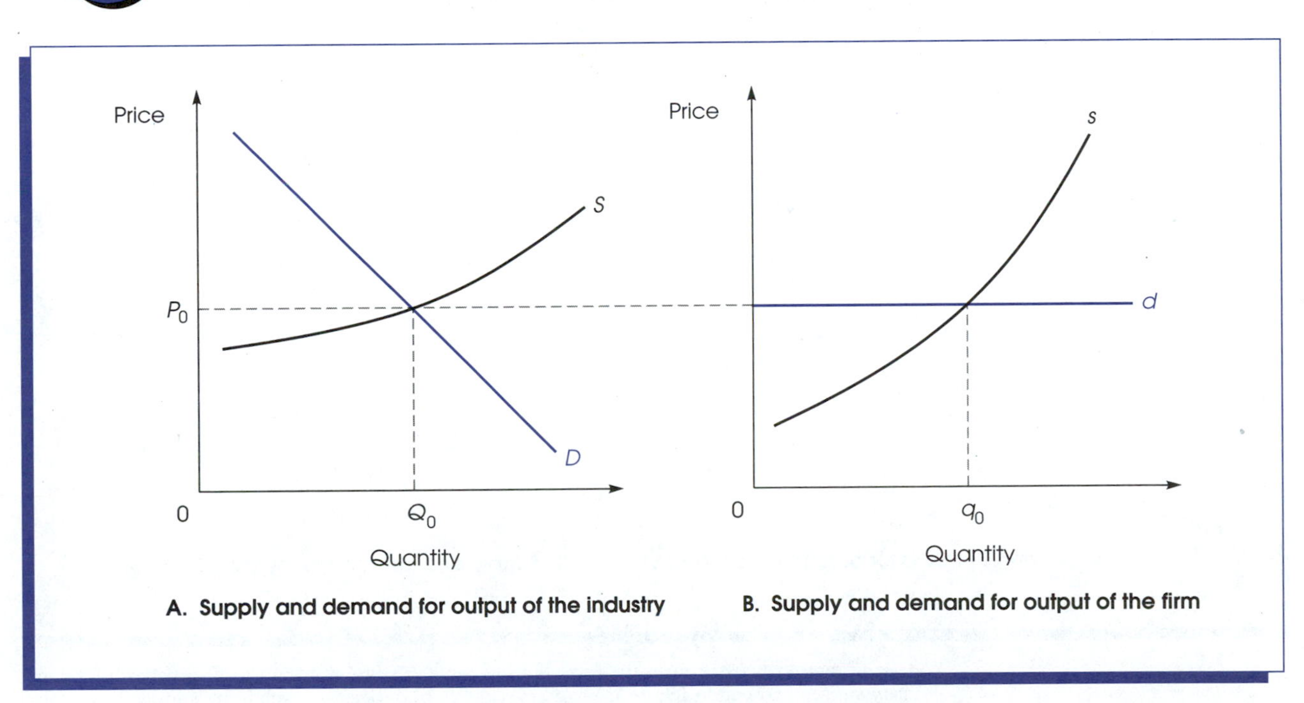

The equilibrium price P_0 is determined by the intersection of the industry's supply curve with the downward-sloping demand curve for the industry's product. The firm faces a horizontal demand curve at this going market price and chooses the quantity q_0 accordingly. The industry-wide quantity Q_0 is the sum of the quantities supplied by all the firms in the industry.

same thing. If an industry is competitive, profit-maximizing firms will be led to the equilibrium outcome—as if by an invisible hand.

Competitive Equilibrium

Exhibit 7–11 illustrates the relationship between the competitive industry and the competitive firm. The industry faces a downward-sloping demand curve for its product. The price P_0 is determined by industry-wide equilibrium, and this same price P_0 is what appears to the individual firm as the "going market price," at which it faces a flat demand curve. The firm then produces the quantity q_0, at which its supply curve S (that is, its marginal cost curve) crosses the horizontal line at P_0.

Exhibit 7-12 A Rise in Marginal Costs

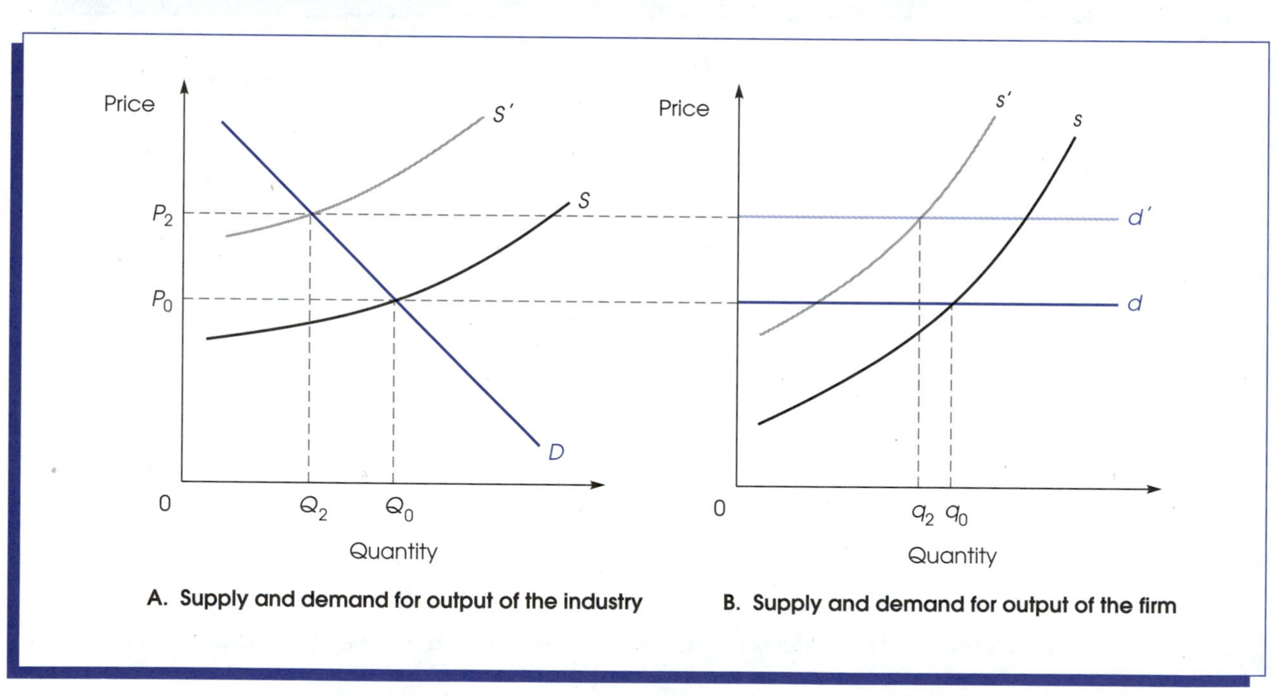

A rise in marginal costs causes the firm's supply curve to shift left from s to s' in panel B. The industry supply curve shifts left from S to S' in panel A, both because each firm's supply curve does and because some firms may shut down. The new market price is P_2. The firm operates at the intersection of s' with its new horizontal demand curve at P_2. Depending on how the curves are drawn, the firm could end up producing either more or less than it did before the rise in costs. (That is, q_2 could be either to the left or to the right of q_0.)

Changes in Fixed Costs

Now we can investigate the effect of a change in costs. Suppose, first, that there is a rise in fixed costs, such as a general increase in the cost of large machinery or a new licensing fee for the industry. What happens to an individual firm's supply curve? Nothing, because marginal cost is unchanged. What about the industry's supply curve? It remains unchanged also, because industry supply is the sum of the individual firms' supplies and these remain fixed. Thus, no curves shift in Exhibit 7–11, so both price and quantity remain unchanged.

This analysis is correct and complete in the short run. However, we will see in Sections 7.5 and 7.6 that in the long run there is more to be said. The reason for this is that in the long run any increase in costs can drive firms from the industry; their exit can then affect prices and quantities.

A Change in Marginal Costs

Next consider the case of a rise in marginal costs, such as a rise in the price of raw materials or the imposition of an excise tax. This immediately raises each firm's marginal cost curve and also causes some firms to shut down. The industry supply curve moves leftward for both of these reasons, and we get a new market equilibrium price of P_2, shown in Exhibit 7–12. Depending on the shapes of the curves, the individual firm's output could go either up or down.

EXERCISE 7.6 Draw graphs illustrating the effect of a fall in marginal costs.

Changes in Demand

Exhibit 7–13 illustrates the effect of an increase in the demand for the industry's product. The new market equilibrium price of P_3 is taken as given by the firm, which increases its output to q_3.

EXERCISE 7.7 Draw graphs illustrating the effect of a fall in demand for the industry's product.

The Industry's Costs

In the short run the competitive industry consists of a fixed number of firms. These firms collectively produce some quantity of output. The total cost of producing that output is the sum of the total costs of all the individual firms.

Suppose that you were appointed the czar of U.S. agriculture and given the power to tell each farmer how much to produce. You would like to maintain the production of wheat at its current level of 1 million bushels per year, but you would like to do this in such a way as to minimize the total costs of the industry. How would you go about this?

The equimarginal principle points the way to the answer. Suppose that the marginal cost of growing wheat is \$5 per bushel at Farmer Black's farm and \$3 per bushel at Farmer White's. Then here is something clever you can do: Order Black to produce one less bushel and White to produce one more. In that way, the industry's total cost is reduced by $2, and the level of output is maintained. You should continue to do this until the marginal costs of production are just equal at both farms.

Indeed, as long as any two farms have differing marginal costs, you can use this trick to reduce total costs. Total costs are not minimized until marginal cost is the same at every farm.

Now, the miracle: In competitive equilibrium, every farmer chooses to produce a quantity at which price equals marginal cost. Since all farmers face the same market price, it follows that all farmers have the same marginal cost. From this we have the following result:

In competitive equilibrium, the industry automatically produces at the lowest possible total cost.

Students sometimes think that this result follows from firms' attempts to minimize their costs. But no firm has any interest in the costs of the industry as a whole. The minimization of

Exhibit 7-13 A Change in Demand

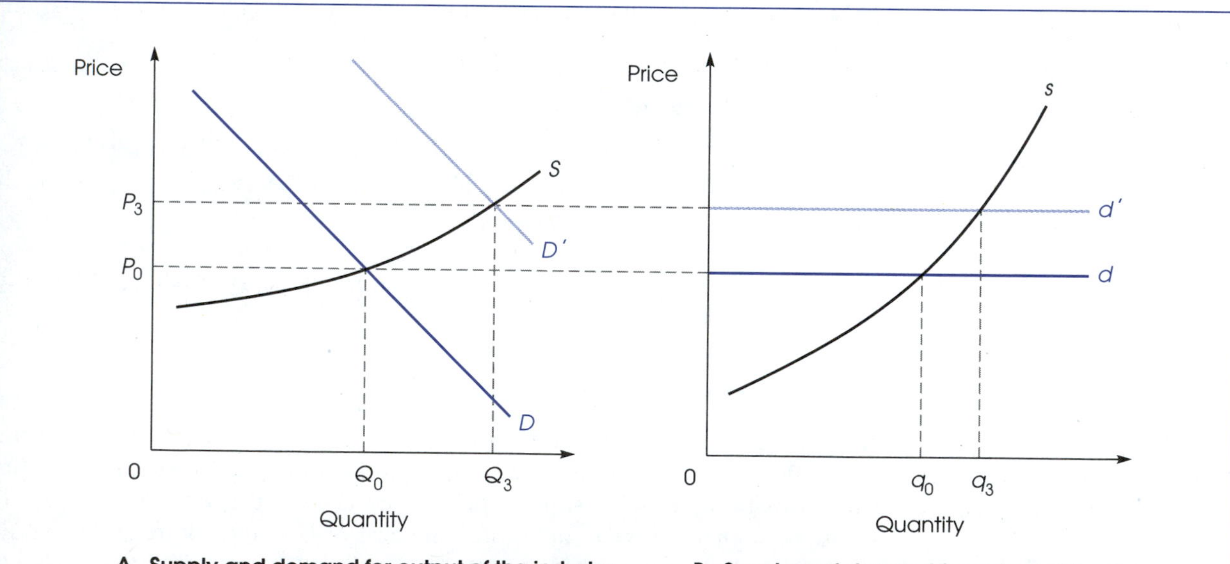

An increase in the demand for the industry's output raises the equilibrium price to P_3 and the firm's output to q_3.

industry-wide costs is a feature of competitive equilibrium that is not sought by any individual firm.

What is the marginal cost to the industry of producing a unit of output? You might think that this question is unanswerable, because the industry consists of many firms, each with its own marginal cost curve. How are we to decide which firm to think of as producing the "last" unit of output in the industry?

The answer to the last question is that it doesn't matter. We have just seen that in competitive equilibrium, the cost of producing the last unit of output is the same at every firm. That cost is the industry's marginal cost of production.

At each point along its supply curve, the competitive industry produces a quantity that equates price with marginal cost. Therefore, the industry's supply curve is identical to the industry's marginal cost curve, just as each individual firm's supply curve can be identified with its own marginal cost curve.

7.3 The Competitive Firm in the Long Run

Long-Run Costs and Supply

In the long run, the firm wants to operate at a point where Price = Marginal cost, for all of the same reasons that it wants to do so in the short run. The only difference is that in the long run it is long-run marginal cost rather than short-run marginal cost that matters. So just as the firm's short-run supply curve coincides with its short-run marginal cost curve, its long-run supply curve coincides with its long-run marginal cost curve.

In the long run, the firm has the option to leave the industry if its profits are negative, which happens when the price of output falls below the average cost of production. Therefore, the part of the long-run marginal cost curve that lies below long-run average cost is not part of the firm's supply curve. Exhibit 7–14 shows the picture.

The competitive firm's long-run supply curve is identical to that part of its long-run marginal cost curve that lies above its long-run average cost curve.

Comparing Short-Run and Long-Run Supply Response

A restaurant produces hamburgers, using inputs that include ground beef, short-order cooks, and kitchen grills. How does this restaurant respond to a rise in the price of hamburgers? In the short run, it can increase quantity by purchasing more beef and hiring more cooks. The resulting quantity of hamburgers is recorded on the short-run supply curve.

In the long run, however, the restaurant might decide to expand its operation by purchasing more grills. Typically, this means that quantity increases by more in the long run than it does in the short run. In other words, the long-run supply curve is more elastic than the short-run supply curve.

Exhibit 7–15 shows the picture. The restaurant has sold hamburgers at a going price of P_0 for a long time, and has thus adjusted the number of grills so

Exhibit 7-14 The Competitive Firm's Long-Run Supply Curve

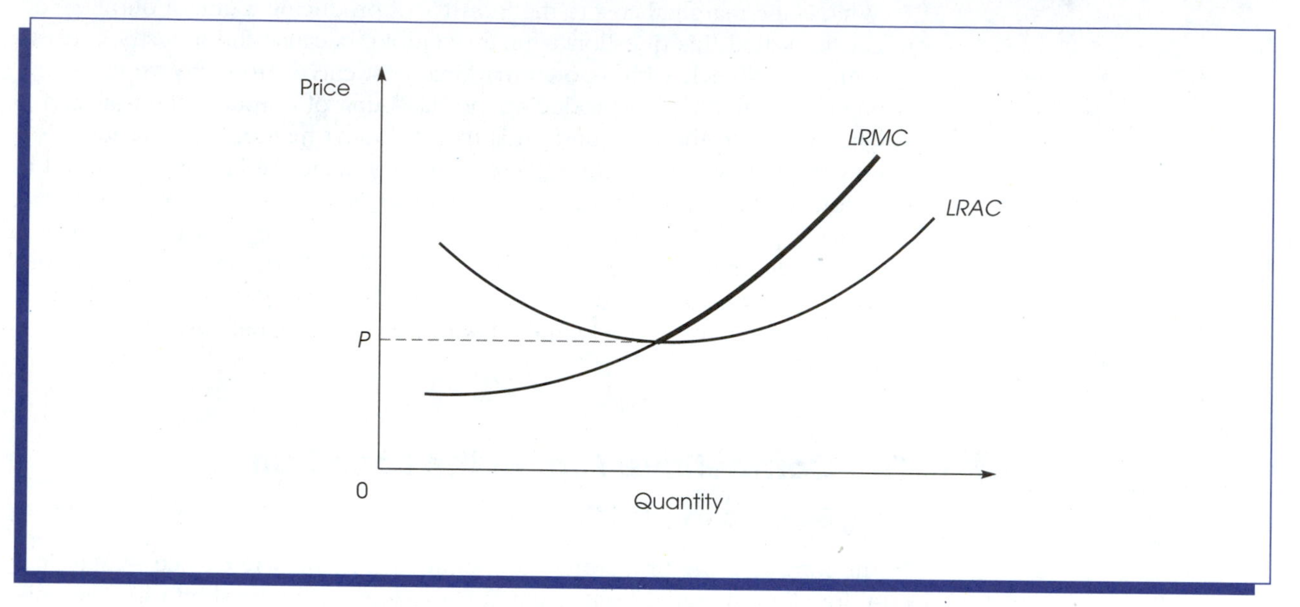

Unless the price is high enough to cover all of its costs, the firm will leave the industry in the long run. Therefore, the long-run supply curve is that portion of the long-run marginal cost curve that lies above the long-run average cost curve. At prices below *P*, the firm leaves the industry and produces zero.

as to produce Q_0 hamburgers at the lowest possible cost. The quantity Q_0 can be read from the long-run supply curve. Since the kitchen hardware is all in place, Q_0 is the quantity read from the short-run supply curve as well.

Now suppose that the price rises to P_1. In the short run, with the number of grills fixed, quantity rises to Q_1, which we can read off the short-run supply curve. In the long run, after the facilities are expanded, quantity rises further, to Q_1'. With its expanded kitchen equipment, the firm has a new short-run marginal cost curve and hence a new short-run supply curve, called S' in the exhibit. Notice that S' must go through the new supply point at (P_1, Q_1').

7.4 An Introduction to the Competitive Industry in the Long Run

Understanding the competitive industry means understanding the interactions among four curves: supply and demand at the industry level and supply and demand at the firm level. We already have good long-run theories for three of those curves: Industry-wide demand is derived from individual tastes as in Chapter 4; the firm's supply curve coincides with (a part of) its long-run marginal cost curve; and the demand curve for the firm's product is flat at the going market price. That leaves the industry supply curve. Our immediate problem is to understand that curve.

Exhibit 7-15 Long-Run and Short-Run Supply Responses

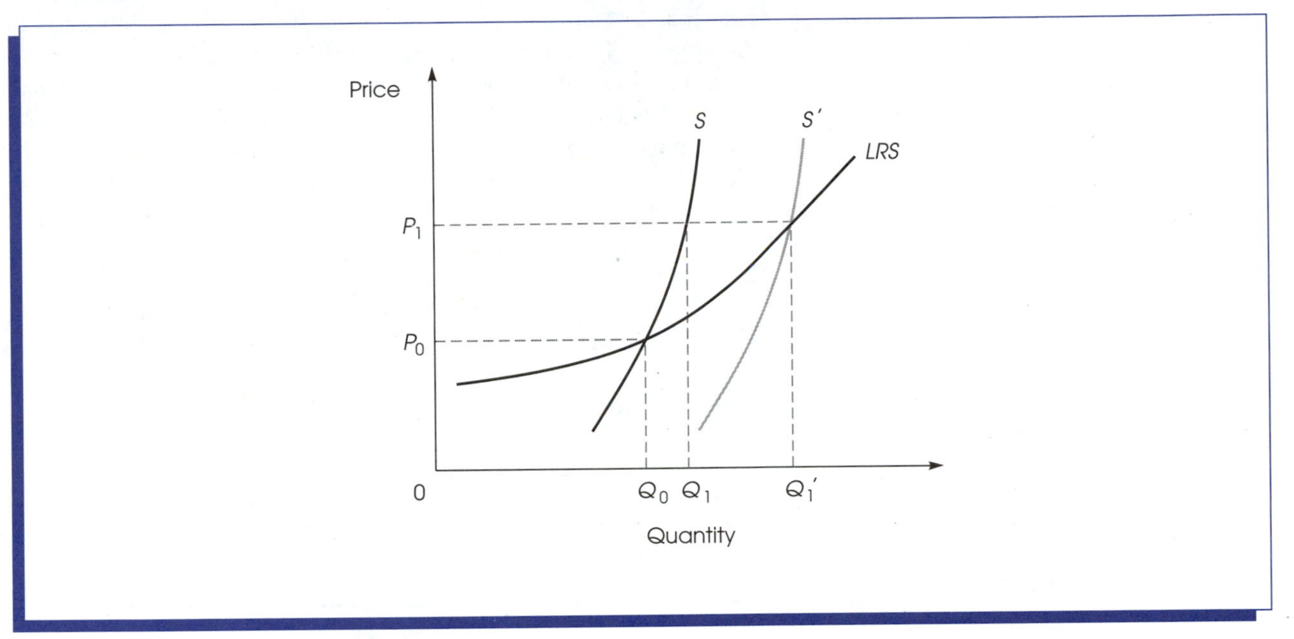

In long-run equilibrium at P_0, the firm is on both its long-run and short-run supply curves. A change in price, to P_1, has the immediate effect of causing the firm to move along its short-run supply curve S to the quantity Q_1'. In the long run, the firm can vary its plant capacity (for example, a hamburger stand can install more grills) and move along its long-run supply curve *LRS* to Q_1'. With the new plant capacity, the firm has a new short-run supply curve S'. In the new equilibrium at price P_1 and quantity Q_1, the firm is again on both its long-run and short-run supply curves.

In the short run, we derived the industry supply curve by adding up the supply curves of individual firms. In the long run we can't do that because it ignores the effects of entry and exit. It makes no sense to add supply curves from "all the firms" when firms are constantly appearing and disappearing.

To account for entry and exit, a good theory of long-run industry supply must account for the *cause* of entry and exit, namely profits. Firms enter an industry when there is an opportunity to earn a positive profit, and they exit when their profits are negative. So the first thing we have to understand is profit.

Profit

Profit equals revenue minus cost. When you use this definition, remember to use the word *cost* in its economic sense, to include forgone opportunities.

Accounting Profit versus Economic Profit

Every day, Bert the newspaper carrier buys 100 newspapers at 15¢ apiece and sells them for a quarter. Every day, his identical twin brother Ernie buys 100 cups of lemonade at 5¢ apiece and sells them for a dime at his lemonade stand.

If Bert and Ernie ask their accountant to calculate their profits, here's what he'll tell them: Bert has $25 in revenue (from selling 100 newspapers at 25¢ apiece) and $15 in costs (from buying 100 newspapers at 15¢ apiece). Therefore his profit is $25 − $15 = $10. Ernie has revenue of $10 (from selling 100 cups of lemonade at 10¢ apiece) and costs of $5 (from buying 100 cups of lemonade at 5¢ apiece). Therefore his profit is $10 − $5 = $5.

But if Bert and Ernie ask an economist—rather than an accountant—to calculate their profits, they'll get very different answers. The economist will point out that by delivering newspapers, Bert passed up an opportunity to earn $5 by running a lemonade stand like Ernie's. That forgone opportunity is a cost, which must be subtracted from Bert's profit. So according to the economist, Bert's profit is not $10, but only $5.

The recalculation of Ernie's profits is even more depressing. To earn $5 at his lemonade stand, Ernie passed up an opportunity to earn $10 delivering newspapers. Subtracting that cost, the economist calculates that Ernie's profit is *minus* $5.

Let's summarize all these calculations in a table:

	Bert's Profit	Ernie's Profit
Accountant's Calculation	$10	$5
Economist's Calculation	$5	$(−5)

Although their calculations differ, the economist and the accountant agree on the one crucial point: Bert earned more profit than Ernie. If your skills are identical to Bert and Ernie's, and you're looking for advice on how to maximize your profits, the accountant and the economist will both give you the same advice: start a paper route like Bert's, not a lemonade stand like Ernie's.

Accounting profit Total revenue minus those costs that an accountant would consider.

Economic profit Total revenue minus all costs, including the opportunity cost of being in another industry.

To avoid confusion, we sometimes speak of the difference between **accounting profit** and **economic profit**. Accounting profit is total revenue minus those costs that an accountant would consider. Economic profit is total revenue minus *all* costs, including the opportunity cost of being in another industry.

When noneconomists use the word *profit*, they usually mean accounting profit. But in an economics course or a book about economics, *profit* means economic profit.

The Zero Profit Condition

Now let's think about how much (economic) profit Bert and Ernie can reasonably expect to earn in the long run.

Given the previous table, Ernie won't want to stay in the lemonade business. He'd prefer to switch to newspaper delivery. But now suppose that there are many newspaper carriers, all identical to Bert, and many lemonade stands, all identical to Ernie's. Then as lemonade sellers switch to newspaper delivery, the price of lemonade is bid up—which means higher profits for the lemonade stands that remain in the industry. At the same time, the price of newspapers is bid down—which lowers the profits of newspaper carriers.

The process continues until the newspaper industry and the lemonade industry are equally attractive—that is, until profits in both industries become equal. But if profits in both industries are equal, then (by the economist's calculation), they must be zero. For example, if everyone in both industries earns \$8 a day in accounting profit, then every newspaper carrier forgoes an opportunity to earn \$8 a day running a lemonade stand. Subtracting that \$8 opportunity cost leaves an economic profit of zero.

You might be tempted to ask why a firm would bother to operate at all if it earns zero profit. The answer is that if a firm closed down completely, it would earn a *negative* profit. In the above example, a firm that fails to sell either newspapers *or* lemonade earns a profit of \$(−8).

The argument for zero profits contains a hidden assumption: It assumes that all newspaper carriers are equally efficient, and likewise for lemonade sellers. If we drop that assumption, the conclusion can change. Suppose, for example, that there's one exceptionally efficient newspaper carrier—call him Grover. Grover has extra-strong muscles that allow him to pedal his bicycle twice as fast and deliver twice as many papers in a day. Therefore Grover earns an accounting profit of \$15, even though Bert earns only \$8. In the lemonade industry, where strong legs would have no particular value, Grover would earn \$8, just like everyone else. Then, because he delivers newspapers, Grover's economic profit is \$15 − \$8 = \$7, which is not the same as zero.[2]

So our zero-profit conclusion rests on the assumption that all firms are identical; when this assumption fails (as when Grover's delivery service is more efficient than Bert's), the conclusion can fail also. Therefore the correct statement is:

If all firms are identical, then all firms must earn zero profit in the long run.

The Break-Even Price

Now let's give a more precise illustration of the zero-profit condition.

Floyd the barber faces the (long-run) marginal cost curve shown in Exhibit 7–16A. His total cost includes these marginal costs, as well as the \$8 opportunity cost of running a gas station (which is Floyd's next best opportunity).

The first two columns of Exhibit 7–16B show Floyd's supply curve. The sup-

[2]Not every economist would endorse this calculation. Some would point out that Ernie would be happy to start a newspaper delivery service and hire Grover to do all the work for a salary of up to \$15; by working for himself instead of Ernie, Grover forgoes \$15 and so has an economic profit of zero. Although economists disagree about how to measure Grover's economic profit, that disagreement is a purely semantic one with no consequences for the analysis that will follow.

ply curve is just the marginal cost curve in reverse; the marginal cost of the fifth haircut is $9. Therefore, when the price of haircuts is $9, Floyd provides 5 haircuts.

The next column of Exhibit 7–16B calculates Floyd's total revenue as a function of the market price of haircuts. If haircuts sell for $9, he provides 5 haircuts for a total revenue of $9 × 5 = $45.

The next column is Floyd's total cost curve, which is copied from Exhibit 7–16A.

The final column shows Floyd's profit, calculated by subtracting total cost from total revenue.

QA **Exercise 7.8** Make sure that all of the table entries in Exhibit 7–16B are correct.

The table in Exhibit 7-16B is not at all like the table in Exhibit 5-5, which shows the Tailor Dress Company's profits as a function of the quantity it produces. In Exhibit 5-5, Tailor *chooses* a row in the table in order to maximize its profits. In Exhibit 7-16B, Floyd does not get to choose the row—the row is determined by the going market price.

Notice in Exhibit 7–16 that when the market price of haircuts is below $7, Floyd earns a negative profit, and when the market price of haircuts is above $7, he earns a positive profit. When the market price of haircuts is exactly $7, Floyd's profit is exactly zero.

Break-even price The price at which a seller earns zero profit.

We say that $7 is Floyd's **break-even price**. As long as he sells haircuts at that price, his profit is zero.

If all barbers are identical, all barbers must earn zero profit. Thus if all barbers are identical, the price of a haircut must be $7. Indeed, if haircuts sell for, say, $2, each barber earns a profit of $(−8). (You can find this number in Exhibit 7–16B.) Barbers leave the industry, causing the price of haircuts to rise. That process continues until the price of haircuts reaches $7. Similarly, if haircuts sell for $9, each barber earns a positive profit of $8. New barbers enter the industry until the price of haircuts falls to $7.

Changes in the Break-Even Price

When costs rise, so does the break-even price.

For example, suppose that the opportunity cost of barbering rises from $8 a day to $16 a day. Floyd's profit numbers all drop by $8—in Exhibit 7–16B, the profit column now reads $(−16), $(−13), $(−11). $(−8), $0, $10. Break-even now occurs at a price of $9 per haircut.

For another example, suppose that a new law requires Floyd to pay $18 a day for a barbering license. The profit figures in Exhibit 7–16B all fall by $18, and break-even occurs at a price of $10 per haircut.

For yet another example, Floyd's marginal costs might increase—say, because of an increase in the cost of cleaning solutions for Floyd's barber tools. Then Floyd's supply curve changes, so the total revenue numbers in Exhibit

Exhibit 7-16 Computing the Break-even Price

Quantity	Total Cost (TC)	Marginal Cost (MC)
1	$10	$2 per haircut
2	15	5
3	21	6
4	28	7
5	37	9
6	48	11

A: Floyd's total and marginal cost curves.

Supply		Total	Total	
Price	Quantity	Revenue	Cost	Profit
$2	1	$2	$10	$(−8)
5	2	10	15	(−5)
6	3	18	21	(−3)
7	4	28	28	0
9	5	45	37	8
11	6	66	48	18

B: Calculating Floyd's profit as a function of the price of haircuts.

Table A shows Floyd's total and marginal cost curves. The first two columns of Table B shows his supply curve, the points of which coincide with the points of his marginal cost curve. Total revenue (*TR*) is calculated as price times quantity supplied; total cost (*TC*) is copied from Table A to Table B, and profit is $TR - TC$. Floyd breaks even when the market price is $7. If the price of haircuts is below $7 per haircut, Floyd seeks to exit the industry; if the price is above $7 per haircut, others like Floyd seek to enter.

7–16B change. (The total cost numbers change also.) The profit column needs to be recalculated and the break-even price changes.

Average Cost in the Long Run

Floyd earns zero profit when his total revenue (*TR*) is equal to his total cost (*TC*). Remember that $TR = P \cdot Q$ and $TC = AC \cdot Q$, where P is price, Q is quantity, and AC is average cost. Therefore the zero profit condition is

$$P \cdot Q = AC \cdot Q$$

which is the same thing as

$$P = AC$$

In other words:

If price equals average cost, the firm earns zero profit.

Likewise,

If price is above average cost, the firm earns a positive profit. When price is below average cost, the firm earns a negative profit.

Exhibit 7–17 illustrates all three possibilities. If the market price is P_0, the firm produces quantity Q_0. At that quantity, average cost is above P_0, so the firm's profit is negative. If the market price is P_2, the firm produces quantity Q_2. At that quantity, average cost is below P_2, so the firm's profit is positive. If the market price is P_1, the firm produces quantity Q_1. At that quantity, average cost is equal to P_1, so the firm's profit is zero. In other words, P_1 is this firm's break-even price.

If all firms are identical, then the zero-profit condition holds in the long run. Thus, if all firms are identical, the long-run price must be P_1, and each firm must produce quantity Q_1.

There's something else special about quantity Q_1—it's the quantity at which average cost is minimized. Here's why that must be true: We know that for *every* competitive firm, profit-maximization requires $P = MC$. We know that for a firm earning zero profit, $P = AC$. Putting these equations together, we discover that for a competitive firm earning zero profit, $MC = AC$. But we learned in Section 6.3 that $MC = AC$ just at the bottom of the average cost U.

Exhibit 7-17 **Profit and the Average Cost Curve**

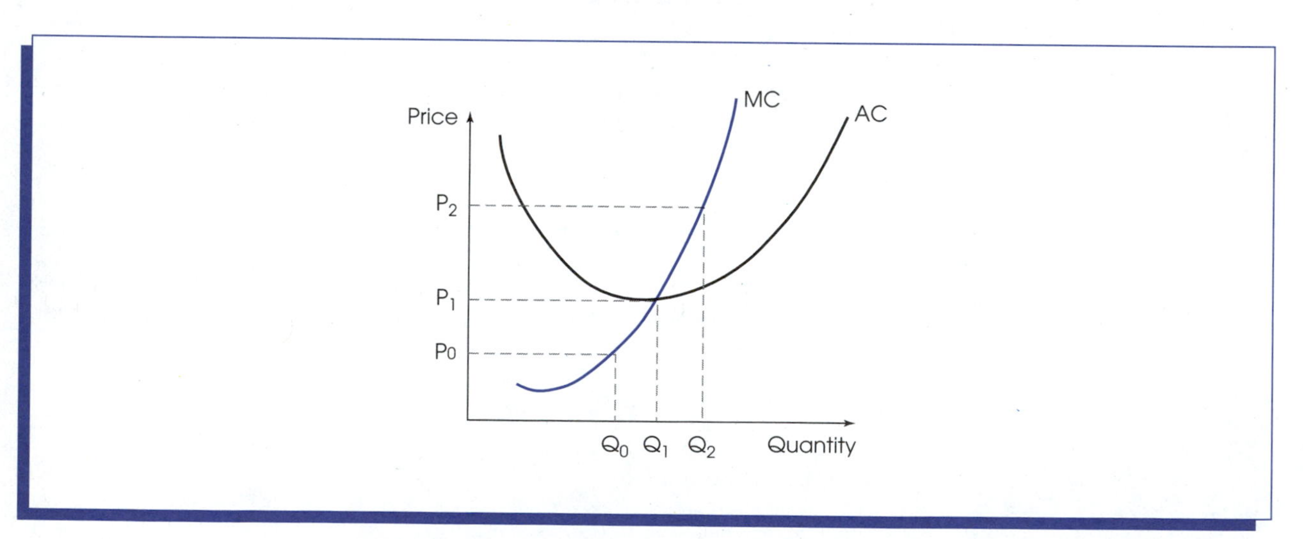

If the market price is P_0, the firm produces quantity Q_0, where average cost is above P_0. Thus the firm's profit is negative. Similarly, if the price is P_2, the firm's profit is positive and if the price is P_1, the firm's profit is zero. At the break-even price P_1, the chosen quantity Q_1 minimizes average cost.

Therefore:

When a competitive firm earns zero profit, it produces at the lowest possible average cost.

The minimization of average cost is *not* a goal of the firm. The firm's only goal is to maximize profit. In Exhibit 7-17, a profit-maximizing firm facing price P_0 or P_2 will not minimize average cost. It is only when the price is P_1—that is, when profits are zero—that average cost is minimized.

EXERCISE 7.9 In Exhibit 7–16, compute Floyd's average cost when the price of a haircut is \$2, \$5, \$6, \$7, \$9, and \$10. Confirm that his average cost is minimized when he is breaking even.

7.5 Constant Cost Industries

Now we are prepared to study the long-run supply curve and long-run competitive equilibrium.

It turns out that there are three types of competitive industries, and we will need separate theories of long-run supply for each. In this section we will study *constant-cost* industries, and in the next section we will study *increasing-cost* and *decreasing-cost* industries.

Definition of a Constant-Cost Industry

Constant-cost industry A competitive industry in which all firms have identical cost curves, and those cost curves do not change as the industry expands or contracts.

A **constant-cost industry** is a competitive industry that satisfies the following assumptions:

Assumption 1: All firms have identical cost curves.

Assumption 2: Those cost curves do not change as the industry expands or contracts.

Assumption 1 is probably true for sidewalk flower vendors and false for breeders of world-class orchids. There are a lot of people who can run sidewalk flower stands about equally well; thus, all of them have the same cost curves. But only very few people have the delicate skills to breed orchids efficiently. Those with fewer skills will find it substantially more costly to produce a given quantity of orchids. (If ½ of your flowers die before you can bring them to market, that adds substantially to the average cost of producing a marketable orchid.)

In general, Assumption 1 will be true in industries that do not require unusual skills, and false in industries where unusual skills are required. Hamburger stands satisfy Assumption 1; gourmet restaurants do not.

Assumption 2 is also probably true for sidewalk flower vendors. If you're selling flowers, there's no reason why the arrival of new competitors should affect your costs. (New arrivals can affect your *profits* by competing for customers, but that's not the same thing as affecting your costs.) However, Assumption 2 is probably false for farmers. Here's why: An influx of new farmers bids up the rental price of *land*, and the rental price of land is one of the costs of farming.

The key difference is this: Sidewalk flower vendors cannot significantly bid up the wholesale price of flowers, because sidewalk flower vendors, taken as a whole, do not use a significant fraction of the world's flowers. Farmers, by contrast, *can* bid up the price of land, because farmers, taken as a whole, *do* use a significant fraction of the world's arable land.

When you think about flower vendors, be sure to distinguish between the retail price of sidewalk flowers (the price at which the vendors *sell* their wares) and the wholesale price of flowers (the price at which vendors *buy* their wares). To affect costs competitors must affect the wholesale price of flowers.

Here's an exception: Suppose that instead of buying their flowers from reputable dealers, the flower vendors pick their flowers from a small public park. Then the arrival of new competitors will make it harder to find flowers in the park, which increases the cost of acquiring flowers. In this case, sidewalk flower vending does not satisfy Assumption 2.

In general, Assumption 2 will be true in industries that are not large enough to affect the price of any input (where inputs are things like wholesale flowers or arable land), and false in industries that are large enough to affect the price of some input. Here the phrase *large enough* must be interpreted relative to the size of the market for the input in question. For example, the jewelry industry is large enough to affect the price of diamonds, because a substantial fraction of the world's diamonds are used in jewelry. By contrast, hamburger stands use a lot of meat, but probably not enough to affect its price: Only a small fraction of the world's meat is used to make fast food hamburgers. Thus hamburger stands, like sidewalk flower vendors, are likely to satisfy Assumptions 1 and 2, and can safely be treated as a constant-cost industry.

Long-Run Supply in a Constant Cost Industry

Suppose that barbershops form a constant-cost industry, and that each firm has a break-even price of $7. (For example, each firm might be just like Floyd's barbershop in Exhibit 7–16.) Let's figure out what the long-run supply curve looks like in this industry.

At any price below $7 per haircut, profits are negative, so all firms exit and the entire industry disappears. Thus at prices below $7, the quantity supplied is zero.

At prices above $7 per haircut, profits are positive, so every firm in the world chooses to become a barbershop. The quantity supplied is effectively infinite, and cannot be displayed on a graph whose horizontal axis is confined to a single sheet of paper or a single blackboard.

At a price of $7 per haircut, all firms are indifferent between barbering and the next best alternative. Thus at a price of $7 per haircut, the firm might supply any quantity of haircuts whatsoever. On the supply curve, the price of $7 corresponds to *every* quantity. Thus the long-run supply curve is flat at $7, as shown in Exhibit 7–18.

In a constant-cost industry, the long-run supply curve is flat at the break-even price.

Is the Long-Run Supply Curve Really Flat?

In a constant-cost industry, the long-run supply curve is flat because of entry and exit: If price goes even a little below the break-even price, every firm exits; if price goes even a little above the break-even price, an unlimited number of firms enter.

Yet when we make arguments that rely on entry and exit, we should remember that we are dealing with processes that take time. In the real world, a

Exhibit 7-18 Long-Run Supply in a Constant-Cost Industry

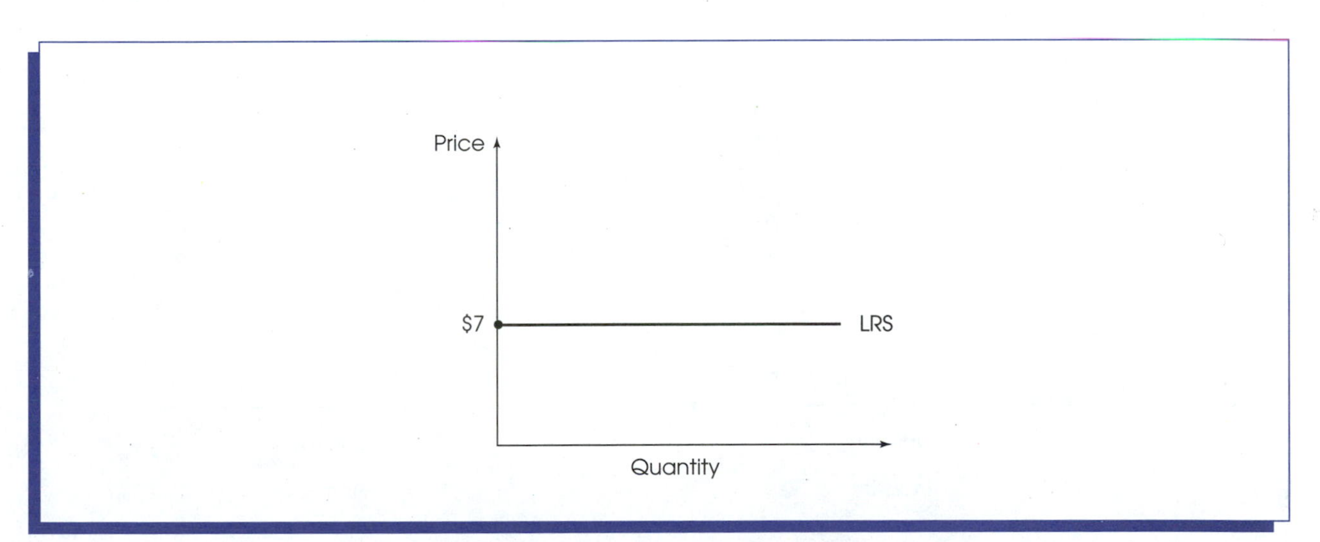

If any number of barbers can break even selling haircuts at $7, then the long-run industry supply curve is flat at $7. At prices below $7, nobody wants to be a barber; at prices above $7, there is an unlimited number of barbers. At a price of $7, all firms are indifferent between barbering and the next best alternative, so there might be any number of firms in the industry—and hence, any quantity of haircuts supplied.

firm cannot instantly convert itself from a clothing store into a cafeteria or a barber shop. If the demand for haircuts rises, barbers may indeed find themselves earning positive profits for quite some time, until other firms have had a chance to enter. It is only after the smoke has cleared and firms have moved into the industry that profits return to zero. Notice that this means that over any period of time too short to allow for entry, the industry supply curve is upward-sloping.

Many economists argue that the long-run zero-profit equilibrium is almost never reached, because demand curves and cost curves shift so often that the entry and exit process never settles down. Although this is arguably true in many industries, the zero-profit condition is often a useful approximation to the truth.

Equilibrium

The relationship between the competitive industry and the competitive firm is the same in the long run as in the short run: The market price is determined

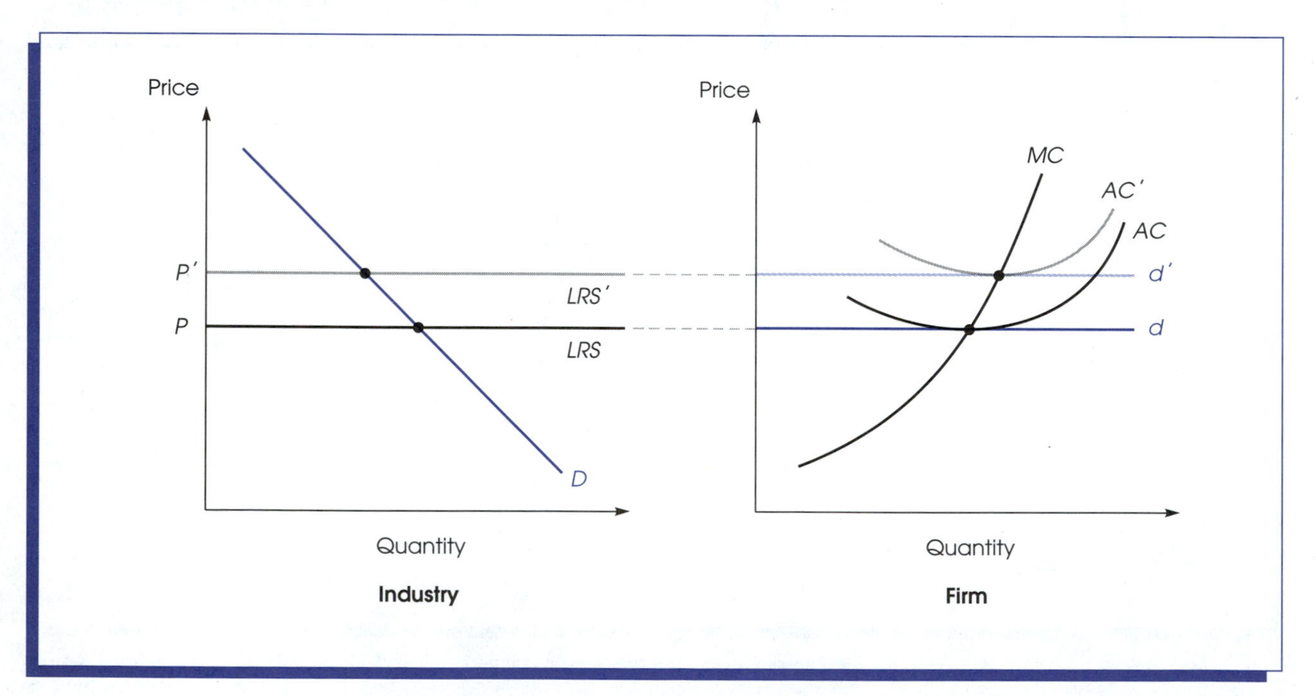

If fixed costs rise, the break-even price rises also, so the long-run industry supply curve rises from *LRS* to *LRS'*. Quantity increases at each individual firm and decreases in the industry. The firm's average cost curve rises from *AC* to *AC'*, indicating that profit is zero in the new equilibrium.

by the intersection of the industry-wide supply and demand curves, and firms face flat demand curves at the market price.

However, the long-run analysis of *changes* in equilibrium differs from the short-run analysis. A key difference is that (in a constant-cost industry) the long-run supply curve is flat at the break-even price, and therefore shifts whenever the break-even price changes.

Here are some examples.

Changes in Fixed Costs

Suppose new legislation requires every barbershop to pay a daily license fee. What happens in the long run?

Exhibit 7–19 shows the answer. The firm's marginal cost curve is unaffected, but the break-even price rises. (For example, if the cost curves are as in Exhibit 7–16, a license fee of $18 a day will cause the break-even price to rise to $10.) Thus, the industry supply curve shifts vertically upward to the level of the new break-even price. Each firm produces more haircuts than before; the industry as a whole now produces fewer.

If each barber cuts more hair, how can the total number of haircuts go down? The answer is that in the long run, the number of barbers must fall. In the short run, such an outcome would be impossible.

There is no way to predict which individual barbers will exit. All we know is that *some* barbers will exit, and exit continues until the price is bid up to its new break-even level. The right half of Exhibit 7–19 shows the situation at one of those barbershops that happens to remain.

In Chapter 6, we argued that in the long run, firms have no fixed costs because they can vary their employment of any factor of production. As long as the firm's costs consist entirely of payments to factors, it is correct to say that the firm has no long-run fixed costs. However, the license fee we've just considered, because it does not vary with output, is a fixed cost even in the long run.

It is important to distinguish a fixed cost from a sunk cost. Although the license fee is a fixed cost for any firm that decides to remain in the industry, it is not yet a sunk cost at the point when the entry/exit decision is being made. Thus, it is relevant to the decision. A cost that is truly sunk, in the sense that it cannot be avoided even by leaving the industry, will not affect anything.

Changes in Marginal Costs

An increase in variable costs has two effects: First, the firm's marginal cost curve shifts upward. Second, the break-even price increases, so the industry supply curve shifts upward. Exhibit 7–20 shows the consequences. The quantity supplied by individual firms might either increase or decrease, while the quantity supplied by the industry must decrease.

There's one special case where we can say more: Suppose that marginal cost shifts upward by the same amount at every quantity (so that the marginal cost curve shifts upward parallel to itself). Then the break-even price rises by that same amount (as does the average cost curve). Consequently, the new equilibrium quantity at the firm is unchanged.

Changes in Demand

Suppose the demand for haircuts increases. At the top of Exhibit 7–21, you can see the long-run consequence. Industry-wide demand shifts rightward. The market price remains unchanged, so nothing changes in the "firm" part of the picture. Individual barbershops continue producing just as before, but the industry-wide quantity of haircuts increases, because of entry.

It is instructive to compare the long run with the short run. At the bottom of Exhibit 7–21 you can see this comparison. The industry is initially in both short-run and long-run equilibrium at the price P_0 and quantity Q_0. The increase in demand initially leads to a movement along the short-run supply curve S to the higher price P_1. Firms now provide q_1 haircuts apiece, for an industry-wide total of Q_1. The higher price leads to positive profits and attracts entry in the long run. Thereupon, the price is bid back down to P_0 and the industry-wide quan-

Exhibit 7-20 A Rise in Variable Costs

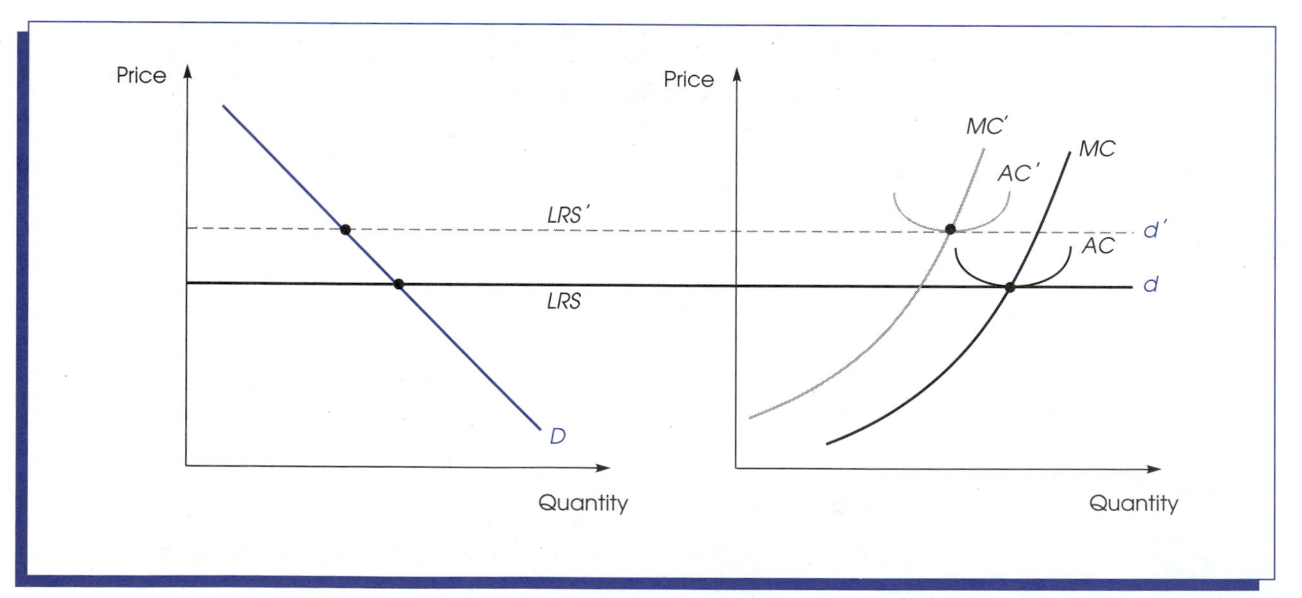

If variable costs rise, the firm's marginal cost curve rises from *MC* to *MC'*. The break-even price rises, so the long-run industry supply curve rises from *LRS* to *LRS'*. The industry quantity falls; the firm quantity can either fall or rise. The average cost curve shifts from *AC* to *AC'* and the firm earns zero profit at the new equilibrium.

Exhibit 7-21 A Rise in Demand

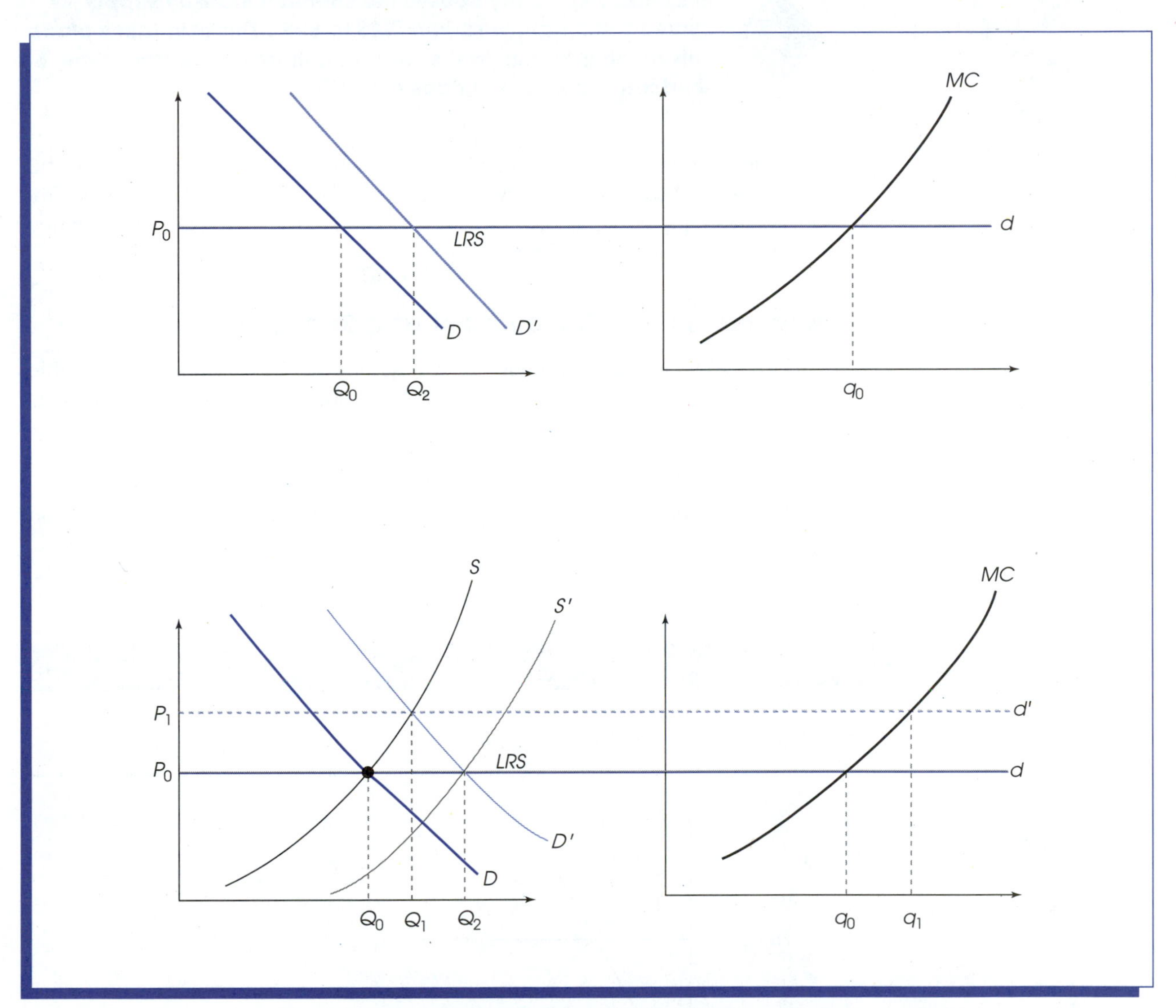

The top of this exhibit shows the long-run effect of an increase in demand for the product of a constant-cost industry. The industry demand curve shifts from D to D'. There is no change in price and hence no change in the "firm" part of the picture. Firms produce exactly as before, but the industry quantity increases. The bottom of the exhibit contrasts the short-run and long-run responses. The industry is initially in both short-run and long-run equilibrium at price P_0. When demand shifts from D to D', the price is bid up to P_1. Firms increase their output from q_0 to q_1, and the industry output rises to Q_1. Now firms earn positive profits, so in the long run there is entry. Entry continues until the price is bid back down to P_0. At this point firms return to producing quantity q_0, and the industry produces quantity Q_2. Entry causes the short-run supply curve to shift rightward to S'. The short-run supply curve shifts in the long run, not in the short run.

tity rises further to Q_2, although individual firms return to the original quantity q_0.

In Exhibit 7-21, entry causes the short-run industry supply curve to shift rightward from *SRS* to *SRS'*. This shift takes place only in the long run; in the short run, there is no entry so the short-run supply curve does not shift.

Notice that entry does *not* cause a shift in the *long-run* supply curve, because the consequences of entry are already *built in* to that curve. But the short-run supply curve ignores the effects of entry, and so it must shift to a new location after entry takes place.

Application: The Government as a Supplier

Suppose your city's government decides there is not enough housing available, and decides to do something about it by building and operating a new apartment complex. Will this policy succeed in increasing the quantity of housing?

In the short run, yes. The new apartment complex causes the short-run housing supply curve to shift to the right. In Exhibit 7–22, you can see that the equilibrium price of housing falls from P_0 to P_1, and the quantity increases from Q_0 to Q_1.

Exhibit 7-22 The Government as a Supplier

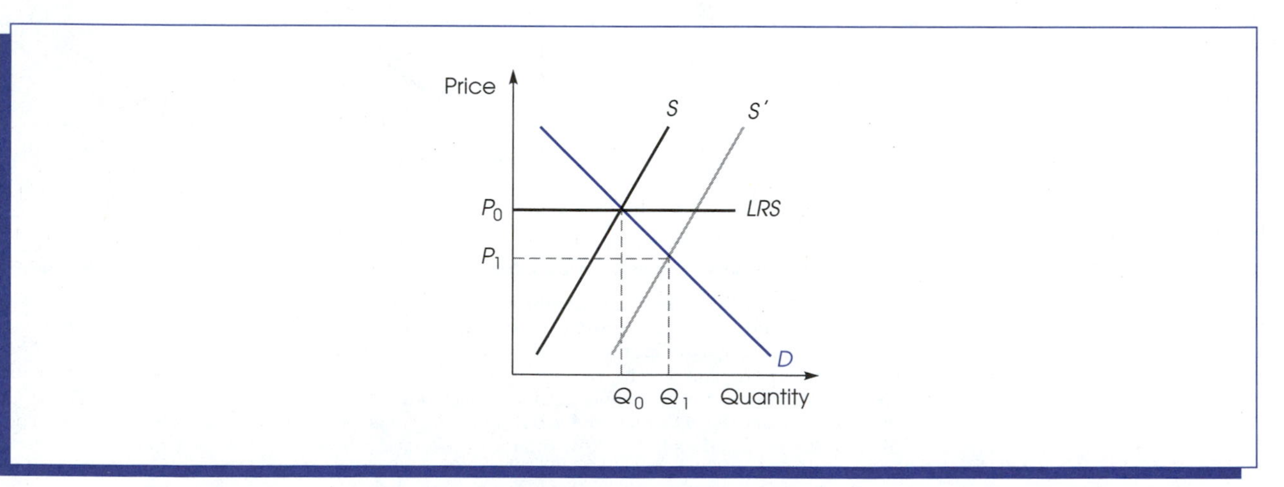

When the government builds an apartment complex, the short-run housing supply curve shifts rightward, but the long-run housing supply curve remains fixed. Thus, the quantity of housing increases from Q_0 to Q_1 in the short run, but returns to Q_0 in the long run.

But the long-run supply curve does not shift. That's because the long-run supply curve is determined by the break-even price. For example, if it costs landlords $400 a month to provide an apartment, then the long-run supply curve is flat at $400 a month.

It follows that in the long run, the price of housing must return to P_0 and the quantity must return to Q_0. That is, in the long run, the number of privately owned apartments withdrawn from the market must just equal the number of new apartments built by the government. (Otherwise, the price would remain below P_0 and landlords would earn negative profits, prompting further exit.) Thus, in the long run, the government's new apartment complex adds exactly nothing to the supply of housing.

7.6 Increasing and Decreasing Cost Industries

We now have a complete theory of the constant-cost industry. But not all industries are constant-cost. In this section, we consider the alternatives.

Definition of an Increasing-Cost Industry

Increasing-cost industry A competitive industry where the break-even price for new entrants increases as the industry expands.

An **increasing-cost industry** is a competitive industry where the break-even price for new entrants increases as the industry expands.

There are two reasons why an industry might be increasing-cost. First, some firms might have higher break-even prices because they are less efficient. Second, an expansion of the industry might bid up the price of some factor of production and thereby raise the break-even price for everyone—as when an expansion of the farming industry bids up the price of land (this is the *factor price effect,* which we also encountered in the short run). In either case, we shall see that the long-run industry supply curve slopes upward.

Less-Efficient Firms

Suppose that Floyd the barber can break even selling haircuts at $7 apiece. His less-efficient cousin Lloyd has to charge $9 per haircut to break even.

When the market price of haircuts is $7, Floyd cuts hair but Lloyd does something else. If the price rises to $9, Lloyd enters the barbering industry. Between them, Floyd and Lloyd cut more hair than Floyd alone. Thus, a higher price of haircuts leads to a greater quantity of haircuts supplied. In other words, the long-run supply curve slopes upward.

The Factor-Price Effect

Suppose instead that Floyd and Lloyd are equally efficient. Either one can break even selling haircuts at $7 apiece.

But suppose also that if Floyd and Lloyd *both* become barbers, they bid up the price of razors—because two barbers demand more razors than one barber. This adds to their costs and makes it impossible for them to continue breaking even at $7. Thus, as long as haircuts sell for $7, only one barber can survive. If the price of haircuts rises to $9, it becomes possible for Floyd and Lloyd to break even simultaneously.

Once again, a higher price of haircuts leads to more haircuts being supplied. Once again, the long-run supply curve slopes upward.

This example is entirely unrealistic, because in reality barbers cannot bid up the price of razors. That's because the entire world population of barbers accounts for only a small fraction of the world's demand for sharpened steel. We've used this example only for easy contrast with earlier examples.

The moral of both Floyd/Lloyd examples is this:

In an increasing-cost industry, the long-run supply curve slopes upward.

An Intermediate Case: A Few Efficient Firms

One case of interest is that in which a few firms are especially efficient and a great number of other firms are essentially identical. In this case, a few efficient firms will be willing to enter the industry even when the price is low, yielding a small but nonzero quantity supplied. When the price rises high enough for the "ordinary" firms to break even, any quantity can be supplied. Thus, the long-run supply curve slopes upward for a short while and then becomes flat, as in Exhibit 7–23. In such an industry, when there is sufficient demand for

Exhibit 7-23 Long-Run Supply with a Few Efficient Firms

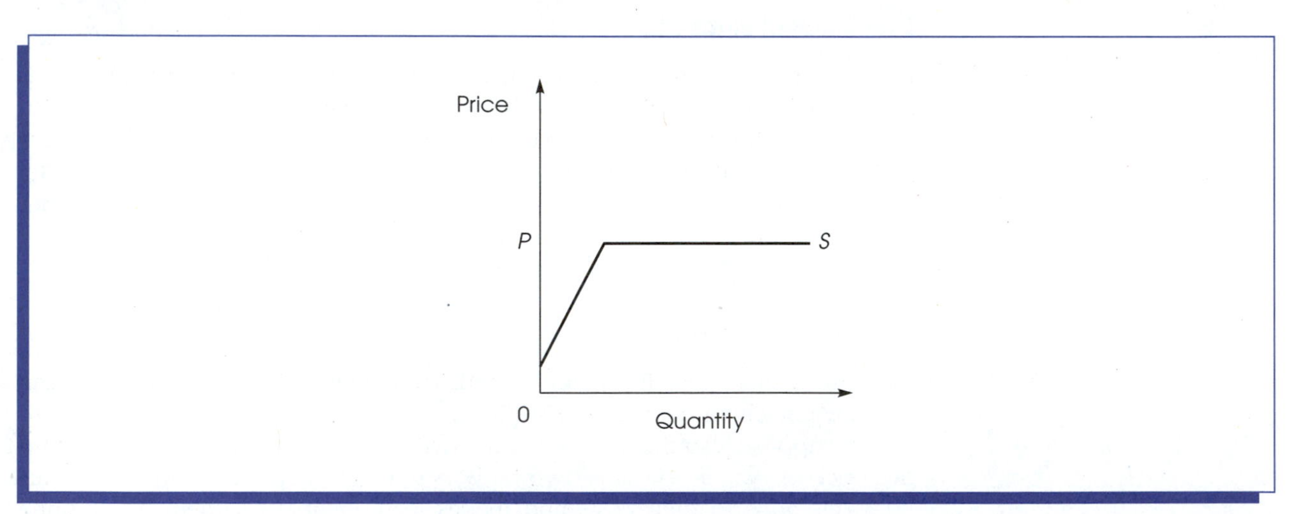

Suppose there are a few exceptionally efficient firms and a great number of identical "ordinary" firms. At low prices, only the efficient firms enter and the quantity supplied is small. At the break-even price of the ordinary firms (P), the supply curve becomes flat.

equilibrium to occur on the flat part of the supply curve, it is usually harmless to assume (for simplicity) that the entire supply curve is flat.

Definition of a Decreasing-Cost Industry

Decreasing-cost industry A competitive industry where the break-even price for new entrants falls as the industry expands.

This site describes how meat processing has the characteristics of a decreasing-cost industry: http://ag.arizona.edu/AREC/WEMC/papers/Today_Tomorrows.html

A **decreasing-cost industry** is a competitive industry where the break-even price falls as the industry expands. Imagine a community with a small number of printers, each of whom makes his own ink. If additional printers enter, it might become profitable for an inkmaker to set up shop, allowing each printer to reduce costs. (We assume that buying from the inkmaker is cheaper than making your own.) Because inkmakers can survive only when there are enough printers to support them, the entry of new printers drives down the cost of printing. Consequently, while 1 printer might have to charge $1 a page to break even, it is conceivable that 10 printers can break even at 50¢ a page. Thus the lower price is associated with a greater quantity supplied, so the long-run supply curve slopes downward.

In a decreasing-cost industry, the long-run supply curve slopes downward.

At the end of Chapter 2, we briefly discussed the gains from trade that are due simply to the scale of operations, as opposed to those that are due to comparative advantage. Decreasing-cost industries provide examples of such gains. Suppose that each of two isolated countries has a small number of printers, insufficient to support an inkmaker. If these two countries begin to trade with each other, the combined number of printers might suffice to bring an inkmaker into the market. By concentrating on the production of ink in large quantities, the inkmaker can produce at a lower average cost than any of the printers can, thereby reducing the average cost of producing books. Residents of both countries can benefit from the savings.

Equilibrium

The analysis of long-run equilibrium in the increasing-cost and decreasing-cost cases is just as in the constant-cost case; the only thing that differs is the shape of the long-run industry supply curve. Several examples are provided in Exhibit 7–24 and Exhibit 7–25.

7.7 Applications

Removing a Rent Control

For an analysis of rent control in Honolulu visit: http://millennianet.com/glondon/conclusion.html

In the town of Llareggub, apartments rent for $400 per month. The town passes a law setting a maximum rent of $200 a month. Some years later the law is repealed. Nothing changes in the interim. Does the rent on apartments return all the way up to its old level of $400 per month?

To analyze this problem, look at Exhibit 7–26. The market is initially in both short-run and long-run equilibrium at a price of $400 and a quantity of Q_2. When the price is artificially lowered to $200, landlords' short-run response is to provide fewer apartments. The new quantity can be read off the short-run supply curve S at a price of $200. (This quantity is not marked on the graph.)

Exhibit 7-24 An Increase in Costs in an Increasing-Cost Industry

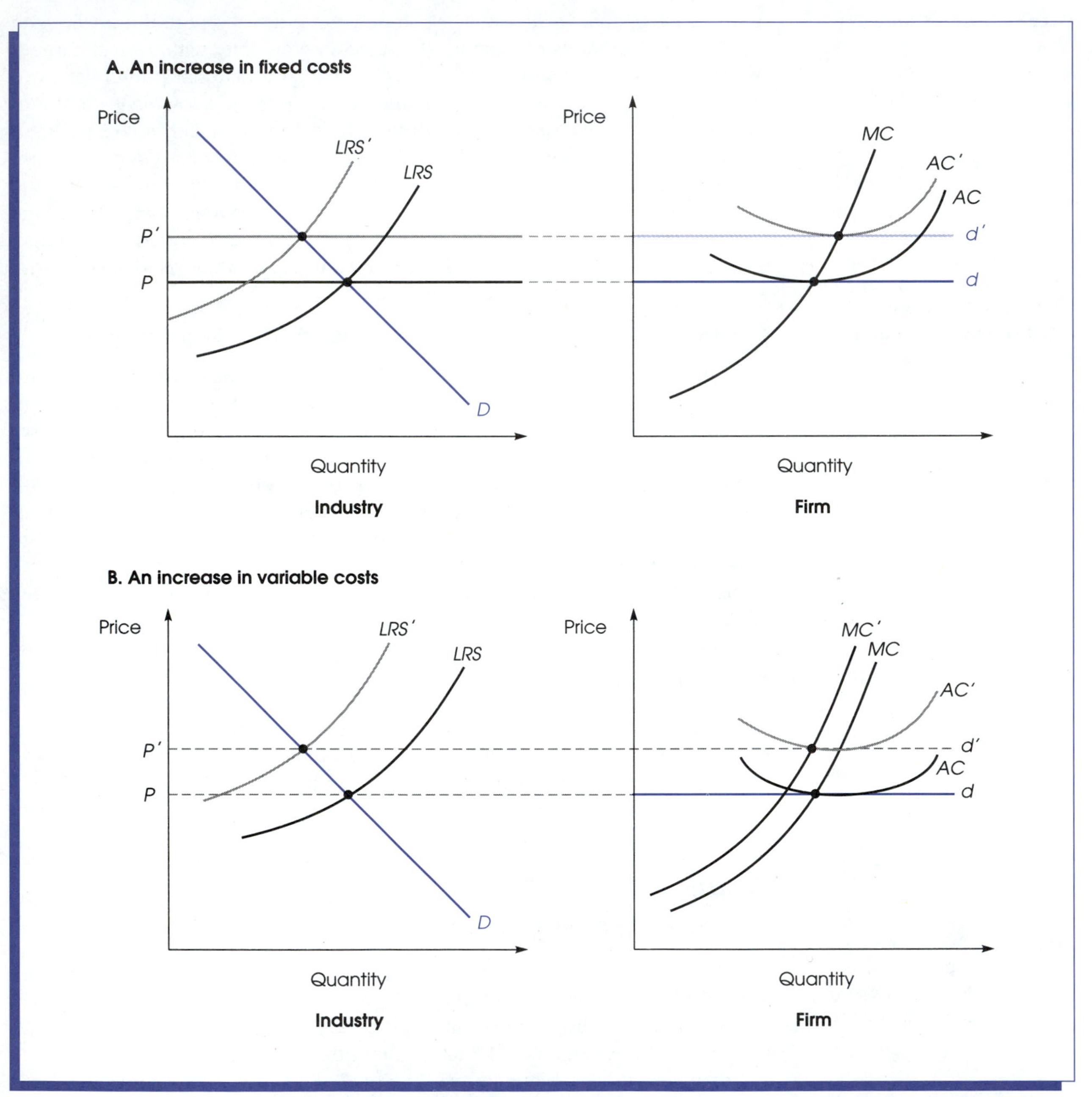

The top panels show an increase in fixed costs and the bottom panels show an increase in marginal costs. In both cases, the break-even price increases so the long-run industry supply curve shifts. The firm's marginal cost curve shifts only in the second of the two examples. In both examples, the price rises and the industry supplies a smaller quantity. In the first example, the firm's quantity surely increases; in the second, the firm's quantity could increase or decrease.

Exhibit 7-25 A Change in Demand

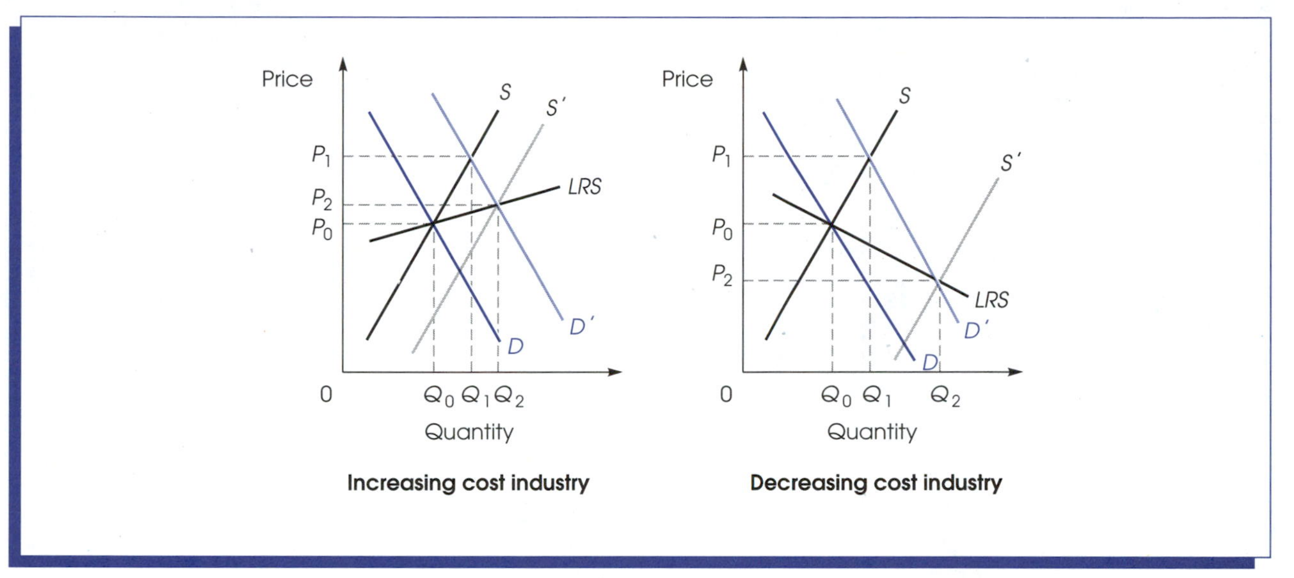

When demand increases, price rises in an increasing-cost industry, but it falls in a decreasing-cost industry. In both cases, the industry-wide quantity increases.

In the long run, as landlords seize additional opportunities to convert apartments to commercial or other uses, or just decide not to keep some existing apartments in adequate repair, the quantity falls still further, to Q_1, which is read off the long-run supply curve at a price of $200.

With the stock of apartments reduced, there is a new short-run supply curve S'. When the rent control is lifted, the new equilibrium is at $500 and a quantity somewhere between Q_1 and Q_2. Thus, the answer to the question "Does the rent return all the way up to $400?" is no; actually, it goes *above* $400.

At $500, landlords earn positive profits and slowly they reconvert commercial buildings to use as apartments. Eventually, the market does return to the old long-run equilibrium at a price of $400 and a quantity of Q_0. The reason for this is quite simple: Neither the demand curve nor the long-run supply curve has shifted, so the equilibrium can't change.

A Tax on Motel Rooms

Consider a town located near an interstate highway, with many essentially identical motels. One day the town imposes a sales tax of $5 per room per night. Who pays the tax?

By far the most important input in the provision of motel services is the physical motel rooms. However, it is not the only input. By hiring a larger maintenance staff, for example, a motel owner may be able to increase the number of rooms he has available on an average night. In the short run, mo-

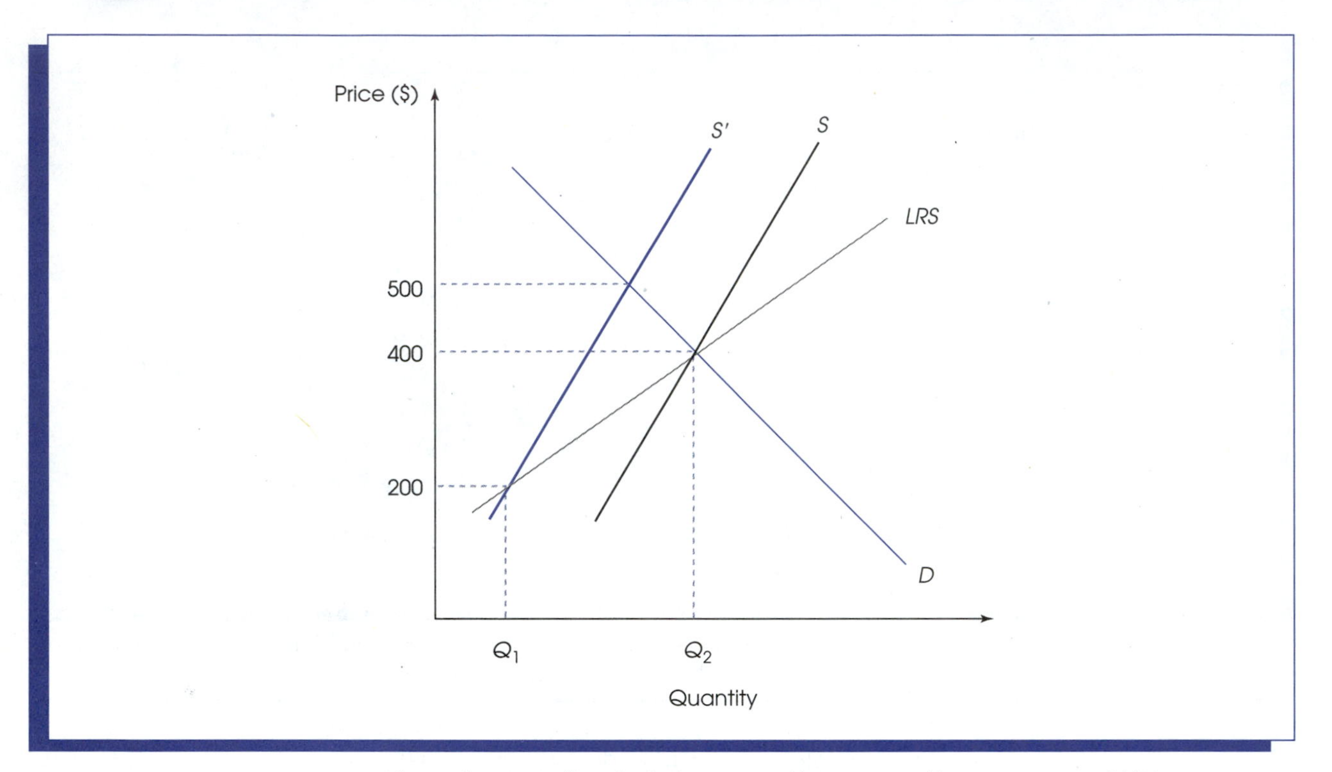

The market is initially in both short-run and long-run equilibrium at a price of $400. A maximum legal rent of $200 is imposed. Eventually, quantity falls to Q_1 and the short-run supply curve falls from S to S'.

When the rent control is removed, the market moves to a new short-run equilibrium at a price of $500, *above* the original uncontrolled price. Eventually, it returns to the long-run equilibrium.

tel rooms are a fixed input and maintenance staff is a variable input. Because of the importance of the fixed input, the short-run supply curve for motel rooms is nearly vertical. Consequently, the tax will be paid mostly by suppliers (motels), as shown in panel A of Exhibit 7–27, where the price falls from P to P', almost the entire amount of the tax.

In the long run, however, the number of motel rooms is variable, because individual motels can expand or contract, because new motels can appear, and because existing motels can convert to other enterprises, say, by becoming coffee shops. Therefore, the long-run industry supply curve is much flatter than the short-run industry supply curve. It is perfectly flat?

Suppose for the moment that the motel industry uses only a small portion of the land near the highway. In this case there is no reason for the construction of the thousandth motel to cost more than the construction of the first motel. Motel rooms are provided by the industry at constant marginal cost, so there is a flat long-run industry supply curve, as shown in panel B of Exhibit

Exhibit 7-27 A Tax on Motel Rooms near a Highway

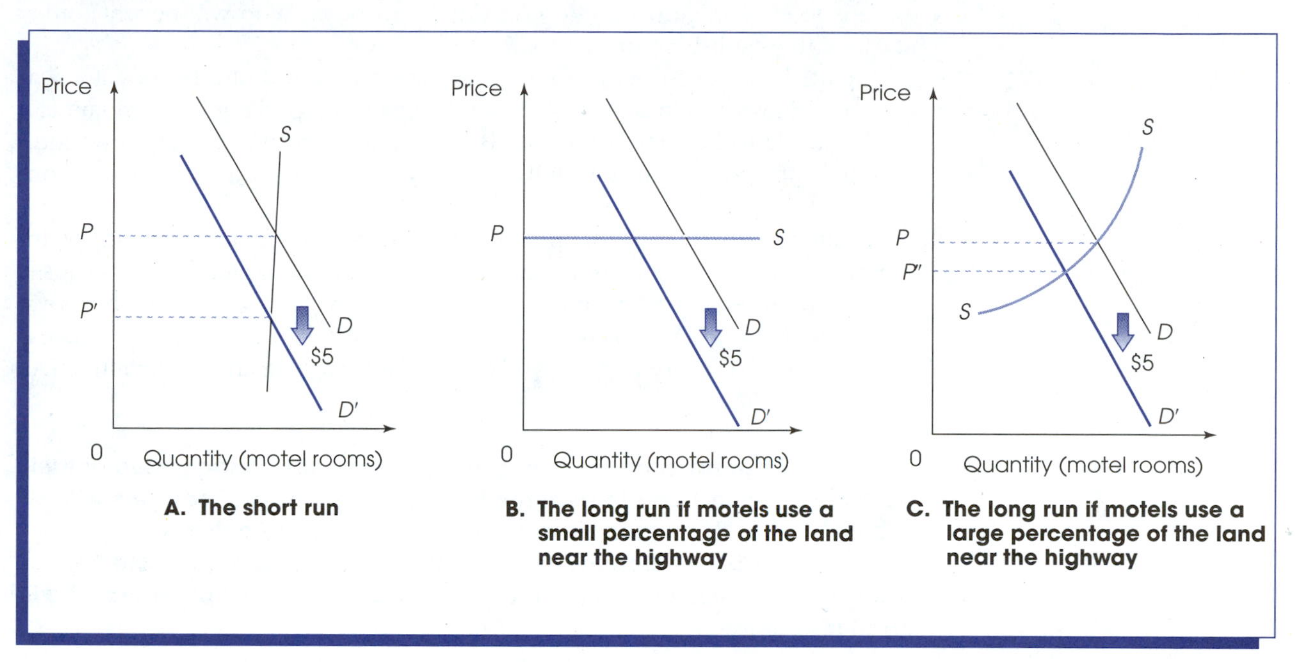

In the short run the number of motel rooms is nearly fixed. (It is not entirely fixed, because the number of rooms available on a given night can be stretched by the use of additional maintenance staff or by other means). As a result, the short-run supply curve is nearly vertical, so a sales tax lowers the price of rooms by almost the full amount of the tax, from P to P' in panel A. The tax burden falls almost entirely on suppliers.

In the long run the lowered price leads to exit from the industry, causing prices to rise until profits are zero again. If the marginal cost of building motels is constant, then price must be bid up to its original level P, as in panel B. Now demanders pay the full burden of the tax.

If, on the other hand, motels use a significant proportion of the land near the highway, then exit will drive down land prices and so drive down the cost of owning a motel. As a result, the new zero profits price will be lower than the original price, at P'' in panel C, though the price does not fall by as much as in the short run.

7–27. In the long run, firms exit from the industry until the price of motel rooms is bid back up to P, and the tax is paid entirely by demanders (travelers).

Suppose, on the other hand, that the motel industry demands a significant fraction of the land near the highway. Then when the industry contracts, the price of land decreases, reducing the marginal cost of owning a motel room. The industry's long-run marginal cost curve is upward sloping (though not as steeply as its short-run marginal cost curve), as shown in panel C of Exhibit 7–27. Therefore, price is bid up from P' in the short run to P'' in the long run, but not all the way back up to P. The tax will be split between suppliers and demanders, with demanders paying much more than they did in the short run.

QA **Exercise 7.10** Illustrate the short-run and long-run effects of a government program that subsidizes motel visits.

Tipping the Busboy

In Carmel, California, there is an organization called the Brotherhood for the Respect, Elevation, and Advancement of Dishwashers. The organization's purpose is to encourage people to give tips to busboys. Who will benefit if they succeed in establishing this custom?

A partial answer is: not busboys. The talents required of a busboy are reasonably widespread in society. A grocery bagger or a parking lot attendant can easily decide to become a busboy. Because there are no (or very few) individuals with special "busboy skills," busboys' services are provided at a constant cost.

It follows that the total compensation of busboys cannot change. If tips increase, wages must decrease by the same amount. The increase in tips causes positive profits; the positive profits cause grocery baggers to become busboys; the entry of the grocery baggers causes wages to fall; and the whole process continues until grocery bagging and busing tables are again equally attractive.

Students sometimes argue that as grocery baggers leave their own industry to become busboys, the wage of baggers will rise. This would be true if bagging were the only other unskilled occupation. But since the new busboys come from many other industries, the number coming from any one other industry is negligibly small.

Another way to make the same point is this: Since potential busboys are all pretty much identical, the supply curve of busboys is a horizontal line at the entry price determined by the condition that busing be just as attractive as bagging. If the supply curve for a good is horizontal, then changes in demand cannot change its price.

If busboys don't gain, who does? Tipping reduces the costs of restaurant owners, who now pay lower wages. Suppose that customers leave a tip of size T at each meal. Then busboys' wages are reduced by T per meal served, which lowers the industry's supply curve by the amount T. The short-run effect is illustrated in panel A of Exhibit 7–28. The fall in costs leads to a fall in the price of restaurant meals, to P_1. Who benefits? The restaurateurs and, ironically, the customers themselves.[3]

In the long run there are two possibilities to consider, both of which are shown in Exhibit 7–28. In each case the long-run supply curve falls by T. If the restaurant industry has constant costs, as in panel B, then the price of a meal drops by exactly T, the full amount of the tip. Although the customers would like to tip the busboys, the entire value of their tips is returned to them in the form of lower meal prices!

The other possibility is that there are increasing costs in the restaurant industry. This would be the case, for example, if the potential entrants have vary-

[3]There may be an additional effect as restaurateurs decide to hire a larger number of busboys at the lower wage. This effect is irrelevant to anything we are considering in this example.

Exhibit 7-28 Tipping the Busboy

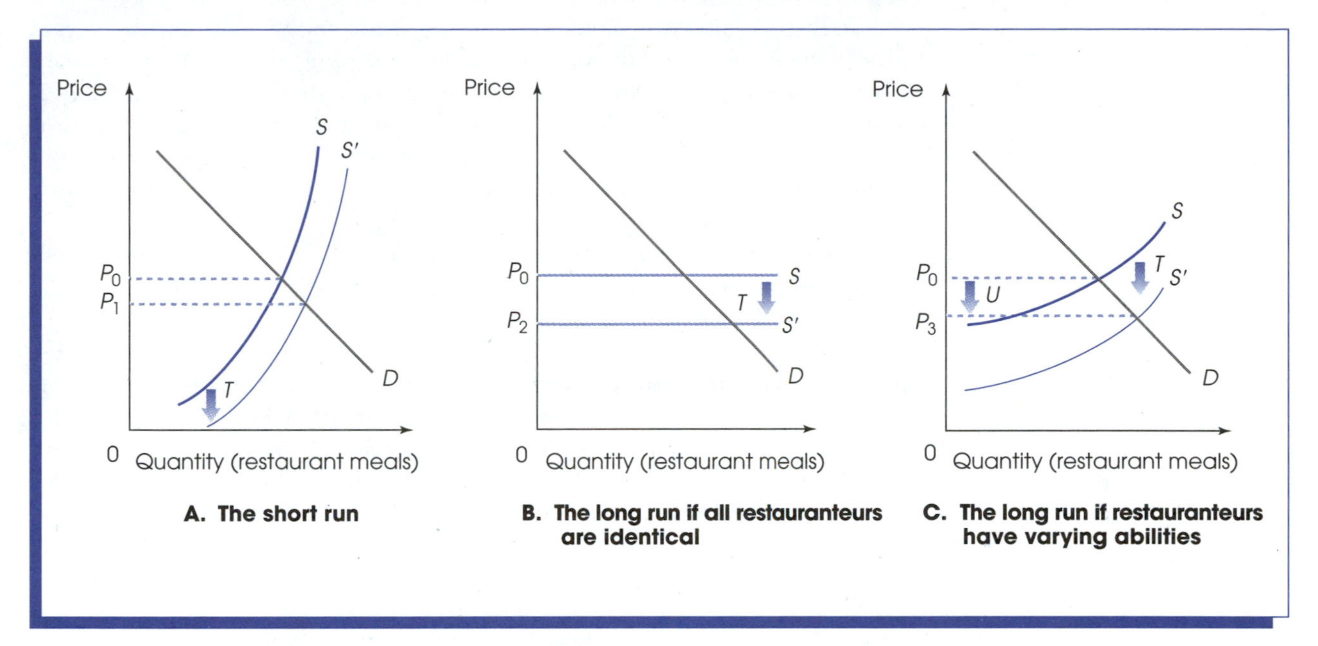

Suppose that people decide to start tipping busboys. Because busing services are provided at constant cost (there are many essentially identical busboys), the total compensation of busboys cannot change. Therefore, wages are reduced by the amount of the tip, T. The marginal cost of serving meals falls by this amount.

In the short run (panel A), price falls, but by less than T. Part of the tip is returned to the customer through the lower price, and the rest goes to the restaurant owner.

In the long run, if all restaurateurs are identical (panel B), entry bids profits back down to zero only when the price of meals falls by the full amount T. We can see this geometrically: The horizontal supply curve falls by T, and the price falls by this full amount.

If not all restaurateurs are identical, then entry by less efficient firms can drive profits to zero even though the price is reduced by less than the full amount of the tip. This is shown in panel C, where the upward-sloping long-run supply curve drops by the amount T, but the price of meals falls by something less, which we label U. Those restaurateurs who were in the industry originally gain rents equal to $T - U$ per meal served (their marginal costs fall by T but their price falls by U, so they gain the difference), while customers get back U in the form of a lower price. The tip is split between the restaurateur and the customer; the busboy gets nothing.

ing aptitudes for restaurant management. That case is shown in panel C. Here the price of restaurant meals drops, but not by the full amount of the tips. The tips are split between the restaurateurs and their customers, with the customers getting back more in the long run than they do in the short run.

7.8 Using the Competitive Model

Exhibits 7–12 and 7–13 illustrate changes in short-run competitive equilibrium; Exhibits 7–19, 7–20, and 7–21 illustrate changes in long-run competitive equilibrium for a constant-cost industry, and Exhibits 7–24 and 7–25 illustrate changes in long-run competitive equilibrium for other sorts of industries. Problems 21 through 56 at the end of the chapter call for you to provide a large number of similar analyses. Here we will list the most important principles to keep in mind when you work problems of this type.

As in the exhibits, you should begin by drawing supply and demand curves for both the industry and the firm. The industry supply curve is always upward sloping in the short run. In the long run it can be either flat (if the industry is constant-cost) or upward sloping (if the industry is increasing-cost). There is also the possibility of a downward-sloping long-run industry supply curve, but we will not discuss that case here. The firm's demand curve should be drawn flat at the price determined by industry-wide equilibrium.

To analyze a change in equilibrium, you must decide how the curves shift. Usually this means thinking about each curve separately. Here are the fundamental principles to keep in mind.

Shifts in the Firm's Supply Curve. The firm's supply curve coincides with its marginal cost curve. Therefore, only a change in marginal costs can affect it. A cost is marginal only if it varies with output. In the short run, marginal costs include labor and raw materials. In the long run, they also include those items of capital equipment that can be varied in the long run. For example, if a restaurant decides to serve more hamburgers, it will use more meat and more waiters in the short run and will expand its kitchen facilities in the long run. Therefore, a change in the price of meat or the wages of waiters causes the firm's supply curve to shift in both the short-run analysis and the long-run analysis, whereas a change in the price of kitchen facilities causes the supply curve to shift only in the long-run analysis. Some costs (e.g., annual license fees) do not vary with output even in the long run, and so do not shift the firm's supply curve even in the long run (unless they cause the firm to exit altogether).

Shifts in the Short-Run Industry Supply Curve. In the short run, the industry supply curve is the sum of the individual firm's supply curves. Therefore, it shifts only if there is a change in supply at the individual firms.

Shifts in the Long-Run Industry Supply Curve. The long-run industry supply curve shifts in response to any change in profitability—unless the change in profitability is due to a change in the price of output, in which case it is reflected by a movement *along*, rather than *of*, the long-run supply curve. However, remember that sunk costs are sunk, so that only future costs are relevant. Costs that have been paid and are irretrievable do not affect future profits, therefore do not affect entry and exit decisions, and therefore do not affect the industry supply curve.

The Individual Firm's Exit Decision: The Constant-Cost Case. In a constant-cost industry, every firm is completely indifferent about whether to remain in the industry. Thus, anything that reduces profits at just one firm must drive that firm from the industry. For example, suppose that newsstands constitute a constant-cost industry and a single newsstand owner is notified of a rent increase. The owner will certainly leave the industry. On the other hand, if *all* newsstand owners are notified of rent increases, then the industry supply curve shifts, some firms exit, the industry-wide price of newspapers rises until zero profits are restored, and any *particular* newsstand might very well remain in business. There is no way to predict which firms exit under these circumstances.

Note again that sunk costs are sunk. A fire at an individual newsstand is not like a rent increase. The costs of the fire are sunk (even if the firm exits, it continues to bear the costs via a reduction in the resale value of its merchandise); the rent increase can be avoided by exit and is therefore not sunk. The fire, therefore, has no effect, while the rent increase drives the firm from the industry.

In an increasing-cost industry, some firms might be particularly efficient and therefore prefer this industry over any of the alternatives. Such a firm might decide to remain in the industry even following an individual rent increase.

Demand Curves. After shifting the firm's and the industry's supply curves, and after deciding whether the firm remains in the industry, determine whether there is any shift in the industry demand curve. Then if there has been a shift in industry equilibrium (due to shifts in either industry supply, industry demand, or both), draw the new firm demand curve as horizontal at the new industry equilibrium price.

Exceptions. The rules listed here will serve you well most of the time. As you work the problems at the end of the chapter, you will find a few exceptions due to unusual circumstances. As always, each problem needs to be considered individually.

summary

A perfectly competitive firm is one that faces a horizontal demand curve for its product; that is, it can sell any quantity it wants to at the going market price. The total revenue curve for such a firm is a straight line through the origin, and the marginal revenue curve is a horizontal line at the going market price. Thus, the marginal revenue curve is identical with the demand curve.

Like any producer, competitive or not, the competitive firm produces, if it produces at all, where marginal cost equals marginal revenue. Since marginal revenue equals price for a competitive firm, we can say that such a firm produces, if it produces at all, where marginal cost equals price. To see what the firm will produce in the short run, we use its short-run marginal cost curve, and to see what it will produce in the long run, we use its long-run marginal cost curve.

In the short run the firm operates only if its revenue exceeds its variable costs. This is the same as saying that the firm operates only if the market price exceeds its average variable cost. Thus, the firm's short-run supply curve is that portion of its marginal cost curve that lies above average variable cost.

A competitive industry is one in which all firms are competitive and any firm can freely enter or exit in the long run.

To derive the short-run industry supply curve, we assume a fixed number of firms and add their quantities supplied at each price. It might then be necessary to modify the industry supply curve to take account of the factor-price effect.

The competitive industry operates at the point where supply and demand are equal, because each individual firm maximizes profits at this point. In competitive equilibrium the total cost of producing any quantity of output is minimized. This is because each firm has the same marginal cost (equal to the market price).

In the long run, the firm operates where price is equal to long-run marginal cost, provided that it earns positive profits. If profits are negative (which happens when price falls below average cost) the firm leaves the industry. Therefore, the firm's long-run supply curve is that part of its long-run marginal cost curve that lies above its long-run average cost curve.

To study long-run equilibrium, we must take account of the possibility of entry and exit. Entry and exit are driven by profit. There are several cases to consider.

One possibility is that the industry is constant-cost, which means that all firms have identical cost curves that do not change when the industry expands or contracts. In this case there is only one price that can prevail: the one at which each firm earns exactly zero profit. That price is called the break-even price. Any higher price would bring entry, bidding the price back down, and any lower price would bring exit, bidding the price back up. Here the industry long-run supply curve is flat.

A second possibility is that the industry is increasing-cost, which means that the break-even price for new entrants increases as the industry expands. This could happen either because new entrants are less efficient than existing firms or because new entrants bid up the price of inputs, causing everyone's costs to increase. In this case the industry supply curve slopes upward.

A third possibility is that the industry is decreasing-cost, which means that the break-even price for new entrants falls as the industry expands. For example, when the industry reaches a certain size, specialized subindustries can be formed. In this case there is a downward-sloping long-run supply curve.

Review Questions

R1. For a competitive firm with an upward-sloping marginal cost curve, explain carefully why the marginal cost curve and supply curve coincide.

R2. When a competitive firm has a U-shaped marginal cost curve, what is its supply curve in the short run? In the long run? Explain why.

R3. What determines the short-run supply curve of a competitive industry?

R4. What determines the demand curve facing a single firm in a competitive industry?

R5. What is the difference between accounting profit and economic profit?

R6. Why must economic profits be zero in the long run if all firms are identical?

R7. Explain why average cost is minimized in long-run zero-profit competitive equilibrium.

R8. What is a constant-cost industry? What is an increasing-cost industry? What is a decreasing-cost industry?

R9. What is the shape of the long-run supply curve in a constant-cost industry? In an increasing-cost industry? In a decreasing-cost industry?

Numerical Exercises

N1. In the widget industry, each firm has fixed costs of $10 and faces the following marginal cost curve:

Quantity	MC
1	$2 per widget
2	4
3	5
4	7
5	11
6	13

The industry-wide demand curve is given by the following chart:

Price	Quantity
$2	60 per widget
4	48
5	36
7	24
11	12
13	0

a. What is the break-even price in this industry?

b. What quantity is produced by each firm?

c. How many firms are in the industry?

Now suppose that the demand curve shifts outward as follows:

Price	Quantity
$2	96 per widget
4	84
5	72
7	60
11	48
13	36

d. In the short run, what is the new price of widgets, and how many does each firm produce?

e. In the long run, what is the new price of widgets and how many does each firm produce?

N2. In the gadget industry, each firm must have one gadget press, regardless of how many gadgets it produces. The cost of a gadget press is the only fixed cost that firms face in this industry. Entry by gadget firms can bid up the cost of gadget presses. The following charts show (1) the demand for gadgets; (2) the marginal cost of producing gadgets at each individual firm; and (3) the cost of a gadget press as a function of the number of firms in the industry.

Price	Quantity Demanded
1	800
2	700
3	600
4	500
5	400
6	300

Quantity	Marginal Cost
1	$1
2	2
3	3
4	4
5	5
6	6

Number of Firms	Cost of Gadget Press
0–75	$6
76–150	10
141–225	15
225–300	18
>300	21

What is the long-run equilibrium price of gadgets? (*Hint:* Start by figuring out, for each price, the number of firms and the profits at each firm.)

N3. Kites are manufactured by identical firms. Each firm's long-run average and marginal costs of production are given by

$$AC = Q + \frac{100}{Q} \text{ and } MC = 2Q$$

where Q is the number of kites produced.

a. In long-run equilibrium, how many kites will each firm produce? Describe the long-run supply curve for kites.

b. Suppose that the demand for kites is given by the formula

$$Q = 8000 - 50P$$

where Q is the quantity demanded and P is the price. How many kites will be sold? How many firms will there be in the kite industry?

c. Suppose that the demand for kites unexpectedly goes up to

$$Q = 9000 - 50P$$

In the short run it is impossible to manufacture any more kites than those already in existence. What will the price of kites be? How much profit will each kite maker earn?

d. In the long run, what will the price of kites be? How many new firms will enter the kite-making industry? How much profit will they earn?

N4. Suppose that a law is passed requiring each kite maker to have one fire extinguisher on the premises. (These are the same kite makers we met in the preceding exercise.) The supply curve of fire extinguishers to kite makers is

$$Q = P$$

For example, at a price of $3, 3 fire extinguishers would be provided. Suppose that the kite industry reaches a new long-run equilibrium.

a. Let F be the number of firms in the kite industry. Explain why each now has long-run cost curves given by

$$AC = Q + \frac{100}{Q} + \frac{F}{Q} \text{ and } MC = 2Q$$

b. How many kites will each firm produce? (You will have to express your answer in terms of F.) How many kites will the entire industry produce? (Again, you will have to express your answer in terms of F.) What will the price of kites be?

c. If the price of kites is P, what is the number of firms F? How many kites will the industry produce in terms of P? Write a formula for the long-run industry supply curve.

d. Suppose, as in Exercise N3, that the demand for kites is

$$Q = 8000 - 50P$$

What will be the price of kites? How many kites will be produced? By how many firms? How much profit does each firm earn?

Problem Set

1. Which of the following are true for all firms? Which are true for competitive firms only? Which are false for all firms?

a. The firm faces a flat demand curve for its product.

b. The firm faces a flat marginal revenue curve.

c. The firm seeks to operate where price equals marginal cost.

   d. The firm seeks to operate where marginal cost equals marginal revenue.

   e. The firm seeks to operate where average cost is minimized.

2. If a competitive firm *fails* to maximize profits, which of the following statements are true and which are false?

   a. Price equals marginal cost.

   b. Price equals marginal revenue.

   c. Marginal cost equals marginal revenue.

3. True or False: A firm that shuts down must be earning negative profits, but a firm that earns negative profits might not shut down.

4. True or False: When price equals marginal cost, profit must equal zero.

5. The Z.Z. Top Company earned zero profit in 1997, but because of a demand shift, the company earned a positive profit in 1998. True or False: The average cost of producing a Z.Z. Top is lower in 1998 than in 1997.

6. Suppose the demand for beer increases. True or False: In the short run, beer makers will not only earn higher total profits, they will also earn higher average profits per can.

7. If a firm's long-run average and marginal cost curves are identical to its short-run average and marginal cost curves, then the firm's shutdown price is always below its break-even price.

8. Books with many mathematical formulas are generally more expensive than similar books written entirely in prose. True or False: Because typesetting is not part of the marginal cost of producing a book, the cost of typesetting mathematical formulas cannot explain this price difference.

9. In the Woody Allen film *Radio Days*, a character who has never been successful in business decides to start a career engraving gold jewelry. He argues that this should be especially lucrative, because the engraver gets to keep the gold dust from other people's jewelry. Comment.

10. True or False: In the long run, a rise in the wages of industrial workers will cause the price of haircuts to rise.

11. If New York City provides better shelters for the homeless, then in the long run homeless New Yorkers will be better off.

12. Suppose there is a fall in the demand for shoes, which are provided by a competitive constant cost industry.

    a. Does the industry-wide quantity change by more in the short run or in the long run? Justify your answer.

    b. Does the quantity provided by each individual shoemaker change by more in the short run or in the long run? Justify your answer.

    c. Do the profits of shoemakers change by more in the short run or in the long run? Justify your answer.

13. Suppose health clinics form a competitive constant-cost industry. One day, the government unexpectedly opens a new clinic, which treats 800 patients a day for free.

a. In the short run, what happens to the number of patients served by private clinics? Does it rise or fall? By more or less than 800 per day?

b. In the long run, what happens to the number of patients served by private clinics? Does it rise or fall? By more or less than 800 per day?

14. Suppose a series of bombings completely destroys several video stores in your neighborhood.

a. What happens to the number of tapes rented by one of the surviving stores in the short run? Illustrate your answer with graphs.

b. What happens in the long run? Why?

15. Every doctor in Coconino County uses disposable tongue depressors to examine patients, and also must keep exactly one X-ray machine in his office. The tongue depressors cost 10¢ each and the X-ray machine can be rented for $100 per year. The county is considering a plan to provide each doctor with free tongue depressors. An alternative plan would provide each doctor with a free X-ray machine.

a. If medicine is a competitive industry in Coconino County, what is the short-run effect of each plan, both for the town as a whole and at each individual doctor's office?

b. If medicine is a competitive constant-cost industry in Coconino County, what is the long-run effect of each plan, both for the town as a whole and at each individual doctor's office?

c. If medicine is a competitive increasing-cost industry in Coconino County, what are the long-run effects of each plan?

16. Suppose the wholesale price of gasoline falls by 50 cents a gallon. Does the retail price fall by more than 50 cents, by 50 cents, or by less than 50 cents?

a. Answer assuming that gas stations constitute a competitive constant-cost industry.

b. Answer assuming that gas stations constitute a competitive increasing-cost industry.

17. Upper, Middle, and Lower Slobbovia are distant countries that do not trade with each other or the rest of the world. In Upper Slobbovia, kites are provided by a competitive constant-cost industry. In Middle Slobbovia, kites are provided by a competitive increasing-cost industry. In Lower Slobbovia, kites are provided by a single monopolist. All three countries have just imposed a new tax on kite producers of $1,000 per firm per year. Rank the three countries in terms of what fraction of this tax is passed on to consumers in the long run. Justify your answer carefully.

18. True or False: In a competitive constant-cost industry, an excise tax is *partly* passed on to demanders in the short run, but *completely* passed on to demanders in the long run.

19. True or False: An excise tax on the product of a decreasing cost industry would raise the price by *more* than the amount of the tax.

20. Suppose gas stations form a competitive constant cost industry, and Gus owns a gas station. Gus is also a good friend of the mayor.

a. Suppose the mayor imposes a $1 excise tax on all gasoline sold in town *except at Gus's station*, where there is no tax. Show the effect on the price and quantity of gas that Gus sells in the short run and in the long run.

b. Suppose the mayor imposes a $1,000 annual license fee to be paid by all gas stations in town *except for Gus's*; Gus gets a free license. Show the effect on the price and quantity of gas that Gus sells in the short run.

c. Suppose that the mayor imposes a $1,000 annual license fee to be paid by all gas stations in town *except for Gus's*; Gus gets a free license. Show the effect on the price and quantity of gas that Gus sells in the long run.

For each of the following situations, decide how the circumstance being described might affect the price and quantity of drinks sold at the Airliner Bar. Answer (a) in the short run, assuming perfect competition; (b) in the long run, assuming that bars are a competitive constant-cost industry; (c) in the long run, assuming that bars are a competitive increasing-cost industry; and (d) in the long run, assuming that bars are a competitive decreasing-cost industry.

21. The wholesale price of liquor goes up.

22. The owners recalculate and discover that the redecoration completed last month actually cost 15% more than they thought it did.

23. A disgruntled customer threatens to sue after being mistakenly served *lye* instead of *rye*. In exchange for a large payoff, the customer offers not only to withhold suit, but also to keep his mouth (or what is left of it) shut about the incident.

24. The same incident occurs as in Problem 23, except that the newspapers have already found out about it.

25. The yearly price of liquor licenses goes up.

26. The city council passes a one-time emergency tax measure, requiring every local tavern owner to immediately contribute $30 to the town treasury.

27. The owners of a neighboring establishment complain about the noise from the Airliner Bar, and they win a court order requiring the bar to compensate them. The court rules that the Airliner Bar must pay the neighbors 5¢ for each drink it serves.

28. A general breakdown of family life leads to a lot more people going out to bars.

29. A wealthy couple decide that they really want to build a house precisely on the site now occupied by the Airliner Bar.

30. There is a general rise in the price of land.

In each of the following situations, determine the effect on the price and quantity of car washes sold at Al's Car Wash. Answer (a) in the short run, assuming perfect competition; (b) in the long run, assuming that car washes are a competitive increasing-cost industry; and (c) in the long run, assuming that car washes are a competitive constant-cost industry.

31. The cost of mechanical car wash equipment goes up.

32. The motel next door to Al's wants to expand and offers to buy him out.

33. One of Al's major pieces of equipment breaks down unexpectedly and needs to be repaired.

34. There is an epidemic of equipment failures at car washes all over town.

35. The mayor declares a one-time only Car Wash Appreciation Day, on which every car wash owner in the city is given $1,000 out of city funds.

36. The mayor declares that Car Wash Appreciation Day will become an annual event.

37. An influential member of the city council invents an automatic car-polishing machine. When the council member discovers that no car wash wants to buy the machine, legislation is pushed through requiring every car wash to own one. (The council member's supply curve for car-polishing machines is upward sloping.)

38. There is a general rise in wage rates.

39. A story on *60 Minutes* reveals that Al subscribes to the deconstructionist school of literary criticism. Workers throughout the city are so revolted that they will not work for Al unless he pays them 50 cents an hour more than they can earn at any other car wash.

40. A large office building is constructed, making it impossible to see Al's Car Wash from the road.

41. The city begins using salt to clear ice off the roads in winter. (Salt causes cars to rust unless it is washed off frequently.)

In each of the following situations, determine the effect on the price and quantity of goose liver sold at Bambi's House of Goose Liver. Answer (a) in the short run, assuming perfect competition; (b) in the long run, assuming that goose liver is a competitive increasing-cost industry; and (c) in the long run, assuming that goose liver is a competitive constant-cost industry.

42. Due to a health scare, the city requires all goose liver purveyors to discard their inventory and replace it with fresh goose liver.

43. An incompetent but enthusiastic health inspector takes office, and is ex-

pected to periodically order all goose liver purveyors to discard their inventory at random times.

44. Bambi's vindictive ex-husband is appointed health inspector, and is expected to fine Bambi $5,000 per year for spurious health violations.

45. Bambi's vindictive ex-husband is appointed health inspector, and is expected to fine Bambi one-tenth of her revenues each year for spurious health violations.

46. A careless employee leaves the freezer door open and all of Bambi's goose liver has to be replaced.

47. A medical journal reports that goose liver can cause cancer.

48. A medical journal reports that goose liver prevents cancer.

49. Bambi's freezer needs to be replaced.

50. Bambi has a fight with the owner of Tiny's Discount Goose Liver Emporium, which supplies all of the goose liver restaurants in town. Consequently, she must now import all of her goose liver from the next county, and must pay additional shipping fees.

51. Bambi and Tiny make up, and as a sign of friendship Tiny agrees to supply Bambi with goose liver at half price from now on.

52. Bambi and Tiny make up, and as a sign of friendship Tiny gives her 100 free pounds of goose liver (but continues to charge the usual price when he orders more).

53. A new law requires all restaurant owners who serve goose liver to pass a course on "The Role of Goose Liver in the Secular Society." The local college charges $500 tuition for this course.

54. There is a fall in the wage rate for restaurant dishwashing services.

55. A new landfill comes to occupy the property next to Bambi's. The odor from the landfill is offensive to customers.

56. A new movie theater opens next door to Bambi's, and is the only movie theater in town that allows movie-goers to bring in their own goose liver instead of buying it at the concession stand.

Internet Exercise

In December 1994 the City of New York reduced the tax rate applied to hotel rooms. The New York City Independent Budget Office has analyzed the impact of this tax reduction, and their report is available on the Internet at the following site (http://www.ibo.nyc.ny.us/pubtax1.html). Access this material and relate it to Exhibit 7–27 in Chapter 7.

chapter 8

Welfare Economics and the Gains from Trade

We now know a great deal about what determines the prices and quantities of goods traded in the marketplace. We learned about the sources of demand curves in Chapters 3 and 4 and about the sources of supply curves in Chapters 5, 6, and 7. We know that a competitive market operates at the point where the supply and demand curves cross.

All of the theory we have developed involves the efforts of individuals and firms to make themselves as well off as possible: Individuals seek the highest possible indifference curve and firms seek the maximum possible profit. These efforts are the reason for trade.

In this chapter we will develop a way to measure the gains from trade. When a consumer purchases a dozen eggs from a farmer, each is better off (or at least not worse off)—otherwise no trade would have occurred in the first place. The question we will address is: How *much* better off are they?

Once we know how to measure the gains from trade, we will be able to study the ways in which these gains are affected by various changes in market conditions. Such changes include taxes, price controls, subsidies, quotas, rationing, and so forth. We will be able to see who gains and who loses from such policies and to evaluate the size of these gains and losses.

Finally, we will learn one of the most remarkable facts in economics: In a competitive equilibrium, the sum of all the gains to all the market participants is as large as possible. This fact, called the *invisible hand theorem*, suggests a normative standard by which market outcomes can be judged. In the appendix to the chapter, we will compare this normative standard with a variety of alternatives.

8.1 Measuring the Gains from Trade

For more on marginal value, demand, and consumer surplus, see: http://www.best.com/~ddfr/Academic/Price_Theory/PThy_Chapter_4/PThy_Chapter_4.html

When a consumer buys eggs from a farmer, each one gains from the trade. Our first task is to devise a method for measuring the extent of these gains.

Consumers' and Producers' Surplus

We begin by considering the gains to the consumer. First, we develop a geometric measure of the value that the consumer places on his purchases.

Marginal Value and Demand

Value The maximum amount that a consumer would be willing to pay for an item.

Consider the buyer of eggs. We begin by asking him how much he values one egg. The **value** of an egg to a consumer is defined as the maximum amount that the consumer would be willing to pay to acquire that egg. Let us suppose that our (very hungry) consumer would be willing to pay up to $15 in exchange for an egg. (In other words, we assume that at any market price less than $15, the consumer would buy the egg, whereas at any market price over $15, he would choose not to buy it.) The value of 1 egg to this consumer is $15.

How much, then, would the consumer value 2 eggs? Presumably, more than $15. But we expect him to value 2 eggs at something less than $30, because somebody who already has an egg places less value on a second egg than on the first. In other words, the *marginal* value of the second egg is something less than $15, and so the total value of the first 2 eggs is something less than $30.

Why does marginal value decrease as the consumer acquires more eggs? Because when he has only 1 egg, he uses it in the one way in which he would most like to use an egg. Perhaps that means that he fries it for breakfast. When he has 2 eggs, he fries the first one and uses the second for whatever he considers to be an egg's second most important use (maybe egg salad for lunch). Even if he uses the second egg together with the first egg to make an omelet, it is reasonable to assume that the second half of his omelet is less valuable to him than the first half.

As the consumer acquires more eggs, their marginal value continues to decrease. Let us assume that these marginal values are as given in Table A in Exhibit 8–1. If the market price is $7 per egg, how many eggs does this consumer buy? He certainly buys a first egg: He values it at $15 and can get it for $7. He also buys a second egg, which he values at $13 and can also get for $7. Likewise, he buys a third egg. The fourth egg, which he values at $7 and can buy for $7, is a matter of indifference; we will assume that the consumer buys this egg as well. The fifth egg would be a bad buy for our consumer; it provides only $5 worth of additional value and costs $7 to acquire. He buys 4 eggs.

EXERCISE 8.1 Add to Table A in Exhibit 8–1 a "Net Gain" column displaying the difference between total value and total cost. Verify that the consumer is best off when he buys 4 eggs.

Exhibit 8-1 Demand and Marginal Value

Table A. Total and Marginal Value

Quantity	Total Value	Marginal Value
1	$15	$15/egg
2	28	13
3	38	10
4	45	7
5	50	5
6	52	2

Table B. Demand

Price	Quantity
$15/egg	1
13	2
10	3
7	4
5	5
2	6

Value per egg ($)
15
13
11
9
7
5
3
1
0
1 2 3 4 5 6
MV
Quantity (eggs)

A

Price per egg ($)
15
13
11
9
7
5
3
1
0
1 2 3 4 5 6
D
Quantity (eggs)

B

At a given market price the consumer will choose a quantity that equates price with marginal value. As a result, his demand curve for eggs is identical with his marginal value curve.

EXERCISE 8.2 How many eggs does the consumer buy when the market price is $5 per egg? Explain why.

There is nothing new in this reasoning; it is just an application of the equimarginal principle. The consumer buys eggs as long as the marginal value of an egg exceeds its price, and stops when the two become equal. In other words, he chooses that quantity at which price equals marginal value. In Table B of Exhibit 8–1 we record the number of eggs the consumer will purchase at each price. Table B is the consumer's demand schedule, and the corresponding graph is a picture of his demand curve for eggs.[1] (Compare this reasoning with the derivation of Farmer Adams's supply curve in Exhibit 7–4.)

The graphs in Exhibit 8–1 display both the consumer's marginal value curve and his demand curve for eggs. The curves are identical, although they differ conceptually. To read the marginal value curve, take a given quantity and read the corresponding marginal value off the vertical axis. To read the demand curve, take a given price and read the corresponding quantity off the horizontal axis.

In fact, what we have learned is not new. The marginal value of an egg, measured in dollars, is the same thing as the consumer's marginal rate of substitution between eggs and dollars: It is the number of dollars for which he would be just willing to trade an egg. In an indifference curve diagram between eggs and dollars, the marginal value is the slope of an indifference curve and the price is the slope of the budget line. We saw in Section 3.2 that the consumer's optimum occurs at a point where the marginal value is equal to the price, and that this is the source of the consumer's demand curve.

Total Value as an Area

Suppose the consumer of Exhibit 8–1 acquires 4 eggs. We would like to depict geometrically their total value. We begin by depicting the $15 in value represented by the first egg. This $15 is the area of rectangle 1 in panel A of Exhibit 8–2. The height of the rectangle is 15, and the width of the rectangle (which stretches from a quantity of 0 to a quantity of 1) is 1. Thus, the area is $15 \times 1 = 15$. The $13 in value that the consumer receives from the second egg is represented by rectangle 2 in the same graph. The height of this rectangle is 13 and its width is 1, so its area is $13 \times 1 = 13$.

The area of rectangle 3 is the marginal value of the third egg, and the area of rectangle 4 is the marginal value of the fourth egg. The total value of the 4 eggs is the sum of the 4 marginal values, or the total area of the 4 rectangles. That is, the total value is $\$(15 + 13 + 10 + 7) = \$45$.

Actually, what we have done is only approximately correct. That is because the marginal value table in Exhibit 8–1 omits some information. It does not show the value of 1½ eggs or 3¼ eggs, for example.[2] In order to consider such quantities, we might make our measurements not in *eggs,* but in *quarter-eggs*. If we do so, the quantity of quarter-eggs bought is 16, and the four rectangles

---

[1]More precisely, the graph is a picture of his *compensated* demand curve. When we talk about "willingness to pay" for an additional egg, we are asking what number of dollars the consumer could sacrifice for that egg and remain equally happy. The points on the marginal value curve all represent points on the same indifference curve for the consumer.

All of the demand curves in this chapter are really compensated demand curves. However, the compensated and uncompensated demand curves coincide when income effects are small, so measurements using the ordinary (uncompensated) demand curve are good approximations for most purposes.

[2]You might think it is impossible to buy just one-quarter of an egg, but this is not so. Remember that every demand curve has a unit of time implicitly associated with it. If our demand curves are *per week,* then the way to buy exactly one-quarter of an egg per week is to buy one every four weeks.

Exhibit 8-2 Total Value

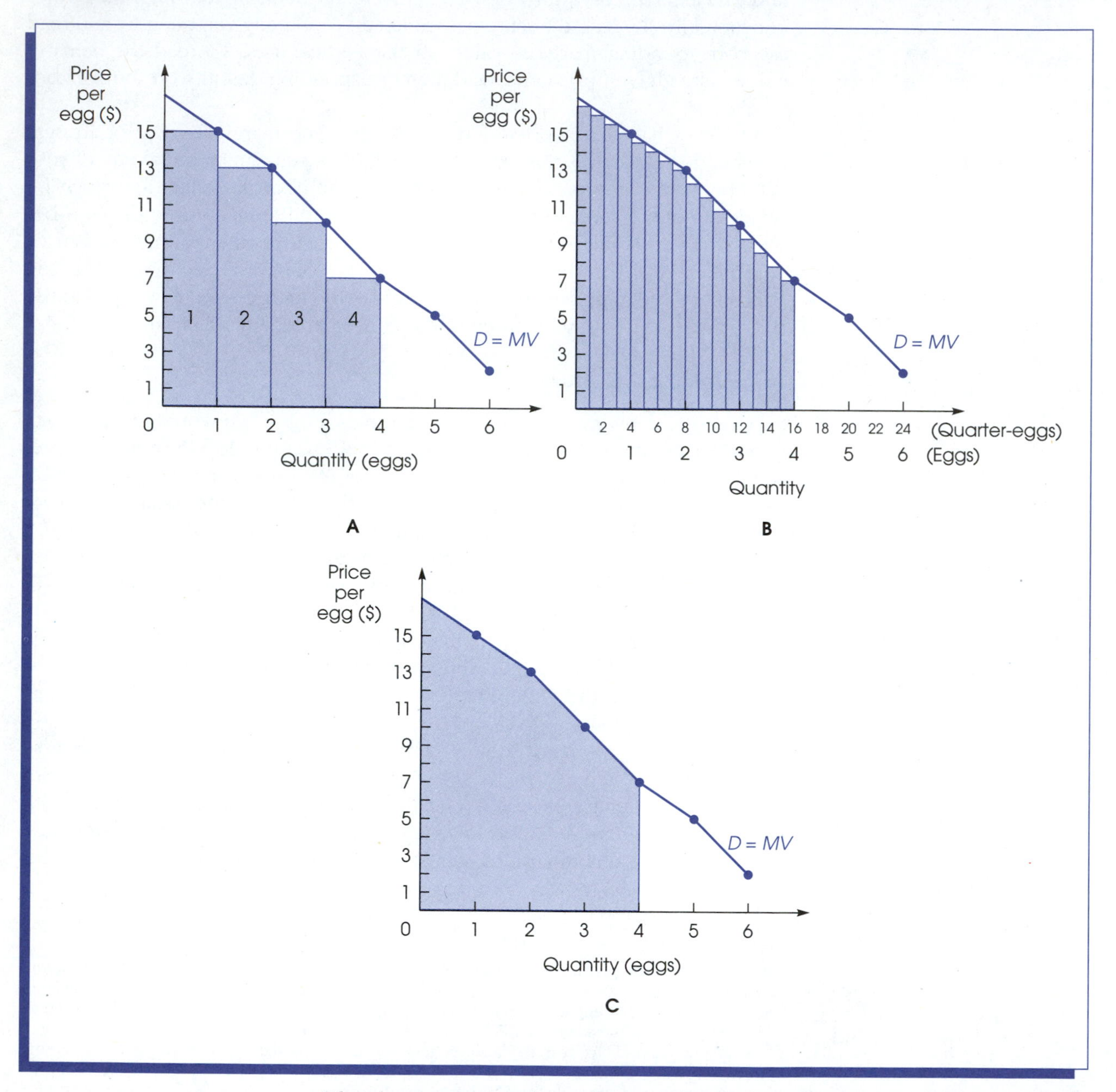

When the consumer buys 4 eggs, their marginal values ($15, $13, $10, and $7) can be read off the demand curve. Their values are represented by the areas of rectangles 1 through 4 in panel A. Therefore, their total value is the sum of the areas of the rectangles, or $45.

We can get a more accurate estimate of total value if we measure eggs in smaller units. Panel B shows the calculation of total value when we measure by the quarter-egg instead of by the whole egg. As we take smaller and smaller units, we approach the shaded area in panel C, which is the exact measure of total value when the consumer buys 4 eggs.

of panel A of Exhibit 8–2 are replaced by the 16 rectangles of panel B, each one-quarter as wide as the original ones. Refining things even further, we could measure quantities in hundredth-eggs, making 400 rectangles. As our fundamental units get smaller, our approximation to the total value of 4 eggs gets better. The total value of the consumer's 4 eggs is exactly equal to the shaded area in panel C.

The total value of the consumer's purchases is equal to the area under the demand curve out to the quantity demanded.[3]

The total value of 4 eggs is completely independent of their market price. Imagine offering the consumer a choice of living in two worlds, both identical except for the fact that in one world he has no eggs and in the other he has 4 eggs. Ask him what is the most he would be willing to pay to live in the second world rather than the first. His answer to that question is the total value that he places on 4 eggs.

The Consumer's Surplus

Access a slide show on demand and consumer surplus at: http://price.bus.okstate.edu/archive/Econ3113_963/Shows/Chapter 4/chap_04.htm

Consumer's surplus The consumer's gain from trade; the amount by which the value of his purchases exceeds what he actually pays for them.

Suppose the market price of an egg is $7. At this price, the consumer of Exhibit 8–1 buys 4 eggs, with a total value of (approximately) $45, which is represented by the entire shaded area in Exhibit 8–3.[4]

When the consumer buys those eggs, his total expenditure is only 4 × $7 = $28—a bargain, considering that he'd have been willing to pay up to $45. That $28 is represented in Exhibit 8–3 by area *B*, which is a rectangle with height 7 and width 4. The extent of the bargain is measured by the difference $45 − $28 = $17, which is area *A*. We call that area the **consumer's surplus** in the market for eggs. It is the total value (to him) of the eggs he buys, minus what he actually pays for them.

In summary, we have

Total Value	=	$A + B$	=	$45
Expenditure	=	B	=	$28
Consumer's Surplus	=	A	=	$17

[3]If you have had a course in calculus, you might be interested to know that we have just "proven" the fundamental theorem of calculus! Think of total value as a function (where quantity is the variable). The marginal value is the addition to total value when quantity is increased by one small unit. In other words, marginal value is the derivative of total value. The area under the marginal value curve out to a given quantity is the integral of marginal value from zero out to that quantity. We have argued that this integral is equal to the total value associated with that quantity. In other words, integrating the derivative brings you back to the original function.

Perhaps you knew the fundamental theorem of calculus but always accepted it as a mysterious fact of nature. If so, thinking about the economics of total and marginal values should give you some real insight into why the fundamental theorem is true.

[4]$45 is the area of the four rectangles in Exhibit 8–2A, which is approximately the same as the shaded regions in Exhibits 8–2C and 8–3. The approximation is good enough that from now on, we will say that the area of the shaded region *is* $45.

Exhibit 8-3 The Consumer's Surplus

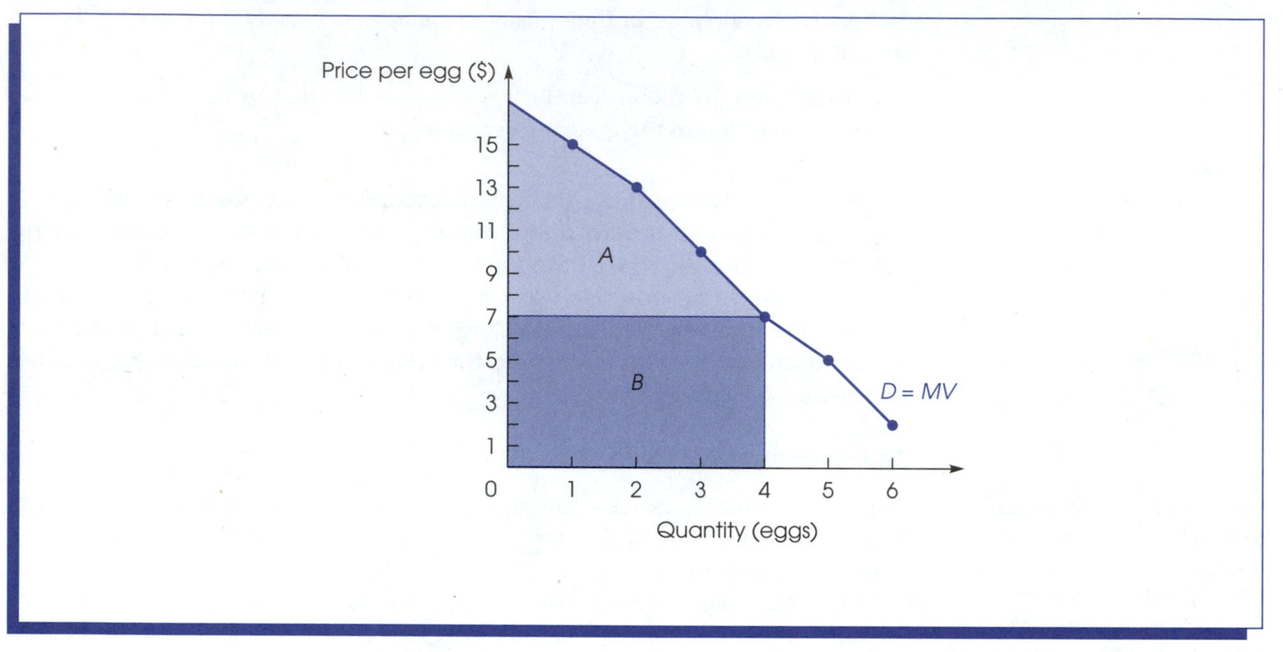

In order to acquire 4 eggs, the consumer would be willing to pay up to the entire shaded area, *A* + *B*. At a price of $7 per egg, his actual expenditure for 4 eggs is $28, which is area *B*. The difference, area *A*, is his consumer's surplus.

This consumer would be willing to pay up to $17 for a ticket to enter a grocery store where he can buy eggs. If the store lets him in for free, it's as if the consumer has received a gift (that is, a free admission ticket) that he valued at $17. You can think of the consumer's surplus as the value of that gift. Geometrically, we have seen that:

The consumer's surplus is the area under the demand curve down to the price paid and out to the quantity demanded.

Notice that the consumer's surplus is measured in units of *dollars*. In general, horizontal distances represent *quantities*, vertical distances represent *prices* (in units of, for example, dollars per egg), and areas represent numbers of *dollars*.

The Producer's Surplus

The consumer is not the only party to a transaction, and not the only one to gain from it. We can also calculate the *producer's* gains from trade. Imagine a producer with the marginal cost curve shown in Exhibit 8–4. Suppose that this producer supplies 4 eggs to the marketplace. What is the cost of supplying these 4 eggs? It is the sum of the marginal cost of supplying the first egg ($1), the marginal cost of the second ($3), the marginal cost of the third ($5), and the marginal cost of the fourth ($7). These numbers are represented by the 4 rectangles in panel A of Exhibit 8–4. Their heights are 1, 3, 5, and 7, and they each have width 1.

As with the consumer's total value, we must realize that the rectangles of panel A provide only an approximation, because we are making the faulty assumption that eggs can be produced only in whole-number quantities. A more accurate picture would include very thin rectangles, and the sum of their areas would be the area labeled *D* in the second panel. This is the cost of providing 4 eggs.[5] Area D is approximately equal to $ (1 + 3 + 5 + 7) = $16.

Exhibit 8–4 The Producer's Surplus

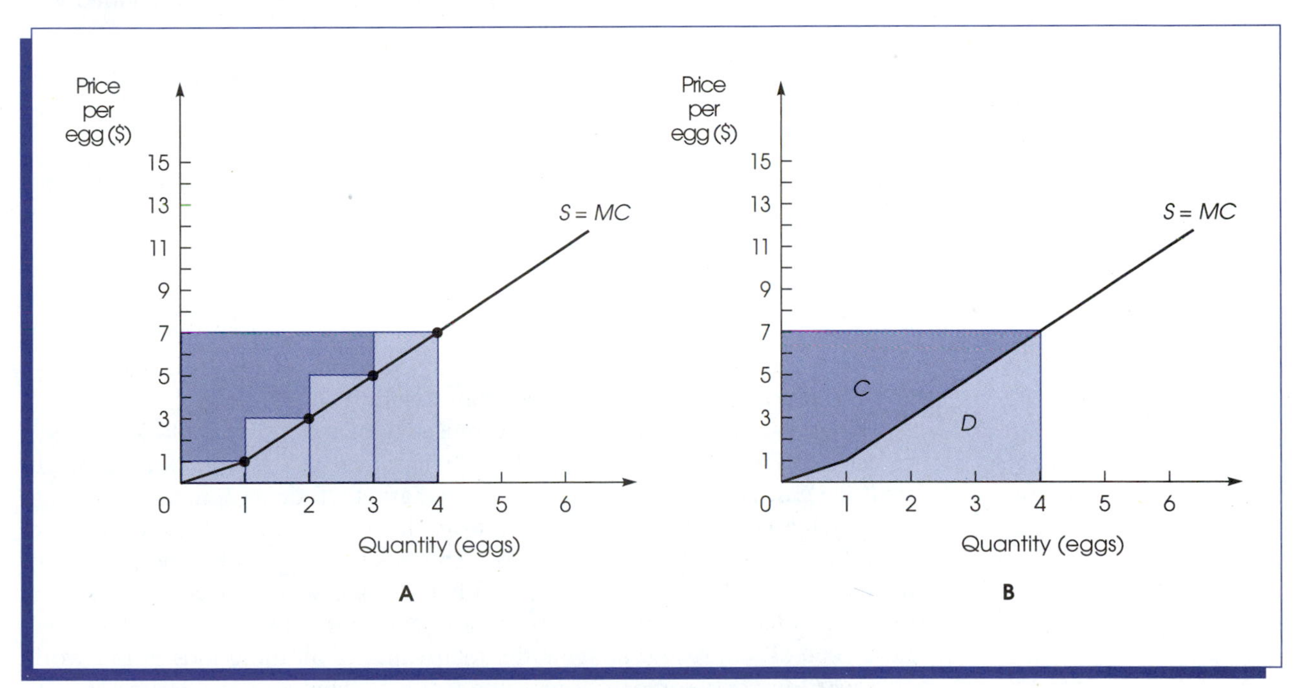

If the producer supplies 4 eggs, his cost is the sum of the 4 marginal costs, which are represented by the rectangles in panel A. If we measure eggs in very small units, we find that an exact measure of his cost is area *D* in panel B. At a market price of $7, revenue is $7 × 4 = $28, which is the area of rectangle *C* + *D*. Thus, the producer's surplus is area *C*.

[5]By adding up the producer's marginal costs, we are excluding any fixed costs that the producer might have. This is because we are considering only how the producer is affected by trade, whereas the producer would incur the fixed costs even without trading. This makes the fixed costs irrelevant to the discussion.

Next we depict the producer's total revenue. This is easy: he sells 4 eggs at \$7 apiece, so his revenue is $4 \times \$7 = \$28$, which is the area of the rectangle $C + D$ in Exhibit 8–4.

Now we can compute the producer's gains from trade: Total revenues are $C + D$ and production costs are D. The difference, area C, is called the **producer's surplus** and represents the gains to the producer as a result of his participation in the marketplace.

Producer's surplus The producer's gain from trade; the amount by which his revenue exceeds his variable production costs.

In this example, we have

Total Revenue	=	$C + D$	=	\$28
− Production Costs	=	D	=	\$16
Producer's Surplus	=	C	=	\$12

This producer would be willing to pay up to \$12 for a license to sell eggs. If no license is required, it's as if the producer has received a gift (that is, a free license) that he valued at \$12. You can think of the producer's surplus as the value of that gift.

If the producer is competitive, his marginal cost curve can be identified with his supply curve. Therefore:

The producer's surplus is the area above the supply curve up to the price received and out to the quantity supplied.

For a noncompetitive producer, we would want to change *supply curve* to *marginal cost curve* in the preceding sentence, but for a competitive producer these are the same thing.

Social Gain

In panel A of Exhibit 8–5 we have drawn both the supply and the demand curve on the same graph. The consumer's surplus is taken from Exhibit 8–3 and the producer's surplus is taken from Exhibit 8–4.

The consumer's and producer's surpluses depicted in Exhibit 8–5 provide a measure of the gains to both parties. Their sum is called the **social gain,** or **welfare gain,** due to the existence of the market. Students sometimes want to know where these gains are coming from: If the consumer and the producer have both gained, then who has lost? The answer is *nobody*. The process of trade creates welfare gains, which simply did not exist before the trading took place. The fact that the world as a whole can be made better off should not strike you as surprising: Imagine the total value of all the goods in the world 100 years ago and compare it with the value of what you see around you today. In a very real sense the difference can be thought of as the sum of all the little triangles of surplus that have been created by consumers and producers over the passage of time.

Social gain or **welfare gain** The sum of the gains from trade to all participants.

There is another way to measure the welfare gains created by the marketplace. Rather than separately computing a consumer's surplus and a producer's surplus, we can calculate the total welfare gain created by each egg. This is shown in panel B of Exhibit 8–5. The first rectangle represents the difference between the marginal value of the first egg and the marginal cost of producing it, which is precisely the welfare gain due to that egg. The height of the

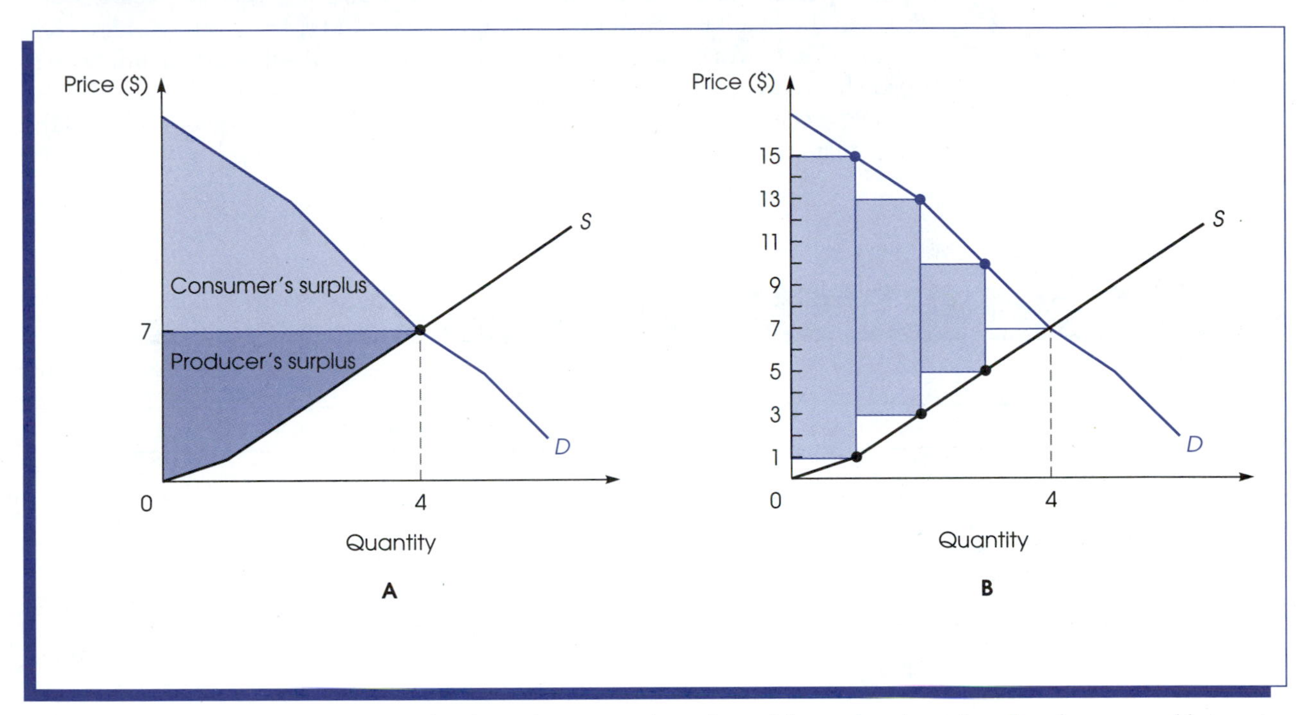

Panel A shows the consumer's surplus and the producer's surplus when 4 eggs are sold at a price of $7. The sum of these areas is the total welfare gain. The second panel shows another way to calculate the welfare gain. The first egg creates a gain equal to the area of the first rectangle, the second creates a gain equal to the area of the second rectangle, and so on. When units are taken to be small, the sum of these areas is the shaded region, which is the sum of the consumer's and producer's surpluses.

rectangle is $15 - 1 = 14$, and its width is 1, giving an area of 14. The second rectangle has a height of $13 - 3 = 10$ and a width of 1, giving an area of 10, which is the welfare gain from the second egg. The welfare gain due to the exchange of 4 eggs is the sum of the 4 rectangles (the fourth "rectangle" has height zero!). As usual, our focus on whole numbers has forced us to approximate: The total welfare gain is actually the entire shaded area between the supply and demand curves out to the equilibrium point.

Notice that the total welfare gain (shown in panel B) is the sum of the consumer's and producer's surpluses (shown in panel A). This is as it should be: All of the gains have to go somewhere, and there are only the consumer and the producer to collect them.

Social Gains and Markets

Next we want to consider markets with more than one consumer and with more than one producer. It turns out that consumers' and producers' surpluses can again be computed in exactly the same way.

Imagine a world with three consumers: Larry, Moe, and Curly. Exhibit 8–6 displays each man's marginal value schedule for eggs. In this world, when the price is $15, Larry buys 1 egg and Moe and Curly each buy 0 eggs. The total quantity demanded is 1. At a price of $13, Larry and Moe buy 1 each and Curly buys 0; the quantity demanded is 2. At a price of $11, Larry buys 1, Moe buys 2, and Curly buys 0 for a total of 3, and so on. The resulting demand curve is also shown in Exhibit 8–6.

The rectangles below the demand curve represent the marginal values of the eggs that are bought. Each rectangle is labeled with the name of the man who

Exhibit 8-6 Consumers' Surplus in the Market

Larry		*Moe*		*Curly*	
Quantity	Marginal Value	Quantity	Marginal Value	Quantity	Marginal Value
1	$15/egg	1	$13/egg	1	$7/egg
2	8	2	11	2	3

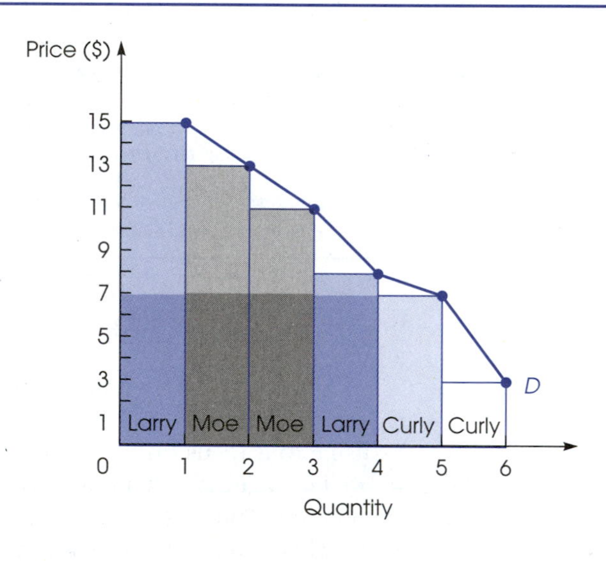

The demand curve is constructed from the marginal value curves of the three individuals. At a price of $7, Larry buys 2 eggs that he values at $15 and $8, Moe buys 2 that he values at $13 and $11, and Curly buys 1 that he values at $7. These marginal values are represented by the first 5 rectangles under the demand curve, each labeled with the appropriate consumer's name. The total value of the 5 eggs to the consumers is the sum of the areas of the first 5 rectangles. The cost to the consumers is the darker area. The consumers' surplus is what remains; it is the area under the demand curve down to the price paid and out to the quantity purchased.

consumes the corresponding egg: The first egg sold is bought by Larry, the second and third by Moe, the fourth by Larry, the fifth and sixth by Curly.

Now suppose that the price of eggs is $7. How many eggs are sold, and what is their total value? Larry buys 2 (the first and fourth), Moe buys 2 (the second and third), and Curly buys 1 (the fifth). The values of these eggs are given by the areas of the corresponding rectangles, and the total value to the consumers is the sum of the 5 areas, which are shaded in Exhibit 8–6. From this must be subtracted the total amount that the consumers pay for the 5 eggs, which is represented by the darker, lower portions of the rectangles. The remaining portion, above the $7 price line, is the consumers' surplus. The consumer's surplus is composed of many rectangles, and each consumer receives some of these rectangles as his share of the welfare gain. But, just as before, the total consumers' surplus is represented by the area under the demand curve down to the price paid and out to the quantity demanded.

An analogous statement holds for producers' surplus. Suppose that three different firms have the marginal cost schedules shown in Exhibit 8–7. The total supply curve is given by the graph. The blue rectangles corresponding to individual eggs are labeled with the names of the firms that produce them. Producers' surplus is given by total revenue (the entire shaded region) *minus* the sum of the areas of these rectangles, out to the quantity produced. That is, the producers' surplus is the gray part of the shaded region in the exhibit. This surplus is divided up among the producers, but the total of all the producers' surplus is still given by the area above the supply curve up to the price received and out to the quantity supplied.

8.2 The Efficiency Criterion

For a summary description of the efficiency standard, in regard to congestion pricing visit: http://www.hhh.umn.edu/Centers/SLP/Conpric/econ.htm

Suppose the government decides to impose a sales tax on coffee and give away the tax revenue (say as welfare payments or Social Security payments). Is that a good or a bad policy?

Both coffee drinkers and coffee sellers will tend to oppose this policy, because a sales tax simultaneously raises the price to demanders and lowers the price to suppliers. On the other hand, the citizens who are slated to receive the tax revenue will tend to favor the policy. How should we weigh the interests of one group against those of another?

Normative criterion A general method for choosing among alternative social policies.

A **normative criterion** is a general method for making this sort of decision. One example of a normative criterion is *majority rule:* Every citizen gets one vote to cast for or against the tax, and we bow to the will of the majority. In this case, the tax will probably be defeated if the coffee buyers and coffee sellers outnumber the tax recipients, and the tax will probably pass if the tax recipients outnumber the buyers and sellers.

One problem with the majority rule criterion is that it allows the slight preference of a majority to overrule the strong preference of a minority. For example, suppose that you and nine of your fellow students vote to burn down your economics professor's house for amusement. By the majority rule criterion, your ten votes in favor of this activity outweigh the professor's one vote against. Nevertheless, most people would agree that burning down the house is a bad thing to do. So there is apparently something wrong with unrestricted majority rule.

Exhibit 8-7 Producers' Surplus in the Market

Firm A		*Firm B*		*Firm C*	
Quantity	Marginal Cost	Quantity	Marginal Cost	Quantity	Marginal Cost
1	$1	1	$5	1	$6
2	3	2	11	2	7

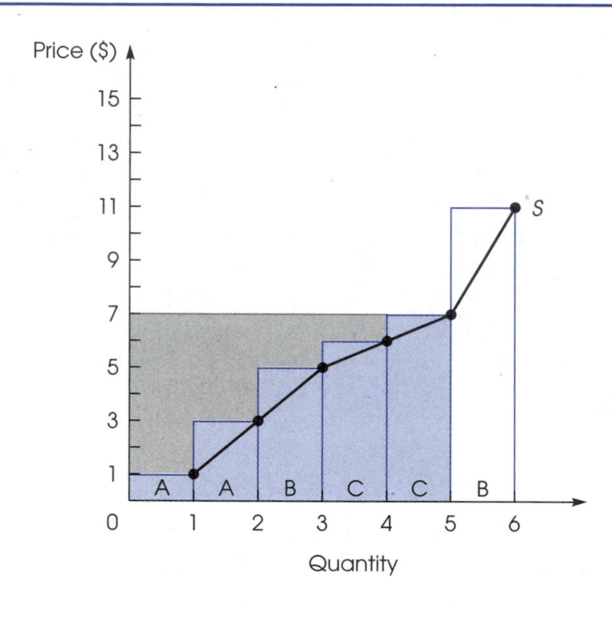

The market supply curve is the industry's marginal cost curve. When the price is $7, Firm A produces 2 items at marginal costs of $1 and $3, Firm B produces 1 at a marginal cost of $5, and Firm C produces 2 at marginal costs of $6 and $7. These costs are represented by the blue rectangles below the supply curve. The revenue earned by producers is the entire shaded region. The gray portion of that region above the supply curve is the producers' surplus.

Efficiency criterion A normative criterion according to which your votes are weighted according to your willingness to pay for your preferred outcome.

An alternative to majority rule is the **efficiency criterion**. According to the efficiency criterion, everyone is permitted to cast a number of votes proportional to his stake in the outcome, where your stake in the outcome is measured by how much you'd be willing to pay to get your way. So, for example, if ten students each think it would be worth $10 to watch the professor's house go up in flames, while the professor thinks it would be worth $1,000 to prevent that outcome, then each of the students gets 10 votes and the professor gets 1,000 votes. The house burning is defeated by a vote of 1,000 to 100.

One advantage of the efficiency criterion is that when it is applied consistently, you'll have the most influence on the issues you care about the most. In the appendix to this chapter, we will consider several alternatives to the efficiency criterion. In this section, we will explore the consequences of accepting the efficiency criterion and applying it to evaluate public policies. This will enable us to judge various policies—such as the sales tax on coffee—to be either "good" or "bad" *as judged by the efficiency criterion*. Of course, it does not follow that those policies are necessarily either good or bad in a larger sense. The efficiency criterion is one possible method of choosing among policies, and it is a method that you might come either to approve or disapprove.

To help you decide whether you like the efficiency criterion, it will be useful to see what it recommends in a variety of specific circumstances. That's what we'll do in this section.

Consumers' Surplus and the Efficiency Criterion

Suppose that we are deciding whether it should be legal to produce, sell, and buy eggs. Among the parties who will be interested in the outcome of this debate are the people who like to eat eggs for breakfast. They'll want to vote for legal egg sales. How many votes should we give them?

The answer, according to the efficiency criterion, is that they should receive votes in proportion to their willingness to pay for the right to buy eggs. That willingness to pay is measured by the consumers' surplus. For example, consider the consumer depicted back in Exhibit 8–3; this consumer receives a number of votes proportional to area *A*.

If we want to know how many votes should be allocated to *all* egg consumers (as opposed to the *single* egg consumer of Exhibit 8–3), we can use the market demand curve to measure the total consumers' surplus. For example, suppose the area under the market demand curve, out to the quantity of eggs consumed, and down to the market price of eggs, is equal to $10,000. Then we know that egg consumers *as a group* should receive 10,000 pro-egg votes. (In other words, each consumer receives a number of votes proportional to his individual consumer's surplus, and we know that the sum of all these numbers is 10,000.)

Likewise, we can use the producers' surplus to compute the number of pro-egg votes cast by egg producers. If there are any anti-egg votes (say, from people who hate living next door to chicken farms), their number is a bit harder to calculate in practice. But in principle, the farmer's neighbors gets a number of votes proportional to what they would be willing to pay to make the chickens go away. (The easiest case is the case where there are no unhappy neighbors; then there might be *zero* votes in favor of banning egg production.)

The Effect of a Sales Tax

Now let's return to the issue of a sales tax on coffee, and evaluate that policy according to the efficiency criterion.

Panel A of Exhibit 8–8 shows the supply and demand for coffee. Panel B shows the same market after a 5¢ per-cup sales tax is placed on consumers. As we know from Chapter 1, this has the effect of lowering the demand curve vertically a distance of 5¢.

Before the sales tax is imposed, the consumers' and producers' surpluses are as shown in panel A. The sum of these is the total welfare gained by all mem-

Exhibit 8-8 The Effect of a Sales Tax

	Before Sales Tax	After Sales Tax
Consumers' Surplus	$A + B + C + D + E$	$A + B$
Producers' Surplus	$F + G + H + I$	I
Tax Revenue	—	$C + D + F + G$
Social Gain	$A + B + C + D + E$ $+ F + G + H + I$	$A + B + C + D$ $+ F + G + I$
Deadweight Loss	—	$E + H$

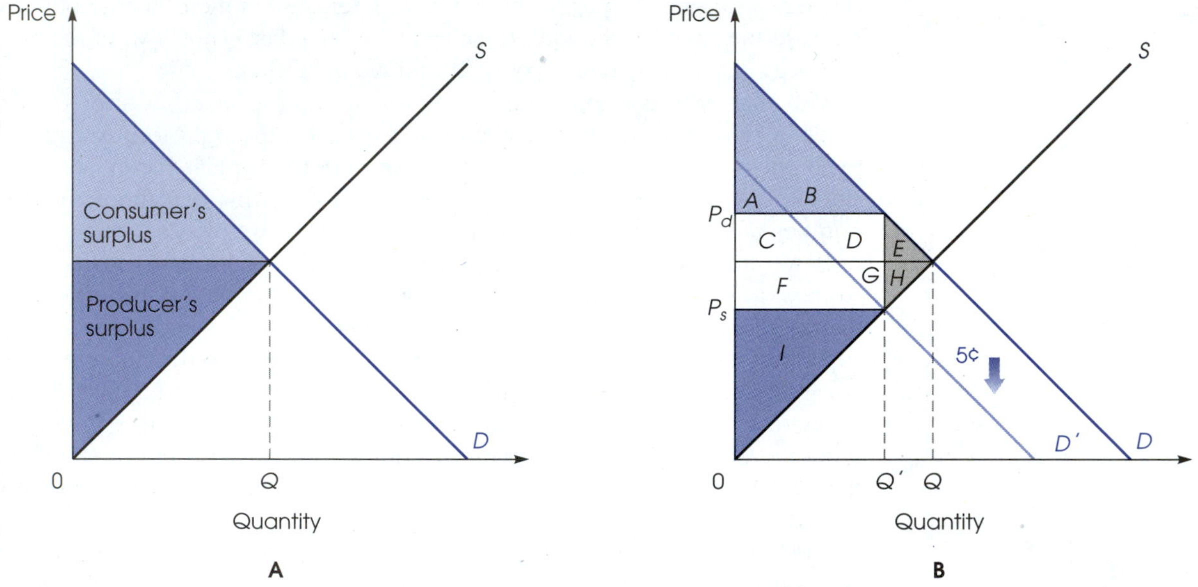

Before the sales tax is imposed, consumers' and producers' surpluses are as shown in panel A. The first column of the chart shows these surpluses in terms of the labels in panel B. The second column shows the gains to consumers and producers after the imposition of the sales tax, and includes a row for the gains to the recipients of the tax revenue. The total social gain after the tax is less than the social gain before the tax. The difference between the two is area $E + H$, the deadweight loss.

bers of society, and we will refer to it as the *social gain*. In terms of the areas in panel B, we have:

$$\text{Consumers' Surplus} = A + B + C + D + E$$

$$\text{Producers' Surplus} = F + G + H + I$$

$$\text{Social Gain} = A + B + C + D + E + F + G + H + I$$

Once the sales tax is imposed, we need to recompute the consumers' and producers' surpluses. The consumers' surplus is the area below the demand curve down to the price paid and out to the quantity demanded. The question now arises: Which demand curve? The answer is: The original demand curve, because this is the curve that reflects the consumers' true marginal values. Which price? The price paid by demanders: P_d. Which quantity? The quantity that is bought when the tax is in effect: Q'. The consumers' surplus is area $A + B$.

In other words, the sales tax causes the consumers' surplus to fall by the amount $C + D + E$. Thus, consumers would collectively be willing to pay up to $C + D + E$ to prevent the tax, and we will eventually allow them to cast $C + D + E$ votes against it.

What about producers' surplus? We need to look at the area above the supply curve up to the price received and out to the quantity supplied. The relevant price to suppliers is P_s and the relevant quantity is the quantity being sold in the presence of the sales tax: Q'. The producers' surplus is I. The tax costs producers $F + G + H$, so we will allow them to cast $F + G + H$ votes against the tax.

We can now make the following tabulation:

	Before Sales Tax	After Sales Tax
Consumers' Surplus	$A + B + C + D + E$	$A + B$
Producers' Surplus	$F + G + H + I$	I
Social Gain	$A + B + C + D + E$ $+ F + G + H + I$	?

What about the social gain after the sales tax is imposed? Can't we find it by simply adding the consumers' and producers' surpluses? The answer is no, because there is now an additional component to consider. We must ask what becomes of the tax revenue that is collected by the government. The simplest assumption is that it is given to somebody (perhaps as a welfare or Social Security payment). Alternatively, it might be spent to purchase goods and services that are then given to somebody. In some form or another, some individual (or group of individuals) ultimately collects the tax revenue, and that individual is part of society. The revenue that the recipients collect is welfare gained.

How much tax revenue is there? The answer: It is equal to the tax per cup (5¢) times the number of cups sold (Q'). Since the vertical distance between the two demand curves is 5¢, the amount of this revenue is equal to the area of the rectangle $C + D + F + G$ (height = 5¢, width = Q'). The recipients of the tax revenue gain $C + D + F + G$ as a result of the tax, and so will be allowed to cast $C + D + F + G$ votes in its favor. The final version of our table is this:

	Before Sales Tax	After Sales Tax
Consumers' Surplus	$A + B + C + D + E$	$A + B$
Producers' Surplus	$F + G + H + I$	I
Tax Revenue	—	$C + D + F + G$
Social Gain	$A + B + C + D + E$ $+ F + G + H + I$	$A + B + C + D + F$ $+ G + I$

The social gain entry is obtained by adding the entries in the preceding three rows. Even after the tax revenue is taken into account, the total gain to society is still less after the tax than it was before. The reduction in total gain is called the **deadweight loss** due to the tax. In this example, the deadweight loss is equal to the area $E + H$. Other terms for the deadweight loss are *social loss, welfare loss,* and *efficiency loss.*

Deadweight loss A reduction in social gain.

Let's tabulate the votes for and against this tax. Consumers cast $C + D + E$ votes against; producers cast $F + G + H$ votes against, and the recipients of tax revenue cast $C + D + F + G$ votes in favor. The tax is defeated by a margin of $E + H$ votes, so, according to the efficiency criterion, the tax is a bad thing.

It is no coincidence that the margin of defeat $(E + H)$ is equal to the deadweight loss. The efficiency criterion always recommends the policy that creates the greatest social gain. If an alternative policy creates a smaller social gain, the difference is equal to the deadweight loss from that policy *and* to the margin by which that policy loses in the election prescribed by the efficiency criterion.

In doing the computations, we have considered three separate groups: consumers, producers, and the recipients of tax revenue. Some individuals might belong to two or even all three of these groups. A seller of coffee might also be a drinker of coffee; a drinker of coffee might be one of the group of people to whom the government gives the tax proceeds. Such an individual receives shares of more than one of the areas in the graph. Someone who both supplies and demands coffee will get a piece of the producers' surplus in his role as a producer and a piece of the consumers' surplus in his role as a consumer. Nevertheless, we keep track of the consumers' and producers' surpluses separately.

Our rejection of the sales tax is based on several hidden assumptions.

First, we assumed that in the absence of the sales tax, the market price would be determined by the intersection of supply and demand. (We used this assumption when we computed the consumers' and producers' surpluses in the "no tax" column.) Although that assumption holds in competitive markets, we will see in Chapter 10 that it need *not* hold when there are firms with monopoly power.

Second, we assumed that the government simply gives away the tax revenue, as opposed to using it for some purpose that is even more valuable. (We used this assumption when we entered the value of tax revenue at $C + D + F + G$.) That's the amount of revenue *collected*, and it's certainly still the value of the revenue if it's simply given away. But if, for example, $C + D + F + G = \$100$, and if the government uses that \$100 to construct a post office that has a value of \$300 (measured by people's willingness to pay for the post office), then our calculation of

social gain in the "after sales tax" column is off by $200. In Chapter 14, we will discuss the circumstances in which governments might be able to spend money more efficiently than individuals can.

Third, we assumed that the production and consumption of coffee does not affect anyone but the producers and consumers. But suppose that coffee producers use heavy machinery that keeps their neighbors awake at night, or that coffee drinkers use styrofoam cups that they throw by the roadside when they're done. Then there should be additional rows in our chart to reflect the concerns of sleep-deprived neighbors and Sunday motorists who prefer not to confront other people's litter. By omitting these rows, we assumed that there are no significant concerns of this kind. In Chapter 13, we will discuss how to incorporate such concerns in the analysis.

In addition to these hidden assumptions, we have made the nonhidden assumption that the efficiency criterion is an appropriate way to judge a policy. If any one of these assumptions is violated, we might need to reconsider the desirability of the sales tax on coffee.

Understanding Deadweight Loss

Exhibit 8–9 presents another view of the deadweight loss. The prices and quantities are the same as in panel B of Exhibit 8–8. At the original equilibrium quantity Q, the social gain is the sum of all the rectangles. At Q', which is the quantity with the tax, the social gain consists of only the color rectangles. The next cup of coffee after Q' would increase welfare if it were produced, because the marginal value it provides (read off the demand curve) exceeds the marginal cost of producing it (read off the supply curve). However, that cup is not produced and an opportunity to add to welfare is lost.

The deadweight loss calculated in Exhibit 8–9 is the same as the deadweight loss calculated in Exhibit 8–8, where it corresponds to the area $E + H$.

If we think of the social gain as a pie divided among various groups, then a tax has two effects: It changes the way the pie is distributed, and it simultaneously changes the size of the entire pie. Thus, in Exhibit 8–8, the pie originally consists of all the lettered areas. The tax reduces the consumers' and producers' pieces. On the other hand, the recipients of the tax revenue, who get nothing in the absence of the tax, now receive a piece of the pie. After adding up everyone's pieces, we find that the total pie has shrunk; the losses to the losers exceed the gains to the winners. The shrinkage in the pie is the deadweight loss.

The deadweight loss is *not* due in any way to the costs of collecting the tax. We have been assuming that these costs are negligible. If, in fact, it is necessary to hire tax collectors, to provide them with office space, and to buy them computers, or if it is costly for citizens to compute their taxes or to deliver them to the government, these are additional losses that are not included in our computation of the deadweight loss.

Exhibit 8-9 Deadweight Loss

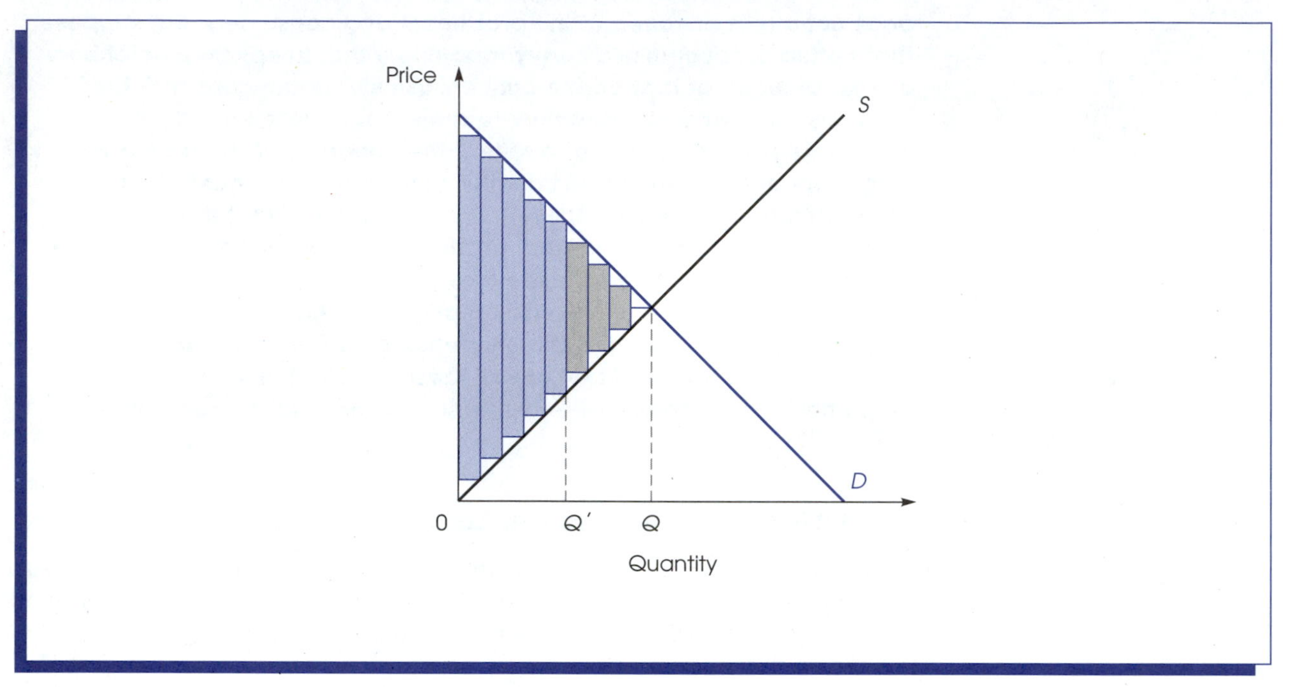

If the market operates at the equilibrium quantity Q, all of the rectangles are included in the social gain. If for any reason the market operates at the quantity Q' (for example, because of a tax), then only the color rectangles are included. The units of output that could create the gray rectangles are never produced, and those rectangles of gain are never created. The gray rectangles, representing gains that could have been created but weren't, constitute the deadweight loss.

EXERCISE 8.3 In Exhibit 8–8 how much does each group of losers lose? How much does each group of winners win? Is the excess of losses over gains equal to the deadweight loss?

A moral of this story is that "taxes are bad"—though not in the sense you might think. You might think that taxes are bad because paying them makes you poorer. True, but collecting them makes somebody else richer. In Exhibit 8–8 the areas $C + D + F + G$ that are paid in taxes do end up in somebody's pocket. Whether this is a good thing or a bad thing depends on whose pocket you care about most. The aspect of the tax that is unambiguously "bad" is the deadweight loss. This is a loss to consumers and producers that is not offset by a gain to anybody.

EXERCISE 8.4 Work out the effects of an *excise* tax of 5¢ per cup of coffee. (*Hint:* We already know that an excise tax has exactly the same effects as a sales tax, so you will know your answer is right if it gives exactly the same results as in Exhibit 8–8.)

Whenever a policy creates a deadweight loss, it is possible to imagine an alternative policy that would be better for everybody. Exhibit 8–10 illustrates such a policy. The graph in the exhibit is the same as in panel B of Exhibit 8–8.

Exhibit 8–10 The Tax Collector versus Robin Hood

	No Tax	With Sales Tax	With Robin Hood Policy
Consumers' Surplus	$A+B+C+D+E$	$A+B$	$A+B+1/2\,E$
Producer's Surplus	$F+G+H+I$	I	$1/2\,H+I$
Tax Revenue	—	$C+D+F+G$	$C+D+1/2\,E+F+G+1/2H$
Social Gain	$A+B+C+D+E+F+G+H+I$	$A+B+C+D+F+G+I$	$A+B+C+D+E+F+G+H+I$
Deadweight Loss	—	$E+H$	

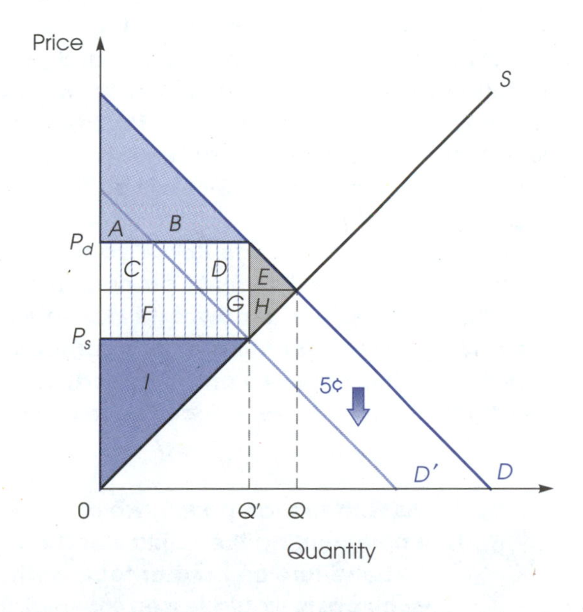

The table shows the effects of three different policies. In the first column there is no tax, in the second column there is a sales tax, and in the third column there is a Robin Hood policy whereby the tax collector unexpectedly takes $C + D + ½ E$ from the consumers, takes $F + G + ½ H$ from the producers, and gives all of the proceeds to the same group that gets the revenue from the sales tax.

Every member of society prefers the Robin Hood policy to the sales tax. Because the Robin Hood policy creates no deadweight loss, it makes it possible to give everyone a bigger share of the social pie.

Suppose that instead of a 5¢ sales tax, we adopt the following plan: One night, without warning, the tax collector breaks into the homes of the consumers and steals an amount of wealth equal to the area $C + D \frac{1}{2} E$. Then he breaks into the homes of the producers and steals the area $F + G + \frac{1}{2} H$. Finally, like Robin Hood, he gives all the proceeds to the people who would have been receiving the tax revenue.

The table in Exhibit 8–10 compares the effects of three different policies. The first and second columns are taken from Exhibit 8–8 and show the welfare gains before and after a tax is imposed. The third column shows the effect of eliminating the tax and instituting the Robin Hood policy.

Compare the second and third columns of the table. You will find that all three groups—consumers, producers, and tax recipients—are happier in the Robin Hood world than in a world with a sales tax. This is possible because the Robin Hood policy creates no deadweight loss; it results in a social gain as great as in the world without taxes. Because there is more surplus to go around, it's not surprising that we can find a way to increase everyone's share. When the pie is bigger, you can always give everyone a bigger piece.

An important feature of the Robin Hood policy is that it is totally unexpected and nobody can do anything to avoid it. If people know in advance, for example, that Robin Hood will be stealing from all producers of coffee, the producers will react to this as they would to a tax, and produce less. Their exact reaction will depend on Robin's exact policy: If he steals more from those who produce more, he is effectively imposing an excise tax, which causes each firm to reduce its quantity. If he steals equally from all producers, the main effect will be to drive some producers out of the industry altogether.

When people anticipate Robin's actions, they will take steps to avoid them. These steps will include producing and consuming less coffee, and this will create a deadweight loss. The only way to avoid a deadweight loss is for the market to produce the equilibrium quantity of coffee, and this happens only if nobody is given a chance to alter his or her behavior in order to reduce the tax burden.

As with the tax policy, we are ignoring any costs involved with implementing the Robin Hood policy (such as Robin's expenditure on burglar tools or the value of his time). Any such costs would lessen the social gain.

Other Normative Criteria

Pareto criterion A normative criterion according to which one policy is better than another when it is preferred unanimously.

The simplest of all normative criteria is the **Pareto criterion**, according to which one policy is "better" than another when it is preferred unanimously. In Exhibit 8–10, this means that the Robin Hood policy is better than the sales tax, because everyone—consumers, producers, *and* recipients of tax revenue—agrees on this assessment. But according to the Pareto criterion, there is no way to decide between the "no tax" policy in the first column and the "sales tax" policy in the second column. Consumers and producers prefer the first, while tax recipients prefer the second. There is no unanimity; therefore the Pareto criterion remains silent.

The great advantage of the Pareto criterion is that its recommendations, when it makes them, are extremely noncontroversial. Who can disagree with the outcome of a unanimous election? The offsetting disadvantage is that the Pareto criterion usually makes no recommendation at all, because unanimity is rarely found.

Potential Pareto criterion A normative criterion according to which any proposal that can be unanimously defeated—even by a candidate not under consideration—should be rejected.

One modification of the Pareto criterion is the **potential Pareto criterion**, according to which any proposal that *could* be unanimously defeated should be rejected—even if the proposal that defeats it is not really in the running. For example, suppose in Exhibit 8–10 that we are asked to choose between the "no tax" proposal in the first column and the "sales tax" proposal in the second. According to the potential Pareto criterion, we should reject the sales tax because it loses unanimously to the Robin Hood proposal in the third column—and that's enough to disqualify it, even if the Robin Hood policy is not under serious consideration.

In all of our examples, the potential Pareto criterion and the efficiency criterion will make identical recommendations. It's easy to see why if you return to the pie analogy: The efficiency criterion says that we should always try to make the total "pie" of social gain as big as possible. The potential Pareto criterion says that if there's a way to make everyone's piece of pie bigger, you're not doing things right. But to say that everyone's piece could be made bigger is the same thing as saying that the pie could be made bigger—so whatever the potential Pareto criterion rejects, the efficiency criterion will reject as well.

Many economists regard the potential Pareto criterion and the efficiency criterion as good rough guides to policy choices, though few would defend it as the sole basis on which to make such decisions. Regardless of your feelings on this issue, calculations of social gains and deadweight losses can still be useful in understanding the consequences of various alternatives. If a policy causes a large deadweight loss, it is at least worth considering whether there is some good way to revise the policy so that the loss can be made smaller.

8.3 Examples and Applications

The machinery of consumers' and producers' surpluses is widely applicable, as the following sequence of examples will illustrate. All of them use just one basic procedure, which is summarized in Exhibit 8–11.

Subsidies

Suppose that the government institutes a new program whereby buyers of home insulation receive a rebate of $50 for every unit of insulation they purchase. This has the effect of shifting the demand curve upward a vertical distance $50, from D to D' in Exhibit 8–12.

With the subsidy, the quantity sold is Q', at a market price of P_S. This is the price suppliers receive for insulation. However, consumers actually pay less,

Exhibit 8-11 Calculating the Consumers' and Producers' Surpluses

You will often be asked to calculate the effects of governmental policies on consumers' and producers' surpluses. Here are some rules to help you:

1. Begin by drawing a supply and demand diagram showing equilibrium both before and after the policy is imposed. Draw horizontal and vertical lines from the interesting points in your diagram to the axes. After a while you will get a feel for which lines to draw and which to omit. It never hurts to draw more than you need.
2. Before you proceed, label every area that is even possibly relevant.
3. When calculating consumers' surplus, use only the demand curve and prices and quantities that are relevant to the consumer. When calculating producers' surplus, use only the supply curve and prices and quantities relevant to the producer.
4. Remember that the demand and supply curves are relevant only because they are equal to the marginal value and marginal cost curves. If for some reason the demand curve should separate from the marginal value curve, continue to use the marginal value for calculating consumers' surplus. Do likewise if the supply curve should separate from the marginal cost curve.
5. Check your work with a picture like Exhibit 8–9: Calculate the social gain directly by drawing rectangles of "welfare gains" for each item actually produced and by summing the areas of these rectangles. The sum should equal the total of the gains to all of the individuals involved.

because they receive a payment of $50 from the government, so that the consumer's actual cost is $P_s - \$50 = P_d$.

To calculate consumers' and producers' surpluses before the subsidy, we use the equilibrium price and quantity. This is shown in the first column of the table in Exhibit 8–12.

After the subsidy, consumers purchase quantity Q' at a price to them of P_d. Their consumers' surplus is the area under the *original* demand curve D out to this quantity and down to this price. We use the original demand curve because it is this curve that represents the true marginal value of insulation to consumers. The intrinsic value of home insulation is not changed by the subsidy. Therefore, the consumers' surplus is the area $A + C + F + G$, as recorded in the second column of the table.

Exhibit 8-12 The Effect of a Subsidy

	Before Subsidy	After Subsidy
Consumers' Surplus	$A + C$	$A + C + F + G$
Producer's Surplus	$F + H$	$C + D + F + H$
Cost to Taxpayers	—	$-(C + D + E + F + G)$
Social Gain	$A + C + F + H$	$A + C + F + H - E$
Deadweight Loss	—	E

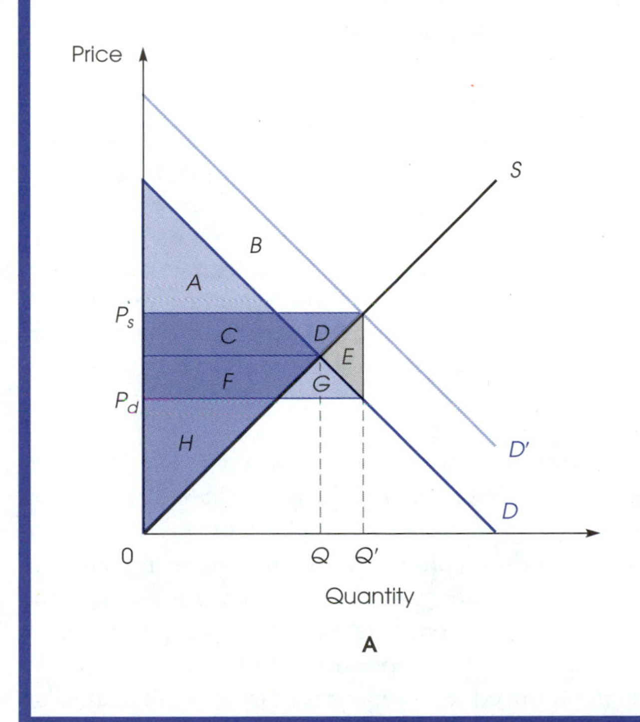

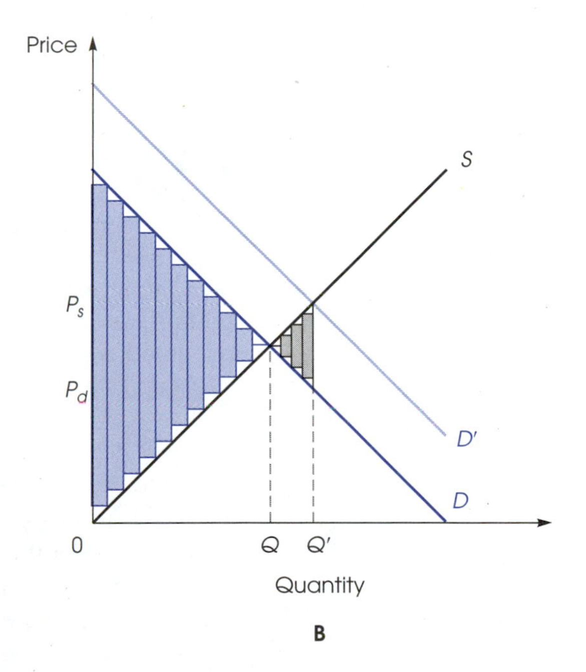

The table shows the gains to consumers and producers before and after the institution of a $50-per-unit government subsidy to home insulation. With the subsidy in effect, there is a cost to taxpayers that must be *subtracted* when we calculate the social gain. We find that the social gain with the subsidy is lower by E than the social gain without the subsidy. E is the deadweight loss.

To check our work, we can consider the social gain created by each individual unit of insulation, shown in panel B. Each unit up to the equilibrium quantity Q creates a rectangle of social gain. After Q units have been produced, we enter a region where marginal cost exceeds marginal value. Each unit produced in this region creates a social *loss* equal to the excess of marginal cost over marginal value; these losses are represented by the gray rectangles, which stop at the quantity Q' that is actually produced. The social gain is equal to the sum of the blue rectangles minus the sum of the gray ones. Since the social gain without the subsidy is just the sum of the blue rectangles, the gray rectangles represent the deadweight loss.

To calculate producers' surplus, we use the quantity Q' and the producers' price P_S. This yields the area $C + D + F + H$, which is also recorded in the table.

We are still not finished. The subsidy being paid to consumers must come from somewhere, presumably from tax revenues. This represents a cost to taxpayers equal to the number of units of insulation sold times $50 per unit. Geometrically, this is represented by the rectangle $C + D + E + F + G$. This cost is a *loss* to the taxpayers, and so must be *subtracted* in the computation of social gain. The deadweight loss of E is the different between social gain before and after the subsidy.

According to the efficiency criterion, the subsidy should be rejected: It gathers $F + G$ votes in favor from consumers and $C + D$ votes in favor from producers, but $C + D + E + F + G$ votes opposed from taxpayers. Thus, it loses by a margin of E, which (noncoincidentally) is the dead weight loss.

EXERCISE 8.5 Verify the calculation of social gain in Exhibit 8–12.

Students often want to know how areas *C* and *F* can be part of both the consumers' surplus and the producers' surplus. The answer is that surplus is not an area at all—the area is just a *measure* of surplus. The fact that you have 12 yards of carpet and your friend has 12 yards of carpet does not mean that you both own the same "yards," only that each of you owns carpeting that can be measured by the same yardstick. The areas of surplus are yardsticks by which we measure different individuals' gains from trade.

Panel B in Exhibit 8–12 provides a way to check our work. The blue rectangles to the left of equilibrium represent gains to social welfare just as in Exhibit 8–9. In this case, however, *more* than the equilibrium quantity is produced. Consider the first item produced after equilibrium. The marginal value of this item to consumers (read off the original demand curve) is *less* than the marginal cost of producing it. The difference between the two is the area of the first gray rectangle. This area therefore represents a net welfare *loss* to society. Similarly, the next item produced represents a welfare loss in the amount of the area of the second gray rectangle, and so on out to the quantity Q'. The total welfare loss is the sum of these rectangles, which is equal to the area E in panel A. Therefore, area E should be the deadweight loss, and the calculation in the table is confirmed.

An alternative way to calculate the consumers' surplus is shown in Exhibit 8–13. For most purposes, it suffices to use either the method of Exhibit 8–12 or that of Exhibit 8–13. Since both always lead to the same answers, you need to master only one of them. However, there will be a few occasions later on in this book where you will find it much easier to use the alternative method of Exhibit 8–13.

Exhibit 8–13 Another Way to Do It

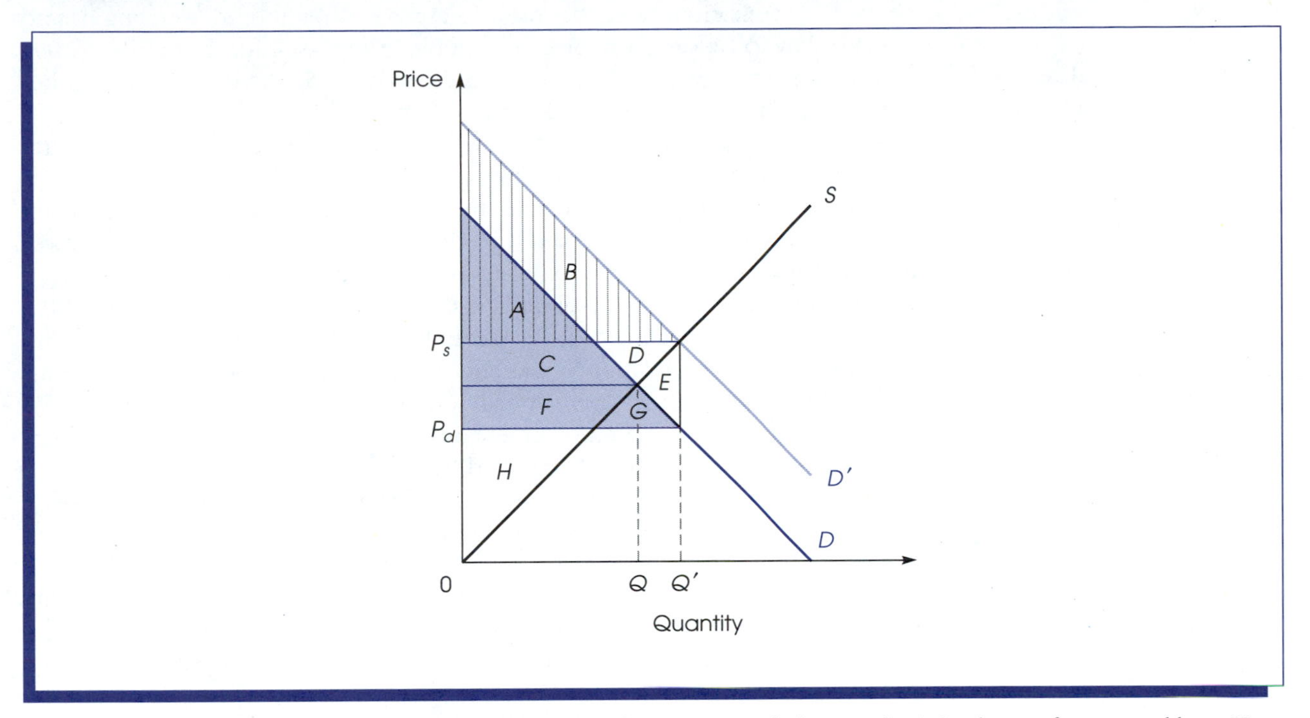

The method that we have been using to calculate social gain is adequate for most problems. However, there is an alternate method that may occasionally be more convenient.

We illustrate with the "subsidy" example from Exhibit 8–12. The graph here is identical to panel A in that exhibit. There are two ways of viewing a \$50 rebate for home insulation. The first way, which we adopted in Exhibit 8–12, is to say that the rebate does not alter the value of home insulation. Consumers benefit from the subsidy by being able to buy insulation at a lower price. This is why we use the *old* demand curve (the true marginal value curve) and the price paid by consumers (P_d) as boundaries for the area of consumer surplus. This gives the shaded area $A + C + F + G$.

An alternative and *equally valid* point of view is to say that a subsidy is like a \$50 bill taped to each unit of insulation. This raises the marginal value of the insulation by \$50. However, we now have to view the insulation as being purchased at the market price P_s. If we said that the insulation has increased in value *and* that the consumer is paying less than market price for his insulation, we would be wrongly double-counting the \$50 rebate.

From the alternative point of view, the consumer surplus is the area under the *new* demand curve down to the *market* price P_s and out to the quantity Q'. That is, the striped area $A + B$.

If both points of view are equally valid, how can they give different answers? The answer is: They don't. In fact, area $A + B$ is equal to area $A + C + F + G$. They have to be equal, because each represents the consumers' surplus calculated correctly, and there can be only one consumers' surplus. If you find that argument unconvincing, try proving directly that the two areas are equal. This is an exercise in high school geometry if you assume all curves are straight lines; it is an exercise in calculus otherwise.

Price Ceilings

Price ceiling A maximum price at which a product can be legally sold.

Effective price ceiling A price ceiling set below the equilibrium price.

A **price ceiling** is a legally mandated maximum price at which a good may be sold. The effect of a price ceiling depends on its level. If the legal maximum is above the equilibrium price that prevails anyway, then the price ceiling has no effect (a law forbidding any piece of bubble gum to sell for more than $2,000 will not change anyone's behavior). An **effective price ceiling** is one set below the equilibrium price, like the price P_0 in Exhibit 8–14.

At the price P_0, producers want to sell the quantity Q_s and consumers want to buy the quantity Q_d. What quantity actually gets traded? The answer is Q_s, because as soon as Q_s units are sold, the sellers pack up and go home. When buyers and sellers disagree about quantity, the group wanting to trade fewer items always wins, because trading stops as soon as either party loses interest.

Another, and very real, possibility must be considered: Since buyers are frustrated, they will be willing to offer prices higher than P_0, and sellers may accept these prices in violation of the law. For purposes of our simple analysis, we will assume that the law is perfectly enforced and this does not occur. We will also assume that the enforcement is costless (otherwise, the cost of enforcement would have to be subtracted from social gain).[6]

The quantity sold is Q_s. What price do consumers pay? You may think the answer is obviously P_0, but this is incorrect. At a price of P_0, consumers want to buy more goods than are available. Therefore, *they compete with each other* to acquire the limited supply. Depending on the nature of the good, this may take the form of standing in line, searching from store to store, advertising, or any of a number of other possibilities. All of these activities are costly, in time, gasoline, energy, and other currency, and these costs must be added to the "price" that consumers actually pay for the item.

How high does the price go? It must go to exactly P_1 in Exhibit 8–14. At any lower price the quantity demanded still exceeds Q_S, and consumers intensify their efforts. Only when the "price" reaches P_1 does the market equilibrate.

Of course, even though P_1 is the price paid by consumers, the price received by suppliers is still P_0. Therefore, we use P_1 to calculate consumers' surplus and P_0 to calculate producers' surplus. In each case the appropriate quantity is Q_S, the quantity actually traded. The computations are shown in Exhibit 8–14.

EXERCISE 8.6 Verify the correctness of the table in Exhibit 8–14.

The deadweight loss calculated in Exhibit 8–14 comes about for two reasons. First, there is the reduction in quantity from Q to Q_S, which leads to a social loss of $C + E$, just as in the case of a tax. However, now there is another sort of loss as well. The value of the time people spend waiting in lines is equal to the value of the time-per-unit-purchased ($P_1 - P_0$) times the quantity of units

[6]Here is an interesting puzzle. Why is it that in "victimless crimes" like prostitution and the sale of drugs, both parties are held criminally liable, whereas in the equally "victimless" crime of violating a price control, only the seller faces legal consequences? For an interesting discussion of this puzzle, see J. Lott and R. Roberts, "Why Comply: One-Sided Enforcement of Price Controls and Victimless Crime Laws," *Journal of Legal Studies* 18 (1989).

Exhibit 8-14 A Price Ceiling

	Before Ceiling	After Ceiling
Consumers' Surplus	$A + B + C$	A
Producers' Surplus	$D + E + F$	F
Social Gain	$A + B + C + D + E + F$	$A + F$
Deadweight Loss	—	$B + C + D + E$

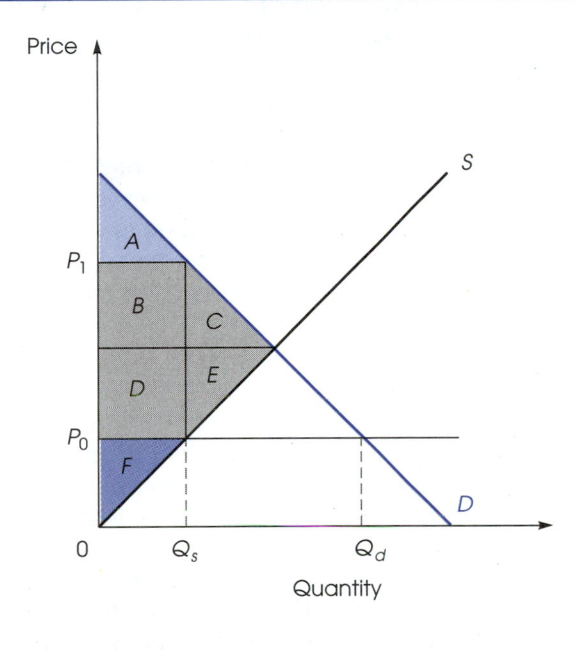

At a maximum legal price of P_0, demanders want to buy more than suppliers want to sell. Therefore, they compete against each other for the available supply, by waiting in line, advertising, and so forth. This increases the actual price to consumers. The full price to consumers must be bid all the way up to P_1 since at any lower price the quantity demanded still exceeds the quantity supplied, leading to increases in the lengths of waiting lines.

The deadweight loss comes about for two reasons. First, there is the reduction in quantity from equilibrium to Q_S. This loss is the area $C + E$. Second, there is the value of the consumers' time spent waiting in line. This is equal to $P_1 - P_0$ times the quantity of items purchased, which is the rectangle $B + D$.

purchased (Q_S), which is the rectangle $B + D$. Taken together, these effects account for the entire deadweight loss.

Notice that from a social point of view there is a great difference between a *price control* that drives the demanders' price up to P_1 and a *tax* that drives the demanders' price up to P_1. Because the revenue from a tax is wealth transferred from one individual to another, it is neither a gain nor a loss to society as a whole. But the value of the time spent waiting in lines is wealth lost and never recovered by anyone.

Some of the deadweight loss can be avoided if there is a class of people whose time is relatively inexpensive. Those people will offer their services as "searchers" or "line-standers" and consumers will pay them up to $P_1 - P_0$ per item for their services. The income to the line-standers, minus the value of their time, is a gain that offsets part of the lost area $B + D$.

Of course, some consumers whose time has low value might stand in line to make their own purchases. We view these consumers as having purchased line-standing services from themselves at the going price of $P_1 - P_0$. Such a consumer earns part of area A as a consumer and part of area $B + D$ as a line-stander.

The reduction in deadweight loss through the use of line-standers doesn't work if too many people have low time values. In that case, all of those people attempt to become line-standers and the lines get longer, so that the value of the time each one spends waiting gets bid back up to $P_1 - P_0$.

Tariffs

Visit the National Center for Policy Analysis at: http://www.public-policy.org/~ncpa/studies/s171/s171.html for more on import tariffs.

Suppose that Americans buy all of their cameras from Japanese companies. It is proposed that a tariff of \$10 per camera be imposed on all such imports and that the proceeds be distributed to Americans chosen at random. What areas must we measure to see whether the tariff makes Americans as a whole better off?

Exhibit 8–15 shows the market for cameras, with both the original and post-tariff supply curves. The table shows the gains to Americans before and after the tariff. These gains are calculated using the pre-tariff price and quantity of P_0 and Q_0 and the post-tariff price and quantity of P_1 and Q_1. Notice that we do not include the producers' surplus, since this is earned by the Japanese companies and the question asks only about the welfare of Americans. If we had been asked about the welfare of the entire world, we would have included producers' surplus in our calculations.

EXERCISE 8.7 Calculate the social gains to the entire world before and after the tariff is imposed.

Now we return to the question: What areas must we measure? The answer is evidently that one must compare area D with area $E + F$. If $E + F$ is bigger, the tariff improves the welfare of Americans; otherwise it reduces their welfare.

In practice, these areas can be estimated if the supply and demand curves can be estimated, and, as we remarked in Chapter 1, there are econometric methods available for this. Therefore, an economist can contribute meaningfully to a debate about tariffs by computing the relevant areas and reporting which policy is better—*provided* that the goal is to maximize Americans' welfare.

Exhibit 8-15 A Tax on Imported Cameras

	Before Tariff	After Tariff
Consumers' Surplus	$A + B + C + D$	A
Tariff Revenue	—	$B + C + E + F$
Social Gain	$A + B + C + D$	$A + B + C + E + F$

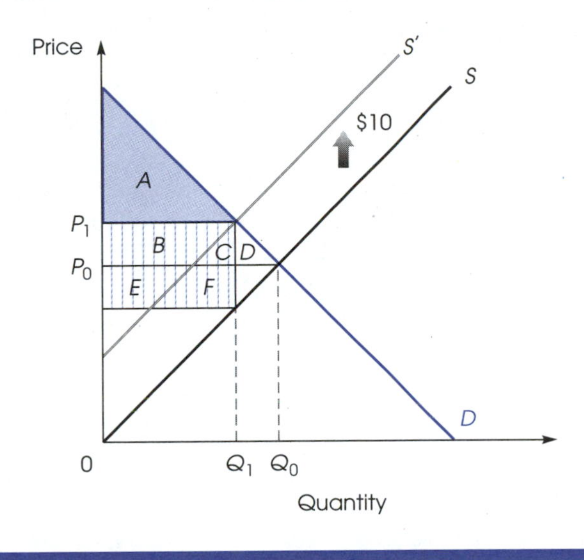

If cameras are supplied by foreigners and purchased by Americans, then a tariff affects Americans through the consumers' surplus and through the tax revenue that it generates.

It is often a reasonable assumption that a country faces flat supply curves for imported items. The reason for this is that Japanese firms sell cameras in many foreign countries, and the United States is only a small part of their market. Thus, changes in quantity that appear big (from our point of view) may in fact correspond only to very small movements along the Japanese supply curves and hence to small changes in price. Exhibit 8–16 shows the analysis of a tariff when the supply curve is flat. In this case you can see that the tariff always reduces Americans' welfare.

Tariffs and Domestic Industries

A more interesting example involves tariffs on a product that is produced both domestically and abroad. Suppose that Americans buy cars from Japan subject to a flat Japanese supply curve at a price P_0, and that domestic car manufacturers have the upward-sloping supply curve shown in panel A of Exhibit 8–17. Assuming that all cars are identical, no consumer will be willing to pay more

Exhibit 8–16 A Tariff on Imported Cameras That Are Elastically Supplied

	Before Tariff	After Tariff
Consumers' Surplus	$A + B + C$	A
Tariff Revenue	—	B
Social Gain	$A + B + C$	$A + B$
Deadweight Loss	—	C

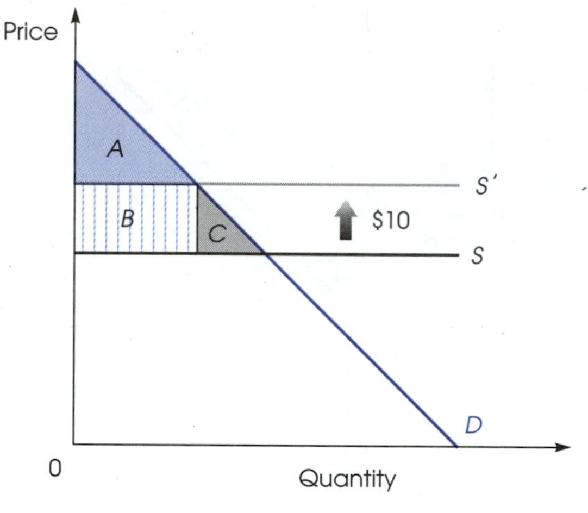

If the United States is a small part of the market to which the Japanese sell cameras, then Americans will face a flat supply curve. In this case a tariff always reduces the welfare of Americans.

than P_0 for a domestic car, because the consumer can always buy an import instead. Therefore, all cars sell at a price of P_O. At this price domestic manufacturers produce Q_0 cars and domestic consumers buy Q_1. The difference, $Q_1 - Q_0$, is the number of imports. Table A in Exhibit 8–17 shows the consumers' and producers' surpluses.

Now suppose that we impose a tariff of \$500 on each imported car. This raises the foreign supply curve \$500 to a level of P_0 + \$500. The price of cars goes up to P_0 + \$500, the quantity supplied domestically goes up to Q_0' (in panel B of Exhibit 8–17), and the quantity demanded falls to Q_1'. The quantity imported falls to $Q_1 - Q_0'$.

In Exhibit 8–17 Table B shows the consumers' and producers' surpluses both before and after the tariff. (The "before" column, of course, simply repeats the calculation from Table A.) What about revenue from the tariff? The number of imported cars is $Q_1' - Q_0'$, and the tariff is \$500 on each of these. Thus, the tariff revenue (which ends up in American pockets) is $(Q_1' - Q_0') \times \$500$,

Exhibit 8-17 A Tariff When There Is a Domestic Industry

Table A

Consumers' Surplus	$A + B$
Producers' Surplus	C
Social Gain	$A + B + C$

Table B

	Before Tariff	After Tariff
Consumers' Surplus	$E + F + G + H + I + J$	$E + F$
Producers' Surplus	K	$G + K$
Tax Revenue	—	I
Social Gain	$E + F + G + H + I + J + K$	$E + F + G + K + I$
Deadweight Loss	—	$H + J$

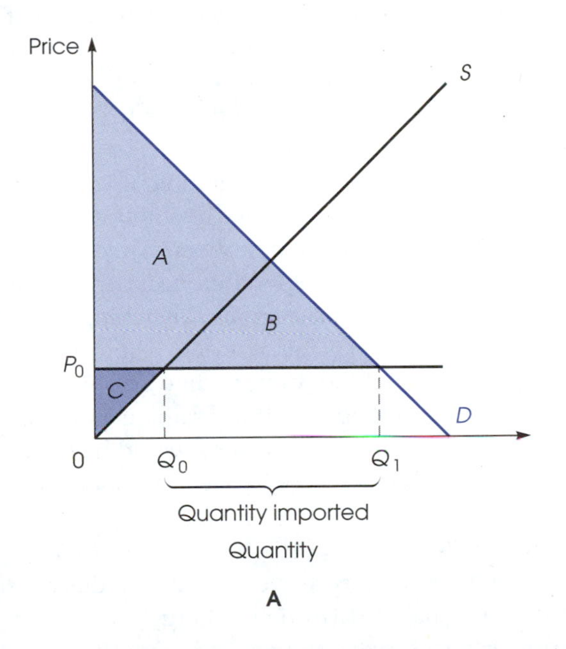

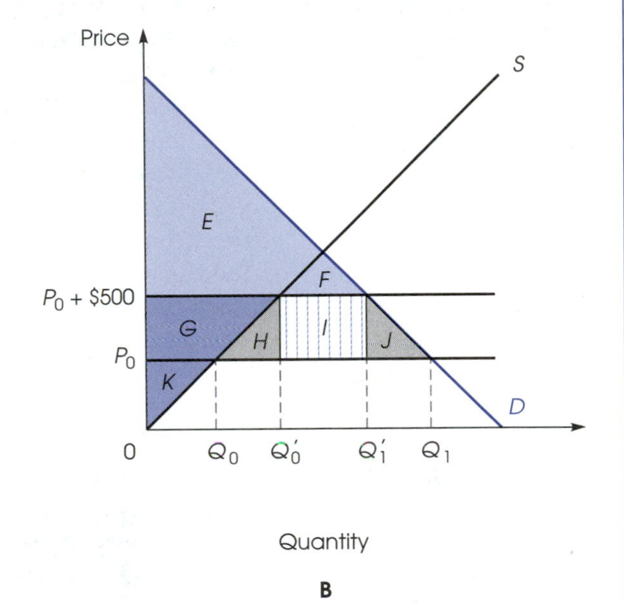

We assume that Americans can buy any number of cars from Japan at the price P_0. The supply curve S shows how many cars American manufacturers will provide at each price. At the price P_0, American producers supply Q_0 cars and American consumers purchase Q_1 cars. The difference, $Q_1 - Q_0$, is the number of cars imported. Table A shows the gains to Americans.

In panel B we see the effect of a \$500 tariff on imported cars. The price of a foreign car rises to $P_0 + \$500$, and the number of imports falls to $Q_1' - Q_0'$. Table B compares gains before and after the tariff. Note that the first column of Table B is identical to Table A except that it uses the labels from panel B rather than panel A. The tariff revenue is computed by observing that the area of rectangle I is $(Q_1' - Q_0') \times \$500$.

and this is the area of rectangle *I*. This is recorded in Table B, along with a comparison of social gains.

We can see that even when there is a domestic industry that benefits from the tariff, and even though the tariff revenue is a gain to the country, tariffs still cause a deadweight loss (we say that they are *inefficient*) because consumers lose more than all other groups gain.

EXERCISE 8.8 Suppose that the government wants to benefit domestic auto producers and the recipients of tax revenue at the expense of car buyers. Devise an efficient (though perhaps impractical) way of doing this that makes everybody happier than a tariff does.

Robbery

For more on the economics of robbery visit: http://www.best.com/~ddfr/Academic/Price_Theory/PThy_Chapter_20/PThy_Chapter_20.html

From the point of view of economic efficiency (that is, the maximization of the total gains to all members of society), a loss to one group that is exactly offset by a gain to another group is a "wash." To one who is interested only in maximizing social gain, such a transfer is neither a good thing nor a bad thing. How, then, should such a one feel about *robbery?*

Many people think that robbery constitutes a social loss equal to the value of what is stolen. Their reasoning is simple but faulty: They notice the loss to the victim without noticing the offsetting gain to the robber. A more sophisticated answer would be that robbery is a matter of indifference, because stolen goods do not disappear from society; they only change ownership.

However, this more sophisticated answer is also wrong. There *is* a social cost to robbery. It is the opportunity cost of the robber's time and energy. The robber who steals your bicycle could, perhaps, with the same expenditure of energy, be building a bicycle of his own. If he did, society would have two bicycles; when he steals yours instead, society has only one. The option to steal costs society a bicycle.

This shows that robbery is socially costly; we still have to ask: *How* costly? To answer this, it is reasonable to treat robbery as a competitive industry: Robbers continue to rob until the marginal cost (in time, energy, and so on) of committing an additional crime is equal to the marginal revenue (in loot). The cost is what interests us, the loot is observable, and we know that the two are equal. So, at the margin, we can reckon the cost of a robbery as approximately equal to the value of what is stolen.

This tells us that the amount stolen is a correct measure of the cost of the last robbery committed. In Exhibit 8–18 we calculate the total social cost of all robberies. Suppose that a robber can expect to earn $\$R$ each time he commits a robbery. Then robbers steal until the marginal cost of stealing is equal to $\$R$; that is, they commit Q robberies. The amount stolen is $\$R \times Q$, the area $A + B$. However, the robbers' total costs are given by the area under the supply curve, A. This cost to the robbers is society's cost as well. Therefore, the total social cost of all robberies (A) is less than the value of what is taken ($A + B$).

Exhibit 8-18 The Social Cost of Robbery

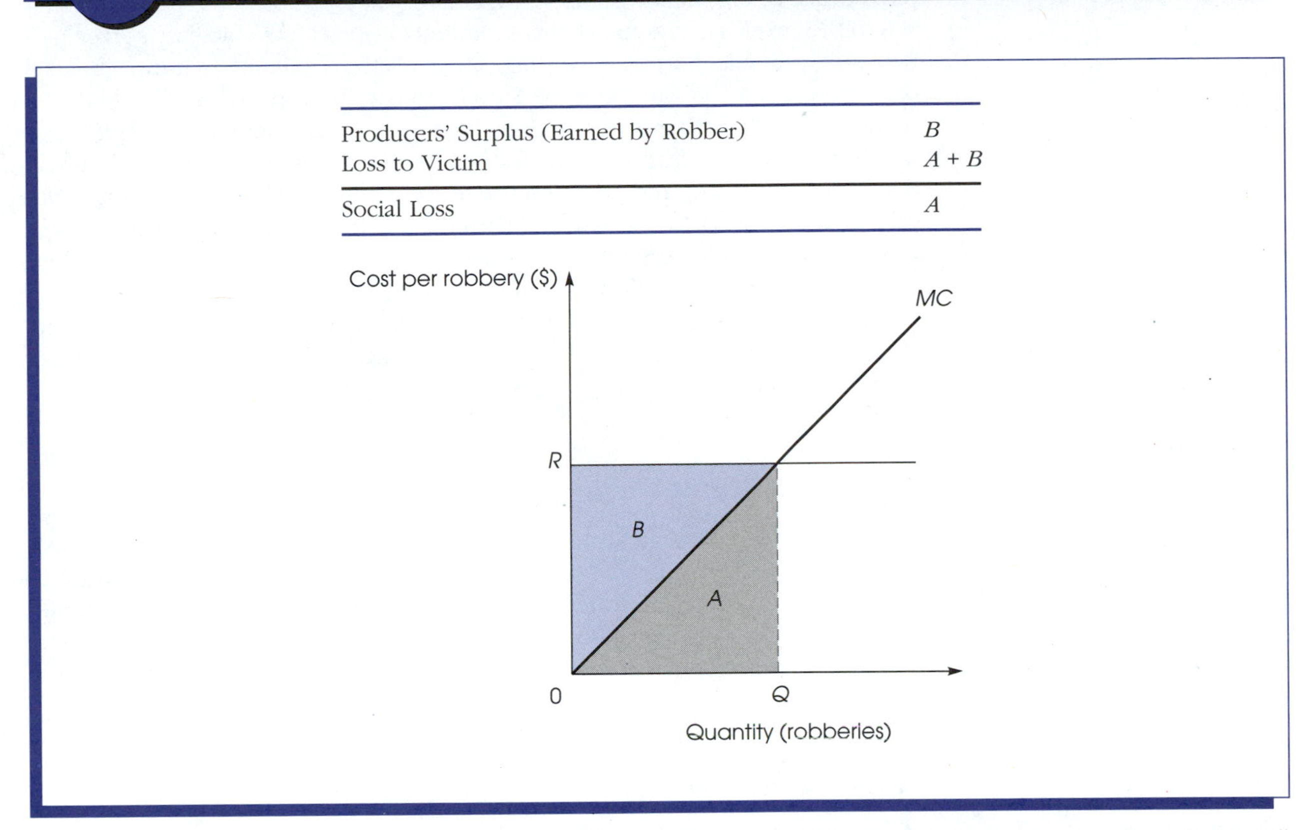

Producers' Surplus (Earned by Robber)	B
Loss to Victim	$A + B$
Social Loss	A

We suppose that a robber can expect to earn $R for each robbery he commits. Then robberies will take place until the robbers' marginal cost (the opportunity cost of their time, energy, and so on) equals $R. The number of robberies committed is Q, and robbers earn a producers' surplus of B. However, victims lose the amount stolen, which is $A + B$. There is a net social loss of A. If society pursues economic efficiency, A is the maximum amount it would be willing to spend to prevent all robberies.

This analysis ignores the very real possibility that people will take costly steps to protect themselves from robbery—installing burglar alarms, deadbolt locks, and the like. These additional costs are also due to the existence of robbery and must be added to area *A* in order to calculate the full social cost of robberies.

The more general lesson of this example is that effort expended in nonproductive activity is social loss. Accountants devising new methods of tax avoidance, lawyers in litigation, lobbyists seeking laws to transfer wealth to their clients, and all of the resources that they employ (secretaries, file clerks, photocopy machines, telephone services, and so on) are often unproductive from a social point of view. Whatever they win for their clients is a loss for their adversaries. In the absence of this activity, all of these resources could be employed elsewhere, making society richer.

On the other hand, some of this seemingly unproductive activity serves hidden and valuable purposes. Suppose that a law is passed requiring that all owners of apple orchards donate $5,000 each to the president's brother. The owners of apple orchards might hire a lobbyist to assist them in having this law overturned. If the effort is successful, apple growers win only what the president's brother loses, and so at one level of analysis the lobbyist's time contributes nothing to the welfare of society. On the other hand, if all orange growers were made very nervous by this law and planned to burn down their orange trees as a precaution against their being next, then the lobbyist saves a lot of valuable orange trees through his efforts. Insofar as redistributing income affects the incentives to engage in productive activities, it can indirectly affect society's welfare.

Theories of Value

We have defined value in terms of consumers' willingness to pay, and we have discovered that the price of an item is equal to its marginal value. Other theories of value have arisen in the history of economics, only to be abandoned when careful analysis revealed them as erroneous. Because such errors are still common in much discussion by noneconomists, it is worth examining them to see why they should be avoided.

The Diamond-Water Paradox

Read about the diamond-water paradox at: http://www.bibliomania.com/NonFiction/Smith/Wealth/Bk1Chap04.html

Many classical economists were puzzled by the so-called diamond–water paradox. How can it be that water, which is essential for life and therefore as "valuable" a thing as can be imagined, is so inexpensive relative to diamonds, which are used primarily for decoration and the production of nonessential goods? If price reflects value, shouldn't a gallon of water be worth innumerable diamonds?

The paradox is resolved when you realize that price reflects not *total* value, but *marginal* value. Exhibit 8–19 depicts the demand curves for water and for diamonds, together with their market prices and the corresponding consumer's surpluses. The marginal value of your first gallon of water is indeed much higher than the marginal value of your first diamond, and this is reflected by the heights of the demand curves at low quantities. But this has nothing to do with the *price* of water; the price is equal to the marginal value of the last bucket consumed, and this may be very low if you consume many gallons.

Read Adam Smith's own words on the labor theory of value at: http://www.bibliomania.com/NonFiction/Smith/Wealth/Bk2Chap03.html

Notice that the total value (the colored area) in the market for water is much higher than in the market for diamonds: If you lost all of your water and all of your diamonds, you would be willing to pay more to retrieve the water than to retrieve the diamonds. In consequence, the consumers' surplus is much higher in the market for water than in the market for diamonds. Exhibit 8–19 shows that there is nothing paradoxical about a low price and a large consumers' surplus existing simultaneously.

Exhibit 8-19 The Diamond-Water Paradox Resolved

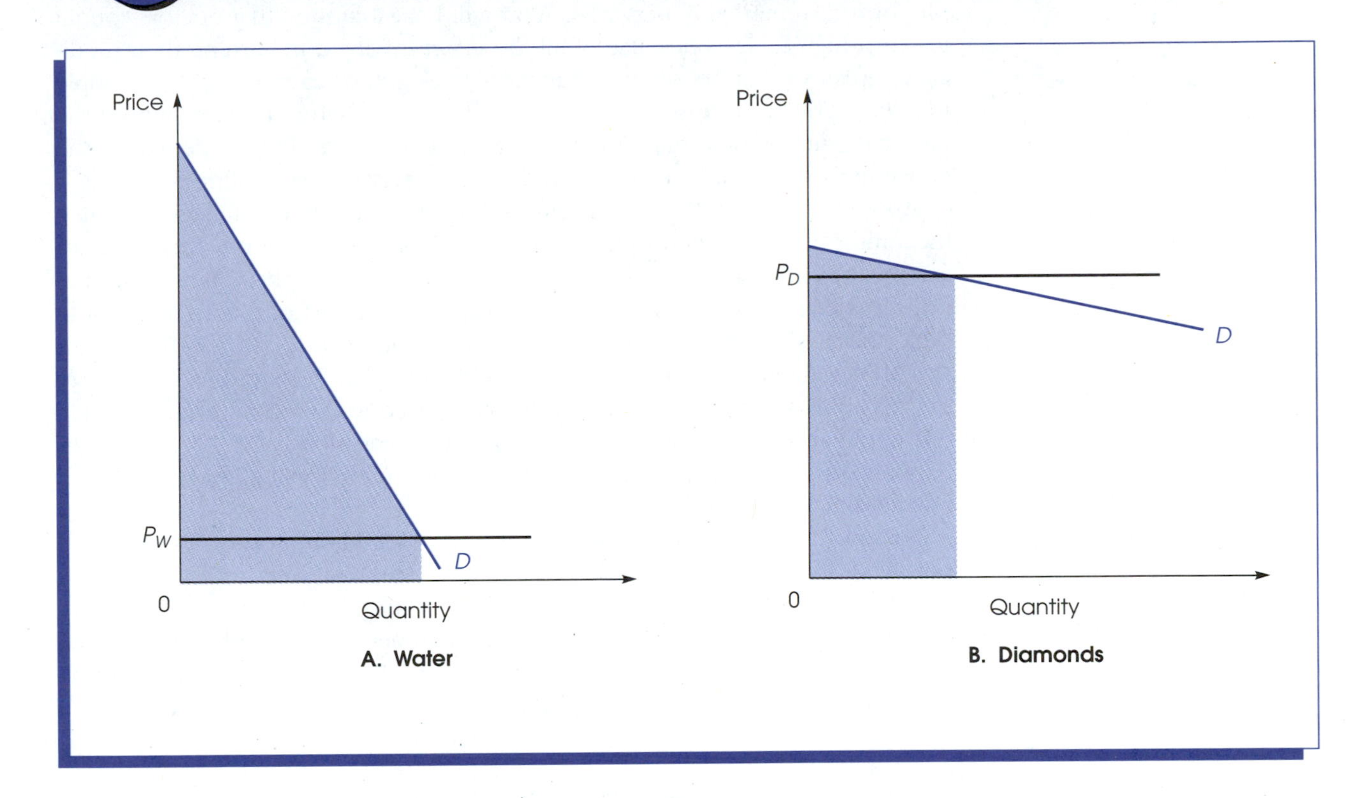

If you had no water and no diamonds, you would be willing to pay far more for a first bucket of water than for a first diamond. Therefore, your marginal value (= demand) curve for water starts out much higher than your marginal value curve for diamonds. At the market prices P_W and P_D, you consume Q_W buckets of water and Q_D diamonds, so that the marginal value of a bucket of water (P_W) is much less than the marginal value of a diamond (P_D).

It is true that the total value of all your water (the shaded area in panel A) is greater than the total value of all your diamonds (the shaded area in panel B). The graphs show that this is perfectly consistent with a low marginal value for water and a high marginal value for diamonds. The price, which is equal to the marginal value, should not be expected to reflect the total value.

The Labor Theory of Value

Labor theory of value The assertion that the value of an object is determined by the amount of labor involved in its production.

The **labor theory of value** is an error that deceived such diverse economists as Adam Smith and Karl Marx. In its simplest form it says that the price of an item is determined by the amount of labor used in its production.[7] In this form it is clearly false: You can expend an enormous quantity of labor digging a gigantic hole in your backyard, and the price that hole commands in the marketplace may be far less than the price of a short story produced by a good

[7]Of course, this is a simpler form than economists have ever believed; typical versions restrict attention to "socially necessary" labor and include the labor of previous generations who built machines used in current production.

writer in an afternoon, sitting at a word processor in an air-conditioned house sipping lemonade.[8]

For a theory so evidently false, the labor theory of value (even in this simple form) is remarkably pervasive. You will hear it argued that doctors "ought to" earn high salaries because of all the effort involved in earning their medical degrees, or that people in occupation A "ought to" earn as much as people in occupation B because they work equally hard. Such arguments ignore the fact that value is determined not by the cost of inputs, but by demand—the consumer's willingness to pay for the good or service being offered.

Another common belief that embodies the labor theory fallacy is that a meaning can be attached to the "book value" of a firm. A firm's "book value" is a measure of what it would cost to produce the actual physical assets of the firm. It is computed, for example, by adding up the cost of the bricks used to build the firm's plants and office buildings, the desks and chairs in the executive offices, the machines along the assembly line, and the letterhead stationery in the cabinets. This book value can be compared to the actual price at which one could acquire the entire firm (say, by purchasing all its stock). It sometimes happens that a firm can be acquired for less than book value, and it is widely believed that this represents a bargain.

Not so. The fact that a factory is built from $1 million worth of bricks does not make that factory worth $1 million, any more than your application of $1 million worth of labor would make a hole in your backyard worth $1 million. If your labor is devoted to the production of something that nobody wants, or if the bricks are glued together to form a factory that produces nothing useful, this will be reflected in the price. What we have here is a *brick theory of value*, different perhaps from the labor theory of value, but perfectly analogous and just as false.

A final example illustrates both the diamond–water and the labor theory paradoxes. It is sometimes argued that something must be wrong with society's values when a baseball player (for example) earns a salary in the high six figures for playing a game that (1) he enjoys anyway and (2) produces little social value compared with something like teaching elementary school, which is far less lucrative. The first point is the labor theory of value again. It errs by assuming that how hard the baseball player works determines the value of what he produces. The second point uses the erroneous reasoning that underlies the diamond–water paradox. It may very well be that teachers (like water) produce far more total social value than star baseball players. But it can be simultaneously true that *one additional teacher* produces less social value than one additional star baseball player. This can be the case, for example, if there are many teachers and few star baseball players. We should not expect the price of a teacher or a baseball player to tell us anything about the total value to society of the two professions.

---

[8]It *is* true, of course, that in a competitive market, price equals marginal cost (and a competitive producer will not choose to dig a hole in his backyard for sale in the marketplace). But marginal cost is not labor cost. Some labor costs may be sunk (and therefore irrelevant), and many relevant costs have nothing to do with labor. The relevant costs, as always, are the opportunity costs—the writer could be writing a movie script instead.

8.4 General Equilibrium and the Invisible Hand

Based on the examples in Section 8.3, you might have begun to suspect that any deviation from competitive equilibrium leads to a reduction in social gain. In this section we will see that this is, in fact, the case.

The Fundamental Theorem of Welfare Economics

Exhibit 8–20 shows the competitive market for potatoes. We can ask two questions about this market, ostensibly as different as questions can be:

1. What is the quantity of potatoes actually produced and sold?
2. Suppose you were a benevolent dictator, concerned only with maximizing the total welfare gains to all of society. What quantity of potatoes would you *order* produced and sold?

Note well the dissimilarity between these questions. One is a question about what *is;* the other is a question about what *ought* to be.

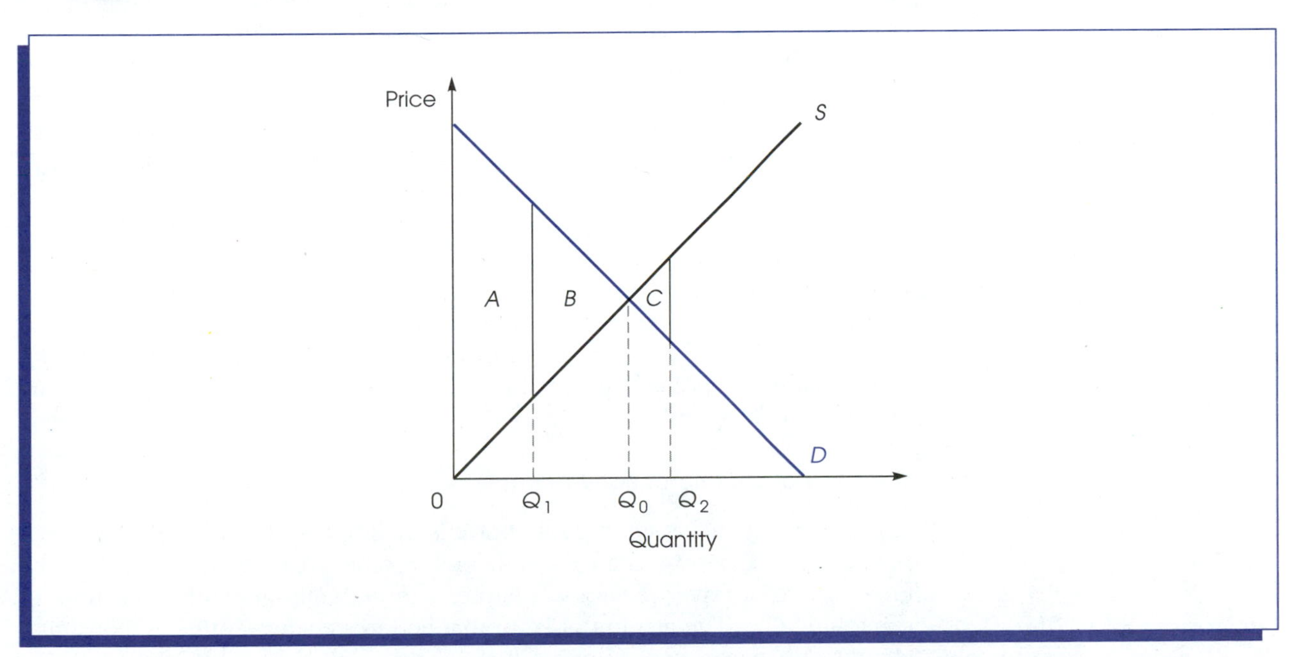

Under competition, the quantity produced is Q_0, where supply equals demand. A benevolent dictator who wanted to maximize social gain would employ the equimarginal principle and order potatoes to be produced to a quantity where marginal cost equals marginal value. This also occurs at quantity Q_0.

If the dictator ordered Q_1 potatoes produced, social gain would be area A; if he ordered Q_2, social gain would be $A + B - C$. The maximum social gain, at Q_0, is $A + B$.

We know the answers to each of these questions. They are:

1. The quantity of potatoes produced and sold is at Q_0, where supply equals demand. We have seen that individual suppliers and demanders, seeking to maximize their own profits and their own happiness, choose to operate at this point.
2. To maximize social gains, you would continue ordering potatoes to be produced as long as their marginal value exceeds the marginal cost of producing them. You would stop when marginal cost equals marginal value, that is, at Q_0.

The choice of Q_0 yields a social gain of $A + B$ in Exhibit 8–20. A despot who made the mistake of ordering only Q_1 potatoes produced would limit social gain to area A. If the same benevolent dictator made the mistake of ordering Q_2, area C would be subtracted from the social gain, since it is made up of rectangles whose areas represent an excess of marginal cost over marginal value.

It is astounding that the two questions have identical answers. The coincidence results from the prior coincidences of the supply curve with the marginal cost curve, and of the demand curve with the marginal value curve.

It is not only astounding that the two answers are identical, but it is fortunate. It means that people living in a competitive world achieve the maximum possible social gain without any need of a benevolent despot. The market alone achieves an outcome that is economically efficient. To say the same thing in different words, competitive equilibrium is Pareto-optimal.

The eighteenth-century economist Adam Smith was so struck by this observation that he described it with one of the world's most enduring metaphors. Of the individual participant in the marketplace, he said: "He intends only his own gain, and he is . . . led by an invisible hand to promote an end which was no part of his intention."[9]

Noneconomists frequently misunderstand what Smith meant by the *invisible hand*. Some think it is a metaphor for an ideology or a philosophical point of view; the notion has even been described as a theological one! In fact, the *invisible hand* expresses what is at bottom a mathematical truth. The point of equilibrium (where competitive suppliers operate "intending only their own gain") is also the point of maximum social gain (an end that is no part of any individual participant's intention).

The Idea of a General Equilibrium

The preceding analysis is striking, but it is incomplete. By participating in the potato market, people change conditions in other markets as well. When he grows more or fewer potatoes, a farmer consequently grows less or more of something else. The amount of labor that he hires changes. When a consumer changes his potato consumption, he probably also changes his consumption of rice, and of butter. At one further remove, any change in the potato market affects the potato farmer's income, which affects his purchases of shoes, which

---

[9]From Book 4 of Smith's monumental work *The Wealth of Nations*, first published in 1776.

affects the market for leather, which affects the market for something else, ad infinitum.

If we really want to understand the welfare consequences of competitive equilibrium in the potato industry, we need to consider its effects in all of these other markets as well. Could it be that by maximizing welfare gains in one market, we are imposing a net welfare *loss* in the totality of all other markets?

It was not until the 1950s, nearly 200 years after Adam Smith, that economists developed the mathematical tools necessary to deal fully with this complicated question. In that decade economists such as Kenneth Arrow, Gerard Debreu, and Lionel McKenzie devised techniques that make it possible to study all the markets in the economy at one time. In this they were advancing a subject called **general equilibrium analysis**, first invented by the nineteenth-century economist Lèon Walras. One of the great and powerful results of general equilibrium theory is that even in view of the effects of all markets on all other markets, competitive equilibrium is still Pareto-optimal. This discovery is usually called the *First Fundamental Theorem of Welfare Economics*, or the *Invisible Hand Theorem*.

General equilibrium analysis A way of modeling the economy so as to take account of all markets at once, and of all the interactions among them.

The Invisible Hand Theorem says, in essence, that in competitive markets, people who selfishly pursue their own interests end up achieving an outcome that is socially desirable. Outside of competitive markets, such good fortune is not to be expected. The governor of Colorado recently told of walking down a suburban street where each homeowner was out blowing leaves onto his neighbor's lawn. Each homeowner acted selfishly, and the outcome was highly undesirable. If the homeowners had all agreed to spend the afternoon watching football, they would have enjoyed themselves more and had the same number of leaves on their lawns at the end of the day. Because the decision to blow leaves takes place outside of the market system, there is no reason to expect it to yield outcomes that are in any sense desirable. In Chapters 10 through 14 we will see many more such examples. The fact that the Invisible Hand Theorem fails so easily in so many contexts makes it utterly remarkable that it succeeds in the particular context of competitive markets.

The Pareto optimality of competitive equilibrium is a deep and wondrous fact about the price system. No analogous statement is true in the absence of competition or in the absence of prices. The Invisible Hand Theorem is a remarkable truth.

An Edgeworth Box Economy

For more on an Edgeworth box economy see: http://www.best.com/~ddfr/Academic/Price_Theory/PThy_Chapter_6/PThy_Chapter_6.html

The Invisible Hand Theorem is true in very complex economies with many participants and many markets, but we will illustrate it (and the basic ideas of general equilibrium analysis) only in the simplest possible case. Assume a world with two people (Aline and Bob) and two goods (food and clothing). We will simplify further by assuming that there is no production in this world; Aline and Bob can only trade the goods that already exist. These assumptions will enable us to present a complete general equilibrium model and to illustrate the Invisible Hand Theorem.

Since there is no production in this world, there is only a fixed, unchangeable amount of food and clothing. In panel A of Exhibit 8–21 we draw a box that has a width equal to the amount of food in existence, and a height equal

Exhibit 8-21 Trade in an Edgeworth Box Economy

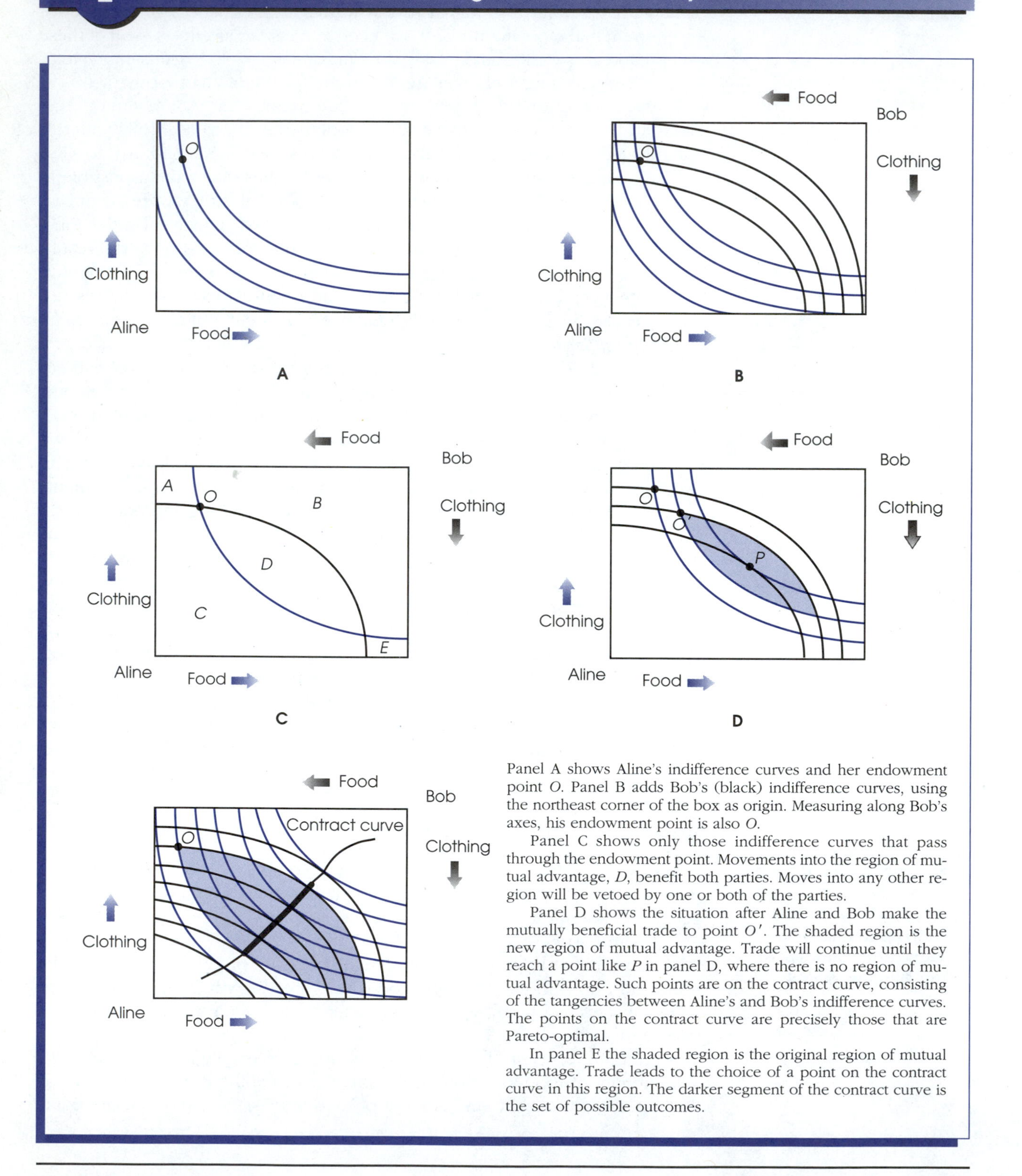

Panel A shows Aline's indifference curves and her endowment point *O*. Panel B adds Bob's (black) indifference curves, using the northeast corner of the box as origin. Measuring along Bob's axes, his endowment point is also *O*.

Panel C shows only those indifference curves that pass through the endowment point. Movements into the region of mutual advantage, *D*, benefit both parties. Moves into any other region will be vetoed by one or both of the parties.

Panel D shows the situation after Aline and Bob make the mutually beneficial trade to point *O*′. The shaded region is the new region of mutual advantage. Trade will continue until they reach a point like *P* in panel D, where there is no region of mutual advantage. Such points are on the contract curve, consisting of the tangencies between Aline's and Bob's indifference curves. The points on the contract curve are precisely those that are Pareto-optimal.

In panel E the shaded region is the original region of mutual advantage. Trade leads to the choice of a point on the contract curve in this region. The darker segment of the contract curve is the set of possible outcomes.

Edgeworth box A certain diagrammatic representation of an economy with two individuals, two goods, and no production.

Endowment point The point representing the initial holdings of an individual in an Edgeworth box.

to the amount of clothing. Such a box is called an **Edgeworth box.**[10] Using the lower left-hand corner as the origin, we draw Aline's indifference curves between food and clothing. We also mark one point of special interest: It is Aline's **endowment point**, *O*, representing the basket of food and clothing that she owns at the beginning of the story.

In panel B we do a strange thing: We turn the entire page upside down, and we draw Bob's (black) indifference curves in the same box. For him, the food axis is the line that Aline views as the top of the box, and the clothing axis is the line that Aline views as the right side of the box.

To plot Bob's endowment point, remember that the width of the box is equal to the sum of Bob's and Aline's food endowments, and that the height is equal to the sum of their clothing endowments. A moment's reflection should convince you that Bob's endowment point (measured along *his* axes) is the same as Aline's endowment point (measured along *her* axes).

Panel C shows a piece of panel B: All but two indifference curves have been eliminated. We have retained only those indifference curves (one of Aline's and one of Bob's) that pass through the endowment point.

Now suppose that Bob and Aline discuss the possibility of trade. Aline vetoes any trade that moves her into region *A, C,* or *E,* since these all represent moves to lower indifference curves from her point of view. Similarly, Bob vetoes any trade that moves him into region *A, B,* or *E.* (Hold the book upside down for help in seeing this!) However, a movement anywhere inside region *D* benefits both Aline and Bob. For this reason region *D* is called the **region of mutual advantage,** and Aline and Bob can arrange a trade that moves them into this area.

Region of mutual advantage The set of points that are Pareto-preferred to the initial endowment.

After moving to a new point inside the region of mutual advantage, Aline and Bob face a new, smaller region of mutual advantage, as shown in panel D. They will move to a new point in this new region and will continue this process until no region of mutual advantage remains. This occurs precisely when they reach a point where their indifference curves are tangent to each other, such as the point *P* in panel D.

A point of tangency between Aline's and Bob's indifference curves is a point from which no further mutually beneficial trade is possible. In other words, such a point is Pareto-optimal; from that point no change can improve both parties' welfare. The collection of all Pareto-optimal points forms a curve, which is called the **contract curve** and is illustrated in panel E.

Contract curve The set of Pareto-optimal points.

We do not know in advance exactly what point Aline and Bob will reach through the trading process. We know only that it will be somewhere within the original region of mutual advantage, and that it will be on the contract curve. The set of possible outcomes is the darker segment of the contract curve shown in panel E.

Competitive Equilibrium in the Edgeworth Box

Our analysis has revealed an infinite variety of possible outcomes for the bargaining process. Next we ask what can happen if Aline and Bob play according to a far more restrictive set of rules. Instead of letting them bargain in what-

[10]The Edgeworth box is named after the nineteenth-century British economist F. Y. Edgeworth.

ever way they choose, we require them to bargain through the mechanism of a price system.

The new rules of the game work this way: Aline and Bob decide on a relative price for food and clothing. At this price, each decides how much of each commodity he or she would like to buy or sell. If their desires are compatible (that is, if Aline wants to buy just as much food as Bob wants to sell), they carry out the transaction. If their desires are not compatible, they decide on a new relative price and try again. This process continues until they find a relative price that "clears the market" in the sense that quantities demanded equal quantities supplied.

Why would Aline and Bob ever agree to such a strange and restricted set of rules? They wouldn't, because two people can bargain far more effectively without introducing the artifice of market-clearing prices. But our interest in Aline and Bob is not personal; we are concerned with them only because we are interested in the workings of much larger markets, and such markets *do* operate through a price mechanism. So we shall force Aline and Bob to behave the way people in large markets behave, hoping that their responses will teach us something about those large markets.

Suggesting a relative price is equivalent to suggesting a slope for Aline's budget line. Once we know this slope, we know her entire budget line. This is because her budget line must pass through her endowment point, in view of the fact that she can always achieve this point by refusing to trade. Bob's budget line (viewed from his upside-down perspective) is the same as Aline's. In panel A of Exhibit 8–22 a relative price has been suggested that leads Aline to choose point X and Bob to choose point Y. The total quantity of food demanded is more than exists in the world; the total quantity of clothing demanded fails to exhaust the available supply. The market has not cleared and a new relative price must be tried. In view of the outcome at the current price, it seems sensible to raise the relative price of food. That is, we try a steeper budget line, as in panel B. This time Aline and Bob both choose the same point Z and the market clears.

Competitive equilibrium A point that everyone will choose to trade to, for some appropriate market prices.

The mutually acceptable point Z in panel B is called a **competitive equilibrium** for this economy. It requires finding a budget line that goes through the original endowment point and leads to the same optimum point for Aline that it does for Bob. It is not immediately obvious that a competitive equilibrium should even exist, but it turns out to be possible to prove this.[11]

The Invisible Hand in the Edgeworth Box

At the competitive equilibrium Z of Exhibit 8–22, Aline's indifference curve is tangent to the budget line, and Bob's indifference curve is tangent to the same budget line. It follows that Aline's and Bob's indifference curves are tangent to each other. This, in turn, means that the competitive equilibrium is a point on the contract curve, that is, it is Pareto-optimal.

[11] In fact, *you* can prove it, if you have had a course in calculus. Define the *aggregate excess demand* for food as the sum of the quantities demanded by Bob and Aline, *minus* the world supply of food. At a price of zero, draw the budget line and compute the aggregate excess demand. Do the same at an infinite price. Now use the Intermediate Value Theorem to complete the proof.

Exhibit 8-22 Competitive Equilibrium in an Edgeworth Box Economy

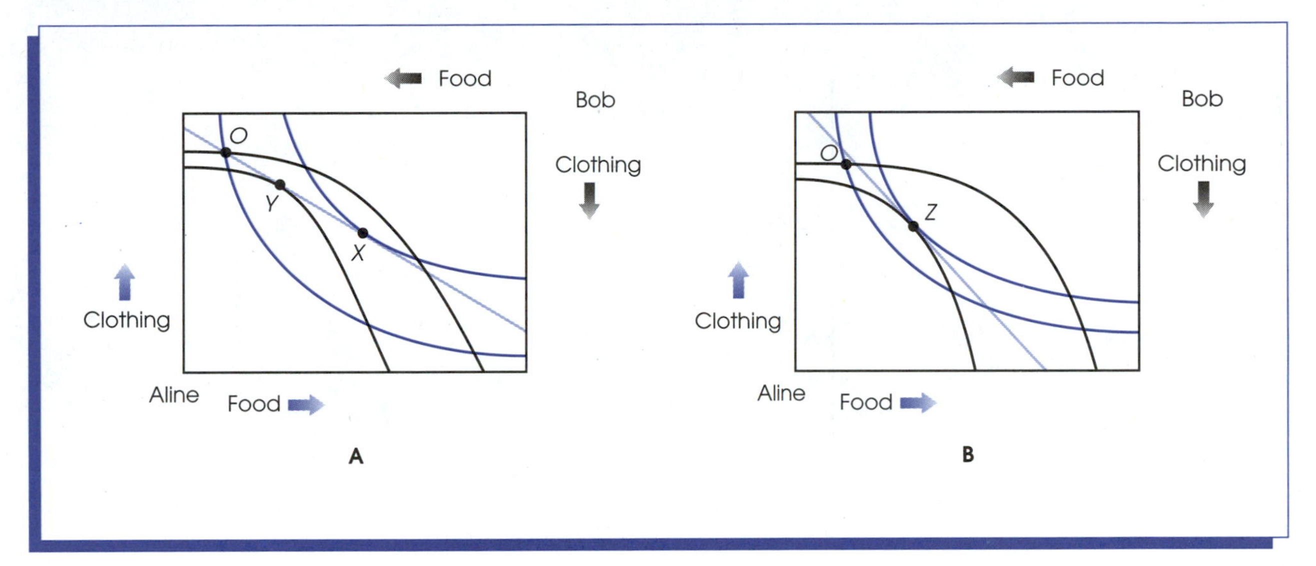

In panel A a relative price has been suggested that leads to the budget line pictured. (This is Aline's budget line from her perspective and Bob's budget line from his.) Aline chooses point X and Bob chooses point Y. But these points are not the same; the quantities that Aline wants to buy and sell are not the same quantities that Bob wants to sell and buy.

In panel B a different relative price has been suggested. At this price Aline's desires are compatible with Bob's. Point Z is a competitive equilibrium.

This reasoning shows that in an Edgeworth box economy, any competitive equilibrium is Pareto-optimal. That is, the Invisible Hand Theorem is true.

We began this section by noticing that competitive equilibrium is Pareto-optimal in the context of a single market. We have just seen that the same is true in the context of an entire economy (albeit an extraordinarily simple economy in which no production takes place). The same is also true in far more complex models involving many markets and incorporating production, though this requires advanced mathematics to prove.

General Equilibrium with Production

In the Edgeworth box economy there is no production. Next we will study general equilibrium in an economy where production is possible.

Robinson Crusoe

Robinson Crusoe lives alone on an island where the only foods he can produce are tomatoes and fish. He grows the tomatoes and catches the fish. Because each activity takes time, he can have more of one only by accepting less of the other.

Exhibit 8–23 shows the various combinations of tomatoes and fish that Robinson could produce in a week. If he grows no tomatoes, he can catch 15

Exhibit 8-23 The Production Possibility Curve

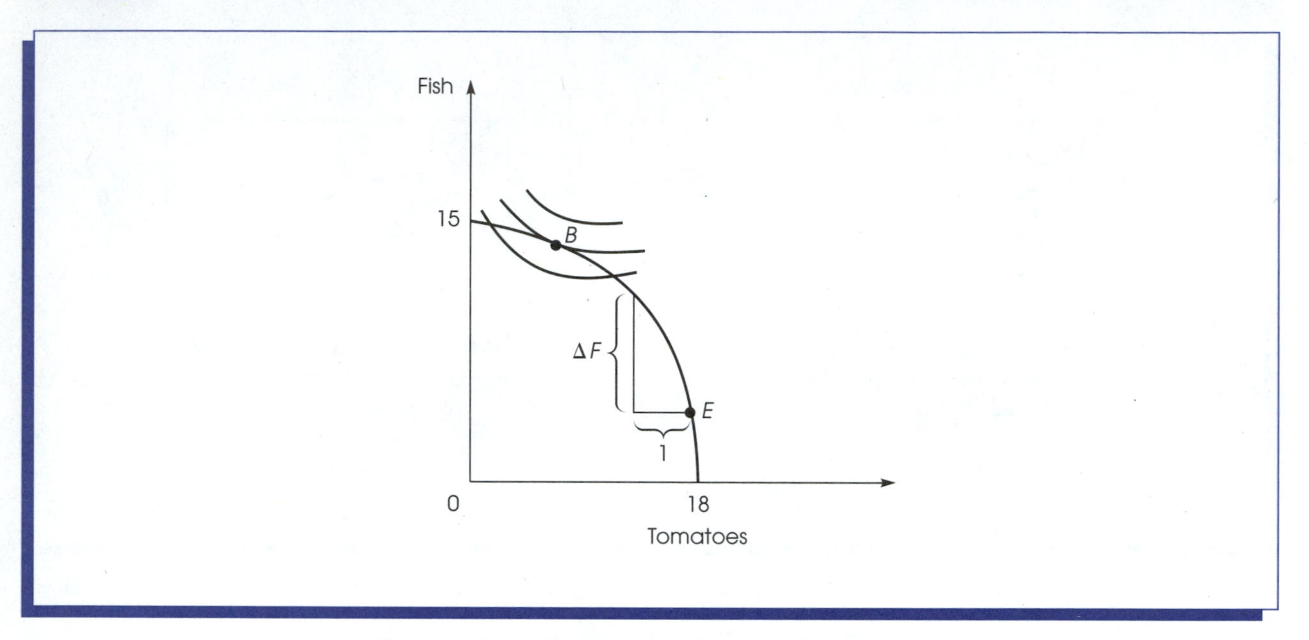

The curve shows the various combinations of tomatoes and fish that Robinson can produce. Its slope shows how many fish he can have in exchange for one tomato and can therefore be thought of as the relative price of tomatoes. At point *E* that relative price is the distance ΔF. Robinson chooses a point of tangency with an indifference curve; that is, he chooses point *B*.

Production possibility curve The curve displaying all baskets that can be produced.

fish. If he catches no fish, he can grow 18 tomatoes. The curve displaying all of his options is called Robinson's **production possibility curve**.

If Robinson starts at point *E* in the diagram and gives up a single tomato, he can catch ΔF additional fish. We can think of ΔF as the relative price of tomatoes in terms of fish. ΔF is also the slope of the production possibility curve at *E*. Therefore, the slope of the production possibility curve is equal to the relative price of tomatoes in terms of fish.

At point *E,* Robinson grows a lot of tomatoes. Because of diminishing marginal returns to farming on a fixed quantity of land, it takes a lot of effort to grow one more tomato. By giving up his last tomato, Robinson frees up a lot of time and catches a large number (ΔF) of fish. By contrast, if Robinson started out at a point near the northwest corner of the production possibility curve, the marginal tomato would require less effort.

Giving it up would only free a small amount of time; moreover, diminishing marginal returns to fishing render that time relatively unproductive. (Notice that Robinson is already catching a lot of fish.) In consequence, the price of a tomato in terms of fish is very low near the northwest corner, just as it is very high near the southeast corner. Remembering that price equals slope, this tells us that:

The production possibility curve bows outward from the origin.

To complete the analysis we must bring Robinson's indifference curves into the picture. Robinson chooses his favorite point on his production possibility curve, which is the tangency *B*. At this point, Robinson equates the relative price of tomatoes (the slope of the production possibility curve) with the marginal rate of substitution between tomatoes and fish (the slope of the indifference curve).

The Open Economy

Open economy An economy that trades with outsiders at prices determined in world markets.

Now suppose that Robinson establishes contact with the natives of a large nearby island. His own island is transformed into an **open economy**, one that can trade with outsiders at prices determined in world markets. The going price of a tomato on this other island is *P* fish dinners.

Robinson now faces two separate choices. First, how should he allocate his time between farming and fishing? Second, how should he allocate his consumption between tomatoes and fish?

We know how to answer the second question. Robinson chooses the tangency between his budget line and an indifference curve. What is his budget line? It is a line with absolute slope *P* (*P* being the relative price of tomatoes) and passing through the point representing Robinson's production. Why must it pass through that point? Because Robinson can always consume at that point by simply not trading with his neighbors. Since that point is available to him, it must be on his budget line.

Panel A of Exhibit 8–24 shows several lines with absolute slope *P*. If Robinson produces either basket *A* or basket *E*, his budget line is the lightest of these. If he produces *B* or *D*, his budget line is the middle one. If he produces *C*, the dark line is his budget line. It is best to have a budget line as far from the origin as possible, so *C* is Robinson's best choice. That is:

Production occurs at the point where the production possibility curve is tangent to a line of slope *P*. The line of tangency becomes the budget line.

Panel B of Exhibit 8–24 shows Robinson's consumption choice. Having produced basket *C*, he has the budget line shown; along this budget line he selects basket *X*. Notice that *X* is superior to the basket *B* that Robinson would consume in the absence of trade. Robinson gains from trade with his neighbors. We can go on to ask: How much does he gain?

Autarkic relative price The relative price that would prevail if there were no trade with foreigners.

World relative price The relative price that prevails in the presence of trade with foreigners.

To answer this question, we must compare two different prices. One is the **autarkic relative price** that would prevail on Robinson's island if there were no trade. With no trade, Robinson would choose point *B* in Exhibit 8–25 and would have the blue budget line. The slope of that line is the autarkic relative price of tomatoes.

The second interesting price is the **world relative price** at which Robinson can trade with his neighbors. Suppose first that the world relative price happens by chance to equal the autarkic relative price. In that case, Robinson's budget line must be tangent to the production possibility curve and parallel to the blue line; that is, his budget line is the blue line itself. He produces at the point *B* and consumes at the point *B*. But this is exactly the same point that

Exhibit 8–24 Production and Consumption with Foreign Trade

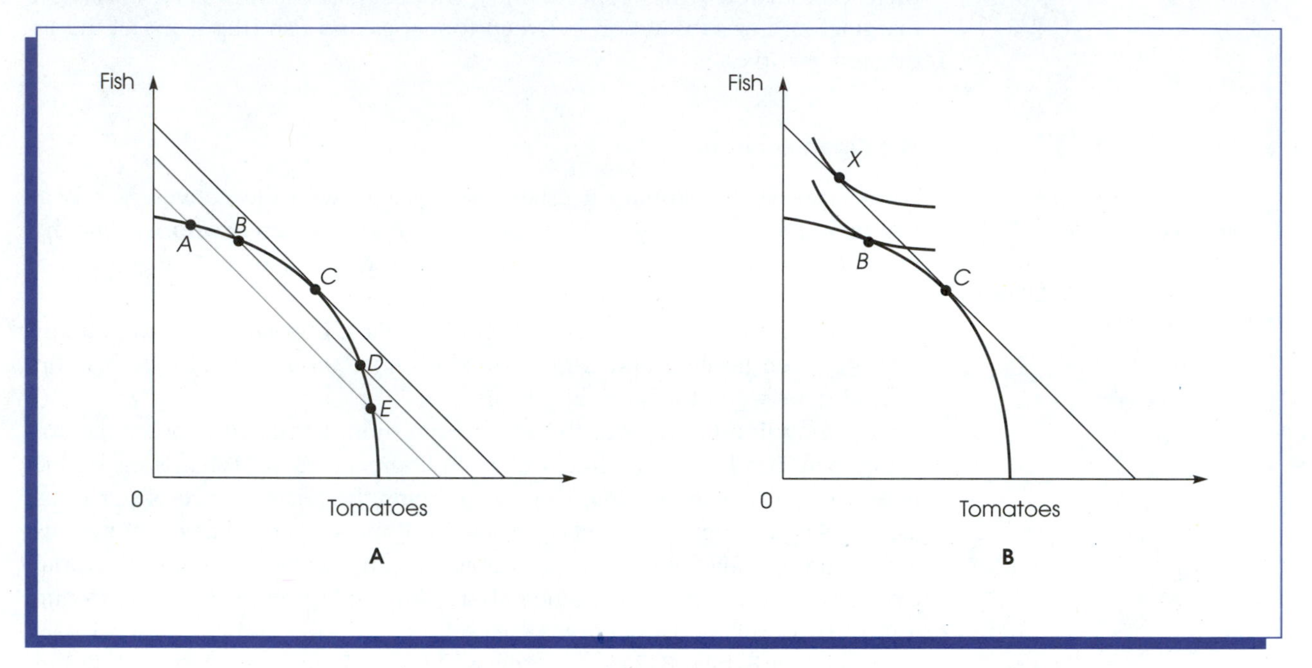

When Robinson can trade with his neighbors at a relative price of *P* fish per tomato, he faces a budget line of absolute slope *P*. All of the lines in panel A have that slope. By choosing a basket to produce, Robinson can choose his budget line from among the lines pictured. If he produces basket *A* or basket *E*, he has the light budget line; if he produces basket *B* or basket *D*, he has the middle budget line; if he produces basket *C*, he has the dark budget line. The dark budget line is the best one to have, so Robinson produces basket *C*. He then trades along the budget line to his optimal basket *X*, shown in panel B. Without trade, Robinson would choose basket *B*. Since basket *X* is preferred to basket *B*, Robinson gains from trade.

Robinson chose in Exhibit 8–23, when there was no opportunity to trade. In other words:

If the autarkic and world relative prices are equal, then there is no gain from trade.

Suppose, alternatively, that the world relative price is given by the slope of the black line in Exhibit 8–25. Then Robinson produces at *C* and consumes at *X*, which makes him happier than if he were to consume at *B*. In this case, he gains from trade.

Next, suppose that the world relative price differs even more from the autarkic relative price, being given by the slope of the gray line in Exhibit 8–25. Then Robinson produces *D* and consumes *Y*, which is better even than *X*.

The more the world relative price differs from the autarkic relative price, the more Robinson gains from trade.

Exhibit 8–25 Autarkic versus World Relative Prices

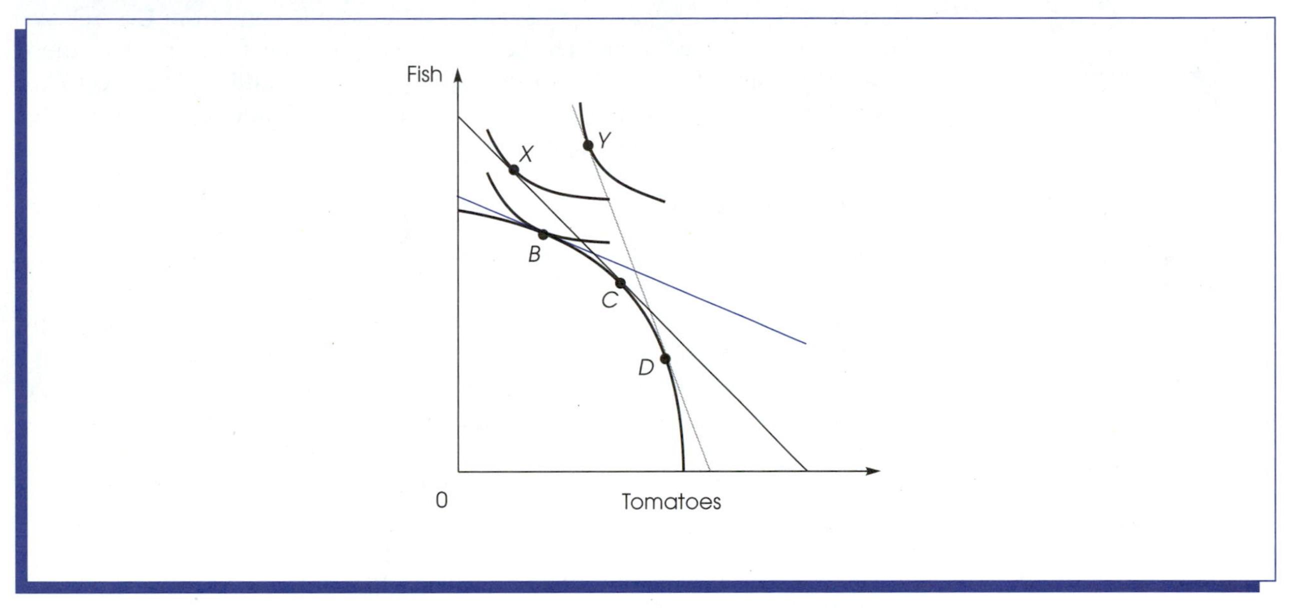

The slope of the blue line represents the autarkic relative price on Robinson's island. If the world relative price is the same as the autarkic relative price, then Robinson both produces and consumes basket *B*, just as he would with no opportunity to trade.

If, instead, the world relative price is given by the slope of the black line, then Robinson produces basket *C* and consumes basket *X*, which is an improvement over basket *B*. If the world relative price goes up to the slope of the gray line, then Robinson produces basket *D* and consumes basket *Y*, which is a further improvement.

The more the world relative price differs from the autarkic relative price, the more Robinson can gain from trade.

EXERCISE 8.9 The black and gray lines in Exhibit 8–25 represent world relative prices that are greater than the autarkic relative price. Draw some budget lines that result when world relative prices are *less* than the autarkic relative price. Check that it remains true that the gains from trade are greater when the world relative price is further from the autarkic relative price.

What determines the world relative price? The answer is: supply and demand by everyone in the world, including Robinson. Thus, the world price is a sort of average of the autarkic relative prices on all of the various islands in Robinson's trading group. If Robinson's supply and demand constitute a large percentage of the world's supply and demand, then his own autarkic relative price counts quite heavily in this average, bringing the world relative price closer to the autarkic one. This, in turn, reduces Robinson's gains from trade.

If, on the other hand, Robinson is an insignificant player in the world market, then there is a greater chance that the world relative price differs substantially from his autarkic one. In this case, Robinson's gains from trade are greater.

All of this serves to illustrate a point we made back in Chapter 2: To gain from trade, it pays to be different from the world. Small countries are more likely to be different from the world than large countries are. Therefore, small countries have more to gain from international trade than large ones do. For many goods, world relative prices do not differ significantly from U.S. relative prices, so the United States has relatively little to gain from trade in these goods. But New Zealand, for example, where the autarkic relative price of wool is quite low, benefits greatly from being able to trade its wool for other goods at the comparatively high world relative price.

The World Economy

We have seen how Robinson Crusoe reacts to world prices, and we have asserted that these world prices are determined by supply and demand. To complete the picture of the world economy, we have only to understand exactly how the world supply and demand curves are determined.

To derive a point on the supply curve for tomatoes, we imagine a price and ask what quantity Robinson supplies. Referring again to Exhibit 8–25, suppose that the blue budget line has absolute slope P. Then Robinson produces basket B, and the quantity of tomatoes he supplies is the horizontal coordinate of this point (whether he supplies them to himself or to someone else is not relevant here). The price P corresponds to this quantity on the supply curve.

To get another point on the supply curve, suppose the black budget line has absolute slope P'. At this price, Robinson produces at point C, and the corresponding quantity of tomatoes is paired with price P' on his supply curve.

A similar procedure generates points on Robinson's demand curve. When the price is P he has the blue budget line and demands a quantity of tomatoes given by the horizontal coordinate of point B. When the price is P', he has the black budget line and demands a quantity given by the horizontal coordinate of point X.

In this way, we can generate Robinson's supply and demand curves for tomatoes. We can do the same for all his trading partners. We get world supply and demand curves by adding the individual supply and demand curves, and these determine a world equilibrium price.

summary

Consumers and producers both gain from trade. Consumers' and producers' surpluses are measures of the extent of their gains.

When the consumer buys a good X, the total value of his purchase is given by the area under his demand curve out to the quantity. This area is the most that he would be willing to pay in exchange for that quantity of X. After we subtract the total cost to the consumer, we are left with the area under his demand curve down to the price paid and out to the quantity consumed. This area is his consumer's surplus. It is the amount that the consumer would be willing to pay in exchange for being allowed to purchase good X.

The producer's surplus is the excess of the producer's revenues over his costs. It is measured by the area above the supply curve up to the price received and out to the quantity supplied.

When there is more than one consumer or more than one producer, the total surplus to all consumers is given by the area under the market demand curve down to the price paid and out to the quantity demanded. The total surplus to all producers is given by the area above the market supply curve up to the price received and out to the quantity sold.

Policies such as taxes or price controls can change prices and quantities and consequently change the consumers' and producers' surpluses. They also sometimes generate tax revenue (which is a gain to somebody) or impose a cost on taxpayers (which is a loss). Social gain is the sum of consumers' and producers' surpluses, plus any other gains, minus any losses. If a policy reduces social gain below what it might have been, the amount of the reduction is known as a deadweight loss.

Whenever there is deadweight loss, it is possible to devise an alternative policy that is Pareto-preferred (that is, preferred by everybody) to the current policy. A policy is said to be Pareto-optimal, or efficient, if no other policy is Pareto-preferred.

The efficiency criterion is a normative criterion asserting that we should prefer policies that maximize social gain, or, equivalently, minimize deadweight loss. Few (if any) would argue that the efficiency criterion should be the sole guide to policy, but many economists consider it reasonable to use it as a rough guideline. When a policy creates large deadweight losses, there may be a Pareto-preferred policy that is actually possible to implement.

The Invisible Hand Theorem states that competitive equilibrium is Pareto-optimal. That is, in a competitive market where each individual seeks only his own personal gains, it turns out to be the case that social gains are maximized. This is true in individual markets, and remains true when the entire economy is taken into account. The Edgeworth box presents an example of a complete economy that can be used to illustrate the workings of the Invisible Hand.

It is also possible to study general equilibrium in economies with production. The opportunity to trade with outsiders confers benefits on the members of such an economy. The more world prices differ from autarkic relative prices, the greater those benefits tend to be.

Review Questions

R1. Explain why a consumer's demand curve is identical to his marginal value curve.

R2. What geometric areas represent the value of the goods that a consumer purchases and the cost of producing those goods? What geometric area represents the social gain from the goods' production, and why?

R3. What geometric areas represent the consumers' and producers' surpluses, and why?

R4. Analyze the effect on social welfare of a sales tax.

R5. Analyze the effect on social welfare of a subsidy.

R6. Analyze the effect on social welfare of a price ceiling.

R7. Analyze the effect on social welfare of a tariff, assuming that the country imposing the tariff constitutes a small part of the entire market.

First answer assuming that the good in question is available only from abroad, then repeat your answer assuming that there is a domestic industry.

R8. "The fact that secretaries are paid less than corporate executives shows that society values secretarial services less than it values the work of executives." Comment.

R9. State the Invisible Hand Theorem. Illustrate its meaning using supply and demand curves.

R10. Explain the difference between the allocation of resources and the distribution of income. With which is the efficiency criterion concerned?

R11. Using an Edgeworth box, illustrate the region of mutual advantage and the contract curve. Explain why trade will always lead to a point that is both in the region and on the curve.

R12. Using an Edgeworth box, illustrate the competitive equilibrium. Explain how you know that the competitive equilibrium is on the contract curve. How does this illustrate the Invisible Hand Theorem?

R13. Show how Robinson Crusoe chooses his consumption point when he is unable to trade. Show how he chooses his production and consumption points when trade becomes an option.

Problem Set

1. True or False: If Jack Daniel's whiskey sells for $10 per bottle and if 1,000 bottles were sold last year, then the total value of those bottles to consumers was $10,000.

2. Suppose that your demand curves for gadgets and widgets are both straight lines but your demand curve for gadgets is much more elastic than your demand curve for widgets. Each is selling at a market price of $10, and at that price you choose to buy exactly 30 gadgets and 30 widgets.

a. From which transaction do you gain more surplus?

b. If forced at gunpoint to buy either an extra gadget or an extra widget, which would you buy?

c. Illustrate the chance in your consumer's surplus as a result of the forced transaction of part b.

3. True or False: If the market price of haircuts falls by 10%, then barbers will lose 10% of their producers' surplus.

4. Adam and Eve consume only apples. Of the following allocations of apples, which are preferred to which others according to (a) the Pareto criterion, and (b) the efficiency criterion?

a. Adam has 12 apples and Eve has 0 apples.

b. Adam has 9 apples and Eve has 3 apples.

c. Adam has 6 apples and Eve has 6 apples.

d. Adam has 0 apples and Eve has 12 apples.

e. Adam has 5 apples and Eve has 5 apples.

5. True or False: If there is a fixed amount of land in Wyoming, then a sales tax on Wyoming land will have no effect on social welfare.

6. In the subsidy example of Exhibit 8–12, devise an alternative program that *everybody* (consumers, producers, and taxpayers) prefers to the subsidy program. If your alternative program involves transfers of wealth, be specific about how *much* wealth must be transferred.

7. The demand and supply curves for gasoline are the same in Upper Slobbovia as in Lower Slobbovia. However, in Upper Slobbovia everybody's time is worth just $1 per hour, while in Lower Slobbovia everybody's time is worth $10 per hour. True or False: If both countries impose a price ceiling on gasoline, the value of time wasted in waiting lines will be higher in Lower Slobbovia than in Upper Slobbovia.

8. In the preceding problem, suppose that there is also a country of Middle Slobbovia, where the value of various people's time ranges between $1 and $10. If Middle Slobbovia imposes a price ceiling on gasoline, how will the value of time wasted in waiting lines compare to the time wasted in Upper and Lower Slobbovia?

9. True or False: A sales tax on a price-controlled item can improve social welfare.

10. There is currently a federal gasoline tax of 4.3 cents per gallon. A United States senator has proposed eliminating this tax, but requiring oil companies to pass all of the savings on to the consumer (by maintaining a new price at the pump that is 4.3 cents lower than the current price). Show the deadweight loss under the current tax and under the senator's plan. Can you tell which is bigger?

11. Suppose that the government sets a price floor in the market for peanut butter. That is, it sets a price above equilibrium, and forbids anyone to sell below this price.

a. If peanut butter manufacturers have no way to compete for customers other than lowering prices, show the deadweight loss associated with this program.

b. Can you think of some ways in which peanut butter manufacturers *could* in fact compete for customers? How does such competition affect the deadweight loss?

12. In the tariff example of Exhibit 8–17, divide the two triangles of deadweight loss into individual rectangles of loss, as in Exhibit 8–9 or panel B of Exhibit 8–12. Give an intuitive explanation of the loss that each of these rectangles represents.

13. Suppose that South Molucca is willing to supply any number of bird cages to Americans at a price of P_0. American bird cage manufacturers have an upward-sloping supply curve that intersects demand at a price above P_0.

a. Explain why the market price for bird cages is P_0. Show how many bird cages Americans buy at this price. Show how many are provided domestically and how many are imported from South Molucca.

b. Show the welfare gain to Americans from the existence of the bird cage market, and show how it is distributed between consumers and producers.

c. Now suppose that a quota is enacted that permits the South Moluccans to sell only Q_0 bird cages per year in America, and that Q_0 is less than the quantity they have been selling to us up until now. Show that there is only one price consistent with Americans wanting to import exactly Q_0 bird cages, and explain why the price of bird cages will rise to that level.

d. Show the new gains to American producers and consumers. Who wins and who loses as a result of the quota? Which is greater—the amount the winners win or the amount the losers lose? Show on your graph the difference between these two quantities.

e. Suppose that the quota is abolished and replaced by a tariff that causes the number of imported bird cages to fall to Q_0. Which Americans prefer the tariff to the quota, and which prefer the quota to the tariff? Which do the South Moluccans prefer—the tariff or the quota?

14. Suppose the U.S. supply and demand curves for automobiles cross at a price of $15,000, but (identical) automobiles can be purchased from abroad for $10,000. Now suppose the government imposes a $2,000 sales tax on every American who buys a car (regardless of whether the car is produced domestically or abroad).

a. What price must Americans pay for cars before the tax is imposed? What price must Americans pay for cars after the tax is imposed? (*Hint:* American suppliers can always sell cars abroad for $10,000, and so will never sell cars for less.) What prices do U.S. producers receive for their cars before and after the tax is imposed?

b. Before and after the tax is imposed, calculate the gains to all relevant groups of Americans. What is the deadweight loss due to the tax?

15. Suppose the U.S. supply and demand curves for automobiles cross at a price of $15,000, but (identical) automobiles can be purchased from abroad for $10,000. Now suppose the government imposes a $2,000 excise tax on every car produced in the United States (regardless of whether the car is sold in the United States or abroad).

a. What price must Americans pay for cars before the tax is imposed? What price must Americans pay for cars after the tax is imposed? (*Hint:* Americans can always buy cars on the world market, and so will never pay more than the world price for a car.) What prices do U.S. producers receive for their cars before and after the tax is imposed?

b. Before and after the tax is imposed, calculate the gains to all relevant groups of Americans. What is the deadweight loss due to the tax?

16. Suppose the U.S. supply and demand curves for automobiles cross at a price of $15,000, but (identical) automobiles can be purchased from abroad for $10,000. Now suppose the government offers a subsidy of $2,000 to each American who buys an imported car. Buyers of domestic cars receive no subsidy.

a. What price do Americans pay for domestic cars before the subsidy is offered? What is the most an American will pay for a domestic car after the subsidy is offered?

b. Given your answer to part a, and given that anyone can buy or sell cars abroad at the world price of $10,000, how many cars will U.S. producers want to sell in the United States.

c. Before and after the subsidy is offered, calculate the gains to all relevant groups of Americans. What is the deadweight loss due to the subsidy?

d. How does your answer change if U.S. producers are prohibited from selling cars abroad?

17. Suppose the U.S. supply and demand curves for automobiles cross at a price of $15,000, but (identical) automobiles can be purchased from abroad for $10,000. Now suppose the government offers U.S. producers a $2,000 subsidy for every car they produce (regardless of whether the car is sold in the United States or abroad).

a. What prices must Americans pay for cars before and after the subsidy is offered? What prices do U.S. producers feel they are receiving before and after the subsidy is offered?

b. Before and after the subsidy is offered, calculate the gains to all relevant groups of Americans. What is the deadweight loss due to the subsidy?

18. Suppose the U.S. supply and demand curves for automobiles cross at a price of $15,000, and that (identical) automobiles can be purchased from abroad for $10,000. Now suppose the government offers a $2,000 subsidy to every American who buys a car (regardless of whether the car is foreign or domestic).

a. At what prices do U.S. producers sell their cars before and after the subsidy is offered? What prices do U.S. consumers feel like they are paying before and after the subsidy is offered?

b. Before and after the subsidy is offered, calculate the gains to all relevant groups of Americans. What is the deadweight loss due to the subsidy?

19. Suppose that an effective price *floor* is established in the market for oranges and that the government agrees to buy any oranges that go unsold at this price. The oranges purchased by the government are discarded.

a. Show the number of oranges purchased by the government.

b. Show the consumers' surplus, the producers' surplus, the cost to the taxpayers, and the social gain both before and after the program is introduced.

c. What is the deadweight loss from this program?

20. Suppose that a law is passed requiring each purchaser of gasoline to present one ration ticket per gallon purchased. A ration ticket cannot be reused. A quantity of ration tickets (*less* than the equilibrium quantity of gasoline) is printed and distributed randomly to citizens, who may buy and sell them freely. Assume that it costs nothing to print and distribute ration tickets. Show on a graph (a) the price of the ration tickets, (b) the consumers' surplus, (c) the producers' surplus, (d) the value of the ration tickets that people receive, and (e) the deadweight loss.

21. In 1992, the French government was subsidizing sales by French wheat farmers. U.S. farmers argued that this created unfair competition. The U.S. president took a tough negotiating stance on behalf of U.S. farmers and convinced the French to cancel the subsidy. Assume that U.S. producers' supply curve crosses U.S. consumers' demand curve at $12 a bushel, that without the subsidy French farmers will sell any quantity of wheat to Americans at $10 a bushel, and that the subsidy leads French farmers to supply any quantity of wheat to Americans at $8 a bushel. Use a graph to illustrate the gains and losses to Americans as a result of the president's success. Did the president increase or decrease the welfare of Americans, and by how much?

22. U.S. farmers sell wheat to the rest of the world at a going price P_0. The U.S. government offers farmers a deal: "If you cut your production in half, then we [the government] will give you an amount of wheat equal to your production cutback. You are then free to sell this wheat as if you'd grown it yourself." (This essentially describes the PIK, or Payment-In-Kind, program, which was in effect in the 1980s.)

a. Assume that the government buys its wheat on the world market. Show the social gains and losses associated with this program.

b. Assume, instead, that the government provides wheat out of stockpiles that it would otherwise destroy. Now recompute the gains and losses.

23. Suppose that the government successfully maintains a price P_0 for wheat that is above the equilibrium price. At this price, consumers want to purchase Q_d bushels of wheat and farmers want to produce Q_s. The way that the government maintains the price P_0 is by offering farmers a cash reward for limiting their production.

a. How much must farmers agree to cut back production in order for the program to be successful?

b. Show on a graph the minimum payment that the government must make to farmers in order for them to agree to the deal.

c. Assuming that the government makes this minimum payment, use your graph to show the gains and losses to consumers, producers, and taxpayers from this arrangement. Calculate the deadweight loss.

24. Suppose that U.S. firms can hire any number of foreign workers at a wage P_0 that is lower than the wage rate at which their demand curve crosses U.S. workers' supply curve.

a. What wage rate will U.S. workers earn? Why? Show on a graph the number of U.S. workers employed, the number of foreign workers employed, and the consumers' and producers' surpluses earned by U.S. workers.

b. Let Q_0 be equilibrium number of U.S. workers that would be hired if there were no foreign workers. Suppose that new legislation requires employers to collectively hire at least Q_0 Americans before they hire any foreigners. What wage rate will be necessary to induce that many Americans to work? Now how many foreigners will firms want to hire? What are the new consumers' and producers' surpluses earned by U.S. workers?

c. Who gains and who loses from this legislation? What, if anything, is the deadweight loss?

25. **True or False:** If all thieves are identical, then the social cost of robbery is equal to the value of the stolen goods.

26. Suppose that it is now between harvests, so that the number of avocados is in fixed supply. There are equal numbers of avocados available in Los Angeles and San Francisco, but the demand curve is much higher in Los Angeles.

a. Compare the prices and quantities of avocados in the two locations.

b. In view of your answer to part a, what will avocado suppliers begin to do? If it is costless to ship avocados, when will this process stop? Why?

c. Draw the demand and supply curves for avocados in the two cities both before and after the process you described in part b. Compare consumers' and producers' surpluses before and after the process takes place.

d. Suppose that it were made illegal to transport avocados from one city to another. Could this benefit consumers? Producers? Society as a whole? What areas would you have to measure to get definitive answers to these questions?

27. The U.S. government has recently taken over a number of failed savings and loan institutions and has acquired a large number of office buildings in the process. It plans to sell all of these buildings. An alternative plan is to sell only some of the buildings, in an attempt to keep the price high. **True or False:** Depending on the shape of the demand curve for office space, the alternative plan could yield more revenue, and hence be socially preferable.

28. Popeye and Wimpy trade only with each other. Popeye has 8 hamburgers and 2 cans of spinach, and Wimpy has 2 hamburgers and 8 cans of spinach. Their indifference curves, somewhat unusually, are all straight lines, Popeye's being much steeper than Wimpy's:

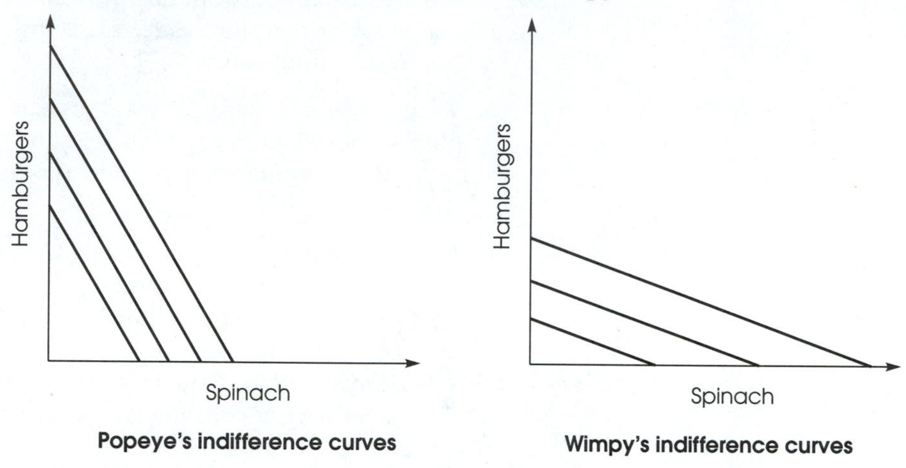

In an Edgeworth box, show the initial endowment, the region of mutual advantage, the contract curve, and the competitive equilibrium.

29. Robinson Crusoe lives alone on an island, producing nuts and berries and trading with people on other islands. If his production possibility curve is a straight line, what can you conclude about the quantities of nuts and berries he will produce?

30. Robinson Crusoe lives alone on an island, producing nuts and berries and trading with people on other islands. True or False: If nuts are an inferior good for Robinson, then his supply curve for nuts must be upward sloping.

Appendix to Chapter 8

Normative Criteria

Suppose that by ordering the execution of one innocent man you could save the lives of five others, equally innocent. Should you do it?

Consequentialist moral theories Moral theories that assert that the correctness of an act can be judged by its consequences.

Consequentialist moral theories assert that the correctness of an act depends only on its consequences. A simple consequentialist position might be that one lost life is less bad than five lost lives, so the execution should proceed.

Other views are possible. You might argue that if the one man to be executed is happy and fulfilled, while the other five lead barely tolerable lives, then it would be better to spare the one and sacrifice the five. This position is still consequentialist, because it judges an action by its consequences: The sacrifice of one happy life versus the sacrifice of five unhappy lives.

There are also moral theories that are not consequentialist. Some are based on natural rights. One could argue that a man has a natural right to live, and that there can be no justification for depriving him of this right, regardless of the consequences. There can be no execution, even if it would save a hundred innocent lives.

In the heated public debate about abortion, both sides have tended to make arguments that go beyond consequentialism. One side defends a "right to choose" while the other defends a "right to life." A strictly consequentialist view would discard any discussion of "rights" and judge the desirability of legalized abortion strictly on the basis of its implications for human happiness. This is not enough to settle the issue; one must still face extraordinarily difficult questions about how to trade off different people's happiness and potential happiness. Consequentialism, like natural rights doctrine, accommodates many precepts and conclusions.

The efficiency criterion is an example of a consequentialist normative theory. Which kind of world is better: One with ten people, each earning $50,000 per year, or one with ten people, of whom three earn $30,000 and seven earn $100,000? According to a strict application of the efficiency criterion, the second world is better, since total income is $790,000 instead of $500,000. The world with more wealth is the better world.

There are many other possible viewpoints, some consequentialist and some not. One might argue that certain people are more deserving of high income than others, and so there is no way to choose between the two income distributions without knowing more about the characteristics of the people involved. Such a position introduces criteria other than the ultimate consequences for human happiness, and so can be characterized as nonconsequentialist.

Judging the desirability of outcomes requires a normative theory. Economics can help us understand the implications of various theories, and perhaps help us choose among them. For the most part, economic analysis tends to focus on the various consequentialist theories. This is not because natural rights doctrines are uninteresting; it just seems to be the case that (so far) economics has less to say about them.

Some Normative Criteria

Here are a few of the normative criteria that economists have thought about.

Majority Rule

According to this simple criterion, the better of two outcomes is the one that most people prefer.

A number of objections can be raised. One is that majority rule does not provide a coherent basis for choosing among *three* or more possible outcomes. Sharon, Lois, and Bram plan to order a pizza with one topping. Their preferences are shown in the following table.

	Sharon	Lois	Bram
First Choice	Peppers	Anchovies	Onions
Second Choice	Anchovies	Onions	Peppers
Third Choice	Onions	Peppers	Anchovies

A majority (Sharon and Bram) prefers peppers to anchovies, a different majority (Sharon and Lois) prefers anchovies to onions, and a third (Lois and Bram) prefers onions to peppers. No matter what topping is chosen, there is some majority that prefers a different one.

A more fundamental objection to majority rule is that it forces us to accept outcomes that almost all people agree are undesirable. If 60% of the people vote to torture and maim the other 40% for their own amusement, a true believer in majority rule is forced to admit the legitimacy of their decision.

A less flamboyant example is a proposed tax policy that would have the effect of increasing 51% of all household incomes by $1 per year while decreasing 49% of all household incomes by $10,000 per year. The majority supports the proposal. Do you think it should be implemented?

The Kaldor-Hicks Potential Compensation Criterion

The British economists Nicholas Kaldor and Sir John Hicks suggest a normative criterion under which a change is a good thing if it would be possible in principle for the winners to compensate the losers for their losses, and still remain winners.

If a policy increases Jack's income by $10, reduces Jill's by $5, and has no other effects, should it be implemented? According to Kaldor–Hicks, the answer is yes, because Jack could in principle reimburse Jill for her loss and still come out ahead. On the other hand, a policy that increases Jack's income by $10 while reducing Jill's by $15 is a bad thing, because there is no way for Jack to reimburse Jill out of his winnings.

In applications like this, the Kaldor–Hicks criterion and the efficiency criterion amount to the same thing. When Jack gains $10 and Jill loses $5, social gains increase by $5, so the policy is a good one. When Jack gains $10 and Jill loses $15, there is a deadweight loss of $5, so the policy is bad.

However, there are potential subtleties that we did not address when we discussed the efficiency criterion in Section 8.1. Suppose that Jack has a stamp collection that he values very highly. Aside from his stamp collection, he owns nothing of great value and in fact barely gets enough to eat. Nevertheless, he would be unwilling to sell his stamp collection for anything less than $100,000. On the other hand, if the collection were taken from him, he would be willing to pay only $100 to get it back; any higher payment would mean starvation.

Jill values Jack's stamp collection at $50,000, regardless of who currently owns it. Should the collection be taken from Jack and given to Jill? If so, she would gain $50,000 in surplus, which is not enough to compensate Jack for his $100,000 loss. The Kaldor–Hicks criterion opposes such a move.

On the other hand, suppose that the stamp collection has already found its way into Jill's hands. If it is restored to Jack, he gains something that he values at $100, not enough to compensate Jill for her $50,000 loss. Kaldor–Hicks opposes this move also.

Thus, we get the somewhat paradoxical result that Jack gets to keep his stamp collection, unless it accidentally finds its way into Jill's hands, in which case Jack is not allowed to get it back.

Such paradoxes did not arise when we applied the efficiency criterion in Section 8.1. Why not? When we experimented with changing government policies, making some people better off and others worse off, we implicitly assumed that there were no resulting income effects on demand. If there are income effects, they cause the demand curve to shift at the moment when the policy is effected. This makes welfare analysis ambiguous: Should we calculate surplus using the old demand curve or the new one?

However, when the changes being contemplated do not affect large fractions of people's income, the Kaldor–Hicks criterion becomes unambiguous and equivalent to the efficiency criterion we have already studied.

The Veil of Ignorance

Let us repeat an earlier question. Is it better for everyone to earn $50,000 or for 70% of us to earn $100,000 while the rest earn $30,000?

The philosopher John Rawls has popularized a way to think about such problems.[1] Imagine two planets. On Planet X everyone earns $50,000; on Planet Y 70% earn $100,000 and the rest earn $30,000. On which planet would you rather be born? Your honest answer reveals which income distribution is morally preferable.

When you choose where to be born, it is important that you not know who you will be. If you knew that you'd be rich on Planet Y, you would presumably choose Y; if you knew you'd be poor on Y you would presumably choose X. But Rawls insists that we imagine making the decision from behind a *veil of ignorance,* deprived of any knowledge of whose life we will live.

A potential problem with the "veil of ignorance" criterion is that there might be honest disagreements about which is the better world. But Rawls contends that such disagreements arise because of different circumstances in our present lives. If we take seriously the presumption of the veil, that we have not yet lived and are all equally likely to live one life as another, then the reasons for disagreement will vanish and we will achieve unanimity. The unanimous decision is the right decision.

Suppose that a potential change in policy would enrich one billionaire by $10,000 while costing eight impoverished people $1,000 each. The efficiency criterion pronounces such a policy a good one. Rawls's criterion probably would not. If you did not yet know whether you were going to be the billionaire or one of the impoverished, it seems likely that you would oppose this policy, on a variety of grounds. First, $10,000 is unlikely to make much difference in a billionaire's life, while a loss of $1,000 can be devastating if you are very poor. Second, it is 8 times more likely that you will be poor than rich. Rawls would argue that behind the veil of ignorance, the vote against this policy would be unanimous. Therefore, the policy is bad.

The veil of ignorance can be used to justify various forms of social insurance, in which income is redistributed from the more to the less fortunate. Some misfortunes do not usually strike until late in life, and we can buy insurance against them at our leisure. But other misfortunes are evident from birth, making insurance impossible. You can't insure against being born into poverty, or with below-average intelligence. There is a plausible case that behind the veil, we *would* insure ourselves, by agreeing that those born into the best circumstances will transfer income to those born into the worst. Since everyone behind the veil would want this agreement, it is a good thing and should be enforced.

The Maximin Criterion

The maximin criterion says that we should always prefer that outcome which maximizes the welfare of the worst-off member of society. Taken to the ex-

---

[1]See J. Rawls, *A Theory of Justice* (Harvard University Press, 1971). A similar idea had appeared in J. C. Harsanyi; "Cardinal Utility in Welfare Economics and the Theory of Risk Taking," *Journal of Political Economy* 61 (1953):434–435.

treme, this means that a world in which everyone is a millionaire, except for one man who has only $200, is not as good as a world in which everyone has only $300 except for one man who has $201.

Perhaps nobody would want to apply the maximin criterion in a circumstance quite so extreme as this. But John Rawls believes that for the most part, souls living behind the veil of ignorance would want the maximin criterion to be applied. This is because people abhor risk, and worry about the prospect of being born unlucky. Therefore, while still behind the veil, their primary concern is to improve the lot of the least fortunate members of society.

According to Rawls, then, the maximum criterion is not really a new criterion at all, but instead prescribes exactly the same outcomes that the veil of ignorance criterion prescribes.[2]

The Ideal Participant Criterion

This is a slight variant on the veil of ignorance criterion, developed by Professor Tyler Cowen for the purpose of thinking about the problem of population, but applicable more generally. (We will briefly address the population problem later in this appendix.) According to this criterion, we should imagine living many lives in succession, one each in the circumstances of every person on earth. The right outcomes are the ones we would choose prior to setting out on this long journey.

In comparing the ideal participant criterion with the more standard veil of ignorance criterion, you might want to consider two critical questions. First, in what circumstances would these criteria lead to the same choices and in what circumstances would they disagree? Second, is there some more fundamental moral principle from which we can deduce a preference for one of the two criteria over the other? So far, economists have not found much to say about either of these issues.

Utilitarianism

Utilitarianism The belief that utility, or happiness, can be meaningfully measured, and that it is desirable to maximize the sum of everyone's utility.

Utilitarianism, a creation of the philosopher Jeremy Bentham, asserts that it is meaningful to measure each person's *utility,* or happiness, by a number. This makes it possible to make meaningful comparisons across people: If your utility is 4 and mine is 3, then you are happier than I am. (By contrast, many mod-

[2]A complete statement of Rawls's position would have to incorporate at least two additional subtleties. First, Rawls believes that from behind the veil, people's first priority would be to design social institutions that guarantee individual liberty. Having narrowed down to this set of institutions, they would then choose among them according to the maximin criterion. Second, Rawls does not want to apply the maximin criterion to particular details of the income distribution or human interactions. He wants to apply it instead to the design of social institutions. Thus, a Rawlsian might focus not on designing the ideal income distribution but rather on designing an ideal tax structure, from which the income distribution would arise. Rawls seeks that tax structure, among all of those that are consistent with individual liberty, which maximizes benefits to the least well-off members of society.

ern economists deny that any precise meaning can be attached to the statement "Person X is happier than Person Y.")[3]

Starting from the assertion that utilities are meaningful, utilitarians argue that the best outcome is the one that maximizes the sum of everybody's utilities. By this criterion, it is often better to augment the income of a poor man than a rich man, because an extra dollar contributes more to the poor man's utility than to the rich man's. This conclusion need not follow, however. One can imagine that the poor man has for some reason a much lower *capacity for happiness* than the rich man has, so that additional income contributes little to his enjoyment of life.

A generalized form of utilitarianism proposes that we assign a *weight* to each person and maximize the *weighted* sum of their utilities. If Jack has weight 2 and Jill has weight 3, then we choose the outcome that maximizes twice Jack's utility plus 3 times Jill's. The source of the weights themselves is left open, or is determined by any of various auxiliary theories.[4]

Under quite general circumstances, it is possible to prove that utilitarianism, with any choice of weights, always leads to a Pareto-optimal outcome, and that utilitarian criteria are the only criteria that always lead to Pareto-optimal outcomes. This is so even if we drop the assumption that it is meaningful to compare different people's utilities.

Fairness

Economists have attempted to formalize the notion of fairness in a variety of ways, usually in the context of allocating fixed supplies of more than one good. In a world with 6 apples and 6 oranges, it seems absurd to insist that Jack and Jill each end up with 3 of each fruit, since Jack might have a strong preference for apples and Jill for oranges. On the other hand, it seems quite unfair for either Jack or Jill to have all of the food while the other one starves. What precisely distinguishes those allocations that we think are equitable?

Envy-free allocation An outcome in which nobody would prefer to trade baskets with anybody else.

A widely studied criterion is that allocations should be **envy-free,** which means that no person would prefer somebody else's basket of goods to his own. Any allocation of apples and oranges is envy-free if neither Jack nor Jill would want to trade places with the other, given the choice.

In an Edgeworth box economy, it is possible to show that if each trading partner starts with equal shares of everything (3 apples and 3 oranges each), then any competitive equilibrium is envy-free. This is an important result, because we already know that any competitive equilibrium is efficient as well; that is, it satisfies the efficiency criterion. This implies that in such an economy, it is always possible to achieve an outcome that is simultaneously efficient and envy-free, satisfying two criteria at once.

---

[3]Utilitarians are not the only ones who believe that they can compare different people's happiness. In order to apply the maximin criterion, for example, it is necessary to make sense of the notion of the "least well-off" member of society.

[4]The primary proponents of utilitarianism among economists were H. Sidgwick and F. Y. Edgeworth (the same Edgeworth of the Edgeworth box). For a very interesting attempt to reconstruct the weights that Sidgwick and Edgeworth had in mind, see M. Yaari, "Rawls, Edgeworth, Shapley, Nash: Theories of Distributive Justice Re-examined," *Journal of Economic Theory* 24 (1981): 1–39.

Optimal Population

What is the right number of people?[5] If large populations imply crowding and unpleasantness, then how much is too much? Would it be better if there were only ten people, each deliriously happy, or if there were 1 billion people, each slightly less happy? Where should we draw the line?

It should first be noted that the implied premise is at least debatable. A 10% increase in the current world population would change a lot of things, some for the better and some for the worse. The new arrivals would consume resources (which is bad for the rest of us) and produce output (which is good for the rest of us); it is unclear whether we'd be better or worse off on balance.

Still, it is probable that beyond some point—though it might be very far beyond the point we're at now—increases in population will make life less pleasant for everyone. At what point does the population become "too big"? The population problem tends to confound the usual normative criteria, which are designed to address the problem of allocating resources among a fixed number of people.

We could adopt the utilitarian prescription, attempting to maximize total utility. A world of 1 billion reasonably happy people is better than a world with 100 extremely happy people, because total utility is higher in the first of these worlds. But the same criterion dictates that a world of 10 trillion people, each leading a barely tolerable existence, can be superior to the world of 1 billion who are reasonably happy. To some economists, this conclusion is self-evidently absurd. Professor Derek Parfit has endowed it with a proper name: He calls it the Repugnant Conclusion.[6] To Parfit and others, any moral theory that entails the Repugnant Conclusion must be rejected. There are others though, who think that the repugnance of the Repugnant Conclusion is far from evident.

An alternative is to maximize average (as opposed to total) utility. In practice, people are probably happier on average when the population is reasonably large (so that there is greater efficiency in production, a wider range of consumer goods, and a better chance of finding love). Therefore, a world of 1 billion might lead to higher average utility than a world of 100, even though a grossly overcrowded world of 1 trillion is worse than either. An objection to the average utility criterion is that it always implies that the world would be a better place if everyone with below-average utility were removed.

Alternatively, we can step behind the veil of ignorance and ask how many of us should be born. The trade-off is this: If the population is too large, the world is an unpleasant place, but if it is too small, most of us never get a chance to live. The conceptual problem here is to decide exactly how many souls there are behind the veil. Is there one for every person who *might* be born? Is that an infinite number? If so, then each has effectively zero chance of being among the finitely many lucky ones who do get born, rendering each indifferent to what the world is like. If instead there is a large, finite number of souls behind the veil, what determines that large, finite number?

---

[5]This entire section owes much to Tyler Cowen's paper "Normative Population Theory," *Social Choice and Welfare* 6 (1989):33–43.

[6]D. Parfit, *Reasons and Persons* (Oxford University Press, 1984).

Tyler Cowen has raised an additional objection to the veil of ignorance criterion. He asks a form of the following question: Suppose that you were offered a bet, whereby there is a 1% chance that 100 duplicate copies of Earth will be created and a 99% chance that all human life will disappear. Would you take the bet? Behind the veil you would, since it actually increases the chance of your birth without changing the average quality of human life. Yet, Cowen argues, the bet is obviously a bad one.[7] Since the veil criterion leads us to choose a bad bet, it must be a bad criterion.

Cowen has argued that the Ideal Participant Criterion is the ideal criterion for considering problems of population. You can read his arguments in the paper cited in the footnote at the beginning of this section. But the issue is very far from unsettled. In a world where we can't agree on what the speed limit should be, a consensus on population size will probably be a long time coming.

Internet Exercise

The efficiency criterion can be used to select mechanisms for resolving problems of congestion in energy, telecommunications, and transportation networks. The following Internet site, maintained by the Hubert H. Humphrey Institute of Public Affairs at the University of Minnesota, provides a summary description of the efficiency standard, and relates this standard to the notion of congestion pricing (http://www.hhh.umn.edu/Centers/SLP/Conpric/econ.htm). After reviewing the material on this Internet site, assess congestion pricing from the perspective of the efficiency criterion. If people could vote on congestion pricing versus the status quo, and if votes were allocated in proportion to dollar impact, would a policy of congestion pricing pass? Why?

[7]It should perhaps be mentioned that what is obvious to Cowen is not obvious to everyone, among them the author of your textbook.

chapter 9

Knowledge and Information

Every night the 1.5 million residents of Manhattan Island go to bed confident that when they awake, they will be able to purchase food, clothing, gasoline, and dozens of other items that are sent to New York City from thousands of miles away. How can Iowa farmers and Texas oil producers know what products to ship to Manhattan and in what quantities? Since each individual supplier makes an independent decision about how much to send, why do residents of the city not find all the stores nearly empty on some days or full to overflowing on others? When New Yorkers want more pork, how do the suppliers of feed corn know to increase production so that the hog farmers can raise more hogs? How is this activity coordinated with the activities of the butchers and truck drivers and refrigerator repairmen who are the hog farmers' partners in the production of pork chops? How *can* it be coordinated, when all of these producers are unknown to each other?[1]

In this chapter we will see how prices serve to convey information so that complex social activities can be organized and implemented. This will extend our understanding of the social role of prices that was developed in Chapter 8. There we saw how the price system acts to allocate resources efficiently by ensuring that appropriate quantities will be produced. Here we will focus on how prices contribute to the efficient production and distribution of those quantities by embodying vast amounts of knowledge not available to any individual. The two effects work together—hand in Invisible Hand—to lead to social outcomes that take account of producers' costs and consumers' preferences in ways that no individual planner could hope to accomplish.

[1]Such questions were raised by the nineteenth-century French economist Frederic Bastiat in his book *Economic Sophisms*, 1873.

9.1 The Informational Content of Prices

Prices and Information

In February 1976 the prestigious journal, *Science*, carried an article titled "Limits to Exploitation of Nonrenewable Resources." It contained this passage:

> To society . . . the profit from mining (including oil and gas extraction) can be defined either as an energy surplus, as from the exploitation of fossil and nuclear fuel deposits, or as a work saving, as in the lessened expenditure of human energy and time when steel is used in place of wood in tools and structures.[2]

Presumably, the "energy surplus" associated with, say, a coal deposit refers to the difference between the energy that can be extracted from the coal deposit on the one hand, and the energy required to excavate it on the other.

By this accounting, a society's choice of energy sources becomes a matter of simple arithmetic. Suppose, for simplicity, that it is necessary to choose between two projects: mining coal (which is located in the eastern half of the United States) and drilling for oil (which is located in the West). Coal mining yields sufficient fuel to provide 1,000 British thermal units[3] of energy per month, but the mining process itself consumes 500 BTUs in the same time period. Oil drilling yields 800 BTUs per month but consumes 200 BTUs. Because the "social profit" from oil (600 BTUs per month) exceeds that from coal (500 BTUs), society should choose to drill for oil.

Alas, the world is not so simple. A subsequent issue of the same journal carried a letter from Harvared economist Robert Dorfman, who elucidated the fallacy. Suppose that the land in the West is the only land suitable for growing hops. A society that drills for oil will then be a society without beer.

Then perhaps it is best to mine coal instead. Or perhaps not—the eastern land might be the best place to raise cattle. On the other hand, the West might be where everyone wants to live, because of its better climate and greater scenic beauty. (See Exhibit 9–1.) What should society do?

A rational choice involves weighing the importance of the alternative uses of land in the different regions of the country. Essentially, there are two ways to do this. One is to empanel a blue-ribbon commission, peopled by experts in mining, agriculture, ranching, housing, and other fields, and to empower this commission to collect evidence about public desires and technological constraints. The panel would inquire into how the eastern land might be made suitable for the growing of hops, and at what cost. It would ask whether there is a way to make beer without hops, or whether beer can be adequately imported, or whether there is some other beverage that might easily take the place of beer. Having settled these questions, it would move on to analogous questions about housing. At some point the commission would issue a report,

---

[2]E. Cook, "Limits to Exploitation of Nonrenewable Resources," *Science* 191 (1976):677–82.

[3]British thermal units, or BTUs, are the basic units in which energy is measured.

Exhibit 9-1 Information and Prices

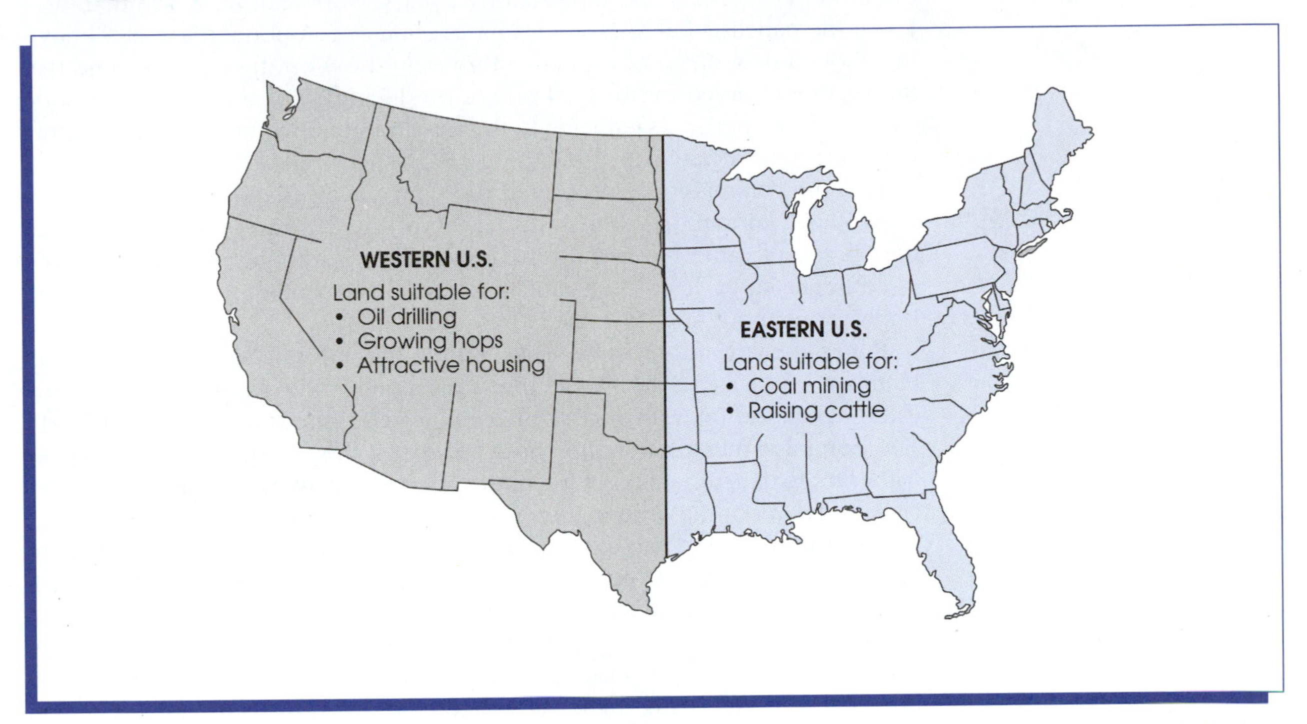

Even if we know that oil drilling produces more energy than coal mining, we still do not have enough information to choose between the two projects. If we drill for oil, we must do without beer and attractive housing, while if we mine coal we must do without beef. The desirability of either alternative depends on the availability of substitutes for beer, western housing, and beef. A blue-ribbon commission can make a disastrously wrong decision if it is missing just one fact. For example, if the commission is unaware of a new breed of cattle that thrives in the West, it might rule out coal mining in the mistaken belief that eastern land is the only source of beef.

However, prices convey the relevant information. The existence of the new breed of cattle drives up the price of western land and drives down the price of eastern land. Although the prices do not reveal the existence of the new breed of cattle, they do reveal that *something* has raised the value of western land and lowered the value of eastern land. This is precisely the kind of information that is needed to choose between the two energy sources.

making the best recommendation it can on the basis of the information it has been able to acquire.

An alternative is to observe the *price* of land in each region. The price of a parcel of land is equal (under competition) to the marginal cost of providing that parcel. Since a cost is nothing but a forgone opportunity, the price is a measure of the value of the land in the most valuable of its alternative uses.

When we observe that an acre of land in the West sells for $1,000 and that an acre in the East sells for $800, we know that someone values the western land at $1,000 per acre and that no one values the eastern land at more than

$800 per acre. The price alone does not reveal the most valuable use of the western land, but it does reveal how much the land is worth in that use.[4]

Which method is more informative? The commission's report, which may fill three bound volumes and represent two years' work, can be worse than useless if the panelists fail to take account of even one important fact. Not knowing about a new breed of cattle that thrives in the West, they recommend that the East be reserved for the vital role of producing beef, and that the West be exploited for energy—sacrificing both beer and good living and unnecessarily impoverishing society.

Had the commissioners observed the high price of land in the West, they would have known that something was afoot—in this case, the owners of the new breed of cattle bidding up the price of land. Although observers of the price might know less about ranching than the commissioners do, they will know more about how to extract energy efficiently.

Prices convey information. They reflect the information available to all members of society (in this case, the small number who know about the new cattle reveal the relevant part of their knowledge through the price of land). The commissioners, no matter how wise and how benevolent, can never gather more than a fraction of the information that may be relevant to their decision—but *all* of that information is reflected in the price.

Prices have at least two other advantages over expert panels. One is that observing prices is free. Expert panels consume resources—lots of resources, if they do their jobs well.

The other advantage of prices is that in addition to conveying information, they also provide appropriate incentives to act on that information. When a price tells you (by being high) that western land is valuable to someone, you will not choose to use it yourself unless it is even more valuable to you.

Here is Dorfman again:

> Clearly, then, social costs cannot be measured in . . . simple physical units. The only adequate measure is what economists call "social opportunity costs," meaning the social value of the alternative commodities that have to be forgone in order to obtain the commodity being produced. Under certain idealized conditions this opportunity cost is measured by the dollars-and-cents cost of producing the commodity. Under realistic conditions the dollars-and-cents production cost is a fair approximation to the social cost. Under almost any conceivable conditions the dollars-and-cents cost is a much better approximation to social cost than the amounts of energy expended or any other simple physical measure.
>
> Energy is indeed a scarce and valuable resource; but . . . there is a good deal more to life . . . than British thermal units.[5]

---

[4]There are exceptions to this rule, as we shall see in Chapter 13.

[5]From *Science*, letter to editor by R. Dorfman, 1976.

The Problem of the Social Planner

Try the following experiment: Ask your friends to name the two ways to get a chicken to lay more eggs. Few will know. The two ways to get a chicken to lay more eggs are to feed it more or to provide it with more heat from blowers that are usually powered by natural gas.[6] In chicken farming natural gas and chicken feed are close substitutes.

Imagine a chicken farm next door to a steel mill. In a typical week each consumes 100 cubic feet of natural gas. The steel mill has no economical alternative production process, and it would have to curtail its operation significantly if natural gas became unavailable. The chicken farmer, at an additional cost of a few cents per day, could switch off the blowers and use more chicken feed.

One day it transpires that only 100 cubic feet of natural gas per week will be available in the future. A benevolent economic planner, seeking only to benefit society, must decide how to allocate this natural gas. Perhaps he observes that the steel mill and the chicken farmer have historically used natural gas in equal quantities, and on this basis he decides that their "needs" for natural gas are roughly equal. He assigns 50 cubic feet per week to the steel mill and 50 cubic feet to the chickens.

As a result, there is a substantial cutback in steel output, to society's detriment. If all 100 cubic feet had been assigned to the steel mill, production would have continued about as before, with the chicken farmer having slightly higher costs and perhaps cutting egg production by a small amount.

Why does the benevolent planner not recognize his mistake? Because he—like the friends you were invited to poll on this question, and almost everybody else except for chicken farmers and the readers of this book—has never remotely suspected that chicken feed can be substituted for natural gas. Why doesn't the chicken farmer tell him? If he did, he would lose his natural gas allocation and his costs would go up—only slightly, to be sure, but the incentive is still to keep mum.

An alternative social arrangement is to abolish the planner, and to allocate the gas via the price system. Now when natural gas becomes more scarce, the price gets bid up. This has two effects on the chicken farmer: He acquires the information that the available natural gas is more valuable to someone else than it is to him, and he acquires an incentive to react accordingly. He puts in an order for some chicken feed.[7]

The Use of Knowledge in Society

See the scholarship on Friedrich Hayek at: http://members.aol.com/gregransom/hayekpage.htm

In 1945, Friedrich A. Hayek (later a Nobel Prize winner) addressed the American Economic Association on the occasion of his retirement as its president.

---

[6]Chickens use calories from feed to produce both eggs and body warmth. A chicken in a heated henhouse can divert more calories to egg production.

[7]Economist, financial planner, and chicken expert Dan Gressel reports that when natural gas prices were controlled in the 1970s, chicken farmers routinely consumed large and socially inefficient quantities of natural gas. When the controls were lifted and prices rose, farmers switched to chicken feed.

The title of his address was "The Use of Knowledge in Society." In it he called attention to the social role of prices as carriers of information, allowing the specialized knowledge of each individual to be fully incorporated in decisions concerning resource allocation. He contrasted this knowledge with so-called scientific knowledge and found it unjustly underrated by comparison:

> A little reflection will show that there is beyond question a body of very important but unorganized knowledge which cannot possibly be called scientific in the sense of knowledge of general rules: *the knowledge of the particular circumstances of time and place.* It is with respect to this that practically every individual has some advantage over all others in that he possesses unique information of which beneficial use might be made, but of which use can be made only if the decisions depending on it are left to him or are made with his active cooperation. We need to remember only how much we have to learn in any occupation after our theoretical training, how big a part of our working life we spend learning particular jobs, and how valuable an asset in all walks of life is knowledge of people, of local conditions, and special circumstances. To know of and put to use a machine not fully employed, or somebody's skill which could be better utilized, or to be aware of a surplus stock which can be drawn upon during an interruption of supplies, is socially quite as useful as the knowledge of better alternative techniques. [Emphasis added.][8]

The special knowledge of the chicken farmer is a sort of knowledge of the particular circumstances of time and place. But Hayek is referring here to knowledge even much more specialized (and inaccessible to the planner) than that: the knowledge of the foreman that a leak in a certain machine can be plugged with chewing gum; the knowledge of a manager that one of the file clerks has a knack for plumbing repairs; the knowledge of a shipper that a particular tramp steamer is half-full. No planner can have access to this knowledge:

> The sort of knowledge with which I have been concerned is knowledge of the kind which by its nature cannot enter into statistics and therefore cannot be conveyed to any central authority in statistical form. The statistics which such a central authority would have to use would have to be arrived at precisely by abstracting from minor differences between the things, by lumping together, as resources of one kind, items which differ as regards location, quality, and other particulars,

[8]F.A. Hayek, "The Use of Knowledge in Society," *American Economic Review* 35 (September 1945): 519–530.

> in a way which may be very significant for the specific decision.[9]

Suppose that you and your friends discover a new science fiction writer whose works you all rush out to buy. It may not occur to you that this requires more linseed plants to be grown in Asia, but it does, because the oil from those plants is used to make the ink to print the books that the stores now want to restock. The Asian linseed farmer is no more aware of the change in your reading habits than you are of your need for his services, but he nevertheless responds by increasing his output. Your increased demand for books causes a rise in the price of linseed and informs the farmer that someone, somewhere, wants more linseed for some reason.

A competing economics textbook begins its first chapter by observing that "the rest of us people" (together with nature) "dominate your life and prevent you from having all you want."[10] However, the authors warn:

> Do not suppose that if we were less greedy, more would be within your grasp. For greed impels us to produce more, not only for ourselves, but, miraculously, more for you too . . .

What the authors have in mind is that other people's greed enables you to offer them incentives to act as you want. It is because the carpenter is "greedy" that you can hire him to build your house.[11] In fact, we can say more. Although greedy neighbors are more likely than apathetic neighbors to respond to your desires, you might imagine that the best possibility is a third one that the authors did not consider: What if the rest of the world were neither greedy nor apathetic, but actively altruistic, attempting to cater to all of your wishes? Although such as world would have obvious advantages, it would also have a less obvious disadvantage: In the absence of a price system, you would be severely limited in your ability to communicate your desires. The farmer in Asia, wanting only to make your life more pleasant, has no criterion by which to choose between producing more linseed or more of some other crop. You have no way of informing him because you don't realize that a yen for science fiction creates a need for more linseed oil—or, if you do realize this, then you don't realize that you also need more glycerin, to make the glue with which the books are bound.

Your need for the selfishness of others stems not just from the fact that it motivates them to respond to your desires—altruism on their part would serve that purpose even better. It also stems from your need to *communicate* those desires. Students—and others who have not previously encountered the idea—generally find it quite surprising that a major role of prices in society is to fulfill this need.

---

[9]Ibid.

[10]A. Alchian and W. Allen, *Exchange and Production: Theory in Use* (Belmont, CA: Wadsworth, 1969).

[11]Adam Smith put this very well. In *The Wealth of Nations*, he said, "It is not from the benevolence of the butcher, the brewer, or the baker that we expect our dinner, but from their regard to their own interest. We address ourselves not to their humanity but to their self-love."

The Costs of Misallocation

We now want to explicitly relate the "informational" aspect of prices to the "equilibrating" aspect that has been stressed in previous chapters. Exhibit 9–2 displays the marginal value curves of three consumers in the market for eggs and the corresponding market demand curve. (The graph and tables are identical to those of Exhibit 8–6.)

The rectangles represent marginal values associated with individual eggs, each labeled with the name of the man who buys the corresponding egg and receives the corresponding value. When the market price is $7 per egg, 5 are sold and the top parts of the shaded rectangles constitute the consumer's surplus.

Exhibit 9-2 The Costs of Misallocation

Larry		*Moe*		*Curly*	
Quantity	Marginal Value	Quantity	Marginal Value	Quantity	Marginal Value
1	$15/egg	1	$13/egg	1	$7/egg
2	8	2	11	2	3

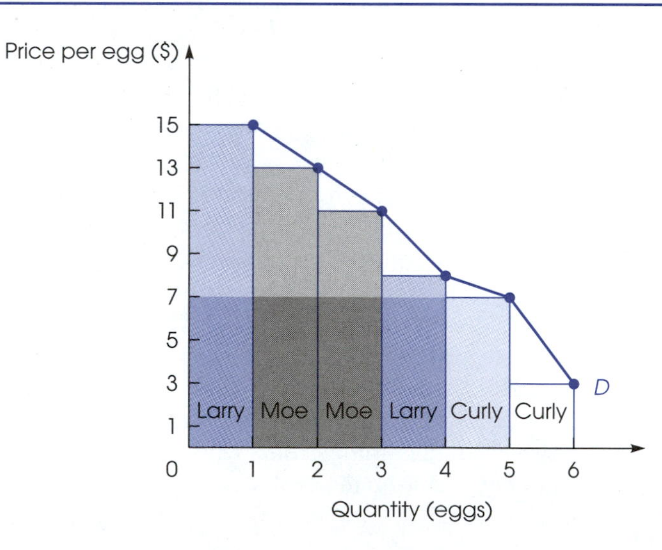

When the market price is $7 per egg, 5 eggs are sold (2 to Larry, 2 to Moe, and 1 to Curly) and their total value (the sum of the shaded rectangles) is $54. If the same 5 eggs were distributed by a mechanism other than the market, the total value might be less. For example, if a social planner gave 2 eggs to Larry, 1 to Moe, and 2 to Curly, the total value would be only $46. In this case, therefore, the usual measures of social gain would overstate the true social gain by $8.

EXERCISE 9.1 Assume a flat supply (= marginal cost) curve at $7 and calculate the total value of the eggs produced, the total cost of producing them, and the social gain. (Assume that eggs can be consumed only in "whole number" quantities for this calculation.)

Now let us reintroduce our benevolent social planner. Although the price system has been abolished he has managed through painstaking research to discover the demand and supply curves for eggs. Plotting both of these on the same graph, he discovers that equilibrium occurs at a quantity of 5. Wishing to maximize social gain and realizing that this is accomplished at equilibrium, he orders 5 eggs to be produced and distributed to consumers.

It appears that the social planner has succeeded in duplicating the workings of a competitive market, but this need not be true and, in fact, is not likely to be. Suppose that the planner orders the 5 eggs to be distributed as follows: 2 to Larry, 1 to Moe, and 2 to Curly. The marginal values of these eggs are equal to the areas of the first, second, fourth, fifth, and sixth rectangles in Exhibit 9–2. In comparison with competition, Moe has lost his second egg (worth $11 to him), and Curly has gained a second egg (worth only $3 to him). There is a net social loss of $8.

EXERCISE 9.2 Calculate the total value and total cost of the 5 eggs distributed by the planner. Compare these with your answer to Exercise 9.1.

In attempting to justify his actions, the social planner might look at the graph in Exhibit 9–2 and argue: "It is clear from this graph that social gain is maximized at a quantity of 5. That is the quantity I ordered produced. Therefore, social gain is maximized." But in actuality the social gain is a sum of 5 rectangles. We compute it by looking at the area under the demand curve out to a quantity of 5, implicitly assuming that it is the sum of the *first* 5 rectangles. This in turn assumes that the 5 eggs are distributed where they will be valued the most. In a competitive market this assumption is justified (Curly simply won't buy a second egg at $7, whereas Moe will). In the absence of a price system, it is not.

What must the social planner do to really maximize welfare? He must give Curly's second egg to Moe instead. (Of course, by doing this, he increases welfare and so can make both parties better off.)

EXERCISE 9.3 Describe explicitly how the social planner can make both Curly and Moe better off.

Now we return to the problem that is the theme of this chapter. How is the planner to *know* that Moe values a second egg more than Curly does? This information is available only to Moe and Curly. Its inaccessibility to the social planner renders him powerless to make improvements.

We can summarize as follows:

When allocation decisions are not made on the basis of price, the traditional measures of social gain (via areas) overstate the actual gains to society. Equivalently, the traditional measures of deadweight loss underestimate the losses.

EXERCISE 9.4 Suppose that the supply curve for eggs is as given in Exhibit 9–3 (which is identical to the curve in Exhibit 8–7). A social planner orders 5 eggs to be produced, 1 by firm A and 2 each by firms B and C. What is the extent of the social loss due to the social planner's failure to perceive that A is the low-cost producer?

example

A Military Draft

Society, through its armed forces, demands military services that are supplied by young people between the ages of 18 and 26. Suppose that the armed forces are able to set a maximum price (below equilibrium) that they will pay for military services, and suppose that they can *compel* young people to supply the quantity of military services that is demanded at that price (Q_d in Exhibit 9–4).

Exhibit 9-3 Planning versus Markets

Firm A		*Firm B*		*Firm C*	
Quantity	Marginal Cost	Quantity	Marginal Cost	Quantity	Marginal Cost
1	$1	1	$5	1	$6
2	3	2	11	2	7

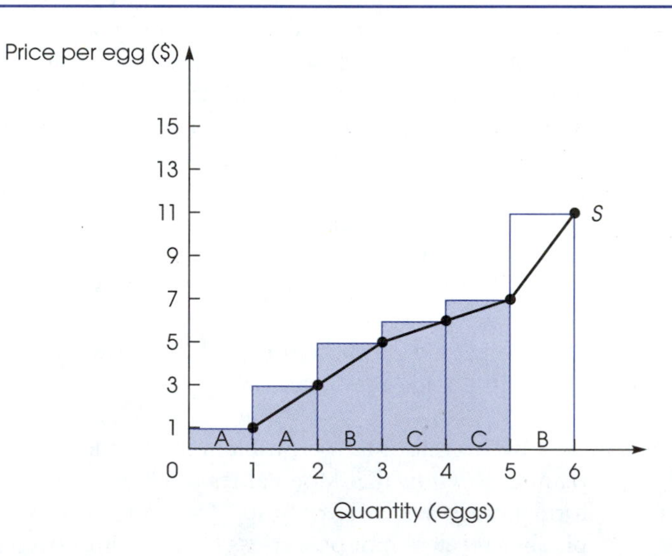

At a market price of $7, 5 eggs are produced in the least costly way possible. If a social planner orders 5 eggs to be produced and fails to realize that the low-cost producer is Firm A, then the total cost of production will be higher than necessary.

The "Draft" column of the table in Exhibit 9–4 shows the distribution of gains; the "Volunteer Army" column shows the gains in equilibrium for comparison.[12]

Exhibit 9–5 elaborates on the reason why the producers' surplus is $F - C - D - E$ in the presence of a draft. Panel A of Exhibit 9–5 reproduces the rele-

Exhibit 9–4 **A Military Draft**

	Volunteer Army	Draft	Limited Draft
Consumers' Surplus	A	$A + B + C + D$	$A + B + C$
Producers' Surplus	$B + F$	$F - C - D - E$	$F - C$
Social Gain	$A + B + F$	$A + B + F - E$	$A + B + F$
Deadweight Loss	—	E	—

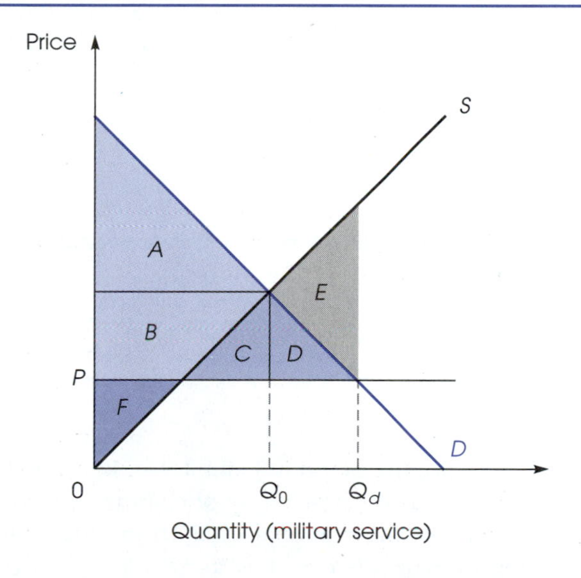

Military services are supplied by young people and demanded by society through the armed forces. The first column shows the gains at equilibrium, with a volunteer army. We assume that the wage rate is set at P, so that more young people are demanded than will volunteer. If the army can draft as many young people as it wants to at the price P, it will choose the quantity Q_d and social gains will be as depicted in the second column. If, on the other hand, the army is permitted to hire only Q_0 young people, social gains will be as in the third column, seemingly eliminating the deadweight loss. This leads to the apparent conclusion that the limited draft is as efficient as the volunteer army. As explained in the text, however, this conclusion is misleading.

[12]By drawing one graph, we are implicitly assuming that all young people would make equally good soldiers. To dispense with this assumption, we could draw several graphs, each showing the demand for soldiers of a different level of quality. None of our conclusions would be substantially altered.

Exhibit 9-5 Computing Producers' Surplus with a Draft

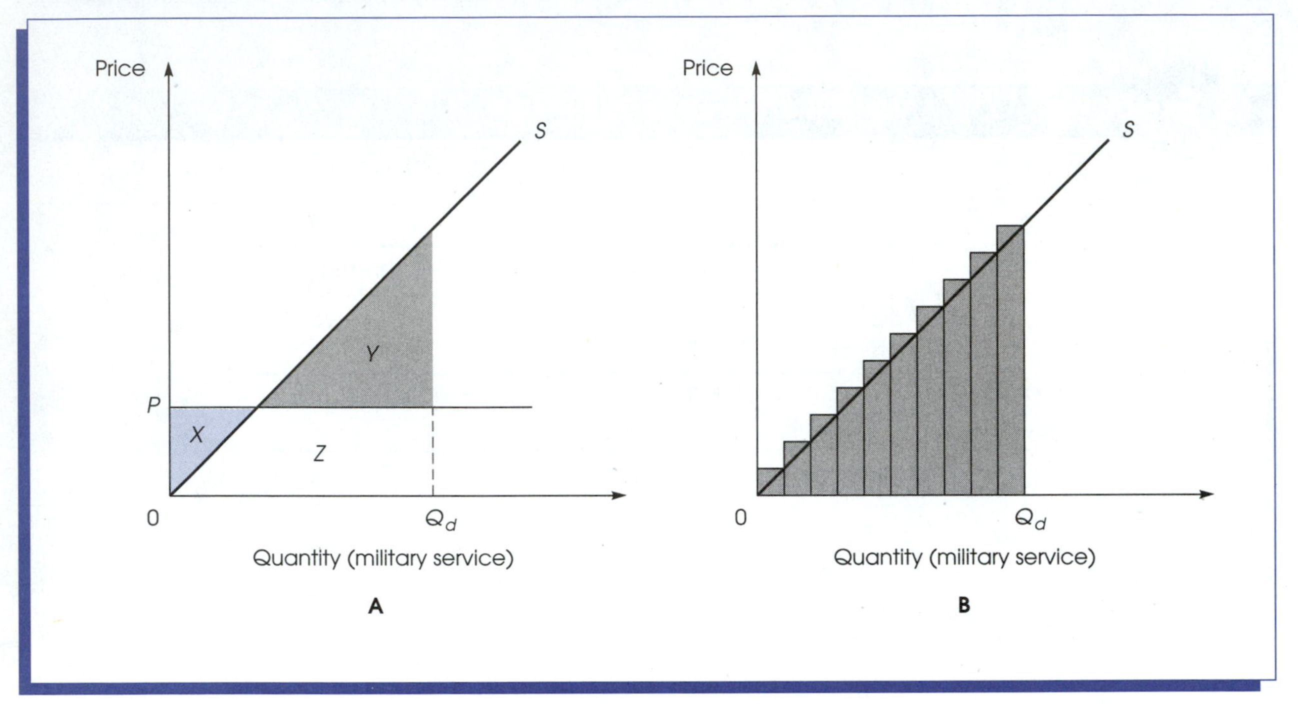

If the army forcibly hires Q_d soldiers at the price P, then soldiers will earn $P \cdot Q_d = X + Z$ in wages. Their opportunity cost of being in the army is the sum of all the rectangles in panel B, which is the same as area $Y + Z$ in panel A. This leaves a producers' surplus of $(X + Z) - (Y + Z) = X - Y$.

vant part of the graph in Exhibit 9–4. Revenue to producers (that is, the wages paid to soldiers) is given by price times quantity, that is, the rectangle $X + Z$. The sum of the marginal costs to producers is the sum of the rectangles in panel B, which is the same as area $Y + Z$ in panel A. The difference is $(X + Z) - (Y + Z) = X - Y$, which is the same as $F - C - D - E$ in Exhibit 9–4.

EXERCISE 9.5 Verify the deadweight loss in Exhibit 9–4 by calculating social gain directly (that is, using rectangles representing marginal value minus marginal cost, without breaking things down into consumers' and producers' surpluses).

Now consider an alternative policy. Suppose that at the same controlled price P, the armed forces can compel services only from that number of young people who would have enlisted voluntarily at the equilibrium price. In Exhibit 9–4 the number of soldiers is Q_0 and the social gains are computed in the "Limited Draft" column of the table. Notice that the measured deadweight loss becomes *zero*.

EXERCISE 9.6 Verify all of the entries in the "Limited Draft" column of the table. Recompute the deadweight loss by a different method and make sure the answers coincide.

Notice that, compared with the volunteer army, the new "limited" version of the draft transfers the amount $B + C$ from young people to the other members of society.

EXERCISE 9.7 Give an economic interpretation of the area $B + C$ in Exhibit 9–4.

Now we are closing in on the main point: Even though the computed deadweight loss is zero, the limited draft is still inferior to the volunteer army from the point of view of economic efficiency. There are social costs associated with the draft that are not captured in our representation of deadweight loss.

Consider the calculation of producers' surplus, which is illustrated anew in Exhibit 9–6. We begin with the total revenue of soldiers and subtract from it the sum of the shaded rectangles. These rectangles are the costs of joining the army for the Q_0 young people who would volunteer at the equilibrium price. But it is unlikely that these are the same young people who are drafted. Instead of drafting the young people represented by rectangles a, b, and c, the authorities may draft those represented by rectangles d, e, and f. The true producers' surplus is reduced by the area $(d + e + f) - (a + b + c)$. The measured producers' surplus—and consequently the measured deadweight loss—is too optimistic.

In concrete terms, what this means is that the Selective Service Board will draft young people who are potentially brilliant brain surgeons, inventors, and economists—young people with high opportunity costs of entering the service—and will leave undrafted some young people with much lower opportunity costs. The social loss is avoided under a voluntary system, in which precisely those with the lowest costs will volunteer.

What if the authorities choose to draft only the low-cost young people? Here, of course, the problem of knowledge becomes insurmountable. Information about individual opportunity costs, available for free under a voluntary system, is available only at high cost and with great uncertainty in the absence of prices. The Selective Service authorities can pass out questionnaires—but who will freely reveal that his costs are low? They can observe people's behavior—but who can observe the difference between two starving novelists in garrets, one with a brilliant vision that needs only careful nurturing to become great literature, the other barren of ideas, frustrated, and ready to quit?

It is often argued that the draft is better for society than a volunteer army because it is less costly. This argument is wrong.[13] The cost of maintaining an army is the sum of the opportunity costs of its soldiers and is independent of the wages paid to those soldiers. Higher wages mean less wealth for taxpayers and more for soldiers, but no more or less for society, to which taxpayers

[13]Of course, there are many other arguments for and against the draft, but their validity does not concern us here.

Exhibit 9-6 Underestimating Deadweight Loss

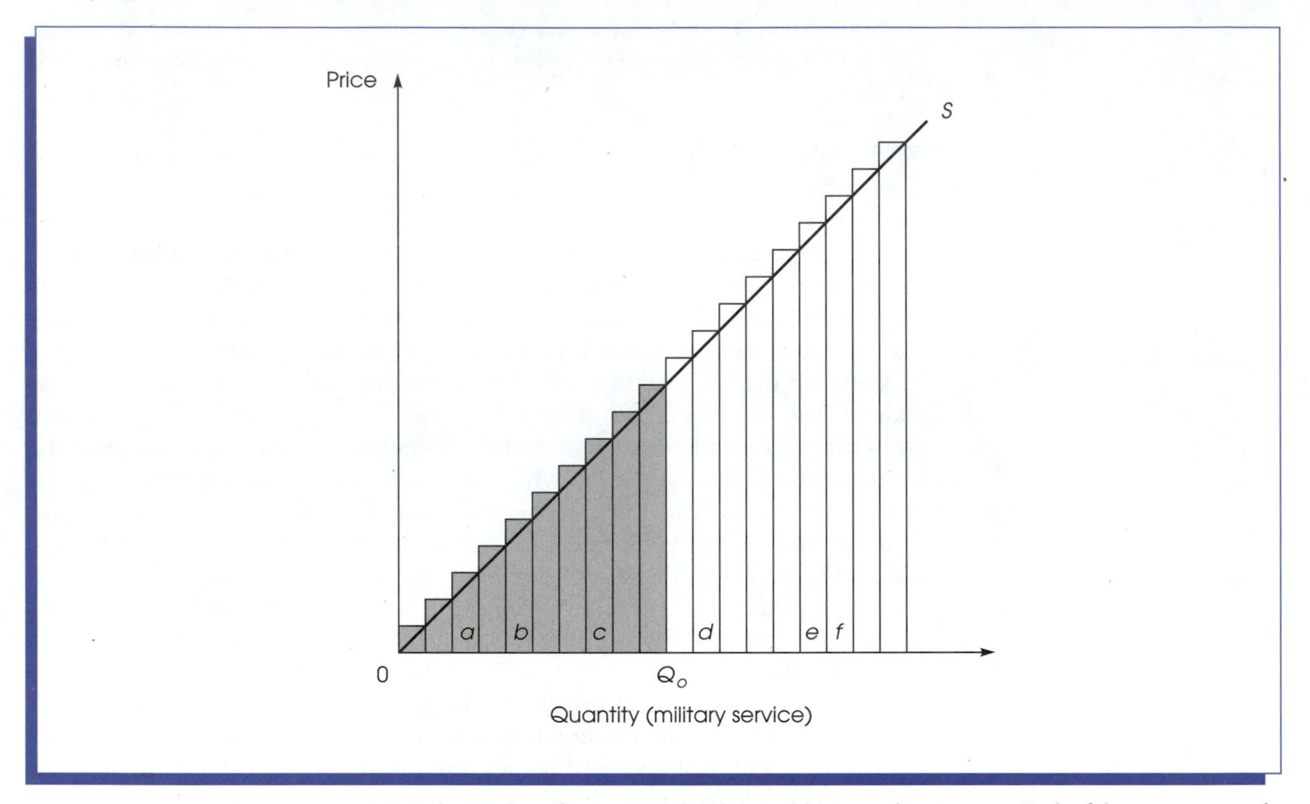

Q_0 is the number of young people who would join a volunteer army. Each of these young people has an opportunity cost of joining that is represented by one of the shaded rectangles. When we compute producers' surplus, we take the total revenue earned by young people and subtract this shaded area.

Under a limited draft, the same number of young people enter the army. However, those who are drafted are not identical to those who would have volunteered. Suppose that the draft board selects the young people represented by rectangles *d, e,* and *f* instead of rectangles *a, b,* and *c*. In that case, social welfare is reduced by the area $(d + e + f) - (a + b + c)$, even though this reduction is ignored in the usual welfare computations. Hence, the measured deadweight loss is overly optimistic.

and soldiers equally belong. There are two ways in which an army can be unnecessarily costly: It can be the wrong size or it can consist of the wrong people. Exhibits 9–4 and 9–6 illustrate these two mistakes.

The Social Role of Rent

Visit the Henry George Institute site on the social function of the rent on land at: http://www.henrygeorge.org/

An issue of great importance in the history of economic thought has been the social function of the rent on land. The nineteenth-century English economist Henry George argued in his book, *Progress and Poverty,* that because the quantity of land is fixed, the payment of rent to landlords serves no economic purpose. Increased demand for land (which, he argued, is an inevitable consequence of population growth) bids up prices, but, unlike in other markets, this increased price calls forth no additional output. Landlords are enriched to no social end.

Rent Payments to a factor of production in excess of the minimum payments necessary to call it into existence. In other words, the producer's surplus earned by the factor.

This analysis, applied to a more general notion of "rent," was a recurrent theme in the writings of Fabian socialism.[14] The **rent** earned by a factor of production is the excess of payments received by that factor over the minimum payments necessary to call it into existence. When Clint Eastwood earns $10 million a picture for starring in movies that he would be willing to star in for $100,000, the difference $9.9 million is rent. In other words, rent is producers' surplus. The lowest annual income that would induce Eastwood to become a movie star is equal to the area under his supply curve out to the quantity of movies he appears in each year. His revenue is a rectangle representing the quantity of movies times the wage per movie. The difference is producers' surplus, or rent.

Exhibit 9–7 shows the markets for land and for Clint Eastwood. We adopt, for the sake of argument, George's assertion that the supply curve for land is vertical.[15] In this case all of the revenue collected by landlords is rent (the shaded area in panel A of Exhibit 9–7). Eastwood's supply curve becomes essentially vertical above a certain price; there is a limit to the number of movies that a person can make in a year. As a result, his revenue (area $A + B$ in panel B) consists almost entirely of rent (the shaded area A). In general:

When a factor is in fixed (or nearly fixed) supply, the revenue it earns will consist entirely (or almost entirely) of rent.

The Fabians argued that there would be no social cost associated with the appropriation of rents by the government. Suppose that landlords were not permitted to collect rent, but were told by the government to allow designated individuals to use their land at a price of zero. Suppose that Eastwood, who now makes two movies per year, were given a government salary equal to area B in panel B of Exhibit 9–7 and ordered to continue making two movies per year. Such confiscation of rents (the Fabians argued) would not affect social welfare.

EXERCISE 9.8 Compute consumers' and producers' surpluses in the markets for land and for Clint Eastwood's services, both before and after the confiscation of rents. Verify that there is no deadweight loss.

The fly in the Fabian ointment is that land is not equally valuable in all uses, and Clint Eastwood is not equally valuable in all movies. Exhibit 9–8 shows the sort of error that can arise in the allocation of land. When landlords earn rents, they let their land to the people who will pay the most for it: those represented

[14] The Fabian Society was a major contributor to British political discourse in the early part of this century. Its most prominent spokesmen were the economists Sidney Webb and George Bernard Shaw.

[15] In fact, this is probably false in any reasonable sense. The relevant market for a given purpose is not land, but "agricultural land" or "land suitable for building," and the like. Such things *can* be created: Irrigation converted the Negev Desert to productive farmland, for example.

by the shaded rectangles. If land is not allocated to precisely those people, there is a diminution in social welfare. If land is not allocated by price, there is no way to identify those people.

Similarly, it matters not only that Clint Eastwood makes two movies per year; it matters *which* movies he makes. Those movie producers who will pay him the highest salary are those who value his talents most highly; that is, those who think that his presence will most enhance people's desire to see their movies. If he works on projects where his talents contribute less, efficiency is lost. Notice that even if Clint is given the freedom to choose his acting assignments, and even in the event that he is entirely altruistic and wants to work only where he is most valuable, he is unlikely to *know* where he is most valuable if the studios cannot bid for his services.

The Fabian literature contains much interesting economic argument, some

Exhibit 9-7 The Rent on Land and the Rent on Clint Eastwood

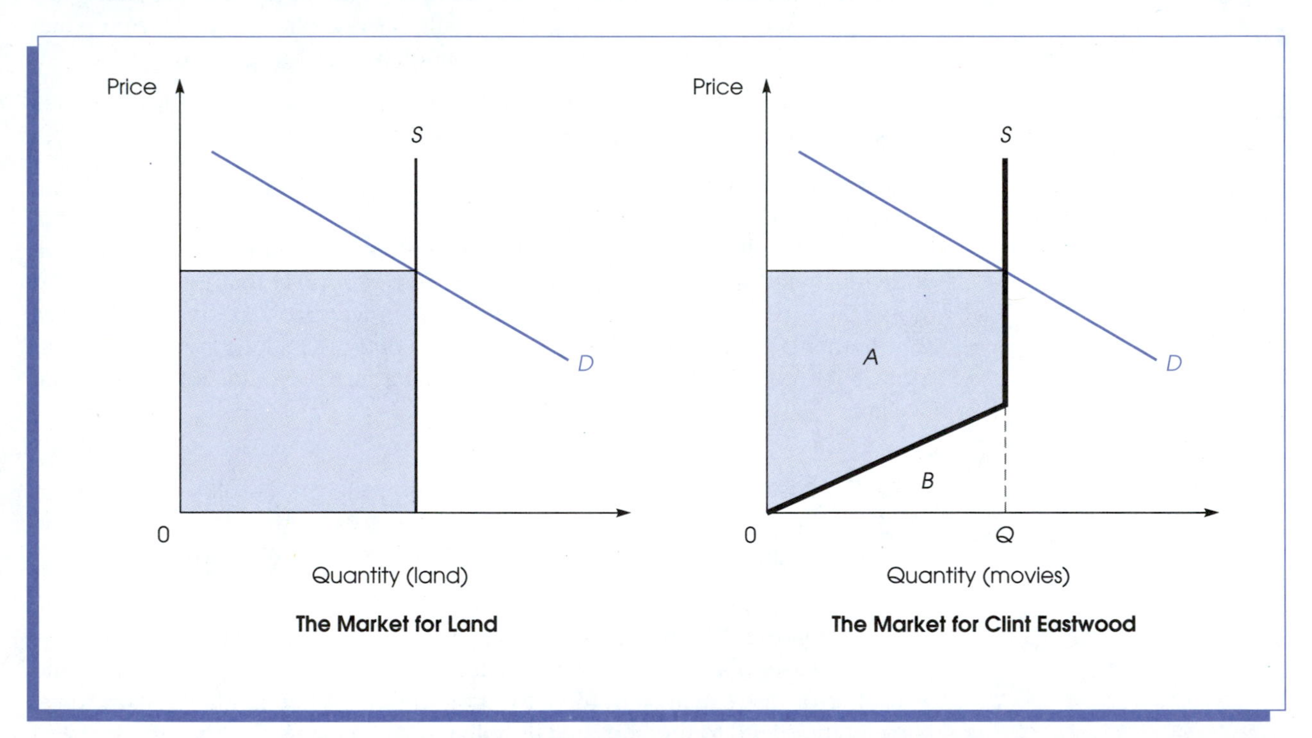

If the supply curve for land is vertical, then all of the revenue earned by landowners is producers' surplus, or rent (the shaded area in panel A). If the supply curve for Clint Eastwood's services becomes vertical at a quantity where the demand price is still very high, then almost all of his income is rent (the shaded area A in panel B). Rent can be interpreted as the amount by which a factor's income exceeds what is necessary to call it into existence. Because the land would exist even if its owners earned no income, all of their income is rent. Because Clint earns $A + B$ for making Q movies, but would be willing to make Q movies if he were paid B to do so, his rent is A.

Exhibit 9-8 The Social Role of Rent

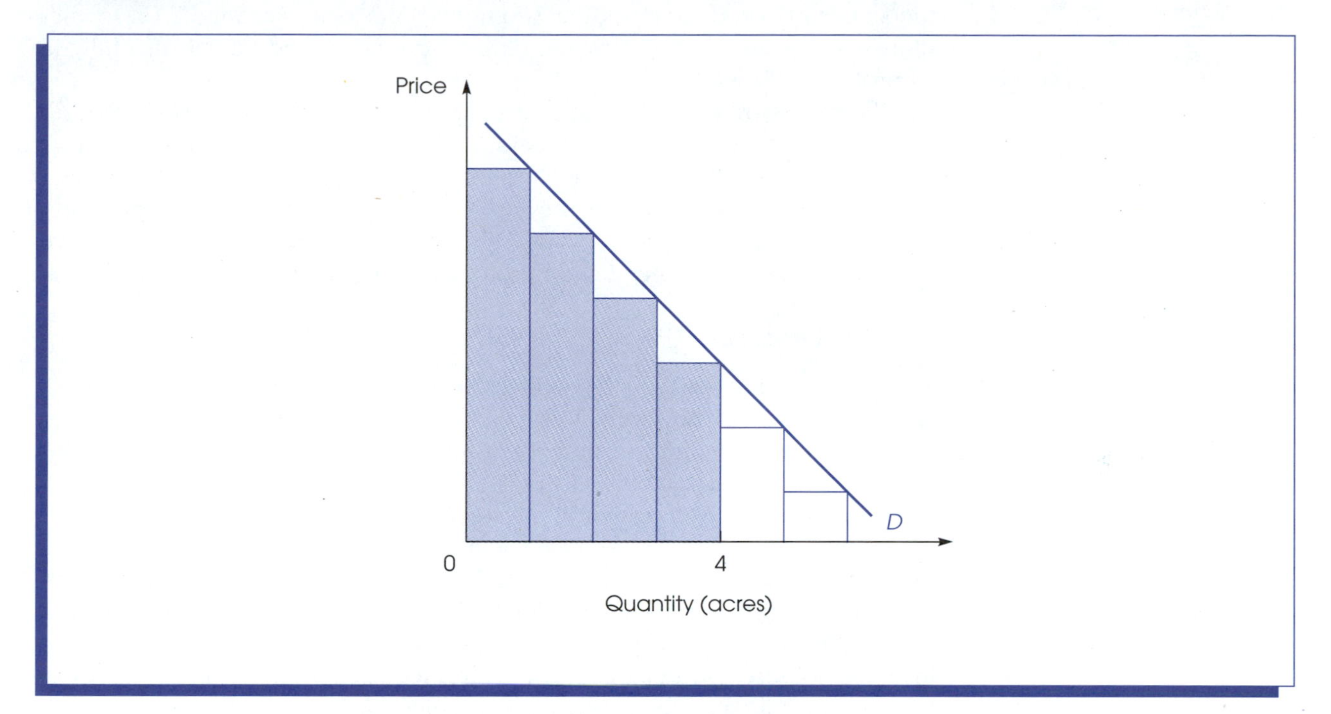

With the supply of land fixed at 4 acres, landlords let those acres to those who value them the most. The total value of the land to its users is the sum of the 4 shaded rectangles. If all rent were confiscated, the 4 acres of land would still exist, which led some thinkers to believe that no social harm would be done. But in fact the confiscation of rents leaves landlords with no incentive to seek out the users represented by the 4 shaded rectangles. Land will be used for less valuable projects, represented by the unshaded rectangles, and social welfare will be diminished.

of it correct, and the tracts by Shaw are both readable and highly entertaining. His *Intelligent Woman's Guide to Socialism and Capitalism* is a rare phenomenon: economic writing by a master of English prose. It is a fertile source of propositions on which you can test out the analytic skills you have been developing in this course. It's also fun to read.

9.2 Financial Markets

Hayek's 1945 article was prescient. Since that time the vision of prices as carriers of information has become ubiquitous in economics. This is especially true in the study of markets for financial securities, such as stock exchanges. Financial markets are extraordinarily efficient processors and disseminators of information. Their informational role affects our understanding of issues ranging from the social allocation of resources to individual investment strategy.

Efficient Markets for Financial Securities

Efficient market A market in which prices fully reflect all available information.

An **efficient market** is one in which prices fully reflect all available information. Here we shall be interested in the markets for financial securities, such as the shares of corporate stock that are traded on stock exchanges. The owner of a share of stock owns a fraction of the corporation and participates fully in its profits and losses.

Efficient securities markets serve an important social function, since they allow firms to make appropriate decisions regarding the allocation of resources (how much to produce, how much to invest in future growth, and so on) and assure investors that the prices they are paying for assets are meaningful indications of those assets' actual value. However, many noneconomists believe that asset markets in general and the stock market in particular are inefficient.

Technical Analysis

The most extreme believers in inefficient markets are the so-called *chartists*, or *technical analysts*. They argue that a careful study of the past prices of a given stock conveys useful information about future prices.

It is easy to see why this analysis cannot be correct if markets are efficient. Suppose that the past behavior of the stock of XYZ Corporation exhibits a pattern that indicates a probable price rise in the near future. That probable price rise is an important feature of XYZ stock, making it more valuable to hold. In an efficient market that higher value will already be reflected in the *current* price. (It is also easy to see the mechanism by which this would occur: Smart investors, observing the pattern, expect a price rise tomorrow and rush out to buy the stock today. This bids up *today's* price.) If the market is perfectly efficient, the chartist cannot expect to profit, because any stock that can be identified as a "good buy" will be expensive—and therefore *not* such a good buy!

There is overwhelming evidence against the chartists.[16] Hundreds of careful statistical studies indicate that knowledge of past price changes contributes nothing to the prediction of future price changes. All of the information contained in the past history of the stock is already embedded in a single number—the current price.

Analysis of Market Conditions

Some dissenters from the efficient-markets hypothesis are less extreme. While admitting the unprofitability of technical analysis, they claim that a more general analysis of market conditions (still making use only of publicly available information) can provide important clues to the savvy investor. This proposition is harder to test than the claims of the chartists, and the empirical evidence is correspondingly less definitive. Nevertheless, the overwhelming majority of researchers in the field, basing their conclusions on decades of empirical work, reject this claim as well. The theoretical basis for this rejection is the same as that for rejecting chartism: Any publicly available information indicating that a

[16]See E. Fama, "Efficient Capital Markets: A Review of Theory and Empirical Work," *Journal of Finance* 25 (May 1970):383–417, for an overview.

stock will soon go up (or down) will cause an immediate shift in demand and an immediate price adjustment, leaving no opportunity for profit.

There is still room for argument over the meaning of the word *immediate*. How quickly do prices adjust to new information? If the adjustment process takes sufficiently long, an observant investor may have time to cash in.

To put the question another way: Prices reflect all available information in the long run, but how long is the long run? Recent evidence supports the hypothesis that the long run is shorter than 30 seconds—that is, all information entering the marketplace is fully incorporated into prices within 30 seconds of its arrival.[17] Hardly comforting news to the investor who analyzes patterns at leisure over a cup of coffee and the daily business page.

Asset Markets and the Royal Head-Flipper

Does this mean that no technical analyst will ever succeed in the stock market? Of course not; some will do well, for the same reasons that some people do well at the roulette wheel. If there are enough such analysts (and there are), a few will even win consistently, by the simple laws of probability. All of these will attribute their success to their singular talents. To them we dedicate a bit of economic folklore: The Fable of the Royal Head-Flipper.

In a faraway land with 64 million inhabitants, the king wished to appoint a royal head-flipper. Calling all of his subjects before him, he gave each one a coin and ordered all to flip. Thirty-two million came up heads and 32 million came up tails. Those who flipped tails were obviously no good at flipping heads and were eliminated from the competition. The remaining 32 million flipped again. When 16 million failed, they too were sent home. On the 25th trial, only 2 remained. They each flipped, and one prevailed. He was appointed the royal head-flipper by the king, who congratulated him with a toast: "Here's to the royal head-flipper, whose prowess has enabled him to flip heads 26 times in a row. According to the royal statistician, the odds against such a feat occurring by chance are a staggering 64 million to 1!"

Black Monday: The Crash of 1987

The events of October 19, 1987, present a major challenge to the economist's faith in efficient markets. On that day the Dow Jones Industrial Average, which measures the value of major stocks that are traded on the New York Stock Exchange, fell by 23%. This followed a week of significant declines; most major indexes of stock values fell by more than 30% in the period from October 14 to October 19. The theory of efficient markets suggests that this astonishing fall in prices must have been a response to some new information about the expected future profitability of almost all publicly traded firms. What could that information have been?

One possible culprit is a bill designed to discourage corporate takeovers by eliminating tax benefits, which was gathering steam in the House of Repre-

---

[17]See L. J. Feinstone, "Minute by Minute: Efficiency, Normality and Randomness in Intra-Daily Asset Prices," *Journal of Applied Econometrics* 2 (1987):193–214.

sentatives. In the week preceding the crash, the success of this legislation seemed increasingly likely. Stock in corporations that were probable takeover targets led the decline, and in fact continued to decline after the crash when the rest of the market was beginning to recover. Other recent news included an unexpectedly large U.S. trade deficit (which measures the excess of current imports over current exports) and a rise in interest rates.

Could this kind of information have led rational investors to revise their estimates of future corporate profits by as much as 30% downward? Nobody is actually sure. One bit of evidence that the crash really was a rational response to new information is that it took five months for the market to recover. Economists are somewhat uncomfortable positing a short burst of irrationality, but become entirely squeamish at the suggestion that irrational behavior could persist for five months.

But the magnitude of the decline cries out for explanation, and a variety of alternatives have been offered. Some, as we have seen, suggest that the fall in prices was an accurate reflection of genuinely new information. The others fall into two broad categories: those that focus on the mechanics of trading and those that attempt to explain how fundamentally rational investors can sometimes move prices in surprising directions.

Business journalists have been nearly unanimous in embracing one of the "mechanical" theories. The villain of this particular theory is *program trading*. Allegedly, large numbers of investors using similar or identical software to guide their decisions were all instructed by their computers to sell at the same moment. A major problem for this theory, and for any other theory that depends on the detailed institutional structure of the New York Stock Exchange, is that the crash was worldwide, and in fact began in Europe. The decline was actually sharper in those countries where computerized trading is a rarity than in those countries where it is common. The most straightforward reading of the evidence suggests that computerized trading actually *mitigated* the severity of the crash.[18]

Other theories try to show how rational investment strategies can sometimes cause prices to change even in the absence of new information. Expectations can be self-fulfilling. If everyone expects prices to rise, then everyone wants to buy and prices do rise; the process then repeats and compounds itself. The resulting **speculative bubble** must eventually burst, resulting in a sudden and sharp decline in prices.[19]

Speculative bubble A situation in which expectations of rising prices cause prices to rise.

Professor Sanford Grossman of the University of Pennsylvania has written extensively on the informational role of prices in financial markets. Recently a number of his writings have been collected in a book, and his introduction to that book specifically addresses the problem of October 1987.[20] He calls at-

---

[18]See *Black Monday and the Future of Financial Markets* (Homewood, IL: Dow Jones-Irwin, 1989), a book compiled by the Mid-America Institute for Public Policy Research and containing analyses by several prominent economists. See especially the chapter by Richard Roll.

[19]In *Black Monday and the Future of Financial Markets*, Lester Telser argues the case that the crash was a burst of a speculative bubble.

[20]S. Grossman, *The Informational Role of Prices* (MIT Press, 1989).

tention to two related new ideas. First, there might be large numbers of investors who are determined not to let their wealth fall below some predetermined level. When a downturn in the market brings them close to that level, they become extremely sensitive to negative fluctuations. Even a slight downward movement in prices can cause many such investors to try to sell simultaneously.

Grossman's second idea is that some traders are better informed than others about real financial conditions. When prices begin to fall, poorly informed traders (and even well-informed traders who aren't sure that they are well informed) cannot be certain whether to attribute the downturn to some genuine bad news that other traders have discovered. The possibility that bad news is in the process of spreading leads them (rationally) to want to sell immediately. This has the effect of exacerbating any downturn. The same process in reverse increases the magnitudes of upturns as well. The net effect is to substantially increase the volatility of stock prices, particularly in the short run. Grossman argues that such a theory is necessary, since observed short-run price volatility appears to be greater than can be accounted for by traditional theory.

The two phenomena that Grossman describes can be mutually reinforcing. A small downturn causes a group of investors to protect their assets by selling stocks. A second group of investors observes this activity and worries that the sellers know something bad, leading them to sell also. This, in turn, causes the first group to sell more, and so forth.

The events of 1987 have generated a lot of discussion about what can be done to prevent future crashes. Much of this discussion fails to address a critical question: Was the crash a good thing or a bad thing? If the fall in stock prices was a response to genuine bad news about future corporate productivity, then it was almost surely a good thing. The signal that it sent to investors was: "Stop diverting so many resources to enterprises that are about to become less productive." The market didn't cause the bad news; it only publicized it while there was still time to limit the damage. If this interpretation is correct, then taking steps to prevent future crashes is like shooting the messenger who comes to alert you that your troops need reinforcements.

9.3 Topics in the Economics of Information

> Everybody bet lots of money on the eggplant, thinking that if a vegetable challenges a live animal with four legs to a race, then it must be that the vegetable knows something.
>
> —D. Pinkwater, *Borgel*

Although the price system routinely accomplishes miracles in the dissemination of information, it also sometimes fails to deliver all that one could hope for. When information is distributed asymmetrically, so that some types of knowledge are more readily available to one group than to another, market outcomes can fail to be Pareto-optimal. Other times, Pareto-optimal outcomes are achieved, but in unexpected ways. In this section, we present a potpourri of examples in which asymmetric information can produce surprising outcomes.

Signaling: Should Colleges Be Outlawed?

Going to college will probably increase your income. Perhaps you will also pick up some useful skills along the way. But even if colleges taught nothing of practical value, and even if employers were fully aware of this deficiency, a college education could still be a path to higher wages.

To see why, let us make the cynical assumption that everything you are taught in school is completely useless. However, the ability to graduate requires a certain level of intelligence and ambition. If employers have no other way to distinguish one high school graduate from another, they will prefer to hire the ones who have gone on to success in college. And that alone can make college a good investment for a bright student.

In this case, going to college is an example of what economists call a *signal.* This means that on the one hand, it produces nothing of any value (such as actual skills or knowledge), but on the other hand its owner reaps rewards because of the information that it telegraphs to others (in this case, it signals employers about your basic abilities).

Signals are socially costly. In our example, the resources spent on college don't increase anyone's productivity and hence constitute pure social waste. Whenever there is social waste, there is room for an improvement that could benefit everybody. Suppose that we closed all the colleges and simply asked each high school graduate whether he *would* have gone to college given the opportunity; suppose also that everybody answered honestly. Employers would have exactly the same information for sorting job candidates that they have today, and bright students would save four years and many thousands of dollars. They could, of course, share part of this windfall with those of their high school friends who never were college material, as a reward for their honesty, making *every* high school graduate better off.

Unfortunately, that social improvement is impossible to achieve as long as colleges are allowed to exist. If we relied strictly on voluntary announcements, then each dull student would have an incentive to misrepresent himself as bright. Employers would have no way to distinguish bright students from dull ones, and the genuinely bright students would return to college in order to signal their truthfulness.

However, we could still increase social welfare by outlawing colleges completely. Employers would no longer be able to distinguish bright students from dull ones, and would treat each student equally, paying them more than if they were known to be bright and less than if they were known to be dull; the gains to one group would balance the losses to the other. And the bright students' losses might be more than compensated by their savings in tuition costs. Thus, both groups of students can gain. Finally employers end up with the same pool of employees as before and pay them the same salary on average. Therefore, employers neither lose nor gain, and social welfare is unambiguously increased.

This discussion implicitly assumes that although bright students are more productive than dull ones, they both perform essentially the same tasks. In fact, employers might prefer to reserve certain tasks for the best and brightest and other tasks for the rest of us. If the signal is abolished, this becomes impossible, so productivity falls and the abolition imposes real social costs. Those costs might or might not outweigh the benefit of removing the costly signal.

So far we have assumed that bright students can survive college and dull students can't. But the same conclusions hold even with a less radical assumption. Suppose instead that any student can survive college, but it is in some way less costly for bright students to survive than for dull ones. For example, bright students need to spend less time studying than dull students, or they have less need to hire tutors for exams and ghostwriters for term papers, or they pay less extra tuition making up courses that they have failed. Then even if we continue to assume that colleges teach nothing of value, the bright students might still choose to go to college.

To see why, suppose that employers are willing to pay more to bright students than to dull ones—enough so that it is worth $10,000 to convince an employer that you are bright. Suppose that it costs a bright student $7,000 to get through college and a dull student $15,000. Then bright students will find the college signal worthwhile, dull students will find that it is not worthwhile, only bright students will go to college, and employers will continue to reward college graduates because the college graduates really *will* be smarter than their non-college-trained contemporaries.

Once again, the college education is pure social waste. If dull students were willing to voluntarily identify themselves, then bright students would still get the better jobs and save themselves $7000 each. This $7000 could be shared to make *everybody* better off. Once again, though, this agreement cannot be maintained because dull students would misrepresent themselves. Only an absolute ban on colleges could have a chance of yielding an actual improvement.

example

Dressing for Success

Signaling behavior is a widespread social phenomenon. "Dressing for success" is a signal. Surely the clothes you wear do not make you a more productive manager, but your ability to choose clothes that are both tasteful and fashionable without being too ordinary is a meaningful signal of your ability to interpret social norms and to be creative within acceptable limits. These are skills that are extremely valuable in business, and it can be rational to invest in displaying them just as it can be rational to invest in an unproductive education that displays your intellect.

Here again it is genuinely rational for the signaler to invest in sending the signal and for the observer to be guided by it. Nevertheless, as with college, everyone could benefit if the signal were abolished. We might all be better off if wearing clothes to job interviews were against the law.

example

Signaling in the Animal Kingdom

The male birds of many species—peacocks and birds of paradise most prominently—have tails that appear to be too long for their own good. Besides requiring nutrients that could be put to other productive uses, the tails are cumbersome and actually impede locomotion. They make the birds more vulnerable to predators.

How could such a characteristic survive the pressures of natural selection? A simple theory is that the tails are part of a signaling equilibrium. Suppose that the healthiest males can bear the burdens of a long tail more cheaply than weaker males can. Suppose also that females have a natural preference for healthy males. (Such a preference would be naturally selected for, because healthy males tend to produce healthy offspring, so a female with this preference has a greater chance of eventually becoming a grandmother.) Then it can be to the reproductive advantage of every male to signal his health with a long tail, even if the tail itself is a burden in everyday life. Females choose the males with the longest tails, and tails get longer over time until the marginal cost of additional growth outweighs the marginal advantage in terms of attracting females.

Such a signaling equilibrium is suboptimal. If all the males agreed to cut their tails in half, the females would still be able to identify the longest tails and would make exactly the same choices as they do now. No valuable information would be lost, and the costs of excessive tail growth would be partly eliminated. Unfortunately for the birds, such an agreement must fall apart. Each individual male would try to cheat by letting his tail grow, and the original signaling equilibrium would soon be restored.

example

The Supply of Jokes

Why do people tell jokes? Frequently it is to entertain their friends. But there are other reasons.

According to *The Wall Street Journal* of January 31, 1997,

> "Jokes still play an important role in the discourse of financial markets, where the sober business of making money is lubricated by fast, topical jokes. "If you're going to be perceived as a great salesman, proving you have information first is really important," says a trader at a small securities firm. "If someone calls you up and starts a joke, and you can finish it, you have the edge. It proves you're plugged in."

If all salesmen could be induced to honestly reveal how "plugged in" they are, they wouldn't have to spend time learning jokes. That would be a welfare improvement. But because there is no mechanism to induce those honest revelations, jokes survive as a signal of general knowledgeability.

Adverse Selection and the Market for Lemons

The seller of a used car typically knows more about its quality than potential buyers do. Professor George Akerlof has demonstrated that under such circumstances, it can be impossible for high quality cars ever to be sold.[21]

Suppose that there are two equally common types of used cars: "good" cars and "lemons." Potential sellers value the good cars at $100 and potential buyers value them at $120. Potential sellers value the lemons at $50 and potential buyers value them at $60. If there were perfect information, there would be separate markets for the two kinds of cars, and all of them would sell.

QA EXERCISE 9.9 What is the possible range of prices at which a good car could sell? What about a lemon?

Suppose for the moment that neither buyers nor sellers can distinguish between a good car and a lemon. Each seller figures that if his car is good, it's worth $100 to him and if not, it's worth $50; taking account of both possibilities, he values the car at $75. Each buyer does a similar calculation, figuring that the car is equally likely to be worth either $120 or $60 and valuing it at $90. All of the cars sell at some price between $75 and $90.

But now suppose instead that the sellers actually know the quality of the cars. We shall see that this simple assumption has drastic consequences.

What can the price of a used car be? Suppose first that it is over $100. At that price, all sellers put their cars up for sale. Buyers, who cannot tell one car from another, value a used car at only $90 and will not pay the asking price. So the quantity supplied (namely, all the cars) exceeds the quantity demanded (namely, zero). There can be no equilibrium price above $100.

Now suppose that the price is above $60 but below $100. In this range, sellers are willing to part with their lemons (which they value at $50), but not their good cars (which they value at $100). Only lemons come on the market. Buyers, realizing this, are willing to pay only $60 (the value that they place on a lemon). Once again the quantity demanded is zero, so we still haven't found an equilibrium.

Suppose a price below $50. At this price, buyers want to buy, but no sellers want to sell. That leaves only one possibility: The market price must be above $50 but below $60. At such a price, sellers supply only lemons and buyers are willing to buy them. But no good car ever changes hands.

If all sellers were truthful about the quality of their cars, social welfare could be improved, since the good cars would find their way into the hands of the buyers, who value them more than the sellers do. Unfortunately, such truthfulness cannot be maintained, because if there is any market at all for good cars, each lemon owner will want to deceptively sell his car in that market to command a higher price.

---

[21] G. Akerlof, "The Market for Lemons: Qualitative Uncertainty and the Market Mechanism," *Quarterly Journal of Economics* 84 (1970):484–500.

Adverse Selection and Insurance Markets

In the lemons market, one group of traders (in this case the sellers) knows more than the other group (the buyers), and each uses his extra information to decide whether to participate in the market. In equilibrium, the "high quality" participants are driven out altogether.

Adverse selection The problem that arises when people know more about their own risk characteristics than others do.

This **adverse selection** problem arises in a variety of contexts, and is particularly acute in the market for insurance. Suppose that everyone has a 1 in 10 chance of becoming sick next year. In that case, insurance companies will sell you $10 worth of insurance (to be paid if you do become sick) for a premium of $1.[22]

Now suppose instead that there are two classes of people: "Healthies," whose chance of getting sick is 1 in 10, and "Sicklies," whose chance of getting sick is 9 in 10. If the insurance company can tell who is who, it charges the Healthies $1 for $10 worth of insurance, and it charges the Sicklies $9 for $10 worth of insurance.

But now suppose also that the insurance company cannot distinguish one group from the other. What does it do? You might think that it offers insurance at some compromise price, such as $5 for $10 worth of insurance. The reason this doesn't work is that at this price the Sicklies all buy large policies, but the Healthies, who think it is unlikely that they'll get sick, buy very little. The Healthies are essentially driven out of the market, just as the sellers of good used cars are driven out of their market. Since most of its customers are now Sicklies, the insurance company loses money selling at a price of $5. It increases the price, and drives away even more of the few Healthies who are still insured. This forces it to increase its price still further. Eventually, only the Sicklies are insured.[23]

But the insurance company can adopt an alternative strategy. It offers two different policies: One provides $10 worth of insurance for $1, but with a limit of $10 worth of insurance per customer. The other provides $10 worth of insurance for $9, which can be purchased in any amount.

Given this choice, Sicklies, who want to be heavily insured, might choose the more expensive policy. A typical Sickly could buy $100 worth of insurance for $90. The Healthies, unwilling to pay such high rates to insure against a low-probability event, choose the cheaper policy. The two groups voluntarily separate themselves, and the insurance company breaks even on each group separately.

The only problem with this solution is that Healthies are prohibited from buying as much insurance as they really want. If they were permitted to buy more, Sicklies would claim to be Healthies and take advantage of the lower rates. The problem would be solved if the Sicklies voluntarily identified them-

---

[22]At these rates, the insurance companies just break even, as they must under competition in the long run. If the companies bear some operating costs in addition to paying claims, those costs will be reflected in the rates as well. In this example, we will keep things simple by ignoring such costs.

[23]It is possible to give a careful proof that no equilibrium can be reached until the Healthies are driven out entirely. The argument, which is not difficult, can be found in M. Rothschild and J. Stiglitz, "Equilibrium in Competitive Insurance Markets: An Essay in the Economics of Imperfect Information," *Quarterly Journal of Economics* 90 (1976): 629–650.

selves, so that the company could sell unlimited insurance to each group. The Sicklies would be no worse off—their insurance premium remains the same even after they are identified—but the Healthies would be happier. As in the lemons market, though, the social optimum is not an equilibrium.

Moral Hazard

People who are insured take more risks than people who aren't. Insurance companies, recognizing this, adjust their rates accordingly.

Suppose that there is a 1 in 10 chance that your uninsured house will burn next year. After you buy insurance, you become laxer about checking for frayed electrical wires and take up smoking in bed. Consequently, the chance of a fire rises from 1 in 10 to 1 in 5.

Which probability is reflected in your insurance rate? The answer is the one that is relevant for insured homeowners, namely, 1 in 5. $10 worth of fire insurance will sell for $2, not $1.

If you could promise to buy insurance and still remain as careful as ever, the company would be able to reduce your premium to $1. Unfortunately, because it can't watch you every minute of the day, the company has no way to know whether you are keeping your promise. This leaves you with no incentive to keep it, which the insurance company realizes. The bottom line is that your standard of care goes down and your insurance premium goes up.

Moral hazard The incentive for an individual to take more risks when insured.

The problem here is called a **moral hazard.** Moral hazards arise when an insured driver is more reckless than an uninsured one, when a homeowner fails to install a security system because he is insured against break-ins, and when a person with health insurance takes more risks on the ski slopes than he otherwise would. If you live in a rented apartment, your rent is probably higher because of moral hazard: Your landlord cannot be certain that you won't scratch the floors or write on the walls and wants to be compensated for his risk.

If the moral hazard were eliminated, insurance rates would fall and everyone could benefit. And in fact, there are some remedies available. Insurance companies can refuse to insure you unless you agree to modify your behavior.

Some homeowner's policies are offered only to those with burglar alarms, and some health insurance is offered only to nonsmokers. However, these remedies are effective only insofar as the company can observe its customers' behavior.

There is another class of remedies in which the insurance company, even though it cannot require good behavior, creates incentives to elicit it. Your fire insurance company cannot require you to install a fire extinguisher, but it can offer to sell you a fire extinguisher at a subsidized price that you are likely to accept.[24] Your health insurance company can make it easier for you to stay healthy by sending you free newsletters about the advantages of diet and exercise.

[24]This doesn't necessarily work without some further restrictions, since it would enable you to buy insurance, go into the fire extinguisher business, and bankrupt the insurance company by buying all your inventory from them.

There is another kind of moral hazard that arises from the insurance company's inability to verify that you have a valid claim. When you report that your insured diamond ring has been stolen, the company might well wonder whether you are telling the truth. Because the company has to be compensated for such risks, theft insurance rates are higher than they would otherwise be.

In cases where the legitimacy of a claim is completely unverifiable, insurance markets might disappear completely. An unexpected fire and an unexpected urge to visit Hawaii can be equally devastating financially, but you can insure against one and not the other. The ashes of your house are easily observable; the depths of your psyche are not.

Students sometimes find it hard to tell the difference between adverse selection and moral hazard. In the adverse selection problem, one group of people *starts out* at higher risk than the other. In the moral hazard problem, people incur additional risks *as a result* of being insured.

Principal-Agent Problems

When you've hired somebody to fix your roof, it is difficult to be sure how good a job he's doing. You can offer to pay extra for more careful work, but you can never be certain that you're getting what you've paid for.

Principal-agent problem
The inability of the principal to verify the behavior of the agent.

When an employer cannot fully monitor his employees' work efforts, we say that there is a **principal-agent problem.** The word *principal* refers to the employer, the word *agent* refers to the employee, and the word *problem* refers to the fact that an opportunity for social gain is being lost. If the employer could be sure of getting what he pays for, he could offer a higher wage for better work, to the benefit of both employer and employee.

In December 1990, the *New York Times* reported the plight of Harriette Ternipsede, a ticket agent at TWA. The airline uses sophisticated computer methods to monitor her performance, and supervisors are alerted instantly if she so much as stands up to stretch her muscles. Mrs. Ternipsede and other workers are taking legal action in an attempt to prevent TWA from keeping such close tabs on them.

It might seem obvious to you that employees would be better off without their supervisors breathing over their shoulders at every moment. But strict supervision does not just allow the employer to observe low productivity; it allows him to observe high productivity too. This in turn enables him to reward high productivity so as to elicit more of it. On the other hand, if monitoring is impossible, employees (except for those with extraordinary motivation) put forth the minimum effort and employers pay accordingly.

Short of perfect monitoring, the market provides a variety of partial solutions to the principal-agent problem. The economists Paul Yakoboski and Kenneth McLaughlin have stressed the importance of productive fringe benefits.[25] Sup-

[25]P. Yakoboski, "Productive Fringe Benefits: Theory and Evidence," Ph.D. Dissertation, University of Rochester, 1990; also P. Yakoboski and K. McLaughin, "The Economics of Productive Fringe Benefits," 1990.

pose you hold a job in which having a $1,000 home computer would increase your productivity by $2,000. In a world of perfect monitoring, you buy the computer and your wages increase by more than enough to compensate you. In a world with no monitoring, your employer is unaware of the productivity increase and does not reward you, so you never buy the computer. In the real world we live in, your employer might buy you a computer as part of your fringe benefit package, offering himself some assurance that it will be put to good use.

Another way to improve employees' performance is to offer them a share of the firm's profits. Unfortunately, the resulting incentives are still far from optimal. An employee who is entitled to 1% of the profits must increase his output by $100 to reap a $1 reward. If the necessary effort costs him $5, he won't undertake it, and an opportunity to increase social welfare by $95 ($100 in extra profits minus $5 in extra costs) is sacrificed.

There is, however, an extreme version of profit sharing, which *does* work perfectly, at least in principle. It requires paying each employee 100% of the firm's profits. Under such a plan, the worker who saves the firm $100 earns $100 for himself. If he can accomplish this at a personal cost of less than $100, he will be entirely self-motivated to do so. There is never any need for the employer to provide additional incentives.

The problem that has probably occurred to you is that the owners of a firm with 8 employees might be reluctant to pay out 800% of their profits in wages. The solution is that each worker pays, up front, a large flat fee in exchange for his job, so that his net compensation is reasonable. Once he starts working, the flat fee becomes a sunk cost and does not affect his incentive to perform.

Why, then, does this scheme strike us as outrageous? Probably because profits depend on a lot of random events, not just on worker performance. An unexpected change in market conditions can cause a large corporation's profits to fluctuate by tens of millions of dollars. It would be a rare worker who was either able or willing to accept that kind of fluctuation in his yearly income. In the absence of large random fluctuations, the 100% profit-sharing plan might work.

Efficiency Wages

For more on efficiency wages see: http://www.uwm.edu/People/drago/effic.asc

Another solution to the principal-agent problem is to punish severely those employees who get caught shirking. Although most shirkers never get caught, the possibility of a sufficiently severe punishment still serves as a strong incentive to perform. Workers respond to the incentive, become more productive, and earn higher salaries.

An impediment to this solution is that there are limits to the employer's ability to punish. Usually the most severe punishment available is termination. If the worker can just move on to an identical job at another firm, this is no punishment at all.

Efficiency wage A wage higher than market equilibrium, which employers pay in order to make workers want to keep their jobs.

To overcome this impediment, the employer might offer an **efficiency wage**; that is, a wage higher than the market equilibrium. This makes the job a particularly desirable one that workers will be reluctant to risk losing.

Now you might think that if *every* employer offers an efficiency wage, then losing your job and having to move on is still no punishment. But this is not correct. The reason is that when employers offer higher wages, they demand less labor. Thus, efficiency wages lead to unemployment. The wage is set higher than the market equilibrium and the quantity of labor demanded is less than the quantity supplied. This in turn means that the worker who loses his job risks not finding another one.

Efficiency wages lead to higher productivity by employed workers who are scared of losing their jobs, but also to unemployment of other potentially productive workers. Many economists believe that efficiency wages should play a significant role in macroeconomic models of unemployment.

Executive Compensation

Learn about performance-based executive compensation at: http://www.pepsico.com/web_pages/resource/financial_info.html

The principal-agent problem is a major factor in the relationship between corporate shareholders and corporate executives. Shareholders want executives to pursue aggressive, creative, and intelligent strategies to maximize corporate profits. Because it is impossible to monitor all of the executives' behavior, it is hard for shareholders to reward good performances and punish bad ones. If General Motors is given the opportunity to build a new electric car that would revolutionize the industry, and if the chief executive officer (CEO) passes up the opportunity out of foolishness or sloth, shareholders might never be aware of his mistake. If, on the other hand, he builds the car and it fails in the marketplace, stockholders are left uncertain whether an intelligent risk happened to turn out badly or whether further marketing research would have revealed the paucity of demand before it was too late. When the CEO spends $10 million to upgrade the executive air fleet, stockholders can never be certain whether the decision was dictated by the best interests of the firm or the personal comfort of the chairman.

As a result, we expect to see executive compensation schemes that reward executives for high performance and punish them for the opposite. The most obvious scheme is to create a close link between the firm's profits and the CEO's salary. This can be accomplished by requiring the CEO to hold a large quantity of the corporation's stock or by paying him an annual bonus that depends on the firm's performance.

A recent study by Professors Michael Jensen and Kevin Murphy reveals that these sorts of incentive pay are substantially less common than one might expect.[26] Typically, CEO wealth changes by just $3.25 for each $1,000 change in shareholder wealth. Of this, $2.50 is due to stock ownership (the median CEO holds just .025% of his firm's common stock) and another 75¢ comes from raises, stock options, and other sources. Moreover, this $3.25 figure has been steadily declining over the last 50 years. Jensen and Murphy argue that CEOs are left with woefully little incentive to guard the shareholders' interests. Consider the CEO who is contemplating a completely wasteful $10 million expen-

---

[26]M. Jensen and K. Murphy, "Performance Pay and Top-Management Incentives," *Journal of Political Economy* 98 (1990): 225–264. See also M. Jensen and K. Murphy, "CEO Incentives—It's Not How Much You Pay, but How," *Harvard Business Review,* May–June 1990, pp. 138–153.

diture on the corporate air fleet. If he holds the typical .025% of corporate stock, then only $25,000 of the $10 million comes out of his own pocket. Jensen and Murphy characterize this as "not much of a disincentive for someone who earns on average $20,000 a week." If, on the other hand, the CEO owns 45% of the stock (like Warren Buffett of the Berkshire Hathaway conglomerate), then the decision costs him personally $4.5 million, which is a much better incentive to avoid waste.

Why do shareholders tolerate a salary structure that motivates executives so poorly? Jensen and Murphy hypothesize that political considerations prevent corporations from paying very high salaries (in real terms, executive salaries are lower now than in the 1930s) and that this makes it difficult to adequately reward excellent performances. An alternative hypothesis is that CEOs actually contribute surprisingly little to shifts in corporate fortunes and that the variation in their rewards is commensurate with their contributions.

We have focused on the problems of motivating executives to expend effort and to avoid waste. Another source of conflict between executives and shareholders involves their attitudes toward risk. The typical shareholder has only a small percentage of his wealth invested in any single corporation. Consequently, he is prepared to have the corporation take on considerable risk in return for the prospect of considerable gains. Even if the corporation goes bankrupt, the shareholder's lifestyle is unlikely to be greatly affected.[27] The executive, by contrast, can have a large personal stake in the corporation's success. Consequently, CEOs are likely to be far more cautious than stockholders might prefer.

How can stockholders induce executives to take on more risk? One way is to limit their stock ownership. This might provide an alternative explanation for the findings of Jensen and Murphy. By decoupling executive compensation from corporate performance, the stockholders sacrifice part of the incentive for executives to work hard and be frugal, but at the same time they create an incentive for executives to take more chances, which is something that stockholders want.

There are other ways to limit a CEO's downside risk. One is to assure him that he is unlikely to be fired if some of his decisions turn out badly—and in fact, Jensen and Murphy report that as low as 4% of CEOs do lose their jobs because of poor performance. Another is to assure him that even if things turn out so badly that he does get fired, he will still receive a substantial severance payment. Such payments are sometimes called *golden parachutes*. Many people cannot understand why corporations pay tens of millions of dollars to former officials who have been fired for poor performance. An answer is that without the implied assurance of such settlements, the successors to those officials would exercise great caution in their decisions, contrary to the interests of the stockholders.

Shielding executives from risk improves their willingness to take chances but damages their incentives to perform responsibly. Is there an alternative way to elicit more risk taking, without such detrimental side effects? Possibly. In general, people with high incomes are more willing to risk large losses. Es-

[27]We will give a more rigorous treatment of attitudes toward risk in Chapter 17.

sentially, this is because a smaller percentage of their income is at risk.[28] Therefore, a simple solution might be to make certain that corporate executives are wealthy. Stockholders can accomplish this easily by paying high salaries. This could partially explain why CEO salaries are as high as they are. When the president of General Motors must decide whether to introduce a new model line, stockholders do not want him unduly influenced by concern about making his next month's mortgage payment.

A Theory of Unemployment

For many decades prior to the 1970s, economists observed a correlation between the rate of inflation and the level of employment. When inflation (the rate of increase in absolute prices) was higher than usual, employment tended to be high also. In periods of low inflation, employment was low. More recently, this relationship has broken down. Many explanations have been offered for these phenomena, although there is no consensus among economists as to which come closest to the truth. Here we will present one possible explanation, of particular interest because it focuses on the informational content of prices. The version we will present is a caricature; a fully articulated model is more appropriate for a course in macroeconomics. In its general outlines, however, the theory we will present has been a highly influential one and has occupied a central role in macroeconomic thinking for the last twenty years.[29]

We know from Chapter 2 that only relative prices are relevant to the determination of equilibrium. If all prices (including wages) were to double tomorrow, markets could remain in equilibrium without any quantity adjustments. If it were known that such a doubling occurred every Wednesday, nothing of any real economic significance would be affected.[30]

Now imagine an unemployed worker. He is unemployed not because there are no jobs available to him but because the only available jobs pay wages lower than he is willing to accept. The highest wage offer he has received has been $8,000 a year, but he is not willing to work for less than $10,000.

One night, while our worker is sleeping, all prices and all wages double. He is awakened the next morning by a telephone call from an employer who says, "I am now prepared to offer you an annual salary of $16,000." Of course, $16,000 today will buy only what $8,000 bought yesterday, so the worker, if he is fully informed, will not accept the position.

But what if he is *not* fully informed? What if he went to sleep unaware of the changes that were to take place in the middle of the night, and, having just been awakened by a telephone call, is still unaware of them? In that case he

---

[28]Chapter 18 elaborates on this point also.

[29]The broad outlines of this theory were sketched around 1968 by Milton Friedman and Edmund Phelps (working independently). The first careful development was by Robert E. Lucas, Jr., in "Expectations and the Neutrality of Money," *Journal of Economic Theory* 4 (1974): 103–124.

[30]There is one important exception to this statement. Briefly, a rise in absolute prices reduces the purchasing power of money, so an expected rise in absolute prices makes it more desirable to hold nonmonetary assets, such as real estate. The increase in demand for these "inflation-proof" assets has real effects. For the current discussion, those effects are irrelevant.

will accept the job, convinced that he will be earning far more than his minimum requirement of $10,000.

Now, after a day on the job, our hero is likely to stop at the supermarket to indulge the temptations of his new economic status. When he sees the prices on the items, he will recognize himself to be the victim of a cruel hoax, and begin the mental task of composing a letter of resignation.

This story suggests a reason why an increase in inflation could lead to an increase in employment. It also suggests that the effect is ephemeral. More importantly, it implies that employment is affected only by *unexpected* inflation. When inflation becomes the norm (as it did in the 1970s), workers can no longer be "fooled" by high absolute wages.

Another important implication is that the increase in employment resulting from an unexpected inflation is not socially beneficial—it is a consequence of deceiving people into working more than they would choose to if they were fully aware of their economic environment.

The fundamental role of inflation in this model is to dilute the informational content of prices. A rise in the nominal wage rate for plumbers may indicate either an increase in demand for plumbers' services or a rise in the general price level. If plumbers know the inflation rate, they can make the distinction. An increased demand for plumbers will lead to a higher relative price for their time and call forth more plumbing services—an example of prices transmitting the necessary information to the appropriate parties. If plumbers are uncertain of the inflation rate, they will be uncertain of the real value of their wages and may provide the "wrong" amount of service from a social point of view. If they underestimate the rate of inflation, they will provide too much plumbing; if they overestimate, they will provide too little.

EXERCISE 9.10 Explain in detail why a plumber who has overestimated the rate of inflation will provide less plumbing service as a result.

Macroeconomists have devoted considerable effort to understanding the ways in which uncertainty about inflation introduces "static" into the price signals that people use to make economic decisions. Much research is devoted to the methods that people use to disentangle valuable information from this static, and to the consequences of the necessary imperfections in these methods. An underlying theme is that society is best served by the accurate dissemination of knowledge, and that prices are the most effective known tool for accomplishing this task.

summary

The price of an item reflects the value of that item to some potential user. It also provides an incentive for others to act on that information. If the item is valuable elsewhere, the high price will tell potential users to search for substitutes.

Prices allow complex economies to be coordinated in ways that take account of vast amounts of knowledge. This knowledge includes what Hayek called the "particular circumstances of time and place." Each individual producer and consumer has access to special information that is not available to anyone else, and prices lead him to use this information in deciding how to allocate resources. A social planner without access to all of this information will allocate resources less efficiently.

The conventional measures of social welfare that were introduced in Chapter 8 make the implicit assumption that all goods are produced by the low-cost producers and distributed to the consumers who value them the most. In the absence of a price system, this assumption may be unjustified, in which case the usual measures of social welfare are overly optimistic.

An efficient market is one in which prices fully reveal all available information. Markets for financial assets appear to provide examples.

When the informational content of prices is diluted, as by an inflation that makes it difficult for people to distinguish absolute from relative price changes, resources are allocated less efficiently. This provides one possible explanation of why the level of employment will change in response to an unexpected inflation but not to an expected one.

When information is distributed asymmetrically, surprising and sometimes inefficient outcomes can result. Examples include signaling equilibria, adverse selection, moral hazard, and principal-agent problems.

Review Questions

R1. A social planner equipped with knowledge of all market supply and demand curves would still lack much of the knowledge necessary to duplicate the functioning of the price system. Give some examples of the knowledge that would lack. How is this knowledge taken into account when prices are used to allocate resources?

R2. Explain why a rise in soldiers' wages does not increase the cost of maintaining an army.

R3. What is the social role of rent? If all rents were confiscated, would there be a consequent loss of efficiency? Why or why not?

R4. What is an efficient market?

R5. "If it is well known that IBM will soon release a new and highly desirable product, then it is a good idea to buy IBM stock." Explain why this statement is wrong.

R6. What is a signaling equilibrium? In what sense is it inefficient?

R7. What is adverse selection? What is inefficient about the equilibria that result from adverse selection?

R8. What is moral hazard? What are some of the ways in which an insurance company can attempt to reduce moral hazard?

R9. Give some examples of principal-agent problems.

Problem Set

1. A race of timid elves passes the time by sneaking out at night, locating machinery that is in disrepair, and fixing it while people are sleeping. The human beneficiaries of this largesse are, of course, surprised and delighted when they discover the elves' handiwork the following morning. **True or False:** If the elves were to start charging for their services, humans would certainly be made worse off.

2. A chemical company is considering locating a plant on the outskirts of a certain town. Although the town welcomes the benefits that this plant will bring, some residents have expressed concern about the possibility of an accident involving toxic chemicals. The city council has met to discuss the matter. Although none of the councilmen has any background in chemistry or engineering, many have strong opinions (some pro and some con) about whether a building permit should be issued. One councilman, who has remained neutral throughout, suggests that the permit be issued if and only if the chemical company can demonstrate the ability (either through its own assets or an adequate insurance policy) to reimburse the townspeople for any damage caused by its factory. Explain his reasoning. Explain why his policy might be expected to lead to a socially optimal decision.

3. In 1993, the Mississippi River flooded, causing widespread devastation and leaving midwesterners desperate to acquire basic necessities such as food and ice (for food storage). Profiteers soon emerged, selling ice for as much as $50 per pound. Editorialists and politicians decried this price gouging and called for an end to it.

    a. Suppose that the authorities had effectively prohibited price gouging. What would have been the effect on the amount of ice brought into the affected area?

    b. Suppose that the authorities had effectively prohibited price gouging and somehow managed to ensure that their action had no effect on the quantity of ice in the area. What would have been the effect on social welfare?

    c. Suppose that a pure altruist in the affected area had come into possesion of a small amount of ice. Explain why he might have charged $50 a pound for it, even if he was completely unconcerned with his own welfare.

    d. Do you think that it would have been a good idea to prohibit price gouging?

4. **True or False:** In a large corporation it is usually better for the central management to make decisions rather than divisional managers, because the central management has access to a wider range of information.

5. Aramis, Porthos, and Athos have the following marginal value schedules for swords:

	Marginal Values		
Number of Swords	Aramis	Porthos	Athos
1	$10	$7	$9
2	8	5	6
3	0	4	2
4	0	3	0

Aramis, Porthos, and Athos are the only buyers of swords in the community, and swords are produced at a constant marginal cost of $6 per sword.

a. If the industry is competitive, how many swords will be produced and at what price will they be sold? Justify your answer.

b. Suppose that a social planner orders 5 swords to be produced, with 4 distributed to Porthos and 1 to Athos. What is the social loss in this situation (compared with competitive equilibrium)? Justify your answer.

6. Evaluate the following methods of providing an army. Rank them in order of preference from the point of view of (a) young people, (b) consumers of military service, and (c) economic efficiency. Assume that the army will be of the same size in all cases.

a. A volunteer army, financed by a tax on all citizens.

b. A draft, with soldiers paid a wage of zero.

c. A volunteer army, financed by a tax on young people.

d. A draft, with soldiers paid a wage of zero but with the proviso that draftees may hire other young people to take their place.

7. Suppose that the supply curve for land is perfectly vertical.

a. True or False: Although the Fabians were wrong to argue that a 100% tax on land rents entails no social loss, it would be *right* to argue that a 99% tax on land rents entails no social loss.

b. Would your answer change if it requires some effort for landlords to locate the highest bidder for their land?

8. The University of Rochester has a fixed number of parking spaces for students on campus. They are currently sold at a price that clears the market. It has been proposed that the price should be lowered and a lottery held to determine who may park on campus. Each winner of the lottery would receive a ticket entitling him to purchase a parking space, and these tickets could be freely bought and sold. The number of winners would be equal to the number of parking spaces.

a. Graph the supply and demand for parking spaces. Show on your graph the price of a ticket. Show the consumers' surplus (earned by parkers), the producers' surplus (earned by the university), and the total value of the tickets to the winners of the lottery. Who gains, who loses, and who is unaffected if this plan is adopted?

b. The nearby University of Retsehcor is identical to the University of Rochester in every way except two. First, nobody at Retsehcor has proposed a lottery plan as at Rochester. Second, someone at Retsehcor has proposed that the university hold a lottery and give cash gifts to randomly chosen students. (An alternative proposal is to simply randomize tuition). Compare the effects of the Retsehcor plan with those of the Rochester plan.

c. An alternative proposal at the University of Rochester would institute the lottery without allowing the resale of tickets. The university would carefully monitor compliance, expelling any lottery winner who allowed his parking spot to be used by anybody else. How would this revision affect welfare if the enforcement mechanism were successful? If it were unsuccessful?

9. Pizza is provided by a competitive industry. Suppose that in a burst of generosity, the producers of pizza decided to continue producing the same quantity as always, but to give their pizzas away for free.

a. Use a graph to show the change in consumer and producer surpluses.

b. Is it possible that (despite what your graph shows) this burst of generosity could make consumers as a group worse off? Why or why not?

10. Santa Claus always gives away exactly 1,000,000 toys per year, at a price of zero. It costs him nothing to produce these toys. There is also a market where toys can be purchased from commercial toy manufacturers.

a. Use a graph to show how the existence of Santa Claus affects the supply of toys, the price of toys, the number of toys that consumers acquire, and the number of toys that are provided by commercial manufacturers.

b. Use your graph to show how Santa affects the consumer surplus in the toy market, and the producer surplus earned by commercial toy manufacturers. (Don't forget that the toys Santa gives away are free.)

c. According your graph, how much does Santa add to social welfare? Explain why this answer may overestimate the true social value of Santa Claus. (*Hint:* How does Santa decide who gets the toys?)

11. No coffee is produced in the United States. Americans can buy as much coffee as they want from foreign producers at a price of $10 per pound. At this price, they buy 1,000 pounds per week. The U.S. government has decided to make coffee available to all U.S. citizens at a price of $3 per pound. It gets the coffee by purchasing it from foreigners.

a. Show the gains and losses to all relevant groups of Americans as a result of this program. Compute the deadweight loss.

b. True or False: The deadweight loss in this problem is entirely attributable to the fact that Americans consume an inefficiently large quantity of coffee.

c. Suppose that the government modifies the program. It will continue to sell coffee at $3, but will provide only 1,000 pounds per week, choosing randomly those citizens who are permitted to buy them. Recompute the deadweight loss by the methods of Chapter 8, and show that it is now zero.

d. What important social costs does the analysis of part (c) overlook?

12. Suppose that a bright student can get through college for a cost of *$A*, a dull student can get through college for a cost of *$B*, and that it is worth *$C* to convince an employer that you are bright. Suppose also that nothing of value is learned in college. In which of the following circumstances would bright students go to college?

a. $C > B > A$

b. $B > C > A$

c. $B > A > C$

13. Ten people with different incomes have applied for membership in an exclusive club. One of the club's criteria in deciding whom to accept is to favor those applicants whose incomes are high relative to other applicants'. Each applicant knows his own income and can reveal it voluntarily by submitting his income tax returns. Also, everyone happens to know that there is exactly one applicant whose income is $10,000, one whose income is $20,000, and so forth up to $100,000. How many applicants reveal their incomes?

14. a. What are some of the consequences of prohibiting insurance companies from charging higher rates to people who are in high-risk groups for AIDS?

b. What are some of the consequences of prohibiting insurance companies from requiring AIDS tests as a precondition for coverage?

15. The government is considering a law that would require all sellers of used cars to provide independent certification of their quality. Make an argument in defense of such a law, from the viewpoint of promoting social welfare.

16. Many insurance companies sell group policies that cover all of the employees at a particular firm, or all of the members of a particular organization. How could this policy help to overcome the problem of adverse selection?

17. If all used cars were required to come with warranties, we might solve an adverse selection problem while creating a moral hazard problem to take its place. Explain.

18. Many insurance companies sell auto insurance that includes a "deductible" of $250 or $500. If you have an accident, your insurance covers all of your costs *minus* the amount of the deductible. The amount that they pay on a typical claim is far more than the amount of the deductible. **True or False:** If the deductible were eliminated, the percentage increase in claim payments would be small. Therefore, since insurance companies must earn zero profits, the percentage increase in premiums would be small as well.

Internet Exercise

The firm Towers Perrin publishes information on executive compensation. Access the Towers Perrin Internet site (www.towers.com). Click the "Publications" button, then scroll down and click the "Perspectives on Management Pay" button. Several full-text issues should be accessible. In a past issue [September 1996] Towers Perrin reported, for example, that only about 27 percent of typical CEO compensation in large US corporations was in the form of salary, while annual and long-term incentive pay made up 66 percent, with the remainder of compensation being in the form of benefits.

Use the information that you find at this site to write a two-paragraph executive summary of current practices in CEO incentive compensation, and relate your findings to the agency problem mentioned in the text.

chapter

10

Monopoly

The OECD site describes anti-monopoly policy in the U.S. and other OECD countries at: http://www.oecd.org/daf/ccp/abs15.htm

Market power or **monopoly power** The ability of a firm to affect market prices through its actions. A firm has monopoly power if and only if it faces a downward-sloping demand curve.

A firm that is not perfectly competitive is said to have **market power**. The decisions of such a firm affect the market price of its output. Another name for market power is **monopoly power**. This term can be misleading, because etymology suggests (and popular usage affirms) that a monopoly is a "single seller," the only firm in its industry. Indeed, many textbooks adopt this definition. However, the condition of being a single seller is difficult to make precise. Coca-Cola Inc. is the only producer of Coca-Cola, but it is not the only producer of cola beverages. Is it a single seller? You might answer this question one way if you think that Pepsi is basically indistinguishable from Coke, and another way if you have a strong preference for one or the other.

We would prefer to avoid having to deal with such difficult questions. Therefore, although the single seller is a good example to keep in mind, we shall use the word *monopoly* in reference to any firm that faces a downward-sloping demand curve for its output.

In the first section of this chapter, we will learn how prices and quantities are determined under monopoly, we will explore the welfare consequences of monopoly pricing, and we will see how these welfare consequences can be affected by government policies. In the second section, we will study some of the sources of monopoly power. In the third section, we will learn about a variety of profitable pricing strategies that are available to a monopolist but not viable under perfect competition.

10.1 Price and Output under Monopoly

In this section, we will learn how a monopolist chooses price and quantity and will examine the welfare consequences of these choices.

Exhibit 10-1 Monopoly Price and Output

Quantity	Price	Total Revenue	Marginal Revenue	Total Cost	Marginal Cost
1 dress	$10/dress	$10	$10/dress	$5	$4/dress
2	9	18	8	10	5
3	8	24	6	16	6
4	7	28	4	23	7
5	6	30	2	31	8
6	5	30	0	40	9
7	4	28	-2	50	10
8	3	24	-4	61	11

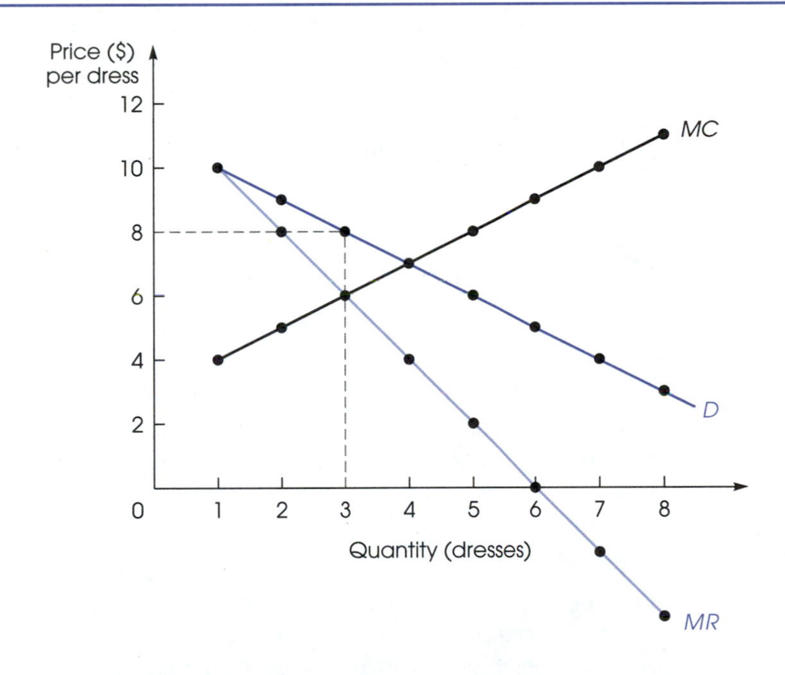

The Tailor Dress Company produces 3 dresses (the quantity at which marginal cost equals marginal revenue) and sells them at a price of $8 apiece. The price is read off the demand curve at a quantity of 3.

Monopoly Pricing

The Tailor Dress Company, which we first met in Chapter 5, is a monopolist. The demand curve for its product, displayed in Exhibit 10–1, is downward sloping. The exhibit also displays Tailor's marginal revenue curve (which can be computed from the demand curve) and its marginal cost curve.

Like any firm, Tailor operates at the point where marginal cost equals marginal revenue; that is, it produces 3 dresses. The price that it charges is the highest price at which demanders will purchase those 3 dresses. This price is \$8 per dress, which can be read off the demand curve at a quantity of 3.

The Monopolist's Marginal Revenue Curve

In Exhibit 10–1 the marginal revenue curve lies everywhere below the demand curve. To understand why, let us compute the marginal revenue when the Tailor Dress Company produces 3 dresses. Suppose that the company has already produced 2 dresses, which can be sold for \$9 each, yielding a total revenue of \$18. When it makes a third dress, two things happen. First, since the price of dresses is now \$8, and since Tailor is making 1 more dress, total revenue goes up by \$8. Second, the first 2 dresses, which could have been sold for \$9 each, can now be sold for only \$8 each, reducing total revenue by \$2. The marginal revenue derived from the third dress is \$8 − \$2 = \$6. The marginal revenue is less than the demand price of \$8.

In general, there are two components to a monopolist's marginal revenue: There is the *price* at which he can sell an additional item (an increment to revenue), and the *price reduction* on earlier items that will now have to be sold at a lower price in order to induce demanders to accept the new quantity (a decrement). Combined, these yield a marginal revenue that is less than the demand price.[1]

EXERCISE 10.1 Compute the two components of marginal revenue at a quantity of 4. Do they add up to the number in the table in Exhibit 10–1?

Notice that a competitive producer faces only the first component of marginal revenue. Because he can sell any quantity at the market price, he does not need to reduce this price when he increases his output. This is why marginal revenue is equal to (demand) price for a competitive producer, although it is always less than that for a monopolist.

example

Passing on a Cost Increase

Suppose that lettuce is supplied at a constant marginal cost of \$1 per head. A change in weather conditions causes the production cost to increase to \$2 per head. In which case will *buyers* feel a greater price increase: when lettuce is supplied competitively, or when it is supplied by a monopolist?

Exhibit 10–2 reveals the surprising answer. Under competition, the upward shift in the marginal cost curve (from MC to MC') moves the competitive equilibrium from point A to point B; the market price rises from \$1 to \$2. The entire increase in marginal cost is passed on to the consumer.

---

[1]If you have had calculus, you may recognize this as an application of the product rule for differentiation. Since Total revenue = Price × Quantity, we can write

$$MR = \frac{dTR}{dQ} = P + Q\frac{dP}{dQ}$$

The term dP/dQ, being calculated along the downward-sloping demand curve, is negative.

Exhibit 10-2 A Rise in Marginal Cost

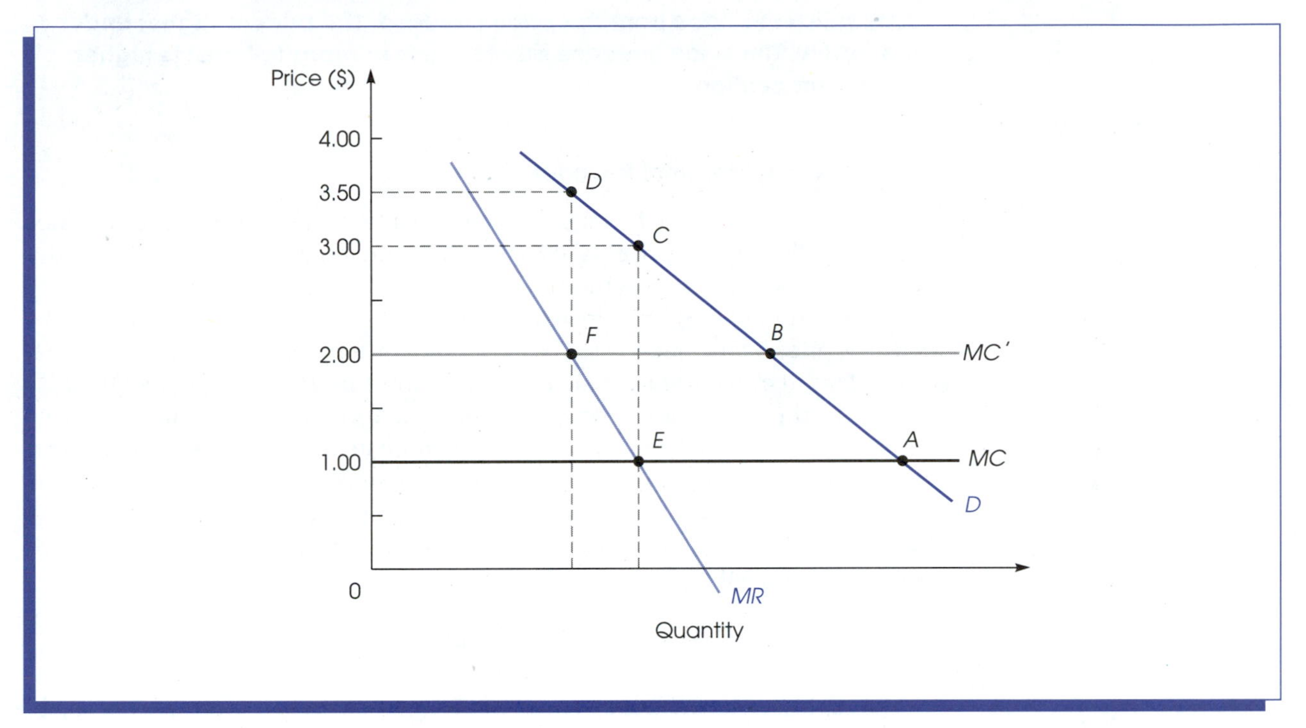

The marginal cost of producing lettuce increases from $1 to $2. Under competition, the equilibrium moves from *A* to *B* and the market price increases by $1. Under monopoly, the monopolist moves from *C* to *D* and the price increases by less than $1. The vertical distance from *C* to *D* must be less than $1, because the vertical distance from *E* to *F* is exactly $1 and the demand curve is flatter than the *MR* curve.

Under monopoly, the price rises from $3 to $3.50 as the monopolist moves from point *C* to point *D*; in this case, only half the price rise is passed on to the consumer. The fact that the consumer pays an extra 50¢ (as opposed to 25¢ or 75¢) is an artifact of the way the demand curve is drawn; if it were drawn differently the price could go up less or more than 50¢. But no matter how the demand curve is drawn, the price always goes up by less than $1.

The reason for this result is that the monopolist always sets marginal cost equal to marginal revenue. When marginal cost increases by $1, quantity must fall by just enough so that marginal revenue increases by $1 as well. But since the demand curve is flatter than the marginal revenue curve, the resulting change in the demand price has to be less than $1.

To put this another way: As quantity falls from Q_M to Q_M', we move back along the marginal revenue curve from *E* to *F*. We simultaneously move back along the demand curve the same horizontal distance from *C* to *D*. Moving along the *MR* curve, we rise a distance $1; moving the same horizontal distance along the (flatter) demand curve, we must rise a distance of less than $1.

Students typically find it surprising that consumers are hit with a greater price increase under competition than they are under monopoly. Don't monopolists charge higher prices than competitors do? To avoid confusion, be very careful to distinguish the *price* from the *price increase*. The price is higher under monopoly. The price increase due to a rise in marginal cost is higher under competition.

Elasticity and Marginal Revenue

A producer facing a downward-sloping demand curve can increase his sales only if he lowers his price. A 1% increase in quantity requires a $1/|\eta|$% decrease in price, where η is the price elasticity of demand. A 1-*unit* increase in quantity, from Q to $Q + 1$, increases quantity by the fraction $1/Q$, and so decreases price by the fraction $(1/|\eta|) \cdot (1/Q)$. Since this is the *fraction* by which price falls, the *amount* by which price falls must be $P \cdot (1/|\eta|) \cdot (1/Q)$.

Using this observation, we can derive a formula for the monopolist's marginal revenue. When he produces one more item, two things happen. First, he collects the price P for that item. Second, he must sell the preceding Q items at a price that is reduced by $P \cdot (1/|\eta|) \cdot (1/Q)$ per item; this reduces his revenue by $[P \cdot (1/|\eta|) \cdot (1/Q)] \cdot Q = P \cdot (1/|\eta|)$. Combining the two effects, we find that marginal revenue is given by

$$MR = P - P \cdot \frac{1}{|\eta|} = P \cdot \left(1 - \frac{1}{|\eta|}\right)$$

From this formula we see that if $|\eta| > 1$, then marginal revenue is positive, whereas if $|\eta| < 1$, then marginal revenue is negative. This makes good sense. For $|\eta| > 1$, a 1% increase in quantity requires a less than 1% increase in price, so that total revenue increases. Since total revenue is increasing, marginal revenue is positive. When $|\eta| < 1$, the opposite is true. Since a typical (downward-sloping) demand curve yields a marginal revenue curve that is positive for small quantities and negative for large quantities (see Exhibit 10–1), we can conclude that a downward-sloping demand curve is elastic when quantity is small and inelastic when quantity is large.

EXERCISE 10.2 In Exhibit 10–1 which is the elastic portion of the demand curve? Which is the inelastic portion?

Because the monopolist chooses the quantity where marginal revenue equals marginal cost and because marginal cost is positive, it follows that at the chosen quantity marginal revenue is positive. Therefore, the monopolist always operates on the elastic portion of the demand curve.

example

Price Increases and Monopoly Power

Several years ago, an unexpected frost killed a substantial portion of the Florida orange crop. The price of oranges rose by so much that the total revenue of orange growers actually increased. At the time, many news reporters and editorialists argued that such a large price increase must be evidence of monopoly power in the orange-growing industry.

Using economic analysis, we can show not only that the conclusion is wrong, but that the exact opposite is true: The orange-growing industry cannot possibly be monopolized. The fall in quantity led to an increase in total revenue, which means that the industry's marginal revenue was negative. (If a fall in quantity increases total revenue, then an increase in quantity reduces total revenue.) The industry was operating on the inelastic portion of its demand curve.

However, we have just seen that a monopolist always operates on the *elastic* portion of his demand curve. It follows that the orange-growing industry cannot be controlled by a monopolist.

To make the same point in different terms: We have learned that a reduction in quantity yields an increase in total revenue. Surely, then, a monopolist who controlled the industry would not have to wait for a frost. He would long ago have reduced the production of oranges until no further reductions were profitable.

The Monopolist Has No Supply Curve

Where is the monopolist's supply curve? Points on the supply curve answer questions such as: "How much would you produce at a going market price of $1?" and "How much would you produce at a going market price of $2?" and so on. These are questions that a monopolist is never asked, because he never faces a going market price. The price is a consequence of the monopolist's actions, rather than a datum to which he must react. Therefore, a monopolist has no supply curve; a supply curve presumes the existence of a going market price.

Welfare

Suppose that the shoe industry is dominated by a monopoly supplier of the "single seller" breed. Suppose also that a competitive shoe industry would produce with the same (industry-wide) marginal cost curve as the monopolist's. Exhibit 10–3 shows the quantities produced by the monopolist (Q_M) and the competitive industry (Q_C) and the prices that they charge. The table shows consumers' and producers' surpluses in each case.

EXERCISE 10.3 Verify the entries in the table in Exhibit 10–3.

From Exhibit 10–3 it is clear that consumers' surplus is reduced by the existence of the monopoly. It is less obvious, but nonetheless true, that producers' surplus is increased. The monopoly producer's surplus exceeds the competitive producers' surplus by the amount $C + D - H$, and your first thought might be that it would be necessary to measure areas in order to determine whether this is positive or negative. Recall, however, that the monopolist is choosing the strategy that will benefit him the most. Since the monopolist could choose the competitive output Q_C but prefers the smaller output Q_M instead, we infer

Exhibit 10-3 Monopoly versus Competition

	Competition	Monopoly
Consumers' Surplus	$A + B + C + D + E$	$A + B$
Producers' Surplus	$F + G + H$	$C + D + F + G$
Social Gain	$A + B + C + D + E + F + G + H$	$A + B + C + D + F + G$
Deadweight Loss	—	$E + H$

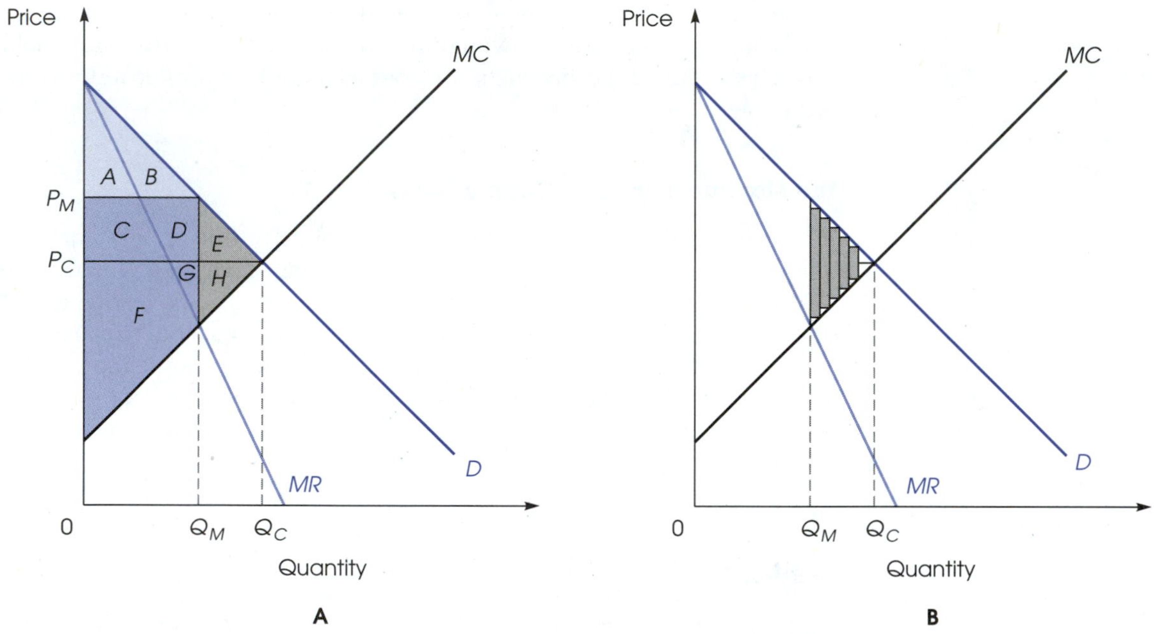

Price, MC, A, B, P_M, C, D, E, P_C, G, H, F, MR, D, 0, Q_M, Q_C, Quantity

A

Price, MC, MR, D, 0, Q_M, Q_C, Quantity

B

The table assumes that a monopoly and a competitive industry would have the same marginal cost curve. The competitive industry produces the equilibrium quantity Q_C and the monopolist produces its profit-maximizing quantity Q_M. Since marginal value still exceeds marginal cost at Q_M, it would be efficient for additional units to be produced. The social gains from additional units after Q_M are represented by the rectangles in panel B. Since the monopolist does not produce those units, those social gains are sacrificed, giving a deadweight loss of $E + H$.

that the producer's surplus is higher at Q_M than at Q_C. In other words, $C + D + F + G > F + G + H$.

Exhibit 10–3 also shows a social welfare loss of $E + H$ due to the existence of the monopoly. This is the amount by which the consumers' losses exceed the producer's gains. It is easy to see the reason for this welfare loss: When output is at Q_M, marginal value still exceeds marginal cost. It is socially beneficial to produce another pair of shoes, creating the first rectangle of social gain shown in panel B of the exhibit. From the viewpoint of efficiency, additional pairs of shoes should be produced, as they would be under competition.

When an item's marginal value exceeds its marginal cost, the competitive producer will always choose to provide it, because he can sell the item for more than it will cost him to produce it. However, the monopolist will not always make the same choice. The monopolist must reason as follows: "It is true that I can sell the next item for more than it will cost me to produce it. But it is also true that producing this item will reduce the price at which I can sell all of the items I've already decided to produce. I have to weigh both of these considerations before deciding to proceed." The second consideration is, of course, irrelevant to the competitor, whose actions do not affect the market price.

Monopoly and Public Policy

What can be done to reduce the efficiency loss due to monopoly? Since the inefficiency results from a reduction in output caused by the monopolist's pursuit of high profits, some might argue that the government should tax away the monopolist's ill-gotten gains, say, by imposing an excise tax. However, this "solution" only reduces efficiency still further. The original problem is that production is less than it should be from a social viewpoint, and the effect of an excise tax is to lower production still further. The tax increases the deadweight loss.

EXERCISE 10.4 Draw the monopolist's demand, marginal revenue, and marginal cost curves both before and after the imposition of an excise tax on his output. Label the areas of deadweight loss both before and after the tax.

Subsidies

The preceding observation suggests that the real solution might be to give the monopolist a *subsidy* per unit of output.

Exhibit 10–4 shows the effect of an "ideal" subsidy, that is, one of exactly the right size to induce the monopolist to supply the competitive quantity Q_C. We know that this quantity maximizes social gain, so the deadweight loss is reduced to zero.

To see how the gains and losses are distributed over society, notice that the ideally subsidized monopolist produces the same quantity at the same price as does a competitive market. Therefore, the consumers' surplus is the same in either case. The monopolist earns both the competitive producers' surplus and the revenue from the subsidy; the latter, of course, comes from the taxpayers.

We can see this distribution in Exhibit 10–4. In the presence of the $\$S$-per-unit subsidy, the monopolist chooses the quantity Q_C and the price P_C. Therefore, the consumers' surplus is $A + B + C + D + E$, just as in competition. To compute the producers' surplus by our usual methods, we would have to draw a horizontal line at the "price received by suppliers," a distance $\$S$ above the price charged in the marketplace. This would clutter the diagram beyond all redemption, so we resort to an alternative method, which was introduced in

Exhibit 10-4 A Subsidized Monopolist

	Competition	Unsubsidized Monopoly	Subsidized Monopoly
Consumers' Surplus	$A + B + C + D + E$	$A + B$	$A + B + C + D + E$
Producers' Surplus	$F + G + H$	$C + D + F + G$	$F + G + H + I + J + K$
Cost to Taxpayers	—	—	$I + J + K$
Social Gain	$A + B + C + D + E + F + G + H$	$A + B + C + D + F + G$	$A + B + C + D + E + F + G + H$

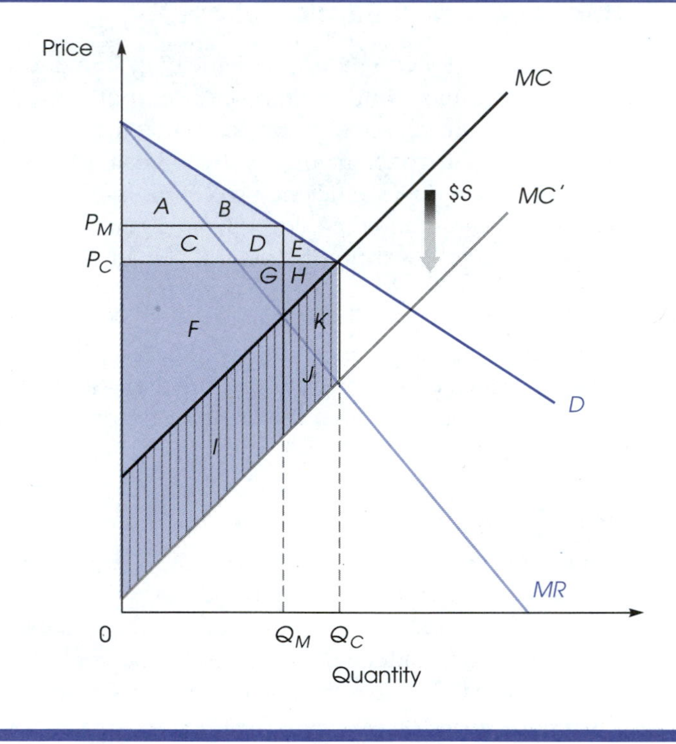

An unsubsidized monopolist produces the quantity Q_M. The subsidy of $\$S$ per unit of output, which lowers the marginal cost curve to MC', is chosen to be of just the right size so that the monopolist will now produce the competitive quantity Q_C. Since the competitive quantity maximizes social gain, the deadweight loss is eliminated. The table confirms that social gain is the same as it would be under competition.

Exhibit 8–13. According to this method, we calculate using the price charged in the marketplace and the new, lower marginal cost curve. This gives a producers' surplus of $F + G + H + I + J + K$. By elementary geometry, the cost to taxpayers, $\$S \times Q_C$, is represented by the area of the trapezoid $I + J + K$. These calculations are shown in the third column of the table in Exhibit 10–4.

The social gain is just what it would be under competition, so the deadweight loss is zero, as we have already argued that it must be.

Of course, this analysis assumes an "ideal" subsidy, which in turn assumes that policy makers are able to discern both the competitive equilibrium quantity and the size of the subsidy needed to call forth that quantity from the monopolist. A more reasonable expectation is that the subsidy will either be too small or too large. If it is too small, it is still certain to be welfare-improving, but perhaps by less than we might hope. If it is too large, it will encourage overproduction. Depending on the size of the subsidy, this could be either less or more detrimental that the underproduction it was designed to replace.

EXERCISE 10.5 Draw diagrams depicting the effects of subsidies that are smaller or larger than the optimal one. Indicate the areas of deadweight loss in each. Compare these areas with the areas of deadweight loss from an unsubsidized monopoly.

Price Ceilings

From an efficiency standpoint, it is desirable to subsidize a monopolist, although the size of the optimal subsidy may be difficult to determine. From a political viewpoint, it can be difficult to generate support for subsidies to a monopolist who is already perceived as wealthier than he "deserves" to be. There is, however, another approach to the "problem" of monopoly.

Consider a price ceiling imposed on a monopolist at the level of the competitive price. This is shown in panel A of Exhibit 10–5. If the price ceiling is perfectly enforced, the monopolist effectively faces a flat demand curve at the price P_C out to the quantity Q_C. This is because no demander can ever offer a price higher than P_C, so that portion of the demand curve that lies above P_C becomes irrelevant to the monopolist's calculations. The new demand curve is as shown in panel B of Exhibit 10–5; it is flat out to Q_C and becomes identical with the old demand curve thereafter. The new marginal revenue curve is shown in panel C of the exhibit: In the region where demand is flat at P_C, we always have marginal revenue equal to P_C (just as in the competitive case). In the region of downward-sloping demand, the original marginal revenue curve is still in effect; thus, the new marginal revenue curve jumps downward at the quantity Q_C.

The monopolist produces the quantity where its new marginal revenue curve meets its marginal cost curve, that is, the competitive quantity Q_C (refer to panel A to see this). Consumers' surplus and producers' surplus are what they would be under competition, and there is no deadweight loss.

EXERCISE 10.6 Give the reasons for the assertions made in the preceding paragraph. In a competitive market, price controls cause social loss due to time spent waiting in line and so on, yet no such social loss takes place in the market pictured in Exhibit 10–5. Why not?

Unfortunately, finding the optimal price ceiling may be no easier for the policy maker than finding the right level of subsidy. In the absence of a competitive market, it is difficult to determine what the competitive price would be. It

Exhibit 10-5 A Price Ceiling

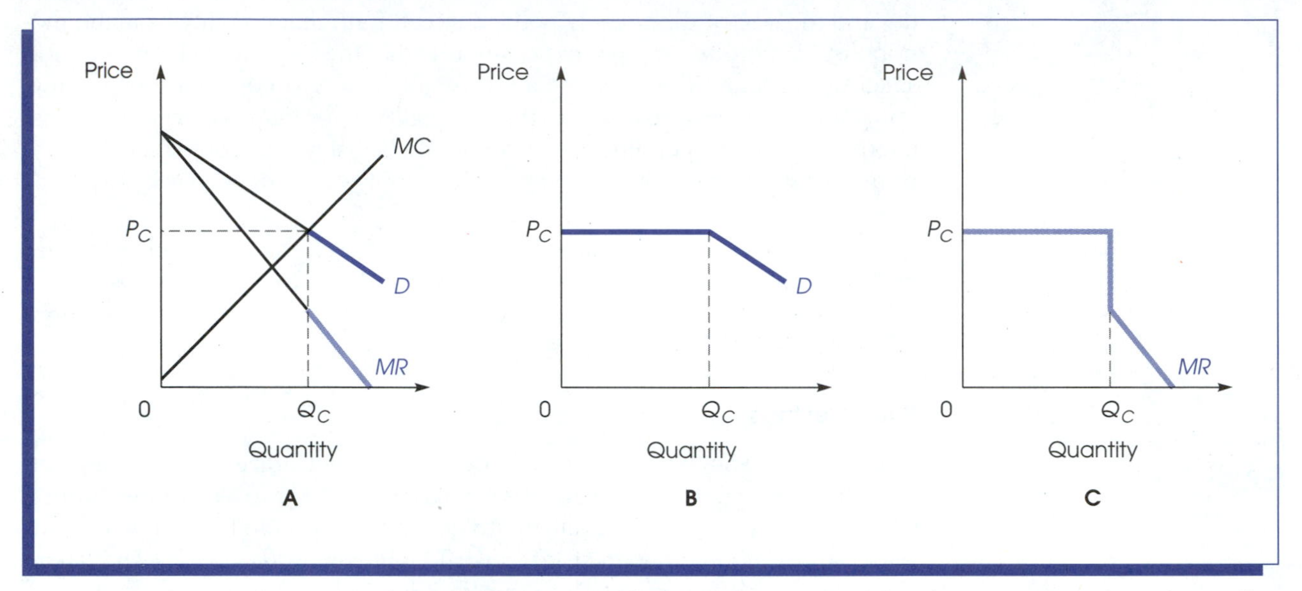

If a monopolist is required by law to charge no more than the competitive price P_C, then it effectively faces the demand and marginal revenue curves shown in panels B and C. It produces at the point Q_C, where marginal cost and marginal revenue are equal.

is therefore possible to set the price ceiling either too high or too low. If it is set too high, its effect will be diminished. Deadweight loss will be reduced but not eliminated altogether. If it is set too low, there will be deadweight loss due to underproduction. If it is set very low, the deadweight loss can be greater than with an unregulated monopoly.

EXERCISE 10.7 Draw diagrams depicting price ceilings that are higher or lower than the optimal one. Show the areas of deadweight loss and compare them with the deadweight losses in the absence of a price control.

Rate-of-Return Regulation

Read about rate-of-return regulation in the electricity industry at: http://www.eia.doe.gov/oiaf/elepri97/comp.html

In practice, many monopolists (such as public utility companies) are required to set prices in such a way that they will earn no more than a "normal" rate of return on their capital investment. That is, they must earn no more than they could by investing the same amount of capital in some other industry; they are required to earn zero economic profits.

It is sometimes argued that this policy is desirable because the goal is to make monopolists behave more like competitors, and competitors earn zero profits in long-run equilibrium. The problem with this argument is that it is not the zero profits aspect of competition that one wishes to reproduce; it is the efficiency aspect. Although efficiency and zero profits are compatible under competition, they are very unlikely to be compatible under monopoly.

Exhibit 10–6 shows two possible configurations of demand, marginal revenue, marginal cost, and average cost curves. In each case the monopolist earns zero profits when it produces the quantity Q_Z and sells at the price P_Z. At this point, price exactly covers average cost. However, in each case the efficient level of output is Q_C, where a competitive industry would produce. In panel A, a monopolist that is required to earn zero profits will produce too much from the viewpoint of efficiency. In panel B, the monopolist will produce too little.

There are additional problems with regulation requiring the monopolist to earn zero profits. One is that such regulation provides the monopolist with no incentive to seek more efficient methods of production. If a new technology would lower the average cost and if the result of this is that the monopolist must lower its price accordingly, then there is no reason for it to adopt the new technology.

A closely related problem is that the owners and managers of the monopoly firm are given an incentive to adopt inefficient policies that benefit themselves personally. Suppose that the president of an electric utility company must decide whether to undertake an expensive redecoration of his office. Ordinarily,

Exhibit 10-6 Zero Profits Regulation of Monopoly

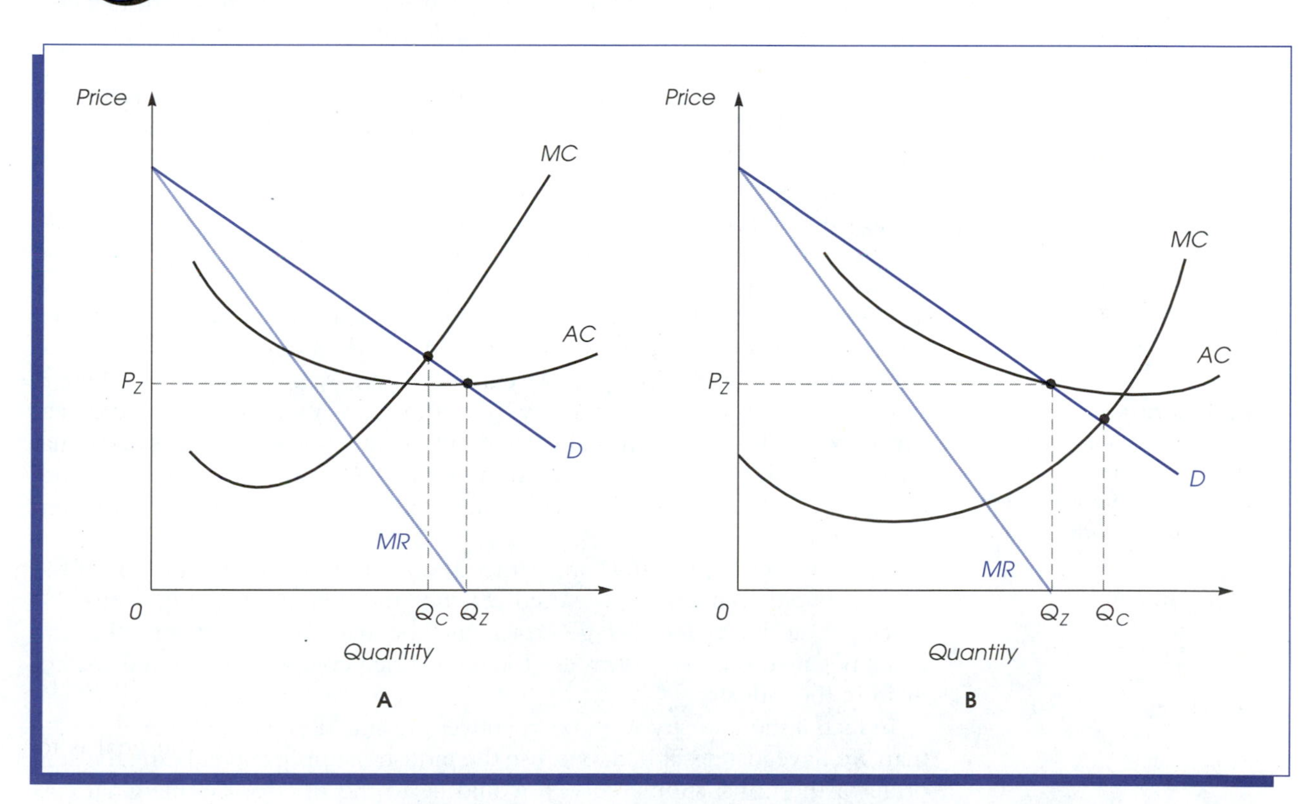

The two panels show two possible configurations of demand, marginal revenue, marginal cost, and average cost curves for a monopolist. If the monopolist is required by law to earn zero profits, it will produce that quantity Q_Z at which the demand price is equal to average cost. The efficient level of output is Q_C, where marginal cost equals demand. As the two panels show, Q_Z could be either greater or less than Q_C.

he would weigh the costs and benefits before proceeding. But if a regulatory agency always constrains the firm to earn zero profits, then the firm will be allowed to raise prices in order to cover the increased costs due to the redecoration. The president will certainly choose to undertake the project, even though it might be socially inefficient.[2]

10.2 Sources of Monopoly Power

We turn now to the question of why monopolies arise in the first place. We will discover that the answers make it necessary to modify our welfare analysis in certain cases.

Natural Monopoly

Suppose you want to produce a new word processing program. Your fixed costs (the costs of developing the software) are likely to be quite high, but your marginal costs (the costs of copying the software onto disks) will be extremely low. In fact, if the software is distributed over the internet, your marginal cost might be essentially zero.

In a competitive market, word processing software would sell at marginal cost—that is, it would be almost free. But at that price, all firms earn negative profits, so nobody is willing to enter the industry. Therefore a competitive market for word processors cannot survive.

By contrast, a monopolist can sell software for substantially more than its marginal cost. Microsoft Word sells for many times the cost of producing an additional copy. Therefore, Microsoft can earn enough to cover its fixed costs, and is willing to remain in business.

Notice that Microsoft's average cost curve is decreasing. To see why, consider an extreme example: Suppose it costs $1,000 to write the software, and suppose it costs exactly zero to run off a copy. Then if Microsoft sells 1 copy, its average cost is $1,000 per copy; if it sells 2 copies, its average cost is $500 per copy; if it sells 3 copies, its average cost is $333.33 per copy, and so on.

Natural monopoly An industry in which each firm's average cost curve is decreasing at the point where it crosses market demand.

Whenever a firm's average cost curve is decreasing at the point where it crosses market demand, we say that there is a condition of **natural monopoly**. This condition is illustrated in Exhibit 10–7. We have just seen that Microsoft is an example of a natural monopoly. We shall now see that, more generally, under conditions of natural monopoly, a competitive industry cannot survive.

If the firm in Exhibit 10–7 were forced to set prices and quantities as if the industry were competitive, it would produce the quantity Q_C at the price P_C. However, at this point average cost is greater than the price P_C, so the firm earns negative profits. If firms are forced to price competitively, none will remain in the industry.

In fact, if the industry were competitive, the situation would be even worse than we have just described, because the industry supply curve, being the sum of all of the firms' supply curves, would lie to the right of the marginal cost

[2] If a period of time elapses between the increase in costs and the firm's securing permission from the regulatory authority to increase its prices, then the firm still has some incentive to keep its costs down.

Exhibit 10-7 Natural Monopoly

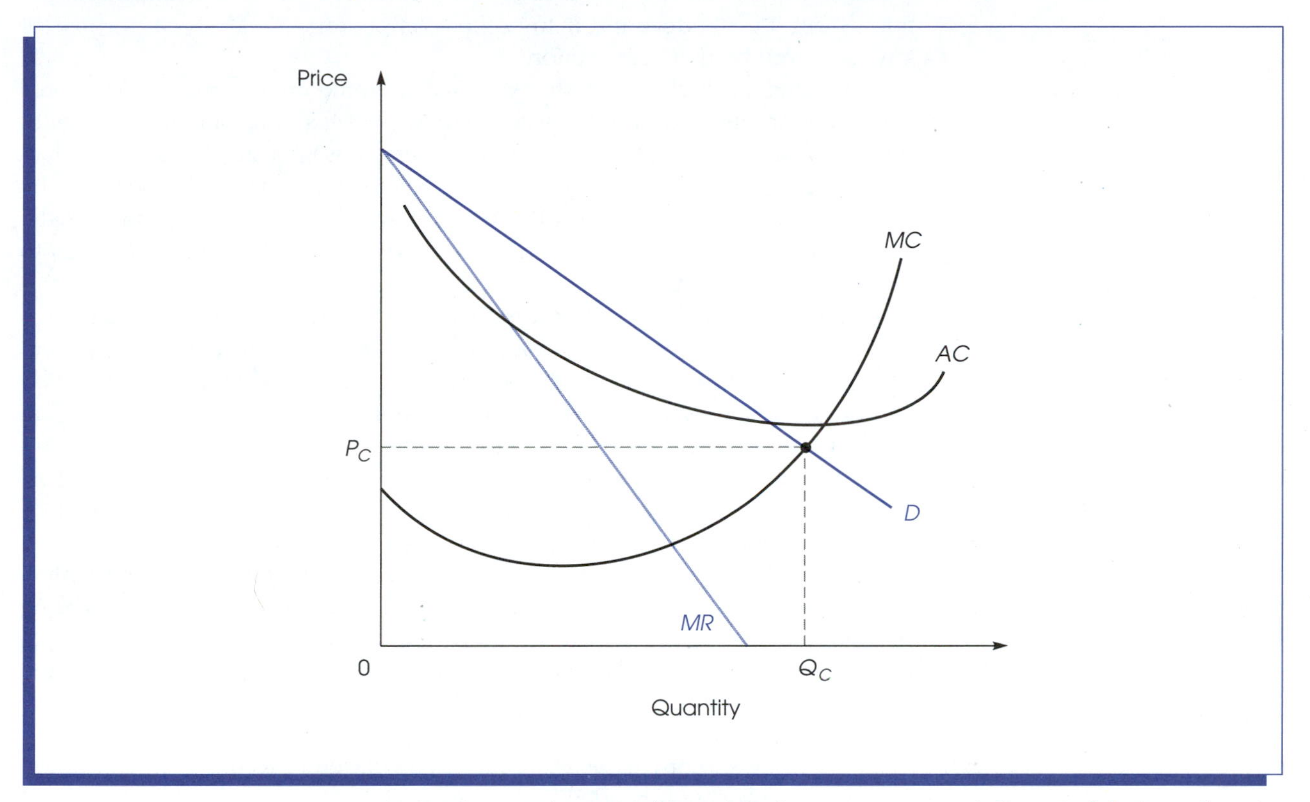

A natural monopoly occurs when each firm's average cost curve is downward sloping at the point where it crosses industry demand. Since marginal cost crosses average cost at the bottom of the U, marginal cost must cross demand at a point where price is below average cost. Thus, if the firm priced competitively, it would earn negative profits.

curve shown in the exhibit. Therefore, the equilibrium price would be even lower than P_C.

It follows that at the competitive price, no firm can cover its costs. A monopoly producer, however, may be able to enter the industry and prosper. The industry can survive only if it is monopolized.

The Welfare Economics of Natural Monopoly

In Section 10.1, we computed the welfare loss due to monopoly by comparing the social gain from a monopolized industry with the social gain available if the industry were perfect competitive. Now we see that in the case of a natural monopoly, the comparison is unfair. It is unfair because such an industry could never survive under perfect competition. So the first observation is that, realistically, the monopoly outcome might be the best we can hope for.

But not always. There can still be competition, even when it is not perfect. You might have noticed that Microsoft, despite its considerable monopoly power, is not the world's only producer of computer software, or even the world's only producer of word processors. Microsoft faces substantial competition from WordPerfect and many other competitors. What social purpose, if any, is served by that competition?

Producing exact clones of Microsoft Word would entail considerable social waste; the producer would duplicate all of Microsoft's development costs without doing anything to reduce the (already very low) marginal cost of producing copies. Still, this activity might have some offsetting social benefits, by putting downward pressure on the price of word processors. As long as the price remains high enough for firms to survive, any price reduction leads to more sales and an increase in social gain.

But that's not the main reason we should be glad that Microsoft has competitors. The main reason we should be glad is that those competitors *don't* produce exact clones. Instead, they're always trying to produce something better than Microsoft—and Microsoft is always trying to stay ahead of them. There might always be monopoly power in the software industry, but firms still compete to capture that monopoly power for themselves—and they do so by finding better ways to serve their customers. That's why word processors get better all the time.

The social value of all that improvement cannot be depicted in our simple graphs, because those graphs illustrate the market for a single, unchanging product. But the fact that we can't draw something doesn't mean it's not important. Even under conditions of natural monopoly, competition can be the consumer's best friend.

Nevertheless, even when competition to innovate benefits consumers, it need not always improve social welfare. We will return to this issue in Section 11.1, in the subsection headed "Tournaments."

Patents

An amicus brief on the economics of intellectual property for a recent U.S. Supreme Court case can be seen at: http://server.berkeley.edu/BTLJ/lvb/econprof.html

Patents are another source of monopoly power with ambiguous welfare consequences. A patent confers a legally protected monopoly for a period of 17 years after the development of a new invention. In the absence of this monopoly, the invention could be copied by others and produced competitively. On the other hand, if there were no patents, the incentive to invent would be much reduced and many inventions might not come into being in the first place. In deciding on the optimal length of a patent, it is necessary to weigh the losses from monopoly production against the gains from promoting inventive activity.

Keep in mind, though, that there is an optimal quantity of inventive activity, and that it is socially undesirable to grant incentives for people to be inventive past the point where the marginal benefits of inventions exceed the marginal gains from inventors' alternative employment. Another factor often ignored is that patents divert creative individuals *away* from making socially valuable innovations that are not patentable. The inventors of the Macintosh computer received many valuable patents; the inventor of the supermarket received none. If the length of patent protection is increased, society will have more inventions like the Macintosh and fewer like the supermarket; it is very hard to judge the optimal mix.

With all of these uncertainties in mind, you should be somewhat skeptical of attempts to estimate the optimal life of patent, but such attempts have been made.[3] Although the results necessarily depend on a number of ad hoc assumptions, they tend to suggest that the existing 17-year limit is a reasonable one.

Resource Monopolies

Monopolies occasionally result when a single firm gains control of a productive input that is necessary to the industry. The most commonly cited example is Alcoa (Aluminum Company of America), which completely dominated the market for aluminum in the first 40 years of this century. Alcoa initially established its monopoly position by acquiring critical patents, but it was able to maintain its position long after the patents expired largely by virtue of owning essentially all of the sources of bauxite (the ore from which aluminum is derived) in the United States.

Legal Barriers to Entry

In many industries, legal barriers to entry constitute a source of monopoly power. We will have more to say on this topic in Section 11.3. Here we will give one brief example. In many states travelers on limited-access highways can visit restaurants and gas stations at "oasis stops" without having to leave the highway. The number of oases is determined by an agency of the state government, which also decides which restaurants will be granted the rights to do business there. Because entry is restricted, these rights confer considerable monopoly power. (In many states the restaurants are subject to price controls, but they still appear to price higher than competitively.) There is a great deal of competition among restaurants to acquire these rights, much of which takes the form of lobbying appropriate government officials and applying other forms of political pressure. This lobbying process itself can consume valuable resources (lobbyists' time, for example) without producing offsetting social gains. The concomitant losses should be *added* to the welfare cost of monopoly, which is therefore underestimated by the methods of Section 10.1.

EXERCISE 10.8 Explain why it would be socially more efficient to legalize bribery of state officials who decide on the placement of roadside restaurants.

Some economists have used the observation of Exercise 10.8 to explain the preponderance of lawyers as members of state and federal legislative bodies. The reason is that it is easier to bribe a lawyer than (for example) a medical doctor. This is not because of any moral superiority on the part of physicians;

[3]One of the most famous attempts is by William Nordhaus, *Invention, Growth and Welfare* (Cambridge, MA: MIT Press, 1969).

it is a purely technological phenomenon. Many of the firms that seek favors from legislators have considerable need for legal services, and they can contrive to hire those services from favored lawyer–legislators at inflated fees. A number of U.S. congressmen from widely scattered parts of the country are associated with previously undistinguished law firms whose business has thrived since one of the partners went to Washington. A small-town medical practice would find it far more difficult to plausibly collect million-dollar fees for services rendered to large corporations thousands of miles away.

10.3 Price Discrimination

Learn about U.S. policy toward price discrimination at: http://www.stolaf.edu/people/becker/antitrust/statutes/clayton.html

The analysis of monopoly pricing in Section 10.1 assumes that the monopolist will sell all of his output at a single price. In this section we will see that, unlike a competitor, a monopolist can benefit by charging different prices for identical items.

example

Monopoly in the Pie Market

Exhibit 10–8 shows the market for Mrs. Lovett's pies. Mrs. Lovett faces a downward-sloping demand curve, so she acts as a monopolist. That is, she produces the quantity Q_0 where marginal cost equals marginal revenue and charges $10 per pie, read off the demand curve.

Mrs. Lovett could sell additional pies if she charged any price less than $10. For example, some customers may approach Mrs. Lovett and offer to buy additional pies at the competitive price of $7. Since this price exceeds Mrs. Lovett's marginal cost, both she and her customers would benefit from such a transaction. That is to say, both the producer's and consumers' surpluses will be increased. Each additional pie beyond Q_0 creates a rectangle of social gain, as in the exhibit. Mrs. Lovett earns the lower portions of these rectangles as additional producer's surplus. Her customers gain the upper portions.

Although the transaction would benefit everyone, it still might not take place. Why not? Because Mrs. Lovett will be willing to market additional pies at the lower price of $7 only on the condition that her customers continue to buy Q_0 high-priced pies. Ideally, Mrs. Lovett would like to market some pies at $10 and other identical pies at $7, and then post a sign in her shop reading: "Please buy as many $10 pies as you are willing to before purchasing any $7 pies." Realistically, she fears that her customers will not cooperate. This fear leads her to produce only Q_0 pies at a single monopoly price of $10.

Conceivably, Mrs. Lovett could attempt some approximation to the scheme she has just rejected. If she believes that the typical customer is willing to buy two pies at $10 each, she can sell pies at "$10 each, 3 for $27." This effectively enables her to sell each customer a third pie for $7 without cutting into the sales of $10 pies.

But this plan, too, has its flaws. First, some of her customers might in fact have been willing to pay $10 for a third pie. A more important (and perhaps fatal) flaw is this: Some customers may buy a third pie for $7, then resell the pie for $9 to somebody else who would have been willing to buy it from Mrs.

Exhibit 10-8 Mrs. Lovett's Pies

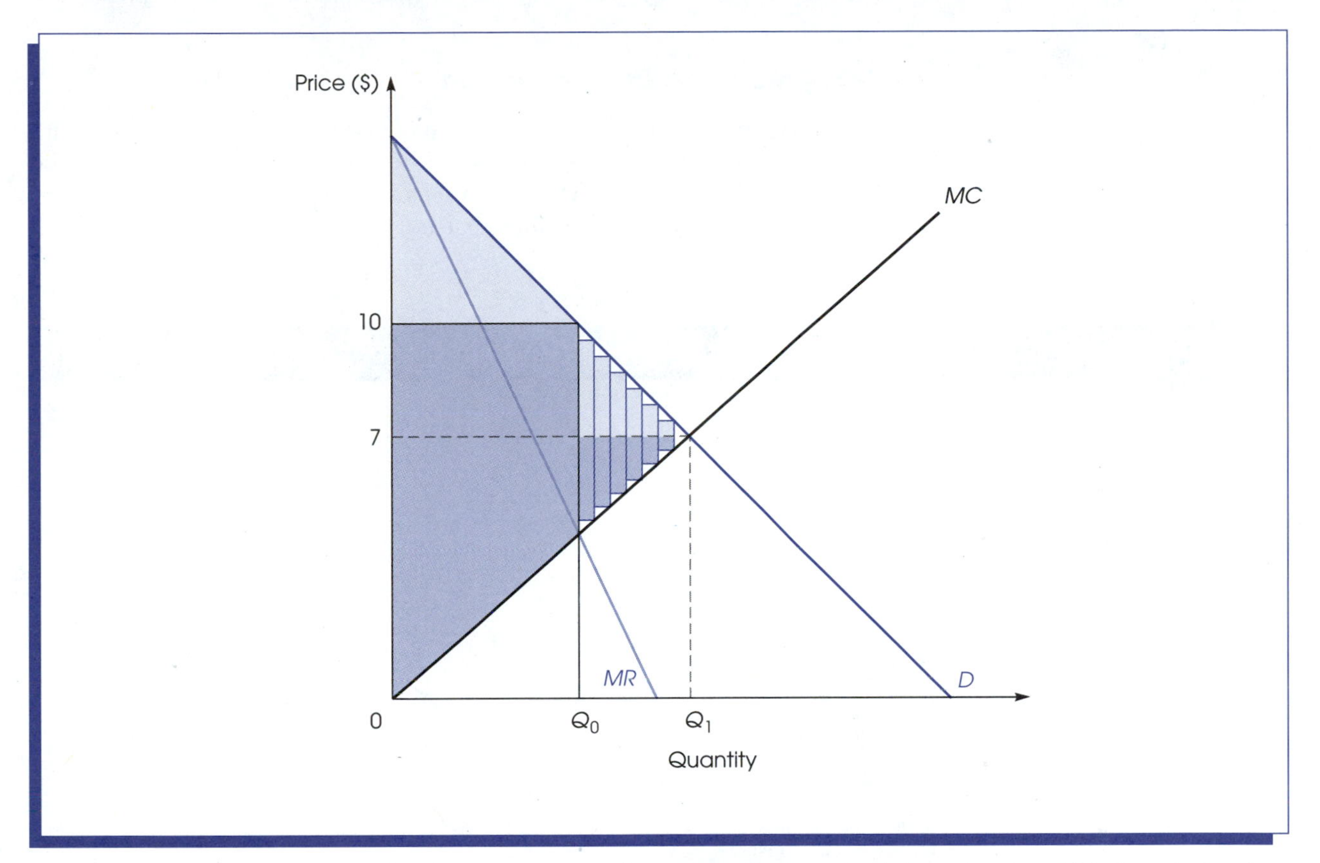

Mrs. Lovett, as a monopolist, produces Q_0 pies and sells them at a price of \$10. Once she has done so, she can still sell additional pies at prices that exceed her marginal cost. For example, at the competitive price of \$7, she could sell an additional $Q_1 - Q_0$ pies, creating additional social gains represented by the rectangles. The upper portions of the rectangles represent additions to consumers' surplus, and the lower portions represent additions to Mrs. Lovett's producer's surplus.

Lovett for \$10. In effect, she makes it possible for her own customers to go into competition with her! We will return to these problems later in this section.

Price discrimination
Charging different prices for identical items.

The act of charging different prices for identical items is known as **price discrimination.** Any monopolist faces the temptation to price discriminate, because he produces where marginal value exceeds marginal cost. Consequently, he can always sell additional items at a price higher than the marginal cost of producing them.

A competitive producer, by contrast, faces no temptation to price discriminate. This is because he can sell any quantity he wants to at the going market price, so there is never any reason for him to sell for less.

In order to price discriminate successfully, a monopolist must be able to prevent the low-priced units from being resold, undercutting his own higher-priced sales. This is easier in some industries than in others. Utility companies offer quantity discounts, for example, because technological barriers prevent a customer from buying lots of cheap electricity and reselling it to his friends at a profit.

First-Degree Price Discrimination

Returning to Mrs. Lovett, we find that there is yet another pricing policy with even greater potential to increase her revenue. Exhibit 10–9 shows again the market for Mrs. Lovett's pies; the curves are exactly as in Exhibit 10–8. The rectangles represent the marginal values that her customers place on pies. Each

Exhibit 10-9 First-Degree Price Discrimination

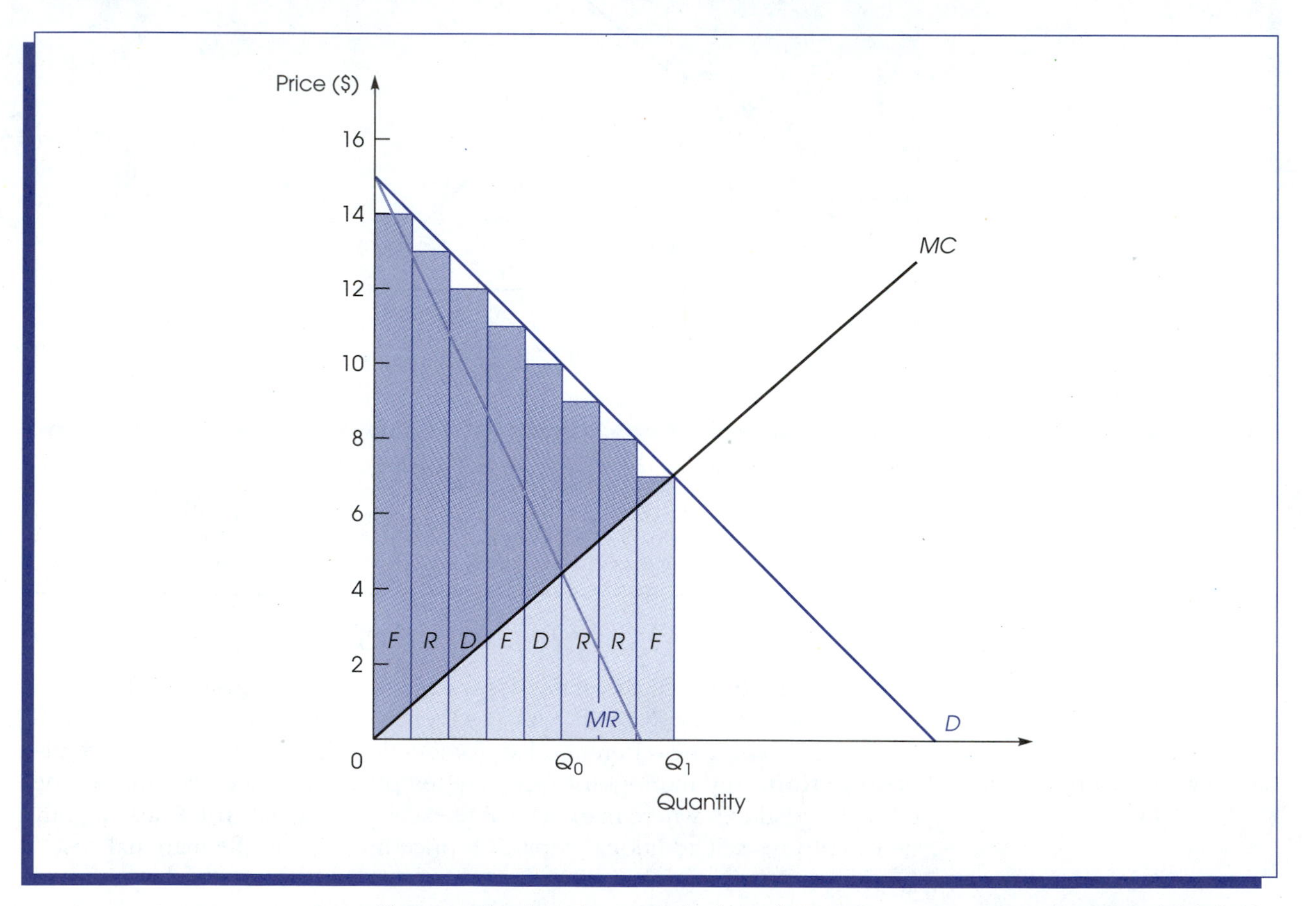

The rectangles show the marginal values of pies to Mrs. Lovett's customers, with each labeled by the initial of the corresponding customer. If she charges each customer the maximum amount that she is willing to pay for a pie, Flicka will have to pay $14 for her first pie, Ricka will pay $13 for her first pie, and so on. Since each customer pays her marginal value for each pie, there is no customers' surplus. All of the surplus is earned by Mrs. Lovett, who gains the entire shaded area.

rectangle is labeled with the initial of the corresponding customer. Flicka has the highest marginal value, valuing her first pie at $14. Ricka values her first pie at $13, Dicka values her first pie at $12, Flicka values her second pie at $11, and so on. If Mrs. Lovett knows all this, she can price her pies as follows: To Flicka the first pie is $14 and the second is $11. To Ricka the first pie is $13. To Dicka . . . and so on.

This scheme allows Mrs. Lovett to capture all of the social gains for herself. Each customer pays the maximum amount she would be willing to pay for each pie, so that she earns no surplus, while Mrs. Lovett gains the shaded areas shown in the exhibit. Mrs. Lovett will sell pies as long as she can collect prices higher than her marginal cost, so she will produce the competitive quantity Q_1. Therefore, there is no deadweight loss.

First-degree price discrimination Charging each customer the most that he would be willing to pay for each item that he buys.

Second-degree price discrimination Charging the same customer different prices for identical items.

This scheme is called **first-degree price discrimination,** to distinguish it from the **second-degree price discrimination** that Mrs. Lovett practiced when she offered quantity discounts. In second-degree price discrimination each customer is offered the same set of prices, although the price may depend on the quantity purchased. In first-degree price discrimination each individual customer is charged the highest price he is willing to pay for each item.

Either form of price discrimination leads to an increase in output and an increase in welfare. Second-degree price discrimination benefits both the producer and the consumers. First-degree price discrimination benefits the producer in two ways. First, it allows him to appropriate the consumers' surplus. Second, it allows him to produce out to the competitive quantity, creating additional welfare gains, all of which go to the producer.

Third-Degree Price Discrimination

Third-degree price discrimination Charging different prices in different markets.

The third and most common form of price discrimination is called **third-degree price discrimination.** This occurs when a seller faces two (or more) identifiably different groups of buyers having different (downward-sloping) demand curves. Such a seller can increase profits by setting different prices for the two groups, provided resales can be prevented.

example

Two Markets for Pies

Consider again Mrs. Lovett, who has discovered a second market for her pies. A grocery store in a large city 200 miles away is willing to buy as many pies as Mrs. Lovett wants to sell at a price of $7 each.[4]

What quantity of pies will Mrs. Lovett provide to her local customers? The ordinary monopoly quantity is Q_0 in Exhibit 10–10. At this quantity, her marginal revenue is $5 per pie. But Mrs. Lovett can always sell pies to the big-city grocery store at a marginal revenue of $7 per pie. Given this, it pays to sell

[4]By coincidence, $7 is also the competitive price in Mrs. Lovett's own hometown. Such remarkable coincidences are not to be expected. We make the assumption for purposes of this example, and only because it helps to keep the graph readable. None of the ideas that we will stress depend on this assumption.

Exhibit 10-10 Third-Degree Price Discrimination with Monopoly in One Market and Competition in Another

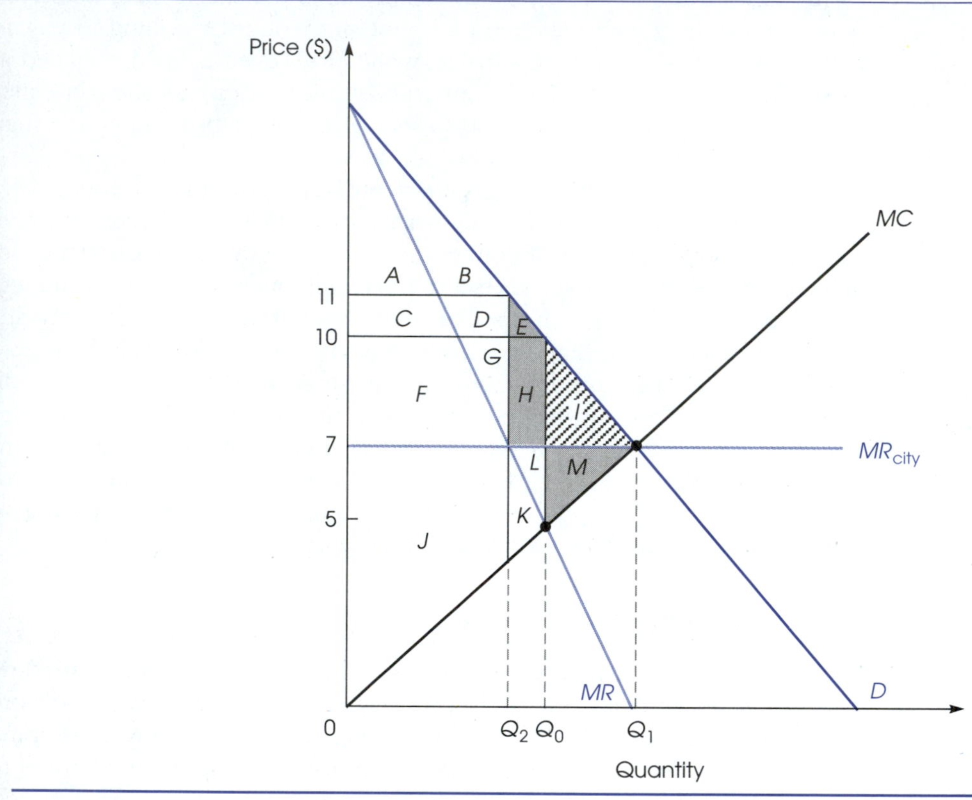

	Competiition	Ordinary Monopoly	Price-Discriminating Monopoly
Consumers' Surplus	$A+B+C+D+E+F+G+H+I$	$A+B+C+D+E$	$A+B$
Producers' Surplus (Local)	$J+K+L+M$	$F+G+H+J+K+L$	$C+D+F+G+J$
Producer's Surplus (City)	—	—	$K+L+M$
Social Gain	$A+B+C+D+E+F+G+H+I+J+K+L+M$	$A+B+C+D+E+F+G+H+J+K+L$	$A+B+C+D+F+G+J+K+L+M$
Deadweight Loss	—	$I+M$	$E+H+I$

The demand and marginal revenue curves are from Mrs. Lovett's hometown market. In the distant city she can sell all of the pies she wants to at the competitive price of $7. In that case she will sell only Q_2 pies at home, as opposed to the ordinary monopoly quantity Q_0. The reason is that she can always earn $7 marginal revenue by selling pies in the city, so that she will not sell pies at home when her marginal revenue there falls below $7. When she sells Q_2 pies at home, she sets a price of $11, higher than the ordinary monopoly price of $10. The table shows what social gains would be if the pie industry were competitive, if Mrs. Lovett were an ordinary monopolist, and if Mrs. Lovett were able to sell pies in both markets at different prices.

In each case the consumers' surplus comes entirely from the local market. There is no consumers' surplus in the city market, because the demand curve there for Mrs. Lovett's pies is flat.

fewer pies locally and more in the big city. Mrs. Lovett will keep transferring pies from the local market to the big-city market as long as the local marginal revenue is less than \$7. This will reduce the local quantity to Q_2 in Exhibit 10–10.

In general:

Any producer selling in two different markets will choose quantities so that his marginal revenue is the same in each market.

The reason for this is that if marginal revenue in Market 1 were higher than marginal revenue in Market 2, the producer could increase his profits by selling one more item in Market 1 and one less in Market 2.

Because Mrs. Lovett sells only Q_2 pies at home, she is able to command a price of \$11 for them. Then she will turn to the big-city market and will sell pies there as long as her marginal revenue (\$7 per pie) exceeds her marginal cost. That is, she will produce Q_1 pies altogether, selling Q_2 of them at home for \$11 each and $Q_1 - Q_2$ of them in the big city for \$7 each.

The table in Exhibit 10–10 shows social gains in three situations: Mrs. Lovett as a competitor, Mrs. Lovett as an ordinary monopolist, and Mrs. Lovett as a price-discriminating monopolist.

If Mrs. Lovett sold only in the local market, the deadweight loss would be $I + M$. When she can sell in both markets and price discriminate, the deadweight loss is $E + H + I$. $E + H$ can be either greater or less than M; therefore, Mrs. Lovett's price discrimination can be either beneficial or detrimental to welfare. On the other hand, it certainly hurts the local consumers.

Of course, like all price discriminators, Mrs. Lovett has to worry about resale. One of her neighbors may get the idea to drive to the city, buy a truckload of pies at \$7 apiece, bring them back and sell them locally for \$10.50. Before long Mrs. Lovett may find that she is no longer a monopolist in her hometown.

A Monopolist in Two Markets

If Mrs. Lovett sells pies both in her hometown and in the big city, then she is a monopolist in one market and a competitor in another. Sometimes a producer is a monopolist in two markets. His behavior will be essentially the same as Mrs. Lovett's. Benjamin Barker is a barber who cuts the hair of both adults and children. Adults have one demand curve and children have another.

Benjamin wants to decide how many haircuts to sell to adults and how many to sell to children. We will call these quantities Q_A and Q_C. Then Benjamin wants to choose Q_A and Q_C so that his marginal revenue in the adults' market, his marginal revenue in the children's market, and the marginal cost to him of producing $Q_A + Q_C$ haircuts are all equal.

EXERCISE 10.9 Explain why Benjamin wants all three of these numbers to be equal. If any two were not equal, how could he alter his behavior to make himself better off? How would this change in his behavior tend to equalize the three quantities?

Exhibit 10-11 shows a graphic method for determining how many haircuts Benjamin will sell to each group. The MR_A and MR_C curves are the marginal

Exhibit 10-11 **Third-Degree Price Discrimination by a Monopolist in Two Markets**

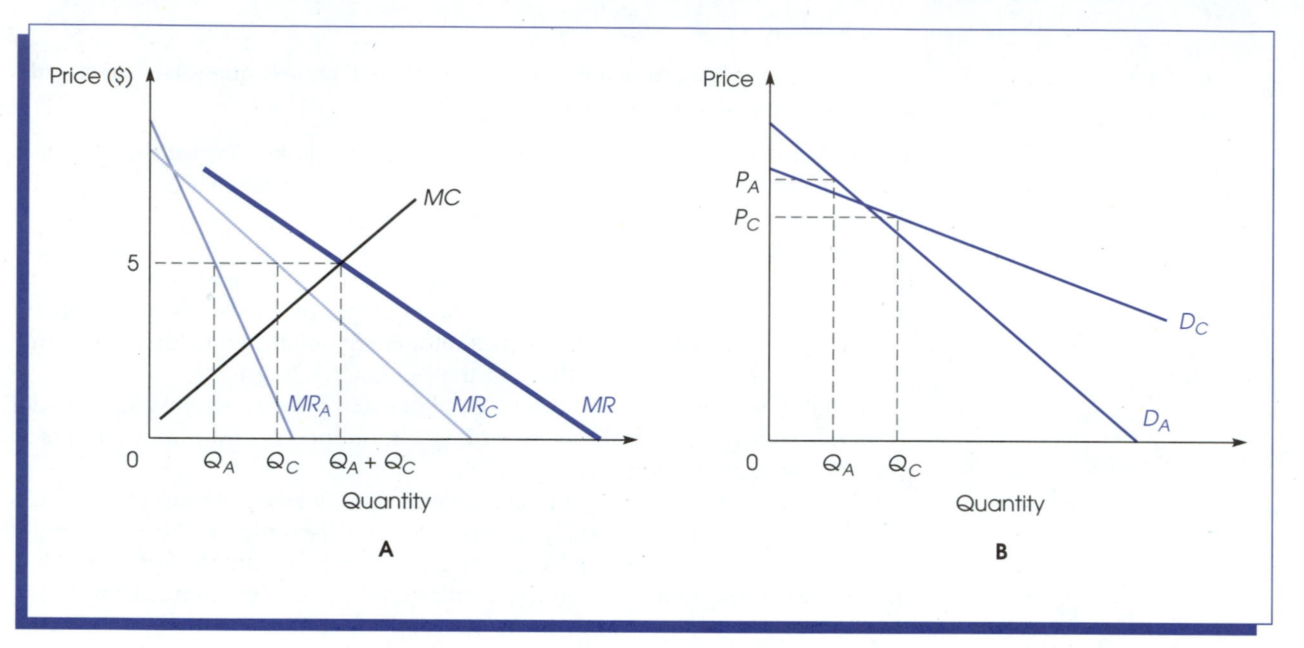

Benjamin Barker sells haircuts to adults and children. The two groups have different marginal revenue curves, labeled MR_A and MR_C in panel A. The heavier curve MR is obtained by horizontally summing the curves MR_A and MR_C. Benjamin produces the quantity $Q_A + Q_C$ where MC crosses MR, selling Q_A haircuts to adults and Q_C to children. He chooses the corresponding prices of the adults' and children's demand curves, which are shown in panel B.

revenue curves that he faces in the adults' and children's markets. The MR curve is obtained by summing MR_A and MR_C horizontally. That is, for any price, read the corresponding quantities off MR_A and MR_C; then add these to get the corresponding quantity on MR.

Benjamin can equalize his marginal cost and both marginal revenues by choosing the quantity where his marginal cost curve MC crosses the MR curve. In the exhibit this means that he produces a total of $Q_A + Q_C$ haircuts, so that his marginal cost is \$5 per haircut. He sells Q_A of these haircuts to adults and Q_C to children, so that his marginal revenue is \$5 per haircut in each market.

Once Benjamin has chosen the quantities Q_A and Q_C, he reads prices off the adults' and children's demand curves, just like any good monopolist. These prices, P_A and P_C, are shown in panel B of Exhibit 10-11.

Elasticities and Price Discrimination

There is an interesting relationship between the prices P_A and P_C in Exhibit 10–11. Write η_A for the elasticity of the adults' demand curve at P_A and η_C for the elasticity of the children's demand curve at P_C. Since the marginal revenue is \$5 in each market, the equation that relates price to marginal revenue says that

$$P_A\left[1-\left(\frac{1}{|\eta_A|}\right)\right] = \$5 \text{ and } P_C\left[1-\left(\frac{1}{|\eta_C|}\right)\right] = \$5$$

It follows that

$$P_A\left[1-\left(\frac{1}{|\eta_A|}\right)\right] = P_C\left[1-\left(\frac{1}{|\eta_C|}\right)\right]$$

From this equation we can see that

$$\text{if } |\eta_C| > |\eta_A|, \text{ then } P_C < P_A$$

whereas

$$\text{if } |\eta_C| < |\eta_A|, \text{ then } P_C > P_A$$

In other words:

The group with the more elastic demand is charged the lower price.

Roughly, this means that the monopolist will charge less in the market where he is closer to being a competitor.

Movie theaters that offer discounts to students and senior citizens are engaging in third-degree price discrimination. So are railroads that sell special "youth passes." In each case a lower price is offered to these customers who are more sensitive to price, which is to say, to those with the more elastic demand. A possible reason for this more elastic demand is that students and senior citizens have either below-average incomes or low values of time. In either case they will be more likely than others to shop around for alternatives when prices go up. This makes it desirable to price discriminate in their favor.

Price Discrimination and Welfare

When a monopolist moves from setting a single price to practicing third-degree price discrimination, his total output might go either up or down. Social welfare can also go either up or down. It is often quite difficult to predict the direction of the change in social welfare. However, under a variety of conditions, it is possible to prove that *if* total output falls, *then* social welfare must fall also. The proof is not easy.[5]

[5]See R. Schmalensee, "Output and Welfare Implications of Monopolistic Third-Degree Price Discrimination," *American Economic Review* 71 (1981):242–247; H. Varian, "Price Discrimination and Social Welfare," *American Economic Review* 75 (1985):870–875; and M. Schwartz, "Third-Degree Price Discrimination and Output: Generalizing a Welfare Result," *American Economic Review* 80 (1990): 1259–1263.

Conditions for Price Discrimination

We can now summarize the conditions necessary to make price discrimination profitable. First, the seller must have some degree of monopoly power. (Thus, wheat farmers never offer senior citizen discounts.) Second, resales must be controllable. Therefore, price discrimination is most often observed in markets for goods that have to be consumed immediately upon purchase, such as education. (Does your college charge different tuitions to different students by offering scholarship aid to some and not to others?) Each of these two conditions applies to any form of price discrimination. Finally, in the case of third-degree price discrimination, some mechanism must be found for offering lower prices to precisely those demanders who are more sensitive to price. (Are those students who get scholarships by and large the ones who would be most likely to go elsewhere—or to not attend college at all—if they had to pay full tuition?)[6]

Examples of Price Discrimination

Discount coupons for supermarket shopping constitute a mechanism for offering a lower price to appropriate consumers. The shoppers who find it worth their while to clip these coupons are those with a relatively low value of time (for example, because their wages are low); by and large, these are the customers with a greater propensity for comparison shopping. The supermarket's ideal pricing policy is, "lower prices to those who would otherwise shop elsewhere." A practical approximation to this ideal is, "lower prices to those with enough free time to clip coupons."

It is important to notice that there would be no point to coupons if everyone redeemed them; in this case the store could just lower its prices and have the same effect. Similarly, there would be no point to coupons if only a random set of customers redeemed them. The point of coupons is that they offer lower prices to precisely those customers who are most sensitive to price.[7]

Manufacturers' rebates (for example, buy a coffeemaker and get a coupon that can be redeemed for $5) work much the same way. They are redeemed by precisely the shoppers who are willing to devote some extra time and energy to recovering a few dollars. These are the same shoppers who are most likely to compare prices at many stores or to decide to do without a coffeemaker altogether.

Promotions that require customers to save game cards, scratch off designated areas to reveal numbers, and the like serve the same purpose. These promotions may appeal primarily to families with children, who can be enlisted to paste, scratch, tear, and cut. It is reasonable to think that those with children are those most likely to be watching pennies in their food budgets.

---

[6]In 1988 MIT sent a letter to parents announcing that it was raising both tuition and the amount of scholarship aid that it would provide. How would the parents have reacted if MIT had announced that it was going to exercise monopoly power more fully through an increase in price discrimination?

[7]In 1996, basketball star Michael Jordan earned over $52 million in salary and endorsement income. It is probable that he does not clip supermarket coupons.

Students sometimes reason that if grocery stores engage in price discrimination, for which monopoly power is a prerequisite, then grocery stores must be monopolies, so we should never use the competitive model when we study them. But, in fact, we use different models to describe different phenomena. Consider a simple analogy from physics: If we want to describe the interactions of several moving balls on a billiard table, it is often safe to assume there is no friction, because friction does not play an important role in the phenomenon under study. But if we want to explain why the balls roll instead of slide, friction suddenly becomes important and we switch to a description that takes account of it. Similarly, when we want to study the determination of prices and quantities in the grocery industry, the assumption of competition may be close enough to truth to yield deep and important insights. When we switch to studying a phenomenon like price discrimination, monopoly power acquires central importance and must be explicitly included in the description.

When you order a pizza and get "free delivery," you are being charged less for a pizza than somebody who picks one up at the take-out counter. (When you take out, you pay for both the pizza and for gasoline, making the effective price of the pizza higher.) People ordering pizzas by telephone have more elastic demand because they can easily hang up the phone and order a pizza elsewhere. Whenever a producer offers "free extras" that only some customers take, you should ask how the extras have been designed to appeal to the more elastic demanders.

Why, for example, do coffee shops in downtown office buildings typically offer free cup lids? Such a coffee shop has two classes of customers: those who work in the building and those who pass by the building on their way to work elsewhere. With regard to the first group, the shop has some monopoly power (people would rather not go outside for coffee). With regard to the second, it is nearly in perfect competition (people walking by can always stop somewhere else for coffee). Therefore, they would like to offer a "free extra"—such as a cup lid—that is taken primarily by those who are walking by.[8]

Many hotels offer rooms at two different prices. Often the only difference between a $50 room and a $60 room is $10. If you call ahead for a reservation, you will get a $50 room. If you walk in at 11 P.M. looking tired, the $50 rooms will all be filled.

Airlines charge less for travelers who are staying over a Saturday night. These are the nonbusiness travelers who are likely to find another mode of transportation, or choose not to travel, when prices are high.

Many jewelry stores will give you a discount on a new watch if you trade in your old watch. The watches they receive as trade-ins are immediately discarded. People who already have watches are effectively charged less than those who don't. Can you see why the first group has the more elastic demand?

[8]This example, invented by Robert Topel of the University of Chicago, is intended to be frivolous. An alternative (and perhaps more plausible) explanation is that cup lids are priced at marginal cost, and the best practical approximation to a marginal cost of .001¢ is zero.

Many furniture stores offer "free delivery." If a delivery ordinarily costs $25 and all customers take advantage of the free delivery, then the price of furniture increases by $25 and the "free delivery" has no real effect.

What, then, is the point of free delivery? A more sophisticated analysis must recognize that if only some customers accept the free delivery, then it can be a form of price discrimination. Professor Robert Michaels of the California State University at Fullerton points out that "free delivery is not free for many buyers." You have to wait at home for the delivery truck and are often not told when to expect it; if you and the driver miss each other, you have to wait a long time for your delivery to be rescheduled. Customers with a low enough opportunity cost to wait at home for a weekday delivery also have a low opportunity cost of shopping and hence more elastic demand for furniture from a particular store. Free delivery (and hence an effectively lower price) is offered to the more elastic demanders.

In each of these examples you should give thought to the question of how resales are controlled. Firms have been known to get very creative about this. Many years ago the Rohm and Haas chemical company produced a compound called methyl methacrylate that was used both in dentistry and industrial production. There were few good substitutes for this compound in dentistry, but there were many in industry. As a result, dentists were charged a much higher price than industrial users; as a further result, industrial users bought cheap and sold to dentists. The marketing directors at Rohm and Haas considered many strategies to combat this activity, one of which was to add arsenic to the compound before selling it in the industrial market. This plan was never implemented, but a closely related one was: They started a *rumor* that they had added the arsenic. This had the desired effect.

Counterexamples

Price discrimination is evidence of monopoly power, and students confronted with so many examples sometimes infer that monopoly power is ubiquitous. It is important, then, to realize that many practices having the appearance of price discrimination are, in fact, something quite different. Price discrimination occurs when the same product is sold at two different prices. Often, a careful examination will reveal that two apparently identical products are actually quite different.

Many restaurants offer a lower price at the salad bar to those who order an entrée. This has the appearance of price discrimination, but an alternative explanation is that people who order entrées tend to take less food at the salad bar. This would explain a lower price on the basis of a lower cost to the restaurant.

Ice cream shops usually charge less for a second scoop than for a first. Is this second-degree price discrimination? Neither the preparation of the cone, nor the opening of the freezer, nor the ringing of the cash register has to be repeated for the second scoop of ice cream. Such factors make serving the second scoop genuinely cheaper for the ice cream shop and provide an alternative explanation.

In fact, almost everything that appears to be price discrimination admits at least one alternative explanation. Alternative theories are available even for the most widely accepted examples, some of which we have used in this book.

Earlier we offered grocery store coupons as an example of price discrimination. A different hypothesis is that coupon-clippers have low values of time and hence can arrange to do their shopping when the store is not crowded. Non-clippers arrive at 5 P.M. on their way home from work, when the store is crowded, adding to general congestion and the lengths of the checkout lines. The non-clippers are therefore genuinely more expensive to serve, and so pay higher prices.

An objection to this new theory is that if grocery stores really want to charge less at certain times of the day, they can just announce discount prices for those who shop at those times. There is no need to introduce the artifice of coupons. A counter to the objection is that time-of-day discounts can be a logistical nightmare: What do you do with the customer who complains that he would have checked out at 2:59 rather than 3:01 if only he had gotten competent service at the meat counter?

In general, economists who are disinclined to believe in substantial monopoly power will welcome this kind of analysis. Those who believe that monopoly power is a significant economic force will be more comfortable with a diagnosis of price discrimination. But in analyzing any particular market, it pays to put prejudice aside and weigh the inherent plausibility of competing theories.

Two-Part Tariffs

The World Bank Describes how two-part tariffs are used in electricity markets at: http://www.worldbank.org/html/fpd/notes/47/47Bacon.html

Disneyland amusement park has substantial monopoly power. How should Disneyland wield that power? Should it charge a low admission price, to draw lots of visitors who will pay monopoly prices for the rides and other attractions? Or should it charge low prices for the rides, to draw lots of visitors who will pay a monopoly price to get in?

Polaroid is the only maker of Polaroid cameras and Polaroid film. Should the company charge a low price for the cameras to increase the demand for high-priced film? Or should it charge a low price for film to increase the demand for high-priced cameras?

Some monopolists—like Disneyland and Polaroid—get to charge their customers twice. There's an initial fee (for admission to the park or the Polaroid camera) and then ongoing charges for the purchase of goods or services (like ride tickets or Polaroid film).

In both examples, the initial fee itself buys you nothing except the right to make future purchases. For the most part, the only reason to enter Disneyland is so you can spend more money after you get inside. And surely the only reason to buy a Polaroid camera is so you can start buying and using film.

There are more examples. Some private dining clubs charge yearly membership fees that entitle the member to buy meals. Banks charge annual fees for credit cards that allow you to borrow money at interest. Neither the membership nor the credit card is of any value until you start using it.[9]

---

[9]With the credit card, as with Disneyland, our assumptions are only approximations to the truth: In reality, some people want to enter Disneyland just to enjoy the atmosphere, and some people want credit cards just for convenience, paying off their full balances each month to avoid all interest charges. But if there are few enough of those unusual people, our analysis will be close to correct.

Exhibit 10–12 Pricing Strategy with a Two-Part Tariff

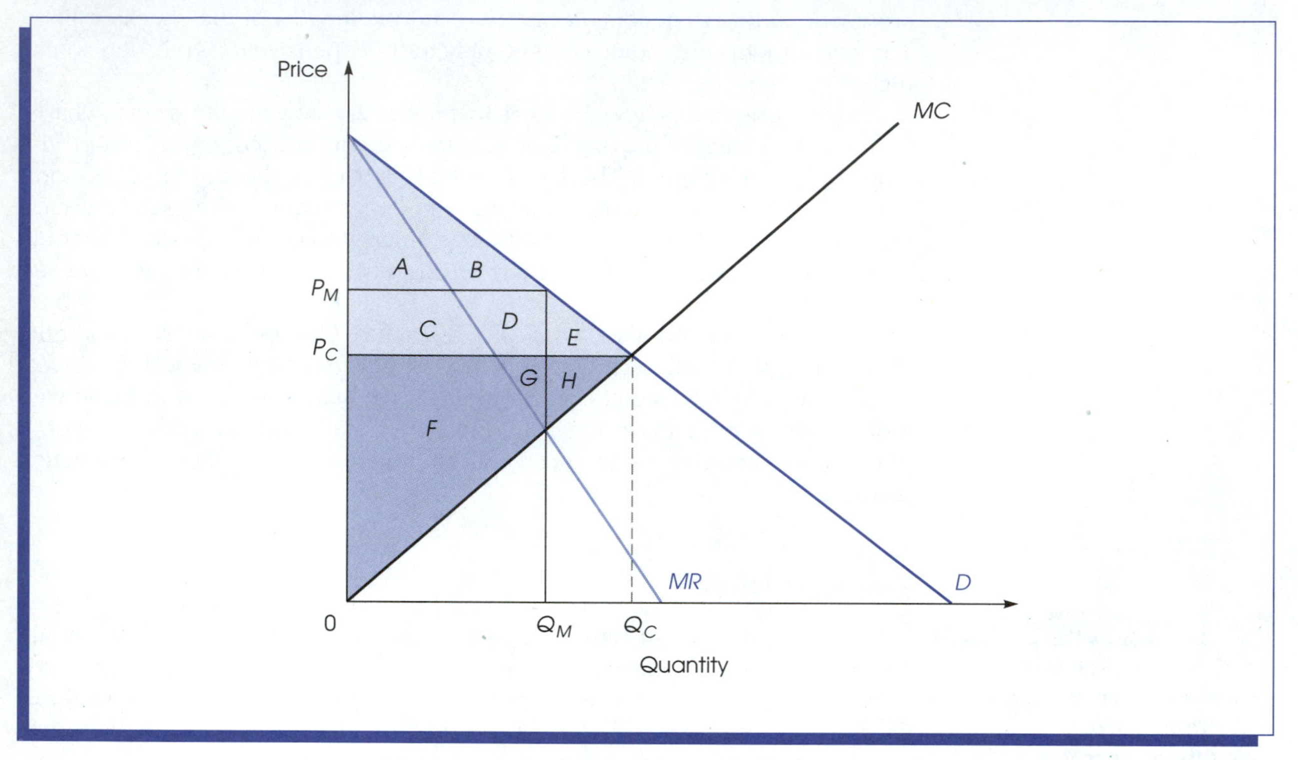

If the firm sells the monopoly quantity Q_M at the monopoly price P_M, it will earn a producer's surplus of $C + D + F + G$ and will be able to charge the consumer $A + B$ as an entry fee. But if it sells the competitive quantity Q_C at the lower price P_c, it will earn the smaller producer's surplus $F + G + H$ while collecting the larger entry fee $A + B + C + D + E$. Under the second strategy, the firm's net earnings are increased by $E + H$.

Two-part tariff An entry fee that allows you to purchase goods or services.

When a firm charges a fee for the right to buy its products, we say that it has set a **two-part tariff**. Most of the time, the word *tariff* refers to a tax on imported goods, but the phrase *two-part tariff* is an exception to the rule. Here the word *tariff* simply means "price."

Setting the Entry Fee

Let's figure out the optimal strategy for a two-part tariff monopolist. Exhibit 10–12 shows the demand, marginal revenue, and marginal cost curves for a firm such as Disneyland or Polaroid. The quantity on the horizontal axis is the quantity of the good that customers purchase *after* they've paid the entry fee; in the case of Disneyland it is the quantity of rides, while in the case of Polaroid it is the quantity of film.

First let's see what happens if the firm charges the monopoly price P_M in Exhibit 10–12. The first observation is that the firm earns $C + D + F + G$ in producer's surplus on the sale of the ride tickets, film, or whatever else it is selling. Now how much will the firm charge consumers for the right to buy those products? The answer, of course, is that it will charge the maximum amount consumers are willing to pay—and that amount is measured by the consumer's surplus, in this case $A + B$. So if the firm charges the price P_M for its products, it will earn $C + D + F + G$ in producer's surplus on the sales, and an additional $A + B$ in admission fees. The total is $A + B + C + D + F + G$. Notice that consumers are left with no surplus at all.

Now let's see what happens if the firm charges the competitive price P_C. Producer's surplus on product sales is reduced to $F + G + H$. But admission fees can be raised $A + B + C + D + E$, giving the firm a total of $A + B + C + D + E + F + G + H$. This is more than it earns at the monopoly price P_M. Once again, consumers are left with no surplus at all. All of the social gain goes to the firm.

So the firm does best by charging a competitive price for its goods. That way, it is therefore not surprising that the firm does best by charging a competitive price—as long as it is collecting all the social gain, it will want that social gain to be as large as possible, and that's accomplished by competitive pricing.

Differences Among Customers

Let's be clear on what it means to charge the full consumer's surplus as an admission fee. Here's an example. Suppose in Exhibit 10–12, that area $A + B + C + D + E$ is equal to \$1,000, and the firm has 100 identical customers. Then each of the 100 customers earns a consumer's surplus of \$10, so the right admission fee is \$10 per customer.

But what if the customers are not identical? Suppose, for example, that one of them earns a consumer's surplus of \$901, while the others earn \$1 each. Then area $A + B + C + D + E$ will still equal \$1,000, but if the monopolist tries to capture this area by charging an admission fee of \$10, it will drive away 99% of its customers!

The problem here is that while the *average* customer earns a consumer's surplus of \$10, it's not true that every customer is average, except in the case where every customer is identical. As long as all (or most) of the customers are *nearly* identical, they will all (or almost all) earn consumer's surpluses of *about* \$10, so an admission fee of just a bit under \$10 will retain all (or most) of the customers and allow the monopolist to earn nearly \$1,000 in admission fees. But when the differences among customers are dramatic, the monopolist cannot capture the bulk of the consumers' surplus in this way. In this case, our conclusion—that the monopolist should price his product competitively—no longer holds.

Two-Part Tariffs and Price Discrimination

When there are significant differences among customers, a monopolist will look for opportunities to price discriminate. For a two-part tariff monopolist, there's a clear strategy for price discrimination: By charging a low entry fee and a high price for the product, the monopolist effectively charges lower prices to the lightest users, and there is a good chance that the lightest users are precisely the ones who will walk away in the absence of a discount.

At Disneyland, for example, those patrons who come only to ride the roller coaster are very different from those who feel a compulsion to go on every ride. Disneyland might reasonably expect that those in the former group will go and find a *different* roller coaster unless they get a discount, while those in the latter group are unlikely to find many good substitutes for Disneyland. Thus, the goal is to target discounts to the roller-coaster-only crowd. This goal is accomplished through a low admission price coupled with a high price for ride tickets; roller-coaster riders buy only one ticket while their more compulsive neighbors buy dozens.

Similarly, if Polaroid charges a low price for cameras and a high price for film, it is effectively charging more to those who take a lot of pictures. The *real* goal is to charge more to those who are willing to pay the most; but by and large, those who are willing to pay the most might be precisely the ones who take the most pictures.

The Bottom Line

A two-part tariff monopolist with identical customers will want to capture as much surplus as possible by setting a low (competitive) price for the product and a high admission fee. A two-part tariff monopolist with very different customers will want to price discriminately by setting a low admission fee and a high price for the product.

The typical firm faces a base of customers who are neither identical nor dramatically different, and therefore will want to compromise between the two strategies; firms with more diverse groups of customers will shade more toward the high admission fee.

Sometimes a firm has to experiment for a while in order to learn how different its customers are. Disneyland has gone through a series of different pricing policies, ranging from free admission and high-priced rides to free rides and high-priced admission.

Popcorn at the Movie Theater

Suppose you own a movie theater, where you have some monopoly power and you make money both at the box office and the popcorn stand. Should you charge a high price for admission and a low price for popcorn, or vice versa?

If your customers are all identical, Exhibit 10–12 provides the answer, interpreting the "price" and "quantity" in that exhibit as the price and quantity of popcorn. By pricing popcorn competitively, you earn a total of $A + B + C + D + E + F + G$ in producer's surplus at the popcorn stand plus admission fees at the box office. If you priced the popcorn at the higher price P_M, you would earn only $A + B + C + D + F + G$. Thus, you should price the popcorn competitively.

People who have not studied economics usually get this wrong. They reason that once customers have entered the theater, the theater owner might as well take advantage of his monopoly power at the popcorn stand. That argument overlooks the fact that higher prices at the popcorn stand must mean either lower prices at the box office or fewer people going to the movies.

What if the customers are very different? Then you might think that you can apply the same reasoning we used for Disneyland and Polaroid cameras, to conclude that popcorn should be priced high and the admission fee should be low in order to price discriminate. But that's not quite right. The case of the movie theater is not exactly like the case of the Polaroid camera, and here's why: A Polaroid camera is valuable *only* because it allows you to buy film, but it's not true that admission to the movie theater is valuable only because it allows you to buy popcorn. Consumers earn surplus just by entering the premises and being allowed to see the movie. A theater owner will want to try to capture some of that surplus. The best way to do so is not apparent from Exhibit 10–12, which shows only the surplus earned at the popcorn stand and not the surplus earned from seeing the movie.

The problem is to charge a high overall price to those who are willing to pay that price and a low overall price to those who would otherwise go to a ball game or stay home and watch TV. *If* the people who especially love going to the movies are the same people who buy a lot of popcorn, then the right strategy is to price discriminate with a high price at the popcorn stand. But if the people who especially love going to the movies are the same people who buy relatively *little* popcorn, then the right strategy can be to price discriminate in their favor with a *low* price at the popcorn stand—even with a price below marginal cost. You will be invited to work out the details of the analysis in Problem 32 at the end of this chapter.

summary

A firm has monopoly power when it faces a downward-sloping demand curve for its product. Such a firm also faces a downward-sloping marginal revenue curve that lies everywhere below the demand curve. Like any producer, the monopoly firm chooses the quantity where marginal cost equals marginal revenue, and then charges the price that corresponds to that quantity on the demand curve.

Because marginal revenue lies below demand, the monopolist chooses a quantity at which marginal cost is less than the consumer's marginal value. Thus, it underproduces from the point of view of social welfare. Various public policies can address this problem. If the monopolist is given a subsidy per unit of output, it will increase production. If a price ceiling is set at the competitive price, the monopolist will essentially face a flat marginal revenue curve and behave like a competitor.

Monopolies arise for various reasons. An industry where each firm's average cost curve is decreasing at the point where it crosses market demand is known as a natural monopoly. If price were set equal to marginal cost in such an industry, profits would be negative and no firms would enter. A monopoly producer, however, may be able to survive since he can charge a price that is higher than marginal cost.

One common source of natural monopoly is the combination of high fixed costs and low marginal costs. However, this is not the only source.

Other sources of monopoly power include patents, the control of resources, and barriers to entry erected by the government.

Sometimes a monopolist can increase its profits by charging different prices for identical items. This practice is known as price discrimination. In first-degree price discrimination, each consumer is charged the maximum he would be willing to pay for each item. If successful, this allows the monopolist to collect all of the social gain for himself, and it provides an incentive to produce the competitive quantity. In practice, perfect first-degree price discrimination is almost never possible, but it can sometimes be approximated.

In second-degree price discrimination, each customer is offered the same set of prices, but prices vary with the items purchased. Quantity discounts can be an example of second-degree price discrimination. However, quantity discounts are not always price discrimination. They can result instead from genuine cost savings to the seller when larger quantities are exchanged.

The most common type of price discrimination is third-degree price discrimination, in which two identifiably different groups of customers are charged different prices. In this case the lower price will go to the group with the more elastic demand curve. Senior citizen discounts at movie theaters are an example.

For price discrimination to be profitable, the firm must have monopoly power, must be able to find a device that discriminates in favor of the appropriate group, and must be able to prevent resales.

Another pricing policy available to some monopolists is a two-part tariff, where the customer is charged a one-time fee for the right to buy goods from the monopolist. If the monopolist prices at marginal cost and sets an entry fee equal to the consumer's surplus, he can maximize social gain and capture all of this gain for himself. However, if different consumers have different demand curves, this strategy requires knowing each consumer's demand curve and setting his entry fee accordingly. In practice, this is usually not possible. Therefore, the monopolist's pricing problem is a difficult one. Pricing at marginal cost creates more gain for him to capture through entry fees. On the other hand, in some cases (like Polaroid film), pricing above marginal cost offers the opportunity to price discriminate. Choosing the right strategy is a complicated matter, involving both the characteristics of the product and the characteristics of the demanders.

Review Questions

R1. Why does a monopolist's marginal revenue curve lie below its demand curve? In what way does this imply that the monopolist will choose an inefficient level of output?

R2. On which part of its demand curve, the elastic or the inelastic, does a monopolist firm always operate? If it were operating on the other part of the demand curve, explain how it could increase profits.

R3. Draw a graph to illustrate the effect on social welfare when a monopolist is subjected to an excise tax. Do the same when it is given an optimal subsidy.

R4. Show the effect of an optimal price ceiling on a monopolist's output.

R5. What are some of the problems with regulating a monopolist's rate of return?

R6. List some of the sources of monopoly power.

R7. How and why must the welfare analysis of monopoly be modified when there is a natural monopoly? When there is a monopoly due to the granting of a patent?

R8. Describe the three types of price discrimination. Give examples of each.

R9. Describe the conditions necessary for successful price discrimination.

R10. What is a two-part tariff?

R11. Why might a monopolist who can charge an entry fee choose to price his product at marginal cost? Why might this strategy fail?

Numerical Exercises

N1. Suppose that a monopolist faces the demand curve

$$Q = a - bP$$

where a and b are constants. Show that his marginal revenue curve is given approximately by the equation

$$MR = \frac{a - 2Q}{b}$$

(This approximation becomes exact when very small units are chosen.)

N2. Suppose that a monopolist sells in two markets with demand curves

$$Q_A = 100 - 10P_A$$
$$Q_B = 8 - 2P_B$$

a. Show that for any given quantity, demand is more elastic in market A than in market B.

b. Suppose that the monopolist produces at zero marginal cost. How much does he supply in each market, and what prices does he charge? (*Hint:* Use the formula for marginal revenue from the preceding problem.)

c. Suppose that the monopolist's marginal cost curve is given by

$$MC = Q/21$$

How much does he supply in each market, and what prices does he charge?

d. Reconcile your answers to parts a, b, and c with the statement in the text that the group with more elastic demand is always charged the lower price.

e. Suppose that the monopolist's marginal cost curve is given by

$$MC = Q/3$$

What will the monopolist do?

N3. A monopoly barber sells haircuts to adults for \$30 and to children for \$10. Let η_A represent adults' elasticity of demand for haircuts and let η_C represent children's elasticity of demand.

a. Explain why $|\eta_A|$ and $|\eta_C|$ must both be greater than 1.

b. Find a formula for η_A in terms of η_C.

c. What is the largest possible value for $|\eta_A|$?

Problem Set

1. **True or False:** Unlike a competitor, a monopolist can charge any price he wants to.

2. **True or False:** One difference between a monopolist and a competitor is that if a monopolist increased his price, he could increase his profits.

3. Suppose that the Airliner Bar is the only bar in town and that new entry is prohibited by law. In each of the circumstances described by problems 21–30 at the end of Chapter 7, determine the effect on the price and quantity of drinks provided at the Airliner.

4. Suppose that Al's Car Wash is the only car wash in town and that new entry is prohibited by law. In each of the circumstances described in problems 31–41 at the end of Chapter 7, determine the effect on the price and quantity of car washes provided by Al's.

5. Suppose that Bambi's House of Goose Liver is the only restaurant in town and that new entry is prohibited by law. In each of the circumstances described by problems 42–56 at the end of Chapter 7, determine the effect on the price and quantity of meals at Bambi's.

6. A monopolistic firm produces widgets at a constant marginal cost of $10 apiece. One day it discovers a new production process that would lower its marginal cost by $1 per widget. Use a graph to show how much its producer's surplus will increase if it adopts the new production process.

7. For a good supplied by a monopolist, how does a sales tax of $1 per item affect the marginal revenue curve?

8. We know that for a competitively supplied good the economic incidence of a tax is independent of the legal incidence; that is, a sales tax and an excise tax of equal magnitudes have exactly the same effects. Is the same thing true for a good supplied by a monopolist?

9. True or False: An excise tax on a monopolist that causes quantity to fall by one unit is just as detrimental to social welfare as an excise tax on a competitive industry that causes quantity to fall by one unit.

10. True or False: If the supply of land is fixed, then it can be equally efficient for land to be supplied by a monopolist or by competitors.

11. Snidely Whiplash owns all the houses in the Yukon Territory, where he charges the residents so much for rent that if he charged any more, they would all leave the territory. The residents (who are all identical) have always shopped at competitive grocery stores. However, Snidely has just bought all the grocery stores in the Territory, and is planning to charge a monopoly price for groceries.

    a. Use a graph to illustrate the market for groceries in the Yukon Territory. On your graph, show how much Snidely will have to cut the rent on houses when he raises the price of food.

    b. Is it a good idea for Snidely to raise the price of groceries? Why or why not?

12. At MacAdam University, all profits from the dining services are used to fund scholarships for the students. True or False: Because the profits are returned to them anyway, students won't care if the dining services charge

monopoly prices. (Assume that all students have the same demand for dining services and all students receive equal shares of the scholarships.)

13. Alcoa is a monopoly producer of the aluminum used to make soda cans. The soda companies that demand those cans all pay the same price. Suppose the soda companies band together and offer Alcoa a cash payment in exchange for Alcoa's setting quantities and prices as if it were a competitive industry. Is there some cash payment that will be acceptable to both the soda companies and to Alcoa? Use a graph to justify your answer by showing the maximum amount the soda companies would offer and the minimum amount Alcoa would accept.

14. Elmer is a monopolist in the carrot industry. His customers have formed an organization that proposes to purchase Elmer's carrot patch and run it for the mutual good of the new owners.

a. Use a graph to show the number of carrots that Elmer produces, and the number of carrots that will be produced if the organization accomplishes its goals.

b. In terms of your graph, suggest an amount that the organization should pay Elmer for his carrot patch. The amount you suggest should be something that Elmer will be happy to accept and that the organization will be happy to pay.

15. Fuzzy dice are produced only by Americans and consumed only by non-Americans. Can an excise tax on fuzzy dice improve the welfare of Americans? If so, use a graph to illustrate the optimal size of the excise tax. If not, use a graph to show why any excise tax must create a deadweight loss for Americans.

16. The following table shows the total cost of producing various quantities of shoehorns and the total value of those shoehorns to consumers. What are the price and quantity produced if the shoehorn industry is competitive? What are they if it is monopolized? What is the extent of the social loss due to the existence of the monopoly? (The answers to all of these questions should be *numbers*. Assume that only a whole number of shoehorns can be produced.)

Q	*TC*	*TV*	*Q*	*TC*	*TV*
1	$1	$9	5	$15	$35
2	3	17	6	21	39
3	6	24	7	28	42
4	10	30	8	36	44

The next four problems all refer to the domestic hatpin industry, which is monopolized. The graph on the next page shows the U.S. demand for hatpins and the monopoly producer's marginal cost curve. There is also a foreign hatpin market, in which the going price of hatpins is $6.

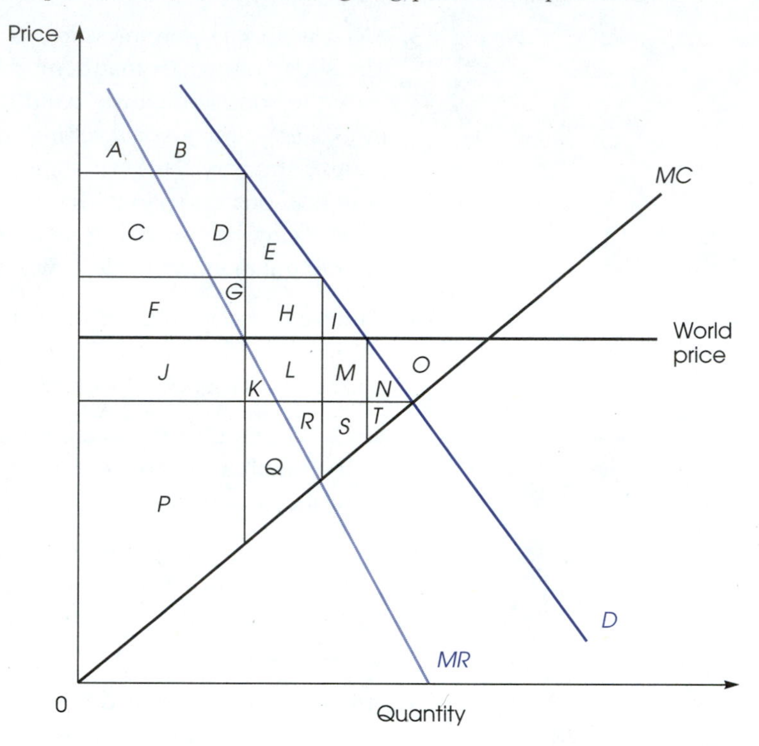

17. Suppose that all Americans are free to buy and sell hatpins in the foreign market. What is the deadweight loss from the existence of the domestic monopoly?

18. Suppose instead that it is illegal to buy or sell hatpins on the foreign market. Now what is the deadweight loss from the existence of the domestic monopoly?

19. Suppose instead that it is illegal to *sell* hatpins to foreigners, but perfectly legal to *buy* them from foreigners. Now what is the deadweight loss from the existence of the domestic monopoly?

20. Suppose instead that it is illegal to *buy* hatpins from foreigners but perfectly legal to *sell* them to foreigners. Now what is the deadweight loss from the existence of the domestic monopoly?

21. True or False: To make a natural monopolist behave more efficiently, subsidies will work better than price controls.

22. True or False: If a natural monopolist is required to earn zero profits, it will produce less than is optimal, but if any other kind of monopolist is required to earn zero profits, it will produce more than is optimal.

23. True or False: A regulated monopoly is more likely to engage in discriminatory hiring practices than is an unregulated monopoly.

24. Bad Ideas Inc. is the world's only manufacturer of disposable sweaters. After a sweater is made, Bad Ideas can attach buttons on the right, making it suitable for men, or on the left, making it suitable for women. No man will wear a woman's sweater and no woman will wear a man's sweater. Bad Ideas faces the following demand and marginal cost schedules for its sweaters:

Quantity	Men's Demand Price	Women's Demand Price	Marginal Cost
1	$10	$24	$1
2	9	16	1.5
3	8	12	2
4	7	9.50	2.5
5	6	4	3
6	5	0	3.5
7	4	0	4
8	3	0	4.5

How many sweaters does it produce? How many does it sell to men, and at what price? How many does it sell to women, and at what price?

25. True or False: Heavy competition among firms for a limited number of customers leads to such devices as discounts for students and senior citizens.

26. Many hotels allow children to stay in their parents' rooms for free. Why?

27. Some Canadian restaurants (especially in tourist areas) will accept U.S. currency at a more favorable exchange rate than the banks will give. Why?

28. In many cities, when three people share a taxicab to exactly the same address, the fare depends on whether the three were traveling together at the time they hailed the cab. Riders who know each other are charged less than those who don't. Why?

29. The Taos Pueblo is an ancient American Indian community in New Mexico that admits tourists. The admission fee is $5 per car plus $5 per camera.

a. Give an explanation of this pricing strategy that is based on price discrimination.

b. Give an explanation of this pricing strategy that is *not* based on price discrimination.

c. Which of your explanations do you believe? Why? What further evidence would help you to decide between your two theories?

30. Many cable television services will allow you to purchase viewing rights to several channels but will not allow you to purchase viewing rights to just one. Why might this be a profit-maximizing strategy for them? What determines the fee for the full cable service?

31. Hughes Tool produces a patented drill bit (thus, it has a monopoly on the bit). Only Hughes Tool can resharpen the bit. Suppose it costs Hughes Tool exactly $100 to resharpen a drill bit.

a. True or False: If all of Hughes Tool's customers value the drill bit equally, then Hughes Tool should charge exactly $100 for a resharpening.

b. True or False: If Hughes Tool's customers differ significantly in how much they value the drill bit, then Hughes Tool should charge exactly $100 for a resharpening.

c. If you see Hughes Tool taking steps to prevent competitors from offering resharpening services, what can you conclude about the diversity of Hughes Tool's customers?

32. Suppose you are the monopoly owner of a movie theater. You can provide popcorn at a marginal cost of 50¢ per bag. It costs you nothing to allow people to enter the theater. You have two customers, Gene and Roger. Gene never buys popcorn under any circumstances. Roger's demand for popcorn is the curve in the following graph:

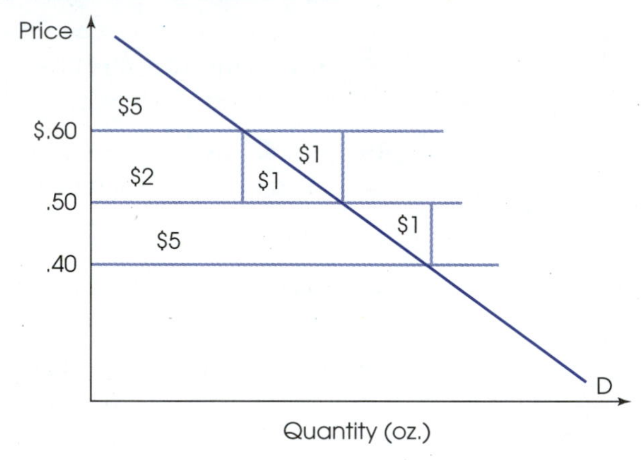

a. Suppose that Gene is willing to pay up to $4 to see the movie and Roger is willing to pay up to $10 to see the movie. How much should you charge for popcorn and how much should you charge for admission to the theater?

b. Suppose that Gene is willing to pay up to $9 to see the movie and Roger is willing to pay up to $10 to see the movie. How much should you charge for popcorn and how much should you charge for admission to the theater?

c. Suppose that Gene is willing to pay up to $25 to see the movie and Roger is willing to pay up to $10 to see the movie. How much should you charge for popcorn and how much should you charge for admission to the theater?

(*Hint:* In each case, consider whether you are better off setting the highest admission price that will attract *one* customer or the highest admission price that will attract *two* customers. Remember to account both for what you earn at the admission booth *and* what you earn (or lose) at the popcorn stand.)

Internet Exercise

In this chapter you have learned about the circumstances under which a monopolist would engage in price discrimination. Access the Internet site maintained by Anthony Becker at (http://www.stolaf.edu/people/becker/antitrust/subject.html). This site contains summaries of U.S. Supreme Court cases involving antitrust. Scroll down to the material on price discrimination to learn more about how U.S. antitrust law relates to price discrimination by reading one or more of the case summaries.

chapter 11

Market Power, Collusion, and Oligopoly

Market power is an elusive goal. It is limited everywhere by the threat of entry. Even a firm producing a unique product with no close substitutes might not be able to engage in monopoly pricing, because the profits that it would earn by doing so would lure entrants and destroy its market position.

But market power can be highly profitable to those who achieve it, and is therefore avidly pursued. In this chapter, we will look first at some of the strategies that firms employ in their quest for a monopoly position. These can include mergers, predatory pricing, and *fair trade* agreements. We will examine each strategy and each strategy's limits. We will also see that activities that appear to be attempts either to gain or to exploit monopoly power are not always what they seem.

Collusion among existing firms is one of the most straightforward and common methods of trying to monopolize a market. It is important enough that we devote an entire section to it, Section 11.2. Using tools from the theory of games, we will see why collusion is often doomed to fail.

We will then see that a collusive arrangement among firms that would ordinarily collapse under its own weight can at times be supported by various forms of regulation. This discussion occupies Section 11.3. While regulation sometimes plays this role, it also plays a variety of others, and there are a great number of theories of the regulatory process. We will survey a few ideas from this large body of thought.

Finally, we will turn from the pursuit of market power to its exercise. We already have (from Chapter 10) a simple model of monopoly behavior, which ignores the firm's need to respond to other firms' actions. In Section 11.4, we will survey some theories of oligopoly that provide a starting point for thinking about industries with small numbers of firms, each enjoying some monopoly power but each affected by the others' behavior. Under this heading, we will consider some classical models of oligopoly and the contemporary theory of contestable markets. In Section 11.5, we will look at the related theory of monopolistic competition, which also tries to model firms that exercise some degree of monopoly power while simultaneously competing with other firms.

11.1 Acquiring Market Power

In this section we will explore some methods that firms either use or are alleged to use in their attempts to acquire and exploit market power. We will explore the limits of these methods, and we will learn that they are not always what they seem.

Read articles on mergers and market power at http://www.pblutah.com/publications/present-index.html

Mergers

The issue of monopoly power arises whenever two firms merge to form a larger firm. Mergers can be roughly classified into two types. **Horizontal integration** combines two or more producers of the same product. An example would be the combination of Ford, Chrysler, and General Motors into a single company. **Vertical integration** combines firms one of which produces inputs for the other's production processes. An example would be the merger of a steel plant with an auto manufacturer.

Horizontal integration A merger of firms that produce the same product.

Vertical integration A merger between a firm that produces an input and a firm that uses that input.

Horizontal Integration

There are essentially two different reasons why firms might want to merge horizontally. First, there may be economies of scale or other increased efficiencies associated with size, so that a larger firm can produce output at a lower average cost. Second, there may be an opportunity for the larger firm to exercise some monopoly power. Of course, both motives may be present in a single merger.

From a welfare point of view, mergers are desirable insofar as they reduce costs, and they are undesirable insofar as they create monopoly power. Exhibit 11–1 illustrates the trade-off. We assume that the industry is initially competitive, with marginal cost curve MC. (The marginal cost curve is drawn horizontally in order to simplify the diagram; nothing of importance depends on this simplification.) If the firms in the industry merge, technical efficiencies will lower the marginal cost curve to MC', but they will also enable the new, larger firm to exercise monopoly power, producing the monopoly quantity Q', where MC' crosses the marginal revenue curve MR.

The welfare consequences of the merger are ambiguous. There is a gain of $F + G$, representing the cost savings due to greater efficiency (the rectangle F

Exhibit 11-1 A Horizontal Merger

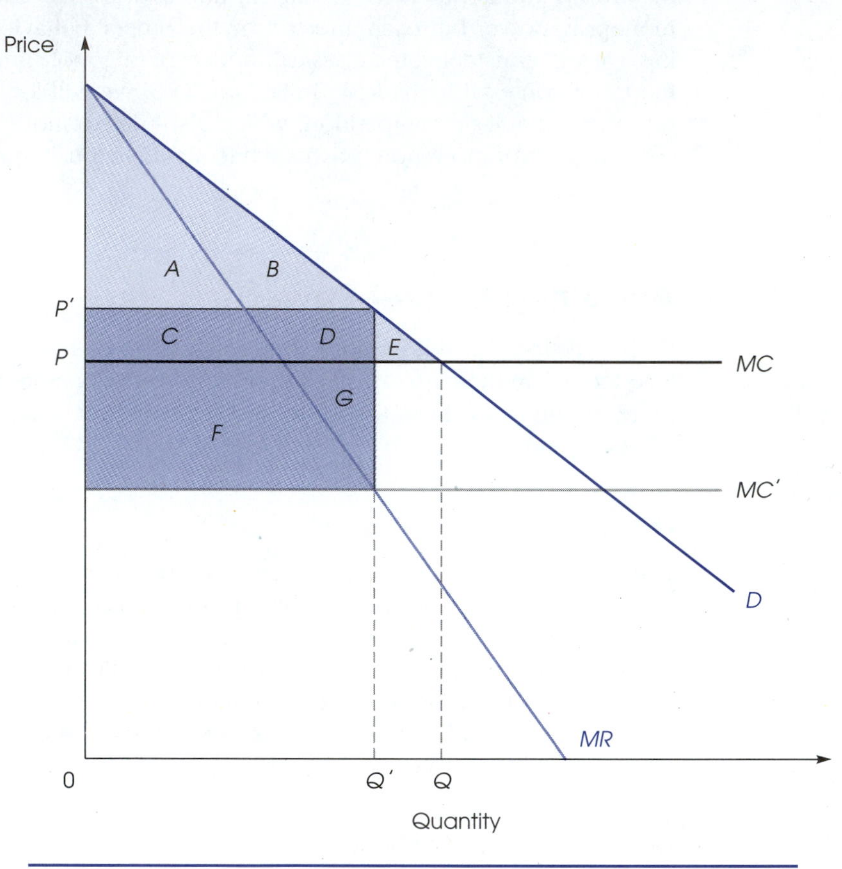

	Before Merger	After Merger
Consumers' Surplus	$A + B + C + D + E$	$A + B$
Producers' Surplus	—	$C + D + F + G$
Social Gain	$A + B + C + D + E$	$A + B + C + D + F + G$

Initially, the industry's marginal cost (= supply) curve is *MC*. If the industry is competitive, it produces the equilibrium output Q at the price P. Because the *MC* curve is horizontal, there is no producers' surplus.

Following a merger, marginal cost is reduced to MC', but the newly created firm has monopoly power and so produces the quantity Q', where MC' crosses the marginal revenue curve *MR*. The monopoly price is P'. The table above computes welfare before and after the merger.

+ G has area equal to Q' times the cost savings per unit). There is also a loss of E, due to the reduction in output. Which of these is greater will vary from one individual case to another.

If MC' is very much lower than MC, then the picture will look like Exhibit 11–2. In this case the monopoly price P' is actually lower than the competitive price P, and both consumers and producers gain from the merger.

EXERCISE 11.1 Suppose that the merger does not reduce costs at all, so that $MC = MC'$. Draw the appropriate graph. In this case does the merger have an unambiguous effect on social welfare?

The analysis here is incomplete if it is possible for another firm to enter the market. Even if the new entrant has the relatively high marginal cost curve *MC*, it can undercut the price *P′*. Sufficiently many such new entrants—or even just the threat of new entrants—will drive the market price back down to *P*.

Antitrust Policies

Learn about aspects of antitrust law and economics at: http://www.findlaw.com/01topics/01antitrust/index.html

The Sherman Act of 1890 and the Clayton Act of 1914 give the courts jurisdiction to prevent mergers that tend to reduce competition. There has been much controversy about exactly what criteria the courts should apply in determining whether a particular merger is illegal.

One viewpoint is that mergers should be prohibited only when they reduce economic efficiency. According to this viewpoint, the court should compare areas in Exhibit 11–1 before deciding whether or not to allow a particular merger. If a merger reduces costs by enough to make the graph look like Exhibit 11–2, then according to this viewpoint the merger should certainly be allowed.

A summary of the *Brown Shoe* case is at: http://www.stolaf.edu/people/becker/antitrust/summaries/370us294.html

In a series of decisions beginning with *Brown Shoe* v. *the United States* (1962), the Supreme Court under Chief Justice Earl Warren explicitly rejected this viewpoint. Instead, the Court placed particular emphasis on the welfare of small firms that are not involved in the merger. The Court held that the Sherman and Clayton acts should be interpreted so as to protect such firms by disallowing mergers that would make it difficult for them to compete. In these cases the Court took the position that a merger could be illegal precisely *because* it would lead to a reduction in costs, lower prices, and increased economic efficiency. The reason is that smaller, less efficient firms would not be able to survive in the new environment, and the Court considered the interests of those firms to be protected by the law.[1]

The most vocal critic of the Warren Court's position has been Judge Robert Bork. In his book, *The Antitrust Paradox*, Bork argues forcefully that the antitrust laws should be interpreted so as to promote economic efficiency (which

---

[1]Among the more important of these cases were *United States v. Vons Grocery* (1966) and *Federal Trade Commission v. Procter & Gamble Co.* (1967). The Court's position was stated quite clearly in *U.S.* v. *Philadelphia National Bank, et al.*: "A merger the effect of which 'may be substantially to lessen competition' is not saved because, on some ultimate reckoning of social or economic debits and credits, it may be deemed beneficial."

Exhibit 11-2 A Horizontal Merger Leading to a Large Cost Reduction

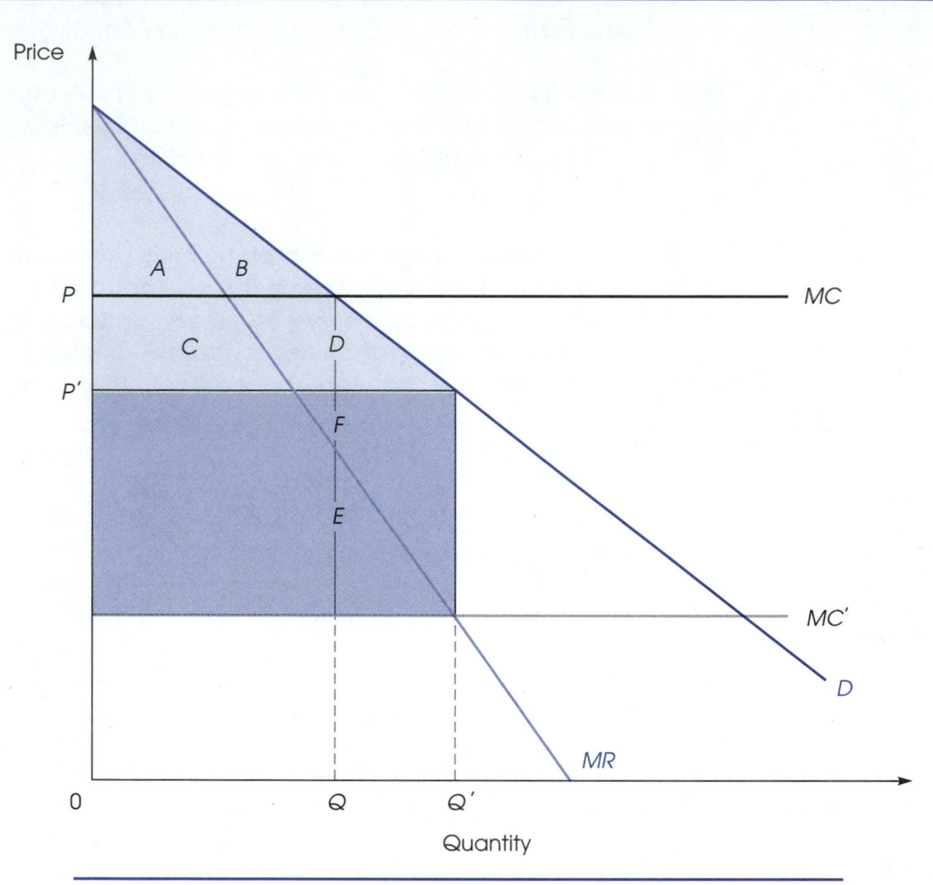

	Before Merger	After Merger
Consumers' Surplus	$A + B$	$A + B + C + D$
Producers' Surplus	—	$E + F$
Social Gain	$A + B$	$A + B + C + D + E + F$

If the competitive industry's marginal cost curve is MC, and if a merger converts the industry into a monopoly with the much lower marginal cost curve MC', then price will fall from P to P', benefiting both consumers and producers.

he calls *consumer welfare*).[2] He argues that the interests of consumers should be given as much weight as the interests of small businesses, and that preventing mergers that would benefit consumers constitutes a misapplication of the law.

Economists disagree about both positive and normative aspects of merger policy. On the positive side, there is disagreement about whether mergers frequently yield substantial cost reductions. Many economists believe that such savings are rare, that most mergers are attempts to monopolize, and that therefore an efficiency standard must oppose almost any merger that leads to higher prices. Other economists believe that mergers are frequently motivated by opportunities to reduce costs rather than to monopolize markets, and these economists are far more inclined to view mergers favorably.

There is also disagreement about the normative question of whether economic efficiency should be the only criterion for determining whether a merger is desirable. Some, like Robert Bork, believe that the courts should concern themselves exclusively with efficiency. However, many economists would give some weight to other criteria, including the distribution of income between consumers and producers, the welfare of small firms, and the desirability of competition for its own sake. The latter group of economists supports more active policies to prevent those mergers that tend to reduce competition.

Vertical Integration

To most noneconomists, all mergers are seen as attempts to monopolize. Yet one surprising result of economic analysis is that both the intent and the effect of vertical integration can be to *reduce* monopoly power.

To see this, imagine a monopoly steel producer, Flemington Steel, which sells its product to a monopoly automobile manufacturer. In Exhibit 11–3, Flemington sets a quantity of Q_M and a price of P_M. Deadweight loss is $E + H$.

Suppose, however, that Flemington Steel acquires ownership of the auto manufacturer. Flemington continues to produce steel and provide it to the auto manufacturer, which is now renamed "Flemington Steel, Auto Division." Flemington earns both the producer's surplus (in its capacity as a steel maker) and the consumers' surplus (in its capacity as an automaker). Therefore, Flemington will no longer be interested in maximizing just producer's surplus (at Q_M); it will instead want to maximize the sum of consumers' and producer's surpluses. Therefore, it will produce at Q_C, creating more steel, more autos, lower costs in the auto industry, and ultimately lower prices to consumers.

Essentially, the effect of the vertical integration is that it enables the monopolist to profit by acting less like a monopolist and more like a competitor. Here is another way to see the same point. Suppose that the firms remained separate but that the automaker offered to pay Flemington a flat fee of $C + D$ in exchange for Flemington's behaving exactly like a competitor. This exchange would make both parties better off.

[2]R. H. Bork, *The Antitrust Paradox: A Policy at War with Itself* (New York: Basic Books, 1978).

Exhibit 11-3 Vertical Integration

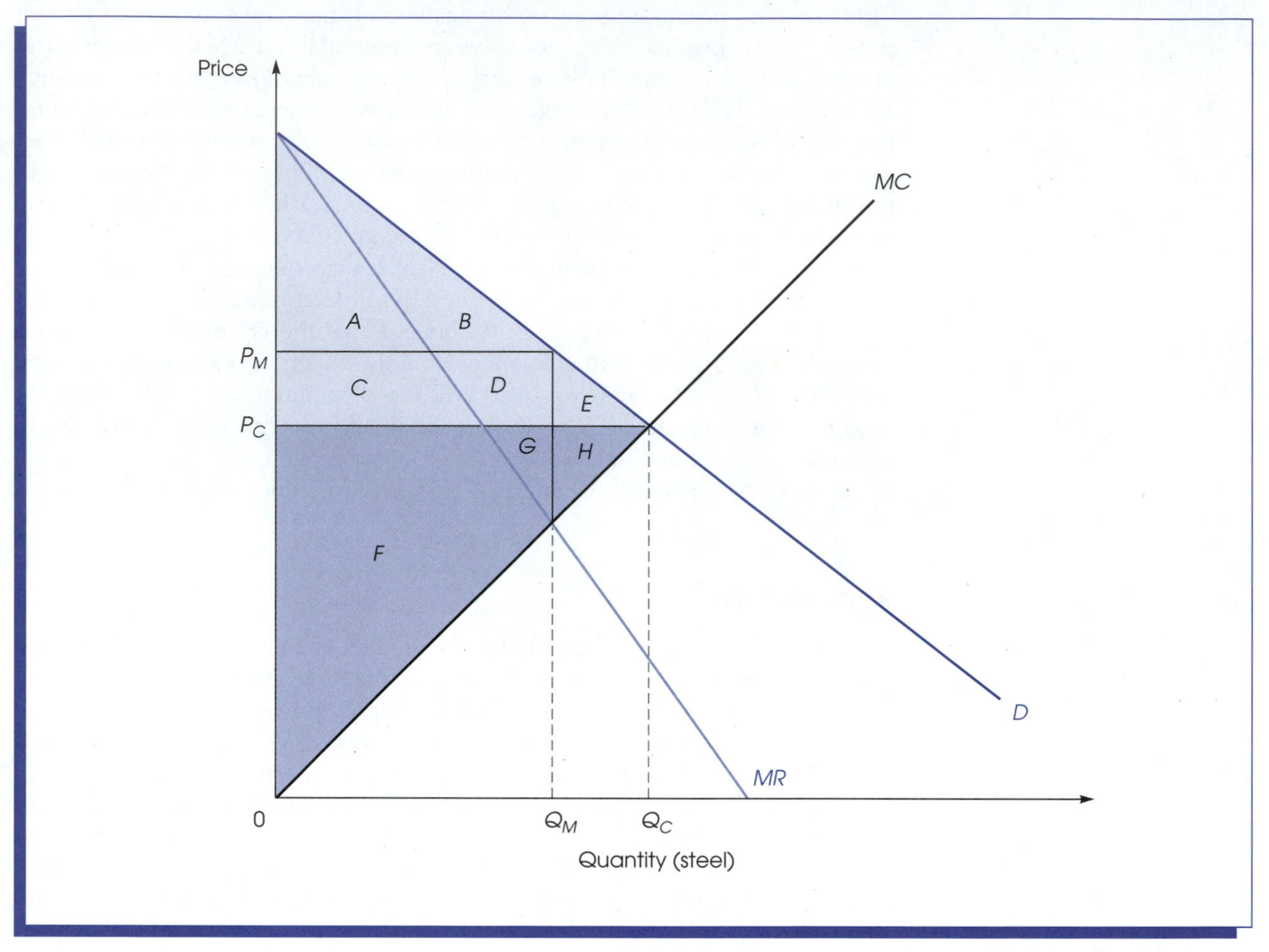

The monopolist Flemington Steel produces Q_M units of steel for sale to a monopoly automaker. This maximizes producer's surplus at $C + D + F + G$ while restricting consumers' surplus to $A + B$.

If Flemington acquires ownership of the automaker, it will earn both the producer's and the consumers' surpluses and will therefore want to maximize the sum of the two. This is accomplished by producing the quantity Q_C of steel, creating a gain equal to the sum of all the lettered areas. Social gain is increased by $E + H$. More steel is produced, more cars are produced, and the price of cars to consumers goes down.

Exercise 11.2 Calculate both consumers' and producer's surpluses after the deal between Flemington Steel and the automaker is struck, and verify that both parties would benefit. What is the smallest flat fee that would make this arrangement benefit both parties? What is the largest?

If such a bribe is mutually beneficial, why does it not take place? One difficulty is that there might be no way for the automaker to prevent Flemington from taking the money and then reneging on the agreement by continuing to charge monopoly prices. Some kind of enforcement mechanism is necessary in order to make the plan work.

When the two firms merge, each can continue going about its business exactly as before, except that there is now a central management with the authority to enforce mutually beneficial contracts. This enables the parties to come to an agreement that increases social gains by prohibiting the exercise of monopoly power.[3]

Vertical Integration and Monopoly Power

Our analysis shows that when a monopoly steel producer acquires a monopoly auto manufacturer, the effect can be to reduce monopoly power. However, vertical mergers happen under a wide variety of conditions. We could ask about the effects of a vertical merger when steel is produced competitively, when autos are produced competitively, or when a competitive automaker can become a monopolist by acquiring steel producers as subsidiaries. It turns out that the theory is very complicated and that much depends on the specifics of market structure, the shapes of demand curves, and the shapes of cost curves. Thus, economic theory does not unambiguously predict whether a vertical merger will increase or decrease monopoly power, whether it will increase or decrease economic efficiency, or whether it will increase or decrease the price of the final product.

Selling to Your Own Subsidiaries

It might be argued that if Flemington Steel acquires ownership of an automaker, then Flemington will be able to force the automaker to buy steel from Flemington, even if this is costlier than buying it elsewhere. According to this argument, vertical integration promotes inefficiency.

However, the argument overlooks the fact that once Flemington owns the automaker, it has every interest in that automaker's maximizing its profits. If the automaker can buy steel elsewhere more cheaply than Flemington can produce it, Flemington will happily tell the automaker to do so.[4]

The argument that a large firm might exploit its vertically integrated subsidiaries surfaced in the Supreme Court's *Brown Shoe* decision. Brown, a shoe manufacturer, sought to merge with Kinney, which both manufactures shoes and sells them in a string of retail stores. Thus, the merger had both horizontal (merging two manufacturers) and vertical (merging a manufacturer with a retailer) characteristics. The Court held that the vertical aspect of the merger would be detrimental, since it would place Brown in the position of being able

[3]This analysis of vertical mergers is far from complete. For example, one might want to take account of the possibility that Flemington can substitute other inputs for steel in its production process. The example here shows that a vertical merger can reduce monopoly power; it does not show that *every* vertical merger reduces monopoly power.

[4]There is an exception: Flemington might prefer to manufacture at high cost rather than buy elsewhere at low cost if it thinks that this strategy can limit the growth of potential future rivals.

to force Kinney to market Brown's shoes in its retail stores. Robert Bork offered the following commentary on this reasoning:

> It completely ignores the fact that whatever considerations of price, quality, style or other matters had led Kinney not to purchase Brown's shoes before the merger would remain just as valid afterward. . . . "Forcing" Kinney to take a product inappropriate for its business would, therefore, cost Kinney at least as much as it would benefit Brown. Since Brown now owned Kinney, it could gain nothing and might well lose from this imagined maneuver.
>
> The problem can be stated in another way. If the Court's naive theory of "forcing" were correct, Brown would not have to acquire Kinney to employ the tactic. Since Brown, in common with almost every enterprise, was already integrated vertically, it could simply set up a separate profit and loss statement for all vertically related manufacturing operations and require each department to "force" more goods at higher prices upon the next, seriatim, all the way to the factory door. The last department might have some trouble selling all those high-priced shoes, but imagine the profits every previous department would report. Nobody has ever explained why this Rube Goldberg mechanism should suddenly become sensible if one more department, a retail outlet, is added and the shoes "forced" upon it.[5]

example

Microsoft versus Netscape

Read more about the Microsoft case at: http://www.findlaw.com/01topics/01antitrust/microsoft.html

In 1997, the U.S. Justice Department took legal action intended to prevent the Microsoft corporation from extending its monopoly power. In the market for operating systems, Microsoft's Windows and its variants had already achieved a substantial monopoly position. But in the market for Web browsers, Microsoft's Internet Explorer was locked in intense competition with its rival Netscape.

The government attacked Microsoft's practice of bundling Internet Explorer with Windows—that is, forcing most Windows users to take Internet Explorer as part of a combined package. According to the government, this bundling was an attempt to extend Microsoft's monopoly power from the market for operating systems to the market for Web browsers. Microsoft disputed the government's analysis, claiming that the bundling was justified because the presence of Internet Explorer improves the performance of Windows.

Economics can't tell us which of those theories is more plausible, but it *can* help us address a related question: If Microsoft succeeds in dominating the browser market, are consumers helped or hurt? The answer depends on what the alternative is, so let's make the question more precise: Are consumers bet-

[5]Bork. *The Antitrust Paradox,* pp. 213–214.

ter off getting their browsers from a Microsoft monopoly or from a Netscape monopoly?

To answer this question, let's make a few simplifying assumptions. First, we assume that Microsoft and Netscape produce browsers of identical quality. Second, we assume that nobody buys an operating system without a browser, and nobody buys a browser without an operating system. (This second assumption could be dropped without changing most of the conclusions that will follow.)

Exhibit 11–4 shows the demand curve for the combined package consisting of an operating system and a Web browser. Suppose first that Microsoft supplies the entire package, and suppose (to keep the diagram simple) that the marginal cost of production is zero. (The assumption of zero marginal cost is

Exhibit 11-4 Microsoft vs. Netscape

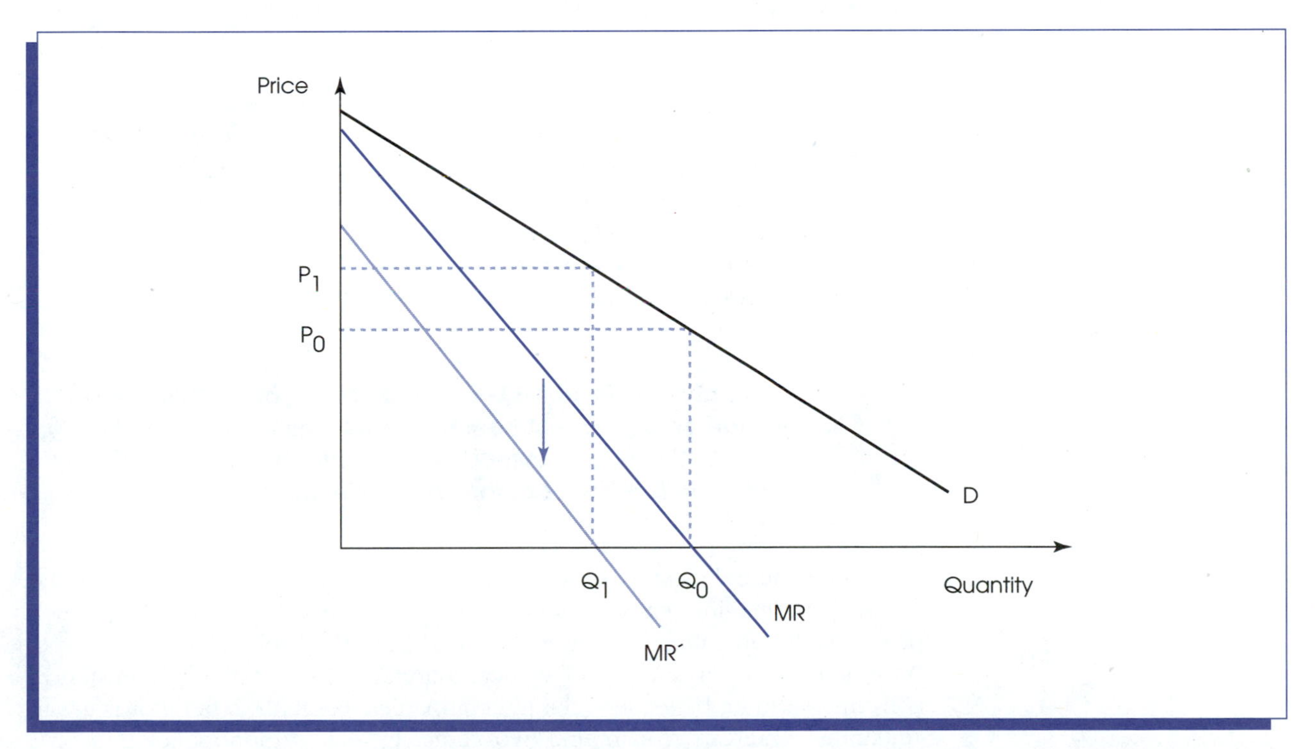

The demand curve D shows the demand for a package consisting of an operating system and a web browser. If Microsoft supplies the entire package (at zero marginal cost), then it sells quantity Q_0 at price P_0. If instead Netscape sells the browser while Microsoft sells the operating system, then Microsoft faces the lower marginal revenue curve MR' and supplies quantity Q_1, pricing the operating system so that the combined package sells for price P_1. Therefore, consumers prefer one combined monopoly to two separate monopolies.

doubly harmless, first because it is close to accurate and second because it has no effect on the conclusions to follow.) Then Microsoft supplies quantity Q_0 (where marginal revenue equals the zero marginal cost) and charges P_0 for the entire package.

Now suppose instead that Netscape supplies the browser while Microsoft supplies the operating system. Then Microsoft does not collect all of the revenue from the combined package; hence, it faces the lower marginal revenue curve MR' in Exhibit 11–4. For example, if Netscape charges $20 for the browser, then Microsoft's marginal revenue curve falls vertically a distance $20 per package.

With Netscape in the picture, Microsoft produces Q_1 operating systems, and prices them so that the combined package sells for a price of P_1. (For example, if Netscape charges $20 for a browser, Microsoft charges $P_1 - \$20$ for an operating system.) Consumers pay a higher total price for the package, and are therefore worse off buying browsers from Netscape than from Microsoft.

Here is the basic idea underlying this analysis: Every time Microsoft raises the price of Windows, it is punished by the loss of some sales. If Microsoft supplies the browser market, then raising the price of Windows is *doubly* punished, with the loss of both a Windows sale and a browser sale. Therefore the price of the package remains lower when Microsoft has both monopolies.

We have determined that consumers prefer a Microsoft monopoly to a Netscape monopoly. We have *not* determined that consumers prefer monopoly to competition. In fact, competition for market share is the main source of innovations; that's why today's browsers are so much better than the ones available just a few years ago. In the next section, on tournaments, we will return to this issue.

The analysis in Exhibit 11-4 is incomplete, because it does not provide an account of how Netscape sets the price of its browser. You will be invited to complete the analysis in Numerical Exercise 2 at the end of the chapter.

This example illustrates anew the virtues of vertical integration. Here's the connection: Imagine that you buy your entire package from Microsoft, which produces the operating system by itself and buys the browser from Netscape. We know from our analysis of vertical integration that in that circumstance, consumers can be better served if the companies merge. In other words, it's in consumers' interests to combine two vertically related monopolies into one, which is exactly the lesson of this example.

The Microsoft-Netscape example is slightly different from the earlier example of Flemington Steel, because Flemington acquired a *competitive* auto industry, whereas here we are

talking about Microsoft "acquiring" a *monopoly* Netscape. But the basic conclusion—that vertical integration tends to reduce monopoly power—remains.

Tournaments

Tournament Competition to dominate an industry by being slightly better than one's rivals.

In some industries, it's both possible and profitable to capture a large share of the market by being slightly better than the competition. Computer software is a good example. Nobody wants to buy the second best word processor, even if it's almost as good as the best. The competition to dominate such an industry is called a **tournament**, because of its winner-take-all aspect.

It's easy to think of industries that are *not* tournaments. Medical care, for example, is not a tournament. The best doctor in the world will never have more than a negligible share of the market, because no doctor has time to see more than a negligible share of the world's patients. By contrast, the best comedian in the world might very well have a substantial portion of the market for comedy CDs, because there is no limit to the number of CDs that can be pressed after a single performance. Thus, the market for comedy can be a tournament.

The key difference between medical care and comedy CDs is that CDs are produced at very low marginal cost. That's what makes it possible to produce enough of them to generate monopoly power. The same is true of software.

In a tournament, players expend resources trying to rise to the top. This works to the advantage of consumers in that industry, because it improves the quality of the products that are offered for sale. Nevertheless, the social cost of those improvements can exceed their value.

For example, let's revisit the example of Microsoft versus Netscape. If either company has a monopoly in the browser market, it has little incentive to innovate. But as long as each is trying to dominate the industry, each keeps offering improvements. Consumers are the big beneficiaries.

However, it does not follow that such competition is socially desirable. Here's an example. Suppose that Microsoft earns $100 million a year from its browser business. Suppose that Netscape can invest $50 million to make a slight improvement, which would allow it to take over the market and earn $105 million (a slightly better product will earn slightly higher revenue). That investment is socially inefficient—it costs $50 million and adds only $5 million to the value of the browsers. But the investment is in Netscape's interest, because it stands to gain $105 million, only $5 million of which is a true addition to social gain (the other $100 million is offset by a $100 million loss to Microsoft).

In addition to Netscape, the winners here are the people who use browsers. The losers are the people who would otherwise have benefited from the $50 million in resources that Netscape spent to make a slight improvement.

In this example, Netscape's tendency to overinvest might be partly offset by the certainty that Microsoft will quickly copy any of Netscape's innovations (and similarly, Microsoft's tendency to overinvest will be partly offset by the certainty that Netscape will behave the same way). But in general, tournaments can lead to inefficiency.

Read about the Wal-Mart predatory pricing case at the Competitive Enterprise Institute site at: http://www.cei.org/update/0696-db.html

Predatory pricing Setting an artificially low price so as to damage rival firms.

Predatory Pricing

Predatory pricing occurs when a firm sets prices so low as to incur losses, forcing its rivals to do the same. If the firm can outlast the competition in the resulting "price war," it may hope to be the only survivor.

Conceivably, a firm could engage in predatory pricing in some markets while continuing to charge normally in others. In this case predatory pricing becomes a form of price discrimination.

Economists disagree about how widespread this practice really is. There are a number of reasons for skepticism. First, there is nothing to prevent the reemergence of rival firms as soon as the would-be monopolist raises his prices. Second, during the period of price warfare, all sides are losing money. The predator's losses, however, are greater: It is he who is attempting to expand his market share, and therefore selling greater quantities at the artificially low price. Indeed, if the other firms "lay low" by producing very little (or even nothing) for a while, they can force the predator to take losses that are enormous compared with their own. Finally, a firm being preyed upon, if it is capable of competing successfully in the long run, can usually borrow funds to get through the temporary period of price cutting. Thus, even a predator whose assets greatly outstrip his rivals' may not have any survival advantage over them.

Despite all of these arguments, there are still reasons to think that predation might sometimes be profitable. The most significant of these is that predation can serve as a warning to future entrants. By driving one rival from the marketplace, the predator can prevent many additional rivals from entering in the first place. This can make predation a sensible strategy, even when the predator's losses from underpricing far exceed his gains from the first rival's elimination.

example

The Standard Oil Company

Historians have traditionally attributed much of the success of the Standard Oil Company to predatory price cutting. Founded in 1870 by John D. Rockefeller, Standard Oil was estimated to supply 75% of the oil sold in the United States by the 1890s. In 1911 Standard Oil (by now reorganized and called Standard Oil of New Jersey) was dissolved by order of the U.S. Supreme Court.

The role of predatory pricing in the Standard Oil case was reexamined by John McGee of the University of Washington in 1958.[6] In a widely quoted article, he argued that no historical evidence supports the assertion that predatory pricing played a major role in Rockefeller's success. Instead, McGee argued, this success could be attributed primarily to a successful policy of buying out rivals. The one-time cost of such buy-outs was substantially less than the cost of predation.

Buy-outs also have the advantage of allowing the would-be monopolist to acquire the rival firm's physical plant and equipment, which at least delays the

[6]John McGee, "Predatory Price Cutting: The Standard Oil (N.J.) Case," *Journal of Law and Economics* 1 (1958): 137–169.

rival's ability to reconstitute himself. A firm that stops producing in response to predatory price cutting still has its factories, ready to go back into production the instant prices are raised.

On the other hand, buy-outs have the disadvantage of actually encouraging new entrants, who may be hoping to be bought out at a favorable price. And a firm that has been "bought" may soon reappear under a new name. It is said that more than a few nineteenth-century businessmen made lifetime careers out of being bought out by John D. Rockefeller.

The Robinson–Patman Act

Additional information on the Robinson-Patman Act can be found at: http://www.lawmall.com/rpa/

Because of the potentially predatory nature of price discrimination, the Robinson–Patman Act of 1938 forbids price discrimination in cases where it tends to "create a monopoly, lessen competition, or injure competitors." This language is sufficiently imprecise as to invite controversy over exactly when price discrimination should be considered predatory. The most widely accepted standard (but by no means the only one) was offered in 1975 by Phillip Areeda and Donald Turner of the Harvard Law School.[7] They argue, among other things, that no price can be considered predatory unless it is below marginal cost. As long as the firm is pricing at or above marginal cost, those rivals who are more efficient (that is, have even lower costs) should be able to survive. Only when the firm prices below marginal cost is there a risk of its driving out a more efficient rival.

The Supreme Court gave its interpretation of the Robinson–Patman Act in the 1967 case *Utah Pie v. Continental Baking Company*. Utah Pie was a small, local company with 18 employees marketing frozen pies in the Salt Lake City area. Continental Baking, Carnation, and Pet were large national producers of a wide variety of food products. Utah Pie alleged that these three giants price-discriminated in an injurious way by selling frozen pies at a lower price in Salt Lake City than they did elsewhere. The Supreme Court agreed.

All parties to the *Utah Pie* case were in agreement that the defendants charged lower prices in Utah Pie's marketing territory than they did outside it. However, this could have resulted from the fact that elasticity of demand for Continental pies was greater in areas where Utah Pie's products were sold. In other words, Continental's actions could have been a simple case of ordinary third-degree price discrimination.

According to the Areeda-Turner rule, the price discrimination could have been considered predatory only if the defendants had priced below marginal cost in the Salt Lake City area. No evidence was offered that they had done so. Thus, the Supreme Court's decision makes deviation from marginal cost an irrelevant criterion in deciding whether a pricing policy can be considered predatory. For this reason economists generally regard *Utah Pie* as a bad decision. By forbidding Continental et al. to undercut Utah Pie's prices, the Court is as likely to have created a local monopoly (in the hands of Utah Pie) as to have prevented one.

---

[7]P. Areeda and D. Turner, "Predatory Pricing and Related Practices Under Section 2 of the Sherman Act," *Harvard Law Review* 88 (1975): 689–733.

In fact, the Supreme Court essentially took the position that the mere fact that the price of pies decreased in Salt Lake City constituted a violation of the Robinson–Patman Act![8] This reinforced the Court's interpretation of the Sherman and Clayton Acts, by reaffirming that benefits to consumers are not considered a defense against the charge of injury to other firms.

Resale Price Maintenance

Resale price maintenance or **fair trade** A practice by which the producer of a product sets a retail price and forbids any retailer to sell below that price.

Resale price maintenance, or **fair trade,** is a practice under which a monopoly supplier sets a retail price for its product and forbids retailers to undercut that price. Retailers who sell below the set price have their supplies cut off in the future. For example, until it lost a Supreme Court case on this and other issues in 1967, the Schwinn Bicycle Company required all sellers of Schwinn bicycles to charge a price that was determined by Schwinn.

Although such a practice might at first appear to be an attempt by the manufacturer to keep prices artificially high, economic analysis suggests otherwise. The price at which consumers will buy Schwinn bicycles is determined by the quantity that Schwinn chooses to produce. If Schwinn wanted to raise prices, the most direct way for it to do so would be to restrict output. And conversely, unless Schwinn restricted output, no fair trade agreement could have enabled Schwinn to sell its bicycles at a price higher than demanders were willing to pay.

Why, then, would manufacturers choose to engage in this practice? A number of explanations have been offered.[9] One is that products like bicycles are displayed in showrooms, where people go to examine them and ask questions about them before making their purchases. If some retailers offered cut-rate prices, customers would first go to the stores with the fancy showrooms and knowledgeable sales forces, ask their questions, make their decisions, and then buy from the discounters. Eventually, those retailers who offered quality service would find that there are no rewards in that activity, and so they would eliminate all of the costly forms of assistance that customers find valuable. Consumers could find themselves worse off, and so could Schwinn, as buyers would now have a greatly reduced incentive to purchase Schwinn bicycles.

Through resale price maintenance, Schwinn ensures that its dealers, who cannot compete with each other by offering lower prices, will instead compete with each other by attempting to offer higher-quality service. Thus, according to this theory, a practice that at first seems designed to establish monopoly power at the expense of consumers can actually be more plausibly explained as a practice designed to make the product more desirable by providing consumers with services that they value.

Exhibit 11–5 illustrates the theory. Suppose that P_0 is the wholesale price at which Schwinn sells its bicycles, and suppose, for simplicity, that retailers have no costs other than purchasing the bicycles from Schwinn. The retailers' marginal cost curve MC is flat at P_0, and if the retail market is competitive, they

---

[8]For more on this point, see Bork, *The Antitrust Paradox*, pp. 386–387.

[9]The explanation we give here was suggested by L. Telser, "Why Do Manufacturers Want Fair Trade?" *Journal of Law and Economics* 3 (1960): 86–105.

Exhibit 11-5 Resale Price Maintenance

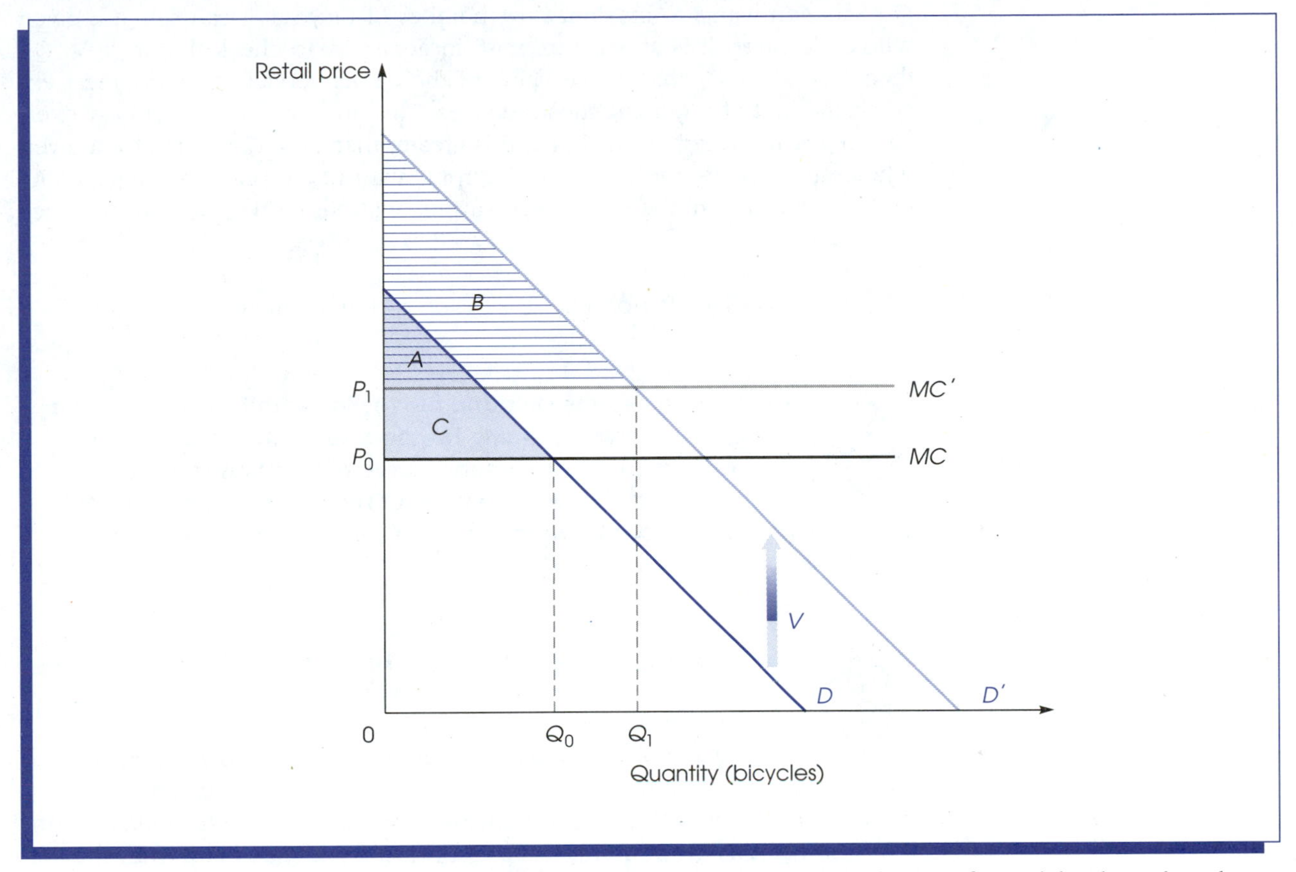

Suppose that Schwinn provides bicycles at a wholesale price of P_0 and that this is the only cost that retailers have. If the demand curve is D, then under competition the quantity sold is Q_0 and consumers' surplus is $A + C$.

If Schwinn maintains a retail price of P_1, dealers compete with each other by offering services that cost $P_1 - P_0$ per bicycle to provide. The value of these services to consumers is some amount V, so that the demand curve moves vertically upward a distance V to D'. The new quantity sold is Q_1.

Since Schwinn chooses to engage in the practice, we can assume that $Q_1 > Q_0$. Elementary geometry now reveals that $V > P_1 - P_0$ (the value of the dealer services exceeds the cost of producing them) and $A + B > A + C$ (consumers' surplus is increased).

---

sell Q_0 bicycles, where MC meets the demand curve D. Now suppose that Schwinn sets a retail price of P_1 and requires all dealers to adhere to this price. Dealers will then compete for customers by providing additional services up to the point where the cost of providing these services is $P_1 - P_0$. This raises their marginal cost curve to MC'.

Exercise 11.3 Explain why dealers provide services exactly up to the point where the cost of providing them is $P_1 - P_0$.

We assume that the dealer services add some quantity V to the value of each bicycle; thus, the demand curve moves vertically upward a distance V to D'. The new quantity sold is Q_1, where MC' meets D'.

Notice that Schwinn would engage in this practice only if Q_1 is greater than Q_0; Schwinn wants to maximize the number of bicycles it can sell at a given wholesale price. It is an easy exercise in geometry to check that if $Q_1 > Q_0$, then $V > P_1 - P_0$; that is, the value of the dealer services to consumers exceeds the cost of providing those services. This, in turn, by another easy exercise in geometry, implies that area B is greater than area C, so that, for a given wholesale price P_0, the consumers' surplus with resale price maintenance $(A + B)$ is greater than the consumers' surplus without resale price maintenance $(A + C)$.

EXERCISE 11.4 Perform the easy exercises in geometry.

Do not confuse the demand curves in Exhibit 11-5 which are the demand curves facing retailers, with the demand curve facing Schwinn. The demand curve facing Schwinn passes through the point (P_0, Q_0) without resale price maintenance, and it moves out to pass through the point (P_0, Q_1) when resale price maintenance is allowed.

The analysis here is incomplete, because it takes the price P_0 as given. In fact, when resale price maintenance makes bicycles more attractive to consumers, the demand curve facing Schwinn moves out, leading Schwinn to set a new, higher price for bicycles. As a result, consumers keep only some of the increase in social welfare, and Schwinn gets the rest. Nevertheless, with the assumptions made here, it is possible to show that even after the price rises, consumer's surplus is still greater with resale price maintenance than without.

The theory that resale price maintenance exists to ensure a high level of service to customers is by no means the only one possible. A variety of other explanations have been offered. Indeed, in the same article where Professor Lester Telser first proposed the "service" argument, he went on to contend that it did *not* apply to resale price maintenance in the light bulb industry, which was the special case that he was attempting to explain.[10] A recent study examined the evidence from a number of legal actions and found that the dealer service argument appears to correctly explain resale price maintenance approximately 65% of the time.[11]

---

[10]This point is reinforced in L. Telser, "Why Should Manufacturers Want Fair Trade II?" *Journal of Law and Economics* 33 (1990):409–417.

[11]P. M. Ippolito, "Resale Price Maintenance: Economic Evidence from Litigation" (1988).

The U.S. antitrust laws, as interpreted by the federal courts, severely limit the exercise of resale price maintenance. In May 1988, the Supreme Court issued a ruling that substantially relaxed these restrictions and made it easier for manufacturers to prevent retailers from offering discounts. In their decision, the justices called explicit attention to the role of resale price maintenance in maintaining high levels of dealer service. Later that week, the *New York Times* editorial page called for new legislation to overturn the effects of the ruling. The editorial called for giving manufacturers the right to "set high standards for service and refuse to supply retailers who don't meet them," while denying manufacturers the right to set prices.[12]

What the *Times* apparently failed to understand is that in the presence of competition among dealers, there is no difference between setting a standard for service and setting a retail price. Given a service standard, the price must rise until it just covers the cost of meeting the standard; given a price, the standard must rise until the cost of meeting it drives profits to zero. To allow manufacturers to set one but not the other is like allowing bathers to select the water level in the left half of the tub while disallowing them to select the water level in the right half. No matter how scrupulously you tried to obey such a law, you'd probably have trouble forcing yourself to forget that when you choose one level, you are automatically determining the other one.

example

Barnes and Noble versus Amazon

Barnes and Noble is a large chain bookstore that offers a comfortable atmosphere for browsing. You can sit in comfortable chairs, sip coffee and listen to music while you contemplate your selections. These amenities are costly to provide, in some ways that are obvious and other ways that are not so obvious. Barnes and Noble rents large amounts of space to give its customers elbow room. It keeps the shelves well-stocked, which not only invites damage and theft, but also requires a substantial financial investment and hence a forgone opportunity to earn interest.

Amazon.com is a Web-based virtual bookstore that offers the convenience of shopping at home. Amazon has fewer expenses than Barnes and Noble: Rather than paying for your elbow room, Amazon invites you to keep your elbows on your desktop. Rather than keeping a large number of books in stock, Amazon orders many books from suppliers only after they have been requested by customers.

Amazon passes some of its cost savings on to the customer. Many popular hardcovers are about 20% cheaper at Amazon. This means you have two choices: Shop in comfort at Barnes and Noble, where you can look at the books before you buy them, or shop at Amazon and save a few dollars.

Unfortunately for Barnes and Noble—and for the people who like to shop there—there's also a third option: Browse at Barnes and Noble and then buy from Amazon. Consumers who behave this way raise Barnes and Noble's costs and therefore reduce the amount of space and comfortable chairs that Barnes and Noble is willing to provide.

---

[12]"Let the Retail Price Be Right," *New York Times* editorial, May 6, 1988.

Under these circumstances, it is plausible that book publishers would want to engage in retail price maintenance—essentially forbidding Amazon to offer discounts, so that the service at Barnes and Noble is not diminished. (Publishers care about the quality of service at Barnes and Noble because it entices people to buy books.)

However, the issue in book publishing is less clearcut than in the case of bicycles or stereo equipment. A discount bike shop or a discount stereo store offers nothing special except discounts. By contrast, Amazon offers a service that many customers value highly: The opportunity to shop without leaving home.

Therefore, publishers probably have mixed emotions about Amazon. On the one hand, it threatens Barnes and Noble and so drives away those readers who will only buy books in comfortable surroundings; on the other hand, it brings in a different class of readers who might never have shopped at Barnes and Noble. Thus, it's not clear whether publishers should want to stifle Amazon's business practices.

11.2 Collusion and the Prisoner's Dilemma: An Introduction to Game Theory

Collusion An agreement among firms to set prices and outputs.

Cartel A group of firms engaged in collusion.

Collusion takes place when the firms in an industry join together to set prices and outputs. The firms participating in such an arrangement are said to form a **cartel.** By restricting each firm's production, the cartel attempts to restrict industry output to the monopoly level, allowing all firms to charge a monopoly price. This maximizes the total producers' surplus of all firms in the industry. If necessary, the resulting profits can then be redistributed among firms so that each gets a bigger "piece of the pie" than it had under competition.

Collusion is an ancient phenomenon. In the tenth century B.C. the Queen of Sheba (near what is now Yemen) held a monopoly position in the shipment of spices, myrrh, and frankincense to the Mediterranean. When Solomon, the king of Israel, entered the same market, "she came to Jerusalem, with a very great train, with camels that bear spices, and very much gold, and precious stones," which could indicate how much she valued the prospect of an amicable agreement to divide the market.[13] More recently, Adam Smith observed:

> People of the same trade seldom meet together, even for merriment and diversion, but the conversation ends in a conspiracy against the public, or in some contrivance to raise prices.[14]

A more contemporary example dates from May 1991, when the Justice Department charged the eight Ivy League universities with illegally colluding to coordinate their financial aid offers. At an annual meeting called Overlap, the Ivy League schools (and fifteen others) negotiated agreements on both a general formula for determining aid offers and the specific amounts that would be offered to individual students. Because of the universities' agreement not to bid

[13] 1 Kings 10:2.

[14] Adam Smith, *The Wealth of Nations.*

against each other, many students paid more for their educations than they would have under competition. The Justice Department argued that this made the Overlap group an illegal cartel.

According to *The Wall Street Journal*, the colleges defended their practices as a way of ensuring that students would not be influenced by financial considerations in choosing a college.[15] This defense was at least novel: If the major auto manufacturers had been caught colluding to fix high prices, they might not have thought to argue that they were performing a public service by ensuring that consumers would not be influenced by financial considerations in choosing a car. But the Justice Department was unimpressed, and the Ivy League schools, without admitting wrongdoing, agreed to cancel Overlap and not to collude in the future.

Game Theory and the Prisoner's Dilemma

Cartels require cooperation. In order to understand the difficulties facing those who would cooperate, we will digress briefly into a topic from the Theory of Games.[16] The particular "game" we will analyze is called the *Prisoner's Dilemma*.

A crime has been committed and two suspects have been arrested. The suspects are taken to the police station and the district attorney meets with each one separately. To each he makes the following offer: "If you each confess, I'll send you both to jail for 5 years. If neither of you confesses, I can still get you on a lesser charge and send you to jail for 2 years each. If your buddy confesses and you don't, you'll get 10 years and he'll get 1. But if *you* are the only one to confess, you'll get off with 1 year while I put *him* away for 10. Now do you confess or don't you?" Each prisoner has to decide without conferring with the other.

Exhibit 11–6 will help you keep track of the district attorney's offer. Prisoner A, by choosing to confess or not confess, selects one of the columns in the table. Prisoner B selects one of the rows.

Let's evaluate the choices available to Prisoner A. What if B has confessed, thereby choosing the first row? Then A's choices are to confess and get 5 years, or to not confess and get 10 years. He should confess.

On the other hand, what if B has not confessed, thereby choosing the second row? Then A's choices are to confess and get 1 year, or to not confess and get 2 years. He should confess.

Needless to say, Prisoner A confesses. Following the same logic, so does Prisoner B. They both end up with 5 years in jail, even though they would have both been better off if neither had confessed.

---

[15]"U.S. Charges Eight Ivy League Universities and MIT with Fixing Financial Aid," *The Wall Street Journal*, May 23, 1991.

[16]This theory was developed in the late 1940s by the mathematician John von Neumann and the economist Oscar Morgenstern. It has had a great deal of influence in economics and political science.

Exhibit 11-6 The Prisoner's Dilemma

		Action of Prisoner A	
		Confess	**Not Confess**
Action of Prisoner B	**Confess**	5 years each	A gets 10 years B gets 1 year
	Not Confess	A gets 1 year B gets 10 years	2 years each

Each prisoner must decide whether to confess or not to confess. Prisoner A reasons that there are two possibilities: Either B confesses, in which case A is better off confessing (so that he gets 5 years instead of 10), or B does not confess, in which case A is better off confessing (so that he gets 1 year instead of 2). Regardless of B's action, A should confess, and regardless of A's action, B should confess. As a result, they each go to jail for 5 years, whereas if neither had confessed they would only have gone to jail for 2 years.

It is easy to misunderstand the point of this example. Students sometimes think that Prisoner A confesses because he is afraid that Prisoner B will confess. In fact, A confesses for a much deeper reason. He confesses because it is his best strategy *regardless* of what B does. Prisoner A would want to confess if he knew that B had confessed, and would also want to confess if he knew that B had not confessed. The same is true for B.

The Prisoner's Dilemma and the Invisible Hand

The Prisoner's Dilemma is an interesting case in which the Invisible Hand Theorem is not true. When each party acts in his own self-interest, the outcome is not Pareto-optimal. If neither confessed, both would be better off. We saw in Chapter 8 that in competitive markets, by contrast, the equilibrium outcome is always Pareto-optimal. The fact that the invisible hand can fail in a simple example like the Prisoner's Dilemma makes its success in competitive markets all the more remarkable.

Solving the Prisoner's Dilemma

How can the Prisoner's Dilemma be solved? Suppose that the prisoners of Exhibit 11–6 are members of a crime syndicate that can credibly threaten to impose severe penalties on anyone who confesses. Then the individual prisoners can be induced not to confess, and both will be better off. Contrary to what your intuition may tell you, they both benefit by being "victims" of coercion.

(More precisely, each benefits from the coercion applied to the other, and this benefit exceeds the cost of the coercion applied to himself.)

Therefore, it is possible that people will prefer to have their options limited in situations that resemble the Prisoner's Dilemma. In China before World War II, goods were commonly transported on barges drawn by teams of about six men. If the barge reached its destination on time (often after a journey of several days), the men were rewarded handsomely. On such a team any given member has an incentive to shirk, in the sense of working less hard than is optimal from the team's point of view. This incentive exists regardless of whether he believes that the others are shirking. Thus, the situation is similar to the Prisoner's Dilemma, with the choices "Confess" and "Not Confess" replaced by "Shirk" and "Don't Shirk." As in the Prisoner's Dilemma, an outside enforcer commanding everyone not to shirk can make everyone better off. In recognition of this, it was apparently common for the bargemen themselves to hire a seventh man to whip them when they slacked off!

The Repeated Prisoner's Dilemma

The Prisoner's Dilemma becomes a far richer problem when the two players expect to meet each other repeatedly in similar situations. Even though Prisoner A can always do better in the current game by confessing, he must also worry about whether his actions today will influence Prisoner B's actions tomorrow.

Suppose that A and B plan to play the Prisoner's Dilemma on three separate occasions: Monday, Tuesday, and Wednesday. You might think that each prisoner would have some incentive not to confess on Monday, so that he develops a reputation for reliability. Let us see whether this is true.

We begin by imagining the situation on Wednesday, which is the easiest day to think about. Since Wednesday is the last day, there are no future games to consider, and the game is just like an ordinary Prisoner's Dilemma. Regardless of what has gone before, each prisoner has the usual incentive to confess.

Now let us imagine the situation on Tuesday. Suppose that on Tuesday Prisoner A does not confess in order to convince Prisoner B that he won't confess on Wednesday. Will Prisoner B believe him? No, because Prisoner B realizes that once Wednesday arrives, Prisoner A will surely want to confess. Since he cannot convince Prisoner B of his goodwill anyway, Prisoner A confesses on Tuesday as well. By the same logic, so does Prisoner B.

Finally, how will the prisoners behave on Monday? Each one knows, by the logic of the preceding paragraph, that the other will confess on Tuesday. Thus, there is no credibility to be gained by not confessing on Monday. Both, therefore, confess on Monday as well.

The same reasoning applies to any repeated Prisoner's Dilemma with a definite ending date. By reasoning backward from that ending date, we see that there is never any incentive to establish a good reputation, since no such attempt can ever be credible.

When there is no definite ending date, the analysis of the repeated Prisoner's Dilemma becomes a subtle and difficult problem.

Tit-for-Tat

In 1984 Professor Robert Axelrod of the University of Michigan announced the results of a remarkable experiment.[17] Axelrod had invited various experts in the fields of psychology, economics, political science, mathematics, and sociology to submit strategies for the repeated Prisoner's Dilemma. Using a computer, he invented one imaginary prisoner with each strategy, and he had each prisoner play against each other prisoner in a 200-round repeated game. Each prisoner also played one 200-round game against a carbon copy of himself, and one 200-round game against a prisoner who always played randomly. The jail sentences from Exhibit 11–5 were translated into points as follows:

Sentence	Points
1 year	5
2 years	3
5 years	1
10 years	0

One of the strategies submitted was called *Tit-for-Tat*. According to the Tit-for-Tat strategy, the prisoner does not confess in the first round. In future rounds he continues not confessing, except that if the opponent confesses, then the Tit-for-Tat player punishes him by confessing in the next round. In subsequent rounds, he returns to not confessing, confessing only once as punishment each time his opponent confesses.

Tit-for-Tat won the tournament decisively. Thereupon, Axelrod organized a new and much larger tournament with 62 entrants. In the second tournament the lengths of games were determined randomly, rather than making them all 200 rounds. Also, all participants in the second tournament were provided with detailed analyses of the outcome of the first tournament, so that they could use these lessons in designing their strategies. Once again, Tit-for-Tat, the simplest strategy submitted, was the decisive winner.

In a final experiment, Axelrod used his computer to simulate future repetitions of the tournament. He assumed that the strategies that did well would be more widely submitted as time went on. Thus, a strategy that did well in the first tournament, like Tit-for-Tat, was replicated many times in the second tournament, whereas strategies that did less well were replicated fewer times. This was intended to mimic evolutionary biology, where those animals that succeed in competition have more offspring in future generations. As the tournament was repeated, one could observe the evolution of various strategies. The chief result was that Tit-for-Tat never lost its dominance.

The success of Tit-for-Tat has a paradoxical flavor, in view of the fact that the backward reasoning of the preceding subsection suggests that there is no gain to acquiring a reputation for playing "reasonably" in a repeated Prisoner's

---

[17]His results are reported in a fascinating book, *The Evolution of Cooperation* (New York: Basic Books, 1984).

Dilemma. The success of Tit-for-Tat seems to rely on just such reputational effects. Thus, we have a puzzle. Economists don't always have all the answers.

The Prisoner's Dilemma and the Breakdown of Cartels

We now return to the topic of cartels. In a cartelized industry, price is set above marginal cost. In order to maintain this price, industry output must be held below the competitive level, and each firm is assigned a share of this production. Because price exceeds marginal cost, any given firm can increase its profits by selling a few more items at a slightly lower price. Of course, this increased output will tend to lower the price and to reduce industry-wide profits. For this reason, a monopolist would resist the temptation to increase output. However, a member of the cartel who "cheats" by increasing his output beyond his allotted share will reap all of the benefits from his action while bearing only some of the costs. He gets all of the additional revenue from the increment to output, whereas everybody shares the losses due to the fall in price.

It follows that a cartel member will be less mindful of the negative consequences of his actions than a single monopolist would be. He tends to cheat when he can get away with it, and so does every other member of the cartel. Eventually, output increases all the way out to the competitive level.

The breakdown of cartels is perfectly analogous to the Prisoner's Dilemma. Imagine two firms, A and B, who have formed a cartel and must decide whether to abide by the agreement or to cheat. They are confronted by the options shown in Exhibit 11–7. Reasoning exactly as in the Prisoner's Dilemma, each firm chooses to cheat, and the cartel breaks down.

If a cartel is to succeed, it needs an enforcement mechanism. That is, it needs a way to monitor members' actions and a way to punish those who

Exhibit 11-7 The Breakdown of Cartels

		Action of Firm A: Cheat	Action of Firm A: Not Cheat
Action of Firm B	Cheat	$5 profit each	A gets $3 profit B gets $12 profit
	Not Cheat	A gets $12 profit B gets $3 profit	$10 profit each

Each member of the cartel must decide whether to cheat by producing more than the agreed-upon output. Cheating will increase the cheater's profits (because price is higher than marginal cost) and decrease the other firms' profits (by driving down the price of the product). It is in each firm's interest to cheat, whether it believes the other firm is cheating or not.

cheat. Since price-fixing agreements are illegal in the United States, the enforcement must be carried out in secret. (Indeed, since the *Madison Oil* case of 1940, the courts have held that even an attempt to fix prices is illegal under the Sherman Act, regardless of whether the attempt is successful.) Whenever you hear it asserted that a cartel has been successful, your first question should be: What is the enforcement mechanism?

example Concrete Pouring and Organized Crime

Throughout the 1980s, the concrete-pouring industry in New York City was dominated by a cartel of six firms called "The Concrete Club." Whenever a project was put out for bids, the Concrete Club chose one of its members to handle that project, and agreed that no member of the Club would attempt to underbid that firm. As a result, the cost of a cubic yard of concrete rose to $85, the highest in the nation.

Without a strong enforcement mechanism, it would be very difficult for a cartel like the Concrete Club to succeed. Not only would its own members be tempted to cheat, but competition from nonmembers would soon drive prices down to the competitive level.

In this case, the enforcement mechanism was provided by New York's organized crime families, who managed the cartel and imposed heavy penalties on cheaters. Competition from outside the cartel was eliminated by the families' control of the Concrete Workers Union, which prevented non-Club members from working on any project involving more than $2 million.[18]

example The International Salt Case

To succeed, a cartel must know when its members are cheating. The International Salt Company may have discovered a creative solution to this monitoring problem. The company distributed a patented machine called the Lixator, which was used to dissolve rock salt. In some areas of the country, Lixators were sold outright; in others, they were leased subject to a requirement that the lessee agree to purchase all of its salt from International. In 1947 the Supreme Court ruled, in effect, that International Salt had attempted to create monopoly power in the market for salt. According to the analysis of two-part tariffs in Section 10.3, this explanation is unlikely to be correct. Instead, that analysis suggests that International was price discriminating by effectively charging heavier users more for a Lixator.

In 1985 John Peterman of the Federal Trade Commission reviewed the evidence and found that the economists' explanation was also suspect.[19] He discovered a clause in the Lixator rental contract that allowed any firm to buy its salt elsewhere if it could find it at a price lower than International's. Thus, International could not have charged more than the going market price for salt; if it had, it wouldn't have sold any.

---

[18]The information in this section is taken partly from J. Cummings and E. Volkman, *Goombata* (Little Brown, 1990) and partly from P. Maas, *Underboss* (HarperCollins, 1997).

[19]John Peterman, "The *International Salt* Case," *Journal of Law and Economics* 22 (1985): 351–364.

What, then, could account for the structure of the Lixator contract? Here is one intriguing possibility. Suppose that salt suppliers were colluding. In that case they would have needed a way to gather information on which suppliers were undercutting the agreement, so that the cheaters could be punished. The Lixator contract, with the clause that Peterman discovered, gave International's own customers an incentive to report low salt prices to International. In this way International could be continually informed of who the price cutters were and how much they were charging.

The Government as Enforcer

When cartels have been successful, the outside enforcer has often been the government. The most candid example in U.S. history is the National Industrial Recovery Act of 1933, under the provisions of which government and industry leaders met together to plan output levels with the explicit purpose of keeping prices artificially high. The act was unanimously declared unconstitutional by the U.S. Supreme Court two years after its inception.

A more subtle channel through which government plays the role of enforcer is the apparatus of the various federal regulatory agencies. You may be surprised to learn that many industries welcome regulation. A firm that wants to be told how much to produce seems as unlikely as a bargeman who wants to be whipped. Yet, like the bargeman, the firm can find itself in a Prisoner's Dilemma where it benefits from having its actions restricted. In the next section we will explore some of the more common forms of regulatory activity.

11.3 Regulation

In the United States, as in most industrialized countries, government regulation touches nearly every aspect of economic activity. Government agencies regulate hiring practices and working conditions, limit entry into professions as diverse as medicine and cosmetology, and dictate environmental standards that affect the design of everything from your car to your showerhead. Regulations are highly varied in their justifications, their effects, and the institutional arrangements through which they are enforced. Many different agencies are empowered to devise and enforce economic regulations. Some of these agencies function independently, while others are subsidiary to an executive department. Also, legislatures often pass specific statutes that are designed with regulatory intent.

Regulation has a wide variety of effects and purposes. Among these are the protection of consumers, the promotion of competition, and even the career interests of the regulators themselves. Another aspect of regulation is that it can sometimes serve to lessen competition in designated industries by introducing the government as the enforcer of a *de facto* cartel.

In the examples that follow, we will emphasize the *cartel enforcement* role of regulation, because that is the aspect of regulation that is relevant to the subject of this chapter. Do not allow this emphasis to mislead you into thinking that other aspects of regulation are less important or less interesting; they are only less germane to this discussion.

Examples of Regulation

Regulating Quantity

Learn about how the federal government regulates quality at the Food and Drug Administration site: http://www.fda.gov/

In the United States, the Interstate Commerce Commission (ICC) regulates railroads and trucking, and the Federal Aviation Administration (FAA) regulates airlines. No trucking company can operate without authority from the ICC and no airline can operate without authority from the FAA.

It has not always been easy to obtain that authority. For many years, the ICC routinely denied applications to enter the trucking industry, and strictly limited the activities of existing firms by specifying the routes they were allowed to serve and the types of freight they were allowed to haul. These strict practices kept the price of trucking services high, and were therefore vocally supported by trucking firms. The FAA was comparably strict about controlling entry by new airlines and the routes that existing airlines were allowed to serve.

Over the past two decades, with the encouragement of both parties in Congress, both the ICC and the FAA have significantly curtailed their regulatory activities. One result is that prices in both industries have fallen substantially—in the case of the airline industry, by about 50% over the past two decades.

But regulatory attempts to limit entry into other industries continue. Recently, the U.S. government has taken steps to limit entry into medical specialties, actually going so far as to pay $100 million to 42 New York hospitals in exchange for their *not* training doctors to become specialists. At around the same time, the University of California hospitals agreed to eliminate 452 residencies. The combined effect will be to raise the price of specialized medical care.

Regulating Quality

Regulation often takes the form of minimum *quality* standards. By preventing goods below a prescribed minimum quality from reaching the marketplace, such regulations increase the market power of those suppliers whose output meets the prescribed standards. You might think that consumers always benefit when the average quality of goods increases, but a moment's reflection will convince you that this need not be the case. Few would prefer to live in a world in which every car had the quality (and the price tag) of a Rolls Royce. Many consumers choose goods of lower quality because they would rather devote more income to other things. The poor choose goods of lower quality more frequently, and they are therefore hurt disproportionately when low-quality goods disappear from the marketplace. A poor man who is permitted to purchase steak but not hamburger might have to eat potatoes instead of meat.

In 1989, there were two kinds of bread widely available in Egyptian retail markets. The lower quality product sold for the equivalent of 0.8 U.S. cents per loaf, while the higher quality product sold for 2¢. By the middle of 1990, the government forced the cheap bread to be withdrawn from the market. For many Egyptians, the results were disastrous. The *New York Times* reported the plight of a family of six, each of whom ate one loaf per meal.[20] Because they

[20] "2 Cent Loaf Is Family Heartbreak in Egypt," *New York Times*, July 9, 1990.

were forced to buy the more expensive bread, the family's food expenses increased by more than $10 per month—a quarter of their income. There is no sense in which this family can be said to have benefited from the new minimum quality standard.

But there are some markets, such as the market for drugs, where low-quality products can be harmful or even fatal. In those markets, many people will instinctively agree that minimum quality standards must be beneficial to consumers. Therefore it can be particularly instructive to investigate such markets to determine the actual effects of regulation.

In the United States, the sale of non-narcotic drugs was largely unregulated until 1938. In that year, the Food and Drug Administration (FDA) first began requiring consumers to obtain a doctor's prescription before buying drugs. Have mandatory prescriptions improved consumers' health? Professor Sam Peltzman of the University of Chicago investigated this question in two ways: 1) by comparing American death rates before and after 1938; and 2) by comparing American death rates with death rates in other countries where prescriptions are still not mandatory. (Except for Argentina and Uruguay, most Latin American countries do not require prescriptions. Neither does Greece, and neither do many countries in Asia.) Peltzman concluded that, while the available evidence is too weak to support a firm conclusion, it appears that mandatory prescriptions do not save lives or lead to other improvements in health.[21]

In 1962, the U.S. Congress passed the *Kefauver Amendments*, which required drug manufacturers to prove that their products are safe and effective; the Kefauver Amendments are enforced by the FDA. To investigate the effect of this regulation, Professor Peltzman looked at the rate of new-product development in the drug industry both before and after 1962, and concluded that the Kefauver Amendments have cost more lives than they have saved.[22]

For nearly 40 years, the Kefauver amendments have saved some lives by protecting consumers from harmful drugs. At the same time, they have cost other lives by delaying the appearance of useful drugs; people have died while drugs that could have saved them were still being tested. Because the cost of testing is a disincentive to innovate, the amendments have probably cost additional lives by reducing the number of new drugs that are developed in the first place. They have also raised the price of existing drugs by reducing the number of substitutes.

Peltzman estimated such costs and benefits by observing the behavior of pharmaceutical companies both before and after 1962. He found that the net effect was overwhelmingly negative. The amendments reduced the number of new drugs entering the marketplace from approximately 41 per year to approximately 16 per year, and they introduced an average delay of two years for a drug to reach the marketplace. In recent years, partly because of studies like Peltzman's and partly in response to the spread of AIDS, the FDA has re-

---

[21] S. Peltzman, "The Health Effects of Mandatory Prescriptions", *Journal of Law and Economics* 30 (1987): 207–238.

[22] S. Peltzman, "An Evaluation of Consumer Protection Legislation: The 1962 Drug Amendments", *Journal of Political Economy* 81 (1973): 1049–1091.

laxed its rules substantially, allowing new and important drugs to be fast-tracked into the marketplace.

The FDA regulates not only the quality of drugs, but also of medical devices and food additives. A few years ago the fast-track program was extended to apply to medical devices. In many areas, though, FDA approval continues to take a long time. It was not until December 1997, after many years of delay, that the FDA appproved irradiation of meat products for controlling disease-causing micro-organisms. The FDA concluded that irradiation is a safe and important tool to protect consumers from food-borne diseases, effectively acknowledging that for several years it had denied consumers access to a safe and effective means of protecting their health. Of course, if irradiation had turned out to be harmful, the years of delay might have been a great blessing to consumers.

Frequently, quality regulations take the form of professional licensing requirements. Your doctor, your lawyer, your cab driver, and your beautician all need licenses to practice. Such requirements can help to establish minimal standards of competence; they can also restrict the number of practitioners and thereby keep prices above the competitive level.

Regulating Information

Another way in which entry to a market can be effectively curtailed is by restricting the ability of consumers to learn about new suppliers. Suppliers who cannot make their existence known are essentially excluded from the market. In practice, this is often accomplished through restrictions on advertising. Professional societies such as the American Medical Association and the American Bar Association have gone to extraordinary lengths to restrict advertising by their members.

Many reasons have been offered to suspect that advertising raises prices. It is sometimes alleged that buyers must "pay for the advertising as well as the product." On the other hand, advertising saves the consumer the cost of having to search for information about available products. Indeed, a buyer who prefers not to pay for advertising always has the option to incur the costs of seeking out a seller who does not advertise and to buy the product at a correspondingly lower price. When buyers do not do this, they reveal that they value the informational content of advertising at a price at least equal to whatever they are paying for it.

In fact, by providing information about a wide array of sellers, advertising can promote competition and might therefore actually *reduce* prices. In 1972 Lee Benham set out to investigate this question in the market for eyeglasses.[23] This market was particularly suitable for study since there is wide variation in advertising restrictions across states. He found that in states where advertising was prohibited, the price of eyeglasses was higher by 25 to 100%. This particularly persuasive empirical study has convinced many economists that the net effect of advertising is often (though surely not always) to lower prices.

---

[23] L. Benham, "The Effect of Advertising on the Price of Eyeglasses," *Journal of Law and Economics* 15 (1972):337–352.

Regulating Prices

Instead of setting quality standards, the government sometimes sets minimum prices below which goods cannot be sold. This excludes the producers of low-quality goods from the marketplace, increasing the demand for those high-quality goods that are close substitutes.

By far the most important example is the federal minimum wage law. Although this law is often presented as protective of the unskilled, it is precisely they whom it excludes from the labor market. At a minimum wage of $4.65 per hour, someone who produces $3.00 worth of output per hour will not be hired to work. Overwhelming empirical evidence has convinced most economists that the minimum wage is a significant cause of unemployment, particularly among the unskilled.

Among the beneficiaries of the minimum wage law are the more highly skilled workers who remain employed and who can command higher wages in the absence of less-skilled competition. These more highly skilled workers tend to be represented by labor unions, which, not surprisingly, tend to support increases in the minimum wage.

Minimum wage laws also have other, less obvious effects. When the federal minimum wage was first proposed in the 1930s, it was heavily supported by the northern textile industry. The reason was that wages were lower in the South than in the North, due partly to a lower cost of living in the South. As a result, northern firms found it difficult to compete. By imposing a federally mandated minimum wage, northern producers hoped to eliminate the advantage held by their southern competition, and indeed hoped to drive the South out of textile manufacturing altogether.

Regulating Business Practices

Laws that prohibit transactions at certain times of the day or week tend to inhibit competition and raise prices. So-called *blue laws* in many states prohibit the sale of various goods on Sunday. This solves a Prisoner's Dilemma for suppliers. Any given supplier must choose between the options "work on Sunday" and "not work on Sunday." Each will choose to work on Sunday whether his competitors are doing so or not; but each prefers to have nobody working Sunday than to have everybody working. Blue laws allow the supplier to watch football on Sunday afternoon without losing his business to a rival. Of course, this boon to suppliers comes at the expense of consumers, for whom Sunday is a convenient shopping day.

An interesting variant of the blue laws was recently in effect in the city of Chicago. Until quite recently it was illegal in Chicago to buy meat after 6 P.M. Repeal was opposed by the butchers' union.

example The Economics of Polygamy

The laws against polygamy provide an instructive example of the effects of output restrictions. We will consider the effect of a law that forbids any man from marrying more than one woman.

We can view men as suppliers of "husbandships," which are purchased by women at a price.[24] This price has many subtle components, including all of the agreements, spoken and unspoken, that married couples enter into. Choices about where to live, how many children to have, who will do the dishes, and where to go on Saturday nights are all contained in the price of the marriage. When husbandships are scarce, men can require more concessions on such issues as conditions of their marriages. For example, if there were only one marriageable man and many marriageable women, the man would be in a position to insist that any woman he marries must agree to attend professional wrestling with him every weeknight (assuming that this is something he values). If one woman will not agree to this price, he can probably find another woman who will.

Thus, the price of a husbandship is higher when husbandships are scarce, and, similarly, the price of a husbandship is low when husbandships are abundant. If each man wanted to marry four women, the price of husbandships would be bid down (or, equivalently, the price of wifeships would be bid up) to the point where men would have to make considerable concessions in order to attract even one wife. It is in the interests of men as producers to restrict output so that this does not happen. Antipolygamy laws accomplish this. Thus, the analysis suggests that laws against polygamy, like other laws restricting output, benefit producers (in this case men) and hurt consumers (in this case women).

Sometimes students argue that no woman in the modern world would want to be part of a multiwife marriage, and that therefore women could not possibly benefit from the legalization of polygamy. But this is incorrect, because even under polygamy those women who wanted to could demand as a condition of marriage that their husbands agree not to take any additional wives. And even if no man took more than one wife, the price of wives would still be higher.

For example, imagine a one-husband one-wife family where an argument has begun over whose turn it is to do the dishes. If polygamy were legal, the wife could threaten to leave and go marry the couple next door unless the husband concedes that it is his turn. With polygamy outlawed, she does not have this option and might end up with dishpan hands.

Another reason why students are sometimes surprised by this conclusion is that they are aware of polygamous societies in which the status of women is not high. But, of course, the difference in polygamy laws is not the only important difference between those societies and our own. The fact that polygamy is legal in many places where women are otherwise oppressed does not constitute an argument that the oppression is caused by polygamy. Our analysis compares the status of women with and without legalized polygamy on the assumption that other social institutions are held constant.

[24]Because we are examining the market for husbands, men are the producers and women the consumers. It would be equally correct to treat the marriage market as a market for wives, in which women are the producers and men the consumers. Since we are investigating the effects of the law that restricts the supply of husbands, it is more convenient to think of "husbandships" rather than "wifeships" as the commodity being traded.

In view of our analysis, it is interesting that polygamy laws are often alleged to "protect" women. It has been observed that laws prohibiting any man from marrying more than one woman are perfectly analogous to laws preventing any firm from hiring more than one black.[25] Surely no one would be so audacious as to claim that the purpose of such a law was to protect blacks.

What Can Regulators Regulate?

In any study of the effects of regulation, it is necessary to ask what regulators actually do. In the last 25 years economists have become increasingly aware that regulators' own descriptions of their activities should not always be taken at face value.

In 1962 George Stigler and Claire Friedland examined the effects of regulation in the electric power industry.[26] They examined electric rates in the years 1912–1937. During these years some states regulated the price of electricity and others did not. Stigler and Friedland found that the presence of regulation had no observable effect on the actual price of electricity. The evidence suggested that the regulatory commission consistently ends up setting the price that the utilities would have chosen anyway.

In 1964 Stigler applied a similar analysis to the regulation of the securities industry by the Securities and Exchange Commission (SEC).[27] The SEC requires issuers of securities (for example, corporate stocks) to make public disclosures of relevant information. If you try to sell stock in a gold mine that has never produced any gold, the SEC will require that this fact be disclosed to potential buyers. Stigler examined the performance of newly issued stocks compared with the performance of the market as a whole, before and after the formation of the SEC in 1934. He found that there was no change in the propensity of newly issued stocks to perform well. It appeared that the SEC made no real difference; there is no evidence that the mix of securities that was offered under regulation differed appreciably from the mix of securities that would have been offered in an unregulated market.

These and other studies have convinced a growing number of economists that an industry should not necessarily be considered regulated just because of the existence of an agency with the formal power to regulate it. In many cases there may be political or other considerations that prevent the agency from ever taking any steps that actually have the effect of altering economic behavior. Whether or not an allegedly "regulated" industry is really regulated in any meaningful sense is an empirical question, one that must be decided on a case-by-case basis.

Creative Response and Unexpected Consequences

Although it can be in the interest of an industry to be regulated, it is almost always in the interest of an individual firm to avoid the effects of regulation when

---

[25] G. Becker, "A Theory of Marriage," *Journal of Political Economy* 81 (1973):813–846.

[26] G. Stigler and C. Friedland, "What Can Regulators Regulate? The Case of Electricity," *Journal of Law and Economics* 82 (1974):S11–S26.

[27] G. Stigler, "Public Regulation of the Securities Market," *Journal of Business* 37 (1964).

Creative response A response to a regulation that conforms to the letter of the law while undermining its spirit.

possible. This often leads firms to engage in **creative response,** behaving in ways that conform to the letter of the law while undermining its spirit. For this reason and others, regulations can have unexpected consequences—sometimes directly contrary to the intentions of the regulators.

Until a few years ago, parents traveling on airplanes were allowed to hold infants on their laps. More recently, parents have been required to buy a separate seat for the infant. This regulation, apparently motivated by a desire to make infants safer, has had exactly the opposite effect as many parents, unwilling to pay for the additional seats, have opted to travel by car instead of by airplane. Because the death rate per mile is about 70 times greater in a car, economists have estimated that the net effect of the regulation has been an increase in the number of infant deaths.

Another striking example concerns the use of pesticides. Certain pesticides are banned because of potential health hazards. But a side effect is to raise the cost of growing fruits and vegetables, thereby raising their price and lowering the quantity demanded. The prominent biologist Bruce Ames has pointed out that the fall in fruit and vegetable consumption is likely to be more damaging to health than the pesticides were.

Sometimes the unexpected consequences of regulation can be unexpectedly delightful. In renaissance Europe, regulations forbade unlicensed actors to speak on stage. According to some historians, the result was the advent of modern pantomime.

Here are some further examples from recent history, to demonstrate how creative responses can undermine the apparent intent of a regulation.

example

Affirmative Action Laws

Affirmative action laws provide an example where a creative response may have led to consequences directly contradictory to the intent of the original legislation. These laws and regulations arose from the observation that black workers were systematically paid less than white workers. They required employers to remedy this imbalance by paying higher wages to black workers.

However, wages are only part of the compensation that a worker receives. Typically, workers receive a variety of valuable fringe benefits as well. One of the most important fringe benefits, especially in entry-level positions, is on-the-job training. Such training enables employees to acquire basic skills that will raise their income later in life. Its value often represents a substantial portion of the employee's total compensation.

Since on-the-job training is largely unobservable to outsiders, employers can adjust its quantity without being found guilty of violating those laws that regulate workers' compensation. Thus, some employers were able to comply with the affirmative action regulations without actually changing the total value of the compensation that they offered to blacks. They simply paid a higher wage, satisfying the regulator, while compensating by offering less on-the-job training. Between the years 1966 and 1974 the *observable* wage differences between blacks and whites were essentially eliminated, but they were partially replaced by *unobservable* differences. For black workers this meant higher starting salaries, less on-the-job training, and lower future wages than before affirmative action.

The net effect of all this on the economic status of blacks could be either positive or negative. In one study Professor Edward Lazear found that the relative economic status of blacks (taking account of all their expected future earnings) was not improved by the affirmative action laws.[28] In fact, his evidence supported just the opposite conclusion—that during the period 1966–1972 the gap between black and white compensation, inclusive of the value of on-the-job training, actually widened.

example

Reasonable Quantities of Sale Items

In the late 1970s the Federal Trade Commission (FTC), which regulates (among other things) against false and deceptive advertising, discovered that one of its regulations led to responses that were counterproductive. The FTC periodically receives complaints about the unavailability of advertised specials. Consumers travel to stores that are advertising items at unusually low prices, only to find that those items are sold out shortly after the commencement of the sale. Understandably, these consumers are annoyed. The FTC responded to these complaints in the mid-1970s by issuing a series of regulations requiring stores to have on hand a "reasonable quantity" of any item that was advertised at a sale price.

To understand the effect of these regulations, it is necessary first to understand the reasons for sales. In many (though certainly not all) cases a store will decide to discontinue stocking a certain item and will want to dispose quickly of its remaining stock. In such cases ordering sufficient additional inventory to have a "reasonable quantity" on hand would contravene the very purpose of the sale. Therefore, one effect of the regulations was that sales of this type were discontinued. In view of this effect, fewer items were offered at sale prices. At the same time, it meant that when there *were* sales, the sale items were usually available.

Throughout the late 1970s the FTC interviewed consumers about their feelings regarding the new rules. On the basis of these interviews, the FTC decided that the rules tended to benefit people with higher incomes at the expense of the poor. People with high incomes have a high value of time; they find it very costly to drive to a store only to discover that the item they are shopping for is out of stock. To them the cost of these fruitless shopping trips outweighs the benefit of having more sales to choose from. People with low incomes have a lower value of time and place greater value on being able to buy at sale prices. They prefer there to be more sales, even if the stores sometimes run out before they get there.

On the basis of this analysis, the FTC rescinded its rules on advertised specials.

Positive Theories of Regulation

Throughout this section we have examined some of the consequences of certain existing regulations. However, we have made no attempt to address the

---

[28]E. Lazear, "The Narrowing of Black-White Wage Differentials Is Illusory," *American Economic Review* 69 (1979):553–564.

question of why some industries are regulated and others are not. We have focused primarily on ways in which regulation might act to limit competition. But we have made no attempt to formulate a general principle concerning when regulations will limit competition and when they will serve some other function, such as promoting economic efficiency.

Many economists think that there is a need for a positive theory of regulation, to predict the circumstances under which various types of regulations arise and what their effects will be. Such a theory would have to explain why the trucking industry is more heavily regulated than the airline industry, why some occupations require professional licenses while others don't, and why electricity prices seem to have been unaffected by regulation. A complete theory would begin with an explicit account of what it is that regulators are trying to accomplish. For example, regulators might be motivated by a desire to redistribute wealth in certain ways, or by a desire to protect consumers from major disasters, or even by a desire to maximize their own power. From such assumptions, one could derive conclusions about when, where, and what types of regulations are most likely to occur.

A theory of this sort might also be used to explain why regulations are selectively enforced. For example, radar detectors are legal in 48 states, despite the fact that their only purpose is to facilitate breaking the law. Why are people permitted to purchase the opportunity to violate speed limits with a reduced probability of punishment?

Various theories are consistent with this observation. If the goal of regulators is to increase economic efficiency, they might want to allow speeding by those whose time is sufficiently valuable. These would be primarily those who find it worthwhile to invest in a radar detector. An alternative theory is that regulators prefer not to antagonize the politically powerful, and that those who are wealthy enough to want radar detectors are also powerful enough to keep the regulators at bay.

Which theory seems more sensible to you? Can you think of other examples that would tend to confirm or refute one of these theories? What alternative theories can you propose?

11.4 Oligopoly

Oligopoly An industry in which individual firms can influence market conditions.

An **oligopoly** is an industry in which the number of firms is sufficiently small that any one firm's actions can affect market conditions. Thus, in an oligopoly each firm has a certain degree of monopoly power. The behavior of such firms depends on many things, including whether they are threatened by potential entry. We will first consider markets in which entry is costless (and therefore an ever-present threat), and then markets in which the number of firms is fixed.

Contestable Markets

Contestable market A market in which firms can enter and exit costlessly.

A market in which firms can enter and exit costlessly is called a **contestable market**.[29] A commonly cited example is the market for airplane service on a

[29]The theory of contestable markets is surveyed by its founders in W. Baumol, S. Panzard, and R. Willig, *Contestable Markets and the Theory of Industry Structure* (San Diego: Harcourt Brace Jovanovich, 1982).

particular route, say, from Houston to Dallas. The owner of an airplane that is currently flying back and forth between Houston and San Antonio can easily move into the Houston-to-Dallas market if there is a profit opportunity, and can easily return to the Houston-to-San Antonio market at any time.

In a contestable market, even a single firm producing a unique product with no close substitutes might not be able to engage in monopoly pricing, because the profits that it would earn by doing so would lure entrants and destroy its market position. Exhibit 11–8 illustrates the position of a monopolist threatened by potential entry. Assuming all firms are identical, their entry price will be P_0.

EXERCISE 11.5 Explain why firms would enter if the market price of output were P_0 but would not enter at any lower price.

It follows that the market price cannot be higher than P_0, since any higher price will attract entry. At this price the firm will produce the quantity Q_0. The market will demand Q_1, which may be several times Q_0. If, for example, Q_1 is

Exhibit 11-8 A Contestable Market

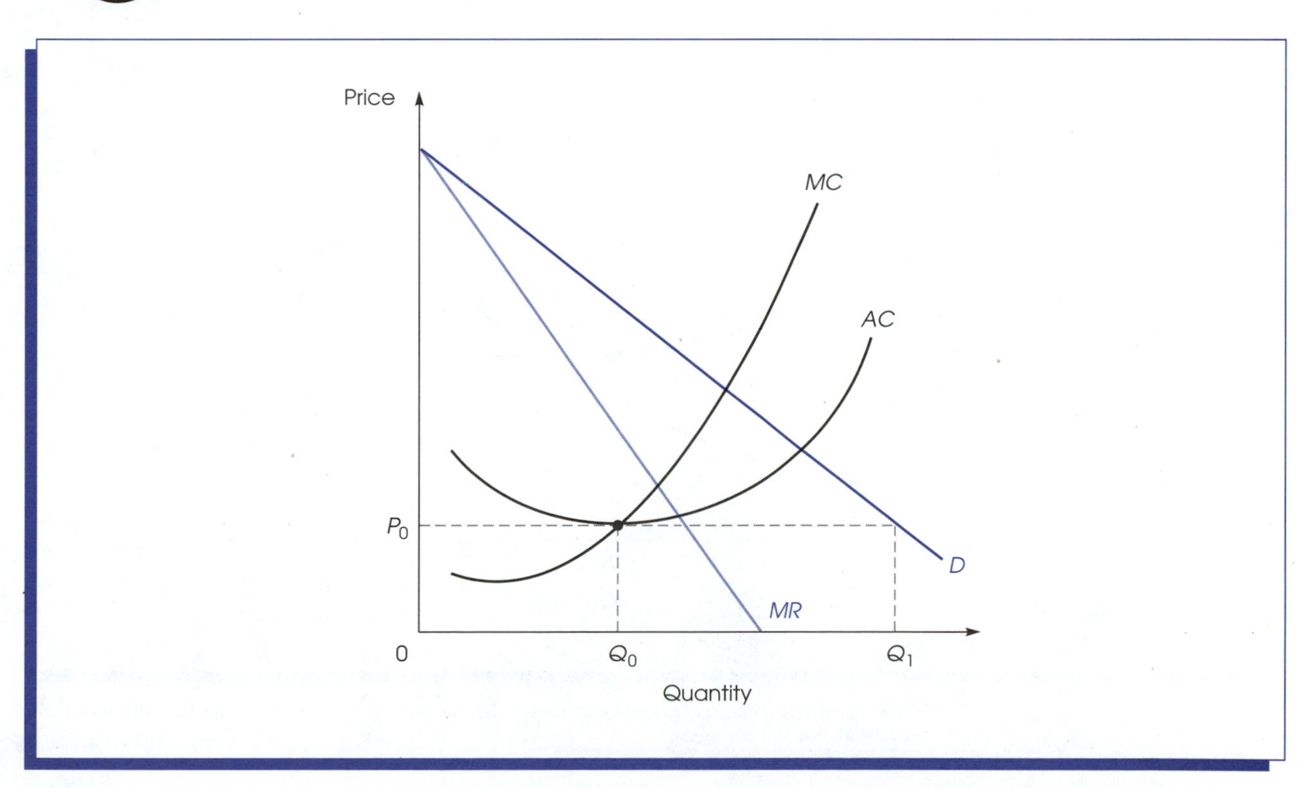

If the market is contestable, firms will enter at any price above P_0. Therefore, the market price cannot be higher than P_0, because any higher price would attract entry. At this price the firm supplies Q_0 units of output and the market demands Q_1. Thus, there is room in the industry for Q_1/Q_0 firms.

twice Q_0 there will be room for a second firm to imitate exactly the actions of the first firm without exhausting market demand. If Q_1 is seven times Q_0, there will be room for seven firms altogether. In general, the number of firms that actually enter will be equal to Q_1/Q_0, each producing Q_0 items at a price of P_0, which equals both average and marginal cost.[30] In other words, potential entry will force firms to behave as competitors, even if there are very few firms.

In a contestable market with identical firms whose average cost curves cross the industry demand curve in the region where they are upward sloping, price, average cost, and marginal cost are all equal.

Contestable Markets and Natural Monopoly

There is also the possibility of natural monopoly in a contestable market. That is, the firm's average cost curve might still be downward sloping where it crosses industry demand. This is shown in Exhibit 11–9. In this case, a

Exhibit 11-9 Natural Monopoly in a Contestable Market

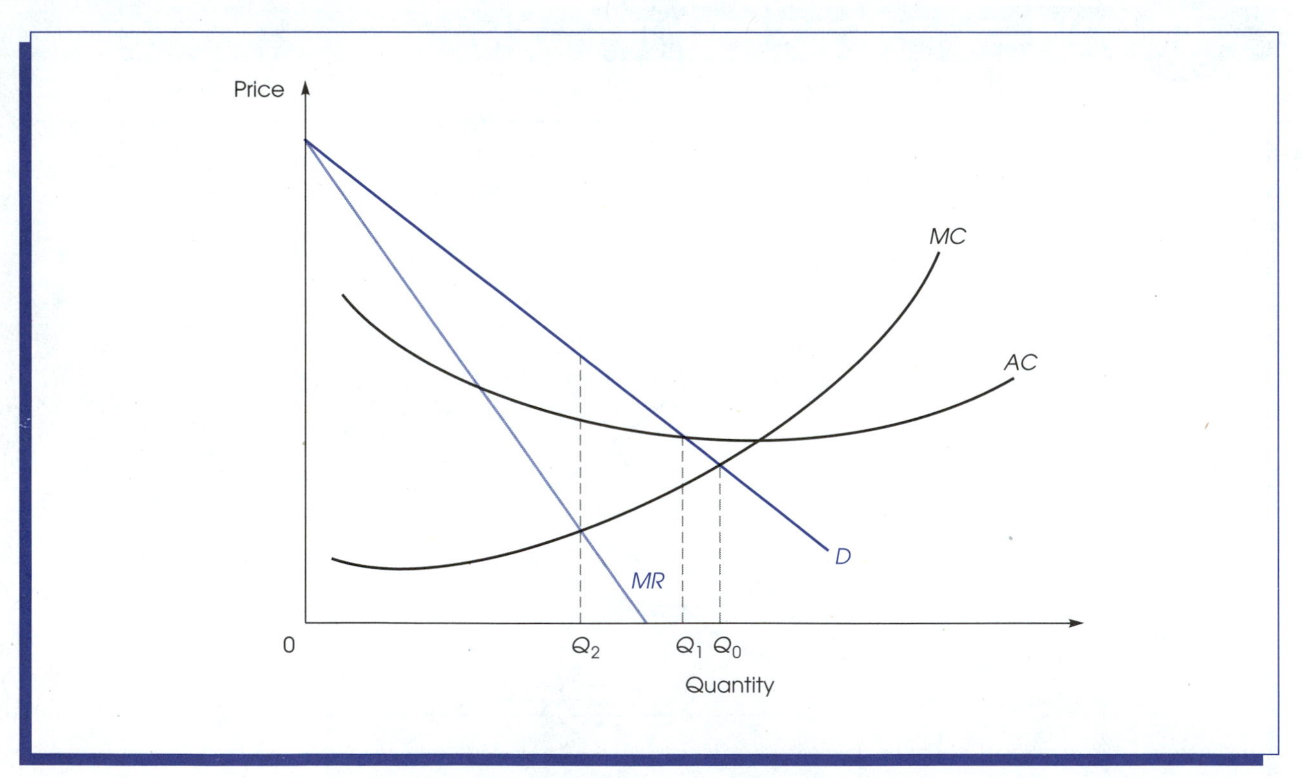

If the market is contestable, a natural monopolist must set output at Q_1 so that it earns zero profits and avoids attracting entry.

[30]There is a slight problem related to the fact that Q_1/Q_0 may not be exactly equal to an integer, in which case we expect the number of firms to be either the integer just above or just below Q_1/Q_0.

monopoly producer cannot operate at the "competitive" point Q_0, because his profits there would be negative. On the other hand, if he follows the usual monopoly pricing rule of setting marginal cost equal to marginal revenue (producing Q_2), he may earn positive profits and lure other firms into the industry. The threat of entry forces him to operate at the zero profits point Q_1.

Oligopoly with a Fixed Number of Firms

When there is no threat of entry, the behavior of an oligopoly is more difficult to predict. One possibility is the formation of a cartel. As we have seen, the Prisoner's Dilemma guarantees that there are forces tending to undermine the success of cartels. On the other hand, cartels are really *repeated* Prisoner's Dilemmas, since firms produce output every day. We have also seen that the outcome of repeated Prisoner's Dilemmas is hard to predict.

When there is no collusion, each firm's actions depend on the actions that it expects the other firms to take. Therefore, the way in which firms form their expectations about each other's behavior is a crucial ingredient in modeling oligopoly. We will examine two different models that proceed from different assumptions about expectation formation. In one, the **Cournot model**,[31] firms take their rivals' output as given. In the other, the **Bertrand model**,[32] firms take their rivals' prices as given.

Cournot model A model of oligopoly in which firms take their rivals' output as given.

Bertrand model A model of oligopoly in which firms take their rivals' prices as given.

The Cournot Model

To simplify the analysis, we will assume an industry with exactly two identical firms having the flat marginal cost curve shown in Exhibit 11–10. We will also assume a straight line demand curve, so that marginal revenue has exactly twice the slope of demand. A monopoly would produce the quantity Q_M and a competitive industry would produce the quantity Q_C. Because of what we have just said about the slopes of the curves, we must have

$$Q_M = \frac{1}{2} Q_C$$

Now let us see what the two firms will produce. Suppose that Firm B produces the quantity Q_B and Firm A makes the assumption that this quantity will never change. Then Firm A views itself as a monopolist in the market for the remaining quantity. That is, Firm A is a monopolist in a market where the zero quantity axis is the blue vertical line in Exhibit 11–10, and the demand curve is the color part of the industry demand curve. In such a market the marginal revenue curve is the color curve MR_A parallel to the industry marginal revenue curve MR. Firm A produces the quantity Q_A, where $MC = MR_A$. Since this is the

[31]For the nineteenth-century French mathematician Augustin Cournot.

[32]For the nineteenth-century French economist Joseph Bertrand.

Exhibit 11-10 The Cournot Model of Oligopoly

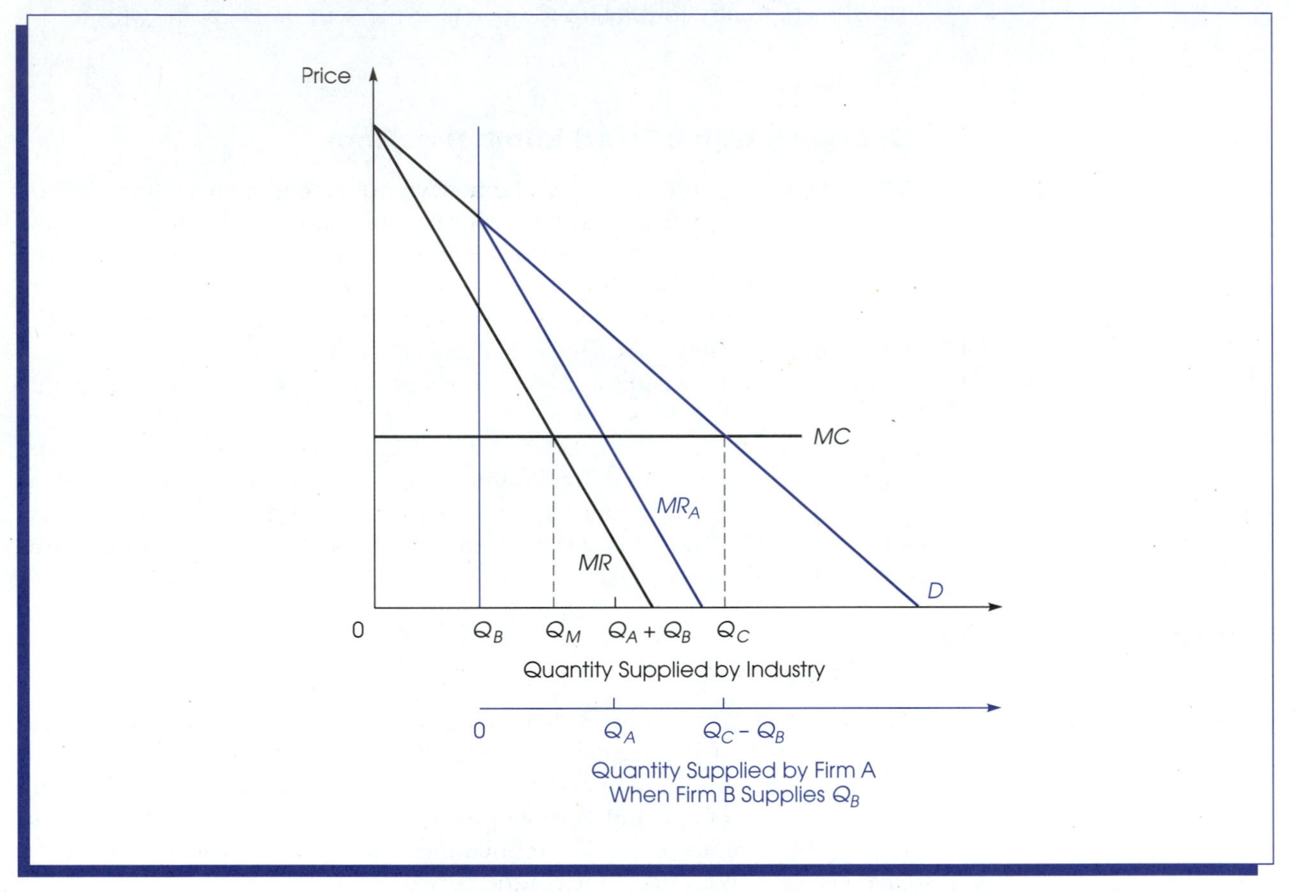

We assume that two identical firms have the flat marginal cost curve *MC* and face a market demand curve *D*. A competitive industry would produce the quantity Q_C. A monopolist would produce the quantity $Q_M = \frac{1}{2} Q_C$, where *MC* crosses the marginal revenue curve *MR*.

If Firm A assumes that Firm B will always produce quantity Q_B, then Firm A views itself as a monopolist in the market for the remaining quantity. The demand curve in that market is the blue part of the market demand curve, measured along the blue axis. The marginal revenue curve is the blue curve MR_A. Firm A produces the monopoly quantity Q_A, which is half the competitive quantity ($Q_C - Q_B$). Combining this fact with the equation $Q_A = Q_B$ (which follows from the fact that the firms are identical), we compute that $Q_A = Q_B = \frac{1}{3} Q_B = Q_C$. Thus, the industry output is $\frac{2}{3} Q_C$, less than the competitive output but more than the monopoly output.

monopoly quantity, it must lie halfway between Firm A's zero quantity axis at Q_B and the competitive point $Q_C - Q_B$. That is,

$$Q_A = \frac{1}{2}(Q_C - Q_B)$$

We can also write one additional equation. Since it is assumed that Firms A and B are identical, it is reasonable to expect that they will produce equal quantities of output. This gives us the equation

$$Q_A = Q_B$$

Putting the two equations together, we get

$$Q_A = \frac{1}{2}(Q_C - Q_A)$$

which can be solved for Q_A, giving

$$Q_A = \frac{1}{3}Q_C$$

In other words, each firm produces ⅓ of the competitive quantity, so that between them they produce ⅔ of the competitive quantity. This is more than the monopoly output, which is only ½ of the competitive quantity.

The Bertrand Model

The Bertrand model has the same flavor as the Cournot model. In the Cournot model, each firm assumes that its rivals will never change quantity. In the Bertrand model, each firm assumes that its rivals will never change price.

As long as price exceeds marginal cost, an oligopolist in the Bertrand model will always want to undercut his rivals by offering a slightly lower price. Since he assumes that his rivals will not meet this price cut, it follows that he will be able to capture the entire market for himself. This is a profitable strategy. The tiniest of price cuts leads to a sizable increase in sales, and all of these sales are at a price that exceeds marginal cost.

Bertrand oligopolists will continue to undercut one another until price falls to marginal cost. Thus, according to Bertrand, price and output will be the same under oligopoly as they are under competition.

Criticism of the Cournot and Bertrand Models

Many economists are uncomfortable with both the Cournot and the Bertrand models of oligopoly, because each model posits that firms make incorrect assumptions about their rivals' behavior. In the Cournot model, firms assume that their own choice of output will not affect their rivals' choices, despite the fact that they know that their rivals' choices are affecting their own. The same is true in the Bertrand model regarding prices instead of quantities.

This criticism highlights the major difficulty that economists face when they attempt to model oligopoly behavior. The assumptions that firms make about one another's behavior are crucial elements in the determination of their own behavior, and the economist must therefore presume to know something about those assumptions. If the assumptions turn out to be incorrect, firms should become aware of this fact over time, invalidating the model. In the real world we expect that oligopolists have at least reasonably accurate information about how their rivals behave, and we would like our models to reflect that fact. Unfortunately, satisfactory models with this property have proven difficult to construct. In much recent research, game theory has proved to be an increasingly effective tool.

11.5 Monopolistic Competition and Product Differentiation

Product differentiation The production of a product that is unique but has many close substitutes.

One strategy for acquiring some degree of monopoly power in a market that is basically competitive is called **product differentiation.** As its name implies, this strategy involves producing a product that differs sufficiently from the output of other producers that some consumers will have a distinct preference for it. Crest and Colgate both produce toothpaste, but they do not produce identical products. The two products are close substitutes, and neither can be priced very differently from the other without a substantial loss of market share. At the same time, there are some consumers with a very strong preference for one or the other brand, so that each firm faces a demand curve that is at least slightly downward sloping.

Products with brand names are product differentiated simply by virtue of having different brand names. But other characteristics can differentiate them as well. The location at which a product is sold can differentiate it from others. A 7-Eleven two blocks from your house is not the same to you as a 7-Eleven a mile and a half away, although they are probably close substitutes.

Monopolistic Competition

Monopolistic competition The theory of markets in which there are many similar but differentiated products.

The theory of markets in which there are many similar but differentiated products is called the theory of **monopolistic competition.** The first panel of Exhibit 11–11 illustrates the conditions facing a monopolistically competitive firm. Suppose that the firm is currently charging price P and selling quantity Q. The demand curve d shows how much the firm can sell at any given price on the assumption that all other firms continue to charge the original price P.

EXERCISE 11.6 Explain why you might expect the curve d to be quite elastic compared with the demand curve facing an ordinary monopolist.

The quantity Q is determined by the condition that $MC = mr$, where MC is the firm's marginal cost curve and mr is the marginal revenue curve associated with d. In panel A of the exhibit, the firm is earning positive profits, since the price P exceeds average cost at quantity Q.

In the long run these profits will attract entry by other firms selling similar products. As a result, the demand curve facing the firm will shift downward, to d' in panel B of Exhibit 11–11. The firm produces quantity Q' and charges price P'. At this point price and average cost are equal, so that profits are zero and there is no further entry.

At the long-run equilibrium quantity Q', the demand curve must touch the average cost curve to give zero profits. You might wonder why we have drawn the curves tangent rather

Exhibit 11-11 Monopolistic Competition

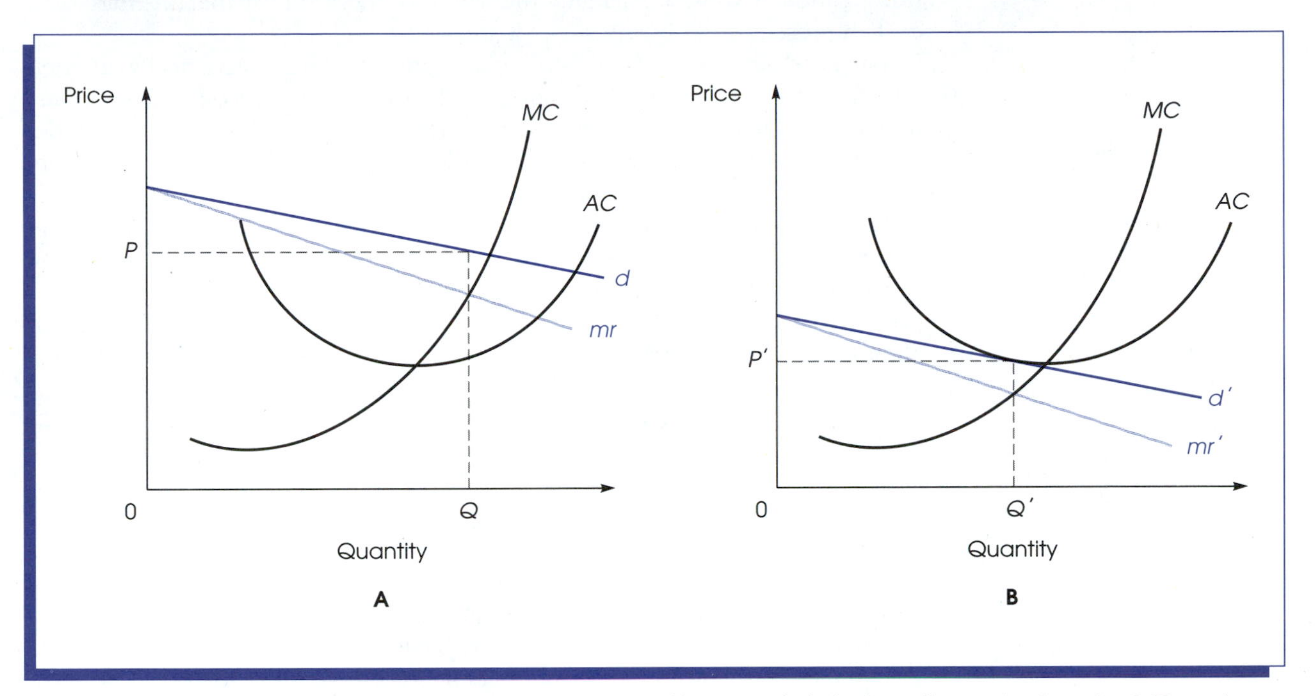

Panel A shows a short-run equilibrium in which the firm sells quantity Q at price P. Here price exceeds average cost, so the firm earns positive profits. In the long run, entry drives the demand curve facing this firm down to d' in panel B, where the firm is just able to earn zero profits by selling quantity Q' at price P'.

than crossing. The reason is that if the curves crossed, the firm could earn positive profits by producing a quantity slightly less than Q'. But we know that Q', the zero profits point, is also the point of maximum profits, since it is the point where $MC = mr$. Thus, it cannot be correct to draw the average cost curve actually crossing demand.

Welfare Aspects of Monopolistic Competition

In Exhibit 11–11 we can see that price is set above marginal cost by a monopolistic competitor, so that the level of output is suboptimal. On the other hand, since we expect monopolistic competitors to face quite elastic demand curves, the deviation of output from the competitive level might not be too great.

A related issue is that a monopolistic competitor, as shown in Exhibit 11–11, does not produce at the minimum point of his average cost curve. Indeed, he cannot do so, since in long-run equilibrium he produces at a point of tangency between his average cost curve and his downward-sloping demand curve. It follows that if a monopolistically competitive industry were replaced by a competitive one, the same output could be produced at lower cost.

It is sometimes argued that monopolistically competitive firms tend to invest more in advertising and other methods of luring each other's customers than is socially optimal. Insofar as such practices simply shift customers from one firm to another without changing the nature of the products that are sold, their costs represent unnecessary social losses.

Balanced against all of this is the observation that monopolistically competitive industries do provide consumers with something that competitive industries do not, namely, differentiated products. Although Burker King and McDonald's are already similar, many people would be unhappy if one of them became exactly like the other.

How can we weigh the inefficiencies associated with monopolistic competition on the one hand against the benefits of product differentiation on the other? Although many economists have strong beliefs about the relative importance of these phenomena, there is not yet any general theory available that allows us to answer such a question in a definitive way.

The Economics of Location

Depending on market conditions, firms may choose either to exaggerate or to minimize their differences. An amusing example involves two ice cream vendors on a beach. Suppose that the beach is a straight line one mile long and that bathers are distributed evenly along it. There are two ice cream vendors, indistinguishable except for location, and each bather will patronize the vendor nearest him. Where will the vendors locate?

Exhibit 11–12 shows the initial positions of the vendors. Given these positions, vendor A will soon realize that he can have more customers if he moves to the right. As long as he stays to the left of vendor B, he will retain all of the customers to his own left, and he can acquire more by moving a bit to the right. Similarly, vendor B has much to gain and nothing to lose by shifting to the left. The only possible equilibrium is for the two vendors to locate right next to each other, exactly at the half-mile mark!

EXERCISE 11.7 What would happen if the vendors started out next to each other but somewhere other than at the halfway point?

Exhibit 11-12 Ice Cream Vendors on a Beach

A B

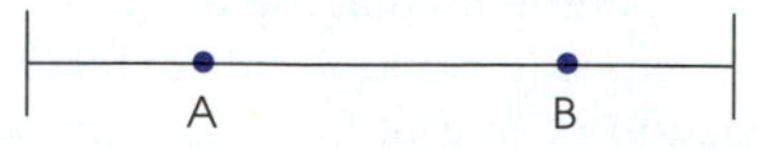

If the vendors start out in the locations shown, each will move toward the center in an attempt to gain more customers. The equilibrium is reached when they are located right next to each other and can move no farther.

Perhaps this example provides a metaphor for the behavior of the two major U.S. political parties. With voters distributed on a continuum from left to right, and voting for the party "closest" to themselves, the parties will behave just as the ice cream vendors do. Do you believe that this metaphor captures a significant feature of reality?

summary

This chapter surveys a number of examples and models in which firms exercise or attempt to exercise various degrees of monopoly power.

Horizontal mergers can both reduce production costs and create monopoly power, and therefore they have ambiguous welfare consequences. Vertical mergers can have the effect of reducing the exercise of monopoly power, since no monopolist would want to extract monopoly profits from one of its own subsidiaries.

In order to eliminate rivals, a firm might engage in the practice of predatory pricing, or it might attempt a strategy of buying out its rivals. Each of these strategies is severely limited. In the case of predatory pricing, there is the threat that rivals will resurface after prices are raised. In the case of buy-outs, new rivals are attracted to the industry by the prospect of being bought out.

When the firms in an industry can collude, they increase producers' surplus and thus can improve each firm's welfare through a system of side payments. However, as in the Prisoner's Dilemma, each individual firm has an incentive to cheat. The reason is that a cartel sets price higher than marginal cost, so that each firm will want to sell more than it is supposed to under the cartel agreement. Therefore, cartels tend to break down unless there is a good enforcement mechanism.

In addition to its other purposes, government regulation can serve as an enforcement mechanism for a cartel. Regulations restrict output in many ways. Professional licensing, minimum quality standards, minimum prices, advertising restrictions, and blue laws can all serve to restrict output and keep prices high. However, there is some evidence that the power of regulators to alter market conditions is sometimes less than it seems.

In contestable markets, entry and exit are costless. Even when there is only one firm in a contestable market, that firm must earn zero profits because of the threat of entry.

The Cournot and Bertrand models apply to oligopolies with a fixed number of firms. In the Cournot model, firms take their rivals' output as given and end up producing more than the monopoly quantity but less than the competitive quantity. In the Bertrand model, firms take their rivals' prices as given and end up producing the competitive quantity.

Under monopolistic competition, firms produce differentiated products. Each firm's product is unique but is similar to those of other firms. Thus, each firm faces a downward-sloping but nevertheless quite elastic demand curve. In the long run, entry forces profits to zero, which implies that firms must *not* be operating at the point of minimum average cost. The negative welfare consequences of this must be balanced against the gains to consumers from having a wide variety of product options, but economists have developed no good general theory of the welfare consequences of monopolistic competition.

Review Questions

R1. What is the distinction between a horizontal merger and a vertical merger?

R2. Under what circumstances is a horizontal merger welfare-improving?

R3. What are some of the advantages and disadvantages to a firm in engaging in predatory pricing? In a strategy of buying out rivals?

R4. Explain why resale price maintenance might be expected to benefit consumers.

R5. Why do both prisoners confess in the Prisoner's Dilemma? In what sense is the outcome not Pareto-optimal? How could both prisoners be made better off?

R6. Explain the analogy between the Prisoner's Dilemma and the breakdown of cartels.

R7. Why might the firms in an industry want to be regulated?

R8. What determines the number of firms in a contestable market?

R9. Explain carefully how output is determined in a Cournot oligopoly.

R10. Explain carefully how price is determined in a Bertrand oligopoly.

R11. What disturbing feature do the Bertrand and Cournot models have in common?

R12. Explain carefully how price and output are determined under monopolistic competition.

R13. Explain why, in a long-run monopolistically competitive equilibrium, average cost is never minimized.

Numerical Exercises

N1. Suppose that a monopoly steel producer produces steel at zero marginal costs, and sells to a monopoly automaker at a price P_{steel}. The automaker has no costs other than the cost of steel, which is converted into cars at the rate of one ton of steel to one car. There is no other way to produce a car than to use a ton of steel. The demand for cars is given by $Q_{cars} = 100 - P_{cars}$.

- **a.** For a given price of steel, what quantity of cars will the automaker produce in order to maximize profits? (*Hint:* The function $-Q^2 + kQ$, with k constant, is maximized at $Q = k/2$.)
- **b.** What is the equation for the automaker's demand curve for steel?
- **c.** How much steel is produced? At what price? How many cars are produced? At what price?
- **d.** If the steel producer acquires ownership of the automaker, how many cars are produced? At what price?

N2. Suppose that Microsoft is the only producer of operating systems and Netscape is the only producer of Web browsers. Suppose also that nobody wants an operating system without a web browser and nobody wants a Web browser without an operating system. Suppose that both firms produce at zero marginal cost, and that the demand for a package consisting of an operating system and a browser is given by $Q = 100 - P$.

- **a.** Suppose that Microsoft and Netscape take each others' prices as given. What is the price of an operating system? What is the price of a browser?
- **b.** Suppose instead that Microsoft first announces a price for its operating

system; then Netscape takes this price as given and sets a price for its browser. Now what is the price of an operating system? What is the price of a browser?

c. Suppose that Microsoft merges with Netscape. Now what is the price for a package consisting of an operating system and a browser?

N3. Dr. Miles is a monopolist who sells a type of patent medicine through competitive retailers. The demand curve for this patent medicine is given by $Q = 100 - 2P$, where P is the price and Q is the number of bottles sold.

a. If Dr. Miles has zero marginal cost, how many bottles of medicine will he sell and at what price? Calculate the consumers' surplus. Calculate Dr. Miles's producer's surplus.

b. Now suppose that retailers are able to provide their customers with valuable services by explaining how the medicine is to be used, what ailments it is effective against, and so on. By incurring a cost of C in time and effort per bottle sold, the retailer can provide services that consumers value at V per bottle sold, where V is given by $V = 5C - C^2$. What is the socially optimal amount of service per bottle for retailers to offer? What is the cost of this service?

c. Now suppose that retailers who offer services do not sell any additional medicine, because customers accept the services and then shop elsewhere, buying from a cut-rate supplier who offers no services. To combat this, Dr. Miles institutes a fair trade agreement under which he will sell at a wholesale price of P_0 but retailers must charge a retail price of P_1. Retailers have no other costs. Explain why retailers will incur costs of service equal to $C = P_1 - P_0$. What is the socially optimal value for C?

d. Taking C as given, write the equation of the new demand curve that retailers face after Dr. Miles institutes fair trade. Write the equation of the new demand curve Dr. Miles faces. In view of his wanting to face the highest possible demand curve, what value will Dr. Miles choose for C?

e. Using your answers to part d, calculate the new price P_0 that Dr. Miles will charge, the new quantity sold, the new consumers' surplus, and the new producer's surplus.

Problem Set

1. Consider a competitive industry where the demand and supply curves are straight lines of equal absolute value, and the supply curve goes through the origin. If all of the firms in the industry merge into one, the new firm will be able to produce at zero marginal cost. On efficiency grounds, should the merger be allowed?

2. Suppose that a monopoly supplier selling in two distinct markets wants to price discriminate. How might the monopolist benefit from a vertical merger?

3. Candy makers sometimes print retail prices directly on the wrappers. Is this a form of resale price maintenance? If so, what are its benefits? If not, what is the reason for the practice?

4. Suppose that a monopoly firm introduces a policy of resale price maintenance. Under the "special services" theory of resale price maintenance, would the firm's output increase or decrease? Conversely, suppose that the purpose of the resale price maintenance is to enforce a cartel among the dealers. Now would the firm's output increase or decrease?

5. Many firms employ salesmen who are assigned exclusive territories. No salesman may enter another's territory and attempt to sell the manufacturer's product there. Construct a theory to explain why firms adopt this practice. Does your theory suggest what kinds of products will be sold in this way and what kinds will not be?

6. Suppose that bicycle dealers serve their customers by providing fancy showrooms and knowledgeable sales forces to answer questions, but that only a small number of customers value these services. Show that in this case, resale price maintenance can cause an increase in bicycle sales but a *decrease* in social welfare.[33]

7. Suppose that airplane flights are provided at a constant marginal cost P_C. (That is, the marginal cost curve in the airline industry is flat at the price P_C.) If there were a single monopoly airline, it would sell tickets at the higher price P_M. Suppose that the government requires all airlines to charge the price P_M and forbids new entry into the airline industry.

   a. Show the consumers' surplus, the producers' surplus, and the deadweight loss.

   b. Now suppose the airlines discover that they can make themselves more attractive to customers by offering costly "extras" ranging from in-flight movies to the scheduling of frequent flights that better accommodate travelers' schedules. By how much does the marginal cost curve rise and why?

   c. In part b, what happens to the demand for airline flights? Recalculate the consumers' and producers' surpluses.

   d. In part c, is it possible that the net social gain could be greater than it is under competition? (*Hint:* Which additional services would be offered under competition and which would not?)

8. True or False Resale price maintenance can be good for consumers because it means there will be more dealer services. Thus, if the marginal value of dealer services decreases rapidly, then the benefits of resale price maintenance are reduced.

9. Offer some alternative theories to explain why manufacturers want fair trade. How might you go about testing your theories vis-á-vis the one out-

[33]This is a hard problem. It is based on an analysis by W. S. Comanor in "Vertical Price Fixing, Vertical Market Restrictions, and the New Antitrust Policy," *Harvard Law Review* 98 (1985):984–1002.

lined in the text? Do they have different implications about what sorts of products might be sold under these conditions, or about what industry structures are most conducive to fair trade?

10. The firms that sell personal computers have never banded together to form a cartel. True or False We may infer from this that at least one firm would fail to benefit from a successful cartel.

11. In many industries workers are required to belong to a union and to pay union dues, even if they would prefer not to. True or False Workers would be better off it each one could choose for himself whether to belong to the union.

12. True or False When all firms in an industry charge the same price, this is evidence of collusion.

13. In the example of Exhibit 11–1, suppose that the firms merge, but the market is contestable. What quantity does the merged firm produce, and at what price? Do any new firms actually enter?

14. Suppose that there are exactly N identical firms in an industry, all with flat marginal cost curves. Industry demand is linear. How much does each firm produce, compared with the competitive quantity, under the Cournot assumption that each takes its rivals' outputs as given? How much does the industry produce? What happens to industry output as N gets large? (*Hint:* Follow carefully the argument that is given in the text for the case $N = 2$.)

15. Consider an industry where there are two firms having identical flat marginal cost curves. Price and output in the industry are determined as follows: First Firm 1 announces how much it will produce; then Firm 2 decides how much to produce; then the industry's output is sold at a price read off the industry demand curve.

a. Is the industry output greater or less than it would be under Cournot behavior?

b. Which firm is better off: Firm 1 or Firm 2?

16. Suppose there are three ice cream vendors on the beach depicted in Exhibit 11–12. How will they locate themselves in equilibrium?

17. Suppose there are four ice cream vendors on the beach depicted in Exhibit 11–12. How will they locate themselves in equilibrium? What can you say if there are five vendors? What if there are more than five?

18. a. Suppose that two ice cream vendors are located on a circular beach that goes all the way around a lake. How will they locate themselves in equilibrium?

b. Suppose instead that there are three ice cream vendors on the same circular beach. How will they locate themselves in equilibrium?

Internet Exercise

The U.S. Supreme Court has ruled on a number of cases involving resale price maintenance. Access the following Internet site maintained by Anthony Becker: (http://www.stolaf.edu/people/becker/antitrust/subject.html). Find the section that summarizes U.S. Supreme Court cases dealing with resale price maintenance, and read the summary for Albrecht v. Herald Co. (1968), and State Oil v. Khan (1997). Describe how the antitrust doctrine applied by the Court to resale price maintenance has changed, and relate this change to the economic analysis of resale price maintenance in the chapter you have just read.

chapter 12

The Theory of Games

If you had to be a pig, would you rather be a strong pig or a weak pig? Sometimes it pays to be weak.

The biologist John Maynard Smith reports an experiment where two pigs are kept in a box with a lever at one end and a food dispenser at the other.[1] When the lever is pushed, food appears at the dispenser.

If the weak pig pushes the lever, the strong pig waits by the dispenser and eats all the food. Even if the weak pig races to the dispenser and arrives before the food is gone, the strong pig pushes the weak pig away. The weak pig is smart enough to figure this out, so it never bothers pressing the lever in the first place.

On the other hand, if the strong pig pushes the lever, the weak pig waits by the dispenser and gets most of the food. But the strong pig can race to the dispenser and shove the weak pig aside before it has entirely finished eating, and then help itself to the leftovers. This makes it worthwhile for the strong pig to push the lever.

For more on game theory and economics, access David Levine's site: http://levine.sscnet.ucla.edu/

The outcome is that the strong pig does all of the work, and the weak pig does most of the eating.

Strategic situations can yield surprising outcomes. The Prisoner's Dilemma of Chapter 11 provides one example; the pigs in a box provide another. In this chapter we will study the **theory of games** (or **game theory** for short), which allows us to catalog many of those outcomes and to discuss both their positive and their normative aspects.

Theory of games or **game theory** A system for studying strategic behavior.

[1]John Maynard Smith, *Evolution and the Theory of Games* (Cambridge, MA: Cambridge University Press, 1982).

12.1 Game Matrices

In this section we will introduce game matrices and show how they can be used to systematically analyze strategic situations.

Pigs in a Box

Game matrix A diagram showing one player's strategy choices across the top, the other player's along the left side, and the corresponding outcomes in the appropriate boxes.

Consider the pigs from the introduction to this chapter. We represent the pigs' dilemma by a **game matrix** as in Exhibit 12-1. Across the top we list the possible strategies of the strong pig, who can either push the lever or wait by the food dispenser. Along the left side we list the possible strategies of the weak pig, who has the same options.

In each of the four boxes of the matrix we show the consequences of the pigs' behavior. We assume that the food dispenser yields 100 calories worth of food, and that pushing the lever burns 10 calories. We assume also that pigs care only about calories (which is presumably why they are called pigs).

If both pigs decide to push the lever, then they both run to the dispenser, where the strong pig shoves the weak pig aside and eats all of the food. The net gain is 90 calories for the strong pig (100 calories worth of food minus 10 calories burned pushing the lever) and *minus* 10 calories for the weak pig, who pushes the lever and runs but gets no food. The upper left-hand box in the exhibit shows this outcome.

Exhibit 12-1 Pigs in a Box

Weak pig's strategy	Strong pig's strategy: Push lever	Strong pig's strategy: Wait by dispenser
Push lever	Strong pig gets 90 calories Weak pig gets −10 calories	Strong pig gets 100 calories Weak pig gets −10 calories
Wait by dispenser	Strong pig gets 15 calories Weak pig gets 75 calories	Strong pig gets 0 calories Weak pig gets 0 calories

The dispenser gives 100 calories worth of food, and it requires 10 calories to push the lever. If both pigs arrive at the dispenser simultaneously, only the strong pig eats. But if the weak pig waits at the dispenser while the strong pig pushes the lever, he can eat ¾ of the food before the strong pig arrives. The game matrix shows the pigs' rewards for each combination of strategies.

The lower left-hand box is the only Nash equilibrium. Starting from any other box, at least one of the pigs would want to change his strategy.

If the strong pig waits by the dispenser while the weak pig pushes the lever, the strong pig gets all 100 calories worth of food and the weak pig loses 10 calories, as shown in the upper right-hand box.

If the strong pig pushes the lever while the weak pig waits by the dispenser, the weak pig is able to consume 75 calories before the strong pig arrives and takes the remaining 25, leaving him with a net gain of 15 after subtracting the 10 that he burns by pushing the lever. This is the outcome in the lower left-hand box.

And finally, if both pigs wait by the dispenser, then nobody gets to eat anything at all, as indicated in the lower right-hand box.

Choosing Strategies

In the introduction to this chapter, we argued that the pigs will end up in the lower left-hand box, which is to say that the strong pig will push the lever while the weak pig waits by the dispenser and gets most of the food. Let us see how we can use the game matrix to reach this conclusion systematically.

When the strong pig selects a strategy, he decides which column of the matrix both pigs will occupy. When the weak pig selects a strategy, he decides on a row. There are four possible outcomes, represented by the four boxes of the game matrix. For each outcome, we can ask this question: If this *were* the outcome, would either pig want to change his mind? If one or both pigs *would* want to change their minds, then we can rule out that outcome as a possibility.

For example, suppose for the moment that we are in the upper left-hand box, where both pigs push the lever. If the strong pig changes his mind and waits by the dispenser, we move to the upper right-hand box, while if the weak pig changes his mind we move to the lower left-hand box. Would the strong pig want to change his mind? The answer is yes: By moving from the upper left to the upper right he gains 10 calories. *This is already enough to rule out the upper left-hand box.*

Would the weak pig want to change his mind? The answer is yes again: By moving from the upper left to the lower left he gains 10 calories (or more precisely, he avoids losing 10 calories). This by itself would *also* be enough to rule out the upper left. So the upper left is ruled out for each of two separate reasons: If that were the outcome, the strong pig would change his mind *and* the weak pig would change his mind.

Next suppose that we are in the upper right-hand box. Would the strong pig want to change his mind and move to the upper left? No; he prefers the upper right, gaining 100 calories instead of 90. Would the weak pig want to change his mind and move to the lower right? Yes; he can then avoid losing 10 calories. So we rule out the upper right on the grounds that the weak pig would change his mind.

What about the lower right? The weak pig would not want to change rows, but the strong pig *would* want to change columns. Because the strong pig wants to change his mind, this outcome can also be ruled out.

EXERCISE 12.1 In the lower right corner, how much would the weak pig lose by changing rows? How much would the strong pig gain by changing columns?

Finally, consider the lower left. Starting from here, the weak pig has the option to move up a box, reducing his calorie intake from 75 to −10; this option is not attractive. The strong pig has the option to move to the right, reducing his net calorie intake from 15 to 0; this is not attractive either. Neither pig changes his mind, and the pigs remain in the lower left-hand box.

Nash equilibrium An outcome from which neither player would want to deviate, taking the other player's behavior as given.

Any outcome that survives this process of elimination is called a **Nash equilibrium** outcome. An outcome is a Nash equilibrium if neither player would want to deviate from it, taking his opponent's behavior as given. The phrase *taking his opponent's behavior as given* is an important one here. Starting in the lower left, the strong pig *would* want to deviate provided he thought that for some crazy reason the weak pig was going to deviate too and he could end up in the upper right. But as long as the strong pig assumes that the weak pig is going to stick to his strategy of waiting by the food dispenser, he has no desire to change his own strategy.

The Prisoner's Dilemma Revisited

The Prisoner's Dilemma of Chapter 11 is already represented by a game matrix, which we reproduce in Exhibit 12–2. We argued in Chapter 11 that the prisoners land in the upper left-hand box. Let us confirm this conclusion using the techniques we've just developed.

Suppose the prisoners were in the upper right-hand box, with B confessing and A not confessing. If B switches strategies, we move down a row, increasing B's prison term; therefore B does *not* want to switch. But if A switches strategies, then we move a column to the left, where A's prison term falls from

Exhibit 12-2 The Prisoner's Dilemma

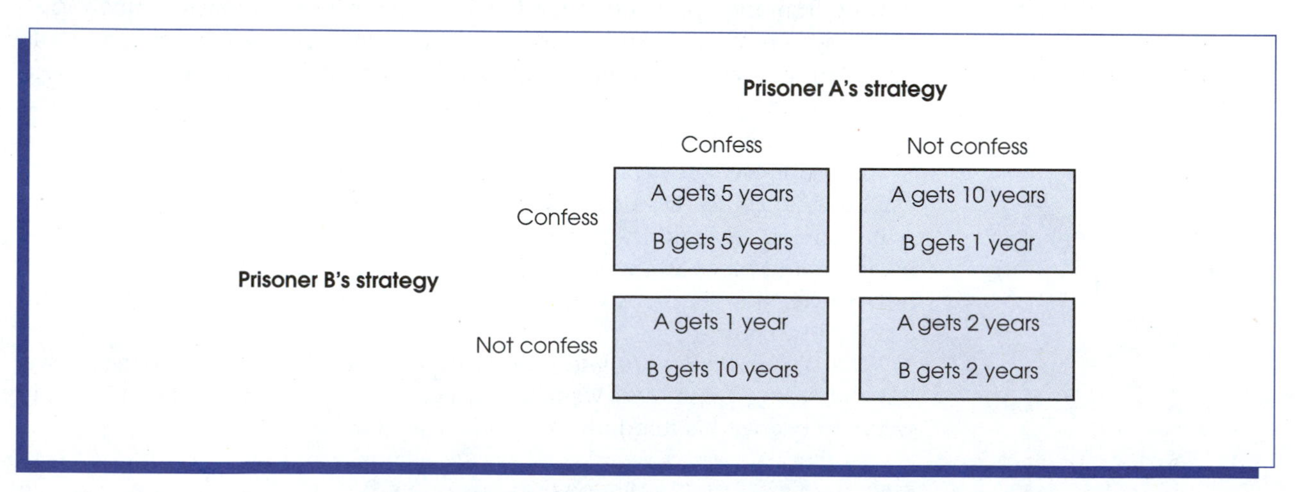

Prisoner B's strategy	Prisoner A's strategy: Confess	Prisoner A's strategy: Not confess
Confess	A gets 5 years B gets 5 years	A gets 10 years B gets 1 year
Not confess	A gets 1 year B gets 10 years	A gets 2 years B gets 2 years

The prisoners face the same dilemma as in Chapter 11. The only Nash equilibrium is in the upper left-hand corner, this is also the only square that is not Pareto-optimal.

10 years to 5; therefore A *does* want to switch. Because at least one of the prisoners wants to switch, the upper right-hand box is *not* a Nash equilibrium.

It's worth noting that the pigs in a box were out to *maximize* their calorie intake, while the prisoners are out to *minimize* their jail sentences. In all of the other examples of this chapter, the goal will be to maximize outcomes (as the pigs do) rather than to minimize them (as the prisoners do).

QA EXERCISE 12.2 Explain why the lower left-hand box and the lower right-hand box are not Nash equilibria. In each case, which prisoner wants to switch?

Dominant Strategies

In Chapter 11, we pointed out that Prisoner A would want to confess *regardless* of his beliefs about Prisoner B's behavior. If Prisoner B is known to be confessing (placing us in the top row), then Prisoner A has a choice between getting a sentence of 5 years by confessing or getting a sentence of 10 years by not confessing. If Prisoner B is known to be not confessing (placing us in the bottom row), then Prisoner A has a choice between getting a sentence of 1 year by confessing or getting a sentence of 2 years by not confessing. Either way, Prisoner A prefers to confess.

Dominant strategy A strategy that a player would want to follow regardless of the other player's behavior.

Confessing in the Prisoner's Dilemma is called a **dominant strategy** for Prisoner A, because he would want to follow that strategy regardless of what Prisoner B was up to. Confessing is also a dominant strategy for Prisoner B. When both prisoners follow their dominant strategies, we reach the Nash equilibrium outcome where both confess.

Pigs in a Box Revisited

Sometimes a player has no dominant strategy. Let us return to the pigs of Exhibit 12–1. Should the strong pig push the lever or wait by the dispenser?

It depends on what he thinks the weak pig is doing. If the weak pig can be counted on to push the lever, then the strong pig should wait by the dispenser; but if the weak pig waits by the dispenser, then the strong pig should push the lever.

We can see this in the game matrix. If the weak pig pushes the lever we are in the first row. The strong pig can push (for a gain of 90) or wait (for a gain of 100); it is better to wait (that is, to choose the second column). But if the weak pig waits by the dispenser, we are in the second row. The strong pig can push (for a gain of 15) or wait (for a gain of 0); it is better to push (that is, to choose the first column).

Before the strong pig can choose his strategy, he'd like to know what the weak pig is going to do. This means that the strong pig has no dominant strategy. If he had a dominant strategy, he would not need to inquire about the weak pig's behavior before deciding on his own.

The weak pig, by contrast, *does* have a dominant strategy: It should wait by the dispenser regardless of how the strong pig behaves. If the strong pig pushes (choosing the first column), then the weak pig can push (for a gain of −10) or wait (for a gain of 75); it is better to wait (that is, to choose the second row). If the strong pig waits (choosing the second column), then the weak pig can push (for a gain of −10) or wait (for a gain of 0); it is still better to wait (that is, to choose the second row).

Dominant Strategies versus Nash Equilibria

When both players have dominant strategies, as in the Prisoner's Dilemma, there is one and only one Nash equilibrium. In the Nash equilibrium, both players play their dominant strategies.

But Nash equilibria can exist even when one or both players have no dominant strategy. In the "pigs in a box" example of Exhibit 12–1, the strong pig has no dominant strategy, but the lower-left corner is still a Nash equilibrium.

To keep track of the differences in these concepts, continue to focus on the pigs. We know that it is a dominant strategy for the weak pig to wait by the dispenser; in terms of the game matrix this means that the weak pig will always choose the second row.

Now suppose that we are in the lower-left box (where the strong pig is pushing the lever) and consider the following two questions:

1. Would the strong pig want to change strategies, given that he knows the weak pig will choose the second row?
2. Might the strong pig want to change strategies if he wasn't sure what the weak pig will do?

The answer to question 1 is no. Once the second row is chosen, the strong pig certainly prefers the first column to the second. Neither the strong pig nor the weak pig wants to change, so the lower left is a Nash equilibrium.

The answer to question 2 is yes. If the strong pig thought that the weak pig had (foolishly) chosen the first row, then he would want to switch to the second column. His choice of columns depends on what he thinks the weak pig is doing, so he has no dominant strategy.

The Battle of the Sexes

Exhibit 12–3 shows a game that is usually called the *Battle of the Sexes*.

Fred prefers to go to boxing matches and Ethel prefers to go to the opera, but they both like doing things together. If they go their separate ways, both are miserable. The game matrix puts numerical values on Fred and Ethel's happiness (which economists sometimes call *utility*). If Fred goes to the opera while Ethel goes to the boxing match, they each earn zero units of utility; if Fred goes to the boxing match while Ethel goes to the opera, they each earn 1 unit.

But if Fred and Ethel attend the boxing match together, then Fred earns 5 units of utility while Ethel earns 3 just by being with Fred; if they attend the opera together, then Ethel earns 5 units of utility and Fred earns 3 just by being with Ethel.

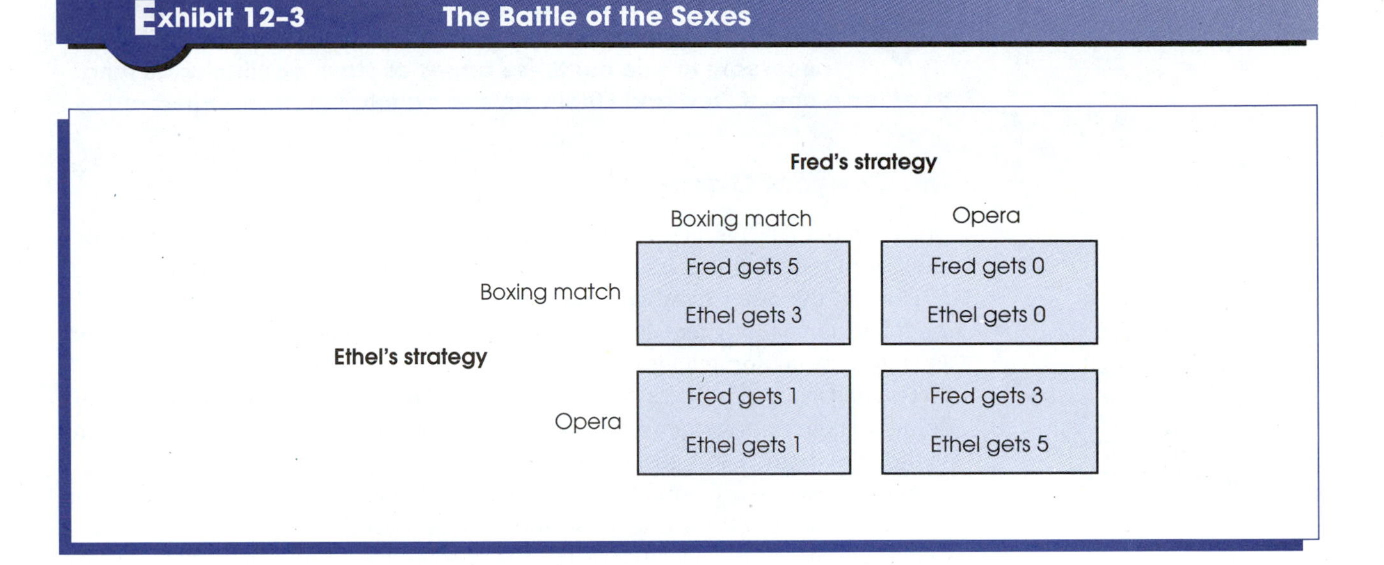

Exhibit 12-3 The Battle of the Sexes

		Fred's strategy	
		Boxing match	Opera
Ethel's strategy	Boxing match	Fred gets 5 Ethel gets 3	Fred gets 0 Ethel gets 0
	Opera	Fred gets 1 Ethel gets 1	Fred gets 3 Ethel gets 5

Fred likes boxing and Ethel likes opera, but they both like to be together. The upper-left and lower-right corners are Nash equilibria.

Does Fred have a dominant strategy in this game? If he thinks that Ethel is going to the boxing match, he prefers to be at the boxing match, while if he thinks that Ethel is going to the opera, he prefers to be at the opera. This means that he has no dominant strategy. Neither does Ethel.

What about Nash equilibria? Suppose that Fred and Ethel both go to the boxing match (the upper left-hand corner). Would Fred want to switch to the opera, knowing that Ethel is going to the boxing match? The answer is no. And would Ethel want to switch to the opera knowing that Fred is going to the boxing match? No again. So this outcome is a Nash equilibrium.

The lower right-hand corner (both going to the opera) is also a Nash equilibrium. But the two outcomes where Fred and Ethel go their separate ways are *not* Nash equilibria, because in either of these situations both Fred and Ethel would want to switch.

Suppose that Fred goes to the boxing match while Ethel goes to the opera (the lower left-hand box). Then, given Ethel's plans, Fred prefers to switch, and, given Fred's plans, Ethel prefers to switch. You might wonder whether Ethel would reason a little more deeply. "I know that as long as I am going to the opera, Fred will want to switch to the opera as well, so I think that I'll just head over to the opera and wait for him to follow along." It is true that Ethel might think this way, but such reasoning is not relevant to the question of whether this outcome is a Nash equilibrium. Given Fred's intention to attend the boxing match, Ethel does want to switch. This rules out the lower left-hand corner as a Nash equilibrium.

From the lower left-hand box (or from the upper right-hand box) both Fred and Ethel want to switch (each taking the other's behavior as given). This is more information than necessary to rule out these boxes as Nash equilibria; as long as at least one of Fred and Ethel wants to switch, the box is ruled out.

The Copycat Game

Dot's brother Ditto is a copycat. If Dot watches television, Ditto wants to watch television, too. If Dot goes out to play in the yard, then so does Ditto.

Dot, on the other hand, always wants to be by herself. She's happy watching television as long as Ditto is out in the yard, and happy in the yard as long as Ditto is watching television.

The matrix in Exhibit 12–4 shows Dot and Ditto's game. As long as they are doing something together, Ditto gets 5 units of utility and Dot gets 0. As long as they are apart, Ditto gets 0 units of utility and Dot gets 5.

Are there any Nash equilibria in this game? Consider the upper left-hand corner. If Dot and Ditto are both watching television, Ditto sees no reason to switch columns—but Dot wants to switch rows by going out to the yard. So the upper left-hand corner is not a Nash equilibrium. Neither is any other corner.

EXERCISE 12.3 Explain why the upper right, lower left, and lower right corners are not Nash equilibria.

Exhibit 12–4 The Copycat Game

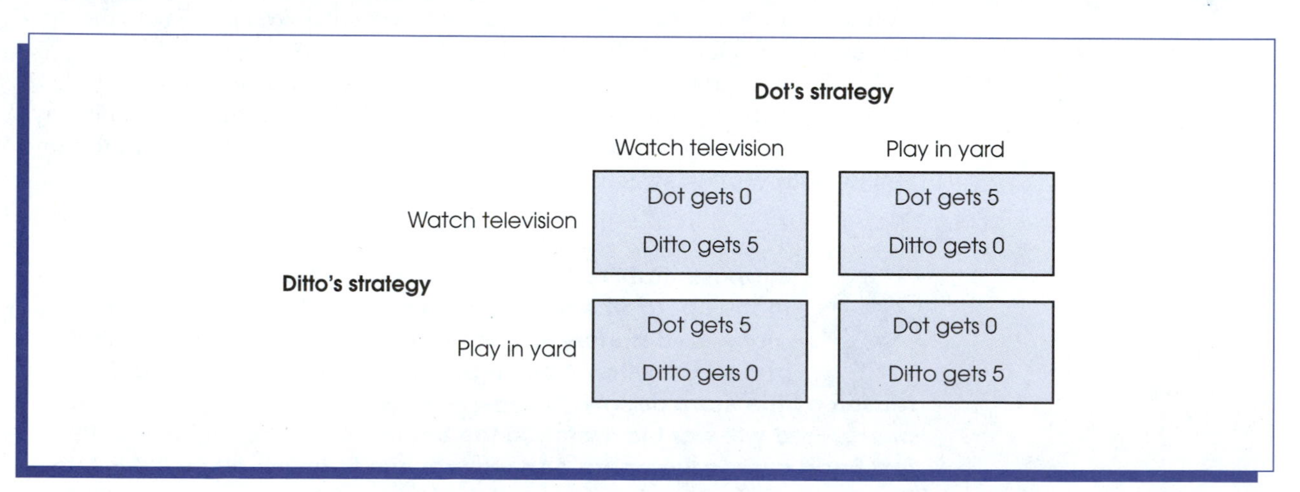

		Dot's strategy	
		Watch television	Play in yard
Ditto's strategy	Watch television	Dot gets 0 Ditto gets 5	Dot gets 5 Ditto gets 0
	Play in yard	Dot gets 5 Ditto gets 0	Dot gets 0 Ditto gets 5

Dot is happy as long as she is alone; Ditto is happy as long as he is with Dot. There is no Nash equilibrium in this game.

Nash Equilibrium as a Solution Concept

Solution concept A rule for predicting how games will turn out.

A **solution concept** is a rule for predicting how games will turn out when they are played. Nash equilibrium is one of the most popular solution concepts; that is, economists like to posit that when people play games, they end up in Nash equilibria. There are, however, some reasons to be uncomfortable with Nash equilibrium as a solution concept.

One problem is that some games, like the Battle of the Sexes, have more than one Nash equilibrium. There is no way to predict which Nash equilibrium is more likely.

Another problem is that some games, like the Copycat Game, have no Nash equilibrium at all. If Dot and Ditto start out watching television together, Dot will go out to the yard, whereupon Ditto will follow her out, whereupon Dot will come back in, whereupon Ditto will follow her in, whereupon. . . . There is nothing in the Nash equilibrium concept to tell us where this process will end.

example

The Price of Car Insurance

A 19-year-old male who drives a five-year-old Chevrolet Caprice will pay about $1,800 a year for car insurance if he lives in Columbus, Ohio. That same 19-year-old male will pay about $2,500 if he lives in Detroit, $4,000 if he lives in Philadelphia, and $5,000 if he lives in Los Angeles! What can account for such enormous differences in price?

In a provocatively titled essay,[2] two economists have drawn attention to the "game" where each driver decides whether to buy insurance. They argue that observed price differences can be attributed to multiple Nash equilibria in this game.

Suppose, for example, that very few drivers buy insurance. Then insured drivers, when they have accidents, will usually have to collect from their own insurance companies—the other party will typically be uninsured. Therefore insurance becomes very expensive, so few drivers want to buy it. In other words, uninsured motorists cause high insurance prices, and high insurance prices cause uninsured motorists. This is an example of a Nash equilibrium: Everyone behaves rationally, taking everyone else's behavior as given.

On the other hand, suppose that most drivers buy insurance. Then insurance becomes cheaper and therefore, most drivers want to buy it. Again, we have a Nash equilibrium.

When a game has more than one Nash equilibrium, it's difficult to predict which of the equilibria will actually occur. But once an equilibrium is reached, it tends to remain stable. So if, for any reason, Columbus fell into the "bad" equilibrium while Philadelphia fell into the "good" equilibrium, it's not surprising that these equilibria would maintain themselves over time.

---

[2]E. Smith and R. Wright, "Why is Automobile Insurance in Philadelphia So Damn Expensive?" *American Economic Review* 82 (1992), 756–772.

example **Social Status**

The average American earns almost $30,000 a year, according to official statistics, the average citizen of Mali earns about $100. The latter figure is surely misleadingly low, but the fact remains that there are enormous differences in income across countries. No economist has succeeded in giving a complete account of those differences. Most partial explanations rely on differences in tastes (for example, people with a strong preference for saving will be wealthier in the long run) and differences in available technology. But recently, a number of economists have pointed to the possibility of multiple equilibria.

One intriguing story is that the relevant game is the mating game—the "game" in which people select marriage partners. To see how this can be relevant, let's imagine two stylized extremes.[3]

First, imagine a society where the richest people get the most desirable mates. In that society, people will be motivated to save, not just to acquire better mates for themselves, but also to acquire better mates for their children. And as long as all your neighbors play that strategy, you'll want to play it, too. In other words, we have a Nash equilibrium.

Now imagine a society where mates are allocated according to social status, which is inherited from your parents independent of wealth. In such a society, low-status people might try to attract high-status mates by acquiring a lot of wealth. But this strategy is discouraged if it dooms your children to even lower status. So *if* the "rules of the game" are that children of such "mixed marriages" have the lowest status of all, then there can be a Nash equilibrium in which people save very little.

Notice that even if the two societies are populated by identical people, their incomes will evolve very differently. A society that lands in either of the two equilibria will tend to remain there.

These highly stylized examples are far too simplistic to explain all the differences between the United States and Mali, but they do demonstrate that it's possible for multiple Nash equilibria to occur in this context, and therefore that multiple equilibria might play an important role in understanding why some countries are so much wealthier than others.

Mixed Strategies

The Copycat Game has no Nash equilibrium. How might we expect Dot and Ditto to select their strategies in this game?

If Ditto can predict Dot's behavior, he will simply mimic it; therefore it is important for Dot to keep Ditto off guard. One way for her to do this is to flip a coin. On heads, she watches television and on tails she plays in the yard. Because her behavior is now totally unpredictable, Ditto can do no better than to flip his own coin and hope that it lands the same way Dot's does.

Notice that it is important to both Dot and Ditto that their coins be *fair coins*, with heads and tails equally probable. If Dot's coin is weighted so that she is more likely to watch television than to play outside, then Ditto will throw his

---

[3]The example to follow is based on H. Cole, G. Maulath and A. Postlewaite, "Social Norms, Savings Behavior and Growth", *Journal of Political Economy* 100 (1992), 1092–1125.

coin away and watch television, giving him a better than even chance to win the game. And likewise, if Ditto's coin is weighted, then Dot has an opportunity to discard her own coin and follow a strategy that puts the odds on her side.

The Copycat Game is quite symmetric, in the sense that there is always a "winner" with 5 utils and a "loser" with 0. In a game with less symmetry, Dot and Ditto might prefer to flip weighted coins, sacrificing some unpredictably in exchange for improving the chances of their preferred outcomes. We can view each possible weighting as an alternative strategy. (That is, "flip a fair coin" is one strategy; "flip a coin that comes up heads two-thirds of the time" is another; "flip a coin that comes up heads three-fourths of the time" is still another.) We call these options **mixed strategies,** as opposed to the **pure strategies** illustrated in Exhibit 12–3. If mixed strategies are allowed, then it is possible to prove under quite general circumstances that a Nash equilibrium must exist.

Mixed strategy A strategy that involves a random choice among pure strategies.

Pure strategy A single choice of row (or column) in the game matrix.

In the remainder of the chapter, we will restrict our attention to games in which only pure strategies are allowed.

Pareto Optima

Nash equilibrium is a *positive* (as opposed to normative) concept; it is designed to predict what *will* happen as opposed to enabling us to discuss what *ought* to happen. In this section, we will discuss the normative side of game theory.

Look again at Fred and Ethel, who played the Copycat Game in Exhibit 12–4; this game is reproduced at the top of Exhibit 12–5. In Exhibit 12–5, each

Exhibit 12-5 The Battle of the Sexes Revisited

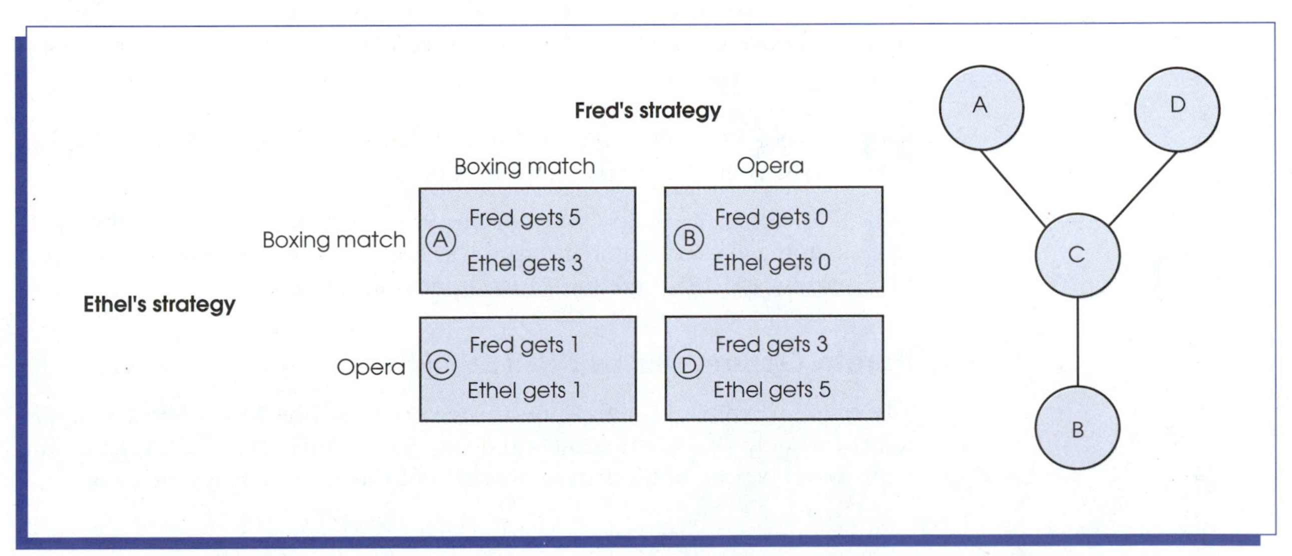

The tree shows that outcomes A and D are Pareto-preferred to C and B, and C is Pareto-preferred to B. A and D are Pareto optima, because nothing sits above them in the tree.

of the four outcomes has been labeled with a letter (from A through D) for easy reference.

Fred and Ethel disagree about the desirability of the various outcomes; for example, Fred thinks outcome A is better than outcome D, while Ethel thinks just the opposite. But there are certain things they both agree on. For example, both agree that outcome C (where Fred and Ethel each get 1) is better than outcome B (where they both get 0).

Pareto improvement or **Pareto-preferred outcome** A change to which nobody objects.

Because Fred and Ethel are unanimous in this judgment, we say that moving from B to C is a **Pareto improvement**, or that C is **Pareto-preferred** to B. In general, a change is a Pareto improvement if nobody objects to it.[4]

Similarly, outcomes A and D are both Pareto improvements over B; nobody would object to a move from B to A or from B to D. A move from A to D is *not* a Pareto improvement, because Fred would object, and a move from D to A is not a Pareto improvement, because Ethel would object.

To the right of the game matrix in Exhibit 12–5, we have arranged the four outcomes in a "tree," where upward movements represent Pareto improvements. A, C, and D are all Pareto improvements over B, so A, C, and D all sit higher than B in the tree. Likewise, A and D both sit above C. But A sits neither above nor below D, because A is not a Pareto improvement over D and D is not a Pareto improvement over A.

Pareto-optimal outcome An outcome that allows no possibility of a Pareto improvement.

We say that an outcome is **Pareto-optimal** if nothing sits above it in the tree. In this example, outcomes A and D are Pareto-optimal. From a normative point of view, we can think of outcomes that are *not* Pareto-optimal as "bad" outcomes. Outcome C, for example, is "bad" in the sense that both Fred and Ethel would prefer to climb higher in the tree, though they might disagree about whether it would be better to climb to A or to D.

Exhibit 12–6 revisits the pigs in a box from Exhibit 12–1. Here outcome B is Pareto-preferred to outcome A and outcome D is Pareto-preferred to outcome C, but there are no other instances of Pareto improvements. Thus, the "tree" breaks into two pieces, one of which shows B above A and one of which shows D above C. The Pareto-optimal outcomes are at the tops of the trees: B and C.

EXERCISE 12.4 Explain why B is not Pareto-preferred to C or D. Explain why C is not Pareto preferred to A or B.

EXERCISE 12.5 Build a tree for the Prisoner's Dilemma of Exhibit 12–2, keeping in mind that in this game, a shorter prison sentence is better than a long one. What are the Pareto optima in this game?

Pareto Optima versus Nash Equilibria

The pigs in Exhibit 12–1 have two Pareto optima (the lower left and upper right) but only one Nash equilibrium (the lower left). The Nash equilibrium happens to be one of the Pareto optima. But this is not always the case.

[4]In some books, the phrase *Pareto improvement* is reserved for a change to which nobody objects *and* at least one person prefers.

Exhibit 12-6 Pigs in a Box Revisited

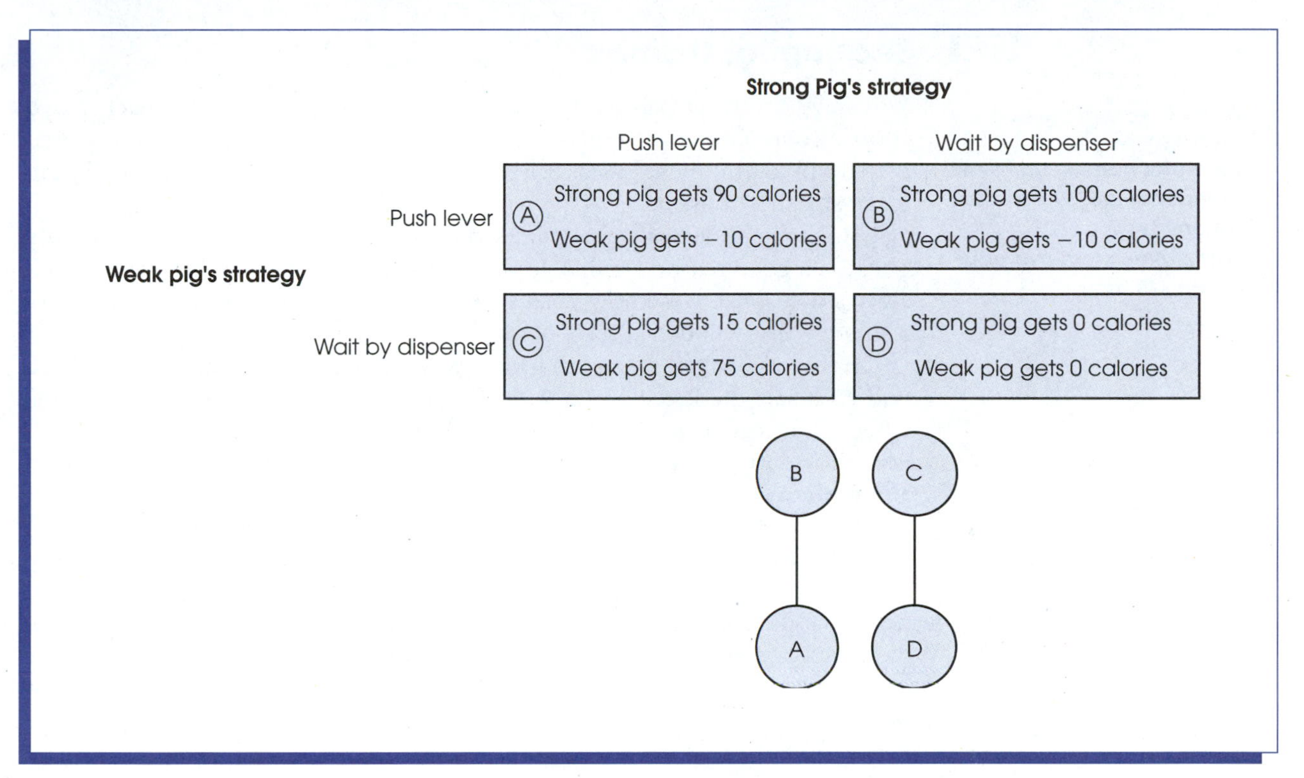

B is Pareto-preferred to A, and C is Pareto-preferred to D. B and C are the Pareto optima.

Consider the Prisoner's Dilemma of Exhibit 12–2. Here we have already seen that the only Nash equilibrium occurs in the upper left. This outcome is not Pareto-optimal, because a shift to the lower right would benefit both prisoners. In fact, the Nash equilibrium is the only outcome that is not Pareto-optimal.

QA **Exercise 12.6** Explain why the upper right box in the Prisoner's Dilemma is Pareto-optimal.

QA **Exercise 12.7** Explain why the lower left box in the Prisoner's Dilemma is Pareto-optimal.

In the Battle of the Sexes (Exhibit 12–3), both of the Nash equilibria (in the upper left and lower right) are Pareto-optimal. Starting in the upper left, any other square would be worse for Fred and starting in the lower right, any other square would be worse for Ethel. Neither of the other two squares is Pareto-optimal.

EXERCISE 12.8 Explain why neither of the other two squares is Pareto-optimal.

12.2 Sequential Games

To read more about sequential games, go to the site maintained by Nicholas Economides: http://raven.stern.nyu.edu/networks/5.html

You have probably played the game of "scissors, paper, rock." Each player chooses one of three strategies (scissors, paper, or rock) and then the winner is determined by these rules: Scissors "cut" paper, paper "covers" rock, and rock "smashes" scissors.

Usually both players are required to choose their strategies simultaneously. There is a good reason for this. If players took turns, the second player would always win. Once you know what your opponent is doing, it is easy to choose a strategy that will defeat him.

On the other hand, there are games where it pays to go first instead of second. Consider the Battle of the Sexes (Exhibit 12–3), where Fred and Ethel disagree about where to spend the evening but want above all to be together. If Fred moves first, by going to the boxing match and waiting for Ethel to follow along, then she is sure to do so, giving Fred his most preferred outcome. If Ethel moves first by going to the opera, Fred follows her and Ethel wins.

In the games of Section 12.1, we have always assumed that both players must choose their strategies simultaneously. In this section, we will assume instead that there is a first player, who chooses a column in the game matrix, and then a second player, who chooses a row. This will require a new way of thinking about the outcome. We will illustrate the new method with some examples.

An Oligopoly Problem

Kodak and Fuji produce photographic film. Suppose that there are no other significant firms in this industry, so that Kodak and Fuji constitute an oligopoly. Industry-wide profits depend on industry-wide output according to the following table:

Quantity (rolls of film day)	Profits (dollars per day)
100	32
125	35
150	30
175	21
200	10

Moreover, the profits are divided in proportion to the firms' output. Thus, if one firm produces 100 rolls of film while the other produces 75 rolls (a ratio of 4 to 3), then the $21 profit is divided in the same ratio ($12 for one firm and $9 for the other).

Exhibit 12–7 shows the game matrix, where each company can produce either 50, 75, or 100 rolls of film.

Exhibit 12-7 An Oligopoly Problem

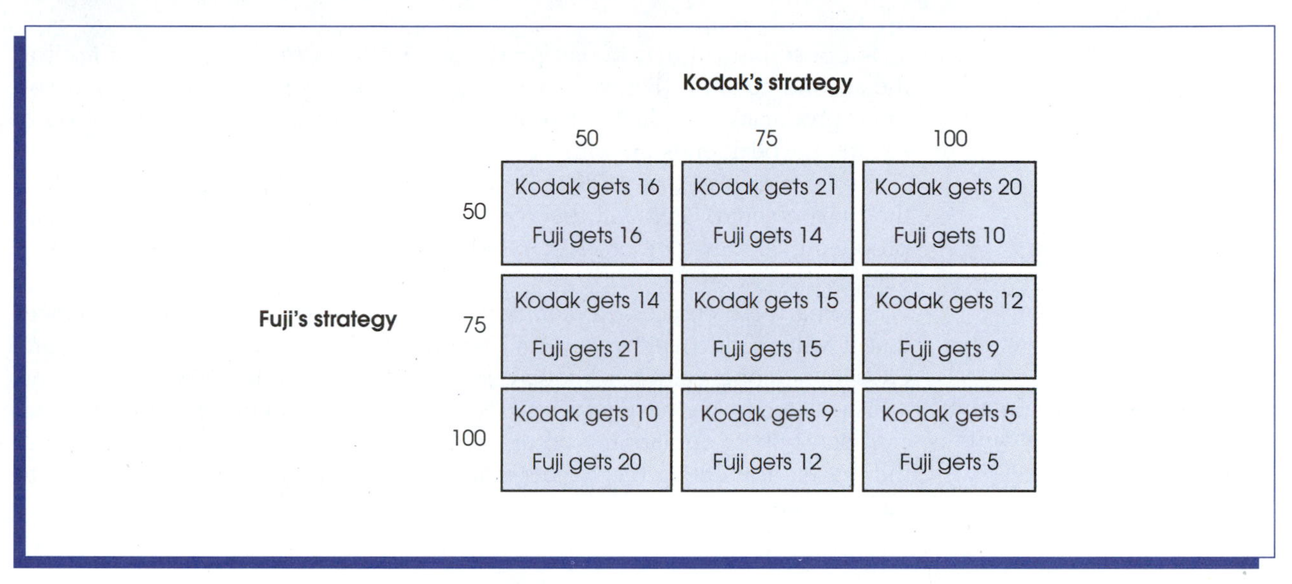

Fuji's strategy \ Kodak's strategy	50	75	100
50	Kodak gets 16 Fuji gets 16	Kodak gets 21 Fuji gets 14	Kodak gets 20 Fuji gets 10
75	Kodak gets 14 Fuji gets 21	Kodak gets 15 Fuji gets 15	Kodak gets 12 Fuji gets 9
100	Kodak gets 10 Fuji gets 20	Kodak gets 9 Fuji gets 12	Kodak gets 5 Fuji gets 5

The only Nash equilibrium is in the center square, where Kodak and Fuji each earn profits of 15. But if the game is played sequentially and Kodak moves first, then Kodak announces a policy of producing 100 rolls of film. Fuji's best response is to produce 50, leading to the upper left-hand square.

The outcome of this game depends very much on how the game is played. Suppose first that the companies are able to collude, maximizing their joint profits and splitting them afterward. Then they will produce 125 rolls of film, for the maximum possible profit of $35.

Suppose instead that each company takes its rival's output as given and chooses its own output accordingly. In the language of game theory, this means that the companies achieve a Nash equilibrium in Exhibit 12–7. In the language of Chapter 11, we called the same thing a *Cournot equilibrium*. A Cournot equilibrium is nothing but a Nash equilibrium in a game where each company chooses its quantity.

In Exhibit 12–7 the only Nash equilibrium is the center square. If each firm makes 75 rolls of film, neither wants to deviate. Kodak recognizes that dropping its output to 50 rolls would lower its profits from $15 to $14 and raising its output to 100 rolls would lower its profits from $15 to $12. Fuji recognizes the same thing.

QA **EXERCISE 12.9** Explain why no other square in Exhibit 12–7 is a Nash equilibrium.

But now let's change the rules of the game. Suppose that Kodak is able to announce its output before Fuji gets to make a move. Now what will Kodak do?

Kodak needs to think through the consequences of each possible strategy. Suppose that Kodak produces 50 rolls of film (committing itself to the first column). Fuji will then pick its favorite square in the first column, producing 75 rolls for a profit of $21 (beating $16 and $20 in the other squares). Kodak ends up with $14 profit.

Suppose instead that Kodak produces 75 rolls of film (committing itself to the second column). Fuji will then pick its favorite square in the second column, producing 75 rolls for a profit of $15 (beating $14 and $12 in the other squares). Kodak ends up with $15 profit.

Suppose instead that Kodak produces 100 rolls of film (committing itself to the third column). Fuji will then pick its favorite square in the third column, producing 50 rolls for a profit of $10 (beating $9 and $5). Kodak ends up with $20 profit.

Among these choices, Kodak likes the last one best. So Kodak announces that it will produce 100 rolls, Fuji responds by producing 50, and the game ends in the upper right-hand square, where Kodak earns twice what Fuji earns.

Stackelberg equilibrium An equilibrium concept that arises when one player announces his strategy before the other.

The outcome we have just described is called a **Stackelberg equilibrium.** A Stackelberg equilibrium occurs when one player commits to a strategy at the outset, accounting for the fact that the second player will choose an optimal response.

The Importance of Commitment

Suppose that Kodak announces it will produce 100 rolls of film and Fuji responds by producing 50 rolls as in the Stackelberg equilibrium of Exhibit 12–7. Once Fuji has agreed to produce only 50 rolls, Kodak wants to deviate.

It is better for Kodak to produce 75 rolls for a profit of $21 than 100 rolls for a profit of $20.

So if Kodak moves first and Fuji moves second, then Kodak wants to change its move. If Kodak does change its move, and if Fuji foresees this, then Fuji goes ahead with plans to produce not 50 rolls of film but 75. (After all, Kodak will eventually place it in the middle column, where Fuji's optimal strategy is not 50 but 75.) The firms end up at the Nash equilibrium in the center instead of the Stackelberg equilibrium in the upper right. Kodak's profits fall from $20 to $15.

This means that Kodak is better off if it can commit itself to producing 100 rolls and assure Fuji that it is never going to back down from that commitment. This might surprise you. You might think that a firm is better off leaving itself some flexibility to deal with unforeseen contingencies. But that is not always so.

Consider the game of chicken, where two cretins drive their cars directly at each other until one of them loses by swerving. If you can absolutely guarantee that you will never swerve, you are a sure winner at this game. If you leave yourself the leeway to swerve in case your opponent is crazier than you are, then your opponent will have an incentive to *become* crazier than you are and you are liable to lose. The way to win the game of chicken is to disable your steering column and make sure your opponent is aware of it.

summary

Strategic situations can be represented by game matrices, showing the outcome that results from each combination of strategies that the players can choose.

A Nash equilibrium is an outcome from which neither player would deviate, taking the other's behavior as given. A game can have one Nash equilibrium, no Nash equilibrium, or many Nash equilibria.

A dominant strategy is a strategy that a player would want to adopt regardless of his beliefs about the other player's strategy choice. The Prisoner's Dilemma is an example of a game where both players have dominant strategies.

One outcome is a Pareto improvement over another if it makes at least one player better off without making any player worse off. An outcome is Pareto-optimal if it allows no Pareto improvements.

There can be Nash equilibria that are not Pareto-optimal, and there can be Pareto optima that are not Nash equilibria.

When games are played sequentially instead of simultaneously, the Nash equilibrium is no longer a natural solution concept. Instead, we use the Stackelberg equilibrium, where the first player calculates the second player's responses to each of his possible strategies and then chooses the strategy that will yield him the best outcome. In a sequential game, it can be advantageous to go first or advantageous to go second, depending on the particular game.

In some games it is important to be able to commit to following a strategy even if better options become available. By committing, you can sometimes convince your opponent to behave in ways that are advantageous to you.

Problem Set

The problems in this problem set refer to the following game matrices. In each case, Jack chooses "left or right" and Jill chooses "up or down." The outcomes show how many buckets of water are rewarded.

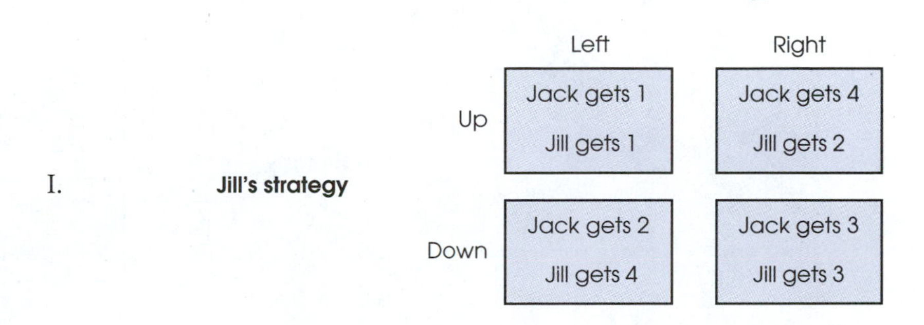

II.

Jill's strategy	Jack's strategy: Left	Jack's strategy: Right
Up	Jack gets 1 Jill gets 1	Jack gets 2 Jill gets 4
Down	Jack gets 4 Jill gets 2	Jack gets 3 Jill gets 3

III.

Jill's strategy	Jack's strategy: Left	Jack's strategy: Right
Up	Jack gets 1 Jill gets 1	Jack gets 4 Jill gets 4
Down	Jack gets 2 Jill gets 2	Jack gets 3 Jill gets 3

IV.

Jill's strategy	Jack's strategy: Left	Jack's strategy: Right
Up	Jack gets 2 Jill gets 2	Jack gets 4 Jill gets 1
Down	Jack gets 1 Jill gets 4	Jack gets 3 Jill gets 3

V.

Jill's strategy	Jack's strategy: Left	Jack's strategy: Right
Up	Jack gets 1 Jill gets 3	Jack gets 3 Jill gets 1
Down	Jack gets 4 Jill gets 2	Jack gets 2 Jill gets 4

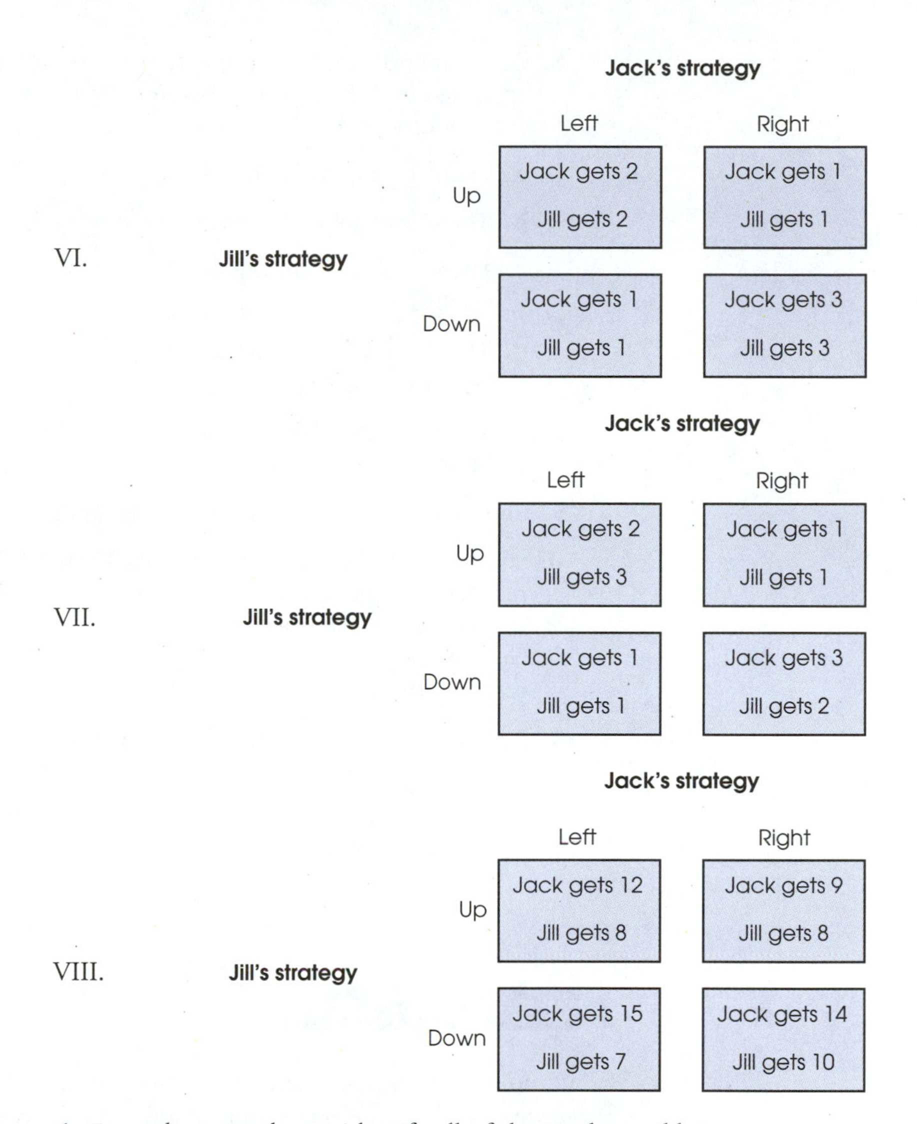

1. In each game above, identify all of the Nash equilibria.
2. In each game above, identify all of the Pareto optima.
3. In each game above, does Jack have a dominant strategy? Does Jill?
4. In each game above, what happens if Jack goes first?
5. In each game above, what happens if Jill goes first?
6. For each game above, create a reasonable story (like those that go with the exhibits in the text) that might lead to these numbers appearing in the matrix.
7. Create a "tree" showing which outcomes are Pareto-preferred to which in the Kodak–Fuji game of Exhibit 12–7.

8. Can you find examples of games (either among those that have appeared in the chapter or by creating them yourself) with the following characteristics?

   a. There are no Nash equilibria.

   b. There is exactly one Nash equilibrium, but it is not Pareto-optimal.

   c. There is more than one Nash equilibrium, but none of them is Pareto-optimal.

   d. There is more than one Nash equilibrium, and all of them are Pareto-optimal.

   e. There is more than one Nash equilibrium, and some are Pareto-optimal while others are not.

9. Can there be a game with no Pareto optimum?

10. Suppose that the games of Exhibits 12–1, 12–2, 12–3, and 12–4 were played as sequential games. In each case, suppose that the player who chooses a column goes first. What are the outcomes of these games? Now suppose that the player who chooses a row goes first. In which cases do the outcomes change?

11. **True or False** In a sequential game where the second player has a dominant strategy, he will always adopt that strategy.

12. **True or False:** In a sequential game where the first player has a dominant strategy, he will always adopt that strategy.

Internet Exercise

While many strategic situations studied by economists are *positive-sum games*—such as the gains from trade realized from market exchange—there are also strategic situations in which the gains and losses sum to zero, called *zero-sum games*. Access David Levine's zero-sum game Internet site (http://levine.sscnet.ucla.edu/Games/zerosum.htm). Practice your game theory skills by using Levine's interactive zero-sum game solver.

c h a p t e r 13

External Costs and Benefits

For more on externalities see the slide shows at the site maintained by Steve Hackett: http://www.humboldt.edu/~envecon/ppt/423/index.html

External costs and benefits, or **externalities** Cost and benefits imposed on others.

Negative externalities External costs.

Positive externalities External benefits.

In previous chapters, we have analyzed the gains from trade that accrue to voluntary participants in transactions. However, many transactions involve involuntary participants as well. The neighbors who breathe the smoke from a factory, the naturalist who deplores the "harvesting" of whales, the shoppers who enjoy the spectacle of department store Christmas displays—all are incurring costs or benefits from transactions that took place without their involvement. Such costs and benefits are said to be **external** and are collectively referred to as **externalities**. External costs (like the factory smoke) are called **negative externalities** and external benefits (like the pleasure from the Christmas decorations) are called **positive externalities**.

In this chapter we will study a variety of examples of externalities. We will see how externalities can be a source of economic inefficiency, and we will study some approaches to combating such inefficiencies.

13.1 Costs Imposed on Others

We will begin with a simple example of an externality: the noise from a confectioner's machinery disrupts the practice of the doctor next door. After examining the social consequences of this externality, we will present a simple policy prescription: If the confectioner is taxed for making noise, then he will produce less of it, and this can improve social welfare. In the remaining sections of the chapter we will criticize this policy prescription, and we will see that the problem is less simple than it might appear.

Exhibit 13-1 Private Costs versus Social Costs

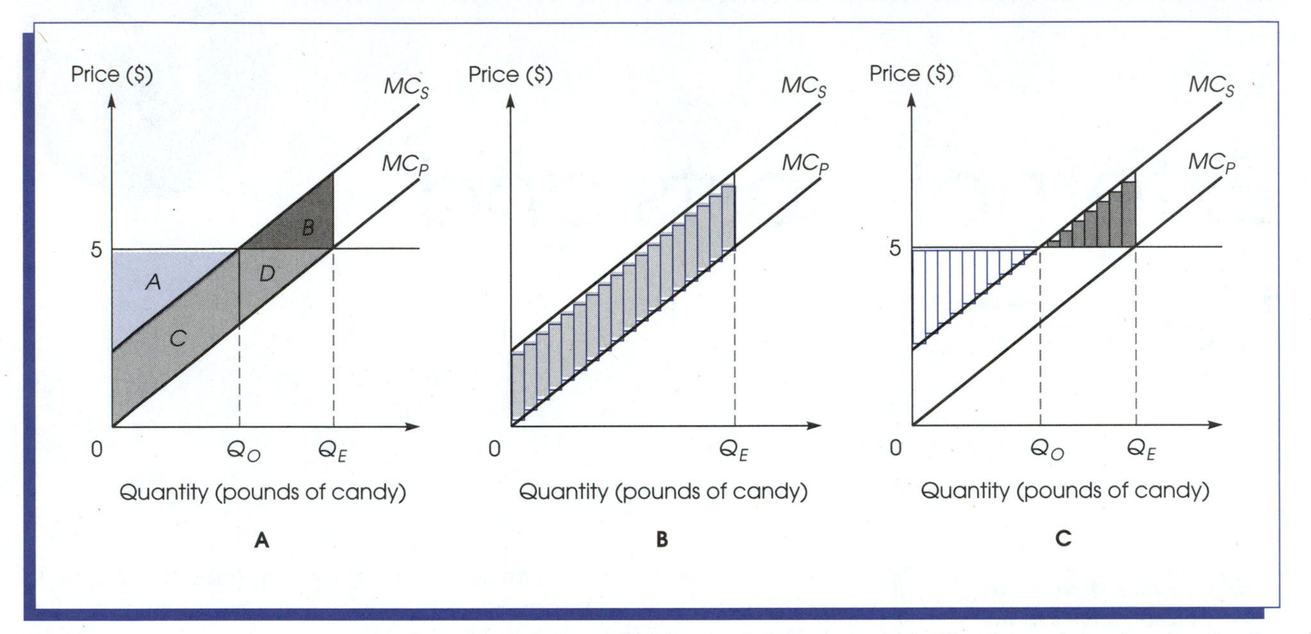

Bridgman, a confectioner, has the marginal cost curve MC_P. When he produces chocolate, he also imposes external costs on Sturges. The cost to society of producing candy is the sum of Bridgman's private cost MC_P and the external costs borne by Sturges. The curve MC_S shows this full social cost.

At a market price of $5, Bridgman produces Q_E pounds of candy. Each pound produced imposes on Sturges a marginal external cost represented by one of the rectangles in panel B. The total external cost is the sum of these rectangles, which is area $B + C + D$ in panel A.

Bridgman earns a producer's surplus equal to $A + C + D$. Subtracting the externality imposed on Sturges, we find a net social gain of $A - B$. The reason for this result is demonstrated in panel C. Each pound of candy up to Q_o creates a social gain equal to one of the unshaded rectangles. Each pound of candy after Q_o creates a social loss equal to one of the shaded rectangles. The net social gain is the sum of the unshaded rectangles minus the sum of the shaded ones, or $A - B$.

The Doctor and the Confectioner

Panel A of Exhibit 13–1 shows the market for Bridgman's Chocolate Confectionery, which sells candy in a competitive market at a going price of $5 per pound. In his business Bridgman uses machinery that creates noise and vibration disturbing to Doctor Sturges, a general practitioner with an office next door. The noise constitutes a negative externality imposed by the confectioner on the doctor, who is unable to consult with patients while the noise is in progress.

Private marginal costs Those costs of a decision that are borne by the decision maker.

Social marginal costs All of the costs of a decision, including the private costs and the costs imposed on others.

The curve labeled MC_P reflects Bridgman's marginal costs (cost of chocolate and other ingredients, cost of running the machinery, and so forth). Because these costs are paid by Bridgman himself, we call them **private marginal costs**. The curve MC_S includes both the private costs borne by Bridgman and the external costs imposed on Sturges. Thus, it includes all costs borne by all members of society. We call these **social marginal costs**. At any given quantity the marginal external cost (Sturges's lost income, and perhaps psychological strain as well) is represented by the vertical distance between the two marginal cost curves.

Because Bridgman does not care about the cost imposed on Sturges, his supply curve is his private marginal cost curve. Equilibrium occurs at the quantity Q_E. To evaluate the welfare aspects of this equilibrium, we must measure the extent of the externalities. The externalities created by the production of successive pounds of candy are measured by the areas of the rectangles in panel B of Exhibit 13–1. The total externality is the sum of these areas; it is the area between the private and social marginal cost curves, out to the quantity produced. In panel A, this is the area $B + C + D$.

QA EXERCISE 13.1 Explain why the rectangles in panel B give the correct measure of the externality.

Now we can evaluate the social gain. There is no consumer's surplus because the demand curve is flat (although a similar analysis would hold without this assumption). Producer's surplus is $A + C + D$. Externalities detract from welfare and so must be subtracted from the social gain. The net social gain is Producer's surplus − Externalities = $(A + C + D) - (B + C + D) = A - B$.

EXERCISE 13.2 Verify the previous two sentences.

The social gain can also be computed directly without reference to its individual components. The demand curve depicts the marginal values of successive pounds of candy (in this case, their marginal values are all $5), and the social marginal cost curve depicts the marginal cost *to society as a whole* of providing those pounds. Part of the social marginal cost is the cost of raw materials and other factors of production; in other words, it is the private marginal cost borne by Bridgman. The remainder is noise damage to Sturges's medical practice, nerves, and psyche.

Each pound prior to Q_O provides $5 worth of value to consumers while costing society less than $5 to produce. For each of these pounds, the excess of value over cost (that is, the social gain) is represented by one of the unshaded rectangles in panel C of Exhibit 13–1. Pounds of candy from Q_O to Q_E cost society more than they are worth to consumers; the resulting social losses are represented by the shaded rectangles. Net social gain is the sum of the unshaded rectangles minus the sum of the shaded ones. This is the same answer we got before; it is area $A - B$ in panel A of the exhibit.

The Pigou Tax

Society would be best off if Bridgman agreed to produce candy only as long as its marginal value exceeds its *social* marginal cost. This would lead him to produce Q_O pounds of candy, yielding a social gain equal to area A in Exhibit 13–1. (In terms of panel C, society would gain the unshaded rectangles without losing the shaded ones.) Unfortunately, Bridgman produces candy as long as its marginal value exceeds his *private* marginal cost, which leads him to produce out to Q_E. If he could be induced to take account of the costs imposed on Sturges, he would choose the efficient level of output Q_O.

A tax can provide the appropriate incentive. Suppose that Bridgman were subject to a tax equal to the amount of the damage he imposes on his neighbor. In that case any noise-related losses to Sturges would become a part of Bridgman's private costs. We say that Bridgman **internalizes** these costs, meaning that they now fully enter his decision-making process. This would cause the private marginal cost curve MC_P in Exhibit 13–1 to move directly on top of the social marginal cost curve MC_S. With such a tax, quantity will fall to Q_O. The externality will be reduced to *C* (the area between the two marginal cost curves out to the new quantity produced). Tax revenue will exactly equal the amount of the costs imposed on Sturges.

Internalize To treat an external cost as a private cost.

QA EXERCISE 13.3 Explain why the tax causes the MC_P curve to coincide with the MC_S curve.

Exhibit 13–2 shows the new distribution of social gains. The graph there is identical to panel A of Exhibit 13–1. When Bridgman is taxed, he produces the quantity Q_O and gains a producer's surplus of *A*. The externality imposed on Sturges is *C*. The tax revenue is also *C*. (There are two ways to verify that area *C* is the tax revenue. The first is to use high school geometry. The second is to remember that Bridgman is being taxed an amount exactly equal to the externality that he imposes, so that the total tax revenue must equal the total external cost *C*.)

A tax that requires Bridgman to pay an amount equal to the externality is called a **Pigou tax** (or, sometimes, a **Pigovian tax**) in honor of the British economist A. C. Pigou, who studied such questions in his influential book *The Economics of Welfare*.[1] The Pigou tax leads to a socially optimal level of output regardless of who gets the tax revenue. One possibility, which appeals to many people's sense of fairness, is that the tax revenue could be given to Sturges. The proceeds of the tax are just sufficient to compensate him for being subjected to the noise from Bridgman's machinery.

Pigou tax or **Pigovian tax** A tax equal to the amount of an externality.

An equivalent strategy is to institute a rule of law under which Bridgman is **liable** for his actions. This means that Sturges would have a legal right to be compensated by Bridgman for damages due to the noise. Such a liability rule is equivalent to a Pigou tax on Bridgman with the proceeds given to Sturges.

Liable Legally responsible to compensate another party for damage.

Another way to describe this liability rule is to say that Sturges is granted a **property right** to the noise-free air around his office. As the owner of this air, he is entitled to charge Bridgman for its use as a noise receptacle.

Property right The right to decide how some resource shall be used.

A Pigou tax on Bridgman with proceeds assigned to Sturges, a legal arrangement assigning liability to Bridgman, and an assignment of property rights to Sturges are three different ways of describing essentially the same thing. Regardless of how it is described, this arrangement ensures that Bridgman will consider the effects of the noise from his machinery when he decides how much to produce. The social costs of production will all become private costs; in other words, all of the externalities will be internalized. As a result,

[1]New York: Macmillan, 1920.

Exhibit 13-2 A Pigou Tax

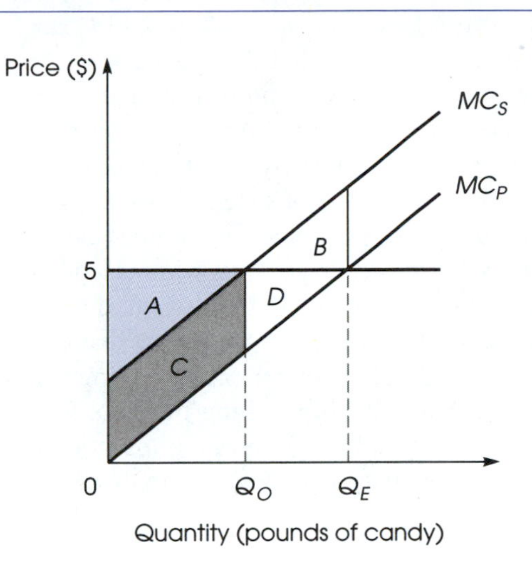

	Without Pigou Tax	With Pigou Tax
Gains to Bridgman:		
Producer's Surplus	$A + C + D$	A
Losses to Sturges:		
Noise Damage	$B + C + D$	C
Tax Revenue	—	C
Social gain	$A - B$	A

A Pigou tax requires Bridgman to pay an amount equal to the external cost that he imposes on Sturges. Since each pound of candy entails a marginal external cost equal to the distance from MC_P to MC_S, the Pigou tax on each pound is also equal to that distance. When the tax is imposed, MC_P moves up to MC_S, Bridgman cuts back production from Q_E to Q_O, and social gains are distributed as in the table.

Bridgman will stop producing when marginal *social* costs equals marginal value, which is the socially efficient level of production.[2]

[2]The Invisible Hand Theorem tells us that competitive markets maximize social welfare. Exhibit 13–1 seems to present a counterexample. But, in fact, the reason why the equilibrium in Exhibit 13–1 is suboptimal is precisely that a market is lacking, namely, the market for air! When nobody owns the air, it can be neither bought nor sold. When Sturges acquires property rights to the air and is reimbursed for noise damage, he is "selling" the use of this air to Bridgman at a competitive price. Once again the introduction of markets leads to an optimal outcome.

The Incompleteness of Pigou's Analysis

For many years all economists believed that Pigou's analysis of the problem of externalities was essentially the final word on the subject. In particular, they believed that the Pigou tax was the correct way to achieve a socially optimal outcome. However, in 1960 Ronald Coase, a law professor and legal scholar, taught economists that there is far more to say about the problem of externalities.[3] Coase demonstrated both that Pigou's analysis is incomplete and that it can lead to incorrect conclusions. There are situations in which a Pigou tax is unnecessary, and many situations in which it is actually counterproductive.

Transactions cost Any cost of negotiating or enforcing a contract.

Coase's analysis of externalities requires the notion of **transactions costs**. A transactions cost is a cost of negotiating or enforcing a contract. If you hire someone to repair your roof, transactions costs might include the time spent locating an appropriate handyman, time or energy spent haggling over a price, the cost of hiring an inspector to make sure that the job has been done correctly, and the potential costs of filing a lawsuit if the roofer fails to make repairs as promised. Anything that interferes with people's ability to make mutually beneficial bargains is a transactions cost.

Coase's analysis of Pigou's analysis of externalities led him to two conclusions.

1. In the absence of transactions costs, Pigou's arguments are wrong.
2. In the presence of transactions costs, Pigou's arguments are still wrong, but for a different reason.

In Section 13.2, we will see how Coase was led to the first of these conclusions, and in Section 13.3 we will see how he was led to the second.

13.2 The Coase Theorem

In this section, we will study Coase's criticism of Pigou in the case where there are no transactions costs. We will begin by reconsidering our analysis of the dispute between Sturges and Bridgman.

The Doctor and the Confectioner Revisited

Read more about the Coase Theorem at David Friedman's site: http://www.best.com/~ddfr/Academic/Coase_World.html

Consider again the dispute between Sturges and Bridgman, and refer to Exhibit 13–2. Equilibrium output is Q_E. Optimal output is Q_O. This means that at Q_O the social "pie" is bigger than at Q_E (in fact, it is A instead of $A - B$). When the pie is bigger, everyone can have a bigger piece. In the absence of transactions costs, both Sturges and Bridgman have an incentive to agree to an arrangement whereby Q_O is produced and the "winner" reimburses the "loser" by enough to make *both parties* better off.

[3]His arguments appear in R. H. Coase, "The Problem of Social Cost," *Journal of Law and Economics* 3 (1960): 1–4.

For example, suppose that Sturges offers Bridgman a payment equal to the area $D + \frac{1}{2} B$ in exchange for Bridgman's agreement to produce only Q_O pounds of candy instead of Q_E. Then Sturges benefits, since he reduces the noise damage by $D + B$ in exchange for a payment of only $D + \frac{1}{2} B$. And Bridgman benefits, since he receives the payment of $D + \frac{1}{2} B$ in exchange for sacrificing only D in producer's surplus.

EXERCISE 13.4 What is the smallest amount Bridgman would accept in exchange for cutting output to Q_O? What is the largest amount Sturges would offer him to do so?

Side Payments

What other kinds of arrangements might Bridgman and Sturges negotiate? Assume that every time Bridgman produces a pound of candy, he imposes \$2 worth of costs on Sturges. This means that in Exhibit 13–2, the MC_S curve lies a vertical distance \$2 above the MC_P curve. Under these conditions, Sturges will offer to pay Bridgman up to \$2 for each pound of candy that Bridgman does *not* produce. We will refer to this \$2 per pound as a "side payment" or "bribe" (though our use of the word *bribe* is not intended to signify that the payment is in any sense dishonest or underhanded).

Now whenever Bridgman produces a pound of candy, he must forgo a \$2 bribe from Sturges. The forgone opportunity becomes part of Bridgman's marginal cost, and enters his production decision in exactly the same way that a tax would. For purposes of choosing a quantity, Bridgman acts as if his marginal cost curve has risen a vertical distance \$2. His new *private* marginal cost curve coincides with the *social* marginal cost curve MC_S!

The table in Exhibit 13–3 shows the social accounting. The first two columns reproduce the accounting from Exhibit 13–2. The third column shows what happens if the Pigou tax is removed but Sturges can offer bribes. Bridgman treats MC_S as his private marginal cost curve and produces Q_O pounds of candy. Since he cuts his production from Q_E to Q_O, Sturges pays him $(Q_E - Q_O) \times \$2 = B + D$. In the table, we have entered this bribe as both a gain to Bridgman and a loss to Sturges; its net contribution to social welfare is a wash. Still there is a net social gain of B that results from the reduction in both candy and noise. Who gets this gain? An examination of the columns in Exhibit 13–3 reveals that it all goes to Bridgman. His gains increase from $A + C + D$ to $A + B + C + D$, while Sturges's losses stay fixed at $B + C + D$.

When Bridgman is offered a \$2/pound bribe, he uses the MC_S curve to choose his quantity. But when we calculate Bridgman's producer's surplus, we use his MC_P curve, since this reflects his actual business expenses. It is the area above the MC_P curve that shows Bridgman's surplus from being in the candy business.

We began this example by observing that Sturges is willing to pay *up to* \$2 per pound to prevent Bridgman from producing candy. The accounting of Ex-

Exhibit 13-3 Side Payments Cause Externalities To Be Internalized

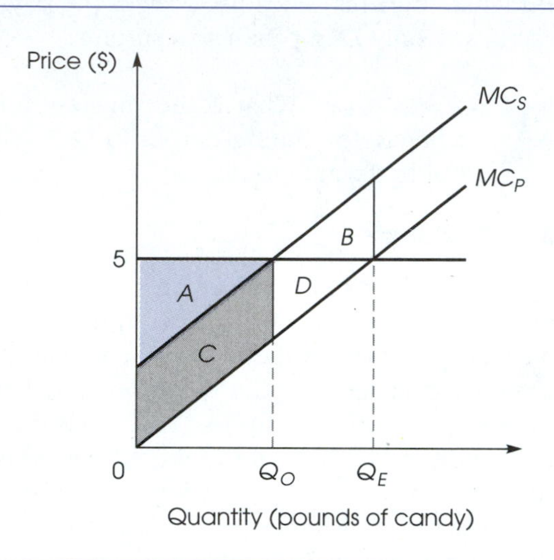

	Original	With Pigou Tax	With Bribes
Gains to Bridgman:			
Producer's Surplus	$A + C + D$	A	$A + C$
Payment from Sturges	—	—	$B + D$
Losses to Sturges:			
Noise Damage	$B + C + D$	C	C
Payment to Bridgman	—	—	$B + D$
Tax Revenue	—	C	—
Social gain	$A - B$	A	A

The graph is as in Exhibit 13–2. Each time Bridgman produces a pound of candy, he imposes a $2 externality on Sturges. In the absence of transactions costs, Sturges offers Bridgman $2 for each pound of candy that he does *not* produce.

Now whenever Bridgman makes a pound of candy he forgoes a $2 bribe. This additional cost shifts his MC_P curve up a distance $2 until it lies on top of MC_S. He reduces his output to Q_O, just as he would under a Pigou tax. Therefore, social gain must increase to A, just as it does under a Pigou tax. The social accounting is displayed in the third column of the table.

hibit 13–3 assumes that he pays *exactly* $2 per pound. In actuality, he might be able to bargain Bridgman down a bit, in which case some of the gains we've attributed to Bridgman becomes gains to Sturges. This is essentially what happened in the example preceding Exercise 13.4, where Sturges offered a lump sum payment of $D + \frac{1}{2} B$, which Bridgman accepted.

Regardless of the details of his arrangement with Sturges, it will always be the case that Bridgman can extract up to $2 additional bribe for each additional

Coase Theorem In the absence of transactions costs, all externalities are internalized, regardless of the assignment of property rights.

pound of candy that he agrees not to produce. The forgone opportunity to collect this bribe is a cost of production that acts exactly like a Pigou tax.

We can now state the **Coase Theorem**, in two equivalent forms:

In the absence of transactions costs, private costs equal social costs.

That is, all externalities are automatically internalized, because forgone bribes act exactly like Pigou taxes. Equivalently:

In the absence of transactions costs, the assignment of property rights (or liability rules) has no effect on social welfare.

That is, a socially efficient outcome will be reached regardless of how property rights are assigned. In our example, the property right to noise-free air is at issue. The second and third columns of the table in Exhibit 13–3 correspond to two choices of property rights. A Pigou tax (which assigns the property right to Sturges) leads to an output of Q_O and a social gain of A. On the other hand, if Bridgman is given the property right, allowing him to make all the noise he pleases, then Sturges will bribe him to produce the quantity Q_O and the social gain will still be A.

The Coase Theorem is often summarized by saying that the assignment of property rights "does not matter." This means that the choice of property rights does not affect economic efficiency. On the other hand, it certainly does matter to Sturges and Bridgman, as you can see by inspecting the second and third columns of the table in Exhibit 13–3. Sturges prefers to collect the Pigou tax; Bridgman prefers to get bribed.

Alternative Solutions

We have argued that in the absence of transactions costs, private costs rise to equal social costs, regardless of how property rights are allocated. In the case of Bridgman and Sturges, this leads to an output of Q_O and a social gain of A. Moreover, this output is optimal in the sense that A is the largest social gain possible. But our analysis is still incomplete, because there may be other alternatives, even more desirable than reducing Bridgman's output. Perhaps Bridgman can acquire more modern machinery that can't be heard from Sturges's office. Perhaps Sturges can move his office to the other side of his house. Perhaps Bridgman or Sturges, or both together, can erect a sound barrier between their properties.

Any of these alternatives would eliminate the discrepancy between private and social costs by reducing social costs rather than by raising private costs as a Pigou tax would. In Exhibit 13–3 the MC_S curve would move down to lie on top of the MC_P curve, since the externality would be eliminated. In this case Bridgman would produce Q_E pounds of candy, and the social gain from his operation would increase from A to $A + C + D$.

However, each of these solutions is costly. The cost of moving Sturges's office cannot be measured by any area in Exhibit 13–3. If that cost is less than $C + D$, the move is a more efficient solution than any scheme for reducing output to Q_O. If Bridgman can buy a new machine more cheaply than Sturges can move, then that solution is more efficient yet.

The Coase Theorem extends to these other possibilities as well. In the absence of transactions costs, Sturges and Bridgman will find the most efficient of all possible solutions and agree to a system of reimbursements or "bribes" that will make them both better off. This is so regardless of how property rights are initially allocated. The most efficient outcome could be either a cutback in production to Q_O or some scheme for eliminating or reducing noise damage. There is no way to determine this outcome from the information available in the graph.

To illustrate this point, let us suppose that the possibilities have been narrowed to two: Either Sturges quits practicing medicine or Bridgman stops producing candy.[4] In order to see how the allocation of property rights will affect this decision, we need to make some assumptions about the value of Bridgman's and Sturges's respective businesses. We will present two examples, using different assumptions.

Example 1

Suppose that Bridgman values his confectionery business at $100, reflecting the income that he earns selling candy. Suppose that Sturges earns so much as a doctor that he values his medical practice at $200. These values then also represent the costs to Bridgman and Sturges of leaving their respective industries.

Suppose first that Sturges has the property right, so that he can demand that Bridgman stop making noise. Then Bridgman will be forced out of business and Sturges will be able to practice medicine in peace and quiet.

Now imagine a change in the law. The property right is reassigned to Bridgman, so that he is allowed to make all the noise he wants. Will he continue to produce candy? In the absence of transactions costs, the answer is no. Sturges is willing to pay up to $200 as a bribe in exchange for Bridgman's closing up shop. For any amount over $100, Bridgman is willing to close. This leaves room for a mutually acceptable payment of, say, $150. Sturges offers this to Bridgman, who accepts it and retires. Each gains $50 more than he would have if Bridgman had exercised his property right. Sturges avoids the loss of a $200 business in exchange for a $150 payment; Bridgman adds $150 to his wallet while sacrificing only $100 worth of income by giving up his business.

Thus, regardless of whether Sturges or Bridgman has the property right, Bridgman will stop producing candy and Sturges will resume his medical practice. The change in the law has no effect on the amounts of medical care and candy that are produced. These outcomes are shown in the first row of the table in Exhibit 13–4.

---

[4]For purposes of this example, we assume that all other solutions have already been rejected as less desirable. In particular, we are assuming that it is less costly for Bridgman to go out of business altogether than to cut back his production to Q_O. This would be the case if an output of Q_O does not allow Bridgman to earn enough to cover his fixed costs. Nothing of importance depends on this assumption. Its only purpose is to keep the example manageable.

Example 2

In this example, we reverse the numbers so that Bridgman's business is worth $200, whereas Sturges's is worth $100.

If Bridgman has the property right, he will continue to make candy. Suppose, alternatively, that Sturges has the property right and can order Bridgman to quit. Will he do so? No. Bridgman will offer up to $200 to Sturges in exchange for permission to continue making noise. Sturges will sell this permission for any amount over $100. Thus, Bridgman pays Sturges some amount between $100 and $200 (say $150) and stays in business. Regardless of who has the property right, Bridgman continues to make candy, and Sturges stops practicing medicine.

Once again, changing the law does not affect the quantities of candy or of medical care. These outcomes are summarized in the second row of the table in Exhibit 13–4.

Comparing the Examples

In Exhibit 13–4 the rows of the table correspond to the two examples, which represent alternative possible economic conditions. The columns correspond to the two possible assignments of property rights, which are alternative pos-

Exhibit 13-4 Alternative Assignments of Property Rights

	Sturges Has Property Right	Bridgman Has Property Right
Example 1: Bridgman's Candy Business Worth $100; Sturges's Medical Practice Worth $200	Sturges forces Bridgman to quit. Society gets medical care, no candy.	Sturges bribes Bridgman $150 to quit. Society gets medical care, no candy.
Example 2: Bridgman's Candy Business Worth $200; Sturges's Medical Practice Worth $100	Bridgman bribes Sturges $150. Sturges retires. Society gets candy, no medical care	Bridgman makes noise, forcing Sturges to retire. Society gets candy, no Medical care.

The two rows correspond to two different assumptions about the values of Bridgman's candy business and Sturges's medical practice. In each example, we ask what happens if Sturges is given the property right (enabling him to force Bridgman to stop making noise) and what happens if Bridgman is given the property right (enabling him to make all the noise he wants). From a social point of view, the allocation of property rights does not matter in either example.

sible legal conditions. The social outcome (will society have candy or will it have medical care?) is determined solely by the economic conditions. The choice of column does not affect the outcome.

Of course, this simply illustrates the Coase Theorem: In the absence of transactions costs, the assignment of property rights does not matter from the point of view of economic efficiency. It does, of course, matter to Sturges and to Bridgman.

EXERCISE 13.5 Verify that under either set of economic conditions, Sturges is $150 richer with the property right than without it, and the same is true of Bridgman.

Sturges and Bridgman are the names of two real people who were involved in a dispute very similar to the one we have described. The real-world dispute ended up in court, where the judges ruled in the doctor's favor. They did so under the mistaken impression that they were affecting the actual workings of the economic system. They thought that they were voting for medical care over candy. Instead, they were only voting for Sturges over Bridgman. Their decision enriched Sturges at Bridgman's expense, but (assuming no transactions costs) it had no effect on which economic activity was actually pursued.

The Coase Theorem: A Summary

At this point we can summarize the main points of this section. A classically trained "Pigovian" economist might look at Exhibit 13–1 and say, "The socially optimal outcome is for Bridgman to produce Q_O. We must impose a tax to induce that outcome." Assuming no transactions costs, Coase tells us that the economist is wrong on *both* counts.

First, Q_O may not be the socially optimal outcome. It might be better to eliminate the noise problem in any of a wide variety of ways. These alternatives include, but are not limited to, one or the other party moving or abandoning his business. (Other possibilities we have already referred to include the construction of sound barriers and the like.)

Second, whatever outcome is socially optimal will be reached with or without a tax, via a bargain between the parties that improves everyone's welfare.[5]

The Coase Theorem with Many Firms

Everything we have said about Bridgman's individual firm applies as well to entire industries. Exhibit 13–5 shows the competitive market for sprockets, which are produced in factories that emit noxious smoke. The industry supply curve is the MC_P curve reflecting producers' cost. The MC_S curve reflects these costs, plus the costs of smoke damage to the neighboring homeowners. Market equilibrium is at quantity Q_E and price P_E. A Pigou tax equal to the amount of the externality imposed on homeowners will move the MC_P curve up to the

[5]Throughout this section, we have assumed no transactions costs. In Section 13.3, we will study Coase's objections to the Pigovian analysis in the case where transactions costs play a significant role.

Exhibit 13-5 A Pigou Tax in a Competitive Industry

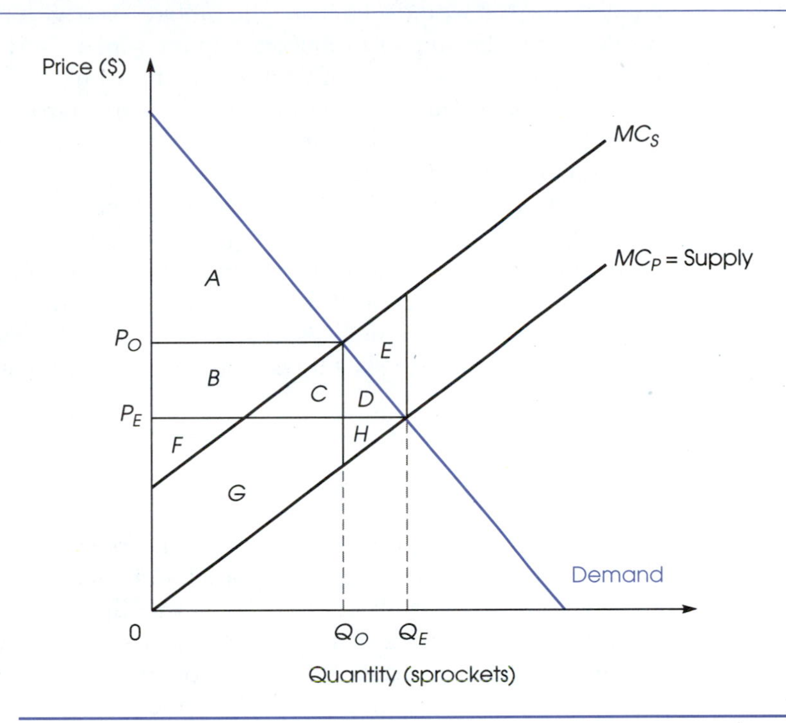

	With No Tax	With Pigou Tax
Gains		
Consumers' Surplus	$A + B + C + D$	A
Producers' Surplus	$F + G + H$	$B + F$
Tax Revenue	—	$C + G$
Losses:		
Smoke Damage	$C + D + E + G + H$	$C + G$
Social gain	$A + B + F - E$	$A + B + F$

Sprockets are produced competitively in factories that emit noxious smoke. The table below gives the Pigovian analysis of social welfare. However, there are two ways in which the analysis is incomplete. First, it does not consider the possibility of an alternative arrangement under which MC_S is lowered to MC_P, perhaps through the instillation of pollution control equipment or the relocation of either the factories or the homes. Second, if there are no transactions costs between factories and homeowners, then forgone bribes will act exactly like a Pigou tax even when there is no tax explicitly imposed.

MC_S curve, leading to the socially optimal output Q_O being sold at a price P_O. The table displays the gains and losses.

Here again, Coase would raise two objections. First, there may be a solution we haven't thought of. Perhaps the factories could install pollution control equipment that would eliminate the smoke damage. Then optimal output would be Q_E, the sum of producers' and consumers' surpluses would be $A + B + C + D + F + G + H$, and the social gain would be $A + B + C + D + F + G + H$ minus the cost of installing pollution control equipment. This gain might be either more or less than the social gain of $A + B + F$ shown in the second column of the table in Exhibit 13–5.

Second, the optimal outcome, whatever it may be, will be achieved in a world without transactions costs regardless of what taxes are imposed. It should be said, however, that transactions costs probably do play a significant role in an example such as this one, because many different homeowners are affected by the smoke. The logistical problem of getting these homeowners together to jointly bribe the factory owners already constitutes a formidable transactions cost.

The Pigou Tax Reconsidered

If transactions are costless, then the Coase Theorem tells us that the Pigou tax is unnecessary. In fact, we can say more: If only *some* transactions are costless, it is possible for the Pigou tax to be positively harmful.

To see why, suppose in Exhibit 13–5 that sprocket producers and homeowners can transact costlessly. Then by offering side payments, homeowners will bid the MC_P curve up to the level of the MC_S curve. Now suppose that a Pigou tax is imposed, with the revenue collected by some third party. This will move the MC_P curve up higher yet, so that it now lies *above* the MC_S curve! The number of sprockets produced will be *less* than the optimal quantity Q_O.[6]

The problem here is that producers receive a double incentive to reduce their output. When the production of a sprocket causes \$2 worth of damage, the producer is both charged \$2 tax and made to forgo a \$2 bribe, raising his costs by \$4. This extra incentive causes him to continue cutting back on output even after the social optimum has been reached.

If *all* parties, including consumers and the recipients of tax revenue, can enter the negotiations, then the social optimum is achieved with or without a Pigou tax. It is always possible to arrange a system of side payments that will benefit everyone when the size of the social pie is maximized. However, the example here shows that when some but not all of the parties can negotiate, the Pigou tax can actually reduce social welfare.[7]

---

[6]The problem does not occur if the Pigou tax is paid to the homeowners rather than a third party. If the homeowners are reimbursed for the pollution, they are indifferent to how much pollution occurs and will therefore not offer bribes.

[7]This point seems to have first been clearly exposited by Ralph Turvey in "On Divergences Between Social Cost and Private Cost," *Economica* 30 (1963):309–313.

example

The Nature Conservancy

For more about the activities of the Nature Conservancy, access their site at: http://www.tnc.org/

Environmental pollution is often cited as an example of an externality that cannot be bargained away because of high transactions costs. It is alleged that the large number of people affected suffices to negate any possibility of negotiating side payments. There is undoubtedly much truth in this assertion, but it is far from entirely true.

In Arlington, Virginia, a charitable organization called the Nature Conservancy solicits funds from the public and uses those funds exactly in the way that Coase would predict. It purchases land in ecologically significant areas and maintains that land to preserve threatened species and places of special beauty. Its current holdings comprise 2.8 million acres in 4,100 locations. In making its purchases, the Conservancy bids against other potential users of the land, forcing those other potential users to take account of the land's ecological significance.

At the same time, because it pays market prices, the Conservancy must take account of the value of the land in its alternative (nonecological) uses. When a parcel of land has exceptional value in other uses, the price of the land is high and the Conservancy is less likely to acquire it. Thus, from a social point of view, the Conservancy's approach has a distinct advantage over, for example, legally mandating that landowners follow policies that are oriented toward conservation.

Unfortunately, even those who value conservation highly have an incentive to "free ride" on the efforts of groups like the Nature Conservancy, so that the actual level of contributions may inadequately reflect the true demand for conservation. Nevertheless, the organization has been extraordinary successful. In 1997, it received private contributions of over $150 million. The Nature Conservancy's success is a striking reminder that seemingly insurmountable transactions costs can be at least partially overcome.

External Benefits

Everything we have said about external costs has its analogue regarding external benefits. Suppose that Nabisco can produce a cookie at a (private) marginal cost of 5¢. At the same time, the factory produces a pleasant aroma worth 2¢ to motorists driving by. Then the cookie is produced at a social marginal cost of only 3¢; part of the private costs are returned to society via the external benefit from the aroma. In the presence of external benefits, the social marginal cost curve lies below the private marginal cost curve, and too few cookies are produced.

Just as a Pigou tax internalizes external costs, so a "Pigou subsidy" equal to the benefits conferred on others can internalize external benefits, leading to an efficient level of output. However, the Coase Theorem applies in this case as well. In the absence of transactions costs, the recipients of the benefit will offer a bribe in exchange for greater production, and this bribe will operate just like a Pigou subsidy.

example

The Fable of the Bees

The USDA provides an overview of contract pollination services at: http://gears.tucson.ars.ag.gov/home/edwards/leaf549.htm

An interesting real-world example is what Professor Steven Cheung has called *The Fable of the Bees*.[8] In the literature of economics, the standard example of a positive externality is the interaction between apple growing and beekeeping. When these two activities are carried on in close physical proximity, one might expect each to confer benefits on the other. More apple trees mean more honey; more bees mean more cross-pollination and eventually more apples. Pigou would have argued (and his disciples did argue) that this situation must result in suboptimal levels of output in both activities. An apple grower stops planting new trees as soon as the marginal cost of planting exceeds his private marginal benefit, failing to consider that further trees would benefit his neighbor. The beekeeper performs a similar unfortunate calculation. Both could be made better off by a system of taxes and subsidies that encouraged them to consider their neighbor's welfare as part of their own.

Cheung investigated the accuracy of this fable by interviewing apple growers and beekeepers. He found that, contrary to the expectations of Pigou style economists and exactly as Coase would have predicted, there is an elaborate system of contracts under which the two groups reimburse each other with "bribes" for increasing output to the socially optimal levels.[9] The evidence that such contracts exist is not hard to find; Cheung pointed out that one need only look in the Yellow Pages under nectar and pollination services. Never-the-less, a generation of economists had somehow managed to deny that such contracts were possible.

EXERCISE 13.6 State an appropriate moral for *The Fable of the Bees*.

Income Effects and the Coase Theorem

According to the Coase Theorem, assignments of property rights do not matter from the point of view of economic efficiency. In the example of Exhibit 13–4 an even stronger statement can be made. Not only does a change in property rights have no effect on economic efficiency, it also has no effect on the amounts of medical care and candy that are produced. The "resource" consisting of the air around Bridgman's confectionery and Sturges's office is allocated either to the production of candy (via its use as a "dumping ground" for Bridgman's noise) or to the production of medical care (via its use as a quiet, conducive environment in which Sturges can practice), depending on where it is most valuable and regardless of who has the property rights.

We will refer to this outcome as the *Strong Coase Theorem:*

***Strong Coase Theorem:* In the absence of transactions costs, the assignment of property rights has no effect on the allocation of resources.**

[8] S. Cheung, "The Fable of the Bees: An Economic Investigation," *Journal of Law and Economics* 16 (1973):11–34.

[9] He also discovered that, contrary to a widespread assertion in economic literature, apples produce almost no honey. Therefore, he extended his investigation to include many other plants.

The Strong Coase Theorem is not universally true. Suppose that a law were passed requiring all classical music lovers to give half of their wealth to people who like rock and roll. Although this is just a change in property rights, the demand for classical records would fall, the demand for rock records would rise, and resources formerly allocated to producing classical music would be reallocated to the production of rock. However, although the allocation of resources has changed, it is still efficient (that is, Pareto-optimal). Rock fans are happier, classical music lovers are less happy, but social welfare is still being maximized *given* the new wealth distribution. This is an example of what we will call the *Weak Coase Theorem:*

***Weak Coase Theorem:* In the absence of transactions costs, the assignment of property rights does not affect the *efficiency* of resource allocation (though it might cause resources to be diverted from one efficient allocation to another).**

The Weak Coase Theorem is always true. The Strong Coase Theorem is true whenever the reallocation of property rights does not change people's wealth enough to have significant effects on market demand curves. (In other words, the redistribution of income that results from the change in property rights should have negligible income effects.)

Notice that changes in the assets of *firms* do not affect the validity of the Strong Coase Theorem. Only changes in the assets of individuals are relevant, because individuals are the source of demand curves. For the Strong Coase Theorem to fail, there must be large changes in the wealth of enough individuals to make a significant difference in the relevant market.

In Exhibit 13–4 a shift in property rights from Sturges to Bridgman makes Bridgman richer. If Bridgman loves candy, this could raise the demand for candy and cause more candy production; if he loves medical care, it could bring about more medical care. (For that matter, if Bridgman loves carrots, it will raise carrot production.) The fact that Bridgman is a *producer* of candy is irrelevant to how demands will shift. In any event, Bridgman as a consumer is undoubtedly such an insignificant part of either market that no real change will come about.

example

The Reserve Clause in Baseball

Read more about the economics of the reserve clause in baseball at: http://hubcap.clemson.edu/~sixmile/sports/1_22.htm

Before 1972 all major league baseball players had contracts containing a *reserve clause.* The reserve clause forbade the player from attempting to sell his services to any other team. If the Chicago White Sox wanted to acquire a player from the New York Yankees, the White Sox had to buy that player's contract from the Yankees. They could not simply offer him a higher salary to try to lure him away.

In the 1970s the reserve clause was substantially weakened, and now a number of players are *free agents* who can sell their services to the highest bidder. At the time it was argued that the weakening of the reserve clause would enable the wealthiest teams to buy up all of the best players. Let us subject this assertion to some economic analysis.

The weakening of the reserve clause is a transfer of property rights. Player's services, which used to belong to the teams they played for, now belong to the players themselves. The Coase Theorem suggests that such a transfer of property rights should not affect the allocation of players to teams.

Consider a player, Frank DeMeyer, who currently plays for the New York Yankees. Having DeMeyer on the team is worth $100,000 to the Yankees. This is because his presence increases the Yankees' revenue by $100,000. He would be worth only $75,000 to the Chicago White Sox.

Under the reserve clause, the Yankees will not sell DeMeyer for any amount less than $100,000, and the White Sox will not offer any amount more than $75,000. No exchange takes place, and DeMeyer continues to play for the Yankees.

On the other hand, suppose that DeMeyer becomes a free agent. Then the Yankees will offer him up to $100,000 to play for them. This is because he can produce an additional $100,000 in revenue for the Yankees and has nothing to do with whether the Yankees are rich or poor. The White Sox will offer DeMeyer up to $75,000. If DeMeyer maximizes his salary, he will play for the Yankees. Thus, free agency has no effect on where DeMeyer plays.

We have implicitly made the simplifying assumption that DeMeyer receives no salary under the reserve clause. If he receives $20,000 in salary, then the Yankees will value his contract at $80,000, not $100,000, and the White Sox will value his contract at $55,000. However, the conclusion that he continues to play for the Yankees does not change.

EXERCISE 13.7 Assume that DeMeyer is worth $100,000 to the Yankees and $150,000 to the White Sox. For whom does he play under the reserve clause? For whom does he play under free agency?

Now let's throw in a complication. Suppose that DeMeyer hates living in New York, so much so that he would be willing to pay up to $50,000 to move to the White Sox. Under free agency, DeMeyer will move. The White Sox offer him $75,000 and the Yankees offer him $100,000. The additional $25,000 he can earn in New York is not enough to overcome his $50,000 preference for Chicago.

Under the reserve clause, DeMeyer will also move. The White Sox are willing to buy him from the Yankees for $75,000. In addition, DeMeyer himself is willing to "bribe" the Yankees up to $50,000 in exchange for their agreeing to sell him. Thus, the Yankees can collect a total of $125,000 for letting DeMeyer go. Since he is worth only $100,000 to the Yankees, DeMeyer ends up in Chicago.

This example illustrates the Strong Coase Theorem. The reallocation of property rights that results from free agency has no effect on where DeMeyer plays.

EXERCISE 13.8 Suppose that DeMeyer is willing to pay only $10,000 to live in Chicago. Where does he play under free agency? Where does he play under the reserve clause?

Finally, let's throw in one additional complication. Suppose that DeMeyer's demand for living in Chicago depends upon his income. When he is a poor reserve player, he is willing to pay only $10,000 to live in Chicago, but when he is a rich free agent, he is willing to pay $50,000. Now under the reserve clause, the Yankees can collect a total of only $85,000 for DeMeyer ($75,000 from the White Sox plus a $10,000 bribe from DeMeyer himself) and will not sell. In this case, DeMeyer continues to play for the Yankees. Under free agency, the $25,000 difference in salary offers does not compensate DeMeyer for his $50,000 preference for Chicago, and so he plays for the White Sox.

The preceding paragraph shows how income effects enter the analysis. A change in property rights can affect the allocation of resources (the resource here being DeMeyer) only if it alters incomes in such a way as to change the demand for some resource (in this case DeMeyer's demand to live in Chicago). In such cases, the Strong Coase Theorem fails, but the Weak Coase Theorem is still true. Either allocation of resources is efficient, given DeMeyer's income.

How does free agency affect the allocation of players to teams? If players' preferences about where to live are unaffected by their incomes, then it does not affect the allocation. Otherwise, it increases the wealth of players and makes it more likely that they will choose the teams that they personally value playing for. This means that with the advent of free agency, it is the teams that are desirable to players, not the wealthy teams, that gain an advantage.

13.3 Transactions Costs

In the presence of transactions costs, it might not be possible to negotiate side payments leading to efficient outcomes. Thus, the Coase Theorem need not hold. However, even when there are positive transactions costs, the traditional Pigovian analysis of externalities is incomplete and can lead to wrong conclusions.

Example: Trains, Sparks, and Crops

Railway engines create sparks, and these sparks sometimes set fire to crops planted near the tracks. A large number of farmers are affected, and transactions costs prevent deals from being struck between these farmers and the railroad. If the railroad company is not liable for the ensuing damage, it will not consider the effects of this damage in deciding how many trains to run. A liability rule requiring the railroad to indemnify the farmers (in other words, a Pigou tax with proceeds assigned to the farmers) would provide such an incentive. There would be less rail service but more wheat and corn, which appears to be a social improvement.

The Coase Theorem says that if there were no transactions costs, this argument would be wrong because even without a Pigou tax, farmers would offer side payments to the railroad in exchange for running fewer trains. The railroad would be bribed into cutting back to the optimal level of rail service regardless of liability rules. But Coase made another, equally important point: When there *are* transactions costs, the conclusion that the railroads should be made liable may still be wrong, though for a different reason.

The flaw in the argument is that we do not know the cheapest way to prevent the fires. Suppose that farmers, at very little cost to themselves, can move their crops back a few feet from the railway bed, out of all danger from sparks. This would remove the externality and increase the social gain from the running of the railroad. However, if the railroad reimburses the farmers for all damage done, the farmers have no incentive to move their crops. Crops will be planted and burned, and fewer trains will be run because of the cost of reimbursement. If farmers were made to bear the losses from fires, they would move their crops, to society's benefit.

Exhibit 13–6 shows the picture, which should be familiar: It is identical to panel A of Exhibit 13–1. If the railroad is liable, it runs Q_O trains and the social gain is A. If the railroad is not liable and the farmers move their crops, the social marginal cost curve falls to the level of the private marginal cost curve, Q_E trains are run, and the social gain is $A + C + D$ minus the cost of moving the crops. If the cost of moving them is small, the latter is the better solution.

Exhibit 13-6 Sparks from Railroads

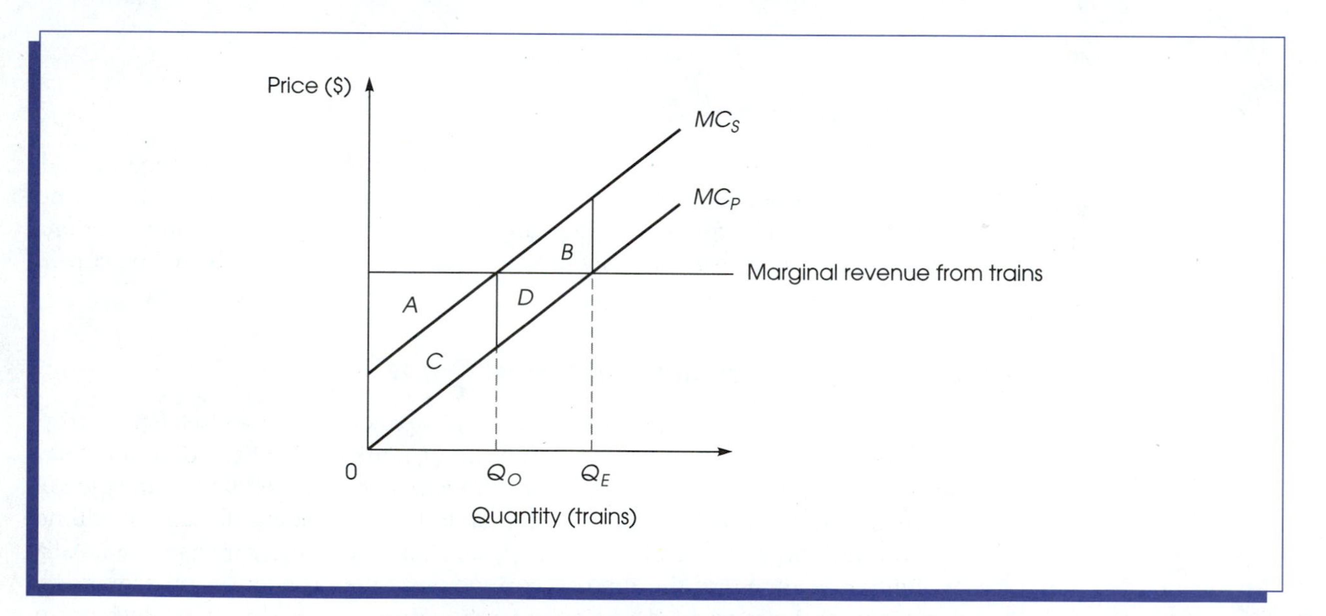

Because railway engines emit sparks that sometimes set fire to crops, the social marginal cost of running trains exceeds the private marginal cost. If the railroad is not liable, it runs Q_E trains and social gain is $A - B$. If the railroad is made liable, it takes account of all costs and runs Q_O trains, for a social gain of A. Thus, the standard Pigovian analysis suggests that the railroad should be liable.

But this analysis overlooks other possibilities. Suppose that the railroad is not liable and that as a result the farmers decide to move their crops away from the tracks. Then the externality is eliminated. Q_E trains are run (which is now the social optimum) and social gain is $A + C + D$ minus the cost of moving the crops. This gain could be more or less than the gain of A that comes about when the railroad is liable. Thus, the graph does not reveal the efficient solution.

Does this mean that the railroad should not be liable for its actions? Not necessarily. Suppose that the railroad can cheaply install safety equipment that will prevent sparks from being thrown by the engines. If the railroad has no liability for fire damage, it will have no incentive to install this equipment. Once again, it is possible that the low-cost solution has been sacrificed.

Exhibit 13–6 simply does not contain the information necessary to determine how property rights should be allocated. (The property right in question is the right to the unencumbered use of the land adjacent to the tracks—either for agriculture or for spark disposal.) Whoever has the property right has no incentive to seek a solution to the problem. If farmers can move their crops very cheaply, then it is most efficient for the railroad to have the property right so that farmers will have the incentive to move their crops. If the railroad can install safety equipment very cheaply, then it is more efficient for the farmers to have the property right so that the railroad will have the appropriate incentive.

In cases such as this one, courts often concern themselves (or profess to concern themselves) with questions of economic efficiency. If a judge has efficiency foremost in his mind, then he must attempt to determine which party can solve the problem at the lowest possible cost and make that party bear the costs of the damage (that is, the property right should be assigned to the other party). Unfortunately, this can be difficult. If the judge asks the railroad whether it can prevent spark damage at a relatively low cost (planning to make the railroad bear this cost if the answer is yes), the railroad has every incentive to conceal the truth by claiming that controlling the sparks would be prohibitively expensive. The farmers have the same incentive to exaggerate the cost of moving their crops.

When there is a great deal of uncertainty about the costs of various solutions, a judge may be well advised to assign property rights according to some secondary criterion and then to attempt to reduce transactions costs between the parties. If he can do so (say, by appointing a spokesman for the farmers and facilitating negotiation between this spokesman and the railroad company), then any mistake in the initial allocation of property rights will tend to be mitigated by the action of the Coase Theorem.

The Reciprocal Nature of the Problem

In Exhibit 13–6, the choice to run Q_E trains when there are crops planted near the railroad tracks is not socially optimal. The market's failure to produce the optimal outcome is due to the divergence between private and social costs. A Pigou tax remedies this divergence by shifting the private marginal cost curve upward. Coase's observation is that the divergence can be remedied equally well by moving the social marginal cost curve downward (for example, by having the farmers move their crops).

Why did economists in the Pigovian tradition fail to recognize the alternative remedy? Coarse argues that the error arises from the mistaken notion that the railroad is the "cause" of the fires, and therefore must curtail its activities if the damage is to be reduced. In actuality, the railroad is no more the cause of the fires than the crops are. Although it is true that if there were no railroads, there would be no fires, it is equally true that if there were no crops there would be no fires. Ultimately, the problem is caused by the fact that the railroad and the farmers are attempting to use the same land for two different purposes and this is no more one party's fault than it is the other's. Either party might be in possession of the cheapest means of dealing with the problem.

Every case of externalities is similarly reciprocal in nature. The neighborhood residents denounce the owner of a polluting factory; the owner might respond that there would be no externality if it weren't for the existence of the neighbors. The factory owner can mitigate the problem through cutbacks in production or pollution-control equipment; the neighbors can contribute equally well to a solution by moving away. Each of these options has a cost.[10] If the factory owner is allowed to pollute without penalty, he has no incentive to reduce pollution. If the neighbors are fully compensated by the factory for damage to their lungs and houses, they have no incentive to move away. Either liability rule might cause the elimination of the low-cost option; the "right" liability rule depends on the actual costs.

It is often argued that the pollution of a lake or river is an economic problem that must be solved, especially if the water would otherwise be available for recreation. If the pollution is curtailed and the lake is reclaimed, it makes equal sense to say that the boaters and fishermen are the source of a problem in that they cause a reduction in the output of a socially valuable product. Which is worth more, the additional product or the boating and fishing? There is no way to tell without examining actual costs and benefits.

Nonsmokers like to view cigarette smoke as a cost imposed on them unfairly by smokers. The problem, however, is a reciprocal one: It is caused by smokers and nonsmokers wanting to use the same air for two different purposes. Conceivably, it could be cheaper (that is, less unpleasant) for the nonsmokers to wear gas masks than for the smokers to curtail their smoking.

Automobiles sometimes hit pedestrians, injuring or killing them. The problem is caused by cars and people being in the same place at the same time; it can be partially alleviated by more care on the part of drivers or by more care on the part of pedestrians. In the 1970s the state of California, seeking to give appropriate incentives to drivers, made them legally responsible for any injury they caused to pedestrians. As a result, pedestrians had a greatly reduced incentive to take precautions, and they do, in fact, take fewer precautions. Whether the net effect has been to reduce accidents is unclear.

Sources of Transactions Costs

Read about the sources of transactions costs in economic development projects at: http://www.worldbank.org/html/fpd/notes/95/95summary.html

An understanding of the nature of transactions costs can be useful to one who is attempting to reduce them. The following series of examples illustrates some of the sources from which transactions costs are likely to arise.

---

[10]Of course, the cost of moving does not consist only of the fees paid to the moving companies; it includes the value of the dissatisfaction generated by leaving one's friends and gathering places as well.

example

Mining Safety and the Principal-Agent Problem

Coal mining is an inherently dangerous activity. Mining companies are able to reduce the frequency of injury to miners by the purchase of various types of safety equipment. If the companies are liable for injuries sustained on the job, they will have an obvious incentive to invest in such equipment until the marginal cost of one more unit of equipment is equal to the marginal benefit of that unit in terms of accident prevention. If, on the other hand, the companies bear no liability, you might at first think that they will have no incentive to make any investment in safety. The Coase Theorem suggests that this conclusion is wrong: Miners (who will now have to bear the costs of their own injuries) will be willing to "bribe" the company to buy safety equipment in the optimal amount. The most convenient form of such a bribe is for the miners to accept a lower wage. This is, of course, equivalent to a direct payment from the miners to the mining company.

Now suppose that there is another way to improve mining safety, which involves precautions taken by the miners themselves in the course of their underground activity. If miners bear the costs of their own injuries, they will engage in an appropriate level of precautionary activity. Alternatively, suppose that miners are fully reimbursed for all injuries by the mining company. In this case there appears to be no incentive for miners to take appropriate care. (If they are reimbursed but not fully, then they will take some care but less than the optimal amount.)

In the absence of transactions costs, however, the Coase Theorem suggests that the company itself will offer to pay the miners a bonus in exchange for their agreement to behave cautiously. Both sides benefit, as the miners collect the bonus and there are fewer injuries whose cost the company must bear.

But, unfortunately, there is no way to guarantee that an individual miner will live up to his part of the bargain. There is nothing to stop a miner from collecting the bonus and then behaving recklessly underground, where there is no one to observe him, knowing that he will be compensated by the company for any injury he sustains.

The fact that the miner's behavior is *unobservable* constitutes a transactions cost that can prevent the enforcement of the optimal contract. If all liability is with the company, and if precautionary behavior by miners is totally unobservable, then there will be no precautionary activity, regardless of what the optimal level might be.

In our simplified model of the mining industry, the most efficient liability rule is one that relieves owners of all responsibility to compensate miners for injuries. This in no way affects the incentives of owners to provide safety equipment, because their workers can still bribe them into behaving optimally. It also has the advantage of giving workers appropriate incentives, which they would not otherwise have because of the transactions costs involved in observing their behavior.[11]

---

[11]An interesting aspect of this choice of liability rule is that in the long run miners themselves will be indifferent to which rule is chosen (unlike Sturges and Bridgman, who cared very much). The reason is that entry and exit from the mining industry will eventually leave mining just as attractive (or just as unattractive) as the alternative occupations.

Whenever one party contracts to pay another to behave in a certain way, we call the first party a *principal* and the second an *agent*. If the mine owner attempts to pay the workers for behaving cautiously, then the owner is the principal and the workers are the agents. We say that a *principal-agent problem* arises when the principal cannot verify that the agent is abiding by the bargain, as in this example.[12]

In general, if A's behavior is observable and B's is not, then, in the absence of other transactions costs, it is efficient for B to bear the costs of damage resulting from interactions between A and B. This gives B the appropriate incentives; A has them already because of the Coase Theorem.

example

AIDS and Blood Transfusions

The recipients of blood transfusions sometimes contract infectious diseases as a result. AIDS is the most significant example. Who should bear the costs of such illnesses, the patient or the doctor?

In the absence of transactions costs, the placement of liability would not matter. If doctors were liable, they would adopt appropriate standards of safety in order to avoid lawsuits; if patients were liable (as, in fact, they legally are), they would offer higher fees to doctors and elicit the same standard of safety.

Here we face a close analogy with mining accidents. The patient's behavior is perfectly observable: A simple test reveals whether he has contracted AIDS. The doctor's behavior, however, is not. Thus, there is a principal-agent problem. If a patient pays extra for blood that is 99% certain to be AIDS-free and is instead given blood that is 95% certain to be AIDS-free, he is likely never to know the difference, whether or not he eventually becomes ill. If he does contract AIDS and suspects the doctor of cheating him, he will have great difficulty proving his suspicion. The inability to monitor doctors' compliance is a transactions cost that suggests that doctors should bear the liability for transfusion-induced illnesses.

We have been assuming that a transfusion patient is unlikely to contract AIDS in any other way. Without this assumption, our analysis must be modified. Suppose that doctors are fully liable when their patients develop AIDS. Then a recent transfusion recipient has reduced incentives to avoid other activities that may lead to the disease. If he contracts AIDS through riotous living, he can blame the doctor and be compensated. As a result, he may engage in such activities to a greater than optimal degree. The unobservability of the patient's behavior constitutes an argument for patient liability.

If doctors are liable to transfusion patients who contract AIDS, then some doctors will have to pay for patients who get the disease elsewhere. Although this might strike you as "unfair," the argument we have made does not concern this unfairness. It concerns only the inefficiency that arises if incentives are distorted so that the number of AIDS cases ends up being either more or less than optimal.

---

[12]Principal-agent problems were introduced in a different context in Chapter 9.

Incomplete Property Rights

Transactions costs also arise when property rights are ill-defined or nonexistent. Not knowing who owns something makes it difficult to bargain over its use. If Jack owns a tree that is worth more to Jill than to him, he will sell it to Jill. If Jill owns the tree and values it more than Jack does, she will keep it. If the tree belongs to some third party, he will sell it to whoever values it the most. In any event, the tree ends up in the hands of whoever values it the most, regardless of who owns it initially—provided *someone* owns it initially.

Suppose, alternatively, that there are no property rights to trees, and that a tree belongs to the person who takes it. The tree is worth $3 to Jack and $5 to Jill. Nevertheless, if Jack is first to spot the tree, he will claim it for his own. If Jack had a well-defined property right, he could agree to sell the tree to Jill; unfortunately, unless he uses the tree immediately, Jill will claim it for her own. Jack takes the tree for himself.

You might think that Jack could call Jill on the phone, warn her that he is about to claim the tree, and offer to leave it standing for her if she will pay him $4. Unfortunately, Jack has 13 identical cousins, all named Jack, each of whom is prepared to present Jill with the same threat. To save the tree for herself, she would have to pay $13 \times \$4 = \$52$, or $47 more than it is worth to her. She passes up this opportunity, and the tree goes to one of the Jacks, who values it less than Jill does.

The lack of property rights in trees can present other problems as well. In the absence of property rights, nobody will plant or nurture trees, even though the benefit from doing so may exceed the cost. Another difficulty arises if Jill values a tree most for its decorative beauty. A tree left standing is a tree left vulnerable to expropriation, so Jill uses the tree for firewood, reducing its value to her and creating a social loss.

Liability Rules as Incomplete Property Rights

In Section 13.2 we treated liability rules and property rights as different ways to describe the same thing. In the examples considered there, this was an accurate depiction. In other instances, however, liability rules can better be viewed as *incomplete* property rights.

Consider again Bridgman the confectioner and Sturges the doctor. Bridgman makes noise damaging to Sturges's practice. If Bridgman is granted the right to make noise, we say either that he has a property right to the air or that there is a liability rule in his favor.

However, we must distinguish between two different legal situations. Is it *Bridgman* personally who is granted a right to the air, or is it *confectioners in general* who have this right? In the first case, any other confectioner who wants to make noise in the neighborhood must first purchase the right from Bridgman. And Bridgman will take Sturges's desires into account, because Sturges will offer to pay him *not* to sell the right to a confectioner.

But if all confectioners, just by being confectioners, acquire the right to make noise, and hence the opportunity to be bribed by Sturges, then some people in other industries might become confectioners just in order to collect these bribes. As a result, there will be overproduction of candy, because the bribes from Sturges constitute a subsidy and an artificial incentive to enter the candy industry. Similarly, there will be a suboptimal number of doctors, as each potential doctor recognizes that he will be subject to such extortion and takes this into account in his decision about whether to enter the profession.

The reason for the inefficiency here is that when the air belongs to confections generally, it does not really belong to anybody. Like the tree in the forest, it belongs to whoever takes it. If the efficient use of the air is to sell it to Sturges as a quiet zone, this outcome cannot be achieved, because after Sturges pays Bridgman to keep quiet, he will still have to contend with Bridgman's 13 identical cousins, all named Bridgman.

As long as the number of firms in each industry is fixed, a liability rule is the same as a property right. But if the number of practitioners in either industry can change, then the liability rule is likely to convey only a partial property right and hence can lead to inefficiency.[13]

Free Riding

Free riders People who benefit from the actions of others and therefore have reduced incentives to engage in those actions themselves.

Another important source of transactions costs is the problem of **free riders.** Suppose that a factory causes pollution that adversely affects the lives of 50 families. The families would like to take up a collection to bribe the owner of the factory so that he will reduce the scale of his operation. There are logistical difficulties involved in communicating with so many people at one time, but we shall suppose that these have been overcome. Each family would be willing to pay $100 to reduce pollution and is therefore asked to contribute $100 to the fund. However, each family reasons as follows: "We don't know whether the other families are contributing their share. If they are, the fundraising drive is bound to be successful even without our contribution. Everyone else will pay and we will share in the benefits; we can 'ride for free' while others pay the fare. Another possibility is that the other families aren't paying, in which case our $100 certainly won't be enough of a bribe to make a significant difference. Either way, let's not contribute."

You might recognize this reasoning; it is precisely that of the prisoners in the Prisoner's Dilemma. It is rational reasoning on the part of each individual family, but it prevents the socially optimal contract from being reached, and as such can be counted as a transactions cost. An alternative view is that this is just another example of ill-defined property rights: If property rights to the newly clean air were well established, those who have bought it could demand payment from other families who make use of it.

13.4 The Law and Economics

Historically, English and U.S. courts have often expressed a desire to adopt liability rules and systems of property rights that have the effect of fostering eco-

[13]The importance of this distinction between property rights and liability rules was clarified by H. E. Frech III in "The Extended Coase Theorem and Long Run Equilibrium: The Nonequivalence of Liability Rules and Property Rights," *Economic Inquiry* 17 (1974): 254–268. There has been much confusion among both economists and legal scholars about this issue. Frech points out that in most of the examples that are used to illustrate the Coase Theorem (such as the case of Bridgman and Sturges), there are fixed numbers of participants, so that liability rules and property rights are equivalent.

Common law The system of legal precedents that has evolved from court decisions.

nomic efficiency. The system of legal precedents that has evolved from centuries of court decisions is known as the **common law.** The common law promotes efficiency both when it directly creates incentives for problems to be solved in the least expensive way and when it acts to reduce transactions costs so that the parties to a dispute can reach low-cost solutions not directly observable by the court.

The Law of Torts

Torts Acts that injure others.

Links to law and economics resources on the Internet are available at the following FindLaw site: http://www.findlaw.com/lawecon/

The law of torts provides some interesting examples. A **tort** is an action that intentionally or unintentionally causes damage to another party. Once this damage has been done, there is generally no way to rectify it. If you hit a pedestrian with your car, causing him injury and six months' lost income, those costs become sunk at the moment of the accident. Regardless of whether the court orders you to pay for these damages, the damages still exist. The court can redistribute income, but it cannot change the size of the social pie. In this sense, it seems that the court's decision is irrelevant to social welfare.

However, this view fails to take account of how the court's decision affects the future behavior of others. While a ruling in favor of the pedestrian will not affect social welfare in the current case, it will send a signal to future drivers in similar situations that they are likely to be held liable as well, and it may affect their behavior in ways that have important social consequences.

Standards of Liability

Negligence A defendant's failure to take precautions whose cost is less than the damage caused by an accident multiplied by the probability that the accident will occur.

The common law assigns liability according to different standards in different sorts of cases. One standard is the standard of **negligence.** Under this standard a defendant is held liable for the costs of an accident if those costs, multiplied by the probability of the accident occurring, exceed the cost at which he could have prevented the accident.[14] Suppose that your barbecue grill sets fire to your neighbor's garage, causing $1,000 worth of damage, and that the court determines that there was initially a 25% chance of the fire's getting started. Then you are negligent (and hence liable under a negligence standard) if you could have taken safety precautions to prevent the fire at a cost to you of less than $250; you are not negligent if those same precautions would have cost more than $250. This standard encourages low-cost precautions while discouraging precautions whose cost exceeds their value.

There is a problem with the negligence standard, however. Suppose that you can prevent fires at a cost of $200, while your neighbor can fireproof his garage at a cost of $100. In this case a negligence standard will hold you liable for fire damage, leaving your neighbor no incentive to implement the true low-cost solution. For this reason the negligence standard is often modified by allowing a defense of **contributory negligence,** under.which the plaintiff (that is, the accident victim) cannot collect for damages in cases where he himself

Contributory negligence A plaintiff's failure to take precautions whose cost is less than the damage caused by an accident multiplied by the probability that the accident will occur.

[14]The legal literature defines negligence in a variety of ways. At least to a rough approximation, the definitions are all equivalent (although to an economist not trained in the law, some of them seem vague to the point of incomprehensibility). The one we are adopting here was stated explicitly by Judge Learned Hand when he decided the case of *United States* v. *Carroll Towing Co.*, 159 F.2d 169, 173 (2d Cir. 1947).

could have prevented the accident at a cost less than the cost of the accident multiplied by the probability of occurrence.[15]

The contributory negligence standard can also lead to inefficient outcomes. Continue to assume a $1,000 fire that had a 25% chance of occurring. Suppose that you could prevent the accident at a cost of $100, while your neighbor could fireproof his garage for $200. Under contributory negligence, he cannot collect for damages, so you have no incentive to guard against starting fires, even though it would be efficient for you to do so.

There is another reason why a negligence standard, with or without the allowance of contributory negligence, can lead to an outcome that is socially undesirable. Suppose that your barbecuing has a 25% chance of causing a $1,000 fire, which cannot be prevented at any reasonable cost *so long as you continue to barbecue*. But suppose that the cheapest way to prevent the fire is for you to give up barbecuing altogether, which would cause you only $75 worth of regret. This $75 figure is known only to you and is completely unobservable to the court. Therefore, as long as you continue to take all other reasonable precautions, the court cannot find you negligent just for operating a barbecue, and you are left with no incentive to switch to indoor cooking.

Strict liability Liability that exists regardless of whether the defendant has been negligent.

The problem can be solved by scrapping negligence and instituting a standard of **strict liability,** according to which barbecue owners are liable for all fires involving barbecues, regardless of whether there is negligence. The good news about a strict liability standard is that if you expect to cause more damage than your barbecue is worth to you, you will give it up voluntarily. The bad news is that it leaves your neighbor with absolutely no incentive to take any precautions against a fire.

We can illustrate the relative merits of negligence and strict liability by considering the law that governs auto accidents. Suppose that only negligent drivers are held liable for the accidents they cause. Then pedestrians have appropriate incentives to be cautious; the pedestrian who darts recklessly into traffic will not be compensated for injuries and will therefore think twice before darting in the first place.

On the other hand, under a negligence standard, drivers make socially inappropriate calculations about whether to drive in the first place. Suppose that a trip to the grocery store gives you $1 worth of consumers' surplus, and that, on average, such trips cause $2 worth of damage to others via accidents *that do not involve your own negligence*. Under a negligence standard, you are not liable for that damage and hence do not treat it as a private cost. You will choose to drive to the store even though it is socially inefficient. But under a standard of strict liability, you are liable for all accident damage and will therefore make the socially correct decision to forgo the trip.

In general, negligence can provide incentives for people to take appropriate precautions once an activity (like driving or crossing the street) is underway, whereas strict liability can provide incentives for people to make appropriate decisions about whether to undertake the activity in the first place.

---

[15]As with our definition of negligence, our definition of contributory negligence is one among several roughly equivalent definitions that appear in the legal literature.

Criminal Penalties and Punitive Damages

In 1989, the *Exxon Valdez* oil tanker went aground off Prince William Sound in Alaska, creating an oil spill of historic proportions. Exxon spent between $2 and $3 billion settling lawsuits and cleaning up the mess. However, government prosecutors argued that Exxon should pay *additional* penalties, in excess of the damage that the oil spill had actually caused. These penalties were effected by charging Exxon with a *criminal* act and assessing a $100 million fine. Exxon agreed not to contest this fine.

In 1991, Federal Judge Russel Holland overturned Exxon's agreement with the government, arguing that the criminal penalty should be far greater, so as to send a message that environmental spills will not be tolerated. What are the efficiency consequences of Judge Holland's ruling?

Let us suppose that an oil tanker traveling in the vicinity of Prince William Sound can be expected to cause, on average, $1 million worth of damage. (Most tankers cause almost no damage; an occasional tanker causes a great deal of damage; we assume that the average damage is $1 million.) In that case, it is efficient for Exxon to employ such tankers when and only when the resulting net benefits exceed $1 million. If Exxon is responsible for the full costs of oil spills, it has every incentive to make efficient choices.

But if an oil spill results in both full liability for the damage *and* a criminal penalty, then Exxon's private costs are driven *above* social costs and it will employ fewer tankers than are socially optimal. A more dramatic way to put this is that there will be *too few* oil spills. The optimal number of oil spills is likely not to be zero, given the costs of prevention (e.g., shipping much less oil). But the prospect of a sufficiently large criminal penalty could drive Exxon out of using tankers altogether, to the net detriment of society. Indeed, Judge Holland made his intentions clear on this matter when he suggested that the criminal penalty be increased so as to avoid sending the message that "spills are a cost of doing business that can be absorbed."[16]

Punitive damages Additional charges levied against one who commits a tort as punishment for his behavior.

Liability together with criminal penalties can raise private cost above social cost, with the result that too little of an activity is undertaken. A closely related institution that can similarly raise private cost above social cost is the assessment of **punitive damages**, under which someone who has committed a tort must pay to the victim a sum *greater* than the actual damage, as punishment for his actions. Punitive damages are most often assessed when a tort is judged to have been intentional, or a result of grossly wanton misconduct.

Suppose that you are planning to build a dam in an area where there is some possibility that the dam will break and the resulting flood will damage the property of those living nearby. The larger the dam, the less likely it is to break. The courts have determined that it is negligent to build a dam under 15 feet high. Thus, if you build a 12-foot dam and it breaks, you are negligent and liable for the full damage to surrounding property.

Now suppose that you believe that a 12-foot dam can be expected to cause, on average, about $1 million worth of property damage via flooding. You also

[16]Judge Holland did go on to express skepticism about the wisdom of the law that he felt bound to enforce.

believe that by building a 12-foot dam instead of a 15-foot dam, you can save $2 million in building costs. Assuming that your estimates are correct, it is efficient for you to build the smaller dam, and under a negligence standard you will choose to do so. However, a negligence standard combined with large criminal penalties or punitive damages could deter you from making the efficient choice and induce you to build a 15-foot dam instead.

If judges knew as much about dams as people who build dams know about dams, there would be no problem: In this example, building an efficient 12-foot dam would not have been deemed negligent in the first place. Because judges sometimes make mistakes—and because they tend to have less information available to them than people who are actively involved in making economic decisions—it is desirable for dam builders to "override" judges' wisdom by accepting the penalties for negligence when they believe it is efficient to do so. Criminal penalties or punitive damages can deter the dam builder from making the best use of his specialized information and professional judgment.

In cases like this, punitive damages are rarely assessed, so that legal doctrine does encourage efficient behavior. Next we will learn about a positive theory of the common law that predicts that such outcomes are to be expected.

A Positive Theory of the Common Law

Judge Richard Posner, of the Seventh Circuit Court of Appeals, argues that, as a matter of historical fact, the common law has tended to embody standards that encourage economic efficiency.[17] Posner presents this viewpoint as a *positive* (as opposed to normative) theory of the common law. That is, he argues that the positions of the courts can be predicted on the basis of the assumption that they are attempting to promote efficiency. Of course, he makes no attempt to argue that every court decision fits this mold, but he does make the case that the broad outlines of legal doctrine, and the directions in which those doctrines evolve over time, are consistent with this positive theory.

Law students are frequently told that the key question in tort law is "Whose ox is being gored?" This is a shorthand way to say that the law cares who loses and who wins whenever there are losses and gains to be distributed. Posner's efficiency theory maintains to the contrary that the law's chief concern is only to minimize the number of gored oxen, without regard to who owns them. Or, if it is costly to prevent gorings, then the law is concerned with optimizing (not minimizing) their number; gorings should be prevented until the marginal benefit of preventing another is equal to the marginal cost of preventing it.

Posner and his disciples believe that the efficiency theory of the common law can be applied not only to the law of torts, but to other areas of law such as the law of contracts and the law of property. We will consider just two of their many examples. One, the doctrine of *general average*, determines the distribution of losses from disasters at sea. The other, the doctrine of *respondeat superior*, determines an employer's liability for the conduct of his employees.

[17]You can read his arguments in "A Theory of Negligence," *Journal of Legal Studies* 1 (1972): 29, in his book *Economic Analysis of Law* (Little, Brown, 1972), and in *The Economic Structure of Tort Law* by William Landes and Richard Posner (Cambridge, MA: Harvard University Press, 1987). Many of the examples in this section are adapted from these sources.

example

General Average

General average The rule of law that dictates the division of losses when cargo is jettisoned to prevent a disaster at sea.

When ships encounter peril at sea, cargo sometimes has to be quickly thrown overboard. If you are unlucky enough to own that cargo, should you bear the loss alone, or should you be partially reimbursed by the other cargo owners and the owners of the ship? The legal principle of **general average** dictates that losses should be divided proportionately according to each person's share in the venture. If the ship itself is worth $25,000 and the cargo is worth $75,000, then the entire venture is worth $100,000 and the shipowner pays for 25% of the losses. If $3,000 worth of the cargo belongs to you, then you pay for 3% of the losses, regardless of whose belongings are jettisoned.

It is easy to see how this arrangement promotes efficiency. If the owner of the jettisoned cargo bore all of the loss, the captain would simply toss the heaviest items, or those most conveniently at hand, without regard to their value (as long as they didn't belong to him). General average gives him an incentive to be more prudent, insofar as he acts as an agent for the owner of the ship. The captain is unlikely to discard a passenger's $60,000 gold bar if he knows that it will cost his own shipping company $15,000.

Not only does general average give the captain an incentive to behave responsibly; in many instances it gives exactly the *right* incentive. When the captain tosses out your $10,000 jeweled paperweight, he increases the probability of the ship's survival. That increased probability has some dollar value V. The social benefit from tossing the paperweight is V, and the social cost is $10,000. If the captain has a 25% stake in the venture, then his private benefit from tossing the paperweight is $V/4$ (because ¼ of everything that is saved belongs to him) and his private cost is $2,500 (because of the law of general average). His self-interested calculation (toss the paperweight if and only if $V/4 > \$2,500$) leads to the same outcome as if all social costs and benefits were accounted for (toss the paperweight if and only if $V > \$10,000$).

example

Respondeat Superior

Respondeat superior The liability of an employer for torts committed by his employees.

According to the legal doctrine of **respondeat superior**, employers are liable for torts committed by their employees. For example, if you get a job delivering pizza, and you run down a pedestrian in the course of carrying out your duties, the pedestrian can successfully sue your employer. However, respondeat superior does not usually apply when the victim is a fellow employee. If you run down one of your co-workers in the parking lot, he *cannot* successfully sue the employer. How do these rules help to promote economic efficiency?

The doctrine of respondeat superior creates an incentive for the employer to select employees whom he believes to be cautious, and to oversee their activities. Although it might be more efficient for the burden of care to fall entirely on the employee, thus eliminating the costs of oversight, it is unfortunately the case that liability for accidents cannot deter an employee who has no money. Thus, in cases where the employer is much wealthier than the employee, respondeat superior at least ensures that someone will have an incentive to take appropriate safety precautions.

However, if respondeat superior applied to fellow workers as well, then workers would have no incentive to avoid the company of other workers whom they know to be habitually careless. Employees would be less likely to take extra precautions when the reckless drivers were working. They would also have no incentive to report the behavior of such employees to the employer. (Once the habitual carelessness has been reported, the employer does become liable.) The difference between the random pedestrian and the fellow employee is one of transactions costs. Because a pedestrian cannot be expected to know that a particular pizza truck driver is careless, he cannot negotiate with him to drive less recklessly. This high transactions cost makes it necessary to place liability in such a way as to create incentives to solve the problem, and respondeat superior can accomplish this. But fellow employees often have detailed information about each other's behavior, and this information may not be fully available to the employer. By eliminating the employer's liability in cases involving fellow employees, the law encourages workers to use this socially valuable information in an appropriate way.

Normative Theories of the Common Law

Posner's positive theory of the common law asserts that the law seeks economic efficiency. A closely related normative theory asserts that the law *should* seek economic efficiency.

A number of authors have proposed changes in the existing system of tort law, often arguing that goals other than economic efficiency should be given greater weight. One of the most eloquent of these is Professor Richard Epstein of the University of Chicago School of Law.[18] Epstein argues that the negligence system should be largely replaced by a system of strict liability. He argues, contrary to Coase, that it is indeed *possible* to develop a consistent set of criteria according to which we can say who is the "cause" of an injury and, contrary to Posner, that it is *desirable* to make this determination and to assign liability accordingly.

Good Samaritan Rule A bystander has no duty to rescue a stranger in distress.

As an example, Epstein considers the **Good Samaritan Rule**. According to this rule, a bystander has no duty to rescue a stranger in trouble, even when he can do so at low cost to himself. If you are walking along the beach carrying a life preserver and see a man drowning, the law does not require you to save him. This rule seems not to conform to the logic of efficiency, since the benefits of the rescue would clearly exceed the costs. Epstein offers this rule as evidence that the common law is not so concerned with efficiency as Posner believes it to be. From a normative point of view, he believes that the rule is a good one, because the bystander is not the cause of the drowning. He argues both that the principles embodied in the Good Samaritan Rule are applied more widely than many scholars believe, and that it would be a good thing if they were applied more widely still.

---

[18]R. Epstein, "A Theory of Strict Liability," *Journal of Legal Studies* 2 (1973): 151 and *A Theory of Strict Liability: Toward a Reformulation of Tort Law* (San Francisco: Cato Institute, 1980).

Optimal Systems of Law

An important role for the legal system is to maintain a system of well-defined property rights. We have seen that uncertainty about property rights can be an important source of inefficiency. For this reason courts are often well advised to adopt standards that are simple and well understood, even when more complicated rules appear to provide more appropriate incentives. The gain from clarity may suffice to justify a more straightforward legal standard.

Consider traffic lights, which constitute a method of allocating the property rights to an intersection. When you are stopped by a red light and there are obviously no cars coming in the opposite direction, property rights have been allocated inefficiently. You have an immediate use for the intersection, but the right has been granted to others who have no use for it. Nevertheless, the law does not allow you to enter the intersection. If it did, there would be ambiguity about when you could and could not take advantage of this exception, and that ambiguity could lead to an increase in the number of accidents. The law accepts inefficient outcomes in some cases in order to have the most efficient possible *system* of outcomes.

Another example is the "reasonable man" standard in tort law, where negligence is judged not by the actual costs of preventing a given accident, but by the typical costs of preventing similar accidents in similar circumstances. In individual cases this may lead to inefficient outcomes, but it has the salutary effect of making it easier to judge whether you or your neighbor is legally responsible for preventing his garage from catching fire. You may not be aware of his individual cost of fireproofing, but you are likely to be aware of the typical costs of fireproofing. The resulting clarification of property rights tends to ensure that at least *someone* will prevent fires, even if not always in the ideal way. Such approximations are often all that could be asked of the legal system by any reasonable man.

summary

An external cost is a cost imposed on others, such as the damage to neighboring homes from a polluting factory. External costs can lead to a divergence between private costs and social costs, and hence to inefficiency. The reason for the inefficiency is that producers equate marginal benefit to their private marginal cost, whereas the efficient outcome is where marginal benefit equals social marginal cost.

An externality is said to be internalized when the source of the externality counts it as part of his private costs in the course of making decisions. Pigou argued that the way to internalize an externality is to impose a tax (known as a Pigou tax) equal to the amount of the external cost.

Coase found a number of problems with Pigou's analysis. First, in the absence of transactions costs, bargaining will lead to an optimal outcome even when there is no Pigou tax. Second, in the presence of transactions costs, a Pigou tax (or an equivalent property right or liability rule) eliminates the incentives for one party or the other to seek a low-cost solution to the problem. Coase also argued that it makes no sense to identify one party or the other as the "cause" of the externality; externalities arise when two parties want to use the same resource for two different purposes.

Coase's first point is called the Coase Theorem. In its strongest form it says that a reassignment of property rights or a change in liability rules has no effect on the way resources are allocated. However, there are a few important exceptions. First, if there are no transactions costs between a polluting factory and its neighbors, a Pigou tax can actually reduce social welfare by inducing the factory to underproduce. However, this objection vanishes when the proceeds of the Pigou tax are paid to the neighbors, or when the recipients of the tax revenue can costlessly enter the negotiations. Second, a redistribution of property rights affects the distribution of income, possibly changing demand curves and thereby affecting the allocation of resources. Third, many liability rules convey only incomplete property rights and therefore create artificial incentives to enter or leave an industry.

Transactions costs arise when behavior is not observable, when property rights are incomplete, when free ridership problems occur, and in many other situations. In all of these cases Coase's second point applies. That is, the allocation of property rights has important implications for economic efficiency via its effects on the incentive structure.

A court can attempt to promote efficiency by assigning rights so as to create appropriate incentives. Unfortunately, the court may be unaware of the costs of various alternatives, and hence unable to determine what incentives are appropriate. An alternative approach is for the court to attempt to reduce transactions costs. If transactions costs are sufficiently low, the Coase Theorem guarantees an efficient outcome regardless of how rights are assigned. In some cases the court's decision itself can affect transactions costs. For example, the unobservability of someone's behavior becomes a transactions cost when he is awarded a right that leads others to attempt to bribe him. (Giving miners the right to be compensated for injuries is an example.)

Posner argues that the law of torts, with its emphasis on the negligence standard, has evolved to promote economic efficiency.

Review Questions

R1. What is a Pigou tax? Explain how it works.

R2. Under what circumstances and in what sense do assignments of property rights "not matter"?

R3. State the Coase Theorem and explain what it means.

R4. Why might it be undesirable to make a railroad liable for the damage its trains cause to neighboring crops? Why might it be desirable? What sorts of information are necessary for determining the optimal liability rule?

R5. What is a principal–agent problem? Give some examples. How does the existence of a principal–agent problem affect the optimal choice of liability rule?

R6. How do incomplete property rights lead to inefficiency? In what way are many liability rules examples of this phenomenon?

R7. What is negligence? What is strict liability? What are some of the ways in which these standards can be conducive or nonconducive to economic efficiency?

Problem Set

1. Suppose that Japanese cars and American cars are identical from the viewpoint of their owners, but that Japanese cars cause harmful pollution while American cars do not. Each American owner of a Japanese car imposes $1,000 worth of pollution costs on his neighbors. Suppose that the U.S. supply and demand curves for cars cross at a price of $10,000, but Americans can buy as many cars as they want to from Japan at $7,000 apiece.

a. Draw a diagram to illustrate the social gain from the market for cars. Be sure to show gains and losses to all relevant groups of Americans.

b. Now suppose that the government imposes a tariff of $1,000 on all Japanese cars sold in the United States. Once again illustrate the social gain, making sure to include all relevant groups of Americans.

c. Does the tariff increase or decrease social welfare? By how much?

2. In the preceding problem, suppose that instead of imposing a $1,000 tariff on Japanese cars, the government imposes a sales tax of $1,000 on *all* cars sold in the United States whether foreign or domestic.

a. Explain why U.S. producers must still receive $7,000 for every car they sell. How much must U.S. consumers now pay for a car?

b. Illustrate the social gain, including gains to all relevant groups of Americans.

c. Is the sales tax better or worse than the tariff of problem 1? Is it better or worse than doing nothing at all?

3. In problem 1, suppose that instead of imposing a tariff on Japanese cars, the government offers a $1,000 subsidy to each American who buys an American car. (To prevent abuse of the subsidy, U.S. consumers are not allowed to resell their cars abroad.) What price do U.S. producers receive for cars? What price do U.S. consumers pay? Does the subsidy increase social gain? By how much?

4. People who suffer from mange can purchase either of two cures: Mange-Away, which is made in the United States and sold by producers who have an upward-sloping supply curve, or Look-Ma-No-Mange, which is made in Mexico and available in any quantity at $5 per dose. The supply curve for Mange-Away crosses the (U.S.) demand curve for mange cures at a price of $8 per dose.

To the individual mange sufferer, Mange-Away and Look-Ma-No-Mange are interchangeable products. But although Mange-Away cures the disease, it also leaves the patient contagious to others. Look-Ma-No-Mange both cures the disease *and* renders the patient noncontagious; thus, every user of Look-Ma-No-Mange confers $1 worth of external benefits on his neighbors.

In order to encourage people to use more Mexican Look-Ma-No-Mange, the government has imposed a sales tax of $1 per dose on American Mange-Away.

a. Before the tax is instituted, how much can U.S. producers charge for Mange-Away? After the tax is instituted, how much can U.S. producers charge for Mange-Away? Does the tax have any effect on the amount that U.S. consumers must pay for mange cures?

b. Use a graph to show the quantities of Mange-Away and Look-Ma-No-Mange that Americans buy both before and after the tax is instituted.

c. Use your graph to show how the tax on Mange-Away affects the welfare of all relevant groups of Americans, including the neighbors of potentially contagious mange sufferers and the recipients of tax revenue.

d. Does the tax on Mange-Away create a net social loss or a net social gain? Of how much?

5. Widgets are provided by a single monopolist, whose production process pollutes the surrounding environment. The U.S. government is thinking about breaking the monopoly up into a large number of small firms, who would then form a competitive industry. The small firms would use exactly the same production process as the large firm; thus, a breakup would not affect either the private or the social marginal cost curve. Conditions in the industry are summarized by the following graph.

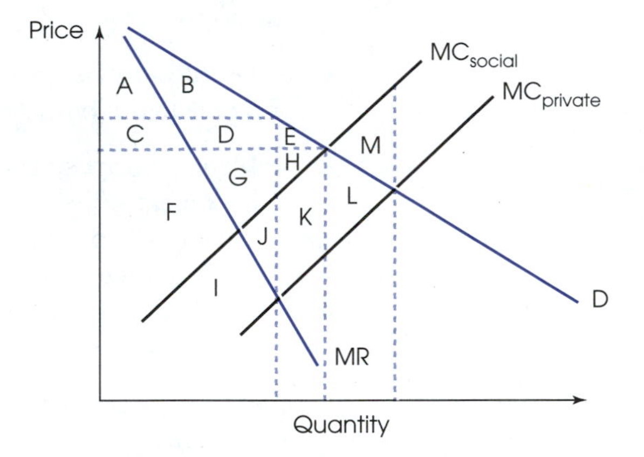

Suppose that you are called upon to advise the government as to whether breaking up the monopoly would improve social welfare. A magic oracle offers to reveal to you the exact numerical values of any *three* labeled areas in the graph. To help you give accurate advice, which three areas would you choose? Why?

6. Suppose that reckless driving imposes costs (in the form of medical bills) on both the drivers themselves and on pedestrians. Each mile of reckless driving costs drivers $1 and pedestrians $0.25. The marginal value to drivers of their reckless driving is indicated by the downward-sloping curve in the following figure:

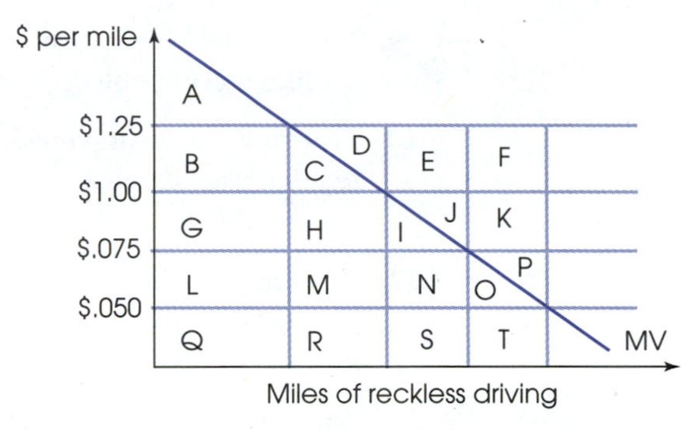

a. In terms of labeled areas on the graph, what is the social gain from reckless driving?

b. Suppose that you could require drivers to pay all the pedestrians' medical bills. According to the graph, how much would social gain increase?

c. Explain why, from the viewpoint of economic efficiency, requiring drivers to pay for pedestrians' medical bills might nevertheless be a mistake.

In the remainder of this problem, suppose that drivers can acquire air bags that reduce the cost (to them) of their reckless driving from $1 per mile to $0.50 per mile. The cost to pedestrians remains $0.25 per mile, regardless of whether drivers use air bags, and pedestrians pay their own medical bills.

d. Suppose you want to predict whether having air bags will increase or decrease drivers' medical costs. Which areas would you want to measure and compare?

e. Suppose you want to know whether air bags will increase or decrease the social gains from reckless driving. Which areas would you want to measure and compare?

f. Suppose you want to know how much drivers would be willing to pay for air bags. Which areas would you want to measure?

g. Suppose you are interested in maximizing social gain, so that you want drivers to buy air bags if and only if the social benefits of the air bags exceeds their cost. You cannot tax reckless driving, but you can tax air bags. How much should you tax them?

7. True or False Monopolies lead to inefficient allocation of resources. Externalities lead to inefficient allocation of resources. Therefore, a firm that is both a monopoly *and* a source of negative externalities is an especially serious social problem.

8. True or False If a new law requires married men to do at least half the housework, then a lot of men will have to do more housework than they do today.

9. **True or False:** In the absence of transactions costs, every monopolist would act like a competitor.

10. **True or False:** If universities were made liable to their students for the effects of assaults that occur on campus, the number of such assaults might go up.

11. Farmer Jones keeps rabbits; Farmer Smith grows lettuce on adjoining land. The rabbits like to visit Farmer Smith. **True or False** Farmer Jones should reimburse Farmer Smith for the damage, since it is caused by the rabbits.

12. The City of Rochester is thinking of expanding its airport. The expansion will increase travelers' consumers' surplus by $100 and airlines' producers' surplus by $200, while taxpayers only $50. However, the expanded airport will be much noisier. Hearing the noise would impose a $10 cost on each of the airport's 30 neighbors. Can you tell whether the expansion would improve social welfare? Why or why not?

13. Suppose that you are the judge in the lawsuit described in the article below. Under various assumptions, discuss the senses in which your decision "matters" and the senses in which it might not. Which of your assumptions seems most reasonable to you?

Bee Trial Brings Up Sticky Insect Mess

If you stay in this business long enough, sooner or later you deal with everything. This column, for example, is about insects depositing waste material—forgive the euphemism—on cars.

The issue comes up because in Macomb, Illinois, there is a lawsuit that charges that bees did $25,000 worth of damage to the paint on new cars by dropping their waste on them.

Anyway, the Macomb suit alleges that as much as 1.5 million bees were brought to a clover field across the road from a line of new car dealerships. The suit says the beekeeper and the landowner "should have known that said bees would rise up out of their hives and travel the short distance to the Mac Ford [or Kelly Pontiac] lot to deposit the fecal excrement upon said automobiles. Bee waste, it seems, contains acid that eats through automotive paint, right down to the bare metal, according to Bob Allen, a co-owner of Mac Ford.[19]

Now suppose that the "victim" is not a car dealer but a large collection of motorists whose cars are attacked whenever they drive by the area. How would your answer change? What are some of the important factors that you would take into account in making your decision?

---

[19]*Chicago Tribune*, 1985.

14. Suppose that you are attempting to study for your economics final and are distracted by noise from your roommate's stereo. In some dormitories, there are rules allowing you to throw the stereo out the window under these circumstances. In other dormitories, roommates are allowed to play their stereos as much as they want to without punishment.

a. In what sense does it not matter what the rules are in your particular dormitory? In what sense does it matter?

b. Suppose that instead of just you and your roommate, there are many students making noise, and each of them disturbs many other students. In what sense do the rules now matter more than they used to?

c. In case (b), what sorts of considerations would go into formulating the most efficient rule? Is it possible that the most efficient rule would lead to inefficient outcomes some of the time? Explain.

15. A factory is located next to a laundromat, and soot from the factory accumulates on the freshly washed clothes, significantly reducing demand for the laundromat's services. The owner of the laundromat asks the court to prevent the factory from emitting soot.

a. Assuming that there are no transactions costs between the owners of the two business, which among the following are affected by the court's decision and which are not? *(i)* The number of goods produced at the factory. *(ii)* The prices at the laundromat. *(iii)* The wealth of the factory owner. *(iv)* The wealth of the laundromat owner. Explain *briefly*.

b. Now suppose instead that transactions costs make it impossible for the owners of the two business to negotiate with each other. Assume that the court is interested in fostering efficiency. Give an example of a circumstance where it would be a mistake to rule *against* the laundromat. Give an example of a circumstance where it would be a mistake to rule *for* the laundromat.

16. The workers at a certain firm are exposed to radiation. This exposure can cause birth defects if the workers have children in future years. (If they don't have children, no health problems arise.) Some ex-workers have had children with birth defects and then sued the firm for large sums of money.

a. Under what circumstances, and in what sense, does it not matter how the court rules in these lawsuits?

b. Suppose that after an employee leaves the firm, all contracts between the employee and the firm become unenforceable. Now does it matter how the court rules?

c. Suppose that the firm is considering a policy that requires all employees to be sterilized as a condition of employment. How does this possibility affect your analysis?

d. Suppose that the firm is forbidden by law to adopt the policy described in part (c). How does this affect your analysis?

17. Suppose that judges in property disputes universally adopted a policy of holding an auction and awarding property rights to the highest bidder. In what ways would this tend to promote or retard efficiency? (The idea behind this problem comes from Benjamin Pualwan.)

18. True or False: The availability of liability insurance to drivers reduces their incentive to drive carefully, with the result that there are more accidents. Insurance is therefore detrimental to welfare.

19. The text suggests an argument for imposing strict liability on doctors whose transfusion patients contract AIDS, and it also suggests a counter argument. Taking account of both arguments, and additional arguments of your own, what do you think would be the efficient liability standard in such cases?

20. True or False: If the courts enforce a negligence standard in determining liability for auto accidents, then people will take too many car trips.

21. A radical revision of accident law has been proposed. The proposal is that every individual who is within one mile of an auto accident when it occurs must pay a fine equal to the sum of all of the damages. No attempt will be made to determine who was responsible for the accident; everyone who was in the vicinity must pay the full amount. However, anyone who bears any personal costs as a result of the accident is permitted to deduct those costs from his fine. Evaluate the efficiency aspects of this proposal.

22. Betty hires Veronica to build an addition to Betty's house. They agree on a price and Veronica begins the job. After the work is partially completed, Betty changes her mind and decides that the addition is worth less than the price she has agreed to, and announces that she will not pay for the job. Veronica then sues Betty for breach of contract.

Under these circumstances, a court can order Betty to pay either *reliance damages* or *expectations damages*. "Reliance damages" means a sum of money sufficient to make Veronica as well off as if she had never signed the contract. "Expectation damages" means a sum of money sufficient to make Veronica as well off as if the contract has been fulfilled.

Let A stand for the costs that Veronica has incurred so far, let B stand for the total cost of building an addition, let C stand for the amount Betty originally promised to pay, and let D stand for the value that Betty places on having the job completed now that she has changed her mind about its worth.

a. How much will Betty have to pay Veronica under a rule of reliance damages? How much will Betty have to pay Veronica under a rule of expectation damages?

b. How much does Betty lose if she fulfills the contract?

c. Assuming that courts assess reliance damages, write down an inequality that expresses the condition under which Betty will break the contract. Do the same for expectations damages.

d. Write down an inequality that expresses the condition under which it is efficient for Betty to break the contract.

e. Which rule induces Betty to behave efficiently: reliance damages or expectation damages?

23. In the situation of the preceding problem, suppose that courts want to choose a standard (either reliance damages or expectation damages) that induces efficient behavior. Having worked the preceding problem, judges are aware that one of these standards results in contracts being broken when and only when it is efficient for them to be broken. (And, having worked the problem, they know *which* standard has this property.) Does it follow that this is the standard they should adopt?

Internet Exercise

The chapter discussed the welfare losses that occur due to negative externalities in otherwise well-functioning competitive markets. If you have access to a computer with Excel, you can download an interactive simulation of negative externalities in a competitive market. To get this simulation, go to the following Internet site maintained by Steve Hackett: (http://www.humboldt.edu/~envecon/e423sim.htm). This simulation allows you to input different marginal external costs and see how they impact the welfare properties of competitive markets.

chapter 14

Common Property and Public Goods

In Chapter 13 we learned how incomplete property rights can lead to inefficiency. Here we will examine some important special cases. One is the theory of common property, which is property that has no owner. An example is a lake where anybody can fish and for which nobody has the authority to charge an admission fee. Another topic is the theory of public goods, which are goods that, once produced, are costlessly available for use by others. An example is a streetlight you install in front of your house, which illuminates your neighbor's properties for free.

Each of these theories is a topic in the theory of externalities. The user of a common property resource imposes a negative externality on other users, so that such property tends to be overused. The producer of a public good creates a positive externality, so that such goods tend to be underproduced. We will explore the nature of these problems and will examine some potential solutions as well.

14.1 The Tragedy of the Commons

The Springfield Aquarium

For more on the tragedy of the commons, and possible solutions for the case of marine fisheries, visit: http://www.cei.org/ebb/fish.html

The small town of Springfield has a large city park that never gets crowded. Unfortunately, picnics in the park are pretty much the only recreational activity available in Springfield, and people have begun hankering to expand their options. Therefore, the town council wants to build an aquarium, financed by tax dollars and offering free admission. The aquarium will be small but excellent, and it is anticipated that it will always be crowded.

How much should the citizens of Springfield be willing to pay for their aquarium? That is, how much pleasure will the aquarium bring them? If Springfielders all have identical tastes, the remarkable answer is: Zero! If the aquarium costs so much as one penny to build, it is a bad idea.

How can this be true? To analyze the problem, we first measure the dollar value of a picnic in the park. Suppose that each picnic is worth $2. (Here is where we use the assumption that everyone's tastes are identical: We assume that the same $2 figure applies to everybody. Without this assumption, the analysis would be a bit more complicated.) Next we measure the dollar value of visiting the aquarium. Suppose that this value is $3.

Under these circumstances aquarium-goers are happier than picnickers. The obvious consequence is that people start canceling their picnics and plan trips to the aquarium instead. As they do so, the aquarium becomes more crowded, and therefore less desirable. The value of a visit to the aquarium is now only $2.50.

You can probably foresee what comes next: Since the aquarium remains more desirable than the park, additional people skip the park and go to the aquarium. The crowds get even larger and the aquarium less desirable still. The process continues until an aquarium visit is worth only $2—neither more nor less than a picnic. But now the aquarium is worth nothing at all to the Springfielders. It makes them no more happy than a picnic, and picnics have always been available for free. Any resources spent to build the aquarium have been completely wasted.

Suppose that despite this argument, the aquarium gets built. Suppose also that two years later, a popular new television program about a school of Ninja Guppies inspires everyone in Springfield to learn more about fish. Does this increase the value of their aquarium? Unfortunately not. It certainly increases the value of *seeing the fish,* but it increases the size of the crowds as well. As before, the crowds must grow until an aquarium visit is no more fun than a picnic.

Common property Property without a well-defined owner.

The aquarium is an example of **common property;** it has no owner and there are no restrictions on its use. Consequently, it is overused, to the point where it is of no value to anyone. All of the consumer's and producers' surpluses that the aquarium might have provided have vanished. Economists call this phenomenon the **dissipation of rents,** or, more poetically, the **tragedy of the commons.**

Dissipation of rents or **tragedy of the commons** The elimination of social gains due to overuse of common property.

An important assumption has been slipped under the rug. We have assumed that the value of a picnic in the park is $2 for everyone. In particular, we have assumed that a picnic on Sunday is worth the same amount to people who are still cleaning ants out of Saturday's picnic basket as it is to people who have not picnicked in a year. If we assume instead that the value of a picnic depends on how much recent picnicking you've done, then the analysis becomes substantially more complicated, but dissipated rents remain the dominant theme.

For further reading on common property, access the Lincoln Institute site: http://www.lincolninst.edu/landline/1997/march/commonp.html

Admission Fees

What if the town decides to charge an aquarium admission fee of $1 per patron? The cost of a visit is now $3 (a forgone $2 picnic plus a $1 admission fee), and the size of the crowd readjusts downward so that the value of a visit is equal to the $3 cost. Aquarium-goers are still no happier than they were at the park.

Does this mean that the situation is no better than before? It does not mean that, and here is why: The revenue that the town collects is a social benefit that did not exist when the aquarium was free. All of that revenue is pure social gain, since it comes at nobody's expense: Those who pay the fee are fully compensated for it by the smaller crowds.

How can social gain be manufactured out of nothing at all? The answer is that each person who visits the aquarium imposes externalities on everyone whose elbows he jostles or whose view he obstructs. Because of these externalities, the free-admission equilibrium is inefficient. An admission fee acts as a Pigou tax that discourages overuse of the aquarium and increases the size of the social pie.

What is the best admission fee for the town to set? Since the only social gains in this situation are the revenues from the admission fee, the efficient fee is the one that maximizes those revenues. The socially optimal behavior for the town council is to behave like a profit-maximizing firm.

A Graphical Analysis

Exhibit 14–1 shows the value of an aquarium visit as a function of the crowd size. The first two columns in the table show that if only 1 person is present, he values his visit at $10; if 2 are present, they value their visits at $9 each, and so forth. If 10 are present, they value their visits at only $1 each. The numbers in the "value of a visit" column can also be thought of as the private marginal benefit that each new visitor gains from going to the aquarium.

The next column shows the total value of all aquarium visits. These numbers are constructed by multiplying the value of each visit times the size of the crowd. The final column shows the social marginal benefit due to each new visitor.

Notice that there is a discrepancy between private and social marginal benefits. For example, when the fourth visitor enters the aquarium, his private marginal benefit is $7 but the social marginal benefit is only $4. The $3 difference is accounted for by the externalities that his presence imposes on each of the first three visitors. The value of their visits is reduced by $1 apiece, from $8 to $7, for a total external cost of $3.

EXERCISE 14.1 When the sixth visitor enters, what is the difference between his private marginal benefit and the social marginal benefit? What accounts for the difference?

The marginal cost of adding a visitor is a picnic forgone, or $2. We will assume that it costs the town nothing to let the visitor walk through the aquarium, so that this $2 is both the private marginal cost and the full social marginal cost.

In the absence of an admission fee, the crowd grows until the private marginal benefit is equal to the $2 private marginal cost. The crowd size is 9 and there is no social gain.

Exhibit 14-1 The Dissipation of Rents

Crowd Size	Value of a Visit	Total Value of Visits	Social Marginal Benefit
1	$10/visitor	$10`	$10/visitor
2	9	18	8
3	8	24	6
4	7	28	4
5	6	30	2
6	5	30	0
7	4	28	−2
8	3	24	−4
9	2	18	−6
10	1	10	−8

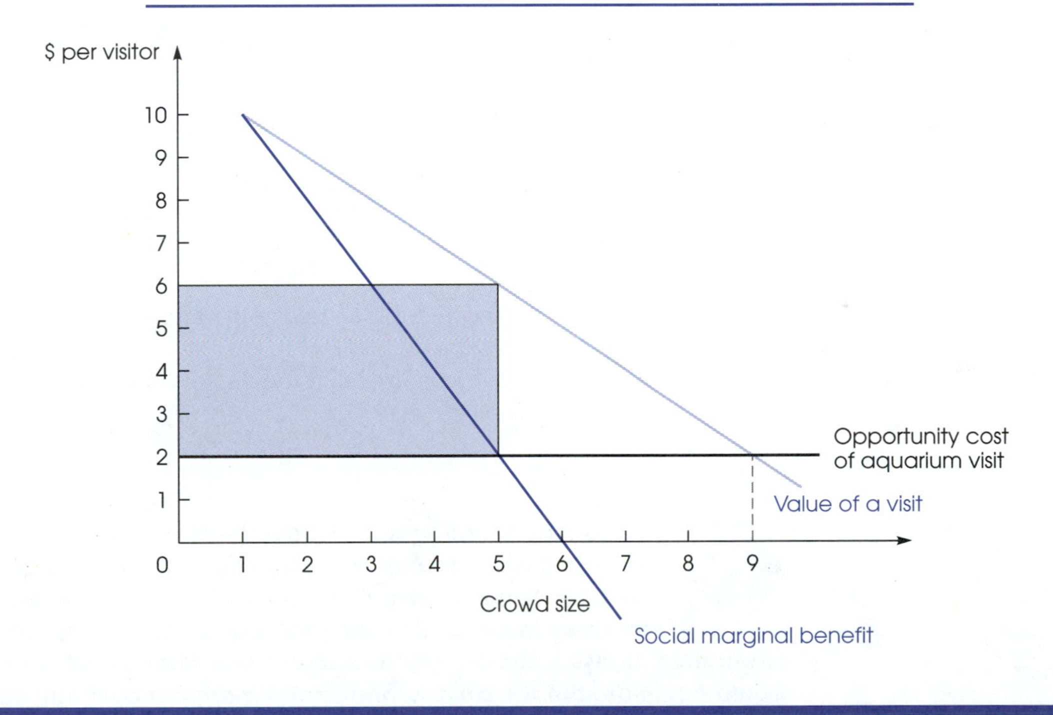

Each visitor to the aquarium lowers the value of all other visitors' visits. Therefore, the social marginal benefit of adding a visitor is less than the value of his visit. If there is no admission fee, and the opportunity cost of a visit is $2, then 9 visitors enter, and there is no social gain. Rents are completely dissipated, and the aquarium is of no value to anybody.

If only 5 people come to the aquarium, each gains $4 (the $6 value of his visit minus his $2 opportunity cost). The social gain of $20, represented by the shaded area, is the largest possible. A $4 admission fee would ensure this optimal outcome.

The social optimum is achieved when the *social* marginal benefit is equal to the \$2 marginal cost, at a crowd size of 5. At this crowd size, the difference between private marginal benefit and social marginal benefit (that is, the externality) is \$6 − \$2 = \$4. Therefore, the optimum can be achieved by imposing a Pigou tax—that is, an admission fee—of \$4. This raises the private cost of a visit to \$2 + \$4 = \$6, and the crowd stops growing when it reaches its optimal size of 5. The social gain is the sum of the admission fees, or 5 × \$4 = \$20, which is represented by the shaded area in the exhibit.

To check that we really have achieved a social optimum, we can compute what would happen if the admission fee were something different. If the fee is \$8, then the private cost of a trip to the aquarium is \$2 + \$8 = \$10 per person, and only 1 visitor attends. The town collects a total of \$8 in fees. If the fee is \$7, the private cost is \$9 per person, and 2 visitors attend. The town collects \$18. Continuing in this way, we can generate a table:

Admission Fee	Crowd Size	Social Gain
\$8	1	\$ 8
7	2	14
6	3	18
5	4	20
4	5	20
3	6	18
2	7	14
1	8	8
0	9	0

EXERCISE 14.2 Check all of the entries in the table.

An examination of the table confirms that the \$4 admission fee generates the largest possible social gain.

Throughout the analysis, we have treated crowding as something that *reduces the benefit* of visiting the aquarium. It would be equally correct to treat crowding as something that *increases the cost* of visiting the aquarium. Under the alternative analysis, the private and social marginal benefit curves would coincide, but the private and social marginal cost curves would diverge. For example, when the fifth person enters the aquarium, he lowers its value to the first four visitors by \$1 each, so the social marginal cost of the fifth visitor is \$6 (\$2 private marginal cost plus \$4 in externalities). The alternative analysis would result in a different graph, but the same numerical conclusions.

However, it is important not to double count. It is correct to count crowding as a reduction in benefit (as we have chosen to do in this text) or to count it as an increase in cost (as suggested in the paragraph above). It is *not* correct to treat it as both simultaneously.

Property Rights

We have seen that if the Springfield aquarium were privately owned, all social gains would go to the owner in the form of entrance fees. To maximize these gains, the owner would set a $4 admission fee, ensuring the optimal crowd size of 5. Under private ownership, the socially efficient outcome is achieved automatically.

Indeed, any well-defined allocation of property rights leads to the socially efficient outcome. If it were feasible for visitors to demand compensation from others who jostled them or blocked their views, all of the externalities would be internalized and the crowd would adjust to its optimal size. In this scenario, property rights are allocated to some of the visitors rather than an aquarium owner. As always, it doesn't matter (for efficiency) who has the property rights as long as they are assigned and enforced.

But when there are no property rights at all—as when the town operates the aquarium and allows anyone to use it—we face the tragedy of the commons. In this example, rents are dissipated completely, and the aquarium might as well not exist.

It Can Pay To Be Different

Consider again an aquarium with free admission. In our original analysis, we assumed that everyone values picnics at $2. Thus, we were implicitly assuming that everyone has identical tastes. Under this assumption, we discovered that the aquarium has no social value.

But now let us modify our assumption and suppose that tastes differ. Some Springfielders don't share their neighbors' enthusiasm for picnics; others are particularly keen on watching fish; still others are unusually serene about large crowds. Any of these people might have a positive preference for the aquarium over the park and can benefit from its presence. That benefit is a real social gain, and it means that the rents from the aquarium are not entirely dissipated.

Whether or not tastes differ, this much remains true: The marginal aquarium-goer is indifferent between the park and the aquarium. If he weren't, the crowd would grow and he wouldn't be marginal anymore. If everyone is identical to the fellow at the margin, then everyone shares his indifference and the aquarium is worthless. But if people are *not* all identical, the aquarium can yield positive social gains.

Unfortunately, even in this case the outcome is suboptimal. The crowd still grows until its marginal member has equated his private cost to his private benefit. That last entrant to the aquarium would be just as happy at the park, where he wouldn't be in other people's way. Moving him to the park would be a clear social improvement, but he has no incentive to move. An admission fee can provide the right incentive.

A Graphical Analysis

Suppose that people differ in their enjoyment of picnics, so that some face higher opportunity costs than others when they visit the aquarium. Then the marginal cost of adding a visitor is upward sloping, as in Exhibit 14–2. The rea-

Exhibit 14-2 Gains from an Aquarium Whose Visitors Are Not Identical

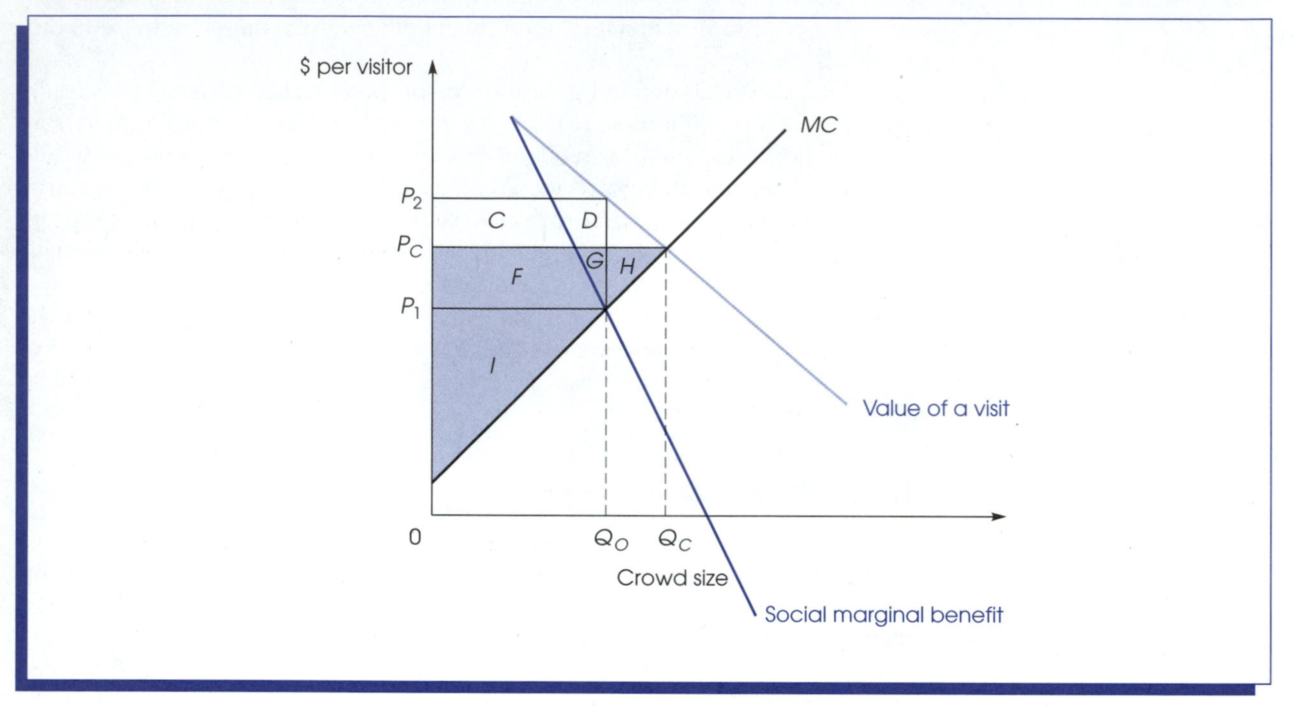

The *MC* curve shows the cost of adding additional visitors to the aquarium. Visitors enter until the later entrant's visit has a value equal to his opportunity cost. This occurs at Q_C. Each visitor values his visit at P_C, and the total surplus is $F + G + H + I$. If it were possible to control entry, the optimal crowd size would be Q_O, and surplus would be $C + D + F + G + I$. An admission fee of $P_2 - P_1$ yields this optimal outcome, with I going to visitors as surplus and $C + D + F + G$ going to the owner as revenue.

son for the upward slope is that the first visitor is the one with the lowest opportunity cost, the second has a slightly higher opportunity cost, and so on.

Visitors arrive until the marginal visitor is just indifferent between entering the aquarium and going to the park; this occurs at a quantity Q_C.

The visitors earn a total surplus of $F + G + H + I$. (This area can be divided into rectangles, each representing the excess of a visitor's benefit, which is always P_C, over his opportunity cost.)

There would be more surplus if visitors stopped arriving when the marginal cost of entry equaled the marginal social benefit, at quantity Q_O. Here the surplus is $C + D + F + G + I$. This optimum can be achieved via an admission fee of $P_2 - P_1$.

If the aquarium were run by a private competitor (competing with other aquariums), $P_2 - P_1$ is exactly the admission fee the owner would set. To discover this directly would require a little work, but we can jump to the conclusion because we know that competitive markets maximize social gains and that social gains are maximized by this admission fee.

Under competition, then, the number of visitors is Q_O, the value of a visit is P_2, and the price of a visit is $P_2 - P_1$. Each visitor earns a surplus of P_1 minus his opportunity cost. The total surplus to visitors is area I.

At the same time, the owner collects revenue equal to $C + D + F + G$. The social gain, consisting of visitors' surplus plus the owner's revenue, is $C + D + F + G + I$, the largest possible.

Common Property

The International Association for the Study of Common Property site provides access to a "virtual library" on common property: http://www.indiana.edu/~iascp/

Common property is overused. At a common-property aquarium, the crowds grow too large. Rents are dissipated. This much we have seen. But there are still other problems associated with common property. One problem is that nobody has any incentive to maintain or improve that which is commonly owned. Imagine a large forest where many people come to cut trees. There might very well be nobody with the incentive to plant and tend new trees, because the planter has no well-defined property rights. Thus, we have two separate problems: First, if loggers impose externalities on each other, there will be too many loggers. Second, if planters have no rights to the fruit of their labors, there will be too few planters.

Fishery Common property.

The most frequently cited example of a common-property resource is a lake stocked with fish. This example is cited so frequently, in fact, that economists sometimes refer to any commonly owned property as a **fishery**. Here the dissipation of rents and the lack of maintenance can be especially acute, because a fish caught today is a fish that does not reproduce tomorrow. As a result, the fish can be overharvested to the point of extinction. The whaling industry presents an important instance (whales are not fish, but whaling is a fishery). The imminent extinction of various species is a direct result of the fact that nobody owns the whales. In the timber industry, by contrast, trees are constantly replenished precisely because they are owned.

It is interesting to contrast the fate of elephants with the fate of cattle. Elephants are hunted for their ivory and, like whales, face possible extinction. It is sometimes claimed that the world's demand for ivory is the source of the problem. But the world's demand for meat far exceeds its demand for ivory, and nobody worries that cattle might become extinct. The key difference is that elephants are common property, and cattle are not.

Optimal Activity Levels

Before we leave this subject, there is one further subtlety worth mentioning. There is a sense in which even an admission fee fails to completely alleviate the tragedy of the commons. The reason is this: Even though the admission fee can limit the number of entrants, it does nothing to limit people's activity after they have entered. Even at an aquarium where the crowd size is already optimal, there might be further social improvements if visitors could be induced to spend more time at the snack bar and less time standing in front of other visitors at the exhibits. To overcome this problem, the owner would have to be able to charge people separately for every activity that imposes externalities.

If you have ever been to Disneyland, you have directly observed this sort of inefficiency. There is a fee to enter the park, without which congestion would dissipate rents. But there are no fees for the individual rides, as a result of which people queue up for the popular rides without regard to the costs (in waiting time) that they are imposing on others. The result can be waits of several hours, which would be alleviated by well-defined property rights.[1,2]

This is not a complete analysis of the problem. The next question to ask is: If the pricing system at Disneyland is so inefficient, why don't they change it? The same question occurs for ski lift tickets: Why do resorts sell tickets on a daily basis rather than a per-ride basis, since the former creates long lines that skiers would be willing to pay to avoid? These questions are difficult, but they have been addressed.

example

Splitting the Check

Suppose that you are eating dinner at a restaurant as part of a party of 10.[3] It comes time to decide whether to order dessert. You are surprised to discover that the dessert selections are very expensive, all priced at $10, whereas the most you would be willing to pay is $2. Of course, you choose to pass up dessert.

Now the waiter arrives at the table and announces that he forgot to keep separate checks, and as a result will present one bill, which will be split 10 ways. Suddenly the dessert takes on the characteristics of common property: You can have it without paying the full cost. In fact, ordering a $10 dessert will raise everyone's bill, including your own, by only $1. You order dessert. This decision is individually optimal, regardless of what everyone else is doing.

Now, as it happens, everyone else at the table has the same preferences as you do and reasons in exactly the same way. Everyone orders dessert. You end up paying $10 (a $1 share of each of 10 desserts) and getting a dessert that you value at $2.

Perhaps this inefficient outcome should be referred to as the "tragedy of the compotes."

EXERCISE 14.3 Find a better pun.

---

[1]As always, it doesn't matter who has these rights. If the park claimed them, it could set appropriate prices to discourage inefficient overuse of the rides. If the customers had well-defined, enforceable property rights, the people behind you in line could bribe you to leave, so that only those who valued the rides highly enough to justify the cost would remain.

[2]See R. Barro and P. Romer, "Ski-Lift Pricing, with Applications to Labor and Other Markets," *American Economic Review* 77 (1987):875-890.

[3]This example is adapted from D. Weimer and A. Vining, *Policy Analysis: Concepts and Practice*, Chapter 3 (Englewood Cliffs, NJ: Prentice-Hall, 1989).

example

Bumblebees and Property Rights

Often, several species of bumblebees compete for nectar from the same flowers.[4] The nectar is a common-property resource, so each species has an incentive to extract more nectar than is optimal from the viewpoint of all the bees. A system of contracts limiting each species' harvesting would improve each species' welfare.

Evolution has provided an excellent substitute for such a system of contracts. In small locales only a few species of bees tend to be abundant, and these species tend to have tongues of widely varying lengths (typically, there are three species: one very short-tongued, one long-tongued, and one medium-tongued). These differences cause the bees to favor different flowers. Short-tongued bees cannot reach the nectar in flowers with deep corollas; on the other hand, a long tongue can be a clumsy liability on a short-corolla flower.

As a result, each species specializes in taking nectar from particular sorts of flowers. Tongue lengths allocate property rights, and the bees avoid dissipating rents from nectar, without which they could not survive.

14.2 Public Goods

Public good A good where one person's consumption increases the consumption available for others.

Nonexcludable good A good that, if consumed by one person, is automatically available to others.

Nonrivalrous good A good that, if consumed by one person, can be provided to others at no additional cost.

Read about the provision of public goods at the following site containing work by Cliff Landesman: http://www.magnolia.net/~leonf/sd/vpopg/vpopg.html

A good is said to be a **public good** if one person's consumption increases the amount available to everybody. The most commonly cited example is national defense. An additional missile built to defend your house automatically defends your neighbor's houses as well. Police protection is another example, as are city parks, streetlights, and television programs (a program broadcast to your set is broadcast to other sets as well).

When called upon to make this definition more precise, economists define public goods in different ways. Some define a public good to be one that is **nonexcludable**, meaning that when one person consumes the good, there is no way to prevent others from consuming it as well. People define a public good to be one that is **nonrivalrous,** meaning that when one person consumes the good, it becomes possible to provide it to others at no additional cost. Yet other people define a public good to be one that is both nonrivalrous and nonexcludable simultaneously.

Common property, such as a fishery, is nonexcludable (anyone can use it) but not nonrivalrous (each fisherman reduces the number of fish available to others). Movie showings in uncrowded theaters are nonrivalrous (once the movie is being shown, it costs nothing to allow others to enter the theater) but not nonexcludable (theater owners can refuse admittance to anyone without a ticket). National defense, police protection, and uncrowded city parks are both nonexcludable and nonrivalrous.

---

[4]This example is taken from the fascinating book *Bumblebee Economics* by Bernd Heinrich (Cambridge, MA: Harvard University Press, 1979).

Some Market Failures

Market failure An occasion on which private markets fail to provide some good in socially efficient quantities.

A **market failure** occurs when private markets fail to provide some good in socially efficient quantities. Nonexcludable and nonrivalrous goods are particularly susceptible to market failures, for reasons we shall now explore.

Nonexcludability

In Section 14.1 we saw how nonexcludability (for example, at an admission-free aquarium) can lead to inefficient crowding. Here we shall concentrate on a different form of inefficiency associated with nonexcludable goods: The market tends to undersupply them.

Suppose that it would cost $300 to install a streetlight that is worth $10 to each of 100 neighbors. The streetlight is socially desirable, but no individual is willing to pay for it. The neighborhood could take up a collection, asking everybody to contribute $3 to a streetlight fund. If the fund-raising drive is successful, the light gets built and everybody benefits. Nevertheless, people are not eager to contribute. Each reasons thus: "I'm not sure whether my neighbors are contributing their share, though I hope they are. But if they aren't, my $3 won't be enough to build the light. And if they are, the light will get built without my $3. Either way, I see no point in contributing."

Free riding Reaping benefits from the actions of others and consequently refusing to bear the full costs of those actions.

This **free riding** is an example of the Prisoner's Dilemma that we met in Chapter 11. Although it is rational behavior for each individual separately, it leads to a socially suboptimal outcome: The streetlight does not get built.

If streetlights were excludable, there would be no problem. The rule would simply be that if you don't contribute, you can't use the light. Unfortunately, there is no way to prevent people from making use of a streetlight once it is lit. This nonexcludability is the source of the free-riding problem.

Nonrivalry

Computer software is expensive to develop but cheap to reproduce. Indeed, copies of sophisticated software can be reproduced at a marginal cost very close to zero. Thus, software is an example of a nonrivalrous good.

What is the efficient price for a software package once it has been produced? The answer is zero. At any higher price, some people who want the software will decide not to buy it. Since it would cost nothing to make the software available to everybody, it is inefficient to deny it to anybody.

The same is true of seats in an uncrowded movie theater. If the $5 admission fee keeps people away, there is a pure social loss. It would cost the theater owner nothing to allow people to sit in the unused seats.

Unfortunately, if nonrivalrous goods were really priced at zero, nobody would produce them. The software manufacturers and theater owners must set positive prices for their goods or there will be no goods to sell. These nonzero prices mean that nonrivalrous goods, if they are produced at all, are produced in inefficiently small quantities.

The Provision of Public Goods

Because nonexcludable and nonrivalrous goods are supplied inadequately by the marketplace, they are often provided by the government. If it would cost

$300 to build a streetlight that 100 neighbors value at $10 apiece, we have seen that the market can fail to provide the streetlight. A government, however, can assess a tax of $3 per neighbor and use the proceeds to build the light, yielding a clear gain in social welfare.

On the other hand, alternative mechanisms can sometimes accomplish the same job through the marketplace. In principle, an ambitious entrepreneur could buy all 100 houses in the neighborhood for their current market value, install the streetlight at a cost of $300, and then resell each house for $10 more than he paid for it—since we already know that a house near a streetlight is worth $10 more than a house that is in the dark at night.

For something as small as a streetlight, this kind of plan might be more trouble than it's worth—unless the enterpreneur already owns the houses. A builder who has just constructed a housing development will voluntarily install streetlights at his own expense if he thinks their value to potential buyers exceeds their cost. If the builder is a shrewd judge of preferences, he will provide such public goods in optimal quantities, without any need for the government to take action.

example

Clean Air

Cleantown and Grimyville are identical in every way except for air quality. The Grimyville Steel Plant accounts for the difference.

People moving in from out of state can rent apartments in either Cleantown or Grimyville. Why does anyone choose Grimyville? For one reason and one only: The rents are lower. In fact, the rents are just enough lower so that people are indifferent between the two towns. If people weren't indifferent, there would be migration between the two towns and rents would adjust until people *were* indifferent.

Grimyville Steel is capable of producing clean air by installing filters in its smokestacks. The reason it doesn't do so is that clean air is nonexcludable; there is no way to make the beneficiaries pay for it. This is just the sort of transactions cost that we often encountered in Chapter 13.

Because the market does not provide clean air in adequate quantities, the Grimyville City Council has ordered Grimyville Steel to clean up its act under penalty of law. The results have been remarkable: Grimyville's air is now indistinguishable from Cleantown's.

Of course, Grimyville's rents are also now indistinguishable from Cleantown's. So who benefits from the clean air legislation? Certainly not the apartment dwellers. Originally, they had a choice between living in Grimyville and Cleantown, and between the two they were indifferent. Now they have a choice between living in two copies of Cleantown. This makes them no worse off than before, but no better off either.[5]

The only beneficiaries of the clean air legislation are the landlords of Grimyville, who collect all of the benefits in the form of higher rents. It is therefore very easy to determine whether the clean air legislation is efficient: If rents

---

[5]This analysis assumes that everyone's tastes are identical. Without this assumption the analysis is slightly subtler. This theme is taken up in the problems at the end of the chapter.

rise by more than the cleanup costs, then there is a net social gain; if they rise by less, there is a net social loss.

Now the question is: Could the landlords of Grimyville have taken up a collection on their own to bribe Grimyville Steel and make it stop polluting, or to clean up the air in some other way? Surely there would be a free-rider problem here, but not so intractable a free-rider problem as if all the citizens of Grimyville had been beneficiaries. If there are only half a dozen landlords in town, it is conceivable that they could formulate and enforce an agreement that would obligate all of them to contribute to the antipollution fund.

When the benefits of a public good are concentrated among a small number of people, there is a better chance that the good can be provided by coordinated action among the beneficiaries. The point of this example is that a good that at first appears to benefit a very large class (here, all of the residents of Grimyville) may in fact benefit only a much smaller class (here, the Grimyville landlords). In fact, whenever a public good increases the desirability of living in a certain area, its benefits tend to be captured completely by an increase in land values. If the number of landlords is small, the public good can frequently be provided by private action.

The Role of Government

When the benefits of a public good are widespread, private mechanisms can break down and the government plays a role as provider. Governments provide national defense and police services because such goods are nonexcludable. A private army or police force cannot charge for its services and protect only those who pay; an aggressor or criminal deterred is as much a benefit to those who don't contribute as to those who do.

There is, however, a crucial difficulty. How can the government determine when it is optimal to purchase a public good? Suppose that some neighbors believe that the streetlight would be a net benefit to the neighborhood and others don't. One possibility is to conduct a vote on the matter. However, a disadvantage of voting is that it does not allow people to register the strengths of their preferences. If 19 people each value the light at $1 apiece and if one person would be willing to pay $40 to prevent its construction, an election will lead to an overwhelming victory for installing the light, even though installing it is socially undesirable.

Another possibility is for the government to ask people not just whether they want the light but how much it is worth to them to either have it or not have it. This has the disadvantage that people will find it in their interest to exaggerate their preferences. If you want the light at all, you might as well claim that it is worth $1 million to you, just to increase the chance of its being built.

In order to create appropriate incentives, the government might say that your share of the tax burden for installing the streetlight will be proportional to its value to you. This makes it costly to exaggerate the value and discourages overstatements. Unfortunately, it encourages dishonesty of another sort. People will tend to understate their personal valuations so as to shift the tax burden to their neighbors. With everybody understating, there may be a false appearance of insufficient demand to justify installing the lamp.

In order for the government to provide public goods in appropriate quantities, it must find ways of gathering information that is initially available only to private individuals with no incentives to reveal it. One possible source of such information is the price of private goods that are similar in nature to the public good being contemplated. For example, suppose that the good under consideration is a dam that will make water available to surrounding farmland. If the farmers are currently purchasing water through a private mechanism, the price of that water is a good indication of its value to farmers.

The more common situation, however, is one in which no such easily observable good exists. The surprising fact is that in such a case it is often possible, by the clever structuring of incentives, to induce people to reveal their true demand for a public good.

Before describing such a mechanism, we present as puzzles two other situations in which there exist surprising mechanisms to elicit the revelation of privately held information. In each case try to figure out the scheme that works before looking at the answer later in this section.

Puzzle No. 1. In Joseph Conrad's novel, *Typhoon*, each of 200 men on a ship has stored several years' wages in his own personal strongbox. The ship encounters bad weather, the boxes are smashed, and all the coins are mixed together. The captain gathers up all the coins and wants to return them to the men, giving each the number of coins to which he is rightfully entitled. Each man knows how many coins were his, but nobody knows how many belong to anybody else. Obviously, each man, if asked, will exaggerate his fair share. How can the coins be returned to their owners?[6]

Puzzle No. 2. Property taxes are levied in proportion to the value of people's homes. Ideally, each individual would be taxed a given fraction of the valuation that he personally places on his house. In practice, this is assumed to be equal to the market value of similar houses. Because no two houses are alike, taxing agencies devote considerable resources to examining individual houses and assessing their values. Homeowners often protest these assessments, leading to costly disputes. How can the tax collector costlessly determine the true value of an individual house (keeping in mind that only the owner himself is initially in possession of this information)?

In interpreting Puzzle No. 2, keep in mind that the value a homeowner places on his home might be very different from its market value.

Schemes for Eliciting Information

The town of Springfield is thinking of installing a streetlight, and the local newspaper has been lobbying for it very hard. Mayor June is interested to

[6]The analogy between this problem and the theory of public goods was suggested by Gene Mumy in "A Superior Solution to Captain MacWhirr's Problem," *Journal of Political Economy* 89 (1981). The solution he proposed was substantially more complicated (though identical in spirit) to the one that we will give.

know just how much Ed the Editor really values a streetlight, and doesn't trust him to tell the truth if he is asked outright. So the mayor has thought of a tricky plan.

Using his pocket calculator, the mayor has generated a random number X, which is recorded in a sealed envelope. He has walked into Ed's office and laid down some terms: "Ed, I want you to tell me how much you really value that streetlight. Whatever answer you give me I will call E. If my secret number X is less than E, I will build the streetlight and I will raise your taxes by X to pay for it. (The mayor has total control of the tax laws in Springfield.) But if X is more than E, then I'm going to forget all about this streetlight thing and leave your taxes as they are."

Now Ed actually values the streetlight at \$47. Since he'll have to pay X in taxes to build it, Ed is thinking "If X is less than \$47, this streetlight is a good deal for me and I hope it gets built. But if X is more than \$47, I hope we can forget all about this streetlight thing."

If you compare the mayor's offer with Ed's silent calculation, you will discover something remarkable: If Ed tells the truth, so that E = \$47, then he is certain to get the outcome he prefers. Faced with the mayor's terms, Ed will choose to tell the truth and the mayor will learn the streetlight's true value.

Reaching the Efficient Outcome

It is not only Ed's opinion that interests the mayor. What the mayor really wants to know is whether it would be efficient to build the streetlight. The light would cost \$300 and it would benefit five people, one of whom is Ed. The problem is to simultaneously discover how much each of the five values the streetlight, and to build it only if the sum of those values exceeds \$300.

Here is the mayor's plan. Instead of walking into Ed's office with a secret number in his pocket, he asks each of the five (Al, Barb, Cassie, Dale, and Ed) to write down an assessment of the streetlight's value. The mayor plans to call these numbers A, B, C, D, and E. He announces to Ed (in advance): "After the envelopes are opened I am going to compare your number E with the number $X = 300 - A - B - C - D$. If X is less than E, I will build the streetlight and charge you X. Otherwise, I will forget about the streetlight."

This is just like the mayor's earlier plan except that the unknown random number X from the mayor's calculator is replaced by the unknown number $X = 300 - A - B - C - D$. Just as before, Ed is induced to tell the truth.

At the same time, the mayor tells Dale that he will decide whether to build the light by comparing Dale's number D with the number $300 - A - B - C - E$. If $300 - A - B - C - E < D$, the mayor will build and charge Dale $300 - A - B - C - E$; otherwise, he will do nothing. Dale, like Ed, is induced to tell the truth.

The mayor makes similar announcements to Cassie, Barb, and Al. In Cassie's case he says he will make a decision by comparing $300 - A - B - D - E$ with C; this leads Cassie to tell the truth, and similarly for Barb and Al.

Now the mayor has made a lot of apparently contradictory promises, but fortunately the contradictions are only apparent. He has told Ed that he will build if and only if $300 - A - B - C - D < E$; he has told Dale that he will build if and only if $300 - A - B - C - E < D$, and so forth. A small amount of algebra reveals that each of these conditions is equivalent to the single condition $A + B + C + D + E > 300$. Therefore, all of the promises are equivalent and can be kept simultaneously.

And something even more wonderful is true: Not only does everyone reveal the truth about his desire for a streetlight, but the light gets built if and only if it is efficient. The inequality $A + B + C + D + E > 300$ says precisely that the light's benefits exceed its costs; and this is precisely the circumstance in which the light gets built.

Clarke tax A tax designed to elicit information about the demand for public goods.

The mayor's tax plan is an example of a **Clarke tax.** The only problem with the Clarke tax is that if the light *does* get built, the mayor has made some promises about how much he will tax everybody, and there is no reason why the tax revenue should happen to just cover the $300 cost of the light: It could turn out to be either too high or too low. Thus, the mayor must be prepared either to turn a profit for the city treasury or to finance the light partly out of city coffers if that becomes necessary. If he is willing to do so, he can simultaneously elicit full information from everybody and guarantee an efficient outcome.

Solutions to Puzzles

The mayor's cleverness solves a problem that initially appears insoluble. Here are some clever solutions to the puzzles from earlier in this chapter.

Solution to Puzzle No. 1 The captain can ask each man to write down the number of coins he started with. He announces that the numbers will be added up, and that if the sum does not match exactly the total number of actual coins, all of the coins will be tossed overboard.

Solution to Puzzle No. 2 Ask each homeowner what his house is worth to him. The values will be made public, and each owner will be required to sell to anyone who offers him more than the stated value of his house. No truthful owner can be hurt by this scheme; he can only be forced to sell to someone he would be willing to sell to anyway.

summary

Commonly owned property is an important source of externalities. There is no way to limit use of the property in order to avoid problems of congestion. Also, there is no incentive to improve the property itself. If all users of the property are identical, then rents will be dissipated completely. This is because people continue to make use of the property until everyone is indifferent regarding its existence. An owner—any owner—will improve social welfare by setting entry fees that discourage overuse and also perhaps by improving the property.

If users of the property vary in their tastes or opportunity costs, then rents are partially, but not completely, dissipated in the absence of ownership.

Because public goods present incentives for free riding, they represent a type of externality. Since individuals will purchase less than the optimal quantity of public goods, public goods are often provided by the government. This makes it desirable for the government to be able to elicit information about how much people value public goods, which presents a problem in view of individuals' incentives to be untruthful. A number of clever schemes have been devised for eliciting truthful responses in a variety of circumstances.

Review Questions

R1. What is the dissipation of rents? Under what circumstances are rents dissipated completely? Under what circumstances are they dissipated partially? Why?

R2. What is a nonrivalrous good? What is a nonexcludable good?

R3. Describe a mechanism that would induce each party to reveal how much he privately values a certain public good.

Numerical Exercises

N1. Each potential user of the Phoenix River Bridge is willing to pay up to \$299 per crossing, provided there are no other cars to slow him down. When there are more cars, willingness to pay goes down. Specifically, when there are N cars per day on the bridge, each user is willing to pay up to (\$300 $- N^2$) to cross.

- **a.** In terms of N, what is the social gain from the existence of the bridge?
- **b.** If there is no bridge toll, how many people cross per day and what is the social gain?
- **c.** What is the optimal number of bridge crossings per day? (To answer this question, you will need either some calculus or some patience with trial and error.)
- **d.** If there is a bridge toll of \$$T$, how many people cross per day? (Answer in terms of T.)
- **e.** What is the optimal bridge toll? How much social gain results when this toll is set? Who gets the benefits?

N2. Let A be the value of a visit to the aquarium and let η be the elasticity of A with respect to the number of visitors. (That is, η is the elasticity of the lightly colored curve in Exhibit 13–1.) Show that the optimal admission fee is $A/|\eta|$.

Problem Set

1. A fisherman at Hardin Lake can catch 20 fish per day, provided he has the lake to himself. Two fishermen can catch 19 fish apiece per day, and three can catch 18 fish apiece per day. Other numbers are given by the table:

Number of Fishermen	Fish per Day per Fisherman
1	20
2	19
3	18
4	17
5	15
6	13
7	10
8	7

The opportunity cost of a day at the lake is 7 fish (that is, the alternative activity is as valuable as 7 fish).

a. How many fishermen come to the lake? How many fish do they catch? What is the social gain from the existence of the lake?

b. What is the optimal number of fishermen at the lake? What is the social gain if this optimum is achieved?

c. What entrance fee leads to the optimal outcome?

2. Happy, Grumpy, Dopey, Sleepy, Sneezy, Doc, and Bashful are miners, who have nothing to do with their time but to go mining. There are no other miners in the vicinity. Each miner can dig in either of two mines. The number of gold nuggets that a miner can find in a day depends both on which mine he is working and how many other miners are present in that mine, as indicated by the following chart:

Number of Miners	Nuggets per day in Mine A	Nuggets per day in Mine B
1	20	30
2	18	27
3	16	24
4	14	21
5	12	18
6	10	15
7	8	12

a. If entry to the mines is free, how many miners work in each mine?

b. At the social optimum, how many miners would work in each mine?

c. What system of entry fees to the mines could bring about that social optimum?

d. Suppose that both mines are owned by a Wicked Queen who can set entry fees. What fees would she set?

3. Two roads go from Hereville to Thereville. One road is very wide and can easily accommodate all the traffic that would ever want to use it, but it is in poor repair and unpleasant to drive on. The other road is in excellent repair and goes through the most scenic areas, but it has only one lane in each direction and easily becomes congested.

a. Explain why, if there are sufficiently many drivers, both roads will be equally pleasant to drive on.

b. How do the private marginal benefits compare for a driver entering the wide road and a driver entering the narrow road? How do the marginal social benefits compare?

c. In view of your answer to part (b), could a social planner reallocate one car in order to make a welfare improvement?

d. How much further reallocation would the planner want to make? How could the same thing be accomplished without a planner?

4. A race of dwarfs lived near a forest where apple trees grew wild. Any dwarf who wanted to could enter the forest and pick apples for himself and his family. One day a giant came, claimed the forest for himself, and began charging the dwarfs for the right to pick apples.

a. Suppose that dwarfs can pick fewer apples when the forest is more crowded. Draw a graph with "Number of dwarfs in the forest" on the horizontal axis and "Apples per dwarf" on the vertical. Draw a curve representing the number of apples picked per dwarf and a curve representing each dwarf's marginal contribution to the apple harvest. Explain intuitively why the latter curve lies below the former.

b. Suppose that all dwarfs have the same opportunity cost to enter the forest. Show on your graph how many dwarfs enter the forest before the giant arrives and how many enter after the giant arrives. Show the giant's revenue.

c. Now drop the assumption that all dwarfs have the same opportunity cost, and assume that some dwarfs' time is more valuable than others'. On the graph you drew for part (a), add the upward-sloping curve that shows the marginal cost of adding dwarfs to the forest. Show the number of dwarfs that enter. Show the producers' surplus that the dwarfs earn as apple-pickers.

d. Continuing to use your graph from part (c), show the optimal number of dwarfs in the forest. Show the entrance fee that achieves this optimal number. Explain why this is the entrance fee that a competitive giant would set.

e. Can the dwarfs be made better off as a result of the giant's arrival and the entry fee? What about society as a whole (consisting of the dwarfs plus the giant)?

f. (This is a difficult problem.) Assuming straight-line curves, and assuming that the giant sets a monopoly price to enter the forest, show that the monopolized forest is more socially efficient than the common-property forest if and only if the "marginal apple harvest" curve is steeper than the dwarfs' marginal cost curve.

5. True or False A communally owned lake is more valuable in a town where everybody is an excellent fisherman than in a town where people vary widely in their fishing ability.

6. Suppose that the town of Springfield establishes an aquarium with free admission, and that all residents of Springfield are identical. True or False: If the population of Springfield is sufficiently small, not all rents will be dissipated.

7. Rollo's Roller Rink is located in a town where everyone is identical. Rollo's is subject to crowding and becomes less pleasant when it is crowded. **True or False:** If Rollo is a monopolist, he will charge exactly the same price as he would under competition.

8. Which of the following are nonexcludable? Nonrivalrous? Both? Neither?

   a. Network TV programming

   b. Cable TV programming

   c. Textbooks

   d. Statues in the park

   e. Water fountains in the park

9. A public radio station soliciting donations argued that its listeners would be irrational not to contribute. "Unless our fund drive is successful," they warned, "we will have to go off the air. Surely you get at least $20 worth of pleasure from listening to our station over the course of a year. Make your $20 pledge now to protect your own self-interest." Comment.

10. Most of the people living on the north side of Boomtown are apartment dwellers who commute into the center of town every day to go to work. The city is considering building a new subway line between the north side and the center of town. True or False: Since the landlords all live on the south side of town, and the employers are all in the center of town, all of the benefits from the new subway will go to the working people on the north side of town.

11. Cleantown and Grimyville are identical except for the inferior air quality in Grimyville. All potential residents have identical tastes. Apartments in Cleantown rent for $300 per month. The cost of breathing Grimyville air is $100 per month. The quantity of apartments in each town is fixed.

    a. Explain why the demand curve for Grimyville apartments is flat at a price of $200 per month. Draw the supply and demand curves for Grimyville apartments and show the consumers' and producers' surpluses.

    b. Suppose that the air in Grimyville is brought up to Cleantown standards. Show the effects of this change on your graph. Show the increase in social gain. Who benefits from the clean air?

12. In the preceding problem, drop the assumption that everyone is identical. Some hate pollution more than others do. The one person in Grimyville who hates pollution the most considers the cost of breathing it to be $100 per month.

a. Explain why the demand curve for Grimyville apartments is downward sloping. At what price does it cross the supply curve? Draw the supply and demand curves for Grimyville apartments and show the consumers' and producers' surpluses.

b. Suppose that the air in Grimyville is brought up to Cleantown standards. Show the effects of this change on your graph. Show the increase in social gain. Who benefits from the clean air? Who loses from it?

13. Suppose that you want to sell your car to one of several people and that you decide to auction it off. You are curious to know the highest price that each of the potential buyers would be willing to pay for the car. You ask each to submit a sealed bid, announcing that the car will go to the high bidder but that he will be charged the amount of the second highest bid. Will the submitted bids be truthful? Why or why not?

14. (This is a difficult problem.) A factory that emits noxious smoke is located near a small cluster of homes. It is up to you to decide whether the factory will have to install pollution-control equipment. A key variable in your decision is the extent of the cost imposed on the homeowners. How can you discover this cost?

Internet Exercise

A problem with the private provision of public goods is that self-interested parties have an incentive to free-ride on the contributions of others. There have been a number of economic experiments designed to study free-riding behavior. Access the Spring 1993 issue of *Classroom Expernomics* at the following Internet site: (http://www.marietta.edu/~delemeeg/expernom/s93.html#hoaas1). The article describes how a classroom activity can be structured to illustrate the social dilemma of providing for public goods.

chapter 15

The Demand for Factors of Production

The Bureau of Labor Statistics site is a good source of information on labor markets: http://stats.bls.gov/

In the preceding 14 chapters we have studied markets for consumption goods. In this and the next two chapters we will study markets for factors of production (also called inputs). Factors of production, such as labor and capital, are supplied by individual households and demanded by firms, which use them to produce output for consumption. In this chapter we will study the firm's demand for inputs.

Firms demand inputs only because they can be used to produce output. Therefore, the value of those inputs depends on conditions in the output market. For example, a farmer's for demand for fertilizer depends on the price at which he can sell his crops. The need to take account of conditions in the output market means that the derivation of the firm's demand for factors will be more subtle than the derivation of the consumer's demand for consumption goods.

The firm's income is paid out to the various factors of production. Workers receive wages, the owners of capital receive rental payments for the use of their facilities, and so forth. In the last section of this chapter we will use our understanding of the firm's factor demand curves to see what determines how the firm's income is distributed.

15.1 The Firm's Demand for Factors in the Short Run

For more on the demand for factors of production, see: http://www.best.com/~ddfr/Academic/Price_Theory/PThy_Chapter_14/PThy_Chapter_14.html

Marginal revenue product of labor The additional revenue that a firm earns when it employs one more unit of labor.

In the short run, only one factor of production is variable, and we will assume that factor to be labor. Thus, we will study the demand for labor on the assumption that the firm uses some fixed quantity of capital.

The Marginal Revenue Product of Labor

Recall from Chapter 6 that the total and marginal product of labor curves are typically shaped like those in the first two panels of Exhibit 15–1. We will also be interested in the **marginal revenue product of labor (MRP_L),** defined as the additional revenue earned by the firm when one additional unit of labor is employed. The marginal revenue product of labor is measured in dollars per unit of labor, whereas the marginal product of labor is measured in units of output per unit of labor.

For a firm in a competitive industry, selling output at a going price P_X, the marginal revenue product of labor is given by

$$MRP_L = P_X \cdot MP_L$$

Given the MP_L curve from Exhibit 15–1 and given the price of output (say, \$7 per unit), we can construct the MRP_L curve simply by changing the units on the vertical axis. We have done so in panel C of the exhibit.

EXERCISE 15.1 If the firm in question were a monopolist in the output market, how would the MRP_L curve differ?

Suppose that the firm can hire labor at a going wage rate of \$25 per unit of labor. How much labor will it hire? As long as additional units of labor yield marginal revenue products in excess of \$25, it will continue hiring. As soon as the MRP_L reaches \$25, it will stop. Therefore, we see from Exhibit 15–1 that the firm will hire 4½ units of labor. In general, at any given wage rate, the firm will want to hire a quantity of labor read from the downward-sloping portion of the MRP_L curve. We can summarize this by saying:

The firm's short-run demand curve for labor coincides with the downward-sloping portion of the MRP_L curve.

The Algebra of Profit Maximization

The amount of labor needed to produce one more unit of output is $1/MP_L$. The cost of that labor is the price per unit of labor (P_L) times the quantity of labor ($1/MP_L$), or P_L/MP_L. Therefore, the marginal cost of producing another unit of output is given by

$$MC = \frac{P_L}{MP_L}$$

When firms maximize profit, they set the price of output P_X equal to marginal cost, or

$$P_X = MC$$

Exhibit 15-1 The Total, Marginal, and Marginal Revenue Products of Labor

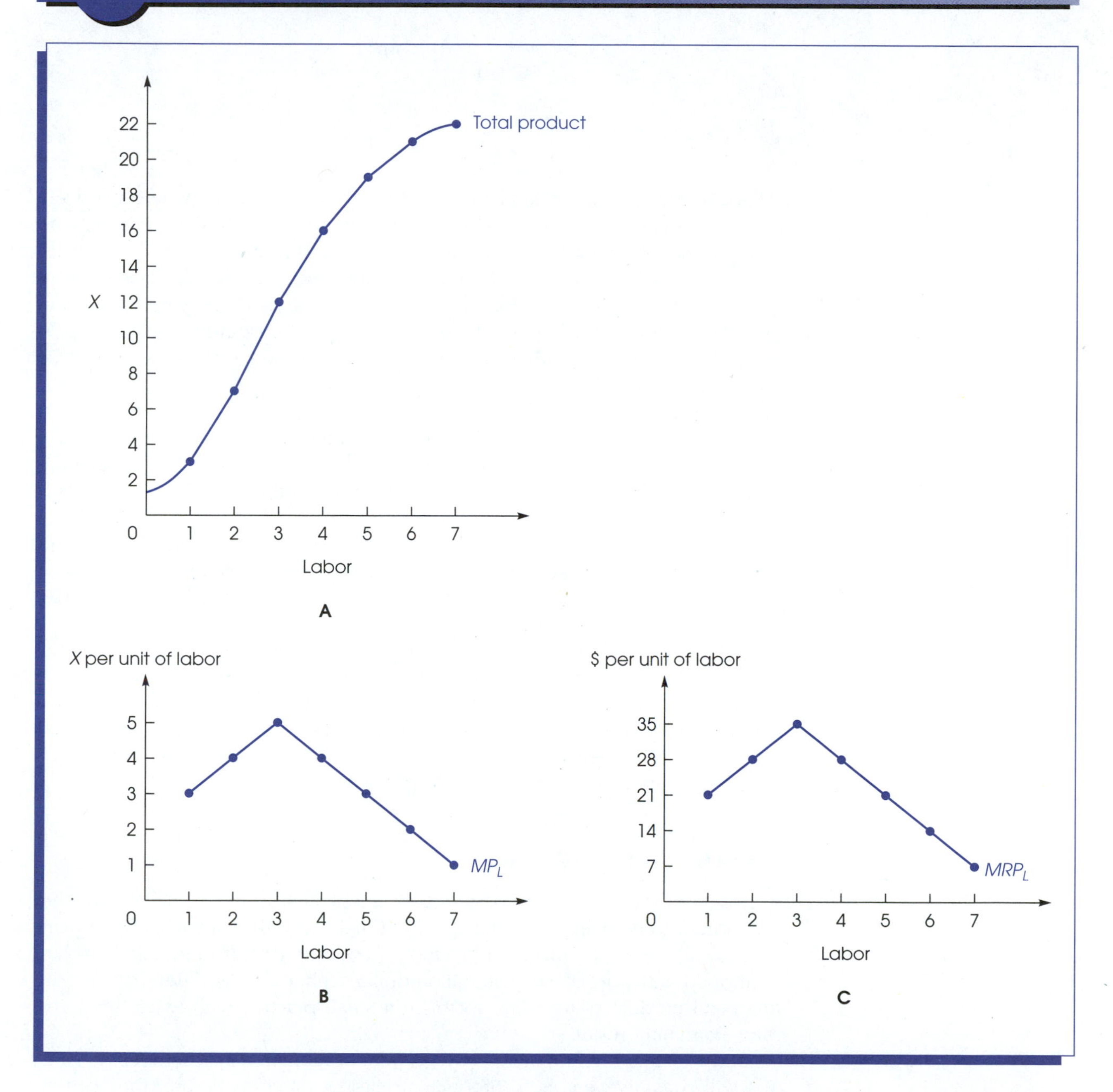

The total product and marginal product of labor (MP_L) curves are as in Exhibit 6–1. The marginal product of labor increases until diminishing marginal returns set in at $L = 3$, and it decreases thereafter. If the firm is competitive and sells its output at $7 per unit, then the marginal revenue product of labor (MRP_L) is given by

$$MRP_L = \$7 \times MP_L$$

Thus, the MRP_L curve can be constructed from the MP_L curve by simply changing the units on the vertical axis, as shown in panel C.

Combining the two displayed equations, we find that profit maximization requires

$$P_X = \frac{P_L}{MP_L}$$

or

$$P_L = P_X \cdot MP_L = MRP_L$$

This confirms that a profit-maximizing firm wants to operate where the wage rate of labor is equal to its marginal product; in other words, the firm's demand curve for labor coincides with the MRP_L curve, as we have already determined.

These equations enable us to relate the firm's behavior in the labor and output markets. First suppose that the wage rate of labor P_L goes up. The equation $MC = P_L/MP_L$ tells us that the firm's marginal cost curve must go up as well. With a higher marginal cost curve, the firm produces less output and so hires less labor. This confirms yet again that the demand curve for labor is downward sloping.

Exhibit 15–2 shows the picture. When the wage rate increases from P_L to P_L' in panel A, the marginal cost curve increases from MC to MC' in panel B. Output falls from Q to Q', and the amount of labor that the firm needs to hire falls from L to L' in panel C. This fall in the quantity of labor demanded could be read equally well directly off the demand for labor curve in panel A.

For an alternative exercise, imagine a change in the price of output P_X (with the wage rate of labor P_L held fixed). Since $P_L = P_X \cdot MP_L$ it follows that MP_L must go down, which requires that L go up.

Exhibit 15–3 shows the picture. The increase in price from P_X to P_X' in panel C yields an increase in output from Q to Q'. This requires more labor, as seen in panel B where the quantity of labor must rise from L to L'. Alternatively, we can argue that the increase in P_X causes an outward shift in MRP_L (since $MRP_L = P_X \cdot MP_L$), as seen in panel A. The quantity of labor demanded rises from L to L', just as we have already seen in panel A.

The Effect of Plant Size

Our entire short-run analysis assumes a fixed plant size (that is, we assume that the firm does not vary its capital usage). It makes a difference what fixed plant size we assume. The marginal product of the 40th doctor in a major hospital equipped with the latest multimillion-dollar technology is different from the marginal product of the 40th doctor in a small practice with two offices and one examining room.

Suppose that the firm increases its capital usage. Then any number of workers will certainly be able to produce at least as much as before (they can always just continue what they were doing before, ignoring the new machinery) and will probably be able to produce more. Therefore, the total product curve can be expected to rise. This does not necessarily imply that the marginal product of labor will rise. In the two panels of Exhibit 15–4, we show two possibilities. In panel A the total product of labor rises while becoming steeper at

Exhibit 15-2 The Market for Labor and the Market for Output

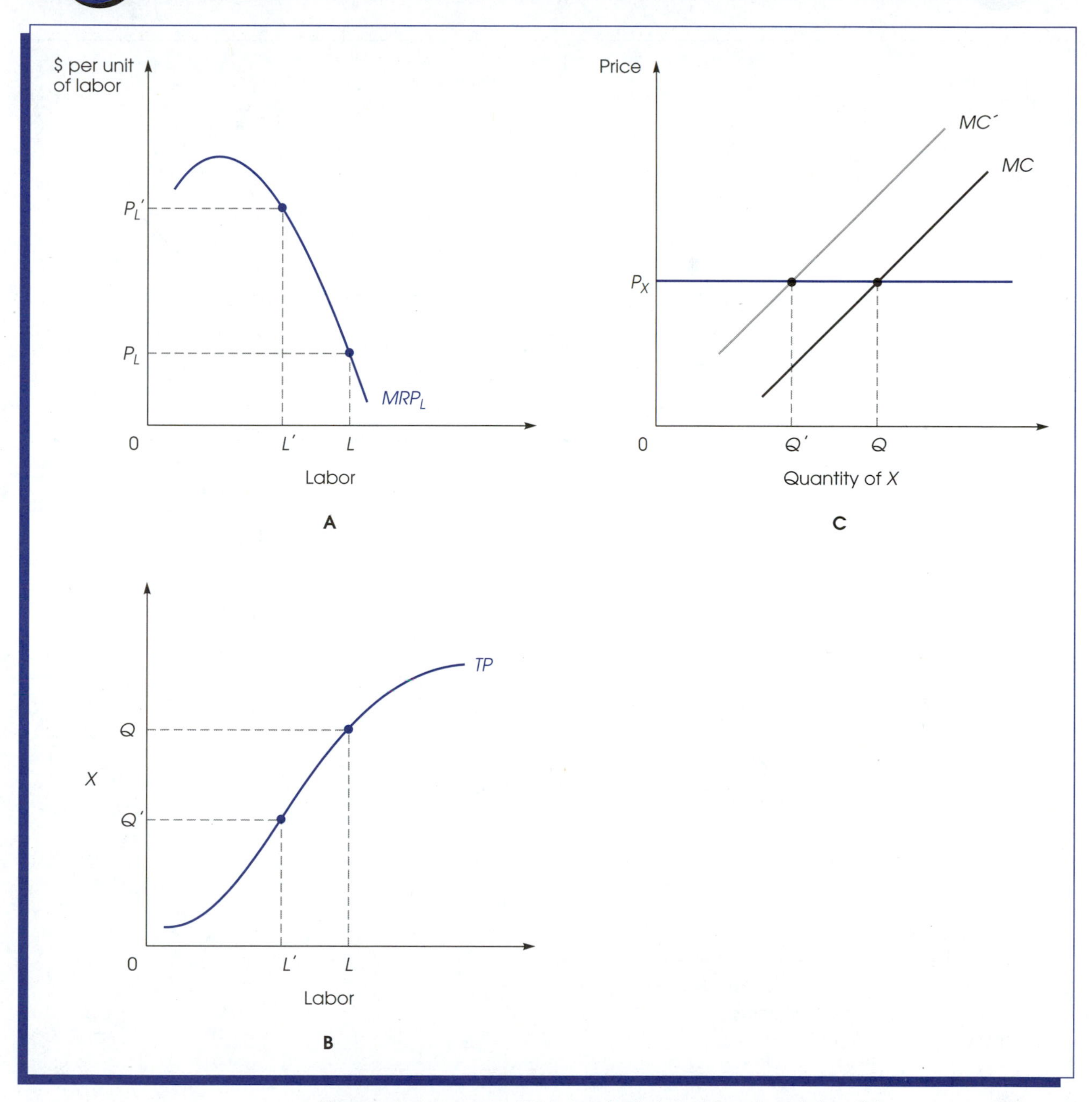

The marginal cost curve, *MC,* in panel C is derived from knowledge of the wage rate of labor, P_L, and the total product of labor curve, *TP,* in panel B. The derivation was given in Chapter 6. Thus, each graph contains some information that is also encoded in the other graphs.

To see the interrelations, notice that when the wage rate is P_L, panel A shows that the firm hires L units of labor, panel B shows that L units of labor will produce Q units of output, and panel C confirms that the firm's output is Q. If the wage rate rises to P_L', the marginal cost curve rises to MC'. Now panel A shows that the firm hires L' units of labor, panel B shows that the firm produces Q' units of output, and panel C confirms this.

Exhibit 15-3 A Rise in the Price of Output

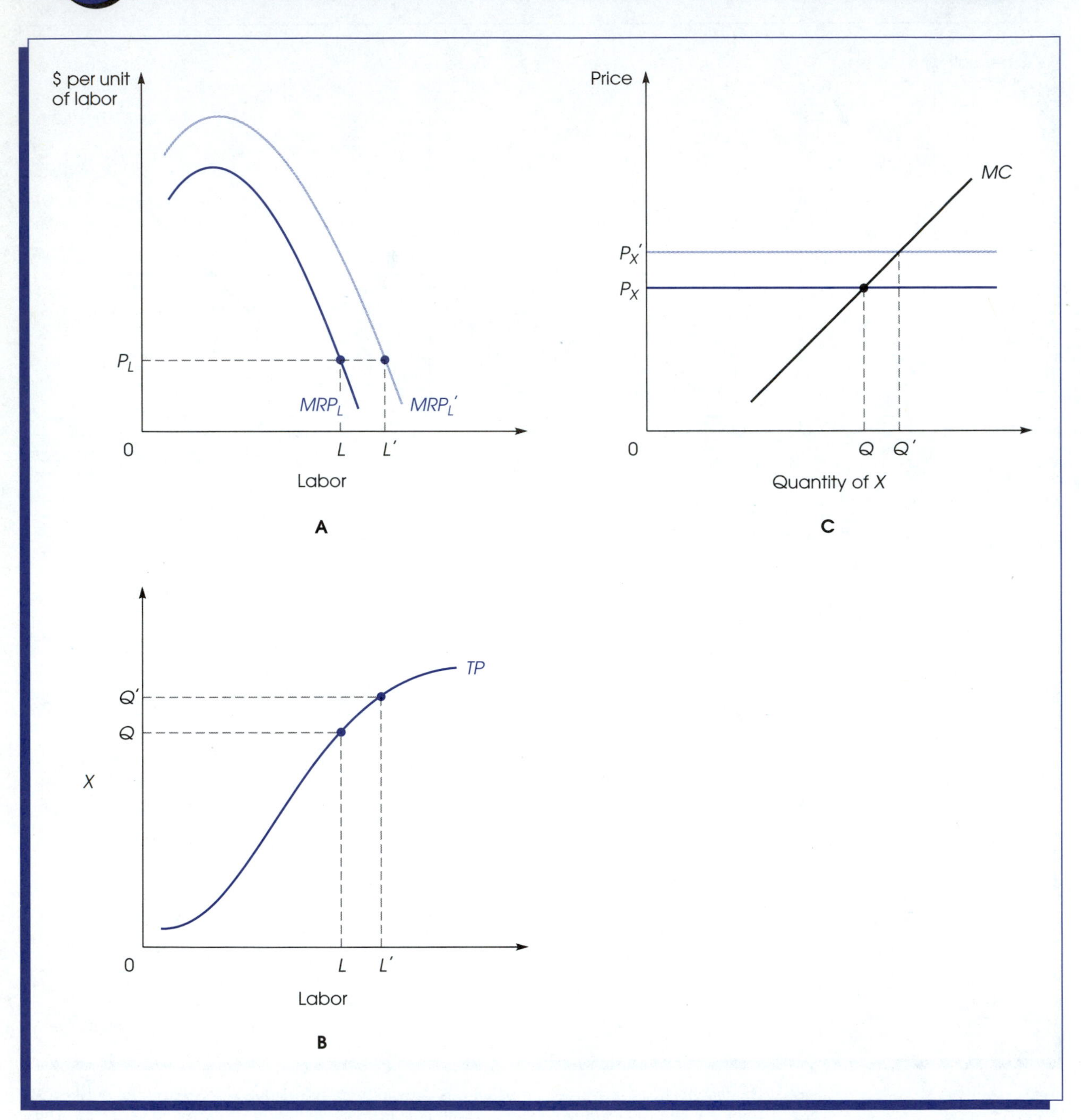

Initially, the price of output is P_X and the wage rate of labor is P_L. The firm hires L units of labor and produces Q units of output. When the price of output rises to P_X', the MRP_L curve shifts out to MRP_L', employment rises to L', and output increases to Q'.

each level of output. In this case the marginal product of labor rises, and therefore so does the competitive firm's demand curve for labor. In panel B the total product of labor rises while becoming shallower at each level of output. This leads to a fall in the marginal product of labor, and so to a fall in the competitive firm's labor demand.

Complements in production Two factors with the property that an increase in the employment of one raises the marginal product of the other.

Substitutes in production Two factors with the property that an increase in the employment of one lowers the marginal product of the other.

In the first case, which is the typical one, we say that labor and capital are **complements in production.** When labor and capital are complements in production, increases in capital make workers more productive at the margin and lead to increases in the demand for labor. In the second case, we say that labor and capital are **substitutes in production.** When labor and capital are substitutes in production, an increase in capital leads to a fall in labor's marginal productivity and decreases the demand for labor. People who worry about "automation" reducing the demand for workers believe that capital and labor are substitutes in production. As an empirical matter, this case seems to be much rarer than it is often believed to be.

Exhibit 15-4 **An Increase in Plant Size**

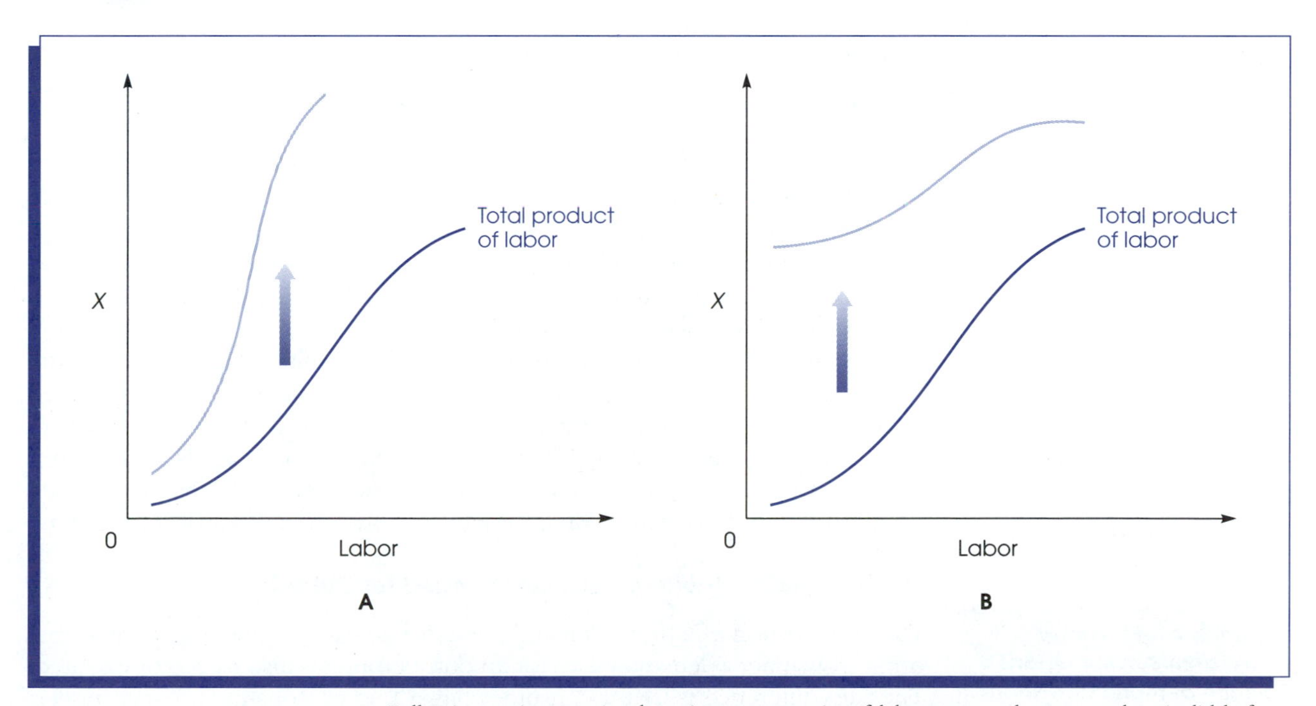

Following an increase in plant size, any quantity of labor can produce more than it did before. Thus, the total product curve shifts upward. Typically, it also becomes steeper, as in panel A, so that the marginal product of labor increases as well. In this case we say that capital and labor are complements in production. But conceivably the total product could rise but become shallower, as in panel B. In this case the marginal product of labor falls because of the increase in plant size; we say that capital and labor are substitutes in production.

A change in plant size is a long-run phenomenon. Thus, when we talk about the marginal product of labor before and after the capital adjustment, we are comparing one initial short-run situation with the new short-run situation that holds following a long-run adjustment.

15.2 The Firm's Demand for Factors in the Long Run

Next we will study the demand for labor in the long run, with both labor and capital treated as variables. (To study the demand for capital, simply interchange the words *capital* and *labor* throughout this section.)

Constructing the Long-Run Labor Demand Curve

Now we will construct the firm's long-run labor demand curve. Throughout the discussion the following are held fixed:

The technology available to the firm (that is, its isoquant diagram).

The rental rate on capital, which we denote by P_K.

The market price of output, which we denote by P_X.

Constructing a Point on the Curve

To find a point on the labor demand curve, we will take a particular wage rate, P_L, as given and see how much labor the firm chooses to employ.

The wage rate P_L determines the slope of the firm's isocosts, which is $-P_L/P_K$. This allows us to draw in the family of isocosts and so to construct the expansion path as in panel A of Exhibit 15–5. In Section 6.3 we saw how the expansion path determines the firm's (long-run) total and marginal cost curves. The long-run marginal cost curve *(LRMC)* in panel B of Exhibit 15–5 is the one that arises from that process. The firm chooses a level of output, Q_0, so as to maximize its profits. It then looks to the Q_0-unit isoquant and finds the least-cost way of producing Q_0 units. That least-cost way is the basket labeled *A* in panel A. The firm hires the basket of inputs represented by *A*. This basket includes L_0 units of labor. Therefore, a wage rate of P_L leads to the firm's demanding L_0 units of labor. This entire process allows us to construct a single point on the firm's demand curve for labor, shown in panel C of the exhibit.

The Demand for Inputs versus the Demand for Output

The USDA's Economic Research Service reports on the demand for various agricultural commodity inputs can be seen at: http://www.econ.ag.gov/

The construction of a firm's demand curve for a factor is similar in spirit to that of the consumer's demand curve for an output, but it is also more complicated. The key difference is that a consumer has a budget constraint. Given prices, we can determine that budget constraint and find the basket he consumes. A firm, by contrast, has no budget constraint. Instead, it has an infinite family of isocost lines, and it could choose to operate on any one of them. In order to find out what basket of inputs the firm chooses, we must refer to another market, the market for output (that is, we must use panel B in Exhibit 15–5). The

Exhibit 15-5 Constructing a Point on the Labor Demand Curve

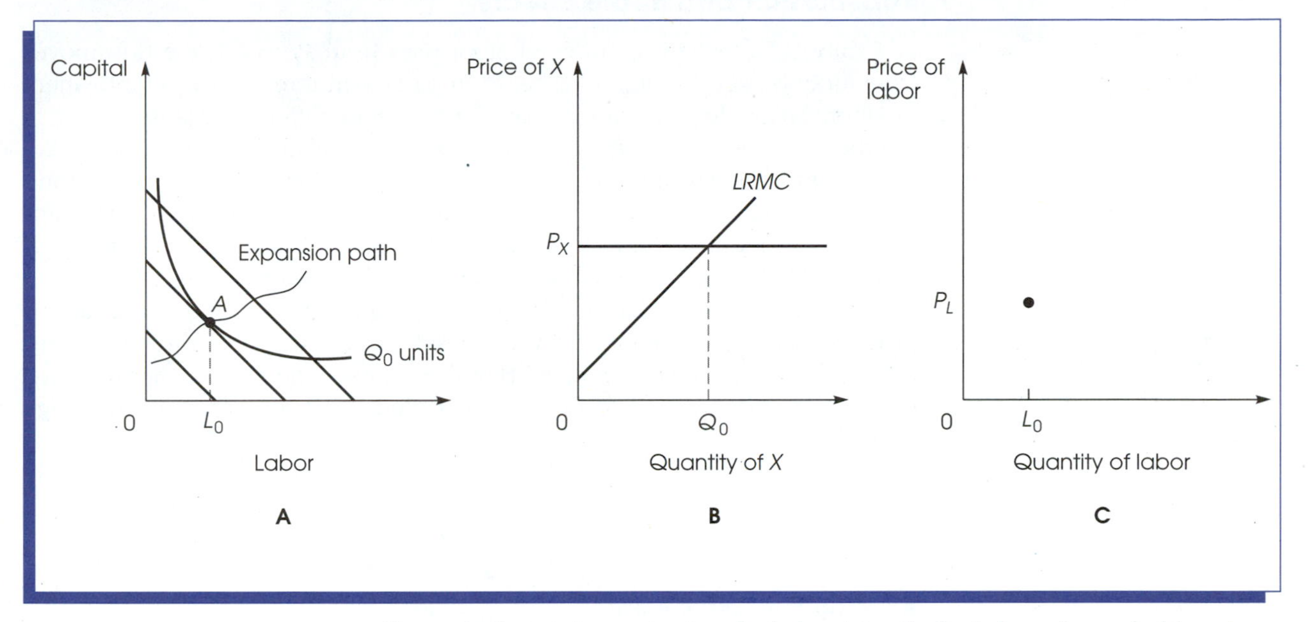

The graphs illustrate the construction of a single point on the firm's demand curve for labor, shown in panel C. The isoquant in panel A and the output price, P_X, shown in panel B are given and are independent of the wage rate. Now we assume a wage rate P_L. This enables us to draw the isocosts in the first panel, which have slope $-P_L/P_K$. These in turn determine the expansion path, also shown in panel A. Using panel A, we can derive the firm's long-run marginal cost (= long-run supply) curve, *LRMC*, using the methods of Section 6.3. Panel B determines the firm's output, which is Q_0. We now return to panel A to see that when the firm produces the quantity Q_0, it chooses the basket of inputs *A*, and this basket contains L_0 units of labor. Finally, we conclude that the wage rate P_L corresponds to the quantity of labor L_0, and we record this fact in panel C.

Derived demand Demand for an input, which depends on conditions in the output market.

firm's demand curve for a factor of production is called **derived demand** because it is partly derived from information external to the market for the factor itself.

A Change in the Wage Rate

Continuing with the example of Exhibit 15–5, suppose that the price of labor rises, to P_L'. This causes all of the isocosts to become steeper, as in panel A of Exhibit 15–6, yielding a new expansion path shown in blue. The new expansion path leads to new (long-run) total and marginal cost curves. Suppose that the new marginal cost curve is the curve *LRMC'* in panel B of Exhibit 15–6. Then the firm reduces output to Q_1 and chooses an input basket where the Q_1-unit isoquant is tangent to an isocost. The new basket is the one labeled *B* in panel A of Exhibit 15–6. The quantity of labor demanded is L_1. This gives a second point on the firm's demand curve for labor, shown in panel C of the exhibit.

Continuing in this way, we can generate as many points as we want and can connect them to get the firm's labor demand curve.

Substitution and Scale Effects

In Exhibit 15–6, when the price of labor rises from P_L to P_L', the firm moves from input basket *A* to input basket *B*. In particular, it reduces its employment of labor. This reduction comes about for two quite different reasons.

One reason is that labor is now more expensive relative to capital, so it pays to use less labor and more capital in producing any given quantity of output. In other words, the expansion path in panel A of the exhibit has shifted upward and to the left. (Instead of passing through *A*, it now passes through *B* and *C*.) This is called the **substitution effect** of the wage change.

Substitution effect When the price of an input changes, that part of the effect on employment that results from the firm's substitution toward other inputs.

The other reason is that the firm now faces higher costs and consequently produces less output, so that it wants less of every factor of production, including labor. We see this in panel B of the exhibit, where the higher marginal cost curve causes output to fall. This is called the **scale effect** of the wage change.

Scale effect When the price of an input changes, that part of the effect on employment that results from changes in the firm's output.

The substitution and scale effects of a change in the wage rate are closely analogous to the substitution and income effects that a consumer experiences in response to a change in the price of a consumption good.

An Imaginary Experiment

In order to separate the substitution effect from the scale effect, we can conduct a hypothetical experiment. Suppose that the price of labor were to rise from P_L to P_L' but that the firm kept its output fixed at Q_0. (The experiment is hypothetical because the firm would *not,* in fact, keep its output fixed at Q_0.) In that case, where would the firm operate? It would want to be on its new expansion path but to remain on the Q_0-unit isoquant. That is, it would move to point *C* in panel A of Exhibit 15–6.

The movement from point *A* to point *C* is a pure substitution effect. The scale effect, which results from changes in the firm's output level, has been totally eliminated by assuming that the firm holds its output level constant.

Now, in fact, the firm does not hold its output level constant. Instead it moves to point *B*. The "move" from the hypothetical point *C* to the firm's actual new basket *B* is due entirely to the change in output from Q_0 to Q_1. It is the scale effect. To summarize:

The firm's movement from A to B can be thought of as a movement along the isoquant from A to C (called the *substitution effect*), followed by a movement along the expansion path from C to B (called the *scale effect*).

Direction of the Substitution Effect

When the price of labor rises, the substitution effect is a movement along an isoquant to a tangency with a new, steeper isocost. It must be a movement to the left. This is because isoquants become steeper to the left and shallower to the right. In panel A of Exhibit 15–6 this means that point *C* is to the left of point *A* and this represents a basket with less labor.

Exhibit 15-6 A Rise in the Wage Rate

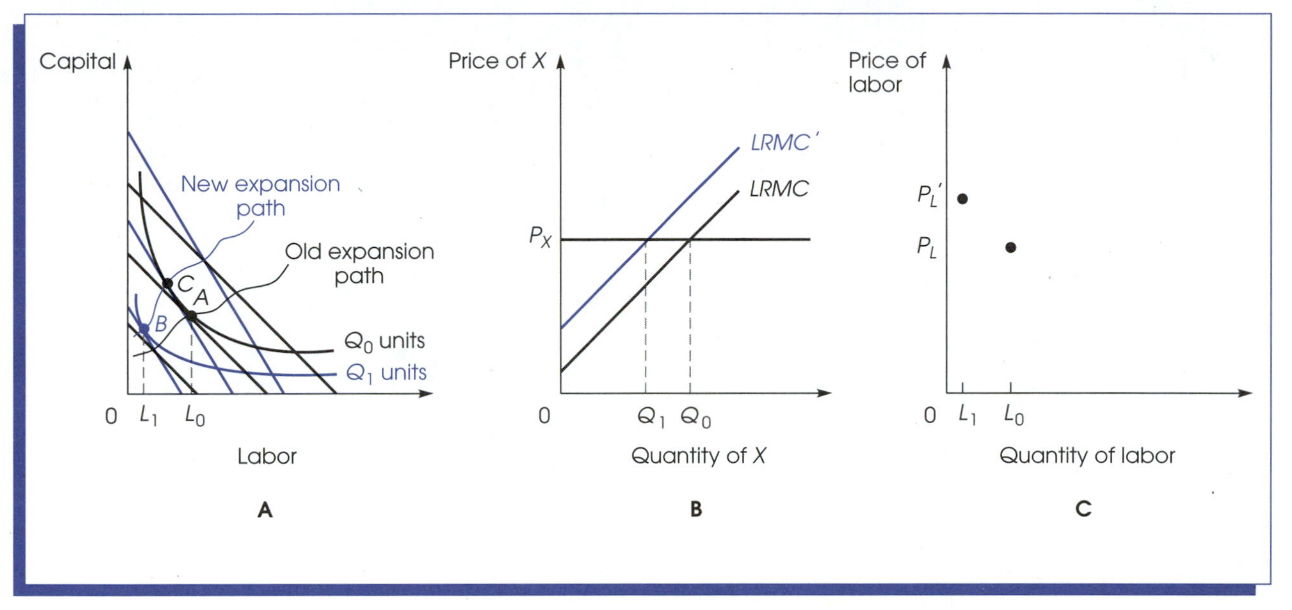

Beginning with the situation in Exhibit 15–5, we assume that the wage rate now rises from P_L to P_L. The new curves are the colored ones. First we get new isocosts (with slope $- P_L'/P_K$) and a new expansion path in panel A. This yields a new marginal cost curve, *LRMC'*, and a new quantity of output, Q_1, in panel B. The firm chooses a point on its expansion path where it can produce Q_1 units of output, namely, *B* in panel A. Thus, it hires L_1 units of labor, generating the new point on the demand curve that is shown in panel C.

The substitution effect of a rise in the wage always reduces the firm's employment of labor.

Direction of the Scale Effect

An increase in the wage rate raises the firm's long-run total cost curve. However, this could happen in either of two ways. The long-run total cost curve could both rise and become steeper. In this case, because marginal cost is equal to the slope of total cost, and because that slope has increased, long-run marginal cost will rise. Alternatively, the long-run total cost curve could rise and become shallower, in which case long-run marginal cost will fall. The two possibilities are illustrated in Exhibit 15–7.

Panel A of Exhibit 15–7 is by far the more usual case. Here a rise in the wage leads to a rise in marginal cost, as was assumed in Exhibit 15–6. Thus, in Exhibit 15–6 output falls, from Q_0 to Q_1. Therefore, the scale effect is a movement along the expansion path to a lower isoquant and so must be a movement to the left. Recall that in Exhibit 15–6 the scale effect is the movement from point *C* to point *B*. Because *B* is to the left of *C*, the scale effect reduces the employment of labor, thereby reinforcing the substitution effect.

Exhibit 15-7 **Two Possible Effects of a Rise in the Wage Rate**

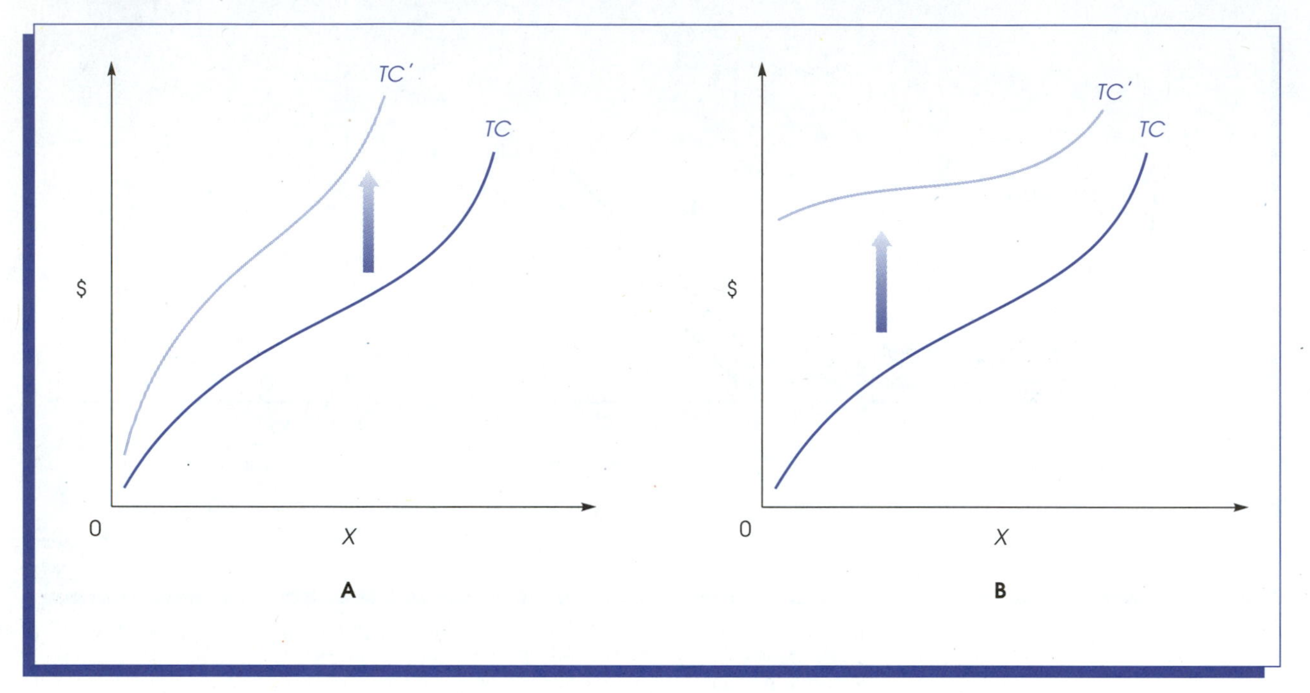

A rise in the wage rates raises the firm's long-run total cost curve, *TC*, to a new level, *TC′*. Usually, *TC′* is steeper than *TC*, as in panel A. In this case the firm's long-run marginal cost curve moves upward and output decreases, as in panel B of Exhibit 15–6. However, it is possible that *TC′* could be shallower than *TC*, as in panel B. In this case long-run marginal cost is reduced and output increases. When the latter case occurs, we say that labor is a regressive factor.

Regressive factor A factor with the property that an increase in its wage rate lowers the firm's long-run marginal cost curve.

However, it is also possible that the rise in the wage rate could lead to an increase in total cost of the sort shown in panel B of Exhibit 15–7 and hence to a fall in the marginal cost curve. If so, we say that labor is a **regressive factor.** For example, the rise in wages might make it profitable for the firm to build a highly automated factory, allowing it to produce at very low marginal cost. This case is shown in Exhibit 15–8, where output rises from Q_0 to Q_2 in panel B. Because of the rise in output, the scale effect is a rightward move, from point *C* to point *B′* in panel A. That is, the scale effect causes the firm to employ more labor than it otherwise would.

Combining the Substitution and Scale Effects

Exhibits 15–6 and 15–8 show two possibilities, corresponding to the two panels of Exhibit 15–7. In each case the substitution effect, from point *A* to point *C*, is a movement to the left. In Exhibit 15–6, which is the usual case, the scale effect, from *C* to *B*, is a further movement to the left. Thus, we can conclude that *B* must lie to the left of *A*, which is to say that the quantity of labor demanded decreases in response to a rise in the wage rate. That is, in this case the demand curve for labor surely slopes down.

In Exhibit 15–8, where labor is a regressive factor, the substitution and scale effects work in opposite directions. The substitution effect reduces the quantity of labor demanded, whereas the scale effect increases it. That is, C is to the left of A, but B' is to the right of C. Where is B' with respect to A?

From what we can see in the diagram, there is no way to tell for sure whether B' is to the left or to the right of A. However, as a matter of mathematical fact, B' must lie to the left of A. That is, for a regressive factor the substitution effect must be greater than the scale effect. The proof of this is a bit subtle. If you are very talented mathematically, you will learn a lot from trying to discover it.

We can summarize by saying that in any case a rise in the wage rate leads to a fall in the quantity of labor demanded. Put another way:

The competitive firm's demand curve for labor (or any other factor of production) always slopes down.

Exhibit 15-8 A Rise in the Wage of a Regressive Factor

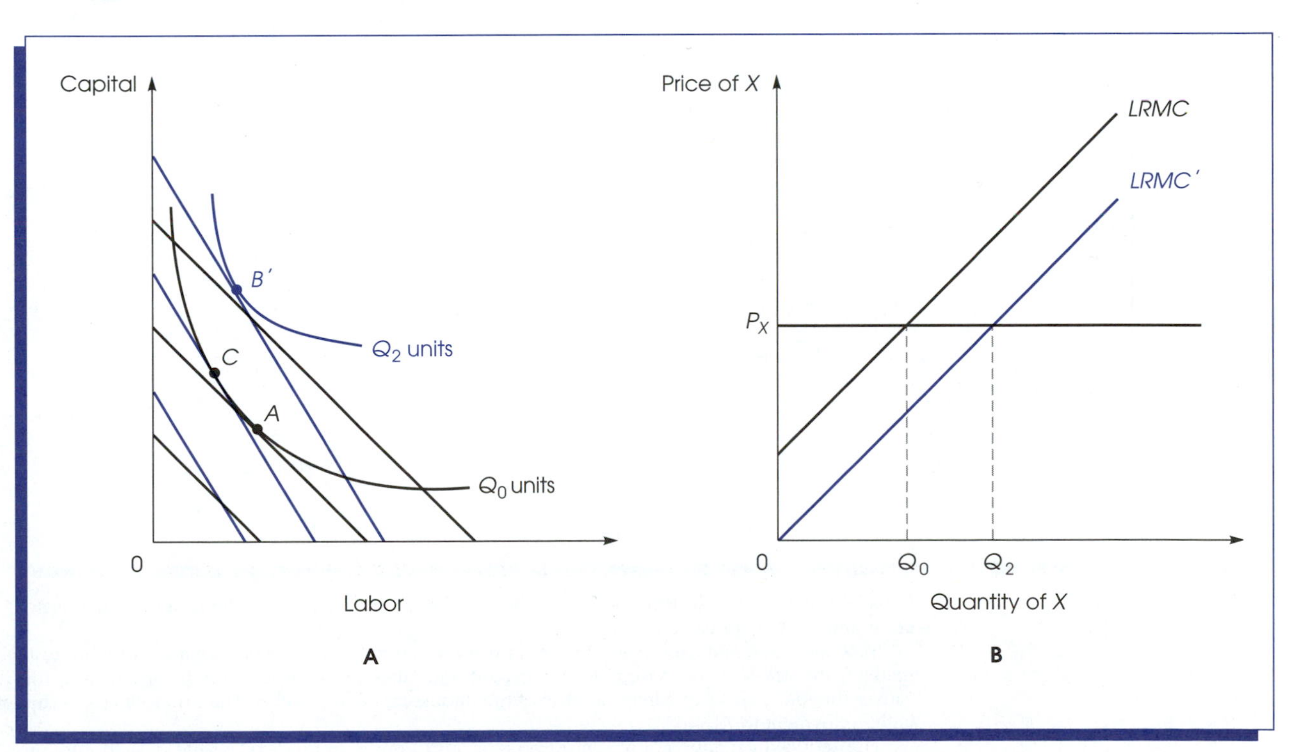

If labor is a regressive factor, then a rise in the wage rate leads to a fall in marginal cost and an increase in output, from Q_0 to Q_2. Therefore, the firm moves from point A on the Q_0-isoquant to point B' on the higher Q_2-isoquant. The move can be decomposed into a substitution effect (the move from A to C) and a scale effect (the move from C to B').

In fact, the same statement is also true for a monopoly firm's demand curve for labor.

In the case of consumer goods, which we studied in Section 4.3, we had to admit the theoretical possibility of a Giffen good, for which the consumer's demand curve would slope up. However, there is not even a theoretical possibility of a Giffen *factor.* A firm's derived demand curves for factors of production must slope down.

Relationships Between the Short Run and the Long Run

We began this section by studying the case in which labor is the only variable input, and we argued that the firm's demand curve for labor is just the down-

Exhibit 15-9 Labor Demand in the Short Run and the Long Run

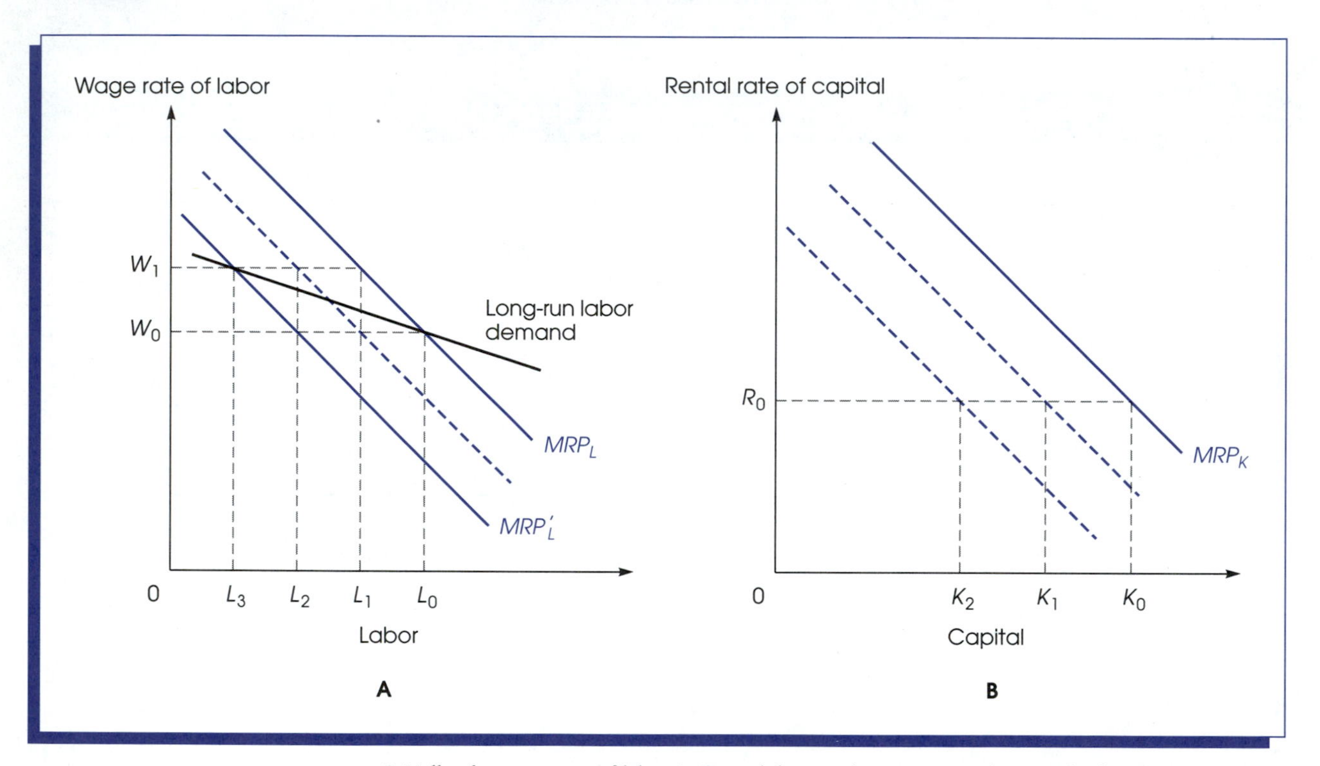

Initially, the wage rate of labor is W_0 and the rental rate on capital is R_0. The firm hires L_0 units of labor and K_0 units of capital.

Now the wage rate rises to W_1. In the short run the firm reduces its employment of labor to L_1 read off the MRP_L curve. Assuming that capital and labor are complements in production, this causes the MRP_K curve to fall to the level of the middle curve in panel B. The firm reduces its capital employment to K_1.

The reduced capital employment lowers the MRP_L curve to the level of the dashed curve in panel A, causing labor employment to fall to L_2. This lowers the MRP_K still further, causing capital employment to fall to K_2, and the process repeats. Eventually the MRP_L curve settles at the new level MRP_L'. Here the firm hires L_3 units of labor. Thus the long-run labor demand curve (in black) shows that a wage of W_1 corresponds to the quantity L_3 of labor employed.

ward-sloping part of the MRP_L curve. We then moved on to the more complicated case in which two factors are variable, and we derived the firm's demand curve for labor via the more complicated process depicted in Exhibit 15–6. What is the relationship between these two approaches to labor demand?

The answer is that in the long run the MRP_L curve shifts because of adjustments in the employment of capital. For example, consider the effect of a rise in the wage when labor and capital are complements in production. Exhibit 15–9 shows the adjustment process. Initially, the wage rate of labor is W_0 and the rental rate on capital is R_0. At these prices, the firm hires L_0 units of labor (chosen from the MRP_L curve) and K_0 units of capital (chosen from the MRP_K curve).[1]

When the wage rises to W_1, the firm's short-run response is to move along the MRP_L curve and reduce the employment of labor to L_1. The reduction in labor reduces the marginal product of capital, so that the MRP_K curve moves down to the middle curve in panel B. In the long run the firm reduces its capital employment to K_1, causing the marginal product of labor to fall to the dashed curve in panel A. This causes employment to fall further, to L_2. This in turn leads to a further reduction in the marginal product of capital, which leads to even less capital employed, which reduces the marginal product of labor still further, and so on. After many iterations the marginal product of labor settles down, as indicated in panel A, and the final level of employment is L_3.

In the long run, therefore, the firm hires L_3 units of labor when the wage is W_1. Thus, on the long-run labor demand curve, shown in black, the wage W_0 corresponds to L_0 and the wage W_1 corresponds to L_3.

The adjustment process described here requires, in principle, an infinite number of steps. But since the firm can foresee the outcome of these infinitely many steps, it can simply move directly to the new level of employment without actually stopping at each step along the way.

15.3 The Industry's Demand Curve for Factors of Production

The industry's demand curve for factors of production can be approximated by adding the demand curves of the individual firms. However, this overlooks an important complication. When the wage rate goes up, in the usual case all firms' marginal cost curves move up. As a result, the industry supply curve shifts and the price of output rises. This in turn means that firms will not reduce output by as much as they would if price remained constant. The substitution effect is unchanged, but the scale effect is lessened. Firms reduce their employment of labor by less than Exhibit 15–6 predicts. On similar grounds, a

[1]Instead of using P_K and P_L for the prices of capital and labor, we are writing R and W. The only reason for this is that we want to be able to use numerical subscripts, which look ugly when appended to P_K and P_L.

fall in the wage leads to a smaller increase in employment than one would expect from our study of individual firms. The bottom line is that the industry's demand curve for a factor tends to be less elastic than the sum of the demand curves from the individual firms in the industry.

Finally, in any discussion of the demand for labor (or any input), it should be remembered that labor is demanded by many different industries. All the corresponding industry demand curves must be added together to get "the" demand curve for labor.

Monopsony

An article by Robert Valletta of the San Francisco FRB relates the theory of a labor market monopsony to the employment effects of a minimum wage: http://www.frbsf.org/econrsrch/wklyltr/el97-34.html

Throughout this chapter we have assumed that firms take factor prices as given. This is equivalent to saying that for each factor the firm faces a supply curve that is horizontal at the market wage rate. However, there remains the possibility that a single firm could account for a substantial portion of the market for some factor. In this case the quantity demanded by the firm affects that factor's wage rate. The firm faces an upward-sloping supply curve for that factor.

Monopsonist A buyer who faces an upward-sloping supply curve.

The most extreme example occurs if there is some factor of production that is demanded by only one firm. In that case the firm in question is a "single buyer," just as a monopolist might be a "single seller." A single buyer is called a **monopsonist**. However, just as we use the word *monopolist* to describe any seller who faces a downward-sloping demand curve, so we shall use the word *monopsonist* to describe any buyer who faces an upward-sloping supply curve.

To a monopsony demander of labor, the cost of hiring an additional unit of labor exceeds the wage rate. The reason for this is that when the monopsonist hires an additional worker, there are two ways in which his costs increase: (1) he must pay the new worker's wage and (2) he bids up the wages of all workers.

Marginal labor cost The cost of hiring an additional unit of labor.

As a result, the monopsonist faces a **marginal labor cost** (MLC) curve that lies everywhere above the labor supply curve that he faces. He maximizes profits by choosing that quantity where the marginal revenue product of labor and the marginal cost of labor are equal; then he pays a wage read off the supply curve at that quantity. The process is illustrated in Exhibit 15–10.

Do not confuse MLC, which is the cost of hiring one additional unit of labor, with *MC*, which is the cost of producing one additional unit of output.

The monopsonist hires fewer workers and pays a lower wage than would be the case if many firms competed to hire labor. Under competition there would be a going wage rate of W_C in Exhibit 15–10, and employment would be L_C.

How Widespread Is Monopsony?

In order for a firm to have monopsony power, it must constitute a substantial portion of the demand for some factor. Therefore, even a firm that is unique

Exhibit 15-10 Monopsony

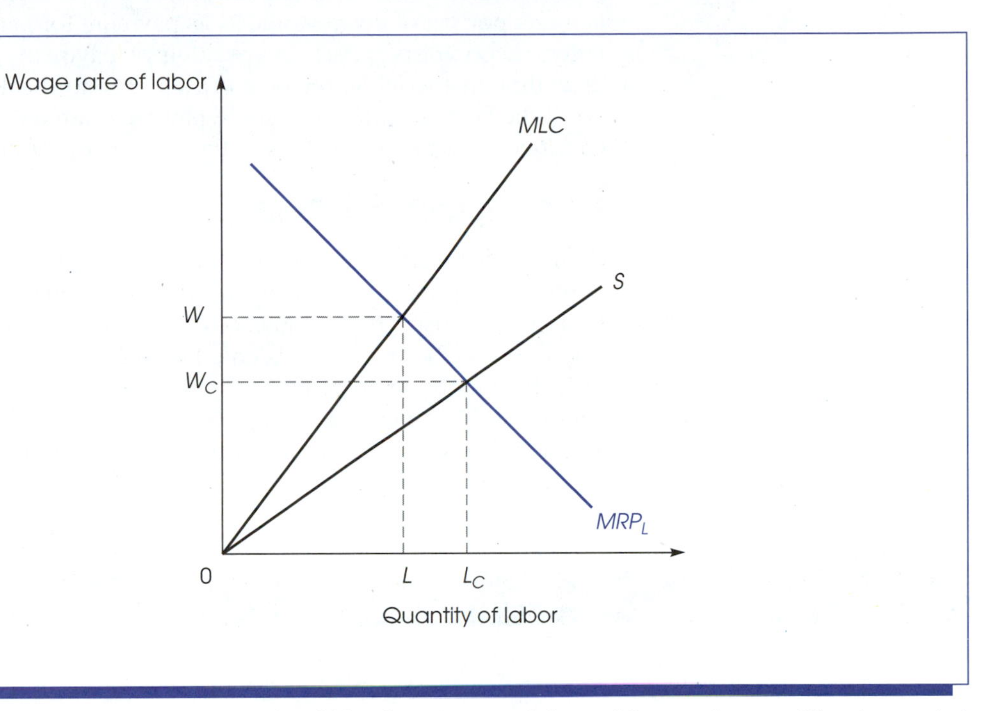

A monopsony demander of labor faces an upward-sloping labor supply curve *(S)* and a marginal labor cost (*MLC*) curve that lies everywhere above *S*. He hires *L* units of labor (where MRP_L = *MLC*) and pays the wage *W* that he reads off the supply curve at that quantity.

In an industry with many firms, the going price for labor would be W_C, and each firm would face a flat supply curve at this price. L_C units of labor would be hired.

in its industry has no monopsony power, provided that there are firms in *other* industries competing with it for the use of factors.

For example, suppose that all of the major auto manufacturers were to merge into one giant firm. At first, this firm could well have monopsony power in the market for autoworkers, who would have no other employer competing to hire their valuable skills. However, if the giant auto firm were to exercise this monopsony power to keep wages low, some autoworkers would eventually decide to acquire other skills and to sell their services elsewhere—say, as shipbuilders. In the long run the single automaker competes in the labor market with all of the firms in the shipbuilding industry and in countless other industries besides.

The same is true when a single employer dominates a certain geographic area. Although the employer may have some monopsony power in the short run, he may be unable to exercise that power without causing some of the area's residents to move elsewhere. Ultimately, he competes for the local workers with employers all over the world.

15.4 The Distribution of Income

Firms hire factors of production and combine them to create output. This output generates revenue, or income, for the firm. Each factor of production receives a portion of this revenue as its payment for participating in the firm's activity. (Economists persist in speaking of payments to factors of production, even though it would often be more accurate to speak of payments to the *owners* of the factors.) After all of these payments are made, any remaining revenue (positive or negative) accrues to the owners of the firm in the form of profit.

Factor Shares and Rents

From the first part of this chapter, we know that when labor markets are competitive, the price of any factor is equal to its marginal revenue product. If a firm or an industry hires L units of labor at a wage rate of $P_L \cdot L$. Therefore, we can say that labor's income is equal to $MRP_L \cdot L$.

If the supply curve of labor to this firm or industry is upward-sloping, the suppliers of labor earn a producers' surplus, or rent, equal to area B in Exhibit 15–11. Labor's income is the sum of areas B and C, so that only a portion of this income can be considered rent.

Exhibit 15-11 Labor's Share of Income

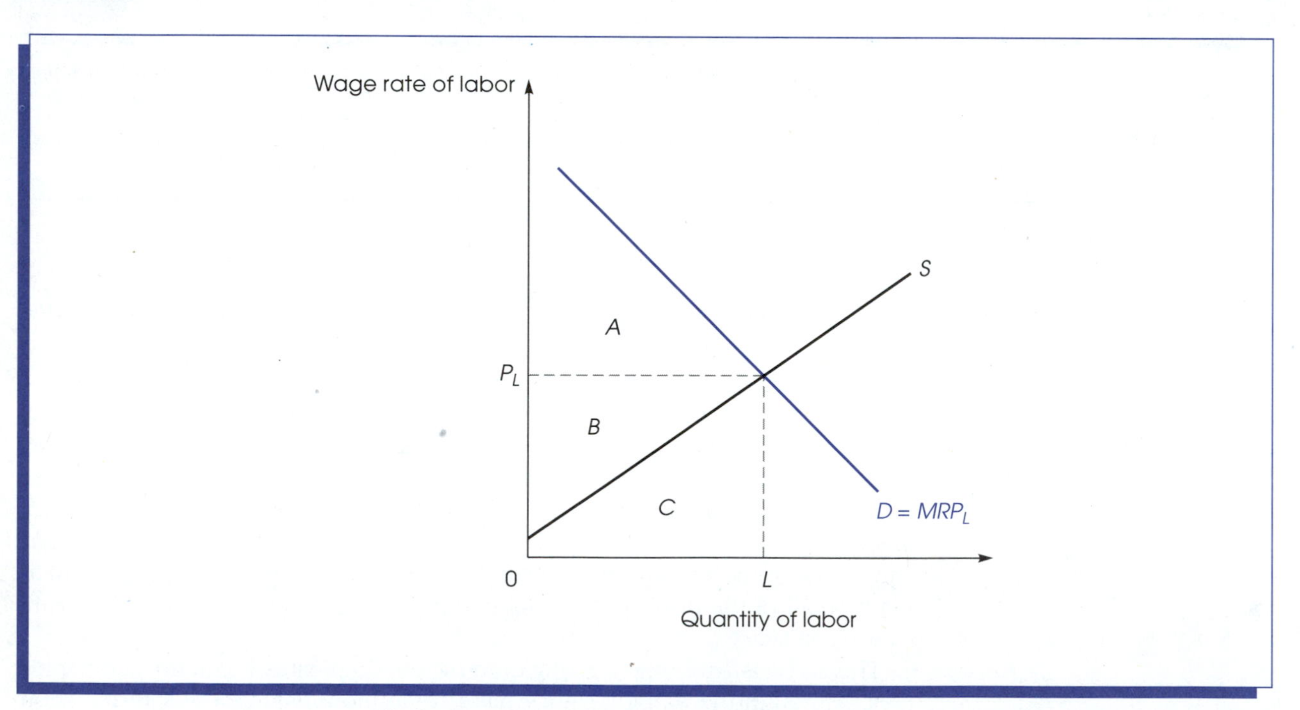

The firm or industry hires L units of labor at the wage P_L and earns a total revenue of $A + B + C$. Of this revenue, labor receives a share equal to $P_L \cdot L = B + C$. Of this, area C covers workers' opportunity costs and area B is earned as rent.

Do not confuse the word *rent*, meaning producers' surplus, with the rental (that is, wage) paid by the firm to hire a factor of production. The factor earns a producers' surplus equal to the payment it receives from the firm *minus* its opportunity costs. Only when the factor supply curve is perfectly vertical does the rental payment consist entirely of rent.

The area $A + B + C$ under the MRP_L curve in Exhibit 15–11 is equal to the total revenue of the firm or of the industry. (The area can be broken into rectangles representing the revenue from the first unit of labor employed, the revenue from the second unit, and so on.) Because labor receives $B + C$, the remaining area A must represent the sum of the payments to all other factors, plus any profits that are earned.

What is true of labor is also true of every other factor. Capital earns an income of $MRP_K \cdot K$, of which some portion is rent. There are also intangible factors like "entrepreneurial ability" that are typically supplied by the owners of the firm. Although such factors are not explicitly on the payroll, they should be viewed as implicitly receiving a wage equal to their marginal revenue product. If the owner supplies E units of entrepreneurial ability, with a marginal revenue product of MRP_E, then we think of the firm as paying the owner an income of $MRP_E \cdot E$ in his capacity as a factor of production.

Inputs like entrepreneurial ability are often supplied quite inelastically. The owner of a shoe store has a great deal of knowledge about the specific workings of his own enterprise. Such knowledge is a factor of production that would be much less valuable in any alternative use. As a result, he might supply almost all of this knowledge to his own business, regardless of whether he earns a high or a low wage by doing so. Thus, the supply curve for the owner's entrepreneurial services is very inelastic, so that a large portion of the income earned by these services tends to be rent.

Profit

The sum of the factor payments may be less than, equal to, or greater than the revenue of the firm. If the factor payments are less than the firm's revenue, then the difference is profit and accrues to the owner of the firm. If the factor payments exceed the firm's revenues, the firm takes a loss, sometimes called a negative profit, equal to the difference. This loss comes from the pocket of the firm's owner.

Notice that in our analysis the owner of the firm receives two very different kinds of payments. (They are different to the economist, although an accountant or a businessman would see no reason to distinguish them.) First, there is the income that he earns as the supplier of certain factors of production. Much of this income is usually a rent, or a producer's surplus. Second, there is the profit remaining after the firm has made all of its factor payments (including the ones to the owner).

As was discussed briefly in Chapter 7, many economists would prefer not to think of specialized skills, such as knowledge of the workings of a particular shoe store, as factors of production that are hired by the firm. They would prefer to think of the firm as earning positive profits due to the existence of these factors. The two analyses use different words but describe the same outcomes.

Returns to Scale

In long-run equilibrium, it can be shown mathematically that when production is subject to decreasing returns to scale (that is, when average cost is increasing), factor shares add up to less than the firm's total revenue (so that the firm has a positive profit); when production is subject to constant returns to scale (that is, when average cost is flat), factor shares add up to the firm's revenue exactly (so that profit is zero); and when production is subject to increasing returns to scale (that is, when average cost is decreasing), factor shares add up to more than the firm's revenue (so that profit is negative).

In long-run competitive equilibrium, the firm operates at the minimum point of its average cost curve, where returns to scale are constant. Therefore, profits are zero, as we already know from Chapter 7.

However, Professor Paul Romer of the University of California at Berkeley argues that in many industries firms experience increasing returns to scale over the entire relevant range.[2] The reason is that many important inputs (unlike the labor and capital we have considered in this chapter) are *nonrivalrous:* Once produced, there is no limit to how much they can be used. A firm that produces one specialized software program to install on a manager's computer can allow other managers to install the same program at essentially no additional cost.

A firm that has one specialized software program but doubles all of its other inputs (number of computers, number of managers, number of factories, etc.) might be expected to double its output. If the firm really doubles *all* of its inputs by constructing a second specialized software program, then it should *more* than double its output. This is precisely the definition of increasing returns to scale.

If increasing returns are truly a common phenomenon, they present a major challenge to the standard competitive model of the firm. A competitive firm that experiences increasing returns must earn negative profits after all factors shares are paid out. In such circumstances, we should not expect to see any competitive firms.

Producers' Surplus

In earlier chapters we talked about the producer's surplus earned by firms. It is often useful to think of producers' surplus in that way. However, in a more careful analysis, we recognize that at least part of the producers' surplus is actually earned by the factors that the firms employ.

[2]P. Romer, "Are Nonconvexities Important for Understanding Growth?" *American Economic Review* 80 (1990):97–107.

The Distribution of Rent

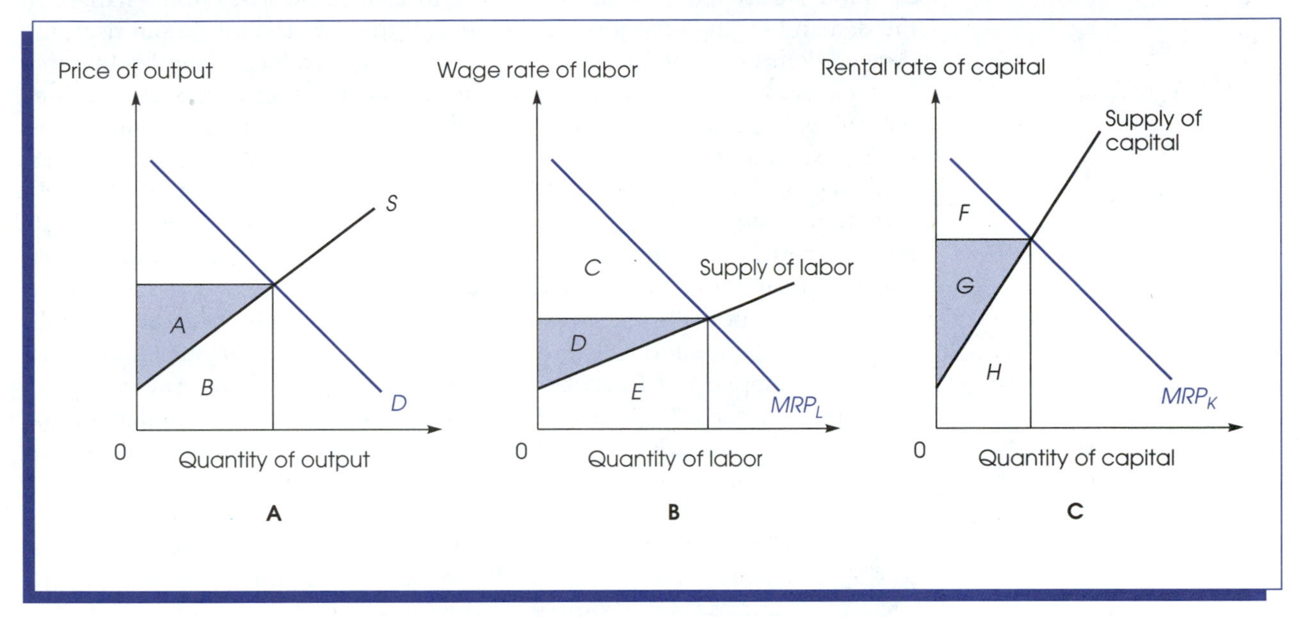

In long-run zero profits equilibrium, the industry's total revenue (given by $A + B = C + D + E = F + G + H$) is paid out to factors. Since labor's total wages are $D + E$ and the total rental payments to capital are $G + H$, we have $A + B = (D + E) + (G + H)$. Producers' surplus in the industry is equal to A, of which workers get D and owners of capital get G. Therefore, $A = D + G$.

In fact, in long-run competitive equilibrium, firms earn zero profits. This means that all of the producers' surplus that we have previously attributed to the firms is actually paid out to factors.

Exhibit 15–12 shows the relationship between the industry-wide markets for output, labor, and capital when each firm earns zero profits. The firms earn total revenue equal to $A + B$ in the output market, of which A is producers' surplus. (The firms' total revenue is also equal to $C + D + E$ in panel B and to $F + G + H$ in panel C.) This revenue is distributed to workers, who earn $D + E$ in panel B, and to the owners of capital, who earn $G + H$ in panel C. Since we assume that firms earn zero profits, these factor payments must exactly account for the firms' total revenue. That is, $(D + E) + (G + H) = A + B$.

The portion of total revenue that is producers' surplus is exactly A, of which D is earned by workers and G is earned by the owners of capital. Therefore, $A = D + G$. If profits were nonzero, then area A would include those profits in addition to $D + G$.

Of course, when there are more than two factors of production, rents are divided among all of them, not just capital and labor.

Who Benefits?

Factors that are supplied relatively inelastically (the most extreme case being a fixed factor) earn more rents than those supplied more elastically. As a result, the more nearly fixed factors have more to gain (or to lose) from changes in the demand for the output of the industry. If the demand for output rises, the derived demand for all inputs rises. This increases producers' surplus by more for those factors with inelastic supply curves than for other factors. By the same reasoning, these factors bear most of the loss when the demand for output falls.

For example, professional football games are produced with many inputs, including professional quarterbacks and footballs. The supply of quarterbacks is quite inelastic, because the particular skills of a quarterback have relatively few alternatives uses that are anywhere near as valuable. Therefore, quarterbacks earn substantial rents. (That is, their wage bills far exceed their opportunity costs.) Footballs are supplied much more elastically, because the skills needed to produce footballs are also useful in a variety of other industries. Therefore, suppliers of footballs earn comparatively little rent. Any change in the public's demand for football games will have a much greater effect on the fortunes of quarterbacks than it will on the fortunes of football manufacturers.

What matters in this example is not the fact that quarterbacks' wages are high, but that their supply curve is inelastic. Suppose, for example, that all quarterbacks could equally well earn $500,000 a year as movie stars. Then, over a substantial range, the supply curve for quarterbacks would be flat (perfectly elastic) at $500,000 per year. In this case the wage would be high, but there would be no producers' surplus. And, in fact, in this case quarterbacks would not be hurt if the public completely lost interest in football. Changes in the industry's fortunes are felt most by those factors that are inelastically supplied, *not* by those factors whose wage bills are high.

Some factors are fixed in the short run and variable in the long run. An increase in the price of output benefits these factors more in the short run than in the long run. For example, in the short run there are a fixed number of recording studios capable of producing compact discs. A rise in the price of compact discs will raise revenue in the recording industry, and in the short run this increased revenue will largely be paid as rent to the owners of the recording studios. In the long run, however, more recording studios can be built, and the owners of existing recording studios will not continue to reap this windfall benefit.

Short-term rents due to inelastic short-run supply are sometimes called **quasi-rents.**

Quasi-rents Producers' surplus earned in the short run by factors that are supplied inelastically in the short run.

Finally, we should note that the owners of the factors of production are the same individuals and households that are the consumers in the economy. In earlier chapters we maintained a careful distinction between the consumers' surplus earned by individuals and the producers' surplus earned by firms. Now we see that the producers' surplus is actually earned by the same individuals who are earning the consumers' surplus. All gains from trade ultimately accrue to individuals. Who else is there to benefit?

summary

A factor's marginal revenue product is defined as the amount of additional revenue the firm can earn by employing one more unit of that factor. The equimarginal principle implies that the firm's demand curve for the factor will be identical with the downward-sloping portion of the factor's marginal revenue product curve.

An increase in employment of one factor will usually raise the marginal productivity of other factors, and hence it will raise the firm's demand curve for other factors. In this case we say that the factors are complements in production. It is also possible that an increase in the employment of one factor will reduce the marginal productivity of other factors, in which case we say that the factors are substitutes in production.

In the long run a change in the wage rate of labor will cause the firm to change its employment of both labor and capital. The firm's marginal cost curve will change, leading to a change in output as well.

In the hypothetical case in which the firm does *not* adjust output, the change in the wage rate leads to a movement along an isoquant, known as the substitution effect. The substitution effect is always in the expected direction: A rise in the wage rate reduces the quantity of labor demanded, and a fall in the wage rate increases the quantity demanded.

The scale effect of a wage change is that part of the change in employment that is due to the change in output. It is a movement along the new expansion path. The scale effect is usually in the same direction as the substitution effect, but it can go in the opposite direction, in which case we say that labor is a regressive factor. For a regressive factor, however, the substitution effect is always larger than the scale effect. Thus, even for a regressive factor the firm's labor demand curve must slope downward.

The firm's revenues are paid out to the factors of production, with each factor earning a wage equal to its marginal revenue product. Among these payments may be payments to the firm's owners for the use of specialized factors such as particular skills. After all these payments are made, whatever remains is the firm's profit. In long-run competitive equilibrium, profits are zero, so the factor payments exactly exhaust the firm's income.

Payments to factors minus the factors' opportunity costs are the factors' producers' surplus, or rent. The firm's producer's surplus (the area above the firm's supply curve up to the price and out to the quantity supplied) is the sum of all these factor rents plus the firm's profit, if any. Thus, the producers' surplus that we have attributed to firms in previous chapters is actually distributed as factor rents.

The more inelastically supplied the factor, the greater the percentage of its income that is rent. Thus, inelastically supplied factors benefit the most from the existence of the industry, and they stand to gain or lose the most when the industry's fortunes wax or wane.

Review Questions

R1. What is the relationship between marginal product and marginal revenue product?

R2. Draw total and marginal product diagrams to show how a rise in the price of output affects the employment of labor.

R3. Draw total and marginal product diagrams to show how an increase in plant size affects the employment of labor.

R4. Explain how to construct a point on the firm's long-run demand curve for labor.

R5. Define the substitution and the scale effects of an increase in the wage rate. What can be said about their directions?

R6. Define monopsony. Does a monopsonist employ more or less labor than a firm that hires workers competitively? Why?

R7. In long-run competitive equilibrium, the firm's total revenue is equal to the sum of its factor payments. Why?

R8. What is the relationship between the producers' surplus measured above the firm's supply curve for output and the producers' surpluses measured above the factors' supply curves for their services?

R9. A factor that is supplied perfectly elastically to an industry has nothing to gain or lose from changes in the price of output. Explain why, first using graphs and then giving the verbal interpretation.

R10. A factor that is supplied perfectly inelastically to an industry earns rents equal to its entire wage bill. Thus, such a factor participates heavily in the industry's fortunes, be they good or bad. Explain why, first using graphs and then giving the verbal interpretation.

Numerical Exercises

N1. Consider a firm that produces according to the production function

$$Q = \sqrt{KL}$$

where Q is the firm's output and K and L are the quantities of capital and labor that it employs. With this production function, the slope of an isoquant at the point (L, K) is given by $-K/L$.

a. Suppose that the going wage rate of labor is W, and the going rental rate on capital is R. What is the slope of an isocost? If the firm uses K units of capital and L of labor in long-run equilibrium, derive a formula for K in terms of L, W, and R. Derive a formula for L in terms of K, W, and R. (*Hint:* In long-run equilibrium, the firm operates at a point where the slope of an isocost and the slope of an isoquant are equal.)

b. Using the production function and the result of part (a), write a formula for L in terms of Q, W, and R, and a formula for K in terms of Q, W, and R.

c. Write a formula for the total cost of producing Q units of output.

d. Describe the firm's long-run marginal cost curve.

e. In long-run equilibrium, what must the price of output be? Would you have had enough information to answer this question if your answer to part (d) had been different than it was?

f. In terms of Q, how much does the firm

pay out to labor and to capital? What is its total revenue? What is its profit?

N2. Consider a perfectly competitive industry with many identical firms, each producing according to the production function

$$Q = \sqrt{KL}$$

Labor and capital are supplied to the industry according to the supply curves $L = W$ and $K = 4R$.

a. Suppose that the industry produces Q units of output, using K units of capital and L of labor. Write a formula for L in terms of Q, W, and R and for K in terms of Q, W, and R.

b. Write two equations expressing the conditions of equilibrium in the two factor markets. Use these equations to get a numerical value for W/R. (*Hint:* Divide one equation by the other.)

c. Show that the industry's long-run total cost curve is given by

$$Q = P$$

(*Hint:* Make use of your answers from N1.)

d. Suppose that the demand curve for the industry's output is given by

$$Q = 1{,}5000 - P$$

What are the price and quantity of output? How much labor is hired, and at what wage? How much capital is rented, and at what rental rate?

e. Under the conditions of part (d), calculate the producers' surplus in the output market. How much producers' surplus is earned by labor and how much by capital? How much profit is earned by firms? Is your answer consistent with your answer to Numerical Exercise N1(f)?

Problem Set

1. True or False: A rise in the demand for apples has no effect on the productivity of apple pickers, and hence no effect on the demand for apple pickers.

2. True or False: If the demand curve for a product is vertical, then any rise in the wage rate could be passed on entirely from firms to customers, without any fall in production. Thus, a rise in the wage rate would not reduce employment, either in the short run or in the long run.

3. True or False: If labor and capital are complements in production, then the long-run labor demand curve is more elastic than the short-run labor demand curve.

4. a. Prepare graphs like those in Exhibit 15–9 to illustrate the relationships between short-run and long-run labor demand when capital and labor are substitutes in production.

b. In this case is the short-run labor demand curve more or less elastic than the long-run labor demand curve?

5. a. Use Exhibit 15–9 to show that when labor and capital are the only inputs and when they are complements in production, the long-run labor demand curve must slope downward.

b. Use the graphs you prepared for Problem 4(a) to show that when labor and capital are the only inputs and when they are substitutes in production, the long-run labor demand curve must slope downward.

6. True or False: The industry demand curve for a regressive factor is likely to be more elastic than the sum of the firms' demand curves.

7. True or False: The isocosts of a monopsonist in the labor market are not straight lines.

8. Use a graph to demonstrate the social welfare consequences of monopsony.

9. True or False: If there is monopsony in the labor market, a minimum wage law can lead to increased employment.

10. Suppose that labor and capital are both supplied perfectly inelastically to the U.S. economy.

a. Show the producers' surplus earned by *capital* on a graph of the marginal product of *labor*. Explain where you make use of the fact that the supply of capital is perfectly inelastic.

b. Suppose that General Motors moves one of its plants to South Korea, increasing the number of workers who can be combined with U.S. capital. Show the gains and losses to (1) U.S. workers, (2) U.S. owners of capital, and (3) South Korean workers.

c. Does the plant's relocation help or hurt Americans as a whole?

11. True or False: If firms earn zero profits and if labor and capital are the only inputs, then a rise in wages must be bad for the owners of capital.

12. True or False: If firms earn zero profits and if labor and capital are the only inputs, then labor and capital must be complements in production. (*Hint:* Make use of your answer to the preceding problem.)

13. Suppose that there are exactly three factors of production: skilled labor, which is represented by unions; unskilled labor, which is not represented by unions; and capital. Currently, skilled labor earns $15 per hour and unskilled labor earns $5 per hour. Legislation has been proposed to establish a minimum wage of $10 per hour for all workers, and this legislation has been strongly endorsed by the unions.

Assuming that the unions act in the best interest of their members, can you determine whether skilled and unskilled labor are complements or substitutes in production? What about capital and unskilled labor? Can you predict how the owners of capital will feel about the legislation?

14. In order to promote economic expansion, the town of Hyde Park has declared certain areas of the city to be "no-tax zones." Businesses located in these areas are exempt from all city taxes. As a result, many new firms have started up, each of which rents offices and machinery and hires many workers.

In the long run, which of the following groups are likely to benefit from the existence of the no-tax zones: the owners of firms, the customers of the firms, landowners in the no-tax zones, the producers of machinery, the workers?

Internet Exercise

Agricultural commodities such as wheat and other grains are important factors of production. The Internet site for the Economic Research Service of the United States Department of Agriculture provides information about the demand for these inputs at (http://www.econ.ag.gov/). For example, review a colorful slide show to learn about baseline global demand for agricultural commodities projected to 2005 at: (http://www.econ.ag.gov/briefing/baseline/webshow.htm).

chapter

16

The Market for Labor

There are two types of decision makers in the economy: individuals and firms. Individuals supply factors of production, such as labor, to firms, and demand output in return. Firms demand factors of production, use them to produce output, and supply that output to individuals.

In Chapters 3 and 4 we studied the demand for output by individuals and in Chapters 5 through 7 we studied the supply of output by firms. In Chapter 15 we studied the demand for inputs by firms; now in this chapter and the next we will complete the picture by studying the supply of inputs by individuals.

The Bureau of Labor Statistics provides information on employment trends and occupational outlook at the following Internet site: http://stats.bls.gov/emphome.htm

In a competitive economy all prices and quantities are determined by the intersections of supply and demand curves. We know that the firm's supply of output and demand for inputs depend on available technology (encoded in marginal product curves, isoquants, and the like) and that the individual's demand for output depends on his tastes (encoded in indifference curves). Now we will discover that the individual's supply of inputs also depends on his tastes. It follows that ultimately all prices and quantities are determined by just two things: the technology available to firms and the tastes of individuals.

We will begin in Section 16.1 by studying individual labor supply curves, and then in Section 16.2 we will study equillibrium in the labor market. Sections 16.3 and 16.4 survey two special topics related to labor markets: Why do some people earn more than others? and: What are the extent, causes, and effects of discrimination in labor markets?

16.1 Individual Labor Supply

Individuals supply labor to the market at a price called the wage rate of labor. We will begin by deriving an individual's labor supply curve.

Consumption versus Leisure

Leisure All activities other than labor.

Consumption All goods other than leisure.

Each individual is endowed with 24 hours per day that he can allocate between labor and leisure. Labor consists of working in the marketplace for the going wage. **Leisure** consists of all other activities. Thus, leisure includes time spent on the beach, but it also includes time spent in productive activities such as going to school or looking for a better job.

There are two goods relevant to the labor supply decision. One is leisure, and the other is **consumption**. The word *consumption* is used to represent all the goods that can be purchased in the marketplace. Thus, it plays the same role that "all other goods" plays in the derivation of individual demand curves. Consumption stands for all goods other than leisure.

Consumption is often measured in dollars. We will find it more convenient to measure consumption in terms of the output good that the worker is producing. Thus, if he is a sausage maker, we will measure all consumption in terms of sausages.

It is often useful to pretend that there is only a single consumption good in the economy, so that all workers receive their wages in the form of this single good.

Indifference Curves

We can draw indifference curves between leisure and consumption, and we will choose to draw them with the leisure axis running *from right to left*. This is pictured in panel A of Exhibit 16–1. Because it is not possible to have more than 24 hours of leisure per day, we have drawn a vertical barrier at the 24-hour mark. The number of hours that the individual devotes to labor is given by 24 minus the number of hours he devotes to leisure. This is indicated in the graph by the second row of labels on the horizontal axis.

In panel B of Exhibit 16–1 we have reproduced panel A without the right-hand vertical axis and with only the labor markings on the horizontal. This panel depicts the individual's indifference curves between labor and consumption. They are upward sloping, reflecting the fact that labor is considered undesirable. The slope of an indifference curve at any point is the amount of consumption needed to just compensate the worker for an additional hour of labor. It is the marginal value of leisure, measured in terms of consumption.

In Exhibit 3-16, where we studied the effects of a head tax and an income tax, we ran the leisure axis from left to right, rather than from right to left, as we will in the present chapter. The choice of a direction for the axis is purely a matter of convenience and does not affect the substantive analysis in any way.

EXERCISE 16.1 Use the observation of the preceding sentence to explain why the indifference curves become steeper as you move up and to the right.

Consumption versus Leisure

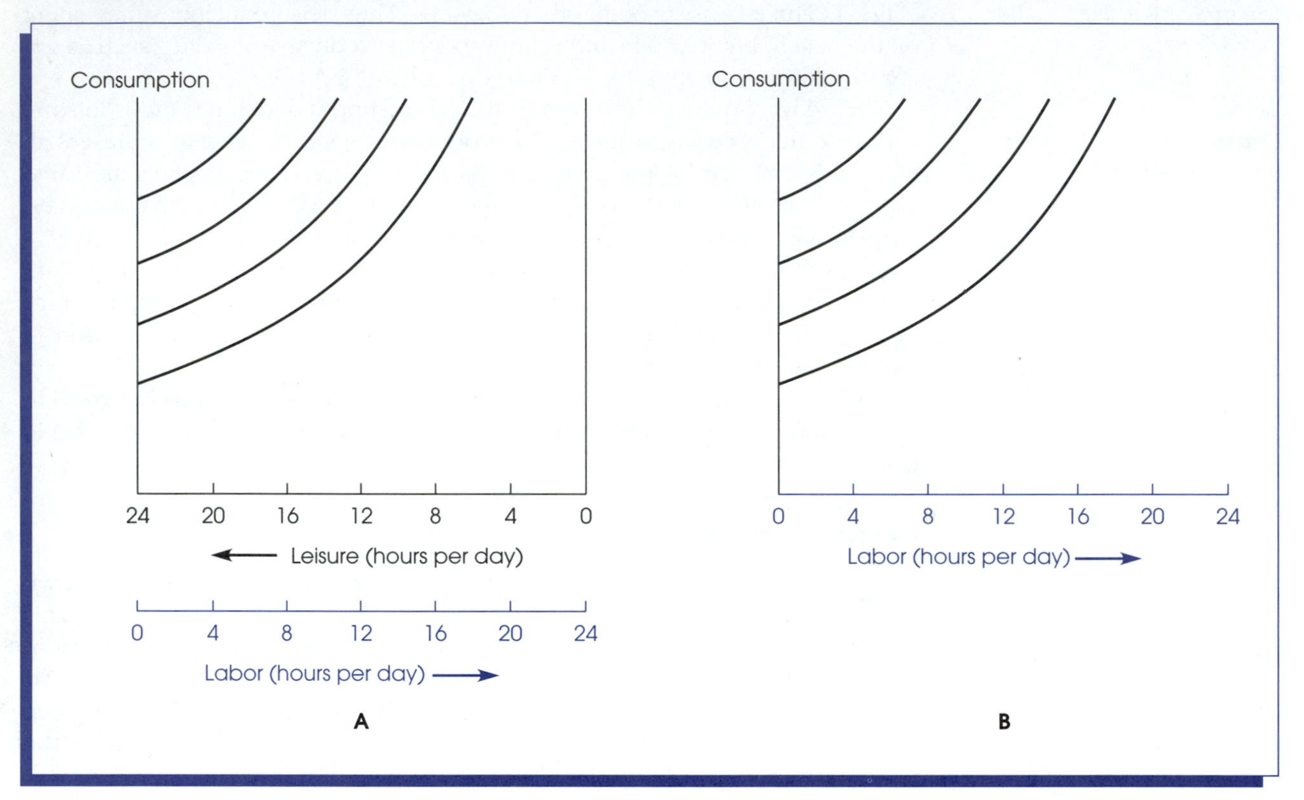

Panel A shows indifference curves between the two goods leisure and consumption, with the leisure axis running from right to left. Because of the reversed axis, the indifference curves appear to slope upward.

The alternate axis in panel A is the labor axis, since the amount of labor supplied per day is always 24 hours minus the amount of leisure taken. Panel B is a duplicate of panel A, with the leisure axis eliminated and only the labor axis shown.

Nonlabor income Income from sources other than wages.

In Exhibit 16–2 we have added the budget constraint. When the individual does not work at all, he earns an income of C_0. This **nonlabor income** is a return to some asset owned by the individual, such as an apple tree, a portfolio of stocks, a small business, or a pension. The slope of the budget line is equal to the wage, which we call W. If consumption is measured in sausages, then W is measured in sausages per hour. Each additional hour of labor yields W additional units of consumption.

The worker chooses his optimum point, which is at a tangency between an indifference curve and the budget line (point P in the exhibit). At the wage W the worker supplies L units of labor. At point P the wage rate (the slope of the budget line) is equal to the marginal value of leisure.

Exhibit 16–2 The Worker's Optimum

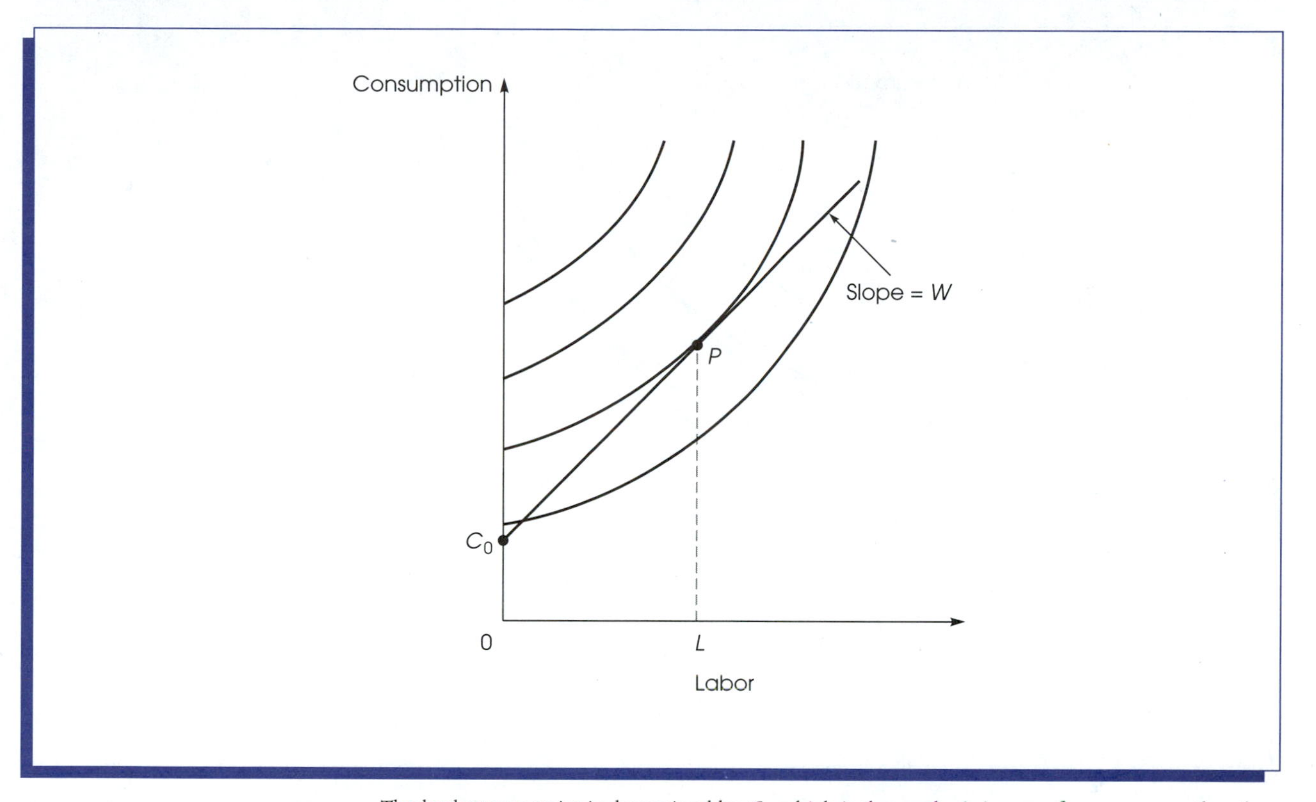

The budget constraint is determined by C_0, which is the worker's income from sources other than labor, and the wage rate W, which gives the slope of the budget line. The optimum is at P, where the worker supplies L units of labor. Here the wage rate (the slope of the budget line) is equal to the marginal value of leisure (the slope of the indifference curve).

EXERCISE 16.2 Justify the worker's choice on economic grounds: If the wage were either more or less than the marginal value of leisure, how could the worker improve his position?

Changes in the Budget Line

The worker's budget line changes if either his nonlabor income C_0 or his wage rate W changes. We will now study how the worker's optimum is affected by each of these possibilities.

Changes in Income

Exhibit 16–3 shows the effect of an increase in the worker's nonlabor income from C_0 to C_1. The new optimum is at P'. If both consumption and leisure are normal (as opposed to inferior) goods, then the worker will choose more of

Exhibit 16-3 An Increase in Nonlabor Income

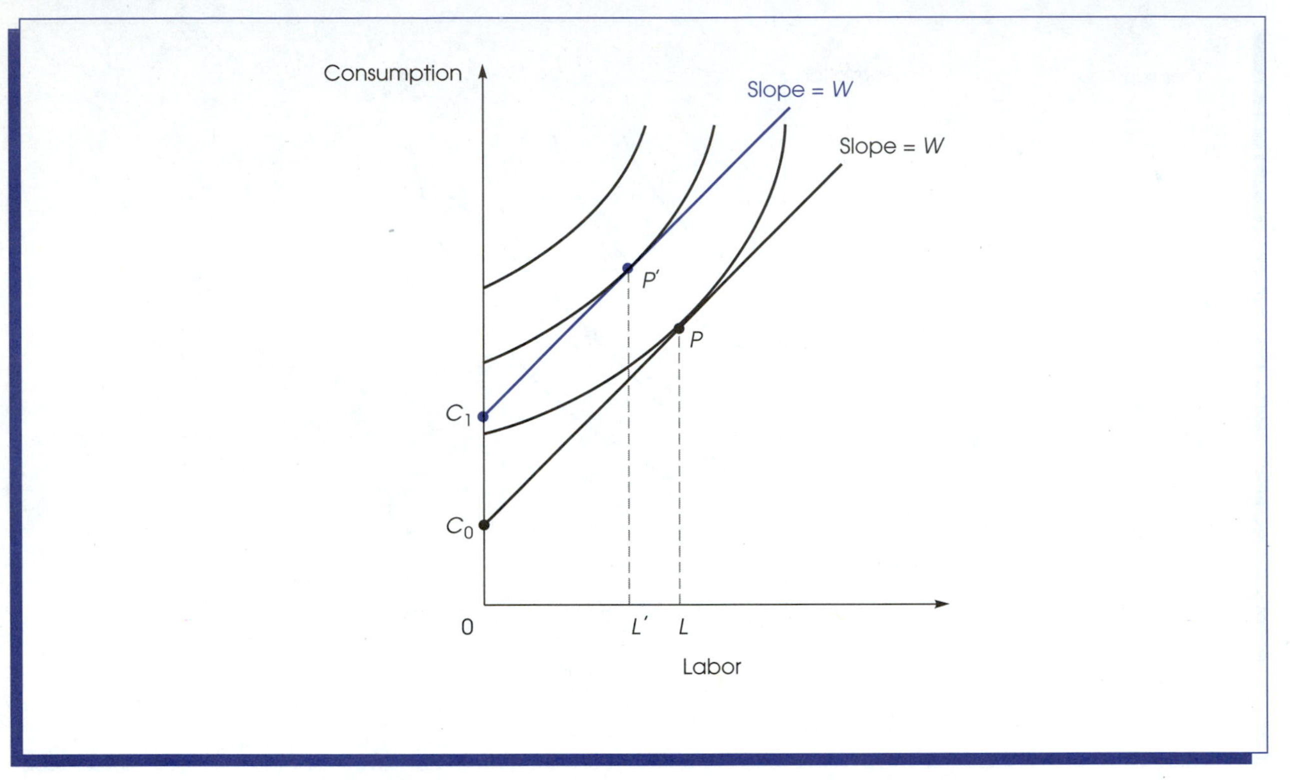

When nonlabor income increases from C_0 to C_1, the worker's budget line shifts upward parallel to itself. The new optimum is at point P'. If consumption and leisure are both normal (as opposed to inferior) goods, then P' lies above and to the left of P. Thus, an increase in nonlabor income leads to increased consumption and less labor supplied. The quantity of labor that this worker supplies falls from L to L'.

each in response to his higher income; that is, P' will be above and to the left of P. Although it is logically possible for P' to be either below or to the right of P, we will assume that the income effects work in the expected directions, as in the exhibit. With this assumption:

An increase in nonlabor income leads to a fall in the quantity of labor supplied.

An Increase in the Wage Rate

Suppose that the wage rises from W to W' while nonlabor income stays fixed. This has the effect of making the budget line steeper. Since there is no change in nonlabor income, the budget line swings through its intercept with the vertical axis. Exhibit 16–4 shows two possible outcomes. The optimum basket moves from P to Q in panel A of the exhibit or from P to R in panel B.

Exhibit 16-4 A Rise in the Wage Rate

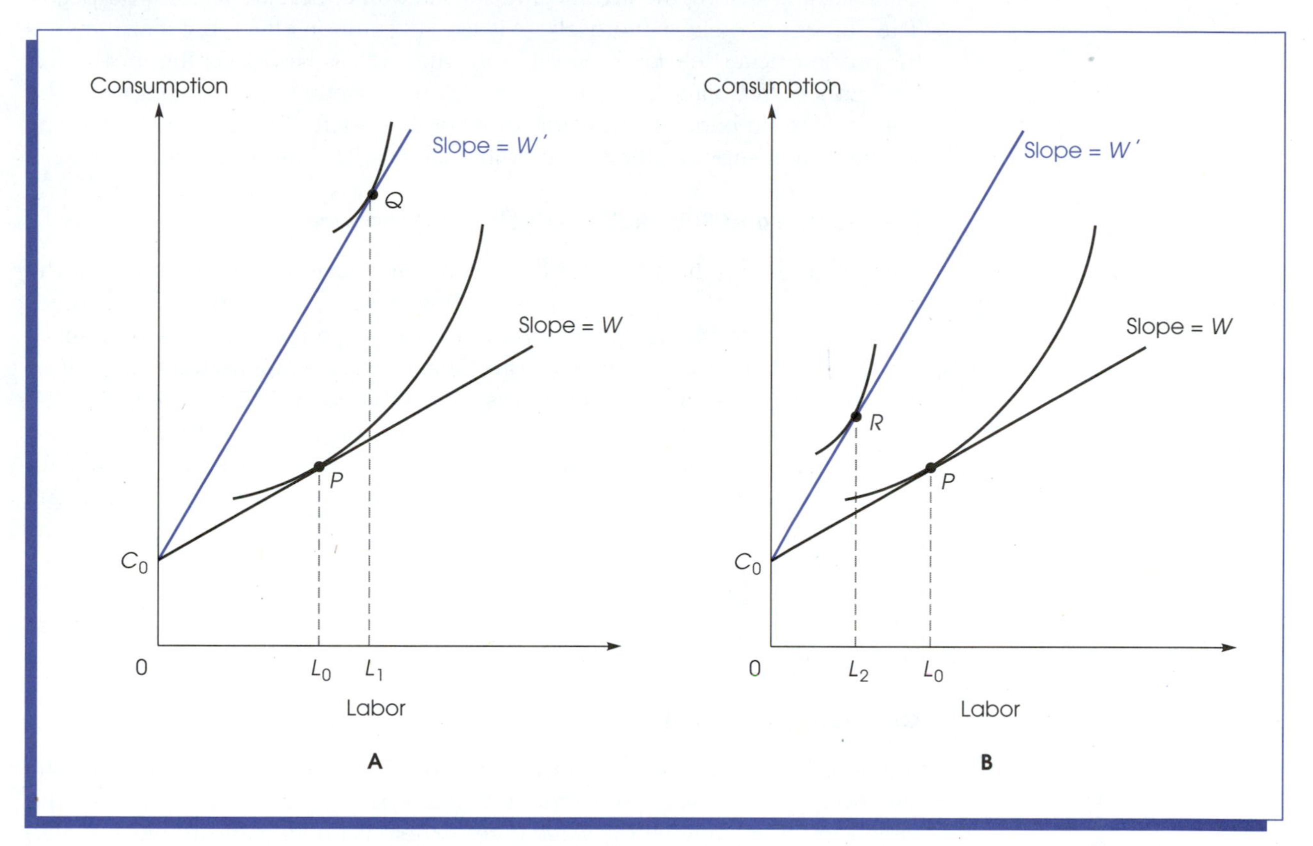

An increase in the wage, from W to W', causes the budget line to swing counterclockwise around the intercept C_0. Depending on the slope of the indifference curves, the new optimum could be at a point like Q, where more labor than before is supplied, or at a point like R, where less labor is supplied.

Income and Substitution Effects

When the wage goes up, there is both a substitution effect and an income effect. The substitution effect is that an additional hour of leisure is now more expensive in terms of forgone consumption. To say the same thing another way, additional consumption is now less expensive in terms of forgone leisure. In consequence of the substitution effect, the worker chooses more consumption and less leisure. Since he chooses less leisure, he supplies more labor.

The rise in the wage also has an income effect in that it makes suppliers of labor better off. As in Exhibit 16–3, we assume that both consumption and leisure are normal goods, so that the income effect leads the worker to choose more of both. Since the income effect leads the worker to choose more leisure, he supplies less labor.

Both the income and substitution effects lead to an increase in consumption (an upward movement in the consumer's optimum). These effects reinforce each other, and we can conclude that the new optimum (*Q* or *R* in the two panels of Exhibit 16–4) will be higher than the old optimum (*P* in either panel).

Regarding leisure, the income and substitution effects are at cross-purposes. The higher wage elicits more labor via the substitution effect, but it also makes the worker richer, eliciting more leisure (hence less labor) via the income effect. Either effect can dominate, so that the new optimum can be either to the right of *P* (as in panel A of Exhibit 16–4) or to the left of *P* (as in panel B). The worker might supply either more or less labor when the wage rate increases.

The Income and Substitution Effects via Geometry

We can use a graph to sort out the income and substitution effects. After the wage rises from W to W', we imagine a downward adjustment in the worker's nonlabor income that just compensates for the wage increase, leaving him on the same indifference curve as before. This gives a compensated budget line, shown in blue in each of the panels in Exhibit 16–5. We now imagine the movement to the new optimum as taking place in two steps: from P to Q' to Q in panel A or from P to R' to R in panel B. The first movement is the substitution effect and must be upward and to the right (it is a movement along an indifference curve to a steeper point). The second movement is the income effect, as in Exhibit 16–3, which is a movement upward and to the left.

In panel A, the substitution effect is greater than the income effect, while in panel B the reverse is true. Thus, in panel A the wage increase leads to more labor supplied and in panel B the wage increase leads to less labor supplied.

Comparing the Two Effects

Which is larger, the income effect or the substitution effect? First, consider the situation when the wage is very low. In that case, the worker supplies very little labor (for example, if the wage is zero, there is no incentive to work at all!). Therefore, a change in the wage has little effect on the worker's income, so the income effect is negligible. It follows that at low wages, the substitution effect dominates the income effect, as in panel A of Exhibit 16–5. Therefore:

When the wage is very low to begin with, an increase in the wage leads to an increase in labor supplied.

When the wage rate is high, both the income and the substitution effects can be substantial. Therefore, at high wage rates there is no way to tell which effect will dominate.

The Worker's Supply of Labor

Deriving the Labor Supply Curve

From graphs like those in Exhibit 16–4, we can derive the labor supply curves of individuals. Exhibit 16–6 depicts the labor supply curves of the two individuals whose indifference curves appear in Exhibit 16–4. Both curves slope upward at low wages, reflecting the dominance of the substitution effect over the income effect. The second curve "bends backward" at higher wages, to re-

Exhibit 16-5 Income and Substitution Effects

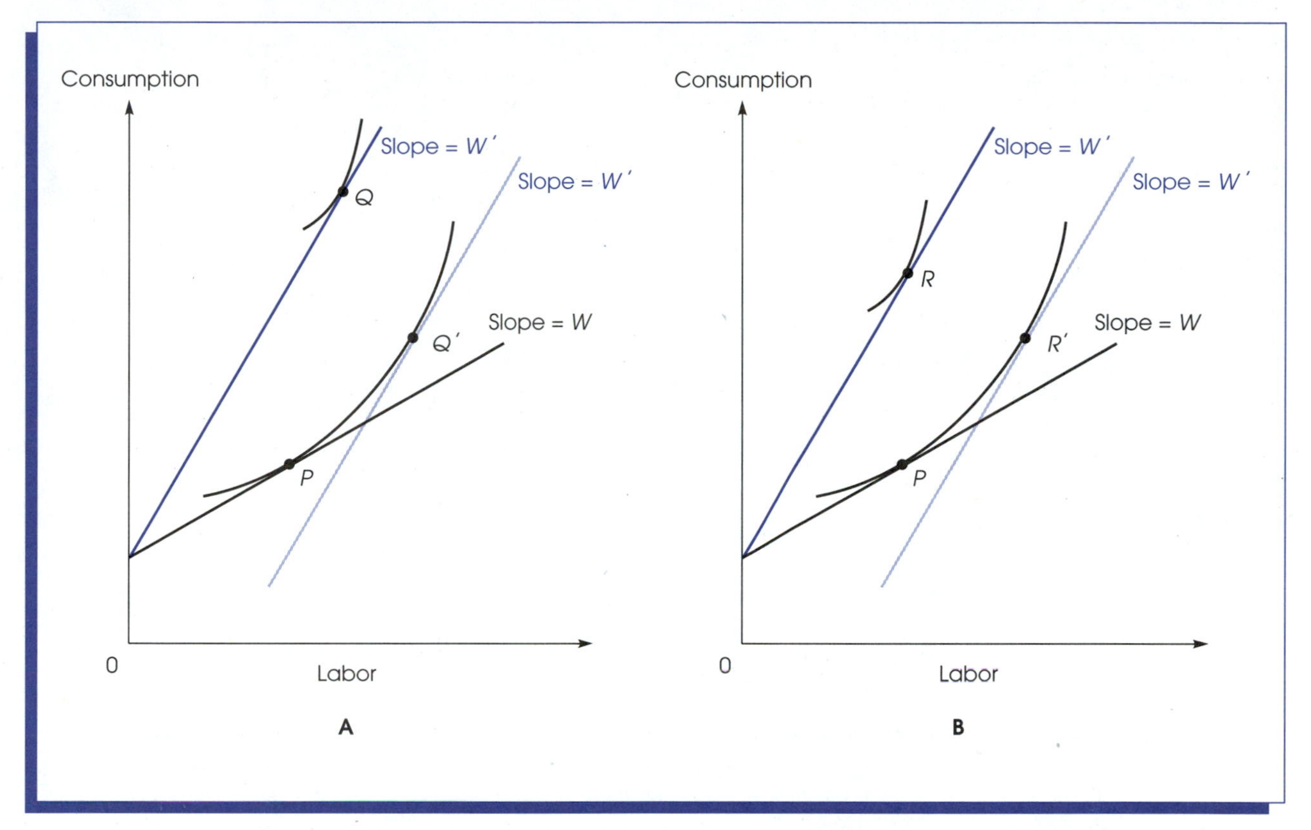

The effect of a wage increase can be decomposed into a substitution effect followed by an income effect.

When the wage goes up, we pretend that the worker loses just enough nonlabor income to keep him on his original indifference curve. In either panel this yields the light blue budget line. The substitution effect is from P to Q' in panel A or from P to R' in panel B; it is a movement along the indifference curve and leads to more labor supplied.

The income effect is from Q' to Q in panel A or from R' to R in panel B. It leads to less labor supplied.

In panel A the substitution effect dominates the income effect, so that more labor is supplied after the wage increase. In panel B the opposite is true.

flect the fact that for this individual the income effect eventually comes to dominate the substitution effect. An individual's labor supply curve might or might not be backward bending.

Using the Labor Supply Curve

Changes in wage rates correspond to movements along the labor supply curve, whereas changes in other things, such as nonlabor income, correspond to shifts of the curve.

Since the early days of the Industrial Revolution, wage rates have increased

Exhibit 16-6 The Individual's Labor Supply Curve

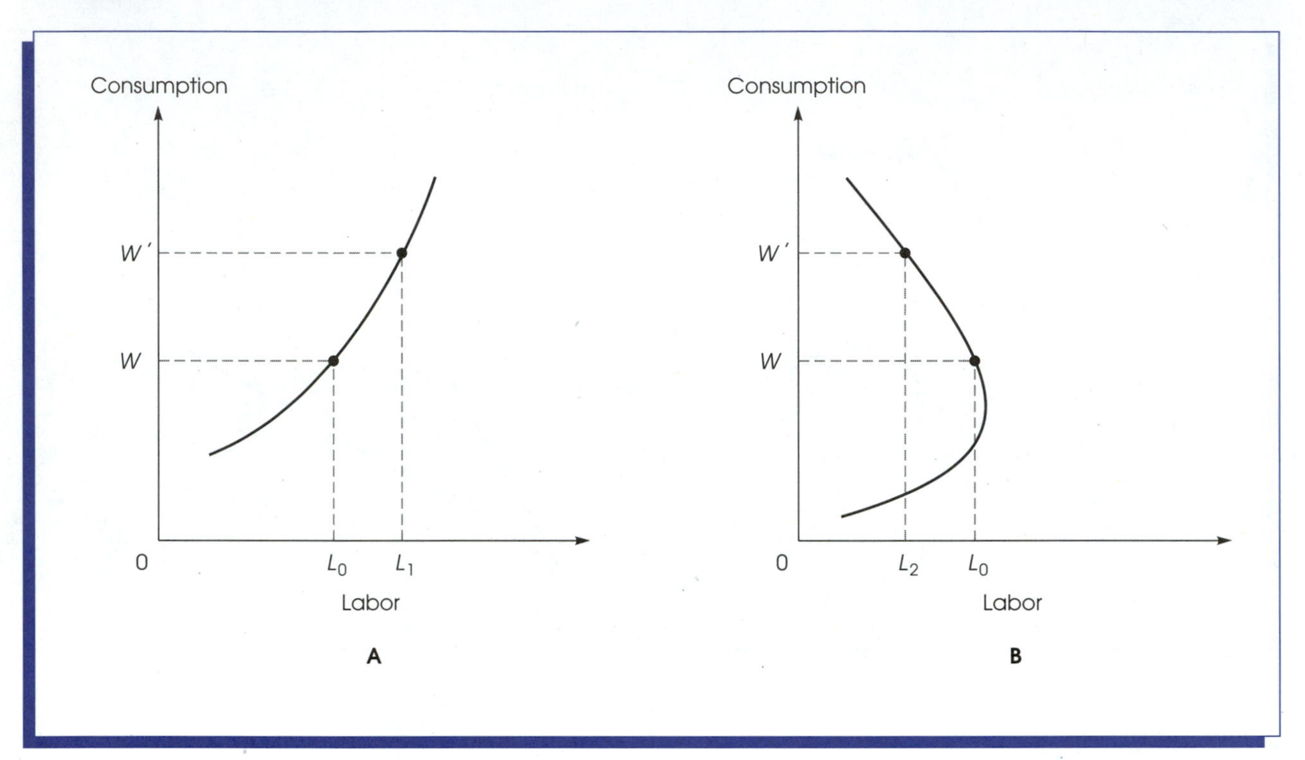

The graphs show the labor supply curves of the two individuals whose indifference curves are depicted in Exhibit 16–4. The enlarged points here are derived from the points *P*, *Q*, and *R* in that exhibit.

substantially and, at the same time, the quantity of labor supplied has decreased. The 60-hour workweeks that were common for unskilled laborers 100 years ago are uncommon today. This evidence is consistent with a backward-bending labor supply curve. However, there is an alternative explanation. Along with the increase in wages has come a substantial increase in nonlabor income. As you can see from Exhibit 16–3, an increase in nonlabor income leads to less labor supplied at any given wage; that is, it causes the labor supply curve to shift leftward. Thus, the fall in hours worked might be explained by an upward-sloping labor supply curve that has shifted leftward, as in Exhibit 16–7.

A Digression: The Demand for Sleep

Traditionally we view the worker as dividing his time between just two activities: work and leisure. Of course, there are many different leisure activities, so the "leisure" axis in Exhibit 16–1 is really a sort of "all other activities" axis, analogous to the "all other goods" axis that we introduce in the theory of the

Exhibit 16-7 A Rise in the Wage Accompanied by a Rise in Nonlabor Income

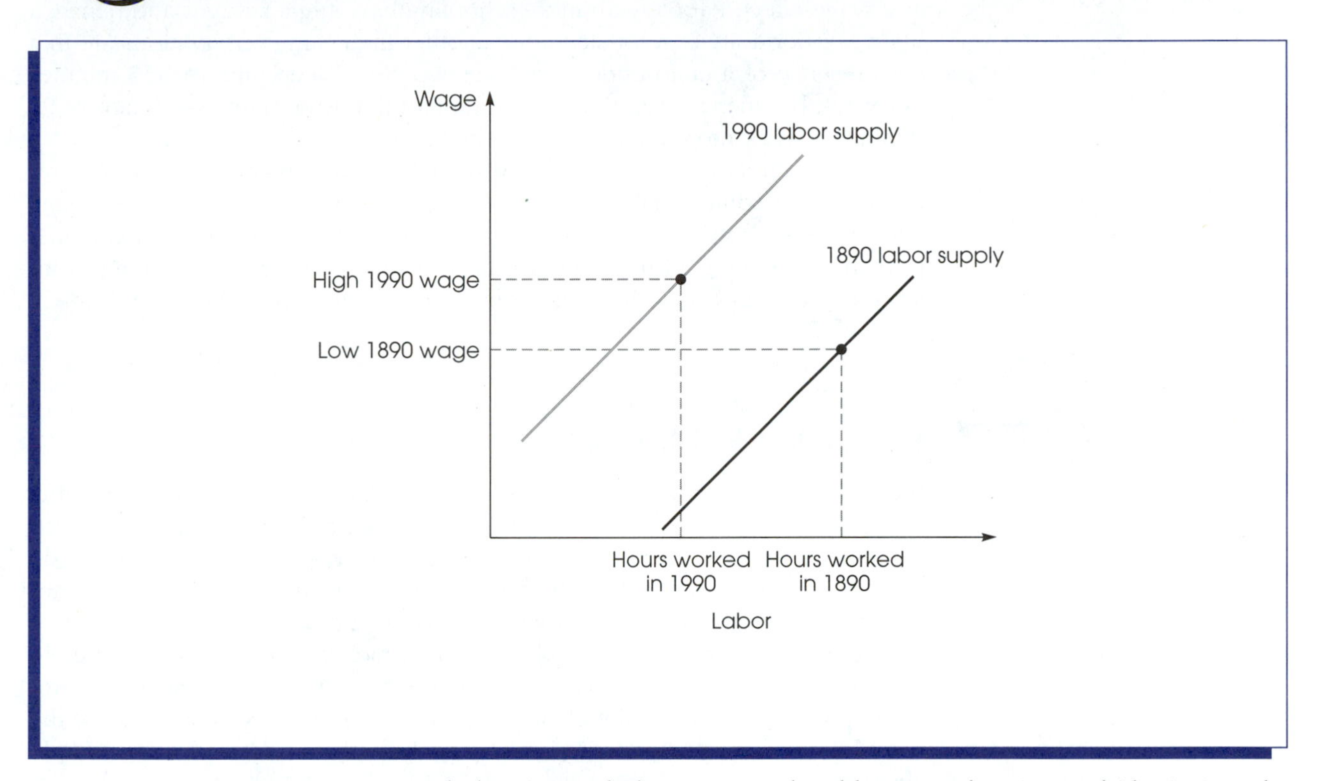

Over the last 100 years both wage rates and nonlabor income have increased. The rise in nonlabor income causes the labor supply curve to shift leftward, as shown. This could explain the observed fall in the quantity of labor supplied.

consumer.

Among leisure activities, *sleep* stands out for two reasons. First, it is by far the most time-consuming. Second, time spent sleeping can have an effect on productivity and hence on the worker's wage rate. This makes sleep unlike most of the other goods we have studied: Merely by consuming it, you can change the relative price (in terms of leisure hours) of the goods that you earn in the marketplace.

Because of sleep's unique characteristics, Professors Jeff Biddle and Daniel Hamermesh have proposed that it be treated as a separate good in the theory of labor supply.[1] Thus, workers have a budget constraint in three dimensions instead of two, the three dimensions representing consumption, sleep, and waking leisure. Moreover, the amount of time spent sleeping causes the budget constraint to change.

In addition to working out the theory of the demand for sleep, Biddle and

[1]J. Biddle and D. Hamermesh, "Sleep and the Allocation of Time," *Journal of Political Economy* 98 (1990):922–942.

Hamermesh present evidence on how sleep time is related to wage rates. Among other things they found that more educated people sleep less (by about 14 minutes per week for each year of additional schooling). They interpret this as a wage effect: People with more schooling have higher wages and hence, a higher opportunity cost for sleep. Some other interesting observations are that the presence of a child under 3 reduces women's sleep time by 153 minutes per week but men's sleep time not at all; and that Protestants sleep almost 90 minutes a week more than Roman Catholics do.

Looking directly at the effects of wage rates and nonlabor income, the authors discern some notable differences between men and women. As wage rates increase, both men and women sleep less, but men devote the extra time primarily to waking leisure while women devote it primarily to working. Nonlabor income appears to have no effect on the sleep habits of men or women.

16.2 Labor Market Equilibrium

We have now constructed a single individual's labor supply curve. Repeating this construction for each individual separately and then adding up, we can construct a market labor supply curve. At any given wage, we read each individual's quantity supplied from his own supply curve; then we add these quantities to get the quantity of labor supplied to the market.

There is also a market demand for labor, which we know from Chapter 15 coincides with the MRP_L curve. Putting the supply and demand curves together, we can find the point of labor market equilibrium. Now we can use the machinery of supply and demand to analyze the effects of some simple changes.

To carry out the exercises of this section, we will assume that the labor supply curve is upward sloping.

Changes in Nonlabor Income

Part A of Exhibit 16–8 illustrates what happens when a single worker experiences an increase in nonlabor income, such as an unexpected inheritance. The labor market (depicted in the left-hand panel) is in equilibrium at the wage W. The individual worker, who is a competitive supplier in the labor market, then faces a flat demand curve for his services at that wage. His initial supply curve is s in the right-hand panel and he supplies L units of labor.

When he learns about his inheritance, the worker feels wealthier and decides to work less, so his labor supply curve shifts back to s'. Because he represents an insignificant part of the market, the market curves in the left-hand panel do not move, and neither does the flat demand curve d. The worker now supplies L' units of labor instead of L.

Part B of the same exhibit illustrates what happens when many workers experience a simultaneous increase in their nonlabor income. This could happen for a variety of reasons. Perhaps a lasting peace in the Middle East brings down the price of oil (which effectively increases the wealth of oil consumers); perhaps the same lasting peace leads to a reduction in U.S. military expenditures

Exhibit 16-8 An Increase in Nonlabor Income

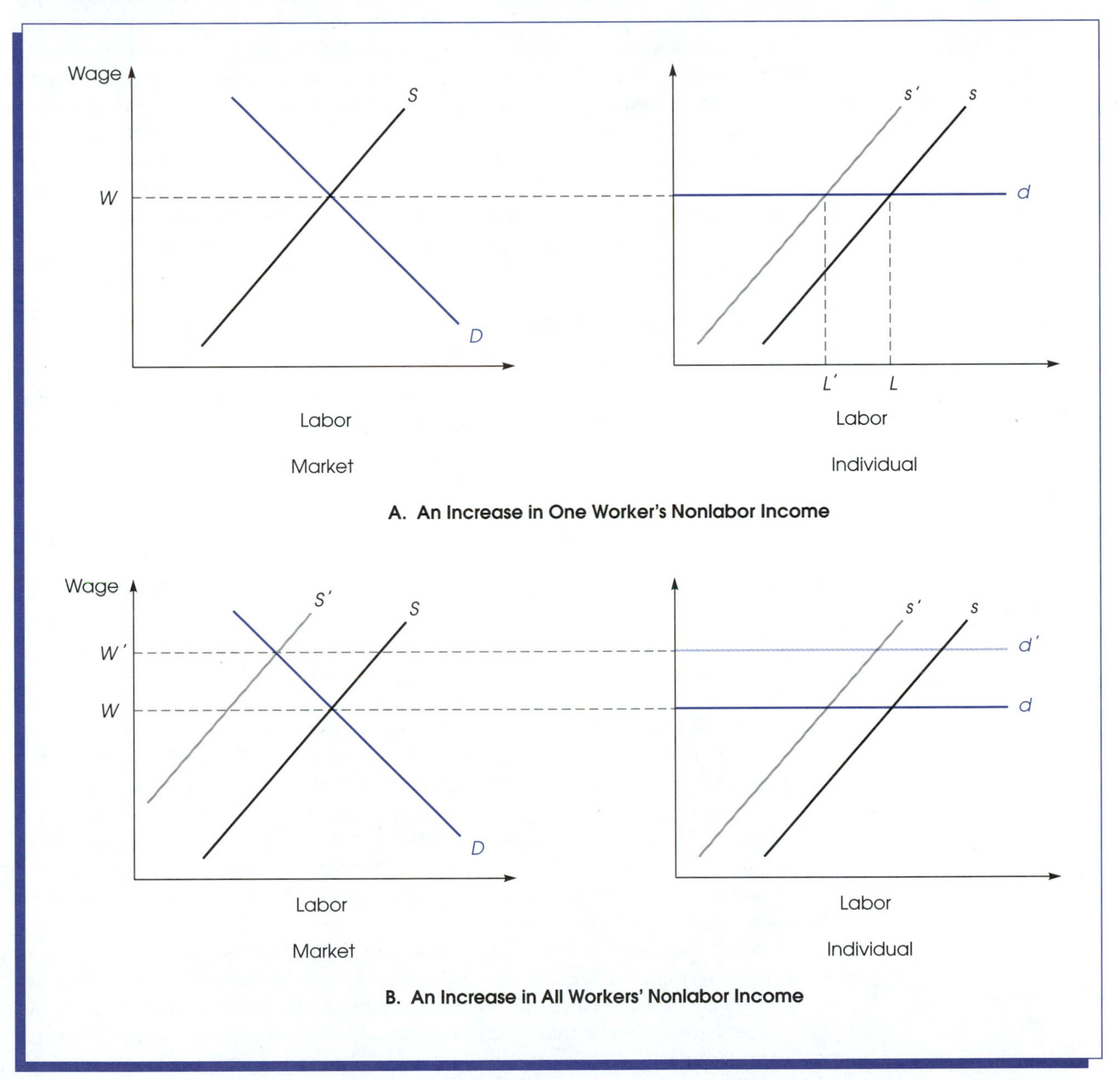

Part A depicts the effect of an increase in a single worker's nonlabor income. The market is in equilibrium at a wage of *W*. The worker faces a flat demand curve at that wage. When his income increases, the worker's supply curve shifts back from *s* to *s*′ and his quantity of labor supplied falls from *L* to *L*′.

Part B depicts the effect of a simultaneous increase in all workers' nonlabor income. The individual supply curve shifts back from *s* to *s*′ as before. Since *all* workers' supply curves shift, the market supply curve shifts back also, from *S* to *S*′. The wage rises from *W* to *W*′. The quantity of labor supplied to the market falls; the quantity supplied by a given individual can either rise or fall.

and a consequent reduction in taxes; perhaps (as happened in 1991) Rocky and Bullwinkle are released on videotape, yielding a widespread improvement in standards of living. Now the individual supply curve in the right-hand panel shifts back from s to s' as before. The new wrinkle is that the shift in supply occurs for every individual, not just one, and therefore, the market supply curve shifts back as well, from S to S' in the left-hand panel. The market wage rises from W to W'. The total quantity of labor supplied to the market certainly falls, but a given worker, moving from the intersection of s and d to the intersection of s' and d', can either increase or decrease the quantity he supplies.

To sum up, a marketwide increase in nonlabor income can lead to either an increase or a decrease in any one individual's working hours, but the *average* or "representative" worker must decide to work less. We know this because the total quantity of labor supplied to the marketplace must fall.

Changes in Productivity

Read more about the determinants of changes in labor productivity at the following site maintained by the National Science Foundation: http://www.nsf.gov/sbe/sber/sociol/works1a.htm

Workers can be made more productive in many ways, including technological advances (like faster computers, which improve the productivity of office workers), improvements in the weather (which improves the productivity of agricultural workers), or unexpected disasters (which can improve the productivity of medical personnel).

Panel A of Exhibit 16–9 shows the effect of an increase in marginal productivity. The labor demand curve, which coincides with the MRP_L curve, shifts rightward from D to D' in the left-hand panel. The market wage rises from W to W' and the flat demand curve for the services of an individual worker rises accordingly, from d to d' in the right-hand panel. Each individual worker supplies more labor than before.

That analysis holds workers' nonlabor income fixed. But when there is an economy-wide increase in productivity, such as analysis is likely to be incomplete, because workers' nonlabor income is likely to rise. Here's why: When workers become more productive, the value of capital increases. (For example, a factory employing highly productive workers is worth more than a factory employing less productive workers.) Therefore the owners of capital experience an increase in nonlabor income. But in many cases, the owners of capital include the workers themselves: Farmers own tractors; plumbers own plumbing tools; and many workers own stock in corporations that in turn own all sorts of capital equipment.

Therefore, a general increase in productivity is likely to yield an increase in workers' nonlabor income. In that case, Panel A in Exhibit 16–9 must be replaced by Panel B. Here the demand for labor shifts out, just as in Panel A, but at the same time, the market and individual labor supply curves shift leftward, as in Exhibit 16–8. The wage rate increases, but the quantity of labor supplied, both by the entire market and by the individual, moves ambiguously.

Temporary Changes in Productivity: Intertemporal Substitution

In March 1989, the *Exxon Valdez* oil tanker ran aground in Alaska, creating an oil spill of historic proportions. Clean-up operations were urgent, so the marginal productivity of Alaskan workers quickly jumped up.

Exhibit 16-9 An Increase in Marginal Productivity

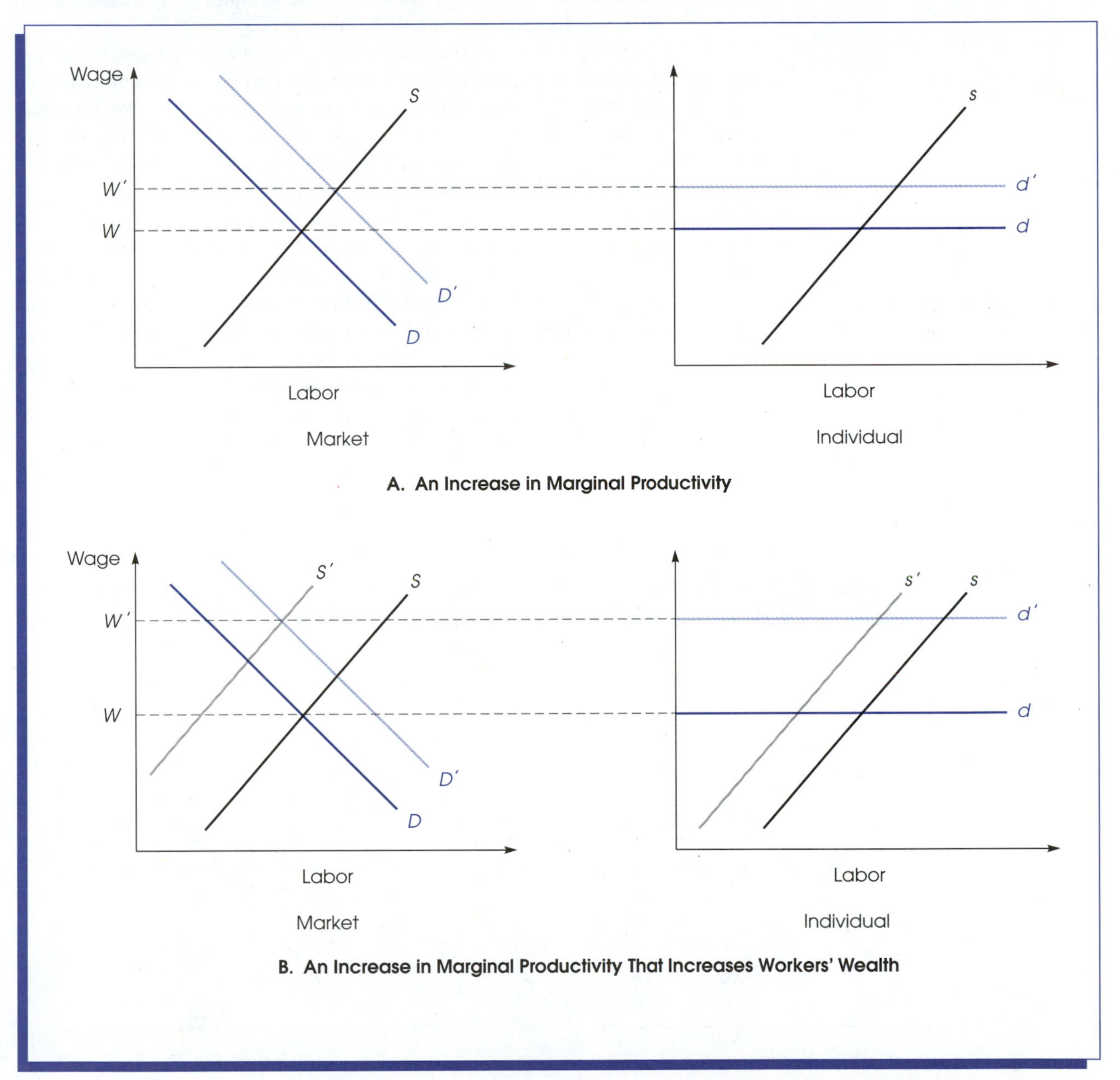

A. An Increase in Marginal Productivity

B. An Increase in Marginal Productivity That Increases Workers' Wealth

Part A shows the effect of an increase in marginal productivity. The market demand for labor moves out from *D* to *D′*; the wage increases from *W* to *W′*; and the quantity of labor supplied, both by the market and by the individual, increases.

Part B shows the effect of an increase in marginal productivity that causes an increase in workers' nonlabor income (by increasing the value of the capital that they own). Demand in the left-hand panel moves out as in part A. Supply in both panels moves back as in part B of Exhibit 16–8. The wage increases from *W* to *W′*, and the quantity of labor supplied, both by the market and by the individual, moves ambiguously.

According to Panel A, of Exhibit 16–9, there should have been increases in both the wage rate and the quantity of labor supplied by each worker. Both these predictions were borne out. Wages quickly rose (from about $9 an hour to about $10.60 an hour), and at the same time, the average workweek shot up from about 35 hours a week to about 49 hours a week.

What is surprising here is not that the average workweek increased, but that it increased so dramatically. In fact, Alaskan wages had been as high as $10.60 an hour just a few years earlier, but at that time average workweeks were just slightly more than 40 hours a week. To put this another way, the average worker's labor supply curve, which had recently passed through ($10.60,40), now passed through ($10.60,49). So the labor supply curve must have shifted far to the right in 1989. What could have caused that shift?

The answer is that the high productivity of Alaskan workers was *temporary*. When there is a temporary opportunity to earn high wages, workers often rush to take advantage of it, working extra hard during the brief window of opportunity and postponing leisure time. (For example, people who sell Christmas trees tend to work very hard in December and compensate by relaxing in January.) Such behavior is called **intertemporal substitution.**

Intertemporal substitution Working additional hours during temporary periods of high productivity.

Intertemporal substitution leads to a rightward shift in the labor supply curve, as shown in Exhibit 16–10. The labor demand curve in the left-hand

Exhibit 16-10 A Temporary Increase in Marginal Productivity

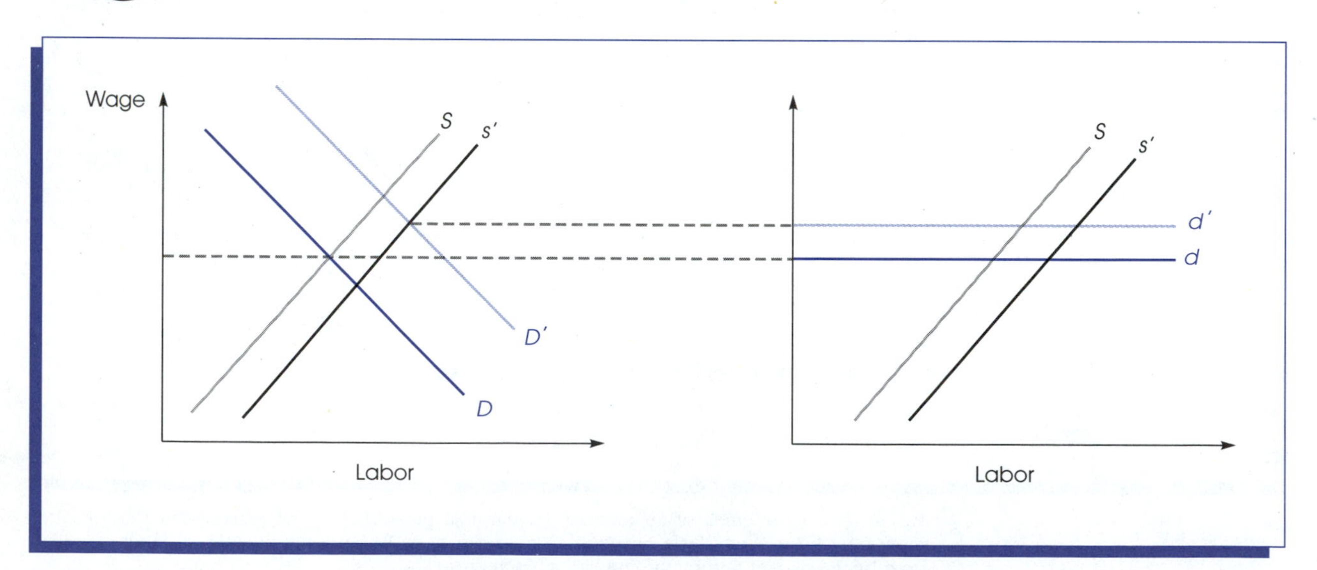

When the marginal product of labor increases *temporarily*, individual labor supply curves shift rightward as workers rush to take advantage of the brief opportunity to earn high wages. As a result, employment rises by more than if the increase were permanent.

panel shifts rightward as workers become more productive, just as in Panel A of Exhibit 16–9. But now, because the opportunity to earn high wages is temporary rather than permanent, laborers rush to take advantage of this brief opportunity and their labor supply curves also shift rightward. The rightward shift in individual labor supply (in the right-hand panel) implies a rightward shift in the market-wide labor supply (in the left-hand panel).

Because the demand and supply curves both shift rightward in the left-hand panel of Exhibit 16–10, it appears that the equilibrium wage rate can either rise or fall. But a fall in the equilibrium wage rate would be inconsistent with the story we've been telling: The entire reason the supply curve shifts is so that workers can take advantage of temporarily high wages. This can happen only if wages *are* temporarily high; thus, the new (temporary) equilibrium must be higher than the old equilibrium to which the market will eventually return.

The conclusion is that, because of intertemporal substitution, a *temporary* increase in productivity has a much bigger effect on employment than a *permanent* increase in productivity. Therefore, intertemporal substitution might be an important factor in determining the severity of recessions (that is, temporary periods in which average income is low, and, typically, unemployment is high).

16.3 Differences in Wages

We have discussed the determination of "the" market wage. Yet it is a common observation that different people earn different wages. In this section we will discuss some of the reasons for these differences.

The National Science Foundation has produced a comprehensive study of human capital, which you can read at the following Internet site: http://www.nsf.gov/sbe/sber/sociol/works1.htm

Human Capital

Human capital Productive skills.

A firm that hires an employee is often hiring not just raw *labor*, but an entire package of productive skills. Some of those skills, like intelligence, may be innate, whereas others, like education and training, are the result of investments by the employee earlier in life. Such skills can productively be viewed as a form of capital, which we will call **human capital.**

We have seen in Section 15.4 that the revenues of the firm are divided among the productive inputs, with each earning its marginal product. A worker who brings both labor and human capital to an enterprise earns both the wage rate for his labor and the market rate of return for his skills. In practice, he usually receives the sum of these returns in a single paycheck, the size of which is described as his *wage*. Of course, workers with different amounts of human capital will earn differing returns.

The use of the word *capital* here is more than just a loose metaphor. As we will see in Chapter 17, capital consists of productive resources that have themselves been produced by forgoing consumption at earlier times. This description fits human capital perfectly. When you attend college, you forgo current consumption, both by making tuition payments that could be used for other things and by allocating time to your studies that could otherwise be spent earning income. The sum of these costs is an investment in human capital.

In the short run, human capital is a fixed factor (its supply curve is vertical). For this reason, payments to human capital are a form of rent. The difference between the earnings of a college graduate and those of an unskilled laborer constitute the rent on human capital.

In the long run, people can vary their investments in human capital. As more investment takes place, the costs (like college tuition) are driven up and the rents to human capital are driven down. People will continue to invest until the marginal cost and marginal benefit from a unit of human capital are equal.

If all people can make equally productive use of an education, then everyone will be indifferent between becoming educated and not becoming educated. This is because the cost of an education will exactly offset the benefits. (If the benefits of going to college exceed the costs, additional people will enter college until this is no longer the case.) If, on the other hand, people are endowed with varying quantities of other skills (like intelligence or perseverance) that make education more productive, then those who have unusually large endowments of these other skills can benefit from education.

Signaling

In Chapter 9, we discussed the phenomenon of *signaling*, whereby a college education can lead to higher wages even without contributing to productivity, provided that it helps employers identify people with intelligence and perseverance. Education can lead to higher wages either by adding to human capital or by performing a signaling function; in practice, both aspects are surely present.

Education as Consumption

We have used education as an example of an investment in higher wages. We have suggested two ways in which this could happen. Perhaps education is a way to acquire human capital; perhaps it is a signal of certain innate skills; perhaps it is some combination of the two.

In fact, highly educated people do earn higher wages than do less highly educated people. However, there is yet another possible explanation for this. Rather than education causing high wages, perhaps high wages cause education.

Suppose that people actually enjoy going to college and view it as a consumption good. Then we expect people with greater wealth to consume more of this good. Just as richer people buy more Rolls Royces, so richer people buy more education. No one would suggest that because rich people drive Rolls Royces, buying a Rolls Royce will make you rich.

Undoubtedly, education is partly investment and partly consumption. To some extent, people purchase it to raise their incomes, and to some extent they purchase it because they enjoy it. Here is a question to ponder: What observable data would help you determine what percentage of educational spending is pure consumption?

Compensating Differentials

Another reason for differences in observed wage rates is that some jobs are more pleasant or less pleasant than others. When there is a large class of equally talented workers available to each of several occupations, these workers must be indifferent as to which occupation they choose.

QA EXERCISE 16.3 Why must the workers be indifferent among occupations? If they were not indifferent, what would happen?

There are many reasons why one occupation might be inherently less pleasant than another. In some occupations the work itself is unpleasant, in others the people employed command less respect, and in still others there are greater degrees of risk. In order for workers to remain indifferent, the less pleasant occupations must pay more. We can view the wage in the less pleasant occupation as the sum of the market wage determined elsewhere plus an additional payment to compensate the worker for the unpleasant aspects of his job. This additional payment is known as a **compensating differential**.

Compensating differential
A wage adjustment that comes about in equilibrium to compensate for a particularly pleasant or unpleasant aspect of a job.

Other occupations are unusually attractive. An employee in such an occupation earns less than one in a more typical job, the compensating differential being negative. For example, many positions offer workers the opportunity to invest in human capital at a cost much lower than the usual market rate. This comes about when an employee, in the course of performing his duties, acquires skills that he will later be able to sell in the marketplace. Such on-the-job training occurs at every level of skill. A postdoctoral instructor in physics at a top university is gaining valuable skills that will increase his marketability in later life, in exchange for which he accepts a wage that might be less than his marginal product. A clerk in a bookstore is observing and learning the business, gaining the skills necessary to be a manager or to open his own shop someday. Again, he pays for this opportunity through a lower wage.

Although on-the-job training is important at every level, it is particularly important at the very bottom of the career ladder, where the skills that are mastered (fundamentals such as knowing the importance of showing up for work on time and how to get along with co-workers) will be useful in any future occupation. In entry-level positions, on-the-job training is often a substantial portion of the employee's total compensation.

Access to Capital

Wages would also differ if workers had access to capital of differing qualities. A secretary in New York City using the latest word processor might be more productive at the margin than a secretary using a manual typewriter in a locality with no electricity.

In making this argument, it is important not to confuse total productivity with marginal productivity. The lone secretary with the manual typewriter in a developing country can certainly be more productive *at the margin* than the 100,000th word-processing New Yorker. In fact, as long as people can move from country to country, wages will tend to become equal everywhere over time because of people leaving the low-wage countries to enter the high-wage countries. This equalization of wages implies an equalization of marginal products. Therefore, the access of different workers to different sorts of capital can explain wage differences in the long run only if there are barriers to the mobility of workers, such as immigration restrictions.

However, even immigration restrictions fail to explain wage differences across countries. If wages are lower in Mexico than in the United States, we at first expect Mexican workers to cross the border until wages are equalized. Then we are reminded that the immigration laws prevent this. But now we should expect U.S. firms to move their capital across the border into Mexico to take advantage of the low wages there. This will raise wages in Mexico and reduce wages in the United States, and the flow of capital across the border should continue until wages are equalized.

We do see some phenomena like this. In recent years, for example, many firms have relocated from the northern to the southern United States to take advantage of lower wage rates. But there has been nothing like the international movement of capital that one would expect on the basis of standard economic theory. Why not?[2]

An answer to this riddle might be found in the external effects of human capital accumulation.[3] When you invest in training or education, you increase not only your own productivity, but that of your fellow workers, through a variety of complicated interactions between you and them. Perhaps some of your new knowledge rubs off in conversations around the water cooler. Perhaps you are more likely to make suggestions or to have ideas that other workers can imitate or that will inspire them to formulate related new ideas of their own. These interactions need not be confined to your own workplace. To paraphrase Adam Smith, people of the same trade seldom meet together, even for merriment and diversion, without the conversation ending in a mutually beneficial exchange of ideas and methods or in some contrivance to increase efficiency.

Through such mechanisms, your accumulation of human capital can raise the productivity not only of your co-workers and of other workers in your industry, but also of the physical capital with which you interact. In that case those owners of physical capital who locate themselves in areas with large concentrations of highly trained people will reap a share of these external benefits. They might be willing to pay higher wages, or higher land rents, in exchange for such an opportunity. Consequently, the difference between land rents in, say, Manhattan and a more remote location might be a tolerably good measure of the value of those external benefits.

If human capital investment yields significant positive externalities, then there will be too little of it. People invest in human capital only up to the point where the marginal cost is equal to the marginal increase in their own pro-

---

[2]This riddle was posed by Robert E. Lucas, Jr., in a recent series of lectures titled "On the Mechanics of Economic Development," *Journal of Monetary Economics* 21 (1988). The answer we will propose is also taken from those lectures, although it is offered there as a clue to the solution of a much deeper riddle, namely: Why do different countries have different levels of economic development and different rates of growth?

[3]An alternative possible answer is that after adjusting for human capital differences, Mexican wages really *aren't* any lower than U.S. wages.

ductivity, without taking account of how their investment affects the productivity of others. This observation constitutes an efficiency-based argument for subsidizing investments in human capital, such as education. If, as we have argued, differences in land rents measure the value of human capital externalities, then the size of such rent differentials could be used in a calculation of the size of the optimal subsidy.

16.4 Discrimination

The following Internet site maintained by the Russell Sage Foundation contains an article by Philip Moss and Chris Tilly that investigates employment problems experienced by black men: http://epn.org/sage/rstill.html

The average black person earns less than the average white person, and the average woman earns less than the average man. Parts of these differentials are easy to account for. The average black is about 6½ years younger than the average white, and younger workers generally earn less than older workers do. A larger percentage of blacks live in the South, where wages are lower generally. Women are more likely than men to have studied sociology instead of engineering.

Economists disagree about whether such factors can account for all of the observed wage differentials. The alternative hypothesis is that the differentials are partly due to discrimination. The existence of discrimination is difficult to measure. One must ask not: "Do blacks earn less than whites do?" but: "Do blacks earn less than whites *with comparable market characteristics* [education, experience, age, etc.] do?"[4] The question is empirical but difficult to settle, because of the difficulty of measuring all of the relevant market characteristics.

The government agencies charged with administering the civil rights and affirmative-action laws have devised various statistical tests for discrimination. When discrimination is found, the firms are required to take remedial action. Many economists have been skeptical of the value of the particular tests that are used, on the grounds that the tests fail to take account of genuine differences in productivity. In the 1970s the Department of Health, Education, and Welfare (HEW) analyzed the employment patterns at universities with the aid of such tests, and it required significant changes in hiring practices on the basis of what it found.[5] Interestingly, an academic turned the tables on HEW. George Borjas reported in 1978 that the very same statistical tests, when applied to data on HEW's own employment practices, appeared to reveal a pattern of discrimination that HEW would have found unacceptable at any university.[6]

[4]The real question is: "Do blacks earn less than do whites with the same marginal product?" In view of the difficulty of measuring marginal product directly, we hope to approximate it with a mix of observable market characteristics.

[5]The Department of Health, Education, and Welfare has since been renamed the Department of Health and Human Services.

[6]G. Borjas, "Discrimination in HEW: Is the Doctor Sick or Are the Patients Healthy?" *Journal of Law and Economics* 21 (1978):97–110.

Theories of Discrimination

If there is discrimination, employers engage in it at a cost. If blacks earn lower wages than equally productive whites, any employer who hires whites forgoes an opportunity to hire equally productive black labor at a lower wage.

In fact, a relatively small number of nondiscriminating employers could suffice to eliminate all wage differentials, even if the majority of employers discriminate. Suppose that 80% of employers are discriminatory and are unwilling to pay blacks more than half their marginal product. Suppose that the remaining 20% of employers are indifferent between hiring whites and hiring blacks, and that these 20% are enough to employ all of the blacks in the economy. Then as long as blacks are paid less than their marginal product, the nondiscriminating firms will hire more of them. This will continue, bidding up the price of black labor, until blacks are earning their full marginal product, just as whites are.

It is sometimes alleged that employers discriminate not out of any genuine distaste for a particular group, but as a strategy to employ that group at a lower wage. Such a strategy would require the cooperation of thousands of employers and would be subject to exactly the same pressures that cause cartels to break down. Any individual employer could gain by cheating. In fact, such a strategy is far more implausible than a cartel, because a cartel requires cooperation only by the firms in a single industry, whereas the "fake discrimination" ploy requires the cooperation of all firms that hire labor.

One theory of discrimination says that while employers might be indifferent between hiring whites and blacks, they nevertheless discriminate because their white employees have a distaste for associating with blacks. Whenever a black is hired, the employer must increase the white workers' wages or they will leave the firm. Thus, because it is especially costly for employers to hire blacks, the demand for blacks is lower and they receive lower wages. If this theory is correct, employers should be able to benefit by hiring all-black work forces, paying the lower black wage without having to worry about the effect on white employees. Employers will adopt this strategy until black wages are bid up to the level of white wages. Thus, the theory predicts a heavily segregated work force, with some all-white firms and some all-black firms, but no wage differentials.

Considerable sophistication is needed to find a theory consistent with sustained wage differentials in the face of profit maximization by even some employers. Since most theories predict a tendency toward complete segregation, it is necessary to postulate a force opposing that tendency in order to get realistic results. One possibility is that blacks and whites have different skills, and that those skills are complementary in production. In this case it would pay to combine black and white workers even if it required paying a premium to the whites. Another possibility is to develop a theory of the costs of changing personnel, so that an employer who would ultimately benefit from an all-black work force will find it optimal to stretch the adjustment out over a long period of time.[7]

---

[7]See K. Arrow, "Some Models of Racial Discrimination in the Labor Market" in A. Pascal (ed.), *Racial Discrimination in Economic Life* (RAND Corporation, 1972), for a survey and detailed discussion of such theories. The first serious attempt by an economist to study questions related to discrimination was in G. Becker, *The Economics of Discrimination* (Chicago: University of Chicago Press, 1957).

Wage Differences Due to Worker Preferences

Some apparent discrimination undoubtedly results from the preferences of the workers themselves. Here is an example of how this might come about.

When a worker seeks a job, he or she typically receives several offers at different salaries. Suppose that men and women typically receive the same range of offers, but that men on average are more inclined to accept their highest-paying offer, whereas women apply many other criteria in making their choice. In this case statistics will show that women earn less than men do, even though men and women both receive exactly the same salary offers on average.

Why might men be more inclined than women to accept their highest-paying offers? One reason is that most married men are trained for more lucrative occupations than their wives are. Thus, if a married couple must live together in the same city, they usually maximize their total family income by moving to the city where the husband has the brightest prospects.

Imagine, for example, a couple in which the husband is a movie director and the wife a professor. The husband is offered a $100,000 job in California and a $50,000 job in Massachusetts. The wife is offered a $10,000 job in California and a $20,000 job in Massachusetts. In this case the couple maximizes its income by moving to California, where their combined salaries are $110,000 instead of $70,000. The wife will earn $10,000, whereas most male professors (who are not married to movie directors) will live in Massachusetts and earn $20,000.

Statistics will show that female professors generally earn less than their male counterparts do, while perhaps failing to show the reason why. The point of this example is not its empirical significance, which at any rate is unclear.[8] The point is that wage differentials can result from supply decisions (by workers) as well as from demand decisions (by employers) through subtle mechanisms that might not be apparent to the researcher. This is why questions about discrimination are so hard to settle.

Human Capital Inheritance

If it is argued that blacks earn less than whites only because of inferior human capital, one must still attempt to account for this interracial difference in human capital. A common explanation is that human capital is largely inherited (we learn much from our parents' skills and attitudes) and that blacks have inherited less because of past discrimination. Of course, this is scant comfort to a black worker who is informed that he earns less than his white colleagues not because he is black, but because his parents were. Yet it surely does make a difference whether blacks and other groups are suffering only from past discrimination or from present discrimination as well. Although two diseases have the same symptoms, the prescribed medications could differ substantially.

Although past discrimination, via human capital inheritance, might play a role in determining the current incomes of blacks, it is at least reasonably certain that this is not true of women. Black people tend to have mostly black an-

---

[8]For some evidence, see R. Frank, "Why Women Earn Less: The Theory and Estimation of Differential Overqualification," *American Economic Review* 68 (1978):360–373.

cestors, but women have only the same percentage of female ancestors that their brothers do.

summary

Individuals supply labor to firms, which produce outputs that individuals demand. Labor supply, like output demand, depends on the tastes of individuals.

Thus, we need to study the individual's indifference curves between consumption and labor. We can begin by drawing his indifference curves between consumption and leisure, which are both goods, and then reversing the leisure axis.

The budget line is determined by nonlabor income (which gives the intercept) and the wage rate (which gives the slope). Once we have the indifference curves and the budget line, we can determine how much labor is supplied.

An increase in nonlabor income corresponds to a parallel shift of the budget line. We always assume that consumption and leisure are both normal goods, so that after a rise in nonlabor income, consumption increases and less labor is supplied.

A rise in an individual worker's wage rate has both an income effect and a substitution effect. The substitution effect, which is a movement to a steeper part of the original indifference curve, results in more labor supplied. The income effect, which is a movement to a higher indifference curve, results in less labor supplied. Either effect could dominate. When wages are low, however, income effects are small, so at least at low wages the substitution effect dominates. Thus, at low wages the individual's labor supply curve slopes upward, whereas at high wages it could either continue to slope upward or it could bend backward.

Combining the worker's labor supply curve with the firm's labor demand curve (and remembering that the labor demand curve is the MRP_L curve) we can find the market equilibrium and study how it changes in response to changing market conditions. A rise in nonlabor income leads to a leftward shift in labor supply. A rise in marginal productivity leads to a rightward shift in labor demand. If the rise in marginal productivity increases the nonlabor income of workers (by increasing the value of the capital that they own) then it leads to a leftward shift in labor supply as well.

When wage changes are perceived to be temporary, intertemporal substitution takes place. That is, the labor supply curve shifts to reflect workers' response to their perception that the situation is temporary. If wages are perceived to be temporarily high, workers will reschedule their current vacation plans for later, if wages are perceived to be temporarily low, workers will reschedule their future vacation plans for today. Thus, it is possible that even small wage changes, if perceived to be temporary, could yield very large changes in employment. This is consistent with what we know of the history of recessions.

Different workers receive different wages for different reasons. Often, a portion of the worker's paycheck is not really a wage at all, but a return on human capital. Workers can benefit by having access to capital of differing qualities, including their colleagues' human capital, from which they receive external benefits. Some workers receive positive compensating differentials for work that is especially pleasant, or negative ones for work that has special advantages.

There are substantial wage differences between blacks and whites and between men and women. Many factors, including discrimination, might be part of the explanation. Most of these factors, including differences in human capital, are very difficult to measure, making it hard to determine the significance of discrimination. Some wage differences result from the choices of workers themselves, as when married women choose to live in the cities where their husbands can earn the highest wage, rather than in the cities where they themselves can earn the highest wage. Economists do not know how important a role such phenomena play in determining wage differences.

Review Questions

R1. Explain the income and substitution effects of a rise in an individual's wage. Which causes him to work less, and why?

R2. Under what circumstances can we be sure that the substitution effect will outweigh the income effect? What implications does this have for the shape of the individual's labor supply curve?

R3. What are the possible shapes for an individual's labor supply curve? Interpret them in terms of income and substitution effects.

R4. Draw a diagram with two panels depicting the supply and demand for labor both in the market as a whole and for an individual worker.

R5. In the preceding question, how is the supply curve affected by a change in nonlabor income? How is the demand curve affected by a change in productivity?

R6. Will employment fall more in response to a permanent fall in wages or in response to a temporary fall? Why?

R7. List some reasons why different people earn different wages.

R8. List some theories that might explain wage differences between blacks and whites. How might you go about testing some of these theories? What problems might you run into?

Problem Set

1. True or False: If an individual suddenly found that he needed less sleep per night than previously, his consumption would go up.

2. Jack can work up to 8 hours a day at a wage rate of W and as much more as he wants at the higher overtime rate of W'. He chooses to work 10 hours. Jill can work as many hours as she wants at a wage of W''. Jack and Jill have the same tastes, the same assets, and are equally happy. What can you conclude about the size of W'' compared with W and W'? What can you conclude about the number of hours Jill works?

3. Suppose that all people have identical tastes and identical talents, but that those who attend college become more productive and hence earn higher wages. On the other hand, college students have to pay tuition.

a. Explain why college graduates and nongraduates must be equally happy. (*Hint:* What would happen to tuition if they weren't?) Use this observation and an indifference curve diagram to illustrate the equilibrium tuition cost.

b. True or False: Because college graduates earn higher wages, they might choose to work fewer hours than nongraduates.

4. Dick recently received a substantial inheritance from his aunt, and immediately started working more hours at his job. If Dick's wage rate increases, can you predict what will happen to the number of hours that he works? Justify your answer.

5. Jane recently received a substantial inheritance from her aunt, and immediately started working fewer hours at her job. If Jane's wage rate increases, can you predict what will happen to the number of hours that she works? Justify your answer.

6. Leisure is an inferior good for Horace.

a. Use indifference curves to show the income and substitution effects of an increase in Horace's wage rate.

b. Could Horace's labor supply curve be backward bending? How do you know?

7. Hortense earns a wage of $10 per hour and chooses to work 35 hours per week. One day, her employer tells her that while he will continue to pay her $10 an hour for her first 35 hours each week, he will now pay her $15 per hour for any additional hours beyond the first 35.

a. Illustrate Hortense's situation with indifference curves.

b. True or False: Hortense might choose to continue working exactly 35 hours per week.

8. Car wash attendants currently earn $5 per hour and choose to work 50 hours per week. A law has just been passed requiring car washes to pay double wages for any hours in excess of 40 per week. The law does not, however, apply to any other occupations.

a. Explain why car wash attendants must remain on the same indifference curve. What must happen to their basic wage rate?

b. True or False: Car wash attendants will certainly now work more hours than they did previously.

9. True or False: A man who earns his entire income in wages will respond more sharply to a rise in the wage than will a man whose income is mostly from property.

10. True or False: Workers who like their jobs will be more productive at the margin than those who don't.

11. Suppose that an unexpected blight wipes out a large portion of this year's agricultural harvest. What happens to the wage rate, the amount of labor supplied to the marketplace, and the amount of labor supplied by any given individual?

12. Suppose that a tornado destroys a large number of major factories.

a. What is the effect on the demand for labor?

b. If the factories are owned by workers (say through stock ownership), what is the effect on the supply of labor?

c. What is the effect on the wage rate, the amount of labor supplied to the marketplace, and the amount of labor supplied by any individual?

13. Suppose that an epidemic kills half the workers in an industry that produces goods for export. What is the effect on the wage rate, the amount of labor supplied to the marketplace, and the amount of labor supplied by any individual surviving worker?

14. In the preceding problem, suppose that instead of being produced for export, the good being manufactured is sold to the very workers who produce it. How does your answer change?

15. True or False: If the capital stock is fixed and if the level of output is fixed, then a rise in the marginal productivity of labor benefits the owners of capital.

16. How would the wage rate and the level of employment be affected by the invention of a costless pill that made it unnecessary for anyone to sleep?

17. Contrast the effects on employment, output, and wages of (a) a year of bad weather resulting in low agricultural productivity and (b) nuclear contamination that lowers agricultural productivity permanently.

18. Contrast the effects on employment, output, and wages of (a) an income tax that is expected to be in effect for one year and (b) an income tax that is expected to be permanent.

19. The current federal tax law allows deductions for the depreciation of physical capital. True or False: One effect of this deduction is to reduce the average level of education.

Internet Exercise

There is extensive labor market material available on the Internet for various career areas. A good place to start is the Yahoo! job site: (http://www.yahoo.com/Business_and_Economy/Employment/Jobs). You can search both demand-side "help-wanted" postings as well as submit your resume and enter the Internet labor supply. If you find that there are few job listings in your career area, or if you are interested in considering alternative careers, you may want to read the Occupational Outlook Handbook, available at the following Internet site maintained by the Bureau of Labor Statistics: (http://stats.bls.gov/ocohome.htm).

chapter 17

Allocating Goods over Time

Markets enable people to trade one kind of good for another. In some markets, you can trade an apple for some oranges. In others, you can trade an apple today for some apples tomorrow. In everyday language, the consumer who trades apples for oranges is a "seller" of apples and the consumer who trades apples today for apples tomorrow is a "lender" of apples. But there is no essential difference between the two transactions. In each case the consumer is faced with a market price (for the lender, the relevant price is the interest rate) and must decide how much to buy or sell at that price. Therefore, many of the tools of consumer theory—most specifically the machinery of indifference curves—can also explain borrowing and lending.

In the first two sections of this chapter, we will emphasize the simple observation that an interest rate is nothing but a measure of relative price. In Section 17.2 we will see that this deceptively simple idea has some extraordinarily powerful applications.

Having come to understand the meaning of interest rates, we will turn to the question of how they are determined. We will answer this question in Section 17.3, using a simple supply and demand model. To simplify the discussion, we will assume that there is no technology available for converting current goods into future goods.

In Section 17.4 we will relax that assumption. This will enable us to study the market for capital and to increase our understanding of the determination of interest rates. However, one thing we will discover is that, despite the artificial assumptions of Section 17.3, many of its conclusions remain true in a far more general context.

17.1 Bonds and Interest Rates

When you trade an apple for some oranges, you are called a *seller* of apples, and the number of oranges that you receive is determined by the *relative price* at which you sell. When you trade an apple today for some apples tomorrow, you are called a *lender* of apples and the number of apples that you receive tomorrow is determined by the *interest rate* at which you lend. Lending is a kind of selling, and an interest rate is a measure of relative price.

By the same token, *borrowing* an apple is precisely the same thing as buying an apple today and paying for it with apples tomorrow. Borrowing is a kind of buying.

In any trade, you are simultaneously a seller and a buyer. If you trade apples for oranges, you are both a seller of apples and a buyer of oranges. If you lend an apple today in exchange for some apples tomorrow, you are both a seller of apples today and a buyer of apples tomorrow. A borrower is both a buyer of apples today and a seller of apples tomorrow.

There is one important difference between buying oranges and buying tomorrow's apples. When you buy an orange, you get to hold it in your hand. When you buy an apple for delivery tomorrow, you hold only a promise. That promise might be strictly oral, it might be written down on a piece of paper, or it might be recorded on a computer disk. Another word for that promise is a **bond**. A bond is a promise to pay.

Bond A promise to pay at some time in the future.

We have said that a lender simultaneously sells apples today and buys apples tomorrow. More precisely, he sells apples today and buys a *promise* of apples tomorrow; that is, he buys a bond.

A lender is the buyer of a bond.

By the same token, a borrower buys apples today in exchange for his promise to deliver apples tomorrow; he buys the current apples that the lender sells and sells the bond that the lender buys.

A borrower is the seller of a bond.

Relative Prices, Interest Rates, and Present Values

There are a number of financial calculators available on the Internet that can be used to compute present value, many of which are listed at the following Internet site: http://www.yahoo.com/Computers_and_Internet/Hardware/Calculators/Online_Calculators/Financial/

Suppose that you lend an apple at an interest rate of 10% (= .10) per day. Tomorrow you receive 1.10 apples in return, so the relative price of an apple today in terms of apples tomorrow is 1.10.

More generally, if the interest rate is r per day, then the relative price of an apple today in terms of an apple tomorrow is $1 + r$. So even though an interest rate is not exactly the same thing as a relative price, it is closely related to a relative price. To go from the interest rate to the relative price, just add 1; to go from the relative price to the interest rate, just subtract 1.

EXERCISE 17.1 If 1 apple today can be traded for 2 apples tomorrow, what is the relative price of 1 apple today? What is the interest rate?

Present Values

Present value Relative price in terms of current consumption.

The **present value** of a future delivery is its relative price in terms of current goods. If the interest rate is 50% per day, or $r = .50$, then the relative price of an apple today is 1.5 apples tomorrow. Consequently, the relative price of an apple tomorrow in terms of apples today is 1/1.5 = ⅔; we say that the present value of an apple tomorrow is equal to ⅔ apple today.

Because the relative price of today's apples in terms of tomorrow's is always given by $1 + r$, it follows that the relative price of tomorrow's apples in terms of today's is given by $1/(1 + r)$. If r is 10% (= .10), this works out to about .91. An apple tomorrow is worth .91 apple today.

Another way to say this is that a bond promising 1 apple tomorrow can be purchased for a price of .91 apple today.

The price of a bond is equal to the present value of what it promises to deliver.

Thus, a bond that promises 1 apple tomorrow sells for a price of $1/(1 + r)$ apples today. Notice that high values of r correspond to low bond prices. If $r = .50$, then the bond sells for ⅔ = .67 apple today (which grows to 1 apple tomorrow at the interest rate of 50%), whereas if $r = .10$ the bond sells for .91 apple today (which grows to 1 apple tomorrow at the interest rate of .10).

Face value The amount that a bond promises to pay.

Discount The face value of a bond minus its current price.

Maturity date The date on which a bond promises a delivery.

The **face value** of a bond is the number of future apples that it guarantees. A bond is said to sell at a **discount** equal to the difference between its face value and what it sells for today. Thus, if the interest rate is .50, a bond promising 1 apple tomorrow will sell for ⅔ apple today; the face value is 1 apple and the discount is ⅓ apple. If the interest rate is .10, a bond promising 10 apples tomorrow will sell for 9.1 apples today; the face value is 10 apples and the discount is .9 apple.

The **maturity date** of a bond is the date on which it promises a delivery. All of the bonds we have considered so far have maturity dates of "tomorrow."

QA EXERCISE 17.2 If the interest rate is .25, what are the price, face value, and discount of a bond that promises 5 apples tomorrow?

example

Treasury Bills

To learn more about Treasury bills and other Treasury securities, access the following Internet site maintained by the U.S. Treasury Department: http://www.publicdebt.treas.gov/sec/sec.htm

When the U.S. government borrows, it does so by issuing bonds called Treasury bills. Treasury bills are issued with a fixed face value and maturity date and then auctioned to the highest bidder. Thus, the size of the discount (and consequently, the interest rate) is determined by the outcome of the auction.

For example, suppose that on January 1, 1993, the Treasury issues a bond reading, "We promise to pay $10,000 on January 1, 1994." The Treasury holds a regular weekly auction at which this bond will be offered for sale. Suppose that after much bidding you are able to purchase this bond for $9,500. This bond has sold at a $500 discount: you have lent $9,500 to the Treasury and will receive $10,000 back. Because you earn $500 in interest, the annual interest rate is $500/$9,500 ≈ 5.26%.

After you purchase the bond, you are entitled to resell it to anybody for whatever price you mutually agree upon. The government will make the final payment to whoever holds the bond on its maturity date. Thus, the value of the bond could vary quite a bit between the date of purchase and the date of maturity. For example, suppose that immediately after you purchase the bond, the market rate of interest rises to 12%. Then the value of the bond falls to $10,000 × 1/(1 + .12) ≈ $8,928.57.

Students sometimes want to know the direction of causality: Does a change in the interest rate cause the price of the bond to change, or does a change in the bond price cause the interest rate to change? The answer is that the interest rate and the bond price are two different descriptions of exactly the same thing, and therefore neither can be said to cause the other. The interest rate r is *defined* by the condition that the price of current consumption in terms of future consumption is $1 + r$. It is just a restatement of the definition to say that the price of future consumption in terms of current consumption (that is, the price of a bond) is $1/(1 + r)$.

The More Distant Future

If we know the daily interest rate r, then we can compute the present value of an apple delivered two days from now. An apple delivered two days from now is worth $1 + r$ apples tomorrow, and each apple tomorrow is worth $1 + r$ apples today. Therefore, an apple delivered two days from now has a present value of

$$\frac{1}{(1+r)} \times \frac{1}{(1+r)} = \frac{1}{(1+r)^2}$$

apples today. By the same reasoning, an apple delivered n days in the future has a present value of $1/(1 + r)^n$ apples today.

EXERCISE 17.3 If the daily interest rate is 50%, what is the present value of an apple delivered two days from now? of an apple delivered three days from now?

EXERCISE 17.4 Suppose that the daily interest rate is currently 10%, but that tomorrow it will rise to 20%. What is the present value of an apple delivered two days from now?

EXERCISE 17.5 Suppose that the daily interest rate is 10%. What is the present value of an apple delivered yesterday?

Coupon Bonds

We can also discuss the present value of a basket consisting of several apple deliveries on different dates. Suppose that on Monday Guildenstern promises that he will deliver to Rosencrantz 2 apples on Tuesday, 3 on Wednesday, and 1 on Friday. The present value of this multiple promise is the sum of the present values of the individual promises it comprises. That is, the present value is

$$\left(2 \times \frac{1}{(1+r)}\right) + \left(3 \times \frac{1}{(1+r)^2}\right) + \left(1 \times \frac{1}{(1+r)^4}\right)$$

apples today (today being Monday). With $r = 10\%$ (= .10), this works out to about 4.98 apples today.

Guildenstern's multiple promise is another example of a bond. A bond of

Coupon bond A bond that promises a series of payments on different dates.

this sort is sometimes called a **coupon bond**. The reason for the terminology is that Guildenstern might seal his promise by providing a set of "coupons," such as those in Exhibit 17–1.

Perpetuities

Perpetuity A bond that promises to pay a fixed amount periodically forever.

A **perpetuity** is a promise to pay some fixed amount annually forever. A perpetuity is like a coupon bond with an infinite number of coupons.

Imagine a perpetuity that pays you \$1 per year forever, starting one year hence. The present value of such a perpetuity in dollars is:

$$\frac{1}{(1+r)} + \frac{1}{(1+r)^2} + \frac{1}{(1+r)^3} + \frac{1}{(1+r)^4} + \ldots$$

Perhaps you know how to sum such an infinite series. If not, don't panic. There is a sneaky way to compute the value of a perpetuity without using advanced mathematics.

If you place a dollar in the bank and leave it there forever, it will earn $\$r$ every year in interest, which you can withdraw and spend as you please. In other words, you can trade your dollar for a perpetuity of $\$r$ per year. Thus, a perpetuity of $\$r$ per year has a price—or present value—of exactly \$1. It follows that a perpetuity of \$1 per year must have a present value of exactly $1/r$ dollars. Our infinite series must sum to $1/r$.

For example, if the interest rate is 10%, then a perpetuity paying \$1 per year has a present value of \$1/.10 = \$10. In other words, \$10 today can be traded for \$1 per year forever. And indeed it can: Deposit \$10 in the bank forever and withdraw the interest each year. Or, if you prefer, you can make the opposite exchange: Trade a \$1 annual perpetuity for \$10 today by borrowing \$10 and paying a \$1 interest charge each year.

Exhibit 17–1 A Coupon Bond

THIS COUPON GOOD FOR 2 APPLES DELIVERED ON TUESDAY

THIS COUPON GOOD FOR 3 APPLES DELIVERED ON WEDNESDAY

THIS COUPON GOOD FOR 1 APPLE DELIVERED ON FRIDAY

A coupon bond is a promise to make a series of payments at specified dates in the future. To seal his promise, the seller of a coupon bond might issue a set of coupons such as those above.

EXERCISE 17.6 At an interest rate of 5%, what is the present value of a perpetuity that pays $1 per year forever?

Bonds Denominated in Dollars

A bond that promises to pay 1 apple next year must sell for $1/(1 + r)$ apples today, where r is the annual interest rate. However, relatively few bonds promise to deliver apples. Far more often, they promise dollars. Such bonds are said to be *denominated* in dollars.

When bonds are denominated in dollars, there is a new complication to consider. We usually assume that an apple delivered in the future is identical to an apple delivered today in every respect except for the date of delivery. The same is *not* true of dollars. A dollar delivered in 1990 had far less purchasing power than one delivered in 1980 because of *inflation:* a general rise in the absolute price level, or, in other words, a fall in the value of the dollar.

Suppose that you deposit $1 in the bank today at 5% annual interest, so that next year your balance is $1.05. If there is simultaneously a 5% inflation rate, how much has your purchasing power really grown? The answer is that it has not grown at all. You will be able to buy no more apples with your $1.05 next year than you can with your $1 this year.

Nominal rate of interest The relative price of current dollars in terms of future dollars, minus 1.

Real rate of interest The relative price of present consumption goods in terms of future consumption goods, minus 1.

We distinguish between the **nominal interest rate** at which your *dollars* grow and the **real interest rate** at which your *purchasing power* grows. In the example just considered, you earned a nominal rate of 5% but a real rate of 0%. When a bond is denominated in dollars, the quoted interest rate is a nominal rate; when a bond is denominated in some real good, such as apples, the quoted interest rate is a real rate.

There is a simple equation relating the nominal interest rate i, the inflation rate π, and the real interest rate r. Your money grows at rate i, of which π is necessary just to keep up with inflation. The real growth rate in your purchasing power is equal to the remainder:

$$r = i - \pi$$

or

$$i = r + \pi$$

There are a variety of different firms that rate bond default risk; you can access a list of such rating services at the following Internet site: http://www.yahoo.com/Business_and_Economy/Companies/Financial_Services/Investment_Services/Market_Information_and_Research/Bonds/Bond_Ratings/

EXERCISE 17.7 Suppose that your bank account pays 8% interest on your money and that inflation is 5%. What nominal interest rate are you earning? What real interest rate are you earning?

In general, it is *real* interest rates that are of real interest in microeconomics, and whenever we speak of "the" interest rate we will mean the real interest rate. In times of zero inflation, the real and nominal interest rates will be the same.

Default Risk

A bond is a promise to pay, and throughout this section we have assumed that promises are always kept. Those economists (perhaps a minority) who have been in love know better. The buyer of a bond that promises an apple tomorrow is buying not an apple tomorrow but a *chance* of receiving an apple tomorrow. When he thinks the chance is smaller, he will pay less for the bond. Thus, everything we have said about the pricing of bonds applies literally only to cases in which the lender feels quite certain that his bond will be redeemed.

A less trustworthy borrower has to sell bonds at a greater discount in order to attract lenders. This is why different bonds carry different rates of interest.

Default risk The possibility that the issuer of a bond will not meet obligations.

Risk premium Additional interest, in excess of the market rate, that a bondholder receives to compensate him for default risk.

The possibility that a borrower will fail to meet his obligations is known as a **default risk.** The higher the default risk, the higher will be the interest rate that the borrower has to pay in order to attract lenders. The additional interest that the borrower receives because of the default risk is called a **risk premium.** We will have more to say on the subject of risk and its effect on asset prices in Chapter 18.

Treasury Bills: A Risk-Free Asset?

It is widely believed that Treasury bills carry essentially no default risk, and that the U.S. Treasury has never defaulted on its obligations. This is untrue. For example, the Treasury defaulted on bill #GS7-2-179-46-6606-1 in 1984.

In order to purchase a Treasury bill at auction, the investor (that is, the buyer of the bond) must submit a payment equal to the full face value of the bond. Following the auction the discount is supposed to be returned to the investor immediately. For example, suppose that you want to buy a Treasury bill that promises to pay $20,000 six months from now. To do so, you submit a check for $20,000 before the auction is held. If the bill sells at auction for $19,000, your discount of $1,000 should be returned to you immediately following the auction.

One unfortunate investor followed this procedure on August 14, 1984. His discount, approximately $1,100, was not returned. Following a series of inquiries, the Treasury took the remarkable position that although the default was entirely due to its own clerical errors, there was a strong possibility that the errors were irreparable and that the discount would never be paid. It required nearly nine months, considerable expense on the investor's part, and the intervention of several senators and congressmen before the Treasury met its obligation. Even then, the Treasury refused to pay interest for the nine months in which it unlawfully held the funds.

The frequency of such occurrences is not known. This particular investor went on to write a textbook in price theory, yielding a bit more publicity than might ordinarily be expected. If there are many more such cases, and if they become well known, then the risk premium on Treasury bills will grow, so that the price of the bills will fall.

17.2 Applications

Suppose your company has the opportunity to undertake an investment project that requires $100 in expenditure today but will return revenues of $50 a year for three years, beginning two years from now. Is the project a good one?

Suppose that you buy a used car and the dealer offers you a choice of payment plans. You can make three annual payments of $400 each (beginning immediately) or you can pay nothing down and then two payments of $635 each (beginning one year from today). Which is better?

Present values give us a standard of comparison for different payment streams. If you are offered a choice between a new car and a Hawaiian vacation, and if you have easy access to resale markets, you should always take the one with the higher market value—even if it's not the one you really want. If the car is worth $10,000 and the vacation is worth $8,000, you can take the car, sell it, buy the vacation, and still have $2,000 left over. So it is with payment streams. After choosing the one with the highest present value, you can always make a sequence of market trades that converts your choice to any of the others and leaves you with extra money in your pocket.

If the market interest rate is 10%, then your company's investment project has a present value of $113.04 (this is the present value of three annual payments of $50, beginning in two years). Since the project only costs $100 to undertake, it is a good one. But if the interest rate is 15%, the project's present value is only $99.27, and not worth the $100 cost.

EXERCISE 17.8 Using a calculator, verify the numbers in the preceding paragraph.

At an interest rate of 10%, three annual car payments of $400 each, beginning immediately, have a present value of $1,094.21, whereas two payments of $635 each beginning next year have a present value of $1,102.07. The first plan is better. But, if the interest rate is 15%, the first set of payments has a present value of $1,050.28 and the second set has a present value of only $1,032.33. In this case, you should choose the second plan.

EXERCISE 17.9 Using a calculator, verify the numbers in the preceding paragraph.

Knowing how to calculate present values and recognizing that a present value is nothing but a relative price are the keys to understanding a wide variety of issues. In the remainder of this section we offer several examples.

Valuing a Productive Asset

Suppose that you are thinking of buying a tree that will produce 10 apples per year forever. How much is the tree worth? The answer is the present value of a perpetuity of 10 apples per year. If the interest rate is 10%, the tree is worth 100 apples. In a competitive environment, the tree will sell for exactly that price (at any higher price there are no buyers and at any lower price there are no sellers).

Dividends Streams of benefits.

The goods produced by a productive asset are called **dividends.** In this case, the dividends are the apples.

The value of a productive asset is equal to the present value of the stream of dividends that it produces.

Corporate Stocks

Economists distinguish between productive assets such as apple trees and *financial assets* such as corporate stocks and bonds. A share of corporate stock (which is usually nothing but a piece of paper) produces nothing. Instead, it conveys the right to collect a share of the dividends from productive assets that the corporation owns. If General Enterprises owns productive assets yielding dividends worth $100 per year, and if you own 1% of General Enterprises' stock, then you are entitled to receive dividends of $1 per year.

Dividends can be paid in either of two forms. One possibility is that General Enterprises can take the $100 and convert it into cash for distribution among the shareholders. The other possibility is that General Enterprises can take the $100 that it earns and use it to purchase a new productive asset, such as an apple tree. Since the stockholders all share in ownership of the apple tree, the value of their stocks increases accordingly.

Accountants and stockbrokers distinguish between the two forms of distributing dividends. They call the cash payment a *dividend* and the apple tree purchase *growth*. To an economist, however, this is a distinction without a difference. It is easy enough for a shareholder to convert one to the other. If General Enterprises opts for growth (increasing the value of your shares by $1) and you would rather have the cash, you can simply sell $1 worth of your stock. If the company makes a cash payment and you'd rather have growth, you can simply take your cash payment and use it to buy more stock. Regardless of whether the company's income is initially distributed through cash payments or the purchase of new assets, the economist calls the benefit to the stockholder a *dividend*.

Using the economist's definition of a dividend, we can assert that:

The value of a financial asset is equal to the present value of the stream of dividends that it provides.

One problem with this "law" is that in many cases nobody can confidently predict the stream of dividends that an asset will provide. A more careful statement would be that the value of a financial asset is equal to the present value of its *expected* stream of dividends, recognizing that there is some uncertainty surrounding any expectation. Even one more qualification is needed: Because shareholders do not like risk, greater uncertainty about performance tends to depress the value of a stock (just as default risk depresses the value of a bond).[1] Often, the present value of the expected stream of dividends is a good approximation to the stock's value; adding in an adjustment for risk makes the approximation better.

Valuing Durable Commodities: Is Art a Good Investment?

Sotheby's provides information on assessing the value of art and other collectibles at the following Internet site: http://www.sothebys.com:80/Collector/emerge4.html

Some assets, like apple trees, yield dividends in the form of physical commodities. Others yield dividends in the form of services. Typically, these assets are durable commodities such as sofas, cars, or houses.

How much is a sofa worth? Suppose that the sofa lasts for four years before wearing out. During this time it yields a stream of benefits that you value at $100 per year. That is, $100 per year is the most you would be willing to pay to use the sofa. The present value of those services is the same as the present

[1] Even this needs to be qualified. We shall see in Chapter 18 that some risks can be "diversified away." It is only the undiversifiable part of the risk that requires compensation.

value of a coupon bond that pays $100 per year for four years. At 10% interest, this comes to about $349.[2] If you can buy the sofa for less than $349, you should grab the opportunity; if not, you are better off without it.

What is the market price of the sofa? The price is equal to the sofa's value to the marginal buyer. If the marginal buyer values the sofa's services at $100 a year, its price is $349. If he values its services at more or less than $100 a year, its price is more or less than $349.

The same principle applies to any durable commodity, such as a work of art. Paintings yield dividends because people like to look at them; the value of seeing the painting is the dividend. The price of a painting is the present value of those dividends.

Suppose you are given the opportunity to purchase a painting that you expect to hold for four years and then sell. During the four years that you hold the painting, it yields dividends that the market values at $100 per year. At the end of four years, you expect that the painting can be sold for $1,500. (This $1,500 is in turn a reflection of the dividends that the painting is expected to yield in the years after you sell it.) Assuming a 10% interest rate, the present value of this stream of payments is $1,373.21, and this will be the market value of the painting.

Now suppose that your personal pleasure from looking at this particular painting is only worth $50 per year. The stream of payments that you get if you buy it is $50 per year for four years and then a selling price of $1,500. The present value of this stream of payments is only $1,198.86. If you buy the painting, you will pay $1,373.21 for something that you value at $1,198.86. You shouldn't buy it.

What if for some reason the expected selling price four years from now rises from $1,500 to $2,500? Should this affect your decision? The market price of the painting rises to equal the present value of $100 per year for four years followed by a single payment of $2,500; your personal valuation rises to equal the present value of $50 per year for four years followed by a single payment of $2,500. The market price is $2,056.22 and your personal valuation is $1,881.88. You still shouldn't buy.

In general, any change in the expected future selling price adds the same amount to both the market price and your personal valuation and therefore makes the painting neither more nor less attractive to purchase than it was before.[3] If the dividends that you collect from looking at the painting exceed the market value of those dividends, then you will do well to buy the painting. Otherwise, you won't.

The bottom line, then, is that you should use the same rule when you shop for art that you use when you shop for clothes or food: Buy what you like. More precisely, buy those things that you value more than the market does.[4]

[2] To simplify the calculation, we assume that each year's benefits are all collected at the beginning of the year.

[3] An exception would occur if you acquired access to information that was not publicly available, so that your personal expectation of the selling price changed while the market's remained constant.

[4] This is not to deny the possibility of remarkable luck, good or bad, that happens when the market's expectation of future prices turns out to be wrong. It says only that you cannot reasonably *expect* to come out ahead unless you value the dividends at more than their market price.

Should You Pay with Cash or Credit?

Imagine that you've decided to spend $100 for a new suit of clothes. Several methods of finance are available. First, you can withdraw $100 from your bank account and pay for the purchases up front. Second, you can charge the purchases to your credit card and settle the debt a year from now. In this case, the credit card bill to be paid next year is $110, assuming a 10% interest rate.

There is also a third option—you can charge the $100 to your credit card with no intention of *ever* paying off the debt. Instead, you make a $10 interest payment to the finance company, every year forever.

Now the question is: Which payment scheme do you prefer? The answer is: Since they all have the same present value ($100 in each case), the options are all equally desirable. To verify this, let us assume that you start with $1,000 in the bank and compute your financial status one year from now under each of the three options.

If you pay for the clothes up front, your bank balance falls to $900, which earns $90 interest (continuing to assume a 10% interest rate) over the course of the year. One year from today your balance is $990.

If you charge to your credit card and pay next year, you leave $1,000 in the bank, which grows to $1,100 over the course of the year. You then withdraw $110 to pay the credit card bill, and your balance is again $990.

Finally, under the plan where you charge to your credit card and never pay the debt, your bank balance grows to $1,100, of which you withdraw $10 to make your first annual interest payment, leaving $1,090. Of this, there is $100 that you dare never withdraw, since the income that it yields is necessary to make your future credit card payments of $10 per year. This leaves you with a usable balance of $990, exactly as in the first two cases.

In other words, all three plans leave you equally wealthy, as we knew they must.

In this discussion we made the simplifying assumption that you pay the same interest rate on your credit card that you earn at the bank. Typically, these rates differ because you are a somewhat less reliable credit risk than your bank is. In that case, a complete analysis of the optimal financing plan would depend on the particulars of your other options and your opportunity costs. But the moral remains that any preference between cash and credit must be due to *differences* in interest rates. Just because you must pay interest on your credit card loans is not enough to make them undesirable.

Government Debt

Instead of buying your own clothes, you might imagine hiring a purchasing agent to buy them for you. The agent has two decisions to make: How much should he spend on various sorts of clothes, and how (by spending your cash or by using your credit card) should he finance the purchases?

Regarding the first decision, your agent's choices might please or displease you very much. If he comes home with $5,000 worth of winter boots and you live in Florida, you might start looking for a new purchasing agent. Regarding the second decision, as we have just seen, the choice is largely a matter of indifference.

The government is like a purchasing agent. On your behalf, it purchases post offices, public radio programs, and strategic missiles. It decides how much to spend on all of these items, and then it decides how to finance them. Among the options, it can pay cash (which it gets by taxing you immediately), it can use "credit" to defer the payment (by borrowing money and taxing you in the future to pay the debt), or it can pay on credit and never pay off the debt (by borrowing money and taxing you annually to make the interest payments).

The parable of the clothes buyer suggests that while you might care very much about what the government spends your money on, and about how much it spends, you will be indifferent among the various methods of finance.

In fact, the argument is far *more* convincing in the case of the government than it is in the case of the clothes buyer. In the case of the clothes buyer, we assumed that the interest rate at which you borrow (the credit card rate) is equal to the interest rate at which you lend (the bank rate). We acknowledged that this equality was unlikely to hold in practice and that therefore the conclusion was only approximately true.

However, when the government borrows on your behalf, it does so by selling Treasury bills, and the interest rate that it pays is the Treasury bill rate. You can earn the same rate on your savings by the simple expedient of buying Treasury bills.

When the government borrows $1 to buy a paper clip, it is often alleged that taxpayers end up paying more than $1: A year down the line, they are taxed not only $1 to pay for the paper clip but also 10¢ to pay for interest on the loan. In exchange for that interest payment, goes the argument, the taxpayers receive nothing at all.

The argument is certainly wrong. Taxpayers *do* get something of value in exchange for their 10¢ interest payment. They get the right to pay for the paper clip one year hence instead of today, enabling them to keep $1 in the bank for one additional year and thereby earn 10¢ additional interest on their bank accounts. They spend 10¢ to get 10¢ and are made neither better nor worse off by the transaction.

Keep in mind that the purchase of the paper clip can certainly make taxpayers either more or less happy than they were before. It is only the choice between paying cash and incurring debt that is a matter of indifference.

This entire discussion goes to show that at a given prevailing interest rate, government debt is of no consequence to the taxpayer. However, it does not address another, more interesting question: Can government debt cause the prevailing interest rate to change? We will return to this question in Section 17.3.

"Planned Obsolescence"

Larry's Light Bulb Company can produce light bulbs that burn for 1,000 hours or light bulbs that burn for 3,000 hours. The cost of production is the same in either case. Which kind of light bulb should Larry produce?

Many people think that Larry should produce the inferior light bulbs. They argue that if the average bulb is used 1,000 hours per year, the 3,000-hour bulbs will have to be replaced only once every three years, whereas the 1,000-hour bulbs will have to be replaced once every year, resulting in three times as many sales for Larry.

It is not hard to see that this reasoning cannot be correct if light bulbs are produced competitively. If Larry's competitors have access to the same technology that he does, he will be driven out of business as soon as somebody else decides to produce the better bulb.

However, this argument is actually beside the point. In fact, it is in Larry's interest to make the better bulbs regardless of whether he is a competitor, a monopolist, or anything in between.

To see the reason for this, notice that light bulbs are valuable only because they can be used to produce light. Suppose that customers use each light bulb to produce 1,000 hours of light per year, and that they value an additional year's worth of light at \$5. Then the price of a 1,000-hour light bulb will be \$5. To compute the price of a 3,000-hour light bulb, think of the bulb as providing \$5 worth of service this year, \$5 worth next year, and \$5 worth the year after that. The present value of this service is

$$\$5 + \frac{\$5}{(1 + r)} + \frac{\$5}{(1 + r)^2}$$

where r is the yearly interest rate. When $r = .10$, a little arithmetic reveals that this expression is equal to \$13.68, which is the price consumers will be willing to pay for a light bulb.

Larry has a choice between manufacturing a light bulb that he can sell for \$5 and manufacturing a light bulb that he can sell for \$13.68. Each costs him the same to produce. It isn't hard to see what choice he should make.

It is often alleged that firms, and particularly monopolies, engage in the practice of "planned obsolescence," whereby goods are intentionally designed to wear out more quickly than necessary, without any justification in terms of costs of production. We have just seen that as long as customers are aware of differences in quality, there is never incentive for any firm to engage in this practice. A profit-maximizing firm will always make a longer-lived product, provided that the additional cost of manufacturing such a product is less than the present value of the additional stream of benefits that it provides. (Larry makes the better light bulb as long as its production cost exceeds the production cost of the cheaper bulb by less than \$8.68.)

This decision rule for firms is economically efficient from a social point of view. The cost of providing longevity is weighed against its benefits. Because some of the benefits are delayed, they should be assessed at their present values.

Try the following experiment. Ask 25 of your friends what a camshaft is. Now have your friends ask their grandfathers. You will find that the percentage of correct answers is much higher among the grandfathers. Most of today's grandfathers learned what a camshaft was about 40 years ago when they had to have theirs repaired, often repeatedly. Most of today's college students will never have that experience. When car manufacturers learned how to make camshafts that lasted, they put their knowledge to work.

Artists' Royalties

Prior to 1990, when artists sold their works, they relinquished any right to benefit from future increases in their value. Sydney J. Harris, formerly a syndicated columnist, argued repeatedly that artists should share in the benefits when their paintings appreciate. Specifically, he proposed that whenever a painting is resold, the artist should receive a percentage of the increase in value since the last sale. We will evaluate the effect of this proposal from the artist's point of view.

When the artist first sells the painting, its price is equal to the present value of the stream of benefits that it will provide to future owners. At least this is the case if the stream of benefits can be foreseen. More realistically, we should allow for some uncertainty as to how the painting will be valued in the future. The price of the painting will be equal to the present value of the *expected* stream of benefits. We will study expectations and uncertainty more rigorously in Chapter 18.

Suppose an art lover buying an oil painting expects to derive \$10 per year in pleasure from looking at the painting for each of this year and next year, and then expects to be able to sell the painting for \$50. (This \$50 is his estimate of how the next buyer will value the future stream of benefits two years from now.) In that case, he will be willing to pay a price of

$$\$10 + \frac{\$10}{(1 + r)} + \frac{\$50}{(1 + r)^2}$$

where r is the rate of interest.

Now suppose that the "Harris Plan" is enacted into law. The buyer is required to pay the artist 20% of the painting's resale price. In that case, the buyer can keep only \$40 when he resells the painting, and its present value to him is reduced to

$$\$10 + \frac{\$10}{(1 + r)} + \frac{\$40}{(1 + r)^2}$$

This is a reduction of $\$10/(1 + r)^2$ from what the painting was worth before the Harris Plan was enacted. The current price of the painting will fall by $\$10/(1 + r)^2$, which is a loss to the artist.

On the other hand, when the painting is resold for \$50 in two years, the artist will receive a royalty of 20%, or \$10. The present value of that royalty is $\$10/(1 + r)^2$. From the artist's point of view, the benefits of the Harris Plan are equal to its costs. He is indifferent to whether it is enacted.

The foregoing supposes that the buyer is correct in his expectation that he can sell the painting in two years for \$50. Suppose he turns out to be wrong. Suppose the artist's reputation blossoms, and the painting is sold for \$100, on which the artist's royalty is \$20. The present value of that royalty is $\$20/(1 + r)^2$. The Harris Plan has benefited this artist. The initial value of his painting fell by $\$10/(1 + r)^2$, but this is offset by a future royalty with twice that present value.

Another possibility is that the buyer has been too rosy in his expectations. Suppose that in two years the artist has been forgotten, and his painting sells for only \$15. The royalty is \$3, with a present value of $\$3/(1 + r)^2$. This is insufficient to offset the initial price reduction of $\$10/(1 + r)^2$. This artist is a loser under the Harris Plan.

Who gains and who loses? The average artist—the one whose career turns out about as expected—just breaks even. The artist whose career goes much better than expected is a winner, and the artist who is less successful than expected is a loser. Thus, the Harris Plan is a way to transfer income from unsuccessful artists to successful artists.

Old Taxes Are Fair Taxes

One hundred fifty years ago, Coconino County imposed an annual tax of \$10 per acre on all landowners. Landowners to this day grumble about the tax. The mayor has decided that the tax represents an unfair burden and has called for its repeal, to correct a historical injustice.

Although the tax might have been a great injustice, repealing the tax is unlikely to correct it. When the tax was imposed, the value of an acre of land plummeted by exactly $\$10/r$, the value of a perpetuity of \$10 per year. Any land sold in the last 150 years has been sold at the new depressed value.

Exhibit 17–2 shows the market for land in Coconino County 150 years ago. After the tax was imposed, the demand curve fell by $\$10/r$ per acre. The price fell from P to $P - \$10/r$. Producers' surplus fell from $C + D + E$ to just E. Consumers' surplus remained constant at $A + B$. Buyers of land lost nothing as a result of the tax; its burden fell completely on the sellers.

Any parcel of land in Coconino County that has been sold at any time in the last 150 years is now owned by somebody who was fully compensated for the infinite stream of future taxes through a reduced purchase price. If the tax is removed now, the current owners will receive a windfall, as the price of the land rises back to P and its total value increases by $C + D$. The full burden of the tax is still being borne by the heirs of the original owners, now probably scattered and unidentifiable.

The Pricing of Exhaustible Resources

A resource is *exhaustible* if every unit consumed today implies that one less unit will be available in the future. Oil is often said to be an exhaustible resource. The coal available from a given mine is a good example.

When a resource is exhaustible, the forgone opportunity to use it in the future becomes a part of the cost of consuming it today. Suppose that coal sells competitively at a going price of P_0 today and is expected to sell at a price of P_1 tomorrow. Suppose also that the cost of digging out any particular nugget of coal is the same on each day. Then any nugget dug out and sold today entails a forgone opportunity to dig out and sell that same nugget tomorrow. The forgone profit on that nugget is $P_1 - MC$, where MC is the marginal cost of physically removing the coal from the ground. The present value of that forgone opportunity is $(P_1 - MC)/(1 + r)$.

The full marginal cost of removing and selling a pound of coal is equal to

Exhibit 17-2 Old Taxes Are Fair Taxes

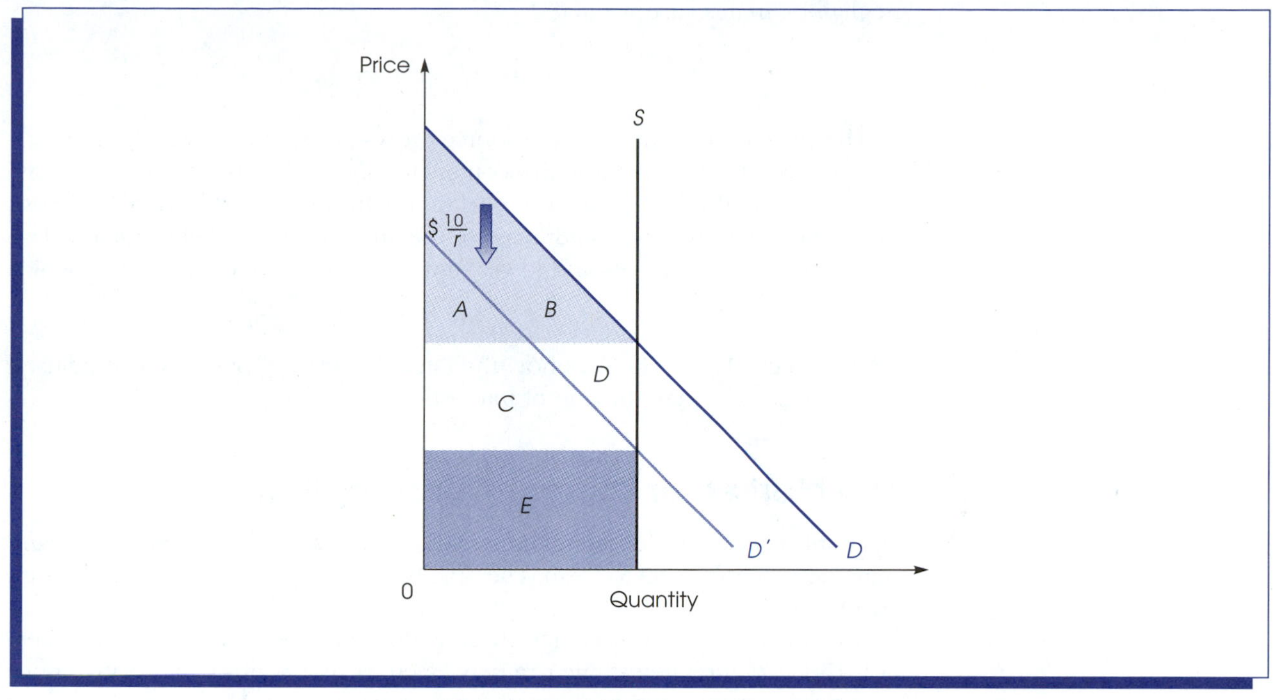

The graph shows the market for land in Coconino County 150 years ago, when an annual \$10-per-acre tax on landholdings was first instituted. The demand curve fell by \$10/*r* per acre, and because of the vertical supply curve, the price fell by \$10/*r*. The landowners of Coconino County suffered a loss in producers' surplus of $C + D$. The buyers of land lost nothing. The price of the land that they bought was reduced by enough to compensate them for the infinite stream of future taxation.

If the tax is repealed, everyone who has bought Coconino County land in the last 150 years will reap a windfall gain. Except in those cases where the land has never changed hands, the winners will be people who were never hurt by the tax in the first place.

---

the sum of the marginal cost of digging it out and the present value of the forgone opportunity to sell it tomorrow. This comes to

$$MC + \frac{P_1 - MC}{1 + r}$$

A competitive producer will choose a quantity where the current price is equal to this full marginal cost, or

$$P_0 = MC + \frac{P_1 - MC}{1 + r}$$

Now a little algebra shows that

$$P_1 = P_0 \cdot (1 + r) - r \cdot MC$$

This equation predicts the price of an exhaustible resource next year in terms of its price this year, the interest rate, and the marginal cost of production.

The equation is particularly simple and intuitive when marginal costs are negligible. In this case we get

$$P_1 = P_0 \cdot (1 + r)$$

The price of the exhaustible resource grows at exactly the rate of interest.

There is a great deal of intuitive content to this result. If the price were growing faster than the rate of interest, coal in the ground would be a good investment and mine owners would increase the amount of coal left unmined. This would raise current prices and lower future prices, reducing the rate at which prices grow.

EXERCISE 17.10 Explain how the rate of growth of prices would adjust if it were less than the rate of interest.

17.3 The Market for Current Consumption

Up until now, we have been taking market interest rates as given and examining how people react to them. The time has come to ask what determines interest rates.

The answer lies in our earlier observation (near the very beginning of Section 17.1) that the interest rate can be viewed as a measure of the relative price of current consumption in terms of future consumption. More precisely, if the daily interest rate is r, then the price of an apple today is $1 + r$ apples tomorrow. Knowing the interest rate is the same thing as knowing the relative price. Price is determined by demand and supply. Thus, we must examine the demand and supply for current consumption.

The Consumer's Choice

When we want to study how people allocate their consumption between apples and oranges, we begin with an indifference curve diagram in which apples appear on the horizontal axis and oranges appear on the vertical. When we want to study how people allocate their consumption between apples today and apples tomorrow, we begin with an indifference curve diagram in which apples today appear on the horizontal axis and apples tomorrow appear on the vertical. The indifference curves of Ken the Consumer are shown in Exhibit 17–3.

Endowment The basket of goods that somebody starts with, prior to any trading.

We assume that Ken has an **endowment** of 6 apples today and 6 apples tomorrow. These are the apples that Ken starts with, prior to any trading. Perhaps they come from an apple tree in his backyard, or maybe he has a job that pays a wage of 6 apples per day. Point A represents Ken's endowment.

Time Preference

As we know from consumer theory, the absolute slope of Ken's indifference curve represents the marginal value to Ken of an apple today, measured in

Exhibit 17-3 The Consumer's Preferences

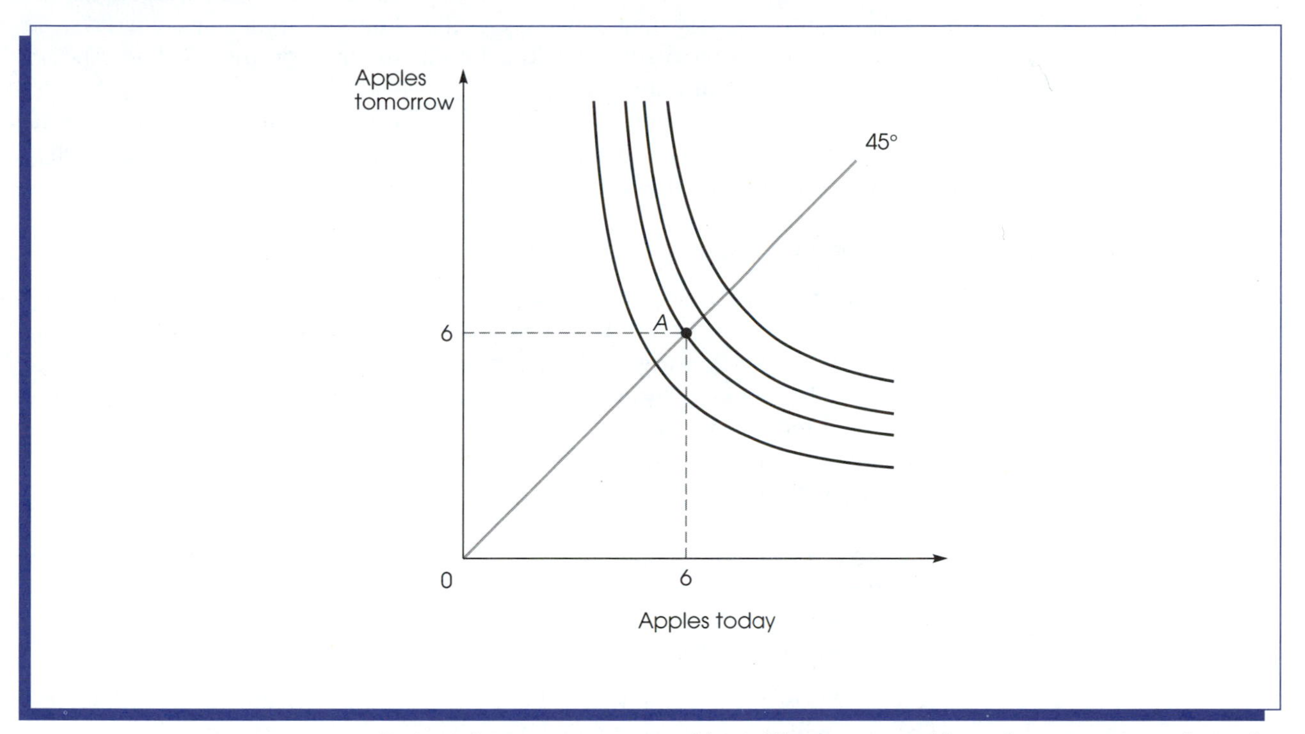

Ken's preferences are represented by indifference curves. The endowment point *A* depicts his holdings before he does any trading. In this example the endowment point is on the 45° line, which means that he is endowed with the same number of apples each day. Under these circumstances we expect that Ken values 1 additional apple today more than 1 additional apple tomorrow. Therefore, at a point like *A*, the absolute value of the slope of the indifference curve is greater than 1.

terms of apples tomorrow. For a variety of reasons, we expect this slope to be greater than 1. That is, we think that 1 additional apple today is worth more to Ken than 1 additional apple tomorrow.

One reason for this expectation is our belief that people are naturally impatient and would prefer to eat now rather than later. Another reason is that Ken is unsure what the future will bring: Since he might be hit by a truck before tomorrow ever comes, he might never get to enjoy tomorrow's apple. Yet a third reason is that an apple once eaten yields a lifetime's worth of pleasant memories. An apple eaten today yields one more day of these pleasures than does an apple eaten tomorrow.

Without committing ourselves fully or exclusively to any of these combinations, we will assume that Ken prefers 1 more apple today to 1 more apple tomorrow, or, in other words, that the absolute slope of his indifference curve at point *A* is greater than 1.

If Ken had a different endowment, say with 100 apples today and 2 tomorrow, we might have a different expectation. In these circumstances, 1 additional apple today is not likely to be very valuable to Ken. Our belief that his indifference curve has absolute slope greater than 1 is predicated on the fact that his initial endowment contains equal numbers of apples on both days. Geometrically, this means that his initial endowment is on the 45° line. The 45° line is illustrated in Exhibit 17–3.

Our assumption, then, is this: At points on the 45° line, Ken's indifference curves have slopes that are greater than 1 in absolute value. Off the 45° line, this assumption need not hold.

Opportunities

Suppose that Ken is given the opportunity to borrow or lend at a market interest rate of 10%. That is, he can buy and sell "apples today" at a relative price of 1.10 apples tomorrow. This means that he faces a budget line with absolute slope 1.10. We also know that his budget line must pass through his endowment point *A*, since he can achieve point *A* by simply not trading at all. The slope and a point are all we need to draw the budget line. It is illustrated in panel A of Exhibit 17–4.

If the interest rate were to change, Ken's budget line would rotate around point *A*, becoming steeper for a rise in the interest rate or flatter for a fall in the interest rate.

The Consumer's Optimum

Ken chooses the point where his budget line is tangent to an indifference curve, which is point *B* in panel A of Exhibit 17–4. At this point he consumes 8 apples today and 3.8 tomorrow. Ken achieves this outcome by borrowing 2 apples to add to his endowment of 6 today; tomorrow he pays back the loan with 2.2 apples out of his endowment of 6 tomorrow.

Ken's neighbor Barb has the same endowment as Ken and the same budget line, but she has different preferences. Panel B of Exhibit 17–4 shows that Barb chooses point *C*, with 5 apples today and 7.1 tomorrow. She achieves this by lending 1 apple out of her endowment of 6 today and collecting 1.1 apples to add to her endowment of 6 tomorrow.

The two panels of Exhibit 17–4 illustrate that, depending on preferences, the consumer's optimum could occur on either side of the initial endowment, and therefore he might decide either to borrow or to lend. However, if the interest rate had been 0%, giving the budget lines a slope of -1, then we know that both Ken and Barb would have been borrowers, consuming more than 6 apples today. The reason is that both Ken and Barb have indifference curves whose slopes at point *A* exceed 1 in absolute value; this forces the tangency to occur below and to the right of *A*.

The Demand for Current Consumption

We can use panel A of Exhibit 17–4 to generate a point on Ken's demand curve for current consumption. The exhibit tells us that when the interest rate is 10%,

Exhibit 17–4 The Consumer's Choice

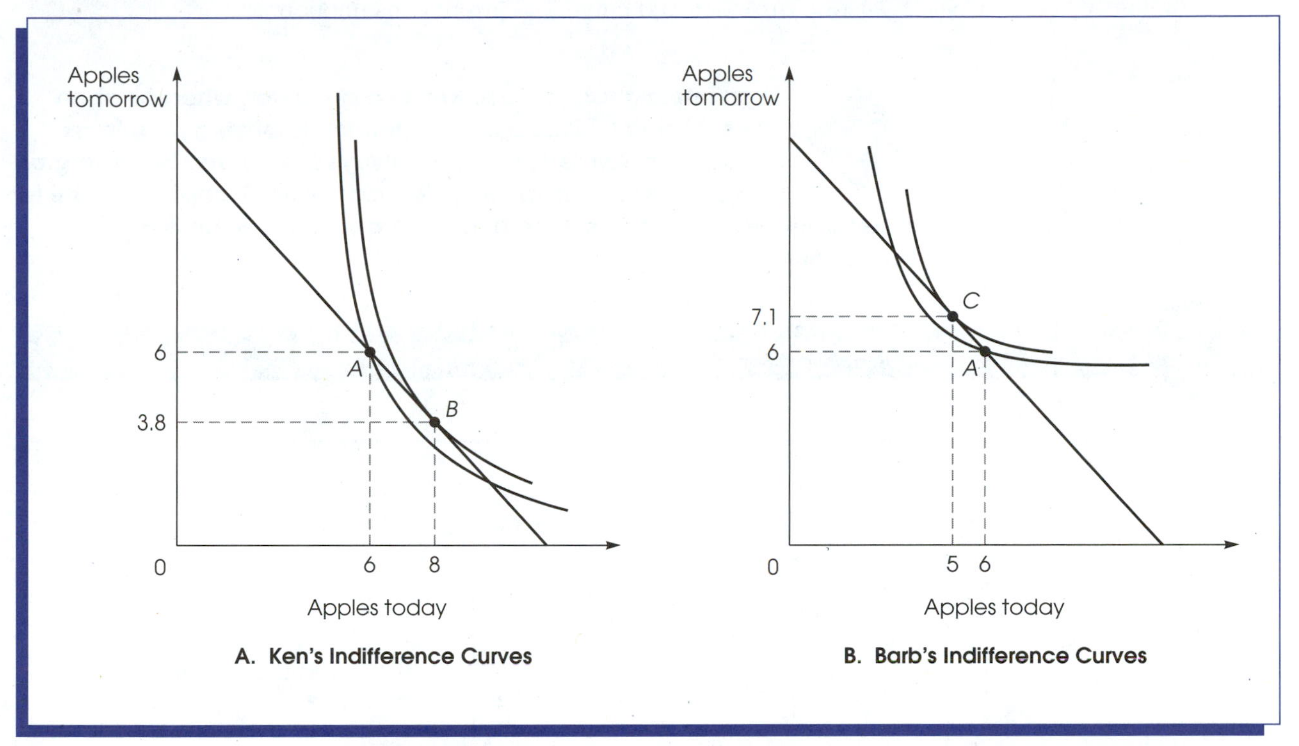

Ken and Barb start with the same initial endowment of 6 apples today and 6 apples tomorrow, at point *A*. They can each borrow and lend at a market interest rate of 10%, giving them identical budget lines of slope −1.10. Ken's preferences lead him to choose point *B*, which he achieves by borrowing 2 apples. Barb's preferences lead her to choose point *C*, which she achieves by lending 1 apple.

Ken demands 8 apples today. This information is recorded by point *B′* in panel B of Exhibit 17–5.

We can generate additional points in the same way. To see how much Ken would demand to borrow at an interest rate of 5%, first draw the corresponding budget line, which passes through his endowment point *A* with an absolute slope of 1.05. This line is drawn in color in panel A of Exhibit 17–5. (The drawing is not to scale!) Ken chooses point *C*, where he consumes 9 apples, of which 3 must be borrowed (since his endowment contains only 6). This information is recorded by point *C′* in panel B of the exhibit.

Generating a series of points in this manner and connecting them, we can derive Ken's entire demand curve for current consumption.

At some interest rates, Ken will not want to borrow at all, but to lend. Suppose that the interest rate rises to 25%. The corresponding budget line, shown in light color in panel A of Exhibit 17–5, passes through the endowment point *A* with absolute slope 1.25. The tangency is at point *D*, so that Ken wants to consume only 5 apples today, meaning that he seeks to lend an apple. Point D' in panel B records the information.

EXERCISE 17.11 By examining panel B of Exhibit 17–4, generate a point on Barb's demand curve for current consumption.

At an interest rate of 10%, Ken is a borrower, whereas at an interest rate of 25%, he is a lender. In classifying people as borrowers or lenders, we refer always to their *net* borrowing or lending. If Ken borrows 3 apples and lends 1 apple, then he is a net borrower of 2 apples. If he borrows 2 and lends 6, he is a net lender of 4.

Exhibit 17-5 Ken's Demand for Current Consumption

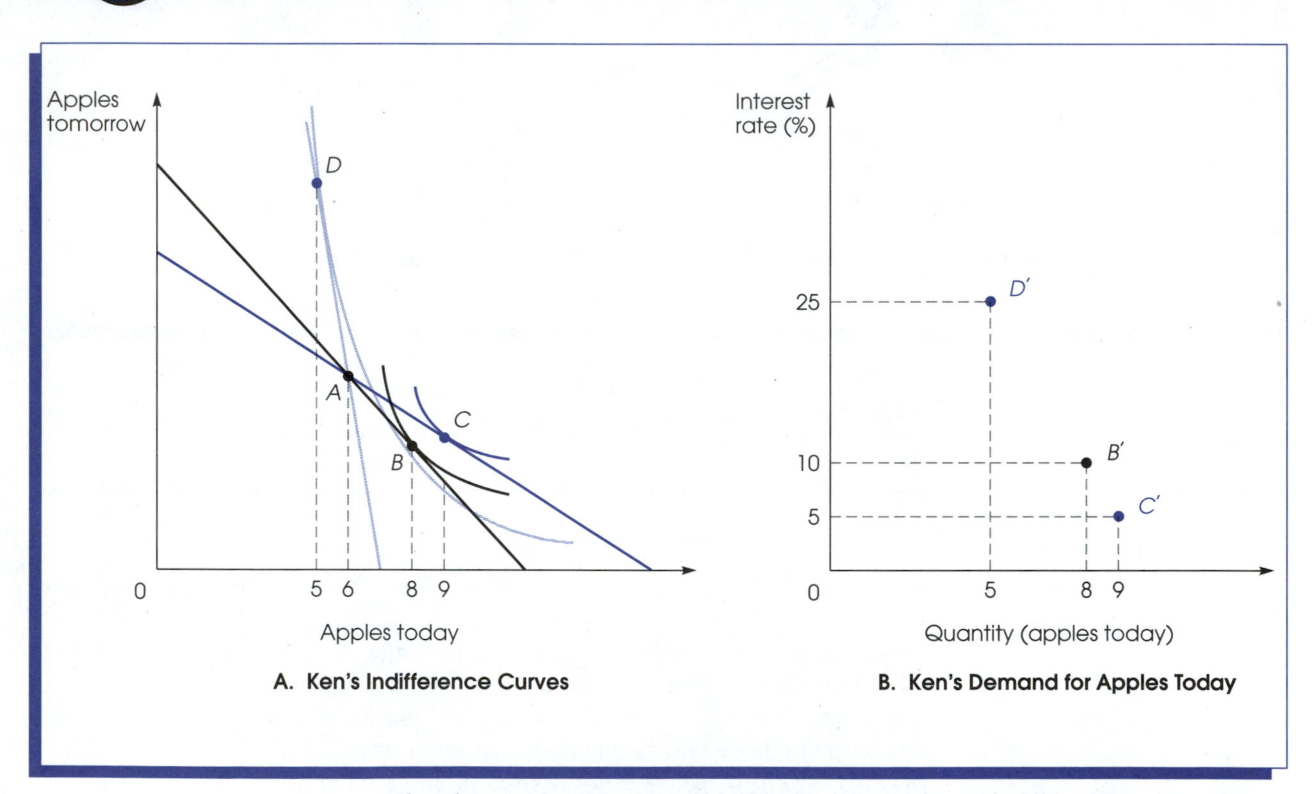

When the interest rate is 10%, Ken has the black budget line with slope −1.10, passing through his endowment point A. Ken chooses basket B, where he consumes 8 apples today, of which 6 come from his endowment and 2 must be borrowed. Point B' in panel B shows that when the interest rate is 10%, Ken eats 8 apples today.

When the interest rate is 5%, Ken's budget line pivots through point A to become the color line with slope −1.05. He chooses point C, eating 9 apples today (of which 3 are borrowed). This information is recorded by point C' in panel B.

At some interest rates, Ken chooses to be not a borrower but a lender. When the interest rate is 25%, he has the light-color budget line with slope −1.25 and chooses point D. He consumes only 5 apples, lending 1 apple out of his endowment of 6. This information is recorded by point D' in panel B.

If Ken's endowment includes 6 apples today and he wants to eat 8 apples today, he must become a net borrower of 2 apples. Whether he accomplishes this by borrowing 2 and lending none or by borrowing 9 and lending 7 is of little consequence.

The vertical axis in panel B of Exhibit 17–5 is labeled with an interest rate, whereas the vertical axis for a demand curve should be labeled with a price. However, we know that interest rates can be converted to relative prices simply by adding 1. Therefore, it is legitimate to think of the interest rate axis as nothing but a relabeled price axis, and to think of the curve through *B*′ and *C*′ as a demand curve.

Having generated Ken's demand curves for current consumption, we can repeat the exercise for Barb and every other member of the economy. We can add all the demand curves to generate a market demand curve.

The Supply of Current Consumption

In this section, we will assume that the supply of current consumption is fixed: A certain number of apples fall from apple trees and must be eaten immediately. There is (by assumption) no way to save an apple until tomorrow and no way to increase the number of apples in the harvest. Therefore, the supply curve for current apple consumption is *vertical*.

In Section 17.4 we will relax the assumption that the quantity of current consumption is fixed. However, the flavor of the conclusions we draw will not be changed. By working first with the simplest possible model, we will get a good feeling for the nature of equilibrium.

Equilibrium

We can find the market demand curve for current consumption by adding individual demand curves, each of which is derived by the method of Exhibit 17–5. We have a market supply curve that is vertical at the quantity of apples that happen to fall from the trees. Market equilibrium is determined by the intersection of the supply and demand curves. In Exhibit 17–6, the number of apples in the harvest is Q_0 and the equilibrium interest rate turns out to be 7%.

Equilibrium and the Representative Agent

Equilibrium is determined by the intersection of supply and demand. Here we will pursue an alternative approach to the determination of equilibrium. Of course, both methods must lead to the same conclusion, but depending on circumstances one or the other can be easier to apply.

Representative agent
Someone whose tastes and assets are representative of the entire economy.

We reintroduce a fictional character who is called the **representative agent** and is a sort of "average" of all the people in the economy. Let us give our representative agent a name and call her Rebecca Representative.

Do you think Rebecca is a net borrower or a net lender? A bit of reflection

Exhibit 17-6 Equilibrium

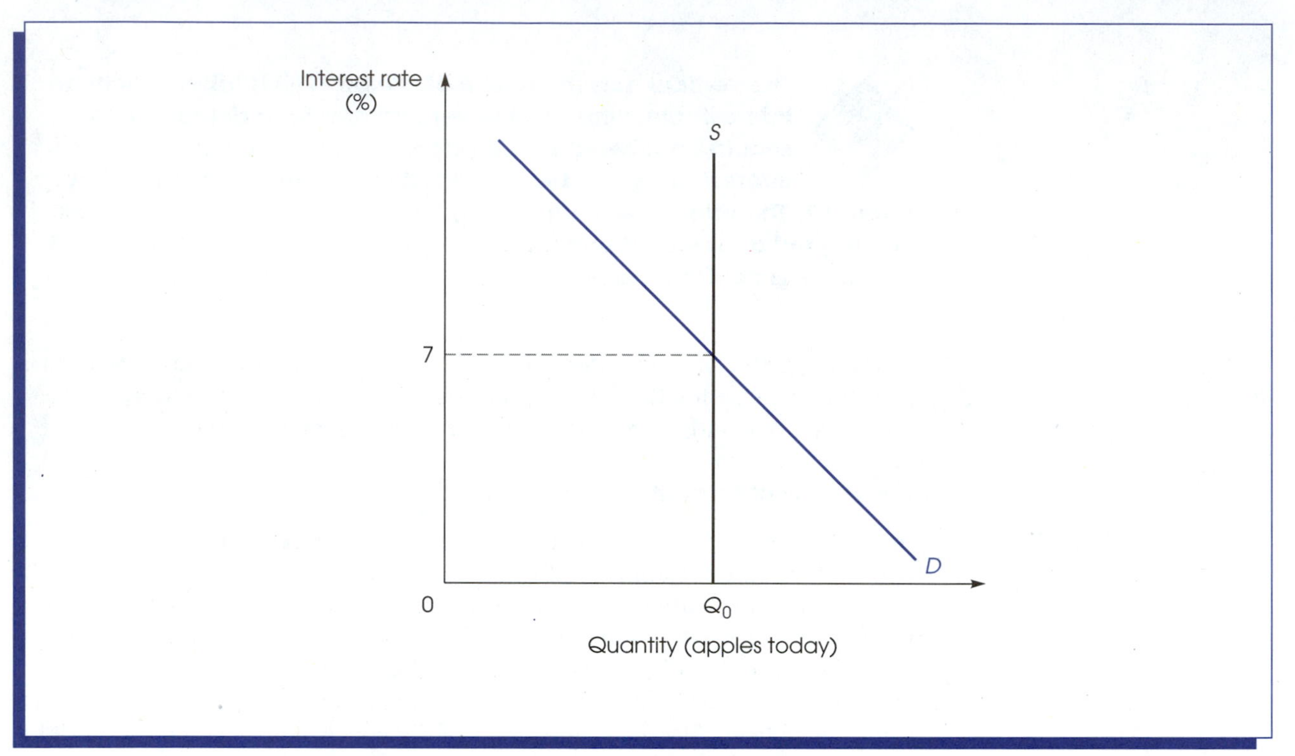

The demand curve is the sum of individual demand curves, each derived by the method in Exhibit 17-5. The supply curve is vertical at the quantity of apples in the harvest. The equilibrium interest rate in this example is 7%.

reveals that she can be neither. Every dollar borrowed is a dollar lent, so the total of all borrowing in the economy must just equal the total of all lending. The average borrower borrows exactly the same amount that the average lender lends. Since Rebecca is an average of all the borrowers *and* all the lenders, she borrows exactly the same amount that she lends. That is, her net borrowing (or net lending) is exactly zero. Another way to say this is that Rebecca consumes exactly her endowment point.

Drawing Rebecca's indifference curves and endowment point as in Exhibit 17–7, we can deduce what her budget line must be. Since she chooses to consume her endowment, her budget line must be tangent to an indifference curve at that point. This tells us the slope of her budget line. In Exhibit 17–7, Rebecca's indifference curve happens to have slope -1.07 at the endowment point E. Therefore, the necessary budget line also has absolute slope 1.07. We can now infer that the equilibrium interest rate is 7%.

To compute the the market interest rate, find the absolute slope of the representative agent's indifference curve at the endowment point, and subtract 1.

Exhibit 17-7 The Representative Agent

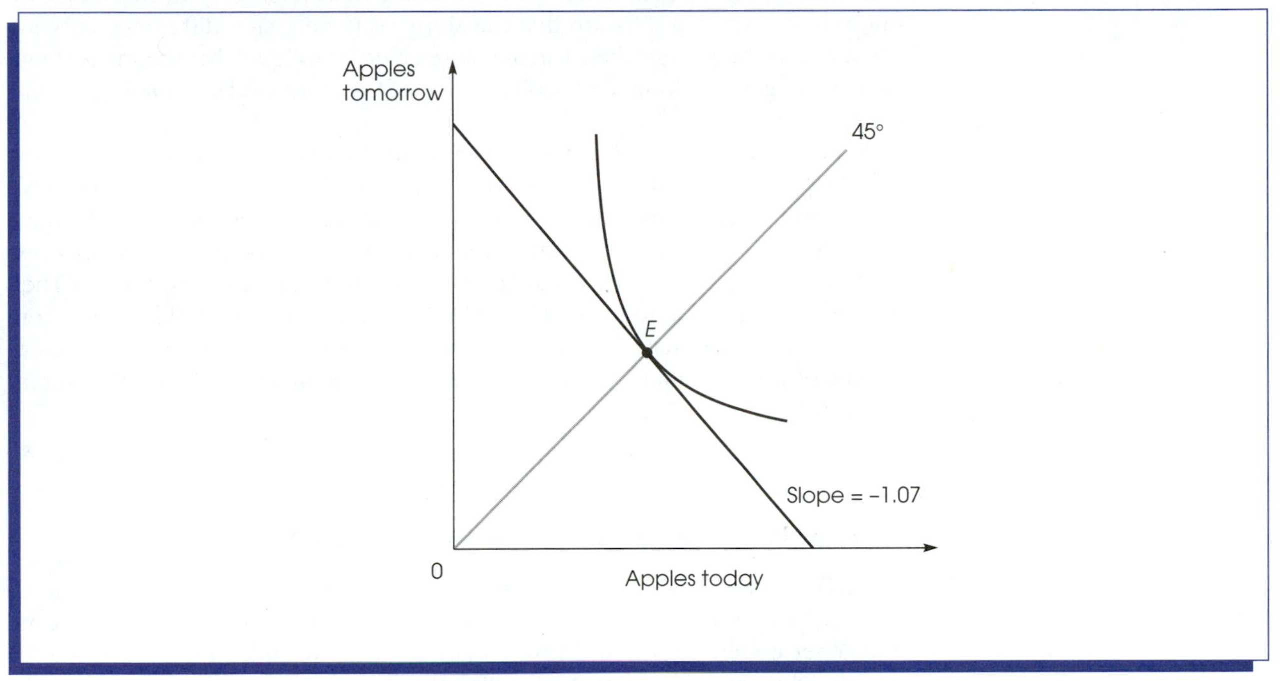

Rebecca Representative's endowment point E happens to be on the 45° line. At that point her indifference curve has slope -1.07. Because the representative agent can be neither a borrower nor a lender, her budget line must be tangent to her indifference curve at the endowment point. Therefore, the budget line has slope -1.07 and the equilibrium interest rate is 7%.

To understand this argument better, try thinking about what happens if the interest rate is less than 7%. Rebecca's budget line through point E is then flatter than in the exhibit, and her optimum lies to the southeast of E. Rebecca wants to be a net borrower, consuming more than her current endowment. Since she is the representative agent, this means that people on average want to consume more than their current endowments. The quantity of current consumption demanded exceeds the quantity supplied, so the interest rate must rise.

EXERCISE 17.12 Explain what happens when the interest rate is greater than 7%.

We can calculate the equilibrium interest rate either by seeking the intersection of supply and demand or by calculating the slope of the representative agent's indifference curve at her endowment point. Because both procedures are correct, they must yield the same answer.

Why Interest Rates Are Positive

In Exhibit 17–7, we assumed that Rebecca Representative's endowment point is on the 45° line. This is a reasonable assumption, tantamount to assuming that one day's apple harvest is no better or worse than another's. In that case, we know from earlier discussion that the slope of Rebecca's indifference curve at point *E* must be greater than 1 in absolute value. It follows that the interest rate (which we get by taking the absolute value of the slope and subtracting 1) must be positive.

If Rebecca's endowment were elsewhere, this would not have to be the case. Suppose that Rebecca starts with 100 apples today and expects to receive only 1 apple tomorrow. (This is not just a statement about a single individual; since Rebecca is the representative agent it means that people *on average* expect their apple trees to produce far less tomorrow than they do today.) Then her endowment is far to the southeast in the indifference curve diagram, where the curves are very flat. The absolute slope of her indifference curve at the endowment point might then have a value of only .3, making the equilibrium interest rate $-.7 = -70\%$.

Why Low Interest Rates Are Not Better than High Ones

Politicians often talk about the urgency of bringing down interest rates, to make it easier for people to increase their current consumption of houses, cars, and other commodities. And lower interest rates are indeed a good thing for people who are net borrowers. On the other hand, it is equally clear that lower interest rates are a bad thing for people who are net lenders: If you are saving for your retirement by lending money to a bank, you will want the interest rate to be as high as possible.

When interest rates fall, helping borrowers and hurting lenders, does the good outweigh the bad? or vice versa? When you reflect on the fact that every dollar borrowed is a dollar lent, you will see that the good and the bad exactly cancel. Every penny that a borrower gains from lower interest rates is a penny that a lender loses.

Put another way, the representative agent is neither a net borrower nor a net lender and therefore neither gains nor loses from a change in interest rates. Since the representative agent is the typical participant in the economy, people on average are neither helped nor hurt when interest rates change.

Because an interest rate is an equilibrium price, it cannot change without a reason: There must be either a change in supply or a change in demand. That change in supply or demand must, in turn, be caused by some outside disturbance. Typically, that disturbance has either good or bad effects in addition to its effect on interest rates. Therefore, interest rate changes tend to be *accompanied* by changes in welfare, but the changes in welfare are not *caused* by the changes in interest rates.

Changes in Equilibrium

To calculate the effects of a change in market conditions, we can use either supply and demand curves or the method of the representative agent. We will carry out a few exercises illustrating both techniques.

A Brighter Future

Suppose that a breakthrough in agricultural technology makes it clear that apple trees will become more productive in the future. Although each tree was initially expected to produce 6 apples per day every day, we now expect the trees to produce 6 apples today and 8 tomorrow. How will the equilibrium interest rate change?

To answer this question, we can consult either the market supply and demand curves or the representative agent's indifference curves. The two approaches are illustrated in the two panels of Exhibit 17–8.

Exhibit 17-8 An Increase in the Future Apple Supply

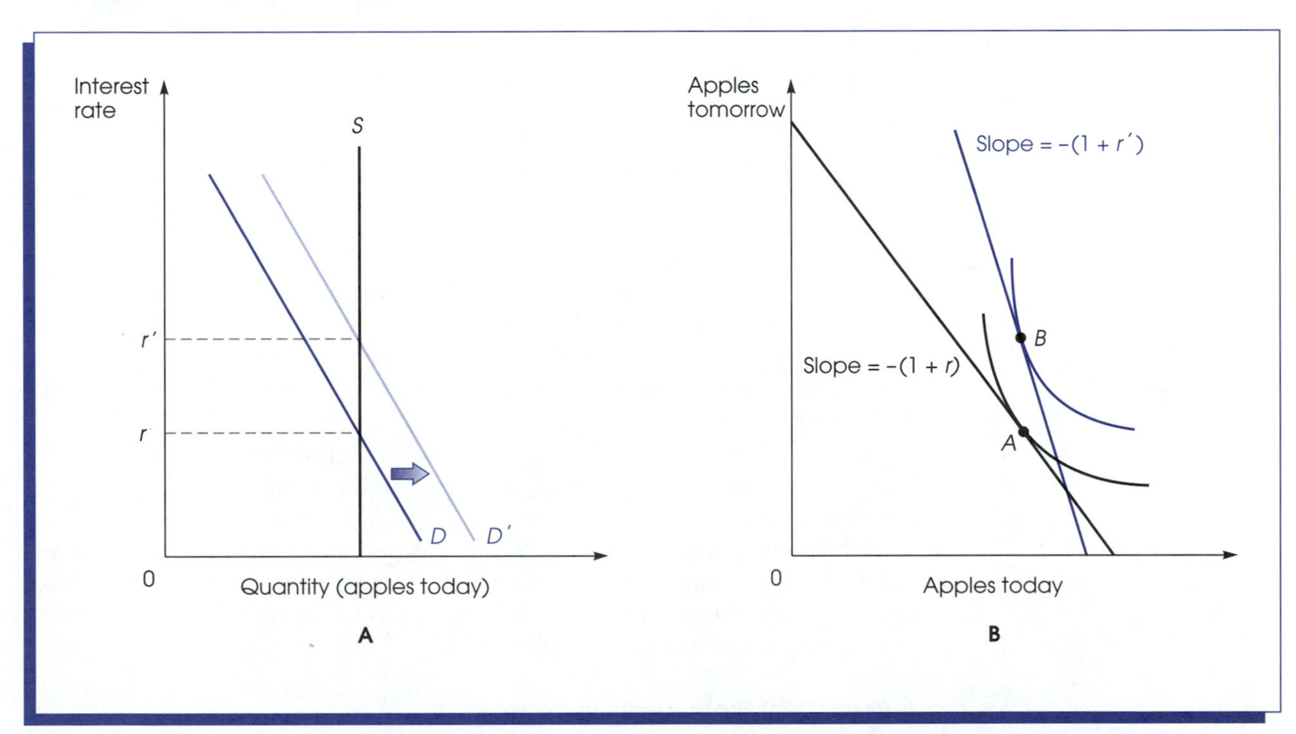

An increase in the future apple supply moves the representative agent from point A to point B in panel B, increasing wealth and hence increasing the demand for all noninferior goods, including apples today. The demand curve shifts outward in panel A and the equilibrium interest rate rises from r to r'.

The representative agent's budget line shifts from the black line (with absolute slope $1 + r$) to the color line (with absolute slope $1 + r'$). The fact that the color line is steeper confirms the observation that r' is greater than r.

When word gets out that apple harvests will improve in the future, people feel wealthier immediately. Assuming that current consumption is a normal good (as opposed to an inferior good), the demand curve shifts out. The outward shift in demand reflects the fact that when you hear that your future income will increase, you want to start spending part of it today.

The supply of current apples is unchanged. Therefore, the market interest rate rises from r to r' in panel A of Exhibit 17–8.

Panel B derives the same outcome from Rebecca Representative's point of view. As soon as she hears the good news about tomorrow's apple harvest, Rebecca's endowment point shifts upward from point A to point B. At the higher point B, we expect the indifference curve to be steeper. In fact, it is possible to show that the indifference curve at B is steeper, provided that we maintain our assumption that current consumption is a normal good. (Verifying this assertion is a somewhat challenging exercise, recommended to the ambitious student.) Therefore, Rebecca's new budget line, tangent at B instead of A, must be steeper. In fact, the slope of her original (black) budget line is $-(1 + r)$, while the slope of her new color budget line is $-(1 + r')$, where r and r' are the same equilibrium interest rates that we found in panel A. That the color line is steeper than the black one confirms that $r' > r$. When the future turns brighter, the interest rate increases.

A Brighter Present

Suppose that this year's apple harvest is unusually large (8 apples per tree instead of the expected 6) through some stroke of good luck that is not expected to persist.

Exhibit 17–9 illustrates. As in the preceding example, people feel wealthier and increase their demand for current consumption. At the same time, the supply of current consumption is increased because of the good apple harvest. It appears from the picture in panel A that the new interest rate r'' could be either below or above the old interest rate r. However, this is a case where an examination of the representative agent's indifference curves actually yields more information.

Turning to panel B, we see that Rebecca Representative's endowment moves rightward from point A to point C. At points farther to the right we expect that the indifference curves become flatter. (This can be proved if you start with the assumption that future consumption is not an inferior good.) Therefore, the color budget line with slope $-(1 + r'')$ is flatter than the black budget line with slope $-(1 + r)$. It follows that r'' is less than r. When the present turns brighter, the interest rate falls.

A Permanent Productivity Increase

Suppose that apple trees, having always produced 6 apples per year, suddenly begin producing 8 apples per year on a permanent basis, beginning immediately. As in panel A of Exhibit 17–9, the demand and supply curves for current consumption both shift rightward and the diagram does not reveal whether the new interest rate is higher or lower than the old. An examination of the representative agent's situation does not relieve the ambiguity. In Exhibit 17–10, we see that Rebecca Representative's endowment point moves from (6,6) to (8,8),

Exhibit 17-9 An Increase in the Current Apple Supply

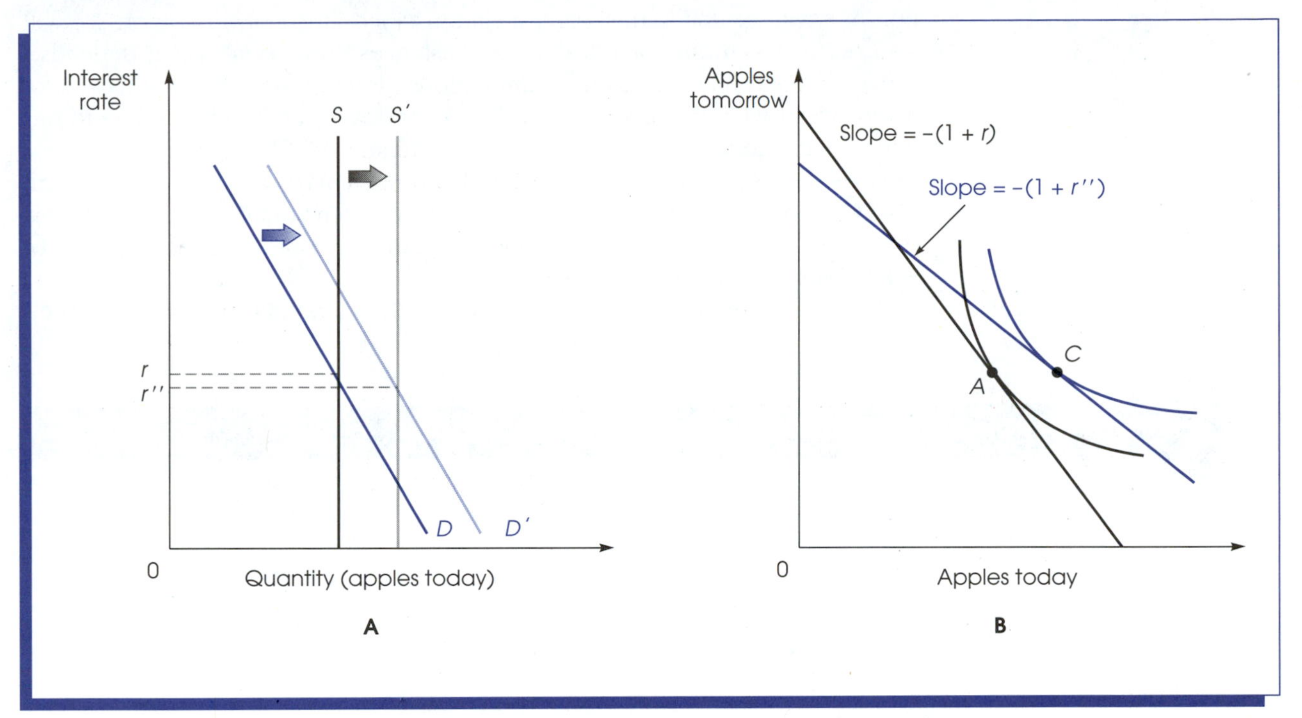

Because people are wealthier when the current apple supply increases, demand increases as well. The supply and demand graph in panel A does not reveal whether the new equilibrium interest rate, r'', is greater or less than the old interest rate r. However, we can make this determination on the basis of Rebecca Representative's indifference curves. Her endowment moves from point *A* to point *C*, so her budget line changes from the black line to the flatter color line. As the slope of the budget line determines the equilibrium interest rate, we conclude that the interest rate falls.

where there is no particular reason to believe that the indifference curve has become either shallower or steeper.

It is common, especially in macroeconomics, to make the additional assumption that at various points along the 45° line, the indifference curves all have the same slope. (Indifference curves with this property are called *homothetic* near the 45° line.) In this case the black and the blue budget lines in Exhibit 17–10 are parallel, and the change in productivity has no effect on the interest rate.

Government Debt Revisited

When the government wants to spend money, it can either raise taxes immediately or it can borrow, in which case it issues an implicit promise to raise taxes in the future. We saw in Section 17.2 that as long as the market interest rate remains fixed, taxpayers are indifferent between the two methods of finance. Government *spending* can be either good or bad, but government *debt* is a matter of indifference.

In the discussion in Section 17.2, we left open the question of whether government debt can affect the interest rate itself. Here we will take up that question. We will see that in the simplest circumstances, the answer is "no". We will also see that in more complicated circumstances, the answer is, "it depends." If that strikes you as depressingly ambiguous, don't despair. We will have a lot to say about what the answer depends *on*, and we will therefore come to understand the conditions necessary for government debt to matter.

Consider Terry Taxpayer, whose indifference curves are shown in Exhibit 17–11. Terry lives in a world where the market interest rate is 10%, so that his (black) budget line between current and future consumption has a slope of −1.10. His endowment point is marked *A*.

Terry's government has decided to spend $1 wastefully.[5] It can do so in ei-

Exhibit 17-10 A Permanent Productivity Increase

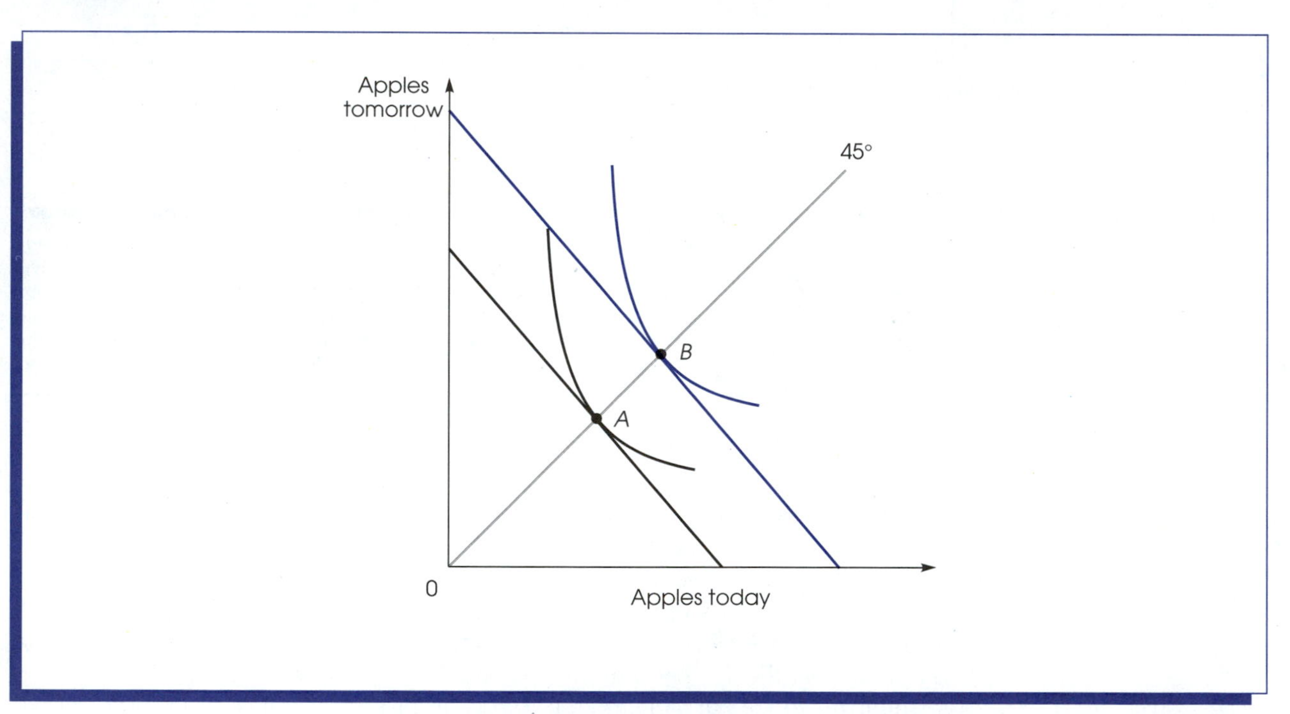

When apple trees become permanently more productive, effective immediately, Rebecca Representative's endowment point moves from *A* to *B* along the 45° line. The interest rate could either rise or fall.

If Rebecca's indifference curves are homothetic, the slope of the indifference curves at *A* and at *B* are equal, and there is no change in the interest rate.

[5]We assume that the spending is wasteful to simplify the discussion of how Terry's endowment point shifts. If the spending is productive, a similar analysis yields identical conclusions.

Exhibit 17-11 Taxation versus Borrowing

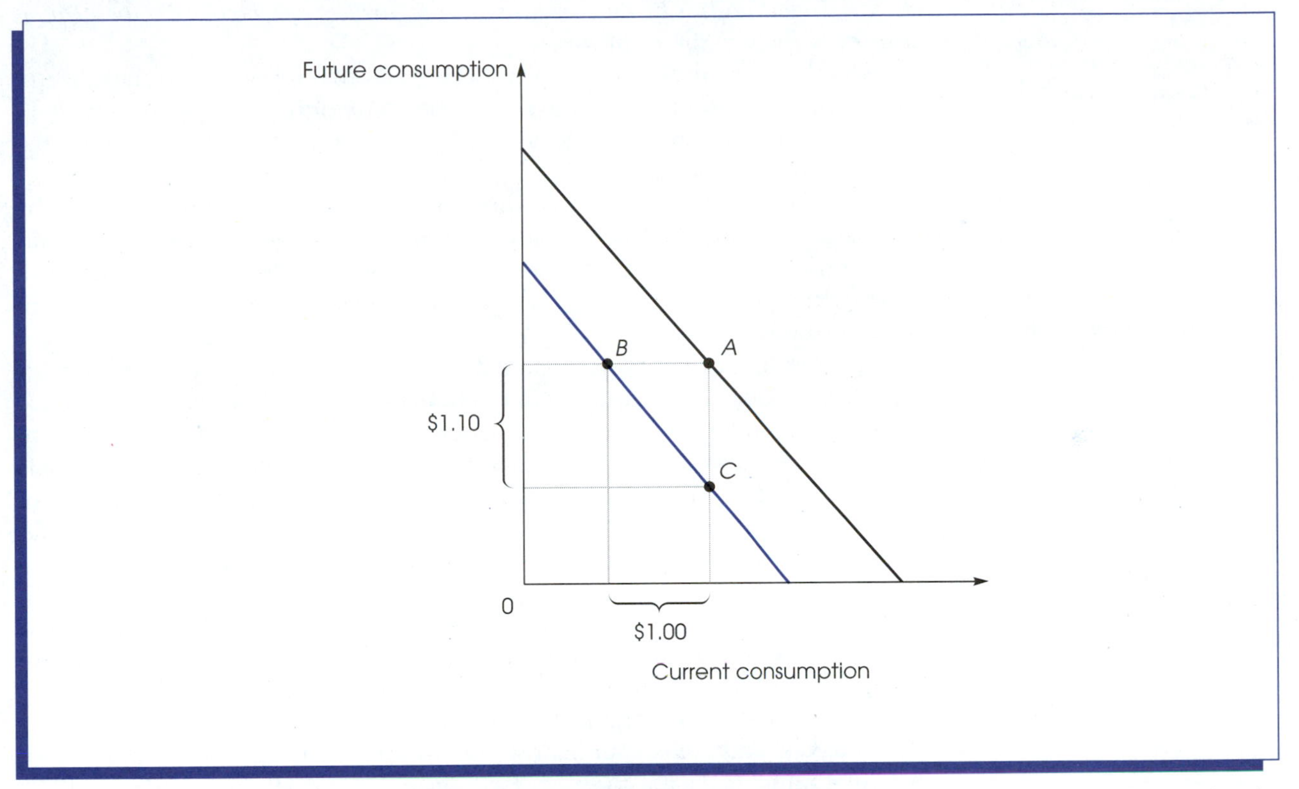

Terry Taxpayer starts with an endowment of *A*, faces an interest rate of 10%, and therefore has the black budget line with slope -1.10. If the government taxes him $1 to finance wasteful spending, his endowment falls to *B* and his budget line moves in to the line shown in color. If the government borrows $1 to finance wasteful spending. Terry is taxed $1.10 in the future, so his endowment falls to *C* and his budget line is again the line shown in color.

Because each plan leaves Terry with the same color budget line, each plan leads to the same demand for current consumption. Each plan also leads to the same supply of current consumption. Therefore, each plan leads to the same market interest rate.

ther of two ways. One is to raise Terry's current taxes by $1, shifting his endowment point $1 to the left, to point *B*. The other is to borrow and raise Terry's future taxes by $1.10, shifting his endowment point down $1.10 to point *C*.

If the government raises current taxes, Terry's new budget line is the line with slope −1.10 through his new endowment point *B*. If it borrows, his new budget line is the line with slope −1.10 through his new endowment point *C*. But these are two descriptions of the same line; it is shown in color in the exhibit.

Either plan—taxation or borrowing—causes Terry's current consumption demand to fall, since his budget line shifts in from the black to the blue. Because the blue budget line is the same in either case, either plan leads Terry's demand to fall by the same amount.

What is true of Terry is true of all other taxpayers and hence of the market as a whole: *Government spending causes the demand for current consumption to fall. Demand falls by the same amount regardless of whether the spending is financed by taxation or by debt.*

For another perspective on Ricardian Equivalence, read what economist William Vickrey has to say (fallacy #9) at the following Internet site maintained by Columbia University: http://www.rain.org/~jjgelles/vickrey15.htm

Now let us turn our attention from demand to supply. When the government spends $1 to purchase and then wastes $1 worth of goods, the supply of current consumption falls by exactly $1 worth, regardless of where the government finds the $1.

Therefore, the two plans cause the supply of current consumption to fall by the same amount. We have already seen that both cause the demand for current consumption to fall by the same amount. We may conclude that they both lead to the same market interest rate. It doesn't matter whether the government taxes or borrows.

Ricardian Equivalence Theorem The statement that government borrowing has no effect on wealth, consequently no effect on the demand for current consumption, and consequently no effect on the interest rate.

This result, sometimes summarized in the slogan "Deficits don't matter," is called the **Ricardian Equivalence Theorem.**[6] The Ricardian Equivalence Theorem is undoubtedly true as a matter of mathematical fact under the simple circumstances we have described here. A more interesting question is whether it is true in the world in which we live. Regarding this question, there is no consensus among economists. Some believe that there are important differences between our world and the world of Terry Taxpayer. We will now consider two of those differences.

One possible difference is that taxpayers in the real world, unlike Terry, might not be savvy enough to recognize that when the government borrows today, it must increase taxes tomorrow. Suppose that you start at point *A* in Exhibit 17–11 and the government borrows $1, implicitly promising to raise your future taxes. This shifts your endowment to point *C*. But if you fail to take notice that future taxes must rise, you will believe that your endowment is still at *A* and will therefore not change your current consumption demand. This contrasts with what happens under taxation, where your endowment point is shifted to *B*, you realize what is happening, and you reduce your current consumption demand accordingly. Under this scenario, borrowing has no effect on demand while taxation shifts demand downward; the interest rate is therefore higher under borrowing than it is under taxation.

According to this scenario, government debt fools people into thinking they are richer than they really are. That hypothesis is very much at odds with the spirit of microeconomics, in which the assumption of rationality plays a central role. As a result, many economists are quite uncomfortable with the notion that such misperceptions could be a significant factor in the determination of interest rates. However, there is insufficient empirical evidence to rule out the possibility.

The second possibly important difference between Terry's world and ours arises from default risk. Suppose, contrary to the picture in Exhibit 17–11, that Terry Taxpayer, because of his poor credit history, is unable to borrow at the market interest rate of 10%, but only at the higher rate of 25%. Then his bud-

[6] In honor of the nineteenth-century economist David Ricardo.

get line is not really the line shown in Exhibit 17–11, but something much steeper. Taxation shifts Terry's endowment to *B*, leaving him with a budget line through *B* that is steeper than the one in the exhibit and therefore passes below *C*. On the other hand, borrowing shifts Terry's endowment to *C*, and leaves him with a steep budget line through *C*.

In this case the "government borrowing" budget line through *C* is higher than the "current taxation" budget line through *B*. Terry is richer when the government borrows for him at 10% than when he has to borrow for himself at 25%. Therefore, he demands more current consumption when the government borrows. Since government borrowing means higher current consumption demand, it also means a higher interest rate.

It is sometimes argued that default risk is especially important in view of the finiteness of life. People who would like to borrow and obligate their children to pay the debt are unable to do so, because there is no legal mechanism by which the children can be bound to fulfill their parents' obligations. The certainty of default on such debts makes the interest rate on them essentially infinite. Government borrowing reduces this rate from infinity to something on the order of 10%.

On the other hand, this is a significant consideration only if there are a significant number of people who would really like to live well at their children's expense. The commonly observed phenomenon of parents working hard in order to leave bequests to their children (or for that matter, in order to send them to college) is evidence to the contrary.

The current thinking of most economists is that Ricardian Equivalence must hold—government debt does not matter—unless either misperceptions or default risks are of serious consequence. There is great controversy over the question of whether these phenomena in fact *are* of serious consequence. However, these are very concrete questions that are amenable to empirical investigation, and one is entitled to hope that the controversies surrounding them will be resolved long before the end of the next century.

17.4 Production and Investment

In Section 17.3, we treated the number of apples available today and tomorrow as fixed and unchangeable. Any individual was able to shift consumption from one period to another by borrowing or lending, but for the economy as a whole such transfers were impossible.

A more complete model should take account of opportunities for current goods to be converted into future goods on an economy-wide basis. There are many ways to do this. The simplest is *storage*. An apple placed in the refrigerator today becomes an apple available for consumption tomorrow. An economy equipped with refrigerators can choose to consume fewer apples today in exchange for additional apples tomorrow—not just for some individuals, but for the economy as a whole.

Even more importantly, there is the possibility of *production*. Grain can be either eaten today or planted to produce even more grain tomorrow. Much production involves the use of machinery and other capital equipment, which must itself be produced. To produce capital, people must forgo the opportunity to produce goods for current consumption. People can choose whether to spend their time picking apples or planting apple trees. In the first case there are more apples today; in the second, more apples tomorrow.

In fact, understanding the decision to invest in producing capital is the key to this entire subject. We now turn to the market for capital.

The Demand for Capital

Recall that the word *capital* in economics always refers to goods that are inputs to the physical production process. An apple tree, which is used in the production of apples, is an example of capital.

In this section, we will measure the value of goods and the value of capital in terms of dollars. As always, those dollars are just stand-ins for physical goods.

The Marginal Product of Capital

The *marginal product of capital (MPK),* first introduced in Chapter 6, is the additional output available when one additional unit of capital is employed. There are many possible units in which to measure the MPK. We shall measure it as a percentage of the cost of the capital. If it costs $10 to plant a tree that produces $1 worth of apples each year, we will say that the MPK is 10%. If it costs $200 to plant a tree that produces $50 worth of apples per year, we will say that the MPK is 25%.

Typically, the marginal product of capital decreases as more capital is added. Holding all other inputs fixed, the 100th apple tree adds less to the harvest than the 99th does, because the orchards become crowded, the water and nutrients must be shared, and the apple-pickers have only a limited amount of time. This observation is not new; we made it first in Chapter 6.

The Marginal Product of Capital versus the Interest Rate

Suppose that the market interest rate is 10% and the marginal product of capital is 15%. Then there is an easy way to make a profit. Borrow $100 and use it to plant a tree that produces $15 worth of apples per year. Each year, harvest the fruit from your tree, make a $10 interest payment, and pocket the remaining $5.

This is a no-lose proposition, and everybody wants to undertake it. As they do, two things happen. First, because everybody wants to borrow and nobody wants to lend, there is upward pressure on the interest rate. Second, all the new apple trees drive down the marginal product of capital. The interest rate and the MPK move closer together, and the process continues until they are equal.

The same sort of thing happens if the numbers are initially reversed. Suppose that the market interest rate is 15% and the marginal product of capital is 10%. Now nobody is willing to borrow to plant apple trees. Of course, people might still want to borrow for other reasons, so the interest rate need not fall. However, as old apple trees die off, there is no incentive to replace them. Over time, the number of apple trees (that is, the quantity of capital) falls, and so the

Exhibit 17-12 The Demand for Capital

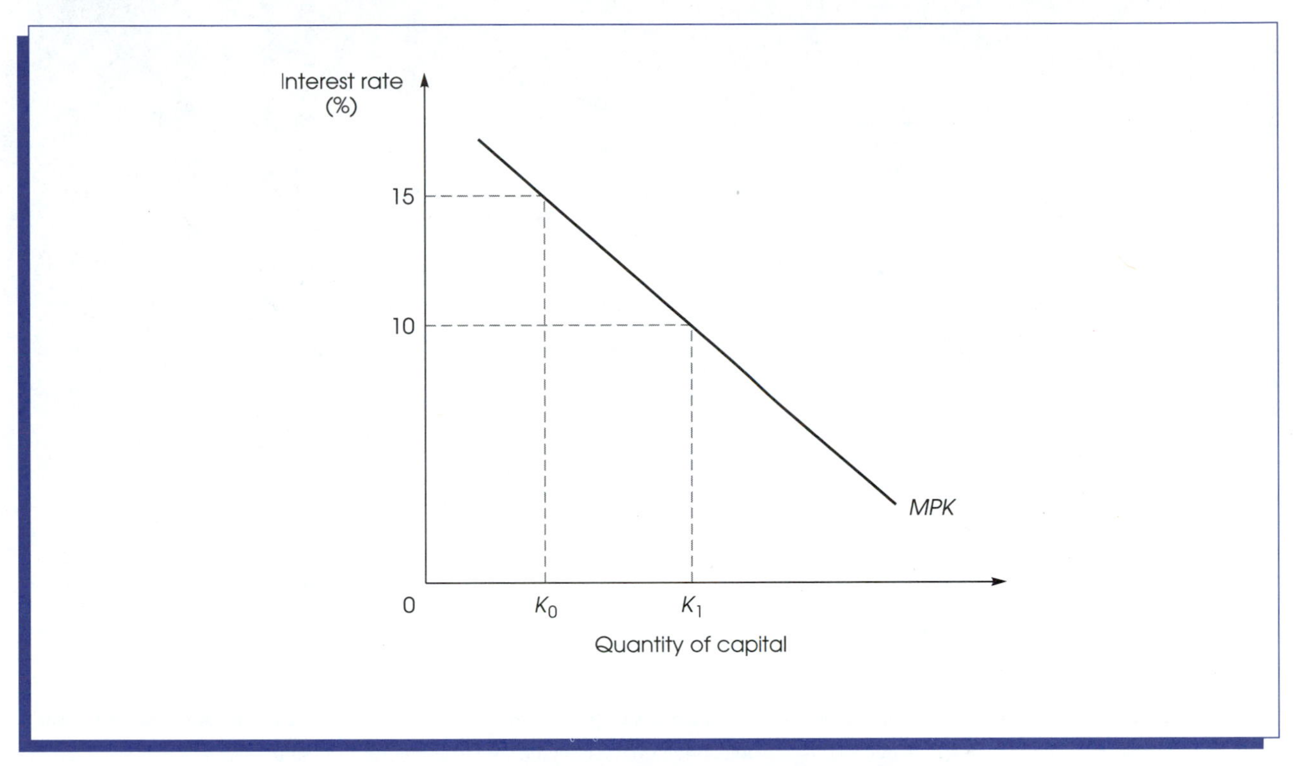

Suppose that the market interest rate is 10% but the marginal product of capital is 15% (so that the quantity of capital must be K_0). Then everybody wants to borrow to invest in capital. The quantity of capital increases and the marginal product of capital falls. This process continues until the quantity of capital reaches K_1, and the marginal product of capital is equal to the interest rate of 10%.

This argument shows that in equilibrium, the *MPK* must be equal to the interest rate. Put another way, the *MPK* curve is the demand curve for capital.

MPK rises. Eventually, the interest rate and the MPK are brought back to equality. This tells us the following:

In equilibrium, the quantity of capital adjusts until the interest rate is equal to the marginal product of capital.

There is another way to view this proposition. To a planter, the price of capital is measured by the interest rate, since meeting expenses means either borrowing or forgoing the opportunity to lend. We saw in Chapter 15 that the demand curve for a factor of production is equal to its marginal product curve. Exhibit 17–12 shows the MPK curve. If the rate of interest is 10%, then the quantity of capital demanded is K_1. The quantity of capital adjusts until the MPK is equal to the interest rate.

Exhibit 17–13 A Brighter Future

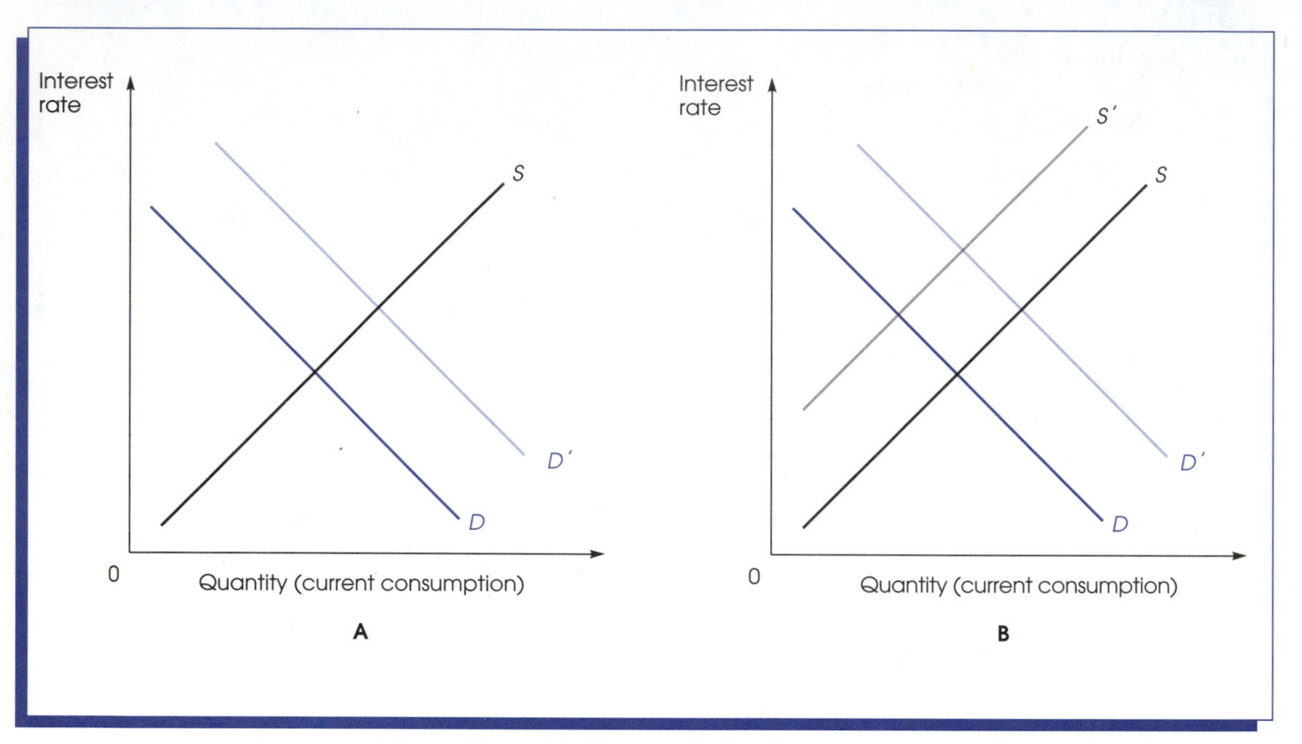

When the future looks brighter, the demand for current consumption increases. If the expected future windfall is unrelated to the productivity of capital, then there is no change in the supply of current consumption. If capital is expected to be more productive, the demand for capital increases, so the supply of current consumption falls.

In either case, the interest rate rises, though it rises by more in the second case. In the first case current consumption increases, whereas in the second case current consumption moves ambiguously.

The Supply of Current Consumption

Imagine a world with $10 worth of resources that can be devoted either to consumption or to the production of capital. If producers demand $2 worth of capital, then there is $8 left for current consumption. If they demand $7 worth of capital, then there is only $3 left for current consumption. The more capital that is demanded, the less current consumption is supplied.

We know from Exhibit 17–12 that the demand for capital slopes downward as a function of the interest rate. It follows that the supply of capital slopes upward as a function of the interest rate. When the interest rate is low, much capital is demanded and few resources are available for current consumption. When the interest rate is high, little capital is demanded and many resources are available for current consumption.

Equilibrium

In Exhibit 17–5, we derived the demand curve for current consumption, and in subsequent exhibits we made extensive use of this demand curve. There is no need to modify our theory of demand. However, throughout Section 17.3, we adopted a very naive theory of the supply for current consumption: We assumed that it was vertical. In an economy with production and capital investment, we now know that the supply curve can slope upward.

It turns out that this new observation does not necessitate any change in our earlier conclusions. We learned in Exhibit 17–8 that a brightening of the future causes the interest rate to rise; we learned in Exhibit 17–9 that a current bumper crop causes the interest rate to fall. All of this remains true when the supply curve slopes upward, although the magnitudes of the shifts might be different.

By way of example, Exhibit 17–13 illustrates two scenarios in which something happens to make the future look brighter. In scenario A, it is discovered that people will be wealthier next year for some reason that has nothing to do with the productivity of capital. In scenario B, it is discovered that capital will be more productive than previously thought.

In either case, people are wealthier, so the demand curve for current consumption shifts out. In the first case, there is no change in the marginal product of capital, and so no change in the demand for capital, and so no change in the supply of current consumption. In the second case, the MPK, and consequently the demand for capital, goes up; when more resources are demanded for capital, fewer are supplied for current consumption. That is why the supply curve in panel B shifts back.

In each scenario the interest rate rises (just as it did in Exhibit 17–8), though it rises by more in the second case. In the first case, current consumption increases, while in the second, current consumption moves ambiguously.

summary

The interest rate is a measure of the relative price of current consumption in terms of future consumption. More precisely, the relative price of current consumption is $1 + r$, where r is the interest rate.

The relative price of future consumption in terms of current consumption is $1/(1 + r)$. This is also called the present value of a unit of future consumption. A bond that promises a unit of future consumption will sell today for the price $1/(1 + r)$.

Present values can be used to assign a value to any income stream and to compare the desirability of different income streams. The stream with the higher present value can always be traded for the stream with the lower present value, with something extra left over.

A consumer chooses between current and future consumption by seeking a tangency between his budget line and an indifference curve. The budget line has a slope of $-(1 + r)$ and passes through the consumer's endowment point. Using the machinery of indifference curves, we can derive the consumer's demand for current consumption. Adding up over all consumers, we can derive the market demand for current consumption.

The simplest assumption about the supply of current consumption is that it is fixed; that is, there is no way to convert current consumption to future consumption. In that case the market supply curve for current consumption is vertical.

The equilibrium interest rate occurs at the intersection of supply with demand. The same equilibrium can be found from the condition that the representative agent must voluntarily consume his endowment. If the slope of his indifference curve at the endowment point is $-(1 + r)$, then r must be the equilibrium interest rate.

In an economy where current consumption can be converted to capital, the quantity of capital always adjusts until the marginal product of capital is equal to the interest rate. When the interest rate is high, there is little capital demanded, so the quantity of current consumption supplied is high. When the interest rate is low, there is a lot of capital demanded, so the quantity of current consumption supplied is low. From these considerations, we derive an upward-sloping supply curve for current consumption. This can be combined with the demand curve for current consumption that was derived earlier to find the market equilibrium.

Review Questions

R1. What is the relationship among (a) the present value of an apple delivered tomorrow, (b) the price of a bond having a face value of one apple and a maturity date of tomorrow, and (c) the rate of interest?

R2. If you can either buy a house for $10,000 or rent the same house for $1,000 per year, should you buy or rent? In what way does your answer depend on the interest rate?

R3. Is the buyer of a bond a borrower or a lender?

R4. What is the present value of a perpetuity that pays $1 per year forever?

R5. What determines the value of a productive asset?

R6. What determines the value of a financial asset?

R7. What determines the value of a durable commodity?

R8. Explain why the purchaser of a new suit of clothes is indifferent between paying now and paying by credit card, provided that he can borrow and lend at the market interest rate.

R9. Explain why the taxpayer is indifferent between higher current taxes and government borrowing.

R10. In general, will the price of an exhaustible resource grow at a rate higher or lower than the rate of interest? Why? Under what circumstances will it grow at exactly the rate of interest?

R11. Explain how to derive a point on the consumer's demand curve for current consumption.

R12. What assumptions lead to a vertical supply curve for current consumption?

R13. Explain how the equilibrium interest rate can be computed from an examination of the representative agent's indifference curves.

R14. Explain why the marginal product of capital must equal the interest rate in equilibrium.

R15. Explain why, when there are opportunities for capital investment, the supply curve for current consumption slopes upward.

Problem Set

1. **True or False:** When the interest rate falls, people want to borrow more, and the additional borrowing tends to drive the interest rate back up.

2. **True or False:** If the interest rate and the price of bonds both rise simultaneously, the quantity of borrowing could go either up or down.

3. John bought a refrigerator and sold it three years later for exactly what he paid for it. **True or False:** It cost John nothing to have the use of the refrigerator for three years.

4. Under the U.S. patent law, an inventor can be granted a patent that confers the exclusive right to produce and market his invention for 17 years. After that time, anybody can produce and market the invention. Assume that the annual profits that can be earned from the invention never change, and that the interest rate is 10%. **True or False:** A 17-year patent is approximately 80% as valuable as a patent that lasts forever.

5. You have just been informed that you have two years to live and are considering a night of debauchery to take your mind off the news. The consequence of such behavior is eternal damnation, beginning on the date of your death. One year of fire and brimstone is equal in unpleasantness to the loss of $\$P$. The interest rate is r.

   a. How pleasant would a night of sin have to be in order to be worth the cost?

   b. Which is more likely to deter you from sinning: a doubling of the torments of the underworld, or a halving of the interest rate?

6. Suppose that apartments in San Francisco typically sell for $300,000 and rent for $1,500 a month. The market interest rate is 10%. **True or False:** The market must be anticipating a rise in apartment rentals at some time in the future.

7. **True or False:** If a house in New York and a house in California are identical in every way except for the fact that the California house is susceptible to being destroyed by earthquakes, then the California homeowner must earn a greater rate of return than the New York homeowner to compensate him for the risk. Therefore, houses in California will increase in value more rapidly than houses in New York.

8. Textbook publishers typically issue new editions every three years, in order to keep copies of the old edition from circulating on the used-textbook market. Suppose that each student keeps his or her textbook for one year and values his possession of the textbook at $20 for that year. Suppose also that a new edition is no more intrinsically valuable than an old edition, but that the appearance of a new edition makes the old edition worthless. The market interest rate is 10%.

   a. If new editions cause old editions to become completely obsolete, what is the price of a new textbook?

b. If the publisher issued just one edition of each book and credibly promised never to issue another one, what would be the price of a new textbook?

c. If it is possible to issue a promise as in part (b), and if it is costly to bring out new editions, what is the publisher's optimal strategy?

d. Suppose that publishers would like to issue a promise as in part (b), but that there is no way for them to legally bind themselves to keeping the promise. If students suspect publishers of dishonesty, what will be the price of a new textbook? Now what is the publisher's optimal strategy?

e. True or False: Even though publishers voluntarily bring out new editions every three years, they might be better off if they were legally forbidden to do so.

9. True or False: The government's responsibility to bail out failed savings and loan institutions is monumentally expensive. But the longer they delay, the more expensive it will be, since interest charges continue to build.

10. George F. Will, a humor columnist for the *Washington Post,* notes that interest payments on the federal debt in a recent year were equal to approximately one-half of all personal income tax receipts. He concludes that this represents "a transfer of wealth from labor to capital unprecedented in U.S. history. Tax revenues are being collected from average Americans and given to the buyers of U.S. government bonds—buyers in Beverly Hills, Lake Forest, Shaker Heights, and Grosse Point, and Tokyo and Riyadh."

Suppose it were the case that the *Washington Post* employed a columnist who viewed thinking as part of his job. What might such a columnist reply?

11. Explain exactly what is wrong with the following argument: If the government buys me a suit of clothes with borrowed money and never pays off the debt, then my grandchildren will be taxed to make interest payments even though they have never seen the clothes. Therefore, government borrowing allows me to live high on the hog at my grandchildren's expense.

12. **a.** Jeeter owes $1,000 on his student loan. The debt is growing at the market interest rate of 10%. Jeeter would like to pay off the loan now, but the bank will not allow him to do so until five years from now. What strategy can Jeeter follow that is equivalent to paying off the loan today?

b. Jeeter is also concerned about his share of the national debt, which he reckons to be $10,000. He wishes that the government would just tax him today and pay off the debt, so that the accumulation of interest will not cause him to have to pay even more tomorrow. What would you suggest that Jeeter do?

13. Write a brief letter in response to the following column:[7]

DEAR ANN LANDERS: This is going to seem like a terrifically trivial problem compared to most you receive, but I've got to get it off my chest.

I'm sure almost every woman in America has gone through this slow burn. You spend two or three bucks for a pair of new pantyhose, and within a week, you have a big ugly runner and have to throw the pair away. Or, they're so stretchy they droop down around your knees and run within the week. Or, they're so NON-stretchy you can't get 'em up above your knees, and they still run within the week!

Why can't the hosiery manufacturers figure out how to make a nylon stocking that fits with a proper degree of stretch and doesn't fall to shreds in six days? Isn't nylon supposed to be one of the toughest substances made by man?

To put this into economic focus: Wanda Worker spends two bucks on nylons every week. That's over a hundred dollars a year, not to mention the aggravation and time spent running to the drugstore on a lunch hour to replace the pair that self-destructed on her way to work.

As I said, Ann, it seems terrifically trivial, but it's maddening. You have contacts all over. Will you please ask somebody who is big in hosiery manufacturing what gives—besides my stockings, that is.

Ladder Legs in Lima, Ohio

Ann says: You really hit a hot button! I contacted four of the leading hosiery manufacturers, and I have never heard so much double-talk, triple-talk and fancy ways of saying "no comment." All those contacted by my office asked that they not be identified—and would I please not name their companies. I am respecting their wishes.

But, of this you can be sure:

The hosiery industry has a mighty sweet thing going and has no intention of letting go. We have been ripped off, if you will pardon the pun, for lo, these many years, ladies. And they will continue to rip us off because the no-run nylons, which they know how to make, would put a serious crimp in their sales. In other words, we are at the mercy of a conspiracy of self-interest.

My advice is this: Shop around. Low-priced, good-fitting nylons are out there. (I wear them myself, and they

[7]Permission granted by Ann Landers and Creators Syndicate.

look as good as the top-dollar variety. Sorry, I can't publish the brand name.) For daily wear, buy nylons with reinforced toe and heel. One final way to get a leg up: If you rip one stocking, cut it off and sew on the good stocking from another pair that similarly failed you.

14. In New York City, every taxicab driver must own a license (called a medallion) to drive a cab. The city has issued a fixed number of medallions, and they are traded on the open market. Because the number of medallions is small, the price of cab rides is higher than it otherwise would be. Suppose that the city decides to abolish the medallion program and allow free entry to the taxicab industry. True or False The owners of medallions will be just as well off after the program is abolished as if it had never existed.

15. True or False If a monopolist owned an exhaustible resource, he would control its availability so that the price rose faster than the rate of interest.

16. True or False A net borrower is always made worse off by a rise in the rate of interest.

17. Herman has an income of \$2 this year and will have an income of \$3 next year. At the current rate of interest he chooses neither to borrow nor to lend. True or False If the interest rate goes up, Herman will become a lender and be better off.

18. Contrast the effects on the interest rate of (a) a year of bad weather resulting in low agricultural productivity and (b) nuclear contamination that permanently lowers agricultural productivity.

19. Contrast the effects on current consumption and the interest rate of (a) a tax on production that is expected to be in effect for one year only and (b) a tax on production that is expected to be permanent. Assume in each case that the proceeds from the tax will be completely wasted.

20. Suppose that the interest rate is 12%, and that the representative agent's tastes are such that the interest rate would have to rise to 20% to get him to voluntarily cut current consumption by \$1,000. Suppose now that there is a war that destroys \$1,000 worth of consumption goods for every agent in the economy. True or False The interest rate must rise to 20% to restore equilibrium.

21. The discussion surrounding Exhibit 17–11 suggests that when the government spends \$1 wastefully, it does not matter (for determining the equilibrium interest rate) whether the government gets the \$1 by taxation or by borrowing. Draw a similar diagram to show that the same conclusion holds when the government spends \$1 productively, say by using it to purchase \$1 worth of goods for Terry Taxpayer.

22. Repeat problem 21 assuming that the government manages to spend the \$1 *super* productively, using it to provide Terry Taxpayer with goods that he values at \$2.

23. True or False: When the government spends \$1, the equilibrium interest rate is unaffected by whether the dollar is spent wastefully or productively.

24. Felix G. Rohatyn, a well-known financier, published a letter on the editorial page of the *New York Times* on July 1, 1990. He wrote:

> I was startled and dismayed by [an earlier *Times* editorial] supporting Government borrowing as the appropriate way to deal with the bailout of bankrupt savings and loan institutions. Borrowing may be politically expedient; it is, however, wrong, from both an economic and moral point of view. The straightforward, and least damaging, way to deal with this fiasco, is to pay off the $130 billion loss with a temporary three- to four-year surcharge on income taxes.
>
> The economics are simple:
>
> (1) Borrowing will turn a $130 billion loss into a $500 billion drain over 20 to 30 years. It will maintain pressure on the credit markets and lead to higher interest rates. It will add $10 billion to $15 billion annually in interest costs to the Federal budget deficit, when interest costs constitute, after defense, the largest Federal expenditure. It will require continued high inflows of foreign capital. It will squeeze out badly needed domestic programs.
>
> (2) A three- to four-year temporary tax surcharge will eliminate $300 billion to $400 billion in interest costs and contribute to lower interest rates and capital costs. This will foster economic growth. The tax will not have negative economic impact because the bailout is basically a transfer program from taxpayers to depositors.
>
> (3) A basic economic principle justifies borrowing only for assets with a useful life. Nothing is more remote from that definition than borrowing to finance losses that have already been incurred.
>
> The moral issue is even simpler. Borrowing burdens the next generation with repayment of our foolishness and burdens lower-income Americans with the interest costs. The income tax puts the burden where it belongs: on the present generation and on higher-income Americans.

a. Find at least one elementary economic error per each paragraph.

b. Focus on the "basic economic principle" articulated under point 3. In an indifference curve diagram, show what happens if, after you have optimized, a tragedy destroys a substantial chunk of your current consumption. Is it better to reduce your consumption by that full amount in the current period? Or is it better to spread out the loss over the present and future by "borrowing to finance losses that have already been incurred"?

c. Suppose that the government does follow Mr. Rohatyn's advice and raises current taxes to meet the costs of the bailout in what is essentially the immediate present. How might individual taxpayers adjust their private borrowing and lending? Will the costs really be paid in the present, or will they be spread out over time despite the government policy? Explain why the Rohatyn plan might have no effect on any important economic variable.

d. Suppose that contrary to your argument in part (c), the Rohatyn plan does have a real effect, either because people are unable to borrow as much as they would like at the market interest rate or because they are insufficiently sophisticated to borrow their way through the higher tax years. In that case, does the Rohatyn plan make people better off or worse off?

25. True or False: When the interest rate goes up, investment becomes more desirable.

26. Your local shoemaker can buy a hammer for $10 that will last forever and increase his profits by $1.50 per year. You are thinking of purchasing the house that you currently rent for $10,000 per year. What is the most you would pay for the house?

27. Suppose that scientists discover a new method of harnessing nuclear fusion as a practical energy source. At the moment, the method is still on the drawing boards, but it is clear that within 10 years this discovery will be the basis of a technological revolution. What happens to the interest rate?

28. Suppose that an increase in world tensions makes it more likely than before that there will soon be a nuclear war that destroys all life on earth. What happens to the interest rate?

29. Suppose that an increase in world tensions makes it more likely than before that there will be a nuclear war within 10 years. Such a war would kill half the world's population and destroy 90% of the world's physical wealth. What happens to the interest rate?

30. Consider an agricultural society in which seeds can either be planted immediately to produce food almost instantly or stored for planting next year to produce food then. Suppose that this society becomes convinced that the weather will improve dramatically next year. Show the effects on the amount of food produced this year and on the interest rate.

Internet Exercise

It was shown in the preceding chapter that changes in interest rates affect the price of bonds, and that these price changes reflect the time value of money. To gain additional practice in computing bond prices and understanding the time value of money, access one of the financial calculators available at the following Internet site: (http://www.yahoo.com/Computers_and_Internet/Hardware/Calculators/Online_Calculators/Financial/). For example, suppose that a bond will generate a payout of $1,000 five years from the present. If we ignore default risk, then by what percentage (and in what direction) will the current price of the bond change if interest rates fall from 8 percent to 6 percent?

chapter 18

Risk and Uncertainty

State of the world A potential set of conditions.

The future brings surprises. A rainstorm can change the price of wheat. A fire can destroy your house. The invention of the automobile can make you rich if you own rubber plantations, or wipe you out if you manufacture buggy whips.

Your wealth tomorrow depends on the **state of the world.** Examples of alternative states of the world are "rain" versus "sunshine," "fire" versus "no fire," and "cars invented" versus "cars not invented."

Markets abound for transferring wealth from one state of the world to another. By placing a bet that it will rain, you increase your wealth in the rainy state of the world while decreasing your wealth in the sunny state. (Of course, you will occupy only one of these states, but at the time you place the bet you don't know which it will be.) Purchasing fire insurance is a mechanism for increasing your wealth in the "fire" state at the expense of decreasing your wealth (by the amount of the insurance premium) in the "no fire" state. Organized markets in stocks and commodities afford numerous opportunities for transferring wealth between states of the world.

In this chapter we will begin by studying the individual's choice about how much wealth to transfer from one state of the world to another and the determination of the equilibrium price at which he can do so. We will then examine some of the particular markets in which such transactions take place.

18.1 Attitudes Toward Risk

When there are two alternative states of the world, we can use diagrams like those in Exhibit 18–1 to represent your wealth in each of them. The horizontal axis measures your wealth in one state, and the vertical axis measures your wealth in the other. Suppose that your total wealth is $100 but that it will be

Exhibit 18-1 States of the World

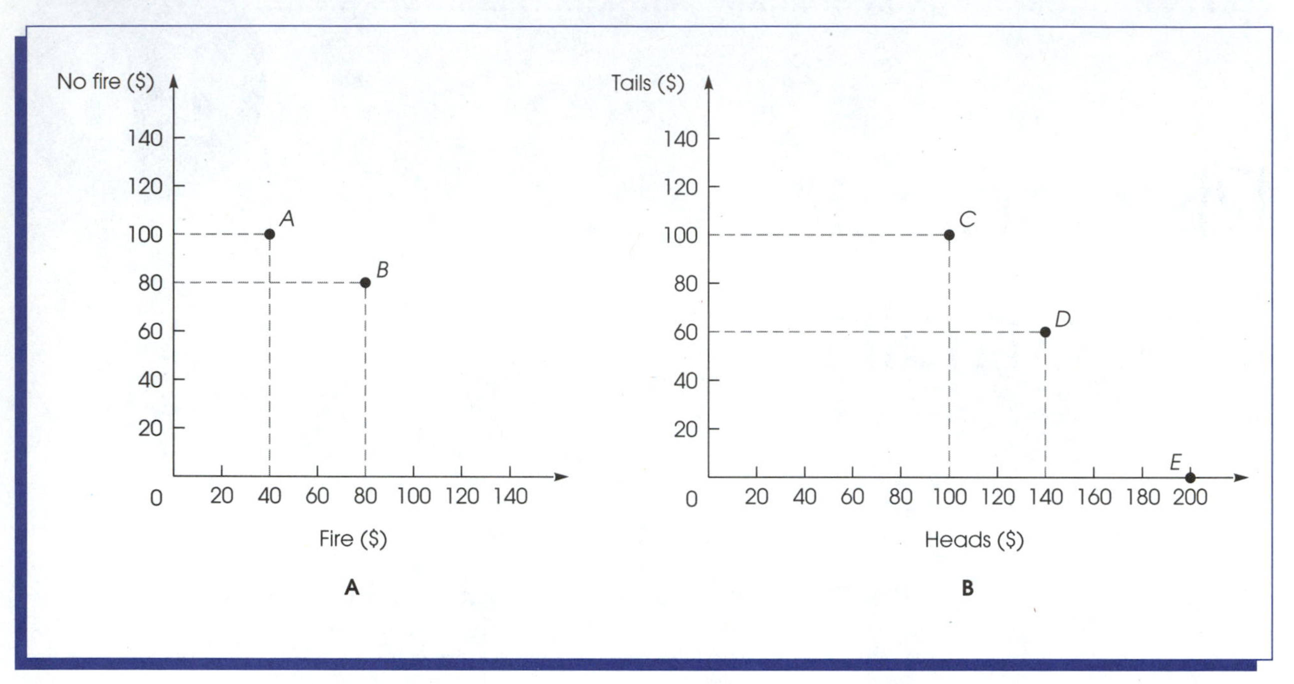

In either panel the two axes represent your wealth in alternative states of the world. Panel A considers the states in which your house is destroyed by fire and in which it is not. Suppose that your wealth is initially $100 but that it will be reduced to $40 in the event of a fire. Then your position is represented by point *A*. Now suppose that for $20 you purchase an insurance contract that will return $60 in the event of a fire. Then your new position is represented by point *B*, where your wealth is $80 in either state of the world.

Panel B considers the two possible outcomes of a coin toss. If your initial wealth is $100 and if you do not bet on the outcome of the toss, then your position is represented by point *C*. If you wager $40 that the coin will come up heads, you move to point *D*.

There are a variety of different quizzes you can take on the Internet to help determine your own attitude toward risk. The following site contains a quiz developed by the Massachusetts Mutual Life Insurance Company: http://www.massmutual.com/Pm/personal/RiskQuiz.htm

reduced to $40 if there is a fire. In that case your position is represented by point *A* in panel A of Exhibit 18–1.

Now suppose that for $20 you purchase an insurance contract that entitles you to collect $60 in the event of a fire. Then if there is no fire, your wealth is reduced to $80, whereas if the fire occurs your wealth is also $80 ($40 plus $60 insurance payment minus $20 to buy the insurance in the first place). Thus, your new position is represented by point *B*.

For another example, suppose that you are a gambler, that you have total assets of $100, and that you have just bet $40 that a certain tossed coin will come up heads. The possible states of the world are "heads" and "tails." In case of heads your wealth is $140; in case of tails it is $60. Your position is represented by point *D* in panel B of Exhibit 18–1. If you don't place the bet, your wealth is $100 regardless of whether the coin comes up heads or tails, and your position is represented by point *C*.

QA **EXERCISE 18.1** What bet would you have to place to move to basket *E* in Exhibit 18–1?

We can think of each of the points in Exhibit 18–1 as a *basket of outcomes,* and we can use indifference curves to represent an individual's preferences among these baskets. However, these baskets of outcomes differ in an important way from the baskets of consumer goods that we studied in Chapter 3. When you own a basket of apples and oranges, you can consume both apples and oranges. But when you own a basket of outcomes, you get only one of the outcomes. Once the state of the world has been determined, we do not need indifference curves to tell us which baskets are preferable to which others. After the coin comes up heads, everyone will agree that point *D* is better than point *C* in panel B of Exhibit 18–1. Or after it comes up tails, everyone will agree that *C* is better than *D*.

Ex ante Determined before the state of the world is known.

Ex post Determined after the state of the world is known.

When we talk about preferences between baskets of outcomes, we are referring to the preferences of someone who does not yet know what the state of the world will be. Such preferences are called **ex ante** preferences, as distinguished from the **ex post** preferences of someone who has already learned the state of the world. If we say that Clarence prefers *D* to *C,* we mean that he would choose to bet $40 on heads rather than not bet at all, if he were asked *before* the coin was flipped.

Characterizing Baskets

Before drawing budget constraints and indifference curves, we need to introduce two concepts that describe important characteristics of any basket of outcomes. One of these is the expected value of a basket; the other is its riskiness.

Expected Values

Expected value The average value over all states of the world, with each state weighted by its probability.

The **expected value** of a basket is given by the formula

$$\begin{pmatrix}\text{Probability}\\ \text{of state 1}\end{pmatrix} \times \begin{pmatrix}\text{Wealth in}\\ \text{state 1}\end{pmatrix} + \begin{pmatrix}\text{Probability}\\ \text{of state 2}\end{pmatrix} \times \begin{pmatrix}\text{Wealth in}\\ \text{state 2}\end{pmatrix}$$

For example, suppose that your basket of outcomes is represented by point *A* in panel A of Exhibit 18–1, and that the probability of a fire is .25 (so that the probability of "no fire" is .75). Then the expected value of your wealth is

$$(.25 \times \$40) + (.75 \times \$100) = \$85$$

In panel B of Exhibit 18–1, if we assume that the coin is unbiased, meaning that it has probability .50 of coming up heads and probability .50 of coming up tails, then the expected value of basket *D* is

$$(.50 \times \$140) + (.50 \times \$60) = \$100$$

EXERCISE 18.2 If the coin is unbiased, what is the expected value of basket C? If the coin is weighted so that it comes up heads two-thirds of the time, what are the expected values of baskets C and D? What if the coin is weighted so that it comes up tails two-thirds of the time?

If you repeat the same gamble a large number of times, the average outcome will be approximately equal to the expected value of the gamble. It is possible to formulate this statement more precisely and to prove it mathematically. The careful mathematical formulation is known as the **law of large numbers.**

Law of large numbers
When a gamble is repeated many times, the average outcome is the expected value.

Suppose that state 1 occurs with probability P_1 and state 2 occurs with probability P_2 (so that $P_1 + P_2 = 1$). Then along any line with slope $-P_1/P_2$, all bas-

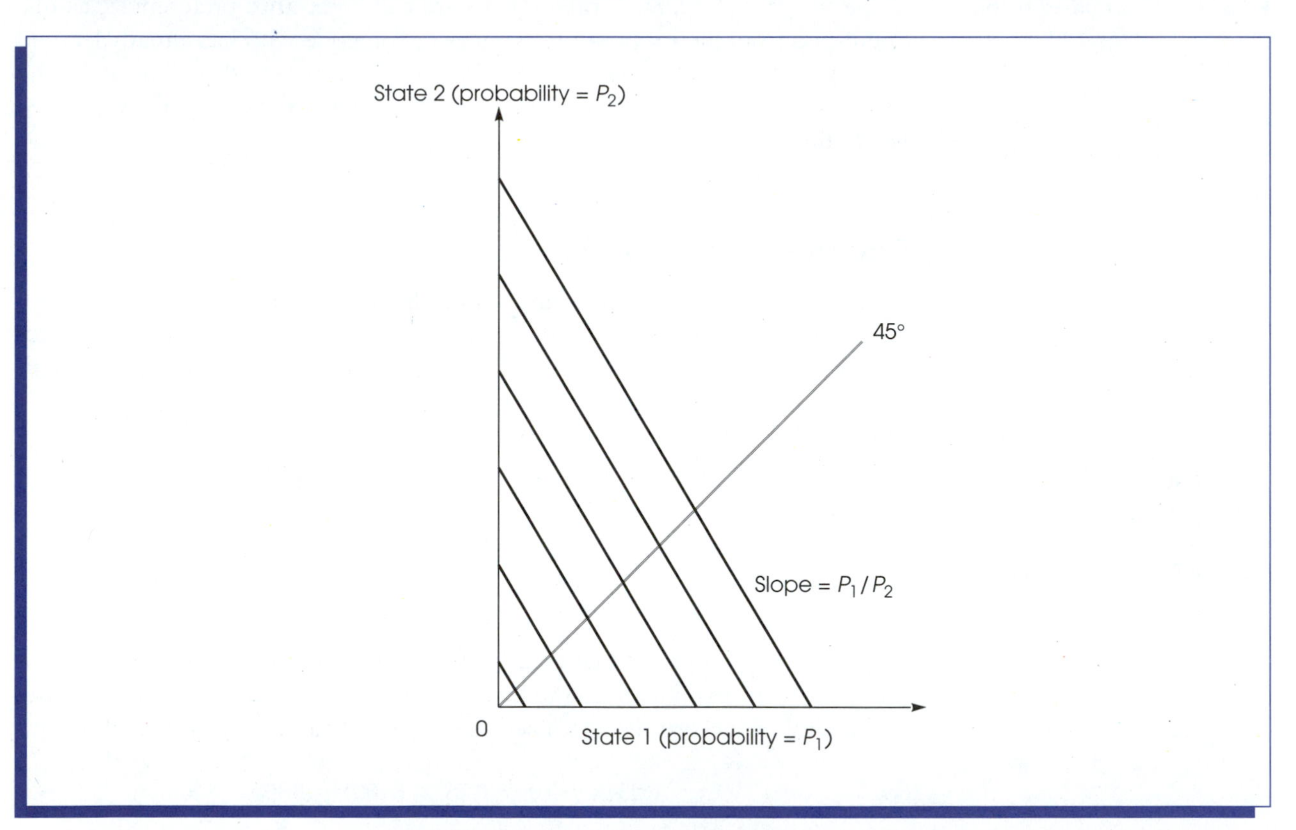

If the probability of state 1 is P_1 and the probability of state 2 is P_2 (so that $P_1 + P_2 = 1$), then all of the baskets along a line of slope $-P_1/P_2$ have the same expected value. The graph shows a family of such lines.

The baskets along the 45° line are risk-free, because a person holding such a basket will have the same wealth in either state of the world. Moving along an iso-expected value line away from the 45° line in either direction, the baskets become successively riskier.

kets have the same expected value. A family of such "iso-expected value" lines is illustrated in Exhibit 18–2.

EXERCISE 18.3 In panel B of Exhibit 18–1, what do the iso-expected value lines look like if the coin is unbiased? If the coin comes up heads two-thirds of the time? If it comes up tails two-thirds of the time? In each case, which point lies on the higher line, *C* or *D*? Are your answers consistent with your calculations in Exercise 18.2?

Riskiness

Riskiness Variation in potential outcomes.

Risk-free Having the same value in any state of the world.

Baskets differ not only in expected value but also in **riskiness.** Baskets on the 45° line (shown in Exhibit 18–2) are referred to as **risk-free,** because individuals who hold them know with certainty what their wealth will be regardless of the state of the world. Moving away from the 45° line along an iso-expected value line, the baskets become riskier, carrying more uncertainty about what the future will bring. In panel B of Exhibit 18–1 baskets *C* and *E* have the same expected value, but a person holding basket *C* knows for certain what his wealth will be, whereas a person with basket *E* could come away with either twice as much wealth or with nothing at all.

Opportunities

Suppose that you enter a gambling parlor with $100 in your pocket. Bets are being taken on a coin flip. If you place no bets, your wealth is $100 in either state of the world. This is your endowment, and it is represented by point *C* in Exhibit 18–3. Suppose that you are invited to express your opinion about how the coin will turn up, and to bet as much as you would like on the outcome. By betting $50 on tails, you can move yourself to point *X,* where your wealth is $150 if you win or $50 if you lose. Other bets can get you to any of the points on the black line shown in Exhibit 18–3. By placing bets, you can trade your endowment for any point along that line. In other words, it is your budget line.

EXERCISE 18.4 What would your budget line look like if you were permitted to bet only on heads?

The gambling parlor offers you the opportunity to trade dollars in the heads state of the world for dollars in the tails state at a relative price of 1. This price is reflected in the slope of the budget line, which is 1 in absolute value.

Other prices are also possible. Suppose that you are offered the opportunity to bet on tails and given *odds* of 2 to 1. This means that for every $1 you bet, you win $2 if tails comes up (but you still lose only $1 if the outcome is heads). Suppose that you are allowed to take either side of this bet: You can bet either on tails at odds of 2 to 1, or on heads, in which case you must grant odds of 2 to 1. You now have an opportunity to trade dollars between the heads state of the world and the tails state of the world. The relative price is 2 "tail-dollars" per "head-dollar." By betting $25 on tails, you can move from point *C* to point *Y* in Exhibit 18–3. In so doing, you are selling 25 head-dollars and receiving 50 tail-dollars in return. Alternatively, you could buy head-dollars and sell tail-

Exhibit 18-3 Opportunities

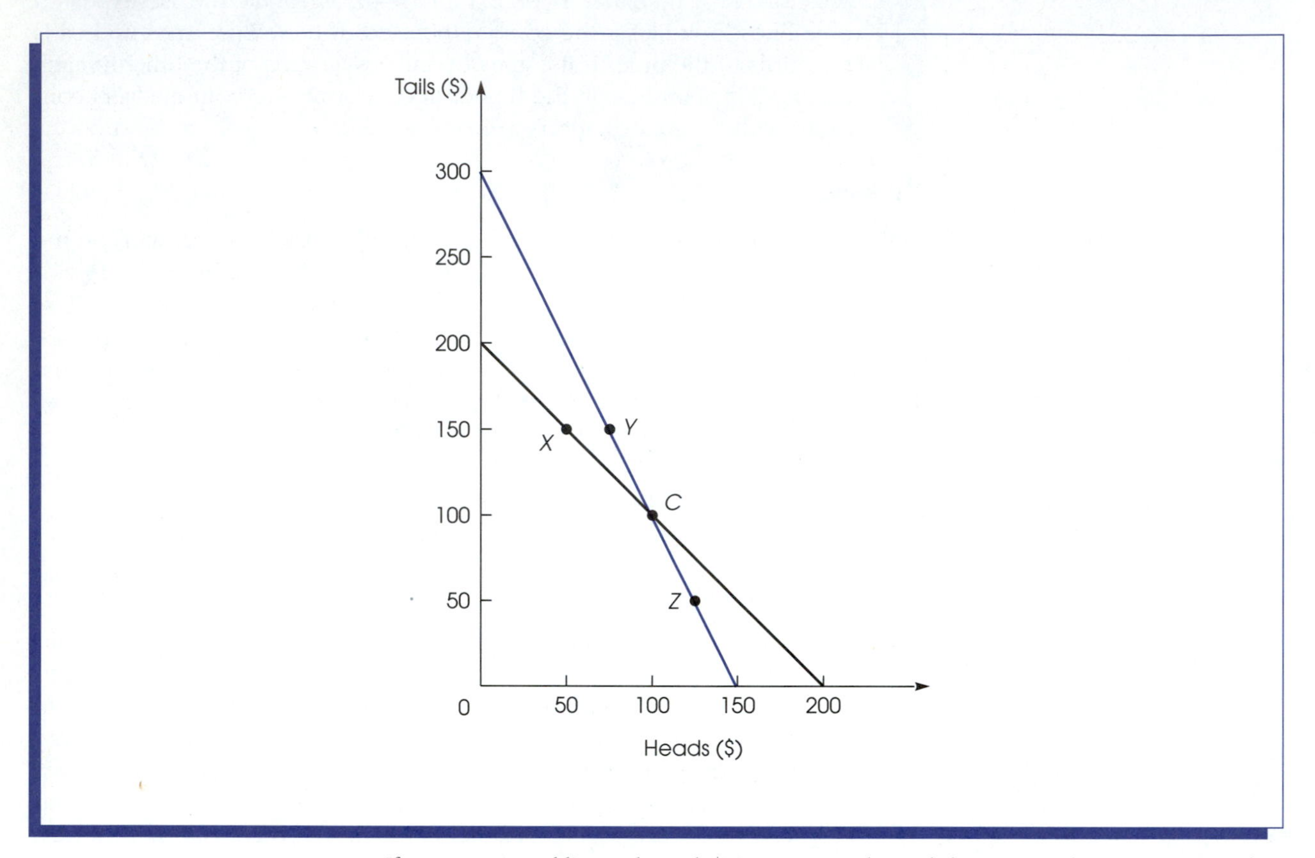

If you enter a gambling parlor with $100 in your pocket and choose not to bet on a coin toss, then your wealth will be $100 in either state of the world. Thus, you achieve point *C* without trading—point *C* is your endowment. By betting on either heads or tails at even odds, you can achieve any basket along the black budget line, such as *X*. If the odds are such that tails bettors receive 2 to 1 payoffs, you can achieve any point on the color budget line. The odds give the relative price of wealth in the tails state in terms of wealth in the heads state, and they therefore determine the slope of the budget line.

dollars, moving to a point like *Z*. Your budget line is the color line in Exhibit 18–3, with an absolute slope of 2, reflecting the relative price of tail-dollars in terms of head-dollars.

Fair Odds

Fair odds Odds that reflect the true probabilities of various states of the world.

Odds are said to be **fair odds** if they reflect the actual probabilities of the two states of the world. An unbiased coin is equally likely to come up heads or tails, so the fair odds on the toss of such a coin are 1 to 1. A weighted coin might be twice as likely to come up heads as to come up tails, in which case the fair odds are 2 to 1 for those who bet on tails.

EXERCISE 18.5 What are the fair odds on a bet that the roll of a die will turn up 1? What are the fair odds on a bet that it will turn up 4 or less? What are the fair odds on a bet that it will turn up an even number?

What is so fair about fair odds? The answer is that at fair odds the expected value of any bet is the same as the expected value of not betting at all. In other words, if two parties bet with each other repeatedly at fair odds, neither will come out very far ahead or very far behind in the long run. If a coin comes up heads twice as often as it comes up tails, and if the payoff for betting on heads is half the payoff for betting on tails, then each party's wins and losses will just cancel out.

When an individual is offered fair odds, any gamble has the same expected value as any other. Therefore:

When an individual is offered fair odds, his budget line coincides with an iso-expected value line.

Preferences and the Consumer's Optimum

The Frequent Gambler

A gambler who bets frequently with the goal of maximizing his winnings is concerned only with the expected values of his wagers. This is because any wager, when it is repeated sufficiently often, returns its expected value on average. In panel B of Exhibit 18–1, if the coin is unbiased, points *C, D,* and *E* all have the same expected value and hence are equally attractive to the frequent, repetitive gambler. If he holds basket *C* every day, he comes away with $100 every day. If he holds basket *E* every day, he comes away with $200 half the time and $0 the other half. Over time, this averages out to the same $100 per day that he can have with basket *C*.

The frequent gambler is indifferent between two baskets of equal expected value, regardless of the risk associated with each. We say that this is because he can **diversify** his risk by playing repeatedly so that he is guaranteed to win the expected value of any gamble in the long run.[1]

Diversify To reduce risk.

When someone's preferences among baskets are determined solely on the basis of their expected values, we describe those preferences as **risk-neutral.** From the definition of risk neutrality, we can see this:

Risk-neutral Caring only about expected value.

The indifference curves of a risk-neutral individual are identical with the iso-expected value lines.

Risk Neutrality

We have seen that the frequent gambler is risk-neutral. Conceivably, some infrequent gamblers might be risk-neutral as well.

Consider a risk-neutral person who is given the opportunity to play at fair odds. Because he is risk-neutral, his indifference curves are the iso-expected value lines. Because the odds are fair, his budget line is the iso-expected value

[1]This assumes that he can always borrow enough to keep playing after he is wiped out by a run of bad luck—or by a single turn of bad luck after a large bet.

Exhibit 18-4 Risk Neutrality

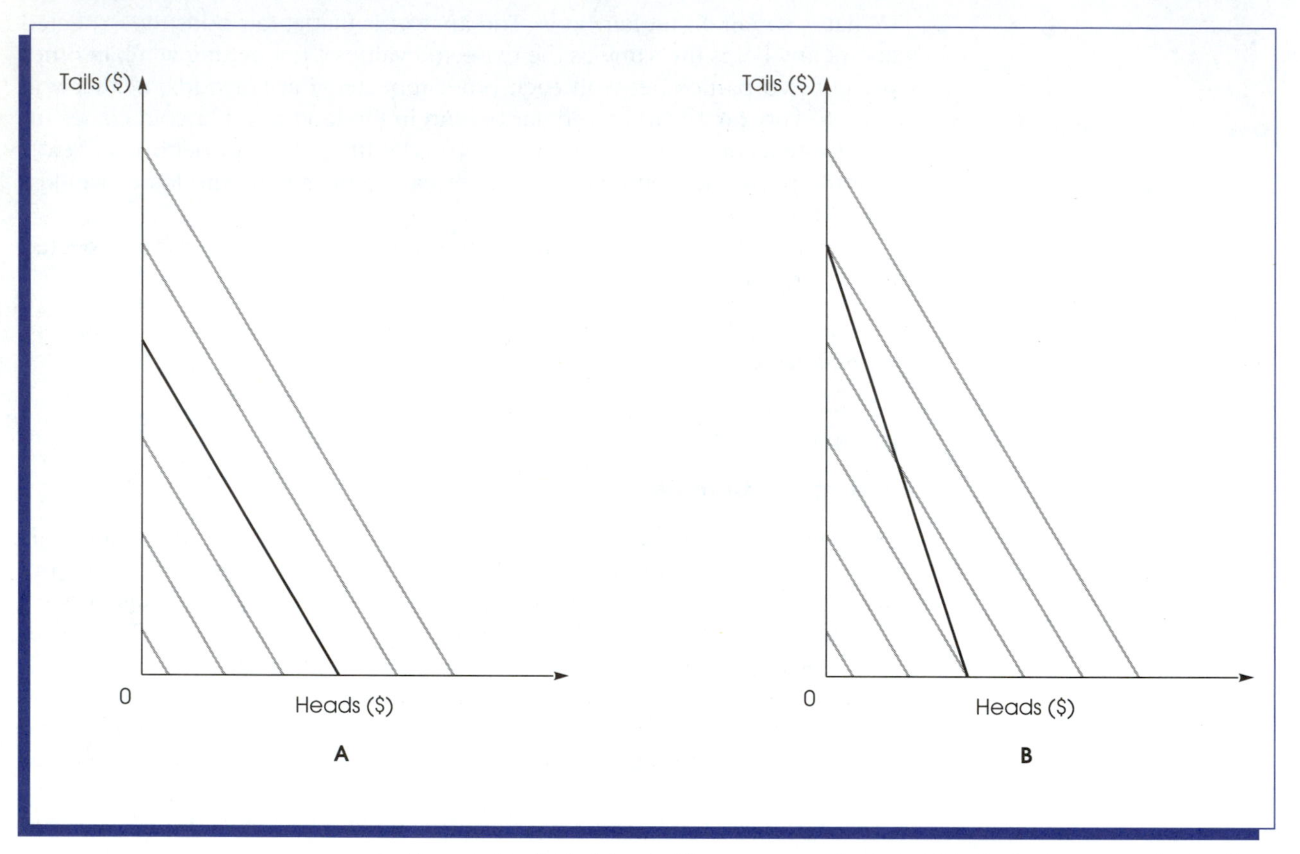

A risk-neutral individual has indifference curves that coincide with the iso-expected value lines, shown in gray in both panels. When he is offered fair odds, his budget line coincides with one of the indifference curves, as in panel A. In that case the individual is indifferent among all of the options available to him. When he is offered any odds other than fair odds, his budget line has a different slope than his indifference curves, like the black budget line in panel B. In that case he will always choose a corner and bet everything he has on one outcome or the other.

line through his endowment. The picture is as in panel A of Exhibit 18–4, where the gray iso-expected value lines are the indifference curves, and the black budget line coincides with one of them. This individual is indifferent among all of the points on his budget line. Thus:

At fair odds, a risk-neutral individual is indifferent as to how much he bets.

Suppose that the risk-neutral person has an opportunity to play at other than fair odds. This rotates his budget line through his endowment, either clockwise, if the new odds favor betting on tails, or counterclockwise, if the new odds favor betting on heads. The first possibility is illustrated in panel B of Exhibit 18–4. As you can see, he now chooses a point on the vertical axis, where his wealth becomes zero in the event that the coin turns up heads.

A risk-neutral individual faced with unfair odds will bet everything he owns on one or the other outcome.

Unlike all of the indifference curves we have encountered previously, the indifference curves of this chapter depend on more than just tastes. They depend also on the probabilities associated with the two states of the world. If a fair coin is replaced by a biased coin, a gambler might change his mind about the desirability of various wagers, even though his underlying tastes have not changed.

Risk Aversion

Now let us consider the preferences of someone who is not a frequent gambler. To such a person, the riskiness of his basket can be a significant consideration. He does not expect his gains and losses to cancel out in the long run.

Risk-averse Always preferring the least risky among baskets with the same expected value.

Many people are **risk-averse.** This means that among baskets with the same expected value, they choose the one that is least risky. Consequently, when offered fair odds, they choose the basket that equalizes their incomes in both states of the world. Such baskets are located on the 45° line.

The two panels of Exhibit 18–5 show the indifference curves of typical risk-averse individuals facing fair odds. In panel A the individual has an initial wealth of $100 and is offered the opportunity to bet on a coin toss at fair odds. His optimum point occurs right on the 45° line, at this endowment point *P*. He places no wager.

Panel B shows the situation of a risk-averse person whose wealth is $100, which is reduced to $40 if there is a fire. His endowment is at point *A*. We will assume that "fire" occurs with probability .25, so that "no fire" occurs with probability .75.

Suppose that it is possible to buy fire insurance for $1. The insurance pays $4 in the event of fire, and the homeowner can buy as many units of this insurance as he wants to. Buying insurance is exactly like betting that there will be a fire. If there is no fire, he loses his $1. If there is a fire, there is a net gain of $3 (a $4 insurance payment minus the $1 cost of the insurance). Therefore, this particular insurance policy offers 3-to-1 odds when the homeowner bets that a fire will take place. These happen to be the fair odds, because the probability of "no fire" (.75) is 3 times the probability of "fire" (.25).

The homeowner's budget line has an absolute slope of ⅓, reflecting the odds of 3 to 1. Because the homeowner is assumed to be risk-averse, he always eliminates risk when he can bet at fair odds. That is, he chooses the point where his budget line crosses the 45° line, at point *Q* in panel B of Exhibit 18–5. At this point the homeowner is guaranteed that his wealth will be $85 regardless of whether or not the fire occurs. His indifference curves must be like those in the graph, with the optimum at *Q*.

EXERCISE 18.6 Exactly how much insurance does the homeowner buy?

Exhibit 18–5 Risk Aversion

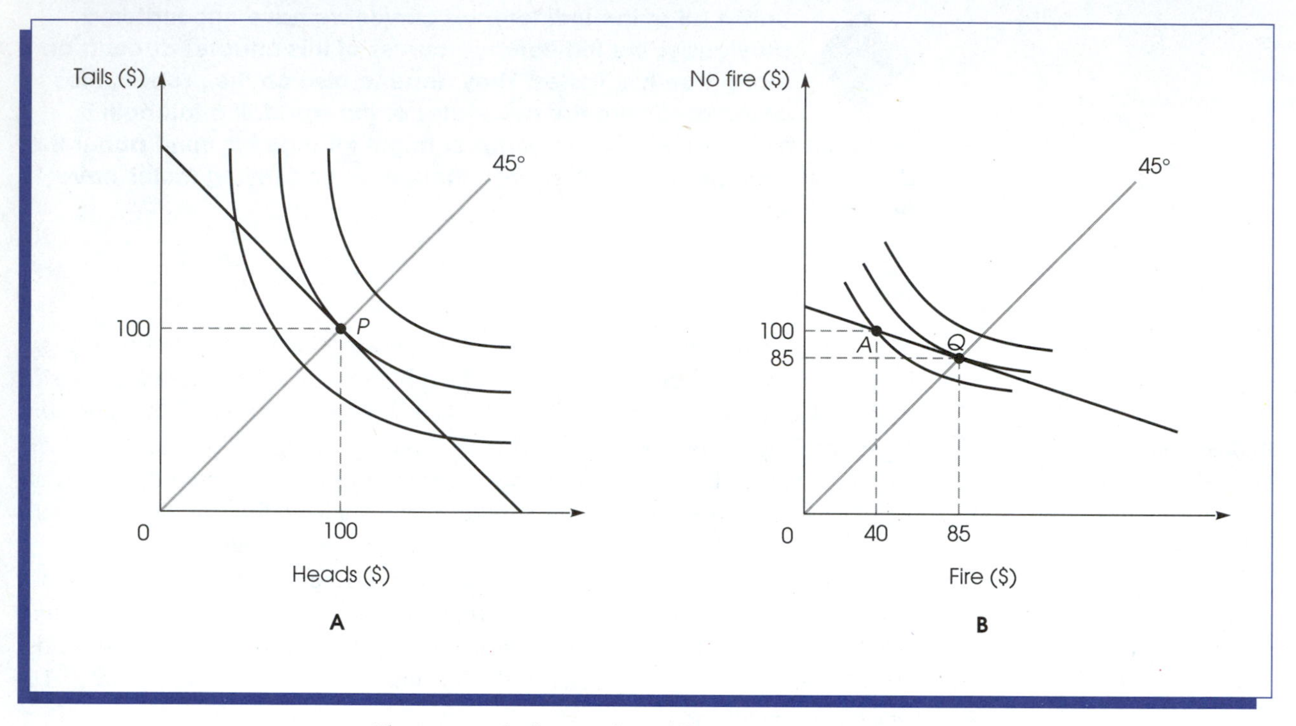

The two panels illustrate the indifference curves of individuals facing fair odds. In panel A the individual has initial wealth of $100 and is offered the opportunity to bet at even odds on the toss of a fair coin. His endowment is at point *P*, which is already on the 45° line. This is also his optimum, so he places no wager.

In panel B the individual has initial wealth of $100, which will be reduced to $40 in the event of a fire. His endowment is at point *A*. We assume that the probability of "no fire" is 3 times as great as the probability of "fire." Thus, the fair odds for an insurance policy are 3 to 1, and we assume that such a policy is available. This gives the illustrated budget line, which crosses the 45° line at (85,85). Since he is risk-averse, his optimum is at *Q*. He achieves this point by purchasing $15 worth of insurance.

Risk Preference

Risk-preferring Always preferring the most risky among baskets with the same expected value.

Another type of individual is **risk-preferring.** Given a choice between a "sure thing" and a lottery with the same expected value, he chooses the lottery. Such an individual has indifference curves as shown in Exhibit 18–6. They become tangent to the fair-odds budget lines at points along the 45° line, but this is because the individual considers any such point to be the *worst* he can do when trading at fair odds. You can see from Exhibit 18–6 that a risk-preferring person always chooses a lottery in which he risks sacrificing everything he owns in exchange for a chance at great wealth.

It is also possible for an individual to be risk-preferring in some situations and risk-averse in others. Consider an individual with the indifference curves and budget line shown in Exhibit 18–7. Starting from an endowment at point

A, he indulges his risk preference by gambling to get to either point *B* or point *C*. At that point, risk aversion becomes dominant and he gambles no further.

Are criminals risk preferrers? To find out, read David Friedman's essay at the following Internet site: http://www.best.com/~ddfr/Academic/Are_Criminals_Risk_Preferrers/Are_Crim_Risk_Pref.html

Which Preferences Are Most Likely?

Attitudes toward risk typically vary with income. At very low levels of income, people are probably risk-preferring. To see the reason for this, suppose that \$5 per year is the minimum income necessary for survival. In that case, an income of \$3 per year is no more valuable than an income of zero. Somebody earning \$3 per year would be willing to gamble, even at very unfavorable odds, for a chance to earn enough to stay alive.

Even at higher levels of income, we sometimes observe risk preference for similar reasons. If you are determined to purchase a particular sailboat for \$20,000 and if your current assets total \$19,000, you might be willing to take a very risky bet as long as it offered some chance to win \$1,000.

Exhibit 18-6 Risk Preference

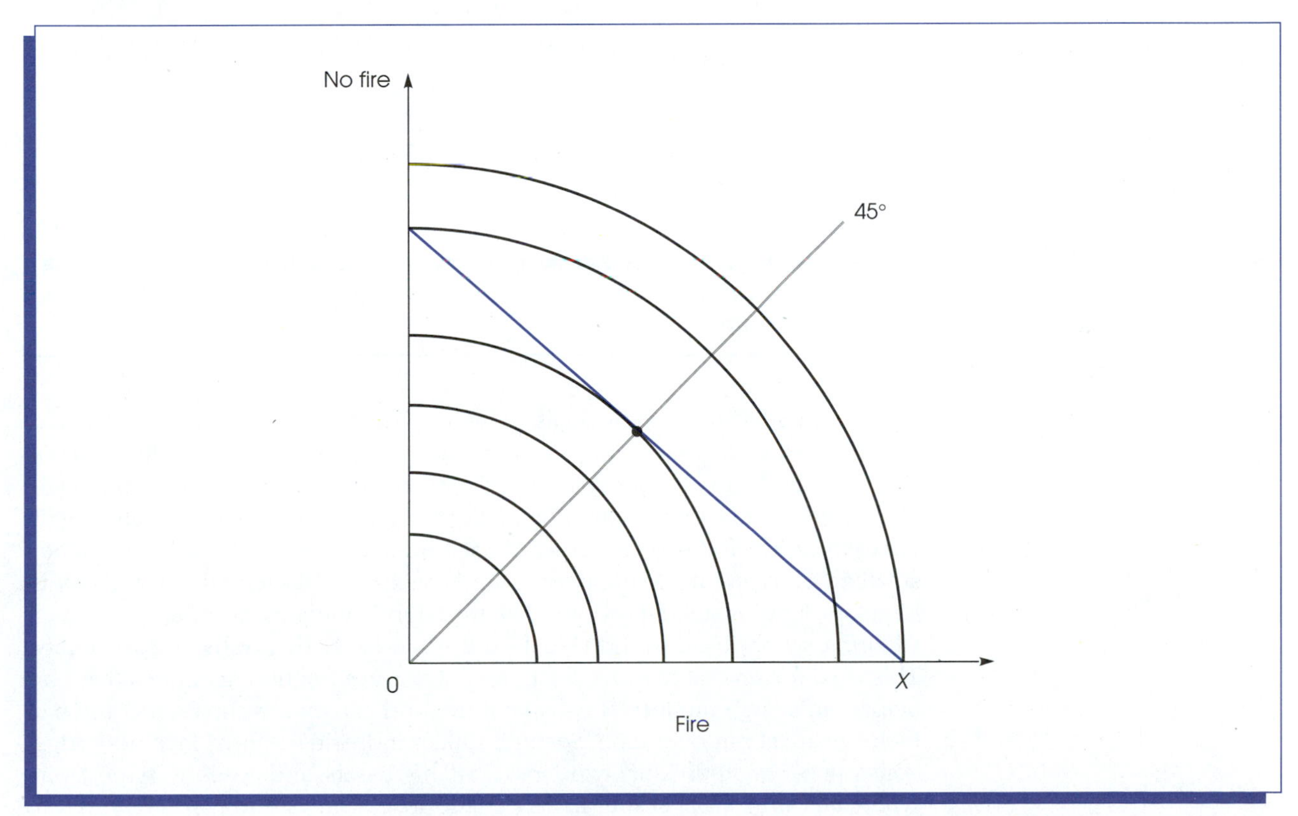

The risk-preferring individual always chooses a corner solution, regardless of the odds he faces. This individual chooses point *X*, where his wealth becomes zero if there is no fire. He can accomplish this by spending all of his income on fire insurance, hoping for a fire that will make him rich.

Exhibit 18-7 Risk Preference and Risk Aversion Combined

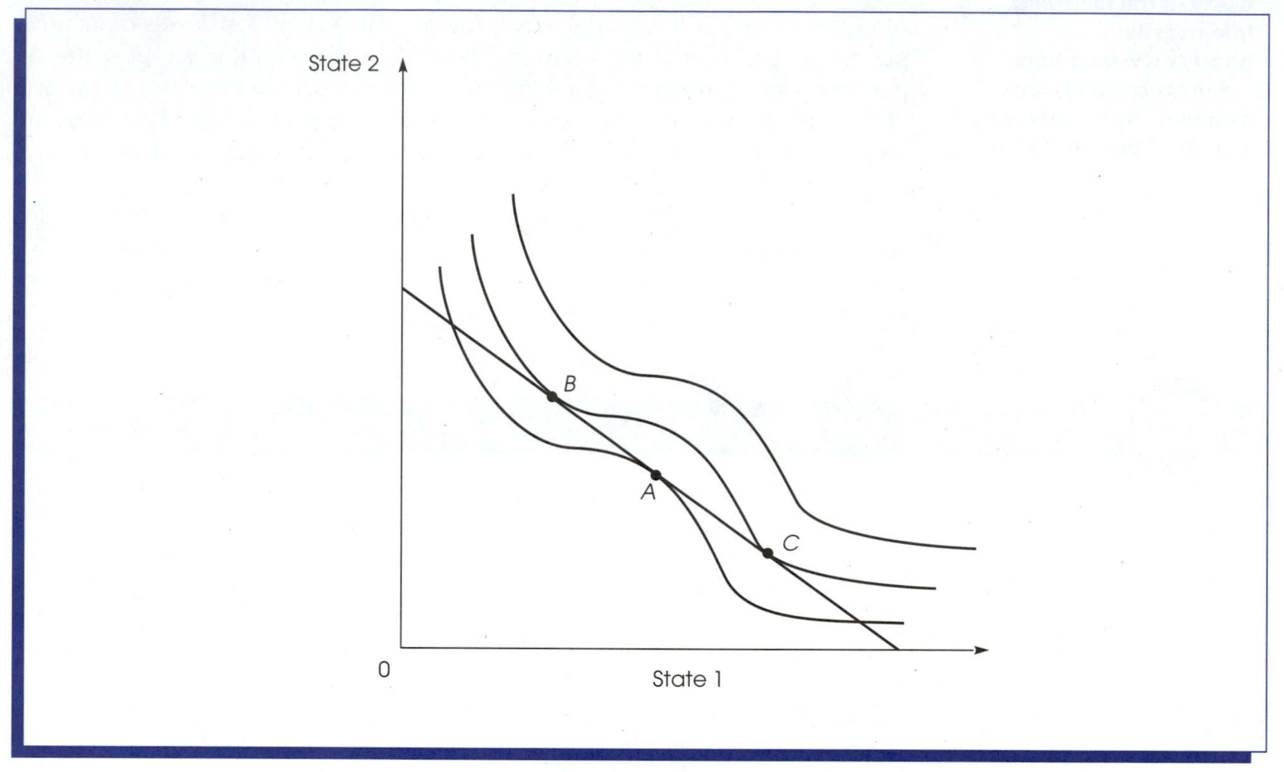

The same individual can exhibit both risk preference and risk aversion at different points on his indifference curve map.

Nevertheless, most individuals exhibit some degree of risk aversion over most ranges of income. A person earning $20,000 per year is unlikely to be willing to trade a year's income for a 50-50 chance at $40,000, or even a 50-50 chance at $50,000. On the other hand, the same person might very well be willing to trade $20 for a 50-50 chance at $50, or $2 for a 50-50 chance at $5. When small amounts are involved, people tend to exhibit risk-neutral behavior. With large amounts at stake, however, risk aversion is the general rule.

Firms, as opposed to individuals, are more likely to exhibit risk neutrality. This is so for several reasons. First, many firms are frequent gamblers that participate in a large number of risky ventures and can expect their good and bad luck to cancel out over time. Second, unlike individuals, firms face no budget constraints. An individual who risks all his assets and loses is wiped out, whereas a firm that risks all its assets and loses can often borrow enough to continue operating. (Of course, the firm must convince lenders that it is showing good business sense in the long run.)

Those firms that are corporations have an additional reason for risk-neutral behavior. Corporate stockholders are able to diversify their risks by holding small amounts of stock in many different companies. Once diversified, they, like the frequent gambler, earn approximately the expected value of the return on their overall portfolios. For this reason the stockholders are interested only in maximizing expected return, and they want the corporation to behave in a risk-neutral way.

Gambling at Favorable Odds

Often we encounter opportunities to gamble at better than fair odds. Suppose that you own a restaurant and have the opportunity to run an advertising campaign that has a 50-50 chance of success. If the campaign succeeds, your profits (net of advertising costs) will increase by $2,000, whereas if it fails, you will lose $1,000. Since success and failure are equally likely, and since the gain from success exceeds the loss from failure, the odds are better than fair. If you run the campaign, you increase the expected value of your wealth. For another example, suppose that you have the opportunity to buy a ticket to a concert that you will enjoy with probability .75. The ticket costs $1, and you receive $2 worth of pleasure if the concert turns out to be good. Thus, if the concert is bad, you lose $1, and if it is good, you gain $1 ($2 in enjoyment minus $1 for the ticket). Since the concert is more likely to be good than bad, the odds on this gamble are also favorable.

EXERCISE 18.7 For each of the opportunities described in the preceding paragraph, what odds would be fair? What are the actual odds? What is the expected value of your winnings if you gamble?

We have already seen that a risk-neutral person always accepts any wager in which the odds are better than fair, and that he wagers as much as he possibly can at such odds. What does a risk-averter do? Does the prospect of a positive expected gain entice him to gamble, or does his risk aversion prevent him from gambling?

Consider an example. Suppose that you are risk-averse, have assets totaling $5, and have the opportunity to gamble at 3-to-1 odds on the toss of an unbiased coin. If you bet $1 on heads, then you either lose $1 (if tails comes up) or win $3 (if heads comes up).

Your budget line is then the black line in Exhibit 18–8. Your endowment is at point *A*, where you keep your $5 no matter how the coin turns up. We know that if you were offered the fair odds of 1 to 1, you would not bet at all, so the absolute slope of the indifference curve at *A* must be 1. It follows that the budget line cuts through the indifference curve, as shown in the exhibit.

By betting $1, you move from point *A* to point *B*, which is an improvement. Thus, if your only options are to bet $1 or to not bet at all, you choose to bet.

Suppose, alternatively, that the house rules require you to bet either $3 or nothing at all. A $3 bet would move you to point *C*, which is less desirable than point *A*. Thus, in this case you would prefer not to bet.

Therefore, the exhibit demonstrates this principle:

A risk-averse person, offered the opportunity to place a sufficiently small bet at favorable odds, always accepts. If only offered the opportunity to place a very large bet at favorable odds, he always declines.

Exhibit 18-8 Gambling at Favorable Odds

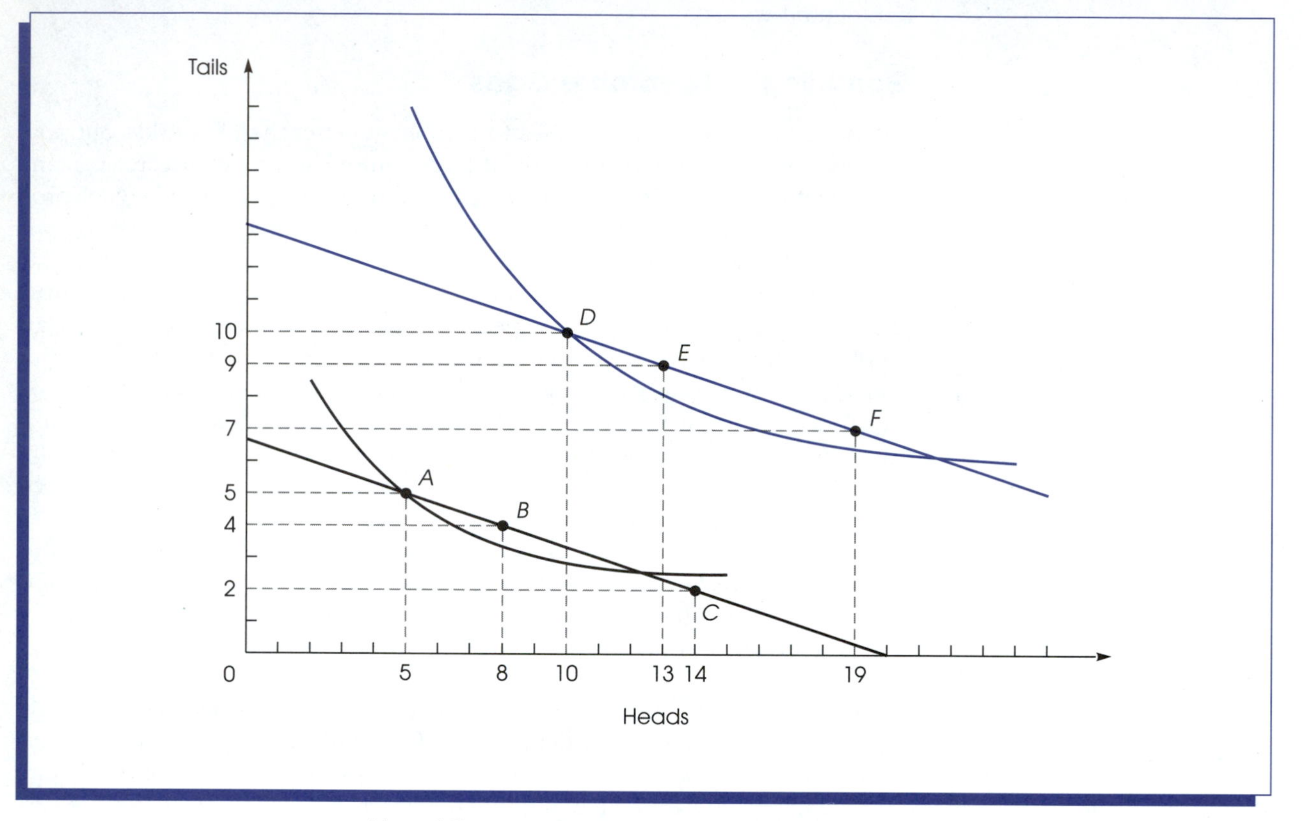

The indifference curves are those of a risk-averter facing the opportunity to bet on the toss of an unbiased coin. His initial wealth is $5, so that point *A* is his endowment. Because he is risk-averse, the absolute slope of the indifference curve at *A* must reflect the fair odds of 1 to 1; in other words, it has an absolute slope of 1.

This individual is invited to bet on heads at the favorable odds of 3 to 1. By betting $1, he moves to point *B*, which he prefers to point *A*. If he bet $3, he would move to point *C*, which he likes less than point *A*. Thus, if he is allowed to place the small bet of $1, he will do so, but if he must place the large bet of $3, he will decline.

Suppose that this individual has an increase in wealth, to $10. Then his endowment moves to point *D*. From point *D* a $1 bet moves him to point *E*, and a $3 bet moves him to point *F*. Either of these is an improvement over point *D*, and if offered either option, he will accept it. With greater initial wealth, he is willing to accept the $3 bet that he previously considered too large. However, he will continue to reject much larger bets.

The largest bet that a risk-averter would be willing to make depends on his wealth. Suppose that instead of starting with $5, you started with $10. In that case your endowment would be at point *D* in Exhibit 18–8. A $1 wager at the favorable odds of 3 to 1 brings you to point *E*, and a $3 wager brings you to point *F*. Either of these is preferable to point *D*. Thus, even if the house rules require the relatively large $3 wager, you still choose to bet.

The indifference curves of Exhibit 18–8 are typical. As a risk-averter acquires more wealth, he is willing to enter into larger wagers at favorable odds. However, there is always a limit to what size wager he will accept. Even with the initial wealth of $10, a person with the indifference curves of Exhibit 18–8 will not bet $5 on heads.

Risk and Society

What are the added risks associated with travel? See an illustrative example of quantitative risk assessment at the following Internet site maintained by the Illinois Mathematics and Science Academy: http://www.imsa.edu/team/spi/SADVI/sadvi97/riskexample.html

Societies, like corporations, must decide when to undertake risky projects. Just as risk-averse stockholders can prefer the corporations they own to behave risk-neutrally, so risk-averse citizens can prefer the societies they inhabit to behave risk-neutrally in some respects. In a society that undertakes a large number of independent investment projects, citizens will be best off in the long run if those projects are evaluated risk-neutrally. However, the individual entrepreneurs who actually decide how to allocate resources often have much personal wealth at stake, so that risk aversion enters their decisions.

In some cases, however, entrepreneurial initiatives are intensely personal. In the 1950s Joseph Wilson (later the head of the Xerox Corporation) had a vision of the copying machine as a tool that would transform U.S. business. At the time few shared his vision. Entrepreneurial visions arise every day, and most do not succeed. Should such visions be pursued?

Suppose that Wilson had a 1 in 100 chance of succeeding in his project. Then from a social point of view, the project should be undertaken if the benefits from a success would be more than 100 times the losses from a failure. The frequency with which such projects arise in society justifies a risk-neutral calculation. But visions are the property of individuals, and individuals are risk-averse. From Wilson's point of view, a mere 100-to-1 payoff would not have sufficed. In order to induce him to risk a substantial fraction of his personal wealth for a 1% chance of success, Wilson might have required the prospect of a 500-fold multiplication of his wealth.

From a social point of view, risk-averse individuals underinvest in risky projects. The existence of corporations helps to solve this problem, since, as we have seen, the shareholders, with diversified portfolios, will encourage appropriate risk-taking. However, intensely personal visions cannot always be effectively pursued by large corporations. In such cases only the prospect of great personal fortune will induce individuals to take great risks. A society that attempted to limit the amassing of great wealth might be a society without copying machines.

18.2 The Market for Insurance

Many markets have developed to facilitate transfers of risk from one party to another. In this and the next two sections we will examine a few of these markets. We have already alluded to the insurance market in Section 18.1. Panel A of Exhibit 18–1 depicts the endowment of a homeowner facing the possibility of a fire. In Exhibit 18–5 we can see how the homeowner, when facing a given price, decides how much insurance to buy. But what determines the market price of insurance?

Insurance companies are highly diversified. If each individual house catches fire with probability .25, you must experience considerable uncertainty about whether yours will be one of those that burn. By contrast, a company that insures 1,000 houses can be sure that almost exactly 250 of them will burn. If there were no other considerations, an insurance company that offered fair odds would just break even. Any insurance company offering less than fair odds would earn profits, causing entry to the insurance industry, and driving the odds down until they were fair. Thus, a $1 insurance policy must buy a $4 payoff in case of fire.[2]

There are, however, other considerations. For one thing, there are costs involved with running an insurance company—costs of maintaining an office, a sales force, an actuarial staff to estimate probabilities, assessors to estimate actual damages when they occur, and so forth. A firm offering fair odds could not cover these costs and would not survive. The odds must be tilted in the company's favor by enough so that these basic operating costs can be met.

However, more interesting and more important reasons exist as to why insurance is not offered at fair odds. In discussing them, we can safely ignore the relatively minor issue of operating costs.

Imperfect Information

First, there are problems of information, such as *moral hazard* and *adverse selection,* which are discussed in Section 9.3. The moral hazard problem arises when people behave more recklessly because they are insured; this means that insurance companies must offer odds that are adjusted accordingly.

The adverse selection problem arises when fair odds are different for different people (as when some are more naturally susceptible to disease than others, which affects the fair odds for health insurance) and the insurance company is unable to tell who is who.

As in Section 9.3, assume that some people are "Healthies," with a 1 in 10 chance of becoming ill, while others are "Sicklies," with a 9 in 10 chance of becoming ill. If the insurance company could distinguish one group from the other, it would offer the appropriate odds to each group. If it can't tell the difference, then it can't simply offer odds that are appropriate for Healthies, because Sicklies will purchase the insurance and bankrupt the company.

The discussion in Section 9.3 suggested a solution: Offer two policies, one at "Healthy" odds and one at "Sickly" odds, but limit the quantity of Healthy insurance that any one person can buy. If the quantity is chosen correctly, each group will voluntarily purchase the right kind of insurance.

With the machinery of this chapter, we can show exactly how the limit is chosen. In panel A of Exhibit 18–9, Healthies and Sicklies both have endowment point *A*. The black budget line shows fair odds for Healthies and the blue line shows fair odds for Sicklies. If Sicklies are offered insurance at fair odds, they choose point *Q* on the blue indifference curve. The point where the blue indifference curve crosses the black budget line is labeled *R*.

---

[2]With this policy you lose $1 when there is no fire, and you gain $3 (the $4 payoff minus the $1 premium) if there is a fire. Therefore, the policy offers the fair odds of 3 to 1.

People who purchase insurance at Healthy fair odds move down along the black budget line from *A*. If purchases are limited so that nobody is allowed to move past *R*, then no Sickly ever chooses Healthy insurance. By purchasing Sickly insurance, the Sickly can achieve point *Q*, which is preferred to any point between *A* and *R* on the black budget line.

Healthies, on the other hand, who have a different family of indifference curves, might very well choose Healthy insurance. Panel B of Exhibit 18–9 shows that a Healthy would rather buy a limited quantity of Healthy insurance, achieving point *R*, than an unlimited quantity of Sickly insurance, which allows the Healthy to achieve point *X*.

Exhibit 18-9 Adverse Selection

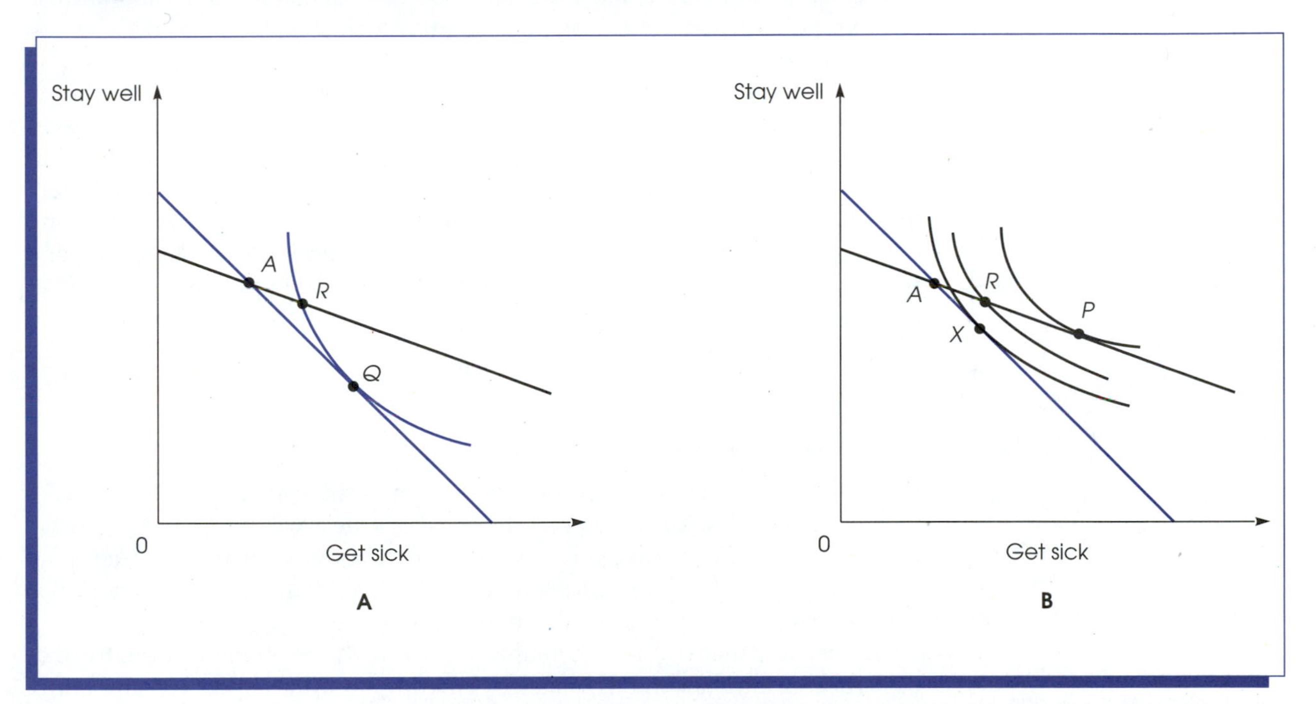

Healthies and Sicklies both have endowment point *A*. The black budget line represents fair odds for Healthies and the blue budget line represents fair odds for Sicklies. If Sicklies buy Sickly insurance, they choose the quantity to achieve point *Q*, on the blue indifference curve in panel A. The point where that curve crosses the black budget line is labeled *R*.

The insurance company offers both types of insurance, but limits the quantity of Healthy insurance so that the purchaser cannot move past point *R* on the black budget line. Sicklies voluntarily choose Sickly Insurance, because they prefer point *Q* to any point between *A* and *R* along the black line.

Healthies, meanwhile, might have the black indifference curves shown in panel B and choose the limited Healthy insurance, since they prefer point *R* to anything they can achieve on the blue budget line.

If Sicklies voluntarily identified themselves, the company could offer unlimited quantities of each type of insurance to the appropriate group. Sicklies would still achieve point *Q*, and Healthies would achieve point *P*.

Of course, if Sicklies voluntarily revealed their identities, the insurance company could offer each form of insurance in unlimited quantities to the appropriate group. Sicklies would still achieve point *Q*, and Healthies would be better off, achieving *P* instead of *X*. But, as discussed in Section 9.3, such voluntary revelation cannot be sustained in equilibrium.[3]

Uninsurable Risks

Uninsurable risk A risk that cannot be diversified.

Another reason why fair-odds insurance is not always available is that some risks are **uninsurable risks** because they cannot be diversified. This occurs when a large number of people are all adversely affected in the same state of the world.

Suppose that you and your friend must each carry a $10 bill through a bad neighborhood at different times. You can insure against robbery by agreeing that if either one is robbed, the other will ease the burden by paying $5 to the victim. But if you are traveling together, so that if one is robbed the other will also be robbed, then there is no advantage to such a contract and no way you can insure each other.

An insurance company brings together many people, its customers, who effectively insure each other against individual disasters. But a collective disaster cannot be insured against by everybody simultaneously. You cannot buy fair-odds insurance against a nuclear disaster. The insurance company is risk-neutral when it insures 1,000 people against a .25 chance of fire, because it knows that it will have to pay off in only 250 cases. It is no longer risk-neutral, and will not offer fair-odds insurance, when it insures 1,000 people against a .25 chance of a nuclear disaster, because there is a .25 chance that it will have to pay off in 1,000 cases.

18.3 Futures Markets

Learn about currency futures and options at the following Internet site maintained by the Chicago Mercantile Exchange: http://www.cme.com/market/currency/index.html

Suppose that you are a farmer, planting wheat in the spring to be harvested in the fall. You do not know whether the price of wheat will be $3 or $4 a bushel next fall, and you are therefore uncertain both about your future wealth and about the optimal amount of planting to do. If you are risk-averse, you will want to insure against the possibility of a low price.

Futures contract A contract to deliver a specified good at a specified future date for a specified price.

In practice, this is often accomplished through the medium of a **futures contract.** A futures contract is an agreement to deliver a specified amount of something (in this case wheat) at some future date (in this case next fall) for a price agreed upon today. If the low price of $3 and the high price of $4 are equally likely, then a "fair odds" delivery price is $3.50. By signing a contract to deliver at this price, you can reduce your risk without sacrificing expected value. At the same time, the buyer of the contract is able to insure against a high price, which is the unfavorable state of the world from the buyer's point of view.

---

[3]The discussion of adverse selection is based on M. Rothschild and J. Stiglitz, "Equilibrium in Competitive Insurance Markets: An Essay in the Economics of Imperfect Information," *Quarterly Journal of Economics* 90 (1976):629–650. Rothschild and Stiglitz show that the solution in Exhibit 18–9 is the only possible equilibrium, although there might be no equilibrium at all.

Futures market The market for futures contracts.

Spot market The market for goods for immediate delivery.

Spot price Price in the spot market.

The market for futures contracts is called the **futures market** for short. The market for wheat for immediate delivery is called the **spot market.** The **spot price** of wheat is the price of wheat in the spot market; in other words, it is simply what we would ordinarily call "the" price of wheat.

Speculation

Nonfarmers can also sell futures contracts. Suppose that in July wheat for September delivery is selling at $3.50 per bushel. You, however, believe that next September the spot price of wheat is likely to be only $3.25. In that case, you can sell a futures contract for $3.50, wait until September, and then buy a bushel of wheat for $3.25 to deliver in fulfillment of your contract. You will earn a profit of 25¢. On the other hand, if you are in error and the spot price next September turns out to be $3.75, then you will have to buy at that price and will end up with a net loss of 25¢.

Speculator One who attempts to earn profits in the futures market by predicting future changes in supply or demand.

Somebody who tries to outguess the market and earn profits by buying and selling futures contracts is called a **speculator.** Next we will see that when speculators are successful, they have the effect of improving economic efficiency.

Suppose that it is now February. A certain amount of grain is stored in grain elevators, and this is the only source of grain for this month and the next. The sellers (that is, the elevator owners) must decide how much to sell in February and how much to save for sale in March. Panel A of Exhibit 18–10 shows the February demand curve for grain. Panel B shows (in dark blue) the expected March demand curve as foreseen by the sellers. Sellers choose to supply Q_F bushels in February and save Q_M bushels to supply in March. (If they are risk-averse, they sell futures contracts now, promising delivery of Q_M bushels in March.) These quantities are chosen so that the equilibrium prices in the two months are equal. In Exhibit 18–10 the equilibrium price in each month is P_0.

To see why the equilibrium prices must be equal, let us see what would happen if the expected March spot price exceeded the current price. Sellers, sensing a profit, would save more grain for next month, reducing Q_F and increasing Q_M. This would have the effect of raising the current price and reducing the March price and would continue until the two prices were equal.

EXERCISE 18.8 Explain what happens if the current price exceeds the expected March spot price.

Actually, sellers equate the current price not to the March price, but to the present value of the March price. We are assuming that the interest rate is small enough so that, for practical purposes, a dollar delivered in March is worth as much as a dollar delivered in February. We are also ignoring storage costs, which, if significant, would make suppliers willing to provide grain at a lower price today than tomorrow. These assumptions simplify the analysis but do not affect the welfare conclusions.

Exhibit 18-10 Speculation

Case 1: Speculator Right

Without Speculator:	**With Speculator:**
February welfare: $A + B + D$	February welfare: $A + B + C + D + E$
March welfare: $F + I + M + N$	March welfare: $F + I + M$
Total: $A + B + D + F + I + M + N$	Total: $A + B + C + D + E + F + I + M$

Gain due to speculator: $C + E - N$

Case 2: Speculator Wrong

Without Speculator:	**With Speculator:**
February welfare: $A + B + D$	February welfare: $A + B + C + D + E$
March welfare: $F + G + H + I + J + K + L + M + N$	March: $F + G + I + J + M$
Total: $A + B + D + F + G + H + I + J + K + L + M + N$	Total: $A + B + C + D + E + F + G + I + J + M$

Loss due to speculator: $H + K + L + N - C - E$

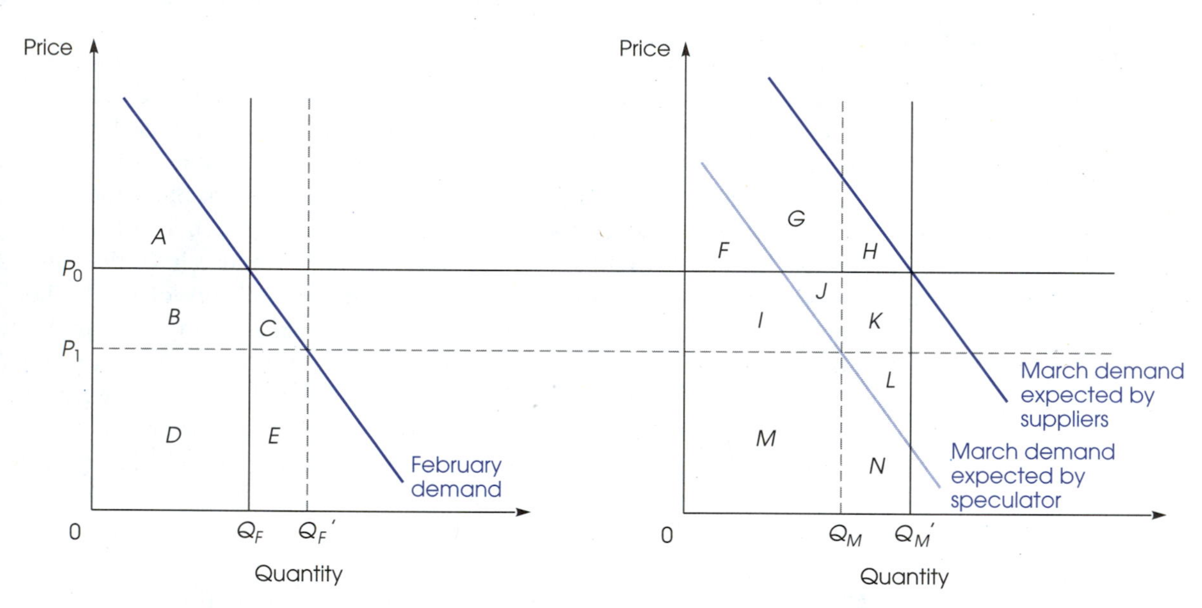

A. Supply and demand for February grain

B. Supply and demand for March grain

The February demand curve for grain is shown in panel A. Suppliers expect the March demand curve to be the dark blue curve in panel B. Thus, they supply Q_F bushels in February and Q_M bushels in March, where these quantities are chosen to make the prices equal. The price in either month is P_0.

Now a speculator arrives on the scene, believing that the March demand curve will be the light blue curve in panel B. Thus, he offers to sell March futures contracts, driving down the price of March grain and leading suppliers to sell more in February and less in March. The quantities adjust to Q_F' and Q_M'.

The table shows the welfare analysis, first when the speculator proves to be right and then when he proves to be wrong. In each case we must use the appropriate March demand curve—the light blue one if the speculator is right and the dark blue one if he is wrong. If the speculator is right, his arrival increases welfare, and if the speculator is wrong, his arrival decreases welfare.

Now suppose that there arrives on the scene a speculator who believes that the market has made a mistake and that the March demand curve will be lower than everyone else expects. He believes that the March demand curve will be the light blue demand curve shown in panel B of Exhibit 18–10. Anticipating a profit, he sells futures contracts, planning to fulfill them by buying cheap wheat on the spot market in March.

The speculator's advertised willingness to provide March wheat at less than the going price of P_0 drives down the expected price of March wheat and along with it the price of a March futures contract.

With the discovery that March wheat is selling for less than P_0, grain suppliers sell more wheat today and save less for March, moving the vertical February supply curve to the right and the vertical March supply curve to the left. This process continues until the speculator no longer perceives any profit to be earned by undercutting the price of March wheat, that is, until the quantities have moved to Q_F' and Q_M' and the price has fallen to P_1.

Speculation and Welfare

The table in Exhibit 18–10 calculates the change in welfare due to the arrival of the speculator, first on the assumption that he is right about the March demand curve and then on the assumption that he is wrong. The marginal cost of providing grain that is already in storage has been taken to be zero, so social welfare is simply the area under the demand curve. To calculate March welfare, we must use the actual March demand curve, which is the light blue curve if the speculator is right and the dark blue curve if he is wrong.

To understand the gains and losses better, keep in mind that the distance from Q_F to Q_P' must equal the distance from Q_M' to Q_M. (Either of these distances is the amount of additional grain sold in February instead of March.) From this it is easy to see that N is less than $C + E$, so the speculator really increases social welfare when he is right. Similarly, $C + E$ is less than $H + K + L + N$, so the speculator really decreases social welfare when he is wrong.

Society gains when a speculator correctly alerts it to a coming drop in demand by bidding down the price of futures contracts. This information enables people to increase their current consumption, in recognition of the fact that grain will be less valuable at the margin tomorrow than it is today. Similarly, a speculator who correctly forecasts an increase in tomorrow's demand bids up the price of futures contracts, alerting people today that wheat will be more valuable tomorrow and ought to be conserved.

When the speculator guesses the future correctly, he earns profits and he increases social welfare. When he guesses incorrectly, both he and society lose. By and large, we expect successful speculators to increase the level of their speculative activity over time, and unsuccessful speculators to eventually drop out of the market. Therefore, it is a reasonable expectation that the majority of existing speculators serve a welfare-improving function.

18.4 Markets for Risky Assets

Many assets are valued not for their uses in consumption but for their potential to increase their owners' wealth. Corporate stocks are a prime example;

real estate is another. The owner of a stock is often entitled to a stream of dividends of uncertain size. In addition, the value of the stock itself might rise or fall. Both the dividends and the changes in the stock price are referred to as **returns** to the owner of the stock. The expected present value of these returns is called the **expected return** to the stock owner.

Returns Gains to the holder of a financial asset, including dividends and increases in the asset's value.

Expected return The expected value of returns.

A risk-neutral stockholder cares only about expected returns. A risk-averse stockholder cares also about the certainty with which those returns will be realized. Such a stockholder is not indifferent between a stock that returns $5 next year for certain and one that returns either $0 or $10 next year with 50-50 probabilities, even though the expected returns are the same in each case.

The risk associated with a given stock can be described by a number called the **standard deviation** in its returns, abbreviated by σ (the Greek letter *sigma*). If you have taken a statistics course, you know a precise definition of the standard deviation. What you need to know here is that σ is a measure of the *spread* in possible outcomes. A stock that returns $5 with certainty has σ = $0. A stock that returns either $0 or $10 with equal probability has σ = $5. A stock that returns either −$5 or $15 with equal probability has σ = $10.

Standard deviation A precise measure of risk.

We shall henceforth measure expected returns and standard deviations as percentages of current asset values. Thus, a stock that currently sells for $10 and is expected to return $5 (either by increasing in value or by paying dividends) has an expected return of 50%. If the $5 return is certain, then σ = 0%. If the return might be either −$5 or $15, then σ − 100%, because $10 is 100% of $10.

People who buy financial assets in the hope of increasing their wealth are often referred to as **investors.** The language is unfortunate, because the purchase of existing stocks, bonds, and real estate does not constitute investment in the sense of Chapter 17. Economists generally reserve the word *investment* to describe the creation of new factors of production. Nevertheless, we will bow to popular usage and refer to the purchaser of stocks as an "investor."

Investors Buyers of risky assets.

Portfolios

An investor is interested not only in the characteristics of individual stocks; he is also interested in the characteristics of **portfolios,** or combinations of several stocks. In order to compare the characteristics of a portfolio with those of the stocks it comprises, let us consider some examples.

Portfolios Combinations of risky assets.

Read more about portfolio theory as it relates to financial markets at the following Internet site: http://www.contingencyanalysis.com/glossarymodernportfoliotheory.htm

Exhibit 18–11 displays the characteristics of three stocks, each now selling for $10. The stocks are General Air-Conditioning (GAC), General Surfboards (GSB), and General Snowshoes (GSS). The value of each stock tomorrow depends on the state of the world: Either an ice age begins or it doesn't. Exhibit 18–11 shows what will happen to each stock in each state of the world. It also shows the expected return and the standard deviation for each stock, computed on the assumption that the probability of an ice age is .50.

For each stock the expected return is the average of the returns in the two states of the world, and the standard deviation (σ) is equal to the absolute value of the difference between the expected return and either of the possible actual returns. For instance, the possible returns to General Surfboards are −40% and 120%. The average of these is 40%, which is the expected return.

Exhibit 18-11 Expected Returns and Standard Deviations

Stock	Current Value	Value If Ice Age Comes	Value If No Ice Age Comes	Expected Return	σ
General Air-Conditioning (GAC)	$10	$5 (Return = −50%)	$25 (Return = 150%)	50%	100%
General Surfboards (GSB)	10	6 (Return = −40%)	22 (Return = 120%)	40	80
General Snowshoes (GSS)	10	25 (Return = 150%)	5 (Return = −50%)	50	100

The table displays the characteristics of three hypothetical stocks. There is a 50% chance of an ice age beginning tomorrow, and each stock's value tomorrow depends on whether the ice age actually arrives. For each stock the expected return is the average of the two possible returns. For each stock the standard deviation is the absolute value of the difference between its return if the ice age arrives and its expected return.

The possible returns of −40% and 120% differ from the expected return of 40% by exactly 80% in absolute value, so for General Surfboards $\sigma = 80\%$.

We can now compute the returns and standard deviations on various portfolios. Consider first a portfolio consisting of one share each of General Air-Conditioning and General Surfboards. Such a portfolio has a current value of $20 and could either go down to $11 (the sum of the values of the two stocks if the ice age arrives) or go up to $47 (the sum of the values if the ice age fails to arrive). These outcomes constitute returns of either −45% or +135%. The expected return is 45% and the standard deviation is 90%.

EXERCISE 18.9 Verify the numbers in the preceding paragraph.

If you are rash enough to generalize on the basis of this single example, you might be tempted to conclude that the expected return and standard deviation of a portfolio are computed by taking the average expected return and the average standard deviation of the constituent stocks. If you succumbed to such a temptation, you would be right regarding the expected return, but wrong regarding the standard deviation.

Consider a portfolio consisting of one share each of General Air-Conditioning and General Snowshoes. The current value of such a portfolio is $20. In the event of an ice age, its value will be $5 + $25 = $30, and in the event of no ice age, its value will be $25 + $5 = $30. Such a portfolio earns a 50% return with certainty. Its standard deviation is zero.

A portfolio consisting of General Air-Conditioning and General Snowshoes is completely diversified. Whenever one of its constituent stocks goes up, the other goes down. As a result, all of the risk is eliminated and σ is equal to zero. In general, the standard deviation of a portfolio is given by the average of the standard deviations of the individual stocks, *minus* a correction term for any diversification that takes place. Because of this correction term, we can say:

The standard deviation of a portfolio is *at most* equal to the average standard deviation of the individual stocks.

By contrast:

The expected return to a portfolio is *exactly* equal to the average expected return of the individual stocks.

We have seen an example of a completely undiversified portfolio (GAC and GSB) and of a completely diversified portfolio (GAC and GSS). It is also possible to construct a portfolio that is partially, but not completely, diversified. Consider the portfolio that combines one share of General Surfboards with one share of General Snowshoes. This portfolio, initially worth $20, will either go up to $31 or go up to $27. The possible returns are 55% and 35%. The expected return is 45% (the average of the expected returns on the two stocks). The standard deviation is 10%, much less than the average of the standard deviations on the two stocks, but still not zero because the diversification is not complete.

The Geometry of Portfolios

Any individual stock, and any portfolio, can be represented by a point in a diagram, as in Exhibit 18–12. The points labeled *GSB* and *GSS* represent the stocks General Surfboards and General Snowshoes from Exhibit 18–11.

It is possible for two different stocks to occupy the same position in the diagram. General Air-Conditioning is represented by the same point that represents General Snowshoes.

There is a geometric construction of the portfolio that combines two given stocks. Consider the portfolio consisting of GSB and GSS. We begin by locating the midpoint of the line segment that connects the stocks. That point is labeled *X* in Exhibit 18–12. It represents a portfolio with the average of the two expected returns and the average of the two standard deviations. Since there is some diversification, the portfolio's standard deviation is less than the average of the two stocks' standard deviations. Thus, the portfolio is represented by a point some distance to the left of *X*. The size of the leftward shift depends on the amount of diversification. In this case we find that the combined portfolio is located at point *D*.

EXERCISE 18.10 What point represents the portfolio consisting of GAC and GSS?

Two portfolios can be combined to make a new portfolio, using the same geometric prescription that is used to combine two stocks.

The Efficient Set

In panel A of Exhibit 18–13 there are hypothetical dots representing all of the stocks that might be available at a given time. The shaded area represents all of the available portfolios. Any available stock must be in the shaded region,

Exhibit 18-12 The Geometry of Portfolios

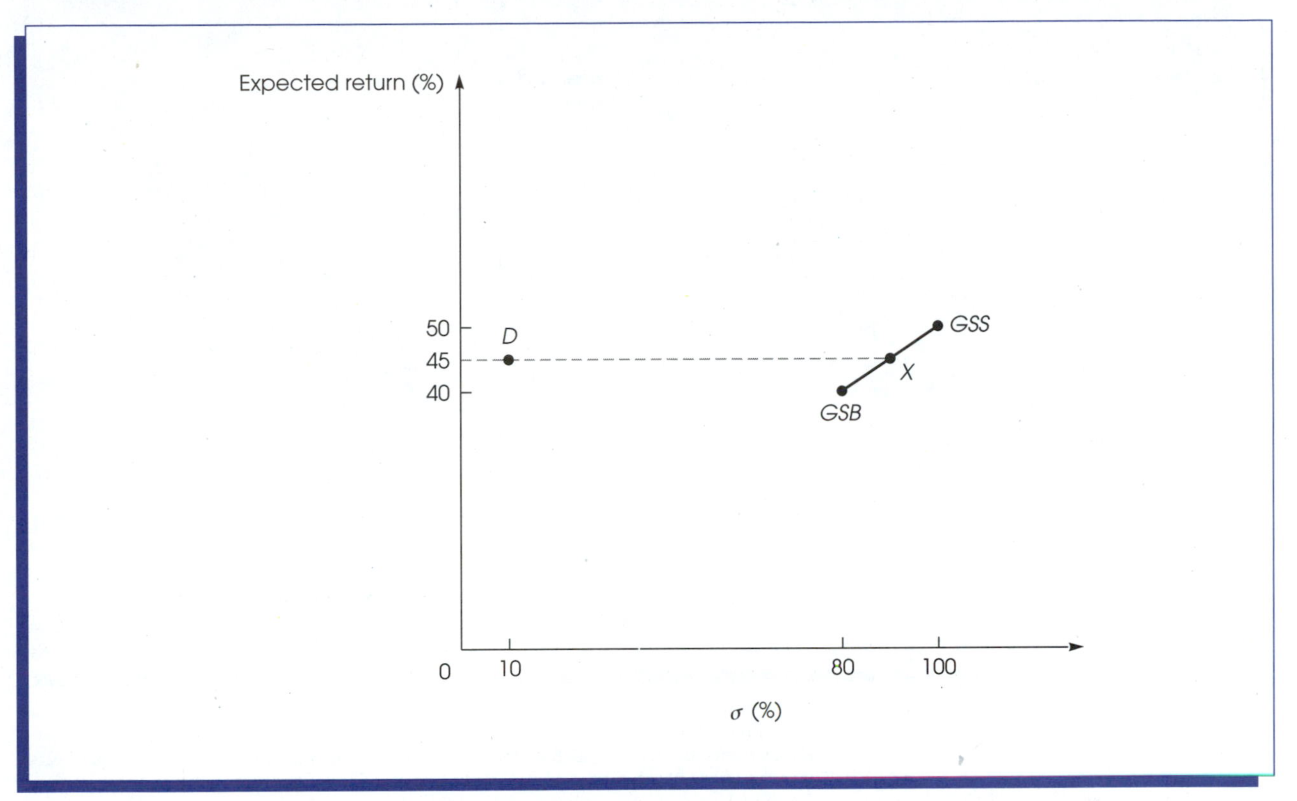

Every stock, and every portfolio, is represented by a point in the diagram. The points *GSS* and *GSB* represent General Snowshoes and General Surfboards, which are described in Exhibit 18–11.

The point *X,* which is midway between the stocks *GSS* and *GSB,* represents an asset with the average of their expected returns and the average of their standard deviations. The portfolio containing *GSS* and *GSB* has the average expected return but a smaller standard deviation. Thus, it is represented by a point directly to the left of *X,* namely, *D.*

because one can always hold a portfolio consisting of that stock alone. We have also darkened the northwest boundary of the shaded region.

It is no accident that the northwest boundary is shaped as it is. Panel B suggests another shape, which we shall argue is impossible. If the boundary were shaped as in panel B, then there would be portfolios represented by points *E* and *F.* Combining these portfolios yields a new portfolio, which must be represented either by point Y or by some point to its left. Some such point must therefore be in the shaded region, which is not true. Therefore, the shape depicted in panel B is impossible.

Efficient set The northwest boundary of the set of all portfolios.

Efficient portfolio A portfolio in the efficient set.

The northwest boundary of the shaded region in Exhibit 18–13 is called the **efficient set,** or the set of **efficient portfolios.** These are the only portfolios that a risk-averse individual would ever hold. The reason is that from any other

Exhibit 18–13 The Efficient Set

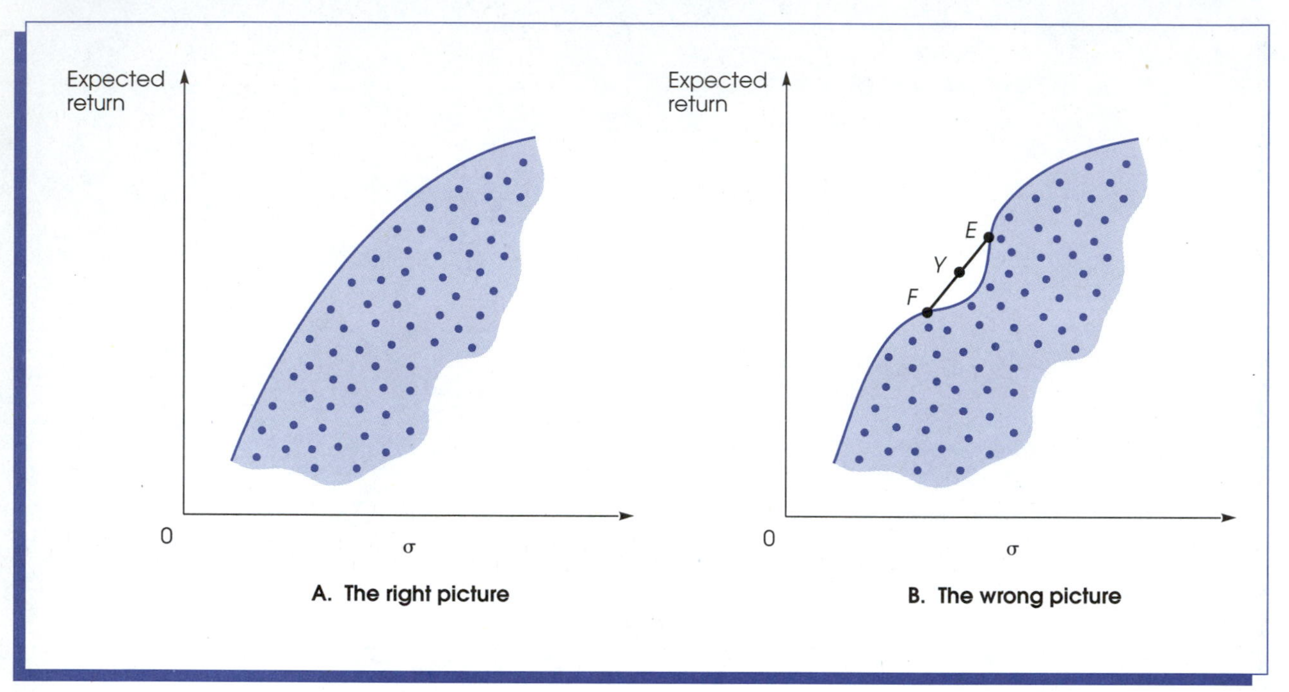

The dots represent the stocks available in the marketplace, and the shaded region represents all of the portfolios that can be constructed from those stocks. The picture must look like panel A and cannot look like panel B. In panel B the portfolio that combines portfolios *E* and *F* must be located at *Y* or to the left of *Y*, where the picture shows no portfolios. Therefore, the picture is wrong.

In panel A, which is the correct picture, the northwest boundary of the shaded region is the efficient set. No investor would choose a portfolio that is not in the efficient set.

point in the shaded region the investor can always move either upward (increasing expected returns) or to the left (decreasing risk) or both. Because both upward and leftward movements are desirable to the risk-averse investor, he would never remain at a point that was off the efficient set.

The Investor's Choice

Because the risk-averse investor views expected return as a "good" and standard deviation as a "bad," his preferences among portfolios are represented by indifference curves such as those shown in Exhibit 18–14. He chooses among the portfolios in the efficient set (also shown) so as to be on the highest possible indifference curve (in this case "highest" means "most northwesterly"). That is, he will pick the portfolio where the efficient set is tangent to an indifference curve, as at point *P* in Exhibit 18–14.

Exhibit 18-14 The Investor's Choice

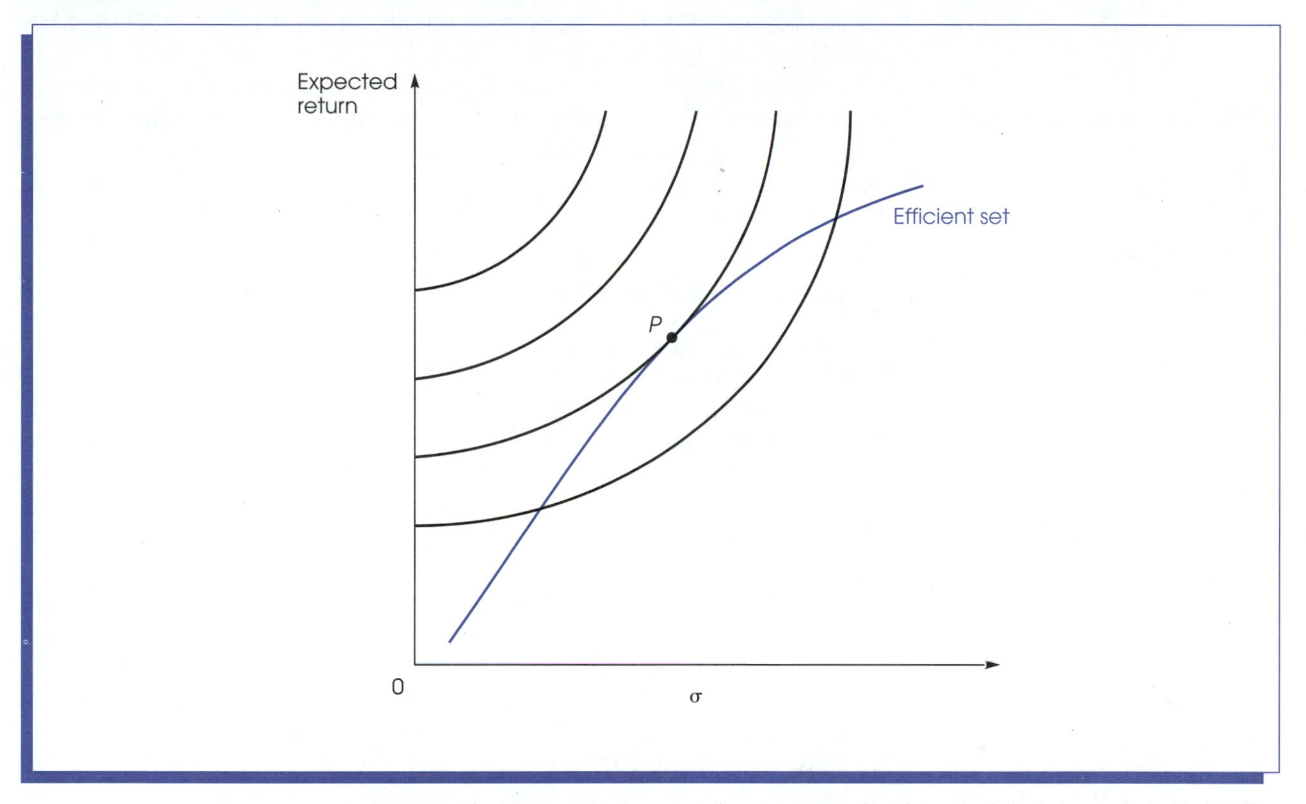

Because the investor views expected return as good and standard deviation as bad, his indifference curves are shaped as shown. Of the portfolios in the efficient set, this investor selects the one on the "highest" (most northwesterly) indifference curve, which is at the tangency *P*.

In practice, "choosing" portfolio *P* is not as easy as we have made it sound. Even though we know that some portfolio has the expected return and standard deviation associated with point *P* in Exhibit 18-14, actually constructing that portfolio—determining the particular combination of stocks from which it is built—can require considerable skill. For this reason, investors often find it in their interest to hire a professional *portfolio manager* to help them construct the portfolio they have chosen.

In asserting that the investor will choose point *P*, we have assumed that expected return and standard deviation are the only characteristics of his portfolio that concern him. Conceivably, he could be concerned with other, more subtle, statistical features as well. Suppose that portfolio *A* could return −6%, −2%, 0%, 2%, or 6%, all with equal probability. Portfolio *B* could return −4%

or 4%, each with equal probability. Both portfolios have the same expected return (0%) and the same standard deviation (4%). (If you know the precise definition of standard deviation, you should check this.) Therefore, both portfolios occupy the same position in the graph of Exhibit 18–14. Consequently, the theory embodied in that graph must assume that the investor is indifferent between these two portfolios.

Capital asset pricing model A model that assumes that investors care only about expected return and risk, where risk is measured by standard deviation.

The assumption that the investor cares only about expected return and standard deviation is the key assumption of the **capital asset pricing model,** which is often used to study markets for risky assets. A body of empirical evidence indicates that this assumption is not far wrong. We will continue to pursue its implications.

Introduction of a Risk-Free Asset

Suppose now that in addition to all of the stocks shown in Exhibit 18–13, a risk-free asset is available. It is often asserted that U.S. Treasury bills constitute such an asset (but see the end of Section 17.1 for some contrary evidence). Whatever this risk-free asset might be, it is represented by a point on the vertical axis, like *R* in Exhibit 18–15.

Let us see what happens when the risk-free asset is combined with a portfolio of stocks. Suppose that an investor holds half of his wealth in the form of stock portfolio *A* and half in the form of the risk-free asset *R*. Then his overall portfolio is represented by the point *X*, midway between *A* and *R*. (A risk-free asset cannot contribute to diversification, so the combined portfolio is represented by *X* rather than some point to the left of *X*.) Similarly, if the investor holds three-fourths of his wealth in portfolio *A* and one-fourth in the risk-free asset *R*, then his overall portfolio is represented by the point *Y*, three-fourths of the way along the line from *R* to *A*.

In general, the investor can achieve any point along the line segment from *R* to *A* by combining portfolio *A* with the risk-free asset. Similarly, he can achieve any point along the line segment from *R* to *B*, or from *R* to any other existing portfolio. The uppermost of these line segments, connecting *R* with *M*, contains the most desirable combinations.

Under some circumstances the investor can move past *M* along the same line. This is possible when he can hold a *negative* amount of the risk-free asset *R*. For example, if *R* is a Treasury bill and if the investor is able to borrow at the Treasury bill rate, then such borrowing is equivalent to holding a *negative quantity of Treasury bills*. (*Borrowing* equals *selling bonds* equals buying bonds in negative quantities.) Assuming that this is possible, the investor can achieve any point along the line passing through *R* and *M*. This line is called the **market line.**

Market line The line through a risk-free asset and tangent to the efficient set.

Market portfolio The point of tangency between the market line and the efficient set.

The market line is the line through *R* that is just tangent to the efficient set. The **market portfolio** is the portfolio represented by the point where the market line touches the efficient set. In Exhibit 18–15 point *M* represents the market portfolio.

There might be more than one market portfolio, since several portfolios can occupy the same position in the graph.

With the availability of the risk-free asset, an investor is no longer restricted to the old efficient set. He can reach any point on the market line by holding

Exhibit 18-15 A Risk-Free Asset

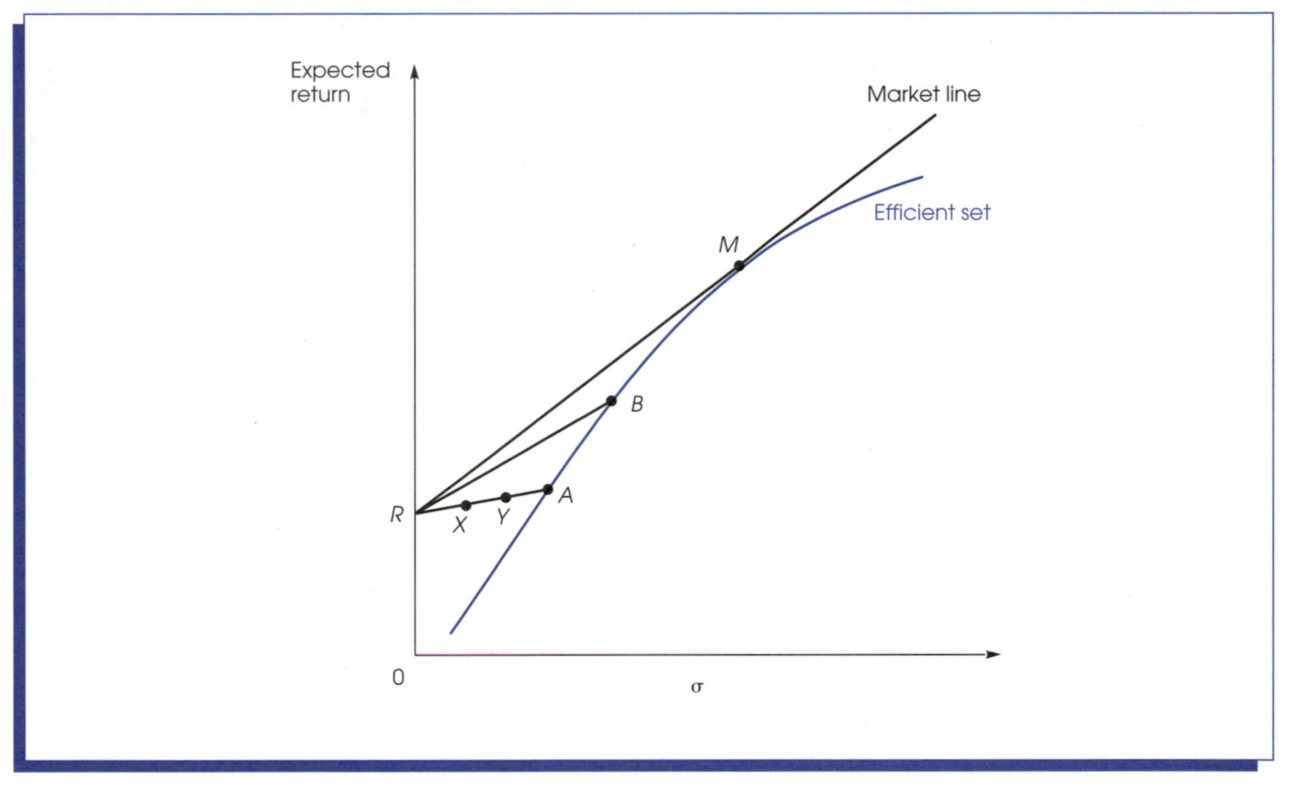

Point R represents a risk-free asset, possibly a Treasury bill. The investor can achieve any point along the illustrated line segments by combining R with portfolios such as A, B, and M. For example, combining R and A in equal amounts yields point X. The line connecting R and M contains the most desirable possibilities; it is called the market line. If R can be held in negative amounts (say by borrowing), then it is possible to move beyond point M along the market line.

No investor would ever want to be off the market line. Therefore, every investor wants to hold a portfolio consisting partly of R and partly of a market portfolio M.

an appropriate combination of risk-free assets and shares of the market portfolio. These options are always preferable to points on the efficient set. For example, an investor holding portfolio A in Exhibit 18–15 could move either directly upward to the market line, increasing his expected return, or directly leftward to the market line, decreasing his risk.

Investors choose only points on the market line. Points on the market line are obtained by combining the risk-free asset R with the market portfolio M. Therefore:

A rational investor always holds a portfolio that combines the risk-free asset with the market portfolio in some proportions.

Exhibit 18-16 **The Investor's Choice Revisited**

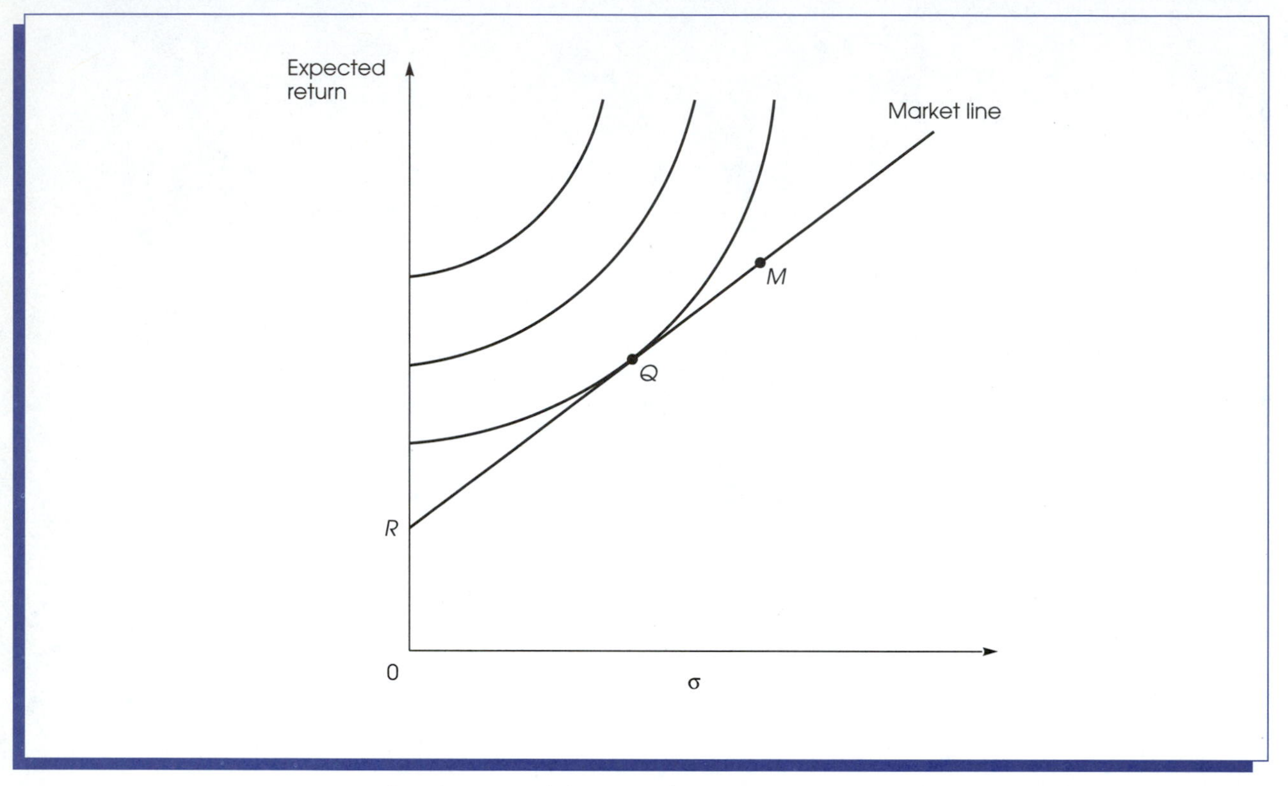

When there is a risk-free asset, the investor is no longer restricted to the old efficient set. He can now reach any point on the market line by combining the risk-free asset with the market portfolio in appropriate proportions. This investor chooses proportions that enable him to reach point *Q*.

The investor can never do better than to be on the market line. Thus, his portfolio of risky assets will always be the market portfolio. There is never any reason to hold any other portfolio of risky assets.

To see what proportions the investor will choose, we must examine his indifference curves. In Exhibit 18–16 the investor chooses proportions that enable him to reach point *Q*.

Constructing a Market Portfolio

What happens if we create a giant portfolio consisting of all of the risky assets in the economy? Since every asset is held by somebody, this is the same thing as adding up all of the individual investors' portfolios. Since each investor holds a market portfolio at point *M* in Exhibit 18–15, we are adding up many portfolios, all at point *M*. The result must be a portfolio at *M*, or a portfolio to the left of *M* if there is further diversification. But we see from Exhibit 18–15 that there are no portfolios to the left of *M*. It follows that our giant portfolio is itself at point *M*. In other words:

A portfolio that consists of all of the risky assets in the economy, held in proportion to their existing quantities, must be a market portfolio.

The individual investor wants to hold a combination of two assets: the risk-free asset and a market portfolio. But how is he to construct a market portfolio? Actually, we have just described one: the portfolio consisting of all of the assets in the economy. An individual investor can hold a miniaturized copy of this portfolio by holding all of the risky assets in proportion to their existing quantities. By choosing an appropriate mix of this particular market portfolio and the risk-free asset, he can reach point *Q* in Exhibit 18–16, which is his individual optimum.

Unfortunately, practical considerations prevent the investor from really holding all of the risky assets in proportion to their existing quantities. A shopping center in Dubuque, Iowa, might represent a .0001% share of the nation's economy. It is unrealistic to suggest that .0001% of an investor's portfolio should consist of shares in this shopping center. Typically, practical considerations make it necessary for an investor to approximate the market portfolio with a very small number of assets. To some extent he can alleviate this problem by holding shares in mutual funds that in turn hold shares in a large and highly diversified collection of assets. Also, the services of a portfolio manager can be helpful.

18.5 Rational Expectations

In this section we will examine how prices are set in a market where suppliers have to make decisions in the face of uncertain demand. We will discover that equilibrium prices depend very much on the way in which suppliers form their expectations. We will also discover an important reason why economists studying such markets are liable to make predictions that are drastically wrong.

A Market with Uncertain Demand

Suppose that lettuce is sold in a central marketplace. Each day lettuce farmers must decide how much lettuce to load onto their trucks and bring to the market. If they knew what the price was going to be, this decision would be easy. They would simply bring lettuce until the marginal cost of supplying another head was equal to the price. Unfortunately, demand, and therefore price, fluctuates from day to day. The best that farmers can do is to form an *expectation* of the price. The amount they bring to market on a given day is given by an upward-sloping "supply curve," as shown in panel A of Exhibit 18–17. The difference between this curve and a true supply curve is that in this case the vertical axis measures not price, but expected price, which we denote by the symbol P_E.

When the farmers actually arrive at the marketplace, the supply curve for lettuce is vertical. The quantity of lettuce is equal to what the farmers have irrevocably decided to bring with them, and all of the lettuce must be sold or it

Exhibit 18-17 Expectations and Supply

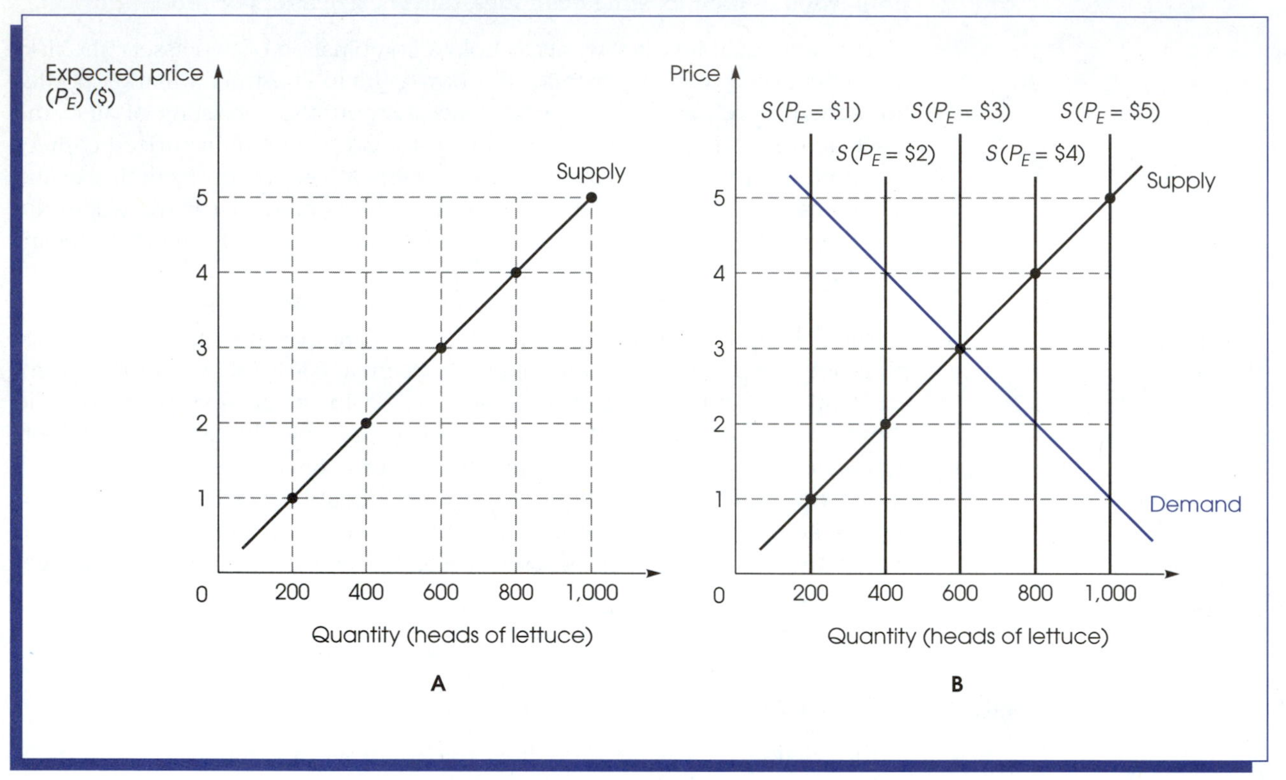

The curve in panel A shows how much lettuce the farmers bring to market at each expected price. It is like a supply curve, except that it depends on expected price rather than actual price.

When the farmers arrive at the market, the supply curve is vertical. The position of the vertical supply curve depends on the farmers' expectation of the price. Panel B shows the supply curve from panel A superimposed on several possible vertical supply curves. The actual price depends on the expected price (which determines the vertical supply curve) and the actual demand.

will rot. The location of the vertical supply curve depends on the farmers' expectation of price at the time they start out in the morning. According to Exhibit 18–17, if the farmers expect a price of $1, the supply is 200 heads of lettuce; if they expect a price of $2, the supply is 400 heads, and so forth. Panel B of the exhibit shows the curve from panel A together with the various possible vertical supply curves, each labeled with the corresponding expected price.

Panel B of Exhibit 18–17 also shows the demand curve for lettuce on a particular day. The market price depends both on the location of this demand curve and on what expectation the farmers have when they start out. If the farmers expect a price of $2, they bring 400 heads of lettuce to market and the actual price is $4. If they expect a price of $4, they bring 800 heads and the actual price is $2. If they expect a price of $3, they bring 600 heads and the actual price is $3. Only in this last case does the farmers' expectation prove to be correct.

EXERCISE 18.11 What is the actual price of lettuce if the farmers expect a price of $1? If they expect a price of $5?

Each day demand is different. Suppose, for example, that the curves D_1 and D_2 in Exhibit 18–18 represent the lower and upper limits of demand. Some days demand is as low as D_1, some days it is as high as D_2, and on the average day it is given by the demand curve D_{Average} between them. If farmers consistently expect a price of $1, they will find that the actual price is sometimes

Exhibit 18-18 Rational Expectations

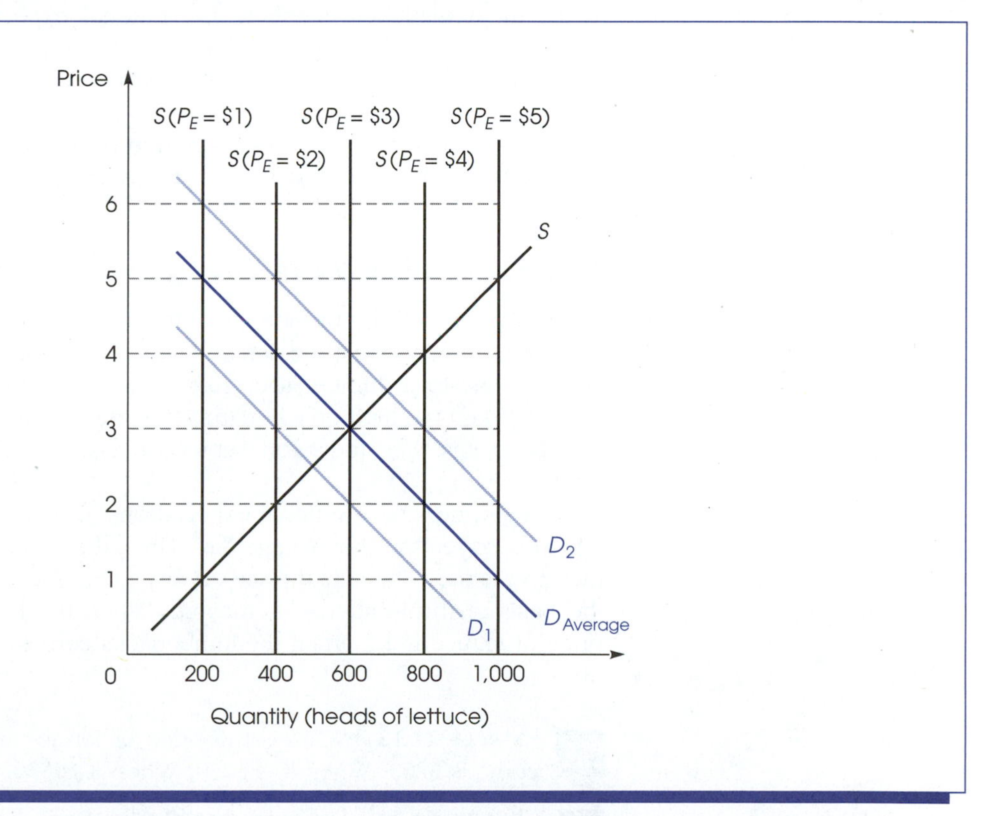

Demand fluctuates between D_1 and D_2; it is D_{Average} on the average day. If farmers expect lettuce to sell at $1, they bring 200 heads of lettuce to market and the price on the average day is $5 (where D_{Average}, crosses the quantity 200). The farmers' expectation is systematically wrong.

If, on the other hand, the farmers expect lettuce to sell at $3, they bring 600 heads of lettuce to market and the price on the average day is $3. Thus, the expectation of a $3 price is correct on average; we say that it is a rational expectation.

as low as $4, sometimes as high as $6, and about $5 on the average day. In other words, they will consistently find that their predictions are drastically wrong.

Exercise 18.12 Explain how farmers' expectations are confounded if they consistently expect a price of $5.

Now, farmers are not omniscient; nobody expects them to make correct predictions all the time. But farmers are not foolish either, and when their predictions are consistently off in a systematic way, we expect them to revise those predictions. Farmers who expect a price of $1 will consistently find that they have underestimated, and therefore they will not persist in their belief.

A similar argument can be made about any expected price except for an expected price of $3. If farmers expect a price of $3, then the price will be as low as $2 some days, as high as $4 other days, and $3 on average. Farmers will have no reason to revise their expectations either upward or downward. In this case we say that the farmers have **rational expectations.**

Rational expectations
Expectations that, when held by market participants, lead to behavior that fulfills those expectations on average.

An expectation is rational when it does not lead to systematic, correctable errors in prediction. Nevertheless, a rational expectation is not always, nor even usually, a correct expectation. In our example the price might be $2 half of the time and $4 half of the time, in which case the rational expectation of $3 will *never* be correct.

Geometrically, the rational expectation occurs where the average day's demand curve crosses the farmers' upward-sloping supply curve.

Why Economists Make Wrong Predictions

Now let us embellish our model by making an assumption about why demand fluctuates. Suppose that the demand for lettuce is strictly determined by the income of the local lumberjacks. Exhibit 18–19 shows some possible demand curves. When the lumberjacks earn $100, the demand curve is D_{100}; when they earn $150, it is D_{150}, and so on. Let us also assume that on the average day lumberjacks earn $150.

If the farmers have rational expectations, they always expect a price of $3, which is correct on the average day. Thus, they always bring 600 heads of lettuce to market. The actual price on any given day is perfectly predictable on the basis of the lumberjacks' income. When the lumberjacks earn $100, the price of lettuce is $2; when the lumberjacks earn $150, the price is $3; and so on.

Exercise 18.13 What is the price of lettuce when the lumberjacks' income is $200? When it is $250? When it is $300?

Exercise 18.14 Suppose that the lumberjacks' income averaged $250. What would be the rational expectation of the price of lettuce? How many heads of lettuce would farmers bring to the market? What would be the actual price when the lumberjacks earned $100? When they earned $200? When they earned $300?

Exhibit 18-19 Lumberjacks' Income and the Price of Lettuce

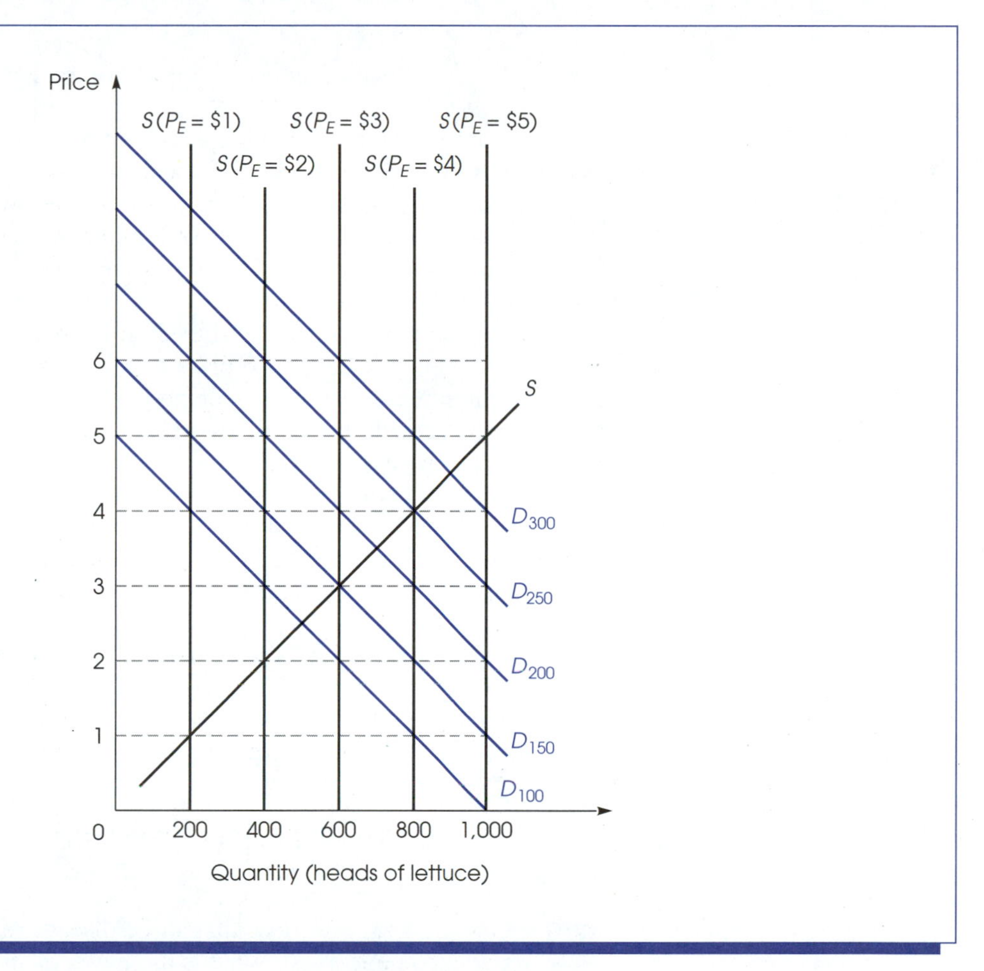

The demand curve for lettuce depends on the lumberjacks' income. When their income is $100, the demand curve is D_{100}; when their income is $150, the demand curve is D_{150}; and so on. Initially, the lumberjacks earn $150 on average. Thus, the rational expectation of the price is $3 (where D_{150} crosses the upward-sloping supply curve), so farmers supply 600 heads of lettuce. When the lumberjacks really do earn $150, the rational expectation is fulfilled. On days when the lumberjacks earn $250, the price of lettuce is $5.

Now a paper mill arrives, raising the lumberjacks' income to $250 on average. The new rational expectation for the price is $4. Farmers bring 800 heads of lettuce to market. On an average day the lumberjacks earn $250 and the price of lettuce is $4.

An econometrician extrapolating from past experience would predict that on days when the lumberjacks earn $250, the price of lettuce is $5. Thus, he would predict that when the paper mill arrives, the price of lettuce will go up to $5 on average. But he is wrong, because past experience is no longer relevant. When farmers have rational expectations, the additional lettuce that they bring to market invalidates the old relationship between the lumberjacks' income and the price of lettuce.

Suppose now that an econometrician comes to study this market. He is pleased to discover that he can predict the price of lettuce on the basis of the lumberjacks' income, as detailed in the preceding paragraph. He might even be so bold as to summarize his knowledge in an equation:

$$\text{Price of lettuce} = \frac{1}{50} \times \text{Lumberjack's income}$$

For example, since the lumberjacks earn \$150 on average days, the price of lettuce is $1/50 \times \$150 = \$3$ on average days, which is correct.

One day a paper mill is built in the area. The owners of the mill announce that they will be purchasing a lot of lumber. As a result, the lumberjacks' income will now average \$250 per day. What does the econometrician predict about the price of lettuce?

Drawing on past experience, the econometrician knows that lumberjack income of \$250 implies a lettuce price of \$5. Thus, he predicts that the price of lettuce will now be \$5 on the average day.

But what actually happens? By examining Exhibit 18–19, you can see that the new rational-expectations price of lettuce is \$4 (where supply crosses the new average demand curve D_{250}). Farmers now bring 800 heads of lettuce to market each day. When the lumberjacks earn \$250, on the average day the price of lettuce is \$4, not \$5 as the econometrician predicted.

Where did the econometrician go wrong? All past experience supports his equation. It has always been true in the past that on days when the lumberjacks earn \$250, the price of lettuce is \$5. What happened is that the arrival of the paper mill caused farmers to change their expectations and bring a different amount of lettuce to market. This, in turn, invalidated the econometrician's equation. The correct new equation is

$$\text{Price of lettuce} = \left(\frac{1}{50} \times \text{Lumberjack's income}\right) - \$1$$

EXERCISE 18.15 Suppose that a tree disease reduces the lumberjacks' average income to \$100. What is the new equation for the price of lettuce?

example

Tweedledum and Tweedledee

Tweedledum and Tweedledee have identical skills and have therefore always had identical incomes. In years when their skills are in demand, their incomes are both high, and at other times their incomes are both low. An econometrician, having carefully collected data, can confidently assert the truth of the equation

$$\text{Tweedledee's income} = \text{Tweedledum's income}$$

If he can observe Tweedledum's income, the econometrician can use his equation to predict Tweedledee's income, and he will always be right.

One day Tweedledee hired just such an econometrician to advise him on how to increase his income. The econometrician, having discovered the above equation, advised Tweedledee, "It's simple. Your income is always the same as Tweedledum's income, so if you want your income to rise, just give all of your money to Tweedledum." Tweedledee tried it, but it didn't work.

This simple example illustrates that even when equations predict very well, they can be entirely useless as guides to policy. The reason is that changes in policy can invalidate the equations.[4] The equality between Tweedledee's and Tweedledum's incomes existed for a *reason*; because their incomes were derived from selling identical skills in the marketplace. The econometrician's suggestion leads to behavior that eliminates this reason for equality, and as a result the equality itself disappears.

Similarly, we can imagine the econometrician of the preceding subsection advising farmers to try to attract a paper mill to the area, promising that the price of lettuce will rise to $5. When it rises to only $4, the farmers are disappointed, just like Tweedledee. Again the reason is that the policy change eliminates the reason underlying the validity of the very equation that was used to justify the policy change.

The example of Tweedledee and Tweedledum illustrates that this problem with policy evaluation can occur even in exceptionally simple examples. The lumberjacks/lettuce example illustrates that the problem is particularly likely to arise in the presence of rational expectations, since changes in policy lead to changes in those expectations and hence to changes in behavior.

Rational expectations play a central and exciting role in modern macroeconomics, although they are fundamentally a microeconomic concept.[5] Two important areas of research are the attempt to understand the ways in which econometricians can be led astray in their predictions and the development of new econometric techniques that are appropriate for studying markets in which expectations are rational.

summary

In many cases an individual's wealth depends on the state of the world. It is possible to transfer income from one state of the world to another in a variety of ways. The gambler who bets that a tossed coin will turn up heads transfers income from the state of the world in which tails comes up to the state of the world in which heads comes up. The homeowner who buys fire insurance transfers income from the state of the world in which his house is undamaged to the state of the world in which his house burns down. The investor who buys a share of stock in a company that makes digital tapes transfers income from the state of the world in which digital tape technology is unsuccessful in the marketplace to the state of the world in which digital tapes completely replace compact discs.

[4]This point was made forcefully in R. E. Lucas, Jr., "Econometric Policy Evaluation: A Critique," in *The Phillips Curve and Labor Markets*, vol. 1 of Carnegie-Rochester Conference Series on Public Policy, Karl Brunner and Allan H. Meltzer, eds. (Amsterdam: North Holland, 1976), pp. 19–46.

[5]Rational expectations were introduced by the economist John Muth to study problems in agricultural economics.

There are thus many ways that an individual can distribute his income across states of the world. We can draw indifference curves to illustrate his preferences among these distributions. The indifference curves depend both on the consumer's tastes and on the probabilities of the various states of the world.

A risk-neutral individual is one who always chooses the lottery with the highest expected value, without regard to risk. We expect a frequent gambler to be risk-neutral, since his good and bad luck wash out over time. For someone who is risk-neutral, the indifference curves are straight lines whose absolute slope is the ratio of the probabilities of the states of the world. When he is offered the opportunity to gamble at fair odds, the risk-neutral person is indifferent among all of the opportunities on his budget line. When offered the opportunity to gamble at favorable odds, he will always bet everything he has.

In many situations we expect people to be risk-averse. Among baskets with the same expected value, a risk-averter always chooses the one with no risk, that is, the one on the 45° line. Thus, at points along the 45° line the risk-averter's indifference curves have an absolute slope that reflects the fair betting odds. When offered the opportunity to bet at favorable odds, the risk-averter always accepts a small wager, but never a large one. Usually, an increase in income will increase the size of the largest wager that the risk-averter will accept at given odds.

Many markets exist to facilitate the transfer of risk across individuals. One is the market for insurance. In a world of perfect information, much insurance would be offered at fair odds (except for a slight tilting in favor of the insurance company to allow it to cover its costs). However, there are important reasons why we do not observe this practice. Among these are moral hazard and adverse selection, which were introduced in Chapter 9. Another problem is that some risks are undiversifiable, hence uninsurable.

The futures market is another market for transferring risk. It enables farmers to reduce their risks by contracting now for the prices of future deliveries. It also creates the opportunity for speculation, which is welfare-improving when speculators are right and detrimental to welfare when speculators are wrong.

The stock market is yet another market for trading risky assets. In addition to individual stocks, investors can hold portfolios, created by combining various stocks in different proportions. The portfolio consisting of two stocks in equal proportions has the average expected return but may have less than the average standard deviation (riskiness), because of diversification.

By combining the market portfolio (which consists of all of the risky assets in the economy held in proportion to their actual quantities) with a risk-free asset, the investor can create a portfolio that is superior to any other given portfolio in terms of risk and expected return. Thus, the only portfolio of risky assets that an investor would ever want to hold is the market portfolio. In practice, however, it is necessary to approximate this portfolio, which can require considerable expertise.

When there is uncertainty about the future, people may form rational expectations, which are expectations that are correct on the average day. If there is a change in circumstances, such as the arrival of a new industry or a change in some government policy, then the rational expectations may change, and consequently so may people's behavior. As a result, equations that have always predicted accurately in the past may prove drastically wrong following a policy change.

Review Questions

R1. Describe the indifference curves of (a) a person who is risk-neutral, (b) a person who is risk-averse, and (c) a person who is risk-preferring.

R2. Under what circumstances might a person be expected to be risk-neutral? Why is a firm more likely to be risk-neutral than an individual?

R3. Explain why the stockholders and the executives of a corporation might have different preferences with regard to the corporation's behavior toward risk. Describe some possible remedies and their pros and cons.

R4. What is moral hazard? Give some examples.

R5. What is adverse selection? Give some examples.

R6. Describe a possible equilibrium in an insurance market with adverse selection. In what sense is it suboptimal?

R7. What is an uninsurable risk? Give some examples.

R8. Explain what a futures contract is. How can a farmer or the owner of a grain elevator use futures contracts to eliminate risk?

R9. Explain what happens to the current and future supply of wheat when a speculator expects the price to fall. In what circumstances is this socially beneficial?

R10. What is the efficient set of portfolios? Explain why it is shaped as it is.

R11. Explain why the market portfolio is the only portfolio of risky assets that any investor would want to hold.

R12. What determines the daily equilibrium price in a market where demand fluctuates and suppliers have rational expectations?

R13. Explain how the arrival of a paper mill can cause a change in the relationship between lumberjacks' income and the price of lettuce.

Problem Set

1. According to Dr. Johnson, "He is no wise man who will quit a certainty for an uncertainty." Comment.

2. True or False: If nothing is worth dying for, then going to war is irrational.

3. Whenever John is offered the opportunity to take either side of a bet in which the odds are even slightly unfair, he invariably does bet something. True or False: John is certainly not risk-averse.

4. Jill likes to bet on heads when the odds are fair, but will bet on tails only if offered very favorable odds. Draw her indifference curves.

5. True or False: A risk-preferring person will always bet, no matter how much the odds are against him.

6. Bookmakers organize betting on football games in the following way: First, they determine a "point spread" that one team is expected to beat with 50-50 probability. Then bettors are allowed to bet on whether the team will beat the spread. They may take either side of the bet, and are offered slightly unfavorable odds either way. Show the budget line faced by the bettors. What will a risk-averse bettor do in these circumstances? What will a risk-preferring bettor do? Can you think of any reason why a risk averter might still bet?

7. **True or False:** If "sickly" people could insure against illness at the same rates available to healthy people, they would end up preferring illness to good health.

8. **True or False:** Speculators are less harmful to society than they at first appear, because they sometimes err in forecasting the future and their losses due to these errors compensate the rest of us for their gains when they are right.

9. Suppose that it is known for certain that the demand for wheat this year is identical to the demand for wheat next year. This year's wheat crop of 100 tons has just been harvested. Everybody believes that next year's wheat crop, which has already been planted, will also be 100 tons. Now a speculator arrives on the scene, convinced that next year's crop will be only 80 tons.

   a. If wheat can be stored costlessly, what will the speculator do? What happens to this year's wheat supply and to next year's? (If it helps you, assume an interest rate of 0%.)

   b. How long does the speculator continue this activity? What is this year's wheat supply when he is finished? What is next year's wheat supply when he is finished if he turns out to be right? What is it if he turns out to be wrong?

   c. Use a graph to show the social gains with and without a speculator, on the assumption that the speculator is right. If he is right, does he improve social welfare?

   d. Use a graph to show the social gains with and without a speculator, on the assumption that the speculator is wrong. If he is wrong, does he improve social welfare?

10. **True or False:** Nobody would ever hold a stock that was below the efficient set, since there is always an alternative with less risk or greater expected return.

11. Suppose that exactly half of all terrorists who take hostages kill their hostages. The government is considering a new policy under which all terrorist kidnappings will be met with massive military force intended to kill the kidnapper immediately. Unfortunately, it is estimated that in 90% of cases, the victim will die in the assault. **True or False:** Obviously, one drawback of this plan is that more hostages will die.

12. In New York State, the drinking age is 18. Studies show that 18-year-old

drivers have a much higher crash rate than do 16- and 17-year-olds. The same studies indicate that if the drinking age were raised to 19, 30% of all crashes by 18-year-olds could be prevented, saving 25 to 35 lives per year. *The New York Times* has editorialized that the drinking age should be raised to 19, as 25 to 35 lives would be well worth saving. Assuming that all of the numbers in the studies are correct, comment on the *Times's* assertion that raising the drinking age would save 25 to 35 lives per year.

13. Suppose that in reality the number of cars demanded, Q, depends on the real interest rate, r, according to an equation of the form

$$Q = Ar + B$$

where A and B are constants. An econometrician believes that the number of cars demanded depends on the *nominal* interest rate, i, and uses data to estimate the coefficients C and D in the equation

$$Q = Ci + B$$

a. Express the estimated coefficients C and D in terms of the "true" coefficients A and B and the inflation rate, π.

b. Explain why this model will make good predictions as long as the inflation rate is constant.

c. Suppose that it is considered desirable to raise the demand for cars and that the government can affect i by adopting policies that lead to a change in π. What will the econometrician advise?

d. When the new policy is adopted, what happens to C and D? Explain why the recommended policy won't work.

Internet Exercise

As was mentioned in the chapter, individuals vary widely in terms of their risk preference, and thus will make different choices when confronted with a particular risky situation. Risk preference is also an important aspect of financial planning. There are a number of Internet sites where you can take a quiz that provides information on your own attitude toward financial risk. One is the Internet site mentioned earlier in the chapter that is maintained by the Massachusetts Mutual Life Insurance Company (http://www.massmutual.com/Pm/personal/RiskQuiz.htm). How might one's attitude toward financial risk change with age?

chapter 19

What is Economics?

19.1 The Nature of Economic Analysis

Bill Goffe's RFE site provides one of the most comprehensive sources of information for economists on the Internet, including economic data, government statistics, working papers, courseware, research and policy institute links, on-line journals, and job information, among others: http://wueconb.wustl.edu/EconFAQ/EconFAQ.html

Economics is one of several sciences that attempt to explain and predict human behavior. It is distinguished from the other behavioral sciences (psychology, anthropology, sociology, and political science) by its emphasis on rational decision making under conditions of scarcity. Economists generally assume that people have well-defined goals and preferences, and that they allocate their limited resources so as to maximize their own well-being in accordance with those preferences.

Stages of Economic Analysis

Much of economic analysis can be divided into three stages. First, we make explicit assumptions about people's goals and about the constraints on their behavior. This allows us to formulate an economic problem: Within the limits imposed by the constraints, what is the best way to achieve the goals? Second, we determine the solutions to these problems, and we see how the solutions vary in response to changes in the constraints. We assume that the individuals under study can also solve their economic problems and that they behave accordingly. We describe this by saying that the individuals *optimize*. Third, we examine the interactions among individuals: Each person's behavior affects each other person's constraints. In view of these interactions, we are often able to conclude that there is only one possible outcome in which all individuals are simultaneously optimizing. Such an outcome is called an *equilibrium*.

We shall now examine each of these stages in more detail.

Formulating the Individual's Economic Problem

The first step in economic analysis is to make explicit assumptions about individuals' desires and the nature of the constraints that they face. For example, we assume that a consumer has indifference curves that are convex toward the origin and must select a market basket that is within his budget line. Or we assume that a competitive firm wants to maximize profits and must sell its output and purchase its inputs at fixed market prices. Or we assume that a worker views both leisure and consumption as desirable, but can consume no more than he earns in the marketplace.

Each of the agents in these examples faces an economic problem: a choice among competing alternatives. The consumer can eat more eggs and drink less wine, or he can eat fewer eggs and drink more wine, but once he has allocated his entire income he cannot have more of both. The firm can reduce its costs by cutting back production, but it must accept a reduction in revenues as the consequence if it does. The worker can earn more income, or he can improve his suntan, but he must choose between the two.

The problem of an economic actor is to decide how to allocate scarce resources among competing ends. Such trade-offs can always be expressed in terms of *costs,* which is another word for forgone opportunities. The cost of eating an egg is forgoing some amount of wine; the cost of increasing a firm's revenues is (at least partly) measured by the price of inputs; the cost of a day's wages is a forgone day at the beach. Therefore, we can say that the first step in economic analysis is to make explicit assumptions about both the desirability and the cost of various alternatives.

Optimization

The second step in economic analysis is to solve the agent's economic problem. The solution can typically be expressed in terms of the crucial principle of *equimarginality:* If an activity is worth pursuing at all, then it should be pursued until the marginal cost is equal to the marginal benefit. The consumer should buy eggs until the marginal value of an additional egg is equal to the marginal value of the wine that he could trade it for. (This is another way of saying that he should move along his budget line until it is just tangent to an indifference curve.) The firm should produce until its marginal cost is equal to its marginal revenue. It should select an input combination that equates the marginal product of a dollar's worth of labor to the marginal product of a dollar's worth of capital. The worker should relax until the marginal cost in forgone wages is equal to the marginal benefit of relaxation—or, in other words, he should work until the marginal income from working is equal to the marginal cost in forgone leisure.

The economist assumes that people act according to the principle of equimarginality. This is often expressed by saying that the economist assumes that people are *rational.* Indeed, it has been said that a student becomes a true economist on the day when he fully understands and accepts the principle that people equate costs and benefits at the margin. In Section 19.2 we will address the question of whether the economist's assumption is a reasonable one. Here we will pursue its consequences.

In addition to solving the individual's optimization problem, the economist also asks how the solution would change if the constraints changed. For example, in modeling a consumer's behavior, the economist notes first that the consumer's optimum occurs at a point where the budget line is tangent to an indifference curve, but he is also interested in how this tangency moves when there is a shift in the budget line due to a change in prices or a change in income. Although the real-world consumer needs to choose only a single consumption basket, the economist imagines how the consumer would behave in a variety of hypothetical circumstances and predicts the basket that the consumer would choose in each situation. The consumer's demand curve is an example of the economist's solution to a family of optimization problems. The demand curve in Exhibit 4–8 shows that *if* the price of X is \$6, the consumer's optimal basket will contain 2 units of X; *if* the price is \$3, his optimal basket will contain 3 units; and so forth.

A competitive firm's supply curve constitutes another example of how the economist expresses his solutions to a family of optimization problems. The point corresponding to a price of P shows that quantity at which the firm can equate marginal cost with marginal revenue, given that it is constrained to sell at the market price of P. As the constraint (that is, the price) varies, so does the solution to the problem (that is, the corresponding quantity).

Equilibrium

Solving the optimization problem tells the economist how people respond to various constraints. In order to predict their behavior, he must still determine what constraints are actually in force. The key here is that each individual's actions affect the options available to others. One of the constraints faced by a competitive firm is that it cannot sell its wares at a price higher than consumers will pay. That price is determined by the actions of other firms and of the consumers themselves, all of whom are solving their own optimization problems. Those optimization problems, in turn, involve constraints that are partly the result of the original firm's actions.

In Section 18.3 we saw the same thing in a slightly different context; Farmer Brown attempts to maximize profit under conditions of uncertainty; the constraints that he faces are the probabilities associated with various market prices; these constraints are themselves determined by the amount of wheat that other farmers bring to market, in other words, by the solutions to other farmers' optimization problems. And the entire process comes full circle, because the optimization problems faced by the other farmers include constraints that are partly the result of the actions of Farmer Brown.

In some sense the various optimization problems being solved by economic agents must have solutions that are compatible with each other. This requirement, known as an *equilibrium condition,* enables the economist to "solve" his model and make predictions about actual behavior. Consumers choose an optimal basket given the market prices that they face; firms supply a profit-maximizing mix of goods given those same market prices. In order for the quantity demanded by consumers to equal the quantity supplied by firms, prices cannot be arbitrary. In many circumstances there is only one equilibrium price that equates supply and demand.

Economists use many different equilibrium conditions. A *Nash equilibrium* is one in which each individual optimizes, taking the actions of other individuals as his constraints. The prisoners of Exhibit 11–6 achieve a Nash equilibrium when both confess. A *Walrasian equilibrium* is one in which each individual optimizes, taking market prices as given. The supply and demand diagrams of Chapter 1 illustrate Walrasian equilibria.

The third step in most economic analyses is the choice of an equilibrium condition and a study of the resulting equilibria: Do any exist? How many are there? How can they be computed? How will they change in response to changes in exogenous variables? (An *exogenous variable* is one that is taken to be determined outside the economic model under consideration. For example, the tastes of consumers and the technology available to firms are often treated as exogenous variables.[1]

Other Aspects of Economic Analysis

The economic study of human behavior consists largely of analyzing problems in the way we have just described: First, specify agents' goals and the nature of their constraints; second, solve the corresponding optimization problems (usually employing the equimarginal principle); and third, impose an equilibrium condition to find out what particular constraints agents must be facing and to describe their behavior.

Not all economic analysis can be fit into this simple mold, however. For example, economists are often concerned with modeling the process by which an equilibrium is achieved. This is known as the study of *economic dynamics*. On the other hand, that process is often most productively viewed as the solution to another, more subtle problem of optimization and equilibrium.

Economics also provides tools for analyzing the desirability of outcomes according to various criteria. The efficiency criterion introduced in Chapter 8 is one of the most popular, but economists can and do consider many other criteria as well.

The Value of Economic Analysis

In this book you have seen many examples of economic models. What do such models teach us? Some economic models are intended to reflect certain aspects of the world with sufficient accuracy to allow the economist to make precise numerical predictions. Such models are obviously of interest to anyone who must make decisions today that will be appropriate tomorrow. The shoemaker wants to know what the price of shoes will be next week; the policymaker wants to know how a tax on gasoline will affect the price of cars, or how a "comparable worth" law will affect the average size of firms.

Often, economic models are insufficient to make numerical predictions, but they do allow us to predict directions of change. Using the economic models in this book, you can predict that a tax on shoes will raise the price of shoes, reduce the quantity of shoes traded, and reduce economic efficiency. You can also predict a range for the possible price rise (at least zero and no more than the amount of the tax). A more precise model, incorporating more information

[1]The process of studying how equilibria change in response to changes in exogenous variables is known as *comparative statics*. When you solved Problem 11 at the end of Chapter 1, you were performing an exercise in comparative statics.

about the supply and demand curves, would allow a more precise prediction, but even the rough prediction of the simple model is obviously of interest.

There is also a large class of economic models whose assumptions and conclusions are essentially untestable. Consider the Edgeworth box of Chapter 8. We used this box to describe the outcome of a situation in which exactly two people trade exactly two goods and are constrained to use the artificial medium of a price system in doing so. Outside of an experimental laboratory, no such situation would ever be observed.

Why, then, does the Edgeworth box interest us? The answer is that economists are often interested in understanding the outcomes of real-world situations involving bargaining. Many of these situations are far too difficult to model precisely or to think about in their entirety. But an economist who has studied a wide variety of bargaining models develops a strong "seat of the pants" intuition for what *sorts* of things are likely to affect the outcome. After years of studying abstract models—each one abstract in its own way—the economist develops a sense that certain factors matter in certain ways and others don't matter at all. This intuition is the most powerful tool an economist has for understanding the world, but he can only develop it by first understanding simplifications of the world such as the Edgeworth box.

For example, consider the proposition that the economic incidence of a tax is independent of its legal incidence. In Chapter 1, we proved this proposition under certain conditions—markets are competitive, all taxes are either sales or excise taxes, taxes are flat rate (5¢ per cup) as opposed to something more complicated, and so forth. Economists have examined the impact of taxation in a wide variety of models, each with its own special assumptions, and keep getting the same result: The legal incidence of taxation does not matter. Not only does the economist observe the pattern here, but he begins to develop an intuition into *why* this result obtains in such a wide variety of circumstances. When the economist is asked to comment on the impact of a complicated taxation scheme in the real world, even though it might be the case that none of his models fits the situation exactly, he can predict with confidence that the legal incidence of the tax is irrelevant. He can do so because he understands why it is irrelevant in his models, and he can see that the same intuition is applicable in the case at hand.

Here is another, more general example: The economist's intuition always reminds him of the importance of incentives. Noneconomists are often skeptical that a rise in the price of gasoline will cause people to drive significantly less, that a tax on labor will reduce employment, or that rent controls will reduce the quantity and quality of housing. The economist knows these things to be true. His knowledge derives largely from his study of models of *other* markets, which have revealed the general principle that incentives matter.

In coming to understand the world by first understanding a potpourri of abstract models, the economist is no different from the physicist or any other scientist. Ask a physicist what will happen to your body if you slam on your brakes while going around a curve at 60 miles per hour. He will tell you, with sufficient accuracy to convince you not to do it. He will do so even if he has never written down or studied the physics of the particular situation you are describing. He is able to do so because he has studied the physics of a large number of models, each of which captures some important aspects of the situation, and has observed the common features of what these models predict. In the process he has developed a feel for the sorts of cause-and-effect relationships that are likely to hold. The kind of knowledge embodied in that "feel" is a large part of any successful science.

19.2 The Rationality Assumption

Models start with assumptions. Economic models start with the assumption of rational behavior, usually in the sense that actors accurately solve their optimization problems so as to maximize their well-being within the limits allowed by the constraints (that is, scarcities) with which they must contend. This assumption characterizes economic models. It is perfectly possible to study human behavior productively without assuming rationality, but then one isn't doing economics.

The Role of Assumptions in Science

Students are sometimes uncomfortable with the assumption of universal rationality. Often they point out that the assumption is clearly false, and they are surprised that their economics professors don't seem particularly concerned about this. But the fact of the matter is that all assumptions made in all sciences are clearly false. Physicists, the most successful of scientists, routinely assume that the table is frictionless when called upon to model the motions of billiard balls. They assume that the billiard balls themselves are solid objects. They assume that objects fall in vacuums. They study the behavior of electric charges that are localized at mathematical points and that interact only with a small number of other charges, as if the rest of the universe did not exist.

All scientists make simplifying assumptions about the world, because the world itself is too complicated to study. All such assumptions are equally false, but not all such assumptions are equally valuable. Certain kinds of assumptions lead consistently to results that are interesting, nonobvious, and at some level testable and verifiable. Other kinds of assumptions do not. In any given problem it is important to make simplifying assumptions of the sort that have proved to be successful in the past. It is usually equally important that the model be *robust;* that is, the exact statements of the assumptions should not enter in a crucial way, so that slightly different assumptions would still lead to the same conclusion.

To a large extent, *learning to be an economist consists of learning to make the right simplifying assumptions*. Indeed, we could replace the word *economist* with *physicist* or *anthropologist* or more generally with *scientist,* and this statement would still be true. Unfortunately, no one has ever succeeded in expressing a set of rules for determining the difference between a good and a bad simplification. You undoubtedly discovered this to your frustration when you began working the problems in this book. Often, the problems require assumptions, and often your assumptions probably seemed as good to you as any others, but your teacher did not agree. If you were successful in the course, you gradually developed a sense for what is and what is not the right approach to a problem. If you go on in economics, you will continue to develop this sense, which is what will make you an economist.

All We Really Need: No Unexploited Profit Opportunities

The rationality assumption in economics continues to disturb some students at a far more visceral level than the frictionless planes that other sciences assume. It seems plausible that a world without friction could resemble our own world in important ways, but students find it much more difficult to believe that the behavior of perfectly rational individuals could bear much resemblance to the behavior of the people they encounter in their everyday life. (This difficulty is particularly pronounced among students who live in dormitories!)

It is a misconception, however, to believe that a world in which most people are irrational would have to function very differently from a world in which everyone is rational. Imagine a world in which most people are irrational most of the time, but where enough people are rational enough of the time so that there are *no unexploited profit opportunities.* Such a world would function very similarly to one in which everyone is rational. Rather than give a general argument for this proposition, let us examine an illustrative example.

example

The Law of One Price

Economists believe in the *law of one price,* which says that identical goods will sell for identical prices (here *identical* means identical in all relevant characteristics, including, for example, time of delivery). It is easy to believe that this law would hold in a world of perfectly rational individuals. But it also holds in a world with no unexploited profit opportunities. Why? Because if you value two identical goods at different prices, your neighbor can make money by selling you one and buying from you the other. In the course of doing this, he and others like him will cause the prices of the goods to change and will keep doing this until all of the profit opportunities have been exploited—that is, until the prices of the goods are equal.

Application: The Pricing of Call Options

To learn more about call options, access the following Internet site maintained by PrimeCanadian Futures: http://www.primefutures.com/knowledge37.html

You may think that the law of one price is a very trivial sort of example. Yet it can be applied to solve very nontrivial problems. One example is the pricing of *call options.*

A call option is a piece of paper entitling you to buy a share of some specified stock at some future date for some prespecified price. These pieces of paper are traded in organized markets called options markets. Exhibit 19–1 shows an example of a call option.

Suppose that it is now January 1, 1996, and General Motors stock is selling at $1.00 per share. Suppose also that on January 1, 1997, it will surely be selling for either $.50 per share or $1.50 per share. Suppose finally that the going rate of interest is 25%. How much should you pay for the call option?

The first thing to ask is what the option will be worth a year from today. If the stock goes up $1.50, then your option will enable you to purchase 10 shares (worth $15) for a price of $10; in other words, it will be worth $5. If the

Exhibit 19-1 A Call Option

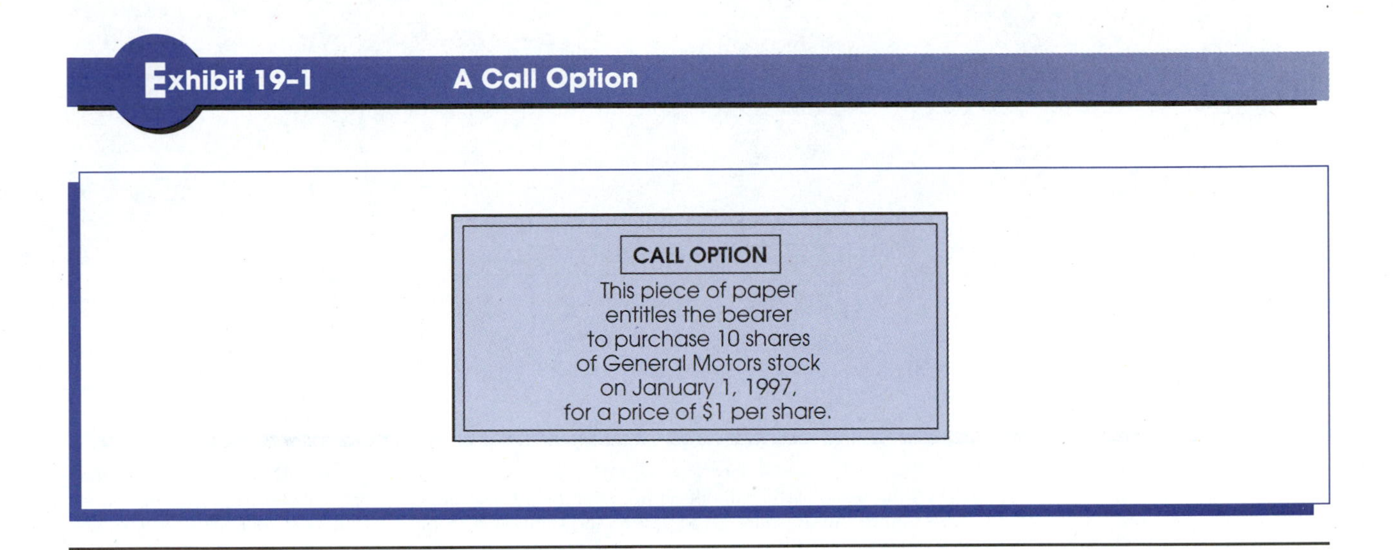

stock goes down to $.50, then you will choose not to exercise your option, so that it is worth zero. In Exhibit 19–2 we record the possibilities.

What is the call option worth today? You might suspect that this depends on the probability that the value of the stock will go up. You might think that if the stock is almost certain to go up, then the option is worth nearly $5, whereas if it is almost certain to go down, then the option is worth nearly zero. However, this is not correct.

To see why, and to price the call correctly, consider your friend Jeeter, who does not deal in options at all, but who adopts a strategy of borrowing $2 to buy 5 shares of stock. What will Jeeter's investment portfolio be worth a year from today? If the stock goes up, his 5 shares are worth $7.50, from which he must subtract $2.50 in order to repay his $2 debt with interest. In other words, his portfolio is worth $5. If the stock goes down, his 5 shares are worth $2.50, from which he must still subtract $2.50, so his portfolio is worth zero. In other words, *Jeeter's portfolio is identical to your call option* in the sense that it will have the same value as your option regardless of what happens to the price of the stock.

Now, by the law of one price, the call option must sell for the same amount of money that it would take to follow Jeeter's strategy. That strategy requires a net outlay of $3 (he takes in $2 in borrowed funds and lays out $5 to buy the 5 shares of stock). Therefore, the call option also sells for $3.

We have just seen a highly streamlined example of the *Black-Scholes Option Pricing Model,* which is used to predict real-world option prices with remarkable accuracy.[2] The model not only assumes that all investors are rational; it also assumes that they are extraordinarily clever: Whenever an option is offered, all of the market participants conjure up imaginary friends with portfolios that are identical to the option in order to price it correctly. In fact, even

[2]This model first appeared in F. Black and M. Scholes, "The Pricing of Options and Corporate Liabilities," *Journal of Political Economy* 81 (1973):637–654.

Exhibit 19-2 **Values of a Call Option**

Value of GM Stock on 1/1/97	Value of Call Option on 1/1/97
$1.50	$5
.50	0

We assume that on January 1, 1997, GM stock will surely sell for either $1.50 or $.50. The table shows the value of the call option from Exhibit 19–1. If the GM stock sells for $1.50, the option allows you to buy 10 shares at $1 apiece and to make a $5 profit. If the GM stock sells for $.50, the call option is worthless.

more is assumed. In the full-blown model, prices change continuously and stocks can go up or down by arbitrary amounts (as opposed to our example, where we allowed only two possible future values). In this case, solving the model requires knowledge of a sophisticated area of mathematics called the "Ito calculus." Most professors of mathematics have never heard of the Ito calculus, but Black and Scholes assume that all investors are whizzes at it.

How can such an unrealistic model possibly make accurate predictions? (If your answer is that it can't, be reminded that it does.) The answer is that although the model appears to invoke universal rationality, its conclusions actually follow from the much weaker assumption that there are no unexploited profit opportunities. The few people in the market smart enough to exploit all of the profit opportunities cause prices to behave as if everyone were perfectly rational—and had a Ph.D. in mathematics besides. The same sort of phenomenon occurs in many economic models.

Why don't Canadian marketers use Canadian celebrities? Read David Menzies' explanation at the following Internet site maintained by Marketing Online: http://www.marketingmag.ca/Content/33.96/retail33.html

19.3 What Is an Economic Explanation?

Economists like to look for puzzling phenomena and see whether they can be explained on the basis of rational behavior. Explanations that have implications beyond the case at hand are especially desirable, since they can be tested in other circumstances. Here are a few examples.

example Celebrity Endorsements

Why are there celebrity endorsements? Why is a stereo system advertised by radio personality Paul Harvey worth more than the same stereo system without a famous name attached to it?

One possible explanation is that buyers are either irrational or very foolish: They don't recognize that endorsements carry no information about product quality and are gulled into believing that because Paul Harvey is a famous and accomplished radio announcer, any stereo that he advertises is likely to be of high quality.

To an economist such an explanation is unsatisfactory. Economists insist on seeking explanations that are grounded in rational behavior. There are two reasons for this insistence. First, on the basis of his past experience, the economist is aware of the power and wide applicability of economic analysis, which presumes rationality. Second, by attempting to extend such analysis into realms where it first appears inapplicable, the economist tests the limits and the durability of his theories.

Imagine a physicist sitting in his garden who notices that a baseball lying on the grass has risen of its own accord and has begun to hover three feet off the ground. He could "explain" this phenomenon by abandoning his former insistence on the universality of gravitation, or he could attempt to find an explanation that is consistent with all of his previous experience. His gut will lead him to the second course of action. Perhaps it will eventually turn out that the laws of gravitation *are* wrong, but it is most productive to begin with the assumption that there must be some less radical solution to the problem.

If physicists abandoned their theories so easily, physics could never progress. The first physicist to have observed a helium-filled balloon would have admitted that there was no gravity, and the true physics of the situation would not have been discovered. By attempting to fit unfamiliar phenomena into familiar patterns, we arrive at deeper understandings of both the patterns and the phenomena.

So the economist is unwilling to abandon rationality quite so easily. Another easy "solution" presents itself: Perhaps people have a *taste* for wearing celebrity-endorsed clothing. They don't expect higher quality from the endorsed products; they just like wearing products that have been endorsed.

This solution is marginally better than the first one, but only marginally. The objection is that it's just too easy. Any human action can be explained on the basis of someone's having had a taste for that action. If we allow ourselves this easy out, we will never seek for deeper explanations.

The physicist could explain the floating baseball by saying that all of the laws of gravitation are true, but that this one baseball happens to contain a unique antigravity substance that is activated only at 2 P.M. on Tuesdays (or whatever time the physicist happens to be making his observation). We expect our physicists to work harder for their pay. We should expect the same of our economists.

Here is an *economic* explanation of celebrity endorsements: New firms enter the marketplace with different strategies. Some plan to make a quick killing by selling shoddy products and then getting out. Others plan to offer products of high quality, which is expensive for them at first, and to be successful by earning a good reputation that will pay off in future years. Firms of the second type would like to let you know that they are of the second type. One way for them to do so is to hire a celebrity at a very high price. This conveys the information that the firm plans to be around a long time—long enough to earn back its investment in celebrity advertising.

Whether or not this is the correct explanation, it is at least an economic one. It says that firms and individuals face certain constraints, one of which is the inability of firms to issue binding promises that they are not fly-by-nights, and that they optimize within the limits that these constraints impose. They convey the information expensively, which is better than not conveying it at all.

The explanation also has testable implications, which is an extremely desirable feature. It suggests that firms whose reputations are already well established should invest less in celebrity endorsements than firms that are just starting up, and that firms producing products whose quality is easily verified at the time of purchase should invest less in celebrity endorsements than those firms producing products whose quality is revealed only after a long period of use. Real-world observations can now be used to confirm or contest the theory.

example The Size of Shopping Carts

Celebrity endorsements are a puzzle, and economists love puzzles. Another puzzle that is very popular among some economists concerns the size of shopping carts. Shopping carts today are larger than they were 20 years ago. Why?

It has sometimes been suggested that the larger shopping carts constitute an attempt on the part of grocery store managers to induce shoppers to make more purchases. The idea is that shoppers are embarrassed to enter the checkout line with a half-full cart.

Not only does this fail as an economic explanation, it fails as any kind of explanation at all! In order to explain a new phenomenon, one must address the issue of why it arose when it did and not earlier. The "embarrassment" theory is a theory of why shopping carts should always be big, not one of why they should grow bigger.

Here is a menu of economic explanations, which might or might not be correct.

Over the past 20 years, large numbers of women have entered the marketplace, and relatively few households now have a member who engages in housework (including shopping) on a full-time basis. Therefore, people want to allocate less time to shopping and they accomplish this by reducing the number of trips to the store, while buying in larger quantities each time they go. Hence the need for larger shopping carts.

Or: Starting again with the observation that changes in family structure have led to people to want to economize on their shopping trips, we observe that one response has been for supermarkets to carry a wider range of items. It is now possible to shop for groceries, pharmaceutical products, and even small appliances under one roof. This enables the shopper to spend less time running from store to store, but it also necessitates larger shopping carts.

Or: Large shopping carts, and the wide aisles that are necessary to accommodate them, have always been desirable luxury items. They are also expensive, since wide aisles mean that stores must occupy more land. As shoppers have become wealthier over the past few decades, they have become increasingly willing to pay higher prices in exchange for wider aisles and bigger carts.

Can you suggest other theories? Can you think of any evidence that would help you choose among the ones suggested here?

example

Why Is There Mandatory Retirement?

Read more about mandatory retirement issues at the following Internet site maintained by the American Association of Retired People: http://www.sarp.org/wwstand/mandret.html

In 1986 the U.S. Congress severely restricted the practice of mandatory retirement. The fact that it was necessary to pass legislation to curtail this practice is an indication of its popularity. What made mandatory retirement so popular?

Professor Edward Lazear raised this question in a 1979 article, in which he examined the inadequacies of various traditional explanations.[3] Most of those traditional explanations rely on the assertion that workers' productivity declines significantly after a certain age and that employers deal with this through mandatory retirement. However, this cannot be a complete explanation. Among workers of any given age, there is wide variability in productivity. Employers do not refuse to hire the less productive workers; they simply pay them lower wages. Thus, "low productivity" cannot be a full explanation of why employers want to eliminate older workers completely.

Lazear offers an alternative explanation of mandatory retirement. Suppose that a worker is employed by a given firm for his entire working life. In competition, the worker receives a stream of wages whose present value is equal to the present value of his lifetime marginal product. There are many ways in which he can receive this stream of wages. Under Plan A the worker might be paid $20,000 each year, whereas under Plan B he receives less than $20,000 in some years and more than $20,000 in other years. Both the firm and the worker will be indifferent between Plan A and Plan B provided the two streams of wages have the same present value.

Now suppose that the worker agrees to acquire special skills that involve working harder but make him worth $30,000 per year to the company. In exchange for this, the firm pays him a higher wage, and both parties benefit. However, there is a catch: There is no way for the worker to guarantee in advance that he will really perform as promised. If he is paid on Plan A and if his salary is raised from $20,000 per year to $29,000 per year, the firm must be concerned that he will work at the old level of effort for a year, collect the $29,000, and then skip town.

Suppose, alternatively, that the worker is paid under a form of Plan B in which he is paid much less than his marginal product when he is young and much more than his marginal product when he is old. Now the contract to acquire special skills is enforceable: The worker must actually perform before he is compensated. The firm has its guarantee, and both parties benefit since the mutually beneficial contract can now be enforced.

Only one problem remains. The worker agrees to be paid less than he is worth to the firm while he is young in exchange for being paid more than he is worth when he is old. The firm will agree to such an arrangement only if it has a definite ending date. Hence the need for mandatory retirement.

You are invited to consider this explanation of the prevalence of mandatory retirement in light of Lazear's criticisms of other explanations. To what extent does Lazear's explanation avoid those problems? To what new criticisms is it

---

[3]E. Lazear. "Why Is There Mandatory Retirement?" *Journal of Political Economy* 87 (1979): 1261–1284.

susceptible? Is it, on balance, an improvement over other theories? Can you advance a new theory that makes even more sense?

Notice that if Lazear's story, or anything like it, is true, then both employers and employees benefit from mandatory retirement. It is true that any employee approaching his retirement would prefer to be allowed to continue working. But it is also true that the same employee, at the beginning of his working life and taking into account his entire lifetime earnings, is better off when he can commit himself to accepting mandatory retirement than when he cannot. The abolition of mandatory retirement reduces the ability of workers to offer guarantees of performance, reduces the willingness of firms to pay for such guarantees, and thereby reduces both the lifetime productivity and the lifetime compensation of workers.

There is an important moral to be drawn here: In evaluating public policy toward a social institution, it is necessary first to ask why that institution arose. It is impossible to know whether mandatory retirement is a good or a bad thing—by *any* criterion—without knowing why it exists in the first place. Social practices do not arise in vacuums; they arise because somebody finds them useful. It is incumbent upon the critic of these practices to understand who finds them useful and why before discarding them.

example Why Rock Concerts Sell Out

Tickets for major entertainment events such as Rolling Stones concerts predictably sell out well in advance. Television news programs show footage of hopeful ticket buyers lined up for blocks, and even camping out overnight so as not to lose their place in the ticket line. Clearly, if the promoters raised their prices they would still sell out. Why, then, do they not raise their prices?

A possible answer is that all of those overnight campers are good publicity for a rock group. A problem with this theory is that it seems like it would be equally good publicity to sell a lot of tickets at very high prices. If people think, "This group must be great; people camped out just to see them," would they not also think, "This group must be great; people paid hundreds just to see them"?

Another possible answer is that promoters are not interested in selling just concert tickets. They are also interested in selling T-shirts, CDs, and all of the other paraphernalia associated with rock groups. Typically, teenagers buy more of these paraphernalia than adults do. Also typically, teenagers are more willing to camp out overnight to buy a ticket than adults are. So by setting prices low and assuring long lines, the promoters also assure themselves of young audiences and lucrative T-shirt sales.

example "99¢ Pricing"

We close with one more example of an attempt to offer an economic explanation of an apparently "irrational" phenomenon. Consider the following letter to Ann Landers:

DEAR ANN LANDERS: I read your letter to E. A. in Riverside, the man who wanted to know why stores charge odd prices, such as 99 cents, $1.99, $29.99, etc. You answered: "It's a sales gimmick that's been around forever."

I am a 10-year-old boy and I think I have a better answer.

Around 1875, Melville Stone owned a newspaper named the *Chicago Daily News*. The price was a penny. Circulation was good, but after a while it began to drop off. He found that it was because pennies were in short supply. Mr. Stone persuaded Chicago merchants to sell their merchandise for a penny below the regular price. This put more pennies in circulation and it helped save the paper.

My source is: "Why Didn't I Think of That?" by Webb Garrison.

—N. C. Reader

Dear N.C.: When I receive a letter like this from a 10-year-old boy, it gives me fresh hope for the youth of this country. Thanks for writing.[4]

Ann's own explanation ("It's a sales gimmick . . ."), which is also the explanation given by most noneconomists, relies on irrational consumers and therefore doesn't conform to the rules of the economic game. Unfortunately, her correspondent's explanation is far worse, since it makes no sense from any point of view, economic or not. The child psychologist Jean Piaget has determined that most children begin to master the principle of conservation at about age 7. By the age of 8, they understand, for example, that when water is poured from a short, thick container into a tall thin container, the quantity of water does not change. One might then expect a 10-year-old to recognize that when a penny changes hands, there are neither more nor fewer pennies in circulation than there were previously.

Here is a suggestion for an economic explanation of how the pricing scheme in question developed. Around the same time that Melville Stone was trying to boost the circulation of the *Chicago Daily News,* the cash register was invented. It was now much easier for store owners to prevent their employees from stealing, because the register kept records of each purchase. However, a sale is recorded only when the register is opened, which would be necessary only if it were required to make change. A clerk can quietly slip a $20 bill into his pocket if the price of the item is $20, but he must ring up the sale and open the register if he has to give a penny in change.

Rationality Revisited

These examples illustrate one further point about the rationality assumption. To a large extent, the assumption of rationality is nothing more than a commitment to inquire sympathetically into people's motives. When we see people flocking to buy clothes endorsed by celebrities, or when we see concert promoters "underpricing" their tickets, we have a choice. Either we can remark—wistfully or cynically, according to our temperament—on the inadequacy of human nature, or we can ask, "How might such behavior be serving someone's purposes?" The first option offers the satisfaction of exempting oneself from the great mass of human folly. The second offers an opportunity to learn something.

[4]Permission granted by Ann Landers and Creators Syndicate.

Adopting the rationality assumption means pledging to treat all human behavior as worthy of respectful consideration. Rather than dismiss the buyers of stereos endorsed by Paul Harvey as victims of a herd mentality, or the concert promoter as a plodder who fails to see profit opportunities, we force ourselves to think deeply about what their true motives and strategies might be. In the process, we discover possibilities and develop insights that would never arise if we allowed ourselves to simply dismiss as "irrational" anything we failed to understand immediately. By disallowing the easy way out, we commit ourselves to careful and creative analysis of why people behave as they do, which is an excellent habit for any social scientist to cultivate.

19.4 The Scope of Economic Analysis

We began this chapter by saying that economics is the science that studies human behavior by positing rational action in the face of constraints. Traditionally, such reasoning was applied primarily to the trading of goods and services in the marketplace. However, in the last 30 years it has become clear that the economic way of thinking can be productively applied to a wide range of activities both in and out of the marketplace. Economists study love and marriage, the structure of families, medieval agriculture, religious activity, cannibalism, and evolution. By extending their methods into such areas, many of which are dominated by actors who are traditionally supposed to be engaged in nonrational behavior, economists have demonstrated the power of their approach. In this section we will summarize a few of the most exciting nontraditional applications of economics.

Laboratory Animals as Rational Agents

In a series of remarkable experiments, a group of researchers has demonstrated that laboratory animals respond to economic stimuli in the ways that economic theory would predict.[5]

Rats as Consumers

In one experiment rats were permitted to "purchase" root beer and collins mix by pressing levers that caused the liquids to be dispensed. The rats were given fixed incomes (for example, 300 lever pushes per day) and prices (for example, one lever push generates .05 ml of root beer or .1 ml of collins mix). Their consumption patterns were noted. Then the rats' incomes and the prices they faced were varied, so that their behavior could be observed under a variety of budget constraints. The rats' behavior demonstrated downward-sloping demand curves and upward-sloping Engel curves, as an economist would expect.

Moreover, the rats' consumption patterns were internally consistent in the sense predicted by economic theory. For example, panel A of Exhibit 19–3 il-

[5] J. H. Kagel, R. Battalio, H. Rachlin, L. Green, R. Basmann, and W. R. Klemm, "Experimental Studies of Consumer Demand Behavior Using Laboratory Animals," *Economic Inquiry* 13 (1975):22–38; see also R. Battalio, L. Green, and J. H. Kagel, "Income-Leisure Tradeoffs of Animal Workers," *American Economic Review* 71 (1981):621–632.

Rats as Rational Consumers

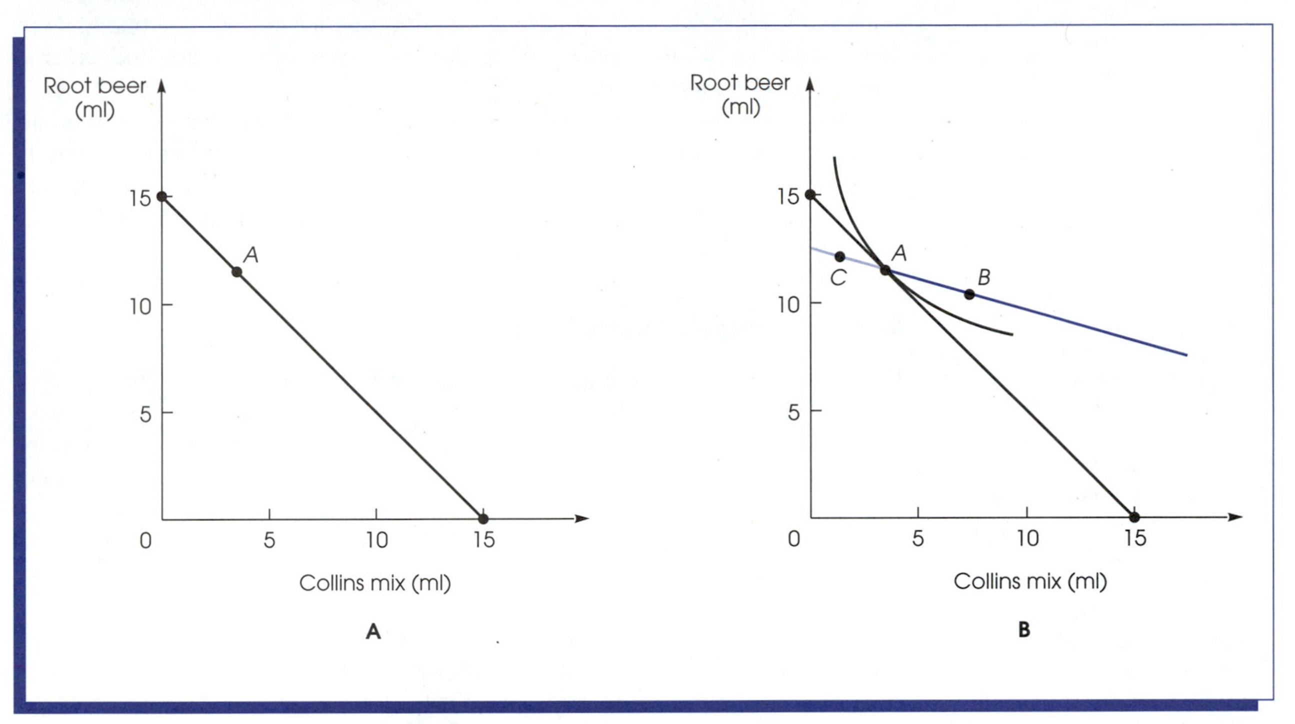

In panel A a rat with the black budget line chose point *A*. Prices and his income were then adjusted so that he now had the color budget line in panel B. According to economic theory, the rat must now choose a point like *B* (on the darker part of the new line) rather than a point like *C* (on the lighter part). The reason is that if an indifference curve were tangent at *C*, it would have to cross the original indifference curve. In fact, the rat chose point *B*, confirming the economic prediction.

lustrates one rat's consumption point when given an income of 300 lever presses and facing prices of 1 press per .05 ml for both liquids. The rat chose point *A*. His income and prices were then adjusted to give him the color budget line shown in panel B. If the rat was a rational maximizer, with an indifference curve tangent to the first budget line at *A*, then his new optimum would have to occur at a point below *A* on the new budget line. In fact, he chose point *B*, confirming this prediction.

Pigeons as Suppliers of Labor

In a later experiment, pigeons were required to earn their incomes (in this case, food) by pecking a response key. Their behavior was observed under variations in both wage rates (amount of food per peck) and nonlabor income (free food delivered at regular intervals). The pigeons demonstrated all of the expected substitution and income effects. In particular, when their nonlabor income was fixed, their labor supply curves were backward bending, as you would expect after having read Section 16.1 of this book.

In one version of the experiment, pigeons were initially presented with no nonlabor income, so that their budget line was as shown in panel A of Exhibit 19–4. They chose point *D*. Then their wages were lowered, while they were simultaneously given just enough nonlabor income to give them the color budget line shown in panel B. Assuming that the pigeons are rational maximizers, they must now choose a point on the darker portion of the color line, such as point *E*, and, in fact, they do so.

Often noneconomists argue that economists are far too optimistic in their assumption that people have sufficient intelligence to respond appropriately to subtle changes in prices and income. The next time you find yourself in conversation with such a noneconomist, you can ask him whether he thinks that most human beings are as intelligent as rats and pigeons.

Altruism and the Selfish Gene

Read an economic working paper (by Ilan Eshel, Larry Samuelson, Avner Shaked) on the relative success of altruists in a social-evolutionary context at the following Internet site maintained by the Center for Economic Learning and Social Evolution (University College London): http://ada.econ.ucl.ac.uk/papers/avnesh.htm

There is a growing literature on the interface and analogies between economics and biology.[6] One area of mutual interest is the study of *altruism*. Economists have long been aware that people choose to give gifts to others, especially to their children and other close relatives. Perhaps you would not be in college if it weren't for this phenomenon. Such behavior can be explained by saying that people have a "taste" for it, but as we have noted before, economists are distinctly uncomfortable with this kind of glibness. So we must look deeper.

Recently, biologists have begun to explore the notion that altruism is a result of purely selfish (nonaltruistic) behavior on the part of the genetic material that is the true medium for natural selection. If you are carrying a certain gene, then there is a 50% chance that your child is carrying the same gene. The gene's survival probability is enhanced if you behave in a way that improves the survival prospects of your children. Now suppose that some particular gene has the effect of making you feel altruistic toward your children. Then that gene will gain an evolutionary advantage and tend to propagate.[7]

Economists have explored some of the consequences of altruistic behavior in the family. For example, suppose that the household is headed by an altruistic parent who gives bequests to the children in such a way as to equalize the children's "incomes," where these incomes include all of the things that are important to a child. If one child is more satisfied than the others, then the parent will tend to give more attention, presents, and so forth to the other children (and consequently less to the satisfied one) until the situation becomes more equal.

Now suppose that the family contains a "Rotten Kid" who is thinking of stealing his sister's marbles. Suppose also that the theft of the marbles would be economically inefficient, either because he values them less than she does

---

[6]See, for example, J. Hirshleifer, "Economics from a Biological Viewpoint," *Journal of Law and Economics* 20 (1977):1–52; and G. Tullock, "Biological Externalities," *Journal of Theoretical Biology* 33 (1971):565–576.

[7]For a fascinating account of this fascinating approach to biology, see R. Dawkins. *The Selfish Gene* (New York: Oxford University Press, 1976). The book's proposed explanations of puzzles in animal behavior are very much in the spirit of economics.

Exhibit 19-4 Pigeons and Labor Supply

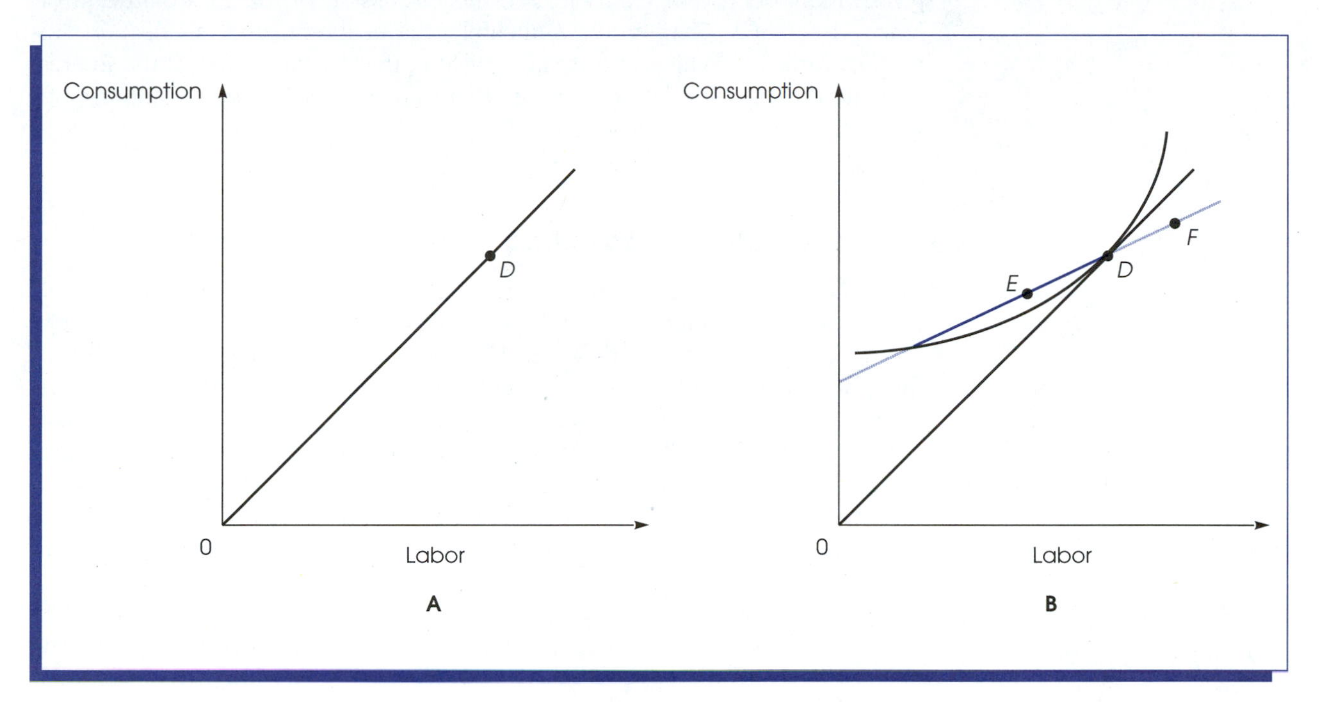

In panel A a pigeon with the black budget line chose point D. His wage and his nonlabor income were then adjusted so that he had the color budget line. According to economic theory, the pigeon must now choose a point like E (on the darker part of the new line) rather than a point like F (on the lighter part). The reason is that if an indifference curve were tangent at F, it would have to cross the original indifference curve. In fact, the pigeon chose point E, confirming the economic prediction.

or because some marbles are likely to be lost in the struggle over their ownership. The Rotten Kid might be deterred from stealing the marbles if he feared being found out and punished by the parent. But more remarkably, he will not steal the marbles even if the parent is totally unable to observe or discover the theft. The reason is that the reduction in his sister's level of satisfaction will cause the parent to divert resources to the sister and away from the Rotten Kid, even though the parent has no idea of the reason why the sister has seemed so unhappy lately. The economic inefficiency of the theft means that there will be a smaller social surplus to divide among the children, and an equal share of a smaller pie is not an improvement from the Rotten Kid's own point of view.

This "Rotten Kid theorem" is due to Professor Gary S. Becker, whose book on the economic analysis of family life is a highly recommended (but somewhat technically sophisticated) source of novel and clever economic argument.[8]

[8]G. S. Becker, *A Treatise on the Family* (Cambridge, MA: Harvard University Press, 1981).

The analysis of altruism is by no means a frivolous pursuit. The extent to which parents care about their children's welfare is an important component in understanding savings behavior, responses to taxation, and responses to government debt. (For example, see the discussion of the Ricardian Equivalence Theorem in Chapter 17.) Ultimately, the economic analysis of these important variables (which in turn are critical in the determination of the interest rate and the rate of inflation, among other things) must rest on an understanding of behavior in the household.

The Economics of Scattering

In medieval Europe many small farmers held their land in scattered plots. This means that a typical farmer would own three or four small plots of land at considerable distances from each other. Historians and economists are puzzled by this phenomenon, which seems to entail unnecessary inefficiencies. (Here is an inefficiency you might not have thought of: With so many small plots, there are many more boundaries between neighbors, and consequently many more externalities. Farmers sometimes remove rocks from their own land near the boundary and toss them onto their neighbor's land. With scattering, almost all land is near a boundary, and a lot of energy gets spent tossing rocks back and forth.)

Many explanations have been offered for scattering. Professor Donald McCloskey has examined these explanations and found them wanting from the economist's viewpoint (he is also the source of the parenthetical observation in the preceding paragraph).[9] He has suggested an alternative. Farming communities are subject to localized disasters. Wind, rain, or fire can destroy all of the crops in one part of town while leaving those in other parts untouched. If there is no organized market for insurance, a rational farmer will be willing to accept the inefficiencies of scattering in exchange for the corresponding reduction in risk. With scattered plots, he will grow less in the average year, but he is much less likely to face a year in which all of his crops are destroyed.

It is sometimes argued that medieval and modern man differ so radically that the economic models developed in the nineteenth and twentieth centuries for understanding behavior in industrialized societies are not useful tools in the study of the distant past. McCloskey's work indicates the opposite: Peasants in the Middle Ages were willing to pay a price for a reduction in risk, just as economic theory would predict (see Chapter 18 of this book), and the price that they were willing to pay was a reasonable one, given the risks involved.

If economic theory applies to rats and pigeons, then surely we should expect it to apply to human beings in situations very different from our own. The scope of economic analysis is being extended every day. This is an exciting time to be studying economics.

---

[9]D. McCloskey, "The Open Fields of England: Rent, Risk and the Rate of Interest, 1300–1815," in D. Galenson, ed., *Markets in History: Economic Studies of the Past* (Cambridge University Press, 1989). This article makes fascinating reading, and applies many of the ideas you have learned in this course both to draw striking conclusions about the past and to refute alternative theories.

Problem Set

1. Reexamine Problem 24 at the end of Chapter 3. What agents are involved in this problem? What are they maximizing and what are their constraints? When you work the problem, at what point are you solving an optimization problem? At what point are you computing an equilibrium?

2. Look back at various other problems in this book. Which are primarily concerned with optimization problems? Which with equilibria? Which with both?

3. Suppose that General Motors stock is currently selling for $\$S$ per share, that one year from today it will either have gone up to $\$U$ or down to $\$D$. and that the annual interest rate is r. You are offered a call option that will allow you to buy GM stock next year at a price of $\$C$, where C is between U and D. In terms of S, U, D, r, and C, what is the value of this call option?

4. True or False: Television sets will be more expensive in an area with great reception and lots of channels than in an area served by only one channel, which comes in poorly.

5. Why do banks construct elaborate buildings with Greek columns? Does your explanation show why supermarkets don't do the same thing? Does it predict which banks are most likely to construct such buildings?

6. True or False: *Good Housekeeping* tests products and awards its Seal of Approval to those found to be of high quality. Manufacturers who have been judged worthy of the seal must still pay to display it. By being selective about how it awards the seal, the magazine has acquired a reputation for trustworthiness, which makes the seal a valuable commodity. Consider the proposition that Paul Harvey awards the use of his name in the same selective way that *Good Housekeeping* awards its seal, and that his endorsement is valuable for that reason. Contrast this proposition with the explanation offered in the chapter. In what ways does one seem more reasonable than the other? What could you observe in the real world to test the truth of either proposition?

7. Evaluate the explanation of mandatory retirement given in the chapter.

8. Criticize the explanation of "99¢ pricing" given in the chapter. Can you think of an alternative economic explanation? What could you observe in the real world to help establish or refute the validity of the text's explanation?

9. Criticize the Rotten Kid theorem.

10. Suppose that McCloskey's theory of scattering is correct. What exogenous social developments would tend to reduce the preponderance of scattering? How would the amount of scattering be related to the interest rate?

11. Consider the following alternative theory of scattering: Every time a farmer dies, his land is divided among his children, creating several small plots.

Whenever there is a marriage, the ownership of several of these plots becomes merged. What flaws are there in this theory? Is it consistent with rational behavior on the part of the peasants? Is it more or less plausible from that point of view than McCloskey's theory?

In the remaining problems, construct theories to explain the phenomena described. Try to base your theories on rational behavior. In each case describe some additional predictions of your theory, and present some ways that you could use real-world observations to test it.

12. Women spend more on medical care than men do.

13. Blockbuster movies generate long lines at the ticket counter, but theater owners don't raise prices for blockbusters.

14. Baseball tickets are priced in such a way that the box seats almost always sell out long before the bleachers do.

15. Ski resorts charge for lift tickets on a per-day rather than a per-ride basis, and there are often long lines at the lifts.

16. Firms lay off workers rather than reduce their salaries.

17. When workers go on strike, the firm loses profits and the workers lose wages. If the strike were called off, the two parties would have a bigger pie to divide between them. Nevertheless, there are strikes.

18. People prefer to bet on the sports teams they are rooting for than on the opposing teams.

19. Following an earthquake, sales of earthquake insurance go up.

20. Some items are sold in English auctions (where the item is offered for sale at a low price and buyers bid the price up until only one buyer is left). Others are sold in Dutch auctions (where the item is offered at a high price and the seller calls out successively lower prices until a buyer steps in).

Can you construct a theory that will predict which sort of auction will be used for which sort of item? Does your theory take into account the incentives that buyers have to attend the auction in the first place?

21. Many societies have strict taboos against baby selling.

22. People give each other gifts that they are not sure the recipient will like, even though they could as easily give cash instead. (Saying that a gift shows you took the time to shop is no answer, since cash shows you took the time to earn the money.)

23. People voluntarily leave tips in restaurants, even when they know they won't be returning.

24. People give to charitable organizations and to political causes.

25. Over half the electorate turns out to vote for presidential elections, even though the probability of any individual's changing the outcome is negligibly small.

26. Car manufacturers will sometimes offer a $500 rebate on a new car rather than take $500 off the sales price. This is so even though reducing the price would lower the sales tax and thus benefit the consumer by more than $500.

27. People in rural communities are often unhappy about the switch to daylight saving time, since they tend to wake up very early (say at 5:30 A.M.) and under daylight saving time it is dark at that hour. A solution would be to continue waking up at the "old" 5:30 A.M. (which is renamed 6:30 A.M. under daylight saving time). But this solution is not implemented.

28. In the United States, a hotel room for two people usually costs less than twice as much as a hotel room for one person, whereas in England a room for two often costs exactly twice as much as a room for one.

29. *(This problem was suggested by Marvin Goodfriend.)* Governments are engaged in the business of redistributing income through the tax system. At the same time, private individuals are prohibited by law from redistributing income (via strong-arm tactics, breaking and entering, extortion, and the like). Thus, the government maintains and enforces a monopoly in the income redistribution market, and there is a general agreement, among both economists and noneconomists, that this is a good thing. But economists generally oppose government monopolies in other areas, such as the postal service. Are they being inconsistent?

Internet Exercise

It was observed in the chapter that altruism may be consistent with self-interested behavior in the context of an evolutionary model. In contrast, in static economic models, altruism is usually seen as being irrational because it is inconsistent with the maximization of utility based on personal consumption. As a consequence, static economic models predict such behavior as free-riding on the voluntary provision of public goods. The following Internet site contains a description of a role-playing classroom economic experiment on public goods (http://www.marietta.edu/~delemeeg/expernom/s93.html#hoaas1). How does the structure of the role-playing exercise reflect the key characteristics of providing for a public good? How do different subject pools affect the degree of free-riding behavior? Compare these subject pool effects with those described in William Herbaugh's research with children at the following Internet site: (http://harbaugh.uoregon.edu/papers/kidalt/kidalt.htm).

Appendix A

Calculus Supplement

This appendix briefly reviews the material of the textbook in the language of calculus. There are sections corresponding to most of the textbook chapters, and most have some brief exercises at the end.

Chapter I

1. Demand and supply. Demand and supply are functions that convert prices to quantities. For a given price P, the demand and supply functions are defined by setting $D(P) =$ the quantity that demanders wish to buy at price P, and $S(P) =$ the quantity that suppliers wish to sell at price P.

When the price changes from P_1 to P_2, the quantity demanded changes from $D(P_1)$ to $D(P_2)$, but the function D remains unchanged. A *change in demand* refers to a change in the function D itself. Similarly for supply.

Because the output from a demand or supply function represents a quantity, it is often denoted by the letter Q. Thus, if we are discussing demand we write

$$Q = D(P)$$

and if we are discussing supply we write

$$Q = S(P)$$

Of course, when we discuss supply and demand simultaneously, we cannot use the same symbol to denote the output from both functions. In that case we usually write

$$Q_d = D(P)$$

$$Q_s = S(P)$$

to distinguish the quantity demanded Q_d from the quantity supplied Q_s.

2. Derivatives. The fact that the demand curve slopes downward is expressed by the inequality

$$D'(P) < 0$$

or

$$\frac{dQ_d}{dP} < 0$$

The fact that the supply curve slopes upward is expressed by the inequality

$$S'(P) > 0$$

or

$$\frac{dQ_s}{dP} > 0$$

3. Equilibrium. The equilibrium price is the price P at which $D(P) = S(P)$, and the equilibrium quantity is this common value. The assumptions $D'(P) < 0$ and $S'(P) > 0$ ensure the uniqueness of the equilibrium.

4. Taxation. Suppose that the demand for lettuce is given by the function $Q_d = D_0(P)$. When a sales tax equal to T per head of lettuce is imposed, the demander must pay $P + T$ to acquire a head of lettuce. Thus, the new demand function is given by the formula $D_1(P) = D_0(P + T)$. The graph of D_1 is identical to the graph of D_0 translated downward a distance T.

Similarly, an excise tax of T per head of lettuce causes the supply function $S_0(P)$ to be replaced by the new function $S_1(P) = S_0(P + T)$. The graph of S_1 is identical to the graph of S_0 translated upward a distance T.

Continue to write D_0 and S_0 for the original demand and supply functions. A sales tax leads to the equilibrium price P_{sales} where

$$D_1(P_{\text{sales}}) = S_0(P_{\text{sales}})$$

and an excise tax leads to the equilibrium price P_{excise} where

$$D_0(P_{\text{excise}}) = S_1(P_{\text{excise}})$$

Substituting the expressions for D_1 and S_1 gives

$$D_0(P_{\text{sales}} + T) = S_0(P_{\text{sales}})$$
$$D_0(P_{\text{excise}}) = S_0(P_{\text{excise}} - T)$$

It is easy to check that if P_{sales} satisfies the first equation, then $P_{\text{excise}} = P_{\text{sales}} + T$ satisfies the second equation. Moreover, there is only one solution to each equation because D_0 is decreasing and S_0 is increasing. It follows that we must have $P_{\text{excise}} = P_{\text{sales}} + T$.

Under a sales tax, demanders pay $P_{\text{sales}} + T = P_{\text{excise}}$ and suppliers get P_{sales}. Under an excise tax, demanders pay P_{excise} and suppliers keep $P_{\text{excise}} - T = P_{\text{sales}}$. Therefore, the sales and excise taxes are equivalent.

Exercises

1. Let $S(P)$ and $D(P)$ be the supply and demand functions for apples. Suppose that an excise tax of T is imposed and the post-tax equilibrium price for apples is P. Treating P as a function of T, use the equation

$$D(P) = S(P - T)$$

and the chain rule to derive a formula for the derivative dP/dT.

Answer: $$\frac{dP}{dT} = \frac{S'(P - T)}{S'(P - T) - D'(P)}$$

2. In problem 1, let P_{sellers} be the price that sellers actually receive for the items they sell. Use the result of problem 1 and the equation

$$P_{\text{sellers}} = P - T$$

to derive and simplify a formula for the derivative dP_{sellers}/dT.

Answer: $$\frac{dP}{dT} = \frac{D'(P)}{S'(P - T) - D'(P)}$$

3. Let $S(P)$ and $D(P)$ be the supply and demand functions for apples. Suppose that a sales tax of T is imposed and the post-tax equilibrium price for apples is P. Treating P as a function of T, use the equation

$$D(P + T) = S(P)$$

and the chain rule to derive a formula for the derivative dP/dT.

4. In problem 3, let P_{buyers} be the price that buyers actually pay for the items they buy. Use the result of problem 3 and the equation

$$P_{\text{buyers}} = P + T$$

to derive and simplify a formula for the derivative dP_{buyers}/dT.

5. Explain how your solutions to problems 1 through 4 illustrate the proposition that the economic incidence of a tax is independent of its legal incidence.

Chapter 3

1. Families of indifference curves. A single indifference curve is defined by a single equation in X and Y. A *family* of indifference curves must be defined by a *family* of equations. The easiest way to do this is to specify a function of two variables $U(X, Y)$ and to consider the family of equations

$$U(X, Y) = C$$

where C is any constant. Thus, for example, one indifference curve is given by $U(X, Y) = 1$, another by $U(X, Y) = 2$, and so forth.

When the indifference curves are described in this way, it is clear that they fill the plane (for every (X, Y), $U(X, Y)$ has *some* value, and (X, Y) is on the corresponding indifference curve) and that they never cross (for every (X, Y) $U(X, Y)$ has only *one* value, and so (X, Y) is on only one indifference curve). The other properties of indifference curves follow from some assumptions on U. A set of assumptions sufficient to guarantee the desired properties is:

$$\frac{\partial U}{\partial X} > 0 \tag{1}$$

$$\frac{\partial U}{\partial Y} > 0 \tag{2}$$

$$\frac{\partial^2 U}{\partial X^2} < 0 \tag{3}$$

$$\frac{\partial^2 U}{dY^2} < 0 \tag{4}$$

$$\frac{\partial^2 U}{\partial X^2} \cdot \frac{\partial^2 U}{\partial Y^2} - \left(\frac{\partial^2 U}{\partial X \partial Y}\right)^2 > 0 \tag{5}$$

2. Properties of indifference curves. To see what our assumptions imply about the indifference curves, fix a constant C and look at the indifference curve defined by $U(X, Y) = C$. This curve is also the graph of the function $Y = f(X)$, where f is implicitly defined by the formula

$$U(X, f(X)) = C$$

The chain rule gives

$$\frac{\partial U}{\partial X}(X, f(X)) + \frac{\partial U}{\partial Y}(X, f(X)) \cdot \frac{df}{dX}(X) = \frac{dC}{dX} = 0$$

so that

$$\frac{df}{dX} = -\frac{\partial U / \partial X}{\partial U / \partial Y} < 0$$

(The final inequality follows from assumptions (1) and (2).) In other words, indifference curves slope downward.

By differentiating both sides of the formula

$$\frac{\partial U}{\partial X}(X,f(X)) + \frac{\partial U}{\partial Y}(X,f(X)) \cdot \frac{df}{dX}(X) = 0$$

we find that

$$\frac{\partial^2 U}{\partial X^2}(X,f(X)) + 2 \cdot \frac{\partial^2 U}{\partial X \partial Y}(X,f(X)) \cdot \frac{df}{dX}(X) + \frac{\partial^2 U}{\partial Y^2} \cdot \left(\frac{df}{dX}(X)\right)^2$$
$$= -\frac{\partial U}{\partial Y}(X,f(X)) \cdot \frac{d^2 f}{dX^2}(X)$$

For a given value of X, the left side of this equation is equal to the value of the quadratic function

$$(t) = \frac{\partial^2 U}{\partial X^2}(X,f(X)) + 2 \cdot \frac{\partial^2 U}{\partial X \partial Y}(X,f(X)) \cdot t + \frac{\partial^2 U}{\partial Y^2}(X,f(X)) \cdot t^2$$

at the point $t = (df/dX)(X)$. Assumptions (3) and (5) imply that the quadratic function takes only negative values.* Thus, we know that $-(\partial U/\partial Y)(X, f(X))$ $(\partial^2 f/\partial X^2)(X)$ is negative. Together with assumption 1 this allows us to conclude that $(d^2 f/dX^2)$ is everywhere positive. In other words, indifference curves are convex.

To summarize, we have shown that when the indifference curves are described by the formulas $U(X, Y) = C$, and when U satisfies assumptions (1) through (5), we may conclude that indifference curves fill the plane, never cross, slope downward, and are convex.

3. The marginal rate of substitution and the consumer's optimum. According to the chain rule, the slope of the indifference curve at the point (X, Y) is given by

$$-\frac{\partial U/\partial X}{\partial U/\partial Y}$$

evaluated at (X, Y). The absolute value of this slope is the marginal rate of substitution between X and Y.

The consumer's budget constraint is given by the equation

$$P_X \cdot X + P_Y \cdot Y = I$$

where P_X, P_Y, and I are constants. Its graph is the equation of the straight line through $(0, I/P_Y)$ and $(I/P_X, 0)$; the slope of this line is $-P_X/P_Y$.

*Assumption (3) implies that $Q(0) < 0$. Assumption (5) implies that Q has no real roots. By the intermediate value theorem, a continuous function that takes one negative value and has no real roots must take only negative values.

In order to attain the highest possible indifference curve, the consumer maximizes $U(X, Y)$ subject to the budget constraint. There are two ways to solve this problem. One is to view it as a constrained maximization problem in the two variables X and Y so that the method of Lagrange multipliers applies. However, there is a much more elementary alternative. Using the budget constraint, we solve for Y and get

$$Y = \frac{I}{P_Y} - \frac{P_X}{P_Y} \cdot X$$

Then we are reduced to solving a maximization problem in one variable: namely: Maximize

$$U\left(X, \frac{I}{P_Y} - \frac{P_X}{P_Y} \cdot X\right)$$

The first order condition is

$$\frac{\partial U}{\partial X} = \frac{P_X}{P_Y} \cdot \frac{\partial U}{\partial Y}$$

or

$$\frac{\partial U/\partial X}{\partial U/\partial Y} = \frac{P_X}{P_Y}$$

That is, the consumer selects the point on the budget constraint at which the marginal rate of substitution and the relative price of X are equal. This has good intuitive content, as described in the textbook.

To verify that we have found a maximum, it is necessary to verify the second-order condition as well. Although it is geometrically obvious that we have indeed found a maximum (see, for example Exhibit 3-9 in the textbook), you might want to verify the second-order condition directly, using assumptions (1) through (5).

Exercises

1. Suppose that your indifference curves between X and Y are given by the family of equations $U(X, Y) = C$ where $U(X, Y) = X^{1/2} \cdot Y^{1/2}$.

a. Does U satisfy the conditions 1 through 5 of section 1?
Answer: Yes.

b. Compute the slope of your indifference curve passing through the point (X, Y) at that point, as a function of X and Y.
Answer: Y/X.

c. Show that your indifference curves are convex.

d. Suppose that the price of X is \$1, the price of Y is \$2, and your income is \$10. What basket of goods do you buy?
Answer: $X = 5$, $Y = 2\frac{1}{2}$.

e. Repeat part (d) if the price of X goes up to \$5.
Answer: $X = 1$, $Y = 2\frac{1}{2}$.

f. Repeat part (d) if your income goes up to $20.

2. Repeat problem 1 with the function U replaced by $U(X, Y) = X^{1/4} \cdot Y^{1/4}$.

Chapter 4

1. The Engel Curve. We will continue to assume that the consumer's indifference curves are the curves $U(X, Y) = C$ for some fixed function U.

In order to see how the consumer reacts to changes in income, we hold the prices of X and Y fixed; that is we treat P_X and P_Y as constants. We can always choose to measure Y in units that make $P_Y = 1$ (for example, if Y is Coca-Cola and it sells for 50¢ per can, then we will declare one "unit" of Coca-Cola to consist of two cans). This allows us to adopt the abbreviation $P = P_X$; that is, P is the relative price of X in terms of Y.

At any given level of income I, the consumer decides what quantity of X to purchase. We will denote this quantity by $E(I)$. $E(I)$ is chosen to maximize

$$U(E(I), I - PE(I))$$

That is, $E(I)$ satisfies the first-order condition

$$U_1(E(I), I - PE(I)) = PU_2(E(I), I - PE(I)) \qquad \textbf{(6)}$$

where we have abbreviated

$$U_1 = \frac{\partial U}{\partial X} \quad U_2 = \frac{\partial U}{\partial Y}$$

The function $E(I)$ implicitly defined by equation (6) is the consumer's Engel curve for X.

By differentiating equation (6) with respect to I, we can find the slope of the Engel curve. You should verify that

$$E'(I) = \frac{-U_{12} + PU_{22}}{U_{11} - 2PU_{12} - P^2U_{22}} \qquad \textbf{(7)}$$

As an example, suppose that there are constants α and β such that

$$U(X, Y) = X^\alpha Y^\beta$$

Then you should be able to verify that the equation of the Engel curve is given by

$$E(I) = \frac{\alpha I}{(\alpha + \beta)P}$$

That is, in this case the consumer's Engel curve is a straight line through the origin with slope $\alpha/((\alpha + \beta) \cdot P)$.

2. The demand curve. The consumer's demand curve D is derived in a similar way, by treating I as a constant and noting that the consumer maximizes $U(X, I - PX)$ by setting $X = D(P)$ where $D(P)$ satisfies

$$U_1(D(P), I - PD(P)) = PU_2(D(P), I - PD(P)) \tag{8}$$

The function D implicitly defined by equation (8) is the consumer's demand curve.

For example, if the indifference curves are given by

$$U(X, Y) = X^{\alpha} Y^{\beta}$$

then the demand curve for X is given by

$$D(P) = \frac{\alpha I}{(\alpha + \beta)P}$$

Although the right-hand expression looks exactly like the expression for the Engel curve, we are now treating P as the independent variable and I as a constant. Thus, the demand curve in this case is a hyperbola.

By differentiating equation (8) with respect to P, we can find the slope of the demand curve. You should verify that

$$D'(P) = \frac{U_{12}D(P) - PU_{22}D(P) + U_2}{U_{11} - 2PU_{12} + P^2U_{22}} \tag{9}$$

3. The compensated demand curve. We can also derive an expression for the compensated demand curve $D_c(X)$. Suppose the consumer starts out on the indifference curve $U(X, Y) = C$. In order to derive the compensated demand curve, we pretend that regardless of how the price P changes, the consumer is constrained to remain on the same indifference curve. Thus, for any price P, the consumer selects quantities $X = D_c(P)$ and $Y = f(P)$ such that

$$U(D_c(P), f(P)) = C \tag{10}$$

Differentiating this with respect to P, we find that

$$f'(P) = \frac{U_1D_c'}{U_2} = PD_c' \tag{11}$$

(The last equality results from the fact that the consumer still maximizes by setting $U_1 = PU_2$.)

From the fact that the consumer is maximizing subject to the price P, we have

$$U_1(D_c(P), f(P)) = PU_2(D_c(P), f(P)) \tag{12}$$

The function D_c is defined implicitly by this together with equation (10). Differentiating equation (12) with respect to P and substituting for $f'(P)$ as per equation (11), we get

$$D_c' = \frac{U_2}{U_{11} - 2PU_{12} + P^2U_{22}} \quad \textbf{(13)}$$

We have noted earlier that the denominator in this expression must be negative in consequence of equations (3) and (5), and the numerator is positive by equation (2). It follows that $D_c'(P)$ is unambiguously negative; the compensated demand curve must be downward-sloping.

4. Substitution and income effects. There is an interesting consequence of equations (7), (9) and (13). Combining them, we find that for any given P and I, we have

$$D'(P) = D_c'(P) - D(P)E'(I) \quad \textbf{(14)}$$

(In interpreting this equation, keep in mind that the functions D and D_c depend on I and that the function E depends on P.) This says that when P changes, the corresponding change in quantity demanded can be decomposed into two parts: first a movement along the compensated demand curve (the substitution effect) and then an additional movement whose size depends on the slope of the Engel curve (the income effect). If the Engel curve is upward sloping (that is, if X is a normal good), then equation (14) shows that both components are negative—the income effect reinforces the substitution effect, so the demand curve must slope downward. If the Engel curve is downward sloping, then $D'(P)$ has one negative component and one positive component—the income effect works counter to the substitution effect. In this case, it is at least theoretically possible for the demand curve to slope upward—the case of a Giffen good.

5. Elasticities. The income elasticity of demand for a commodity is

$$\frac{I}{Q} \cdot \frac{dQ}{dI}$$

where dQ/dI is the derivative of the Engel curve, calculated in expression (7). An equivalent expression is

$$\frac{d(\log Q)}{d(\log I)}$$

Likewise we define the price elasticity of demand to be

$$\frac{P}{Q} \cdot \frac{dQ}{dP}$$

where dQ/dP is the derivative of the demand function calculated in expression (9). An equivalent expression is

$$\frac{d(\log Q)}{d(\log P)}$$

The compensated price elasticity of demand is

$$\frac{P}{Q_c} \cdot \frac{dQ_c}{dP}$$

where dQ_c/dP is the derivative of the compensated demand function calculated in expression (13). An equivalent expression is

$$\frac{d(\log Q_c)}{d(\log P)}$$

6. The Slutsky Equation.* If we multiply equation (14) through by $P/D(P) = P/E(I)$; we get

$$\begin{pmatrix}\text{Elasticity of the} \\ \text{ordinary demand curve}\end{pmatrix} = \begin{pmatrix}\text{Elasticity of the} \\ \text{compensated demand curve}\end{pmatrix} + P \cdot E'(I)$$

The last term on the right can be rewritten as

$$\frac{P \cdot E}{I} \cdot \begin{pmatrix}\text{Elasticity of the} \\ \text{Engel curve}\end{pmatrix}$$

and $\frac{P \cdot E}{I}$ can be interpreted as the fraction of his income that the consumer spends on X. Thus, we have

$$\begin{pmatrix}\text{Elasticity of the} \\ \text{ordinary demand curve}\end{pmatrix} = \begin{pmatrix}\text{Elasticity of the} \\ \text{compensated demand curve}\end{pmatrix} - \begin{pmatrix}\text{Fraction of income} \\ \text{spent on } X\end{pmatrix} \cdot \begin{pmatrix}\text{Elasticity of the} \\ \text{Engel curve}\end{pmatrix}$$

The preceding equation is called the *Slutsky equation*. It shows, for example, that if the fraction of his income that the consumer spends on X is small, then the elasticities of the ordinary and compensated demand curves are approximately equal.

Exercises

1. Suppose that indifference curves are given by the family of equations $U(X, Y) = X^{1/2} \cdot Y^{1/2} = C$, the price of X is \$1, the price of Y is \$2, and income is \$10. One day the price of X goes up to \$2. What happens to consumption of X? How much of this change is due to the substitution effect and how much is due to the income effect?
   Answer: Consumption falls from 5 to 2½. The fall from 5 to $\sqrt{7.5} \approx$ 2.¯4 is the substitution effect and the remainder is the income effect.
2. Repeat problem 1 with the function U replaced by

$$V'(x) - C'(x) = C$$

*This is a topic not covered in the body of the textbook.

Chapter 5

1. A farmer's problem. Consider a farmer who must decide how many acres of land to spray for insects. If he sprays x acres, the value of the crops saved is given by the function $V(x)$. The rate at which V grows as additional acres are sprayed is given by the derivative $V'(x)$, which we call the *marginal value* of the crops saved, or the *marginal benefit* from spraying. In general, the word *marginal* in economics means refers to a first derivative.

When one acre is a small part of the total area under consideration. $V'(x)$ can be well approximated by the quantity $V(x) - V(x - 1)$. The latter expression is used as the definition of marginal value in the textbook, but the more precise definition is $V'(x)$.

Suppose that the cost of spraying x acres is given by the function $C(x)$. The farmer's goal is to maximize the quantity $V(x) - C(x)$, which he accomplishes by setting

$$V'(x) - C'(x) = 0$$

In other words, he sets

$$V'(x) = C'(x)$$

or, in still other words, he chooses that quantity at which marginal benefit is equal to marginal cost.

If a constant is added to the function C, then that same constant is subtracted from the function $V - C$. The addition or subtraction of a constant cannot change the location of the maximum, and therefore the number of acres sprayed will not change. Put another way, the addition of the constant does not change the derivative C' and hence the quantity at which $V' = C'$ does not change.

Of course, the function C can change in many ways other than by the addition of a constant, and in general other such changes in C will affect the farmer's actions.

2. Firms and profit maximization. A firm seeks to maximize its profits, which are defined as revenues minus costs. The firm must select a quantity of output to produce. Let us denote the total revenue derived from producing and selling Q units of output by $TR(Q)$, and the total cost of producing and selling Q units of output by $TC(Q)$. Let $D(P)$ be the demand curve for the firm's product. Then since $D^{-}1(Q)$ is the maximum price at which the firm can sell Q units of output, it follows that

$$TR(Q) = Q \cdot D^{-1}(Q)$$

The firm seeks to maximize

$$TR(Q) - TC(Q)$$

which it accomplishes by selecting the quantity Q, at which

$$TR'(Q) - TC'(Q) = 0$$

or

$$TR'(Q) = TC'(Q)$$

If the TC function changes by the addition of a constant, then the derivative TC' is unchanged and consequently so is the profit-maximizing quantity. Put another way, the addition of a constant to TC simply subtracts a constant from the profit function $TR - TC$, and the subtraction of a constant cannot change the location of the maximum.

Other sorts of changes in TC can change the optimal output level, as can changes in TR. Since we have already seen that $TR(Q) = Q \cdot D^{-}1(Q)$, it follows that any change in TR must arise from a change in the demand function D.

Exercises

1. A firm faces the demand function $D(P) = 100 - 2P$ and the total cost function $TC(Q) = Q^2$. How much does it produce and at what price?
   Answer: $Q = 16\frac{2}{3}$, $P = 41\frac{2}{3}$.
2. A firm faces the demand function $D(P) = P^{-1/2}$ and the total cost function $TC(Q) = Q^2$. How much does it produce and at what price?

Chapter 6

1. Short-run costs. In the short run, we take the firm's capital usage to be fixed at some quantity, so that total product TP is a function only of labor L. The marginal product of labor is $MP(L) = TP'(L)$.

To find the short run total cost of producing Q units of output, note that it is necessary to employ $TP^{-1}(Q)$ units of labor so that the total cost of production is

$$P_K \cdot K_0 + P_L \cdot TP^{-1}(Q)$$

where P_K and P_L are the hire prices of capital and labor. Differentiating this total cost function, we find that the firm's short run marginal cost curve is given by

$$MC(Q) = \frac{1}{MP_L(L)}$$

where L is the quantity of labor used in the production of Q units of output. We define the firm's *variable cost* (VC) to be $P_L \cdot L$, its *average cost* (AC') to be TC/Q and its *average variable cost* (AVC) to be VC/Q. To find the relations among these cost curves, note for example that

$$\begin{aligned}\frac{dAC}{dQ} &= \frac{d(TC/Q)}{dQ} \\ &= \frac{Q\dfrac{dTC}{dQ} - TC}{Q^2} \\ &= \frac{MC}{Q} - \frac{AC}{Q}\end{aligned}$$

From this we conclude that when AC is minimized (so that dAC/dQ is zero), we must have $MC/Q = AC/Q$, or equivalently, $MC = AC$. In other words, the bottom of the U-shaped average cost curve occurs where MC crosses AC. A similar calculation holds with AC replaced by AVC.

The same equation shows that when MC is below AC, dAC/dQ is negative so that AC is downward sloping, and when MC is above AC, dAC/dQ is positive, so that AC is upward sloping.

2. Isoquants and the production function. The technology available to a firm is specified by its *production function* $f(L, K)$, which tells how much output the firm can produce using L units of labor and K units of capital. We assume that the production function satisfies the analogues of properties (1) through (5) which were assumed for the utility function. The isoquants are then the graphs of the various curves $f(L, K) = C$ where C is any constant.

Along the isoquant $f(L, K) = C$, K is implicitly defined as a function $g(L)$. Using the chain rule to differentiate both sides of the formula

$$f(L, g(L)) = C$$

we find that the slope of the isoquant is

$$g'(L) = \frac{\partial f/\partial L}{\partial f \partial K} \tag{15}$$

As we will see in the next paragraph, $\partial f/\partial L$ and $\partial f/\partial K$ can be interpreted as the marginal products of labor and of capital.

3. Long-run costs. In the long run, both capital and labor can be varied. The firm seeks to maximize the output that it can produce at any given cost. For a given expenditure E, the firm can hire any basket of inputs (L, K) such that

$$P_L \cdot L + P_K \cdot K = E$$

Let us rewrite this as

$$K = \frac{E}{P_K} - \frac{P_L \cdot L}{P_K}$$

Then the firm's problem is to maximize

$$f\left(L, \frac{E}{P_K} - \frac{P_L \cdot L}{P_K}\right)$$

Differentiating with respect to L, we find that the firm chooses those quantities L of labor and $K = (E - P_L \cdot L)/ P_K$ of capital at which

$$f_1(L, K) - \frac{P_L}{P_K} \cdot f_2(L, K) = 0$$

or equivalently

$$\frac{f_1(L, K)}{f_2(L, K)} = \frac{P_L}{P_K} \quad \textbf{(16)}$$

That is, the firm chooses an input mix at which the ratio of the marginal products is equal to the ratio of the input prices. Since the ratio of the marginal products is the absolute slope of the isoquant (that is, it is the marginal rate of technical substitution), and since the input price ratio is the absolute slope of the isocosts, it follows that the firm operates at a tangency between an isoquant and an isocost. There are many such tangencies, one for each level of expenditure. The curve formed by these tangencies is the *expansion path*. The expansion path is the graph of equation (16).

For an alternative viewpoint, we can envision the firm minimizing cost for any given level of output. Thus, if $K = g(L)$ is the equation of the isoquant corresponding to the given output, the firm's problem is to minimize

$$P_L \cdot L + P_K \cdot g(L)$$

Differentiating, we find that the firm operates where $g'(L) = -P_L/P_K$; in view of equation (15) this is the same condition as described by equation (16).

For a given quantity of output Q, let $L_0(Q)$ and $K_0(Q)$ be the quantities of inputs that the firm employs in order to produce Q units at the lowest possible cost. Then the functions L_0 and K_0 are determined implicitly by the equations

$$\frac{f_1(L_0(Q), K_0(Q))}{f_2(L_0(Q), K_0(Q))} = \frac{P_L}{P_K}$$

$$f(L_0(Q), K_0(Q)) = Q$$

The first of these equations says that the firm is on its expansion path and the second says that it produces quantity Q. Differentiating the second equation yields

$$f_1(L_0(Q), K_0(Q)) \cdot L_0'(Q) + f_2(L_0(Q), K_0(Q)) \cdot K_0'(Q) = 1$$

Combining this with first equation gives

$$f_1(L_0(Q), K_0(Q)) \cdot \left(L_0'(Q) + \frac{P_K}{P_L} \cdot K_0'(Q) \right) = 1 \tag{17}$$

The long-run total cost of producing Q units of output is

$$LRTC(Q) = P_L \cdot L_0(Q) + P_K \cdot K_0(Q)$$

Thus, the long-run marginal cost is given by

$$\begin{aligned} LRMC(Q) &= P_L \cdot L_0'(Q) + P_K \cdot K_0'(Q) \\ &= P_L \cdot \left(L_0'(Q) + \frac{P_K}{P_L} \cdot K_0'(Q) \right) \\ &= \frac{P_L}{f_1(L_0(Q), K_0(Q))} \end{aligned} \tag{18}$$

(The last equality follows from equation (17).)

A similar calculation shows that we also have

$$LRMC(Q) = \frac{P_K}{f_2(L_0(Q), K_0(Q))}$$

Here is a slightly different way to view the long-run total cost curve: For each quantity of capital K, let $SRTC_K(Q)$ be the short-run total cost curve that results when the firm uses K units of capital. In the long run, the firm chooses K to minimize its costs, so

$$LRTC(Q) = \min_K SRTC_K(Q)$$

Thus, the long-run total cost curve lies below all of the short-run total cost curves.

4. Returns to scale. For any given L and K, define

$$\Gamma = \frac{L \cdot f_1(L,K) + K \cdot f_2(L,K)}{f(L,K)}$$

Then we say that the production function f exhibits constant, decreasing or increasing *returns to scale* at (L,K) according to whether Γ is equal to, less than, or greater than 1.

Suppose that both inputs are increased by the same proportion h, so that the new quantities of labor and capital are $(1 + h)L$ and $(1 + h)K$. Then for h small we have

$$\begin{aligned} f((1+h)L, (1+h)K) &= f(L + hL, K + hK) \\ &\approx f(L, K) + hLf_1(L, K) + hKf_2(L, K) \\ &= (1 + \Gamma \cdot h) \cdot f(L, K) \end{aligned}$$

In other words, the proportional change in output is equal to, less than, or greater than the proportional change in the inputs depending on whether f exhibits constant, decreasing or increasing returns to scale. This is the definition given in the textbook.

A case of particular interest is that of a *homogeneous* production function. A homogeneous production function is defined to be one for which Γ is a constant independent of K and L. In this case we say that Γ is the *degree of homogeneity* of the function f, or that f is *homogeneous of degree* Γ. As an immediate consequence of the definition in the textbook, a homogeneous function of degree 1 exhibits constant returns to scale, and a homogeneous function of degree less than (greater than) 1 exhibits decreasing (increasing) returns to scale.

5. Returns to scale and the long-run average cost curve. We can relate the returns to scale to the slope of the long-run average cost curve. The slope of the long-run average cost curve is

$$\frac{dLRAC}{dQ} = \frac{d(LRTC/Q)}{dQ} = \frac{(dLRTC/dQ)\cdot Q - LRTC}{Q^2} = \frac{(LRMC - LRAC)}{Q}$$

Thus long run average cost is flat, increasing, or decreasing depending on whether *LRAC* is equal to, less than, or greater than *LRMC*. To investigate this we consider the ratio *LRAC/LRMC*. We have

$$\begin{aligned} \frac{LRAC(Q)}{LRMC(Q)} &= \frac{(P_L \cdot L_0(Q) + P_K \cdot K_0(Q))}{f(L_0(Q), K_0(Q))} \bigg/ \frac{P_L}{f_1(L_0(Q), K_0(Q))} \text{ (by (18))} \\ &= \frac{L \cdot f_1(L_0(Q), K_0(Q)) + f_2(L_0(Q), K_0(Q))}{f(L_0(Q), K_0(Q))} \text{ (by (16))} \end{aligned}$$

Since the final term in the right-hand series of equations is none other than Γ, we see that

$$\text{When } \Gamma \text{ is } \left\{\begin{matrix}\text{equal to}\\ \text{less than}\\ \text{greater than}\end{matrix}\right\} 1,\ LRAC \text{ is } \left\{\begin{matrix}\text{equal to}\\ \text{less than}\\ \text{greater than}\end{matrix}\right\} LRMC \text{ and therefore } \left\{\begin{matrix}\text{flat}\\ \text{increasing}\\ \text{decreasing}\end{matrix}\right\}$$

In other words, constant returns to scale imply a flat *LRAC,* decreasing returns to scale imply an increasing *LRAC,* and increasing returns to scale imply a decreasing *LRAC.*

6. Relations between the short run and the long run. Given the long-run production function $f(L, K)$, and given a fixed quantity of capital K_0, we derive the short-run production function

$$TP(L) = f(L, K_0)$$

Thus, the marginal product of labor is given by

$$MP(L) = TP'(L) = \frac{\partial f}{\partial L}(L, K_0)$$

Let $C(Q, K)$ be the cost of producing Q units of output using K units of capital (together with however much labor is necessary). Thus, for fixed K, $SKTC(Q) = C(Q, K)$ is the short-run total cost curve, and short-run marginal cost is given by

$$SRMC(Q) = \frac{\partial C}{\partial Q}(Q, K)$$

Now for any given Q let $K_0(Q)$ be the quantity of capital that allows Q units of output to be produced at the lowest cost. Then $LRTC(Q) = C(Q, K_0(Q))$ is the long-run total cost curve, and long-run marginal cost is given by

$$LRMC(Q) = \frac{\partial C}{\partial Q}(Q, K_0(Q)) + \frac{\partial C}{\partial K}(Q, K_0(Q)) \cdot K_0'(Q)$$

Since $K_0(Q)$ is determined by the first-order condition

$$\frac{\partial C}{\partial K}(Q, K_0(Q)) = 0$$

it follows that in long-run equilibrium (where $K = K_0(Q)$), we have

$$SRMC(Q) = LRMC(Q)$$

Interpreting marginal cost as the slope of total cost, this tells us that the short-run and long-run total cost curves are tangent where they touch. A similar argument applies to the short-run and long-run average cost curves.

Exercises

1. Suppose that a firm's production function is given by $f(L, K) = L^{\alpha}K^{\beta}$, where α and β are positive constants and both α and β are less than 1. When $K = 1$, write down the firm's (short-run) total product and marginal product of labor functions, and its short-run marginal cost function, assuming that the wage rate of labor is 1. Repeat with $K = 2$. Does the firm experience diminishing marginal returns to labor?

Answer: With $K = 1$, $TP_L = L^\alpha$, $MP_L = \alpha L^{\alpha-1}$, and $MC = \frac{1}{\alpha L^{\alpha-1}}$.

2. In problem 1, write down the equations for the 1-unit and 2-unit isoquant.
Answer: The 1-unit isoquant is $L^\alpha K^\beta = 1$.
3. When the price of labor is W and the price of capital is R, what combination of inputs does the firm in problem 1 use to produce 1 unit of output? 2 units of output? Q units of output?
Answer: For 1 unit of output,

$$L = \left(\frac{\alpha R}{\beta W}\right)^{\beta/\beta+\alpha} \text{ and } K = \left(\frac{\beta W}{\alpha R}\right)^{\alpha/\beta+\alpha}$$

4. In problem 1, write down the equations for the firm's long-run total cost and marginal cost curves.

$$\textit{Answer: } LRTC(Q) = (CR^\beta W^\alpha Q)^{1/\alpha+\beta} \text{ where } C = \left[\left(\frac{\alpha}{\beta}\right)^\beta + \left(\frac{\beta}{\alpha}\right)^\alpha\right]$$

5. In problem 1, suppose that $\alpha + \beta < 1$. Does the production function exhibit decreasing, constant, or increasing returns to scale? Repeat under the assumption that $\alpha + \beta = 1$, and then under the assumption that $\alpha + \beta > 1$.
6. Repeat problems 1 through 5 with the production function replaced by

$$f(L, K) = (L^\alpha + K^\alpha)^{\beta/\alpha}$$

Chapter 7

1. The competitive firm. A competitive firm is one that takes prices as given; that is, its own actions do not affect the market price of its product. For a competitive firm, total revenue is given by the simple formula $TR(Q) = P \cdot Q$, so that marginal revenue is the constant function $MR(Q) = P$.

For a competitive firm, the profit maximizing rule $MC = MR$ simplifies to $MC = P$. That is, the firm produces that quantity Q for which $MC(Q) = P$. The exception is that there are some circumstances in which the firm might choose to shut down. It is shown in the text that the firm shuts down precisely if $P < AVC$. Thus, the competitive firm's supply curve is completely specified by the equation

$$S(P) = \begin{cases} MC^{-1}(P) \text{ if } P \geq \min(AVC) \\ 0 \text{ if } P < \min(AVC) \end{cases}$$

This can be interpreted as a description of either the firm's short-run or long-run supply curve. To get the short-run cost curve, use the short-run marginal and average variable cost curves. To get the long-run cost curve, use the long-run marginal and average variable cost curves, keeping in mind that in the long run average variable cost is just the same as average cost.*

2. The competitive industry in the short run. In the short run, we take the number of firms in the industry as given. To a first approximation, the industry supply curve is the sum of the individual firms' supply curves. To derive the industry supply curve precisely, it is necessary to take account of the factor-price effect, as discussed in the textbook.

Suppose that there are N firms in the industry, and that the ith firm has the total cost function TC_i. Let Q be the total output of the entire industry. For each of the firms 2, . . ., n, let Q_i be the output of firm i, so that firm 1 produces the quantity

$$Q_1 = Q - \sum_{i=2}^{n} Q_i$$

Then a planner who wanted to minimize the sum of all firms' costs in producing Q units of output would choose the Q_i to minimize the expression

$$TC_1\left(Q - \sum_{i=2}^{n} Q_i\right) + \sum_{i=2}^{n} TC_i(Q_i)$$

Differentiating with respect to Q_i, we see that this requires setting $MC_1(Q_1) = MC_1(Q_1)$ for each i; that is, $MC_1(Q_i)$ must be independent of i. This condition is satisfied automatically in competitive equilibrium, since the ith firm sets $MC_i(Q_i) = P$, and P is independent of i. A competitive industry minimizes the total cost of producing a given quantity.

3. The competitive industry in the long run. In the long run, we assume that there is free entry to the industry. The industry's long-run supply curve reflects this free entry. At any given price, we assume that sufficiently many firms enter to drive profits to zero, and the long-run supply curve shows the quantity that will be produced by that number of firms at the given price. The textbook discusses the various situations in which this could lead to a flat, increasing, or decreasing industry supply curve.

Exercise

1. Work the Numerical Exercises at the end of Chapter 7 in the body of the textbook.

*It is standard to assume that there are no fixed costs in the long run, since in the long run all factors of production are variable. Thus, there are no fixed costs as long as the firm's only costs are factor payments. It is possible to imagine some costs—such as annual license fees—that are fixed even in the long run. In this case, the average variable cost curve differs from the average cost curve, and it is *average* cost, not average variable cost, that determines whether the firm will remain in the industry.

Chapter 8

1. The consumer's surplus. Consider a consumer who has an income of \$$E$ and can purchase good X in the marketplace at a going price of \$$P$ per unit. He will choose to purchase the quantity x_0 depicted in the diagram:

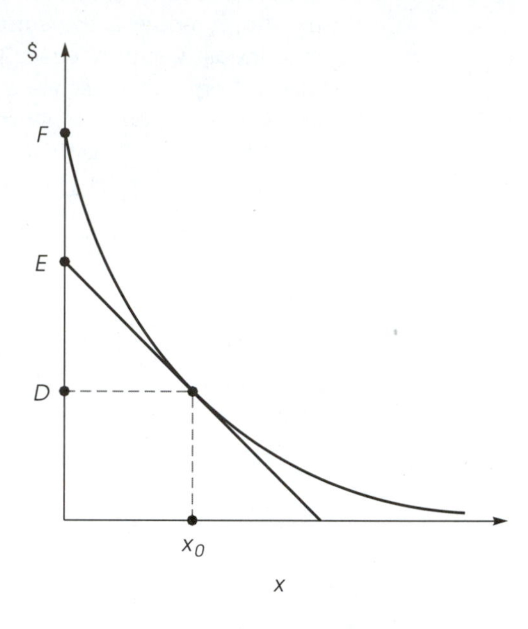

By enabling him to reach the illustrated indifference curve, the existence of the market has made the consumer as well off as if his income had increased to \$$F$. We say that he has earned a *consumer's surplus* of \$(F—E). The equation of the indifference curve can be put in the form $Y = f(X)$. Then the consumer's compensated demand curve is given by the function

$$D_c(P) = (f')^{-1}(-P)$$

The inverse function is

$$D_c^{-1}(X) = -f'(X)$$

The area under the demand curve is the integral of the *inverse* function, since X is the variable on the horizontal axis. Therefore, the area under the compensated demand curve out to the quantity x_0 is given by

$$\int_0^{x_0} f'(X)dX = f(0) - f(x_0) = \$(F - D)$$

This is the total value to the consumer of x_0 units of X, in the sense that if all x_0 units were taken from the consumer and replaced by \$(F—D), the consumer would remain on the same indifference curve.

When the consumer starts with \$$E$ and then trades for the optimal basket O, his total expenditure on good X is \$(E—D). When this is subtracted from the area under the demand curve, we find that the remaining area (that is, the area under the demand curve and out to the quantity x_0, down to the price P) is

$$\$(F - D) - \$(E - D) = \$(F - E)$$

which is precisely the consumer's surplus.*

2. The producer's surplus. The producer's surplus is the excess of his revenue over his variable costs. Since

$$VC(Q) = \int_0^Q MC(x)\,dx$$

it follows that the producer's surplus is the area above the marginal cost curve, out to the quantity supplied and up to the market price, as discussed in the textbook.

3. The invisible hand. Imagine a benevolent planner interested in the welfare of both consumers and producers. Suppose that the planner's goal is to maximize the total welfare gains earned in the market for X. That is, the planner wishes to maximize

$$TV(X) - TC(X)$$

where TV represents total value to consumers and TC represents total cost to producers. We have seen that when consumers purchase x_0 units of X, the total value of their purchases is

$$\int_0^{x_0} D_c(X)\,dX$$

Thus, the planner seeks to maximize

$$\int_0^{x_0} D_c(X)\,dX - TC(x_0)$$

Differentiating, we find that the optimum occurs where

$$D_c(x_0) = MC(x_0)$$

or in other words at the point where the demand and supply curves cross. This, of course, is none other than the point of equilibrium. The competitive equilibrium outcome is precisely the outcome sought by the planner.

*When we computed the total value to the consumer of being able to purchase good X, we assumed that the consumer is on the illustrated indifference curve, which is to say that we assumed that the market for good X actually does exist. Our measure of total value is the amount that the consumer would be willing to pay in order to prevent the market from disappearing. The resulting measure of consumer's surplus is called the *equivalent variation*. An alternative approach is to assume that the market for good X does not exist, and to ask how much the consumer would be willing to pay to have the market come into existence. In this case, we would assume that the consumer is on the indifference curve through point E and integrate the corresponding compensated demand curve. The measure of consumer's surplus that arises in this way is called the *compensating variation*.

4. General equilibrium. Consider the Edgeworth Box economy described in the text. There are two individuals (Aline and Bob) and two goods (Food and Clothing). Suppose that Aline's indifference curves are given by the family of equations $U(X, Y) = C$ and that Bob's are given by the family of equations $V(X, Y) = C$, where X is the quantity of food, Y is the quantity of clothing, and C varies over all possible constants.

We assume that the quantities of food and clothing are permanently fixed at X_0 and Y_0.

We will write X and Y for the quantities of food and clothing owned by Aline, so that $X_0 - X$ and $Y_0 - Y$ are the quantities owned by Bob. An *allocation* is a specification of Aline's basket (X, Y) (which then determines Bob's basket as well). An allocation (X, Y) is *Pareto optimal* if no other allocation could make both Aline and Bob better off; that is, (X, Y) is Pareto optimal if there does not exist any allocation (X', Y') such that $U(X', Y') > U(X, Y)$ and $V(X_0 - X', Y_0 - Y') > V(X_0 - X, Y_0 - Y)$.*

We can show that the allocation (X, Y) is Pareto optimal if and only if

$$\frac{\partial U/\partial X}{\partial U/\partial Y}(X, Y) = \frac{\partial V/\partial X}{\partial V/\partial Y}(X_0 - X, Y_0 - Y) \qquad \textbf{(19)}$$

Suppose first that equation (19) fails to hold; we will conclude that (X, Y) cannot be Pareto optimal. We can assume that

$$\frac{\partial U/\partial X}{\partial U/\partial Y}(X, Y) > \frac{\partial V/\partial X}{\partial V/\partial Y}(X_0 - X, Y_0 - Y)$$

Let h and j be small positive numbers such that

$$\frac{\partial U/\partial X}{\partial U/\partial Y}(X, Y) > \frac{j}{h} > \frac{\partial V/\partial X}{\partial V/\partial Y}(X_0 - X, Y_0 - Y)$$

and consider the allocation $(X + h, Y - j)$. We have

$$U(X + h, Y - j) \approx U(X, Y) + h \cdot \frac{\partial U}{\partial X} - j \cdot \frac{\partial U}{\partial Y} > U(X, Y)$$

$$V(X_0 - X - h, Y_0 - Y + j) \approx V(X_0 - X, Y_0 - Y) - h \cdot \frac{\partial V}{\partial X} + j \cdot \frac{\partial V}{\partial Y} > V(X_0 - X, Y_0 - Y)$$

contradicting Pareto optimality.

On the other hand, if equation (19) *does* hold, then it is possible to show that (X, Y) must in fact be Pareto optimal. Indeed, running the above argument backwards shows that no allocation of the form $(X + h, Y - j)$ can be Pareto preferred to (X, Y) when h and j are small. To show the same thing when h and j are arbitrary requires a little work using the convexity of indifference curves. If you are ambitious, you might try to complete the proof.

*Other references use slightly different formulations involving ≥ signs as well as > signs, but if U and V are continuous, the formulations are equivalent.

In competitive equilibrium, both Aline and Bob choose baskets where their marginal rates of substitution between X and Y are equal to the relative price of X in terms of Y. Since they both face the same relative price, it follows that their marginal rates of substitution are equal. But this is precisely the condition of equation (19). We conclude that a competitive equilibrium is Pareto optimal. This is the theorem of the Invisible Hand.

Exercise

1. Aline's indifference curves are given by the family of equations $X^{1/2} \cdot Y^{1/2} = C$ and Bob's by the family of equations $X^{1/4} \cdot Y^{3/4} = C$. Aline owns 2 X's and 5 Y's, while Bob owns 8 X's and 5 Ys. Characterize the Pareto-optimal outcomes (i.e., give the equation of the contract curve) and compute the competitive equilibrium.
Answer: The equation of the contract curve is $3Y(10 - X) = X(10 - Y)$. In competitive equilibrium, Aline has $^{17}\!/_{3}$ X's and $^{85}\!/_{28}$ Y's.

Chapter 10

1. Monopoly pricing. The monopolist, like any producer, has a total revenue function $TR(Q) = Q \cdot P(Q)$ where $P(Q)$ is the maximum price at which demanders will purchase Q items. That is, $P = D^{-1}$, where D is the demand curve for the product. Differentiating, we find that the marginal revenue function is

$$MR(Q) = P(Q) + Q \cdot P'(Q)$$

Since $P'(Q)$ is negative, we conclude that for a monopolist, marginal revenue is always less than the price at which he sells his goods.

Note that $Q \cdot P'(Q) = P \cdot (1/|\eta|)$, where η is the elasticity of the demand curve. Thus, we can write

$$MR = P \cdot \left(1 - \frac{1}{|\eta|}\right) \qquad \textbf{(21)}$$

To maximize profits, the monopolist (like any producer) chooses the quantity at which $MC = MR$. Since $MR < P$, it follows that for a profit-maximizing monopolist, $MC < P$.

2. Price discrimination. Consider a monopolist who sells in two markets. In market A, the inverse to the demand function is $P_A(Q)$ and in market B, the inverse to the demand function is $P_B(Q)$. By selling Q_A items in market A and Q_B items in market B, the monopolist earns a total profit of

$$Q_A \cdot P_A(Q_A) + Q_B \cdot P_B(Q_B) - TC(Q_A + Q_B)$$

By differentiating separately with respect to Q_A and Q_B, we find that the conditions for profit maximization are

$$MR_A(Q_A) = MC(Q_A + Q_B) = MR_B(Q_B)$$

where MR_A and MR_B are the marginal revenue functions in the two market: Combining this observation with equation 20, we discover that

$$\frac{P_A}{P_B} = \frac{\left(1 - \frac{1}{|\eta_A|}\right)}{\left(1 - \frac{1}{|\eta_B|}\right)}$$

where η_A and η_B are the elasticities of demand in the two markets.

Chapter 11

1. Collusion. Suppose that there are N firms in an industry, and that the ith firm has marginal cost curve MC_i. The inverse demand curve for the industry's product is given by the function $P(Q)$. Under competition, firms take the market price as given, so they produce quantities Q_i such that

$$MC_i(Q_i) = P\left(\sum_{i=1}^{N} Q_i\right)$$

This system of N equations in N unknowns determines the quantities Q_t.

Suppose alternatively that the firms collude in order to maximize industry profits. That is, the cartel seeks to maximize

$$\left(\sum_{j=1}^{N} Q_j\right) \cdot P\left(\sum_{j=1}^{N} Q_j\right) - \sum_{j=1}^{N} TC_i(Q_j)$$

The condition for this is that for each i.

$$MC_i(Q_i) = P\left(\sum_{j=1}^{N} Q_j\right) + \left(\sum_{j=1}^{N} Q_j\right) \cdot P'\left(\sum_{j=1}^{N} Q_j\right)$$

Note that the expression on the right is the industry's marginal revenue curve.

2. Cournot oligopoly. Suppose that the N firms in an industry are not able to collude. Then each maximizes its profits subject to the constraints placed upon it by the behavior of other firms. However, this formulation is imprecise and ambiguous. Exactly what aspects of other firms' behavior shall we assume that each firm takes as given? In the *Cournot model* of oligopoly, the assumption is that each firm takes its rivals' *quantities* as given.

Thus, the tth firm attempts to maximize

$$Q_i \cdot P\left(Q_i + \sum_{j\,i} Q_j\right) - TC_i(Q_i)$$

treating each $Q_j (j \neq i)$ as a constant. This leads the firm to set

$$MC_i(Q_i) = P\left(Q_i + \sum_{ij} Q_j\right) + Q_i P'\left(Q_i + \sum_{ij} Q_j\right)$$

These N equations in N unknowns determine the quantities Q_i.

Chapter 15

1. The derived demand for factors of production. In the short run, the firm's demand curve for a factor is the inverse function to that factor's marginal revenue product, as discussed in the text. To derive the demand for labor in the long run, we assume that the firm has the production function $f(L, K)$, and we take as given the price of capital P_K and the price of output P.

At any given wage rate P_L, the firm chooses quantities L of labor and K of capital to maximize its profit

$$P \cdot f(L,K) - P_L \cdot L - P_K \cdot K$$

The first order conditions for a maximum are

$$P \cdot \frac{\partial f}{\partial L}(L,K) = P_L$$

$$P \cdot \frac{\partial f}{\partial K}(L,K) = P_K$$

These two equations in the two unknowns L and K determine the firm's employment of labor and of capital. If (L, K) is a solution to the system, then the quantity L corresponds to the price P_L on the firm's long-run demand curve for labor.

Continuing to hold P_K and P fixed, let $L_0(P_L)$ and $K_0(P_L)$ be the profit-maximizing quantities of labor and capital when the wage rate of labor is P_L. Thus, the functions L_0 and K_0 are implicitly defined by the system

$$P \cdot \frac{\partial f}{\partial L}(L_0(P_L), K_0(P_L)) = P_L$$

$$P \cdot \frac{\partial f}{\partial K}(L_0(P_L), K_0(P_L)) = P_K$$

Differentiating with respect to the variable P_L, we get

$$P \cdot \frac{\partial^2 f}{\partial L^2}(L_0(P_L), K_0(P_L)) \cdot \frac{dL_0}{dP_L}(P_L) + \frac{\partial^2 f}{\partial L \partial K}(L_0(P_L), K_0(P_L)) \frac{dK_0}{dP_L}(P_L) = 1$$

$$P \cdot \frac{\partial^2 f}{\partial L \partial K}(L_0(P_L), K_0(P_L)) \cdot \frac{dL_0}{dP_L}(P_L) + \frac{\partial^2 f}{\partial K^2}(L_0(P_L), K_0(P_L)) \cdot \frac{dK_0}{dP_L}(P_L) = 0$$

Solving this system, we find that

$$\frac{dL_0}{dP_L}(P_L) = \frac{\partial^2 f/\partial K^2}{P \cdot \delta} \tag{21}$$

$$\frac{dK_0}{dP_L}(P_L) = \frac{-\partial^2 f/\partial L \partial K}{P \cdot \delta} \tag{22}$$

where

$$\delta = \left(\frac{\partial^2 f}{\partial K^2} \cdot \frac{\partial^2 f}{\partial L^2} - \left(\frac{\partial^2 f}{\partial L \partial K}\right)^2\right)(L_0(P_L), K_0(P_L))$$

Because we assume that f satisfies the analogues of equations (1) through (5), we know that $\partial^2 f/\partial K^2 < 0$ and that $\delta > 0$. It follows from this and equation (21) that dL_0/dP_L is everywhere negative. That is, the firm's demand curve for a factor of production must be everywhere downward sloping. This is in contrast to the consumer's demand curve for a consumption good, where the Giffen phenomenon is at least a theoretical possibility.

2. Changes in the price of another factor. In the preceding section we held the price of capital fixed and determined how the firm's employment of labor and of capital varied in response to a change in the wage rate of labor. In particular, we derived the equation for the firm's labor demand curve and showed that this curve must slope downward.

Equation (22) shows how the firm's employment of capital changes in response to a change in the wage rate of labor. Since δ is known to be positive, the sign of dK_0/dP_L depends only on the sign of the cross partial derivative $\partial^2 f/\partial L \partial K$. When the cross partial is positive, we say that capital and labor are *complements in production* and when the cross partial is negative we say that capital and labor are *substitutes in production*.

When labor and capital are complements in production, equation (22) shows that an increase in the wage rate of labor leads to a fall in the demand for capital (and similarly, an increase in the rental rate for capital leads to a fall in the demand for labor). When labor and capital are substitutes in production, the reverse is true.

Economists believe that labor and capital are more often complements than substitutes in production. For example, if labor and capital are the only two inputs and if the production function exhibits constant returns to scale, then we can show that labor and capital must be complements in production. To see this, write

$$f = \frac{\partial f}{\partial L} \cdot L + \frac{\partial f}{\partial K} \cdot K$$

and differentiate with respect to L to get

$$\frac{\partial^2 f}{\partial L^2} \cdot L + \frac{\partial^2 f}{\partial K \partial L} \cdot K = 0$$

Since $\partial^2 f/\partial L^2$ is negative, the cross partial must be positive as needed.

3. Changes in the price of output. Holding P_L and P_K fixed, we let the price P of output vary and write $L_0(P)$ and $K_0(P)$ for the profit maximizing levels of labor and capital employment. Beginning with the system

$$P \cdot \frac{\partial f}{\partial L}(L_0(P), K_0(P)) = P_L$$

$$P \cdot \frac{\partial f}{\partial K}(L_0(P), K_0(P)) = P_K$$

we differentiate with respect to P and find

$$\frac{\partial^2 f}{\partial L^2} \cdot \frac{dL_0}{dP} + \frac{\partial^2 f}{\partial L \partial K} \cdot \frac{dK_0}{dP} = -\frac{\partial f}{\partial L}$$

$$\frac{\partial^2 f}{\partial L \partial K} \cdot \frac{dL_0}{dP} + \frac{\partial^2 f}{\partial K^2} \cdot \frac{dK_0}{dP} = -\frac{\partial f}{\partial K}$$

Solving for dL_0/dP and dK_0/dP, we find that

$$\frac{dL_0}{dP} = \frac{1}{\delta} \cdot \left(-\frac{\partial^2 f}{\partial L^2} \cdot \frac{\partial f}{\partial L} + \frac{\partial^2 f}{\partial L \partial K} \cdot \frac{\partial f}{\partial K} \right)$$

$$\frac{dK_0}{dP} = \frac{1}{\delta} \cdot \left(-\frac{\partial^2 f}{\partial K^2} \cdot \frac{\partial f}{\partial K} + \frac{\partial^2 f}{\partial L \partial K} \cdot \frac{\partial f}{\partial L} \right)$$

This shows that when labor and capital are complements in production, an increase in the price of output leads to an increase in the demand for both labor and capital.

4. The distribution of income. In equilibrium, the wage rate of labor is equal to its marginal revenue product $P \cdot \partial f / \partial L$ and the wage rate of capital is equal to its marginal revenue product $P \cdot \partial f / \partial K$. Thus, when labor and capital are the only inputs, the firm's total costs are

$$P \cdot \frac{\partial f}{\partial L}(L, K) \cdot L + P \cdot \frac{\partial f}{\partial K}(L, K) \cdot K$$

The total revenue of the firm is the price of output multiplied by the quantity of output, or

$$P \cdot f(L, K)$$

Finally, the profits of the firm are given by the difference between revenue and cost, or

$$P \cdot f(L, K) - P \cdot \frac{\partial f}{\partial L}(L, K) \cdot L + P \cdot \frac{\partial f}{\partial K}(L, K) \cdot K$$

From this expression we see immediately that a competitive firm earns zero profits if and only if it produces at a point where there are constant returns to scale. If returns to scale are decreasing, then the firm earns positive profits and if returns to scale are increasing, then the firm earns negative profits.

In the long run, one can argue that all firms experience constant returns to scale provided that the production function really includes every factor of production. This is because of the principle that "what a firm does once, it can do twice" discussed in Chapter 6 of the textbook. It follows that when all payments to all factors are considered, the competitive firm earns zero profits in the long run.

Exercise

1. A firm produces according to the production function $f(L,K) = L^{1/4} \cdot K^{1/4}$. Holding fixed the prices of output and of capital, derive the firm's short run and long run labor demand curves. How does the demand for labor vary with the price of capital? With the price of output?
Answer: Fixing the price of output at 1 and the price of capital at P_K, short-run labor demand is

$$\left[\frac{K}{256P_L^4}\right]^{1/3}$$

and long-run labor demand is

$$\frac{1}{16P_K^{1/2}P_L^{3/2}}$$

Chapter 16

1. The supply of labor. To model the supply of labor, we assume that the worker's indifference curves between consumption and labor are given by the family of equations

$$V(L, Y) = \text{constant}$$

where L is labor and Y is consumption. Given a wage rate P_L, the worker who works L hours earns $P_L \cdot L$ units of consumption; thus, he chooses L so as to maximize

$$V(L, C_0 + P_L \cdot L)$$

where C_0 is the worker's non-labor income.

The first order condition for a maximum is

$$\frac{-V_1(L, C_0 + P_L \cdot L)}{V_2(L, C_0 + P_L \cdot L)} = P_L$$

Thus, the labor supply function S is implicitly defined by the equation

$$\frac{-V_1(S(P_L), C_0 + P_L \cdot S(P_L))}{V_2(S(P_L), C_0 + P_L \cdot S(P_L))} = P_L \tag{23}$$

Let L_0 be the total time available to the worker. For example, if we are deriving the supply of labor per day, then $L_0 = 24$ hours. Set $U(X, Y) = V(L_0—L, Y)$ so that X can be thought of as leisure. We assume that U satisfies properties (1) through (5). This guarantees that the first order condition really is sufficient for the existence of a maximum.

The wage rate P_L can be viewed as the price of leisure, and the effect of a change in the wage rate can be decomposed into income and substitution effects, working with the function U just as in Chapter 4. Note that when leisure is a normal good, the income effect leads the worker to consume more leisure, which is the same thing as supplying *less* labor.

2. The representative agent. Suppose that there is a fixed amount of capital in society, and that labor L produces output Y according to the total product function

$$Y = TP(L)$$

In an economy consisting of a single individual, that individual would choose the quantity of his labor input by maximizing the function

$$V(L, TP(L))$$

The first order condition is

$$\frac{-V_1(L, TP(L))}{V_2(L, TP(L))} = TP'(L) \quad \textbf{(24)}$$

Given a wage P_I, each worker supplies a quantity of labor determined by equation (23). Each employer demands a quantity $D(P_1.)$ of labor determined by the condition

$$TP'(D(P_L)) = P_L$$

For the representative agent, the quantity of labor demanded must coincide with the quantity supplied. Call this common quantity L_0. Then the representative agent employs L_0 units of labor, produces $Y_0 = TP(L_0)$ units of output, pays a wage bill of $P_t \cdot L_0$, and earns a non-labor income C_0 equal to the difference between what he produces and his wage bill; that is

$$C_0 = TP(L_0) - P_L \cdot L_0 \quad \textbf{(25)}$$

In equilibrium, L_0 is also the quantity of labor supplied by the representative agent; that is, $S(P_L) = L_0$. Combining this with equation (23) and (25) and comparing with equation (24), we find that in a competitive economy, the representative agent supplies exactly the same amount of labor that he would choose to supply if he lived in isolation.

Chapter 17

1. A two-period model. The simplest way to model the allocation of goods over time is to imagine an individual who lives for two periods. We then treat consumption in period one and consumption in period two as different goods and apply all of the consumer theory that we have developed.

Let C_0 and C_1 denote "consumption today" and "consumption tomorrow." Then the consumer's indifference curves are given by the family of equations

$$U(C_0, C_1) = \text{constant}$$

for some function U satisfying properties (1) through (5). We often assume that U is of the special form

$$U(C_0, C_1) = V(C_0) + \beta \cdot V(C_1)$$

where β is a constant satisfying $0 < \beta < 1$ and V is a function of one variable satisfying

$$V'(C) > 0$$

$$V''(C) < 0$$

Suppose that the consumer is endowed with E_0 units of consumption today and E_1 units of consumption tomorrow. Then if the price of consumption today in terms of consumption tomorrow is $1/(1 + r)$, the present value of the consumer's wealth is

$$E = E_0 + \frac{1}{1 + r} \cdot E_1$$

and his goal is to maximize $V(C_0) + \beta \cdot V(C_1)$ subject to the constraint

$$C_0 + \frac{1}{1 + r} \cdot C_1 = E$$

The first order condition is

$$\frac{V'(C_0)}{V'(C_1)} = \beta \cdot (1 + r)$$

The representative agent must consume his endowment, so for him we have $C_0 = E_0$ and $C_1 = E_1$. If in addition $E_0 = E_1$, then it follows that in equilibrium we must have

$$\beta = \frac{1}{1 + r}$$

Answers to Exercises

Chapter 1

1.1 Demand for coffee rises. It depends on the related good.

1.2 It would probably rise.

1.3 The demand curve would shift downward a vertical distance 5¢. The demand curve would shift upward a vertical distance 10¢.

1.4 The demand curve would shift downward, but not parallel to itself, because the amount of the tax per item varies with the quantity purchased.

1.5 It would fall. It would fall because an increase in the price of leather belts would probably lead to an increase in the price of leather.

1.6 At a price of 40¢ per cup, suppliers get to keep 30¢ per cup and so supply 300 cups (read off the second line of Table A). And so forth.

1.7 Panel A. Price rises and quantity rises.

1.8 The sales tax causes very little change in price if either the demand curve is quite steep or the supply curve is quite flat. Price drops by nearly the whole 5¢ if either the demand curve is quite flat or the supply curve is quite steep.

1.9 Because the vertical distance from S to S' is 5¢ and the vertical distance from E to H is less than this.

1.10 You should shift the supply curve up a vertical distance 2¢ and the demand curve down a vertical distance 3¢. The new price to suppliers is 2¢ less than the new market price and the new price to demanders is 3¢ more than the new market price. If you have drawn your picture correctly, you will find that the new price to suppliers is on the old supply curve, the new price to demanders is on the old demand curve, and the distance between the two is 5¢. Since this can happen at only one place, the effect must be the same as that of the pure 5¢ sales and excise taxes.

Chapter 2

2.1 The relative price of bread is the reciprocal of the relative price of wine. When a number increases, its reciprocal decreases.

2.2 For the carpenter to rewire takes 20 hours, during which time he could perform $20/18 = 10/9$ paneling jobs.

Chapter 3

3.1 B: 4 eggs, 7 root beers. C: 1 egg 2 root beers. D: 4 eggs, 2 root beers.

3.2 Basket A, which has more of everything.

3.3 When you give Jeremy an egg, your stock of eggs is reduced from 7 to 6; when he gives you 4 root beers in exchange, your stock of root beers is increased from 2 to 6.

3.4 Imagine sacrificing one root beer in exchange for some eggs in such a way that the trade leaves you just as happy as you started out. This will bring you to a point on the indifference curve with vertical coordinate 1. The corresponding horizontal coordinate shows how many eggs you have at the end of the exchange; the excess of this quantity over the 7 eggs you started with shows the marginal value (to you) of a root beer.

3.5 If Jack sacrifices 1 egg for 6 root beers, he moves from point *C* to point *D*, staying on the same indifference curve. If Jill sacrifices 1 egg for 1 root beer, she moves from point C to point E, staying on the same indifference curve.

3.6 The consumer values additional clothing highly relative to additional food when he has little clothing and lots of food. Therefore, the indifference curve should be shallower toward the southeast, confirming our belief that indifference curves are convex.

3.7 Because it is on a higher indifference curve. The budget line would have to be flatter, intersecting the *X* axis on a higher indifference curve than where it intersects the *Y* axis.

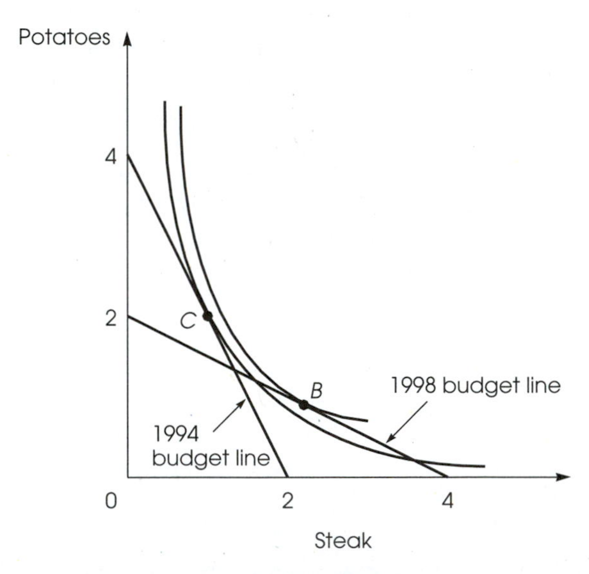

3.9 The figure corresponds to the table in Exhibit 3-13. Here is one of many possible tables that corresponds to the situation in Exhibit 3-12:

Basket	Quantity of *X*	Quantity of *Y*	Old Basket Price (P_X = \$4, P_Y = \$2)	NewBasket Price (P_X = \$3, P_Y = \$4)
P	3	4	\$25	\$20
O	4	2	\$20	\$20

Chapter 4

4.1 The new budget line is shifted southwest from the original line, and parallel to the original.

4.2 No. No. For *Y* to be inferior, point *B* would have to be located vertically below point *A*.

4.3 With an income of $12, the consumer chooses point *C* in panel *A*, and therefore consumes 12 eggs.

4.5 The budget line pivots inward around its X-intercept. If Y is not Giffen, the new optimum is vertically below the original. If Y is Giffen, the new optimum is vertically above the original.

4.6 When the price of *X* is $6, the consumer chooses point *C* in Exhibit 4-8A and therefore consumes 2 eggs.

4.7

The movement from *A* to *D* represents the substitution effect and the movement from *D* to *E* represents the income effect.

4.8 It means that when income rises, quantity of *X* falls; in other words, *X* is an inferior good.

4.9 4.1%. 7.3%. 14%.

Chapter 5

5.1 The numbers decrease in this case because the farmer sprays the most productive acres first and less productive acres later. The total benefit of spraying 3 acres is the sum of the marginal benefits on the first, second, and third acres.

5.2 Because the service is purchased at a constant price of $5 per acre.

5.3 The farmer still sprays 3 acres.

5.4 This affects marginal cost and so it *does* affect the farmer's decision. He now sprays 4 acres instead of 3.

5.5 The total cost of (say) 4 dresses is the sum of the marginal costs of the first, second, third, and fourth dresses. The marginal cost of (say) the fourth dress is the total cost of 4 dresses minus the total cost of 3 dresses.

5.6 \$6.

5.9 Quantity remains 3, price remains \$8, and profit falls to \$3.

Chapter 6

6.3 Six bakers produce 630 cupcakes, so the average product of labor is $630/6 = 105$. Five bakers produce 500 cupcakes, so the marginal product of the sixth baker is $630 - 500 = 130$.

6.4 $540/6 = 90$ and $540 - 500 = 40$.

6.5 For the same reason that when you bowl a below-average game, your bowling average falls. Similarly, if your grade in this course is lower than your grade point average, then your grade point average will fall.

6.8 In the first row, \$3 per unit = \$15 per worker/5 units per worker. And so forth.

6.10 For given quantities L and K of labor and capital, the isoquant through (L, K) shows the maximum quantity of output that can be produced with this basket of inputs. Since there is only one such maximum quantity, there can be only one isoquant through a given point. Since there is always some quantity that can be produced with (L, K), there is always an isoquant through any given point.

6.11 At E, the isocost is steeper than the isoquant so $MRTS_{LK} < P_l/P_K$. If the firm hires one less unit of labor and $MRTS_{LK}$ additional units of capital, it can stay on the isoquant, decrease its labor costs by P_L, and increase its capital costs by only $MRTS_{LK} \cdot P_K$, which is less than the decrease in labor costs. Total costs are decreased by this move, so it is a wise one for the firm. Having moved to the northwest, the firm continues moving in this direction until it reaches the point of tangency C.

6.12 \$145. \$60. \$77.50.

6.13 A 1% increase in output requires more than a 1% increase in all inputs. Therefore, average cost increases when output increases.

6.14 \$115. \$137.50. \$165

6.15 The medium plant is best; the large plant is second best. In the long run the firm chooses the medium plant. At Q_2, the $SRAC_2$ curve is tangent to the $LRAC$ curve.

Chapter 7

7.1 \$20. \$16. \$4.

7.2 3 bushels, because this is the quantity at which price equals marginal cost.

Total Quantity	Marginal Revenue	Marginal Revenue	Total Cost	Cost	Profit
1 bu	\$6	\$6/bu	\$ 1	\$2/bu	\$2
2	12	6	7	3	5
3	18	6	11	4	7
4	24	6	16	5	8
5	30	6	22	6	8
6	36	6	29	7	7

Example 1: Fixed Cost = \$2

Total Quantity	Marginal Revenue	Marginal Revenue	Total Cost	Cost	Profit
1 bu	\$6	\$6/bu	\$22	\$2/bu	−\$16
2	12	6	25	3	−13
3	18	6	29	4	−11
4	24	6	34	5	−10
5	30	6	40	6	−10
6	36	6	47	7	−11

Example 2: Fixed Cost = \$20

With fixed costs of \$2, Farmer Adams produces 5 bushels of wheat and earns an \$8 profit. With fixed costs of \$20, he produces 5 bushels of wheat and earns a profit of −\$10.

7.4 Firm A produces 4, firm B produces 6, firm C produces 7, and the industry produces 17.

7.5 As the output price falls, firms produce less. This bids down the price of inputs and lowers the marginal cost of producing output. Consequently, industry output does not fall as far as it otherwise would.

7.6

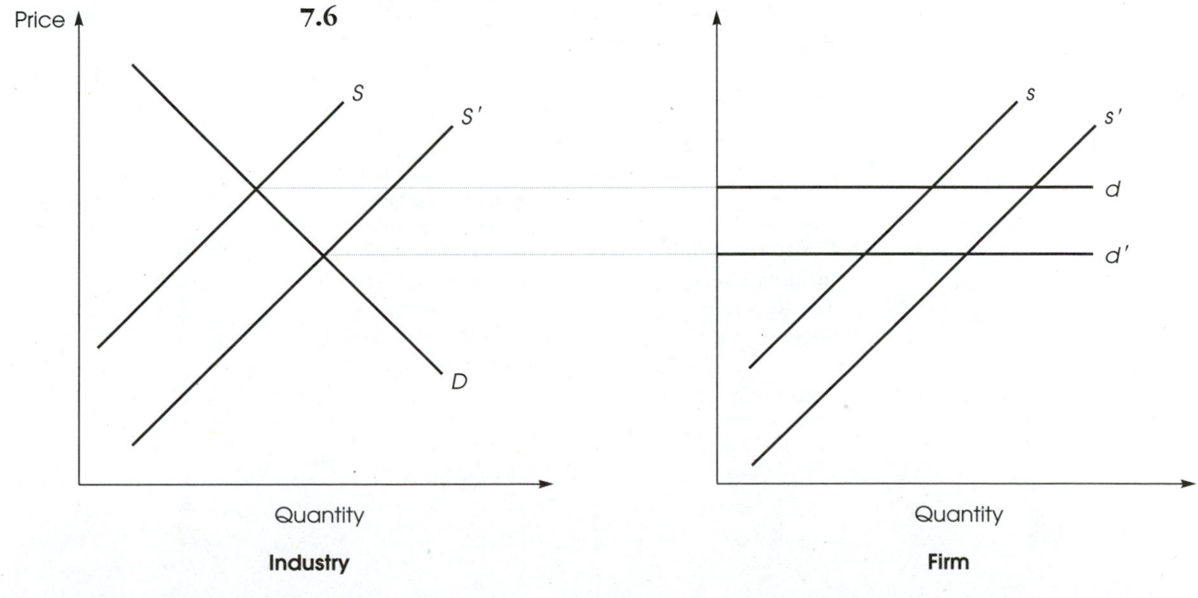

7.7

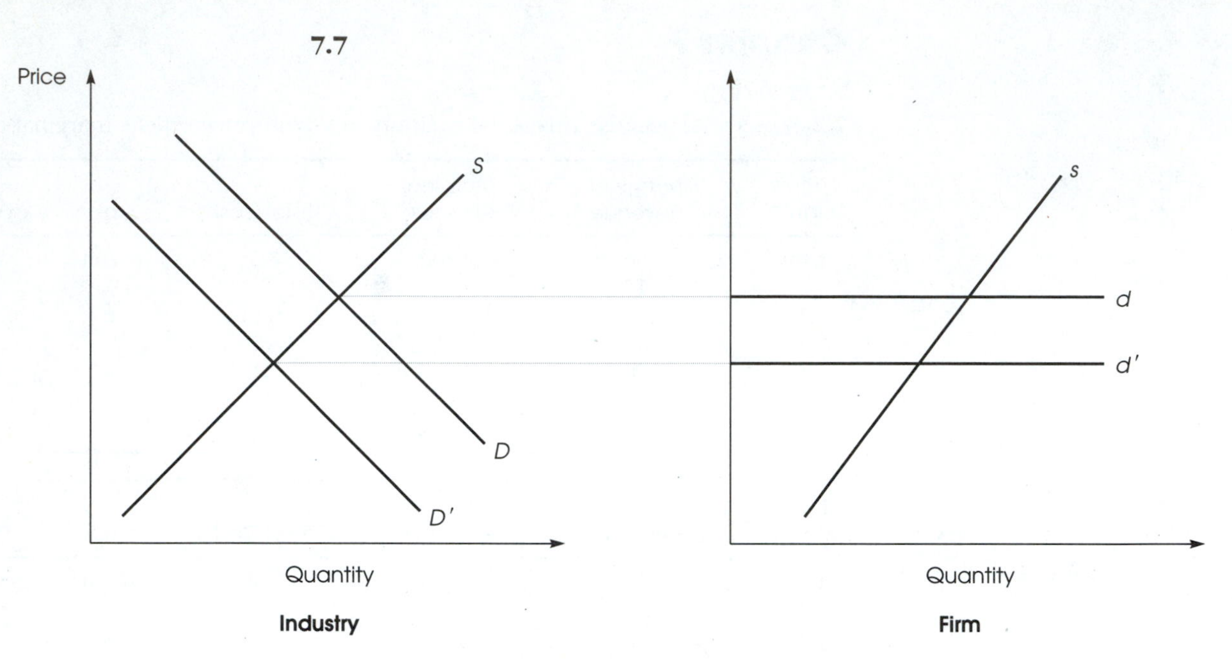

7.9 When the price of a haircut is \$2, Floyd sells 1 haircut at a total cost of \$10 for an average cost of \$10/1 = \$10 per haircut. At price, \$5, \$6, \$7, \$9 and \$10, the corresponding average costs are \$7.50, \$7, \$7, \$7.40 and \$8. When Floyd breaks even (selling 4 haircuts at \$7 a piece) his average cost is minimized (at \$7).

7.10 The demand curve rises, and all effects are the opposite of those shown in Exhibit 7-27.

Chapter 8

8.1 The entries are \$8, \$14, \$17, \$17, \$15, \$10. The largest of these, 17, occurs at a quantity of 4.

8.2 5.

8.3 Consumers lose $C + D + E$. Producers lose $F + G + H$. Tax recipients gain $C + D + F + G$. Yes.

	Before Taxation	With Excise Tax
Consumer Surplus	$A + B + C + D$	A
Producer Surplus	$E + F + G + H + I$	$H + I$
Tax Revenue	—	$B + C + E + F$
Social Gain	$A + B + C + D + E$ $+ F + H + I$	$A + B + C$
Deadweight Loss	—	$D + G$

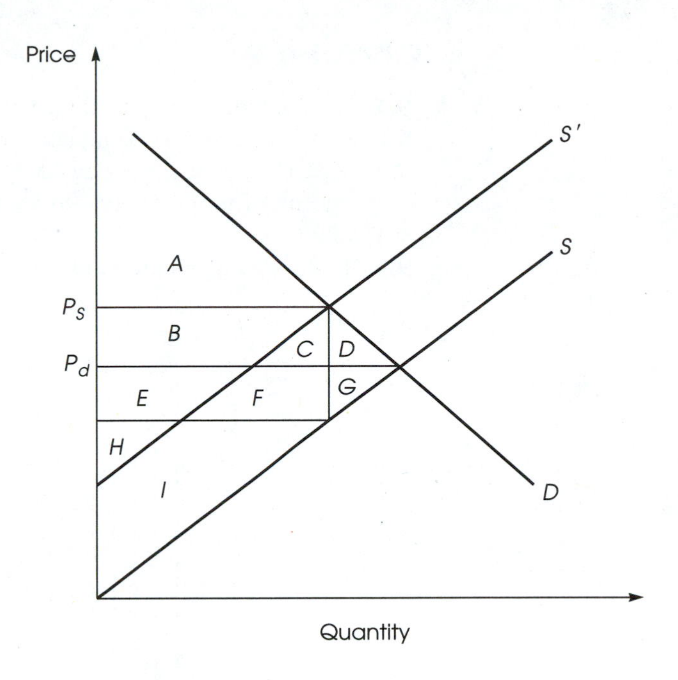

(Warning: these lettered areas are not the same as those in Exhibit 8-8.)

8.7 These calculations would be just like those of Exhibit 8-8.

8.9 In this drawing, the autarkic relative price is the slope of the budget line through *E*. The budget line through *F* results when the world price of tomatoes is slightly lower and the budget line through *G* results when the world price is lower still. As the world price deviates more from the autarkic price, Robinson moves to higher indifference curves and becomes better off.

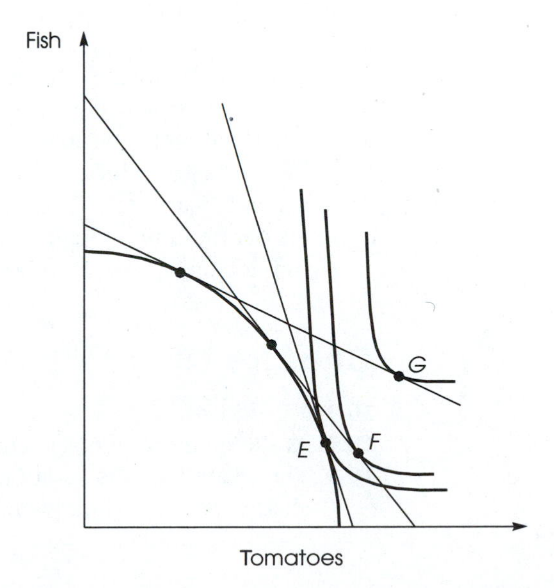

Chapter 9

9.1 Total value = \$54. Total cost = \$35. Social gain = \$19.
9.2 Total value = \$46. Total cost = \$35. Social gain = \$11.
9.3 Give Curly's second egg to Moe. Simultaneously, take from Moe any amount of money between \$3 and \$11 and give it to Curly.
9.4 \$8.
9.5 White rectangles are gains and shaded ones are losses.

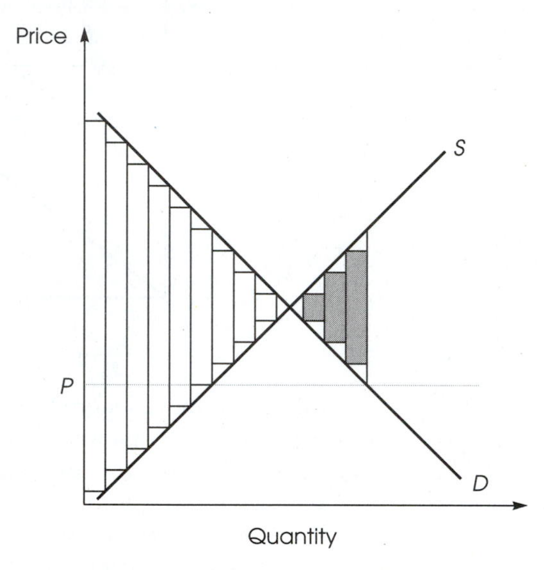

9.7 Under a limited draft, $B + C$ represents the amount by which each soldier's wages are reduced from equilibrium, times the number of soldiers. Thus, it is wealth transferred from soldiers to consumers.
9.9 From \$100 to \$120. From \$50 to \$60.
9.10 The plumber today receives \$100 to fix a leak. \$100 will buy 20 movie tickets at \$5 apiece. Overnight, all prices double, but the plumber thinks they have tripled. Tomorrow, he is offered \$200 to fix the leak. Although \$200 will still buy 20 movie tickets (now at \$10 apiece), the plumber thinks that it will buy only 13.33 movie tickets (which he now believes sell at \$15 apiece). Thus, he thinks he is being offered fewer movie tickets per plumbing repair than he is really being offered. This mistake leads him to supply less plumbing service.

Chapter 10

10.1 \$7 − \$3 = \$4. Yes.
10.2 At the quantity of 6, the curve changes from elastic to inelastic.
10.4 The shaded area is additional deadweight loss due to the excise tax. The shaded areas are deadweight loss.

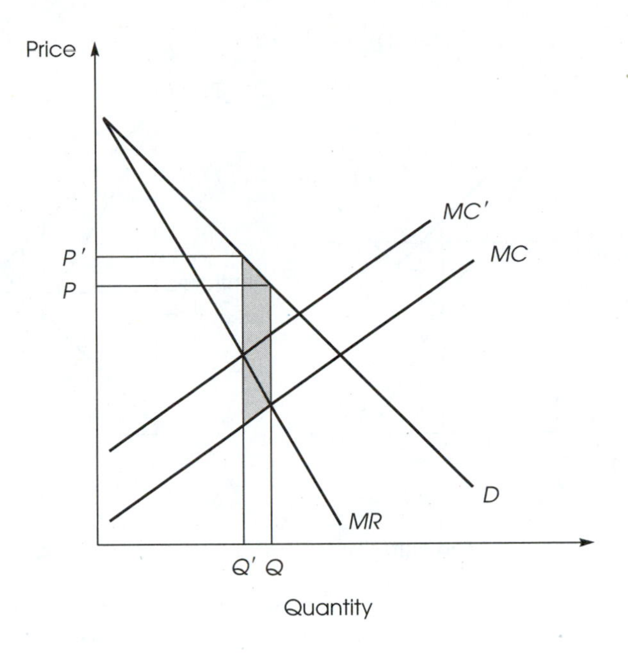

10.5

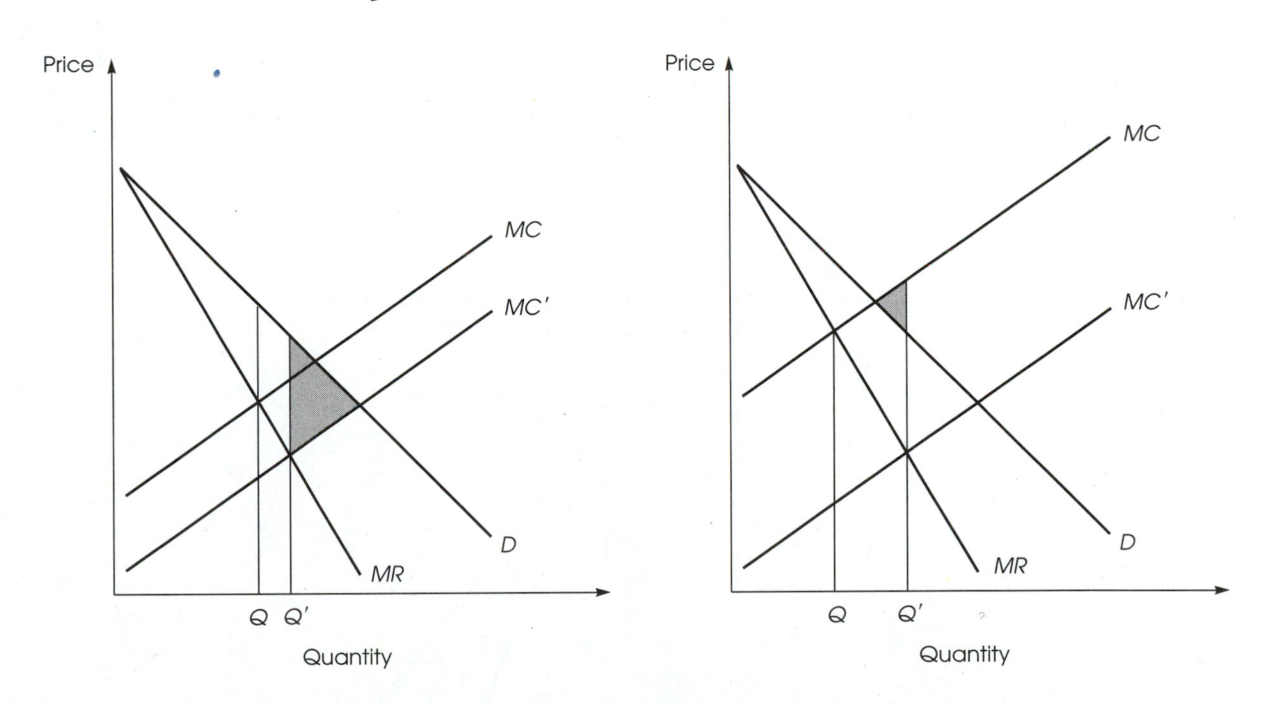

10.6 There are no waiting lines because the monopolist's price and quantity are given by a point on the demand curve. Thus, the quantity demanded is equal to the quantity supplied.

10.7

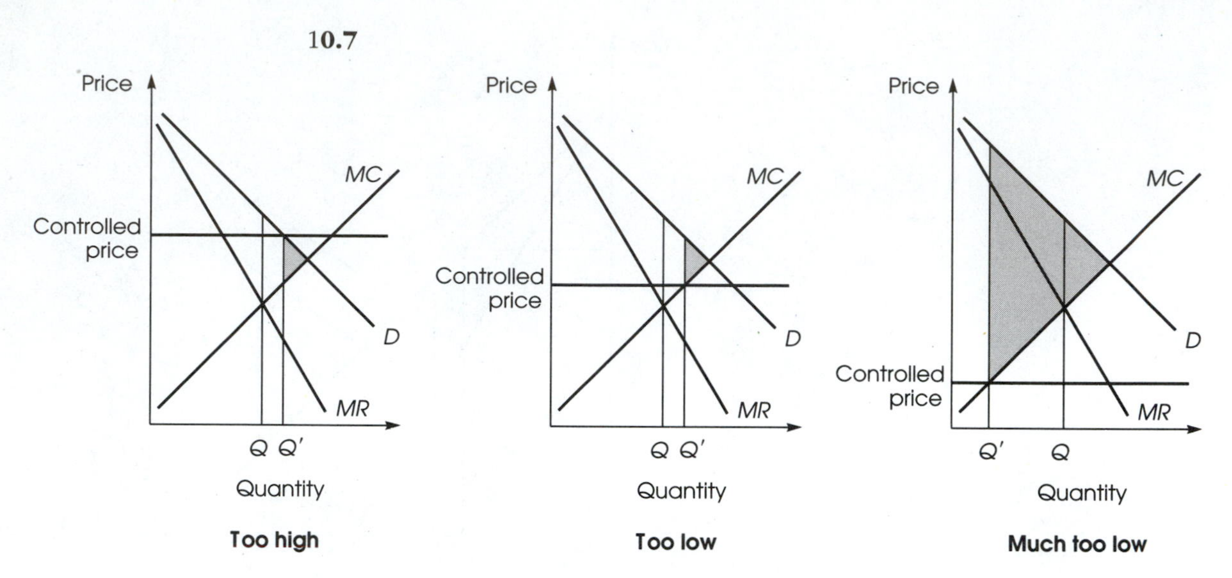

The shaded areas are deadweight loss.

10.8 Lobbying uses up resources. Bribery merely transfers resources from one individual to another.

10.9 If marginal revenue in the adult market is greater than in the children's market, he can sell one more haircut to an adult and one less to a child, increasing his revenue without affecting his cost. Similarly if adults and children are reversed. Thus, Benjamin is never satisfied if the two *MR*'s are different. He also wants $MR = MC$ just like any firm.

Chapter 11

11.1 Social welfare is unambiguously reduced by the merger, from $A + B + C + D + E$ to $A + B + C + D$.

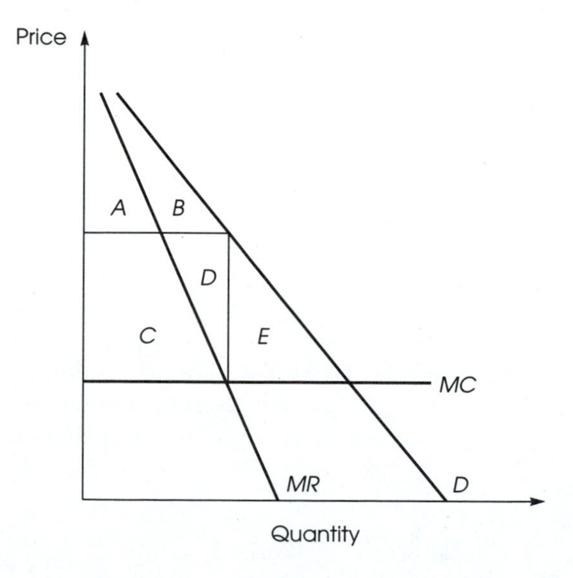

11.2 Flemington would now earn $C + D + F + G + H$ while the automaker earns $A + B + E$. The smallest acceptable fee is $C + D - H$ and the largest is $C + D + E$.

11.3 If they produce anything less in the way of services, then they earn positive profits, leading them to compete with each other for additional customers by increasing the service level.

11.4 To see that $V > P_1 - P_0$, examine the vertical line at Q_1. The portion of this line that stretches from MC to D has length V, which is clearly greater than $P_1 - P_0$. To see that $A + B > A + C$, note that the two triangles are similar, so it suffices to check that the base of $A + B$ is longer than the base of $A + C$. That is, we must check that $Q_1 > Q_0$, which is given.

11.5 At price P_0, firms produce quantity Q_0. At this quantity, average cost is also P_0, so firms earn zero profits.

11.6 Because the other sellers in the marketplace provide close substitutes for the given seller's product.

11.7 The one closer to an endpoint would jump around the other one.

Chapter 12

12.1 10 calories, 15 calories.

12.2 In the lower left, B wants to switch. In the lower right, both want to switch.

12.3 In the upper right, Ditto wants to switch. In the lower left, Ditto wants to switch. In the lower right, Dot wants to switch.

12.4 Because the weak pig prefers both C and D to B. Because the strong pig prefers both A and B to C.

12.5

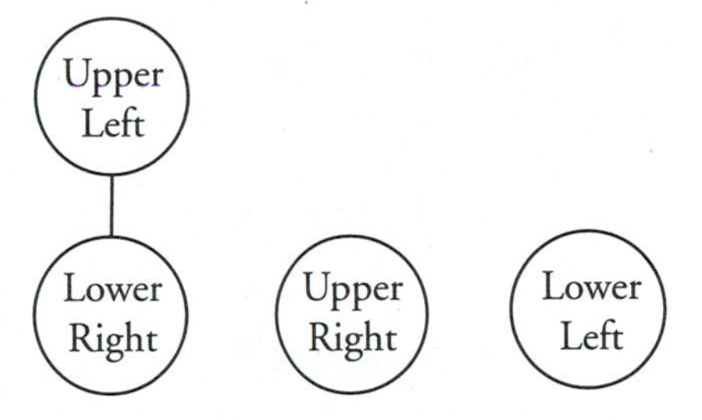

The upper left, upper right and lower left are Pareto optima.

12.6 Because any shift away would hurt B.

12.7 Because any shift away would hurt A.

12.8 In each case, a move to either of the Pareto optima benefits both Fred and Ethel.

12.9 In each case, at least one firm can do better by changing its strategy.

Chapter 13

13.1 Rectangle N has width 1 and height equal to the marginal externality due to the *Nth* unit of output. Therefore, it has area equal to that marginal externality. The sum of the rectangles is equal to the sum of the marginal externalities, which is the total externality.

13.3 The tax shifts MC_P up by the amount of the tax, which is also the amount of the externality. But MC_S already lies above MC_P by the amount of the externality. Thus, the new position of MC_P coincides with the existing position of MC_S.

13.4 D, $D + B$.

13.7 The White Sox. The White Sox.

13.8 New York. New York.

Chapter 14

14.1 The difference is \$5 − \$0 = \$5. The \$5 benefit to the sixth visitor is completely offset by the costs of \$1 apiece that he imposes on each of the first 5 visitors.

Chapter 15

15.1 As labor input increases, so does output, and therefore the output price falls. The effect is to steepen the MRP_t curve.

Chapter 16

16.1 As you move up and to the right you trade away leisure for consumption, so the marginal value of leisure increases.

16.2 If the wage were greater than the marginal value of leisure, the worker could gain by working more. If the wage were less than the marginal value of leisure, he could gain by working less.

16.3 If occupation A were more attractive than occupation B, then workers in occupation B would switch over to occupation A, raising wages in occupation B and lowering them in occupation A. This would continue until the two occupations were equally attractive.

Chapter 17

17.1 2 apples tomorrow per apple today. 100%.

17.2 The price is 4 apples. The face value is 5 apples. The discount is 1 apple.

17.3 .44 apples today. .30 apples today.

17.4 .76 apples today.

17.5 1.10 apples today.

17.6 \$20.

17.7 8%. 3%.

17.11 At an interest rate of 10%, Barb demands 5 units of current consumption.

17.12 Rebecca's budget line is steeper than in the exhibit and her optimum lies to the northwest of point E. She wants to be a net lender, consuming less than her current endowment. Therefore, people on average want to lend and this places downward pressure on the interest rate.

Chapter 18

18.1 Bet $100 on heads.

18.2 The expected value of basket C is always $100, regardless of whether the coin is biased. If the coin comes up heads 2/3 of the time, the expected value of basket D is $113.33. If the coin comes up tails 2/3 of the time, the expected value of basket D is $86.67.

18.3 For an unbiased coin, the iso-expected value lines have slope −1 and *C* and *D* lie on the same line. For a coin that comes up heads 2/3 of the time, the iso-expected value lines are steeper and *D* is on a higher line than *C*. For a coin that comes up tails 2/3 of the time, the lines are shallower and *C* is on a higher line than *D*.

18.4 It would be that portion of the black line in Exhibit 18-3 that lies to the right of point *C*.

18.5 5 to 1 1/2 to 1.1 to 1.

18.6 $15 worth.

18.7 For the advertising campaign fair odds are 1/2 to 1. The actual odds are 1 to 1. The expected winnings are $500. For the concert, fair odds are 1 to 1 and actual odds are 3 to 1. The expected winnings are $.50.

18.8 Owners sell more today and less in March, driving down the current price and driving up the March spot price until the two are equal.

18.10 Expected return is 50%; $\sigma = 0$. Thus, the point is to the left of *GSS* and on the vertical axis.

18.11 $5. $1.

18.12 The actual price is sometimes as high as $2, sometimes as low as $0, and $1 on the average day.

18.13 $4. $5. $6.

18.14 $4. 800 heads. $1. $3. $5.

18.15 Price of lettuce = (1/50) × (Lumberjacks' income) + $.50.

Answers to Problem Sets

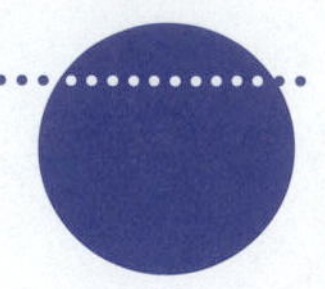

This appendix contains answers, hints, and discussions for many of the end-of-chapter problems throughout the book. In some cases you will find complete answers with reasons. In others you will find answers without reasons; it is still your job to provide the reasons. In still others you will find hints but no answers. In a few cases, you will find complete answers together with additional related discussion that goes beyond what is necessary to answer the problem correctly.

Chapter 1

1. False, in the sense of "not necessarily true." A fuel-efficient car reduces the price of "miles driven," so people choose to drive more miles. More driving with greater fuel efficiency could lead to either an increase or a decrease in the amount of gasoline consumed.

If the demand curve for "miles driven" is particularly steep, do Americans increase or decrease their use of gasoline? What if it is particularly shallow?

5. False. The demand curve for apartments shifts downward; therefore the price falls.

6. *Hint:* What happens to the demand curve for meat? What happens to the equilibrium quantity of meat supplied?

11a. \$1.50. \$3.00. 5 pounds.

12a. Demand rises, so price and quantity both rise.

12d. As farm workers move to the city to earn the higher wages, the supply of corn falls. Price rises and quantity falls. Sometimes students argue that wealthier industrial workers will demand more corn and therefore the demand curve shifts out as well. This is a commendable insight, but it overlooks the fact that those higher wages are paid by employers, who might now *reduce* their demand for corn, offsetting the additional demand by the workers. Therefore, unless we know more about why wages went up, we need not expect the market demand curve to shift.

15. True. When the supply curve shifts up by the amount T of the tax, the new equilibrium point is exactly a distance T above the old equilibrium point. The market price rises by the full amount of the tax.

Students commonly reach the correct answer *true* while offering a reason that is quite mistaken. Their (incorrect) argument is this: A vertical demand curve indicates that demanders will pay any price at all for avocados; therefore suppliers are able to pass the tax on completely without losing any sales. The argument is incorrect because it overlooks the fact that suppliers compete with each other. Any given supplier will indeed lose sales if he fails to match the going market price.

Indeed, to see that the argument cannot possibly be correct, ask yourself why suppliers don't raise their prices *prior* to the tax increase. If suppliers charge $1 originally and $1.25 after the imposition of a $.25 tax, why don't they charge $1.25 (or more) even *before* the tax is imposed? The reason is that price is determined not by individual suppliers, but by the intersection of supply and demand.

25b. The equilibrium wage rate falls by some amount between $200 and $500.

Chapter 2

2. You may conclude that he is confused. If the relative price of widgets in terms of gadgets has risen, then the relative price of gadgets in terms of widgets must have fallen.

7. False. Suppose that the going wage for child labor on farms is $5 per hour. Then the farmer without children must pay $5 to employ someone else's children; the farmer *with* children must forgo $5 per hour (which he could earn by renting his children out to neighboring farmers) to employ his own children. Both face the same cost of $5 per hour.

Some students argue that the farmer with children incurs the costs of feeding, housing, and education. However, it is *not* correct to count these among the costs of putting the children to work, since they must be paid whether the children work or not.

Other students argue that the farmer with children is wealthier at the end of the year since he makes no cash payments to hire labor. Whether or not this is true, it is irrelevant to the question. The question does not ask which farmer is wealthier, it asks only which farmer has higher costs of harvesting. The answer is that both have the same costs.

8. False, in the sense of "not necessarily true." The statement of the problem omits the key information that Mary is a highly skilled neurosurgeon, whereas George can do nothing except type. Mary's greater typing speed does not imply that she has a comparative advantage at typing.

Some students argue that *if* you are an employer who only wants to hire a typist, and *if* George and Mary are available at the same wage rate, then yes, it makes more sense to hire Mary as a typist than to hire George. But even this strained interpretation does not lead to the alleged conclusion. If you can really hire Mary at typist's wages, then you should set her to performing brain surgery, collect her fees as revenue to your firm, and use a small part of that revenue to hire George to do the typing.

14. It goes wrong exactly where it says that in each case there are the same costs for producing, shipping, and marketing the clothes. If a professional middleman can perform some of these tasks more cheaply than Anderson-Little can, then Brand X might be able to pay the middleman more than enough to cover his costs and still deliver the clothes more cheaply than Anderson-Little.

Chapter 3

6.

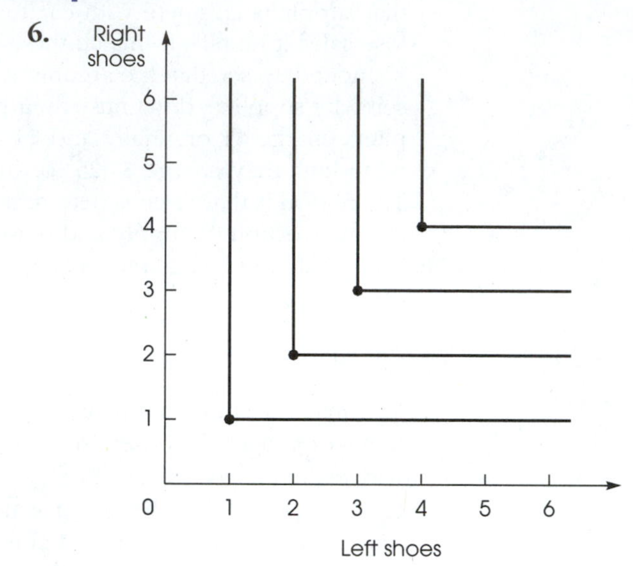

7.

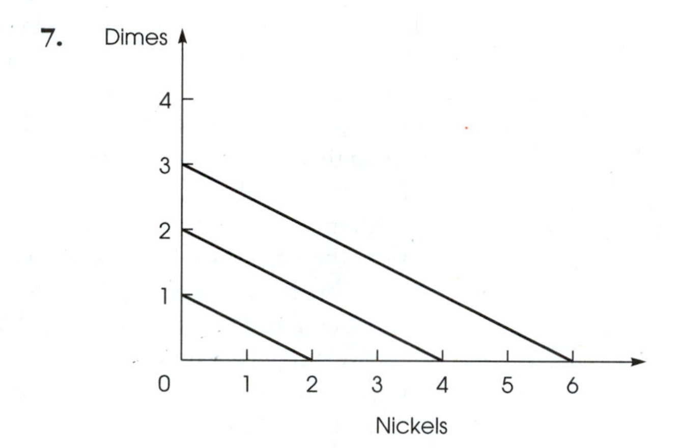

10. You are certainly better off after the changes.

15. You should be able to draw a single family of indifference curves consistent with both Amanda's and Bernard's choices. It is possible that Amanda and Bernard share this family of indifference curves; in other words it is possible (though not certain) that they have identical tastes.

Assuming that Amanda and Bernard *do* have identical tastes, can you determine which of them is happier?

21c. If too much education is available at public schools, then they will be chosen by both poor and rich students. If the purpose is to subsidize the poor at the expense of the rich, this tends to defeat that purpose.

25a. The endpoints are at $120 and 60 miles.

b. The endpoints are at $60 and 120 miles.

c. Your diagram should show that the new car definitely enables you to reach a higher indifference curve; therefore you would buy it.

Chapter 4

2. His Engel curve is a straight line through the origin. His demand curve is a rectangular hyperbola given by the equation PQ = I, where I is his (constant) income.

14b. The substitution effect leads to more speed and less safety, while the income effect leads to more of both. So true.

15f. Somebody whose income is derived entirely from wages feels a greater income effect from a change in the wage rate. Since the income effect works opposite to the substitution effect, such a person will respond less to a wage change than will somebody who has a lot of nonlabor income. Therefore the person whose income is entirely from wages can be expected to have the steeper labor supply curve.

23. It means that when your income goes up, your consumption of the luxury good increases by more than your income does. If your income increases by 1%, your consumption of luxury goods increases by more than 1%. But you cannot increase your consumption of *all* goods by more than 1% without violating the budget constraint. Therefore, not all goods can be luxuries.

In fact, this can be made more precise. When your income increases by 1%, your expenditures must increase by exactly 1% "on average" over all goods.

Thus, the average income elasticity over all goods must be 1. In the averaging process, goods must be weighted by the percentage of your income that you spend on them. Suppose that you consume only X and Y. Write k_x for the fraction of your income that you spend on X, k_Y for the fraction of your income that you spend on Y_1 η_x for your income elasticity of demand for X, and η_Y for your income elasticity of demand for Y. Then we must have

$$k_X\eta_X + k_Y\eta_Y = 1$$

If you want to prove this formula, start with the expressions

$$k_X = P_X X/I$$

$$k_Y = P_Y Y/I$$

$$P_X\Delta X + P_Y\Delta Y = \Delta$$

(First explain what each of these expressions means and why it is true.) Then insert the expressions for k_x, k_y, η_x, and η_Y into the final formula and simplify.

Chapter 5

2. True.

5. False. Exactly the opposite is true. (Be sure you can explain why!)

9. The firm produces four items at $14 apiece.

11. If the area consists entirely of stores, then Wilma is correct. Rents are fixed costs that do not affect prices. The reason that rents are high is that stores are willing to pay a lot for this location, where prices are high. But if many of the buildings in the area are used for office space, or anything other than stores, then Fred might be right. The high rents (caused perhaps by a high demand for office space in this location) have driven some stores out of the area, raising the demand for the products of those that remain, and consequently increasing prices.

Chapter 6

2. 

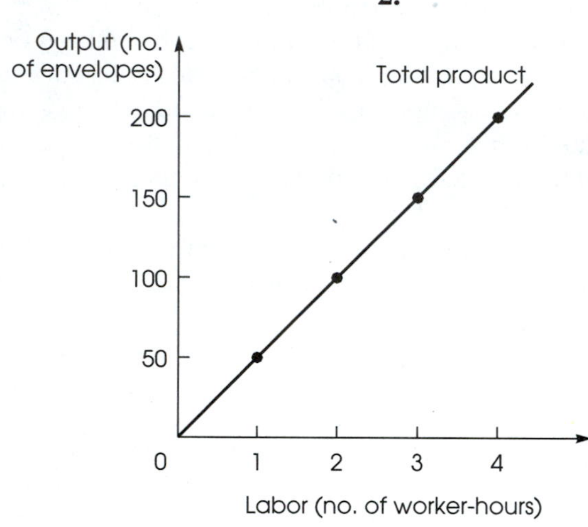

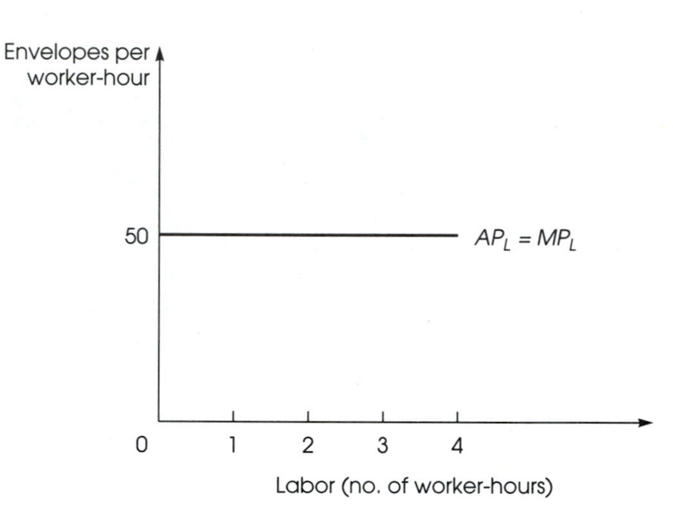

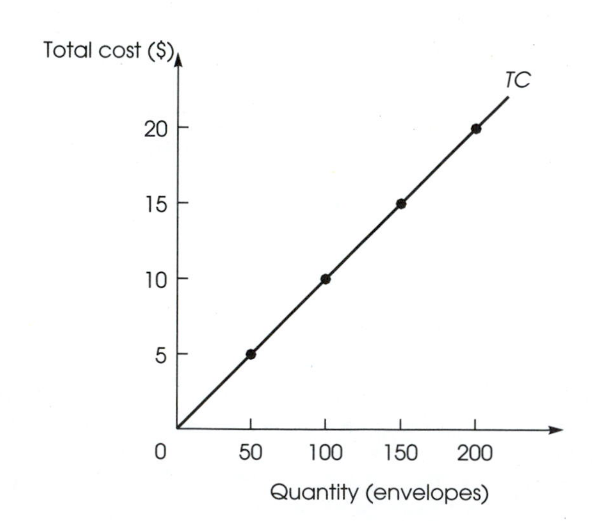

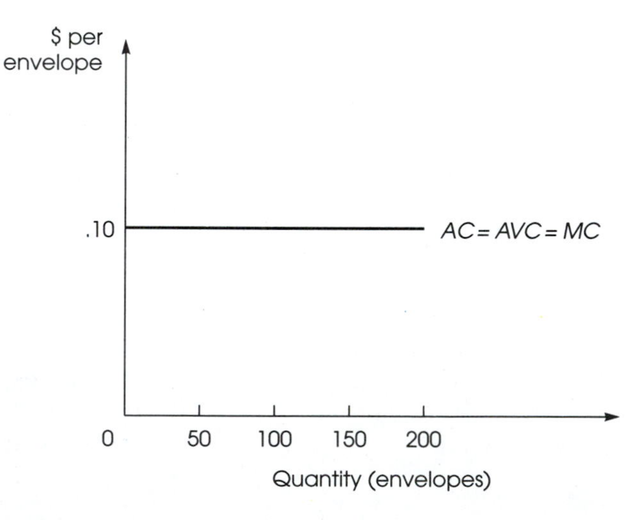

5a. The first two rows look like this:

Quantity	*VC*	*TC*	*AC*	*AVC*
1	$12	$42	$42	$12
2	$20	$50	$25	$10

12.

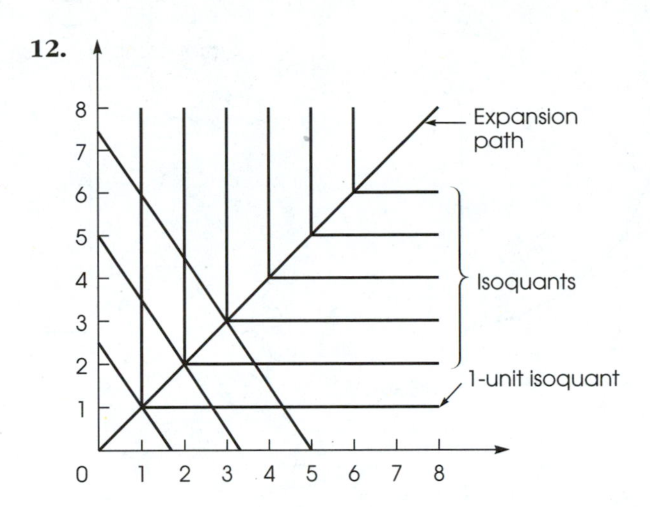
Expansion path
Isoquants
1-unit isoquant
0 1 2 3 4 5 6 7 8

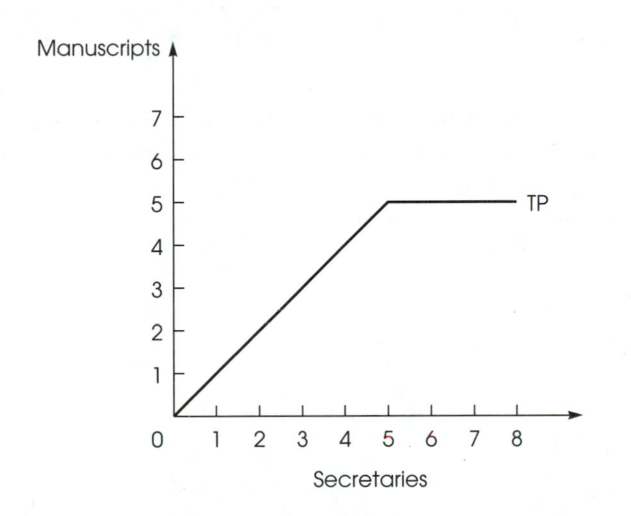
Manuscripts
TP
Secretaries

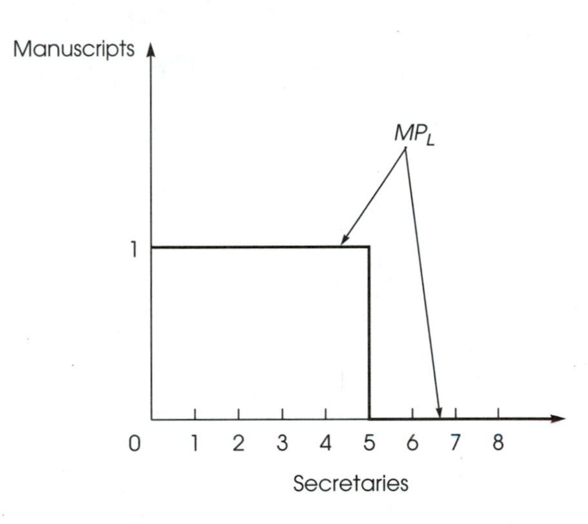
Manuscripts
MP_L
Secretaries

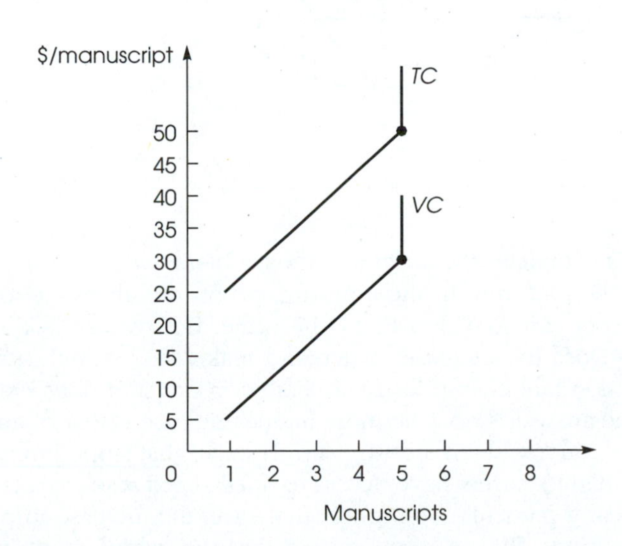
$/manuscript
TC
VC
Manuscripts

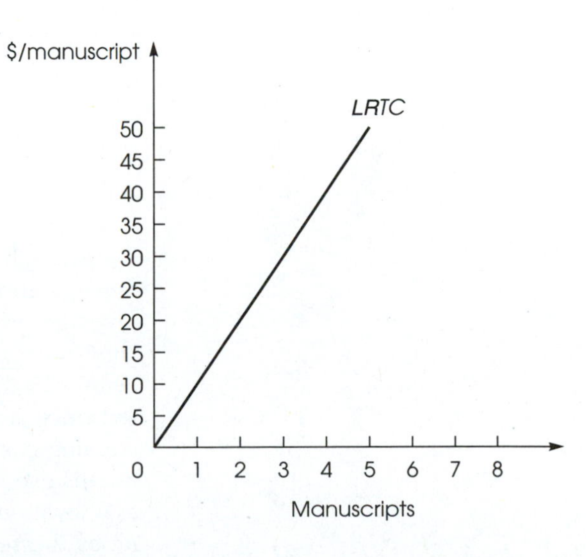
$/manuscript
LRTC
Manuscripts

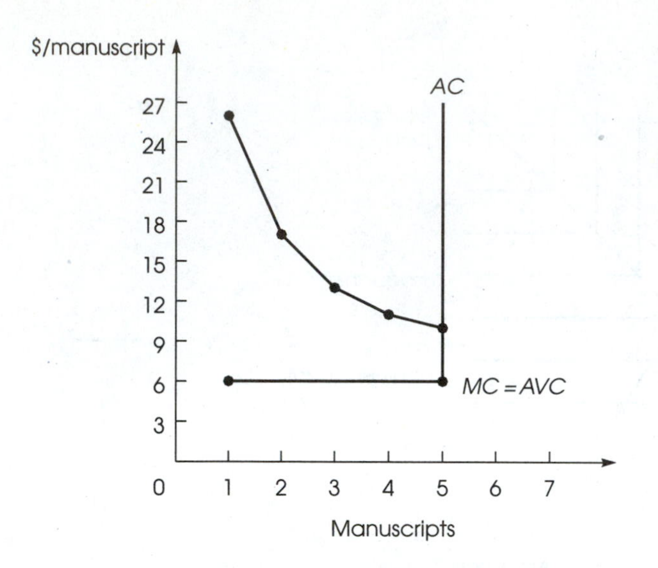

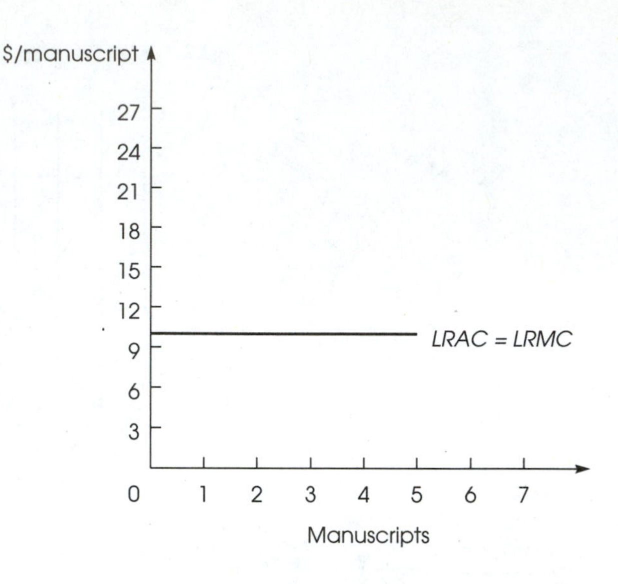

Chapter 7

6. At the initial price P, the beer maker's average profit per can is given by the distance π is the excess of the price per can over the average cost of production. At the new higher price P', the profit per can is π'. Since marginal cost sloped upward more steeply than average cost, π' must be greater than π. Therefore, true.

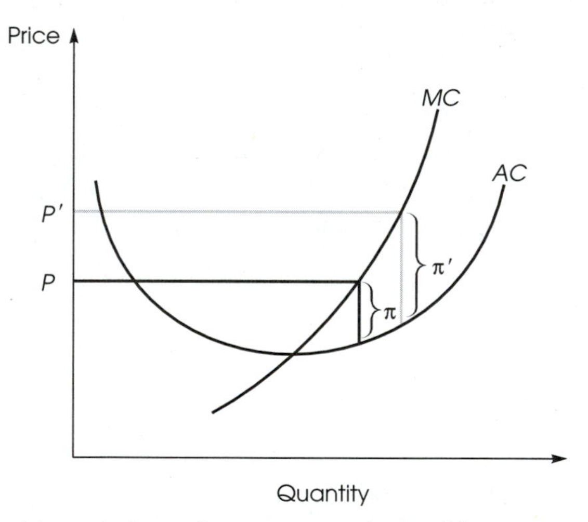

Although this completes the answer to the problem, we will add some remarks about the long run. In the long run, profits are always zero, so "average profit per can sold" must stay the same. But we can ask a related question: Does the increase in demand make beer manufacturers better off? In a constant cost industry, a change in demand does not affect price, so the answer is no. The more interesting case is that of an increasing-cost industry, with an industry supply curve that sloped upward because some manufacturers have access to specialized resources (such as a location near a particular spring). In that case, the increase in price raises the rental rate of these resources, so that the manufacturer who uses them experiences a rise in average cost, from AC to AC' in the graph below. His profits remain zero. However, if the manufacturer happens to *own* the specialized resource as well as using it, then he is certainly better off. Although his profits remain zero, he now collects higher rents (from himself) for the use of his resources.

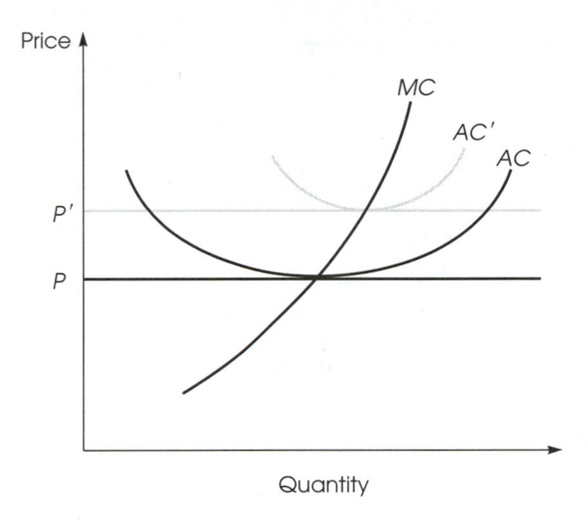

10. True, because in the long run workers must be indifferent between working for industry and cutting hair. To put this another way, the wages of industrial workers are part of the opportunity cost of barbering, so an increase in those wages causes the break-even price (and hence the supply curve) to rise in the barbering industry.

16. The marginal cost of providing a gallon of gasoline has risen by 50¢; thus the supply curves for both the firm and the industry shift vertically upward by 50¢ per gallon. In the constant-cost case, price rises by 50¢ per gallon; in the increasing cost case it rises by less (in the long run).

21a. This is an increase in marginal cost. The following figures show the effects

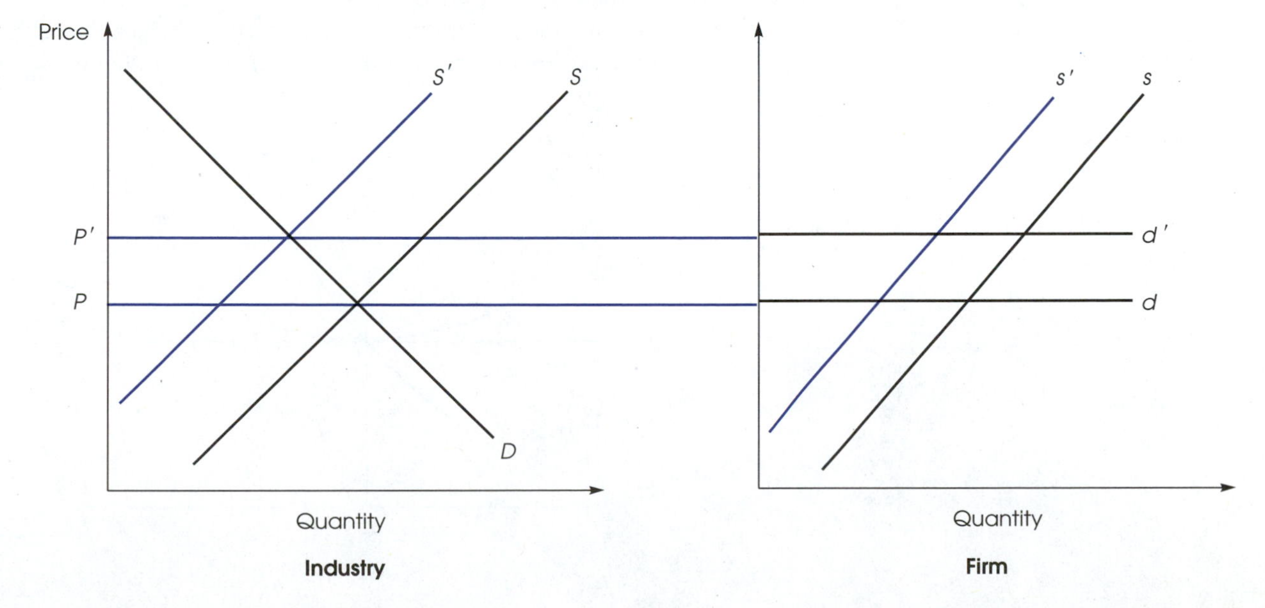

21b.

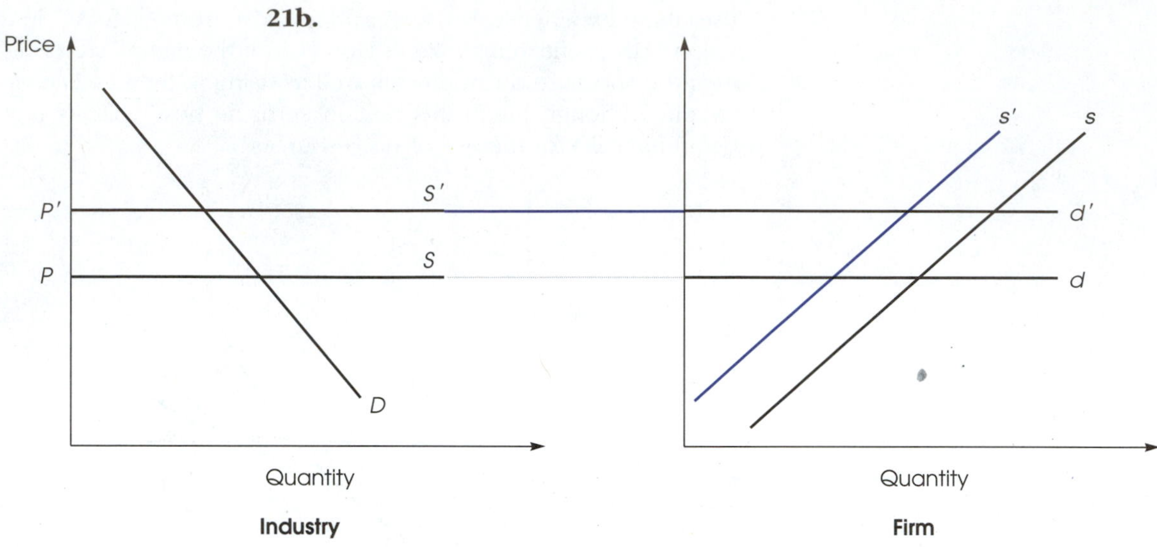

These pictures clearly reveal the direction of price changes and of industrywide changes. The direction of quantity change at the firm could go in either direction.

If you stopped here, you have given a good answer to the problem. However, if we add one more assumption we can say more. The additional assumption is that it takes a fixed quantity of liquor to make a drink, and that there is no substitute (such as a larger quantity of a cheaper type of alcohol) for that fixed quantity. In that case, an analysis just as in the solution to problem 8 reveals that in the short run (part (a)), quantity at the Airline must fall.

Continuing to make our additional assumption, we can also say more about part (c). Observe that the average and marginal cost curves must both rise by exactly the same amount. For example, if it takes one ounce of liquor to make a drink and this cannot be varied, and if the wholesale price increases by 10¢ per ounce, then the average and marginal cost curves both rise by 10¢ per drink. The next picture shows that in this case, the quantity of drinks served at the Airliner will not change.

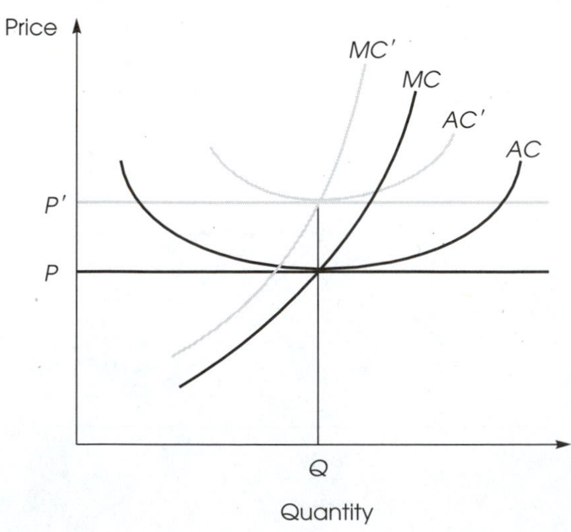

21c. The picture is qualitatively the same as in a).

23. Assuming that the payoff is made, this is a completely sunk cost and affects nothing in either the short run or the long run. The question is: Will the Airliner make the payoff? In parts (a) and (b) the answer is uncertain. But if the industry is constant-cost, as in part (c), then the Airliner is earning zero profits and indifferent about being in the industry. The payoff represents an additional cost, in the face of which the Airliner now prefers to exit. So in part (c), assuming that the industry starts out in long-run equilibrium, the payment is not made and the Airliner leaves the industry.

25a. In the short run this is fixed cost and has no effects.

25b. Each bar's average cost curve moves upward and there is exit from the industry. The Airliner's *marginal* cost curve is not affected. The diagram below shows that the price and quantity at the Airliner both rise (unless, of course, the Airliner is one of those that exit).

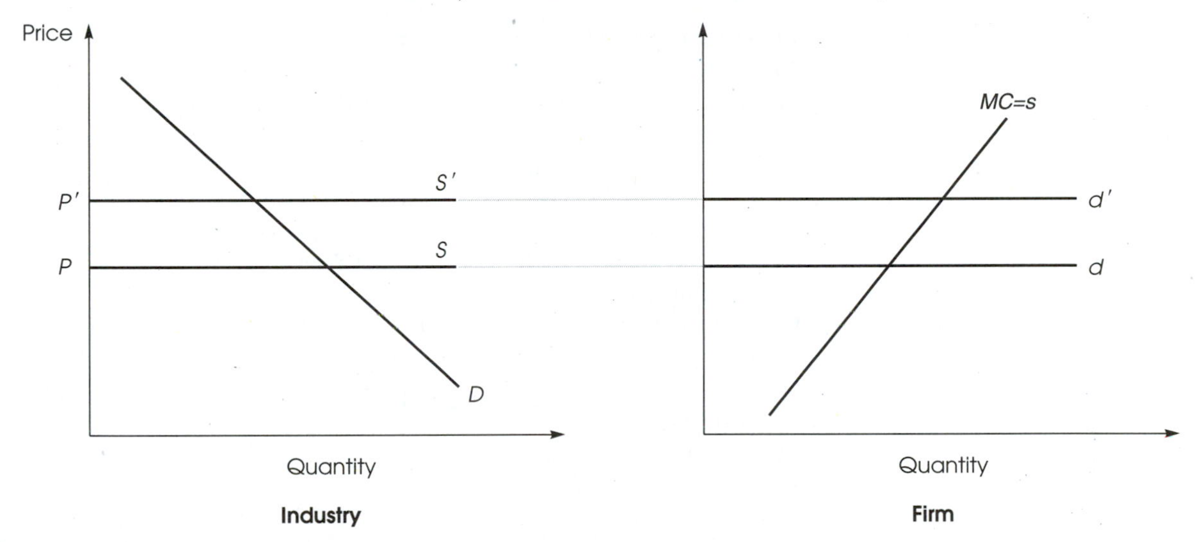

25c. The analysis is similar to part (b). The picture is this:

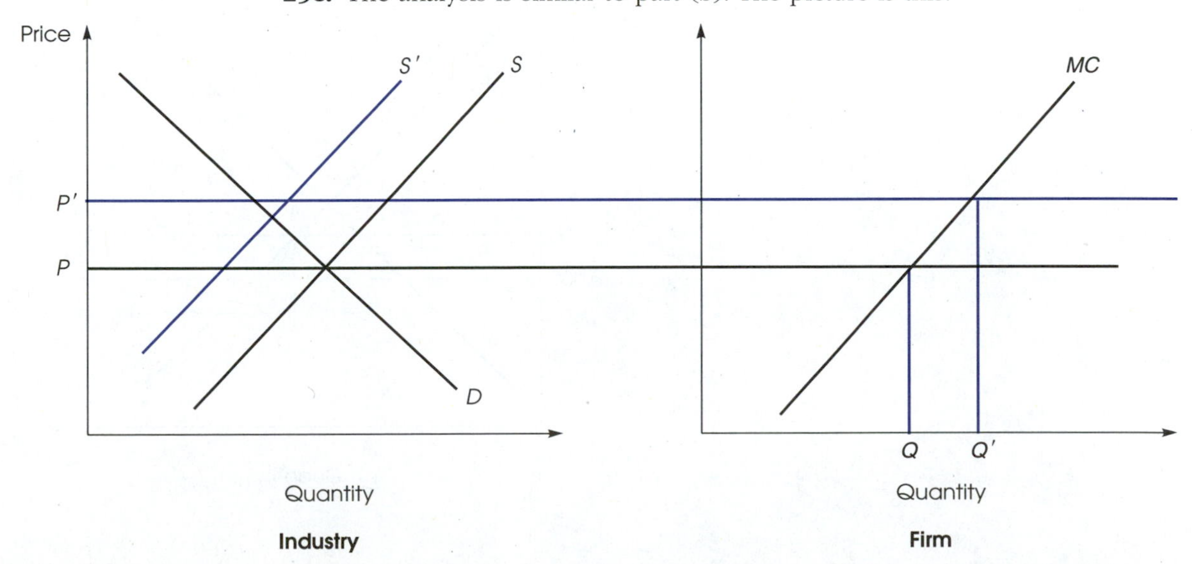

27. *Hint:* This raises short-run and long-run marginal cost at the Airliner only. There is no effect on industry-wide supply or demand.

29. This adds a fixed cost to operating the Airliner (namely the opportunity cost of selling the land). In the short run, there is no effect. In the long run constant-cost case, the Airliner is initially indifferent about its presence in the industry and will certainly exit in response to the increase in costs.

In the long-run increasing cost case, it is possible that the Airliner's owner is earning rents from special resources (such as being in the ideal position for a bar, for example) and prefers to stay in business, sacrificing the purchase offer.

In any of these cases, there is no effect on industry-wide supply or demand.

Chapter 8

2a. From buying the widgets.

2b. A gadget.

4. By the Pareto criterion, c) is better than e) and no other comparisons can be made. By the efficiency criterion, a), b), c) and d) are all equally good, and all better than e).

6. One solution is to give consumers $F + G + ⅓ E$ and give producers $C + D + ⅓ E$, taking the necessary resources from the taxpayers.

7. False. The line lengths adjust so that the value of waiting time is $9 in both countries.

12. The triangle on the left reflects the fact that people purchase foreign cars that could have been produced more cheaply at home. The triangle on the right reflects the fact that people now buy fewer cars. Can you explain why?

14. The shaded area is deadweight loss:

15. The shaded area is deadweight loss:

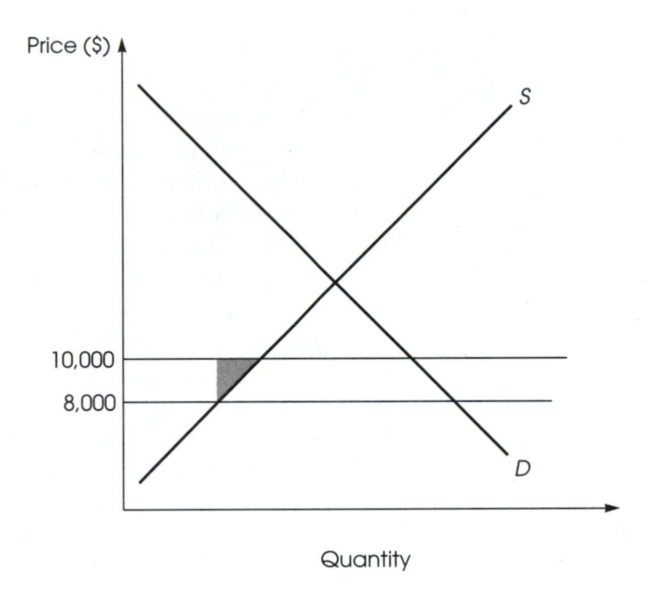

20. True because the demand for committing robberies is horizontal.

22a. The quantity of wheat does not change, so the price does not change. Therefore, there is no effect on consumers. In the diagram below, producers avoid incurring costs of B_1 so B is the gain to producers. The cost

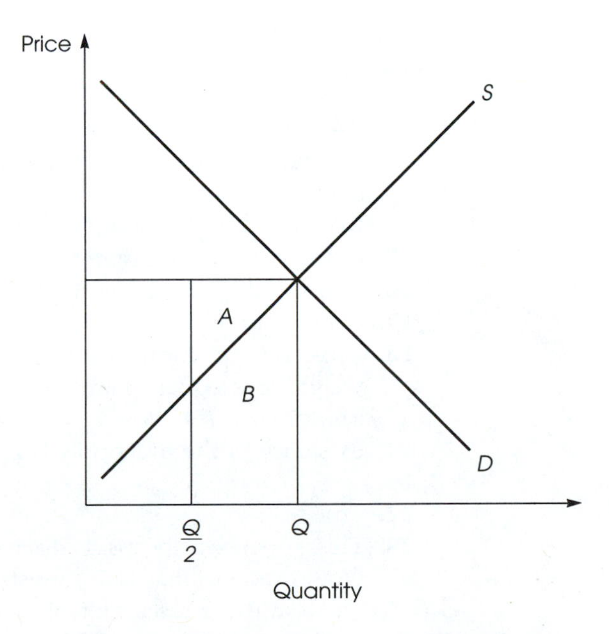

to the government is $A + B$, so the deadweight loss is A.

Why?

Chapter 9

2. None of the council members has the expertise to determine the extent of the risk from the chemical plan; none has the expertise (or the information) to determine the extent of the benefits. It is reasonable to expect that the company owners and their insurers (who are experts at assessing risks) have access to more information than the council has. Under the councilman's proposal, they have the incentive to make use of that information. If the chemical company agrees to bear all of the costs of reimbursement, we may infer that it expects to earn enough from the plant to more than cover those costs. Similarly, if the insurance company is willing to bear the risk in exchange for a price that the chemical company is willing to pay, we may infer that it expects the amount of damage to the townspeople to be less than the gains to the chemical company.

The councilman's suggestion creates an incentive for those with easiest access to the relevant information to analyze that information and act on it in a socially desirable way.

5b. $12.

9b. Consumers could be made worse off if the pizzas are distributed to those who value them relatively little.

13. *Hint:* Suppose that all 3 of the applicants with incomes over $70,000 have revealed their incomes. Your income is exactly $70,000. What will you do?

Chapter 10

1. False, because of the phrase "unlike a competitor." Anybody can charge any price he wants to for anything. However, there is only one profit-maximizing price to charge, and it is foolish to deviate from this price, whether you are a monopolist, a competitor, or anything in between.

7. It drops a vertical distance $1.

16. The social loss from monopoly is $2.

17. There is none.

18. Under competition, the law banning foreign markets creates a deadweight loss equal to area O. Under monopoly, it creates a deadweight loss of $I + M + N + S + T + O$. Thus, the deadweight loss due to the existence of the monopoly is $I + M + N + S + T$.

19. $N + T$.

22. True.

29. This appears to be price discrimination in favor of U.S. tourists, which would require that U.S. tourists have a greater elasticity of demand for meals at these restaurants than the natives do. But this would appear to be the exact opposite of the truth: Tourists, if they are to eat at all, must eat at restaurants, whereas natives have the option of eating at home. Also, tourists are less likely than natives are to know about alternative, out-of-the-way places to eat.

This suggests looking for an explanation that does not involve price discrimination. That is, we must ask why these restaurants find it less expensive to serve tourists than to serve natives. One wild guess is that tourists, for some reason, are better tippers, so that they actually pay more (inclusive of tip) for their meals than the natives pay. Of course, this keeps the staff happy and enables the management to pay lower wages: hence serving tourists helps to keep their costs down.

We repeat that this explanation is a wild guess. If you have a better one, please send it to the author in care of South-Western College Publishing company.

32a. Charge $18 to enter and 50¢ for popcorn.

b. Charge $9 to enter and 60¢ for popcorn.

c. Charge $23 to enter and 40¢ for popcorn.

Chapter 11

2. Conceivably a vertical merger could be used to prevent resales. Suppose that a monopoly steel manufacturer wants to sell cheaply to automakers and expensively to construction firms. The steel firm worries that automakers can buy cheaply and resell to construction firms. But if the steel firm acquires an automaker as a subsidiary, it can sell cheaply to the automaker while ordering it not to engage in resales.

4. It would increase in the first case and decrease in the second.

9. One frequently cited alternative theory is that the manufacturer is acting as an enforcer for a cartel among the dealers. Under what circumstances do you find this theory either more or less plausible than the theory that is elaborated in the textbook?

11. False, because of the Prisoner's Dilemma. Each worker can rationally calculate that his own voluntary contribution is unlikely to be critical in determining the success of the union, and therefore chooses not to join. It is important to notice that workers will elect not to join regardless of whether or not they believe that others are joining. It is possible that all workers could benefit from an outside enforcer who requires them to unionize.

14. The industry output is equal to $N/(N + 1)$ times the output of a competitive industry. When N is large, the Cournot industry's output and the competitive industry's output are approximately equal.

15. The industry output is 3/4 of what it would be under competition, which is greater than what it would be under Cournot behavior. The first firm produces twice as much as the second firm and is better off than the second firm.

Chapter 12

1. I. (Right, Down)

1. III. (Right, Up)

1. V. None.

1. VII. (Left, Up) and (Right, Down)

2. I. (Right, Up), (Left, Down), and (Right, Down)
2. III. (Right, Up)
2. V. (Left, Down) and (Right, Down)
2. VII. (Left, Up) and (Right, Down)
3. I. Yes, Yes.
3. III. Yes, No.
3. V. No. No.
3. VII. No. No.
4. I. (Right, Down)
4. III. (Right, Up)
4. V. (Right, Down)
4. VII. (Right, Down)

Chapter 13

2. This tax is less desirable than the tariff.

6g. The optimal tax is $N + O + P$.

13. Assume first that there are no transactions costs between the beekeeper and the car dealer. In that case, your decision does not matter in the sense that it has no effect on the number of bees that are kept, the procedures used to contain the bees, the number of cars sold, the investment in tents by the car dealer, whether the car dealer will move away, and so forth. It matters in the sense that the beekeeper prefers one decision and the car dealer another.

Alternatively, if there *are* transactions costs, then all of the things that were left unaffected in the preceding paragraph can indeed be affected. A ruling for the car dealer could induce the beekeeper to rein in his bees (say with better netting) or to scale back his operation, while a ruling for the beekeeper could induce the car dealer to erect a tent or to move.

Since there are only two parties and they are in close proximity, the assumption of *no* transactions costs seems the more reasonable.

If a large collection of motorists is involved, the transactions costs can become considerable. It is difficult for the motorists to collectively negotiate with the beekeeper, particularly if different motorists are affected on different days. Many motorists might not even recognize the source of the problem.

In this case, some factors relevant to the decision are: How much would it cost the beekeeper to prevent his bees from flying over the roadway, either by containing them or moving elsewhere? What alternatives are available to motorists? Can they easily take a different route or would it be very costly to do so? How much damage do the bees actually do to the cars, and how much does it cost motorists to cope with this damage, either by having it repaired or by deciding to tolerate it?

18. False. The availability of liability insurance does indeed reduce the incentive to drive carefully, which can indeed result in more accidents. It is nevertheless false that this outcome is necessarily detrimental to welfare. Insurance contracts benefit both the driver and the insurer (otherwise one or the other would not enter the contract). As long as accident victims are fully compensated for their losses, they are not damaged by an increase in the number of accidents. In these circumstances, insurance contracts increase social welfare even as they increase the number of accidents.

In circumstances where accident victims are not fully compensated for their losses, then they are damaged by the additional accidents. This damage might or might not exceed the gains to drivers and insurers, so there could be either a net social gain or a net social loss.

22e. Expectation damages induce Betty to behave efficiently.

23. It does *not* follow that expectation damages are the appropriate standard. Although expectation damages lead to efficient breaches of contract, they might not lead to an efficient number of contracts being signed in the first place. A full analysis of the problem must account for the fact that the number of contracts signed will vary depending on the legal standard that is in force. Such a full analysis is provided by David Friedman in "An Economic Analysis of Alternative Damage Rules for Breach of Contract," *Journal of Law and Economics* 23 (1989). Friedman establishes that either expectation or reliance damages could be more efficient, depending on circumstances.

Chapter 14

1c. The optimal outcome can be achieved with an entrance fee of 8 or 10 fish per day.

2d. She will charge 16 nuggets a day at Mine A and 18 nuggets a day at Mine B.

10. *Hint:* What happens to rental rates on the north side of town?

Chapter 15

7. True. The reason why isocosts are straight lines is that their equations are given by $P_K \cdot K + P_L \cdot L = C$ where P_K, P_L, and C are constants. For a monopsonist in the labor market, P_L is not constant: It varies with his employment of labor. Thus, the isocosts are not straight lines.

11. *Hint:* Graph the MP_L curve. Assume that the wage rate of labor rises from W to W'. Use your graph to illustrate the revenue earned by capital both before and after the wage change. Which is bigger?

12. *Hint:* Graph the MP_K curve. Assume that labor and capital are substitutes in production. Show how MP_K shifts in response to a rise in the wage rate of labor. Use your graph to illustrate the revenue earned by capital both before and after the wage change. Which is bigger? Is your answer consistent with your answer to problem 10? If not, what is the source of the discrepancy?

13. Apparently the union believes that a reduction in the quantity of unskilled labor (as would result from a minimum wage) would increase the demand for the skilled labor that its members supply. Thus, skilled and unskilled labor must be substitutes in production.

To investigate the relationship with capital, begin by dividing inputs into "unskilled labor" and "all other inputs," where the latter includes both skilled labor and capital. When there are zero profits and only two inputs, those inputs must be complements in production (this was shown in problem 10).

This means that a reduction in unskilled labor must reduce the demand for "all other inputs." Therefore, following a reduction in unskilled labor, the demand for either skilled labor or capital must fall. Since we have already agreed that the demand for skilled labor rises, it follows that the demand for capital falls. In other words, unskilled labor and capital are complements in production.

It follows that the owners of capital will oppose the minimum wage.

Chapter 16

2. Jack's budget line has a "kink" at 8 hours and is tangent to an indifference curve at 10 hours. Jill's budget line intersects the consumption axis at the same point as Jack's and is tangent to the same indifference curve. Drawing the picture, you will find that Jane's budget line must be steeper than the initial portion of Jack's but less steep than the later portion; in other words, W' is between W and W'. The same picture should reveal whether Jane works more or fewer than 10 hours.

4. *Hint:* Is leisure a normal or an inferior good for Dick?

9. *Hint:* Which of these men feels a greater income effect when his wage rate changes?

10. False. If workers come to enjoy their jobs, the supply curve of labor shifts out, the quantity supplied increases, and therefore the marginal product of labor decreases. So workers who enjoy their jobs more are *less* productive at the margin than those who enjoy them less.

11. The wage rate falls, less labor is supplied to the marketplace, and a given individual might supply either more or less labor than before.

13. The wage rate rises, less labor is supplied to the marketplace, and a given (surviving) individual supplies more labor than before.

17. One important difference arises from intertemporal substitution. In the circumstance of part (a), there is strong incentive to take one's vacation this year instead of next, whereas that incentive is missing from part (b). You should take account of this difference in determining the effects on wages and the quantity of labor supplied.

19. True, because education is a form of investment in capital. Since the tax break applies to other forms of investment but not to education, investors tend to substitute toward those other forms of investment.

Chapter 17

5b. The halving of the interest rate is the greater deterrent.

12a. Jeeter can purchase a bond for $1,000 at a 10% interest rate and pretend that he has spent the $1,000 to pay off his loan. Five years from today, he simply hands the bond over to the bank. Since the bond and the debt grow at the same rate, the bond covers the debt exactly.

18. The interest rate is higher in the circumstance of (a).

21.

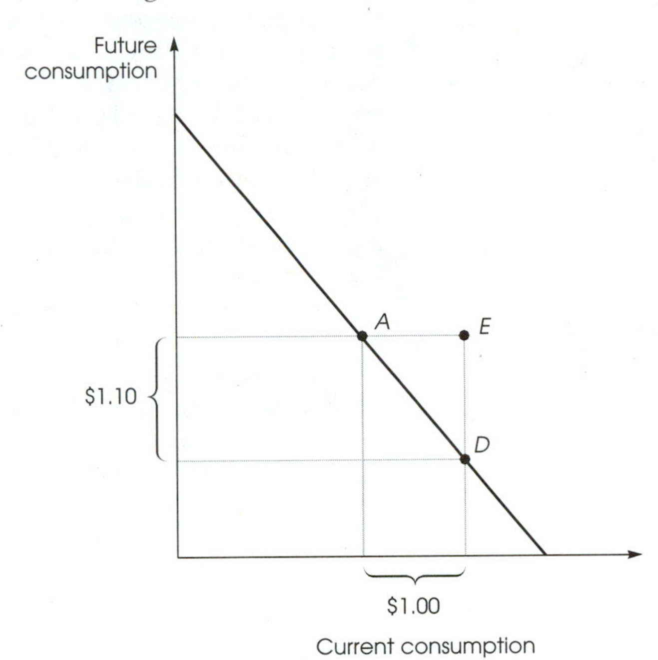

Terry starts with an endowment of A, faces an interest rate of 10%, and therefore has the pictured budget line with slope −1.10. If the government taxes him $1 and then provides him with $1 worth of current consumption, his endowment point remains A (nothing has really changed). If the government borrows $1 to provide Terry with $1 worth of current consumption, it then taxes him $1.10 in the future to repay the debt. Terry's endowment point shifts to D (with $1 more in present consumption and $1.10 less in future consumption). Since Terry's new endowment point is on his original budget line, his optimum consumption basket does not change. Each plan leads to the same demand for current consumption and so to the same equilibrium interest rate.

24. Here are a few observations:

First, Mr. Rohatyn asserts that borrowing will convert a $130 billion loss into a $500 billion drain over 20 or 30 years. In other words, he treats a dollar paid 20 years from now as equal in value to a dollar paid today. If he is really committed to such reasoning, Mr. Rohatyn should be happy to offer you a loan of $200 billion today in exchange for a payback of $300 billion in 20 years. Try writing to him and see if he agrees.

Second, he asserts that one should not borrow to finance losses that have already occurred, and elevates this dictum to "a basic economic principle." On the contrary, people generally prefer to spread their consumption out evenly over their lifetimes rather than having some years of feast and some of famine. (This is why we tend to think of the Great Depression as a bad thing.) It follows that a one-shot unexpected large expense is precisely the sort of thing that ought to be financed by borrowing. Your indifference curve analysis in part (b) should confirm this assertion.

Third, he is wrong in thinking that a short-term tax surcharge would necessarily limit the costs of the bailout to the immediate future. Precisely because people like to smooth out their consumption, they would borrow more (or, equivalently, save less) in the present to get through the temporary period of high taxes. The result would be the same as if the government had done the borrowing.

But not quite. For a variety of reasons, individuals must usually borrow at higher rates than the government does. Therefore, Mr. Rohatyn's proposal comes down to this: Let people attempt to borrow for themselves at high interest rates, rather than let the government borrow for them at lower rates.

Finally, some economists would argue that people are insufficiently sophisticated to borrow their way through the higher tax years (that is, some would argue that people fail to move to the optimum point in the indifference curve diagram). If those economists are right, then Mr. Rohatyn is even further off the mark, since these taxpayers in their naivete will fail to smooth out their consumption streams unless the government leads the way by borrowing for them.

26. $66,666.66

27. The interest rate rises.

Chapter 18

1. The desirability of the trade depends on the possible outcomes of the uncertainty and it depends on the odds. Had the doctor himself been offered the opportunity to trade a certain shilling for a mere 99% chance at a million pounds, he might have reconsidered his position. Indeed, to forgo suicide is to sacrifice the certainty of death for the uncertainties of life, but most of us make this "unwise" choice.

2. False. Even something that is not worth the certainty of death can still be worth some *chance* of death. If this were false, nobody would ever drive a car.

12. Much depends on whether higher crash rates are attributable to age or to lack of driving experience. The *Times* assumes that 18-year-old first-time drivers will crash at the same rate as 18-year-olds with two years' experience, which seems debatable.

Chapter 19

3.

$$\frac{U - C}{D - U} \cdot \left[\frac{D}{1 + r} - \right.$$

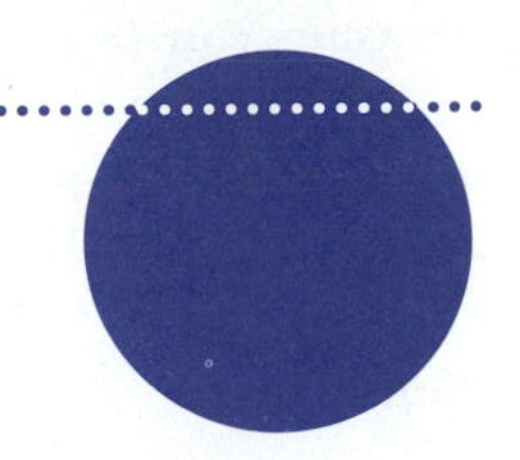

Glossary

Absolute price The number of dollars that can be exchanged for a specified quantity of a given good.

Accounting profits Total revenue minus those costs that an accountant would consider; this excludes the opportunity costs of resources owned by the firm.

Adverse selection The problem that arises when people know more about their own risk characteristics than others do.

Autarkic relative price The relative price that would prevail if there were no trade with foreigners.

Average cost Total cost divided by quantity.

Average product of labor The quantity of output divided by the quantity of labor employed.

Average variable cost Variable cost divided by quantity.

Bertrand model A model of oligopoly in which firms take their rivals' prices as given.

Bond A promise to pay at some time in the future.

Budget line The set of all baskets that the consumer can afford, given prices and his income.

Capital Physical assets used as factors of production.

Capital asset pricing model A model that assumes that investors care only about expected return and risk, where risk is measured by standard deviation.

Cartel A group of firms engaged in collusion.

Clarke tax A tax designed to elicit information about the demand for public goods.

Coase Theorem In the absence of transactions costs, all externalities are internalized, regardless of the assignment of property rights.

Collusion An agreement among firms to set prices and outputs.

Common law The system of legal precedents that has evolved from court decisions.

Common property Property without a well-defined owner.

Comparative advantage The ability to perform a given task at a lower cost.

Compensated demand curve A curve showing how much of a good would be consumed at each possible price if the consumer were income-compensated for all price changes.

Compensating differential A wage adjustment that comes about in equilibrium to compensate for a particularly pleasant or unpleasant aspect of a job.

Competitive equilibrium A point that everyone will choose to trade to, for some appropriate market prices.

Competitive industry An industry in which all firms are competitive and any firm can freely enter or exit.

Complements Goods for which the cross elasticity of demand is negative.

Complements in production Two factors with the property that an increase in the employment of one raises the marginal product of the other.

Composite-good convention The lumping together of all goods but one into a single portmanteau good.

Consequentialist moral theories Moral theories that assert that the correctness of an act can be judged by its consequences.

Constant-cost industry An industry in which all firms have identical costs, which do not change as the industry expands or contracts.

Constant returns to scale A condition where increasing all input levels by the same proportion leads to a proportionate increase in output.

Consumer price index (CPI) The price index officially reported by the U.S. Department of Labor.

Consumer's surplus The consumer's gain from trade: the amount by which the value of his purchases exceeds what he actually pays for them.

Consumption All goods other than leisure.

Consumption goods (or **outputs**) Goods that individuals want to consume.

Contestable market A market in which firms can enter and exit costlessly.

Contract curve The set of Pareto-optimal points.

Contributory negligence A plaintiff's failure to take precautions whose cost is less than the damage caused by an accident multiplied by the probability that the accident will occur.

Convex Bowed in toward the origin, like the curves in panel A of Exhibit 3-7.

Corner solution An optimum occurring on one of the axes when there is no tangency between the budget line and an indifference curve.

Cost A forgone opportunity.

Cost-benefit analysis Analysis of the costs and benefits of various public policies.

Coupon bond A bond that promises a series of payments on different dates.

Cournot model A model of oligopoly in which firms take their rivals' output as given.

Creative response A response to a regulation that conforms to the letter of the law while undermining its spirit.

Cross elasticity of demand The percentage change in consumption that results from a 1% increase in the price of a related good.

Deadweight loss A reduction in social gain.

Decreasing-cost industry An industry in which the cost of production decreases as the industry expands.

Decreasing returns to scale A condition where increasing all input levels by the same proportion leads to a less than proportionate increase in output.

Default risk The possibility that the issue of a bond will not meet his obligations.

Demand A family of numbers that lists the quantity demanded corresponding to each possible price.

Demand curve A graph illustrating demand, with prices on the vertical axis and quantities demanded on the horizontal axis.

Derived demand Demand for an input, which depends on conditions in the output market.

Diminishing marginal returns to labor The circumstance in which each unit of labor has a smaller marginal product than the last.

Discount The face value of a bond minus its current price.

Dissipation of rents or **tragedy of the commons** The elimination of social gains due to overuse of common property.

Diversify To reduce risk.

Dividends Streams of benefits.

Dominant strategy A strategy that a player would want to follow regardless of the other player's behavior as given.

Econometrics A family of statistical techniques used by economists.

Economic incidence The division of a tax burden according to who actually pays the tax.

Economic profits Total revenue minus total cost.

Edgeworth box A certain diagrammatic representation of an economy with two individuals, two goods, and no production.

Effective price ceiling A price ceiling set below the equilibrium price.

Efficiency criterion A normative criterion according to which one policy is better than another if it creates more social gain.

Efficiency wage A wage higher than market equilibrium, which employers pay in order to make workers want to keep their jobs.

Efficient market A market in which prices fully reflect all available information.

Efficient portfolio A portfolio in the efficient set.

Efficient set The northwest boundary of the set of all portfolios.

Elasticity of supply The percentage change in quantity supplied resulting from a 1% increase in price.

Endowment The basket of goods that somebody starts with, prior to any trading.

Endowment point The point representing the initial holdings of an individual in an Edgeworth box.

Engel curve A curve showing, for fixed prices, the quantity of *X* consumed (on the vertical axis) at each level of income (on the horizontal axis).

Entry price The minimum price that would cause a firm to enter a given industry.

Envy-free allocation An outcome in which nobody would prefer to trade baskets with anybody else.

Equilibrium point The point where the supply and demand curves intersect.

Equimarginal principle The principle that an activity should be pursued to the point where marginal cost equals marginal benefit.

Ex ante Determined before the state of the world is known.

Ex post Determined after the state of the world is known.

Excise tax In this book, a tax that is paid directly by suppliers to the government.

Expansion path The set of tangencies between isoquants and isocosts.

Expected return The expected value of returns.

Expected value The average value over all states of the world, with each state weighted by its probability.

External costs and benefits, or **externalities** Costs and benefits imposed on others.

Face value The amount that a bond promises to pay.

Factor-price effect The effect that an expansion of industry output has on the price of a factor of production, thereby raising marginal costs in the industry.

Factors of production (or **inputs**) Goods that are used to produce outputs.

Fair odds Odds that reflect the true probabilities of various states of the world.

Fall in demand A decision by demanders to buy a smaller quantity at each given price.

Fall in supply A decrease in the quantities that suppliers will provide at each given price.

Firm An entity that produces and sells goods, with the goal of maximizing its profits.

First-degree price discrimination Charging each customer the most that he would be willing to pay for each item that he buys.

Fishery Common property.

Fixed cost A cost that does not vary with the level of output; the cost of hiring fixed factors.

Fixed factor of production One that the firm must employ in a given quantity.

Free riders People who benefit from the actions of others and therefore have reduced incentives to engage in those actions themselves.

Free riding Reaping benefits from the actions of others and consequently refusing to bear the full costs of those actions.

Futures contract A contract to deliver a specified good at a specified future date for a specified price.

Futures market The market for futures contracts.

Game matrix A diagram showing one player's strategy choices across the top, the other player's along the left side, and the corresponding outcomes in the appropriate boxes.

General average The rule of law that dictates the division of losses when cargo is jettisoned to prevent a disaster at sea.

General equilibrium analysis A way of modeling the economy so as to take account of all markets at once, and of all the interactions among them.

Giffen good A good for which the demand curve slopes upward.

Good Samaritan Rule A bystander has no duty to rescue a stranger in distress.

Goods Items of which the consumer would prefer to have more rather than less.

Horizontal integration A merger of firms that produce the same product.

Human capital Productive skills.

Income effect When the price of a good changes, that part of the effect on quantity demanded that results from the change in real income.

Income elasticity of demand The percentage change in consumption that results from a 1% increase in income.

Increasing-cost industry An industry in which the cost of production increases as the industry expands.

Increasing marginal cost The condition where each additional unit of an activity is more expensive than the last.

Increasing returns to scale A condition where increasing all input levels by the same proportion leads to a more than proportionate increase in output.

Indifference curve A collection of baskets all of which the consumer considers equally desirable.

Inferior good A good that the consumer chooses to consume less of when his income goes up.

Inflation A continuous rise in the price level.

Internalize To treat an external cost as a private cost.

Intertemporal substitution Adjusting work and vacation times so as to be working when wages are highest.

Investors Buyers of risky assets.

Isocost The set of all baskets of inputs that can be employed at a given cost.

Labor income effect The income effect of a wage change due to the change in the worker's labor income.

Labor theory of value The assertion that the value of an object is determined by the amount of labor involved in its production.

Laspeyres price index A price index based on the basket consumed in the earlier period.

Law of demand The observation that when the price of a good goes up, people will buy less of that good.

Law of large numbers When a gamble is repeated many times, the average outcome is the expected value.

Law of supply The observation that when the price of a good goes up, the quantity supplied goes up.

Legal incidence The division of a tax burden according to who is required under the law to pay the tax.

Leisure All activities other than labor.

Liable Legally responsible to compensate another party for damage.

Long run A period of time over which all factors are variable.

Long-run average cost Long-run total cost divided by quantity.

Long-run marginal cost That part of long-run total cost attributable to the last unit produced.

Long-run supply curve A curve that shows what quantity the firm will supply in the long run in response to any given price.

Long-run total cost The cost of producing a given amount of output when the firm is able to operate on its expansion path.

Marginal benefit The additional benefit gained from the last unit of an activity.

Marginal cost The additional cost associated with the last unit of an activity.

Marginal product of labor The additional output due to employing one more unit of labor (with capital employment held fixed).

Marginal rate of substitution, or **MRS, between X and Y** The value of a consumer's last unit of *X*, measured by the number of additional units of *Y* that would just compensate him for its loss.

Marginal rate of technical substitution of labor for capital The amount of capital that can be substituted for one unit of labor, holding output constant.

Marginal revenue product of labor The additional revenue that a firm earns when it employs one more unit of labor.

Marginal tax rate The amount of income tax you pay on the last dollar that you earn.

Marginal value The marginal rate of substitution of *X* for All Other Goods, often measured in dollars.

Market failure An occasion on which private markets fail to provide some good in socially efficient quantities.

Market line The line through a risk-free asset and tangent to the efficient set.

Market portfolio The point of tangency between the market line and the efficient set.

Market power or **monopoly power** The ability of a firm to affect market prices through its actions. A firm has monopoly power if and only if it faces a downward sloping demand curve.

Maturity date The date on which a bond promises a delivery.

Mixed strategy A strategy that involves a random choice among price strategies.

Money income or **nominal income** Income measured in terms of money.

Monopolistic competition The theory of markets in which there are many similar but differentiated products.

Monopsonist A buyer who faces an upward-sloping supply curve.

Moral hazard The incentive for an individual to take more risks when he is insured.

More efficient Preferred according to the efficiency criterion; able to perform a given task at lower cost: having a comparative advantage.

Nash equilibrium An outcome from which nobody would want to deviate, taking everyone else's behavior as given.

Natural monopoly An industry in which each firm's average cost curve is decreasing at the point where it crosses market demand.

Negative externalities External costs.

Negligence A defendant's failure to take precautions whose cost is less than the damage caused by an accident multiplied by the probability that the accident will occur.

Net demander of labor Someone who demands more labor than he supplies.

Net supplier of labor Someone who supplies more labor than he demands.

Nominal Measured in terms of money.

Nominal rate of interest The relative price of current dollars in terms of future dollars, minus 1.

Nonexcludable good A good that, if consumed by one person, is automatically available to others.

Nonlabor income Income from sources other than wages.

Nonlabor income effect The income effect of a wage change due to the change in the value of the productive assets other than labor that the worker owns.

Nonrivalrous good A good that, if consumed by one person, can be provided to others at no additional cost.

Normal good A good that the consumer chooses to consume more of when his income goes up.

Normative question A question about what *ought* to be.

Oligopoly An industry in which individual firms can influence market conditions.

Open economy An economy that trades with outsiders at prices determined in world markets.

Optimum The most preferred of the baskets on the budget line.

Overshooting A percentage increase in the price level that exceeds the percentage increase in the money supply.

Paasche price index A price index based on the basket consumed in the later period.

Pareto criterion A normative criterion according to which one policy is better than another only if every individual agrees that it is preferable.

Pareto improvement or **Pareto-preferred outcome** A change that helps at least one person without hurting anyone.

Pareto-optimal outcome An outcome that allows no possibility of a Pareto improvement.

Perfectly competitive firm One that can sell any quantity it wants to at some going market price.

Perpetuity A bond that promises to pay a fixed amount periodically forever.

Pigou tax or **Pigovian tax** A tax equal to the amount of an externality.

Point of diminishing marginal returns A level of employment beyond which there are diminishing marginal returns.

Portfolios Combinations of risky assets.

Positive externalities External benefits.

Positive question A question about what *is* or *will be*.

Predatory pricing Setting an artificially low price so as to damage rival firms.

Present value Relative price in terms of current consumption.

Price ceiling A maximum price at which a product can be legally sold.

Price discrimination Charging different prices for identical items.

Price elasticity of demand The percentage change in consumption that results from a 1% increase in price.

Price index A measure of the cost of living, based on changes in the cost of some basket of goods.

Price level The price of goods in terms of money.

Principal-Agent problem The inability of the principal to verify the behavior of the agent.

Private marginal costs Those costs of a decision that are borne by the decision maker.

Producer's surplus The producer's gain from trade; the amount by which his revenue exceeds his variable costs of production.

Product differentiation The production of a product that is unique but has many close substitutes.

Production function The rule for determining how much output can be produced with a given basket of inputs.

Production possibility curve The curve displaying all baskets that can be produced.

Profit The amount by which revenue exceeds costs.

Property right The right to decide how some resource shall be used.

Public good A good where one person's consumption increases the consumption available for others.

Punitive damages Additional charges levied against one who commits a tort as punishment for his behavior.

Pure strategy A single choice of row (or column) in the game matrix.

Quantity demanded The amount of a good that a given individual or group of individuals will choose to consume at a given price.

Quantity supplied The amount of a good that suppliers will provide at a given price.

Quasi-rents Producers' surplus earned in the short run by factors that are supplied inelastically in the short run.

Real Measured in terms of goods.

Real balances The value of money holdings in terms of goods.

Rational expectations Expectations that, when held by market participants, lead to behavior that fulfills those expectations on average.

Real income Income measured in terms of goods.

Real rate of interest The relative price of present consumption goods in terms of future consumption goods, minus 1.

Region of mutual advantage The set of points that are Pareto-preferred to the initial endowment.

Regressive factor A factor with the property that an increase in its wage rate lowers the firm's long-run marginal cost curve.

Relative price The quantity of some other good that can be exchanged for a specified quantity of a given good.

Rent Payments to a factor of production in excess of the minimum payments necessary to call it into existence. In other words, the producer's surplus earned by the factor. Also, a payment made by the firm to hire a factor of production. When the firm and the factor are owned by the same person, we imagine the firm paying the factor its opportunity cost and count this as a rent.

Rental rate The price of hiring capital.

Representative agent Someone whose tastes and assets are representative of the entire economy.

Resale price maintenance or **fair trade** A practice by which the producer of a product sets a retail price and forbids any retailer to sell below that price.

Respondeat superior The liability of an employer for torts committed by his employees.

Returns Gains to the holder of a financial asset, including dividends and increases in the asset's value.

Revenue The proceeds collected by a firm when it sells its products.

Ricardian Equivalence Theorem The statement that government borrowing has no effect on wealth, consequently no effect on the demand for current consumption, and consequently no effect on the interest rate.

Rise in demand A decision by demanders to buy a larger quantity at each given price.

Rise in supply An increase in the quantities that suppliers will provide at each given price.

Risk-averse Always preferring the least risky among baskets with the same expected value.

Risk-free Having the same value in any state of the world.

Risk-neutral Caring only about expected value.

Risk-preferring Always preferring the most risky among baskets with the same expected value.

Risk premium Additional interest, in excess of the market rate, that a bondholder receives to compensate him for default risk.

Riskiness Variation in potential outcomes.

Sales tax In this book, a tax that is paid directly by consumers to the government. Other texts use this phrase in different ways.

Satisfied Able to behave as one wants to, taking market prices as given.

Scale effect When the price of an input changes, that part of the effect on employment that results from changes in the firm's output.

Second-degree price discrimination Charging the same customer different prices for identical items.

Seigniorage The gain to authorities who can print money and spend it to buy goods.

Short run A period of time over which some factors are fixed.

Short-run production function The rule for determining how much output can be produced with a given amount of labor input in the short run (with capital employment held fixed).

Short-run supply curve A curve that shows what quantity the firm will supply in the short run in response to any given price.

Shutdown price The output price below which the firm could no longer cover its average variable costs and would therefore shut down.

Signal An activity that does not directly produce anything socially productive but that conveys information about one's talents, so that it is privately rewarding.

Signaling equilibrium A Nash equilibrium in which signals are employed.

Social gain or **welfare gain** The sum of the gains from trade to all participants.

Social marginal costs All of the costs of a decision, including the private costs and the costs imposed on others.

Solution concept A rule for predicting how games will turn out.

Speculative bubble A situation in which expectations of rising prices cause prices to rise.

Speculator One who attempts to earn profits in the futures market by predicting future changes in supply or demand.

Spot market The market for goods for immediate delivery.

Spot price Price in the spot market.

Stackelberg equilibrium An equilibrium concept that arises when one player announces his strategy before the other.

Standard deviation A precise measure of risk.

State of the world A potential set of conditions.

Strict liability Liability that exists regardless of whether the defendant has been negligent.

Substitutes Goods for which the cross elasticity of demand is positive.

Substitutes in production Two factors with the property that an increase in the employment of one lowers the marginal product of the other.

Substitution effect When the price of a good changes, that part of the effect on quantity demanded that results from the change in the terms of trade between goods; when the price of an input changes, that part of the effect on employment that results from the firm's substitution toward other inputs.

Sunk cost A cost that can no longer be avoided.

Supply A family of numbers giving the quantities supplied at each possible price.

Technologically inefficient A production process that uses more inputs than necessary to produce a given output.

Theory of games A system for studying strategic behavior.

Third-degree price discrimination Charging different prices in different markets.

Torts Acts that injure others.

Total cost The sum of fixed cost and variable cost.

Total product The quantity of output that can be produced with a given input.

Transactions cost Any cost of negotiating or enforcing a contract.

Two-part tariff A pricing strategy in which the consumer must pay a fee in exchange for the right to purchase the product.

Uninsurable risk A risk that cannot be diversified.

Unit isoquant The set of all technically efficient ways to produce one unit of output.

Utilitarianism The belief that utility, or happiness, can be meaningfully measured, and that it is desirable to maximize the sum of everyone's utility.

Value The maximum amount that a consumer would be willing to pay for an item.

Variable cost The cost of hiring variable factors.

Variable factor of production One that the firm can employ in varying quantities.

Vertical integration A merger between a firm that produces an input and a firm which uses that input.

Wage rate The price of hiring labor.

Winner's curse The phenomenon that occurs when the high bidder in an auction discovers that he is the high bidder, and therefore that the item is likely to be worth less than he thought it was.

World relative price The relative price that prevails in the presence of trade with foreigners.

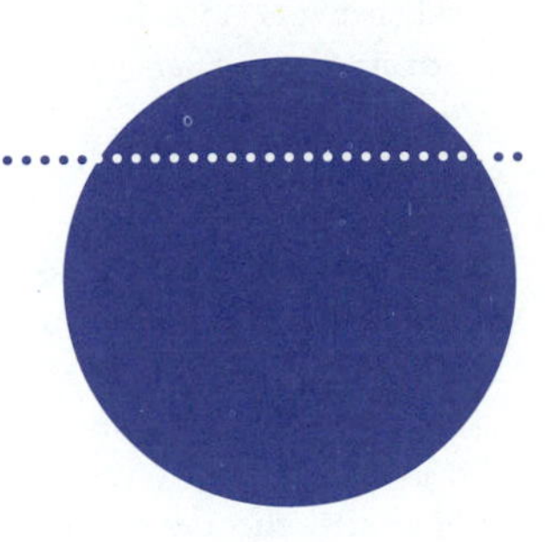

Index

Page numbers in bold refer to definitions. Page numbers followed by *n* indicate footnote references.